T0181996

Lecture Notes in Computer Science   10951

Commenced Publication in 1973
Founding and Former Series Editors:
Gerhard Goos, Juris Hartmanis, and Jan van Leeuwen

Formal Methods

Subline of Lectures Notes in Computer Science

More information about this series at http://www.springer.com/series/7408

Klaus Havelund · Jan Peleska
Bill Roscoe · Erik de Vink (Eds.)

Formal Methods

22nd International Symposium, FM 2018
Held as Part of the Federated Logic Conference, FloC 2018
Oxford, UK, July 15–17, 2018
Proceedings

 Springer

Editors
Klaus Havelund (iD)
NASA Jet Propulsion Laboratory
Pasadena, CA
USA

Jan Peleska (iD)
University of Bremen
Bremen
Germany

Bill Roscoe
University of Oxford
Oxford
UK

Erik de Vink
Eindhoven University of Technology
Eindhoven
The Netherlands

ISSN 0302-9743   ISSN 1611-3349   (electronic)
Lecture Notes in Computer Science
ISBN 978-3-319-95581-0   ISBN 978-3-319-95582-7   (eBook)
https://doi.org/10.1007/978-3-319-95582-7

Library of Congress Control Number: 2018947575

LNCS Sublibrary: SL2 – Programming and Software Engineering

Printed on acid-free paper

This Springer imprint is published by the registered company Springer Nature Switzerland AG
The registered company address is: Gewerbestrasse 11, 6330 Cham, Switzerland

Preface

FM 2018 was held in Oxford as part of FloC during July 15–17, with additional workshops on July 14 and during 18–19. It was a great pleasure to return to one of the spiritual homes of Formal Methods. This was the 22nd of a series stretching back to 1987. We are delighted to present its proceedings, once again published by Springer. FM is a core event for the formal methods community and brings together researchers working on both more theoretical aspects and industrial practice. Once again we had an Industry Day, or I-Day.

In all, there were 110 submitted papers for the main conference of which 35 were accepted, an acceptance rate of 32%. Kim G. Larsen, Annabelle McIver, and Leonardo de Moura gave invited talks. For I-Day, nine presenters were invited to share insights about applications of formal methods in industry.

Seven workshops were associated with FM this year: F-IDE, Overture, QAPL, AVoCS, REFINE, TLA+, and VaVas.

We offer our sincere thanks to all who helped make the conference a success and assisted with the preparation of these proceedings. This includes the FM committee chaired by Ana Cavalcanti, the FloC Organizing Committee led by Moshe Vardi, Daniel Kroening, and Marta Kwiatkowska, as well as the staff and volunteers who supported this event. Naturally, we also thank the Program Committee members and others who put so much effort into ensuring the quality of the program, as well as all authors who submitted papers.

FLoC had many sponsors including Oxford University Computer Science Department, Springer, and Diffblue. We thank them all.

June 2018

Erik de Vink
Jan Peleska
Bill Roscoe
Klaus Havelund

Preface

Organization

Program Chairs

Jan Peleska   University of Bremen, Germany
Bill Roscoe   University of Oxford, UK

Workshop Chairs

Maurice ter Beek   CNR/ISTI, Italy
Helen Treharne   University of Surrey, UK

Industry Day Chairs

Klaus Havelund   NASA Jet Propulsion Laboratory, USA
Jan Peleska   University of Bremen, Germany
Ralf Pinger   Siemens, Germany

Doctoral Symposium Chairs

Eerke Boiten   De Montfort University, UK
Fatiha Zaïdi   Université Paris-Sud XI, France

Organizing Committee

Erik de Vink   Eindhoven University of Technology, The Netherlands
  (General Chair)
Mahmoud Talebi (Website)   Eindhoven University of Technology, The Netherlands

Program Committee

Bernhard K. Aichernig   TU Graz, Austria
Joerg Brauer   Verified Systems International GmbH, Germany
Ana Cavalcanti   University of York, UK
Frank De Boer   CWI, The Netherlands
John Fitzgerald   Newcastle University, UK
Martin Fraenzle   Carl von Ossietzky Universität Oldenburg, Germany
Vijay Ganesh   University of Waterloo, Canada
Diego Garbervetsky   University of Buenos Aires, Argentina
Dimitra Giannakopoulou   NASA Ames Research Center, USA
Thomas Gibson-Robinson   University of Oxford, UK
Stefania Gnesi   ISTI-CNR, Italy

Klaus Havelund	NASA Jet Propulsion Laboratory, USA
Anne E. Haxthausen	Technical University of Denmark, Denmark
Ian J. Hayes	The University of Queensland, Australia
Constance Heitmeyer	Naval Research Laboratory, USA
Jozef Hooman	TNO-ESI and Radboud University Nijmegen, The Netherlands
Laura Humphrey	Air Force Research Laboratory, USA
Fuyuki Ishikawa	National Institute of Informatics, Japan
Einar Broch Johnsen	University of Oslo, Norway
Cliff Jones	Newcastle University, UK
Joost-Pieter Katoen	RWTH Aachen University, Germany
Gerwin Klein	NICTA and The University of New South Wales, Australia
Laura Kovacs	Chalmers University of Technology, Sweden
Peter Gorm Larsen	Aarhus University, Denmark
Yves Ledru	Université Grenoble Alpes, France
Rustan Leino	Amazon Web Services, USA
Elizabeth Leonard	Naval Research Laboratory, USA
Martin Leucker	University of Lübeck, Germany
Michael Leuschel	University of Düsseldorf, Germany
Zhiming Liu	Southwest University, China
Tiziana Margaria	University of Limerick and Lero, Ireland
Mieke Massink	ISTI-CNR, Italy
Annabelle McIver	Macquarie University, Australia
Dominique Mery	Université de Lorraine, LORIA, France
Mohammad Reza Mousavi	University of Leicester, UK
Peter Müller	ETH Zurich, Switzerland
Colin O'Halloran	D-RisQ Software Systems, UK
Jose Oliveira	University of Minho, Portugal
Olaf Owe	University of Oslo, Norway
Sam Owre	SRI International, USA
Jan Peleska	TZI, University of Bremen, Germany
Alexandre Petrenko	CRIM, Canada
Anna Philippou	University of Cyprus, Cyprus
Ralf Pinger	Siemens, Germany
Elvinia Riccobene	University of Milan, Italy
Bill Roscoe	University of Oxford, UK
Grigore Rosu	University of Illinois at Urbana-Champaign, USA
Augusto Sampaio	Federal University of Pernambuco, Brazil
Gerardo Schneider	Chalmers University of Technology, Sweden
Natasha Sharygina	University of Lugano, Switzerland
Ana Sokolova	University of Salzburg, Austria
Jun Sun	Singapore University of Technology and Design, Singapore
Stefano Tonetta	FBK-irst, Italy
Farn Wang	National Taiwan University, Taiwan

Heike Wehrheim	University of Paderborn, Germany
Michael Whalen	University of Minnesota, USA
Jim Woodcock	University of York, UK
Hüsnü Yenigün	Sabanci University, Turkey
Fatiha Zaidi	Université Paris-Sud, France
Gianluigi Zavattaro	University of Bologna, Italy

Additional Reviewers

Abbyaneh, Alireza
Agogino, Adrian
Aldini, Alessandro
Antignac, Thibaud
Antonino, Pedro
Araujo, Hugo
Arcaini, Paolo
Archer, Myla
Asadi, Sepideh
Astrauskas, Vytautas
Avellaneda, Florent
Basile, Davide
Baxter, James
Berger, Philipp
Blicha, Martin
Bodeveix, Jean-Paul
Boudjadar, Jalil
Braghin, Chiara
Bugariu, Alexandra
Byun, Taejoon
Carvalho, Gustavo
Castaño, Rodrigo
Chen, Taolue
Chen, Yu-Ting
Chen, Zhenbang
Chimento, Jesus Mauricio
Ciancia, Vincenzo
Ciolek, Daniel
Colvin, Robert
de Gouw, Stijn
Dodds, Mike
Ehlers, Rüdiger
Eilers, Marco
Even-Mendoza, Karine
Fages, François

Fantechi, Alessandro
Fava, Daniel
Ferrère, Thomas
Foltzer, Adam
Foster, Simon
Gazda, Maciej
Ghasemi, Mahsa
Ghassabani, Elaheh
Gomez-Zamalloa, Miguel
Govind, Hari
Günther, Henning
Hagemann, Willem
Henrio, Ludovic
Holzer, Andreas
Hyvärinen, Antti
Höfner, Peter
Jaafar, Fehmi
Junges, Sebastian
Katis, Andreas
Khakpour, Narges
Kharraz, Karam
Kiesl, Benjamin
Kotelnikov, Evgenii
Kouzapas, Dimitrios
Krings, Sebastian
Kulik, Tomas
König, Jürgen
Laarman, Alfons
Latella, Diego
Legunsen, Owolabi
Lester, Martin Mariusz
Li, Guangyuan
Li, Ian
Liang, Jimmy
Liu, Si

Longuet, Delphine
Lucanu, Dorel
Macedo, Hugo Daniel
Macedo, Nuno
Madeira, Alexandre
Marescotti, Matteo
Markin, Grigory
Matheja, Christoph
Mathur, Umang
Mauro, Jacopo
Mazzanti, Franco
Meinicke, Larissa
Merz, Stephan
Monahan, Rosemary
Mota, Alexandre
Neubauer, Felix
Nguena-Timo, Omer
Nguyen, Huu Nghia
Noll, Thomas
Oortwijn, Wytse
Palmskog, Karl
Pardo, Raúl
Pauck, Felix
Pedro, André
Pena, Lucas
Proenca, Jose
Qu, Hongyang
Robillard, Simon
Scheffel, Torben
Schmidt, Joshua
Schmitz, Malte
Schneider, David
Schoepe, Daniel
Scott, Joe
Sewell, Thomas

Sharma, Arnab
Singh, Neeraj
Steffen, Martin
Stewart, Danielle
Stolz, Volker
Stumpf, Johanna Beate
Swaminathan, Mani
Syeda, Hira
Tabaei, Mitra
Taha, Safouan

Ter Beek, Maurice H.
Ter-Gabrielyan, Arshavir
Thoma, Daniel
Thorstensen, Evgenij
Thule, Casper
Toews, Manuel
Tribastone, Mirco
Tschaikowski, Max
Tveito, Lars
van Glabbeek, Rob

Voisin, Frederic
Winter, Kirsten
Yakovlev, Alex
Ye, Kangfeng
Yovine, Sergio
Zeyda, Frank
Zhao, Liang
Zoppi, Edgardo
Zulkoski, Ed

Contents

FM 2018 Industry Day

Invited Papers

Processing Text for Privacy:
An Information Flow Perspective

Natasha Fernandes, Mark Dras, and Annabelle McIver[✉]

Department of Computing, Macquarie University, North Ryde, Australia
annabelle.mciver@mq.edu.au

Abstract. The problem of text document obfuscation is to provide an automated mechanism which is able to make accessible the content of a text document without revealing the identity of its writer. This is more challenging than it seems, because an adversary equipped with powerful machine learning mechanisms is able to identify authorship (with good accuracy) where, for example, the name of the author has been redacted. Current obfuscation methods are ad hoc and have been shown to provide weak protection against such adversaries. Differential privacy, which is able to provide strong guarantees of privacy in some domains, has been thought not to be applicable to text processing.

In this paper we will review obfuscation as a quantitative information flow problem and explain how *generalised differential privacy* can be applied to this problem to provide strong anonymisation guarantees in a standard model for text processing.

Keywords: Refinement · Information flow
Privacy · Probabilistic semantics · Text processing
Author anonymity · Author obfuscation

1 Introduction

Up until the middle of the nineteenth century it was common for British authors to publish their work anonymously. There were many reasons for the practice, and surprisingly many well-known authors practised it including (as we now know) Alexander Pope, Jonathan Swift, Jane Austen and Daniel Defoe. But can a work ever be entirely anonymous, in the sense that it is not possible to identify the author with full certainty? Authors typically develop their own personal style, and the famous example of the "Federalist papers" showed that the analysis of word frequencies can be used to build compelling evidence to support the identification of authors of anonymous works [22].

Koppel et al. [14] trace the development of techniques from that of Mosteller and Wallace [22] (and earlier) to more recent machine learning methods, which

---

A. McIver—We acknowledge the support of the Australian Research Council Grant DP140101119.

© Springer International Publishing AG, part of Springer Nature 2018
K. Havelund et al. (Eds.): FM 2018, LNCS 10951, pp. 3–21, 2018.
https://doi.org/10.1007/978-3-319-95582-7_1

have taken advantage of the observation that many aspects of style — not only word counts — in writing can be captured by statistical methods. For the last decade, stylometric machine learners have been able to identify authors with accuracy better than 90% from a set of 50 candidates, and have been successfully applied to identification tasks on sets of (anonymous) documents written by tens of thousands of authors.

Methods related to these were employed by researchers working on the 2006 Netflix release of a "deidentified" database of movie reviews in order to allow researchers to work on improving its recommendation systems.

Unfortunately deidentifying data (i.e. removing names) is very different from properly anonymising it and, in this case, privacy researchers were able to demonstrate publicly that Netflix's data contained more information than intended leading to a lawsuit.

There remain many legitimate reasons why an author might want to disguise his or her identity. Indeed could Netflix have done a better job to protect its contributors whilst still preserving the information contained in the reviews well enough to be useful to researchers working on improving Netflix's recommendation systems? In response to the Netflix lawsuit, and other such breaches of privacy, "PAN" a series of scientific events and shared tasks on digital text forensics[1] proposed a task to encourage research into creating systems which are able to truly anonymise. The statement of the task is:

Given a document, paraphrase it so that its writing style does not match that of its original author, anymore.

As an example, consider this extract from George Orwell's *Nineteen Eighty-Four*:

"The object of persecution is persecution. The object of torture is torture. The object of power is power."

It's clear that Orwell's intent was to evoke a sense of shock by the overwhelming use of strong repetition. Another way of saying the same thing might be:

"The aim of persecution, abuse and power is respectively to mistreat, to torture and to control."

which, stripped of of its powerful stylistic ruse, has been rendered into a rather dull opinion.

The range of approaches to "obfuscating" text documents automatically that have been attempted up to and including the PAN task have had limited success. Many of those approaches were inspired by *k-confusability* which articulates the idea of "confusing" some secret with k other things, but turns out to be susceptible to the well-known "linkage" and "intersection" attacks.

Methods based on differential privacy (DP) [10] — which provide some protection from these attacks — have not been attempted to date for this problem.

---

[1] http://pan.webis.de/index.html.

There has been interest for some time in combining DP with machine learning in general (for example, [7]), including recent "deep learning" approaches [1], although applications to text are challenging because of its discrete, complex and unstructured nature. Moreover, a key difference with our application of interest is that we want to conceal the authorship of an individual released document; the goal for DP with machine learning is typically to preserve the privacy of members of the training dataset.

In this paper we link the original goals of the PAN obfuscation task to two theoretical areas in computer science, with the aim of providing a solid foundation for the enterprise and to enable new techniques in theoretical privacy to be applied to this problem.

We explain how this task can be viewed as a problem of Quantitative Information Flow where we describe the result of an obfuscation process as a "channel". In this way we can show upper bounds on the ability of any adversary to determine the real author (whether or not the adversary is using machine learning).

Second, we describe how the novel metrics used in machine learning algorithms for author identification can in fact be used after all to define obfuscators based on differential privacy. The trick is to used *Generalised Differential Privacy* [6] originally used in location-based privacy and which can be used for unstructured data.

2 Text Document Processing

Text documents are processed in many different ways depending on the objective. For example a document might need to be classified in terms of its topic which can be helpful for cataloging in document repositories; or documents can be paraphrased so that domain professionals are able to determine which documents are relevant for their research or report compilation. Statistical and machine learning approaches are the standard way now to tackle these tasks [18]; most recently, approaches falling within the "deep learning" paradigm, using neural networks with many layers, have become dominant and produced state-of-the-art results for many tasks [26].

All these approaches use very different algorithms and representations of documents, but the basic idea is the same, even when the representations and implementations differ: thousands of document samples are analysed to identify important "features" depending on the specific goal of the task. This constitutes the "learning phase" and the result is a "best possible" correlation between categories and the discovered features. Learning algorithms (for classification problems) are evaluated by subjecting the learned correlation to the identification to datasets which are not part of the learning set, and typically counts of correct identification or classification are used to rate the success of the method.

For us the aim is to determine how to obfuscate automatically according to the following constraints:

The result of an obfuscated document must retain as much of the original content in such a way that the author of the obfuscated document cannot be identified.

As a simplification, we focus on the identification of author, and (separately) topic classification (rather than full "content") both of which are examples of "classification problems" in machine learning.

2.1   Representing Documents for Topic Classification and Author Identification

In machine learning documents are transformed into representations that have been found to enable the discovery of features which perform well on a particular classification task. A very simple representation is to choose the word components of a document, so for example,

"The object of persecution is persecution" can be represented by the set:

$$\{\text{"}The\text{"}, \text{"}object\text{"}, \text{"}of\text{"}, \text{"}persecution\text{"}, \text{"}is\text{"}\}. \tag{1}$$

This, of course has lost some useful details such as the number of times that words appear; an alternative richer representation is a "bag of words" which, in this case, retains the repetition of *"persecution"*:

$$\{\!|\text{"}The\text{"}, \text{"}object\text{"}, \text{"}of\text{"}, \text{"}persecution\text{"}, \text{"}persecution\text{"}, \text{"}is\text{"}|\!\}. \tag{2}$$

Even though it still loses a lot information from the original sentence, such as word order, it turns out that the the bag of words representation is still very useful in topic classification, where correlations between topics and the types and frequency of words can be used to assign a topic classification to a document. It can also be used in some stylometric analysis where authors can be correlated with the number of times they use a particular word — in the identification of the authors of the Federalist papers, it was discovered that Hamilton only used "while" whereas Madison preferred "whilst", and used "commonly" much more frequently than did Hamilton.

More recent, widely used author identifiers use "character n-gram" representation for documents. The *n-gram* representation transforms a document into a list of each subsequence of characters of length n, including (sometimes) spaces and punctuation. Such a character 3-gram representation of our example is:

$$\langle \text{"}The\text{"}, \text{"}he\text{"}, \text{"}eo\text{"}, \text{"}ob\text{"}, \text{"}obj\text{"}, \text{"}bje\text{"}, \text{"}jec\text{"}, \text{"}ect\text{"}, \text{"}ct\text{"} \dots \rangle. \tag{3}$$

This representation seems to capture things like systematic punctuation and common word stems, all of which can characterise an author. A particular character n-gram-based method of interest is the one developed by Koppel et al. [15]. This method uses character 4-grams (but without spaces) to classify authorship on a document set consisting of blog posts from thousands of authors, and achieve in excess of 90% precision with 42% coverage for a 1000-author dataset.

On account of its strong performance and suitability for large author sets, and the fact that it underpins the winning systems of PAN shared tasks on author identification [13,24], this algorithm is one of the standard inference attackers used in the PAN obfuscation task. This is therefore the authorship identification algorithm we use in the rest of this paper.

2.2 Privacy Versus Utility

Obfuscating a document means changing the words somehow, and with the use of machine learning as an adversary (as in author identification) or as a friend (as in topic identification) we can see that the bag of words (2) or n-gram representation (3) will be affected.

What we would like is to be able to show that for any adversary whether or not they are using the n-gram representation that the obfuscation method reduces their ability to identify authors, whereas using a state-of-the-art method based on a bag of words representation the topic identification remains almost as it was before obfuscation.

To deal with the former, we shall follow Alvim et al. [2] to model a privacy mechanism as an information flow channel; for the latter we will use generalised differential privacy to show how to preserve topicality using an appropriate metric for "meaning".

3 Channels, Secrets and Information Flow

A *privacy mechanism* produces observations determined by secret inputs; the elements of the channel model for information flow are inputs of type $\mathcal{X}$, observations of type $\mathcal{Y}$ and a description of how the inputs and observations are correlated. For any set $\mathcal{S}$ we write $\mathbb{D}\mathcal{S}$ for the set of discrete distributions on $\mathcal{S}$.

A *channel* between $\mathcal{X}$ and $\mathcal{Y}$ is a (stochastic) matrix whose $\mathcal{X}$-indexed rows sum to 1. We write the type of such channels/matrices as $\mathcal{X}{\rightarrow}\mathcal{Y}$ and for $C\colon \mathcal{X}{\rightarrow}\mathcal{Y}$ its constituents are elements $C_{x,y}$ at row x and column y that gives the conditional probability of output y from input x, the x'th row $C_{x,-}$ and the y'th column $C_{-,y}$. Any row $C_{x,-}$ of $C\colon \mathcal{X}{\rightarrow}\mathcal{Y}$ can be interpreted as an element of $\mathbb{D}\mathcal{Y}$.

A *secret* is a distribution in $\mathbb{D}\mathcal{X}$; initially we call such secrets priors, by which we mean that the adversary might have some prior knowledge which means that knows some secret values are more likely than others, however the fact that his knowledge is represented as a distribution means that he does not know for sure. The mechanism modelled by a channel C produces a correlation between the inputs and the observables.

Given a channel $C\colon \mathcal{X}{\rightarrow}\mathcal{Y}$ and prior $\pi\colon \mathcal{X}$ the joint distribution $J\colon \mathbb{D}(\mathcal{X}{\times}\mathcal{Y})$ is given by $J_{x,y}:=\pi_x C_{x,y}$. For each y the column $J_{-,y}$, the adversary can update his knowledge a-posteriori using Bayesian reasoning that revises the prior: i.e. normalising $J_{-,y}{}^2$ to give the posterior induced on π by that y. We write $\pi\rangle C$ for

---

^{2} If several distinct y's produce the same posterior, they are amalgamated; if there is y with zero marginal probability, it and its (undefined) posterior are omitted.

the joint distribution J, and $\overrightarrow{J}: \mathbb{D}\mathcal{Y}$ for the (right) marginal probability defined $\overrightarrow{J}_y := \sum_{x:\mathcal{X}} J_{x,y}$. For each observation y we denote the corresponding posterior $J^y := \overrightarrow{J} / \overrightarrow{J}_y$.

There are two operations on channels which we will use to model two attacks on privacy.

Definition 1. *Let* $C: \mathcal{X} \to \mathcal{Y}_1$ *and* $D: \mathcal{X} \to \mathcal{Y}_2$ *be channels. We define the sequential composition* $C; D: \mathcal{X} \to (\mathcal{Y}_1 \times \mathcal{Y}_2)$ *as follows:*

$$(C; D)_{x,(y_1,y_2)} \quad := \quad C_{x,y_1} \times D_{x,y_2}.$$

Sequential composition allows the adversary to amalgamate his knowledge about the secret which is leaked from bth C and D.

The second operator models the situation where a channel leaks information about a secret from $\mathcal{X}$ which has an interesting correlation wth a second secret $\mathcal{Z}$. The adversary can then use channel $C: \mathcal{X} \to \mathcal{Y}$ to deduce some information about the second secret!

Definition 2. *Given channel* $C: \mathcal{X} \to \mathcal{Y}$ *and joint distribution* $Z: \mathbb{D}(\mathcal{Z} \times \mathcal{X})$ *expressing an interesting correlation between two secret types* $\mathcal{Z}$ *and* $\mathcal{X}$*, we define the* Dalenius composition $Z \cdot C: \mathcal{Z} \to \mathcal{Y}$ *defined by "matrix multiplication":*

$$(Z \cdot C)_{z,y} \quad := \quad \sum_{x:\mathcal{X}} Z_{z,x} \times C_{x,y}.$$

Dalenius composition[3] can be used the model the risk posed by mechanisms that inadvertently release information about a second secret that is known to be correlated with secrets associated with the mechanism.

3.1   Vulnerability Induced by Gain-Functions

When a channel publishes its observables, the most important concern is to determine whether an adversary can do anything damaging with the information released. We can investigate an adversary's ability to use the information effectively using the idea of "vulnerability" [4], a generalisation of entropy, no longer necessarily e.g. Shannon, and whose great variety allows fine-grained control of the significance of the information that might be leaked [4,5].

Given a secret-space $\mathcal{X}$, vulnerability is induced by a *gain function* over that space, typically g of type $\mathbb{G}_\mathcal{W}\mathcal{X} = \mathcal{W} \to \mathcal{X} \to \mathbb{R}$, for some space of *actions* $w: \mathcal{W}$. When $\mathcal{W}$ is obvious from context, or unimportant, we will omit it and write just $g: \mathbb{G}\mathcal{X}$. Given g and w (but not yet x) the function $g.w$ is of type $\mathcal{X} \to \mathbb{R}$[4] and

---

[3] Named after Tore Dalenius who pointed out this risk in statistical databases [9].

[4] We write dot for function application, left associative, so that function g applied to argument w is $g.w$ and then $g.w.x$ is $(g.w)$ applied to x, that is using the Currying technique of functional programming. This convention reduces clutter of parentheses, as we see later.

can thus be regarded as a random variable on $\mathcal{X}$. As such, it has an expected value on any distribution π over $\mathcal{X}$, written $\mathcal{E}_\pi\, g.w := \sum_{x:\,\mathcal{X}} g.w.x \times \pi_x.$[5]

Once we have x, the (scalar) value $g.w.x$ is simply of type $\mathbb{R}$ and represents the gain to an adversary if he chooses action w when the secret's actual value is x. A particularly simple example is where the adversary tries to guess the exact value of the secret. His set of actions is therefore equal to $\mathcal{X}$, with each action a guess of a value; we encode this scenario with gain function bv defined

$$bv.w.x = (1 \text{ if } w = x \text{ else } 0), \tag{4}$$

so that the adversary gains 1 if he guesses correctly and 0 otherwise. A special case of this is when an attacker tries to guess a property of the secret (rather than the whole secret). For example let $\sim$ be an equivalence class over secrets, and suppose that the attacker tries to guess the equivalence class. The guesses $\mathcal{W}$ now correspond to equivalence classes, and:

$$bv_\sim.w.x = (1 \text{ if } x \in w \text{ else } 0). \tag{5}$$

A gain function $g: \mathbb{G}\mathcal{X}$ induces a g-vulnerability function $V_g: \mathbb{D}\mathcal{X} \rightarrow \mathbb{R}$ so that $V_g[\pi]$ for $\pi: \mathbb{D}\mathcal{X}$ is the maximum over all choices $w: \mathcal{W}$ of the expected value of $g.w$ on π, that is $\max_w(\mathcal{E}_\pi\, g.w)$. In the simple 1-or-0 case above, the vulnerability V_{bv} is called the *Bayes vulnerability*; it is one-minus the Bayes-Risk of Decision Theory, and it gives the maximum probability of an adversary guessing the secret if his prior knowledge about it is π.

We can now use g-vulnerability to determine whether the information leaked through a channel is helpful to the adversary.

Definition 3. *Given a prior $\pi \in \mathbb{D}\mathcal{X}$, a channel $C: \mathcal{X} \twoheadrightarrow \mathcal{Y}$ and gain function $g: \mathbb{G}\mathcal{X}$, we define the* average posterior vulnerability *as*

$$V_g[\pi\rangle C] \quad := \quad \sum_{y:\,\mathcal{Y}} \overrightarrow{J}_y \times V_g[J^y] \,,$$

where $J := (\pi\rangle C)$.

For each observation, the posterior J^y is the adversary's revised view of the value of the secret; the posterior is actually more vulnerable because the adversary can choose to execute a different action (compared to his choice relative to the prior) to optimise the vulnerability $V_g[J^y]$. The posterior vulnerability $V_g[\pi\rangle C]$ is then his average increase in gain. Comparing $V_g[\pi\rangle C]$ and $V_g[\pi]$ then gives an idea of how much information the adversary can usefully use relative to the scenario determined by g.

In this paper we shall use the *multiplicative g-leakage*, defined by

$$\mathcal{L}_g(C) \quad := \quad V_g[\pi\rangle C]/V_g[\pi] \,, \tag{6}$$

---

[5] In general we write $\mathcal{E}_\pi\, f$ for the expected value of function $f: \mathcal{X} \rightarrow \mathbb{R}$ on distribution $\pi: \mathbb{D}X$.

which gives the relative increase in gain. Moreover the leakage measure exhibits an important robust approximation which will be relevant for privacy mechanisms in text processing.

Theorem 1. [4] *Let* $C: \mathcal{X} \to \mathcal{Y}$ *be a channel, and let* $u: \mathbb{D}\mathcal{X}$ *be the uniform prior over* $\mathcal{X}$. *Then for all priors* π *and non-negative gain functions* g *we have that:*

$$V_g[\pi \rangle C]/V_g[\pi] \quad \leq \quad V_{g_{bv}}[u \rangle C]/V_{g_{bv}}[u] \ .$$

A final theoretical idea which will be useful for our application to privacy is that of *security refinement*. If $C \sqsubseteq D$ (defined below) then D is more secure than C in any scenario, because D's posterior vulnerability relative to any gain function is always less than C's and therefore the information D releases is less useable than the information released by C.

Definition 4. *Let* $C: \mathcal{X} \to \mathcal{Y}^1$, *and* $D: \mathcal{X} \to \mathcal{Y}^2$ *be channels. We say that* $C \sqsubseteq D$ *if*

$$V_g[\pi \rangle C] \quad \geq \quad V_g[\pi \rangle D] \ ,$$

for all gain functions g *and priors* π.

We can use security refinement to express compositionality properties.

Theorem 2. [3,19] *Let* C, D, E *be channels and* $Z: \mathbb{D}(\mathcal{Z} \times \mathcal{Y})$ *be a correlation between secret types* $\mathcal{Z}$ *and* $\mathcal{X}$. *The following inequalities hold.*

1. $C \sqsubseteq D \quad \Rightarrow \quad C; E \sqsubseteq D; E$
2. $C \sqsubseteq D \quad \Rightarrow \quad Z \cdot C \sqsubseteq Z \cdot D$

3.2   Privacy Mechanisms as Channels

A privacy mechanism is normally modelled as a function $\mathcal{K}$ which, given a value x from a secret set $\mathcal{X}$, outputs some observable value $y: \mathcal{Y}$. The exact output could be determined by a probability distribution which, in an extreme instance such as redaction, could be a point distribution without any randomness applied.

Traditional approaches to privacy are founded on a principle we call "confusablity". Roughly speaking a mechanism imbues privacy by ensuring that the real value of the secret could be confused amongst several other values. In this section we examine confusability in terms of information flow to show how simple confusability mechanisms provide weak privacy.

3.3   Attacks on Simple Confusability

Traditional approaches to privacy in text programming use the idea of *k-anonymity* [25], which is related to confusability.

Definition 5. *A channel* $C \in \mathcal{X} \to \mathcal{Y}$ *is k-confusable if for each column* y *(observable), the entries* $C_{x,y}$ *are non-zero for at least* k *distinct values of* x.

Although k-confusable seems like a nice, straightforward property, it has some problems when combined with prior knowledge, and k-confusable mechanisms are susceptible to *intersection* and *linkage attacks*.

Intersection Attacks. A mechanism that is k-confusable separates the values of the secret into two subsets (for each observation): one for secret values that are still possible, and one for values which are not possible.

An *intersection* attack refers to the scenario where two different mechanisms are used, one after another. An adversary is able to combine the information flow from both mechanisms to deduce more about the value of the secret than he can from either mechanism separately. For example define two channels as follows. Let $\mathcal{X} := \{x_0, x_1, x_2, x_3\}$ and $\mathcal{Y} = \{y_0, y_1\}$.

$$C_{x_i, y_j} := (i = j \bmod 2) \tag{7}$$
$$D_{x_i, y_j} := 1 \text{ iff } (j = 0 \wedge i < 2) \vee (j = 1 \wedge i \geq 2). \tag{8}$$

Both C and D are 2-confusable since C divides the secret into two equivalence classes: $\{x_0, x_2\}$ and $\{x_1, x_3\}$, whereas D divides it into $\{x_0, x_1\}$ and $\{x_2, x_3\}$. Thus if only C or D is used then indeed the secret is somewhat private, but if both are used one after the other then the secret is revealed entirely, since the adversary can identify the secret by locating it simultaneously in an equivalence class of C and of D.

We can, model such a scenario by the sequential composition of the two mechanisms separately, i.e. the mechanism of an intersection attack is modelled by $C; D$. The susceptibility of k-confusable mechanisms to intersection attacks is summed up by a failure of compositionality for k-confusability.

Lemma 1. *k-confusability is not preserved by to sequential composition.*

Proof. We use the counterexample described above: C and D defined respectively at (7) and (8) are 2-confusable but $C; D$ is not 2-confusable.

Lemma 1 implies that mechanisms based on k-confusability are vulnerable to intersection attacks, a flaw that has been pointed out elsewhere [11].

Linkage Attacks. A *linkage attack* can be applied when the adversary has some prior knowledge about how some secret $\mathcal{Z}$ is correlated to another secret $\mathcal{X}$. When information leaks about $\mathcal{X}$ through a channel $C \colon \mathcal{X} \rightarrow \mathcal{Y}$ the adversary is able to deduce something about $\mathcal{Z}$. A simple example of this occurs when for example secret z has value z_0 exactly when x has value x_1 or x_2, and z has value z_1 otherwise. In this example z and x are *linked* through the correlation defined

$$Z_{z_i, x_j} := (i = j \bmod 2). \tag{9}$$

In this case, since the mechanism C defined above at (7) leaks whether x is in $\{x_0, x_2\}$ or $\{x_1, x_3\}$, this information put together with correlation Z leaks the value of z exactly. Even though C is 2-confusable.

Dalenius composition $Z \cdot C$ now models such linkage attacks, combining correlations with information flows to yield a mechanism describing the leaks about a correlated secrets. As for intersection attacks, we see that k-confusability fails compositionality with respect to Dalenius composition.

Lemma 2. *k-confusability is not preserved by Dalenius composition.*

Proof. We observe that C defined above at (7) is 2-confusable but that $Z \cdot C$ is not 2-confusable (for z), where Z is defined at (9).

Lemma 2 implies that privacy that relies on k-confusability is vulnerable to attacks that can use prior knowledge.

3.4   Universal Confusability

We can avoid intersection attacks and linkage attacks by strengthening k-confusability to "universal confusability".

Definition 6. *We say that a channel C is* universally confusable *if it is k-confusable for all $k \geq 1$.*

A channel is universally confusable if all its entries $C_{x,y}$ are non-zero. This means that for any posterior reasoning, the channel will maintain any extent of confusability that was already present in the prior. In fact universal confusability is (somewhat) robust against intersection and linkage attacks, because the strong confusability property is compositional with respect to sequential and Delanius composition. Universal confusability is particularly important for text processing because all kinds of unforeseen and unexpected correlations can be learned and used, even if they are too strange to understand.

3.5   Differential Privacy

We turn to the question of how to implement mechanisms that are universally confusable; the answer is given by *differential privacy*, which not surprisingly was defined to defend against linkage and intersection attacks.

The definition of an *ϵ-differentially private mechanism* is normally described as a function of type $\mathcal{X} \to \mathbb{D}\mathcal{Y}$, satisfying the following constraint. Let $dist: \mathcal{X} \times \mathcal{X} \to \mathbb{R}_{\geq 0}$ be a distance function, then for all $x, x' \in \mathcal{X}$ with $dist(x, x') \leq 1$, and properties α, we must have:

$$\mathcal{K}.x(\alpha)/\mathcal{K}.x'(\alpha) \quad \leq \quad e^{\epsilon}. \tag{10}$$

In fact, as has been pointed out by Alvim et al. [2] the mechanism $\mathcal{K}$ corresponds to a channel in $C^{\mathcal{K}}: \mathcal{X} \to \mathcal{Y}$ where the rows are defined by $C^{\mathcal{K}}_{x,y} := \mathcal{K}.x(Y = y)$. From (10) it is clear that $C^{\mathcal{K}}$ is strongly confusable because if any non-zero entry was present, the multiplicative constraint would fail to hold.

Moreover we can also obtain an upper bound for the scenario of an attacker trying to use the information leaked to guess the secret, in the sense that the following leakage bound holds [4]. For any prior π,

$$\begin{aligned} &\text{The probability of correctly guessing the secret after applying } \mathcal{K} \\ \leq \quad &V_{bv}[\pi \rangle C^{\mathcal{K}}] \\ \leq \quad &\text{Sum of the column maxima of } C^{\mathcal{K}} \times V_{bv}[\pi]. \end{aligned}$$

What this means is that even if the attacker uses machine learning to try to deduce properties about the original data, its ability to do so is constrained by this upper bound.

As an example, suppose there are three possible values a secret can take, drawn from x_a, x_b, x_c, each a distance 1 apart from eachother.[6] A differentially private mechanism $\mathcal{K}$ could release three possible results, say a, b, c, with corresponding channel:

$$C^{\mathcal{K}}_{x_i j} \quad = \quad 1/2 \quad \textit{if } i = j \text{ , else } 1/4.$$

Here $\mathcal{K}$ is $\log 2$-differentially private, since the maximum of $\mathcal{K}.x(\alpha)$ is at most $\max_{j, i' \in a, b, c} C^{\mathcal{K}}_{x_i j} / C^{\mathcal{K}}_{x_{i'} j} \leq \frac{1}{2} / \frac{1}{4} = 2$.

Unfortunately we cannot apply the original definition of differential privacy (10) to text documents because, unlike databases, texts are highly unstructured. Indeed the applicability of differential privacy to text documents has been dismissed [8, 23]. We propose instead to use a generalisation of differential privacy that can apply to unstructured domains, suggesting that we can after all find an obfuscation mechanism based on generalised differential privacy. The trick to generalising differential privacy is to use a general distance function as follows.

Definition 7. [6] *Let* $\mathcal{K} \colon \mathcal{X} \to \mathbb{D}\mathcal{Y}$, *and let* $dist \colon \mathcal{X} \times \mathcal{X} \to \mathbb{R}_{\geq 0}$ *be a distance function on* $\mathcal{X}$. *We say that* $\mathcal{K}$ *is* ϵ-differentially private *with respect to* $dist$ *if, for all properties* α, *we must have:*

$$\mathcal{K}.x(\alpha) / \mathcal{K}.x'(\alpha) \quad \leq \quad e^{\epsilon \times dist(x, x')}.$$

Definition 7 says that a mechanism imbues privacy by confusing the exact value of a secret x with other values x' with a level proportional to $dist(x, x')$. Thus if x, x' are "close" (as measured by $dist$) then it's quite likely that they could be confused, but if they are far apart, then they would be less likely, although still possibly, be confused.

Putting this together with the channel theorem above, means if we choose ϵ so that $e^{\epsilon \times d(x, x')}$ is as close to 1 as we can make it, then the chance of distinguishing x from x' becomes extremely small.

Even if we do no know the channel matrix exactly, we are still able to obtain a bound on the information leakage.

Theorem 3. *Let* $\mathcal{K}$ *be an* ϵ- *generalised differentially private mechanism wrt. metric* d. *Then for any gain function* g,

$$\mathcal{L}_g(C^{\mathcal{K}}) \quad \leq \quad e^{\epsilon \times d^*},$$

where $d^* := \max_{x, x' \in \mathcal{X}} d(x, x')$.

---

[6] These could, for example, correspond to different possible data values in a database.

3.6   Privacy Versus Utility

Information leakage on its own, in the case that it is large, implies that the probability of determining some property of the system will be high; if the upper bound is small, then it implies the mechanism does not leak very much information about anything. When we bring utility into the mix what we want is that the mechanism leaks a lot of information about a property which is not deemed sensitive, but keeps secret some other property that is deemed private. Not surprisingly there are constraints as to how much both requirements can be served simultaneously, however differential privacy can be used as a way to randomise whilst preserving some modicum of utility. We first use some notions from Quantitative Information flow to understand the trade-off between privacy and utility.

Let $\sim_A$ and $\sim_T$ represent two equivalence classes on a set of (secret) data $\mathcal{S}$. We want to release the equivalence class $\sim_T$ but keep $\sim_A$ private using some mechanism M. We can determine how successful we are by measuring the leakage with respect to the two equivalence classes, where we use a specialised version of vulnerability based on the scenario where an adversary tries to guess which equivalence class.

Definition 8. *M is ϵ-hiding wrt. $\sim_A$ if*

$$\mathcal{L}_{bv_{\sim_A}}(M) \leq 1 + \epsilon \ ,$$

where $bv_{\sim_A}$ is defined at (5) and leakage is defined at (6).

The maximum chance of an adversary guessing which equivalence class of $\sim_A$ the secret is for an ϵ-hiding mechanism is bounded above by $(1 + \epsilon) \times V_{bv_{\sim_A}}[\pi]$, giving a robust privacy guarantee on $\sim_A$.

Definition 9. *M is Δ-revealing wrt. $\sim_T$ if*

$$1 + \Delta \leq \mathcal{L}_{bv_{\sim_T}}(M) \ ,$$

where $bv_{\sim_T}$ is defined at (5) and leakage is defined at (6).

The best chance of an adversary guessing which equivalence class of $\sim_T$ the secret is for a Δ-revealing mechanism could therefore be *as much as* $(1+\Delta) \times V_{bv_{\sim_T}}[\pi]$.

Theorem 4. *If $M_1 \sqsubseteq M_2$ then the following applies:*

- *If M_1 is ϵ-hiding of $\sim_A$ then so is M_2*
- *If M_2 is Δ-revealing of $\sim_T$ then so is M_1*

Note that when data is provided to the user in a different representation, such as character n-grams, this is called "post-processing"; as noted elsewhere [4] post-processing is an instance of refinement, thus, as Theorem 4 indicates the action of transforming documents into either character n-grams or some other representation provides more privacy and less accuracy for utility.

Next we can look at some constraints between privacy and utility.

Theorem 5. *If* $\sim_A \subseteq \sim_T$ *and* M *is both* ϵ *hiding for* $\sim_A$ *and* Δ *revealing for* $\sim_T$ *(both under a uniform prior) then* $\Delta \leq \epsilon$.

Proof. Note that $\mathcal{L}_{bv_{\sim_T}}(M)$ is equal to $V_{\sim_T}[u\rangle M]/V_{\sim_T}[u]$. But this is bounded above by $N \times V_{\sim_A}[u\rangle M]/V_{\sim_T}[u]$, where N is the size of the maximum equivalence class of $\sim_T$. But now $V_{\sim_T}[u]$ is equal to $N/|\mathcal{S}|$, thus $leakage of bv_{\sim_T}(M)$ is bounded above by $N \times V_{\sim_A}[u\rangle M] \times |\mathcal{S}|$ which is equal to $\mathcal{L}_{bv_{\sim_A}}(M)$. The result now follows.

In particular if $\sim_A = \sim_T$ then revealing any of $\sim_T$ will reveal the same about $\sim_A$. In general if $\sim_A$ is finer than $\sim_T$ (as equivalence relations) revealing the equivalence class for $\sim_T$ almost exactly, already reveals quite a lot about the equivalence classes of $\sim_A$

Consider however the following example where there are four secret values: $\{a, b, c, d\}$. Suppose we have equivalence classes of $\sim_T$ are $\{\{a, b\}, \{c, d\}\}$ and for $\sim_T$ are $\{\{a, c\}, \{b, d\}\}$. The mechanism given by

$$M_{x,y} \quad := \quad 1 \; if \; \begin{pmatrix} x \in \{a, b\} \wedge y = 0 \\ \vee \; x \in \{c, d\} \wedge y = 1 \end{pmatrix} \quad else \; 0 \; .$$

has maximum leakage 2, and is 1-revealing wrt. $\sim_T$ and 0-revealing wrt. $\sim_A$; this means that the adversary has maximum chance of 1 of guessing $\sim_T$, but minimal chance of $1/2$ of guessing $\sim_A$.

This suggests that where $\sim_A$ represents equivalence classes over authors, and $\sim_T$ represents equivalence classes over topics, if enough different authors write on the same topic, there is a good chance of being able to disguise the writing style whilst remaining in the same topic.

4   Generalised Differential Privacy and Obfuscation

We can start to bring to bear the above observations to our simplified PAN obfuscation task. In particular we explore whether there are mechanisms whose properties can be understood from the perspective of generalised differential privacy. In our simplified version we imagine that we are already working with a bag-of-words (*BoW*) representation and our mechanism $\mathcal{K}$ will produce another (randomised) bag-of-words representation, i.e.

$$\mathcal{K} : BoW \rightarrow \mathbb{D}BoW.$$

Unlike our example above, we can no longer work with clear, a priori equivalence relations for authorship ($\sim_A$) and topic ($\sim_T$). Instead we use, as is done in machine learners, similarity relationships for categorising topics and identifying authors. For topicality we use a metric based on a learned distance between "Word2Vec word embeddings" and its lifting to documents via the "Earth Movers distance" [16], and for authorship we use the "Ruzicka metric". Both have been found experimentally to provide good results in author identification and topic classification.

Word2Vec [21] is a representation of words as a vector of values which, roughly speaking, captures relationships between words in terms of their meanings. Since this is a learned representation its accuracy depends very much on the quality of the documents. Remarkably the representation supports a metric[7] which captures similarity in meaning between words. For example Word2Vec embeddings put "queen" and "monarch" close together, but "monarch" and "engineer" far apart. Using the distance between words defined on Word2Vec representations as a base, the Earth Mover's distance can then be defined to compare documents for topicality. An example is given at Fig. 1.

Definition 10. *Let d, d' be documents represented as bags of words. Define $|d - d'|_T$ to be the word mover's distance between the movement based on the distance between Word2Vec word embeddings.*

Informally, given two documents d, d' represented as bags of words, we let R be a "move relation" so that $R_{w,w'} \in [0, 1]$ represents the proportion of $w \in d$ that corresponds to $w' \in d'$. R is set up so that for each $w' \in d'$, we have $\sum_{w \in d} R_{w,w'} = 1$, and for each $w \in d$, we have $\sum_{w \in d} R_{w',w} = 1$. The cost of the move is given by $\sum_{w,w'} R_{w,w'} \times dist(w, w')$, and the word mover's distance is then the minimum over all such move relations.

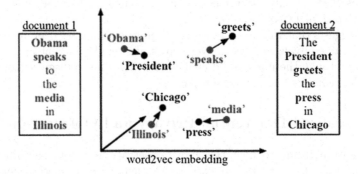

Fig. 1. Depiction of a move relation defining the Word Mover distance [16]

Definition 11. *Let d, d' be documents and d_T be its representation as a a character n-gram vector. In this representation, the vector is composed of discovered "features" which are experimentally found to be good for grouping similar writing styles together. With this in place, we define $|d - d'|_A := (1 - \frac{\sum_i \min |d_i - d'_i|}{\sum_j \max |d_j - d'_j|})$.*

---

[7] There are several ways to define distance between word embeddings, but "cosine similarity" seems to be a popular one; this isn't a metric, but can be used to define one.

Documents close in the $|\cdot|_A$ metric are likely to be authored by the same author. To obtain a mechanism $\mathcal{K}$ which has a privacy guarantee on obfuscation, we would have the following:

$$\mathcal{K}(d)(\alpha)/\mathcal{K}(d')(\alpha) \ \leq \ e^{\epsilon \times dist(d,d')},$$

for *dist* an appropriate metric. Since this has the form of a differentially private mechanism it would be somewhat resistant to linkage and intersection attacks. Similar to Theorem 3, among distances no more than some fixed K, and $\epsilon \approx 1/10K$ then the right-hand side shows that the entries in each column of the channel for those documents are approximately 1.1, thus suggesting that all such documents would be confused with eachother.

It can also be shown [20] that using the Laplace distribution combined with a given metric *dist* it is possible to define a mechanism M so that the output remains close to the input x with high probability (proportional to ϵ) when measured using *dist*.

4.1   Experiments

Using the above observations as a guide, we designed a simple mechanism using *BoW* representations based on Definition 10 designed therefore to preserve topicality. The idea is to use an underlying Laplace mechanism combined with the Word2Vec distance independently applied to each word in the input bag of words.

Next we tested the results, both for privacy and for topicality; our hypothesis was that randomising directly on words would mean that the character n-gram representation would be changed sufficiently to hide stylistic traits. Moreover,

Dataset	Accuracy	Obfuscation Accuracy		
Reuters	Baseline	Scale=0.1	Scale=0.2	Scale=0.5
Raw	71.1	-	-	-
Content-Words	68.5	67.9	67.9	41.7
BOW-1000	65.9	62.1	63.5	41.9
BOW-500	64.1	61.7	62.1	40.9
BOW-200	47.9	46.9	48.5	27.1
BOW-50	23.9	20.0	19.0	6.2
Fan fiction	Baseline	Scale=0.1	Scale=0.2	Scale=0.5
Raw	70.6	-	-	-
Content-Words	67.7	67.7	67.6	4.9
BOW-1000	48.0	35.3	40.2	2.0
BOW-500	46.1	34.3	34.3	5.9
BOW-200	36.3	19.6	18.6	8.8
BOW-50	13.7	4.9	4.9	1.0

Fig. 2. Results for authorship attribution over the various unobfuscated and obfuscated test sets. Uniformly randomly assigning authorship would have an accuracy of 1% over 100 possible authors for the Fan fiction dataset, and 5% over 20 authors for the Reuters dataset.

Dataset	Accuracy	Obfuscation Accuracy		
Reuters	Baseline	Scale=0.1	Scale=0.2	Scale=0.5
Raw	81.4	-	-	-
Content-Words	81.4	81.6	81.0	71.9
BOW-1000	80.4	80.8	80.8	75.2
BOW-500	79.2	79.4	79.4	70.7
BOW-200	76.0	76.0	76.0	66.7
BOW-50	66.3	67.9	68.1	61.7
Fan fiction	Baseline	Scale=0.1	Scale=0.2	Scale=0.5
Raw	82.4	-	-	-
Content-Words	83.3	79.4	79.4	54.9
BOW-1000	83.3	77.5	76.5	57.8
BOW-500	81.4	80.4	81.4	63.7
BOW-200	79.4	71.6	71.6	53.9
BOW-50	60.8	49.0	49.0	46.1

Fig. 3. Results for topic classification over the various unobfuscated and obfuscated test sets. Classification accuracy is significantly lower for scale = 0.5, which corresponds to more obfuscation. However, accuracy is still well above the 'random' baseline of 20%.

our theoretical approach shows only that where documents close in topicality can be confused, so therefore can their authors. Authors that are only known for their work on a single topic cannot be confused with authors who write on entirely different subjects.

To test the results we needed large collections of documents written by different authors, and representing a number of different topics. We were able to use one standard dataset from the Natural Language Processing (NLP) literature; a second data set was constructed by us.

1. The Reuters RCV1 dataset is a standard dataset used in language processing tasks, and consists of over 800,000 Reuters news articles separated into various topics [17]. Although not originally constructed for author attribution work, it has been used previously in this domain by making use of the <byline> tags inside articles which designate article authors [22]. The dataset was chosen because it contains documents of reasonable length, which is required for successful author identification. In addition, this dataset is similar to the dataset on which the Word2Vec vectors used in this experiment were trained on, and thus we would expect high quality outputs when using Word2Vec with this data.

2. Our second data set consisted of "Fan fiction" samples[8]. This data set therefore consists of stories collected over the 5 most popular book-based topics. Fan fiction has been used previously in PAN author attribution tasks, and is suitable for this task because of the content length of the texts and the diversity of authorship styles present in these texts, as stylistic writing qualities are important in this domain.

---

[8] https://www.fanfiction.net.

For each of the documents in the data sets we used our obfuscation mechanism described above to a bag of words representation. We then used appropriate machine learners to try to categorise the results by author and (separately) by topic. In each case we applied the same machine learning techniques to the original (bag of words representations) of the documents to provide a baseline with which to compare.

In Fig. 2 we can see the result of obfuscation: with increasing randomness (as measured by Scale) the ability to identify the author becomes harder, as compared to the Baseline (i.e. unobfuscated documents). This is compared to Fig. 3 which we can see preserves the topicality very well — which is to be expected because of the use of the Laplace mechanism based on Word2Vec.

5 Conclusions and Future Work

This paper has brought two conceptual ideas together to provide some foundations for privacy mechanisms in text document processing. We used generalised differential privacy based on metrics used in machine learning as a way to create a mechanism, and noted how to understand the privacy that it provides in terms of generalised differential privacy cast in terms of channels for quantitative information flow.

We also observed experimentally that the mechanism seems to preserve topicality well, whilst achieving good privacy. We note here that although we have not provided a mechanism that produces human-readable documents, the mechanism still maintains a variety of words, which fits with the spirit of the PAN obfuscation task.

There is, of course, a long way to go before we have a true summarisation mechanism that is private; with this foundation we have the tools to understand the extent of privacy in future obfuscation mechanisms as they become available.

While the approach outlined in this paper used a simple Word2Vec embedding substitution mechanism over a bag of words representation, there is very promising recent work that uses deep learning to generate paraphrased text, taking text as input. For instance, [12] gives a method for producing syntactically controlled adversarial paraphrases for text: paraphrases that have the goal of confounding a machine learner, which in our context would be an inference attacker; an alternative approach based on generative adversarial networks is described by [27]. Incorporating a DP mechanism, along the lines of the one presented in this paper, is one possible avenue to solving the original obfuscation problem presented in Sect. 2.

References

1. Abadi, M., Chu, A., Goodfello, I., McMahan, H.B., Mironov, I., Talwar, K., Zhang, L.: Deep learning with differential privacy. In: Proceedings of the 2016 ACM SIGSAC Conference on Computer and Communication Security (CCS 2016), pp. 303–318, Vienna, Austria, 24–28 October (2016)

2. Alvim, M.S., Chatzikokolakis, K., Degano, P., Palamidessi, C.: Differential privacy versus quantitative information flow. CoRR, abs/1012.4250 (2010)
3. Alvim, M.S., Chatzikokolakis, K., McIver, A., Morgan, C., Palamidessi, C., Smith, G.: Additive and multiplicative notions of leakage, and their capacities. In: IEEE 27th Computer Security Foundations Symposium, CSF 2014, Vienna, Austria, 19–22 July, 2014, pp. 308–322. IEEE (2014)
4. Alvim, M.S., Chatzikokolakis, K., Palamidessi, C., Smith, G.: Measuring information leakage using generalized gain functions. In: Proceedings of the 25th IEEE Computer Security Foundations Symposium (CSF 2012), pp. 265–279, June 2012
5. Alvim, M.S., Scedrov, A., Schneider, F.B.: When notall bits are equal: Worth-based information flow. In: Proceedings of the 3rd Conference on Principles of Security and Trust (POST 2014), pp. 120–139 (2014)
6. Chatzikokolakis, K., Andrés, M.E., Bordenabe, N.E., Palamidessi, C.: Broadening the scope of differential privacy using metrics. In: De Cristofaro, E., Wright, M. (eds.) PETS 2013. LNCS, vol. 7981, pp. 82–102. Springer, Heidelberg (2013). https://doi.org/10.1007/978-3-642-39077-7_5
7. Chaudhuri, K., Monteleoni, C., Sarwate, A.D.: Differentially private empirical risk minimization. J. Mach. Learn. Res. **12**, 1069–1109 (2011)
8. Cumby, C., Ghani, R.: A machine learning based system for semi-automatically redacting documents. In: Proceedings of the Twenty-Third Conference on Innovative Applications of Artificial Intelligence (IAAI) (2011)
9. Dalenius, T.: Towards a methodology for statistical disclosure control. Statistik Tidskrift **15**, 429–44 (1977)
10. Dwork, C., Roth, A.: The algorithmic foundations of differential privacy. Found. Trends Theor. Comput. Sci. **9**(3–4), 211–407 (2014)
11. Ganta, S.R., Kasiviswanathan, S.P., Smith, A.: Composition attacks and auxiliary information in data privacy. In: Proceedings of the 14th ACM SIGKDD International Conference on Knowledge Discovery and Data Mining, pp. 265–273. ACM (2008)
12. Iyyer, M., Wieting, J., Gimpel, K., Zettlemoyer, L.: Adversarial example generation with syntactically controlled paraphrase networks. In: North American Association for Computational Linguistics (to appear, 2018)
13. Khonji, M., Iraqi, Y.: A Slightly-modified GI-based Author-verifier with Lots of Features (ASGALF). In: Working Notes for CLEF 2014 Conference (2014)
14. Koppel, M., Schler, J., Argamon, S.: Computational methods in authorship attribution. JASIST **60**(1), 9–26 (2009)
15. Koppel, M., Schler, J., Argamon, S.: Authorship attribution in the wild. Lang. Resour. Eval. **45**(1), 83–94 (2011)
16. Kusner, M.J., Sun, Y., Kolkin, N.I., Weinberger, K.Q.: From word embeddings to document distances. In: Proceedings of the 32nd International Conference on Machine Learning, pp. 957–966 (2015)
17. Lewis, D.D., Yang, Y., Rose, T.G., Li, F.: RCV1: a new benchmark collection for text categorization research. J. Mach. Learn. Res. **5**, 361–397 (2004)
18. Manning, C.D., Schütze, H.: Foundations of Statistical Natural Language Processing. MIT Press, Cambridge, MA, USA (1999)
19. McIver, A., Meinicke, L., Morgan, C.: Compositional closure for bayes risk in probabilistic noninterference. In: Abramsky, S., Gavoille, C., Kirchner, C., Meyer auf der Heide, F., Spirakis, P.G. (eds.) ICALP 2010. LNCS, vol. 6199, pp. 223–235. Springer, Heidelberg (2010). https://doi.org/10.1007/978-3-642-14162-1_19

20. McSherry, F., Talwar, K.: Mechanism design via differential privacy. In: Proceedings of the 48th Annual IEEE Symposium on Foundations of Computer Science (FOCS), pp. 94–103. IEEE (2007)
21. Mikolov, T., Sutskever, I., Chen, K., Corrado, G.S., Dean, J.: Distributed representations of words and phrases and their compositionality. In: Burges, C.J.C., Bottou, L., Welling, M., Ghahramani, Z., Weinberger, K.Q. (eds.) Advances in Neural Information Processing Systems, vol. 26, pp. 3111–3119. Curran Associates Inc. (2013)
22. Mosteller, F., Wallace, D.L.: Inference in an authorship problem: a comparative study of discrimination methods applied to the authorship of the disputed federalist papers. J. Am. Stat. Assoc. **58**(302), 275–309 (1963)
23. Sánchez, D., Batet, M.: C-sanitized: a privacy model for document redaction and sanitization. J. Assoc. Inf. Sci. Technol. **67**(1), 148–163 (2016)
24. Seidman, S.: Authorship Verification Using the Imposters Method. In: Working Notes for CLEF 2013 Conference (2013)
25. Sweeney, L.: k-anonymity: a model for protecting privacy. Int. J. Uncertainty, Fuzziness Knowl. Based Syst. **10**(5), 557–570 (2002)
26. Young, T., Hazarika, D., Poria, S., Cambria, E.: Recent trends in deep learning based natural language processing. CoRR, abs/1708.02709 (2017)
27. Zhao, Z., Dua, D., Singh, S.: Generating natural adversarial examples. In: International Conference on Learning Representations (2018)

20 Years of *Real* Real Time Model Validation

Kim Guldstrand Larsen(✉), Florian Lorber, and Brian Nielsen

Department of Computer Science, Aalborg University, Aalborg, Denmark
{kgl,florber,bnielsen}@cs.aau.dk

Abstract. In this paper we review 20 years of significant industrial application of the UPPAAL Tool Suite for model-based validation, performance evaluation and synthesis. The paper will highlight a number of selected cases, and discuss successes and pitfalls in achieving industrial impact as well as tool sustainability in an academic setting.

1 Introduction

In 1995 the first release of the real-time verification tool UPPAAL [43] was presented – together with a number of other emerging tools such as HyTeCH and Kronos – at the very first TACAS conference [15]. Soon after the tool was used for off-line verification of a number of *real* (i.e. industrially used) protocols, where real-time aspects were of essence. Today, in 2018, the most recent branches of UPPAAL are applied for on-line optimization of home automation and traffic control systems. In this short note, we aim to recall some of the success stories of UPPAAL over the years in terms of industrial applications, discuss what it takes to achieve lasting industrial take-up as well as reflect on the influence on the development of the tool from industrial feedback.

An overview of the most important case studies which will be discussed whithin this paper can be found in Fig. 1.

The remainder of the paper will be structured as follows: first, in Sect. 2, we will give an overview of the UPPAAL tool family. Then, in Sect. 3 we will present our major use cases in the context of verification. Afterwards, in Sect. 4, we present our case studies in the area of testing and in Sect. 5 we will present cases in which we used UPPAAL for scheduling and controller synthesis. Finally, in Sect. 6, we will present the most important lessons we learned while working on the presented case studies.

2 The UPPAAL Tool Suite

This section will give an overview over the UPPAAL tool family, its components and their main purposes.

Work supported by Innovation Center DiCyPS, DFF project ASAP, and the ERC Advanced Grant Project Lasso.

© Springer International Publishing AG, part of Springer Nature 2018
K. Havelund et al. (Eds.): FM 2018, LNCS 10951, pp. 22–36, 2018.
https://doi.org/10.1007/978-3-319-95582-7_2

Usecase	Tool	Goal	Partners	Outcome
PACP	UPPAAL	Verification	Philips	Significant tool improvement
BRP	UPPAAL	Verification	Philips, Twente University	Protocol verified
BOP	UPPAAL	Verification	Bang & Olufsen	Bug found and corrected
BOPC	UPPAAL	Verification	Bang & Olufsen	Frequency limits identified
FR	UPPAAL	Verification	FlexRay Consortium	Improved fault-tolerance guarantees
FW	UPPAAL	Verification	Radboud University	Sound timing restrictions identified
GC	UPPAAL	Verification	MECEL, Uppsala University	Several requirements verified
HPS	UPPAAL	Verification	Herchel & Planck	Schedulability of task-set established
NMN	UPPAAL	Verification	Neocortec	Energy performance of protocol
D	UPPAAL TRON	Testing	Danfoss	Demonstration of feasibility of online testing
NN	UPPAAL YGGDRASIL UPPAAL CORA	Testing	Novo Nordic	Two times industrial takeup
G	UPPAAL YGGDRASIL	Modelling, Testing	Grundfos	Interest provoked - new collaboration
S	UPPAAL TIGA	Controller Synthesis	Skov	Synthesis of zone-based controller
H	UPPAAL TIGA	Controller Synthesis	Hydac, ULB, ENS Cachan	Improved controller
BPNS	UPPAAL STRATEGO	Scheduling	GomSpace	Battery life improvement of a satellite
HA	UPPAAL STRATEGO	Controller Synthesis	Seluxit	Intelligent floor heating
ICTL	UPPAAL STRATEGO	Controller Synthesis	Municipality of Køge	Efficient traffic controller

Fig. 1. Industrial use cases using UPPAAL.

UPPAAL. The underlying formalism of UPPAAL is that of timed automata with the tool providing support for model checking of hard real-time properties. Since the introduction of the tool in 1995, significant effort have been put into development and implementation of improved datastructures and algorithms for the analysis of timed automata. Besides the several advances with respect to the verification engine, significant effort has over the years been put on the graphical interface of the tool (e.g. [8]), and on the modelling side the introduction of user-defined, structured datatypes and procedures has undoubtedly made the tool significantly more usable in modeling real control programs and communication protocols [7].

UPPAAL CORA. Motivated by the need for addressing (optimal) usage of resources, priced timed automata were introduced in 2001. [4,9] (independently) demonstrated decidability of cost-optimal reachability. Soon after, an efficient priced extension of the symbolic datastructures used in UPPAAL was implemented in the branch UPPAAL CORA. Combined with a symbolic A* algorithm UPPAAL CORA turned into a new generic tool for cost-optimal planning which was competitive to traditional OR methods such as Mixed-Integer Linear Programming [39].

UPPAAL TRON. In 2004 the branch UPPAAL TRON was introduced offering the possibility of performing on-line conformance testing of *realistic* real-time systems with respect to timed input-output automata [41,45]. UPPAAL TRON implements a sound and (theoretically) complete randomized testing algorithm, and uses a formally defined notion of correctness to assign verdicts: i.e. relativized timed input/output conformance providing a timed extension of Jan Tretmans ioco [52]. Using online testing, events are generated and simultaneously executed on the system under test.

UPPAAL YGGDRASIL. is an off-line test case generator integrated into the main UPPAAL component. It aims at creating a test suite for edge coverage in a three phase process, which includes testing according to user-specified test purposes, random testing, and afterwards reachability analysis towards uncovered transitions. The tool enables the user to associate test code with transitions and locations, which is integrated into the test case whenever a trace traverses them. This enables UPPAAL YGGDRASIL to create test scripts in any desired language, which can be executed directly by the chosen execution engine.

UPPAAL TIGA. In 2005 - encouraged by suggestions from Tom Henzinger – the branch UPPAAL TIGA was released, allowing for control strategies to be synthesized from timed games, i.e. two-player games played on timed automata [6,16]. The branch implements an efficient symbolic on-the-fly algorithm for synthesizing winning strategies for reachability, safety as well as Büchi objectives and taking possible partial observability into account [17]. The branch marks a disruptive direction with respect to development of control programs for embedded systems: rather than manually developing the control program with subsequent model checking (and correction), UPPAAL TIGA provides a fully automatic method for deriving a correct-by-construction control program.

ECDAR. In 2010 the branch ECDAR was introduced supporting a scalable methodology for compositional development and stepwise refinenemet of real-time systems [29,30]. The underlying specification theory is that of timed I/O automata being essentially timed games (with inputs being controllable, and outputs being uncontrollable) equipped with suitable methods for refinement checking (in terms of an alternating simulation between two timed game specifications), consistency checking, logical as well as structural composition. For a full account of ECDAR we refer the reader to the tutorial [28].

UPPAAL SMC. One of the most recent branches of the UPPAAL tool suite – UPPAAL SMC introduced in 2011 – allows for performance evaluation on the expressive formalisms of stochastic hybrid automata and games [26,27], and has by now been widely applied to analysis of a variety of case studies ranging from biological examples [25], schedulability for mixed-critical systems [14,22], evaluation of controllers for energy-aware buildings [19], social-technical attacks in security [31], as well as performance evaluation of a variety of wireless communication protocols [53,53]. For a full account of UPPAAL SMC we refer the reader to the recent tutorial [24].

UPPAAL STRATEGO. from 2014 [20,21] is the most recent branch of the UPPAAL tool suite that allows to generate, optimize, compare and explore consequences and performance of strategies synthesized for stochastic priced timed games (SPTG) in a user-friendly manner. In particular, UPPAAL STRATEGO comes with an extended query language, where strategies are first class objects that may be constructed, compared, optimized and used when performing (statistical) model checking of a game under the constraints of a given synthesized strategy.

3   Verification

The early development of UPPAAL was highly driven by colleagues in the Netherlands using the tool for automatic verification of industrial protocols. During a time-span of only a few years this resulted in a huge performance improvement reducing both time- and space-consumption with over 99%.

Philips Audio Control Protocol (PACP). Before the release of UPPAALBosscher, Polak and Vaandrager had in 1994 modelled and verified a protocol developed by Philips for the physical layer of an interface bus that connects the various devices of some stereo equipment (tuner, CD player,...). Essentially – after a suitable translation – the model of the protocol is a timed automata. Whereas the first proof in [13] was manual, the first automated verification of the protocol was done using the tool HyTech. Later, automated – and much faster – verifications were obtained using UPPAAL and Kronos. However, all these proofs were based on a simplification on the protocol, introduced by Bosscher et. al. in 1994, that only one sender is transmitting on the bus so that no bus collisions can occur. In many applications the bus will have more than one sender, and the full version of the protocol by Philips therefore handles bus collisions. Already in the autumn of 1995 an automatic analysis of a version of the Philips Audio Control Protocol with two senders and bus collision handling was achieved using UPPAAL 0.96. To make the analysis feasible a notion of *committed location* was introduced (to remove unnecessary interleavings) and the analysis was carried out on a super computer, a SGI ONYX machine [11]. The total verification time was 8.82 hrs using more 527.4 MB. It is interesting to note that using UPPAAL 3.2 the same verification was reduced to only 0.5 sec using 2.5 MB of memory. In any case, the success in 1996 was a true milestone in the development of UPPAAL as this version of the protocol was orders of magnitude larger than the previously considered version with only one sender, e.g. the discrete state-spaces was 10^3 times larger and the number of clocks and channels in the model was also increased considerably.

Bounded Retransmission Protocol (BRP). In parallel with the collaboration with the group of Vaandrager, a group from Twente University (D'Argenio, Katoen, Reus and Tretmans) was also applying – and seriously testing – the first versions of UPPAAL. In particular, they successfully modelled and verified the Bounded Retransmission Protocol, a variant of the alternating bit protocol introduced by Philips. In [18] it is investigated to what extent real-time aspects are important to guarantee the protocol's correctness using UPPAAL and the Spin model checker.

B&O Protocol (BOP). In 1996, we were ourselves approached by Bang & Olufsen with a request of "analysing their proprietary IR Link protocol". The protocol, about 2800 lines of assembler code, was used in products from the audio/video company Bang&Olufsen throughout more than a decade, and its purpose was to control the transmission of messages between audio/video components over a single bus. Such communications may collide, and one essential purpose of the protocol was to detect such collisions. The functioning was highly dependent on real-time considerations. Though the protocol was known to be faulty (in the sense that messages were lost occasionally), the protocol was too complicated in order for the company to locate the bug using normal testing. However - after 4–5 iterations refining the model of the protocol - an error trace was automatically generated using UPPAAL and confirmed in the actual implementation of the protocol. Moreover, the error was corrected and the correction was automatically proven correct, again using UPPAAL [36].

B&O Powerdown control (BOPC). [35] Our first collaboration with Bang & Olufsen was very much characterized as a reverse engineering exercise of an existing protocol: the only documentation of the protocol was the 2800 lines of assembler code together with 3 flow-charts and a (very) knowledgeable B&O engineer. In our second collaboration with the company, modelling and verification in UPPAAL was carried out in parallel with the actual implementation of a new real-time system for power-down control in audio/video components. During modeling 3 design errors were identified and corrected, and the following verification confirmed the validity of the design but also revealed the necessity for an upper limit of the interrupt frequency. The resulting design was later (seamlessley) implemented and incorporated as part of a new product line.

Whereas the above collaborative projects with B&O were very successful, neither UPPAAL nor model-driven development were taken-up in the company. An obvious reason could the immaturity (and lack of GUI) of the tool back then. However, in retrospect, an other equally likely reason is the fact that we were spending (all) our effort in collaborating with technicians in the company and not on marketing our tool and "disruptive" methodology to decision-makers in the company.

Flexray (FR). As part of the German DFG project AVACS[1] the FlexRay protocol was modeled and verified using UPPAAL. Flexray is a standard, developed by a cooperation of leading companies in the automotive industry, as a robust communication protocol for distributed components in modern vehicles. Developed by the FlexRay Consortium, a cooperation of leading companies including BMW, Bosch, Daimler, Freescale, General Motors, NXP Semiconductors, and Volkswagen, FlexRay was first employed in 2006 in the pneumatic damping system of BMW's X5, and fully utilized in 2008 in the BMW 7 Series. The FlexRay specification was completed in 2009 and is widely expected to become the future standard for the automotive industry. In [34] a timed automata model of its physical layer protocol is presented, and UPPAAL is used to automatically prove fault tolerance under several error models and hardware assumptions. In particular, it is shown that the communication system meets, and in fact exceeds, the fault-tolerance guarantees claimed in the FlexRay specification.

Firewire (FW). The IEEE 1394–1995 serial bus standard defines an architecture that allows several components to communicate at very high speed. Originally, the architecture was designed by Apple (FireWire), with more than 70 companies having been involved in the standardisation effort. In [50] a timed automata model of the leader election protocol is presented and its correctness is established using UPPAAL. In particular, it is shown that under certain timing restrictions the protocol behaves correctly. The timing parameters in the IEEE 1394 standard documentation obey the restrictions found in this proof.

MECEL Gear Controller (GC). In [44] an application of UPPAAL to the modelling and verification of a prototype gear controller was developed in a joint project between industry and academia. In particular, the project was carried out in collaboration between Mecel AB and Uppsala University. Within the project, the (timely) correctness of the controller was formalized (and verified) in 47 logical formulas according to the informal requirements delivered by industry.

Herchel & Planck Schedulatilibity (HPS). In the danish project DaNES, we collaborated with the company Terma on using timed automata model checking as a more exact method for establishing schedulability of a number of periodic tasks executing on a single CPU under a given scheduling policy. In particular a fixed priority preemptive scheduler was used in a combination with two resource sharing protocols, and in addition voluntary task suspension was considered.

---

[1] http://www.avacs.org.

In [46] schedulability was established under the assumption of exact computation times of the tasks. In [23] non-deterministic computations times were considered; depending on the size of the computation time interval, schedulability
was either verified (using UPPAAL) or refuted (using the concrete search engine
of UPPAAL SMC).

4 Testing

Our research on model-based test generation for timed (event recording)
automata started with the thesis work around 1996–2000 in [47]. The approach
aimed at covering timed equivalence classes defined through the clock guards
of the timed automata. It assumed strictly deterministic systems, and its scalability was limited by the analysis techniques of the time. It thus had limited
industrial applicability [48,49].

Later (2002–2004), inspired by [32,52], we developed the online testing tool
UPPAAL TRON [3]. This approach could effectively handle non-determinism in
both the specification (due to abstraction) and system under test (due to uncertainties in scheduling, execution times, timing, etc.), scaled to large models, and
provided response times low enough for many practical cases [5,42,51]. Online
testing generates effective randomized long tests, but coverage must be evaluated post-mortem and cannot be guaranteed a priori. Moreover, it is difficult to
repeat the precise same test and inspect the set of test cases (might be required
by certification bodies).

Our first work on offline test-case generation (with Uppsala University) appeared [37] in 2003. Here we showed how to interpret witness traces generated by
the UPPAAL model-checker as test cases for the sub-class deterministic output
urgent timed automata. Specifically, we showed how to generate the test cases
with the minimum duration that satisfied a given test purpose formulated as
a reachability property by exploiting UPPAAL's fastest witness trace generation
feature. We furthermore formulated coverage as a reachability question, giving
the ability to generate (time optimal) tests that guarantee meeting common
coverage criteria. This work led to the UPPAAL COVER tool (no longer developed)
and UPPAAL YGGDRASIL.

The Danfoss Case (D). We applied and evaluated UPPAAL TRON on an embedded controller supplied by the company Danfoss' Refrigeration Controls Division
around year 2003–2004 [42]. The target device was a stable product of a refrigerator controller for industrial and large supermarket installations. As computer
scientists we did not have domain expertise, and it soon became clear that the
supplied documentation (high-level requirements and user manuals) was insufficient for us to build accurate models. Hence, we ended up formulating a hypothesis model, running the test, and refining the model when the test failed. The
final model consisted of 18 concurrent components (timed automata), 14 clock
variables, and 14 discrete integer variables, and was thus quite large for the time.
When confronting the refined model with Danfoss engineers, they too were surprised about certain aspects of its behavior, and needed to have that confirmed

by other developers. Although we found no confirmed defects, the case showed that our techniques were practically applicable, and effective in finding discrepancies between specified and observed behavior. Encouraged by these results, both parties continued the collaboration on automated testing. At the end, our testing approach was not included in their new test setup that emphasized a new test harness for automated execution of manually defined scripts. Retrospectively, the gap between our method and their established development processes and tools was too big.

The Novo Nordic Case (NN). The first version of UPPAAL YGGDRASIL was developed in 2007–2009 specifically to support a collaboration with Novo Nordic for model-based GUI testing for medical devices. This version used UPPAAL CORA as back-end, and operated in a 3 step process inspired by the company's needs: (1) Generating a separate test sequence for each user defined (supposedly critical) test purpose, (2) using UPPAAL's search heuristics for optimizing model (edge) coverage considering constraints on the maximum lengths of the test cases, and (3) generating targeted test cases for each of the remaining uncovered transitions. The actual test case code was generated from model-annotations that the test engineers added to the model issuing appropriate GUI commands and assertions. Initially, the models were made using UML state-charts (and then translated into the UPPAAL syntax) due to the engineers familiarity with this notation. It is important to remark that the engineers had no prior experience with formal modelling, and models were made for illustrative purposes using Microsoft Visio. Even then, making models that now had a tangible and formal meaning required a substantial training period. First the models were jointly developed assisted by the tool developer, and later only by company engineers with ordinary support.

This approach reduced the time used on test construction from upwards of 30 days to 3 days spent modelling and then a few minutes on actual test generation. At the same time, coverage was easier to establish than in the manual approach, and script maintenance greatly reduced. Later again, the company started using the UPPAAL-editor directly, circumventing a heavy (and costly) UML tool. The approach was thus successfully embedded within the company. Unfortunately, that development team was dissolved as part of a company restructuring a year later, and the competence was no longer used.

MBAT. Since the original UPPAAL YGGDRASIL was tailormade for this collaboration, and since it used the UPPAAL CORA engine that is also no longer being developed, it ended up in a non-usable state. Recently, as part of the EU Artemis MBAT (Combined Model-based Testing and Analysis) project, we re-architected the tool, and integrated it into — and shipped with — the main branch of UPPAAL, such that it now (1) uses the normal search engine, and (2) uses the graphical editor to create the needed annotations, and (3) provides a GUI widget for creating the test case configurations.

UPPAAL YGGDRASIL was applied to a case-study [38], and evaluated positively by a few consortium member companies. However, the collaboration did not result in commercial exploitation, partly because the project came to an end, and partly because we did not have an established company that could sell the licenses, and required maintenance, training, and consultancy.

MBAT also facilitated further developments for tool interoperability that is seen as crucial for large companies owning hundreds of various software development tools. That included prototyping of Open Services for Lifecycle Collaboration (OSLC)[2] adaptors for UPPAAL, and prototyping of Functional Mock-up Interfaces (FMI)[3] co-simulation interfaces. So it is regretful that this source of funding for Artemis/ECSEL industrial collaboration at a European scale ceased, as the Danish government halted national co-funding.

Grundfos (G). Grundfos is a major Danish company and world renowned for its pump products. In a recent meeting in the context of the DiCyPS project[4], we discussed different possible topics for further evaluation, including model-based testing. Based on our positive experiences with Danfoss (whose refrigerator controllers at an abstract level are similar to Grundfos pump controllers) we presented all the benefits/strengths of online model-based tested. However, it was when we presented offline testing that their interest was really triggered. They in particular liked our idea of modelling each of their requirements, using this (combined) model to automatically generate test scripts, and executing these on their existing test harness. Hence, there is a strong fit with their existing testing process and equipment. Also they believed that the (formalized) requirement models could be a valuable documentation complementing the existing design documentation. Hence, we decided to focus the collaboration on this approach, and postpone online testing.

In the first phase, we (university/tool provider/academics) perform the modelling and test case generation in order to prepare the tool and evaluate the method, for this particular case. We have identified an interesting, non-trivial subsystem of a newly developed pump controller exhibiting core functionality. If this stage is successful we plan to train selected Grundfos engineers and evaluate their experiences. Since the collaboration is ongoing, we cannot report on the outcome here.

5   Planning, Scheduling and Synthesis

Within its newer branches, the UPPAAL tool suite allows for the usage of prices and stochastic elements, in order to enable various features, such as cost-optimal reachability, optimal scheduling or synthesis of strategies. The first practical step in this direction was made in 2002, with the initial release of UPPAAL CORA. UPPAAL CORA was developed as part of the VHS and AMETIST projects, and uses *linear priced timed auomata* (LPTA) for reachability problems, searching for paths with the lowest accumulated costs. The idea behind UPPAAL STRATEGO

---

[2] https://open-services.net.

[3] http://fmi-standard.org.

[4] National Innovation Fund supported project on Data-Intensive Cyber-Physical Systems.

came up in the CASSTING project. It was released in 2014, and facilitates the generation, optimization, comparison as well as consequence and performance exploration of strategies for *stochastic priced timed games* (SPTGs) in a user-friendly manner. The tools were since applied in several case studies, such as optimal planning of missions for battery-powered nano-satellites [12], efficient heating in home automation [40] or traffic light scheduling [33]. Below we will give an overview of the three mentioned case studies.

Battery-Powered Nano-Satellites (BPNS). This case study focused on the battery consumption of a GOMX-3 satellite built by the company GomSpace. It contains several antennas, solar panels and a battery. Depending on the scheduling of the different tasks of the satellite, the deterioration of the battery may vary significantly, depending on, for instance, the depth the battery is discharged to before reloading it. UPPAAL STRATEGO was used to analyze different battery usage profiles, to optimize the lifetime of the satellite. This was done via a wear score function, which ranked the profiles according to their impact on the battery life. Additionally, the satellite was modelled as an SPTG in an abstract way. It could choose between the four different experiment types with different strains on the battery. Using the reinforcement learning approach implemented in UPPAAL STRATEGO we could near-optimize the scheduling of the experiments with respect to both the battery life and the number of experiments performed.

Home Automation (HA). In [40] we collaborated with the Danish company Seluxit within the European project CASSTING. Our focus was on using timed games to synthesize a controller for a floor heating system of a single family house. Each room of the house has its own hot-water pipe circuit, which is controlled based on the room temperature. The original system used a simple "Bang-Bang"-like strategy, which turned the heating on if the temperature fell below a certain threshold, and turned it back off if it exceeded another threshold. Our goal was to use weather forecast information to synthesize an improved control strategy. Due to the state-space explosion caused by the number of control modes, we could not apply UPPAAL STRATEGO directly. To cope with this, we proposed a novel online synthesis methodology, which is periodically called and learns an optimal controller for a limited timeframe. We further improved this approach by applying compositional synthesis, making it scalable enough for the study. The controller could access the weather forecast for the next 45 minutes, and used that information to shut down or start the valves much earlier than other controllers, resulting in substantial energy savings and increased comfort.

Intelligent Control of Trafic Light (ICTL). Within the Innovation Center DiCyPS we used UPPAAL STRATEGO for the synthesis of an efficient traffic control strategy. The controller gains information about the traffic via radar detectors and aims at optimizing the total traffic flow in a given traffic light junction. The strategy optimizes the total delay, the queue length and the number of times the vehicles have to stop. Again the synthesis is done online, this time in 5 second intervals, during which the next operation of the traffic light is calculated. We investigated an existing intersection in the municipality of Køge,

Denmark, and simulated it with the open source tool SUMO and the commercial tool VISSIM. The strategy computed by UPPAAL STRATEGO could be integrated into these tools, to analyze the behaviour based on randomly generated traffic scenarios. We evaluated the strategies in comparison to a static controller and a so called Loop controller, under three types of traffic szenarios with low, medium and maximal traffic. For low traffic, all controllers performed very similar, with the Loop controller showing the best results and for medium traffic, all performed equally. However, for high traffic, UPPAAL STRATEGO outperformed both other controllers significantly, essentially halving the expected waiting time [33].

6   Lessons Learned

Based on 20 years of practical experience in using UPPAAL on industrial case studies – as illustrated by the list of case studies given in the previous sections – we believe that a number of lessons may be learned.

It is important to have a dedicated team consisting of committed developers and inquisitive researchers in order to develop efficient and usable tools. In addition, the tools developed must have an interface and functionality which fits the use-case company's tool-chain, development method, and knowledge.

> Formal methods tools must fit development methodology applied by industry.

Having the tool developer applying it in close interaction with the industrial user – e.g. through collaborative projects – gives a strong incentive for achieving alignment with and impact on industrial methodology. The tool developer can then strive to align the tool and the industrial verification workflow, both by adapting the tool and by influencing the used methods.

> Industrial impact requires an *evolution of both their methods and our tools*, potentially in several iterations of collaboration.

The exact formal notations need not be a show-stopper, as long as the notation used is engineer friendly, and supported by a well-designed user-interface. Using a familiar notation is helpful in reducing the entry barrier and learning curve.

> Use of engineer friendly, yet formal, notation increases chances of impact.

Sustaining use may be difficult in a dynamic industrial environment, and requires several collaborations and/or repeated introduction. Follow-up projects can benefit this greatly.

> Sustained industrial use needs repeated committed collaboration.

Tool development needs to be continuously sustained beyond the first case-study and paper-publication. This requires committed developers, continuous maintenance including bug fixing, making enhancements of usability, functions, performance, and performing testing, release management, license serving, ... This is obviously time consuming and requires financial support. More importantly, because formal tools often require specialized expertise knowledge, few of these tasks can be subcontracted to a generic software engineer. Hence, also academic recognition and rewards are needed for such developments that do not readily result in publications.

> Tool development needs to be continuously sustained. This requires increased academic recognition to tool developers.

On the other hand, we ourselves only made few serious attempts at commercializing our tools beyond selling licenses. This is likely because we are researchers at heart.

> Industrial impact could be increased by offering tools and consultancy on commercial terms through spin-out companies.

Finally:

> A successful case study is not the same as industrial impact.

References

1. Proceedings of the 18th IEEE Real-Time Systems Symposium (RTSS 1997), 3–5 December 1997. IEEE Computer Society, San Francisco (1997)
2. Third International Conference on the Quantitative Evaluation of Systems (QEST 2006), 11–14 September 2006. IEEE Computer Society, Riverside (2006)
3. Mikucionis, M., Larsen, K.G., Nielsen, B.: T-uppaal: online model-based testing of real-time systems. In: Grunbacher, P. (ed.) 19th IEEE International Conference on Automated Software Engineering (ASE 2004) Proceedings, pp. 396–397, United States, IEEE Computer Society Press (2004). ISSN; 1068–3062
4. Alur, R., La Torre, S., Pappas, G.J.: Optimal paths in weighted timed automata. In: Benedetto and Sangiovanni-Vincentelli [10], pp. 49–62
5. Asaadi, H.R., Khosravi, R., Mousavi, M.R., Noroozi, N.: Towards model-based testing of electronic funds transfer systems. In: Arbab, F., Sirjani, M. (eds.) FSEN 2011. LNCS, vol. 7141, pp. 253–267. Springer, Heidelberg (2012). https://doi.org/10.1007/978-3-642-29320-7_17
6. Behrmann, G., et al.: UPPAAL-tiga: time for playing games!. In: Damm, W., Hermanns, H. (eds.) CAV 2007. LNCS, vol. 4590, pp. 121–125. Springer, Heidelberg (2007). https://doi.org/10.1007/978-3-540-73368-3_14
7. Behrmann, G., David, A., Larsen, K.G., Håkansson, J., Pettersson, P., Yi, W., Hendriks, M.: UPPAAL 4.0. In: Third International Conference on the Quantitative Evaluation of Systems (QEST 2006) [2], 11–14 September 2006, Riverside, California, USA, pp. 125–126
8. Behrmann, G., David, A., Larsen, K.G., Pettersson, P., Yi, W.: Developing UPPAAL over 15 years. Softw. Pract. Exper. **41**(2), 133–142 (2011)

9. Behrmann, G., Fehnker, A., Hune, T., Larsen, K.G., Pettersson, P., Romijn, J., Vaandrager, F.W.: Minimum-cost reachability for priced timed automata. In: Benedetto and Sangiovanni-Vincentelli [10], pp. 147–161
10. Di Benedetto, M.D., Sangiovanni-Vincentelli, A. (eds.): HSCC 2001. LNCS, vol. 2034. Springer, Heidelberg (2001). https://doi.org/10.1007/3-540-45351-2
11. Bengtsson, J., et al.: Verification of an audio protocol with bus collision using UPPAAL. In: Alur, R., Henzinger, T.A. (eds.) CAV 1996. LNCS, vol. 1102, pp. 244–256. Springer, Heidelberg (1996). https://doi.org/10.1007/3-540-61474-5_73
12. Bisgaard, M., et al.: Battery-aware scheduling in low orbit: the GoMX–3 case. In: Fitzgerald, J., Heitmeyer, C., Gnesi, S., Philippou, A. (eds.) FM 2016. LNCS, vol. 9995, pp. 559–576. Springer, Cham (2016). https://doi.org/10.1007/978-3-319-48989-6_34
13. Bosscher, D., Polak, I., Vaandrager, F.: Verification of an audio control protocol. In: Langmaack, H., de Roever, W.-P., Vytopil, J. (eds.) FTRTFT 1994. LNCS, vol. 863, pp. 170–192. Springer, Heidelberg (1994). https://doi.org/10.1007/3-540-58468-4_165
14. Boudjadar, A., David, A., Kim, J.H., Larsen, K.G., Mikucionis, M., Nyman, U., Skou, A.: Degree of schedulability of mixed-criticality real-time systems with probabilistic sporadic tasks. In: 2014 Theoretical Aspects of Software Engineering Conference, TASE 2014, Changsha, China, 1–3 September 2014, pp. 126–130. IEEE Computer Society (2014)
15. Brinksma, E., Cleaveland, W.R., Larsen, K.G., Margaria, T., Steffen, B. (eds.): TACAS 1995. LNCS, vol. 1019. Springer, Heidelberg (1995). https://doi.org/10.1007/3-540-60630-0
16. Cassez, F., David, A., Fleury, E., Larsen, K.G., Lime, D.: Efficient on-the-fly algorithms for the analysis of timed games. In: Abadi, M., de Alfaro, L. (eds.) CONCUR 2005. LNCS, vol. 3653, pp. 66–80. Springer, Heidelberg (2005). https://doi.org/10.1007/11539452_9
17. Cassez, F., David, A., Larsen, K.G., Lime, D., Raskin, J.-F.: Timed control with observation based and stuttering invariant strategies. In: Namjoshi, K.S., Yoneda, T., Higashino, T., Okamura, Y. (eds.) ATVA 2007. LNCS, vol. 4762, pp. 192–206. Springer, Heidelberg (2007). https://doi.org/10.1007/978-3-540-75596-8_15
18. D'Argenio, P.R., Katoen, J.-P., Ruys, T.C., Tretmans, J.: The bounded retransmission protocol must be on time!. In: Brinksma, E. (ed.) TACAS 1997. LNCS, vol. 1217, pp. 416–431. Springer, Heidelberg (1997). https://doi.org/10.1007/BFb0035403
19. David, A., Du, D., Larsen, K.G., Mikucionis, M., Skou, A.: An evaluation framework for energy aware buildings using statistical model checking. Sci. China Inf. Sci. 55(12), 2694–2707 (2012)
20. David, A., et al.: On time with minimal expected cost!. In: Cassez, F., Raskin, J.-F. (eds.) ATVA 2014. LNCS, vol. 8837, pp. 129–145. Springer, Cham (2014). https://doi.org/10.1007/978-3-319-11936-6_10
21. David, A., Jensen, P.G., Larsen, K.G., Mikučionis, M., Taankvist, J.H.: UPPAAL STRATEGO. In: Baier, C., Tinelli, C. (eds.) TACAS 2015. LNCS, vol. 9035, pp. 206–211. Springer, Heidelberg (2015). https://doi.org/10.1007/978-3-662-46681-0_16
22. David, A., Larsen, K.G., Legay, A., Mikučionis, M.: Schedulability of Herschel-Planck revisited using statistical model checking. In: Margaria, T., Steffen, B. (eds.) ISoLA 2012. LNCS, vol. 7610, pp. 293–307. Springer, Heidelberg (2012). https://doi.org/10.1007/978-3-642-34032-1_28

23. David, A., Larsen, K.G., Legay, A., Mikucionis, M.: Schedulability of herschel revisited using statistical model checking. STTT **17**(2), 187–199 (2015)
24. David, A., Larsen, K.G., Legay, A., Mikucionis, M., Poulsen, D.B.: Uppaal SMC tutorial. STTT **17**(4), 397–415 (2015)
25. David, A., Larsen, K.G., Legay, A., Mikucionis, M., Poulsen, D.B., Sedwards, S.: Statistical model checking for biological systems. STTT **17**(3), 351–367 (2015)
26. David, A., et al.: Statistical model checking for networks of priced timed automata. In: Fahrenberg, U., Tripakis, S. (eds.) FORMATS 2011. LNCS, vol. 6919, pp. 80–96. Springer, Heidelberg (2011). https://doi.org/10.1007/978-3-642-24310-3_7
27. David, A., Larsen, K.G., Legay, A., Mikučionis, M., Wang, Z.: Time for statistical model checking of real-time systems. In: Gopalakrishnan, G., Qadeer, S. (eds.) CAV 2011. LNCS, vol. 6806, pp. 349–355. Springer, Heidelberg (2011). https://doi.org/10.1007/978-3-642-22110-1_27
28. David, A., Larsen, K.G., Legay, A., Nyman, U., Traonouez, L., Wasowski, A.: Real-time specifications. STTT **17**(1), 17–45 (2015)
29. David, A., Larsen, K.G., Legay, A., Nyman, U., Wąsowski, A.: ECDAR: an environment for compositional design and analysis of real time systems. In: Bouajjani, A., Chin, W.-N. (eds.) ATVA 2010. LNCS, vol. 6252, pp. 365–370. Springer, Heidelberg (2010). https://doi.org/10.1007/978-3-642-15643-4_29
30. David, A., Larsen, K.G., Legay, A., Nyman, U., Wasowski, A.: Timed I/O automata: a complete specification theory for real-time systems. In: Johansson, K.H., Yi, W. (eds.) Proceedings of the 13th ACM International Conference on Hybrid Systems: Computation and Control, HSCC 2010, Stockholm, Sweden, 12–15 April 2010, pp. 91–100. ACM (2010)
31. David, N., David, A., Hansen, R.R., Larsen, K.G., Legay, A., Olesen, M.C., Probst, C.W.: Modelling social-technical attacks with timed automata. In: Bertino, E., You, I. (eds.) Proceedings of the 7th ACM CCS International Workshop on Managing Insider Security Threats, MIST 2015, Denver, Colorado, USA, 16 October 2015, pp. 21–28. ACM (2015)
32. de Vries, R.G., Tretmans, J.: On-the-fly conformance testing using SPIN. STTT **2**(4), 382–393 (2000)
33. Eriksen, A.B., Huang, C., Kildebogaard, J., Lahrmann, H., Larsen, K.G., Muniz, M., Taankvist, J.H.: Uppaal stratego for intelligent traffic lights. In: ITS European Congress (2017)
34. Gerke, M., Ehlers, R., Finkbeiner, B., Peter, H.-J.: Model checking the flexray physical layer protocol. In: Kowalewski, S., Roveri, M. (eds.) FMICS 2010. LNCS, vol. 6371, pp. 132–147. Springer, Heidelberg (2010). https://doi.org/10.1007/978-3-642-15898-8_9
35. Havelund, K., Larsen, K.G., Skou, A.: Formal verification of a power controller using the real-time model checker UPPAAL. In: Katoen, J.-P. (ed.) ARTS 1999. LNCS, vol. 1601, pp. 277–298. Springer, Heidelberg (1999). https://doi.org/10.1007/3-540-48778-6_17
36. Havelund, K., Skou, A., Larsen, K.G., Lund, K.: Formal modeling and analysis of an audio/video protocol: an industrial case study using UPPAAL. In: Proceedings of the 18th IEEE Real-Time Systems Symposium (RTSS 1997) [1], 3–5 December 1997, San Francisco, CA, USA, pp. 2–13 (1997)
37. Hessel, A., Larsen, K.G., Nielsen, B., Pettersson, P., Skou, A.: Time-optimal test cases for real-time systems. In: Larsen, K.G., Niebert, P. (eds.) FORMATS 2003. LNCS, vol. 2791, pp. 234–245. Springer, Heidelberg (2004). https://doi.org/10.1007/978-3-540-40903-8_19

38. Kim, J.H., Larsen, K.G., Nielsen, B., Mikučionis, M., Olsen, P.: Formal analysis and testing of real-time automotive systems using UPPAAL tools. In: Núñez, M., Güdemann, M. (eds.) FMICS 2015. LNCS, vol. 9128, pp. 47–61. Springer, Cham (2015). https://doi.org/10.1007/978-3-319-19458-5_4

39. Larsen, K., et al.: As cheap as possible: effcient cost-optimal reachability for priced timed automata. In: Berry, G., Comon, H., Finkel, A. (eds.) CAV 2001. LNCS, vol. 2102, pp. 493–505. Springer, Heidelberg (2001). https://doi.org/10.1007/3-540-44585-4_47

40. Larsen, K.G., Mikučionis, M., Muñiz, M., Srba, J., Taankvist, J.H.: Online and compositional learning of controllers with application to floor heating. In: Chechik, M., Raskin, J.-F. (eds.) TACAS 2016. LNCS, vol. 9636, pp. 244–259. Springer, Heidelberg (2016). https://doi.org/10.1007/978-3-662-49674-9_14

41. Larsen, K.G., Mikucionis, M., Nielsen, B.: Online testing of real-time systems using UPPAAL. In: Grabowski, J., Nielsen, B. (eds.) FATES 2004. LNCS, vol. 3395, pp. 79–94. Springer, Heidelberg (2005). https://doi.org/10.1007/978-3-540-31848-4_6

42. Larsen, K.G., Mikucionis, M., Nielsen, B., Skou, A.: Testing real-time embedded software using UPPAAL-TRON: an industrial case study. In: Wolf, W.H. (ed.) EMSOFT 2005, 18–22 September 2005, 5th ACM International Conference on Embedded Software, Proceedings, Jersey City, NJ, USA, pp. 299–306. ACM (2005)

43. Larsen, K.G., Pettersson, P., Yi, W.: UPPAAL in a nutshell. STTT 1(1–2), 134–152 (1997)

44. Lindahl, M., Pettersson, P., Yi, W.: Formal design and analysis of a gear controller. STTT 3(3), 353–368 (2001)

45. Mikucionis, M., Larsen, K.G., Nielsen, B.: T-UPPAAL: online model-based testing of real-time systems. In: 19th IEEE International Conference on Automated Software Engineering (ASE 2004), 20–25 September 2004, Linz, Austria, pp. 396–397. IEEE Computer Society (2004)

46. Mikučionis, M., et al.: Schedulability analysis using uppaal: Herschel-Planck case study. In: Margaria, T., Steffen, B. (eds.) ISoLA 2010. LNCS, vol. 6416, pp. 175–190. Springer, Heidelberg (2010). https://doi.org/10.1007/978-3-642-16561-0_21

47. Nielsen, B.: Specification and Test of Real-Time Systems. Ph.D thesis. Aalborg University (2000)

48. Nielsen, B., Skou, A.: Automated test generation from timed automata. In: Margaria, T., Yi, W. (eds.) TACAS 2001. LNCS, vol. 2031, pp. 343–357. Springer, Heidelberg (2001). https://doi.org/10.1007/3-540-45319-9_24

49. Nielsen, B., Skou, A.: Test generation for time critical systems: tool and case study. In: 13th Euromicro Conference on Real-Time Systems, Delft, The Netherlands, pp. 155–162, June 2001

50. Romijn, J.: A timed verification of the IEEE 1394 leader election protocol. Formal Methods Syst. Des. 19(2), 165–194 (2001)

51. Rütz, C.: Timed model-based conformance testing - a case study using tron: testing key states of automated trust anchor updating (rfc 5011) in autotrust. B.Sc. thesis (2010)

52. Tretmans, J.: A formal approach to conformance testing C-19, 257–276 (1993)

53. van Glabbeek, R.J., Höfner, P., Portmann, M., Tan, W.L.: Modelling and verifying the AODV routing protocol. Distrib. Comput. 29(4), 279–315 (2016)

FM 2018 Main Conference

Deadlock Detection
for Actor-Based Coroutines

Keyvan Azadbakht[1,2(✉)], Frank S. de Boer[1], and Erik de Vink[1,3]

[1] Centrum Wiskunde en Informatica, Amsterdam, The Netherlands
{k.azadbakht,f.s.de.boer}@cwi.nl
[2] Leiden University, Leiden, The Netherlands
[3] Eindhoven University of Technology, Eindhoven, The Netherlands
evink@win.tue.nl

Abstract. The actor-based language studied in this paper features asynchronous method calls and supports coroutines which allow for the cooperative scheduling of the method invocations belonging to an actor. We model the local behavior of an actor as a well-structured transition system by means of predicate abstraction and derive the decidability of the occurrence of deadlocks caused by the coroutine mode of method execution.

Keywords: Deadlock detection · Predicate abstraction · Actor
Cooperative scheduling · Transition system

1 Introduction

Actors [1,15] provide an event-driven concurrency model for the analysis and construction of distributed, large-scale parallel systems. In actor-based modeling languages, like Rebeca [20], Creol [17], and ABS [16], the events are generated by *asynchronous calls* to methods provided by the actors. The resulting integration with object-orientation allows for new object-oriented models of concurrency, better suited for the analysis and construction of distributed systems than the standard model of *multi-threading* in languages like Java.

The new object-oriented models of concurrency arise from the combination of different synchronization mechanisms. By design, the basic *run-to-completion* mode of execution of asynchronously called methods as for example provided by the language Rebeca does not provide any synchronization between actors. Consequently, the resulting concurrent systems of actors do not give rise to undesirable consequences of synchronization like *deadlock*. The languages Creol and ABS extend the basic model with synchronization on the values returned by a method. So-called *futures* [8] provide a general mechanism for actors to synchronize on return values. Creol and ABS further integrate a model of execution of methods based on and inspired by *coroutines*, attributed by Knuth to Conway [6]. This model allows for controlled suspension and resumption of the executing method invocation and so-called cooperative scheduling of another

© Springer International Publishing AG, part of Springer Nature 2018
K. Havelund et al. (Eds.): FM 2018, LNCS 10951, pp. 39–54, 2018.
https://doi.org/10.1007/978-3-319-95582-7_3

method invocation of the actor. In [3,4], this mechanism is used to implement the well-established algorithms for social network simulation.

Both the synchronization mechanisms of futures and coroutines may give rise to deadlock. Futures may give rise to *global* deadlock in a system of actors. Such a global deadlock consists of a circular dependency between different method invocations of possibly different actors which are suspended on the generation of the return value. On the other hand, coroutines may give rise to a *local* deadlock which occurs when all method invocations of a single actor are suspended on a Boolean condition. In this paper we provide the formal foundations of a novel method for the analysis of such local deadlocks.

To the best of our knowledge, our work provides a first method for deciding local deadlocks in actor-based languages with coroutines. The method itself is based on a new technique for predicate abstraction of actor-based programs with coroutines, which aims at the construction of a well-structured transition system. In contrast, the usual techniques of predicate abstraction [5] aim at the construction of a *finite* abstraction, which allows model checking of properties in temporal logic. In [9], a restricted class of actor-based programs is modeled as a well-structured transition system. This class does not support coroutines and actors do not have a global state specifying the values of the global variables.

Methods that utilize different techniques aiming at detection of global deadlocks in various actor settings include the following. The work in [19] uses ownership to organize CoJava active objects into hierarchies in order to prevent circular relationships where two or more active objects wait indefinitely for one another. Also data-races and data-based deadlocks are avoided in CoJava by the type system that prevents threads from sharing mutable data. In [7], a sound technique is proposed that translates a system of asynchronously communicating active objects into a Petri net and applies Petri net reachability analysis for deadlock detection. The work that is introduced in [11] and extended in [14] defines a technique for analyzing deadlocks of stateful active objects that is based on behavioural type systems. The context is the actor model with wait-by-necessity synchronizations where futures are not given an explicit "Future" type. Also, a framework is proposed in [18] to statically verify communication correctness in a concurrency model using futures, with the aim that the type system ensures that interactions among objects are deadlock-free.

A deadlock detection framework for ABS is proposed in [12] which mainly focuses on deadlocks regarding future variables, i.e., await and get operations on futures. It also proposes a naive annotation-based approach for detection of local deadlocks (await on Boolean guards), namely, letting programmers annotate the statement with the dependencies it creates. However, a comprehensive approach to investigate local deadlocks is not addressed.

Our approach, and corresponding structure of the paper, consists of the following. First, we introduce the basic programming concepts of asynchronous method calls, futures and coroutines in Sect. 2. In Sect. 3 we introduce a new operational semantics for the description of the local behavior of a single actor. The only external dependencies stem from method calls generated by other actors and the basic operations on futures corresponding to calls of methods of other actors. Both kinds of external dependencies are modeled by *non-determinism*. Method calls generated by other actors are modeled by the non-deterministic scheduling of method invocations. The basic operations on futures are modeled by the corresponding non-deterministic evaluation of the availability of the return value and random generation of the return value itself. Next, we introduce in Sect. 4 a *predicate abstraction* [5,13] of the value assignments to the global variables ("fields") of an actor as well as the local variables of the method invocations. The resulting abstraction still gives rise to an *infinite* transition system because of the generation of *self*-calls, that is, calls of methods of the actor by the actor itself, and the corresponding generation of "fresh" names of the local variables.

Our main contribution consists of the following technical results.

- a proof of the *correctness* of the predicate abstraction, in Sect. 5, and
- *decidability* of checking for the occurrence of a local deadlock in the abstract transition system in Sect. 6.

Correctness of the predicate abstraction is established by a *simulation* relation between the concrete and the abstract transition system. Decidability is established by showing that the abstract system is a so-called well-structured transition system, cf. [10]. Since the concrete operational semantics of the local behavior of a single actor is an *over-approximation* of the local behavior in the context of an arbitrary system of actors, these technical results together comprise a general method for proving *absence* of local deadlock of an actor. A short discussion follow-up in Sect. 7 concludes the paper.

2   The Programming Language

In this section we present, in the context of a class-based language, the basic statements which describe asynchronous method invocation and cooperative scheduling.

A class introduces its global variables, also referred to as "fields", and methods. We use $x, y, z, \ldots$ to denote both the fields of a class and the local variables of the methods (including the formal parameters). Method bodies are defined as sequential control structures, including the usual conditional and iteration constructs, over the basic statements listed below.

Dynamic Instantiation. For x a so-called future variable or a class variable of type C, for some class name C, the assignment

$$x = \textbf{new}$$

creates a new future or a unique reference to a new instance of class C.

Side Effect-Free Assignment. In the assignment

$$x = e$$

the expression e denotes a side effect-free expression. The evaluation of such an expression does not affect the values of any global or local variable and also does not affect the status of the executing process. We do not detail the syntactical structure of side effect-free expressions.

Asynchronous Method Invocation. A method is called asynchronously by an assignment of the form

$$x = e_0!m(e_1,\ldots,e_n)$$

Here, x is a future variable which is used as a unique reference to the return value of the invocation of method m with actual parameters $e_1,\ldots,e_n$. The called actor is denoted by the expression e_0. Without loss of generality we restrict the actual parameters and the expression e_0 to side effect-free expressions. Since e_0 denotes an actor, this implies that e_0 is a global or local variable.

The Get Operation. The execution of an assignment

$$x = y.\texttt{get}$$

blocks till the future variable y holds the value that is returned by its corresponding method invocation.

Awaiting a Future. The statement

$$\texttt{await}\ \ x?$$

releases control and schedules another process in case the future variable x does not yet hold a value, that is to be returned by its corresponding method invocation. Otherwise, it proceeds with the execution of the remaining statements of the executing method invocation.

Awaiting a Boolean Condition. Similarly, the statement

$$\texttt{await}\ \ e$$

where e denotes a side effect-free Boolean condition, releases control and schedules another process in case the Boolean condition is false. Otherwise, it proceeds with the execution of the remaining statements of the executing method invocation.

We describe the possible deadlock behavior of a system of dynamically generated actors in terms of *processes*, where a process is a method invocation. A process is either *active* (executing), *blocked* on a get operation, or *suspended* by a future or Boolean condition. At run-time, an actor consists of an active process and a set of suspended processes (when the active method invocation blocks on a get operation it blocks the entire actor). Actors execute their active processes in parallel and only interact via asynchronous method calls and futures. When an active process awaits a future or Boolean condition, the actor can cooperatively schedule another process instead. A *global* deadlock involves a circular dependency between processes which are awaiting a future. On the other hand, a *local* deadlock appears when all the processes of an actor are awaiting a Boolean condition to become true. In the following sections we present a method for showing if an initial set of processes of an individual actor does *not* give rise to a local deadlock.

3   The Concrete System

In order to formally define local deadlock we introduce a formal operational semantics of a single actor. Throughout this paper we assume a definition of a class C to be given. A typical element of its set of methods is denoted by m. We assume the definition of a class C to consist of the usual declarations of global variables and method definitions. Let $Var(C)$ denote all the global and local variables declared in C. Without loss of generality we assume that there are no name clashes between the global and local variables appearing in C, and no name clashes between the local variables of different methods. To resolve in the semantics name clashes of the local variables of the different invocations of a method, we assume a given infinite set Var such that $Var(C) \subseteq Var$. The set $Var \backslash Var(C)$ is used to generate "fresh" local variables. Further, for each method m, we introduce an infinite set $\Sigma(m)$ of renamings σ such that for every local variable x of m, $\sigma(x)$ is a fresh variable in Var, i.e. not appearing in $Var(C)$. We assume that any two distinct $\sigma, \sigma' \in \bigcup_m \Sigma(m)$ are *disjoint* (Here m ranges over the method names introduced by class C.) Renamings σ and σ' are disjoint if their ranges are disjoint. Note that by the above assumption the domains of renamings of *different* methods are also disjoint.

A process p arising from an invocation of a method m is described formally as a pair (σ, S), where $\sigma \in \Sigma(m)$ and S is the sequence of remaining statements to be executed, also known as *continuation*. An actor configuration then is a triple (Γ, p, Q), where Γ is an assignment of values to the variables in Var, p denotes the active process, and Q denotes a set of suspended processes. A configuration is *consistent* if for every renaming σ there exists at most one statement S such that $(\sigma, S) \in \{p\} \cup Q$.

A computation step of a single actor is formalized by a transition relation between consistent actor configurations. A structural operational semantics for the derivation of such transitions is given in Fig. 1. Here, we assume a given set Val of values of built-in data types (like Integer and Boolean), and an infinite set R of references or "pointers". Further, we assume a global variable $refs$ such that $\Gamma(refs) \subseteq R$ records locally stored references.

We proceed with the explanation of the rules of Fig. 1. The rule <ASSIGN> describes a side effect-free assignment. Here, and in the sequel, $e\sigma$ denotes the result of replacing any local variable x in e by $\sigma(x)$. By $\Gamma(e)$ we denote the extension of the variable assignment Γ to the evaluation of the expression e. By $\Gamma[x = v]$, for some value v, we denote the result of updating the value of x in Γ by v.

<ASSIGN>

$$\frac{}{\begin{array}{c}(\Gamma,(\sigma,x=e;S),Q)\rightarrow\\(\Gamma[x\sigma=\Gamma(e\sigma)],(\sigma,S),Q)\end{array}}$$

<NEW>

$$\frac{r\in R\backslash\Gamma(refs)}{\begin{array}{c}(\Gamma,(\sigma,x=\texttt{new};S),Q)\rightarrow\\(\Gamma[refs=\Gamma[refs]\cup\{r\}],(\sigma,x=r;S),Q)\end{array}}$$

<GET-VALUE>

$$\frac{v\in Val}{\begin{array}{c}(\Gamma,(\sigma,x=\ y.\texttt{get};S),Q)\rightarrow\\(\Gamma[x\sigma=v],(\sigma,S),Q)\end{array}}$$

<GET-REF>

$$\frac{r\in R}{\begin{array}{c}(\Gamma,(\sigma,x=\ y.\texttt{get};S),Q)\rightarrow\\(\Gamma[refs=\Gamma(refs)\cup\{r\}],(\sigma,x=r;S),Q)\end{array}}$$

<REMOTE-CALL >

$$\frac{\Gamma(y\sigma)\neq\Gamma(\texttt{this})}{\begin{array}{c}(\Gamma,(\sigma,x=y!m(\bar{e});S),Q)\rightarrow\\(\Gamma,(\sigma,x=\texttt{new};S),Q)\end{array}}$$

<LOCAL-CALL>

$$\frac{\Gamma(y\sigma)=\Gamma(\texttt{this})}{\begin{array}{c}(\Gamma,(\sigma,x=y!m(\bar{e});S),Q)\rightarrow\\(\Gamma[\bar{z}\sigma'=\Gamma(\bar{e}\sigma)],(\sigma,x=\texttt{new};S),Q\cup\{(\sigma',S')\})\end{array}}$$

<IF-THEN>

$$\frac{\Gamma(e\sigma)=true}{\begin{array}{c}(\Gamma,(\sigma,\texttt{if}\ e\ \{S'\}\ \texttt{else}\ \{S''\};S),Q)\rightarrow\\(\Gamma,(\sigma,S';S),Q)\end{array}}$$

<IF-ELSE>

$$\frac{\Gamma(e\sigma)=false}{\begin{array}{c}(\Gamma,(\sigma,\texttt{if}\ e\ \{S'\}\ \texttt{else}\ \{S''\};S),Q)\rightarrow\\(\Gamma,(\sigma,S'';S),Q)\end{array}}$$

<WHILE-TRUE>

$$\frac{\Gamma(e\sigma)=true}{\begin{array}{c}(\Gamma,(\sigma,\texttt{while}\ e\ \{S'\};S),Q)\rightarrow\\(\Gamma,(\sigma,S';\texttt{while}\ e\ \texttt{do}\ \{S'\};S),Q)\end{array}}$$

<WHILE-FALSE>

$$\frac{\Gamma(e\sigma)=false}{(\Gamma,(\sigma,\texttt{while}\ e\ \{S'\};S),Q)\rightarrow(\Gamma,(\sigma,S),Q)}$$

<AWAITB-TRUE>

$$\frac{\Gamma(e\sigma)=true}{\begin{array}{c}(\Gamma,(\sigma,\texttt{await}\ e;S),Q)\rightarrow\\(\Gamma,(\sigma,S),Q)\end{array}}$$

<AWAITB-FALSE>

$$\frac{\Gamma(e\sigma)=false\qquad(\sigma',S')\in Q}{\begin{array}{c}(\Gamma,(\sigma,\texttt{await}\ e;S),Q)\rightarrow\\(\Gamma,(\sigma',S'),(Q\cup\{(\sigma,\texttt{await}\ e;S)\})\backslash\{(\sigma',S')\})\end{array}}$$

<AWAITF-SKIP>

$$\frac{}{\begin{array}{c}(\Gamma,(\sigma,\texttt{await}\ x?;S),Q)\rightarrow\\(\Gamma,(\sigma,S),Q)\end{array}}$$

<AWAITF-SCHED>

$$\frac{(\sigma',S')\in Q}{\begin{array}{c}(\Gamma,(\sigma,\texttt{await}\ x?;S),Q)\rightarrow\\(\Gamma,(\sigma',S'),(Q\cup\{(\sigma,\texttt{await}\ true;S)\})\backslash\{(\sigma',S')\})\end{array}}$$

<RETURN>

$$\frac{(\sigma',S')\in Q}{(\Gamma,(\sigma,\texttt{return}\ e),Q)\rightarrow(\Gamma,(\sigma',S'),Q\backslash\{(\sigma',S')\})}$$

Fig. 1. Concrete transition relation

The rule <NEW> describes the non-deterministic selection of a fresh reference not appearing in the set $\Gamma(refs)$. The rule <GET-VALUE> models an assignment involving a get operation on a future variable y which holds a value of some built-in data type by an assignment of a random value $v \in Val$ (of the appropriate type). The rule `<GET-REF>` models an assignment involving a get operation on a future variable y which holds a reference by first adding a random value $r \in R$ to the set $\Gamma(refs)$ and then assign it to the variable x (note that we do *not* exclude that $r \in \Gamma(refs)$).

It should be observed that we model the local behavior of an actor. The absence of information about the return values in the semantics of a get operation is accounted for by a non-deterministic selection of an arbitrary return value. Further, since we restrict to the analysis of local deadlocks, we also abstract from the possibility that the get operation blocks and assume that the return value is generated.

The rules regarding choice and iteration statements are standard. The rule `<REMOTE-CALL>` describes an assignment involving an external call ($\Gamma(y\sigma) \neq \Gamma(\mathbf{this})$, where $y\sigma$ denotes y, if y is a global variable, otherwise it denotes the variable $\sigma(y)$). It is modeled by the creation and storage of a new future reference uniquely identifying the method invocation. On the other hand, according to the rule `<LOCAL-CALL>` a local call ($\Gamma(y\sigma) = \Gamma(\mathbf{this})$) generates a new process and future corresponding to the method invocation. Here it is implicitly assumed that the renaming $\sigma' \in \Sigma(m)$ is different from σ and all the other renamings in Q. Further, by $\Gamma[\bar{z}\sigma' = \Gamma(\bar{e}\sigma)]$ we denote the simultaneous update of Γ which assigns to each local variable $\sigma'(z_i)$ (i.e., the renamed formal parameter z_i) the value of the corresponding actual parameter e_i with its local variables renamed by σ, i.e., the local context of the calling method invocation. For technical convenience we omitted the initialization of the local variables that are not formal parameters. The body of method m is denoted by S'.

The rule `<AWAITB-TRUE>` describes that when the Boolean condition of the await statement is true, the active process proceeds with the continuation, and `<AWAITB-FALSE>` describes that when the Boolean condition of the await statement is false, a process is selected for execution. This can give rise to the activation of a disabled process, which is clearly not optimal. The transition system can be extended to only allow the activation of enabled processes. However, this does not affect the results of this paper and therefore is omitted for notational convenience.

The rule `<AWAITF-SKIP>` formalizes the assumption that the return value referred to by x has been generated. On the other hand, `<AWAITF-SCHED>` formalizes the assumption that the return value has not (yet) been generated. Note that we transform the initial await statement into an await on the Boolean condition "true". Availability of the return value then is modeled by selecting the process for execution. Finally, in the rule `RETURN` we assume that the return statement is the last statement to be executed. Note that here we do not store the generated return value (see also the discussion in Sect. 7).

In view of the above, we have the following definition of a local deadlock.

Definition 1. *A local configuration (Γ, p, Q) deadlocks if*

> *for all $(\sigma, S) \in \{p\} \cup Q$ we have that the initial statement of S is an await statement* await *e such that $\Gamma(e\sigma) = false$.*

In the sequel we describe a method for establishing that an initial configuration does not give rise to a local deadlock configuration. Here it is worthwhile to observe that the above description of the local behavior of a single actor provides an over-approximation of its actual local behavior as part of *any* system of actors. Consequently, absence of a local deadlock of this over-approximation implies absence of a local deadlock in *any* system of actors.

4   The Abstract System

Our method of deadlock detection is based on predicate abstraction. This boils down to using predicates instead of concrete value assignments. For the class C, the set $Pred(m)$ includes all (the negations of) the Boolean conditions appearing in the body of m. Further, $Pred(m)$ includes all (negations of) equations $x = y$ between reference variables x and y, where both x and y are global variables of the class C (including this) or local variables of m (a reference variable is either a future variable or used to refer to an actor.)

An abstract configuration α is of the form (T, p, Q), where, as in the previous section, p is the active process and Q is a set of suspended processes. The set T provides for each invocation of a method m a logical description of the relation between its local variables and the global variables. Formally, T is a set of pairs (σ, u), where $u \subseteq Pred(m)$, for some method m, is a set of predicates of m with fresh local variables as specified by σ. We assume that for each process $(\sigma, S) \in \{p\} \cup Q$ there exists a corresponding pair $(\sigma, u) \in T$. If for some $(\sigma, u) \in T$ there does not exist a corresponding process $(\sigma, S) \in \{p\} \cup Q$ then the process has terminated. Further, we assume that for any σ there is at most one $(\sigma, u) \in T$ and at most one $(\sigma, S) \in \{p\} \cup Q$.

We next define a transition relation on abstract configurations in terms of a strongest postcondition calculus. To describe this calculus, we first introduce the following notation. Let $L(T)$ denote the set $\{ u\sigma \mid (\sigma, u) \in T \}$, where $u\sigma = \{ \varphi\sigma \mid \varphi \in u \}$, and $\varphi\sigma$ denotes the result of replacing every local variable x in φ with $\sigma(x)$. Logically, we view each element of $L(T)$ as a conjunction of its predicates. Therefore, when we write $L(T) \vdash \varphi$, i.e., φ is a logical consequence (in first-order logic) of $L(T)$, the sets of predicates in $L(T)$ are interpreted as conjunctions. (It is worthwhile to note that in practice the notion of logical consequence will also involve the first-order theories of the underlying data structures.) The strongest postcondition, defined below, describes for each basic assignment a and local context $\sigma \in \Sigma(m)$, the set $sp_\sigma(L(T), a)$ of predicates $\varphi \in Pred(m)$ such that $\varphi\sigma$ holds after the assignment, assuming that all predicates in $L(T)$ hold initially.

For an assignment $x = e$ we define the strongest postcondition by

$$sp_\sigma(L(T), x = e) = \{ \varphi \mid L(T) \vdash \varphi\sigma[e/x], \varphi \in Pred(m) \}$$

where $[e/x]$ denotes the substitution which replaces occurrences of the variable x by the side effect-free expression e. For an assignment $x = $ new we define the strongest postcondition by

$$sp_\sigma(L(T), x = \texttt{new}) = \{ \varphi \mid L(T) \vdash \varphi\sigma[\texttt{new}/x], \varphi \in Pred(m) \}$$

The substitution $[\text{new}/x]$ replaces every equation $x = y$, with y distinct from x, by *false*, $x = x$ by *true*. It is worthwhile to note that for every future variable and variable denoting an actor, these are the only possible logical contexts consistent with the programming language. (Since the language does not support de-referencing, actors encapsulate their local state.)

For an assignment $x = y.\text{get}$ we define the strongest postcondition by

$$sp_\sigma(L(T), x = y.\text{get}) = \{\, \varphi \mid L(T) \vdash \forall x.\varphi\sigma,\ \varphi \in Pred(m) \,\}$$

The universal quantification of the variable x models a non-deterministic choice for the value of x.

Figure 2 presents the structural operational semantics of the transition relation for abstract configurations. In the <ASSIGN> rule the set of predicates u for each $(\sigma', u) \in T$, is updated by the strongest postcondition $sp_{\sigma'}(L(T), (x = e)\sigma)$. Note that by the substitution theorem of predicate logic, we have for each predicate φ of this strongest postcondition that $\varphi\sigma'$ will hold after the assignment $(x = e)\sigma$ (i.e., $x\sigma = e\sigma$) because $L(T) \vdash \varphi\sigma[e/x]$. Similarly, the rules <GET> and <NEW> update T of the initial configuration by their corresponding strongest postcondition as defined above.

In the rule <REMOTE-CALL> we identify a remote call by checking whether the information $\text{this} \neq y\sigma$ can be added consistently to $L(T)$. By $T \cup \{(\sigma, \varphi)\}$ we denote the set $\{\, (\sigma', u) \in T \mid \sigma' \neq \sigma \,\} \cup \{\, (\sigma, u \cup \{\varphi\}) \mid (\sigma, u) \in T \,\}$. In the rule <LOCAL-CALL> the set of predicates u of the generated invocation of method m consists of all those predicates $\varphi \in Pred(m)$ such that $L(T) \vdash \varphi[\bar{e}\sigma/\bar{z}]$, where $\bar{z}$ denotes the formal parameters of m. By the substitution theorem of predicate logic, the (simultaneous) substitution $[\bar{e}\sigma/\bar{z}]$ ensures that φ holds for the generated invocation of method m. Note that by definition, $L(T)$ only refers to fresh local variables, i.e., the local variables of m do not appear in $L(T)$ because for any $(\sigma, u) \in T$ we have that $\sigma(x)$ is a fresh variable not appearing in the given class C. For technical convenience we omitted the substitution of the local variables that are not formal parameters. The renaming σ', which is assumed not to appear in T, introduces fresh local variable names for the generated method invocation. The continuation S' of the new process is the body of method m. The generation of a new future in both the rules <REMOTE-CALL> and <LOCAL-CALL> is simply modeled by the $x = \text{new}$ statement.

By <IF-THEN>, the active process transforms to the "then" block, i.e. S', followed by S, if the predicate set $L(T)$ is consistent with the guard e of the if-statement. (Note that as $L(T)$ is in general not complete, it can be consistent with e as well as with $\neg e$.) The other rules regarding choice and iteration statements are defined similarly. By <RETURN> the active process terminates, and is removed from the configuration. A process is selected from Q for execution. Note that the pair $(\sigma, u) \in T$ is not affected by this removal.

The rules <AWAIT-TRUE> and <AWAIT-FALSE> specify transitions assuming the predicate set $L(T)$ is consistent with the guard e and with $\neg e$, respectively. In the former case, the await statement is skipped and the active process continues, whereas in the latter, the active process releases control and a process

<ASSIGN>
$$\frac{T' = \{\, (\sigma', sp_{\sigma'}(L(T), (x = e)\sigma)) \mid (\sigma', u) \in T\,\}}{(T, (\sigma, x = e; S), Q) \to (T', (\sigma, S), Q)}$$

<GET>
$$\frac{T' = \{\, (\sigma', sp_{\sigma'}(L(T), (x = y.\mathtt{get})\sigma)) \mid (\sigma', u) \in T\,\}}{(T, (\sigma, x = y.\mathtt{get}; S), Q) \to (T', (\sigma, S), Q)}$$

<NEW>
$$\frac{T' = \{\, (\sigma', sp_{\sigma'}(L(T), (x = \mathtt{new})\sigma)) \mid (\sigma', u) \in T\,\}}{(T, (\sigma, x = \mathtt{new}; S), Q) \to (T', (\sigma, S), Q)}$$

<REMOTE-CALL>
$$\frac{L(T) \cup \{\mathtt{this} \neq y\sigma\} \not\vdash false}{(T, (\sigma, x = y!m(\bar{e}); S), Q) \to (T \cup \{(\sigma, \mathtt{this} \neq y)\}, (\sigma, x = \mathtt{new}; S), Q)}$$

<LOCAL-CALL>
$$\frac{L(T) \cup \{\mathtt{this} = y\sigma\} \not\vdash false \qquad u = \{\, \varphi \mid L(T) \vdash \varphi[\bar{e}\sigma/\bar{z}],\ \varphi \in Pred(m)\,\}}{\begin{array}{c}(T, (\sigma, x = y!m(\bar{e}); S), Q) \to \\ (T \cup \{(\sigma', u)\} \cup \{(\sigma, \mathtt{this} = y)\}, (\sigma, x = \mathtt{new}; S), Q \cup \{(\sigma', S')\})\end{array}}$$

<IF-THEN>
$$\frac{L(T) \cup \{e\sigma\} \not\vdash false}{\begin{array}{c}(T, (\sigma, \mathtt{if}\ e\ \{S'\}\ \mathtt{else}\ \{S''\}; S), Q) \\ \to (T \cup \{(\sigma, e)\}, (\sigma, S'; S), Q)\end{array}}$$

<IF-ELSE>
$$\frac{L(T) \cup \{\neg e\sigma\} \not\vdash false}{\begin{array}{c}(T, (\sigma, \mathtt{if}\ e\ \{S'\}\ \mathtt{else}\ \{S''\}; S), Q) \\ \to (T \cup \{(\sigma, \neg e)\}, (\sigma, S''; S), Q)\end{array}}$$

<WHILE-TRUE>
$$\frac{L(T) \cup \{e\sigma\} \not\vdash false}{\begin{array}{c}(T, (\sigma, \mathtt{while}\ e\ \mathtt{do}\ \{S\}'; S), Q) \\ \to (T \cup \{(\sigma, e)\}, (\sigma, S'; \mathtt{while}\ e\ \mathtt{do}\ \{S'\}; S), Q)\end{array}}$$

<WHILE-FALSE>
$$\frac{L(T) \cup \{\neg e\sigma\} \not\vdash false}{\begin{array}{c}(T, (\sigma, \mathtt{while}\ e\ \mathtt{do}\ \{S'\}; S), Q) \\ \to (T \cup \{(\sigma, \neg e)\}, (\sigma, S), Q)\end{array}}$$

<AWAIT-TRUE>
$$\frac{L(T) \cup \{e\sigma\} \not\vdash false}{(T, (\sigma, \mathtt{await}\ e; S), Q) \to (T \cup \{(\sigma, e)\}, (\sigma, S), Q)}$$

<AWAIT-FALSE>
$$\frac{L(T) \cup \{\neg e\sigma\} \not\vdash false \qquad (\sigma', S') \in Q}{(T, (\sigma, \mathtt{await}\ e; S), Q) \to (T \cup \{(\sigma, \neg e)\}, (\sigma', S'), (Q \cup \{(\sigma, \mathtt{await}\ e; S)\}) \backslash \{(\sigma', S')\})}$$

<AWAITF-SKIP>
$$\begin{array}{c}(T, (\sigma, \mathtt{await}\ x?; S), Q) \\ \to (T, (\sigma, S), Q)\end{array}$$

<AWAITF-SCHED>
$$\frac{(\sigma', S') \in Q}{\begin{array}{c}(T, (\sigma, \mathtt{await}\ x?; S), Q) \to \\ (T, (\sigma', S'), (Q \cup \{(\sigma, \mathtt{await}\ true; S)\}) \backslash \{(\sigma', S')\})\end{array}}$$

<RETURN>
$$\frac{(\sigma', S') \in Q}{(T, (\sigma, \mathtt{return}\ e), Q) \to (T, (\sigma', S'), Q \backslash \{(\sigma', S')\})}$$

Fig. 2. Abstract transition system

from Q is activated. Similar to the concrete semantics in the previous section, in
`<AWAITF-SKIP>` and `<AWAITF-SCHED>`, the active process non-deterministically
continues or cooperatively releases the control. In the latter, a process from Q
is activated.

We conclude this section with the counterpart of Definition 1 for the abstract
setting.

Definition 2. *A local configuration* (T, p, Q) *is a (local) deadlock if*

for all $(\sigma, S) \in \{p\} \cup Q$ *we have that the initial statement of S is an await
statement* `await` e *such that* $L(T) \cup \{\neg e\sigma\} \not\vdash false$.

5   Correctness of Predicate Abstraction

In this section we prove that the concrete system is simulated by the abstract
system. To this end we introduce a simulation relation $\sim$ between concrete and
abstract configurations:

$$(\Gamma, p, Q) \sim (T, p, Q), \text{ if } \Gamma \models L(T)$$

where $\Gamma \models L(T)$ denotes that Γ satisfies the formulas of $L(T)$.

Theorem 1. *The abstract system is a simulation of the concrete system.*

Proof. Given $(\Gamma, p, Q) \sim (T, p, Q)$ and a transition $(\Gamma, p, Q) \rightarrow (\Gamma', p', Q')$, we
need to prove that there exists a transition $(T, p, Q) \rightarrow (T', p', Q')$ such that
$(\Gamma', p', Q') \sim (T', p', Q')$.

For all the rules that involve the evaluation of a guard e, it suffices to observe
that $\Gamma \models L(T)$ and $\Gamma \models e$ implies $L(T) \cup \{e\} \not\vdash false$.

We treat the case $x = e$ where e is a side-effect-free expression (the others
cases are treated similarly). If $p = (\sigma, x = e; S)$, where e is a side-effect-free
expression, then $\Gamma' = \Gamma[(x = e)\sigma]$. We put $T' = \{ (\sigma', sp_{\sigma'}(L(T), (x = e)\sigma)) \mid
(\sigma', u) \in T \}$. Then it follows that $(T, p, Q) \rightarrow (T', p', Q')$. To prove $\Gamma' \models L(T')$
it remains to show for $(\sigma, u) \in T$ and $\varphi \in sp_{\sigma'}(L(T), (x = e)\sigma)$ that $\Gamma' \models \varphi\sigma'$:
Let $(\sigma, u) \in T$ and $\varphi \in sp_{\sigma'}(L(T), (x = e)\sigma)$. By definition of the strongest
postcondition, we have $L(T) \vdash \varphi\sigma'[(x = e)\sigma]$. Since $\Gamma \models L(T)$, we have $\Gamma \models
\varphi\sigma'[(x = e)\sigma]$. Since $\Gamma' = \Gamma[(x = e)\sigma]$, we obtain from the substitution theorem
of predicate logic that

$$\Gamma' \models \varphi\sigma' \iff \Gamma \models \varphi\sigma'[(x = e)\sigma]$$

and hence we are done.   □

We conclude this section with the following observation: if the initial abstract
configuration (T, p, Q) does not give rise to a local deadlock then also the configuration (Γ, p, Q) does not give rise to a local deadlock, when $\Gamma \models L(T)$. To see
this, by the above theorem it suffices to note that if (Γ', p', Q') is a local deadlock and $\Gamma' \models L(T')$ then (T', p', Q') is a also a local deadlock because for any
$(\sigma, \text{await } e; S) \in \{p'\} \cup Q'$ we have that $\Gamma' \not\models e\sigma$ implies $L(T') \cup \{\neg e\sigma\} \not\vdash false$.

6   Decidability of Deadlock Detection

The abstract local behavior of a single actor, as defined in the previous section, gives rise, for a given initial configuration, to an infinite transition system because of dynamic generation of local calls and the corresponding introduction of fresh local variables. In this section we show how we can model an abstract system for which the transition relation is computable as well-structured transition system and obtain the decidability of deadlock detection for such abstract systems. To this end, we first provide a canonical representation of an abstract configuration which abstracts from renamings of the local variables by means of *multisets* of *closures*. A closure of a method m is a pair (u, S), where S is a *continuation* of the body of m and $u \subseteq Pred(m)$. (Here $Pred(m)$ denotes the set of predicates associated with m as defined in Sect. 3). The set of continuations of a statement S is the smallest set $Cont(S)$ such that $S \in Cont(S)$ and $\epsilon \in Cont(S)$, where the "empty" statement ϵ denotes termination, and which is closed under the following conditions

- $S'; S'' \in Cont(S)$ implies $S'' \in Cont(S)$
- if $e \ \{S_1\}$ else $\{S_2\}; S' \in Cont(S)$ implies $S_1; S' \in Cont(S)$ and $S_2; S' \in Cont(S)$
- while $e \ \{S'\}; S'' \in Cont(S)$ implies S'; while $e \ \{S'\}; S'' \in Cont(S)$.

Note that for a given method the set of all possible closures is finite. We formally represent a multiset of closures as a function which assigns a natural number $f(c)$ to each closure c which indicates the number of occurrences of c. For notational convenience we write $c \in f$ in case $f(c) > 0$.

In preparation of the notion of canonical representation of abstract configurations, we introduce for every abstract configuration $\alpha = (T, p, Q)$ the set $\bar{\alpha}$ of triples (σ, u, S) for which $(\sigma, u) \in T$ and either $(\sigma, S) \in \{p\} \cup Q$ or $S = \epsilon$.

Definition 3. *An abstract configuration* (T, p, Q) *is canonically represented by a multiset of closures* f, *if for every method* m *and closure* (u, S) *of* m *we have*

$$f((u, S)) = |\{ \sigma \mid (\sigma, u, S) \in \bar{\alpha} \}|$$

(where $|V|$ *denotes the cardinality of the set* V*).*

Note that each abstract configuration has a unique multiset representation. For any multiset f of closures, let $T(f)$ denote the set of predicates $\{\exists v \mid (v, S)^n \in f\}$, where $\exists v$ denotes the existential quantification of all the local variables appearing in the conjunction of the predicates of v. The following lemma states the equivalence of a set of closures and its canonical representation.

Lemma 1. *Let the abstract configuration* (T, p, Q) *be canonically represented by the multiset of closures* f. *Further, let* $(\sigma, u) \in T$, *where* $\sigma \in \Sigma(m)$, *and* $\varphi \in Pred(m)$. *It holds that*

$$L(T) \vdash \varphi\sigma \ iff \ \{u\} \cup T(f) \vdash \varphi$$

Proof. Proof-theoretically we reason, in first-order logic, as follows. For notational convenience we view a set of predicates as the conjunction over its elements. By the Deduction Theorem we have

$$L(T) \vdash \varphi\sigma \text{ iff } \vdash L(T) \rightarrow \varphi\sigma$$

From the laws of universal quantification we obtain

$$\vdash L(T) \rightarrow \varphi\sigma \text{ iff } \vdash \forall X(L(T) \rightarrow \varphi\sigma)$$

and

$$\vdash \forall X(L(T) \rightarrow \varphi\sigma) \text{ iff } \vdash \exists X L(T) \rightarrow \varphi\sigma$$

where X denotes the set of local variables appearing in $L(T) \setminus \{u\sigma\}$. Note that no local variable of X appears in $\varphi\sigma$ or $u\sigma$.

Since any two distinct $v, v' \in L(T)$ have no local variables in common, we can push the quantification of $\exists X L(T)$ inside. That is,

$$\vdash \exists X L(T) \rightarrow \varphi\sigma \text{ iff } \vdash \{ \exists X v \mid v \in L(T) \} \rightarrow \varphi\sigma$$

No local variable of X appears in $u\sigma$, therefore we have

$$\vdash \{ \exists X v \mid v \in L(T) \} \rightarrow \varphi\sigma \text{ iff } \vdash u\sigma \wedge \{ \exists X v \mid v \in L(T) \} \rightarrow \varphi\sigma$$

Again by the Deduction Theorem we then have

$$\vdash u\sigma \wedge \{ \exists X v \mid v \in L(T) \} \rightarrow \varphi\sigma \text{ iff } \{u\sigma\} \vdash \{ \exists X v \mid v \in L(T) \} \rightarrow \varphi\sigma$$

Clearly $u\sigma \vdash \exists u$ and $\exists X v$ is logically equivalent to $\exists v$, for any $v \in L(T) \setminus \{u\sigma\}$. So, we have

$$\{u\sigma\} \vdash \{ \exists X v \mid v \in L(T) \} \rightarrow \varphi\sigma \text{ iff } \{u\sigma\} \vdash \{ \exists v \mid v \in L(T) \} \rightarrow \varphi\sigma$$

Since f represents (T, p, Q) we have that $T(f) = \{ \exists v \mid v \in L(T) \}$. Renaming the local variables of $u\sigma$ and $\varphi\sigma$ then finally gives us

$$\{u\sigma\} \vdash \{ \exists v \mid v \in L(T) \} \rightarrow \varphi\sigma \text{ iff } \{u\} \vdash T(f) \rightarrow \varphi$$

which proves the lemma.   □

We next define an ordering on multisets of closures.

Definition 4. *By $f \preccurlyeq f'$ we denote that $f(c) \leqslant f'(c)$ and $f'(c) = 0$ if $f(c) = 0$.*

In other words, $f \preccurlyeq f'$ if all occurrences of f belong to f' and f' does not add occurrences of closures which do not already occur in f. The following result states that this relation is a well-quasi-ordering.

Lemma 2. *The relation $f \preccurlyeq f'$ is a quasi-ordering such that for any infinite sequence $(f_n)_n$ there exist indices $i < j$ such that $f_i \preccurlyeq f_j$.*

Proof. First observe that for a given class there is only a finite number of closures. We show that the proof for the standard subset relation for multisets also holds for this variation. Assume that for some set X of closures we have constructed an infinite subsequence $(f'_n)_n$ of $(f_n)_n$ such that $f'_i(c) \leqslant f'_j(c)$, for every $c \in X$ and $i < j$. Suppose that for every $c \notin X$ the set $\{\, k \mid f'_j(c) = k, \, j \in \mathbb{N} \,\}$ is bounded. It follows that there exists an f'_k which appears infinitely often in $(f'_n)_n$, since there exists only a finite number of combinations of occurrences of closures in $\bar{X} = \{\, c \mid c \notin X \,\}$. On the other hand, if there exists a $d \notin X$ such that set $\{\, k \mid f'_j(d) = k, \, j \in \mathbb{N} \,\}$ has no upperbound then we can obtain a subsequence $(f''_n)_n$ of $(f'_n)_n$ such that $f''_i(c) \leqslant f''_j(c)$ for every $c \in X \cup \{d\}$ and $i < j$. Thus, both cases lead to the existence of indices $i < j$ such that $f_i \preccurlyeq f_j$. □

From the above lemma it follows immediately that the following induced ordering on abstract configurations is also a well-quasi-ordering.

Definition 5. *We put* $(T, (\sigma, S), Q) \preccurlyeq (T', (\sigma', S), Q')$ *iff* $f \preccurlyeq f'$, *for multisets of closures* f *and* f' *(uniquely) representing* $(T, (\sigma, S), Q)$ *and* $(T', (\sigma', S), Q')$, *respectively.*

We can now formulate and prove the following theorem which states that this well-quasi-ordering is preserved by the transition relation of the abstract system.

Theorem 2. *For abstract configurations* α, α', *and* β, *if* $\alpha \to \alpha'$ *and* $\alpha \preccurlyeq \beta$ *then* $\beta \to \beta'$, *for some abstract configuration* β' *such that* $\alpha' \preccurlyeq \beta'$.

Proof. The proof proceeds by a case analysis of the transition $\alpha \to \alpha'$. Crucial in this analysis is the observation that $\alpha \preccurlyeq \beta$ implies that $\alpha = (T, p, Q)$ and $\beta = (T', p, Q)$, for some T and T' such that

$$L(T) \vdash \varphi\sigma \iff L(T') \vdash \varphi\sigma'$$

for renamings $\sigma, \sigma' \in \Sigma(m)$, where m is a method defined by the given class C, such that $(\sigma, u, S) \in \bar{\alpha}$ and $(\sigma', u, S) \in \bar{\beta}$, for some closure (u, S) and predicate φ of the method m. This follows from Lemma 1 and that $f \preccurlyeq f'$ implies $T(f) = T(f')$, where f and f' represent α and β, respectively. Note that by definition, f' does not add occurrences of closures which do not already occur in f. □

It follows that abstract systems for which the transition relation is computable are well-structured transition systems (see [10] for an excellent explanation and overview of well-structured transition systems). For such systems the *covering* problem is decidable. That is, for any two abstract configurations α and β it is decidable whether starting from α it is possible to cover β, meaning, whether there exists a computation $\alpha \to^* \alpha'$ such that $\beta \preccurlyeq \alpha'$. To show that this implies decidability of absence of deadlock, let α be a *basic* (abstract) deadlock configuration if α is a deadlock configuration according to Definition 2 and for any closure (u, S) there exists *at most one* renaming σ such that $(\sigma, u, S) \in \bar{\alpha}$. Note that thus $f(c) = 1$, for any closure c, where f represents α. Let Δ denote the set of all basic deadlock configurations. Note that this is a finite set. Further, for every (abstract) deadlock configuration α there exists a basic deadlock configuration $\alpha' \in \Delta$ such that $f \preccurlyeq f'$, where f and f' represent α and α', respectively. This is because the different renamings of the same closure do not affect the definition of a deadlock. Given an initial abstract configuration α, we now can phrase presence of deadlock as the covering problem of deciding whether there exists a computation starting from α reaching a configuration β that covers a deadlock configuration in Δ.

Summarizing the above, we have the following the main technical result of this paper.

Theorem 3. *Given an abstract system with a computable transition relation and an abstract configuration α, it is decidable whether*

$$\{\, \beta \mid \alpha \rightarrow^* \beta \,\} \cap \{\, \beta \mid \exists \beta' \in \Delta \colon \beta' \preccurlyeq \beta \,\} = \emptyset \tag{1}$$

Given this result and the correctness of predicate abstraction, to show that an initial concrete configuration (Γ, p, Q) does *not* give rise to a local deadlock, it suffices to construct an abstract configuration $\alpha = (T, p, Q)$ such that $\Gamma \models L(T)$ and for which Equation (1) holds. Note that we can construct T by the constructing pairs (σ, u), where $u = \{\phi \in Pred(m) \mid \Gamma \models \phi\sigma\}$ (assuming that $\sigma \in \Sigma(m)$).

7   Conclusion

For future work we first have to validate our method for detecting local deadlock in tool-supported case studies. For this we envisage the use of the theorem-prover KeY [2] for the construction of the abstract transition relation, and its integration with *on-the-fly* reachability analysis of the abstract transition system.

Of further interest, in line with the above, is the integration of the method of predicate abstraction in the theorem-prover KeY for reasoning *compositionally* about general safety properties of actor-based programs. For reasoning about programs in the ABS language this requires an extension of our method to *synchronous* method calls and *concurrent object groups*.

References

1. Agha, G.: Actors: A Model of Concurrent Computation in Distributed Systems. The MIT Press, Cambridge (1986)
2. Wasser, N., Hähnle, R., Bubel, R.: Abstract Interpretation. Deductive Software Verification – The KeY Book. LNCS, vol. 10001, pp. 167–189. Springer, Cham (2016). https://doi.org/10.1007/978-3-319-49812-6_6
3. Azadbakht, K., Bezirgiannis, N., de Boer, F.S.: Distributed network generation based on preferential attachment in ABS. In: Steffen, B., et al. (eds.) SOFSEM 2017. LNCS, vol. 10139, pp. 103–115. Springer, Cham (2017). https://doi.org/10.1007/978-3-319-51963-0_9
4. Azadbakht, K., Bezirgiannis, N., de Boer, F.S., Aliakbary, S.: A high-level and scalable approach for generating scale-free graphs using active objects. In: Proceedings of the 31st Annual ACM Symposium on Applied Computing, pp. 1244–1250. ACM (2016)

5. Ball, T., Majumdar, R., Millstein, T., Rajamani, S.K.: Automatic predicate abstraction of C programs. In: Conference on Programming Language Design and Implementation, pp. 203–213 (2001)
6. Conway, M.E.: Design of a separable transition-diagram compiler. Commun. ACM **6**(7), 396–408 (1963)
7. de Boer, F.S., et al.: A petri net based analysis of deadlocks for active objects and futures. In: Păsăreanu, C.S., Salaün, G. (eds.) FACS 2012. LNCS, vol. 7684, pp. 110–127. Springer, Heidelberg (2013). https://doi.org/10.1007/978-3-642-35861-6_7
8. de Boer, F.S., Clarke, D., Johnsen, E.B.: A complete guide to the future. In: De Nicola, R. (ed.) ESOP 2007. LNCS, vol. 4421, pp. 316–330. Springer, Heidelberg (2007). https://doi.org/10.1007/978-3-540-71316-6_22
9. de Boer, F.S., Jaghoori, M.M., Laneve, C., Zavattaro, G.: Decidability problems for actor systems. In: Koutny, M., Ulidowski, I. (eds.) CONCUR 2012. LNCS, vol. 7454, pp. 562–577. Springer, Heidelberg (2012). https://doi.org/10.1007/978-3-642-32940-1_39
10. Finkel, A., Schnoebelen, Ph.: Well-structured transition systems everywhere!. Theoret. Comput. Sci. **256**(1), 63–92 (2001)
11. Giachino, E., Henrio, L., Laneve, C., Mastandrea, V.: Actors may synchronize, safely! In: 18th International Symposium on Principles and Practice of Declarative Programming, pp. 118–131 (2016)
12. Giachino, E., Laneve, C., Lienhardt, M.: A framework for deadlock detection in core ABS. Softw. Syst. Model. **15**(4), 1013–1048 (2016)
13. Graf, S., Saidi, H.: Construction of abstract state graphs with PVS. In: Grumberg, O. (ed.) CAV 1997. LNCS, vol. 1254, pp. 72–83. Springer, Heidelberg (1997). https://doi.org/10.1007/3-540-63166-6_10
14. Henrio, L., Laneve, C., Mastandrea, V.: Analysis of synchronisations in stateful active objects. In: Polikarpova, N., Schneider, S. (eds.) IFM 2017. LNCS, vol. 10510, pp. 195–210. Springer, Cham (2017). https://doi.org/10.1007/978-3-319-66845-1_13
15. Hewitt, C.: Description and theoretical analysis (using schemata) of planner: a language for proving theorems and manipulating models in a robot. Technical report, Massachusetts Institute of Technology Cambridge Artificial Intelligence Lab (1972)
16. Johnsen, E.B., Hähnle, R., Schäfer, J., Schlatte, R., Steffen, M.: ABS: a core language for abstract behavioral specification. In: Aichernig, B.K., de Boer, F.S., Bonsangue, M.M. (eds.) FMCO 2010. LNCS, vol. 6957, pp. 142–164. Springer, Heidelberg (2011). https://doi.org/10.1007/978-3-642-25271-6_8
17. Johnsen, E.B., Owe, O., Creol, I.C.Yu.: A type-safe object-oriented model for distributed concurrent systems. Theoret. Comput. Sci. **365**(1–2), 23–66 (2006)
18. Kamburjan, E., Din, C.C., Chen, T.-C.: Session-based compositional analysis for actor-based languages using futures. In: Ogata, K., Lawford, M., Liu, S. (eds.) ICFEM 2016. LNCS, vol. 10009, pp. 296–312. Springer, Cham (2016). https://doi.org/10.1007/978-3-319-47846-3_19
19. Kerfoot, E., McKeever, S., Torshizi, F.: Deadlock freedom through object ownership. In: 5th International Workshop on Aliasing, Confinement and Ownership in Object-Oriented Programming (2009)
20. Sirjani, M.: Rebeca: theory, applications, and tools. In: de Boer, F.S., Bonsangue, M.M., Graf, S., de Roever, W.-P. (eds.) FMCO 2006. LNCS, vol. 4709, pp. 102–126. Springer, Heidelberg (2007). https://doi.org/10.1007/978-3-540-74792-5_5

An Algebraic Approach for Reasoning About Information Flow

Arthur Américo[1]($\boxtimes$), Mário S. Alvim[1], and Annabelle McIver[2]

[1] Universidade Federal de Minas Gerais, Belo Horizonte, Brazil
aamerico@dcc.ufmg.br
[2] Macquarie University, Sydney, Australia

Abstract. This paper concerns the analysis of information leaks in security systems. We address the problem of specifying and analyzing large systems in the (standard) channel model used in quantitative information flow (QIF). We propose several operators which match typical interactions between system components. We explore their algebraic properties with respect to the security-preserving refinement relation defined by Alvim et al. and McIver et al. [1,2].

We show how the algebra can be used to simplify large system specifications in order to facilitate the computation of information leakage bounds. We demonstrate our results on the specification and analysis of the Crowds Protocol. Finally, we use the algebra to justify a new algorithm to compute leakage bounds for this protocol.

1 Introduction

Protecting sensitive information from unintended disclosure is a crucial goal for information security. There are, however, many situations in which information leakage is unavoidable. An example is a typical password checker, which must always reveal some information about the secret password—namely whether or not it matches the input provided by the user when trying to log in. Another example concerns election tallies, which reveal information about individual votes by ruling out several configurations of votes (e.g., in the extreme case of an unanimous election, the tally reveals every vote). The field of *Quantitative Information Flow* (QIF) is concerned with quantifying the amount of sensitive information computational systems leak, and it has been extremely active in the past decade [3–9].

In the QIF framework, systems are described as receiving *secret inputs* from a set of values $\mathcal{X}$, and producing *public*, or *observable*, *outputs* from a set $\mathcal{Y}$. Typical secret inputs are a user's identity, password, or current location, whereas public outputs are anything an adversary can observe about the behavior of the system, such as messages written on the screen, execution time, or power consumption. A system is, then, modeled as an *(information-theoretic) channel*, which is a function mapping each possible pair $x \in \mathcal{X}$, $y \in \mathcal{Y}$ to the conditional probability $p(y \mid x)$ of the system producing output y when receiving input x. Channels abstract

© Springer International Publishing AG, part of Springer Nature 2018
K. Havelund et al. (Eds.): FM 2018, LNCS 10951, pp. 55–72, 2018.
https://doi.org/10.1007/978-3-319-95582-7_4

technicalities of the system, while retaining the essentials that influence information leakage: the relation between secret input and public output values.

The QIF framework provides a robust theory for deriving security properties from a system's representation as a channel. However, obtaining an appropriate channel to model a system is often a non-trivial task. Moreover, some channels turn out to be so large as to render most security analyses unfeasible in practice.

In this paper we provide an algebra for describing (larger, more complex) channels as compositions of other (smaller, simpler) channels. For that, we define a set of operators, each corresponding to a different way in which components can interact in a system—namely, *parallel* composition, *visible choice* composition, and *hidden choice* composition. We prove a series of algebraic properties of these operators, and use such properties to simplify system specifications so that bounds on the information leakage of a compound system can be inferred from the information leakage of its components. In this way, we allow for leakage analyses of systems which would be intractable with traditional QIF techniques.

This compositional approach seems particularly natural for modeling security protocols, which often involve interactions among various entities. Consider, for instance, the well-known *Dining Cryptographers* anonymity protocol [10]. A group of n cryptographers has been invited for dinner by the NSA (American National Security Agency), who will either pay the bill, or secretly ask one of the cryptographers to be the payer. The cryptographers want to determine whether one among them is the payer, but without revealing which one. For that, they execute the following protocol. In a first phase all participants form a circle, and each tosses a coin and shares the result only with the cryptographer on his right. In a second phase, each cryptographer computes the exclusive-or of the two coins tosses he observed (interpreting *heads* as 0 and *tails* as 1), and publicly announces the result. The only exception is the paying cryptographer (if any), who announces the negation of his exclusive-or. In a third phase, the cryptographers compute the exclusive-or of all announcements. One of them is the payer if, and only if, the result is 1. It has been shown that, if all coins are fair, no information is leaked about who the paying cryptographer is [10].

Despite the Dining Cryptographers relative simplicity, deriving its channel can be a challenging task. Since each of the n cryptographers can announce either 0 or 1, the size of the output set $\mathcal{Y}$, and, consequently, of the channel, increases exponentially with the number of cryptographers. The problem is worsened by the fact that computing the probabilities constituting the channel's entries is not trivial. The algebra

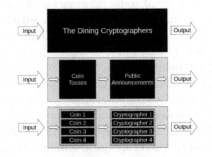

Fig. 1. Schematic representation of the Dining Cryptographers protocol as: (i) a monolithic channel (top); (ii) a composition of two channels (middle); and (iii) a composition of eight channels (bottom).

we introduce in this paper allows for an intuitive and compositional way of building a protocol's channel from each of its components. To illustrate the concept, Fig. 1 depicts three alternative representations, using channels, for the Dining Cryptographers with 4 cryptographers and 4 coins. In all models, the input is the identity of the payer (one of the cryptographers or the NSA), and the output are the public announcements of all cryptographers. The top model uses a single (enormous) channel to represent the protocol; the middle one models the protocol as the interaction between two smaller components (the coins and the party of cryptographers); the bottom one uses interactions between even smaller channels (one for each coin and each cryptographer).

The main contributions of this paper are the following.

- We formalize several common operators for channel composition used in the literature, each matching a typical interaction between system components. We prove several relevant algebraic and information-leakage properties of these operators.
- We show that the substitution of components in a system may be subject to unexpected, and perhaps counter-intuitive, results. In particular, we show that overall leakage may increase even when the new component is more secure than the one it is replacing (e.g., Theorems 5 and 6).
- We show how the proposed algebra can be used to simplify large system specifications in order to facilitate the computation of information leakage bounds, given in terms of the g-leakage framework [1,2,9,11].
- We demonstrate our results on the specification and analysis of the Crowds Protocol [12]. We use the proposed algebra to justify a new algorithm to compute leakage bounds for this protocol.

Detailed proofs of all of our technical results can be found in an accompanying technical report [13].

Plan of the Paper. The remainder of this paper is organized as follows. In Sect. 2 we review fundamental concepts from QIF. In Sect. 3 we introduce our channel operators, and in Sect. 4 we provide their algebraic properties. In Sect. 5 we present our main results, concerning information leakage in channel composition. In Sect. 6 we develop a detailed case study of the Crowds protocol. Finally, in Sect. 7 we discuss related work, and in Sect. 8 we conclude.

2   Preliminaries

In this section we review some fundamentals from quantitative information flow.

Secrets, Gain Functions and Vulnerability. A *secret* is some piece of sensitive information that one wants to protect from disclosure. Such sensitive information may concern, for instance, a user's password, identity, personal data, or current location. We represent by $\mathcal{X}$ the set of possible *secret values* the secret may take.

The *adversary* is assumed to have, before observing the system's behaviour, some *a priori* partial knowledge about the secret value. This knowledge is modeled as a probability distribution $\pi \in \mathbb{D}\mathcal{X}$, where $\mathbb{D}\mathcal{X}$ denotes the set of all probability distributions on $\mathcal{X}$. We call π a *prior distribution*, or simply a *prior*.

To quantify how *vulnerable* a secret is—i.e., how prone it is to exploitation by the adversary—we employ a function that maps probability distributions to the real numbers (or, more in general, to any ordered set). Many functions have been used in the literature, such as *Shannon entropy* [14], guessing-entropy [15], Bayes vulnerability [16], and *Rényi min-entropy* [6]. Recently, the *g-leakage* [1] framework was proposed, and it proved to be very successful in capturing a variety of different scenarios, including those in which the adversary benefits from guessing part of secret, guessing a secret approximately, guessing the secret within a number of tries, or gets punished for guessing wrongly. In particular, the framework has been shown to be able to capture all functions mentioned above [9]. In this framework, a finite set $\mathcal{W}$ of *actions* is available to the adversary, and a *gain-function* $g : \mathcal{W} \times \mathcal{X} \to [0,1]$ is used to describe the benefit $g(w,x)$ an adversary obtains when he performs action $w \in \mathcal{W}$, and the secret value is $x \in \mathcal{X}$. Given an appropriate gain-function g, the secret's *(prior) g-vulnerability* is defined as the expected value of the adversary's gain if he chooses a best possible action,

$$V_g[\pi] = \max_{w \in \mathcal{W}} \sum_{x \in \mathcal{X}} \pi(x)g(w,x),$$

and the greater its value, the more vulnerable, or insecure, the secret is.

Channels and Posterior Vulnerabilities. In the QIF framework, a system is usually modeled as an *(information theoretic) channel* taking a *secret input* $x \in \mathcal{X}$, and producing a *public*, or *observable*, *output* $y \in \mathcal{Y}$. Each element of $\mathcal{Y}$ represents a behaviour from the system that can be discerned by the adversary. Formally, a channel is a function $C : \mathcal{X} \times \mathcal{Y} \to \mathbb{R}$ such that $C(x,y)$ is the conditional probability $p(y \mid x)$ of the system producing output $y \in \mathcal{Y}$ when input is $x \in \mathcal{X}$.

A channel C together with a prior π induce a joint probability distribution p on the set $\mathcal{X} \times \mathcal{Y}$, given by $p(x,y) = \pi(x)C(x,y)$. From this joint distribution we can derive, for every $x \in \mathcal{X}$ and $y \in \mathcal{Y}$, the marginal probabilities $p(x) = \sum_y p(x,y)$ and $p(y) = \sum_x p(x,y)$, and the conditional probabilities $p(x \mid y) = p(x,y)/p(y)$ and $p(y \mid x) = p(x,y)/p(x)$. Note that $p(x) = \pi(x)$ and, if $p(x) \neq 0$, $p(y \mid x) = C(x,y)$.

By observing the output produced by the system, the adversary can update his knowledge about the secret value. More specifically, if the system outputs $y \in \mathcal{Y}$, an adversary can update the prior π to a revised *posterior distribution* $p_{X|y} \in \mathbb{D}\mathcal{X}$ on $\mathcal{X}$ given y, defined for all $x \in \mathcal{X}$ and $y \in \mathcal{Y}$ as $p_{X|y}(x) = p(x \mid y)$.

Example 1. Let $\mathcal{X} = \{x_1, x_2, x_3\}$ and $\mathcal{Y} = \{y_1, y_2, y_3, y_4\}$ be input and output sets. Let $\pi = (1/2, 1/3, 1/6)$ be a prior, and C be the channel below. The combination of π and C yield a joint probability p, according to the tables below.

C	y_1	y_2	y_3	y_4
x_1	$1/6$	$2/3$	$1/6$	0
x_2	$1/2$	$1/4$	$1/4$	0
x_3	$1/2$	$1/3$	0	$1/6$

$\xrightarrow{\pi}$

p	y_1	y_2	y_3	y_4
x_1	$1/12$	$1/3$	$1/12$	0
x_2	$1/6$	$1/12$	$1/12$	0
x_3	$1/12$	$1/18$	0	$1/36$

By summing the columns of the second table, we obtain the marginal probabilities $p(y_1) = 1/3$, $p(y_2) = 17/36$, $p(y_3) = 1/6$ and $p(y_4) = 1/36$. These marginal probabilities yield the posterior distributions $p_{X|y_1} = (1/4, 1/2, 1/4)$, $p_{X|y_2} = (12/17, 3/17, 2/17)$, $p_{X|y_3} = (1/2, 1/2, 0)$, and $p_{X|y_4} = (0, 0, 1)$.   □

The *posterior g-vulnerability* of a prior π and a channel C is defined as the expected value of the secret's g-vulnerability after the execution of the system:

$$V_g[\pi \rangle C] = \sum_{y \in \mathcal{Y}} \max_{w \in \mathcal{W}} \sum_{x \in \mathcal{X}} C(x, y)\pi(x)g(x, w).$$

The *information leakage* of a prior and a channel is a measure of the increase in secret vulnerability caused by the observation of the system's output. Leakage is, thus, defined as a comparison between the secret's prior and posterior vulnerabilities. Formally, for a gain-function g, and given prior π and channel C, the *multiplicative* and the *additive* versions of g-leakage are defined, respectively, as

$$\mathcal{L}_g[\pi \rangle C] = V_g[\pi \rangle C]/V_g[\pi], \qquad \text{and} \qquad \mathcal{L}_g^+[\pi \rangle C] = V_g[\pi \rangle C] - V_g[\pi].$$

Since prior vulnerability does not depend on the channel, we have that

$$\mathcal{L}_g[\pi \rangle C_1] \geq \mathcal{L}_g[\pi \rangle C_2] \;\Leftrightarrow\; \mathcal{L}_g^+[\pi \rangle C_1] \geq \mathcal{L}_g^+[\pi \rangle C_2] \;\Leftrightarrow\; V_g[\pi \rangle C_1] \geq V_g[\pi \rangle C_2],$$

and, hence, the posterior vulnerability of a channel is greater than that of another if, and only if, both multiplicative and additive leakage also are.

Channel Ordering and the Coriaceous Theorem. We now define a common composition of channels, called *cascading*. This operation can be interpreted as the result of a channel post-processing the output of another channel. Formally, given two channels $C : \mathcal{X} \times \mathcal{Y} \rightarrow \mathbb{R}$ and $D : \mathcal{Y} \times \mathcal{Z} \rightarrow \mathbb{R}$, their cascading is defined as

$$(CD)(x, z) = \sum_{y \in \mathcal{Y}} C(x, y)D(y, z),$$

for all $x \in \mathcal{X}$ and $z \in \mathcal{Z}$. If we represent channels as tables, as we did in Example 1, the cascading operation corresponds to a simple matrix multiplication.

An important question in QIF is to decide whether a channel C_2 is always *at least as secure as* a channel C_1, meaning that C_2 never leaks more information than C_1, for whatever choice of gain function g and of prior π. Let us write

$C_1 \sqsubseteq_\circ C_2$ (read as C_2 *refines* C_1) to denote that there exists a channel D such that $C_1 D = C_2$. We write $C_1 \approx C_2$, and say that C_1 is *equivalent* to C_2, when both $C_1 \sqsubseteq_\circ C_2$ and $C_2 \sqsubseteq_\circ C_1$ hold. The *Coriaceous Theorem* [1,2] states that, $C_1 \sqsubseteq_\circ C_2$ if, and only if, $V_g[\pi \rangle C_1] \geq V_g[\pi \rangle C_2]$ for all π, g. This result reduces the comparison of channel security to a simple algebraic test.

The *refinement relation* $\sqsubseteq_\circ$ is a preorder on the set of all channels having the same input set. This preorder can be made into a partial order by using *abstract channels* [2], an equivalence relation that equates all channels presenting same leakage for all priors and gain functions. This partial order coincides with how much information channels leak, being the least secure channel (i.e., the "most leaky" one) at its bottom, and the most secure (i.e., the "least leaky") at its top.

3 Operators on Channel Composition

We shall say that two channels are *compatible* if they have the same input set. Given a set $\mathcal{X}$, we denote by $\mathcal{C}_\mathcal{X}$ the set of all channels that have $\mathcal{X}$ as input set. Two compatible channels with same output set are said to be of the *same type*.

In this section we introduce several *binary operators*—i.e., functions of type $(\mathcal{C}_\mathcal{X} \times \mathcal{C}_\mathcal{X}) \to \mathcal{C}_\mathcal{X}$—matching typical interactions between system components, and prove relevant algebraic properties of these operators. We refer to the result of an operator as a *compound system*, and we refer to its arguments as *components*.

3.1 The Parallel Composition Operator ∥

The *parallel composition operator* ∥ models the composition of two independent channels in which the same input is fed to both of them, and their outputs are then observed. By *independent*, we mean that the output of one channel does not interfere with that of the other. This assumption, while not universal, captures a great variety of real-world scenarios, and is, hence, of practical interest.

For example, *side-channel attacks* occur when the adversary combines his observation of the system's output with some alternative way of inferring information about the secret (e.g., by observing physical properties of the system execution, such as time elapsed [17,18] or change in magnetic fields [19]). In such attacks, the channel used by the adversary to infer information about the secret can be modeled as the composition of a channel representing the program's intended behaviour in parallel with a channel modeling the relation between the secret and the physical properties of the hardware.

Definition 1 (Parallel composition operator ∥). *Given compatible channels* $C_1 : \mathcal{X} \times \mathcal{Y}_1 \to \mathbb{R}$ *and* $C_2 : \mathcal{X} \times \mathcal{Y}_2 \to \mathbb{R}$, *their* parallel composition $C_1 \parallel C_2 :$ $\mathcal{X} \times (\mathcal{Y}_1 \times \mathcal{Y}_2) \to \mathbb{R}$ *is defined as, for all* $x \in \mathcal{X}$, $y_1 \in \mathcal{Y}_1$, *and* $y_2 \in \mathcal{Y}_2$,

$$(C_1 \parallel C_2)(x, (y_1, y_2)) = C_1(x, y_1) C_2(x, y_2).$$

Notice that this definition comes from the independence property, as we have $C_1(x, y_1) C_2(x, y_2) = p(y_1 \mid x) p(y_2 \mid x) = p(y_1, y_2 \mid x)$.

3.2 The Visible Choice Operator $_p\sqcup$

The *visible choice operator* $_p\sqcup$ models a scenario in which the system has a choice among two different components to process the secret it was fed as input. With probability p, the system feeds the secret to the first component, and, with probability $1 - p$, it feeds the secret to the second component. In the end, the system reveals the output produced, together with the identification of which component was used (whence, the name "visible choice").

As an example, consider an adversary trying to gain information about a secret processed by a website. The adversary knows that the website has two servers, one of which will be assigned to answer the request according to a known probability distribution. Suppose, furthermore, that the adversary can identify which server was used by measuring its response time to the request. This adversary's view of the system can be modeled as the visible choice between the two servers, since, although the adversary does not know in advance which server will be used, he learns it when he gets the output from the system.

Before formalizing this operator, we need to define the *disjoint union* of sets. Given any sets $\mathcal{A}$ and $\mathcal{B}$, their disjoint union is $\mathcal{A} \sqcup \mathcal{B} = (\mathcal{A} \times \{1\}) \cup (\mathcal{B} \times \{2\})$.

Definition 2 (Visible choice operator $_p\sqcup$). *Given compatible channels $C_1 : \mathcal{X} \times \mathcal{Y}_1 \to \mathbb{R}$ and $C_2 : \mathcal{X} \times \mathcal{Y}_2 \to \mathbb{R}$, their* visible choice *is the channel $C_1 \,_p\sqcup\, C_2 : \mathcal{X} \times (\mathcal{Y}_1 \sqcup \mathcal{Y}_2) \to \mathbb{R}$ defined as, for all $x \in \mathcal{X}$ and $(y, i) \in \mathcal{Y}_1 \sqcup \mathcal{Y}_2$,*

$$(C_1 \,_p\sqcup\, C_2)(x, (y, i)) = \begin{cases} pC_1(x, y), & \text{if } i = 1, \\ (1 - p)C_2(x, y), & \text{if } i = 2. \end{cases}$$

3.3 The Hidden Choice Operator $_p\oplus$

Similarly to the visible choice case, the *hidden choice operator* $_p\oplus$ models a scenario in which the system has a choice of feeding its secret input to one component (with probability p), or to another component (with probability $1 - p$). In the end, the system reveals the output produced, but, unlike the visible choice case, the component which was used is not revealed. Hence, when the same observations are randomized between the two channels, the adversary cannot identify which channel produced the observation (whence, the name "hidden choice").

As an example, consider statistical surveys that ask some sensitive yes/no question, such as whether the respondent has made use of any illegal substances. To encourage individuals to participate on the survey, it is necessary to control leakage of their sensitive information, while preserving the accuracy of statistical information in the ensemble of their answers. A common protocol to achieve this goal works as follows [20]. Each respondent throws a coin, without letting the questioner know the corresponding result. If the result is heads, the respondent answers the question honestly, and if the result is tails, he gives a random response (obtained, for example, according to the result of a second coin toss). If the coins are fair, this protocol can be modeled as the hidden choice $T \,_{1/2}\oplus\, C$

between a channel T representing an honest response (revealing the secret completely), and a channel C representing a random response (revealing nothing about the secret). The protocol is, hence, a channel that masks the result of T.

Definition 3 (Hidden choice operator $_p\oplus$). *Given compatible channels C_1 : $\mathcal{X} \times \mathcal{Y}_1 \rightarrow \mathbb{R}$ and $C_2 : \mathcal{X} \times \mathcal{Y}_2 \rightarrow \mathbb{R}$, their hidden choice is the channel $C_1\ _p\oplus\ C_2$: $\mathcal{X} \times (\mathcal{Y}_1 \cup \mathcal{Y}_2) \rightarrow \mathbb{R}$ defined as, for all $x \in \mathcal{X}$ and $y \in \mathcal{Y}_1 \cup \mathcal{Y}_2$,*

$$(C_1\ _p\oplus\ C_2)(x,y) = \begin{cases} pC_1(x,y) + (1-p)C_2(x,y), & \text{if } y \in \mathcal{Y}_1 \cap \mathcal{Y}_2, \\ pC_1(x,y), & \text{if } y \in \mathcal{Y}_1 \setminus \mathcal{Y}_2, \\ (1-p)C_2(x,y), & \text{if } y \in \mathcal{Y}_2 \setminus \mathcal{Y}_1. \end{cases}$$

Note that when the output sets of C_1 and C_2 are disjoint the adversary can always identify the channel used, and we have $C_1\ _p\sqcup\ C_2 \approx C_1\ _p\oplus\ C_2$.

3.4 A Compositional Description of the Dining Cryptographers

We now revisit the Dining Cryptographers protocol example from Sect. 1, showing how it can be modeled using our composition operators.

We consider that there are 4 cryptographers and 4 coins, and denote the protocol's channel by *Dining*. The channel's input set is $\mathcal{X} = \{c_1, c_2, c_3, c_4, n\}$, in which c_i represents that cryptographer i is the payer, and n represents that the NSA is the payer. The channel's output set is $\mathcal{Y} = \{0,1\}^4$, i.e., all 4-tuples representing possible announcements by all cryptographers, in order.

Following the scheme in Fig. 1 (middle), we begin by modeling the protocol as the interaction between two channels, *Coins* and *Announcements*, representing, respectively, the coin tosses and the cryptographers' public announcements. Since in the protocol first the coins are tossed, and only then the corresponding results are passed on to the party of cryptographers, *Dining* can be described as the cascading of these two channels:

$$Dining = (Coins)(Announcements).$$

To specify channel *Coins*, we use the parallel composition of channels $Coin_1$, $Coin_2$, $Coin_3$ and $Coin_4$, each representing one coin toss. Letting p_i denote the probability of coin i landing on tails, these channels are defined as on Table 2.

Besides the result of the tosses, *Coins* also needs to pass on to *Announcements* the identity of the payer. We then introduce a fifth channel, $I : \mathcal{X} \times \mathcal{X} \rightarrow \mathbb{R}$, that simply outputs the secret, i.e., $I(x_1, x_2) = 1$ if $x_1 = x_2$, and 0 otherwise. Hence, a complete definition of channel *Coins* is

$Coin_i$	Tails	Heads
c_1	p_i	$1-p_i$
c_2	p_i	$1-p_i$
c_3	p_i	$1-p_i$
c_4	p_i	$1-p_i$
n	p_i	$1-p_i$

Fig. 2. Channel representing toss of coin $Coin_i$.

$$Coins = Coin_1 \parallel Coin_2 \parallel Coin_3 \parallel Coin_4 \parallel I.$$

As we will show in Sect. 4, parallel composition is associative, allowing us to omit parentheses in the equation above.

We now specify the channel *Announcements*, which takes as input a 5-tuple with five terms whose first four elements are the results of the coin tosses, and the fifth is the identity of the payer. For that end, we describe each cryptographer as a channel with this 5-tuple as input, and with the set of possible announcements $\{0, 1\}$ as output set. $Crypto_1$ below describes the first cryptographer.

$$Crypto_1(t_1, t_2, t_3, t_4, x) = \begin{cases} 1, & \text{if } t_4 = t_1 \text{ and } x = c_1, \text{ or } t_4 \neq t_1 \text{ and } x \neq c_1 \\ 0, & \text{otherwise} \end{cases}$$

Channels $Crypto_2$, $Crypto_3$ and $Crypto_4$ describing the remaining cryptographers are defined analogously. Channel *Announcements* is, hence, defined as

$$Announcements = Crypto_1 \parallel Crypto_2 \parallel Crypto_3 \parallel Crypto_4.$$

Note that our operators allow for an intuitive and succinct representation of the channel *Dining* modeling the Dining Cryptographers protocol, even when the number of cryptographers and coins is large. Moreover, the channel is easy to compute: we need only to first calculate the parallel compositions within channels *Crypto* and *Announcements*, and then multiply these channels' matrices.

4 Algebraic Properties of Channel Operators

In this section we prove a series of relevant algebraic properties of our channel operators. These properties are the key for building channels in a compositional way, and, more importantly, for deriving information flow properties of a compound system in terms of those of its components.

We begin by defining a notion of equivalence stricter than $\approx$, which equates any two channels that are identical modulo a permutation of their columns.

Definition 4 (Channel equality). *Let $C_1 : \mathcal{X} \times \mathcal{Y}_1 \to \mathbb{R}$ and $C_2 : \mathcal{X} \times \mathcal{Y}_2 \to \mathbb{R}$ be compatible channels. We say that C_1 and C_2 are equal up to a permutation, and write $C_1 \overset{\circ}{=} C_2$, if there is a bijection $\psi : \mathcal{Y}_1 \to \mathcal{Y}_2$ such that $C_1(x, y) = C_2(x, \psi(y))$ for all $x \in \mathcal{X}$, $y \in \mathcal{Y}_1$.*

Note that, if $C_1 \overset{\circ}{=} C_2$, then $C_1 \approx C_2$.[1]

In remaining of this section, let $C_1 : \mathcal{X} \times \mathcal{Y}_1 \to \mathbb{R}$, $C_2 : \mathcal{X} \times \mathcal{Y}_2 \to \mathbb{R}$ and $C_3 : \mathcal{X} \times \mathcal{Y}_3 \to \mathbb{R}$ be compatible channels, and $p, q \in [0, 1]$ be probability values.

4.1 Properties Regarding Channel Operators

We first establish our operators' associativity and commutativity properties.

Proposition 1 (Commutative Properties)

$$C_1 \parallel C_2 \overset{\circ}{=} C_2 \parallel C_1, \quad C_1 \ _p\sqcup C_2 \overset{\circ}{=} C_2 \ _{(1-p)}\sqcup C_1, \quad \text{and} \quad C_1 \ _p\oplus C_2 = C_2 \ _{(1-p)}\oplus C_1.$$

---

[1] A complete, formal definition of such bijections can be found in an accompanying technical report [13].

Proposition 2 (Associative Properties)

$$(C_1 \parallel C_2) \parallel C_3 \stackrel{\circ}{=} C_1 \parallel (C_2 \parallel C_3), \qquad (C_1 \,_p\sqcup C_2) \,_q\sqcup C_3 \stackrel{\circ}{=} C_1 \,_{p'}\sqcup (C_2 \,_{q'}\sqcup C_3),$$

$$\text{and } (C_1 \,_p\oplus C_2) \,_q\oplus C_3 = C_1 \,_{p'}\oplus (C_2 \,_{q'}\oplus C_3), \text{ s.t. } p' = pq \text{ and } q' = {}^{(q-pq)}/_{(1-pq)}.$$

We now turn our attention to two kinds of channels that will be recurrent building blocks for more complex channels. A *null channel* is any channel $\overline{0}$: $\mathcal{X} \times \mathcal{Y} \to \mathbb{R}$ such that, for every prior π and gain-function g, $V_g[\pi \rangle \overline{0}] = V_g[\pi]$. That is, a null channel never leaks any information. A channel $\overline{0}$ is null if, and only if, $\overline{0}(x,y) = \overline{0}(x',y)$ for all $y \in \mathcal{Y}$ and $x, x' \in \mathcal{X}$. On the other hand, a *transparent channel* is any channel $\overline{I} : \mathcal{X} \times \mathcal{Y} \to \mathbb{R}$ that leaks at least as much information as any other compatible channel, for every prior and gain-function. A channel $\overline{I}$ is transparent if, and only if, for each $y \in \mathcal{Y}$, there is at most one $x \in \mathcal{X}$ such that $\overline{I}(x,y) > 0$. The following properties hold for any null channel $\overline{0}$ and transparent channel $\overline{I}$ compatible with C_1, C_2 and C_3.

Proposition 3 (Null and Transparent Channel Properties)

$$\text{null channel: } (C_1 \parallel \overline{0}) \approx C_1, \ C_1 \sqsubseteq_\circ (C_1 \,_p\sqcup \overline{0}), \ C_1 \sqsubseteq_\circ (C_1 \,_p\oplus \overline{0}).$$

$$\text{transparent channel: } (C_1 \parallel \overline{I}) \approx \overline{I}, \quad (C_1 \,_p\sqcup \overline{I}) \sqsubseteq_\circ C_1.$$

Note that, in general, $(C_1 \,_p\oplus \overline{I}) \not\sqsubseteq_\circ C_1$. To see why, consider the two transparent channels $\overline{I}_1$ and $\overline{I}_2$, with both input and output sets equal $\{1,2\}$, given by $\overline{I}_1(x,x') = 1$ if $x = x'$, and 0 otherwise, and $\overline{I}_2(x,x') = 0$ if $x = x'$, and 1 otherwise Then, $\overline{I}_1 \,_p\oplus \overline{I}_2$ is a null channel, and the property does not hold for $C_1 = \overline{I}_1, \overline{I} = \overline{I}_2$.

We now consider idempotency.

Proposition 4 (Idempotency)

$$C_1 \parallel C_1 \sqsubseteq_\circ C_1, \qquad C_1 \,_p\sqcup C_1 \approx C_1, \qquad \text{and} \qquad C_1 \,_p\oplus C_1 = C_1.$$

Note that $C_1 \parallel C_1 \approx C_1$ holds only when C_1 is deterministic or equivalent to a deterministic channel.

Finally, we consider distributive properties. In particular, we explore interesting properties when an operator is "distributed" over itself.

Proposition 5 (Distribution over the same operator)

$$(C_1 \parallel C_2) \parallel (C_1 \parallel C_3) \sqsubseteq_\circ C_1 \parallel (C_2 \parallel C_3),$$
$$C_1 \,_p\sqcup (C_2 \,_q\sqcup C_3) \approx (C_1 \,_p\sqcup C_2) \,_q\sqcup (C_1 \,_p\sqcup C_3),$$
$$C_1 \,_p\oplus (C_2 \,_q\oplus C_3) = (C_1 \,_p\oplus C_2) \,_q\oplus (C_1 \,_p\oplus C_3).$$

Proposition 6 (Distribution over different operators)

$$C_1 \parallel (C_2 \,_p\sqcup C_3) \stackrel{\circ}{=} (C_1 \parallel C_2) \,_p\sqcup (C_1 \parallel C_3),$$
$$C_1 \parallel (C_2 \,_p\oplus C_3) = (C_1 \parallel C_2) \,_p\oplus (C_1 \parallel C_3),$$
$$C_1 \,_p\sqcup (C_2 \,_q\oplus C_3) = (C_1 \,_p\sqcup C_2) \,_q\oplus (C_1 \,_p\sqcup C_3).$$

Unfortunately, the distribution of $_p\sqcup$ over $\parallel$, $_p\oplus$ over $\parallel$, or $_p\oplus$ over $_p\sqcup$ is not as well behaved. A complete discussion is available in the technical report [13].

4.2   Properties Regarding Cascading

We conclude this section by exploring how our operators behave w.r.t. cascading (defined in Sect. 2). Cascading of channels is fundamental in QIF, as it captures the concept of a system's *post-processing* of another system's outputs, and it is also the key to the partial order on channels discussed in Sect. 2.

The next propositions explore whether it is possible to express a composition of two post-processed channels by a post-processing of their composition.

Proposition 7. *Let* $D_1 : \mathcal{Y}_1 \times \mathcal{Z}_1 \to \mathbb{R}$, $D_2 : \mathcal{Y}_2 \times \mathcal{Z}_2 \to \mathbb{R}$ *be channels. Then,*

$$(C_1 D_1) \parallel (C_2 D_2) = (C_1 \parallel C_2) D^{\parallel},$$

where $D^{\parallel} : (\mathcal{Y}_1 \times \mathcal{Y}_2) \times (\mathcal{Z}_1 \times \mathcal{Z}_2) \to \mathbb{R}$ *is defined, for all* $y_1 \in \mathcal{Y}_1$, $y_2 \in \mathcal{Y}_2$, $z_1 \in \mathcal{Z}_1$, *and* $z_2 \in \mathcal{Z}_2$, *as* $D^{\parallel}((y_1, y_2), (z_1, z_2)) = D_1(y_1, z_1) D_2(y_2, z_2)$.

Proposition 8. *Let* $D_1 : \mathcal{Y}_1 \times \mathcal{Z}_1 \to \mathbb{R}$, $D_2 : \mathcal{Y}_2 \times \mathcal{Z}_2 \to \mathbb{R}$ *be channels. Then,*

$$(C_1 D_1) \,_p\!\sqcup (C_2 D_2) = (C_1 \,_p\!\sqcup C_2) D^{\sqcup},$$

where $D^{\sqcup} : (\mathcal{Y}_1 \sqcup \mathcal{Y}_2) \times (\mathcal{Z}_1 \sqcup \mathcal{Z}_2) \to \mathbb{R}$ *is defined as* $D^{\sqcup}((y, i), (z, j)) = D_1(y, z)$ *if* $i = j = 1$, *or* $D_2(y, z)$ *if* $i = j = 2$, *or* 0 *otherwise, for all* $y_1 \in \mathcal{Y}_1$, $y_2 \in \mathcal{Y}_2$, $z_1 \in \mathcal{Z}_1$, $z_2 \in \mathcal{Z}_2$.

A similar rule, however, does not hold for hidden choice. For example, let C_1 and C_2 be channels with input and output sets $\{1, 2\}$, such that $C_1(x, x') = 1$ if $x = x'$, or 0 otherwise, and $C_2(x, x') = 0$ if $x = x'$, or 1 otherwise. Let D_1 and D_2 be transparent channels whose output sets are disjoint. Then, $(C_1 D_1) \,_{1/2}\!\oplus (C_2 D_2)$ is a transparent channel, but $C_1 \,_{1/2}\!\oplus C_2$ is a null channel. Thus, it is impossible to describe $(C_1 D_1) \,_{1/2}\!\oplus (C_2 D_2)$ as $C_1 \,_{1/2}\!\oplus C_2$ post-processed by some channel. However, we can establish a less general, yet relevant, equivalence.

Proposition 9. *Let* $C_1 : \mathcal{X} \times \mathcal{Y} \to \mathbb{R}$ *and* $C_2 : \mathcal{X} \times \mathcal{Y} \to \mathbb{R}$ *be channels of the same type. Let* $D : \mathcal{Y} \times \mathcal{Z} \to \mathbb{R}$ *be a channel. Then,* $(C_1 D) \,_p\!\oplus (C_2 D) = (C_1 \,_p\!\oplus C_2) D$.

5   Information Leakage of Channel Operators

This section presents the main contribution of our paper: a series of results showing how, using the proposed algebra, we can facilitate the security analysis of compound systems. Our results are given in terms of the g-leakage framework introduced in Sect. 2, and we focus on two central problems. For the remaining of the section, let $C_1 : \mathcal{X} \times \mathcal{Y}_1 \to \mathbb{R}$ and $C_2 : \mathcal{X} \times \mathcal{Y}_2 \to \mathbb{R}$ be compatible channels.

5.1   The Problem of Compositional Vulnerability

The first problem consists in estimating the information leakage of a compound system in terms of the leakage of its components. This is formalized as follows.

The Problem of Compositional Vulnerability: *Given a composition oper-ator* $*$ *on channels, a prior* $\pi \in \mathbb{D}\mathcal{X}$, *and a gain function* g, *how can we estimate* $V_g[\pi \rangle C_1 * C_2]$ *in terms of* $V_g[\pi \rangle C_1]$ *and* $V_g[\pi \rangle C_2]$?

Theorem 1 (Upper and lower bounds for V_g w.r.t. $\|$). *For all gain functions* g *and* $\pi \in \mathbb{D}\mathcal{X}$, *let* $\mathcal{X}' = \{x \in \mathcal{X} \mid \exists w \in \mathcal{W} \ s.t. \ \pi(x)g(w,x) > 0\}$. *Then*

$$V_g[\pi \rangle C_1 \| C_2] \geq \max(V_g[\pi \rangle C_1], V_g[\pi \rangle C_2]), \qquad and$$

$$V_g[\pi \rangle C_1 \| C_2] \leq \min\left(V_g[\pi \rangle C_1] \sum_{y_2} \max_{x \in \mathcal{X}'} C_2(x, y_2), V_g[\pi \rangle C_2] \sum_{y_1} \max_{x \in \mathcal{X}'} C_1(x, y_1)\right).$$

Theorem 2 (Linearity of V_g w.r.t. $_p\sqcup$). *For all gain functions* g, $\pi \in \mathbb{D}\mathcal{X}$ *and* $p \in [0, 1]$,

$$V_g[\pi \rangle C_1 \ _p\sqcup \ C_2] = pV_g[\pi \rangle C_1] + (1 - p)V_g[\pi \rangle C_2].$$

Theorem 3 (Upper and lower bounds for V_g w.r.t. $_p\oplus$). *For all gain functions* g, $\pi \in \mathbb{D}\mathcal{X}$ *and* $p \in [0, 1]$,

$$V_g[\pi \rangle C_1 \ _p\oplus C_2] \geq \max(pV_g[\pi \rangle C_1], (1 - p)V_g[\pi \rangle C_2]), \qquad and$$
$$V_g[\pi \rangle C_1 \ _p\oplus C_2] \leq pV_g[\pi \rangle C_1] + (1 - p)V_g[\pi \rangle C_2].$$

The three theorems above yield an interesting order between the operators.

Corollary 1 (Ordering between operators). *Let* $\pi \in \mathbb{D}\mathcal{X}$, g *be a gain function and* $p \in [0, 1]$. *Then* $V_g[\pi \rangle C_1 \| C_2] \geq V_g[\pi \rangle C_1 \ _p\sqcup C_2] \geq V_g[\pi \rangle C_1 \ _p\oplus C_2]$.

5.2   The Problem of Relative Monotonicity

The second problem concerns establishing whether a component channel of a larger system can be safely substituted with another component, i.e., whether substituting a component with another can cause an increase in the information leakage of the system as a whole. This is formalized as follows.

The Problem of Relative Monotonicity: *Given a composition operator* $*$ *on channels, a prior* $\pi \in \mathbb{D}\mathcal{X}$, *and a gain function* g, *is it the case that* $V_g[\pi \rangle C_1] \leq V_g[\pi \rangle C_2] \Leftrightarrow \forall C \in \mathcal{C}_\mathcal{X}. \ V_g[\pi \rangle C_1 * C] \leq V_g[\pi \rangle C_2 * C]$?

We start by showing that relative monotonicity holds for visible choice. Note, however, that because $V_g[\pi \rangle C_1 \ _p\sqcup C] \leq V_g[\pi \rangle C_2 \ _p\sqcup C]$ is vacuously true if $p = 0$, we consider only $p \in (0, 1]$.

Theorem 4 (Relative monotonicity for $_p\sqcup$). *For all gain functions* g, $\pi \in \mathbb{D}\mathcal{X}$ *and* $p \in (0, 1]$,

$$V_g[\pi \rangle C_1] \leq V_g[\pi \rangle C_2] \Leftrightarrow \forall C. \ V_g[\pi \rangle C_1 \ _p\sqcup C] \leq V_g[\pi \rangle C_2 \ _p\sqcup C].$$

Interestingly, relative monotonicity does not hold for the parallel operator. This means that the fact that a channel C_1 is always more secure than a channel C_2 does not guarantee that if we replace C_1 for C_2 in a parallel context we necessarily obtain a more secure system.[2] However, when the adversary's knowledge (represented by the prior π) or preferences (represented by the gain-function g) are known, we can obtain a constrained result on leakage by fixing only π or g.

Theorem 5 (Relative monotonicity for $\parallel$). *For all gain functions g and $\pi \in \mathbb{D}\mathcal{X}$*

$$\forall \pi'. V_g[\pi' \rangle C_1] \leq V_g[\pi' \rangle C_2] \Leftrightarrow \forall \pi', C. V_g[\pi' \rangle C_1 \parallel C] \leq V_g[\pi' \rangle C_2 \parallel C], \quad and$$
$$\forall g'. V_{g'}[\pi \rangle C_1] \leq V_{g'}[\pi \rangle C_2] \Leftrightarrow \forall g', C. V_{g'}[\pi \rangle C_1 \parallel C] \leq V_{g'}[\pi \rangle C_2 \parallel C].$$

Perhaps surprisingly, hidden choice does not respect relative monotonicity, even when we only consider channels that respect the refinement relation introduced in Sect. 2.

Theorem 6 (Relative monotonicity for $_p\oplus$). *For all $p \in (0,1)$, there are $C_1 : \mathcal{X} \times \mathcal{Y} \to \mathbb{R}$ and $C_2 : \mathcal{X} \times \mathcal{Y} \to \mathbb{R}$ such that*

$$\forall \pi, g. V_g[\pi \rangle C_1] \leq V_g[\pi \rangle C_2] \text{ and } \exists \pi', g', C. V_{g'}[\pi' \rangle C_1\, _p\oplus C] > V_{g'}[\pi' \rangle C_2\, _p\oplus C],$$

The converse, however, is true.

Theorem 7 (Relative monotonicity for $_p\oplus$, cont.). *For all gain functions g, $\pi \in \mathbb{D}\mathcal{X}$ and $p \in (0,1]$,*

$$\forall C. V_g[\pi \rangle C_1\, _p\oplus C] \leq V_g[\pi \rangle C_2\, _p\oplus C] \Rightarrow V_g[\pi \rangle C_1] \leq V_g[\pi \rangle C_2].$$

6   Case Study: The Crowds Protocol

In this section we apply the theoretical techniques developed in this paper to the well-known *Crowds* anonymity protocol [12]. Crowds was designed to protect the identity of a group of *users* who wish to anonymously send requests to a *server*, and it is the basis of the widely used protocols *Onion Routing* [21] and *Tor* [22].

The protocol works as follows. When a user wants to send a request to the server, he first randomly picks another user in the group and forwards the request to that user. From that point on, each user, upon receiving a request from another user, sends it to the server with probability $p \in (0,1]$, or forwards it to another user with probability $1 - p$. This second phase repeats until the message reaches the server.

---

[2] As a counter-example, consider channels $C_1 = \begin{pmatrix} 1 & 0 \\ 1 & 0 \\ 0 & 1 \end{pmatrix}$ and $C_2 = \begin{pmatrix} 1 & 0 \\ 0 & 1 \\ 0 & 1 \end{pmatrix}$. Let $\pi_u = \{1/3, 1/3, 1/3\}$ and $g_{id} : \mathcal{X} \times \mathcal{X} \to [0,1]$ s.t. $g_{id}(x_1, x_2) = 1$ if $x_1 = x_2$ and 0 otherwise. Then, $V_{g_{id}}[\pi_u \rangle C_2] \leq V_{g_{id}}[\pi_u \rangle C_1]$, but $V_{g_{id}}[\pi_u \rangle C_2 \parallel C_1] > V_{g_{id}}[\pi_u \rangle C_1 \parallel C_1]$.

It is assumed that the adversary controls the server and some *corrupt* users among the regular, *honest*, ones. When a corrupt user receives a forwarded request, he shares the forwarder's identity with the server, and we say that the forwarder was *detected*. As no information can be gained after a corrupt user intercepts a request, we need only consider the protocol's execution until a detection occurs, or the message reaches the server.

In Crowds' original description, all users have equal probability of being forwarded a message, regardless of the forwarder. The channel modeling such a case is easily computed, and well-known in the literature. Here we consider the more general case in which each user may employ a different probability distribution when choosing which user to forward a request to. Thus, we can capture scenarios in which not all users can easily reach each other (a common problem in, for instance, *ad-hoc* networks). We make the simplifying assumption that corrupt users are evenly distributed, i.e., that all honest users have the same probability $q \in (0, 1]$ of choosing a corrupt user to forward a request to.

We model Crowds as a channel $Crowds : \mathcal{X} \times \mathcal{Y} \rightarrow \mathbb{R}$. The channel's input, taken from set $\mathcal{X} = \{u_1, u_2, \ldots, u_{n_c}\}$, represents the identity u_i of the honest user (among a total of n_c honest users) who initiated the request. The channel's output is either the identity of a detect user—i.e., a value from $\mathcal{D} = \{d_1, d_2, \ldots, d_{n_c}\}$, where where d_i indicates user u_i was detected—or the identity of a user who forwarded the message to the server—i.e., a value from $\mathcal{S} = \{s_1, s_2, \ldots, s_{n_c}\}$, where s_i indicates user u_i forwarded a message to the server. Note that $\mathcal{D}$ and $\mathcal{S}$ are disjoint, and the channel's output set is $\mathcal{Y} = \mathcal{D} \cup \mathcal{S}$.

To compute the channel's entries, we model the protocol as a time-stationary Markov chain $M = (\mathcal{U}, \boldsymbol{P})$, where the set of states is the set of honest users $\mathcal{U}$, and its transition function is such that $\boldsymbol{P}(u_i, u_j)$ is the probability of u_j being the recipient of a request forwarded by u_i, given that u_i will not be detected.

We then define four auxiliary channels. Transparent channels $I_d : \mathcal{U} \times \mathcal{D} \rightarrow \mathbb{R}$ and $I_s : \mathcal{U} \times \mathcal{S} \rightarrow \mathbb{R}$ are defined as $I_d(u_i, d_j) = 1$ if $i = j$, or 0 otherwise, and $I_s(u_i, s_j) = 1$ if $i = j$, or 0 otherwise; and two other channels $P_d : \mathcal{D} \times \mathcal{D} \rightarrow \mathbb{R}$ and $P_s : \mathcal{S} \times \mathcal{S} \rightarrow \mathbb{R}$, based on our Markov chain M, are defined as $P_d(d_i, d_j) = P_s(s_i, s_j) = \boldsymbol{P}(u_i, u_j)$.

We begin by reasoning about what happens if each request can be forwarded only once. There are two possible situations: either the initiator is detected, or he forwards the request to an honest user, who will in turn send it to the server. The channel corresponding to the initiator being detected is I_d, since in this case the output has to be d_i whenever u_i is the initiator. The channel corresponding to the latter situation is $I_s P_s$—i.e., the channel I_s postprocessed by P_s. This is because, being P_s based on the transition function of M, the entry $(I_s P_s)(u_i, s_j)$ gives us exactly the probability that user u_j received the request originated by user u_i after it being forwarded once. Therefore, when Crowds is limited to one forwarding, it can be modeled by the channel $I_d \ {}_q\oplus I_s P_s$[3], representing the fact that: (1) with probability q the initiator is detected, and the output is generated by I_d; and (2) with probability $1 - q$ the output is generated by $I_s P_s$.

---

[3] To simplify notation, we assume cascading has precedence over hidden choice, i.e., $AB \ {}_p\oplus CD = (AB) \ {}_p\oplus (CD)$.

Let us now cap our protocol to at most two forwards. If the initiator is not immediately detected, the first recipient will have a probability p of sending the message to the server. If the recipient forwards the message instead, he may be detected. Because the request was already forwarded once, the channel that will produce the output in this case is $I_d P_d$ (notice that, despite this channel being equivalent to $I_s P_s$, it is of a different type). On the other hand, if the first recipient forwards the message to an honest user, this second recipient will now send the message to the server, making the protocol produce an output according to $I_s P_s P_s$ (or simply $I_s P_s^2$), since $(I_s P_s^2)(u_i, s_j)$ is the probability that user u_j received the request originated by user u_i after it being forwarded twice. Therefore, when Crowds is limited to two forwardings, it can be modeled by the channel $I_d \,_q\oplus (I_s P_s \,_p\oplus (I_d P_d \,_q\oplus I_s P_s^2))$. Note the disposition of the parenthesis reflects the order in which the events occur. First, there is a probability q of the initiator being detected, and $1 - q$ of the protocol continuing. Then, there is a probability p of the first recipient sending it to the server, and so on.

Proceeding this way, we can inductively construct a sequence $\{C_i\}_{i \in \mathbb{N}^*}$,

$$C_i = I_d \,_q\oplus (I_s P_s \,_p\oplus (I_d P_d \,_q\oplus (\ldots \,_p\oplus (I_d P_d^{i-1} \,_q\oplus I_s P_s^i)\ldots))),$$

in which each C_i represents our protocol capped at i forwards per request. We can then obtain $Crowds$ by taking $\lim_{i \to \infty} C_i$. From that, Theorem 3 and Proposition 2, we can derive the following bounds on the information leakage of Crowds.

Theorem 8. *Let $\{t_i\}_{i \in \mathbb{N}}$ be the sequence in which $t_{2i} = 1 - (1 - q)^{i+1}(1 - p)^i$ and $t_{(2i+1)} = 1 - (1 - q)^{i+1}(1 - p)^{i+1}$ for all $i \in \mathbb{N}$.*
Let $K_m = ((\ldots(I_d \,_{t_0/t_1}\oplus I_s P_s) \,_{t_1/t_2}\oplus \ldots) \,_{t_{2m-1}/t_{2m}}\oplus (I_d P_d^m)$. Then, $\forall m \in \mathbb{N}^*$,

$$V_g[\pi \rangle \lim_{i \to \infty} C_i] \geq t_{2m} V_g[\pi \rangle K_m], \tag{1}$$

$$V_g[\pi \rangle \lim_{i \to \infty} C_i] \leq t_{2m} V_g[\pi \rangle K_m] + (1 - t_{2m})V_g[\pi \rangle I_s P_s^{m+1}], \quad and \tag{2}$$

$$(1 - t_{2m})V_g[\pi \rangle I_s P_s^{m+1}] \leq (1 - q)^{m+1}(1 - p)^m. \tag{3}$$

Equations (1) and (2) provide an effective way to approximate the g-leakage of information of the channel $Crowds$ with arbitrary precision, whereas Equation (3) lets us estimate how many interactions are needed for that.

To obtain K_m, we need to calculate m matrix multiplications, which surpass the cost of computing the m hidden choices (which are only matrix additions). Thus, Theorem 8 implies we can obtain a channel whose posterior vulnerability differs from that of $Crowds$ by at most $(1-q)^{m+1}(1-p^m)$ in $\approx O(mn_c^{2.807})$ time (using the Strassen algorithm for matrix multiplication [23]). Since p is typically high, $(1 - q)^{m+1}(1 - p)^m$ decreases very fast. For instance, for a precision of 0.001 on the leakage bound, we need $m = 10$ when $(1 - q)(1 - p)$ is 0.5, $m = 20$ when it is 0.7, and $m = 66$ when it is 0.9, regardless of the number n_c of honest users.

Therefore, our method has time complexity $O(n_c^{2.807})$ when the number of users is large (which is the usual case for Crowds), and reasonable values of forward probability p, and precision. To the best of our knowledge this method is the fastest in the literature, beating the previous $O(n_c^{3.807})$ that can be achieved by modifying the method presented in [24]—although their method does not require our assumption of corrupt users being evenly distributed.

7   Related Work

Compositionality is a fundamental notion in computer science, and it has been subject of growing interest in the QIF community.

Espinoza and Smith [25] derived a number of *min-capacity* bounds for different channel compositions, including cascading and parallel composition.

However, it was not until recently that compositionality results regarding the more general metrics of *g*-leakage started to be explored. Kawamoto et al. [26] defined a generalization of the parallel operator for channels with different input sets, and gave upper bounds for the corresponding information leakage. Our bounds for compatible channels (Theorem 1) are tighter than theirs.

Recently, Engelhardt [27] defined the *mix operator*, another generalization of parallel composition, and derived results similar to ours regarding the parallel operator. Specifically, he provided commutative and associative properties (Propositions 1 and 2), and from his results the lower bound of Theorem 1 can be inferred. He also proved properties similar to the ones in Proposition 3, albeit using more restrictive definitions of null and transparent channels.

Both Kawamoto et al. and Engelhardt provided results similar to Theorem 5, but ours is not restricted to when one channel is refined by the other.

Just recently, Alvim et al. investigated algebraic properties of hidden and visible choice operators in the context of game-theoretic aspects of QIF [28], and derived the upper bounds of Theorems 2 and 3. Here we expanded the algebra to the interaction among operators, including parallel composition, derived more comprehensive bounds on their leakage, and applied our results to the Crowds protocol.

8   Conclusions and Future Work

In this paper we proposed an algebra to express numerous component compositions in systems that arise from typical ways in components interact in practical scenarios. We provided fundamental algebraic properties of these operators, and studied several of their leakage properties. In particular, we obtained new results regarding their monotonicity properties and stricter bounds for the parallel and hidden choice operators. These results are of practical interest for the QIF community, as they provide helpful tools for modeling large systems and analyzing their security properties.

The list of operators we explored in this paper, however, does not seem to capture every possible interaction of components of real systems. As future work we wish to find other operators and increase the expressiveness of our approach.

Acknowledgments. Arthur Américo and Mário S. Alvim are supported by CNPq, CAPES, and FAPEMIG. Annabelle McIver is supported by ARC grant DP140101119.

References

1. Alvim, M.S., Chatzikokolakis, K., Palamidessi, C., Smith, G.: Measuring information leakage using generalized gain functions. In: Proceedings of CSF, pp. 265–279 (2012)
2. McIver, A., Morgan, C., Smith, G., Espinoza, B., Meinicke, L.: Abstract channels and their robust information-leakage ordering. In: Abadi, M., Kremer, S. (eds.) POST 2014. LNCS, vol. 8414, pp. 83–102. Springer, Heidelberg (2014). https:// doi.org/10.1007/978-3-642-54792-8_5
3. Clark, D., Hunt, S., Malacaria, P.: Quantitative information flow, relations and polymorphic types. J. Logic Comput. **18**(2), 181–199 (2005)
4. Köpf, B., Basin, D.A.: An information-theoretic model for adaptive side-channel attacks. In: Proceedings of CCS, pp. 286–296. ACM (2007)
5. Chatzikokolakis, K., Palamidessi, C., Panangaden, P.: On the Bayes risk in information-hiding protocols. J. Comput. Secur. **16**(5), 531–571 (2008)
6. Smith, G.: On the foundations of quantitative information flow. In: de Alfaro, L. (ed.) FoSSaCS 2009. LNCS, vol. 5504, pp. 288–302. Springer, Heidelberg (2009). https://doi.org/10.1007/978-3-642-00596-1_21
7. McIver, A., Meinicke, L., Morgan, C.: Compositional closure for Bayes risk in probabilistic noninterference. In: Abramsky, S., Gavoille, C., Kirchner, C., Meyer auf der Heide, F., Spirakis, P.G. (eds.) ICALP 2010. LNCS, vol. 6199, pp. 223–235. Springer, Heidelberg (2010). https://doi.org/10.1007/978-3-642-14162-1_19
8. Boreale, M., Pampaloni, F.: Quantitative information flow under generic leakage functions and adaptive adversaries. Log. Methods Comput. Sci. **11**(4) (2015)
9. Alvim, M.S., Chatzikokolakis, K., McIver, A., Morgan, C., Palamidessi, C., Smith, G.: Axioms for information leakage. In: Proceedings of CSF, pp. 77–92 (2016)
10. Chaum, D.: The dining cryptographers problem: Unconditional sender and recipient untraceability. J. Cryptol. **1**(1), 65–75 (1988)
11. Alvim, M.S., Chatzikokolakis, K., McIver, A., Morgan, C., Palamidessi, C., Smith, G.: Additive and multiplicative notions of leakage, and their capacities. In: Proceedings of CSF, pp. 308–322. IEEE (2014)
12. Reiter, M.K., Rubin, A.D.: Crowds: anonymity for web transactions. ACM Trans. Inf. Syst. Secur. **1**(1), 66–92 (1998)
13. Américo, A., Alvim, M.S., McIver, A.: An algebraic approach for reasoning about information flow. CoRR abs/1801.08090 (2018)
14. Shannon, C.E.: A mathematical theory of communication. Bell Syst. Tech. J. **27**(379–423), 625–56 (1948)
15. Massey, J.L.: Guessing and entropy. In: Proceedings of the IEEE International Symposium on Information Theory, p. 204. IEEE (1994)
16. Braun, C., Chatzikokolakis, K., Palamidessi, C.: Quantitative notions of leakage for one-try attacks. In: Proceedings of MFPS. ENTCS, vol. 249, pp. 75–91. Elsevier (2009)
17. Kocher, P.C.: Timing attacks on implementations of Diffie-Hellman, RSA, DSS, and other systems. In: Koblitz, N. (ed.) CRYPTO 1996. LNCS, vol. 1109, pp. 104–113. Springer, Heidelberg (1996). https://doi.org/10.1007/3-540-68697-5_9

18. Brumley, D., Boneh, D.: Remote timing attacks are practical. In: Proceedings of the 12th Conference on USENIX Security Symposium. SSYM 2003, vol. 12, p. 1. USENIX Association, Berkeley (2003)
19. Nohl, K., Evans, D., Starbug, S., Plötz, H.: Reverse-engineering a cryptographic RFID tag. In: Proceedings of the 17th Conference on Security Symposium. SS 2008, pp. 185–193. USENIX Association, Berkeley (2008)
20. Warner, S.L.: Randomized response: a survey technique for eliminating evasive answer bias. J. Am. Stat. Assoc. **60**(309), 63–69 (1965). PMID: 12261830
21. Goldschlag, D.M., Reed, M.G., Syverson, P.F.: Hiding routing information. In: Anderson, R. (ed.) IH 1996. LNCS, vol. 1174, pp. 137–150. Springer, Heidelberg (1996). https://doi.org/10.1007/3-540-61996-8_37
22. Dingledine, R., Mathewson, N., Syverson, P.F.: Tor: the second-generation onion router. In: Proceedings of the 13th USENIX Security Symposium, pp. 303–320. USENIX (2004)
23. Strassen, V.: Gaussian elimination is not optimal. Numer. Math. **13**(4), 354–356 (1969)
24. Andrés, M.E., Palamidessi, C., van Rossum, P., Smith, G.: Computing the leakage of information-hiding systems. In: Esparza, J., Majumdar, R. (eds.) TACAS 2010. LNCS, vol. 6015, pp. 373–389. Springer, Heidelberg (2010). https://doi.org/10.1007/978-3-642-12002-2_32
25. Espinoza, B., Smith, G.: Min-entropy as a resource. Inf. Comput. **226**, 57–75 (2013)
26. Kawamoto, Y., Chatzikokolakis, K., Palamidessi, C.: On the compositionality of quantitative information flow. Log. Methods Comput. Sci. **13**(3) (2017)
27. Engelhardt, K.: A better composition operator for quantitative information flow analyses. In: European Symposium on Research in Computer Security, Proceedings, Part I, pp. 446–463 (2017)
28. Alvim, M.S., Chatzikokolakis, K., Kawamoto, Y., Palamidessi, C.: Leakage and protocol composition in a game-theoretic perspective. In: Bauer, L., Küsters, R. (eds.) POST 2018. LNCS, vol. 10804, pp. 134–159. Springer, Cham (2018). https://doi.org/10.1007/978-3-319-89722-6_6

Towards 'Verifying' a Water Treatment System

Jingyi Wang[1,3], Jun Sun[1(✉)], Yifan Jia[1,4], Shengchao Qin[2,3(✉)],
and Zhiwu Xu[3]

[1] Singapore University of Technology and Design, Singapore, Singapore
sunjun@sutd.edu.sg
[2] School of Computing, Media and the Arts,
Teesside University, Middlesbrough, UK
S.Qin@tees.ac.uk
[3] College of Computer Science and Software Engineering,
Shenzhen University, Shenzhen, China
[4] TUV-SUD Asia Pacific Pte Ltd., Singapore, Singapore

Abstract. Modeling and verifying real-world cyber-physical systems is challenging, which is especially so for complex systems where manually modeling is infeasible. In this work, we report our experience on combining model learning and abstraction refinement to analyze a challenging system, i.e., a real-world Secure Water Treatment system (SWaT). Given a set of safety requirements, the objective is to either show that the system is safe with a high probability (so that a system shutdown is rarely triggered due to safety violation) or not. As the system is too complicated to be manually modeled, we apply latest automatic model learning techniques to construct a set of Markov chains through abstraction and refinement, based on two long system execution logs (one for training and the other for testing). For each probabilistic safety property, we either report it does not hold with a certain level of probabilistic confidence, or report that it holds by showing the evidence in the form of an abstract Markov chain. The Markov chains can subsequently be implemented as runtime monitors in SWaT.

1 Introduction

Cyber-physical systems (CPS) are ever more relevant to people's daily life. Examples include power supply which is controlled by smart grid systems, water supply which is processed from raw water by a water treatment system, and health monitoring systems. CPS often have strict safety and reliability requirements. However, it is often challenging to formally analyze CPS since they exhibit a tight integration of software control and physical processes. Modeling CPS alone is a major obstacle which hinders many system analysis techniques like model checking and model-based testing.

© Springer International Publishing AG, part of Springer Nature 2018
K. Havelund et al. (Eds.): FM 2018, LNCS 10951, pp. 73–92, 2018.
https://doi.org/10.1007/978-3-319-95582-7_5

The Secure Water Treatment testbed (SWaT) built at Singapore University of Technology and Design [28] is a scale-down version of an industry water treatment plant in Singapore. The testbed is built to facilitate research on cyber security for CPS, which has the potential to be adopted to Singapore's water treatment systems. SWaT consists of a modern six-stage process. The process begins by taking in raw water, adding necessary chemicals to it, filtering it via an Ultrafiltration (UF) system, de-chlorinating it using UV lamps, and then feeding it to a Reverse Osmosis (RO) system. A backwash stage cleans the membranes in UF using the water produced by RO. The cyber portion of SWaT consists of a layered communications network, Programmable Logic Controllers (PLCs), Human Machine Interfaces (HMIs), Supervisory Control and Data Acquisition (SCADA) workstation, and a Historian. Data from sensors is available to the SCADA system and recorded by the Historian for subsequent analysis. There are 6 PLCs in the system, each of which monitors one stage using a set of sensors embedded in the relevant physical plants and controls the physical plants according to predefined control logics. SWaT has a strict set of safety requirements (e.g., the PH value of the water coming out of SWaT must be within certain specific range). In order to guarantee that the safety requirements are not violated, SWaT is equipped with safety monitoring devices which trigger a pre-defined shutdown sequence. Our objective is thus to show that the probability of a safety violation is low and thus SWaT is reliable enough to provide its service.

One approach to achieve our objective is to develop a model of SWaT and then apply techniques like model checking. Such a model would have a discrete part which models the PLC control logic and a continuous part which models the physical plants (e.g., in the form of differential equations). Such an approach is challenging since SWaT has multiple chemical processes. For example, the whole process is composed of pre-treatment, ultrafiltration and backwash, de-chlorination, reverse osmosis and output of the processed water. The pre-treatment process alone includes chemical dosing, hydrochloric dosing, pre-chlorination and salt dosing. Due to the complexity in chemical reactions, manual modeling is infeasible. Furthermore, even if we are able to model the system using modeling notations like hybrid automata [11], the existing tools/methods [9,22,23] for analyzing such complicated hybrid models are limited.

An alternative approach which does not require manual modeling is statistical model checking (SMC) [7,16,35]. The main idea is to observe sample system executions and apply standard techniques like hypothesis testing to estimate the probability that a given property is satisfied. SMC however is not ideal for two reasons. First, SMC treats the system as a black box and does not provide insight or knowledge of the system on why a given property is satisfied. Second, SMC requires sampling the system many times, whereas starting/restarting real-world CPS like SWaT many times is not viable.

Recently, there have been multiple proposals on applying model learning techniques to automatically 'learn' system models from system executions and then analyze the learned model using techniques like model checking. A variety of learning algorithms have been proposed (e.g., [4,22,24,25]), some of which require only a few system executions. These approaches offer an alternative way of obtaining models, when having a model of such complex systems is a must. For instance, in [6,19,32,33], it is proposed to learn a probabilistic model first and then apply Probabilistic Model Checking (PMC) to calculate the probability of satisfying a property based on the learned model.

It is however far from trivial to apply model learning directly on SWaT. Existing model learning approaches have only been applied to a few small benchmark systems. It is not clear whether they are applicable or scalable to real-world systems like SWaT. In particular, there are many sensors in SWaT, many of which generate values of type float or double. As a result, the sensor readings induce an 'infinite' alphabet which immediately renders many model learning approaches infeasible. In fact, existing model learning approaches have rarely discussed the problem of data abstraction. To the best of our knowledge, the only exception is the LAR method [32], which proposes a method of combining model learning and abstraction/refinement. However, LAR requires many system executions as input, which is infeasible in SWaT. In this work, we adapt the LAR method so that we require only two long sequences of system execution logs (one for training and the other for testing) as input. We successfully 'verified' most of the properties for SWaT this way. For each property, we either report that the property is violated with a certain confidence, or report that the property is satisfied, in which case we output a model in the form of an abstract Markov chain as evidence, which could be further validated by more system runs or expert review. Note that in practice these models could be implemented as runtime monitors in SWaT.

The remainders of the paper are organized as follows. Section 2 presents background on SWaT, our objectives as well as some preliminaries. Section 3 details our learning approach. We present the results in Sect. 4 and conclude with related work in Sect. 5.

2   Background

In this section, we present the target SWaT system and state our motivation and goals.

System Overview. The system under analysis is the Secure Water Treatment (SWaT) built at the iTrust Center in Singapore University of Technology and Design [20]. It is a testbed system which scales down but fully realized the functions of a modern water treatment system in cities like Singapore. It enables researchers to better understand the principles of cyber-physical Systems (CPS) and further develop and experiment with smart algorithms to mitigate potential threats and guarantee its safety and reliability.

SWaT takes raw water as input and executes a series of treatment and output recycled water eventually. The whole process contains 6 stages as shown in Fig. 1. The raw water is taken to the raw water tank (P1) and then pumped to the chemical tanks. After a series of chemical dosing and a static mixer (P2),

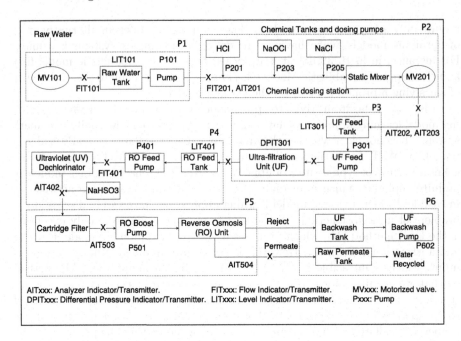

Fig. 1. Six stages of water treatment in SWaT [20].

the water is filtered by an Ultra-filtration (UF) system (P3) and UV lamps (P4). It is then fed to a Reverse Osmosis (RO) system (P5) and a backwash process cleans the membranes in UF using the water produced by RO (P6). For each stage, a set of sensors are employed to monitor the system state. Meanwhile, a set of actuators controlled by the programming logic controller (PLC) are built in to manipulate the state of the physical process. The readings of sensors are collected and sent periodically to the PLC, while the PLC returns a set of actuators values according to the control logics and the current sensor values. For instance, the sensor $LIT101$ is used to monitor the water level of the Raw Water Tank. The PLC reads its value and decides whether to set a new value to the actuators. For example if $LIT101$ is beyond a threshold, the PLC may deactivate the valve $MV101$ to stop adding water into the tank.

SWaT has many built-in safety mechanisms enforced in PLC. Each stage is controlled by local dual PLCs with approximately hundreds of lines of code. In case one PLC fails, the other PLC takes over. The PLC inspects the received and cached sensor values and decides the control strategy to take. Notice that the sensor values are accessible across all PLCs. For example, the PLC of tank 1 may decide whether to start pump $P101$ according to the value of $LIT301$, i.e., the water level of tank 3. In case the controller triggers potential safety violations of the system according to the current values of the sensors, the controller may shut down the system to ensure the safety. The system then needs to wait for further inspection from technicians or experts. Shutting down and restarting

Table 1. Safety properties.

Plant	Sensor	Description	Operating range points
P1	FIT101	Flow Transmitter (EMF)	2.5–$2.6 \, \mathrm{m^3/h}$
	LIT101	Level Transmitter (Ultrasonic)	500–$1100 \, \mathrm{mm}$
P2	AIT201	Analyser (Conductivity)	30–$260 \, \mu\mathrm{S/cm}$
	AIT202	Analyser (pH)	6–9
	AIT203	Analyser (ORP)	200–$500 \, \mathrm{mV}$
	FIT201	Flow Transmitter (EMF)	2.4–$2.5 \, \mathrm{m^3/h}$
P3	DPIT301	DP Transmitter	0.1–$0.3 \, \mathrm{Bar}$
	FIT301	Flow Transmitter (EMF)	2.2–$2.4 \, \mathrm{m^3/h}$
	LIT301	Level Transmitter (Ultrasonic)	800–$1000 \, \mathrm{mm}$
P4	AIT401	Analyser (Hardness)	5–$30 \, \mathrm{ppm}$
	AIT402	Analyser	150–$300 \, \mathrm{mV}$
	FIT401	Flow Transmitter (EMF)	1.5–$2 \, \mathrm{m^3/h}$
	LIT401	Level Transmitter (Ultrasonic)	800–$1000 \, \mathrm{mm}$
P5	AIT501	Analyser (pH)	6–8
	AIT502	Analyser (ORP)	100–$250 \, \mathrm{mV}$
	AIT503	Analyser (Cond)	200–$300 \, \mu\mathrm{S/cm}$
	AIT504	Analyser (Cond)	5–$10 \, \mu\mathrm{S/cm}$
	FIT501	Flow Transmitter	1–$2 \, \mathrm{m^3/h}$
	FIT502	Flow Transmitter (Paddlewheel)	1.1–$1.3 \, \mathrm{m^3/h}$
	FIT503	Flow Transmitter (EMF)	0.7–$0.9 \, \mathrm{m^3/h}$
	FIT504	Flow Transmitter (EMF)	0.25–$0.35 \, \mathrm{m^3/h}$
	PIT501	Pressure Transmitter	2–$3 \, \mathrm{Bar}$
	PIT502	Pressure Transmitter	0–$0.2 \, \mathrm{Bar}$
	PIT503	Pressure Transmitter	1–$2 \, \mathrm{Bar}$

SWaT however is highly non-trivial, which takes significant costs in terms of both time and resource, especially in the real-world scenario. Thus, *instead of asking whether a safety violation is possible, the question becomes: how often a system shutdown is triggered due to potential safety violations?*

In total, SWaT has 25 sensors (for monitoring the status) and 26 actuators (for manipulating the plants). Each sensor is designed to operate in a certain safe range. If a sensor value is out of the range, the system may take actions to adjust the state of the actuators so that the sensor values would go back to normal. Table 1 shows all the sensors in the 6 plants, their operation ranges. The sensors has 3 categories distinguished by their prefixes. For instance, $AITxxx$ stands for Analyzer Indicator/Transmitter; $DPITxxx$ stands for Differential Pressure Indicator/Transmitter; $FITxxx$ stands for Flow Indicator/Transmitter; $LITxxx$ stands for Level Indicator/Transmitter.

SWaT is also equipped with a historian which records detailed system execution log, including all sensor readings and actuator status. Table 2 shows a truncated system log with part of sensors. Each row is the sensor readings at a time point and each row is collected every millisecond. Notice that different sensors may have different collection period. The table is filled such that a sensor keeps its old value if no new value is collected, e.g., $AIT202$ in Table 2. A dataset of SWaT has been published by the iTrust lab in Singapore University of Technology and Design [10, 27]. The dataset contains the execution log of 11 consecutive days (i.e., 7 days of normal operations and another 4 days of the system being under various kind of attacks [10, 27]).

Table 2. A concrete system log with the last column being the abstract system log after predicate abstraction with predicate $LIT101 > 1100$.

$FIT101$	$LIT101$	$MV101$	$P101$	$P102$	$AIT201$	$AIT202$	$AIT203$	$FIT201$	$LIT101 > 1100$
2.470294	261.5804	2	2	1	244.3284	8.19008	306.101	2.471278	0
2.457163	261.1879	2	2	1	244.3284	8.19008	306.101	2.468587	0
2.439548	260.9131	2	2	1	244.3284	8.19008	306.101	2.467305	0
2.428338	260.285	2	2	1	244.3284	8.19008	306.101	2.466536	0
2.424815	259.8925	2	2	1	244.4245	8.19008	306.101	2.466536	0
2.425456	260.0495	2	2	1	244.5847	8.19008	306.101	2.465127	0
2.472857	260.2065	2	2	1	244.5847	8.19008	306.101	2.464742	0

Objectives. As discussed above, each sensor reading is associated with a safe range, which constitutes a set of safety properties (i.e., reachability). We remark that we focus on safety properties concerning the stationary behavior of the system in this work rather than those properties concerning the system initializing or shutting down phase. In general, a stationary safety property (refer to [6] for details) takes the form $S_{\leq r}(\varphi)$ (where r is the safety threshold and φ is an LTL formula). In our particular setting, the property we are interested in is that *the probability that a sensor is out of range (either too high or too low) in the long term is below a threshold.* Our objective is to 'verify' whether a given set of stationary properties are satisfied or not.

Manual modeling of SWaT is infeasible, with 6 water tanks interacting with each other, plenty of chemical reactions inside the tanks and dozens of valves controlling the flow of water. A group of experts from Singapore's Public Utility Board have attempted to model SWaT manually but failed after months of effort because the system is too complicated. We remark that without a system model, precisely verifying the system is impossible. As discussed above, while statistical model checking (SMC) is another option to provide a statistical measure on the probability that a safety property is satisfied, it is also infeasible in our setting.

Thus, in this work, we aim to verify the system by means of model learning. That is, given a safety property, either we would like to show that the property is violated with certain level of confidence or the property is satisfied with certain evidence. Ideally, the evidence is in the form of a small abstract model, at the right level-of-abstraction, which could be easily shown to satisfy the property. The advantage of presenting the model as the evidence is that the model could be further validated using additional data or through expert review. Furthermore, the models can serve other purposes. Firstly, the models could be implemented as runtime monitors to detect potential safety violations at runtime. Secondly, we could also prevent future safety violations by predictive analysis based on the model and take early actions.

3   Our Approach

We surveyed existing model learning algorithms (for the purpose of system verification through model checking) and found most existing model learning approaches [6,19,33] are inapplicable in our setting. The reason is that the real-typed (float or double) variables in SWaT lead to an infinite alphabet. The only method which seems feasible is the recently proposed model learning app-roach called LAR (short for learning, abstraction and refinement) documented in [32], which allows us to abstract sensor readings in SWaT and automatically learn models at a proper level of abstraction based on a counterexample guided abstraction refinement (CEGAR) framework. However, LAR was designed to take many independent execution logs as input whereas we have only few long system logs of SWaT. We thus adapt LAR to sLAR which learns system models from a single long system log instead. In the following, we briefly explain how sLAR works. Interested readers are referred to [32] for the detailed explanation of LAR.

Our overall approach is shown in Fig. 2. Given a training log and a safety property, we first construct an abstract log through predicate abstraction and use a learner to learn a model based on the abstract log. Then, the safety prop-erty is verified against the learned model. If the verification returns true, we report true and output the learned model as evidence. Otherwise, we test the

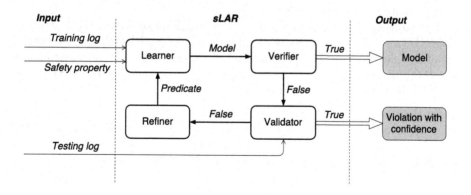

Fig. 2. Overall approach.

property using a validator on the testing log. If the validator finds that the property is violated, we report safety violation together with the level of confidence we achieve. Otherwise, we use a refiner to refine the abstraction and start over from the learner. Although $sLAR$ is based on LAR, our goal of this case study is to verify stationary properties of SWaT and construct a stationary probabilistic model from one single long system log, which is different from LAR. Consequently, the procedures to verify the property and validate the result of the verifier are different. In the following, we present each part of our approach in details.

3.1   The Model

From an abstract point of view, SWaT is a system composed of n variables (including sensors, actuators as well as those variables in the PLC control program) which capture the system status. A system observation σ is the valuation of all variables at a time point t. A system log $L = \sigma_{t_0}\sigma_{t_1}\cdots\sigma_{t_k}$ is a sequence of system observations collected from time point t_0 to t_k. Given a system log L, we write $L(t) = \sigma_t$ to denote the system observation at time t and $L_p(t)$ to denote the system observations before t, i.e., from t_0 to t. In this case study, we use L and L_t to denote the training log and testing log respectively. We also use T_1 and T_2 to denote their lasting time respectively.

Several machine learning algorithms exist to learn a stationary system model from a single piece of system log [6, 24, 33]. However, applying these algorithms directly is infeasible because of the real-typed (float or double) variables in SWaT, since system observations at different time points are almost always different and thus the input alphabet for the learning algorithms is 'infinite'. To overcome this problem, our first step is to abstract the system log through predicate abstraction [29]. Essentially, a predicate is a Boolean expression over a set of variables. Given a system log and a set of predicates, predicate abstraction turns the concrete variable values to a bit vector where each bit represents whether the corresponding predicate is true or false. For example, given a predicate $LIT101 > 1100$, the concrete system log on the left of Table 2 becomes the abstract system log on the right.

The models we learn from the log are in the form of discrete-time Markov Chain (DTMC), which is a widely used formalism for modeling stochastic behaviors of complex systems. Given a finite set of states S, a probability distribution over S is a function $\mu : S \to [0,1]$ such that $\sum_{s \in S} \mu(s) = 1$. Let $Distr(S)$ be the set of all distributions over S. Formally,

Definition 1. *A DTMC $\mathcal{M}$ is a tuple $\langle S, \imath_{init}, Pr \rangle$, where S is a countable, nonempty set of states; $\imath_{init} : S \to [0,1]$ is the initial distribution s.t. $\sum_{s \in S} \imath_{init}(s) = 1$; and $Pr : S \to Distr(S)$ is a transition function such that $Pr(s, s')$ is the probability of transiting from state s to state s'.*

We denote a path starting with s_0 by $\pi^{s_0} = \langle s_0, s_1, s_2, \cdots, s_n \rangle$, which is a sequence of states in $\mathcal{M}$, where $Pr(s_i, s_{i+1}) > 0$ for every $0 \le i < n$. Furthermore, we write $Path^s_{fin}(\mathcal{M})$ to denote the set of finite paths of $\mathcal{M}$ starting with s.

We say that $s_j \in \pi^{s_0}$ if s_j occurs in π^{s_0}. In our setting, we use a special form of DTMC, called stationary DTMC (written as sDTMC) to model the system behaviors in the long term. Compared to a DTMC, each state in an sDTMC represents a steady state of the system and thus there is no prior initial distribution over the states.

Definition 2. *An sDTMC is irreducible if for every pair of states $s_i, s_j \in S$, there exists a path π^{s_i} such that $s_j \in \pi^{s_i}$.*

Intuitively, an sDTMC is irreducible if there is path between every pair of states. For an irreducible sDTMC, there exists a unique stationary probability distribution which describes the average time a Markov chain spends in each state in the long run.

Definition 3. *Let μ_j denote the long run proportion of time that the chain spends in state s_j: $\mu_j = \lim_{n \to \infty} \frac{1}{n} \sum_{m=1}^{n} I\{X_m = s_j | X_0 = s_i\}$ with probability 1, for all states s_i. If for each $s_j \in S$, μ_j exists and is independent of the initial state s_i, and $\sum_{s_j \in S} \mu_j = 1$, then the probability distribution $\mu = (\mu_0, \mu_1, \cdots)$ is called the limiting or stationary or steady-state distribution of the Markov chain.*

In this work, we 'learn' a stationary and irreducible sDTMC to model the long term behavior of SWaT. By computing the steady-state distribution of the learned sDTMC, we can obtain the probability that the system is in the states of interests in the long run.

3.2   Learning Algorithm

After predicate abstraction, the training log becomes a sequence of bit vectors, which is applicable for learning. We then apply an existing learning algorithm in [24] to learn a stationary system model. The initial learned model is in the form of a *Probabilistic Suffix Automata* (PSA) as shown in Fig. 3, where a system state in the model is identified by a finite history of previous system observations. A PSA is an sDTMC by definition. Each state in a PSA is labeled by a finite memory of the system. The transition function between the states are defined based on the state labels such that there is a transition $s \times \sigma \to t$ iff $l(t)$ is a suffix of $l(s) \cdot \sigma$, where $l(s)$ is the string label of s. A walk on the underlying graph of a PSA will always end in a state labeled by a suffix of the sequence. Given a system log $L_p(t)$ at t, a unique state in the PSA can be identified by matching the state label with the suffixes of $L_p(t)$. For example, $\cdots 010$ is in state labeled by 0 and if we observe 1 next, the system will go to state labeled by 01.

To learn a PSA, we first construct an intermediate tree representation called *Probabilistic Suffix Tree* (PST), namely $tree(L) = (N, root, E)$ where N is the set of suffixes of L; $root = \langle \rangle$; and there is an edge $(\pi_1, \pi_2) \in E$ if and only if $\pi_2 = \langle e \rangle \cdot \pi_1$. Based on different suffixes of the execution, different probabilistic distributions of the next observation will be formed. The central question is how deep should we grow the PST. A deeper tree means that a longer memory is

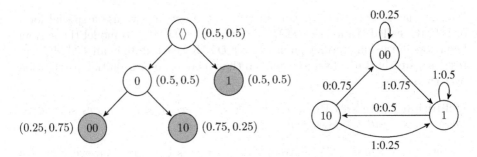

Fig. 3. An example stationary model. The left is the PST representation, where each state is associated with a label and a distribution of the next observation. The right is the corresponding PSA model where leaves are taken as states.

Algorithm 1. *Learn PST*

1: Initialize T to be a single root node representing $\langle\rangle$;
2: Let $S = \{\sigma | fre(\sigma, \alpha) > \epsilon\}$ be the candidate suffix set;
3: **while** S is not empty **do**
4:     Take any π from S; Let π' be the longest suffix of π in T;
5:     (B) If $fre(\pi, \alpha) \cdot \sum_{\sigma \in \Sigma} Pr(\pi, \sigma) \cdot \log \frac{Pr(\pi, \sigma)}{Pr(\pi', \sigma)} \geq \epsilon$
          add π and all its suffixes which are not in T to T;
6:     (C) If $fre(\pi, \alpha) > \epsilon$, add $\langle e \rangle \cdot \pi$ to S for every $e \in \Sigma$ if $fre(\langle e \rangle \cdot \pi, \alpha) > 0$;
7: **end while**

---

used to predict the distribution of the next observation. The detailed algorithm is shown in Algorithm 1. The tree keeps growing as long as adding children to a current leaf leads to a significant change (measured by K-L divergence) in the probability distribution of next observation (line 5). After we obtain the PST, we transform it into a PSA by taking the leaves as states and define transitions by suffix matching. We briefly introduce the transformation here and readers are referred to Appendix B of [24] for more details. For a state s and next symbol σ, the next state s' must be a suffix of $s\sigma$. However, this is not guaranteed to be a leaf in the learned T. Thus, the first step is to extend T to T' such that for every leaf s, the longest *prefix* of s is either a leaf or an internal node in T'. The transition functions are defined as follows. For each node s in $T \cap T'$ and $\sigma \in \Sigma$, let $Pr'(s, \sigma) = Pr(s, \sigma)$. For each new nodes s' in $T' - T$, let $Pr'(s', \sigma) = Pr(s, \sigma)$, where s is deepest ancestor of s' in T. An example PST and its corresponding PSA after transformation is given in Fig. 3. Readers are referred to [24] for details.

3.3   Verification

Once we learn an sDTMC model, we then check whether the learned model satisfies the given safety property. To do so, we first compute the steady-state distribution of the learned model. There are several methods we could use for the calculation including power methods, solving equations or finding eigenvector [2]. The steady-state distribution tells the probability that a state occurs in the long run. Once we obtain the steady-state distribution of the learned model, we could then calculate the probability that the system violates the safety property in the long run by summing up the steady-state probability of all unsafe states. Assume μ is the steady-state distribution, S_u is the set of unsafe states in the learned model and P_u is the probability that the system is in unsafe states in the long run. We calculate the probability of unsafe states as $P_u = \sum_{s_i \in S_u} \mu\{s_i\}$. We then check whether the learned model satisfies the safety property by comparing whether P_u is beyond the safety threshold r. Take the PSA model in Fig. 3 as example. The steady-state distribution over states $[1, 00, 10]$ is $[0.4, 0.31, 0.29]$. States 1 is the unsafe state. The steady-state probability that the system is in unsafe states is thus 0.4.

There are two kinds of results. One is that P_u is below the threshold r, which means the learned model under current abstraction level satisfies the safety requirement. Then, we draw the conclusion that the system is 'safe' and present the learned model as evidence. The soundness of the result can be derived if the learned abstract model simulates the actual underlying model [12]. However, since the model is obtained through learning from limited data, it is not guaranteed that the result is sound. Nevertheless, the model can be further investigated by validating it against future system logs or reviewed by experts, which we leave to future works. The other result is that the learned model does not satisfy the safety requirement, i.e., the probability of the system being in an unsafe state in the steady-state is larger than the threshold. In such a case, we move to the next step to validate whether the safety violation is introduced by inappropriate abstraction [32] or not.

3.4   Abstraction Refinement

In case we learn a model which shows that the probability of the system being in unsafe states in long term is beyond the safety threshold, we move on to validate whether the system is indeed unsafe or the violation is spurious due to over-abstraction. For spuriousness checking, we make use of a testing log which is obtained independently and compute the probability of the system being in unsafe states, which is denoted by P_u^t. The testing log has the same format with the training log. We estimate P_u^t by calculating the frequency that the system is in some unsafe states in the testing log. If P_u^t is larger than the threshold r, we report the safety violation together with a confidence by calculating the error bound [26]. Otherwise, we conclude that the violation is caused by too coarse abstraction and move to the next step to refine the abstraction.

Algorithm 2. Algorithm $CountST(\mathcal{M}_P, L_t)$

1: Augment each transition (s_i, s_j) in $\mathcal{M}_P$ with a number $\#(s_i, s_j)$ recording how many times we observe such a transition in L_t and initialize them to 0;
2: Let t_0 be the first time that $suffix(L_t(t_0))$ matches a label of a state in $\mathcal{M}_P$ and a time pointer $t = t_0$;
3: **while** $t < T_2$ **do**
4:     Refer to $\mathcal{M}_P$ for the current state s_t;
5:     Take $L_t(t+1)$ from L_t and refer to $\mathcal{M}_P$ to get the next state s_{t+1};
6:     Add $\#(s_t, s_{t+1})$ by 1, add t by 1;
7: **end while**

Let N be the total number of states, and n be the number of unsafe states in the testing log. Let $Y = X_1 + X_2 + \cdots + X_N$, where X_i is a Bernoulli random variable on whether a state is unsafe. The confidence of the safety violation report is then calculated as $\alpha = 1 - \mathcal{P}\{Y = n | P_u < r\}$. For example, for property $LIT101 > 1000$, if we observe 1009 times (n) that $LIT101$ is larger than 1000 and the total length of the testing log is 100000 (N), then the estimated P_u^t is $1009/100000 = 0.01009$.

If we conclude that the current abstraction is too coarse, we continue to refine the abstraction by generating a new predicate following the approach in [32]. The predicate is then added to the set of predicates to obtain a new abstract system log based on the new abstraction. The algorithm then starts over to learn a new model based on the new abstract log. Next, we introduce how to generate a new predicate in our setting.

Finding Spurious Transitions. A spurious transition in the learned model is a transition whose probability is inflated due to the abstraction. Further, a transition (s_i, s_j) is spurious if the probability of observing s_i transiting to s_j in the actual system $P_\mathcal{M}(s_i, s_j)$ is actually smaller than $P_{\mathcal{M}_P}(s_i, s_j)$ in the learned model [32]. Without the actual system model, we estimate the actual transition probability based on the testing log. Given the learned model $\mathcal{M}_P$ and the testing log L_t, we count the number of times s_i is observed in L_t (denoted by $\#s_i$) and the number of times the transition from s_i to s_j in is observed L_t (denoted by $\#(s_i, s_j)$) using Algorithm 2. The actual transition probability $P(s_i, s_j)$ is estimated by $\widehat{P}_\mathcal{M}(s_i, s_j) = \#(s_i, s_j)/\#s_i$. Afterwards, we identify the transitions satisfying $P_{\mathcal{M}_P}(s_i, s_j) - \widehat{P}_\mathcal{M}(s_i, s_j) > 0$ as spurious transitions and order them according to the probability deviation.

Predicate Generation. After we obtain a spurious transition (s_i, s_j), our next step is to generate a new predicate to eliminate the spuriousness. The generated predicate is supposed to separate the concrete states of s_i which transit to s_j (positive instances) from those which do not (negative instances). We collect the dataset for classification in a similar way to Algorithm 2 by iterating the testing log. If s_i is observed, we make a decision on whether it is a positive

---

Algorithm 3. Algorithm $sLAR(L, L_t, \mathcal{S}_{\leq r}(\varphi))$

---

1 let P be the predicates in φ;
2 **while** *true* **do**
3   construct abstract trace L_P based on training log L and P;
4   apply Algorithm 1 to learn a stationary model $\mathcal{M}_P$ based on L_P;
5   check $\mathcal{M}_P$ against φ;
6   **if** $\mathcal{M}_P \models \varphi$ **then**
7   report φ is verified, the model $\mathcal{M}_P$;
8   **return**;
9   use the testing log L_t to validate the property violation;
10   **if** *validated* **then**
11   report φ is violated with confidence;
12   **return**;
13   identify the most spurious transitions $\langle s, s' \rangle$ in $\mathcal{M}_P$;
14   collect labeled dataset $D^+(s, \mathcal{M}_P, L_t)$ and $D^-(s, \mathcal{M}_P, L_t)$;
15   apply SVM to identify a predicate p separating the two sets;
16   add p into P;

---

or negative instance by telling whether its next state is s_j. With the labeled dataset, we then apply a supervised classification technique in machine learning, i.e., Support Vector Machines (SVM [1,5]) to generate a new predicate. Then, we add the predicate for abstraction and start a new round.

3.5 Overall Algorithm

The overall algorithm is shown as Algorithm 3. The inputs of the algorithm are a system log L for training, a system log L_t for testing, a property in the form of $\mathcal{S}_{\leq r}(\varphi)$. During each iteration of the loop from line 2 to 16, we start with constructing the abstract trace based on L and a set of predicates P. The initial set of predicates for abstraction is the set of predicates in the property. Next, an abstract sDTMC $\mathcal{M}_P$ is learned using Algorithm 1. We then verify $\mathcal{M}_P$ against the property. If the property is verified, the system is verified and $\mathcal{M}_P$ is presented as the evidence. Otherwise, we validate the verification result using a testing log L_t at line 9. If the test passes, we report a safety violation together with the confidence. Otherwise, at line 13, we identify the most spurious transition and obtain a new predicate at line 15. After adding the new predicate into P, we restart the process from line 2. If SVM fails to find a classifier for all the spurious transitions, Algorithm 3 terminates and reports the verification is unsuccessful. Otherwise, it either reports true with a supporting model as evidence or a safety violation with confidence.

4   Case Study Results

In the following, we present our findings on applying the method documented in Sect. 3 to SWaT. Given the 11 day system log [10], we take the 7 day log under normal system execution and further split it into two parts for training (4 days) and testing (3 days) respectively. The main reason we split them into training and testing log is to avoid over-fitting problem without the testing data. Note that the historian makes one record every second. The training log and testing log contains 288000 and 208800 system observations respectively. The properties we verified are whether the steady-state probability that a sensor runs out of its operating range is beyond or below a threshold. Let P_{train}, P_{learn} and P_{test} be the probability that a sensor is out of operating range in the training log, learned models and the testing log respectively. In our study, we set the threshold r in each property as 20 percent larger than the probability observed in the actual system for a long time, during which the system functioned reliably. The idea is to check whether we can establish some underlying evidence to show that the system would satisfy the property indeed.

The experiment results of all sensors are summarized in Table 3. The detailed implementation and models are available in [30]. The first column is the plant number. Column 2 and 3 are the sensors and their properties to verify which are decided by their operating ranges. The following 4 columns show the probability that a sensor value is out of operating range in the training log, the safety threshold, the probability in the learned model and the probability in the testing log respectively. Column 'result' is the verification result of the given safety properties. 'SUC' means the property is successfully verified. 'FAL' means the property is not verified. 'VIO' means the property is violated. Column 'model size' is the number of states in the learned model. Column ϵ is the parameter we use in the learning parameter. The last column is the running time.

Summary of Results. In total, we managed to evaluate 47 safety properties of 24 sensors. Notice that the sensor from P6 is missing in the dataset. Among them, 19 properties are never observed to be violated in the training log. We thus could not learn any models regarding these properties and conclude that the system is safe from the limited data we learn from. This is reasonable as according to the dataset, the probability violating the property is 0. For the rest 28 properties, we successfully verified 24 properties together with a learned abstract Markov chain each and reported 4 properties as safety violation with a confidence.

We have the following observations from the results. For those properties we successfully verified, we managed to learn stationary abstract Markov chains which closely approximate the steady-state probability of safety violation (evaluated based on the probability computed based on the testing log). It means that in these cases, sLAR is able to learn a model that is precise enough to capture how the sensor values change. Examples are $FIT101 > 2.6$, $LIT301 > 1000$, $LIT301 < 800$ and $LIT401 > 1000$. Besides, it can be observed that the learned abstract models are reasonably small, i.e., usually with less than 100 states and many with only a few states. This is welcomed since a smaller model is easier to

Table 3. Experiment results.

Plant	Sensor	Property	P_{train}	r	P_{learn}	P_{test}	Result	Model size	ϵ	Time
P1	FIT101	>2.6	0.2371	0.2845	0.2371	0.233	SUC	26	0.01	300
		<2.5	0.5092	0.611	0.5092	0.5245	SUC	31	0.01	298
	LIT101	>800	0.1279	0.1535	0.1271	0.1141	SUC	130	0.01	4
		<500	0.1485	0.1782	0.147	0.0977	SUC	54	0.01	2
P2	AIT201	>260	0.6044	0.7253	0.647	1	SUC	2	0.01	31
		<250	0	–	–	–	–	–	–	–
	AIT202	>9	0	–	–	–	–	–	–	–
		<6	0	–	–	–	–	–	–	–
	AIT203	>500	0.0362	0.043	0.0363	0	SUC	2	0.01	27
		<420	0.7654	0.9185	0.7654	1	SUC	2	0.01	32
	FIT201	>2.5	0	–	–	–	–	–	–	–
		<2.4	0.2577	0.3092	0.2567	0.2529	SUC	59	0.01	4
P3	DPIT301	>30	0	–	–	–	–	–	–	–
		<10	0.2006	0.2407	0.1991	0.1799	SUC	119	0.01	4
	FIT301	>2.4	0	–	–	–	–	–	–	–
		<2.2	0.2217	0.266	0.2209	0.1756	SUC	42	0.01	4
	LIT301	>1000	0.134	0.1608	0.135	0.1299	SUC	60	0.01	4
		<800	0.0877	0.1052	0.0876	0.0609	SUC	69	0.01	2
P4	AIT401	>100	0.7156	0.8587	1	1	VIO	2	0.002	35
		<5	0.2844	0.3413	0	1	SUC	2	0.01	33
	AIT402	>250	0	–	–	–	–	–	–	–
		<150	0	–	–	–	–	–	–	–
	FIT401	>2	0	–	–	–	–	–	–	–
		<1.5	0.0117	0.014	0	0	SUC	2	0.01	37
	LIT401	>1000	0.0035	0.0042	0.0037	0.0034	SUC	208	0.002	455
		<800	0.1227	0.1472	0.123	0.079	SUC	70	0.01	2
P5	AIT501	>8	0	–	–	–	–	–	–	–
		<6	0	–	–	–	–	–	–	–
	AIT502	>250	0	–	–	–	–	–	–	–
		<100	0	–	–	–	–	–	–	–
	AIT503	300	0	–	–	–	–	–	–	–
		<200	0	–	–	–	–	–	–	–
	AIT504	>10	0.9983	1	0.9983	1	SUC	2	0.001	37
		<5	0	–	–	–	–	–	–	–
	FIT501	>2	0	–	–	–	–	–	–	–
		<1	0.011	0.0132	0	0	SUC	3	0.01	38
	FIT502	>1.3	0.0356	0.0427	0.0361	0.3241	SUC	9	0.01	15
		<1.1	0.0117	0.014	0	0	SUC	2	0.01	38
	FIT503	>0.9	0	–	–	–	–	–	–	–
		<0.7	0.0117	0.014	0	0	SUC	2	0.01	38
	FIT504	>0.35	0	–	–	–	–	–	–	–
		<0.25	0.0117	0.014	0	0	SUC	2	0.01	38
	PIT501	>30	0.989	1	1	1	VIO	3	0.01	38
		<20	0.011	0.0132	0	0	SUC	3	0.01	38
	PIT502	>0.2	0.989	1	1	1	VIO	3	0.01	37
	PIT503	>20	0.989	1	1	1	VIO	3	0.01	37
		<10	0.011	0.0132	0	0	SUC	3	0.01	38

comprehend and thus more meaningful for expert review or to be used as a run-time monitor. An underlying reason (why a small model is able to explain why a property is satisfied) is perhaps the system is built such that the system modifies its behavior way before a safety violation is possible. Besides, we identify two groups of states which are of special interest. One of them are $FIT401 < 1.5$, $FIT502 < 1.1$, $FIT503 < 0.7$ and $FIT504 < 0.25$. The 4 properties have the same probability 0.0117 of safety violation in the training log and 0 in the testing log. We learn the same models for all of them and P_{learn} equals 0 which is the same as the testing log. We could observe that these sensors have tight connections with each other. Moreover, these sensors are good examples that our learned models generalize from the training data and are able to capture the long run behaviors of the system with P_{learn} equals P_{test}, which is 0. The same goes for the other group of properties, i.e., $FIT501 < 1$, $PIT501 < 20$ and $PIT503 < 10$.

For those properties we reported as safety violations, i.e., $AIT401 > 100$, $PIT501 > 30$, $PIT502 > 0.2$ and $PIT503 > 20$, a closer look reveals that these sensors all have high probability of violation (either 0.7156 or 0.989) in the training log. Our learned models report that the probability of violation in the long term is 1, which equals the probability in the testing log in all cases. This shows that our learned models are precise even though the properties are not actually satisfied.

Discussions. (1) We give a 20% margin for the safety threshold in the above experiments. In practice, the actual safety threshold could be derived from the system reliability requirement. In our experiments, we observe that we could increase the threshold to obtain a more abstract model and decrease the threshold to obtain a more detailed model. For instance, we would be more likely to verify a property with a loose threshold. (2) The parameter ϵ in Algorithm 1 effectively controls the size of learned model. A small ϵ used in the model learning algorithm leads to a learned model with more states by growing a deeper tree. However, it is sometimes non-trivial to select a good ϵ [33]. In our experiment, we use 0.01 as the basic parameter. If we can not learn a model (the tree does not grow), we may choose a more strict ϵ. Examples are $LIT401 > 1000$ and $AIT504 > 10$. This suggests one way to improve existing model learning algorithms. (3) Each sensor has a different collection period and most of them are changing very slowly, thus the data is not all meaningful to us and we only take a data point from the dataset every minute to reduce the learning cost. (4) One possible reason for the safety violation cases is that the system has not exhibited stationary behaviors within 7 days as the probability of safety violations is 1 in the testing data for all these cases.

Limitation and Future Work. Model learning will correctly learn an underlying model in the limit [18,24]. However, since our models are learned from a limited amount of data from a practical point of view, they are not guaranteed to converge to the actual underlying models. One of our future work is how to further validate and update the learned models from more system logs. In general, it is a challenging and interesting direction to derive a confidence for the learned model (as a machine learning problem) or the verification results based on the learned models (as a model checking problem) given specific training data. Or alternatively, how can we derive a requirement on the training data to achieve a certain confidence. Some preliminary results on the number of samples required to achieve an error bound are discussed in [13].

5   Conclusion and Related Work

In this work, we conducted a case study to automatically model and verify a real-world water treatment system testbed. Given a set of safety properties of the system, we combine model learning and abstraction refinement to learn a model which (1) describes how the system would evolve in the long run and (2) verifies or falsifies the properties. The learned models could also be used for further investigation or other system analysis tasks such as probabilistic model checking, simulation or runtime monitoring.

This work is inspired by the recent trend on adopting machine learning to automatically learn models for model checking. Various kinds of model learning algorithms have been investigated including continuous-time Markov Chain [25], DTMC [6,19,31,33,34] and Markov Decision Process [3,18]. In particular, this case study is closely related to the learning approach called LAR documented in [32], which combines model learning and abstraction refinement to automatically find a proper level of abstraction to treat the problem of real-typed variables. Our algorithm is a variant of LAR, which adapts it to the setting of stationary probabilistic models [6].

This case study aims to formally and automatically analyze a real-world CPS by modeling and verifying the physical environment probabilistically. There are several related approaches for this goal. One popular way is to model the CPS as hybrid automata [11]. In [23], a theorem prover for hybrid systems is developed. *dReach* is another tool to verify the δ-complete reachability analysis of hybrid system [9]. Nevertheless, they both require users to manually write a hybrid model using differential dynamic logic, which is highly non-trivial. In [22], the authors propose to learn hybrid models from a sample of observations. In addition, *HyChecker* borrows the idea of concolic testing to hybrid system based on a probabilistic abstraction of the hybrid model and achieves faster detection of counterexamples [15]. *sLAR* is different as it is fully automatic without relying on a user-provided model. SMC is another line of work which does not require a model beforehand [7]. However, it requires sampling the system many times. This is unrealistic for our setting since shutting down and restarting SWaT yield significant cost. Besides, SMC does not provide insight on how the system works but only provides the verification result. Our learned models however can be used for other system analysis tasks.

Several case studies are related to our case study in some way. In [17], the authors applied integrated simulation of the physical part and the cyber part to an intelligent water distribution system. In [8], the authors use model learning to infer models of different software components for TCP implementation and apply model checking to explore the interaction of different components. In [14], a case study on self-driving car is conducted for the analysis of parallel scheduling for CPS. In [21], automata learning is applied in different levels of a smart grid system to improve the power management. As far as we know, our work is the first on applying probabilistic model learning for verifying a real-world CPS probabilistically.

Acknowledgement. The work was supported in part by Singapore NRF Award No. NRF2014NCR-NCR001-40, NSFC projects 61772347, 61502308, STFSC project JCYJ20170302153712968.

References

1. Abeel, T., Van de Peer, Y., Saeys, Y.: Java-ml: a machine learning library. J. Mach. Learn. Res. **10**, 931–934 (2009)
2. Bass, R.F.: Stochastic Processes, vol. 33. Cambridge University Press, Cambridge (2011)
3. Brázdil, T., et al.: Verification of Markov decision processes using learning algorithms. In: Cassez, F., Raskin, J.-F. (eds.) ATVA 2014. LNCS, vol. 8837, pp. 98–114. Springer, Cham (2014). https://doi.org/10.1007/978-3-319-11936-6_8
4. Carrasco, R.C., Oncina, J.: Learning stochastic regular grammars by means of a state merging method. In: Carrasco, R.C., Oncina, J. (eds.) ICGI 1994. LNCS, vol. 862, pp. 139–152. Springer, Heidelberg (1994). https://doi.org/10.1007/3-540-58473-0_144
5. Chang, C.-C., Lin, C.-J.: Libsvm: a library for support vector machines. ACM Trans. Intell. Syst. Technol. (TIST) **2**(3), 27 (2011)
6. Chen, Y., et al.: Learning Markov models for stationary system behaviors. In: Goodloe, A.E., Person, S. (eds.) NFM 2012. LNCS, vol. 7226, pp. 216–230. Springer, Heidelberg (2012). https://doi.org/10.1007/978-3-642-28891-3_22
7. Clarke, E.M., Zuliani, P.: Statistical model checking for cyber-physical systems. In: Bultan, T., Hsiung, P.-A. (eds.) ATVA 2011. LNCS, vol. 6996, pp. 1–12. Springer, Heidelberg (2011). https://doi.org/10.1007/978-3-642-24372-1_1
8. Fiterău-Broştean, P., Janssen, R., Vaandrager, F.: Combining model learning and model checking to analyze TCP implementations. In: Chaudhuri, S., Farzan, A. (eds.) CAV 2016. LNCS, vol. 9780, pp. 454–471. Springer, Cham (2016). https://doi.org/10.1007/978-3-319-41540-6_25
9. Gao, S., Kong, S., Chen, W., Clarke, E.: Delta-complete analysis for bounded reachability of hybrid systems. arXiv preprint arXiv:1404.7171 (2014)
10. Goh, J., Adepu, S., Junejo, K.N., Mathur, A.: A dataset to support research in the design of secure water treatment systems. In: Havarneanu, G., Setola, R., Nassopoulos, H., Wolthusen, S. (eds.) CRITIS 2016. LNCS, vol. 10242, pp. 88–99. Springer, Cham (2017). https://doi.org/10.1007/978-3-319-71368-7_8
11. Henzinger, T.A.: The theory of hybrid automata. In: Inan, M.K., Kurshan, R.P. (eds.) Verification of Digital and Hybrid Systems. NATO ASI Series (Series F: Computer and Systems Sciences), vol. 170, pp. 265–292. Springer, Heidelberg (2000). https://doi.org/10.1007/978-3-642-59615-5_13

12. Hermanns, H., Wachter, B., Zhang, L.: Probabilistic CEGAR. In: Gupta, A., Malik, S. (eds.) CAV 2008. LNCS, vol. 5123, pp. 162–175. Springer, Heidelberg (2008). https://doi.org/10.1007/978-3-540-70545-1_16

13. Jegourel, C., Sun, J., Dong, J.S.: Sequential schemes for frequentist estimation of properties in statistical model checking. In: Bertrand, N., Bortolussi, L. (eds.) QEST 2017. LNCS, vol. 10503, pp. 333–350. Springer, Cham (2017). https://doi.org/10.1007/978-3-319-66335-7_23

14. Kim, J., Kim, H., Lakshmanan, K., Rajkumar, R.R.: Parallel scheduling for cyber-physical systems: analysis and case study on a self-driving car. In: Proceedings of the ACM/IEEE 4th International Conference on Cyber-Physical Systems, pp. 31–40. ACM (2013)

15. Kong, P., Li, Y., Chen, X., Sun, J., Sun, M., Wang, J.: Towards concolic testing for hybrid systems. In: Fitzgerald, J., Heitmeyer, C., Gnesi, S., Philippou, A. (eds.) FM 2016. LNCS, vol. 9995, pp. 460–478. Springer, Cham (2016). https://doi.org/10.1007/978-3-319-48989-6_28

16. Legay, A., Delahaye, B., Bensalem, S.: Statistical model checking: an overview. RV **10**, 122–135 (2010)

17. Lin, J., Sedigh, S., Miller, A.: Towards integrated simulation of cyber-physical systems: a case study on intelligent water distribution. In: 2009 Eighth IEEE International Conference on Dependable, Autonomic and Secure Computing, DASC 2009, pp. 690–695. IEEE (2009)

18. Mao, H., Chen, Y., Jaeger, M., Nielsen, T.D., Larsen, K.G., Nielsen, B.: Learning Markov decision processes for model checking. arXiv preprint arXiv:1212.3873 (2012)

19. Mao, H., Chen, Y., Jaeger, M., Nielsen, T.D., Larsen, K.G., Nielsen, B.: Learning deterministic probabilistic automata from a model checking perspective. Mach. Learn. **105**(2), 255–299 (2016)

20. Mathur, A.P., Tippenhauer, N.O.: SWaT: a water treatment testbed for research and training on ICS security. In: 2016 International Workshop on Cyber-Physical Systems for Smart Water Networks (CySWater), pp. 31–36. IEEE (2016)

21. Misra, S., Krishna, P.V., Saritha, V., Obaidat, M.S.: Learning automata as a utility for power management in smart grids. IEEE Commun. Mag. **51**(1), 98–104 (2013)

22. Niggemann, O., Stein, B., Vodencarevic, A., Maier, A., Büning, H.K.: Learning behavior models for hybrid timed systems. AAAI **2**, 1083–1090 (2012)

23. Platzer, A.: Logical Analysis of Hybrid Systems: Proving Theorems for Complex Dynamics. Springer, Heidelberg (2010). https://doi.org/10.1007/978-3-642-14509-4

24. Ron, D., Singer, Y., Tishby, N.: The power of amnesia: learning probabilistic automata with variable memory length. Mach. Learn. **25**(2–3), 117–149 (1996)

25. Sen, K., Viswanathan, M., Agha, G.: Learning continuous time Markov chains from sample executions. In: Proceedings of the 2004 First International Conference on the Quantitative Evaluation of Systems, QEST 2004, pp. 146–155. IEEE (2004)

26. Sen, K., Viswanathan, M., Agha, G.: Statistical model checking of black-box probabilistic systems. In: Alur, R., Peled, D.A. (eds.) CAV 2004. LNCS, vol. 3114, pp. 202–215. Springer, Heidelberg (2004). https://doi.org/10.1007/978-3-540-27813-9_16

27. SUTD: Swat dataset website. https://itrust.sutd.edu.sg/dataset/

28. SUTD: Swat website. http://itrust.sutd.edu.sg/research/testbeds/secure-water-treatment-swat/

29. Wachter, B., Zhang, L., Hermanns, H.: Probabilistic model checking modulo theories. In: Fourth International Conference on the Quantitative Evaluation of Systems, pp. 129–140. IEEE (2007)
30. Wang, J.: Ziqian website. https://github.com/wang-jingyi/Ziqian
31. Wang, J., Chen, X., Sun, J., Qin, S.: Improving probability estimation through active probabilistic model learning. In: Duan, Z., Ong, L. (eds.) ICFEM 2017. LNCS, vol. 10610, pp. 379–395. Springer, Cham (2017). https://doi.org/10.1007/978-3-319-68690-5_23
32. Wang, J., Sun, J., Qin, S.: Verifying complex systems probabilistically through learning, abstraction and refinement. CoRR, abs/1610.06371 (2016)
33. Wang, J., Sun, J., Yuan, Q., Pang, J.: Should we learn probabilistic models for model checking? A new approach and an empirical study. In: Huisman, M., Rubin, J. (eds.) FASE 2017. LNCS, vol. 10202, pp. 3–21. Springer, Heidelberg (2017). https://doi.org/10.1007/978-3-662-54494-5_1
34. Wang, J., Sun, J., Yuan, Q., Pang, J.: Learning probabilistic models for model checking: an evolutionary approach and an empirical study. In: Int. J. Softw. Tools Technol. Transf., 1–16 (2018). https://doi.org/10.1007/s10009-018-0492-7
35. Younes, H.L.S.: Verification and planning for stochastic processes with asynchronous events. Ph.D. thesis, Carnegie Mellon (2005)

FSM Inference from Long Traces

Florent Avellaneda$^{(\boxtimes)}$ and Alexandre Petrenko$^{(\boxtimes)}$

CRIM, Montreal, Canada
{florent.avellaneda,alexandre.petrenko}@crim.ca

Abstract. Inferring a minimal finite state machine (FSM) from a given set of traces is a fundamental problem in computer science. Although the problem is known to be NP-complete, it can be solved efficiently with SAT solvers when the given set of traces is relatively small. On the other hand, to infer an FSM equivalent to a machine which generates traces, the set of traces should be sufficiently representative and hence large. However, the existing SAT-based inference techniques do not scale well when the length and number of traces increase. In this paper, we propose a novel approach which processes lengthy traces incrementally. The experimental results indicate that it scales sufficiently well and time it takes grows slowly with the size of traces.

Keywords: Machine inference · Machine identification · SAT solver

1 Introduction

Occam's razor is a problem-solving principle attributed to William of Ockham. Also known as the law of parsimony, this principle states that among competing hypotheses, the one with the fewest assumptions should be selected. This simple and natural principle is the base of a lot of work in various areas.

A typical area where this principle is used is the model inference problem. Model inference is the process of building a model consistent with a given set of observations. Since there exists generally an infinite number of consistent models, we choose the simplest following the law of parsimony. When the model to infer is a finite states machine (FSM), we generally use the number of states as the unit of measurement for the complexity. So, the inference in this context consists in finding a minimal FSM consistent with a given set of observation.

Model inference problem has several useful applications such as model-based testing when a model inferred from traces produced by a system executing tests is used to assess the test quality, generate additional tests and model check properties confirmed by the executed tests. The FSM inference from a set of traces is a very active research domain which can be divided into two categories: passive learning (learning from examples) [12,13] and active learning (learning with queries) [4]. In the first category, we have only a set of examples and use it to infer an FSM consistent with this set. Passive FSM inference problem is stated by Kella in 1971 [16] as sequential machine identification. In the second

© Springer International Publishing AG, part of Springer Nature 2018
K. Havelund et al. (Eds.): FM 2018, LNCS 10951, pp. 93–109, 2018.
https://doi.org/10.1007/978-3-319-95582-7_6

category, we use an oracle to ask queries and infer FSM incrementally. The work by Walkinshaw et al. [22] has shown how passive inference algorithms can be used to perform active inference. Based on these results, Smetsers et al. [19] employ SMT solvers to infer DFAs, Mealy machines and register automata.

This paper belongs to the first category: "Given a sample $\mathcal{T}$ and $n \in \mathbb{N}$, does an FSM with n states consistent with $\mathcal{T}$ exist?". Bierman and Feldman address this question [7] by proposing to use a CSP (constraint satisfaction problem) formulation. Later Gold [13] proves that the problem is NP-complete. More than 20 years later Oliveira and Silva [17] develop an algorithm using generic CSP or SMT solvers. Then Grinchtein et al. [14] present a SAT formulation which allows to solve the problem more efficiently, later enhanced by Heule and Verwer [15] by adding auxiliary variables. The method of Grinchtein et al. is less efficient than that of Heule and Verwer, but their incremental approach is interesting, as the time it takes to find a solution grows slowly with the length of a given trace.

It combines the algorithms of Angluin [4] and Biermann and Feldman [7]. As a result, SAT clauses need to be completely rewritten each time new tables as proposed by Angluin are modified. The approach can hardly scale on lengthy traces.

The problem of dealing with long traces is that to infer an adequate model of a component from a set of its execution traces, this set must cover numerous use cases. Intuitively, the more and longer traces are collected from a component under observation the higher the confidence that it is sufficiently representative. Note that in the context of passive inference, we are not controlling the component, as opposed to query learning, aka active inference of FSMs. Unfortunately, multiple lengthy traces pose a problem for the model inference because they significantly increase the time necessary to build a model.

Differently from the existing approaches, our approach does not use the Angluin's tables and builds clauses incrementally, just adding them when a new trace is considered. This allows to use SAT solvers in an incremental way [9]. In incremental SAT solving, the solver processes only newly added formulas, as its state is memorized to accelerate solving.

To process a set of traces incrementally we consider one trace at a time, generate an FSM and verify that it is consistent with the remaining traces. If it is not, choose a trace which is not in the FSM, i.e., a counterexample, and use it to refine the model.

Our incremental inference approach includes in fact two methods for refining conjectures. One is using a prefix and another a suffix instead of processing the whole counterexample trace.

The paper is organized as follows. Section 2 contains definitions. Section 3 provides an overview of passive inference of an FSM from a set of traces based on SAT-solving. In Sect. 4 we present our incremental inference approach together with preliminary experimental results. Section 5 briefly reports on our experience in applying inference in industrial context and Sect. 6 concludes.

2   Definitions

A *Finite State Machine* (FSM) M is a 5-tuple (S, s_0, I, O, T), where S is a finite set of states with initial state s_0; I and O are finite non-empty disjoint sets of inputs and outputs, respectively; T is a transition relation $T \subseteq S \times I \times O \times S$, (s, a, o, s') is a transition.

M is *completely specified* if for each tuple $(s, a) \in S \times I$ there exists a transition $(s, a, o, s') \in T$, otherwise M is *incompletely* specified. We use $\Delta(s, a)$ to denote s' and $\lambda(s, a)$ to denote o. M is *deterministic* if for each $(s, a) \in S \times I$ there exists at most one transition $(s, a, o, s') \in T$, otherwise it is *nondeterministic*. We consider in this paper only deterministic FSMs.

An *execution* of M from state s is a sequence of transitions forming a path from s in the state transition diagram of M. The machine M is *strongly connected*, if the state transition diagram of M is a strongly connected graph.

A *trace* of M in state s is a string of input-output pairs which label an execution from s. Let $Tr(s)$ denote the set of all traces of M in state s and Tr_M denote the set of traces of M in the initial state. Let $\mathcal{T}$ be a set of traces, we say that M is *consistent* with $\mathcal{T}$ if $\mathcal{T} \subseteq Tr_M$. We also say that M is a *conjecture* for $\mathcal{T}$. If all FSMs with fewer states than M are not consistent with $\mathcal{T}$, then we say that M is a *minimal* FSM consistent with $\mathcal{T}$.

We say that two states $s_1, s_1' \in S$ are *incompatible*, if for every two transitions $(s_1, a, o, s_2), (s_1', a, o', s_2') \in T$ it holds that: $o \neq o'$ or s_2 and s_2' are incompatible, denoted $s_1 \not\cong s_1'$. If s_1 and s_1' are not incompatible, then they are *compatible*, denoted $s_1 \cong s_1'$.

3   Passive Inference

Two types of methods solving the problem of learning an automaton from a set of sample traces can be distinguished.

One group constitutes heuristic methods derived from the algorithm of Gold [13] which try to merge states in polynomial time. They are often used in practice because of their efficiency, however, they provide no guarantee for the optimality, since there may exist another way of state merging which provides a resulting machine with a fewer states. Numerous existing heuristic methods allow to infer Mealy machines [21], Moore machines [11] as well as DFA [18].

Another group includes exact algorithms to determine an FSM model with a minimal number of states. This is a much more complicated problem, as it is NP-complete [13], but the minimality may prove to be essential in certain cases. Among existing algorithms for finding a minimal solution, we could mention the algorithm of Heule and Verwer [15] which in our opinion, can be considered as the most efficient currently existing method.

In this paper, we elaborate an approach for the exact FSM inference in an incremental way. It is SAT-solving based and has the advantage of having a low sensibility to the length and number of sample traces.

We rely on the SAT encoding of Heule and Verwer, which we overview in this section, though any other SAT formulation could also be used in our approach.

3.1   Problem Statement

Given a set of traces T generated by an unknown deterministic FSM, we want to find a minimal FSM M consistent with T, i.e., $T \subseteq Tr_M$.

Given T, let $W = (X, x_0, I, O, T)$ be a deterministic acyclic FSM such that $Tr_W = T$. Clearly, W is incompletely specified because the FSM is acyclic. To find an FSM with at most n states consistent with T amounts to determine a partition π on the set of states X into compatible states such that the number of blocks does not exceed n. Clearly, n should be smaller than $|X|$.

This problem can be cast as a constraint satisfaction problem (CSP) [7]. The set of states X is represented by integer variables $x_0, ..., x_{|X|-1}$, such that

$$\forall x_i, x_j \in X : \text{ if } x_i \not\cong x_j \text{ then } x_i \neq x_j$$
$$\text{if } \exists a \in I : \lambda(x_i, a) = \lambda(x_j, a) \text{ then} \qquad (1)$$
$$(x_i = x_j) \Rightarrow (\Delta(x_i, a) = \Delta(x_j, a))$$

Let $B = \{0, ..., n-1\}$ be a set of integers where each integer represents a block of a partition π. Assuming that the value of x_i is in B for all $i \in \{0, ..., |X|-1\}$, we need to find a solution, i.e., an assignment of values of variables in $\{x_0, ..., x_{|X|-1}\}$ such that (1) is satisfied. Each assignment implies a partition of n blocks and thus an FSM with n states consistent with T.

3.2   Encoding as a SAT Problem

The previous CSP formulas can be translated to SAT using unary coding for each integer variable $x \in X$: x is represented by n Boolean variables $v_{x,0}, v_{x,1}, ..., v_{x,n-1}$.

To identify the initial state we have the clause:

$$v_{x_0,0} \qquad (2)$$

It means that the state x_0 should be in the first block.

For each state $x \in X$, we have the clause:

$$v_{x,0} \lor v_{x,1} \lor ... \lor v_{x,n-1} \qquad (3)$$

These clauses mean that each state should be in at least one block.

For each state x and $\forall i, j \in B$ such that $i \neq j$, we have the clauses:

$$\neg v_{x,i} \lor \neg v_{x,j} \qquad (4)$$

These clauses mean that each state should be in at most one block.

The clauses (3) and (4) encode the fact that each state should be in exactly one block.

For every incompatible states $x, x' \in X$ and $\forall i \in B$, we have the clauses:

$$\neg v_{x,i} \lor \neg v_{x',i} \qquad (5)$$

These clauses mean that two incompatible states should not be in the same block.

For every states $x, x' \in X$ such that $\lambda(x, a) = \lambda(x', a)$, and $\forall i, j \in B$, we have a Boolean formula (which can be translated trivially into clauses):

$$(v_{x,i} \wedge v_{x',i}) \Rightarrow (v_{\Delta(x,a),j} \Rightarrow v_{\Delta(x',a),j}) \tag{6}$$

These clauses enforce determinism.

Note that the clauses (5) encode the first line of the CSP constraint (1) and the clauses (6) encode the second line. An existing SAT solver [5,6,10,20] can be used to check satisfiability of the obtained formula.

3.3 Auxiliary Variables

Heule and Verwer [15] propose to use auxiliary variables, replacing formula (6) and add some additional clauses. They provide experimental results which indicate that their encoding is sufficiently efficient. Namely, for $a \in I$ and $0 \leq i, j < n$, variable $y_{a,i,j}$ is introduced for True value means that for any state in block i, the next state reached with input a is in the block j. These variables are used to form the following clauses.

For each transition $(x, a, o, x') \in T$ and for every $i, j \in B$:

$$y_{a,i,j} \vee \neg v_{x,i} \vee \neg v_{x',j} \tag{7}$$

This means that blocks i and j are related for input a if state x is in the block i and its successor x' on input a is in the block j.

For each input symbol $a \in I$, for every $i, h \in B$ and for each $j \in \{h+1, n-1\}$:

$$\neg y_{a,i,h} \vee \neg y_{a,i,j} \tag{8}$$

This means that each block relation can include at most one pair of blocks for each input to enforce determinism.

For each input symbol $a \in \Sigma$ and each $i \in B$:

$$y_{a,i,0} \vee y_{a,i,1} \vee \dots \vee y_{a,i,n-1} \tag{9}$$

This means that each block relation must include at least one pair of blocks for each input to enforce determinism.

For each transition $(x, a, o, x') \in T$ and for every $i, j \in B$:

$$\neg y_{a,i,j} \vee \neg v_{x,i} \vee v_{x',j} \tag{10}$$

This means that once blocks i and j are related for input a and state x is in the block i then its successor x' on input a must be in the block j.

Among these clauses, some are redundant. Nevertheless, their use improves the performance of FSM inference as work in [15] suggests.

3.4   Symmetry Breaking

It is possible that for certain formulations of a SAT formula, some assignments are equivalent, i.e., represent a same solution. In this case, we say that we have a symmetry. A good practice is to break this symmetry [2,3,8] by adding constraints such that different assignments satisfying the formula represent different solutions.

The above formulation can result in a significant amount of symmetry because any permutation of the blocks is allowed. This fact has already been noticed in the literature and the strategy adopted in [1,15] consists in placing each state in a certain subset to a fixed distinct block. To this end, we can use the state incompatibility graph which has $|X|$ nodes and two nodes are connected iff the corresponding states of W are incompatible. Clearly, each state of a clique (maximal or smaller) must be placed in a distinct block. Hence, we can add to the SAT formula clauses for assigning initially each state from the clique to a separate block.

Table 1. Summary for encoding passive inference from ISFSM $W = (X, x_0, I, O, T)$ into SAT. n is the maximal number of states in an FSM to infer, $B = \{0, ..., n-1\}$.

Ref	Clauses	Range
(2)	$v_{x_0,0}$	
(3)	$(v_{x,0} \lor v_{x,1} \lor ... \lor v_{x,n-1})$	$x \in X$
(4)	$(\neg v_{x,i} \lor \neg v_{x,j})$	$x \in X; 0 \le i < j < n$
(5)	$(\neg v_{x,i} \lor \neg v_{x',i})$	$x \not\equiv x'; i \in B$
(7)	$(y_{a,i,j} \lor \neg v_{x,i} \lor \neg v_{x',j})$	$(x, a, o, x') \in T; i, j \in B$
(8)	$(\neg y_{a,i,h} \lor \neg y_{a,i,j})$	$a \in I; h, i, j \in B; h < j$
(9)	$(y_{a,i,0} \lor y_{a,i,1} \lor ... \lor y_{a,i,n-1})$	$a \in I; i \in B$
(10)	$(\neg y_{a,i,j} \lor \neg v_{x,i} \lor v_{x',j})$	$(x, a, o, x') \in T; i, j \in B$

4   Incremental Inference

To alleviate the complexity associated with large sets containing lengthy traces, we propose an approach which, instead of attempting to process all the given traces in the set T at once, iteratively infers an FSM from their subset (initially it is an empty set) and uses active inference to refine it when it is not consistent with one of the given traces. While active inference usually uses a black box as an oracle capable of judging whether or not a trace belongs to the model, we assign the role of an oracle to a set of traces T. Even if this oracle is restricted since it cannot generate traces for all possible input sequences, nevertheless, as we demonstrate, it leads to an efficient approach for passive inference from execution traces.

The proposed approach is elaborated in two methods performing different refinements of a conjecture inconsistent with a given set of traces. Refinement needs to be performed when the shortest prefix ω of a trace in $\mathcal{T}$ which is not a trace of the conjecture is found. The first type of refinement consists in adding ω to the conjecture's initial state which is achieved by formulating the corresponding constraints. We present this method in Sect. 4.1. The second type of refinement consists in adding not ω but its shortest suffix ω' which is not a trace of any state of the conjecture. The suffix ω' is added to some state of the conjecture which is achieved by formulating the corresponding constraints. This method is elaborated in Sect. 4.2.

We provide the results of experimental evaluation of the two methods and discuss them in Sect. 4.3.

4.1 Prefix-Based Method

Let $\mathcal{T}$ be a set of traces (generated by a deterministic FSM). We want to find a minimal FSM consistent with $\mathcal{T}$ iteratively. To do that, we search for an FSM M with at most n states satisfying a growing set of constraints (initially we do not have any constraints). If no solution is found, it means that the state number n is too low. In this case we increase n and start again. If a solution is found and M is consistent with $\mathcal{T}$, then we return this solution. Otherwise, we find the shortest prefix of a trace ω in $\mathcal{T}$ not accepted by M. Then, we use SAT encoding described in the previous section to formulate the constraint that ω has to be a trace of the conjecture.

The approach is formalized in Algorithm 1.

Algorithm 1. Infer an FSM from a set of traces

Input: A set of traces $\mathcal{T}$ and an integer n.
Output: An FSM with at most n states consistent with $\mathcal{T}$ if it exists.
1: $C := \emptyset$
2: **while** C is satisfiable **do**
3:     Let M be an FSM of a solution of C
4:     **if** $\mathcal{T} \subseteq Tr_M$ **then**
5:         **return** M
6:     **end if**
7:     Let ω be the shortest trace in $\mathcal{T} \backslash Tr_M$
8:     $C := C \wedge C_\omega$, where C_ω is clauses encoding the fact that $\omega \in Tr_M$ using Table 1
9: **end while**
10: **return** $false$

Theorem 1. *Given a set of traces $\mathcal{T}$, Algorithm 1 returns an FSM consistent with $\mathcal{T}$ if it exists or false otherwise.*

Proof. If line 5 is reached, then $T \subseteq Tr_M$. So M is consistent with T. If line 10 is reached, then C encoding the fact that all traces of T have to be included in an FSM with at most n states is not satisfiable. So, there is no FSM with at most n states consistent with T. The termination is assured because in each while loop, additional trace of T is considered. When all traces are considered then either there is a solution and $T \subseteq Tr_M$ terminates the function, or there is no solution and the while condition is no longer respected.

Corollary 1. *Let T be a set of traces. If we call Algorithm 1 incrementally by increasing n from n = 1 until an FSM consistent with T is obtained, then it is a minimal FSM consistent with T.*

4.1.1   Example

We illustrate Algorithm 1 with a simple example of a small program, see Algorithm 2.

Let $w = ping/pong.pause/pause.ping/pause.ping/pause.pause/pong.pause/pa$ $use.ping/pause.pause/pong.ping/pause.ping/pause.pause/pause.ping/pause.ping/$ $pause.pause/ping.ping/pong.ping/pong...$ be the only trace in T obtained by random execution of the program.

Algorithm 2

```
 1: while true do
 2:     Event msg = receive();
 3:     if msg == ping then
 4:         send(pong);
 5:     end if
 6:     if msg == pause then
 7:         send(pause);
 8:         while receive() ≠ pause do
 9:             send(pause);
10:         end while
11:         send(pong);
12:     end if
13: end while
```

Initially, we consider as a conjecture the trivial FSM with the empty trace. The shortest prefix trace inconsistent with this conjecture is $ping/pong$, and so, some clauses are added to ensure that the trace $ping/pong$ is accepted. A new conjecture is an FSM with a single state having self-looping transition labeled $ping/pong$. This time, the shortest prefix inconsistent with this conjecture is $ping/pong.pause/pause$. This trace yields new constraints leading to a next conjecture with a single state having two self-looping transitions labeled $ping/pong$ and $pause/pause$. This conjecture is consistent with the two considered traces *ping/pong* and *ping/pong.pause/pause* but still not with the whole *w*. The process continues while the constraints are satisfiable. All the executed steps are illustrated in Fig. 1. A trace beneath a conjecture is a prefix used to obtain the conjecture.

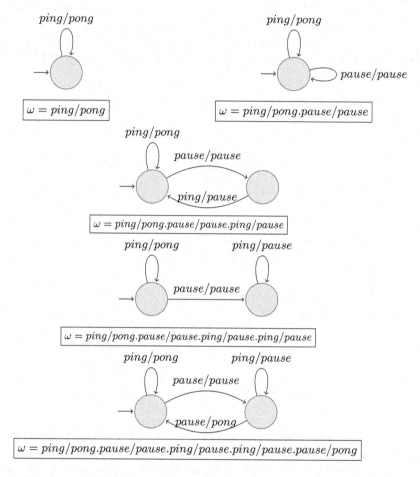

Fig. 1. Inferring an FSM from trace *ping/pong.pause/pause.ping/pause.ping/pause. pause/pong.pause/pause.ping/pause.pause/pong.ping/pong.ping/pong.pause/pause. ping/pause.ping/pause.pause/pong.ping/pong.ping/pong...* with Algorithm 1.

4.1.2 Evaluation

To the best of your knowledge, the approach of Heule and Verwer [15] is currently the most efficient encoding of the FSM inference into SAT. In this section, we provide results of experimental comparison of their approach with ours.

We have implemented the encoding of the inference problem to SAT using the Heule and Verwer's formulas as described in Table 1. We use **H&V** and

Prefix-based to refer to the method of Heule and Verwer and Algorithm 1, respectively.

The prototype was implemented in C++ calling the SAT solver Cryptominisat [20]. The experiments were carried out on a machine with 8 GB of RAM and an i7-3537U processor.

We randomly generate FSMs with seven states, two inputs a and b, and two outputs 0 and 1. Each state s_i is linked to the state $s_{i+1 \ mod \ 8}$ by a transition with input a and a random output to ensure that machines are strongly connected. Then we complete an FSM in a random way. Figure 2 shows an example of such a construction.

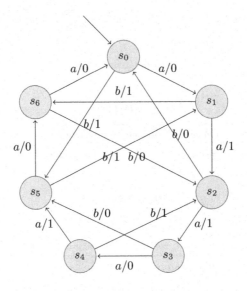

Fig. 2. Example of a random FSM.

Given an FSM, traces of various length are randomly generated. Tables 2 and 3 show time used to infer an FSM from a single trace and 100 traces, respectively. For each length of traces, we calculate the average time used to infer a machine over ten instances.

The results in Tables 2 and 3 indicate that the proposed approach performs much better than that of [15]. Moreover, they show that time used by Algorithm 1 grows very slow when the size of traces increases. This is due to the fact that the approach of [15] uses all the traces at once for inference while our approach is incremental and requires a minimal prefix of a single trace among the given traces in each iteration.

In Tables 4 and 5, we show the results obtained when we push our algorithm to its limits.

Table 2. Seconds to infer an FSM from a trace.

Length	H&V	Prefix-based
1k	2.5	0.2
2k	7.3	0.2
4k	20	0.2
8k	53	0.2
16k	190	0.3
32k	Out of memory	0.5
64k	Out of memory	1.5

Table 3. Seconds to infer an FSM from 100 traces.

Length	H&V	Prefix-based
100	31	<0.1
200	140	<0.1
400	590	<0.1
1k	Out of memory	0.1
10k	Out of memory	3.8

Table 4. Inferring FSM from a single trace with length 100k by Algorithm 1.

# States	Checking $\mathcal{T} \subseteq Tr_M$	SAT Solving	Total
5	3.33 s	0.003 s	3.46 s
6	3.28 s	0.02 s	3.42 s
7	3.28 s	0.076 s	3.48 s
8	3.27 s	0.57 s	3.98 s
9	3.28 s	7.23 s	10.7 s
10	3.28 s	28.6 s	32.0 s

Table 5. Inferring FSM from a single trace with 10 states by Algorithm 1.

Length	Checking $\mathcal{T} \subseteq Tr_M$	Solving SAT	Total
25k	0.17 s	22.9 s	23.2 s
50k	0.79 s	25.1 s	26.0 s
75k	1.83 s	26.4 s	28.3 s
100k	3.28 s	28.6 s	32.0 s

In Table 4, we increase the state number and set the length of generated traces to 100k. In Table 5, we set the state number to 10 and increase the trace length generated by this FSM.

We can see that the time (an average of 100 instances) used by the SAT solver depends on the number of states of the machine to infer, but very little on the length of the traces used. On the other hand, the time to test the trace inclusion depends on the length of a trace, but not on the number of states in the FSM to infer.

It is not surprising that overall time grows rapidly with the number of FSM states to infer (because the problem remains NP-Complete), on the other hand, it is interesting to notice that time grows almost linearly with the length of traces.

4.2   Suffix-Based Method

In the prefix-based method, when a generated conjecture M is inconsistent with T, we use the shortest prefix of a trace to refine the conjecture. Clearly, the longer the prefix the more clauses are added to the constraints. This observation motivates our second method which is using a different refinement.

The idea is that when we find the shortest trace ω which is in T but not in M, we determine a suffix ω' of ω such that ω' is not a trace of any state of the conjecture M. Then if we add the constraint that there exists a state s such that ω' must be accepted by M in state s, thus M is refuted and will be refined. If a refined conjecture which accepts ω' does not accept the whole ω yet then a longer suffix is considered in the next iteration until ω is in Tr_M. When the suffix ω' is shorter than ω, the number of added clauses can be smaller compared to the use of ω.

Theorem 2. *Given a set of traces T, Algorithm 3 returns an FSM consistent with T if it exists or false otherwise.*

Proof. If line 5 is reached, then $T \subseteq Tr_M$ and so M is consistent with T. If line 14 is reached, then all the traces of T cannot be represented by an FSM with n states. The termination is assured because in each while loop, additional suffix of a trace of T is considered. When all suffixes of all traces are considered then either there is a solution and $T \subseteq Tr_M$ terminates the function, or there is no solution and the while condition is no longer respected.

Corollary 2. *Let T be a set of traces. If we call Algorithm 3 incrementally by increasing n from $n = 1$ until an FSM consistent with T is obtained, then it is a minimal FSM consistent with T.*

4.2.1   Example

We illustrate the suffix-based method with the example from Sect. 4.1.1. We use the same trace $w = ping/pong.pause/pause.ping/pause.ping/pause.pause/$ $pong.pause/pause.ping/pause.pause/pong.ping/pause.ping/pause.pause/pause.$

Algorithm 3. Infer an FSM from a set of traces.

Input: A set of traces $\mathcal{T}$ and an integer n.
Output: An FSM with a most n states consistent with $\mathcal{T}$ if it exists.
1: $C := \emptyset$
2: **while** C is satisfiable **do**
3:     Let M be an FSM of a solution of C
4:     **if** $\mathcal{T} \subseteq Tr_M$ **then**
5:         **return** M
6:     **end if**
7:     Let ω be the shortest trace in $\mathcal{T} \backslash Tr_M$
8:     **if** $\exists \omega'$ the shortest suffix of ω such that $\forall s, \omega' \notin Tr(s)$ **then**
9:         $C := C \wedge C'_\omega$, where C'_ω is clauses encoding the fact that $\exists s : \omega' \in Tr(s)$
    using Table 1 without the first constraint.
10:     **else**
11:         $C := C \wedge C_\omega$, where C_ω is clauses encoding the fact that $\omega \in Tr_M$ using
    Table 1.
12:     **end if**
13: **end while**
14: **return** $false$

$ping/pause.ping/pause.pause/ping.ping/pong.ping/pong...$ as the only trace in $\mathcal{T}$ obtained by executing Algorithm 2. Figure 3 shows intermediate conjectures with the suffixes added to obtain them.

4.2.2   Evaluation

Comparing the execution of the two methods on the same trace in Sects. 4.1.1 and 4.2.1, one can notice that the suffix-based method uses instead of a long trace with an event making a conjecture inconsistent just its much shorter suffix with that event. An example of such an event in the trace is $ping/pause$. Intuitively, all things being equal, a suffix could be shorter than a prefix when an event causing inconsistence occurs seldom.

To check this hypothesis, we decided to extend the experiments reported in the last row of Table 2, where a trace of the length 64000 belongs to an FSM randomly generated as explained in Sect. 4.1.2. This time we vary the chances for input b to appear. Table 6 contains the averages of ten instances for each value of probability.

We can see that when all inputs are equiprobable (Line 1 of the Table 6), the second algorithm is a little slower. On the other hand, time used by the prefix-closed method grows when an input rarely appears, but it remains constant with the suffix-closed method, as expected in the hypothesis.

4.3   Discussion

We presented two methods for incremental inference of a minimal FSM consistent with a given set of traces. As could be expected, experimental results

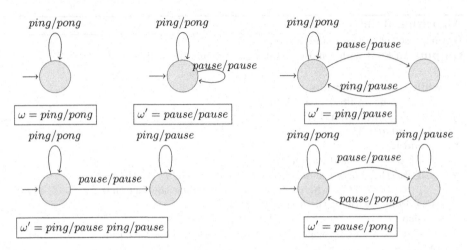

Fig. 3.   Inferring   an   FSM   from   trace   *ping/pong.pause/pause.ping/pause.
ping/pause.pause/pong.pause/pause.ping/pause.pause/pong.ping/pong.ping/pong.
pause/pause.ping/pause.ping/pause.pause/pong.ping/pong.ping/pong...*   with
Algorithm 3

Table 6. Seconds to infer an FSM from a trace with different probabilities of input *b*.

Probability of *b*	Prefix-based	Suffix-based
50%	1.5	2.4
25%	1.4	1.4
10%	1.4	1.4
1%	3.5	1.4
0.5%	6.0	1.5
0.3%	16	1.4
0.2%	90	1.5
0.1%	Out of memory	1.6

indicate that inference from an incrementally growing subset of traces has a big
advantage compared to the classical inference from all the given traces at once,
as in the method of Heule and Verwer [15] when the traces are rather long and
numerous. The reason for that is the proposed approach avoids as long as possible to generate constraints from the whole initial traces, and tries to find instead
their appropriate portions, prefixes, as in the prefix-based method or suffixes, as
in the suffix-based method.

Comparing the two proposed methods, we understand that their efficiency
depends on intricate properties of given traces. Preliminary experiments confirm
our hypothesis that rare key events in a trace may create favorable conditions
for the suffix-based method to perform more efficiently than its counterpart, the
prefix-based method.

5   Industrial Case Study

Our industrial partner provided us with logs of a flight simulator expecting us to produce state machine models of some components involved in the logged executions of the simulator. Models are considered as an important part of documentation, especially for legacy components and components from the third party. They facilitate change impact analysis, regression testing and other tasks of simulator development and maintenance.

The logs are normally collected while executing flight scenarios defined by experts and come in the form of time series of at least 12000 steps.

Clearly, using traditional inference methods directly on time series is out of the question; preprocessing we performed includes their partitioning into smaller time series caused by inputs and replacing time series which are "close" to others such that a limited number of time series become outputs in a state machine model. Vectors of values of input variables present in a log become inputs in the model. In the processed traces their number reaches a dozen. The inferred FSMs have up to ten states.

Flight simulator experts consider the resulting models sufficiently adequate and useful. In this case study log preprocessing turns out to be more challenging and time consuming than the model inference with the prototype we developed. The scalability of the whole approach may, however, be an issue for processing logs resulting from long flight scenarios. The latter need more aggressive preprocessing, e.g., excluding parts where "not much happening", this would favor our suffix-based method which looks for turning events.

6   Conclusion

In this paper we considered the problem of inferring a minimal FSM consistent with a set of long traces. Although this problem has extensively been studied, the efficiency of the existing methods deteriorates quickly with the size of the given traces. We proposed in this paper an approach aimed at dealing with long traces. The need for it comes from the observation that the more and longer traces are collected from a component under observation, the higher the confidence that they are sufficiently representative and would yield an adequate model.

Addressing the scalability issue, we proposed an approach which does not process all the given traces at once, instead it does this incrementally. The idea of processing a set of traces incrementally is to consider one trace at a time, generate an FSM and verify that it is consistent with the remaining traces. If it is not, choose a trace which is not in the FSM, i.e., a counterexample, and use it to refine the model.

Our incremental inference approach includes in fact two methods for refining conjectures. One is using a prefix and another a suffix instead of processing the whole counterexample trace. The approach is SAT-solving based and has the advantage of having a lower sensibility to the length and number of sample traces compared to the existing approaches.

The experimental results indicate that the proposed approach is sufficiently efficient especially for long traces where some inputs occur rather rarely. We plan to perform more experiments to find other ways of improving efficiency.

Acknowledgements. This work was partially supported by MESI (Ministère de l'Économie, Science et Innovation) of Gouvernement du Québec, NSERC of Canada and CAE.

References

1. Abel, A., Reineke, J.: Memin: SAT-based exact minimization of incompletely specified mealy machines. In: 2015 IEEE/ACM International Conference on Computer-Aided Design (ICCAD), pp. 94–101. IEEE (2015)
2. Aloul, F.A., Ramani, A., Markov, I.L., Sakallah, K.A.: Solving difficult SAT instances in the presence of symmetry. In: Proceedings of the 39th annual Design Automation Conference, pp. 731–736. ACM (2002)
3. Aloul, F.A., Sakallah, K.A., Markov, I.L.: Efficient symmetry breaking for boolean satisfiability. IEEE Trans. Comput. **55**(5), 549–558 (2006)
4. Angluin, D.: Learning regular sets from queries and counterexamples. Inf. Comput. **75**(2), 87–106 (1987)
5. Audemard, G., Simon, L.: The glucose SAT solver (2013)
6. Biere, A.: Picosat essentials. J. Satisfiability Boolean Model. Comput. **4**, 75–97 (2008)
7. Biermann, A.W., Feldman, J.A.: On the synthesis of finite-state machines from samples of their behavior. IEEE Trans. Comput. **100**(6), 592–597 (1972)
8. Brown, C.A., Finkelstein, L., Purdom Jr., P.W.: Backtrack searching in the presence of symmetry. In: Mora, T. (ed.) AAECC 1988. LNCS, vol. 357, pp. 99–110. Springer, Heidelberg (1989). https://doi.org/10.1007/3-540-51083-4_51
9. Eén, N., Sörensson, N.: Temporal induction by incremental SAT solving. Electron. Notes Theor. Comput. Sci. **89**(4), 543–560 (2003)
10. Een, N., Sörensson, N.: MiniSat: a SAT solver with conflict-clause minimization. In: 8th SAT-5 (2005)
11. Giantamidis, G., Tripakis, S.: Learning moore machines from input-output traces. In: Fitzgerald, J., Heitmeyer, C., Gnesi, S., Philippou, A. (eds.) FM 2016. LNCS, vol. 9995, pp. 291–309. Springer, Cham (2016). https://doi.org/10.1007/978-3-319-48989-6_18
12. Gold, E.M.: Language identification in the limit. Inf. Control **10**(5), 447–474 (1967)
13. Gold, E.M.: Complexity of automaton identification from given data. Inf. Control **37**(3), 302–320 (1978)
14. Grinchtein, O., Leucker, M., Piterman, N.: Inferring network invariants automatically. In: Furbach, U., Shankar, N. (eds.) IJCAR 2006. LNCS (LNAI), vol. 4130, pp. 483–497. Springer, Heidelberg (2006). https://doi.org/10.1007/11814771_40
15. Heule, M.J.H., Verwer, S.: Software model synthesis using satisfiability solvers. Empirical Softw. Eng. **18**(4), 825–856 (2013)
16. Kella, J.: Sequential machine identification. IEEE Trans. Comput. **100**(3), 332–338 (1971)
17. Oliveira, A.L., Silva, J.P.M.: Efficient algorithms for the inference of minimum size DFAS. Mach. Learn. **44**(1), 93–119 (2001)

18. Oncina, J., García, P.: Identifying regular languages in polynomial time. Adv. Struct. Syntactic Pattern Recogn. **5**(99–108), 15–20 (1992)
19. Smetsers, R., Fiterău-Broştean, P., Vaandrager, F.: Model learning as a satisfiability modulo theories problem. In: Klein, S.T., Martín-Vide, C., Shapira, D. (eds.) LATA 2018. LNCS, vol. 10792, pp. 182–194. Springer, Cham (2018). https://doi.org/10.1007/978-3-319-77313-1_14
20. Soos, M.: Cryptominisat 2.5.0. SAT Race competitive event booklet (2010)
21. Veelenturf, L.P.J.: Inference of sequential machines from sample computations. IEEE Trans. Comput. **2**(C–27), 167–170 (1978)
22. Walkinshaw, N., Derrick, J., Guo, Q.: Iterative refinement of reverse-engineered models by model-based testing. In: Cavalcanti, A., Dams, D.R. (eds.) FM 2009. LNCS, vol. 5850, pp. 305–320. Springer, Heidelberg (2009). https://doi.org/10.1007/978-3-642-05089-3_20

A Weakness Measure for GR(1) Formulae

Davide Giacomo Cavezza$^{(\boxtimes)}$, Dalal Alrajeh, and András György

Imperial College London, London, UK
{d.cavezza15,dalal.alrajeh,a.gyorgy}@imperial.ac.uk

Abstract. In spite of the theoretical and algorithmic developments for system synthesis in recent years, little effort has been dedicated to quantifying the quality of the specifications used for synthesis. When dealing with unrealizable specifications, finding the weakest environment assumptions that would ensure realizability is typically a desirable property; in such context the weakness of the assumptions is a major quality parameter. The question of whether one assumption is weaker than another is commonly interpreted using implication or, equivalently, language inclusion. However, this interpretation does not provide any further insight into the weakness of assumptions when implication does not hold. To our knowledge, the only measure that is capable of comparing two formulae in this case is entropy, but even it fails to provide a sufficiently refined notion of weakness in case of GR(1) formulae, a subset of linear temporal logic formulae which is of particular interest in controller synthesis. In this paper we propose a more refined measure of weakness based on the Hausdorff dimension, a concept that captures the notion of size of the omega-language satisfying a linear temporal logic formula. We identify the conditions under which this measure is guaranteed to distinguish between weaker and stronger GR(1) formulae. We evaluate our proposed weakness measure in the context of computing GR(1) assumptions refinements.

1 Introduction

Specifications provide significant aid in the formal analysis of software supporting tasks such as their verification and implementation. However writing such specifications is difficult and error-prone, often resulting in their incompleteness, inconsistency and unrealizability [27]. Hence providing formal and rigorous support for ensuring their highest quality is of key importance [28]. One crucial quality metric for specifications, which this paper focuses on, is that of weakness in the context of reactive synthesis [2,5,15,21].

Reactive synthesis is concerned with finding a system implementation that satisfies a given specification under all possible environments [36]. When no such implementation exists, a specification is said to be unrealizable [19]. Though there may be many reasons for why a specification is unrealizable, a common cause is an incomplete set of assumptions over the environment behaviour. Several techniques [4,5,15,30] have been proposed in order to compute refinements

© Springer International Publishing AG, part of Springer Nature 2018
K. Havelund et al. (Eds.): FM 2018, LNCS 10951, pp. 110–128, 2018.
https://doi.org/10.1007/978-3-319-95582-7_7

for incomplete assumptions so as to ensure the realizability of a specification. These approaches consider specifications expressed in a subset of linear temporal logic (LTL), namely generalized reactivity of rank 1 (GR(1)) [11–13], for which tractable synthesis methods exist. Their aim is to find the "weakest" assumptions amongst possible alternatives.

Assumption weakness [39] is a feature intended to capture the degree of freedom (or permissiveness) an environment satisfying the assumptions has over its behaviours; generally, weaker assumptions are preferred since they allow for more general solutions to the synthesis problem [18,39]. Existing approaches formalize the weakness relation between assumptions through logical implication [4,39], i.e., a formula ϕ_1 is weaker than a formula ϕ_2 if $\phi_2 \rightarrow \phi_1$ is valid. However, this notion does not fully capture the weakness concept as permissiveness [14]. Consider the simple example of a bus arbiter whose environment consists of three devices that can request for bus access. Let r_i be the binary signal meaning "device i requests access". An assumption like "device 1 requests access infinitely often" (**GF**r_1 in LTL) is intuitively less constraining than "device 2 and 3 request access infinitely often" (**GF**$(r_2 \wedge r_3)$). However, since the two assumptions refer to disjoint subsets of variables, no implication relation holds between the two.

To enable comparison between weakness of specifications as in the case above, we propose a quantitative measure for the weakness of GR(1) formulae (Sect. 4)—based on their interpretation as an ω-language—and a procedure to compute it. The measure builds upon the notion of Hausdorff dimension [41], a quantity providing an indication of the size of an ω-language: the higher the dimension, the wider the collection of distinct ω-words contained in the ω-language (Sect. 5). We show that a sufficient condition for assumptions expressed as invariants to be comparable through our measure is the *strong connectedness* of the underlying ω-language (Sect. 5.1). To compare assumptions containing fairness conditions, we identify and measure a language decomposition based on fairness complements (Sect. 5.2–5.3). We finally demonstrate the use of our proposed weakness measure on a set of assumptions refinement benchmarks (Sect. 6). Though we focus on comparing the weakness of assumptions refinements, the applied scope of our weakness metric can be extended to other contexts, e.g., quantitative model checking, in the form of a measure of the set of behaviors violating some given property (see [6]) and specification coverage as in [8,42].

2   Related Work

The closest notion to our measure is the *entropy* of ω-languages applied by Asarin et al. [6,7] to quantitative model checking. This quantity measures how diverse the ω-words contained in the language of an LTL formula are. However, it is not sufficiently fine-grained to distinguish between weaker and stronger fairness conditions [6]. We will show that our metric based on Hausdorff dimension is capable of making this distinction.

Quality of LTL formulae has also been defined in the context of model verification. The work by Henzinger et al. [25,26] defines a similarity measure between models of LTL formulae so as to render the model checking output quantitative: instead of returning a true/false response, quantitative model checking computes the distance (*stability radius*) of the model from the boundary of the satisfiability region of an LTL property. The scope of our work is different: the measure we propose can be interpreted as the *extension* of such a satisfiability region, which is independent of a specific model to check against.

An alternative way to measure behaviour sets is via probabilities. Probabilistic model checking [24,29] enhances the syntax and semantics of temporal logics (usually *computation tree logic*) with probabilities. This allows for the expressions of properties like "the probability of satisfying a temporal logic formula ϕ by the modelled behaviours is at most p." Further extensions of LTL and/or automata with preference metrics alternative to probabilities have been proposed in [3,10,17,18]. The difference between using such quantities and our proposal is that while all of these measures are additional and depend on arbitrary parameters that may not reflect the true weakness of a logical formula, the measure we propose quantifies a concept of weakness *intrinsic* to the LTL formula itself.

The problem of identifying weakest assumptions appears in the context of assume-guarantee reasoning [20,31,35] for compositional model checking. In order to perform model checking of large systems, those systems are generally broken down to components that can be checked independently for correctness. In this context, one of the challenges is to identify the most general (weakest) assumptions over the environment in which each component operates, such that when they are satisfied, the correctness of the entire system is guaranteed. Assumptions are formalized as transition systems (e.g., modal transition systems) rather than declarative LTL specifications, which is the focus of our work.

3   Preliminaries

Languages and Automata. Let Σ be a finite set of symbols, which we call *alphabet*. A *word* over Σ is a finite sequence of symbols in Σ. An ω *-word* is an infinite sequence of such symbols. A set of words is called a *language*, while a set of ω-words is called an ω-language. A word w is explicitly denoted as a sequence of its symbols $w_1 w_2 \ldots w_n$, or with a parenthesis notation $(w_1, w_2, \ldots, w_n)$, with the symbols separated by commas; the same notation is used for ω-words. The notation w^j denotes the suffix of w starting with w_j.

Given two words v and w, their concatenation is denoted as $v \cdot w$ or simply vw. The same notation is used for the concatenation of a word v and an ω-word w; the concatenation of an ω-word and a word is not defined. Given a set V of finite-length words and a set W of finite-length words or ω-words over the same alphabet Σ, the set $V \cdot W$ is the set of words obtained by concatenating a word in V with a word in W. *Kleene's star operator* yields the set V^* of finite words obtained by concatenating an arbitrary number of words in V. The *omega operator* applied to V yields the set V^ω of ω-words obtained by concatenating a (countably) infinite number of words in V. Naturally, Σ^* and Σ^ω represent, respectively, the set of all finite words and all ω-words over the alphabet Σ. The star and omega operators can also be applied to single finite-length words, like in w^* and w^ω.

Given an ω-language $L \subseteq \Sigma^\omega$, we denote by $A_n(L)$ the set of all $w \in \Sigma^*$ such that w is a prefix of a word in L and $|w| = n$. We also define $A(L) = \bigcup_{n \in \mathbb{N}} A_n(L)$ the set of all the prefixes of ω-words in L. It is possible to define a topology on Σ^ω. For more details, we refer the reader to [41]. In this context, we only need the notions of closed ω-languages and of their closure. An ω-language L is $closed$ if and only if for any ω-word w such that $A(\{w\}) \subseteq A(L)$, $w \in L$. In other words, L is closed if whenever a word w is arbitrarily close (up to a prefix of arbitrary length) to some word in L, then $w \in L$. The $closure$ of an ω-language L, denoted by $\mathcal{C}(L)$, is the smallest closed ω-language that contains L.

The notion of regular ω-languages encompasses ω-languages that allow a finite representation through automata. Formally, we define a $regular$ ω-$language$ as an ω-language which is accepted by a deterministic Muller automaton. A $deterministic$ $Muller$ $automaton$ (DMA) is defined by the quintuple $\mathcal{M} = \langle Q, \Sigma, q_0, \delta, T \rangle$, where Q is a set of states, Σ is the alphabet of the ω-language, q_0 is the initial state, $\delta : Q \times \Sigma \to Q$ is the transition (partial) function and $T \subseteq 2^Q$ is a set (a table) of accepting state sets. Given an ω-word $w \in \Sigma^\omega$, the run induced by w onto $\mathcal{M}$ is a sequence of states $\mathcal{M}(w) = q_0 q_1 \ldots$ such that q_0 is the initial state and $q_i = \delta(q_{i-1}, w_i) \, \forall i \in \mathbb{N}$. Let $\text{Inf}(w) \subseteq Q$ be the set of states occurring infinitely many times in $\mathcal{M}(w)$. Then an ω-word is said to be $accepted$ by $\mathcal{M}$ iff $\text{Inf}(w) \in T$. By extension, the ω-language accepted by $\mathcal{M}$ is the set of ω-words accepted by $\mathcal{M}$.

A $deterministic$ $Büchi$ $automaton$ (DBA) $\mathcal{B}$ is defined in the same way as a DMA except for the acceptance condition, which is stated in terms of a subset of states $F \subseteq Q$. A word w is accepted by $\mathcal{B}$ iff $\text{Inf}(w) \cap F \neq \varnothing$. Given a DBA it is always possible to obtain an equivalent DMA by replacing the Büchi acceptance condition with the table $T = \{Q' \in 2^Q \mid Q' \cap F \neq \varnothing\}$. In Sect. 6 we also refer to nondeterministic automata, where the transition function is replaced by a transition relation and the initial state by a set of initial states.

Linear Temporal Logic and GR(1). $Linear$ $temporal$ $logic$ (LTL) [37] is an extension of Boolean logic with temporal operators. It allows for expressing properties of infinite sequences of assignments to a set $\mathcal{V}$ of Boolean variables. Its syntax and semantics are described in the extended version of this paper [16].

In this paper, we deal with a specific subset of LTL, called $Generalized$ $Reactivity$ (1) (GR(1)), which is largely employed in controller synthesis [12]. This subset makes use of the operators **G** ("always"), which states that its operand formula must hold at each step of a valuation sequence, **F** ("eventually"), which requires its operand formula to hold at some point in the sequence, and **X** ("next"), which states that the operand formula must hold in the state following the one on which the formula is evaluated.

A GR(1) formula over a set of variables $\mathcal{V}$ has the form $\phi = \phi^{\mathcal{E}} \to \phi^{\mathcal{S}}$, where $\phi^{\mathcal{E}}$ and $\phi^{\mathcal{S}}$ are conjunctions of the following units: (i) an *initial condition*, which is a pure Boolean expression over variables in $\mathcal{V}$, denoted by $B^{init}(\mathcal{V})$; (ii) one or more *invariants*, conditions of the form $\mathbf{G}B^{inv}(\mathcal{V} \cup \mathbf{X}\mathcal{V})$, where $B^{inv}(\mathcal{V} \cup \mathbf{X}\mathcal{V})$ denotes a pure Boolean expression over the set of variables in $\mathcal{V}$ and the set of atoms obtained by prepending an $\mathbf{X}$ operator to each variable; and (iii) one or more *fairness conditions* of the form $\mathbf{GF}B^{fair}(\mathcal{V})$.

The semantics of GR(1), as of LTL, are formalized as ω-*words* over the alphabet $\Sigma = 2^{\mathcal{V}}$. The set of ω-words that satisfy a formula ϕ is a regular ω-language [43] denoted by $L(\phi)$.

4 Problem Statement

In this section, we present an axiomatization of weakness of an LTL formula. Hereafter, we denote the weakness measure of the LTL formula ϕ as $d(\phi)$: the higher this measure, the weaker ϕ is, i.e., ϕ_2 is weaker than ϕ_1 if $d(\phi_1) \le d(\phi_2)$.

In settings such as [2,4,39], an LTL formula ϕ_2 is *weaker* than ϕ_1 if and only if $\phi_1 \to \phi_2$ is valid (that is, it is true for any ω-word). Semantically, this translates to language inclusion: namely, ϕ_2 is weaker than ϕ_1 iff $L(\phi_1) \subseteq L(\phi_2)$. This gives us the first axiom of weakness.

Axiom 1. *Given two LTL formulae ϕ_1 and ϕ_2, if $\phi_1 \to \phi_2$, then $d(\phi_1) \le d(\phi_2)$.*

Notice that this criterion defines a partial ordering of specifications: if none of the two formulae implies the other, those are incomparable according to this criterion. However, even for the incomparable case it may be useful to define a preference criterion.

Consider the simple case of two invariants over $\mathcal{V} = \{a, b, c\}$, $\phi_1 = \mathbf{G}(a \wedge b)$ and $\phi_2 = \mathbf{G}c$. Even if the two formulae are incomparable according to implication, i.e., neither one implies the other, it is clear that ϕ_1 allows in some sense fewer behaviors than ϕ_2: at each time step, the former allows for 2 distinct valuations of $\mathcal{V}$ while ϕ_2 allows 4 of them.

Consider the formulae $\phi_3 = \mathbf{G}(a \to \mathbf{X}b)$ and $\phi_4 = \mathbf{G}((a \wedge b) \to \mathbf{X}c)$ instead. Despite neither implying the other, we note that ϕ_3 is more restrictive than ϕ_4 asymptotically: that is, for a large enough n, the number of finite prefixes of length n that satisfy ϕ_3 is less than the number of finite prefixes of length n satisfying ϕ_4 ($\#(L(\phi_3)) < \#(L(\phi_4))$). This can be easily understood if one considers that ϕ_3 poses a restriction to the next symbol in an ω-word whenever a is true (which holds in 4 out of 8 possible valuations of $\mathcal{V}$), while ϕ_4 poses a similar restriction when $a \wedge b$ holds (in 2 out of the 8 valuations).

This means that weakness of a formula should be formalized, in addition to Axiom 1, in terms of the number of finite prefixes it allows. Formally:

Axiom 2. *Given two LTL formulae ϕ_1 and ϕ_2, ϕ_2 is said to be weaker than ϕ_1 if there exists some length $\bar{n}$ such that, for every $n > \bar{n}$, the set of prefixes of length n in $L(\phi_2)$ contains more elements than the set of prefixes of the same length in $L(\phi_1)$, i.e., if $\forall n > \bar{n}$, $\#(A_n(L(\phi_2))) \ge \#(A_n(L(\phi_1)))$, then $d(\phi_1) \le d(\phi_2)$.*

The final desirable property is that a weakness measure be at least as discriminating as implication in case one formula strictly implies the other.

Axiom 3. *Let ϕ_1 and ϕ_2 be such that $\phi_1 \rightarrow \phi_2$ is valid and $\phi_2 \rightarrow \phi_1$ is not. Then $d(\phi_1) < d(\phi_2)$.*

In the next section, we prove that our proposed weakness measure satisfies Axioms 1 and 2. We then show that, although our weakness measure is not guaranteed to satisfy Axiom 3 in general, we are able to guarantee so for a specific class of formulae.

5   Weakness Measure of GR(1) Formulae

Hausdorff dimension and *Hausdorff measure* are basic concepts in fractal geometry and represent a way to define measures of extension—that is, analogous concepts to length, area, volume from classical geometry—for fractals [34]. Staiger [41] pinpointed a homeomorphism between fractals and regular ω-languages and proposed an analogous interpretation of the two quantities as extension measures of ω-languages. Intuitively, given an ω-language L, its Hausdorff dimension quantifies the growth rate of the number of distinct n-long prefixes of words in the language, over the length n of those prefixes. This makes it a good candidate for quantifying weakness: the less constrained the language is, the more prefixes of a fixed length are contained in it, implying a higher Hausdorff dimension.

The formal definition of Hausdorff dimension is tightly related to the notion of Hausdorff measure. The following definitions are given in [40].

Definition 1 (α-dimensional Hausdorff outer measure). *Given a regular ω-language L over an alphabet Σ with cardinality r, and a nonnegative real value α, the α-dimensional Hausdorff outer measure of L is defined as*

$$m_\alpha(L) = \lim_{n \to \infty} \inf_{V \in \mathcal{L}_n} \sum_{v \in V} r^{-\alpha|v|} \tag{1}$$

where $\mathcal{L}_n = \{V \subseteq \Sigma^* \mid V \cdot \Sigma^\omega \supseteq L \text{ and } |v| \geq n \text{ for all } v \in V\}$ is the collection of languages V containing finite words of length at least n and such that every word in L has at least a prefix in V. □

Definition 2 (Hausdorff dimension and measure). *Given an ω-language L, its Hausdorff dimension, denoted by $\dim(L)$, is the (unique) value $\bar{\alpha}$ such that*

$$m_\alpha(L) = \infty \ \ \alpha < \bar{\alpha}$$

$$m_\alpha(L) = 0 \ \ \alpha > \bar{\alpha}$$

The value $m_{\dim(L)}(L)$ is called the Hausdorff measure of L. □

In other words, Hausdorff measure is the limit of the process of approximating the ω-language L by a set V of finite prefixes with length at least n, and weighing each prefix with a quantity $r^{-\alpha|v|}$ that decreases as the prefix length increases. This limit can be finite and positive for at most one value of the α parameter. This value is called *Hausdorff dimension*.

A related concept appearing in the literature is entropy:

Definition 3 (Entropy [34]**).** *Given an ω-language $L \subseteq \Sigma^\omega$ over an alphabet of size r, the* entropy *of L is $H(L) = \limsup_{n \to \infty} \frac{1}{n} \log_r \#(A_n(L))$.*

It has been proved [34] that the Hausdorff dimension has a close relationship with the notion of entropy: Specifically, we have $\dim(L) \leq H(L)$ in general, and $\dim(L) = H(L)$ if L is a closed ω-language. Details on how entropy is computed are given in [16].

When L is not closed, the general algorithm presented in [40,41] provides a more refined intuition of what is actually quantified by Hausdorff dimension, which distinguishes it from entropy. The algorithm is based on computing a Muller automaton $\mathcal{M}_L$ accepting L with set of accepting state sets T_L. For each accepting set $S' \in T_L$ and for each state $s \in S'$, consider the ω-language $C_{S'}$ consisting of all the infinite paths in $\mathcal{M}_L$ starting from s and visiting no states outside S'. It can be shown that this language is closed and its entropy $H(C_{S'})$ is independent of the choice of s [40]. The Hausdorff dimension of L is then

$$\dim(L) = \max_{S' \in T_L} H(C_{S'}). \tag{2}$$

Hausdorff dimension provides an ordering consistent with the weakness notion defined in Sect. 4. We can interpret it as a measure of the asymptotic degrees of freedom of an ω-language: it quantifies how many different evolutions are allowed to an ω-word once its run remains in an accepting subset of the Muller automaton. The example below shows how it differs from entropy.

Example 1. Consider the LTL formula $\phi_1 = \mathbf{FG}a$ over the variable set $\mathcal{V} = \{a\}$ whose Muller automaton is shown in Fig. 1. The accepting sets to which a state belongs are enclosed in curly braces.

Notice that for any $w \in L(\phi_1)$ both valuations of $\mathcal{V}$ are allowed until w reaches the accepting state, and the satisfaction of $\mathbf{G}a$ may be delayed arbitrarily. Therefore, for any finite n, $\#(A_n(L)) = 2^n$, and thereby $H(L(\phi_1)) = 1$.

In this simple DMA, there is only one accepting singleton $\{s_2\}$. Therefore, there is only one $C_{S'} = \{\{a\}^\omega\}$ which allows only the symbol $\{a\} \in 2^{\mathcal{V}}$. This implies $\#(A_n(C_{S'})) = 1$. The Hausdorff dimension is $\dim(L(\phi_1)) = H(C_{S'}) = 0$.

This example demonstrates that the Hausdorff dimension isolates the asymptotic behaviour of $L(\phi_1)$ as it depends only on the condition $\mathbf{G}a$ that is eventually satisfied by any ω-word in the ω-language.   □

The following theorem shows that Hausdorff dimension is consistent with implication (hence satisfying Axiom 1).

Theorem 1. *Given two LTL formulae ϕ_1 and ϕ_2 such that $\phi_1 \to \phi_2$ is valid, then* $\dim(L(\phi_1)) \le \dim(L(\phi_2))$.

Proof. This follows from the language inclusion $L(\phi_1) \subseteq L(\phi_2)$ and the monotonicity of Hausdorff dimension with respect to language inclusion [34].

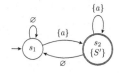

Fig. 1. DMA of $L(\phi_1)$.

Note that Theorem 1 does not exclude the situation where one formula strictly implies another, but the two languages have the same Hausdorff dimension, thus violating Axiom 3. We investigate under which conditions this holds in the context of GR(1) formulae and provide a refined weakness measure that bounds the number of cases in which it can happen.

To this end, in what follows, we introduce a new weakness measure for GR(1) based on Hausdorff dimension. We first analyse the dimension of invariants. We then show that under the condition of strong connectedness, it is possible to distinguish between weaker and stronger invariants, in the implication sense (Sect. 5.1). We show how, under the same condition, this measure fails to capture the impact of conjoining a fairness condition (Sect. 5.2). To overcome this, we define a refined weakness measure for GR(1) formulae that comprises two components: the Hausdorff dimension (*i*) of the whole formula and (*ii*) of the difference language between the invariant and the fairness conditions (Sect. 5.3).

5.1 Dimension of Invariants

Consider the formula $\phi^{inv} = \mathbf{G}B(\mathcal{V} \cup \mathbf{X}\mathcal{V})$. The ω-language $L(\phi^{inv})$ is closed. Hence, the Hausdorff dimension of $L(\phi^{inv})$ coincides with its entropy $H(L(\phi^{inv}))$ and can be computed as the maximum eigenvalue of the adjacency matrix of its Büchi automaton (see [16]). From this equivalence and Definition 3, it is easy to see that in this case Hausdorff dimension satisfies Axiom 2. In general, Theorem 1 may hold for invariants where one is strictly weaker than the other and both have equal dimensions as demonstrated in the following.

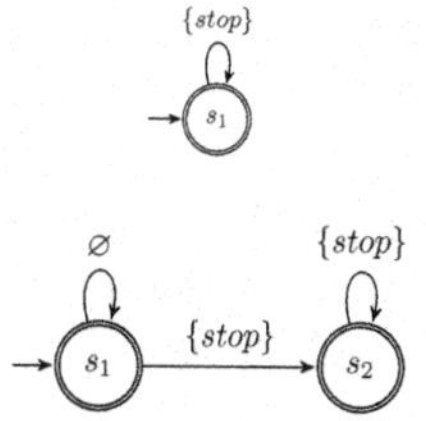

Fig. 2. DBAs of ϕ_1^{inv} (top) and ϕ_2^{inv} (bottom)

Example 2. Consider the variable set $\mathcal{V} = \{stop\}$ and the formulae $\phi_1^{inv} = \mathbf{G}stop$ and $\phi_2^{inv} = \mathbf{G}(stop \to \mathbf{X}stop)$. Their Büchi automata are shown in Fig. 2. Clearly $\phi_1^{inv} \to \phi_2^{inv}$ strictly, however the two languages have the same Hausdorff dimension $\dim(L(\phi_1^{inv})) = \dim(L(\phi_2^{inv})) = 0$.

There exists, however, a subclass of invariants for which the dimension is strictly monotonic with respect to implication. This subclass is characterized through the concept of *strong connectedness* of an ω-language. Hereafter, given a word $w \in A(L)$, we denote by $S_w(L)$ the ω-language formed by the ω-words v such that $wv \in L$ (that is, the suffixes allowed in L after reading w).

Definition 4 (Strongly connected ω-language [34]**).** *An ω-language L is strongly connected if for every prefix $w \in A(L)$ there exists a finite word $v \in \Sigma^*$ such that $S_{wv}(L) = L$.*

In other words, an ω-language is strongly connected if and only if there exists a strongly connected finite-state automaton which represents it [34], i.e., an automaton such that given any pair of states, each of them is reachable from the other. Using this notion, in the next theorem we provide a sufficient condition over invariants for Axiom 3 to be satisfied (the proof is relegated to [16]):

Theorem 2. *Let $\phi_1^{inv} = \mathbf{G}B_1(\mathcal{V} \cup \mathbf{X}\mathcal{V})$ and $\phi_2^{inv} = \mathbf{G}B_2(\mathcal{V} \cup \mathbf{X}\mathcal{V})$ be two non-empty invariants such that $\phi_1^{inv} \rightarrow \phi_2^{inv}$ is valid, $\phi_2^{inv} \rightarrow \phi_1^{inv}$ is not valid and ϕ_2^{inv} is strongly connected. Then $\dim\left(L(\phi_1^{inv})\right) < \dim\left(L(\phi_2^{inv})\right)$.*

An interesting kind of invariant that falls in this class is the *one-state invariant*, one that does not use the $\mathbf{X}$ operator: $\phi_s^{inv} = \mathbf{G}B(\mathcal{V})$ whose DBA is shown in Fig. 3. (For succinctness, the set of valuations that label a transition between the same states is denoted by the Boolean expression characterizing it.) In this case, the Hausdorff dimension has a closed form:

Fig. 3. DBA of a one-state invariant.

$$\dim\left(\phi_s^{inv}\right) = \log_r \#(B(\mathcal{V}))$$

where $r = 2^{\#(\mathcal{V})}$ is the number of valuations of $\mathcal{V}$ and $\#(B(\mathcal{V}))$ is the number of valuations that satisfy $B(\mathcal{V})$. Invariants of this type are clearly strongly connected and satisfy Theorem 2.

Remark 1. Typical examples of GR(1) specifications manually produced, like those of device communication protocols, make use of strongly connected environment assumptions. It is indeed natural to allow environments to be reset to their initial state after some steps. However, when specifications contain "until" operators or response patterns, the procedure to convert them into GR(1) [33] may yield assumptions which are no longer strongly connected. In those cases, a problem similar to that of Example 2 may arise.   □

5.2   Fairness and Fairness Complements

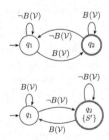

Consider the generic fairness condition $\phi^{fair} = \mathbf{G}\mathbf{F}B(\mathcal{V})$ whose DBA is shown in Fig. 4. This language is not closed: take a symbol $x \in \Sigma$ that does not satisfy $B(\mathcal{V})$ and the ω-word x^ω consisting of infinite repetitions of this symbol. It is clear that $A(\{x^\omega\}) \subseteq A(L(\phi^{fair}))$, but $x^\omega \notin L(\phi^{fair})$. We apply the algorithm in Sect. 5 (cf. Eq. 2) for non-closed languages. A DMA for $L(\phi^{fair})$ can be obtained from the top DBA in Fig. 4: the accepting

Fig. 4. DBA of $L(\phi^{fair})$ (top) and DMA of $L(\phi^{cfair})$ (bottom).

sets are $S_1' = \{q_1, q_2\}$ and $S_2' = \{q_2\}$. It is easy to see that $H(C_{S_1'}) = 1$ and $H(C_{S_2'}) = \log_r \#(B(\mathcal{V})) \leq 1$. Therefore, $\dim\left(L(\phi^{fair})\right) = 1$, independently of $B(\mathcal{V})$. We conclude that fairness conditions are indistinguishable from the *true* constant, which also has dimension 1. To allow for a distinction to be made, we characterize the negation of such formula. We call an LTL formula of the kind $\phi^{cfair} = \mathbf{FG}\neg B(\mathcal{V})$ a *fairness complement*. The DMA of $L(\phi^{cfair})$ is shown in the bottom of Fig. 4. The only accepting set is $S' = \{q_2\}$. (Notice that unlike the top one, this automaton accepts only words that stay forever in q_2 from a certain step on.) The language $C_{S'}$ (see Sect. 5) has an entropy of $\log_r \#(\neg B(\mathcal{V}))$. Hence

$$\dim\left(L(\phi^{cfair})\right) = \log_r \#(\neg B(\mathcal{V}))$$

where $r = 2^{\#(\mathcal{V})}$. Notice that $C_{S'}$ is the language of the formula $\mathbf{G}\neg B(\mathcal{V})$, which is an "asymptotic" condition of ϕ^{cfair}. As observed previously, Hausdorff dimension is strictly monotonic for one-state invariants. Therefore, the weakness of fairness complements can be ranked in terms of the Hausdorff dimension, allowing to compare fairness conditions as follows:

Theorem 3. *Let* ϕ_1^{fair} *and* ϕ_2^{fair} *be two fairness conditions such that* $\phi_1^{fair} \rightarrow \phi_2^{fair}$ *is valid and* $\phi_2^{fair} \rightarrow \phi_1^{fair}$ *is not. Then* $\dim\left(L(\neg\phi_1^{fair})\right) > \dim\left(L(\neg\phi_2^{fair})\right)$.

In other words, the stronger a fairness formula is, the weaker its complement and thereby the higher its dimension.

5.3 Dimension Pairs for GR(1) Formulae

Consider a generic GR(1) formula $\phi = \phi^{init} \wedge \phi^{inv} \wedge \bigwedge_{i=1}^{m} \phi_i^{fair}$. We show through an example that even when ϕ^{inv} is strongly connected, Hausdorff dimension may not distinguish between weaker and stronger fairness conditions in the implication sense (as also pointed out in [6]).

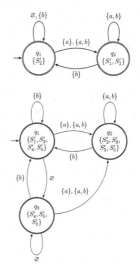

Fig. 5. DMAs of ϕ_1 (top) and ϕ_2 (bottom) of Example 3.

Example 3. Consider the two formulae over the variables $\mathcal{V} = \{a, b\}$: $\phi_1 = \mathbf{G}(a \rightarrow \mathbf{X}b) \wedge \mathbf{GF}a$ and $\phi_2 = \mathbf{G}(a \rightarrow \mathbf{X}b) \wedge \mathbf{GF}b$. The same invariant appears in both, and thereby have the same Hausdorff dimension, but the fairness condition in ϕ_2 is always satisfied when the fairness condition of ϕ_1 is satisfied, by virtue of the invariant itself. However, the ω-word $\{b\}^\omega$ satisfies ϕ_2 but not ϕ_1. So, ϕ_1 implies ϕ_2 but not vice versa.

The language of both formulae is not closed. The Muller automata of ϕ_1 and ϕ_2 are shown at the top and bottom, respectively, in Fig. 5. In both automata, there is an accepting set that covers the entire state space (S_2' in $L(\phi_1)$ and S_6' in $L(\phi_2)$). It is possible to show that the maximum $H(C_{S'})$ of Eq. (2) is achieved exactly for these accepting sets [9,34]. The ω-languages $C_{S'_2}$ in $L(\phi_1)$ and $C_{S'_6}$ in $L(\phi_2)$ both coincide with the language of the invariant alone. Therefore,

$$\dim(\phi_1) = \dim(\phi_2) = \dim(L(\mathbf{G}(a \rightarrow \mathbf{X}b))).$$

To distinguish between the two formulae, we exploit the fact that the complement of a fairness condition is a formula of the kind $\mathbf{FG}B(\mathcal{V})$ which can be compared through Hausdorff dimension. Therefore, we propose a weakness measure which consists of two components: one relating to the whole formula and one measuring the ω-language excluded from the invariant by the addition of the fairness conditions.

Definition 5 (Weakness). *The* weakness *of a GR(1) formula* $\phi = (\phi^{init} \wedge \phi^{inv} \bigwedge_{i=1}^{m} \phi_i^{fair})$, *denoted by* $d(\phi)$, *is the pair* $(d_1(\phi), d_2(\phi))$ *such that* $d_1(\phi)$ *is the Hausdorff dimension of* $L(\phi)$; *and* $d_2(\phi)$ *is the Hausdorff dimension of* $L(\phi^c) = L(\phi^{init} \wedge \phi^{inv} \wedge \bigvee_{i=1}^{m} \phi_i^{cfair})$, *where* $\phi_i^{cfair} = \neg\phi_i^{fair}$. *The following partial ordering is defined based on the weakness measure: If* $d^i = (d_1^i, d_2^i)$, *with* $i \in 1, 2$ *are weakness measures for two GR(1) formulae, then* $d^1 < d^2$ *if* $d_1^1 < d_1^2$ *or* $d_1^1 = d_1^2$ *and* $d_2^1 > d_2^2$.

We apply below this weakness measure to the formulae in Example 3.

Example 4. To compute d_2, let us define $\phi_1^c = \mathbf{G}(a \rightarrow \mathbf{X}b) \wedge \mathbf{FG}\neg a$ and $\phi_2^c = \mathbf{G}(a \rightarrow \mathbf{X}b) \wedge \mathbf{FG}\neg b$. The DMAs of the resulting languages are shown respectively in Fig. 6. Each of them has just one accepting singleton, so the computation of the Hausdorff dimension is straightforward: $\dim(\phi_1^c) = \frac{1}{2}$ and $\dim(\phi_2^c) = 0$. In summary, since ϕ_1 is more restrictive than ϕ_2, the Hausdorff dimension of the ω-language cut out by $\mathbf{GF}a$ is higher than the Hausdorff dimension of the behaviours excluded by $\mathbf{GF}b$.

The following Theorem justifies the use of this dimension pair for weakness quantification when the formulae have the same invariant.

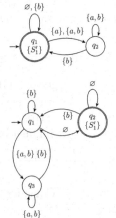

Fig. 6. DMAs of ϕ_1^c (top) and ϕ_2^c (bottom) of Example 4.

Theorem 4. *Let* $\phi_1 = \phi^{inv} \wedge \bigwedge_{i=1}^{m} \phi_{1,i}^{fair}$ *and* $\phi_2 = \phi^{inv} \wedge \bigwedge_{j=1}^{l} \phi_{2,j}^{fair}$, *such that* $\phi_1 \rightarrow \phi_2$ *is valid. Then* $d_1(\phi_1) = d_1(\phi_2)$ *and* $d_2(\phi_1) \geq d_2(\phi_2)$.

Proof. Since ϕ_1 implies ϕ_2, $L(\phi_1) \subseteq L(\phi_2)$. Furthermore, for $i = 1, 2$, $L(\phi_i) = L(\phi^{inv}) \cap L(\bigwedge_{j=1}^{m} \phi_{i,j}^{fair})$. Hence, $L(\phi^{inv}) \backslash L(\bigwedge_{j=1}^{m} \phi_{1,j}^{fair}) \supseteq L(\phi^{inv}) \backslash L(\bigwedge_{j=1}^{l} \phi_{2,j}^{fair})$, i.e., $L(\phi_1^c) \supseteq L(\phi_2^c)$. Then, by monotonicity, $\dim(\phi_1^c) \geq \dim(\phi_2^c)$, finishing the proof. $\square$

Therefore, given two formulae with the same invariant, we deem the formula with lower d_2 weaker.

Regarding formulae with the same d_1 and different invariants, we justify heuristically the same order relation. We first note that the Hausdorff dimension of a countable union of ω-languages, as noted in [41], is

$$\dim\left(\bigcup_i L_i\right) = \sup_i \dim\left(L_i\right).$$

This property is known as the *countable stability* of Hausdorff dimension. This implies that for any formula ϕ, if $d_2(\phi) \leq d_1(\phi)$ then

$$\dim\left(L(\phi^{inv})\right) = \dim\left(L(\phi) \cup L(\phi^c)\right) = \dim\left(L(\phi)\right).$$

So, if for two formulae, ϕ_1 and ϕ_2, we have $d_1(\phi_1) = d_1(\phi_2) > d_2(\phi_1) > d_2(\phi_2)$, then this can be interpreted as the two invariants having the same dimension and the fairness condition of ϕ_1 removing more behaviours than the fairness condition of ϕ_2. In this sense, ϕ_2 is weaker than ϕ_1. This justifies intuitively our weakness definition and the associated partial ordering. In Sect. 6, we illustrate applications of this order relation for comparing GR(1) assumptions.

The computation of $d_2(\phi)$ for a generic ϕ with m fairness conditions can be reduced to the case of a single fairness condition. Based on the countable stability of Hausdorff dimension, we have

$$d_2(\phi) = \sup_{i=1,\dots,m} d_2(\phi^{init} \wedge \phi^{inv} \wedge \phi_i^{cfair}).$$

Furthermore, the case of a single fairness condition can be further reduced to computing the Hausdorff dimension of an invariant by the following theorem.

Theorem 5. *Given a formula* $\phi^c = \mathbf{G}B^{inv}(\mathcal{V} \cup \mathbf{X}\mathcal{V}) \wedge \mathbf{FG}\neg B^{fair}(\mathcal{V})$ *we have*

$$\dim\left(L(\phi^c)\right) = \dim\left(L(\mathbf{G}(B^{inv} \wedge \neg B^{fair}))\right).$$

Proof Sketch (full proof is presented in [16]). Since $L(\phi^c)$ is not closed, the Hausdorff dimension must be computed from a DMA. The proof (given in [16]) consists in showing that the DMA's accepting subsets correspond to the automaton of an ω-language where both B^{inv} and $\neg B^{fair}$ are satisfied at every step. This property is a generalization of the observation made in Sect. 5.2 about the Hausdorff dimension of fairness complements. □

5.4 Initial Conditions

Consider $\phi^{init} = B(\mathcal{V})$. An expression of this form constrains only the first symbol of the ω-words in $L(\phi^{init})$. For the same reason as ϕ^{fair} in Sect. 5.2, $L(\phi^{init})$ is closed, and therefore its dimension can be computed via its entropy. By applying the definition of entropy, it is easy to see that, similarly to the unconstrained language $L(true)$, $\dim\left(L(\phi^{init})\right) = 1$.

Consider now a formula $\phi = \phi^{init} \wedge \phi^{inv}$. A DBA $\mathcal{B}$ for $L(\phi)$ can be computed from a DBA $\mathcal{B}_{inv}$ of $L(\phi^{inv})$ by removing all transitions starting from its initial state whose labels do not satisfy $B(\mathcal{V})$. The resulting automaton may leave out parts of $\mathcal{B}_{inv}$ that are no longer reachable from the initial state. This does not happen if $L(\phi^{inv})$ is strongly connected, as in that case any non-initial state in $\mathcal{B}_{inv}$ is reachable from any other state. In this case

$$\dim(\phi) = \dim\left(\phi^{inv}\right) .$$

This implies that the initial conditions do not affect the Hausdorff dimension and hence cannot be always ordered by our weakness measure. This is acceptable since typically, in applications like assumptions refinement, the focus is in assessing invariants or fairness conditions rather than initial conditions [30].

6   Evaluation

We evaluate here our proposed weakness measure through applications to benchmarks within the assumptions refinement domain, demonstrating its usefulness in distinguishing weakness of different formulae, and discussing the computation time bottlenecks. In [16] we report on our evaluation within another application domain, namely quantitative model checking.

To this aim, we implemented the weakness measure computation for GR(1) specifications in Python 2.7 and made it publicly available in [1]. Our implementation makes use of the Spot tool [22] for LTL-to-automata conversion. We integrated the weakness computation algorithm within two state-of-the-art counterstrategy-guided assumptions refinement approaches [4,15] (the implementations are available in [1]). The outcome of such approaches is a *refinement tree*, a tree structure where each node is associated with a GR(1) formula consisting of a conjunction of environment assumptions; if we denote by ϕ a formula associated with a node, the node's children are of the form $\phi \wedge \psi$, where ψ is a single initial condition, invariant, or fairness condition. Since the goal of such procedures is identifying weakest formulae that describe an environment, our weakness measure can be used to provide a preference ranking of the tree nodes.

We conducted experiments on two benchmarks for GR(1) assumptions refinement, namely the specifications of a lift controller and of the AMBA-AHB protocol for device communications in its versions for two, four and eight master devices [4,12,30]. The lift controller example specifies a controller for a lift with three floors: the Boolean variable b_i denotes the state of the button on floor i; the Boolean variable f_i is true iff the lift is at floor i. For more details on the initial assumptions $\phi^{\mathcal{E}}$ see [4]. The AMBA-AHB protocol provides signals for requesting access to a bus ($hbusreq_i$), for granting access ($hgrant_i$), for signalling the termination of a communication ($hready$), and for identifying the current owner of the bus ($hmaster$). Other signals are detailed in [12]. To our knowledge, the AMBA08 specification is one of the biggest benchmarks available in the field.

In the followings we focus on examples taken from [4,15], and discuss three cases highlighting features of our weakness measure: (i) in the first example, we demonstrate the relationship between weakness and implication; (ii) second, we consider cases when two formulae are not comparable by implication but can be ranked with our measure; and (iii) we discuss the case of formulae equally constraining the environment, which have equal ranking according to our measure. We refer the reader to [1] for the complete results.

Relation Between Weakness and Implication. Consider the lift controller example. Two refinements computed by the automated approach in [15] are: $\phi_1 = \mathbf{G}((\neg b_1 \wedge \neg b_2 \wedge \neg b_3) \rightarrow \mathbf{X}(b_1 \vee b_2 \vee b_3))$; and $\phi_2 = \mathbf{GF}(b_1 \vee b_2 \vee b_3)$. The first forces one of the buttons to be pressed at least every second step in a behaviour. The second forces one of the buttons to be pressed infinitely often in a behaviour. It is clear that ϕ_1 implies ϕ_2. We compare the assumptions obtained by refining the original assumptions with the first one and with the second one: $d(\phi^{\mathcal{E}} \wedge \phi_1) = (0.7746, 0)$ and $d(\phi^{\mathcal{E}} \wedge \phi_2) = (0.7925, 0.5)$. Notice that $d_1(\phi^{\mathcal{E}} \wedge \phi_1) < d_1(\phi^{\mathcal{E}} \wedge \phi_2)$ and this is consistent with the fact that ϕ_1 is stronger than ϕ_2. Consider now the two fairness refinements: $\phi_2 = \mathbf{GF}(b_1 \vee b_2 \vee b_3)$; and $\phi_3 = \mathbf{GF}b_1$. We have $d(\phi^{\mathcal{E}} \wedge \phi_2) = (0.7925, 0.5)$ and $d(\phi^{\mathcal{E}} \wedge \phi_3) = (0.7925, 0.695)$. Here, d_1 is equal for both formulae and $d_2(\phi^{\mathcal{E}} \wedge \phi_2) < d_2(\phi^{\mathcal{E}} \wedge \phi_3)$; this is consistent with the fact that ϕ_2 is weaker than ϕ_3.

Formulae Incomparable via Implication. Consider ϕ_3 above and $\phi_4 = \mathbf{GF}(b_2 \vee b_3)$. Neither implies the other. However, it is reasonable to argue that ϕ_4 is less restrictive than ϕ_3: while ϕ_3 constrains exactly one button to be pressed infinitely often, ϕ_4 allows the extra choice of which one (out of two). This intuition is indeed reflected by our computed weakness metric: $d(\phi^{\mathcal{E}} \wedge \phi_3) = (0.7925, 0.695)$ and $d(\phi^{\mathcal{E}} \wedge \phi_4) = (0.7925, 0.5975)$. This expresses the notion that ϕ_4 removes less behaviours from $\phi^{\mathcal{E}}$ than ϕ_3.

Our weakness measure can help in spotting asymmetries between assumptions that are syntactically equal but constrain semantically different variables. Consider an extended version of the lift controller example given in [16], including the input variable *alarm* and the output variable *stop*: whenever *alarm* is set to high, the lift enters a *stop* state where it does not move from the floor it is at. Computing the weakness of the two refinements $\phi_5 = \mathbf{G}\neg b_1$ and $\phi_6 = \mathbf{G}\neg alarm$ yields $d(\phi^{\mathcal{E}} \wedge \phi^{\mathcal{S}} \wedge \phi_5) = (0.3694, 0.3207)$ and $d(\phi^{\mathcal{E}} \wedge \phi^{\mathcal{S}} \wedge \phi_6) = (0.3746, 0.3346)$. This is consistent with the intuition that the former assumption excludes a part of the desirable system behaviors (all the ones that allow it to reach floor 1), while the latter excludes only the traces ending in the *stop* state, being then a weaker restriction on the combined behaviors of the controller and the environment.

The following two assumptions refinements are computed for the AMBA-AHB case study with two masters: $\psi_1 = \mathbf{G}(\neg hbusreq_1 \vee \mathbf{X}(hready \vee \neg hbusreq_1))$; and $\psi_2 = \mathbf{G}((\neg hgrant_1 \wedge hready \wedge hbusreq_1) \rightarrow \mathbf{X}(\neg hready \vee \neg hbusreq_1))$. As in the case of the lift example, neither formula implies the other. The weakness of the resulting assumptions is: $d(\psi^{\mathcal{E}} \wedge \psi_1) = (0.9503, 0.9068)$ and $d(\psi^{\mathcal{E}} \wedge \psi_2) = (0.9607, 0.9172)$. The refinement ψ_2 is weaker than ψ_1. Such insight into their weakness could be used to guide the refinement approach (e.g., [4,15]) in choosing to only refine those assumptions that may lead to weaker specifications, for instance further refining ψ_2 rather than ψ_1.

Consistency Between Equally Constraining Formulae. Let us consider the AMBA-AHB protocol with eight masters and the two alternative refinements: $\theta_1 = \mathbf{GF}(hmaster_0 \vee \neg hbusreq_1)$; and $\theta_2 = \mathbf{GF}(hmaster_1 \vee \neg hbusreq_2)$. Clearly the two alternatives express the same kind of constraint on different masters. Since the two masters do not have priorities over each other, expectedly the two refinements have the same weakness: $d(\theta^{\mathcal{E}} \wedge \theta_1) = d(\theta^{\mathcal{E}} \wedge \theta_2) = (0.9396, 0.9214)$.

Performance. In order to compare the discriminative power of the weakness measure and implication, we perform an experiment where every pair of refinements from the trees in [15] is compared via both methods. An implication check for the pair of formulae ϕ_1 and ϕ_2 is performed by computing the nondeterministic transition-based generalized Büchi automata (TGBA) [32] of the formulae $\phi_1 \wedge \neg \phi_2$ and $\phi_2 \wedge \neg \phi_1$, and checking whether any of them is empty [38].

We compare the proportion of formulae pairs that have different weakness measure (and thereby can be discriminated via our proposed metric) and the proportion of formulae pairs where one formula strictly implies the other (that can be discriminated via logical implication). Table 1 shows the results: the columns show the total number of nodes in the refinement tree (**#Nodes**), the corresponding number of pairs (**#Pairs**), the percentage of pairs that can be discriminated via implication (**%Impl**) and via weakness (**%Weak**). The table shows that, despite weakness does not capture implication in all cases, it still allows for the discrimination of a larger set of assumptions, by virtue of Axiom 2.

Table 1. Discriminative power of implication and weakness

Case study	#Nodes (k)	#Pairs	%Impl	%Weak
AMBA02	9	36	63.9	88.9
AMBA04	17	136	69.1	79.4

The time taken to compute the weakness measure for each refinement (computed via the approach in [15]) was consistently less than 1 min for the lift controller, AMBA02, and AMBA04 case studies. The time needed on a representative subset of refinements from the AMBA08 example is shown in Fig. 7 as a function of the number of GR(1) conjuncts in the assumptions. The subset comprises a path from the root of the refinement

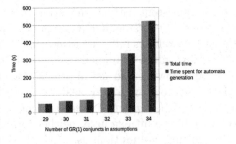

Fig. 7. Execution time of weakness computation for AMBA08

tree (initial assumptions) to one of the
80 leaves. We observed that 79 of the 80 leaves showed similar performance as
the one reported in figure; one of them, instead, took around 5200 s. Notice that
over 99% of the time is spent on DMA computation, and the remaining time is
employed on eigenvalue computation.

In general implication checks require an $O(k^2)$ number of automata computations. On the other hand, for a set of formulae containing at most m fairness
conditions, our weakness measure requires $m + 1$ DMA computations, yielding
$O(mk)$ automata for comparing k formulae. In this respect, the advantage of
our weakness measure resides in the reduced number of DMA computations
with respect to implication.

The price to pay lies in the complexity of the needed automata: while weakness requires deterministic automata, implication can be checked via nondeterministic ones, which are typically faster to compute [23]. However, in the
AMBA08 case we observed that the quadratic growth of implication checks prevailed over the lesser complexity of nondeterministic automata: the value of k
for this case study is 158; while computing all weakness values for the refinement
tree required a total time of 15 hours, in the same amount of time only a small
fraction of the 12,403 formulae pairs could be checked for implication.

7   Conclusion

In this paper we proposed a new measure for assessing the weakness of GR(1) formulae quantitatively and demonstrated its application in the context of weakest
assumptions refinement for GR(1) controller synthesis. We showed that strong
connectedness of invariants is a sufficient requirement to guarantee that our
measure distinguishes between stronger and weaker formulae in the implication
sense. We introduced a component to the measure which allows one to compare formulae with the same dimension based on the weakness of their fairness
conditions. The major limitation of the approach is the need for deterministic
automata to be produced, which induces high computation time because of the
determinization process [23].

As part of our future work, we plan to explore the possibility of refining the
weakness relation by including Hausdorff measure in the definition, since Hausdorff measure can distinguish between stronger and weaker ω-languages in case
they are not strongly connected [34]. We also intend to investigate algorithms for
computing—or approximating at a controlled accuracy—Hausdorff dimension on
nondeterministic automata.

Acknowledgments. The support of the EPSRC HiPEDS Centre for Doctoral Training (EP/L016796/1) is gratefully acknowledged. We also thank our reviewers for their
insightful comments and suggestions.

References

1. https://gitlab.doc.ic.ac.uk/dgc14/WeakestAssumptions
2. Albarghouthi, A., Dillig, I., Gurfinkel, A.: Maximal specification synthesis. ACM SIGPLAN Notices **51**(1), 789–801 (2016)
3. Almagor, S., Avni, G., Kupferman, O.: Automatic generation of quality specifications. In: Sharygina, N., Veith, H. (eds.) CAV 2013. LNCS, vol. 8044, pp. 479–494. Springer, Heidelberg (2013). https://doi.org/10.1007/978-3-642-39799-8_32
4. Alur, R., Moarref, S., Topcu, U.: Counter-strategy guided refinement of GR(1) temporal logic specifications. In: Formal Methods in Computer-Aided Design, pp. 26–33 (2013)
5. Alur, R., Moarref, S., Topcu, U.: Pattern-based refinement of assume-guarantee specifications in reactive synthesis. In: Baier, C., Tinelli, C. (eds.) TACAS 2015. LNCS, vol. 9035, pp. 501–516. Springer, Heidelberg (2015). https://doi.org/10.1007/978-3-662-46681-0_49
6. Asarin, E., Blockelet, M., Degorre, A.: Entropy model checking. In: 12th Workshop on Quantitative Aspects of Programming Languages - Joint with European Joint Conference On Theory and Practice of Software (2014)
7. Asarin, E., Blockelet, M., Degorre, A., Dima, C., Mu, C.: Asymptotic behaviour in temporal logic. In: Joint Meeting CSL/LICS, pp. 1–9. ACM Press (2014)
8. Barnat, J., Bauch, P., Beneš, N., Brim, L., Beran, J., Kratochvíla, T.: Analysing sanity of requirements for avionics systems. Form. Asp. Comput. **28**(1), 45–63 (2016)
9. Berman, A., Plemmons, R.: Nonnegative Matrices in the Mathematical Sciences. Society for Industrial and Applied Mathematics (1994)
10. Bloem, R., Chatterjee, K., Henzinger, T.A., Jobstmann, B.: Better quality in synthesis through quantitative objectives. In: Bouajjani, A., Maler, O. (eds.) CAV 2009. LNCS, vol. 5643, pp. 140–156. Springer, Heidelberg (2009). https://doi.org/10.1007/978-3-642-02658-4_14
11. Bloem, R., Galler, S., Jobstmann, B., Piterman, N., Pnueli, A., Weiglhofer, M.: Specify, compile, run: hardware from PSL. Electron. Notes Theor. Comput. Sci. **190**(4), 3–16 (2007)
12. Bloem, R., Jobstmann, B., Piterman, N., Pnueli, A., Sa'ar, Y.: Synthesis of reactive(1) designs. J. Comput. Syst. Sci. **78**(3), 911–938 (2012)
13. Braberman, V., D'Ippolito, N., Piterman, N., Sykes, D., Uchitel, S.: Controller synthesis: from modelling to enactment. In: International Conference on Software Engineering, pp. 1347–1350. IEEE (2013)
14. Cassandras, C.G., Lafortune, S.: Introduction to Discrete Event Systems. Springer, New York (2008)
15. Cavezza, D.G., Alrajeh, D.: Interpolation-based GR(1) assumptions refinement. In: Legay, A., Margaria, T. (eds.) TACAS 2017. LNCS, vol. 10205, pp. 281–297. Springer, Heidelberg (2017). https://doi.org/10.1007/978-3-662-54577-5_16
16. Cavezza, D.G., Alrajeh, D., György, A.: A weakness measure for GR(1) formulae. CoRR abs/1805.03151 (2018). http://arxiv.org/abs/1805.03151
17. Chatterjee, K., De Alfaro, L., Faella, M., Henzinger, T.A., Majumdar, R., Stoelinga, M.: Compositional quantitative reasoning. In: International Conference on the Quantitative Evaluation of Systems, pp. 179–188 (2006)
18. Chatterjee, K., Henzinger, T.A., Jobstmann, B.: Environment assumptions for synthesis. In: van Breugel, F., Chechik, M. (eds.) CONCUR 2008. LNCS, vol. 5201, pp. 147–161. Springer, Heidelberg (2008). https://doi.org/10.1007/978-3-540-85361-9_14

19. Cimatti, A., Roveri, M., Schuppan, V., Tchaltsev, A.: Diagnostic information for realizability. In: Logozzo, F., Peled, D.A., Zuck, L.D. (eds.) VMCAI 2008. LNCS, vol. 4905, pp. 52–67. Springer, Heidelberg (2008). https://doi.org/10.1007/978-3-540-78163-9_9

20. Cobleigh, J.M., Giannakopoulou, D., Păsăreanu, C.S.: Learning assumptions for compositional verification. In: Garavel, H., Hatcliff, J. (eds.) TACAS 2003. LNCS, vol. 2619, pp. 331–346. Springer, Heidelberg (2003). https://doi.org/10.1007/3-540-36577-X_24

21. D'Ippolito, N., Braberman, V., Sykes, D., Uchitel, S.: Robust degradation and enhancement of robot mission behaviour in unpredictable environments. In: Proceedings of the 1st International Workshop on Control Theory for Software Engineering, pp. 26–33 (2015)

22. Duret-Lutz, A., Lewkowicz, A., Fauchille, A., Michaud, T., Renault, É., Xu, L.: Spot 2.0 — a framework for LTL and ω-automata manipulation. In: Artho, C., Legay, A., Peled, D. (eds.) ATVA 2016. LNCS, vol. 9938, pp. 122–129. Springer, Cham (2016). https://doi.org/10.1007/978-3-319-46520-3_8

23. Esparza, J., Křetínský, J., Sickert, S.: From LTL to deterministic automata. Formal Methods Syst. Des. 49(3), 219–271 (2016)

24. Hansson, H., Jonsson, B.: A logic for reasoning about time and reliability. Formal Aspects Comput. 6(5), 512–535 (1994)

25. Henzinger, T.: From Boolean to quantitative notions of correctness. ACM SIGPLAN Notices 45(1), 157 (2010)

26. Henzinger, T.A., Otop, J.: From model checking to model measuring. In: D'Argenio, P.R., Melgratti, H. (eds.) CONCUR 2013. LNCS, vol. 8052, pp. 273–287. Springer, Heidelberg (2013). https://doi.org/10.1007/978-3-642-40184-8_20

27. Konighofer, R., Hofferek, G., Bloem, R.: Debugging formal specifications using simple counterstrategies. In: Formal Methods in Computer-Aided Design, pp. 152–159 (2009)

28. Kupferman, O.: Recent challenges and ideas in temporal synthesis. In: Bieliková, M., Friedrich, G., Gottlob, G., Katzenbeisser, S., Turán, G. (eds.) SOFSEM 2012. LNCS, vol. 7147, pp. 88–98. Springer, Heidelberg (2012). https://doi.org/10.1007/978-3-642-27660-6_8

29. Kwiatkowska, M.: Quantitative verification: models, techniques and tools. In: Joint Meeting on Foundations of Software Engineering - ESEC/FSE 2015, p. 449. ACM Press (2007)

30. Li, W., Dworkin, L., Seshia, S.A.: Mining assumptions for synthesis. In: International Conference on Formal Methods and Models for Codesign, pp. 43–50 (2011)

31. Lomuscio, A., Strulo, B., Walker, N., Wu, P.: Assume-guarantee reasoning with local specifications. In: Dong, J.S., Zhu, H. (eds.) ICFEM 2010. LNCS, vol. 6447, pp. 204–219. Springer, Heidelberg (2010). https://doi.org/10.1007/978-3-642-16901-4_15

32. Lutz, A.D.: LTL translation improvements in Spot 1.0. Int. J. Crit. Comput.-Based Syst. 5(1/2), 31 (2014)

33. Maoz, S., Ringert, J.O.: GR(1) synthesis for LTL specification patterns. In: Joint Meeting on Foundations of Software Engineering - ESEC/FSE 2015, pp. 96–106. ACM Press (2015)

34. Merzenich, W., Staiger, L.: Fractals, dimension, and formal languages. Informatique théorique et applications 28(3–4), 361–386 (1994)

35. Nam, W., Alur, R.: Learning-based symbolic assume-guarantee reasoning with automatic decomposition. In: Graf, S., Zhang, W. (eds.) ATVA 2006. LNCS, vol. 4218, pp. 170–185. Springer, Heidelberg (2006). https://doi.org/10.1007/11901914_15

36. Pnueli, A., Rosner, R.: On the synthesis of a reactive module. In: Principles of Programming Languages, pp. 179–190 (1989)

37. Pnueli, A.: The temporal logic of programs. In: Annual Symposium on Foundations of Computer Science, pp. 46–57 (1977)

38. Renault, E., Duret-Lutz, A., Kordon, F., Poitrenaud, D.: Three SCC-based emptiness checks for generalized Büchi automata. In: International Conference on Logic for Programming Artificial Intelligence and Reasoning (LPAR), pp. 668–682 (2013)

39. Seshia, S.A.: Combining induction, deduction, and structure for verification and synthesis. IEEE **103**(11), 2036–2051 (2015)

40. Staiger, L.: The hausdorff measure of regular ω-languages is computable. Martin-Luther-Universität, Technical report, August 1998

41. Staiger, L.: On the Hausdorff measure of regular omega-languages in Cantor space. Technical report 1, Martin-Luther-Universität Halle-Wittenberg (2015)

42. Tan, L., Sokolsky, O., Lee, I.: Specification-based testing with linear temporal logic. In: Proceedings of the IEEE International Conference on Information Reuse and Integration, pp. 493–498 (2004)

43. Vardi, M.Y.: An automata-theoretic approach to linear temporal logic. In: Moller, F., Birtwistle, G. (eds.) Logics for Concurrency. LNCS, vol. 1043, pp. 238–266. Springer, Heidelberg (1996). https://doi.org/10.1007/3-540-60915-6_6

Producing Explanations for Rich Logics

Simon Busard$^{(\boxtimes)}$ and Charles Pecheur

Université catholique de Louvain, Louvain-la-Neuve, Belgium
{simon.busard,charles.pecheur}@uclouvain.be

Abstract. One of the claimed advantages of model checking is its capability to provide a counter-example explaining why a property is violated by a given system. Nevertheless, branching logics such as Computation Tree Logic and its extensions have complex branching counter-examples, and standard model checkers such as NuSMV do not produce complete counter-examples—that is, counter-examples providing all information needed to understand the verification outcome—and are limited to single executions. Many branching logics can be translated into the μ-calculus. To solve this problem of producing complete and complex counter-examples for branching logics, we propose a μ-calculus-based framework with rich explanations. It integrates a μ-calculus model checker that produces complete explanations, and several functionalities to translate them back to the original logic. In addition to the framework itself, we describe its implementation in Python and illustrate its applicability with Alternating Temporal Logic.

1 Introduction

Model checking is a verification technique that performs an exhaustive search among the behaviors of a system to determine if it satisfies a given property, usually expressed in a logic [2,10]. *Branching logics*, such as CTL, express properties about the branching structure of the system [12]. Many extensions of CTL have been proposed to take into account other aspects of the verified systems, such as knowledge—with CTLK [28]—, or strategic abilities—with ATL [1]. Such logics can be translated into the *propositional μ-calculus*, a logic based on fixpoint and modal operators [22].

Producing an explanation of the verification outcome is one of the claimed advantages of model checking. But, in the case of branching logics, the explanations can be very rich as, in general, branching logics need branching counter-examples [3]. They have to show different branches of the execution tree of the system to fully explain the truth value of the property. However, current state-of-the-art tools such as NuSMV only produce single executions of the model when explaining why a property is violated [9].

The goal of this paper is to propose techniques and tools to generate, visualize and manipulate explanations for μ-calculus-based logics such as CTL, CTLK and ATL. Let us suppose that someone—the *designer*—uses some logic—the *top-level logic*—to express and verify facts about some system, and wants to develop a

© Springer International Publishing AG, part of Springer Nature 2018
K. Havelund et al. (Eds.): FM 2018, LNCS 10951, pp. 129–146, 2018.
https://doi.org/10.1007/978-3-319-95582-7_8

model checker for it. She can either develop the tool from scratch, or she can translate the models and formulas into another logic—the *base logic*—and use existing tools to solve the model-checking problem.

Many logics can be translated into the μ-calculus, making it a good candidate for a base logic. Nevertheless, when translating her model-checking problem into μ-calculus, the designer has no help to facilitate this translation, in particular, the counter-examples returned by the model checker (if any) are expressed in terms of μ-calculus primitives instead of top-level logic ones. To overcome this limitation and to help designers to quickly develop a model checker with rich counter-examples, this paper proposes a μ-calculus-based framework with rich explanations. The framework provides a μ-calculus model checker that generates rich explanations and functionalities to define how top-level logic formulas are translated into μ-calculus, to control how the μ-calculus explanations are generated, and to translate μ-calculus explanations into top-level logic ones. These functionalities are the following:

1. *Formula aliases* link the formulas stored in the obligations to the top-level logic formulas they represent.
2. The *relational graph algebra* of Dong et al. [15] is provided to transform explanations into the part of the original model they represent.
3. *Obligation and edge attributors* add information to individual nodes and edges of the explanation graph.
4. *Local translation* focuses on the small part that explains a given alias without having to deal with the whole graph at once.
5. *Choosers* can be used to perform interactive or guided generation of explanations. They also introduce the notion of *partial explanations*.
6. *Formula markers* are tags on formulas. Points of interest and points of decision are provided, but other markers can be defined by the designer.

All these functionalities work together to help the designer to produce useful explanations. Figure 1 illustrates the structure of the framework.

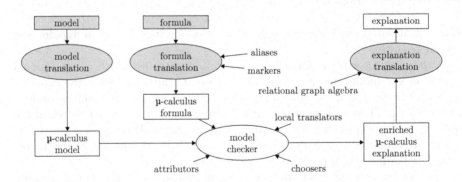

Fig. 1. The structure of the framework. In gray, the parts that the designer has to define; in white, the elements provided by the framework.

The designer first translates the original model and formula into μ-calculus. She can decorate the translated formulas with aliases and markers, and she can also attach attributors, local translators and choosers. The aliases and markers will be present in the obligations in the generated enriched μ-calculus explanation to help the designer with their translation. The attributors and local translators are used by the model checker to add extra information to the generated explanations. The choosers allow the model checker to make the right choices. Finally, the designer translates the enriched explanation back into the top-level logic language thanks to the relational graph algebra.

The features are generic and complement each other: (1) the relational algebra, attributors and local translators manipulate the explanation at different scales; (2) points of decision and choosers work together to produce smaller partial strategies and to select the explanations of interest; (3) points of interest and aliases add information to important formulas.

The remainder of this paper is structured as follows: Sect. 2 presents the propositional μ-calculus. Section 3 describes the framework for μ-calculus-based logics explanations, and Sect. 4 its implementation in Python. Section 5 applies the framework to the case of ATL model checking. Section 6 briefly compares the framework with related work, and Sect. 7 draws conclusions.

2   The Propositional μ-Calculus

The μ-calculus is a logic based on fixpoints [22]. Its formulas follow the grammar

$$\phi ::= true \mid p \mid v \mid \neg\phi \mid \phi \vee \phi \mid \Diamond_i\,\phi \mid \mu v.\ \phi$$

where $p \in AP$ are atomic propositions and $v \in Var$ are variables. For instance, $\Diamond_i\,\phi$ means that *there exists a successor through the transition relation i that satisfies ϕ, that is, a state satisfying ϕ can be reached in one step through the transition relation i.*

We write $\mathcal{L}_\mu$ for the set of μ-calculus formulas. Other operators can be defined in terms of the ones above, such as $\Box_i\,\phi \equiv \neg\,\Diamond_i\,\neg\phi$ and $\nu v.\ \phi \equiv \neg\mu v.\ \neg\phi(\neg v)$.

A variable v is *bound* in ϕ if it is enclosed in a sub-formula $\mu v.\ \psi$ or $\nu v.\ \psi$; otherwise, it is *free*. We sometimes note $\mu v.\ \psi(v)$, $\nu v.\ \psi(v)$, and $\psi(v)$ to stress the fact that ψ contains free occurrences of variable v. We write $\psi[\chi/v]$—or equivalently $\psi(\chi)$ when v is clear from the context—for the μ-calculus formula ψ where every free occurrence of v is replaced by χ. We write $\psi^k(\chi)$ for k nestings of ψ around χ, that is, $\psi^0(\chi) = \chi$ and $\psi^{k+1}(\chi) = \psi(\psi^k(\chi))$.

Any formula $\mu v.\ \psi$ or $\nu v.\ \psi$, must be *syntactically monotone*, that is, all occurrences of v in ψ must fall under an even number of negations. A formula is in *positive normal form* if negations are only applied to atomic propositions and variables. Any syntactically monotone formula can be transformed into an equivalent syntactically monotone formula in positive normal form.

μ-calculus models are Kripke structures $S = \langle Q, \{R_i \mid i \in \Sigma\}, V \rangle$ where (1) Q is a finite set of states; (2) $R_i \subseteq Q \times Q$ are $|\Sigma|$ transition relations;

(3) $V : Q \to 2^{AP}$ labels the states with atomic propositions. We write $q \to_i q'$ for $\langle q, q' \rangle \in R_i$.

µ-calculus formulas are interpreted as sets of states under a given environment. An environment is a function $e : Var \to 2^Q$ associating sets of states to variables. The set of environments is noted $\mathcal{E}$. We write $e[Q'/v]$, for $Q' \subseteq Q$ and $v \in Var$, for the function e' such that $e'(v) = Q'$ and e' agrees with e for all other variables. The semantics of formulas is given by the function $[\![\phi]\!]^S e$. It takes a formula ϕ and an environment e defined at least for the free variables of ϕ, and returns the corresponding set of states. This function is defined as:

$$[\![true]\!]^S e = Q, \qquad\qquad\qquad [\![\neg\phi]\!]^S e = Q \backslash [\![\phi]\!]^S e,$$

$$[\![v]\!]^S e = e(v), \qquad\qquad [\![\phi \vee \psi]\!]^S e = [\![\phi]\!]^S e \cup [\![\psi]\!]^S e,$$

$$[\![p]\!]^S e = \{q \in Q \mid p \in V(q)\}, \quad [\![\mu v.\ \phi]\!]^S e = \bigcap \{Q' \subseteq Q \mid [\![\phi]\!]^S e[Q'/v] \subseteq Q'\}.$$

$$[\![\Diamond i\ \phi]\!]^S e = \{q \in Q \mid \exists q' \in Q \text{ s.t. } q \to_i q' \wedge q' \in [\![\phi]\!]^S e\},$$

3   A µ-Calculus-Based Framework for Rich Explanations

This section presents the µ-calculus-based framework we propose. To illustrate the concepts, we will use the case of ATL model checking, presented in Sect. 3.1. Section 3.2 describes µ-calculus explanations, and Sect. 3.3 presents the functionalities to translate these explanations back to the original logic.

3.1   Translation of ATL Models and Formulas to µ-calculus

ATL formulas are built with atomic propositions and Boolean connectives, as well as coalition modalities $\langle\!\langle\rangle\!\rangle$ and $[\,]$ reasoning about the strategies of groups of agents to enforce temporal objectives specified with the standard **X**, **F**, **G** and **U** temporal operators [1]. For instance, the formula $\langle\!\langle \Gamma \rangle\!\rangle \mathbf{F}\ p$ expresses the fact that agents Γ have a strategy to reach, within a finite number of steps, some goal p, and $[\Gamma]\mathbf{G}\ q$ that they have no strategy to maintain some other goal q forever.

ATL formulas are interpreted over the states of *concurrent game structures* (CGS) $S = \langle Ag, Q, Q_0, Act, e, \delta, V \rangle$ defining the states (Q) and agents (Ag) of the system, what they can do ($e : Ag \to (Q \to (2^{Act} \backslash \varnothing))$), and how the system evolves according to their choices ($\delta : Q \times Act^{Ag} \to Q$).

Given a CGS S, a state q of S, and an ATL formula ϕ, we can translate S into a Kripke structure S', q into a state q' of S', and ϕ into a µ-calculus formula ϕ' such that q satisfies ϕ if and only if q' satisfies ϕ'. To avoid technical details, this section only presents the intuition of the translation and focuses on a small subset of ATL operators. The full translation can be found in [4].

The idea of the translation from a CGS $S = \langle Ag, Q, Q_0, Act, e, \delta, V \rangle$ to a structure $S' = \langle Q', \{R'_i \mid i \in \Sigma\}, V' \rangle$ is to derive, from each state $q \in Q$, each group of agents $\Gamma \subseteq Ag$, and each joint action a_Γ of Γ, a new state q_{a_Γ} representing the fact that Γ chose to play a_Γ in q. For each group $\Gamma \subseteq Ag$, two transition relations are derived from δ: $R_{\Gamma choose}$ links any state $q \in Q$ to the derived states q_{a_Γ} for all possible actions a_Γ of Γ; $R_{\Gamma follow}$ links any derived state q_{a_Γ} to the successors of q restricted to the ones reached if Γ choose a_Γ. Intuitively, the derived structure S' encodes in two steps $(q \rightarrow q_{a_\Gamma} \rightarrow q')$ the one-step transitions of S $(q \xrightarrow{a} q')$. The set Σ of relations names is $\Sigma = \{\Gamma choose \mid \Gamma \subseteq Ag\} \cup \{\Gamma follow \mid \Gamma \subseteq Ag\}$, that is, two transition relations for each group of agents.

Figure 2 presents the CGS of a simple one-bit transmission problem in which a *sender* tries to send a value through an unreliable *link*. The sender can *send* the value or *wait*, and the transmitter can *transmit* the message (if any), or *block* the transmission. In this context, we ask whether *the transmitter has a strategy to never transmit the value*, that is, if q_0 satisfies $\langle\!\langle transmitter \rangle\!\rangle \mathbf{G} \neg sent$.

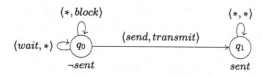

Fig. 2. The CGS of the bit transmission problem. The action pairs are the actions of the sender and the transmitter, respectively. $*$ means *any action of the agent*.

The CGS of this bit transmission problem can be translated into a μ-calculus Kripke structure. Figure 3 presents a part of the translation, focusing on the states derived from q_0; the part about q_1 is not shown. For instance, in q_0, the sender can choose the action *send* to transition to $q_{0_{send}}$. The transmitter's following action can either be *block*, which transitions back to q_0, or *transmit*, which transitions to q_1.

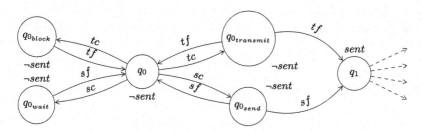

Fig. 3. A part of the translation of the bit transmission CGS. *sc* and *sf* mean *sender chooses* and *sender follows*, *tc* and *tf* mean *transmitter chooses* and *transmitter follows*. Transition relations for the two other groups of agents (no agent, and both agents) are not shown.

ATL formulas can also be translated into μ-calculus formulas. The formula $\langle\!\langle transmitter \rangle\!\rangle \mathbf{G} \neg sent$ is translated as

$$\phi_{ns} = \nu v. \, \neg sent \wedge \Diamond_{trans\ chooses}(\Diamond_{trans\ follows} true \wedge \Box_{trans\ follows} v). \quad (1)$$

The main idea behind this translation is that a state satisfies the second term $\Diamond_{trans\ chooses}(\Diamond_{trans\ follows} \, true \wedge \Box_{trans\ follows} v)$ if there exists an action for *transmitter* that is enabled and such that all choices of the other agents lead to v, that is, if the transmitter can enforce to reach v in one step. Then, a state satisfies ϕ_{ns} if the transmitter can enforce to stay in states satisfying $\neg sent$ forever, that is, if the transmitter has a strategy to enforce $\mathbf{G} \neg sent$.

To explain why an ATL formula ϕ is satisfied by a state q of some CGS S, we want to extract the part of the model starting at q that is responsible for the satisfaction. Furthermore, as such part can be complex and difficult to understand, we want to annotate each state with the sub-formulas of ϕ that are true in that state. For instance, Fig. 4 gives an explanation for why q_0 satisfies $\langle\!\langle transmitter \rangle\!\rangle \mathbf{G} \neg sent$. The explanation shows that, in q_0, the *block* action of the transmitter allows it to prevent the message to be sent.

Fig. 4. An explanation for why the transmitter can prevent the value to be sent.

3.2 μ-Calculus Explanations

A μ-calculus explanation is a graph where nodes are triplets—called *obligations*—composed of a state q of S, a μ-calculus formula ϕ, and an environment e. An edge $\langle\langle q,\phi,e\rangle,\langle q',\phi',e'\rangle\rangle$ encodes the fact that $q \in [\![\phi]\!]^S e$ because $q' \in [\![\phi']\!]^S e'$. In this section, all μ-calculus formulas are considered in *positive normal form*, that is, all negations are applied to atomic propositions or variables only.

More formally, given a Kripke structure $S = \langle Q, \{R_i \mid i \in \Sigma\}, V \rangle$, an explanation is a graph $E = \langle O, T \rangle$ such that the nodes $O \subseteq Q \times \mathcal{L}_\mu \times \mathcal{E}$ are triplets of states of S, μ-formulas and environments, and the edges $T \subseteq O \times O$ link obligations together. The set of successors of o is noted $succ(o) = \{o' \mid \langle o,o'\rangle \in T\}$.

We are interested in explanations that are *adequate*, that is, that effectively show why q satisfies ϕ in environment e. An explanation E is adequate for explaining why $q \in [\![\phi]\!]^S e$ if it is *consistent, matches S*—that is, is composed of elements of S—and $\langle q,\phi,e\rangle \in O$.

An explanation is *consistent* if it exhibits the different parts needed to explain its elements. More formally, let $E = \langle O, T \rangle$ be an explanation and let $o = \langle q,\phi,e\rangle \in O$. o is said to be *locally consistent in E* iff

- $\phi \neq false$;
- if $\phi = true$, then $succ(o) = \varnothing$;
- if $\phi = p$ or $\phi = \neg p$, for $p \in AP$, then $succ(o) = \varnothing$;
- if $\phi = v$ or $\phi = \neg v$, for $v \in Var$, then $q \in e(v)$ (resp. $q \notin e(v)$) and $succ(o) = \varnothing$;
- if $\phi = \phi_1 \wedge \phi_2$ then $succ(o) = \{\langle q, \phi_1, e \rangle, \langle q, \phi_2, e \rangle\}$;
- if $\phi = \phi_1 \vee \phi_2$ then $succ(o) = \{\langle q, \phi_j, e \rangle\}$ for some $j \in \{1, 2\}$;
- if $\phi = \Diamond_i \phi'$ then $succ(o) = \{\langle q', \phi', e \rangle\}$ for some state q';
- if $\phi = \Box_i \phi'$ then, for all $o' \in succ(o)$, $o' = \langle q', \phi', e \rangle$ for some state q';
- if $\phi = \mu v. \psi(v)$, then $succ(o) = \{\langle q, \psi^k(false), e \rangle\}$ for some $k \geq 0$;
- if $\phi = \nu v. \psi(v)$, then $succ(o) = \{\langle q, \psi(\phi), e \rangle\}$.

E is then *consistent* iff all obligations $o \in O$ are locally consistent in E. Intuitively, if $\phi = \mu v. \psi$, then $q \in [\![\phi]\!]^S e$ because q belongs to a finite number of applications of ψ on *false*, that is, $q \in [\![\psi^k(false)]\!]^S e$ for some $k \geq 0$. On the other hand, this idea cannot be applied for $\phi = \nu v. \psi$. In this case, $q \in [\![\phi]\!]^S e$ because it belongs to any number of applications of ψ on *true*. Thus, to explain it, E simply shows that $q \in [\![\psi(\phi)]\!]^S e$ and relies on the fact that the structure has a finite number of states to ensure that the explanation is finite as well.

Furthermore, E matches S iff

1. for all $\langle q', \phi', e' \rangle \in O$, $q' \in Q$;
2. for all $\langle q', p, e' \rangle \in O$, $p \in V(q')$ and for all $\langle q', \neg p, e' \rangle \in O$, $p \notin V(q')$;
3. for all $\langle \langle q', \phi', e' \rangle, \langle q'', \phi'', e'' \rangle \rangle \in T$, either $q' = q''$, or ϕ' belongs to $\{\Diamond_i \phi'', \Box_i \phi''\}$ and $\langle q', q'' \rangle \in R_i$;
4. for all $o' = \langle q', \Box_i \phi', e' \rangle \in O$, $\langle q', q'' \rangle \in R_i$ iff $\exists o'' \in succ(o')$ s.t. $o'' = \langle q'', \phi'', e'' \rangle$.

E matches S if E is part of S: (1) the states of E are states of S; (2) atomic propositions of E are coherent with labels of S; (3) successor states in E are successors in S; (4) the explanation for the $\Box_i$ operator exhibits all successors through R_i.

For instance, Fig. 5 gives an adequate explanation for ϕ_{ns} (of Eq. 1) holding in state q_0 of the μ-calculus structure of the bit transmission problem.

Adequate explanations are necessary and sufficient proofs for why $q \in [\![\phi]\!]^S e$, captured by the following property.

Property 1. Given a Kripke structure $S = \langle Q, \{R_i \mid i \in \Sigma\}, V \rangle$, a state $q \in Q$, a μ-calculus formula ϕ and an environment e, $q \in [\![\phi]\!]^S e$ if and only if there exists an adequate explanation E for $q \in [\![\phi]\!]^S e$.

Proof (Proof Sketch). The left-to-right direction is proved by the generating algorithm of this paper: if $q \in [\![\phi]\!]^S e$, then it generates an adequate explanation for $q \in [\![\phi]\!]^S e$. The other direction can be shown by induction over the structure of ϕ. The main idea is that, if E is adequate for sub-formulas, then local consistency and matching S are sufficient conditions for the formula to be satisfied.   □

Furthermore, we can view adequate explanations as patterns. An explanation E defines an entire set of Kripke structures $\mathcal{K}(E)$ that E matches. E is thus an

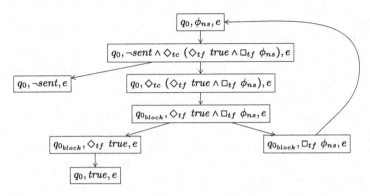

Fig. 5. An explanation for why $q_0 \in [\![\phi_{ns}]\!]^S e$ in the bit transmission problem. tc and tf mean *transmitter chooses* and *transmitter follows*, respectively.

explanation for why all structures of $\mathcal{K}(E)$ satisfy any formula ϕ that E contains. This intuition is formally captured by the following property.

Property 2. Given a consistent explanation $E = \langle O, T \rangle$, for all $\langle q, \phi, e \rangle \in O$, $q \in [\![\phi]\!]^S e$ for all S such that E matches S.

Proof. This property is directly derived from Property 1. If E is consistent, E matches S and $\langle q, \phi, e \rangle \in O$, then E is adequate for $q \in [\![\phi]\!]^S e$. By Property 1, since there exists an adequate explanation for $q \in [\![\phi]\!]^S e$, $q \in [\![\phi]\!]^S e$ is true. □

Finally, we can define an algorithm to generate adequate explanations for μ-calculus formulas, presented in Algorithm 1. It takes a Kripke structure S, a state q of S, a μ-calculus formula ϕ, and an environment e such that $q \in [\![\phi]\!]^S e$, and returns an adequate explanation for $q \in [\![\phi]\!]^S e$. Intuitively, the algorithm starts with an empty explanation and the $\langle q, \phi, e \rangle$ obligation in the *pending* set. Then it considers each obligation $o' \in pending$, adding to O and T the necessary obligations and edges to make o' locally consistent and matching S, and adding to *pending* the newly discovered obligations. It stops the process when all obligations have been made locally consistent in $\langle O, T \rangle$.

3.3   Translating μ-Calculus Explanations

The previous section proposed a structure to explain why a μ-calculus formula is satisfied by a state of some Kripke structure. Nevertheless, as the μ-calculus model checker and explanations are used to solve the model-checking problem of some other top-level logic, the usefulness of such explanations is limited. This section presents the set of functionalities the framework provides to help the designer to translate the μ-calculus explanations back into the top-level logic. They are generic to allow her to easily translate the explanations for logics such as CTL, CTLK, ATL or PDL [16], as well as fair variants such as Fair CTL [13]. First, aliases allow the designer to hide μ-calculus translations behind top-level logic formulas. Second, to ease the translation of explanations back into the

Algorithm 1. $explain(S, q, \phi, e)$

Data: $S = \langle Q, \{R_i \mid i \in \Sigma\}, V \rangle$ a Kripke structure, $q \in Q$ a state of S, ϕ a
    μ-calculus formula, and e an environment such that $q \in [\![\phi]\!]^S e$.
Result: An adequate explanation for $q \in [\![\phi]\!]^S e$.

$O = \varnothing$; $T = \varnothing$; $pending = \{\langle q, \phi, e \rangle\}$
while $pending \neq \varnothing$ **do**

    pick $o' = \langle q', \phi', e' \rangle \in pending$
    $pending = pending \backslash \{o'\}$
    $O = O \cup \{o'\}$
    case $\phi' \in \{true, p, \neg p, v, \neg v\}$: $O' = \varnothing$
    case $\phi' = \phi_1 \wedge \phi_2$: $O' = \{\langle q', \phi_1, e' \rangle, \langle q', \phi_2, e' \rangle\}$
    case $\phi' = \phi_1 \vee \phi_2$
        if $q' \in [\![\phi_1]\!]^S e'$ **then** $O' = \{\langle q', \phi_1, e' \rangle\}$ **else** $O' = \{\langle q', \phi_2, e' \rangle\}$

    case $\phi' = \Diamond_i \phi''$
        pick $q'' \in \{q'' \in Q \mid \langle q', q'' \rangle \in R_i \wedge q'' \in [\![\phi'']\!]^S e'\}$
        $O' = \{\langle q'', \phi'', e' \rangle\}$

    case $\phi' = \Box_i \phi''$: $O' = \{\langle q'', \phi'', e' \rangle \mid \langle q', q'' \rangle \in R_i\}$
    case $\phi' = \mu v. \; \psi$
        $\phi'' = false$; $sat = [\![\phi'']\!]^S e'$
        while $q' \notin sat$ **do**
            $\phi'' = \psi(\phi'')$; $sat = [\![\phi'']\!]^S e'$
        $O' = \{\langle q', \phi'', e' \rangle\}$

    case $\phi' = \nu v. \; \psi$: $O' = \{\langle q', \psi(\phi'), e' \rangle\}$
    $T = T \cup \{\langle o', o'' \rangle \mid o'' \in O'\}$
    $pending = pending \cup (O' \backslash O)$

return $\langle O, T \rangle$

original model language, the framework integrates the relational graph algebra of Dong et al. [15]. This algebra allows the designer to translate the explanation back into the original model language, but it treats the explanation as a whole. To ease the addition of information to individual obligations and edges, the framework also provides the notion of attributors. Finally, local translators are proposed to treat small parts of the given graph.

These functionalities help the designer to translate the μ-calculus explanation into another graph that is closer to the initial model language. Nevertheless, the designer has no control on the initial explanation the algorithm produces. To allow the designer to interfere into the choices the *explain* algorithm makes, the framework provides *choosers*.

Aliases. An alias α is a syntactic function that takes a set of arguments and returns an *aliased* μ-calculus formula. The alias of an aliased formula is then used to hide the latter behind something more intelligible. For instance, the alias $\langle\!\langle\rangle\!\rangle\mathbf{X}(\Gamma,\phi) = \Diamond_{\Gamma choose}(\Diamond_{\Gamma follow} true \wedge \Box_{\Gamma follow} \phi)$ replaces the formula ϕ_{ns} with $\nu v. \neg sent \wedge \langle\!\langle transmitter \rangle\!\rangle \mathbf{X}\ v$.

Relational Graph Algebra. The relational graph algebra of Dong et al. includes operators such as the union $G_1 \cup G_2$ and intersection $G_1 \cap G_2$ of two graphs G_1 and G_2, the selection $\sigma_{f_v, f_e}(G)$ of nodes and edges satisfying a condition, the projection $\pi_{d_v, d_e}(G)$ of nodes and edges on sub-domains d_v and d_e, the grouping $\gamma_{d_v, d_e}(G)$ of nodes and edges, etc. Thanks to this algebra, the designer can transform explanations into other graphs.

Obligation and Edge Attributors. An *attribute* is data associated to explanation nodes and edges, and an *attributor* is a function adding attributes to an obligation or edge. They work as local decorators, in the sense that they deal with obligations and edges one at a time. They can be given to the generating algorithm to be run on every obligation or edge, or they can be attached to individual aliases to be run only on the obligations with instantiations of the aliases, or outgoing edges of these obligations. This improves the performances of decorating the graph when only a few elements must be decorated. In the case of ATL, we can define an attributor to attach to obligations the original CGS state their state derives from.

Local Translation. A local translator is a function taking a relational graph and a particular node as arguments, and updating the graph. The part of the explanation a local translator receives is defined by the alias it is attached to. For instance, with a local translator, we can add edges to an explanation between an obligation labelled with a $\langle\!\langle\rangle\!\rangle\mathbf{X}$ alias and all the original successors of its state. The advantage of such a local translator is that the part of the graph it receives is the one explaining the $\langle\!\langle\rangle\!\rangle\mathbf{X}$ operator only.

Choosers and Partial Explanations. A chooser takes an obligation and a set of possible successors of this obligation and returns a subset of these successors depending on the operator of the formula of the given obligation:

- for $\vee$ and $\Diamond_i$ operators, at most *one* successor must be chosen, to ensure a consistent explanation.
- for $\wedge$ and $\Box_i$ operators, the full explanation shows all successors, but a subset can be returned.
- for the other operators, there is no meaningful choice: there is no successor for *true* formulas, atomic propositions or variables, and there is only one successor for least and greatest fixpoint formulas.

Choosers can guide the explanation generation by choosing particular successors, but also limit the size of the generated explanation by only exploring parts of it. This introduces the notion of *partial explanations*, that is, explanations where some obligations are not fully explained because they lack some successors. The advantage of partial explanations is that the complete explanation can be too large to be generated or understood, so getting a part of it is better than nothing. Furthermore, choosers enable interactive generation of explanations as they can ask the user to resolve some choices.

Markers. They are attached to formulas. The framework provides two types of markers, *points of interest*, and *points of decision*, but new types can be defined by the designer. Points of interest are intended to mark the formulas that are important for the designer. On the other hand, the model checker takes points of decision into account when generating explanations: whenever an obligation formula is marked with such a point, the model checker does not explain it. This produces partial explanations that can be later expanded by the user by forcing the generation of the missing parts.

Thanks to all these features, it is possible to transform the μ-calculus explanation of Fig. 5 for the formula $\langle\!\langle transmitter \rangle\!\rangle \mathbf{G} \neg sent$ and get the explanation of Fig. 6. For this translation, we used:

- aliases to hide μ-calculus formulas behind their ATL counterparts,
- points of interest for marking the formulas that have an ATL counterpart,
- an obligation attributor to extend each obligation with the original state,
- a local translator to add the edge with the action of the transmitter,
- the relational graph algebra to merge nodes together and gather the formulas that the state satisfies.

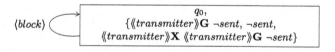

Fig. 6. A translation of the μ-calculus explanation of Fig. 5 using the translation features of the framework.

4 Implementation

The framework has been implemented in Python using PyNuSMV for solving the model-checking problem. PyNuSMV is a library for prototyping symbolic model-checking algorithms based on NuSMV [6]. The implementation and examples are available on http://lvl.info.ucl.ac.be/FM2018/FM2018.

First, to be able to use the framework, the designer has to derive, from the original model, a μ-calculus Kripke structure $S = \langle Q, \{R_i \mid i \in \Sigma\}, V \rangle$. Such a structure is implemented with PyNuSMV as a standard SMV model to which several transition relations R_i are attached.

Second, the framework provides Python classes to define μ-calculus formulas, one for each μ-calculus operator: `MTrue`, `MFalse`, `Atom`, `Variable`, `Not`, `And`, `Or`,

Diamond, Box, Mu, and Nu. With this implementation, μ-calculus formulas do not have to be declared in positive normal form. Instead, the framework lazily derives positive normal forms when needed. This allows the formulas that annotate the obligations to stay as close to the main formula as possible.

Third, most of the features are implemented with Python *decorators*, that is, function annotations that change the function behavior. For instance, aliases are defined as Python functions returning the corresponding μ-calculus formula and decorated with the @alias decorator. The code of Fig. 7 shows a small part of the ATL model checker built with the framework. The CAX function returns the translation of the ⟦agents⟧X formula formula, marked with points of interest and decision, and to which is attached the chosen_action edge attributor.

```
@alias("[{agents}] X {formula}")
def CAX(agents, formula):
    return POD(POI(chosen_action(
            Box(agents + "_choose",
                Or(Box(agents + "_follow", MFalse()),
                    Diamond(agents + "_follow", formula)))
        )))
@edge_attributor
def chosen_action(edge):
    # ...
    return {"action": actions}
```

Fig. 7. A part of the implementation of the ATL model checker built with the framework.

Relational graphs, and generated explanations in particular, are implemented with the Graph class. Nodes and edges of these graphs are implemented with the domaintuple class, a dictionary-like structure where domains of the elements are identified by a name. Each operator of the relational graph algebra is implemented by a method of the Graph class.

The framework allows the designer to efficiently translate an explanation back into the top-level language. Nevertheless, these explanations remain complex and difficult to understand. To help the user in understanding these complex explanations, the implementation also provides a graphical visualization tool. A snapshot of the tool is given in Fig. 8.

The top left part presents the explanation: nodes are depicted in ovals, and edges are depicted as arrows decorated with information in a box. This graph can be moved with the mouse or automatically re-arranged. The information displayed in nodes and edge labels come from the explanation elements themselves. The tool also allows the user to select which keys of the graph elements are displayed, through a right-click menu on the graph area. To enable interactivity, the designer can specify a graphical menu that is displayed whenever the user right-clicks on the element. This can be used, for instance, to expand partial

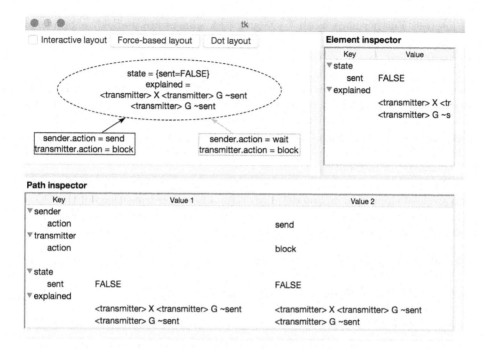

Fig. 8. A snapshot of the visualization tool.

explanations. The top right part of the tool displays the complete information of the selected element (the dashed one on Fig. 8). The bottom part of the tool can display one particular path of the graph, selected by the user.

5   Application to ATL

The objective of this section is to show the usefulness of the framework by applying it to the ATL logic. It describes how explanations for ATL can be obtained, displayed and manipulated thanks to the framework implementation.

The implementation represents a CGS with a standard SMV model to which is attached a set of agents. Each agent has a name and a set of SMV input variables corresponding to its actions. The SMV model itself defines what the agents can do, and how the state of the model evolves according to their actions.

The translation of the CGS acts like a dictionary of transition relations, lazily building these relations when needed. The advantage of this mechanism is that, even if the CGS contains a lot of agents, its implementation builds the transition relations only for the groups of agents appearing in the checked formula. The translation of ATL formulas simply uses the Python classes provided by the framework to define μ-calculus formulas.

To enrich and translate explanations, one alias is declared for each ATL operator. All top-level formulas returned by the aliases are marked as points of interest. Furthermore, both $\langle\!\langle\,\rangle\!\rangle\mathbf{X}$ and $[\![\,]\!]\mathbf{X}$ aliases are marked as points of decision, to be able to generate small partial explanations and to allow the user to expand them as she wishes.

Two attributors add information to obligations and edges of the explanation. The first attributor attaches, to each obligation, the original state its state derives from. This attributor is given to the *explain* algorithm to enrich all obligations. The second attributor stores the actions chosen by the group in the outgoing edge of the obligations labelled with a $\langle\!\langle\,\rangle\!\rangle\mathbf{X}$ or $[\![\,]\!]\mathbf{X}$ aliased formula. This way, the information is more easily accessed by local translators. Figure 7 illustrates these parts of the implementation.

Two local translators are defined, for $\langle\!\langle\,\rangle\!\rangle\mathbf{X}$ and $[\![\,]\!]\mathbf{X}$. They extract, from the two steps of the μ-calculus model, the original one-step transitions of the CGS. The relational graph algebra is used to translate μ-calculus explanations back into ATL ones. The translation:

1. projects the explanation nodes on formulas and original states;
2. groups nodes by their original state;
3. separates unexplained formulas from explained ones;
4. selects edges that are labelled with some actions;
5. keeps the original state and the formulas in nodes, and the actions in edges.

This translation produces explanations such as the one of Figs. 6 and 8.

A chooser is defined to expand partial explanations. When dealing with a $\langle\!\langle\,\rangle\!\rangle\mathbf{X}$ alias, it gets the original actions of the group from the given successors and asks the user to choose one of them through a window. Finally, the visualization tool is used to display and manipulate the translated explanations, as shown in Fig. 8. In particular, it provides, through a right-click menu, the list of unexplained formulas. This menu triggers the expansion of the currently displayed partial explanation, running through the chooser to select the action to play.

6   Related Work

Several authors already proposed solutions to explain why a CTL formula is satisfied by some model. First, some authors proposed structures capturing the part of the model witnessing the satisfaction [3,11,29]. These structures are defined as hierarchies of paths, fitting the CTL semantics. Jiang and Ciardo recently proposed a way to generate such hierarchies of paths with a *minimal* number of states [19]. Other authors proposed more detailed structures, capturing the part of the model, as well as sub-formulas and logical decomposition steps [7,8,18,27,30,31,33]. These different solutions vary in terms of details they provide about the satisfaction—by annotating or not the parts of the counter-example with the sub-formulas they explain—, the fragments of the logic they support—either the full logic or its universal fragment—, and the framework they work in—explicit, game-based, proof-based, BDD-based model checking, or Boolean Equation Systems (BES). All these solutions can be adapted to a BDD-based framework and produced with the framework we propose.

Some solutions have also been proposed in the context of multi-modal logics, adapting and extending the ideas from CTL to richer logics [5,24–26,34]. In this context, MCK, a tool for verification of temporal and knowledge properties, provides several debugging functionalities [17], such as a debugging game inspired by Stirling's games [32] in which the user can try to show why the model-checking outcome is wrong while the system shows her why it is actually right. Such a debugging game can be implemented with adequate choosers.

Finally, several solutions have also been proposed to represent and produce explanations for the μ-calculus [14,20,21,23]. They differ from the ones presented in this paper either by the way they are generated—such as the explanations of Kick [21]—or by the actual framework they rely on.

All these solutions work for particular logics such as CTL, CTLK, the μ-calculus, or are generic solutions with some application to one use case such as BES and their extensions, games, or proofs. But no work proposes a solution to produce explanations and to translate them back into the original language, as the μ-calculus framework of this paper. They either limit themselves to one logic, or they provide generic structures without giving explicit help for applying and translating it into something useful for the end user.

7 Conclusion

In this paper, we described a solution for μ-calculus-based logics explanations. The proposed framework integrates a μ-calculus model checker that generates rich explanations and provides several functionalities to translate them into explanations for a top-level logic such as ATL. It has been implemented with PyNuSMV, taking advantage of Python functionalities such as function decorators to easily describe the different features. The implementation also integrates a graphical tool to visualize, manipulate and explore the explanations.

One of the main advantages of the framework is that many logics can be translated into the μ-calculus, such as CTL, Fair CTL, CTLK, ATL, and PDL. It is thus generic enough to provide model-checking functionalities for all of them. Furthermore, thanks to the framework, the designer does not have to worry about designing and implementing a model checker, nor about generating rich explanations. Nevertheless, she has to translate the top-level models and formulas into μ-calculus. Model translation can be difficult—for instance, the translation from an ATL CGS to a μ-calculus structure is not trivial—and the framework gives no help to complete this task.

The framework features allow the designer to divide the concerns into smaller parts, first dealing with formula translations (with aliases and markers), then with single elements (with attributors), small sub-graphs (with local translation), and with the whole explanation (with the algebra). Furthermore, all the features are useful, as illustrated by the ATL case. In particular, local translators are useless for cases such as CTL, but for ATL, where the model translation is difficult, they can help treating small parts of the explanation separately, instead of having to deal with the whole explanation graph at once. The visualization tool provided by the framework complements the translation features. The latter help the designer to produce useful explanations while the former helps the user visualize, manipulate and explore it.

Finally, the framework supports interactive and guided generation of the explanations through choosers. This can lead to smaller manageable partial explanations that can be interactively expanded, as illustrated by the ATL case.

One of the main drawbacks of the framework is the fact that it produces one single explanation at a time. Representing several explanations at once could help the user to extract the reasons for the satisfaction of the formula more easily. As future work, it would be interesting to explore how we could represent several explanations at once by using binary decision diagrams to represent *sets of obligations* instead of single ones. Furthermore, translating a CGS and an ATL formula into a μ-calculus model and a formula is not an easy task compared to other logics such as CTL and CTLK. One solution to make this particular translation easier is to use the alternating-time μ-calculus [1] as base logic instead of the propositional μ-calculus. Finally, it would be interesting to explore solutions to provide translation functionalities for the model itself. With such translation functionalities, the translation of explanations back into the original language could become automatic.

References

1. Alur, R., Henzinger, T.A., Kupferman, O.: Alternating-time temporal logic. J. ACM **49**(5), 672–713 (2002)
2. Baier, C., Katoen, J.P.: Principles of Model Checking. The MIT Press, Cambridge (2008)
3. Buccafurri, F., Eiter, T., Gottlob, G., Leone, N.: On ACTL formulas having linear counterexamples. J. Comput. Syst. Sci. **62**(3), 463–515 (2001)
4. Busard, S.: Symbolic model checking of multi-modal logics: uniform strategies and rich explanations. Ph.D. thesis, Université catholique de Louvain, July 2017
5. Busard, S., Pecheur, C.: Rich counter-examples for temporal-epistemic logic model checking. In: Proceedings Second International Workshop on Interactions, Games and Protocols, IWIGP 2012, Tallinn, Estonia, 25th March 2012, pp. 39–53 (2012). http://dx.doi.org/10.4204/EPTCS.78.4
6. Busard, S., Pecheur, C.: PyNuSMV: NuSMV as a python library. In: Brat, G., Rungta, N., Venet, A. (eds.) NFM 2013. LNCS, vol. 7871, pp. 453–458. Springer, Heidelberg (2013). https://doi.org/10.1007/978-3-642-38088-4_33
7. Chechik, M., Gurfinkel, A.: A framework for counterexample generation and exploration. In: Cerioli, M. (ed.) FASE 2005. LNCS, vol. 3442, pp. 220–236. Springer, Heidelberg (2005). https://doi.org/10.1007/978-3-540-31984-9_17
8. Chechik, M., Gurfinkel, A.: A framework for counterexample generation and exploration. Int. J. Softw. Tools Technol. Transfer **9**(5–6), 429–445 (2007)
9. Cimatti, A., Clarke, E., Giunchiglia, E., Giunchiglia, F., Pistore, M., Roveri, M., Sebastiani, R., Tacchella, A.: NuSMV 2: an opensource tool for symbolic model checking. In: Brinksma, E., Larsen, K.G. (eds.) CAV 2002. LNCS, vol. 2404, pp. 359–364. Springer, Heidelberg (2002). https://doi.org/10.1007/3-540-45657-0_29
10. Clarke, E.M., Grumberg, O., Peled, D.: Model Checking. MIT Press, Cambridge (1999)

11. Clarke, E.M., Jha, S., Lu, Y., Veith, H.: Tree-like counterexamples in model checking. In: Proceedings of the 17th IEEE Symposium on Logic in Computer Science (LICS 2002), pp. 19–29 (2002)
12. Clarke, E.M., Emerson, E.A.: Design and synthesis of synchronization skeletons using branching time temporal logic. In: Kozen, D. (ed.) Logic of Programs 1981. LNCS, vol. 131, pp. 52–71. Springer, Heidelberg (1982). https://doi.org/10.1007/BFb0025774
13. Clarke, E.M., Emerson, E.A., Sistla, A.P.: Automatic verification of finite-state concurrent systems using temporal logic specifications. ACM Trans. Program. Lang. Syst. 8(2), 244–263 (1986). http://doi.acm.org/10.1145/5397.5399
14. Cranen, S., Luttik, B., Willemse, T.A.C.: Proof graphs for parameterised boolean equation systems. In: D'Argenio, P.R., Melgratti, H. (eds.) CONCUR 2013. LNCS, vol. 8052, pp. 470–484. Springer, Heidelberg (2013). https://doi.org/10.1007/978-3-642-40184-8_33
15. Dong, Y., Ramakrishnan, C.R., Smolka, S.A.: Model checking and evidence exploration. In: Proceedings of the 10th IEEE International Conference on Engineering of Computer-Based Systems (ECBS 2003), pp. 214–223 (2003)
16. Fischer, M.J., Ladner, R.E.: Propositional dynamic logic of regular programs. J. Comput. Syst. Sci. 18(2), 194–211 (1979)
17. Gammie, P., van der Meyden, R.: MCK: model checking the logic of knowledge. In: Alur, R., Peled, D.A. (eds.) CAV 2004. LNCS, vol. 3114, pp. 479–483. Springer, Heidelberg (2004). https://doi.org/10.1007/978-3-540-27813-9_41
18. Gurfinkel, A., Chechik, M.: Proof-like counter-examples. In: Garavel, H., Hatcliff, J. (eds.) TACAS 2003. LNCS, vol. 2619, pp. 160–175. Springer, Heidelberg (2003). https://doi.org/10.1007/3-540-36577-X_12
19. Jiang, C., Ciardo, G.: Generation of minimum tree-like witnesses for existential CTL. In: Beyer, D., Huisman, M. (eds.) TACAS 2018. LNCS, vol. 10805, pp. 328–343. Springer, Cham (2018). https://doi.org/10.1007/978-3-319-89960-2_18
20. Kick, A.: Generation of witnesses for global μ-calculus model checking. Technical report, Universität Karlsruhe, Germany (1995)
21. Kick, A.: Tableaux and witnesses for the μ-calculus. Technical report, Universität Karlsruhe, Germany (1995)
22. Kozen, D.: Results on the propositional mu-calculus. Theor. Comput. Sci. 27, 333–354 (1983). http://dx.doi.org/10.1016/0304-3975(82)90125-6
23. Linssen, C.A.: Diagnostics for Model Checking. Master's thesis, Eindhoven University of Technology (2011)
24. Lomuscio, A., Qu, H., Raimondi, F.: MCMAS: a model checker for the verification of multi-agent systems. In: Bouajjani, A., Maler, O. (eds.) CAV 2009. LNCS, vol. 5643, pp. 682–688. Springer, Heidelberg (2009). https://doi.org/10.1007/978-3-642-02658-4_55
25. Lomuscio, A., Qu, H., Raimondi, F.: MCMAS: an open-source model checker for the verification of multi-agent systems. Int. J. Softw. Tools Technol. Transfer 1–22 (2015). http://dx.doi.org/10.1007/s10009-015-0378-x
26. Lomuscio, A., Raimondi, F.: MCMAS: a model checker for multi-agent systems. In: Hermanns, H., Palsberg, J. (eds.) TACAS 2006. LNCS, vol. 3920, pp. 450–454. Springer, Heidelberg (2006). https://doi.org/10.1007/11691372_31
27. Mateescu, R.: Efficient diagnostic generation for boolean equation systems. In: Graf, S., Schwartzbach, M. (eds.) TACAS 2000. LNCS, vol. 1785, pp. 251–265. Springer, Heidelberg (2000). https://doi.org/10.1007/3-540-46419-0_18

28. Penczek, W., Lomuscio, A.: Verifying epistemic properties of multi-agent systems via bounded model checking. In: Proceedings of the Second International Joint Conference on Autonomous Agents and Multiagent Systems. AAMAS 2003, pp. 209–216. ACM, New York (2003). http://doi.acm.org/10.1145/860575.860609
29. Rasse, A.: Error diagnosis in finite communicating systems. In: Larsen, K.G., Skou, A. (eds.) CAV 1991. LNCS, vol. 575, pp. 114–124. Springer, Heidelberg (1992). https://doi.org/10.1007/3-540-55179-4_12
30. Roychoudhury, A., Ramakrishnan, C., Ramakrishnan, I.: Justifying proofs using memo tables. In: International Conference on Principles and Practice of Declarative Programming: Proceedings of the 2nd ACM SIGPLAN International Conference on Principles and Practice of Declarative Programming, pp. 178–189 (2000)
31. Shoham, S., Grumberg, O.: A game-based framework for CTL counterexamples and 3-valued abstraction-refinement. ACM Trans. Comput. Logic (TOCL) **9**(1), 1 (2007)
32. Stirling, C.: Local model checking games (extended abstract). In: Lee, I., Smolka, S.A. (eds.) CONCUR 1995. LNCS, vol. 962, pp. 1–11. Springer, Heidelberg (1995). https://doi.org/10.1007/3-540-60218-6_1
33. Tan, L., Cleaveland, R.: Evidence-based model checking. In: Brinksma, E., Larsen, K.G. (eds.) CAV 2002. LNCS, vol. 2404, pp. 455–470. Springer, Heidelberg (2002). https://doi.org/10.1007/3-540-45657-0_37
34. Weitl, F., Nakajima, S., Freitag, B.: Structured counterexamples for the temporal description logic ALCCTL. In: 2010 8th IEEE International Conference on Software Engineering and Formal Methods, pp. 232–243. IEEE (2010)

The Compound Interest in Relaxing Punctuality

Thomas Ferrère[(⊠)]

IST Austria, Klosterneuburg, Austria
thomas.ferrere@ist.ac.at

Abstract. Imprecision in timing can sometimes be beneficial: Metric interval temporal logic (MITL), disabling the expression of punctuality constraints, was shown to translate to timed automata, yielding an elementary decision procedure. We show how this principle extends to other forms of dense-time specification using regular expressions. By providing a clean, automaton-based formal framework for non-punctual languages, we are able to recover and extend several results in timed systems. Metric interval regular expressions (MIRE) are introduced, providing regular expressions with non-singular duration constraints. We obtain that MIRE are expressively complete relative to a class of one-clock timed automata, which can be determinized using additional clocks. Metric interval dynamic logic (MIDL) is then defined using MIRE as temporal modalities. We show that MIDL generalizes known extensions of MITL, while translating to timed automata at comparable cost.

1 Introduction

Regular expressions (RE) [20] are a basic notion in computer science. They provide a simple algebraic way to describe finite-state behaviors. Since their introduction in verification and testing, alongside linear temporal logic (LTL) [32], regular expressions have also proven to be a very practical formalism to specify discrete systems behavior [14,36]. Yet not all applications enjoy the synchronous, discrete-time style of modeling captured by finite automata. Modern computerized systems are more asynchronous in nature, calling for a different level of abstraction in which time may no longer be discrete.

Timed automata (TA) [2] are widely regarded as a natural extension of finite-state theory to dense-time. This model of computation uses real-valued variables known as *clocks* to control delays between events. The strength of timed automata, beyond the simplicity of their definition, comes from their theoretical properties: the emptiness problem is solvable in polynomial space, timed regular languages are closed under positive Boolean operations, and their *untiming*

This research was supported by the Austrian Science Fund (FWF) under grants S11402-N23 (RiSE/SHiNE) and Z211-N23 (Wittgenstein Award).

yields back regular languages. However the standard, nondeterministic model (NTA) is not closed under complement, while the deterministic model (DTA) is not closed under concatenation or Kleene star.

Negation is a desirable operation in any specification language. Metric temporal logic (MTL) [21] is a well-studied, established dense-time specification language. Through negation, the set of languages described in MTL is closed under complement. However satisfiability of MTL is non-elementary under the hypotheses of [30], and undecidable in general [3,31]. Timed regular expressions (TRE) [6] constitute an interesting alternative to MTL, both powerful and intuitive. The emptiness of TRE is also decidable in polynomial space, since TRE translate to timed automata in polynomial time [6]. But TRE do not feature a negation operator, which would render them undecidable.

Virtually all negative results in timed systems, such as the undecidability of language inclusion for timed automata, rely on the ability to enforce real delays with infinite precision—some extreme form of *punctuality*. When no semantic restriction is placed on the variability or duration of behaviors, a single unit of time can hold an arbitrary amount of information, which can then be repeatedly transfered from one time unit to the next, encoding Turing computations. A standard way to regain decidability is to bound the variability of behaviors [16,28]. Another, less conventional way is to bound their duration [29].

The syntactic restriction of [3] simply bounds the precision timing constraints—in effect *relaxing punctuality*. Decidability of the resulting metric interval temporal logic (MITL) [3] follows, by translation to timed automata. Subsequently, extensions of MITL with finite automata [17,37] and threshold counting [18] have then been proposed, enjoying special connections with monadic logic [17,19,37]. In this context, our contribution consists in (a) the definition of RE-based variants of MITL for specifying timed behaviors; (b) a simple automaton-based framework in which several results regarding these variants can be derived (Fig. 1).

In particular, we show how to adapt the subset construction of [10] to determinize arbitrary control structures, by introducing the notion of *metric interval automaton* (MIA, Sect. 3). These automata, reminiscent of [5], have a single clock, checked against non-singular timing intervals, and reset after every check. A simple state-elimination argument demonstrates that this model is equivalent to the proposed *metric interval regular expressions* (MIRE, Sect. 3), which therefore translate to deterministic timed automata (Sect. 4). By treating metric interval automata as modalities, we redefine *extended MITL* (EMITL, [37]). Building on our initial results, we propose *metric interval dynamic logic* (MIDL, Sect. 5), equivalent in expressive power, and provide a translation to non-deterministic timed automata (Sect. 6). This translation is compositional, in the style of [26], and does not go through intermediate formalisms such as monadic logic [37] or *event clock* automata [17].

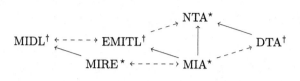

Fig. 1. Translations (- →) and inclusions (→) between formalisms. Closure under Boolean operations (†) and under regular operations (⋆) are indicated in exponent.

2 Preliminaries

In this section, we introduce basic definitions and relevant results. We take the time domain $\mathbb{T} = \mathbb{R}_{\geq 0}$ to be the non-negative reals. Given a set of times $R \subseteq \mathbb{T}$, we write $\mathrm{ch}(R) = \{t \in \mathbb{T} \mid \exists r, r' \in R, r \leq t \leq r'\}$ its convex hull and $t \oplus R = \{t + r \in \mathbb{T} \mid r \in R\}$ its Minkowski sum with some $t \in \mathbb{T}$. We define *timed words* as sequences alternating delays in $\mathbb{T}$ and events in some alphabet Σ. Given a timed word $w = t_1 a_1 \ldots t_n a_n$ we write $w_{i..j}$ its infix $t_{i+1} a_{i+1} \ldots t_j a_j$ between positions $0 \leq i \leq j \leq n$. We denote by $|w| = n$ the size of w and by $\|w\| = \sum_{i=1}^n t_i$ the *duration* of w. The empty word ϵ verifies $|\epsilon| = \|\epsilon\| = 0$.

Automata. Following [2], automata are equipped with a set X of clock variables. A *clock constraint* is a Boolean combination of inequalities of the form $x \bowtie c$, or $x - y \bowtie c$, where $c \in \mathbb{N}$ is a constant, $\bowtie \in \{\leq, <, >, \geq\}$ is a comparison sign, and $x, y \in X$ are clocks. The set of clock constraints over X is denoted $\Phi(X)$. A *valuation* v associates any clock variable $x \in X$ with a delay $v(x) \in \mathbb{T}$. We write $v \models \phi$ when the constraint ϕ is satisfied under clock valuation v.

A *timed automaton* is a tuple $\mathcal{A} = (\Sigma, X, L, S, F, \Delta)$ where L is a set of locations, $S \subseteq L$ is a set of initial locations, $F \subseteq L$ is a set of accepting locations, and $\Delta \subseteq L \times \Sigma \times \Phi(X) \times 2^X \times L$ is a set of edges. A *state* of $\mathcal{A}$ is a pair (ℓ, v) where ℓ is a location in L and v is a valuation over X. For delays $t \in \mathbb{T}$ and events $a \in \Sigma$, transitions $\overset{t}{\rightsquigarrow}$ and $\overset{a}{\rightarrow}$ in $\mathcal{A}$ are defined as the following relations:

- $(\ell, v) \overset{t}{\rightsquigarrow} (\ell', v')$ if $\ell = \ell'$ and $v' = v + t$;
- $(\ell, v) \overset{a}{\rightarrow} (\ell', v')$ if $v \models \phi$ and $v' = v[Z \leftarrow 0]$ for some $(\ell, a, \phi, Z, \ell') \in \Delta$.

Here $v + t$ stands for the valuation such that $(v + t)(x) = v(x) + t$ for all $x \in X$, and $v[Z \leftarrow 0]$ stands for the valuation such that $v[Z \leftarrow 0](x) = 0$ if $x \in Z$, $v(x)$ otherwise. A *run* of automaton $\mathcal{A}$ over the word $w = t_1 a_1 \ldots t_n a_n$ is a sequence $(\ell_0, v_0) \overset{t_1}{\rightsquigarrow} (\ell_0, v_0') \overset{a_1}{\rightarrow} \ldots \overset{t_n}{\rightsquigarrow} (\ell_{n-1}, v_{n-1}') \overset{a_n}{\rightarrow} (\ell_n, v_n)$ of transitions labeled by delays and events in w such that $\ell_0 \in S$, and $v_0(x) = 0$ for all $x \in X$. The language $\mathcal{L}(\mathcal{A})$ is the set of words over which there exists a run of $\mathcal{A}$ ending in an accepting location. We say that $\mathcal{A}$ is deterministic when $S = \{\ell_0\}$ for some ℓ_0, and $\phi_1 \wedge \phi_2$ is unsatisfiable for all $(\ell, a, \phi_1, Z_1, \ell_1) \neq (\ell, a, \phi_2, Z_2, \ell_2) \in \Delta$.

Expressions. We define timed regular expressions (TRE) following [6], but without intersection or projection. They are given by the grammar:

$$\varphi ::= \epsilon \mid a \mid \varphi \cup \varphi \mid \varphi \cdot \varphi \mid \varphi^* \mid \varphi_I$$

where $a \in \Sigma$, and $I \subseteq \mathbb{T}$ is an integer-bounded interval. As customary iterating an expression φ is denoted in exponent, with by convention $\varphi^+ \equiv \varphi^* \cdot \varphi$, and $\varphi^k \equiv \epsilon$ if $k = 0$, $\varphi^k \equiv \varphi^{k-1} \cdot \varphi$ otherwise. Any TRE φ can be associated with a language $\mathcal{L}(\varphi)$ defined inductively as follows:

$$\mathcal{L}(\epsilon) = \{\epsilon\} \qquad\qquad \mathcal{L}(\varphi_1 \cdot \varphi_2) = \{w_1 w_2 \mid w_1 \in \mathcal{L}(\varphi_1), w_2 \in \mathcal{L}(\varphi_2)\}$$

$$\mathcal{L}(a) = \{ta \mid t \in \mathbb{T}\} \qquad\qquad \mathcal{L}(\varphi^*) = \bigcup_{k=0}^{\infty} \mathcal{L}(\varphi^k)$$

$$\mathcal{L}(\varphi_1 \cup \varphi_2) = \mathcal{L}(\varphi_1) \cup \mathcal{L}(\varphi_2) \qquad\qquad \mathcal{L}(\varphi_I) = \{w \mid w \in \mathcal{L}(\varphi), \|w\| \in I\}.$$

The *size* of a TRE φ is the number of atomic expressions it contains. Its *depth* $d(\varphi)$ is the level of nesting of timing constraints in φ, defined by $d(a) = d(\epsilon) = 0$, $d(\varphi \cdot \psi) = d(\varphi \cup \psi) = \max\{d(\varphi), d(\psi)\}$, $d(\varphi^*) = d(\varphi)$, and $d(\varphi_I) = d(\varphi) + 1$.

Theorem 1 (TRE $\Rightarrow$ NTA, [6]). *For any TRE of size m and depth n, one can construct an equivalent timed automaton with n clocks and $m + 1$ locations.*

Logic. Metric temporal logic (MTL) [21] extends LTL [32] by providing the *until* operator with a timing interval. MTL formulas are given by the grammar:

$$\psi ::= a \mid \psi \vee \psi \mid \neg\psi \mid \psi \, \mathcal{U}_I \, \psi$$

where $a \in \Sigma$ and I is an integer-bounded interval. Operators *eventually* and *always* are defined by letting $\Diamond_I \varphi \equiv \top \, \mathcal{U}_I \, \varphi$ and $\Box_I \varphi \equiv \neg \Diamond_I \neg\varphi$. The timing interval $[0, \infty)$ is usually omitted as subscript. Metric interval temporal logic (MITL) [3] is the fragment of MTL where intervals I are *non-singular* ($\inf I < \sup I$).

The semantics $\models$ of MTL and MITL is defined over *pointed words*, pairs (w, i) of timed word w and position $0 < i \leq |w| + 1$, as follows:

$$(w, i) \models a \qquad \text{iff} \qquad w_{i-1..i} = ta \text{ for some } t \in \mathbb{T}$$

$$(w, i) \models \neg\psi \qquad \text{iff} \qquad (w, i) \not\models \psi$$

$$(w, i) \models \psi_1 \vee \psi_2 \qquad \text{iff} \qquad (w, i) \models \psi_1 \text{ or } (w, i) \models \psi_2$$

$$(w, i) \models \psi_1 \, \mathcal{U}_I \, \psi_2 \qquad \text{iff} \qquad (w, j) \models \psi_2 \text{ for some } j > i \text{ such that } \|w_{i..j}\| \in I$$
$$\text{and } (w, k) \models \psi_1 \text{ for all } i < k < j.$$

The language $\mathcal{L}(\psi)$ of formula ψ is defined by $\mathcal{L}(\psi) = \{w \mid (w, 1) \models \psi\}$. The *size* of an MITL formula ψ is the number of temporal operators it contains. Its *resolution* $r(\psi)$ is the maximal relative interval width in ψ, defined by $r(a) = 0$, $r(\psi_1 \vee \psi_2) = \max\{r(\psi_1), r(\psi_2)\}$, $r(\neg\psi) = r(\psi)$, and $r(\psi_1 \, \mathcal{U}_I \, \psi_2) = \max\{r(\psi_1), r(\psi_2), r(\mathcal{U}_I)\}$, where $r(\mathcal{U}_I) = \left\lfloor \frac{\sup I}{\sup I - \inf I} \right\rfloor + 2$ if $\sup I < \infty$, 1 otherwise.

Theorem 2 (MITL $\Rightarrow$ NTA, [3]). *For any MITL formula of size m and resolution n, one can construct an equivalent timed automaton with $2mn$ clocks and 2^{8mn+1} locations.*

3   Metric Interval Regular Expressions

We now introduce *metric interval regular expressions* (MIRE) as TRE of depth 1 and devoid of singular timing intervals. Formally, they are given by the grammar:

$$\varphi ::= \gamma_I \mid \varphi \cdot \varphi \mid \varphi \cup \varphi \mid \varphi^*$$
$$\gamma ::= \epsilon \mid a \mid \gamma \cdot \gamma \mid \gamma \cup \gamma \mid \gamma^*$$

where $a \in \Sigma$ and I is a non-singular, integer-bounded interval. Timing interval $[0, \infty)$ is usually omitted, that is, we write γ in place of $\gamma_{[0,\infty)}$ in MIRE. The *resolution* of a MIRE is defined similarly as for MITL.

Example 1. Consider the expression $(a \cup b \cdot (a^* \cdot b)_{[2,3]})^*$. It describes sequences of events a and b in which every odd occurrence of b is followed by another (even) occurrence of b within 2 to 3 time units.

Automaton Model. We define *metric interval automata* (MIA) as timed automata with a single clock x in which every edge $(\ell, a, \phi, Z, \ell')$ is such that either $Z = \emptyset$ and $\phi = \top$, or $Z = \{x\}$ and $\phi \equiv x \in I$ for some non-singular interval I. Here $x \in I$ is the abbreviated notation for constraint $x \geq c$ when $I = [c, \infty)$, $x \geq c \wedge x \leq d$ when $I = [c, d]$, and similar when I is a (semi-)open interval.

Proposition 1 (MIRE ⇔ MIA). *Every MIRE language is recognizable by MIA, and every MIA language is expressible as MIRE.*

Direction $\Rightarrow$ is a refinement of Theorem 1, and will be proved in Sect. 4. We treat direction $\Leftarrow$ in two steps. Let $\mathcal{A}$ be a MIA. Assume without loss of generality that locations of $\mathcal{A}$ are partitioned into two sets L_0 and L_1, such that edges to L_0 reset the clock while edges to L_1 don't, and initial and final locations of $\mathcal{A}$ lie in L_0. First, we remove all locations in L_1, using the state removal technique in finite automata [35]. This yields an equivalent MIA $\mathcal{A}'$ whose edges are labeled by regular expressions instead of events. Second, we remove clock resets and constraints from $\mathcal{A}'$ by replacing every edge $(\ell, \gamma, x \in I, \{x\}, \ell')$ with $(\ell, (\gamma)_I, \top, \emptyset, \ell')$. We obtain a finite automaton with MIRE labels. We perform again standard state removal to eliminate intermediate locations in L_0. The resulting automaton has only one edge, labeled by a MIRE equivalent to $\mathcal{A}$.

Comparison with MITL. Following Proposition 1, all MIRE properties can be checked using one clock. In contrast, some MITL properties require more than one clock, even when using nondeterminism. For instance the formula $\Box(a \rightarrow \Diamond_{[1,2]} b)$ requires two clocks [25]. In the other direction MIRE feature *untimed* modulo-counting languages, such as $(a^2)^*$, not expressible in MITL. More interestingly, MIRE also feature additional *timed* properties.

Example 2. Consider the expression $\chi \equiv a \cdot ((a^+)_{[1,2]})^+$ over the alphabet $\{a\}$. It describes words w with a subsequence of events a from the first to the last of w such that pairs of adjacent events are separated by 1 to 2 units of time.

We show similarly as in [18] that the language of χ in Example 2 cannot be expressed in MITL. For this, define a family of words (w_n) as follows: $w_0 = \epsilon$, and $w_n = \frac{3}{4} a \, w_{n-1}$ for all $n > 0$. Observe that $w_n \in \mathcal{L}(\chi)$ iff $n > 1$ and n is odd, as illustrated in Fig. 2. In contrast for every MITL formula ψ there exist a bound k such that $w_n \in \mathcal{L}(\psi)$ iff $w_{n+1} \in \mathcal{L}(\psi)$, for all $n \geq k$. This bound is straightforward to obtain by structural induction. Thus, $\mathcal{L}(\chi) \neq \mathcal{L}(\psi)$.

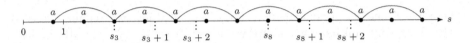

Fig. 2. Timed word w_{13}, with events a occurring at absolute times $s = s_1, s_2, \ldots, s_{13}$. Expression $\chi \equiv a \cdot ((a^+)_{[1,2]})^+$ entails only one possible decomposition of w_{13} as shown. Events at times s_i for i even do not appear in this decomposition but are locally indistinguishable from those at s_j for j odd.

4   From MIRE to Deterministic Timed Automata

In this section, we show that MIRE translate to deterministic timed automata. The first step of the procedure translates a MIRE φ into an equivalent MIA $\mathcal{A}_\varphi$ in a standard way. The second step performs some kind of subset construction to turn $\mathcal{A}_\varphi$ into a deterministic automaton $\mathcal{A}'_\varphi$. Because timed automata have a bounded number of clocks, over a given timed word automaton $\mathcal{A}'_\varphi$ cannot store the set of possible states of $\mathcal{A}_\varphi$ explicitly. To this effect we adapt the notion of approximation of [10] to group in intervals possible clock values in $\mathcal{A}_\varphi$ that have a similar future. We show the soundess of this approximation, and demonstrate how it can be implemented in a deterministic automaton.

Translation to MIA. Automaton $\mathcal{A}_\varphi = (\Sigma, \{x\}, L_\varphi, S_\varphi, \{\ell_\varphi\}, \Delta_\varphi)$ equivalent to the MIRE φ is obtained by structural induction. We assume that automata given by induction hypothesis have disjoint sets of locations, but share the same clock.

- Atomic expressions: $\mathcal{A}_\epsilon$ has its final location ℓ_ϵ marked as initial, and no edge; $\mathcal{A}_a$ further has one edge labeled a from ℓ_ϵ to its final location ℓ_a.
- Disjunction: $\mathcal{A}_{\varphi \cup \psi}$ is obtained by replacing ℓ_φ and ℓ_ψ with $\ell_{\varphi \cup \psi}$ in the component-wise union of $\mathcal{A}_\varphi$ and $\mathcal{A}_\psi$.
- Concatenation: $\mathcal{A}_{\varphi \cdot \psi}$ is defined by letting $L_{\varphi \cdot \psi} = L_\varphi \cup L_\psi \setminus \{\ell_\varphi\}$, $S_{\varphi \cdot \psi} = S_\varphi$ if $\ell_\varphi \notin S_\varphi$, $S_{\varphi \cdot \psi} = S_\varphi \cup S_\psi \setminus \{\ell_\varphi\}$ otherwise, and $\ell_{\varphi \cdot \psi} = \ell_\psi$. The set $\Delta_{\varphi \cdot \psi}$ is obtained from $\Delta_\varphi \cup \Delta_\psi$ by replacing every edge $(\ell, a, \phi, Z, \ell_\varphi)$ with edges $(\ell, a, \phi, Z, \ell')$ for all $\ell' \in S_\psi$.
- Kleene star: without loss of generality, assume that φ^+ is primitive and φ^* is derived as $\epsilon \cup \varphi^+$. Define $\mathcal{A}_{\varphi^+}$ by letting $L_{\varphi^+} = L_\varphi$, $S_{\varphi^+} = S_\varphi$, $\ell_{\varphi^+} = \ell_\varphi$, and $\Delta_{\varphi^+} = \Delta_\varphi \cup \{(\ell, a, \phi, Z, \ell') \mid (\ell, a, \phi, Z, \ell_\varphi) \in \Delta_\varphi, \ell' \in S_\varphi\}$.
- Duration constraint: $\mathcal{A}_{\gamma_I}$ is defined by $L_{\gamma_I} = L_\gamma$, $S_{\gamma_I} = S_\gamma$ if $0 \in I$, $S_{\gamma_I} = S_\gamma \setminus \{\ell_\gamma\}$ otherwise, and $\ell_{\gamma_I} = \ell_\gamma$. The set Δ_{γ_I} is obtained from Δ_γ by replacing every edge $(\ell, a, \top, \emptyset, \ell_\gamma)$ with $(\ell, a, x \in I, \{x\}, \ell_\gamma)$.

Example 2 (Continued). Consider the expression $\chi \equiv a \cdot ((a^+)_{[1,2]})^+$ previously described. Using the above procedure, it translates into the automaton $\mathcal{A}_\chi$ depicted in Fig. 3.

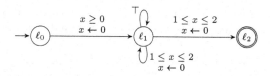

Fig. 3. Automaton $\mathcal{A}_\chi$ translating χ (event labels are omitted).

Parallel Runs. Fix $\mathcal{A}$ a metric interval automaton with clock x. We now treat valuations of x as real values $t \in \mathbb{T}$, and introduce the following definitions. An *interval state* (ℓ, J) pairs a location ℓ with an interval J, representing the set of states $\{(\ell, t) \mid t \in J\}$. A *configuration* is a set of interval states. Transition functions $\overset{t}{\rightsquigarrow}, \overset{a}{\rightarrow}$ between configurations C, D of $\mathcal{A}$ are such that $C \overset{t}{\rightsquigarrow} D$ iff $D = \{(\ell, t \oplus J) \mid (\ell, J) \in C\}$, and $C \overset{a}{\rightarrow} D$ iff $D = \{(\ell', J') \mid \exists (\ell, J) \in C, (\ell, J) \overset{a}{\rightarrow} (\ell', J')\}$. Here, by $(\ell, J) \overset{a}{\rightarrow} (\ell', J')$ we mean that $\mathcal{A}$ has an edge of the form $(\ell, a, \phi, Z, \ell')$ such that $t \models \phi$ for at least one $t \in J$, and $J = J'$ if $Z = \emptyset$, $J = \{0\}$ otherwise. The *parallel run* of automaton $\mathcal{A}$ over some word $w = t_1 a_1 \ldots t_n a_n$ is a sequence of transitions $C_0 \overset{t_1}{\rightsquigarrow} C'_0 \overset{a_1}{\rightarrow} \ldots \overset{t_n}{\rightsquigarrow} C'_{n-1} \overset{a_n}{\longrightarrow} C_n$ labeled by w, where the *initial* configuration C_0 is the set of interval states $(\ell, [0, 0])$ for ℓ initial. All intervals appearing in a parallel run are singular.

Lemma 1. *There exists a run of $\mathcal{A}$ over w finishing in a given location ℓ iff the final configuration of the parallel run of $\mathcal{A}$ over w features ℓ.*

$C_0 \overset{0.5}{\rightsquigarrow}\overset{a}{\rightarrow} \{(\ell_1, [0, 0])\}$

   $\overset{1.3}{\rightsquigarrow}\overset{a}{\rightarrow} \{(\ell_1, [0, 0]),$
       $(\ell_1, [1.3, 1.3]), (\ell_2, [0, 0])\}$

   $\overset{0.3}{\rightsquigarrow}\overset{a}{\rightarrow} \{(\ell_1, [0, 0]), (\ell_1, [0.3, 0.3]),$
       $(\ell_1, [1.6, 1.6]), (\ell_2, [0, 0])\}$

   $\overset{0.2}{\rightsquigarrow}\overset{a}{\rightarrow} \{(\ell_1, [0, 0]), (\ell_1, [0.2, 0.2]),$
       $(\ell_1, [0.5, 0.5]), (\ell_1, [1.8, 1.8]), (\ell_2, [0, 0])\}$

   $\overset{0.9}{\rightsquigarrow}\overset{a}{\rightarrow} \{(\ell_1, [0, 0]), (\ell_1, [0.9, 0.9]), (\ell_1, [1.1, 1.1]),$
       $(\ell_1, [1.4, 1.4]), (\ell_1, [2.7, 2.7]), (\ell_2, [0, 0])\}$

$C_0 \overset{0.5}{\rightsquigarrow}\overset{a}{\rightarrow}\text{-}\overset{\prec}{\text{-}\rightarrow} \{(\ell_1, [0, 0])\}$

   $\overset{1.3}{\rightsquigarrow}\overset{a}{\rightarrow}\text{-}\overset{\prec}{\text{-}\rightarrow} \{(\ell_1, [0, 0]),$
       $(\ell_1, [1.3, 1.3]), (\ell_2, [0, 0])\}$

   $\overset{0.3}{\rightsquigarrow}\overset{a}{\rightarrow}\text{-}\overset{\prec}{\text{-}\rightarrow} \{(\ell_1, [0, 0.3]),$
       $(\ell_1, [1.6, 1.6]), (\ell_2, [0, 0])\}$

   $\overset{0.2}{\rightsquigarrow}\overset{a}{\rightarrow}\text{-}\overset{\prec}{\text{-}\rightarrow} \{(\ell_1, [0, 0.5]),$
       $(\ell_1, [1.8, 1.8]), (\ell_2, [0, 0])\}$

   $\overset{0.9}{\rightsquigarrow}\overset{a}{\rightarrow}\text{-}\overset{\prec}{\text{-}\rightarrow} \{(\ell_1, [0, 1.4]),$
       $(\ell_1, [2.7, 2.7]), (\ell_2, [0, 0])\}$

Fig. 4. The parallel and $\prec$-parallel runs of $\mathcal{A}_\chi$ over w.

Example 2 (Continued). Consider timed word $w = 0.5\,a\,1.3\,a\,0.3\,a\,0.2\,a\,0.9\,a$ and automaton $\mathcal{A}_\chi$. The parallel run of $\mathcal{A}_\chi$ over w is shown in the left part of Fig. 4. Since ℓ_2 appears in the final configuration, we have $w \in \mathcal{L}(\mathcal{A}_\chi)$.

Approximation. We now define an approximation relation (to be correct, a *simulation* relation) between configurations closely matching the one in [10]. Let c, d stand respectively for the largest b and smallest $b - a$ across clock constraints in $\mathcal{A}$ of the form $x \triangleright a \wedge x \triangleleft b$ for some $\triangleright \in \{>, \geq\}$ and $\triangleleft \in \{<, \leq\}$. In the absence of such constraints, take $c = 0$ and $d = \infty$. Approximation relation $\prec$ over configurations will be used to merge intervals either less than d apart, or extend beyond c. It is defined by letting $C \prec D$ when $C \setminus \{(\ell, I), (\ell, J)\} = D \setminus \{(\ell, \mathrm{ch}(I \cup J))\}$ for some $(\ell, I) \neq (\ell, J) \in C$, $(\ell, \mathrm{ch}(I \cup J)) \in D$ such that $\inf J - \sup I < d$ and $\inf I - \sup J < d$, or $\sup(I \cup J) > c$. When all clock constraints are strict (resp. non-strict) we can use $\geq c$ (resp. $\leq d$) instead.

Approximate Parallel Runs. Let us now write $C \xrightarrow{\prec} D$ when D is maximal relative to $\prec$ such that $C \prec^* D$, where $*$ denotes reflexive-transitive closure. A $\prec$-*parallel run* of automaton $\mathcal{A}$ over some word $w = t_1 a_1 \dots t_n a_n$ is a sequence of transitions $C_0 \xrightarrow{t_1} C_0' \xrightarrow{a_1} C_0'' \dashrightarrow \dots \xrightarrow{t_n} C_{n-1}' \xrightarrow{a_n} C_{n-1}'' \dashrightarrow C_n$ labeled by w interleaved with approximations, from the initial configuration C_0. Relation $\prec$ constitutes a faithful abstraction in the sense of the following lemma.

Lemma 2. *For any word w, the set of locations that appear in final configurations of the parallel, and $\prec$-parallel runs of $\mathcal{A}$ over w, are the same.*

The approximation behaves deterministically: for any configuration C of $\mathcal{A}$ there is a unique D such that $C \xrightarrow{\prec} D$. It also ensures the size of configurations also stays bounded. Let $m = |L|$ be the number of locations of $\mathcal{A}$, and let n be the *resolution* of $\mathcal{A}$, defined by $n = \lfloor \frac{c}{d} \rfloor + 2$ if $d < \infty$, 1 otherwise. For any configurations $C \xrightarrow{\prec} D$ of $\mathcal{A}$, we have $|D| \leq mn$.

Example 2 (Continued). The $\prec$-parallel run of $\mathcal{A}_\chi$ over w, shown in the right part of Fig. 4, groups clock values stemming from events number 2 to 5 in w. We check that ℓ_2 appears in the final configuration, and $w \in \mathcal{L}(\mathcal{A}_\chi)$.

Subset Construction. We translate a given MIA $\mathcal{A} = (\Sigma, \{x\}, L, S, F, \Delta)$ to the deterministic timed automaton $\mathcal{A}' = (\Sigma, X', L', S', F', \Delta')$ as follows.

- Clocks: $X' = Y \cup Y'$ with $Y = \{y_1, y_2, \dots, y_{mn}\}$, $Y' = \{y_1', y_2', \dots, y_{mn}'\}$.
- Locations: $L' = 2^{L \times Y \times Y'}$.
- Initial locations: $S' = \{Q_0\}$, where $Q_0 = S \times \{y_1\} \times \{y_1'\}$.
- Accepting locations: $F' = \{Q \in L' \mid Q \cap (F \times Y \times Y') \neq \emptyset\}$.
- Edges: Δ' is built as follows. For every source $P \in L'$, letter a, feasible set of edges $E \subseteq \Delta$, and potential target $Q \in L'$, we construct:
  - constraint $\theta(P, E)$ ensuring that E is exactly the set of edges of $\mathcal{A}$ that can be taken from P;
  - configuration $R(P, E)$ reached when taking such edges;
  - constraint $\lambda_\prec(R, Q)$ ensuring that Q approximates R.

Edges from P to Q are guarded by the conjunction of θ and $\lambda_\prec$, and reset either no clock, one clock in Y, or a pair of clocks in $Y \times Y'$.

Given a valuation v, clock pair $yy' \in Y \times Y'$ represents the interval $[v(y), v(y')]$, location $Q \in L'$ represents the configuration $v(Q) = \{(\ell, [v(y), v(y')]) \mid \ell yy' \in Q\}$.

Edges. We now present in detail the construction of Δ'. For $yy' \in Y \times Y'$ and $\phi \in \Phi(\{x\})$ let $\phi[yy']$ stand for the constraint ϕ in which y (resp. y') replace x in lower (resp. upper) bound comparisons. For any valuation v with $v(y) < v(y')$, we have $v \models \phi[yy']$ iff there exists $t \in [v(y), v(y')]$ such that $t \models \phi$. Now let $P \in L'$ and $a \in \Sigma$. Denote by $\Delta(P, a) \subseteq \Delta$ the set of edges labeled a and whose source location appears in P. Given a subset $E \subseteq \Delta(P, a)$, we define the constraint $\theta(P, E)$ ensuring that edges fired from P upon event a are precisely those in E:

$$\theta(P, E) \equiv \bigwedge\nolimits_{\ell yy' \in P, (\ell, a, \phi, Z, \ell') \in E} \phi[yy'] \wedge \bigwedge\nolimits_{\ell yy' \in P, (\ell, a, \phi, Z, \ell') \in \Delta(P,a) \setminus E} \neg\phi[yy'].$$

Clock resets are temporarily handled using fresh variables y_0 and y'_0, extending sets of clocks to $Y_0 = Y \cup \{y_0\}$, $Y'_0 = Y' \cup \{y'_0\}$ and set of locations to $L'_0 = 2^{L \times Y_0 \times Y'_0}$. The target configuration $R(P, E) \in L'_0$ when firing edges in E from P is defined by letting

$$R(P, E) = \{\ell' yy' \mid \ell yy' \in P, (\ell, a, \top, \emptyset, \ell') \in E\} \cup \{\ell' y_0 y'_0 \mid (\ell, a, \phi, \{x\}, \ell') \in E\}.$$

When $\theta(P, E)$ holds, automaton $\mathcal{A}'$ transits to a configuration that approximates $R(P, E)$. Given configurations $Q, R \in L'_0$, we now define $\lambda_\prec(R, Q)$ ensuring that Q approximates R. We would like that $v \models \lambda_\prec(R, Q)$ iff $v(R) \overset{\prec}{\dashrightarrow} v(Q)$, for all valuations v. But if some clocks share the same value, for a given R there may be more than one Q such that $v(R) \overset{\prec}{\dashrightarrow} v(Q)$. Priority is given to clocks with lowest index. Given indices $i, i', j, j' \in \{0, \dots, mn\}$, $k \in \{i, j\}$ and $k' \in \{i', j'\}$, define

$$\mu_{ii'jj'kk'} \equiv ((y_i - y'_{j'} < c \wedge y_j - y'_{i'} < c) \vee (y_i > d \wedge y_j > d)) \wedge$$
$$(y_i > y_k \vee (y_i = y_k \wedge i \leq k)) \wedge ((y_j > y_k \vee y_j = y_k) \wedge j \leq k) \wedge$$
$$(y'_{i'} < y'_{k'} \vee (y'_{i'} = y'_{k'} \wedge i' \leq k')) \wedge (y'_{j'} < y'_{k'} \vee (y'_{j'} = y'_{k'} \wedge j' \leq k')).$$

For any $\ell \in L$, constraint $\mu_{ii'jj'kk'}$ ensures that $\ell y_i y'_{i'}$ and $\ell y_j y'_{j'}$ should be merged to $\ell y_k y'_{k'}$. The constraint $\lambda_\prec(R, Q)$ is defined as the conjunction of two parts: (1) the disjunction over well-formed chains of merges $i_1 i'_1 j_1 j'_1 k_1 k'_1, \dots, i_h i'_h j_h j'_h k_h k'_h$ from R to Q of conjunctions of μ over the chains; (2) the conjunction of $\neg\mu$ over all possible merges in Q. This guarantees that one such chain is (1) correct and (2) maximal in length. We can now replace temporary variables y_0, y'_0 with available clocks in $Y \cup Y'$. Let us define the set of clocks Z_Q as follows:

– If both y_0 and y'_0 occur in Q, let $Z_Q = \{y_i, y'_{i'}\}$ for $i, i' \geq 1$ the least indices such that $y_i, y'_{i'}$ do not occur in Q;

- If y_0 occurs in Q but not y_0', let $Z_Q = \{y_i\}$ for $i \geq 1$ the least index such that y_i does not occur in Q;
- Otherwise, let $Z_Q = \emptyset$.

We write $\overline{Q} \in L$ to denote the configuration Q in which y_0, y_0' are replaced by clocks in Z_Q. The set of edges of $\mathcal{A}'$ is obtained by letting

$$\Delta' = \{(P, a, \theta(P, E) \wedge \lambda_\prec(R(P, E), Q), Z_Q, \overline{Q}) \mid P \in L', a \in \Sigma, Q \in L_0',$$
$$E \subseteq \Delta(P, a)\}.$$

Theorem 3 (MIRE $\Rightarrow$ DTA). *For any MIRE of size m and resolution n, one can construct an equivalent deterministic timed automaton with $2mn$ clocks and $2^{m^3 n^2 + 1}$ locations.*

Example 2 (Continued). Applying the above procedure to $\mathcal{A}_\chi$, we obtain automaton $\mathcal{A}_\chi'$ of Fig. 5. We use the following simplifications. In $\mathcal{A}_\chi$, any state in location ℓ_1 with clock value above 2 cannot reach ℓ_2. We remove interval states $\ell y y'$ from target configurations of $\mathcal{A}_\chi'$ for any $y \in Y$ such that $y > 2$. Transitions preserve the ordering of non-reset clocks, and we use this to simplify clock constraints. Locations not (co-)reachable are also removed.

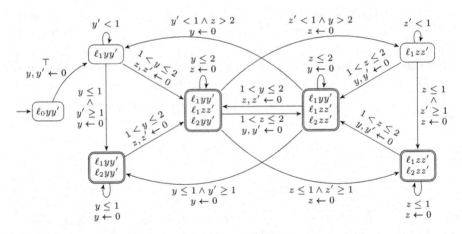

Fig. 5. Automaton $\mathcal{A}_\chi'$ determinizing $\mathcal{A}_\chi$ (event labels are omitted).

5   Metric Interval Dynamic Logic

We now introduce *metric interval dynamic logic* (MIDL) as the dynamic logic of MIRE. It provides linear dynamic logic (LDL) [13,15] with timing constraints.

Syntax. MIDL formulas ψ and expressions φ are given by the grammar

$$\psi ::= a \mid \neg\psi \mid \psi \vee \psi \mid \langle\varphi\rangle\psi$$
$$\varphi ::= \gamma_I \mid \varphi \cdot \varphi \mid \varphi \cup \varphi \mid \varphi^*$$
$$\gamma ::= \epsilon \mid \psi? \mid \gamma \cdot \gamma \mid \gamma \cup \gamma \mid \gamma^*$$

where $a \in \Sigma$ and I is a non-singular integer-bounded interval. The *size* of an MIDL formula is the total size of expressions φ in its modalities $\langle \varphi \rangle$. The *resolution* of MIDL formulas is defined inductively as for MITL.

The form $\langle \varphi \rangle \psi$ is known as *suffix conjunction* and is satisfied when ψ holds at some future time instant such that φ matches the events from now to that time instant. When φ is of the form γ_I for simplicity we write $\langle \gamma \rangle_I \psi$ in place of $\langle \gamma_I \rangle \psi$. Observe that $\langle \varphi_1 \cdot \varphi_2 \rangle \psi \Leftrightarrow \langle \varphi_1 \rangle \langle \varphi_2 \rangle \psi$ and $\langle \varphi_1 \cup \varphi_2 \rangle \psi \Leftrightarrow \langle \varphi_1 \rangle \psi \vee \langle \varphi_2 \rangle \psi$, hence when no star is applied to a timed subexpression, formulas can be rewritten using modalities of the form $\langle \gamma \rangle_I$ only. The form ψ? is known as a *test* and matches any time instant where ψ holds. We also write a in place of a? for any $a \in \Sigma$. Using this convention, MIRE are a fragment of MIDL.

Semantics. The semantics $\models$ of MIDL formulas is defined over pointed words, with the same inductive definitions as MITL in the case of events $a \in \Sigma$ and Boolean connectives $\neg$, $\vee$. The case of suffix implication $\langle \varphi \rangle$ is as follows:

$$(w, i) \models \langle \varphi \rangle \psi \qquad \text{iff} \qquad (w, i, j) \models \varphi \text{ and } (w, j) \models \psi \text{ for some } j \geq i.$$

The semantics $\models$ of MIDL expressions is defined over *bi-pointed words*, triples (w, i, j) of timed word w and positions $0 \leq i \leq j \leq |w|$, as follows.

$(w, i, j) \models \epsilon$	iff	$j = i$
$(w, i, j) \models \psi$?	iff	$j = i + 1$ and $(w, j) \models \psi$
$(w, i, j) \models \varphi_1 \cdot \varphi_2$	iff	$(w, i, k) \models \varphi_1$ and $(w, k, j) \models \varphi_2$ for some k
$(w, i, j) \models \varphi_1 \cup \varphi_2$	iff	$(w, i, j) \models \varphi_1$ or $(w, i, j) \models \varphi_2$
$(w, i, j) \models \varphi^*$	iff	$(w, i, j) \models \varphi^k$ for some k
$(w, i, j) \models \varphi_I$	iff	$(w, i, j) \models \varphi$ and $\|w_{i..j}\| \in I$.

This semantics definition is compatible with that of MIRE and TRE in general. The language $\mathcal{L}(\psi)$ of formula ψ is defined by $\mathcal{L}(\psi) = \{w \mid (w, 1) \models \psi\}$.

Temporal Logic. The *until* operator can be defined in MIDL as the abbreviation $\psi_1 \, \mathcal{U}_I \, \psi_2 \equiv \langle \psi_1 ?^* \cdot \top ? \rangle_I \psi_2$. We also use operators *always* and *eventually* as previously. In general MIDL is more expressive than MITL.

Example 3. Consider the formula $\xi \equiv \Box a \rightarrow \langle \top ?^* \cdot b \cdot \top ?^+ \rangle_{(0,1)} c)$ over the alphabet $\{a, b, c, d\}$. It describes words in which every occurrence of a triggers in the future within less than one time unit an occurrence of b followed by one of c.

A conjecture of [4], proved in [9], states that formulas similar to the one above cannot be expressed in MITL. Replacing b, c by arbitrary formulas, we obtain an instance of so-called *Pnueli modality* [18]. The simpler *threshold counting* modalities $\langle (\top ?^* \cdot \varphi ?)^{k-1} \cdot \top ?^+ \rangle_I \varphi$, requiring that φ holds k times within I time units, already cannot be expressed in MITL for $k > 1$, see [18].

Automata Modalities. Let us define *extended MITL* (EMITL) by adding to MITL the syntactic clause $\psi ::= \mathcal{A}(\psi_1, \ldots, \psi_m)$, where $\mathcal{A}$ is a metric interval automaton over the alphabet $2^{\{\psi_1,\ldots,\psi_m\}}$. The semantics of this clause is such that $(w,i) \models A(\psi_1,\ldots,\psi_m)$ iff the word $t_{i+1}\Psi_{i+1}\ldots t_n \Psi_n$ is accepted by $\mathcal{A}$, where each t_j is the j-th delay in w and each Ψ_j is the subset of formulas amongst $\psi_1,\ldots,\psi_m$ satisfied at position j.

Proposition 2 (MIDL ⇔ EMITL). *Every MIDL translates to an equivalent EMITL formula, and every EMITL translates to an equivalent MIDL formula.*

We translate an MIDL formula into EMITL by recursively replacing every suffix conjunction $\langle\varphi\rangle\psi$ with the modality $A(\psi_1,\ldots,\psi_m,\psi)$, such that $\mathcal{A}$ translates the expression $\varphi \cdot \psi? \cdot (\top?)^*$ in which atomic expressions $\psi_1?,\ldots,\psi_m?,\psi?$ are replaced by compatible subsets of $\{\psi_1,\ldots,\psi_m,\psi\}$.

Example 3 (Continued). Formula $\xi \equiv \Box(a \to (\top?^* \cdot b \cdot \top?^+)_{(0,1)}\, c)$ is rewritten in EMITL as $\xi' \equiv \Box(a \to \mathcal{B})$, where $\mathcal{B}$ is the MIA given in Fig. 6.

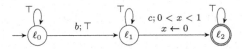

Fig. 6. Automaton $\mathcal{B}$ appearing as subformula in ξ'.

Conversely EMITL translate to MIDL replacing automata $\mathcal{A}(\psi_1,\ldots,\psi_m)$ with suffix conjunctions $\langle\varphi\rangle\neg\langle\top?\rangle\top$, where φ translates $\mathcal{A}$. Here the role of subformula $\neg\langle\top?\rangle\top$ is to recognize the last position in the word.

Expressiveness. Supplementing MITL with automata modalities has been proposed by [37] and [17]. The logic of [37] corresponds to the MIDL fragment where all modalities φ are of the form $\langle\gamma\rangle_I$, equivalently, where no star is applied to a timed expression. We call this fragment *basic MIDL*, and show that it is strictly less expressive. In particular, the MIRE $\chi \equiv a \cdot ((a^+)_{[1,2]})^+$ of Example 2 cannot be expressed as a basic MIDL formula. The family (w_n) of Sect. 3 is not a witness of this fact, since it can be classified for χ using a simple modulo-2 counter. Instead we consider timed words w_n^k, with $k > 0$ events clustered around the events in w_n, as illustrated in Fig. 7. Formally, we let $w_0^k = \epsilon$ and $w_n^k = t_n^k\, a\, w_{n-1}^k$ for all $n > 0$, with delays t_n^k given by $t_n^k = \frac{1}{2} + \frac{1}{4k}$ if $n \equiv 0 \pmod{k}$, $t_n^k = \frac{1}{4k}$ otherwise. We claim that for any basic formula ψ there is a k such that for large enough n either both w_n^k and w_{n+k}^k satisfy ψ, or neither. This disagrees with χ, which recognizes exactly one of w_n^k and w_{n+k}^k.

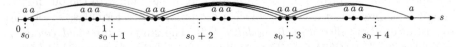

Fig. 7. Timed word w_{18}^3 with events occurring at absolute times $s = s_0,\ldots,s_{17}$. Expression $\chi \equiv a \cdot ((a^+)_{[1,2]})^+$ entails several decompositions of w_{18} as shown. Over words w_n^3 the number of events per interval $[s_i + c, s_i + d]$ for $c < d$ fixed integers and fixed n is either constant or periodic with period 3 as a function of $i < n - 4d$.

6 From MIDL to Nondeterministic Timed Automata

In this section we present a compositional translation of MIDL based on *temporal testers* [26,27,33]. The first step of the procedure turns the MIDL formula into an EMITL formula, and we consider this step implicit. The second step builds testers for every operator of the formula, and composes them together.

Temporal Testers. We introduce the framework of our translation. Let B be a set of Boolean variables. Valuations $u : B \rightarrow \{0,1\}$ are identified with elements of 2^B, under the convention that $u(p) = 1$ iff $p \in u$, for any $p \in B$. In the interest of simplicity, we assume an alphabet of events of the form $\Sigma = 2^A$. We call *timed component* an automaton over an alphabet Σ' of the form 2^B for some $B \supseteq A$. The projection of a timed word $w = t_1 u_1 \ldots t_n u_n$ over variables B onto variables A is defined as $w|_A = t_1(u_1 \cap A) \ldots t_n(u_n \cap A)$. The synchronous product $\mathcal{T}_1 \otimes \mathcal{T}_2$ of timed components $\mathcal{T}_1$ and $\mathcal{T}_2$, defined in the expected way, is such that a timed word w is accepted by $\mathcal{T}_1 \otimes \mathcal{T}_2$ iff w is accepted by both $\mathcal{T}_1$ and $\mathcal{T}_2$ when projected onto their respective variables (see [26] for more details). Let ψ be a formula over $\Sigma = 2^A$ and $\mathcal{T}$ a timed component over $\Sigma' = 2^B$ with output variable $p \in B \setminus A$. We say that $\mathcal{T}[p]$ is a *tester* of ψ when the following conditions hold:

1. For all timed words w over Σ there exists a timed word w' accepted by $\mathcal{T}$ such that w is the projection of w';
2. For all timed words w' accepted by $\mathcal{T}$, and all positions $0 < i \leq |w'|$ it holds $(w', i) \models p$ if and only if $(w', i) \models \psi$.

Compositionality. The construction of a tester $\mathcal{T}_\psi[p]$ for formula ψ is inductive on the structure of ψ. For each subformula ψ' of ψ, we construct a tester for its main subformulas, and compose it with a tester associated to its main operator:

$$\mathcal{T}_{\neg \varphi}[p] = \mathcal{T}_{\neg q}[p] \otimes \mathcal{T}_\varphi[q]$$
$$\mathcal{T}_{\varphi \vee \psi}[p] = \mathcal{T}_{q \vee r}[p] \otimes \mathcal{T}_\varphi[q] \otimes \mathcal{T}_\psi[r]$$
$$\mathcal{T}_{\mathcal{A}(\psi_1, \ldots, \psi_m)}[p] = \mathcal{T}_{\mathcal{A}(q_1, \ldots, q_m)}[p] \otimes \mathcal{T}_{\psi_1}[q_1] \otimes \ldots \otimes \mathcal{T}_{\psi_m}[q_m].$$

Testers for atomic formulas and propositional operators are simple one-state components, with edges labeled by matching valuations of variables. Testers for automata modalities are presented in the rest of this section. An acceptor $\mathcal{A}_\psi$ of $\mathcal{L}(\psi)$ is obtained by product of $\mathcal{T}_\psi[p]$ with a two-state component enforcing that p holds at position 1 in the input word, and projection onto $\Sigma = 2^A$.

Automata Modalities. For a given MIA $\mathcal{A} = (\Sigma, X, L, S, F, \Delta)$, the tester $\mathcal{T}_\mathcal{A}[p]$ predicts at each position whether $\mathcal{A}$ accepts the corresponding suffix, and outputs the prediction in p. If $\mathcal{T}_\mathcal{A}[p]$ predicts that $\mathcal{A}$ accepts the suffix from i, then it creates a *positive obligation* attached to an initial state, and nondeterministically follows one run of $\mathcal{A}$ from this state. If $\mathcal{T}_\mathcal{A}[p]$ predicts that $\mathcal{A}$ rejects the suffix from i, then it creates a *negative obligation* attached to all initial states, and deterministically follows all runs of $\mathcal{A}$ from those states.

Let c and d be the maximum magnitude and minimum width of clock constraints in $\mathcal{A}$, defined as in Sect. 4. We define $\preccurlyeq$ as the approximation relation that verifies $C \preccurlyeq D$ when $C \setminus \{(\ell, I), (\ell, J)\} = D \setminus \{(\ell, \mathrm{ch}(I \cup J))\}$ for some distinct $(\ell, I), (\ell, J), (\ell, K) \in C$, $(\ell, \mathrm{ch}(I \cup J)) \in D$ such that $\sup I \cup J \cup K - \inf I \cup J \cup K < d$ and $K \cap \mathrm{ch}(I \cup J) = \emptyset$, or $\inf K > \inf J > c$.

Approximation $\preccurlyeq$ nondeterministically merges two intervals amongst three within the same window of length d. Assume $\inf J \le \inf K \le \inf H$; after a delay $t \in \mathbb{T}$ if $t \oplus K \subseteq I$ then either $t \oplus J \subseteq I$ or $t \oplus H \subseteq I$. Similar remarks can be made for intervals above c; this settles the correctness of the approximation relative to positive obligations. For negative obligations we see that $\preccurlyeq$ is finer than $\prec$ of Sect. 4. The approximation $\prec$ merges intervals separated by a period less than d, while $\preccurlyeq$ merges intervals lying in a window less than d long.

Let m and n be the number of locations, and resolution of $\mathcal{A}$. Any D such that $C \dashrightarrow^{\preccurlyeq} D$ for some C now has at most $2mn$ interval states.

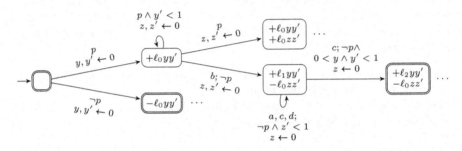

Fig. 8. A few locations and edges of component $\mathcal{T}_B[p]$ (for convenience, the value of p is handled using additional propositional constraints p and $\neg p$).

Subset Construction. We transform the MIA $\mathcal{A} = (\Sigma, X, L, S, F, \Delta)$ into the tester $\mathcal{T}_\mathcal{A}[p] = (\Sigma', X', L', S', F', \Delta')$ defined as follows.

- Clocks: $X' = Y \cup Y'$, where $Y = \{y_1, \ldots, y_{2mn}\}$ and $Y' = \{y'_1, \ldots, y'_{2mn}\}$.
- Locations: $L' = 2^{\{-,+\} \times L \times Y \times Y'}$, sets of (negative, positive) obligations.
- Initial locations: $E' = \{\emptyset\}$.
- Accepting locations: $F' = 2^{(\{-\} \times (L \setminus F) \cup \{+\} \times F) \times Y \times Y'}$, such that all positive (negative) obligations are attached to accepting (rejecting) states.
- Edges: we define $\lambda_{\preccurlyeq}(R, Q)$, Z_Q and $\overline{Q}$ similarly as in Sect. 4, and let

$$\Delta' = \{(P, u, \lambda_{\preccurlyeq}(R, Q) \wedge \theta(P, E), Z_Q, \overline{Q}) \mid P \in L', u \in \Sigma', E \in \Delta(P, u \cap \Sigma),$$
$$R \in R_{u(p)}(P, E), Q \in L'_0\}$$

where $\theta(P, E)$, $\Delta(P, a)$ for $a \in \Sigma$, and $R_i(P, E)$ for $i = 0, 1$ are defined below.

Given $P \in L'$ and $a \in \Sigma$, we denote $\Delta(P, a)$ the set of subsets $E \subseteq \Delta$ such that for all $+\ell x x' \in P$ there exists $\delta = (\ell, a, \phi, Z, \ell') \in E$, and for all

$-\ell x x' \in P$ and $\delta = (\ell, a, \phi, Z, \ell')$, if $\delta \in \Delta$ then $\delta \in E$. The constraint $\theta(P, E)$, defined similarly as in Sect. 4, ensures E contains all feasible edges from negatively marked locations, and one feasible edge from each positively marked location. We denote L'_0 locations of L' with additional variables y_0, y'_0 as previously. Define the target configuration $R(P, E) \in L'_0$ when taking edges E from P as follows: $R(P, E) = \{s\ell' yy' \mid (\ell, a, \top, \emptyset, \ell') \in E, s\ell yy' \in P\} \cup \{s\ell' y_0 y'_0 \mid (\ell, a, \phi, \{x\}, \ell') \in E, s\ell yy' \in P\}$. When the prediction p is false the set of possible target configurations is given by $R_0(P, E) = \{R(P, E)\}$, and when the prediction p is true, given by $R_1(P, E) = \{(R(P, E) \cup \{+\ell y_0 y'_0\}) \mid \ell \in S\}$. This completes the construction of $\mathcal{T}_A[p]$.

Theorem 4 (MIDL $\Rightarrow$ NTA). *For any MIDL formula of size m and resolution n one can construct an equivalent timed automaton $\mathcal{A}_\varphi$ with $4mn$ clocks and $2^{8m^3 n^2 + 1}$ locations.*

Example 3 (Continued). Consider automaton $\mathcal{B}$ of Fig. 6. We illustrate the process of constructing its tester in Fig. 8. After constructing $\mathcal{T}_\mathcal{B}[p]$, we obtain the tester for ξ' as the product $\mathcal{T}_{\xi'}[r] = \mathcal{T}_{\square q}[r] \otimes \mathcal{T}_{a \to p}[q] \otimes \mathcal{T}_\mathcal{B}[p]$. To get an acceptor for ξ, we take the product of $\mathcal{T}_{\xi'}[r]$ with some acceptor of r and project back the result onto alphabet Σ.

7   Discussion

We extended the punctuality relaxation of [3] to timed versions of regular expressions and dynamic logic, generalizing results of [17,37]. The expressions we introduced have a direct connection with automata. Their expressiveness is limited to a small class of one-clock timed automata, also related to *perturbed timed automata* [5]. However in the setting of dynamic logic, such expressions yield an expressive specification language with good decidability properties:

Corollary 1. *The satisfiability of MIDL and the model checking of timed automata against MIDL are EXPSPACE-complete.*

The lower bound follows from the discrete-time case, while the upper bound is obtained by reduction to timed automata language emptiness, see [3]. Decision procedures for MITL have recently been gaining interest, with implementations of [8,12] and formalization by [34]. An interesting direction for future work would be to assess experimentally the efficiency of MIDL decision procedures derived from Corollary 1.

Metric dynamic logic was independently proposed by [7] in the context of monitoring. Extensions of metric temporal logic with regular expressions modalities were also studied by [23]. The logic *MITL+URat* of [23] is equivalent to *basic MIDL* discussed in the present paper. Its modalities $\psi_1 \mathcal{U}_{\gamma,I} \psi_2$ can be written $\langle \gamma \cap (\psi_1?^* \cdot \top?) \rangle_I \psi_2$ (the intersection $\cap$ of untimed expressions γ and $\psi_1?^* \cdot \top?$ can be eliminated in polynomial time) and in the other direction $\langle \gamma \rangle_I \psi$ rewrites into $\top \mathcal{U}_{\gamma,I} \psi$. Both logics are equivalent (and translate in polynomial time) to the *EMITL* of [37]. Complexity of the satisfiability problem was not studied by [37], whose proofs can only give non-elementary upper bounds. The present work improves on the 2EXPSPACE upper bound of [23] by providing a tight EXPSPACE construction. The more general *MITL + Rat* [23] has non-elementary complexity. The position of MIDL in the expressiveness landscape of decidable MTL variants (see also [22]) is a topic for future research.

The family of languages considered in this paper are all recognizable by one-clock *alternating* timed automata (OCATA) [24,30]. Our determinization procedure uses a timed variant of the classical subset construction inspired from [10]. The authors of [10,11] consider the dual problem of eliminating universal non-determinism in OCATA stemming from the translation [30] of MITL formulas. The transition graph in an MIA has more structure than in OCATA stemming from MITL translations, requiring additional clocks to follow states moving to the same location using separate paths. While the emptiness problem for OCATA is decidable over finite words, its complexity is non-elementary [24,30]. Generalizations of this model with Büchi conditions, two-wayness, or silent transitions all lead to undecidability [1]. On the contrary our expressions and logic have elementary decision procedures, which can in principle be extended to handle ω-words, past operators, and continuous-time Boolean signals.

Acknowledgments. I thank Eugene Asarin, Tom Henzinger, Oded Maler, Dejan Ničković, and anonymous reviewers of multiple conferences for their helpful feedback.

References

1. Abdulla, P.A., Deneux, J., Ouaknine, J., Quaas, K., Worrell, J.: Universality analysis for one-clock timed automata. Fundam. Inform. **89**(4), 419–450 (2008)
2. Alur, R., Dill, D.L.: A theory of timed automata. Theor. Comput. Sci. **126**(2), 183–235 (1994)
3. Alur, R., Feder, T., Henzinger, T.A.: The benefits of relaxing punctuality. J. ACM **43**(1), 116–146 (1996)
4. Alur, R., Henzinger, T.A.: Logics and models of real time: a survey. In: de Bakker, J.W., Huizing, C., de Roever, W.P., Rozenberg, G. (eds.) REX 1991. LNCS, vol. 600, pp. 74–106. Springer, Heidelberg (1992). https://doi.org/10.1007/BFb0031988
5. Alur, R., La Torre, S., Madhusudan, P.: Perturbed timed automata. In: Morari, M., Thiele, L. (eds.) HSCC 2005. LNCS, vol. 3414, pp. 70–85. Springer, Heidelberg (2005). https://doi.org/10.1007/978-3-540-31954-2_5
6. Asarin, E., Caspi, P., Maler, O.: Timed regular expressions. J. ACM **49**(2), 172–206 (2002)
7. Basin, D., Krstić, S., Traytel, D.: Almost event-rate independent monitoring of metric dynamic logic. In: Lahiri, S., Reger, G. (eds.) RV 2017. LNCS, vol. 10548, pp. 85–102. Springer, Cham (2017). https://doi.org/10.1007/978-3-319-67531-2_6
8. Bersani, M.M., Rossi, M., Pietro, P.S.: A tool for deciding the satisfiability of continuous-time metric temporal logic. Acta Informatica **53**(2), 171–206 (2016)
9. Bouyer, P., Chevalier, F., Markey, N.: On the expressiveness of TPTL and MTL. In: Sarukkai, S., Sen, S. (eds.) FSTTCS 2005. LNCS, vol. 3821, pp. 432–443. Springer, Heidelberg (2005). https://doi.org/10.1007/11590156_35

10. Brihaye, T., Estiévenart, M., Geeraerts, G.: On MITL and alternating timed automata. In: Braberman, V., Fribourg, L. (eds.) FORMATS 2013. LNCS, vol. 8053, pp. 47–61. Springer, Heidelberg (2013). https://doi.org/10.1007/978-3-642-40229-6_4

11. Brihaye, T., Estiévenart, M., Geeraerts, G.: On MITL and alternating timed automata over infinite words. In: Legay, A., Bozga, M. (eds.) FORMATS 2014. LNCS, vol. 8711, pp. 69–84. Springer, Cham (2014). https://doi.org/10.1007/978-3-319-10512-3_6

12. Brihaye, T., Geeraerts, G., Ho, H.-M., Monmege, B.: MightyL: a compositional translation from MITL to timed automata. In: Majumdar, R., Kunčak, V. (eds.) CAV 2017. LNCS, vol. 10426, pp. 421–440. Springer, Cham (2017). https://doi.org/10.1007/978-3-319-63387-9_21

13. De Giacomo, G., Vardi, M.Y.: Linear temporal logic and linear dynamic logic on finite traces. IJCAI **13**, 854–860 (2013)

14. Eisner, C., Fisman, D.: A Practical Introduction to PSL. Integrated Circuits and Systems. Springer, Heidelberg (2006). https://doi.org/10.1007/978-0-387-36123-9

15. Fischer, M.J.: Propositional dynamic logic of regular programs. J. Comput. Syst. Sci. **18**(2), 194–211 (1979)

16. Furia, C.A., Rossi, M.: MTL with bounded variability: decidability and complexity. In: Cassez, F., Jard, C. (eds.) FORMATS 2008. LNCS, vol. 5215, pp. 109–123. Springer, Heidelberg (2008). https://doi.org/10.1007/978-3-540-85778-5_9

17. Henzinger, T.A., Raskin, J.-F., Schobbens, P.-Y.: The regular real-time languages. In: Larsen, K.G., Skyum, S., Winskel, G. (eds.) ICALP 1998. LNCS, vol. 1443, pp. 580–591. Springer, Heidelberg (1998). https://doi.org/10.1007/BFb0055086

18. Hirshfeld, Y., Rabinovich, A.: An expressive temporal logic for real time. In: Královič, R., Urzyczyn, P. (eds.) MFCS 2006. LNCS, vol. 4162, pp. 492–504. Springer, Heidelberg (2006). https://doi.org/10.1007/11821069_43

19. Hirshfeld, Y., Rabinovich, A.: Expressiveness of metric modalities for continuous time. In: Grigoriev, D., Harrison, J., Hirsch, E.A. (eds.) CSR 2006. LNCS, vol. 3967, pp. 211–220. Springer, Heidelberg (2006). https://doi.org/10.1007/11753728_23

20. Kleene, S.C.: Representation of events in nerve nets and finite automata. Automata Stud., 3–42 (1956)

21. Koymans, R.: Specifying real-time properties with metric temporal logic. Real-Time Syst. **2**(4), 255–299 (1990)

22. Krishna, S.N., Madnani, K., Pandya, P.K.: Metric temporal logic with counting. In: Jacobs, B., Löding, C. (eds.) FoSSaCS 2016. LNCS, vol. 9634, pp. 335–352. Springer, Heidelberg (2016). https://doi.org/10.1007/978-3-662-49630-5_20

23. Krishna, S.N., Madnani, K., Pandya, P.K.: Making metric temporal logic rational. In: Mathematical Foundations of Computer Science, pp. 77:1–77:14 (2017)

24. Lasota, S., Walukiewicz, I.: Alternating timed automata. In: Sassone, V. (ed.) FoSSaCS 2005. LNCS, vol. 3441, pp. 250–265. Springer, Heidelberg (2005). https://doi.org/10.1007/978-3-540-31982-5_16

25. Maler, O., Nickovic, D., Pnueli, A.: Real time temporal logic: past, present, future. In: Pettersson, P., Yi, W. (eds.) FORMATS 2005. LNCS, vol. 3829, pp. 2–16. Springer, Heidelberg (2005). https://doi.org/10.1007/11603009_2

26. Maler, O., Nickovic, D., Pnueli, A.: From MITL to timed automata. In: Asarin, E., Bouyer, P. (eds.) FORMATS 2006. LNCS, vol. 4202, pp. 274–289. Springer, Heidelberg (2006). https://doi.org/10.1007/11867340_20

27. Michel, M.: Composition of temporal operators. Logique et Analyse **28**(110/111), 137–152 (1985)

28. Ničković, D., Piterman, N.: From MTL to deterministic timed automata. In: Chatterjee, K., Henzinger, T.A. (eds.) FORMATS 2010. LNCS, vol. 6246, pp. 152–167. Springer, Heidelberg (2010). https://doi.org/10.1007/978-3-642-15297-9_13
29. Ouaknine, J., Rabinovich, A., Worrell, J.: Time-bounded verification. In: Bravetti, M., Zavattaro, G. (eds.) CONCUR 2009. LNCS, vol. 5710, pp. 496–510. Springer, Heidelberg (2009). https://doi.org/10.1007/978-3-642-04081-8_33
30. Ouaknine, J., Worrell, J.: On the decidability of metric temporal logic. In: Logic in Computer Science, pp. 188–197. IEEE (2005)
31. Ouaknine, J., Worrell, J.: On metric temporal logic and faulty turing machines. In: Aceto, L., Ingólfsdóttir, A. (eds.) FoSSaCS 2006. LNCS, vol. 3921, pp. 217–230. Springer, Heidelberg (2006). https://doi.org/10.1007/11690634_15
32. Pnueli, A.: The temporal logic of programs. In: Foundations of Computer Science, pp. 46–57. IEEE (1977)
33. Pnueli, A., Zaks, A.: On the merits of temporal testers. In: Grumberg, O., Veith, H. (eds.) 25 Years of Model Checking. LNCS, vol. 5000, pp. 172–195. Springer, Heidelberg (2008). https://doi.org/10.1007/978-3-540-69850-0_11
34. Roohi, N., Viswanathan, M.: Revisiting MITL to fix decision procedures. In: Verification, Model Checking, and Abstract Interpretation. LNCS, vol. 10747, pp. 474–494. Springer, Cham (2018). https://doi.org/10.1007/978-3-319-73721-8_22
35. Sipser, M.: Introduction to the Theory of Computation, vol. 2. Thomson Course Technology, Boston (2006)
36. Vardi, M.Y.: From philosophical to industrial logics. In: Ramanujam, R., Sarukkai, Sundar (eds.) ICLA 2009. LNCS (LNAI), vol. 5378, pp. 89–115. Springer, Heidelberg (2008). https://doi.org/10.1007/978-3-540-92701-3_7
37. Wilke, T.: Specifying timed state sequences in powerful decidable logics and timed automata. In: Langmaack, H., de Roever, W.-P., Vytopil, J. (eds.) FTRTFT 1994. LNCS, vol. 863, pp. 694–715. Springer, Heidelberg (1994). https://doi.org/10.1007/3-540-58468-4_191

IPL: An Integration Property Language for Multi-model Cyber-physical Systems

Ivan Ruchkin$^{(\boxtimes)}$, Joshua Sunshine, Grant Iraci, Bradley Schmerl, and David Garlan

Institute for Software Research, Carnegie Mellon University, Pittsburgh, PA, USA
iruchkin@cs.cmu.edu

Abstract. Design and verification of modern systems requires diverse models, which often come from a variety of disciplines, and it is challenging to manage their heterogeneity – especially in the case of cyber-physical systems. To check consistency between models, recent approaches map these models to flexible static abstractions, such as architectural views. This model integration approach, however, comes at a cost of reduced expressiveness because complex behaviors of the models are abstracted away. As a result, it may be impossible to automatically verify important behavioral properties across multiple models, leaving systems vulnerable to subtle bugs. This paper introduces the *Integration Property Language (IPL)* that improves integration expressiveness using modular verification of properties that depend on detailed behavioral semantics while retaining the ability for static system-wide reasoning. We prove that the verification algorithm is sound and analyze its termination conditions. Furthermore, we perform a case study on a mobile robot to demonstrate IPL is practically useful and evaluate its performance.

1 Introduction

Today, complex software systems are often built by multidisciplinary teams using diverse engineering methods [1,2]. This diversity is particularly apparent in *cyber-physical systems* (CPS) where software control interacts with the physical world. For instance, a mobile robot needs to brake in time to avoid collisions, compute an efficient long-term plan, and use a power model of its hardware to ensure it has sufficient energy to complete its missions. To satisfy each of these requirements, engineers may use heterogeneous models that vary in formalisms, concepts, and levels of abstraction. Even though these models are separate, interdependencies naturally occur because they represent the same system.

Mismatches between such implicitly dependent models may lead to faults and system failures. For example, the 2014 GM ignition switch recall was caused by an unanticipated interaction between electrical and mechanical aspects of the ignition switch [3]. This interaction led to the switch accidentally turning off mid-drive and disabling the car's software along with airbags, power steering, and

© Springer International Publishing AG, part of Springer Nature 2018
K. Havelund et al. (Eds.): FM 2018, LNCS 10951, pp. 165–184, 2018.
https://doi.org/10.1007/978-3-319-95582-7_10

power brakes. This mismatch between the electrical, mechanical, and software designs caused dozens of deaths and large financial losses.

To prevent such issues, inconsistencies or contradictions need to be detected by *integrating* the heterogeneous models. This can be done by checking properties that involve multiple models and formalisms, which we term *integration properties*. Model integration is difficult [4] and checking integration properties is often done informally through inspection, and is limited in rigor and outcomes. One way to improve this would be to map diverse semantics and property checks into a single unifying model. Unfortunately, it is hard (and sometimes impossible) to do so, as in the case of unifying stateful and stateless models [5].

A common way to integrate heterogeneous models is to create and relate simplified abstractions. One such abstraction is *architectural views* — behavior-less component models annotated with types and properties [6–8]. Since views are easier to reason about than heterogeneous models, structural consistency checks can be formalized and automated [9]. However, model integration through views sacrifices behavioral expressiveness of integration properties, meaning that sophisticated interactions become uncheckable.

We perceive a *foundational gap* between the limited expressiveness of integration properties and the need to discover complex inconsistencies of several models. State-of-the-art integration approaches are limited in what is exposed from models. Exposing too little leads to insufficiently expressive analysis. Exposing too much leads to limited flexibility and extensibility of integration methods.

To help bridge this gap, this paper introduces the *Integration Property Language (IPL)* – a formal specification and verification method for integration properties based on architectural views. IPL's goal is to systematically express and automatically check properties that combine system behaviors and static abstractions, enabling end-to-end verification arguments over multiple models.

The main design principle behind IPL is to combine first-order logical reasoning across many views with "deep dives" into behavioral structures of individual models as necessary. IPL syntax interleaves first-order quantification over *rigid* constructs (defined by views) and temporal modalities that bind the behavior of *flexible* terms (changing according to models). Built upon existing satisfiability solvers and model checkers, IPL uses a sound reasoning algorithm to modularize the problem into subproblems that respective tools interpret and solve.

This paper makes three contributions: (1) a *formalized modular syntax and semantics of IPL*, instantiated for two modal logics; (2) an *algorithm to verify validity of IPL statements*, with a soundness proof and termination conditions; and (3) a *modeling case study of a mobile robot*, with several integration properties to evaluate practical applicability and performance of the IPL prototype.

The paper is organized as follows. Section 2 introduces an illustrating scenario of integration. Section 3 describes related work. Section 4 gives an overview of the IPL design, while Sect. 5 provides the details of the IPL syntax, semantics, and the verification algorithm. Section 6 provides a case study and a theoretical analysis of the algorithm. We conclude the paper with limitations and future work.

2 Motivating Integration Case

Consider an autonomous mobile robot, such as TurtleBot (http://turtlebot.com), that navigates to a goal location through a physical environment using its map. The environment contains charging stations for the robot to replenish its battery. The robot has an adaptive software layer that monitors and adjusts the execution to minimize mission time and power consumption.

In the design of this system (more detail in Sect. 6.1), we have two models: a power prediction model and a planning model. The power prediction model M_{po} is a parameterized set of linear equations that estimates the energy required for motion tasks, such as driving straight or turning in place. The model is a statistical generalization of the data collected from the robot's executions. Given a description of a motion task, the model produces an estimate of required energy.

The planning model M_{pl} finds a path to a goal by representing the robot's non-deterministic movements on a map, along with their time and power effects, in a Markov Decision Process (MDP) [10]. The model's state includes the robot's location and battery charge. Whenever (re)planning is required, the PRISM probabilistic model checker [11] resolves non-determinism with optimal choices, which are fed to the robot's motion control. Although inspired by M_{po}, M_{pl} is not identical to it because of various modeling choices and compromises, for example it does not explicitly model turns.

These two models interact during execution: M_{po} acts as a safeguard against the plan of M_{pl} diverging from reality and leading to mission failure. M_{pl} only needs to be triggered when the robot is going to miss a deadline or run out of power. Otherwise, the robot avoids running the planner to conserve power[1]. If M_{pl} has overly conservative energy estimates compared to M_{po}, it may miss a deadline due to excessive recharging or taking a less risky but longer route. With overly aggressive estimates, the robot may run out of power.

Integrating these two models means ensuring that their estimates of required energy do not diverge. One threat to integration is the difference in modeling of turns: M_{pl} models turns implicitly, combining them with forward motions into single actions to reduce the state space and planning time. In M_{po} however, turns are explicit tasks, separate from forward motion. This potential inconsistency can be checked with the following integration property: *"the difference in energy estimates between the two models should not be greater than a predefined constant $\overline{err\_cons}$"*. The purpose of this property is to enable end-to-end safety arguments (e.g., not running out of power or arriving before a deadline). Instead of (inaccurately) assuming equivalence of M_{po} and M_{pl}, this property would provide a rigorous estimate of $\overline{err\_cons}$,[2] which can be used to assert that the battery cannot run out because its charge is always greater than $\overline{err\_cons}$.

It is far from straightforward to verify this property. First, the abstractions are different: M_{pl} describes states and transitions (with turns embedded in them),

---

[1] The planner's own power consumption is not modeled, contributing to its inaccuracy.

[2] As we detail later, we use overlines to mark static entities (not changing over time), and underlines to mark behavioral entities (changing over time in model states).

whereas M_{po} describes a stateless relation. Second, there is no single means to express such integration properties formally: PCTL (Probabilistic Computation Tree Logic [11]) is a property language for M_{pl}, but M_{po} does not come with a reasoning engine. Finally, even if these obstacles are overcome, the models are often developed by different teams, so they need to stay separate and co-evolve.

The integration property can be checked in several ways. A direct approach is to develop a "supermodel" containing M_{pl} and M_{po} as sub-models. A supermodel would query M_{po} from each state of M_{pl}. Although accurately detecting violations, this method is not tractable for realistic models of hundreds of thousands of states. Furthermore, the property would be hardcoded in the supermodel implementation, which would need to be developed anew for other properties.

Another approach relies on abstraction of models through *architectural views*. The views are hierarchical arrangements of discrete static instances (architectural elements) with assigned types and properties (defined in Sect. 5.1). Typically, when views are used to integrate multiple models [12], the verification is confined to the views to take advantage of their relatively simple semantics (without temporal behaviors or dynamic computation). One could encode all possible M_{pl} behaviors (i.e., trajectories of locations, turns, and energies) in views, also encoding them as atomic motion tasks of M_{po}. This approach, again, leads to either intractability or approximation (e.g., only recording the number of turns in each path), which in turn would not have soundness guarantees.

In this paper we pursue the integration approach that combines specifications over behaviors and views as necessary. For now, we provide an informal version of the integration property, which will be formalized in the end of Sect. 5.2.

Property 1 (Consistency of M_{po} and M_{pl}). *For any three sequential M_{po} tasks (go straight, rotate, go straight) that do not self-intersect and have sufficient energy, any execution in M_{pl} that visits every point of that sequence in the same order, if initialized appropriately, is a power-successful mission (modulo $\overline{err\_cons}$).*

It is challenging to systematically express and verify such properties while holding the models modular and tractable. Notice how missions in M_{po} need to correspond to missions in M_{pl}; e.g., the initial charge of M_{pl} needs to be within $\overline{err\_cons}$ of the expected mission energy in M_{po}. Specifications like Proposition 1 are enabled by our solution design and the language syntax (Sects. 4 and 5).

3   Related Work

Model Integration. Model-based engineering relies on a variety of formalisms, including synchronous, timed, and hybrid models [5]. When models are similar, it is easier to find unifying abstractions, like in the case of consistency checking for software models [6,13,14] or model refinement [15–17]. We, however, target a broader scope of cyber-physical models that were not intended for integration, leading to more challenging problems [4,18].

Integration approaches for CPS models can be seen along a spectrum from structural (operating on model syntax) to semantic (operating on behavior) ones [19]. One structural approach is to use *architectural views* — abstract component models [7,20]. Views have been extended with physical descriptions for consistency checking via graph mappings [12] and arithmetic constraints [21]. Other recent structural approaches include model transformations [22], ontologies [23], and metamodels [24]. Model transformations are typically forced to either map models to the same semantics or abandon one or more in favor of new meanings. This paper extends the view-based structural approach to write formalized statements that affect many semantic universes.

On the semantic end, one approach is to relate model behaviors directly [25]. Although theoretically elegant, this approach suffers from limited automation and creating inter-model dependencies. Other semantic approaches relate model behaviors through proxy structures. Well-known examples include the Ptolemy II environment [26] and the GEMOC studio [27]. In contrast to these works on heterogeneous simulation, we focus on logical verification of multiple models. Another example is the OpenMETA toolchain for domain-specific language integration [28]. The toolchain contains automated support for verifying individual CPS models (e.g., bond graphs) based on their logically-defined interfaces. OpenMETA's integration language (CyPhyML), however, commits to continuous-trajectory semantics [29], whereas IPL allows arbitrary plug-in behaviors. Our work builds on a prototype of a FOL/LTL contract formalism [30], which we extend by providing a full-fledged language (as opposed to a stitching of two statements) with a sound verification algorithm and a plugin system.

Logics, Satisfiability, Model Checking. This paper is related to quantified Computation Tree Logic (QCTL) [31] and well-researched combinations of first-order logic (FOL) [32] and linear temporal logic (LTL) [33], going back to the seminal work of Manna and Pnueli [34] on first-order LTL, which has been instantiated in many contexts [35,36]. Typically, such work focuses classical properties of logics and algorithms, such as decidability and complexity. We, instead, focus on expressiveness and modularity — practical concerns for CPS. For example, IPL differs from the trace language for object models [36] in that we do not create a full quantification structure in each temporal state. In contrast, IPL is modular with existing models and delegates behavioral reasoning to them.

An ambitious approach is to directly combine arbitrary logics, at the cost of high complexity and limited automation (as in fibred semantics [37]). Even when modular [38], combining logics merges their model structures, which may lead to tractability challenges in practice. We opt to keep models completely separate, thus reducing complexity and overhead.

Our algorithm relies on Satisfiability Modulo Theories (SMT) [39] and model checking [11,40]. To guarantee termination, we limit ourselves to decidable combinations of background theories (like uninterpreted functions and linear real arithmetic) that admit the Nelson-Oppen combination procedure [41]. In practice, modern SMT solvers (e.g., z3 [42]) heuristically solve instances of undecidable theories. In model checking we use the usual conversion of a modal property to an automaton (Buchi, Rabin, ...) and its composition with models [11,43].

4   Integration Property Language: Design

The Integration Property Language (IPL) is intended for model integration, which informally means that models do not contradict each other. We envision the following workflow. An engineer creates or obtains system models for integration. Some of these models will be interfaced through a behavioral property language. The other models will be accessed through static abstractions (views), created by the engineer. Then the engineer writes and checks an integration property over views and behavioral properties using IPL. If the verification fails, the engineer inspects and corrects the models and/or the property. Whenever the models change, their respective views are updated, and properties are reverified.

A primary goal of the IPL design is *applicability* to real-world model integrations. Therefore, our design focuses on these three principles:

1. Expressiveness. To improve expressiveness over state-of-the-art static abstractions, IPL formulas must combine reasoning over views with behavioral analysis of models (e.g., using modal logics). IPL should combine information from several models using first-order logic (quantification, custom functions).

2. Modularity. To support diverse CPS models, IPL should neither be tied to a particular property language or form of model behavior (discrete, continuous, or probabilistic), require the reengineering of constituent models. Thus, IPL should enable straightforward incorporation of new models and property languages.

3. Tractability. To enable automation in practice, verification of IPL specifications must be sound and implementable with practical scalability.

To support these principles, we make the following four design decisions.

A. Model integration by logically co-constraining models. IPL rigorously specifies integration conditions over several models. Logical reasoning is an expressive and modular basis for integration because it allows engineers to work with familiar concepts and tools that are specific to their domains/systems. In this paper, we target two modal logics common in model-based engineering: LTL and PCTL.

B. Separation of structure and behavior. IPL explicitly treats the static (rigid) and dynamic (flexible) elements of models separately. We accomplish this using *views* (defined in Sec. 5.1) that serve as projections of static aspects of behavioral models. This separation enables tractability because static aspects can be reasoned about without the temporal/modal dimension. We support expressiveness by allowing combinations of rigid and flexible elements to appear in the syntax.

C. Multi-step verification procedure. We combine reasoning over static aspects in first-order logic with "deep dives" into behavioral models to retrieve only the necessary values. We preserve tractability by using tools only within individual well-defined semantics, without direct dependencies between models.

D. Plugin architecture for behavioral models. To create a general framework for integration, we specify several *plugin points* — APIs that each behavioral model has to satisfy. While the model itself can stay unchanged, IPL requires a plugin to use their formalism for verification. This way, IPL does not make extra assumptions on models beyond the plugin points, hence enhancing modularity.

To support expression and verification of Proposition 1, we use PCTL with M_{pl} to reason about behaviors and a view V_{po} for reasoning about the static/stateless elements of M_{po}. V_{po} serves as a *task library*, containing all atomic tasks (going straight and rotating in the motivating example) in each location/direction in the given map. Each task is annotated with its properties, such as start/end locations, distance, required time, and required energy. Each task in V_{po} is encoded as a component and contains several properties. Thus, this view allows natural composition of missions as constrained sequences of components.

5 Integration Property Language: Details

This section describes IPL by defining its syntax and formalizing its semantics. After, we provide an algorithm to check whether an IPL formula is valid.

5.1 Concepts and Preliminaries

The concept of an architectural view originates in the field of software architecture [44]. Recently, views have been adapted to represent non-software elements such as sensors and transducers in CPS [9]. We use views to extract information for IPL to analyze without needing to process all the details of models.

Definition 1 (Architectural View). *An* architectural view V *is a hierarchical collection of architectural elements (i.e., components and connectors). Each element has fixed-valued properties, the set of which is determined by its type and values set individually for each element.*

IPL uses views for modeling static, behavior-free projections of models. For example, M_{po} uses a map of locations for its tasks, and it can be exposed in a view (V_{map}) as a set of interconnected components ($\overline{Locs}$). Each component is a location, and connectors indicate direct reachability between them. We use views as an abstraction because of their composability, typing, and extensible hierarchical structure. No dynamic information (e.g., the current battery charge) is put in views so that behavioral semantics are confined to models.

Definition 2 *(Formal View). A* (formal) view V *is a pair of a view signature (Σ_V) and its semantic interpretation (I^V). The signature contains a set of architectural elements ($\mathbb{E}$), their types, properties, sorts/constants, and functions/predicates. The semantic interpretation gives static meaning to the elements in the view signature, independent of state or time.*

We use formal views to define the syntax and semantics of IPL. We establish an isomorphic relationship between the two definitions by converting architectural models to SMT programs, as in prior work [30]. Both definitions of views are used throughout the paper: Definition 1 — for applied modeling (e.g., representing views in the case study), and Definition 2 — for theory behind IPL and verification.

Definition 3 *(Model). A (behavioral) model* M *is a triple of an (interface) signature, an interpretation (I_q^M), and a structure on which it is interpreted. The signature defines symbols of state variables, modal functions/predicates, and a list of name-type pairs for initialization parameters. The parametric structure determines the model's set of behavior traces (*M.trcs*) [43,45].*

Definition 4 *(Model Property Language). For a class of models, a* model property language *is a language for specifying expressions about a model of that class. From these expressions I_q^M produces a value of a type interpretable by views.*

For the rest of this section we consider a fixed set of behavioral models $\mathbb{M}$, with some of them abstracted by a fixed set of views ($\mathbb{V}$). Each view can be seen as some (implicit) function of a model. We consider two specific model property languages: LTL and PCTL, although in principle we are not limited to them.

Shared by models and views, background interpretation I^B evaluates common sorts, constants (e.g., boolean $\top$ and $\bot$), functions (e.g., addition), and predicates (e.g., equality) from background theories (e.g., the theory of equality or linear real arithmetic). Formally, we only allow theories that are decidable [46] and form decidable combinations [41], but in practice it is acceptable to use undecidable combinations for which available heuristics resolve relevant statements.

Formulas will be described over a context of views and models. Syntactically, IPL formulas are written over a *signature* (Σ) that contains symbols from $\mathbb{V}$ and $\mathbb{M}$. Semantically, a formula's context is determined by a *structure* (Γ) that contains interpretations I_q^M, I^V, and I^B along with their domains.

Finally, we make additional assumptions: (i) views are pre-computed and stay up-to-date with models; (ii) views can be translated into finite SMT programs; (iii) once initialized, any model can check/query any statement in its property language; and (iv) models and views share the background interpretation.

5.2   Syntax

To support modularity, we keep track of syntactic terms that cannot be interpreted by either views or models. So we introduce the rigid/flexible separation: *flexible* terms (denoted with underlines, like $\underline{loc}$) are interpreted by I_q^M, and *rigid* terms (denoted with overlines, like $\overline{Tasks}$) are interpreted by I^V. Terms of I^B are used by both models and views (no special notation; e.g., $<$).

To embed model property languages into IPL, the syntax allows model-specific formulas to be defined as "plugins" in the grammar. That is, various property languages are usable inside IPL formulas. Thus, the syntax is split into the *native* (related to views) and *plugin* (related to property languages) parts.

One challenge is that the relation between IPL and model languages is not hierarchical: native formulas contain plugin formulas, but native terms can also appear in plugin formulas. An IPL interpreter should evaluate the native parts when it prepares a model property to verify. Consider Proposition 1 in Sect. 2 where a model evaluating $P_{max=?}$ requires interpreting native IPL term $t_2.startloc$.

We organize the native/plugin syntax as presented in Fig. 1. We define each syntax element (box) on top of symbols in Σ and quantified variables ($\mathbb{V}$). We build two types of subformulas: rigid atomic formulas (RATOM) from rigid terms (RTERM), and flexible atomic formulas (MATOM). Our strategy is to keep flexible and rigid syntax separate until they merge in FORMULA. In this way, we preserve modularity: compound formulas can be deconstructed into simpler ones that are evaluated by either models or views.

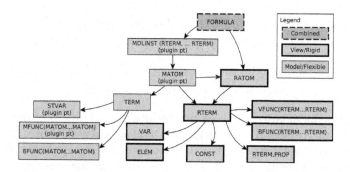

Fig. 1. IPL abstract syntax. Boxes are syntax elements, arrows — syntactic expansions.

A *rigid term* RTERM is either a variable VAR, a constant CONST, an architectural element type ELEM, a property of a rigid term RTERM.PROP[3], a background function BFUNC, or a view function VFUNC. A *rigid atom* RATOM is a logical expression over rigid terms. See the full syntax rules in the online appendix [47].

Behavioral Model Plugin Points. To integrate multiple model formalisms into IPL, the syntax defines four plugin points for model-specific constructs. Each plugin point can be instantiated either with an extensible syntactic form (e.g., a modal expression) or a reference to an existing form (e.g., RTERM). Each behavioral model provides its own syntactic elements for plugin instances.

At the level of *flexible terms* (TERM), two plugin points are *state variables* (STVAR) and *model functions* (MFUNC). Each state variable (e.g., *loc*) is declared

---

[3] Properties are only applicable to architectural elements, references to which can be accessed in a variable or a function. We assume all expressions are well-typed.

as a pair (name, type) to be referenced from IPL. Each model function declares a name, a type, and a list of arguments, each of which is name-type pair.

The third plugin point is *model atom* (MATOM), e.g., the expression $P_{max=?}$. It requires one or several syntactic forms with production rules. In addition to model-specific productions (e.g., temporal modalities), MATOM can use elements RATOM and RTERM from the grammar's rigid side (but not vice versa). A model can, for example, plug in an LTL modal expression and use rigid terms in it.

Behavioral models often have parameters such as initial conditions. To provide parameter values, we introduce the fourth and outermost plugin point:

Definition 5 *(Model Instantiation Clause).* Model instantiation clause *binds rigid terms to model parameters, wrapping* MATOM*:*

$$\text{MDLINST} ::= \text{MATOM}\{|\text{RTERM}_1 \ldots \text{RTERM}_n|\}.$$

The values of RTERM_i are passed as parameters to the behavioral model. Finally, on top of the flexible syntax above, we can define quantification:

Definition 6 *(IPL Formula).* IPL formulas *are logical formulas with first-order quantification over an instantiated model formula or a rigid atom.*

$$\text{FORMULA} ::= \forall \text{VAR} : \text{RTERM} \cdot \text{FORMULA} \mid \text{MDLINST} \mid \text{RATOM} \mid$$
$$\text{FORMULA} \wedge \text{FORMULA} \mid \neg \text{FORMULA}.$$

Illustrating modularity of the syntax, we give two extensions of the grammar: first with Linear Temporal Logic (LTL) [33], and second with Probabilistic Computational Tree Logic (PCTL) [11]. Here we highlight the expansion of MATOM in both plugins, while their full description is in the online appendix [47].

LTL Plugin Syntax. Linear Temporal Logic (LTL) is a logic to express temporal constraints on traces [33]. We embed the usual modalities: until and next.

$$\text{TATOM}_u ::= \text{TATOM } \mathsf{U} \text{ TATOM}, \text{TATOM}_x ::= \mathsf{X} \text{ TATOM},$$
$$\text{TATOM}_a := \text{TATOM} \wedge \text{TATOM}, \text{TATOM}_n := \neg\text{TATOM},$$
$$\text{MATOM} ::= \text{TATOM} ::= \text{RATOM} \mid \text{TERM} \mid \text{TATOM}_u \mid \text{TATOM}_x \mid \text{TATOM}_a \mid \text{TATOM}_n.$$

PCTL Plugin Syntax. We use extended PCTL (its variant used in PRISM) expresses probabilistic constraints over a computation tree, and its models are MDPs and discrete-time Markov chains (DTMCs) [11]. Flexible terms are as in the LTL plugin, but MATOM expands into several layered behavioral atoms.

$$\text{PATHPROP} ::= \text{RATOM} \mid \text{TERM} \mid \text{PATHPROP} \wedge \text{PATHPROP} \mid \neg\text{PATHPROP} \mid$$
$$\text{PATHPROP } \mathsf{U}^{\leq k} \text{ PATHPROP} \mid \mathsf{X} \text{ PATHPROP},$$
$$\text{PPROP} ::= P_{o \sim p}[\text{PATHPROP}], \text{PQUERY} ::= P_{o=?}[\text{PATHPROP}],$$
$$\text{MATOM} ::= \text{PPROP} \mid \text{PQUERY} \mid \text{RWDPROP} \mid \text{RWDQUERY},$$

where $p \in [0,1], \sim \in \{<, \leq, >, \geq\}, o \in \{max, min, \emptyset\}, k \in \mathbb{N} \cup \{\text{inf}\}$.

With the syntax defined, we encode the motivating property (Proposition 1) in IPL below. We use quantification to bind constraints on task sequences in V_{po} (with task attributes *start*, *end*, and expected *energy*) and a PCTL query for M_{pl}.

$$\forall t_1, t_2, t_3 : \overline{Tasks} \cdot t_1.type = t_3.type = \text{STR} \wedge t_2.type = \text{ROT} \wedge \qquad (1)$$

$$t_1.end = t_2.start = t_3.start \ \wedge t_1.start \neq t_3.end \ \wedge \Sigma_{i=1}^{3} t_i.energy \leq \overline{MaxBat} \rightarrow$$

$$P_{max=?}[(\text{F } \underline{loc} = t_2.startloc) \wedge (\text{F } \underline{loc} = t_3.startloc) \wedge$$

$$((\underline{loc} = t_1.start) \ \text{U} \ (\underline{loc} = t_2.start \ \text{U} \ (\underline{loc} = t_3.start \ \text{U} \ \underline{loc} = t_3.end)))]$$

$$\{|\underline{initloc} = t_1.start, \underline{goal} = t_3.end, \underline{initbat} = \Sigma_{i=1}^{3} t_i.energy + \overline{err\_cons}|\} = 1.$$

To summarize, IPL formulas express quantified modal constraints over symbols in Σ. We use quantification outside of flexible atoms to preserve modularity. Further, we extended the flexible part of IPL with two model property languages.

5.3 Semantics

Here we give the meaning to the IPL syntax in terms of structure Γ by reducing a formula to either Γ's model part (I_q^M) or Γ's the view part (I^V), but not both.

Domain Transfer. Interpretation is based on *semantic domains* – collections of formal objects (e.g., numbers) in terms of which syntax elements can be fully interpreted. For IPL we define two domains: the *model domain* (D_M) and the *view domain* (D_V). D_M is associated with I_q^M, and D_V— with I^V.

Definition 7 *(Belonging to semantic domain)*. *Syntactic element s belongs to a semantic domain D if there exists an interpretation I such that $I(s) \in D$.*

Table 1. Semantic domains and transfer in IPL.

View domain D_V	Is transferable	Model domain D_M
VAR	Yes, by value	
ELEM	Yes, by reference	
PROP	Yes, by value	
VFUNC	Yes, by value, if all arguments are transferable. Otherwise, no.	
RTERM	Yes, by value	
$\forall x : X \cdot f$	No	
	No	STVAR
	No	MFUNC
	No	MATOM
	Yes, by value	MDLINST
Constants and BFUNC from background theories. Interpretation I^B.		

$\mathsf{D_M}$ and $\mathsf{D_V}$ are defined in Table 1: the first and third columns contain syntax elements that belong to them. For example, models interpret state variables using their structures, and views can interpret quantified statements using satisfiability solvers. Both domains interpret symbols from background theories (I^B).

The middle column of Table 1 indicates if a syntax element, once interpreted, can be *transferred* to the other domain, i.e., if a bijection between its evaluations and some set in the other domain exists. "By value" is mapping to a constant in the other domain. "By reference" is mapping to an integer ID (e.g., for ELEM, unique integer IDs are generated for referencing in the model). Notice that view domain elements are mostly transferable to the model domain (except quantification). To support modularity, models can only transfer values of MDLINST.

Native semantics. We interpret IPL formulas in the following context: Γ ($\mathbb{V}$, M_i with I_q^M, I^V, and I^B), states q, potentially infinite sequences of states $\omega \equiv \langle q_1, q_2, \ldots \rangle$, and mapping μ of variables to values. Starting from the bottom of Fig. 1 with rigid terms (RTERM), we gradually simplify the semantic context (denoted as the subscript of $[\![ ]\!]$ and on the left of $\models$). The meaning of standard logical operations from FORMULA and RATOM is found in the online appendix [47].

$$[\![\text{CONST}]\!]_\Gamma = I^B(\text{CONST}), [\![\text{VAR}]\!]_\mu = \mu(\text{VAR}), [\![\text{STVAR}]\!]_{\Gamma,q} = I_q^M(\text{STVAR}),$$

$$[\![\text{VFUNC}(r_1, \ldots r_n)]\!]_{\Gamma,\mu} = I^V(\text{VFUNC})([\![r_1]\!]_{\mathsf{V},\mu} \ldots [\![r_n]\!]_{\mathsf{V},\mu}) \quad if \quad r_1 \ldots r_n \in \text{RTERM},$$

$$[\![\text{ELEM}]\!]_{\Gamma,q,\mu} = I^V(\text{ELEM}) = \{e\} \subseteq \mathbb{E}, [\![\text{RTERM.PROP}]\!]_{\Gamma,q,\mu} = I^V(\text{PROP})([\![\text{RTERM}]\!]_{\mathsf{V},\mu}),$$

$$\Gamma, \omega, \mu \models \forall x : r \cdot f \quad iff \quad \Gamma, \omega, \mu' \models f, \text{ where } r \in \text{RTERM},$$

$$f \text{ is either FORMULA or RATOM}, \mu' = \mu \cup \{x \mapsto v\} \text{ for all } v \text{ in } [\![r]\!]_{\Gamma,\mu}.$$

$$\Gamma, \mu \models (a)[\![p_1 \ldots p_n]\!] \quad iff \quad \mathbb{V}, \mathsf{M}([\![p_1]\!]_{\mathsf{V},\mu} \ldots [\![p_n]\!]_{\mathsf{V},\mu}), \mu \models a, \text{ where } a \in \text{MATOM}.$$

We provide a only brief summary of the plugin semantics for LTL and PCTL due to space limitations; for the full semantics see the online appendix [47].

LTL plugin semantics. For LTL the model is a canonical transition system M_{ts} [40]. We evaluate TATOM and FORMULA on a sequence of states (ω). Logical operations and quantifiers are evaluated the same as natively.

$$\Gamma, \omega, \mu \models f \quad iff \quad \Gamma, q, \mu \models f, \text{ where } q \in \omega^{1,1}, f \in \text{TERM}.$$

$$\Gamma \models \text{FORMULA} \quad iff \quad \forall \omega : \mathsf{M}_{ts}.trcs \cdot \Gamma, \omega, \emptyset \models \text{FORMULA}.$$

PCTL plugin semantics. PCTL formulas are evaluated on MDPs (M_{mdp}), or a DTMC M_{dtmc} if we collapse non-determinism [11]. Temporal operators mean the same as in LTL except the bounded until.

For $f \in$ PPROP and RWDPROP, $Prob^\pi(q, f)$ is a probability of f holding after q for policy π from Π:

$$\Gamma, q, \mu \models P_{o \sim p}[f] \quad iff \quad \text{opt}_{\pi \in \Pi} \, Prob^\pi(q, [\![f]\!]_{\Gamma,\mu}) \sim p,$$

$$\Gamma, q, \mu \models R_{o \sim p}[f] \quad iff \quad \text{opt}_{\pi \in \Pi} \, Exp^\pi(q, X_{[\![f]\!]_{\Gamma,\mu}}) \sim p,$$

where $f \in$ PATHPROP; $\sim \in \{<, \leq, >, \geq\}$; $\mathrm{opt}_{\pi \in \Pi}$ is $\sup_{\pi \in \Pi}$ if $o \equiv$ max, $\inf_{\pi \in \Pi}$ if $o \equiv$ min, no-op if $o \equiv \emptyset$; X_f is a random reward variable, Exp^π is its expectation.

Now the semantics of IPL has been fully defined, in a way that formalized Eq. 1 expresses the intent of informal Proposition 1. Formulas are evaluated modularly, by their reduction to subformulas, each of which is interpreted by I^V, I_q^M, or I^B.

5.4 Verification Algorithm

Suppose an engineer needs to verify an integration formula f with a signature Σ against Γ, i.e., check if f is a sentence in the *IPL theory* for Γ.

Problem 1 *(IPL formula validity). Given $f \in$ FORMULA in Σ and a corresponding Γ, decide whether $\Gamma \models f$.*

Below we step through Algorithm 1 that solves Problem 1. The algorithm uses several transformations, all of which are formally defined in the online appendix [47]. The first step is equivalently transforming f to its prenex normal form (PNF, i.e., all quantifiers occurring at the beginning of the formula), denoted $ToPNF(f)$.

Algorithm 1. IPL verification algorithm

1: **procedure** VERIFY(f, M)
2:     $f \leftarrow ToPNF(f)$ ▷ Put the formula into the prenex normal form
3:     $f^{FA} \leftarrow FuncAbst(\hat{f})$ ▷ Replace model instances with functional abstractions
4:     $f^{CA} \leftarrow ConstAbst(\hat{f})$ ▷ Replace model instances with constant abstractions
5:     $\hat{f}^{FA} \leftarrow RemQuant(f^{FA})$ ▷ Remove FA quantifiers
6:     $\hat{f}^{CA} \leftarrow RemQuant(f^{CA})$ ▷ Remove CA quantifiers
7:     $sv \leftarrow$ all μ s.t. $\exists I \cdot I, \mu \models \hat{f}^{FA} \not\Leftrightarrow \hat{f}^{CA}$ ▷ *Saturation:* find all variable values
      that satisfy non-matching abstractions
8:     $I_{sv}^F(F_i(\mu)) \leftarrow [\![\mathrm{MDLINST}_i]\!]_{M,\mu}$ for each $\mu \in sv$ ▷ *Model checking:* run model
      instances to interpret functional abstractions on the above values
9:     **if** $\exists I \cdot I_{sv}^F \subseteq I \wedge I \models \neg f^{FA}$ **then return** $\bot$ ▷ If the FA formula's negation is
      satisfiable given the constructed interpretation, return false
10:    **else return** $\top$ ▷ Otherwise, return true

The next step is to replace occurrences of instance terms $\mathrm{MDLINST}_i$ (interpretation of which is yet unknown to views/SMT) with two kinds of abstractions:
1. *Functional abstraction (FA).* FA replaces $\mathrm{MDLINST}_i$ with uninterpreted functions F_i. The arguments of these functions are the free variables that are present in the syntactic subtree of $\mathrm{MDLINST}_i$. (Below, $\boldsymbol{x} \equiv x_1 \ldots x_n$.)

$$f^{FA} \equiv FuncAbst(f) = Q_1 x_1 : \mathrm{D}_1 \ldots Q_n x_n : \mathrm{D}_n \cdot \hat{f}(\boldsymbol{x}, F_1(\boldsymbol{x}) \ldots F_m(\boldsymbol{x})),$$

2. *Constant abstraction (CA).* CA replaces $\mathrm{MDLINST}_i$ with uninterpreted constants.

$$f^{CA} \equiv C(f) = Q_1 x_1 : \mathrm{D}_1 \ldots Q_n x_n : \mathrm{D}_n \cdot \hat{f}(\boldsymbol{x}, C_1 \ldots C_m).$$

Next, we remove all quantifiers ($RemQuant(f^{FA}) = \hat{f}^{FA}$, $RemQuant(f^{CA})$ $= \hat{f}^{CA}$), replacing all bound quantified variables with free ones.

$$f^{FA} \equiv Q_1 x_1 : D_1 \ldots Q_n x_n : D_n \cdot \hat{f}^{FA}(\boldsymbol{x}), f^{CA} \equiv Q_1 x_1 : D_1 \ldots Q_n x_n : D_n \cdot \hat{f}^{CA}(\boldsymbol{x}).$$

We look for interpretations (I_{sv}^F) of model instances that affect validity of f. I_{sv}^F are characterized by valuations μ of free variables that are arguments for F_i. These interpretations are also subsumed by I^F— a full interpretation of F_i on all possible variable assignments that coincides with semantic evaluation of model atoms: $I^F(F_i(\mu)) = [\![\text{MDLINST}_i]\!]_{\mathsf{M},\mu}$ for any $\mu \in D_1 \times \ldots D_n, i \in [1, m]$.

Instead of constructing full I^F (which requires exhaustive model checking), we determine I_{sv}^F by looking for μ for that make the values of FA and CA differ. In other words, such valuations that it is possible to interpret the two abstractions so that one formula is valid and the other one invalid. That is, we construct a set sv that contains all μ satisfying the *search formula* for f: $\exists I \cdot I, \mu \models \hat{f}^{FA} \not\Leftrightarrow \hat{f}^{CA}$.

In the process of *saturation*, the algorithm enumerates all such μ by iteratively finding and blocking them. With a finite number of μ, it will terminate once the sv is saturated. To terminate, it is sufficient that each D_i is finite, but not necessary: a constrained formula may have finite sv with infinite D_i.

Once variable assignments sv are determined, we can construct I_{sv}^F (a subset of I^F) by directly executing behavioral checking of MDLINST_i on concrete values:

$$I_{sv}^F(F_i)(\mu) = [\![\text{MDLINST}_i]\!]_{\mathsf{M},\mu} \text{ for all } \mu \in sv \text{ and all } i \in [1, m]. \tag{2}$$

Finally, the algorithm performs a validity check by checking satisfiability of the negation of f^{FA}. f is valid iff the check fails to find an interpretation that agrees with I_{sv}^F and satisfies $\neg f^{FA}$. We implemented this algorithm in an IPL IDE based on Eclipse (https://www.eclipse.org), with its source code online (https://github.com/bisc/IPL). More information about the IDE and an illustration of Algorithm 1 on the running example is in the online appendix [47].

6   Evaluation

Here we evaluate IPL from a theoretical (soundness and termination of the algorithm) and practical (checking integration for a mobile robot) standpoint.

To avoid false positives/negatives, IPL verification should produce sound results. We prove that any answer returned by Algorithm 1 is correct with respect to the semantics (independently of the plugins). To be valuable, the algorithm should terminate on practical problems. We hence provide the termination conditions.

We show that interpretations of MDLINST over sv determine the formula's validity. Correctness and termination follow directly from this result in Corollary 2.

Theorem 1. *Absence of flexible interpretations that agree with I_{sv}^F and satisfy $\neg f^{FA}$ is necessary and sufficient for validity of f^{FA} on I^F:*

$$\nexists I \cdot I_{sv}^F \subseteq I \wedge I \models \neg f^{FA} \text{ iff } I^F \models f^{FA}.$$

Proof Sketch. Soundness follows from straightforward instantiation. For completeness, we assume for contraction that $I^F \models f^{FA}$ and instantiate a μ that both satisfies f^{FA} and does not, depending on the interpretation. We show that $\mu \in sv$ to derive a contradiction. Full proof is in the online appendix [47].

Theorem 1 leads to two corollaries (see their proofs in the online appendix [47]).

Corollary 1. *Validity of formula f is equivalent to unsatisfiability* $I_{sv}^F \models \neg f^{FA}$.

$$\mathsf{M} \models f \text{ iff } \nexists I \cdot I_{sv}^F \subseteq I \wedge I \models \neg f^{FA}.$$

Corollary 2. *Algorithm 1 is sound for solving Problem 1. The algorithm terminates if (i) satisfiability checking is decidable, (ii) behavioral checking with* M *is decidable, and (iii) search formula* $\hat{f}^{FA} \not\Leftrightarrow \hat{f}^{CA}$ *has a finite number of satisfying values for free variables (e.g., when quantification domains* D_i *are finite).*

6.1   Case Study: Adaptive Mobile Robot

To assess the practical applicability of IPL, we guided our case study with three questions: 1. What is the role of integration properties in real systems? 2. Can we specify them with IPL? 3. Is IPL verification tractable in practice?

To address these questions, we applied IPL to a system in a case study [48]. The system was chosen to meet the following criteria: it must be a running system to ensure realism, it must be from the CPS domain to ensure fit, it must include multiple models using different formalisms to evaluate IPL's expressiveness, and we had to have access to domain experts to answer questions and assess usefulness. A TurtleBot 2 robot (described in Sect. 2) implemented using the Robot Operating System (ROS) [49] for sensing, localization, and navigation, and a model-based adaptive system for planning the robot's mission-related actions meets all of these criteria. We conducted a historical review with the project's artifacts to discover relevant models and integration properties. The case study models are available online (https://github.com/bisc/IPLProjects).

Our case study focused on a planning model M_{pl} and a power model M_{po} because power is a prominent concern in the system and these two models have a complex dependency. Both models co-evolved throughout the project, and we collected over 10 variants of these models with of varying sophistication.

Integration Properties. An example integration property between M_{pl} and M_{po} is that they must agree on energy spent in various missions; otherwise the robot may run out of power. (A mission is made up of different energy-spending motion tasks such as forward movement, rotation, and charging. A *power-successful mission* can be done with a given initial power budget.)

View Modeling and Verification. To formalize the integration properties, we chose to create a view (V_{po}) for M_{po} and combine it with a behavioral interface to M_{pl}. There are many ways to construct an appropriate view, and we took the route of creating a *task library* — enumerating all relevant atomic tasks.

V_{po} has to agree with M_{pl} on the task primitives, otherwise the integration check will always fail. Each motion command is an architectural element with its own *id*, *startloc*, *endloc*, and *energy* (which is computed by M_{po} given a distance and a speed, hence making V_{po} a correct view for M_{po}). The only requirement for the view is that it contains *all* the objects of interest (here, atomic tasks).

Another view is a map view (V_{map}), containing locations (as components) and their connections. We discovered 5 maps, organized in two categories. The first category contains 9 locations (including 1 charging station) and 9–10 edges. The second category contains 12 locations (including 4) and 13 edges.

Both V_{po} and V_{map} have been created by automated transformations that require the same map artifact. V_{po} requires equations from M_{po} and outputs a library of tasks encoded in the Architecture Analysis and Design Language (AADL) [50]. V_{map} outputs a list of locations in AADL. In total, we generated over 30 variants of views to represent relevant combinations of task primitives.

Using the above view abstractions, we specified dozens of integration property variants (similar to Eq. 1) for various mission features and lengths. In map-related properties, quantified variables iterate over locations. In power-related properties, quantified variable iterate over atomic tasks. Examples of these properties are highlighted in the online appendix [47].

Outcomes. To answer our first question (see top of Sect. 6.1), we discovered that complex integration properties appear when several models contain interrelated data (in our case, locations, connections between them, and energy expenditures for tasks). These properties serve as steps in safety reasoning that would otherwise use oversimplified and unsupported assumptions (e.g., models agree on energy). If these assumptions are not satisfied, the system falls short of its goals. Thus, IPL fills in an important niche of reasoning for multi-model systems.

To answer the second question, we focused on multiple variants of power-related integration properties for M_{po} and M_{pl}. We were able to represent all relevant point-to-point missions up to a bounded number of recharging actions. The end-to-end power-safety argument for the robot relies on these integration properties: if M_{po} has worst-case error $\overline{err\_pow}$, M_{pl} has worst-case error $\overline{err\_mdp}$, the worst-case consistency error is $\overline{err\_cons}$, then to not run out of power, the battery has to have at least $g(\overline{err\_pow}, \overline{err\_mdp}, \overline{err\_cons})$ charge during any execution, where g is some function (addition in simple cases). Thus, we observed that integration properties verify bounds of consistency errors, which are inputs to end-to-end safety arguments.

We discovered several critical inconsistencies in the models we observed: (1) the MDP does not check whether the battery was enough for the last step (thus, in some missions the robot would run out); (2) turn energy was inconsistent making one turn action add energy to the battery (caused by a bug in the model generation code); (3) M_{po} and M_{pl} disagreed significantly in their energy predictions for tasks with near-zero times because of the non-zero y-intersect in M_{po} (recall that it was constructed using regression). We therefore conclude that IPL is capable of finding model inconsistencies in real-world projects.

Performance. We evaluated the performance of the Eclipse-based IPL implementation using the power-related property variants. Specifically, we executed 24 verification runs by varying the number of tasks and the map and toggling the mission features—variable length missions, charging, and rotations. IPL's performance is reasonable for practical purposes, with a remarkably low overhead. Although larger missions with more features led to substantially longer times, IPL finished within several hours. The details are in the online appendix [47].

7 Discussion

This paper makes a significant step towards bridging the semantic gap between heterogeneous CPS models. The Integration Property Language enables systems engineers to specify expressive properties over behavioral and static semantics of multiple models in a way that is both modular and extensible. IPL specifications are soundly checkable with a combination of SMT solving and model checking. The case study showed that IPL can encode relevant real-world integration properties and verify them in reasonable times.

IPL relies on existing views, models, and analysis tools for reasoning. It also shares their limitations on automation and performance. In practice, extra automation or manual effort is required for views to remain up-to-date with models. IPL performance is limited by satisfiability solving for many constraints and quantified variables. Improvements in the state-of-the-art satisfiability and model checking should lead to comparable improvements in the IPL performance.

IPL allows behavioral checking to be carried out independently of where its inputs come from, thereby supporting custom workflows in diverse engineering disciplines. This freedom, however, comes at a cost of expressiveness: we could not allow complete transfer of view functions to D_M (Table 1 allows it only for transferable arguments), which would need callbacks from model checking to views to evaluate a view function. This feedback loop would create a dependency from models to views and negatively impact modularity and extensibility of IPL.

Future work will focus on three areas: (1) incorporating other property languages into IPL and conducting more case studies, (2) handling models (such as Simulink) that are widely used in CPS but do not have a rigorous property language, and (3) an analysis of scalability and effectiveness with respect to other integration methods (e.g., the "supermodel" approach).

Acknowledgments. This material is based on research sponsored by AFRL and DARPA under agreement number FA8750-16-2-0042. The U.S. Government is authorized to reproduce and distribute reprints for Governmental purposes notwithstanding any copyright notation thereon. The views and conclusions contained herein are those of the authors and should not be interpreted as necessarily representing the official policies or endorsements, either expressed or implied, of the AFRL, DARPA or the U.S. Government.

References

1. Mosterman, P.J., Zander, J.: Cyber-physical systems challenges: a needs analysis for collaborating embedded software systems. Softw. Syst. Model. **15**(1), 5–16 (2016)
2. Fitzgerald, J., Larsen, P.G., Pierce, K., Verhoef, M., Wolff, S.: Collaborative modelling and co-simulation in the development of dependable embedded systems. In: Méry, D., Merz, S. (eds.) IFM 2010. LNCS, vol. 6396, pp. 12–26. Springer, Heidelberg (2010). https://doi.org/10.1007/978-3-642-16265-7_2
3. Valukas, A.: Report to board of directors of general motors company regarding ignition switch recalls. Jenner & Block, Technical report (2014)
4. Sztipanovits, J., Koutsoukos, X., Karsai, G., Kottenstette, N., Antsaklis, P., Gupta, V., Goodwine, B., Baras, J., Wang, S.: Toward a science of cyber-physical system integration. In: Proceedings of the IEEE (2011)
5. Alur, R.: Principles of Cyber-Physical Systems. The MIT Press, Cambridge (2015)
6. Dijkman, R.M.: Consistency in multi-viewpoint architectural design. Ph.D. thesis, Telematica Instituut, Enschede, The Netherlands (2006)
7. Maoz, S., Ringert, J.O., Rumpe, B.: Synthesis of component and connector models from crosscutting structural views. In: Proceedings of the 2013 9th Joint Meeting on Foundations of Software Engineering, ESEC/FSE 2013, New York, NY, USA, pp. 444–454. ACM (2013)
8. Reineke, J., Tripakis, S.: Basic problems in multi-view modeling. In: Ábrahám, E., Havelund, K. (eds.) TACAS 2014. LNCS, vol. 8413, pp. 217–232. Springer, Heidelberg (2014). https://doi.org/10.1007/978-3-642-54862-8_15
9. Bhave, A.: Multi-view consistency in architectures for cyber-physical systems. Ph.D. thesis, Carnegie Mellon University, December 2011
10. Howard, R.A.: Dynamic Programming and Markov Processes. Technology Press of the Massachusetts Institute of Technology, Cambridge (1960)
11. Kwiatkowska, M., Norman, G., Parker, D.: Stochastic model checking. In: Bernardo, M., Hillston, J. (eds.) SFM 2007. LNCS, vol. 4486, pp. 220–270. Springer, Heidelberg (2007). https://doi.org/10.1007/978-3-540-72522-0_6
12. Bhave, A., Krogh, B., Garlan, D., Schmerl, B.: View consistency in architectures for cyber-physical systems. In: IEEE/ACM International Conference on Cyber-Physical Systems (ICCPS) (2011)
13. Nuseibeh, B., Kramer, J., Finkelstein, A.: A framework for expressing the relationships between multiple views in requirements specification. IEEE Trans. Softw. Eng. **20**(10), 760–773 (1994)
14. Egyed, A.F.: Heterogeneous view integration and its automation. Ph.D. thesis, University of Southern California (2000)
15. Hoare, C.A.R.: Communicating sequential processes. Commun. ACM **21**(8), 666–677 (1978)
16. Smith, G.: The Object-Z Specification Language. Advances in Formal Methods, vol. 1. Springer, New York (2000). https://doi.org/10.1007/978-1-4615-5265-9
17. Abrial, J.R.: Modeling in Event-B: System and Software Engineering, 1st edn. Cambridge University Press, New York (2010)
18. Karsai, G., Sztipanovits, J.: Model-integrated development of cyber-physical systems. In: Brinkschulte, U., Givargis, T., Russo, S. (eds.) SEUS 2008. LNCS, vol. 5287, pp. 46–54. Springer, Heidelberg (2008). https://doi.org/10.1007/978-3-540-87785-1_5

19. Ruchkin, I.: Integration beyond components and models: research challenges and directions. In: Proceedings of the Third Workshop on Architecture Centric Virtual Integration (ACVI), Venice, Italy, pp. 8–11 (2016)
20. Kruchten, P.: The 4+1 view model of architecture. IEEE Softw. **12**, 42–50 (1995)
21. Rajhans, A., Bhave, A., Loos, S., Krogh, B., Platzer, A., Garlan, D.: Using parameters in architectural views to support heterogeneous design and verification. In: Proceedings of the 50th IEEE Conference on Decision and Control and European Control Conference (CDC) (2011)
22. Marinescu, R.: Model-driven analysis and verification of automotive embedded systems. Ph.D. thesis, Maladaren University (2016)
23. Vanherpen, K., Denil, J., David, I., De Meulenaere, P., Mosterman, P.J., Torngren, M., Qamar, A., Vangheluwe, H.: Ontological reasoning for consistency in the design of cyber-physical systems, pp. 1–8. IEEE, April 2016
24. Torngren, M., Qamar, A., Biehl, M., Loiret, F., El-khoury, J.: Integrating viewpoints in the development of mechatronic products. Mechatronics **24**, 745–762 (2013)
25. Rajhans, A., Krogh, B.H.: Heterogeneous verification of cyber-physical systems using behavior relations. In: Proceedings of the 15th ACM Conference on Hybrid Systems: Computation and Control (HSCC), New York, NY, USA, pp. 35–44. ACM (2012)
26. Lee, E.A., Neuendorffer, S., Zhou, G.: System Design, Modeling, and Simulation using Ptolemy II. Ptolemy.org, Berkeley (2014)
27. Combemale, B., Deantoni, J., Baudry, B., France, R., Jezequel, J.M., Gray, J.: Globalizing modeling languages. Computer **47**(6), 68–71 (2014)
28. Sztipanovits, J., Bapty, T., Neema, S., Howard, L., Jackson, E.: OpenMETA: a model- and component-based design tool chain for cyber-physical systems. In: Bensalem, S., Lakhneck, Y., Legay, A. (eds.) ETAPS 2014. LNCS, vol. 8415, pp. 235–248. Springer, Heidelberg (2014). https://doi.org/10.1007/978-3-642-54848-2_16
29. Simko, G., Lindecker, D., Levendovszky, T., Neema, S., Sztipanovits, J.: Specification of cyber-physical components with formal semantics – integration and composition. In: Moreira, A., Schätz, B., Gray, J., Vallecillo, A., Clarke, P. (eds.) MODELS 2013. LNCS, vol. 8107, pp. 471–487. Springer, Heidelberg (2013). https://doi.org/10.1007/978-3-642-41533-3_29
30. Ruchkin, I., de Niz, D., Chaki, S., Garlan, D.: Contract-based integration of cyber-physical analyses. In: Proceedings of the International Conference on Embedded Software (EMSOFT), New York, NY, USA, pp. 23:1–23:10. ACM (2014)
31. Da Costa, A., Laroussinie, F., Markey, N.: Quantified CTL: expressiveness and model checking. In: Koutny, M., Ulidowski, I. (eds.) CONCUR 2012. LNCS, vol. 7454, pp. 177–192. Springer, Heidelberg (2012). https://doi.org/10.1007/978-3-642-32940-1_14
32. Borger, E., Gradel, E., Gurevich, Y.: The Classical Decision Problem. Springer, Heidelberg (2001)
33. Pnueli, A.: The temporal logic of programs. In: 18th Annual Symposium on Foundations of Computer Science, pp. 46–57, October 1977
34. Manna, Z., Pnueli, A.: The Temporal Logic of Reactive and Concurrent Systems. Springer, Heidelberg (1992). https://doi.org/10.1007/978-1-4612-0931-7
35. Ghilardi, S., Nicolini, E., Ranise, S., Zucchelli, D.: Combination methods for satisfiability and model-checking of infinite-state systems. In: Pfenning, F. (ed.) CADE 2007. LNCS (LNAI), vol. 4603, pp. 362–378. Springer, Heidelberg (2007). https://doi.org/10.1007/978-3-540-73595-3_25

36. Cimatti, A., Roveri, M., Susi, A., Tonetta, S.: Formalizing requirements with object models and temporal constraints. Softw. Syst. Model. **10**(2), 147–160 (2009)
37. Gabbay, D.M.: Fibred semantics and the weaving of logics part 1: modal and intuitionistic logics. J. Symb. Log. **61**(4), 1057–1120 (1996)
38. Konur, S., Fisher, M., Schewe, S.: Combined model checking for temporal, probabilistic, and real-time logics. Theor. Comput. Sci. **503**, 61–88 (2013)
39. Nieuwenhuis, R., Oliveras, A., Tinelli, C.: Solving SAT and SAT modulo theories: from an abstract Davis-Putnam-Logemann-Loveland procedure to DPLL(T). J. ACM **53**(6), 937–977 (2006)
40. Clarke, E.M., Emerson, E.A., Sistla, A.P.: Automatic verification of finite-state concurrent systems using temporal logic specifications. ACM Trans. Program. Lang. Syst. **8**(2), 244–263 (1986)
41. Nelson, G., Oppen, D.C.: Simplification by cooperating decision procedures. ACM Trans. Program. Lang. Syst. **1**(2), 245–257 (1979)
42. de Moura, L., Bjørner, N.: Z3: an efficient SMT solver. In: Ramakrishnan, C.R., Rehof, J. (eds.) TACAS 2008. LNCS, vol. 4963, pp. 337–340. Springer, Heidelberg (2008). https://doi.org/10.1007/978-3-540-78800-3_24
43. Baier, C., Katoen, J.P.: Principles of Model Checking. The MIT Press, Cambridge (2008)
44. Clements, P., Bachmann, F., Bass, L., Garlan, D., Ivers, J., Little, R., Merson, P., Nord, R., Stafford, J.: Documenting Software Architectures: Views and Beyond, 2nd edn. Addison-Wesley Professional, Boston (2010)
45. Gurfinkel, A., Shoham, S., Meshman, Y.: SMT-based Verification of Parameterized Systems. In: Proceedings of the 2016 24th ACM SIGSOFT International Symposium on Foundations of Software Engineering, FSE 2016, New York, NY, USA, pp. 338–348. ACM (2016)
46. Kroening, D., Strichman, O.: Decision Procedures - An Algorithmic Point of View. Texts in Theoretical Computer Science. An EATCS Series. Springer, Heidelberg (2008). https://doi.org/10.1007/978-3-540-74105-3
47. Ruchkin, I., Sunshine, J., Iraci, G., Schmerl, B., Garlan, D.: Appendix for IPL: an integration property language for multi-model cyber-physical systems (2018). http://acme.able.cs.cmu.edu/pubs/uploads/pdf/fm2018-appendix.pdf
48. Yin, R.K.: Case Study Research: Design and Methods, 4th edn. Sage Publications Inc., Thousand Oaks (2008)
49. Quigley, M., Gerkey, B., Smart, W.D.: Programming Robots with ROS: A Practical Introduction to the Robot Operating System, 1st edn. O'Reilly Media, Sebastopol (2015)
50. Feiler, P.H., Gluch, D.P., Hudak, J.J.: The architecture analysis & design language (AADL): an introduction. Technical report CMU/SEI-2006-TN-011, Software Engineering Institute, Carnegie Mellon University (2006)

Timed Epistemic Knowledge Bases
for Social Networks

Raúl Pardo[1]($\boxtimes$), César Sánchez[2]($\boxtimes$), and Gerardo Schneider[1]($\boxtimes$)

[1] Department of Computer Science and Engineering,
Chalmers | University of Gothenburg, Gothenburg, Sweden
{pardo,gersch}@chalmers.se
[2] IMDEA Software Institute, Madrid, Spain
cesar.sanchez@imdea.org

Abstract. We present an epistemic logic equipped with time-stamps in atoms and epistemic operators, which enables reasoning about the moments at which events happen and knowledge is acquired or deduced. Our logic includes both an epistemic operator K and a belief operator B, to capture the disclosure of inaccurate information. Our main motivation is to describe rich privacy policies in online social networks (OSNs). Most of today's privacy policy mechanisms in existing OSNs allow only *static policies*. In our logic it is possible to express rich *dynamic policies* in terms of the knowledge available to the different users and the precise time of actions and deductions. Our framework can be instantiated for different OSNs by specifying the effect of the actions in the evolution of the social network and in the knowledge disclosed to each user. We present an algorithm for deducing knowledge and propagating beliefs, which can also be instantiated with different variants of how the epistemic information is preserved through time. Policies are modelled as formulae in the logic, which are interpreted over timed traces. Finally, we show that the model checking problem for this logic, and in consequence policy conformance, is decidable.

1 Introduction

Online Social Networks (OSNs) like Facebook, Twitter and Snapchat have exploded in popularity in recent years. According to a recent survey [1] nearly 70% of the Internet users are active on social networks. Some concerns, including privacy, have arisen alongside this staggering increase in usage. Even though several studies [2–5] report that privacy breaches are growing in number, the most popular OSNs do not provide effective mechanisms to express privacy

This research has been partially supported by: the Swedish funding agency SSF under the grant *Data Driven Secure Business Intelligence*, the Swedish Research Council (*Vetenskapsrådet*) under grant Nr. 2015-04154 (*PolUser: Rich User-Controlled Privacy Policies*), the EU H2020 project Elastest (num. 731535), by the Spanish MINECO Project "RISCO (TIN2015-71819-P)" and by the EU ICT COST Action IC1402 ARVI (*Runtime Verification beyond Monitoring*).

policies; virtually all privacy policies are static and cannot express timing preferences, such as referring to points in time or how policies evolve.

In [6] we presented a framework to express a limited version of dynamic privacy policies, based on an *epistemic logic* to characterise what users know. Formulae are interpreted over *social network models* which faithfully represent the social graph of OSNs. The policy language in [6] allows to describe, for example, the following policy *"During the weekend only my friends can see my pictures"*. However, the previous policy simply activates the static policy *"only my friends can see my pictures"* during weekends. Two restrictions of the logic in [6] are the lack of explicit time, and that only a knowledge modality is available, thus implicitly assuming that the information that users are told is true. This assumption is not realistic in social networks as users may also receive and disclose information that is false or inaccurate, which has raised a growing interest in the detection of fake news [7–9]. To address these issues we introduce here a logic that: (1) is tailored for social networks and allows to express properties based on the social connections between users; (2) combines knowledge and belief to differentiate true knowledge and information that may be false; (3) has time-stamps in modalities and atoms, which allows to refer to the timing of events and when information is learnt. Based on this logic, we introduce a novel privacy policy language that addresses the limitations mentioned above.

Some existing logics include these elements separately. For example, [10] includes time-stamps in atoms and in a belief modality, but it lacks a knowledge modality, and it is not suitable for OSNs (their aim was to reason about AGM belief revision). The logic proposed in [11] can reason about how beliefs spread in Twitter, but it does not include time-stamps. Finally, [12] proposes an axiomatisation of an epistemic logic with knowledge and belief, but without time-stamps in modalities or atoms. Section 4 includes a more detailed comparison of related work.

Contributions: In this paper we introduce a novel logic that combines knowledge, belief and time (Sect. 2), tailored to define *dynamic privacy policies* (Sect. 3). More concretely: (1) We extend [6] by equipping atoms and epistemic operators with time instants which allows to derive *learning* and *forget* operators. (2) We equip the logic with *belief* operators, with the restriction that agents cannot believe in something that they know is false, and we define a belief propagation algorithm which guarantees that agents' beliefs are always consistent. This allows us to model OSNs that permit gossiping in which potentially false information can be spread. Analogously, we derive the *accept* and *reject* operators which capture the moment in which an agent starts or stops believing in something. (3) We introduce the notion of *extended knowledge bases* (EKBs), which allow to answer queries of temporal epistemic formulas against the knowledge acquired during a sequence of events, via *timed derivations* labelled with time-windows. This idea allows to instantiate our framework for different OSNs, for example those with eternal memory like Facebook and for ephemeral ones like Snapchat. (4) We prove that the model checking problem for this logic is decidable by providing a model checking algorithm that is also used to check policy conformance.

As a result, policy conformance is also decidable. The purpose of this paper is to present an expressive foundation for developing algorithms for detecting privacy violations and for privacy enforcement. We leave the discussion of specialized efficient algorihtms for future work.

2   A Timed Knowledge Based Logic

We introduce here $\mathcal{KBL_{RT}}$ a knowledge-based first-order logic that includes time-stamped knowledge and belief modalities, and quantification over time-stamps.

2.1   Syntax

Let $\mathcal{T}$ be a *vocabulary* consisting of a set of predicate and function symbols, with some implicit arity, and constant symbols. We assume an infinite supply of variables $x, y, \ldots$ Terms can be built as $s::= c \mid x \mid f(\overrightarrow{s})$ where $\overrightarrow{s}$ is a tuple of terms respecting the arity of f. Let $\mathbb{T}$ denote a set of *time-stamps*, which is required to be a non-Zeno totally ordered set, i.e., there is a finite number of instants between any two given instants. We use time-stamps to mark pieces of information or to query the knowledge of the agents at specific instants. Consider also a set of agents Ag, a set of domains $\mathcal{D}$, and a set of events EVT (e.g., share a post or upload a picture). Similarly, we use $\mathcal{C}$ and Σ to denote special sets of predicate symbols that denote connections (between agents) and permissions.

Definition 1 (Syntax of $\mathcal{KBL_{RT}}$).   *Given agents $i, j \in Ag$ a time-stamp $t \in \mathbb{T}$, an event $e \in EVT$, a variable x, a domain $D \in \mathcal{D}$, predicate symbols $c^t(i,j), a^t(i,j), p^t(\overrightarrow{s})$ where $c \in \mathcal{C}$ and $a \in \Sigma$, the syntax of the real-time knowledge-based logic $\mathcal{KBL_{RT}}$ is inductively defined as:*

$$\varphi::= \rho \mid \varphi \wedge \varphi \mid \neg\varphi \mid \forall t \cdot \varphi \mid \forall x : D \cdot \varphi \mid K_i^t\varphi \mid B_i^t\varphi$$
$$\rho::= c^t(i,j) \mid a^t(i,j) \mid p^t(\overrightarrow{s}) \mid occurred^t(e)$$

The epistemic modalities stand for: $K_i^t\varphi$, agent i knows φ at time t; $B_i^t\varphi$, agent i believes φ at time t. We use the following notation as syntactic sugar $P_i^j a^t \triangleq a^t(i,j)$, meaning that "*agent i is permitted to execute action a to agent j at time t*". For example, $P_{Bob}^{Alice} friendRequest^5$ means that Bob is allowed to send a friend request to Alice at time 5. We use $\mathcal{F_{KBL_{RT}}}$ to denote the set of all well-formed $\mathcal{KBL_{RT}}$ formulae. Our logic introduces the following novel notions that have not been considered in other formal privacy policies languages such as [6,13–15].

- *Time-stamped Predicates.* Time-stamps are explicit in each predicate, including connections and actions. For instance, if Alice and Bob were friends in a certain time period, then the predicate $friend^t(Alice, Bob)$ is true for all t falling into the period, and false for all t outside the period. This can be seen as the *valid time* in temporal databases [16].

- *Separating Knowledge and Belief.* Not all the information that users see in a social network is true. For instance, Alice may tell Bob that she will be working until late, whereas she will actually go with her colleagues to have some beers. In this example, Bob has the (false) belief that Alice is working. Traditionally, in epistemic logic, the knowledge of agents consists on true facts, while beliefs represent plausible information that may be false [17]. For $\mathcal{KBL}_{\mathcal{RT}}$ we combine both modalities in one logic. In the following section we describe how to combine these two.
- *Time-stamped Epistemic Modalities.* Time-stamps are also part of the epistemic modalities K and B. Using time-stamps we can refer to the knowledge and beliefs of the agents at different points in time. For example, $B_{Bob}^{20:00} loc^{19:00}(Alice, work)$ means that Bob beliefs at 20:00 that Alice's location at 19:00 is work.
- *Occurrence of Events.* Being able to determine when an event has occurred allows users to define policies that are activated whenever someone performs an undesired event. Examples of these policies are: "if Alice unfriends Bob, she is not allowed to send Bob a friend request" or "if Alice declines an invitation to Bob's party, then she cannot see any of the pictures uploaded during the party." We introduce $occurred^t(e)$ to syntactically capture the moment when a specific event e occurred.

2.2 Semantics

Real-Time Social Network Models. We introduce formal models to reason about the states and evolution of social networks. These models leverage the information in the social graph [18] —the core data model in most social networks [19–21]. We extend social graphs, which include *agents* (or *users*) and the relationships between them, by adding for each agent a knowledge base, and the set of privacy policies that the agent has activated. We build upon a previous version of this framework [6], increasing substantially the expressiveness of privacy policies (see Sect. 3).

Definition 2 (Social Network Models). *Given a set of formulae $\mathcal{F} \subseteq \mathcal{F}_{\mathcal{KBL}_{\mathcal{RT}}}$, a set of privacy policies Π, and a finite set of agents $Ag \subseteq \mathcal{AU}$ from a universe $\mathcal{AU}$, a social network model (SNM) is a tuple $\langle Ag, \mathcal{A}, KB, \pi \rangle$, where*

- *Ag is a nonempty finite set of nodes representing the agents in the social network;*
- *$\mathcal{A}$ is a first-order structure over the SNM, consisting of a set of domains, a set of relations, a set of functions and a set of constants interpreted over their corresponding domain.*
- *$KB : Ag \to 2^{\mathcal{F}}$ is a function retrieving a set of (time-stamped) basic facts of an agent, which are stored in the agent's knowledge base; we write KB_i for $KB(i)$;*
- *$\pi : Ag \to 2^{\Pi}$ which returns the privacy policies of an agent; we write π_i for $\pi(i)$.*

In Definition 2, the shape of the relational structure $\mathcal{A}$ depends on the social network. We represent the connections—edges of the social graph—and the permission actions between social network agents as families of binary relations, respectively $\{C_i\}_{i\in C} \subseteq Ag \times Ag$ and $\{A_i\}_{i\in \Sigma} \subseteq Ag \times Ag$ over the domain of agents. We use $\mathcal{D}$ to denote the set of domains. The set of agents Ag is always included in the set of domains. We use $\mathcal{SN}_{\mathcal{RT}}$ to denote the universe of all possible social network models.

Evolution of Social Network Models. The state of a social network changes by means of the execution of *events* from the set EVT. For instance, in Facebook, users can share posts, upload pictures, like comments, etc. We use traces to capture the evolution of the social network. A *trace* is a finite sequence $\sigma = \langle(SN_0, E_0, t_0), (SN_1, E_1, t_1), \ldots, (SN_k, E_k, t_k)\rangle$ such that, for all $0 \leq i \leq k$, $SN_i \in \mathcal{SN}_{\mathcal{RT}}$, $E_i \subseteq EVT$, and $t_i \in \mathbb{T}$. We use $\mathbb{T}_\sigma = \{t \mid (SN, E, t) \in \sigma\}$ for the set of time-stamps of σ. We impose some conditions to traces so that they accurately model the evolution of social networks. We say that a trace is *well-formed* if it satisfies the following conditions:

1. Time-stamps are strictly ordered from smallest to largest, that is, for any i, j with $0 \leq i < j \leq k$ it follows that $t_i < t_j$.
2. Successor states are the result of events. We use $\rightarrow$ for the transition relation defined as $\rightarrow \subseteq \mathcal{SN}_{\mathcal{RT}} \times 2^{EVT} \times \mathbb{T} \times \mathcal{SN}_{\mathcal{RT}}$ ($\rightarrow$ can be specified using small step operational semantics as we show in [15] for an untimed version of this framework). We write $SN_1 \xrightarrow{E,t} SN_2$ if SN_2 is the result of the set of events $E \in EVT$ happening in SN_1 at time t. We allow E to be empty, in which case $SN_1 = SN_2$.
3. For each $\xrightarrow{E,t}$ the set of events E must only contain independent events. Two events are independent if, when executed sequentially, their execution order does not change their resulting state. Formally, e and e' are independent whenever for every state SN_0 and time t, the state SN_2 and SN_2' obtained as $SN_0 \xrightarrow{\{e\},t} SN_1 \xrightarrow{\{e'\},t} SN_2$ and $SN_0 \xrightarrow{\{e'\},t} SN_1' \xrightarrow{\{e\},t} SN_2'$ satisfy that $SN_2 = SN_2'$. This definition can be easily extended to sets of events in the expected way.

We use $\mathcal{WFT}$ to refer to the set of well-formed traces. We assume that there is a function predecessor $pred : \mathbb{T} \to \mathbb{T}$ that takes a time-stamp and returns the previous time-stamp in the trace. Analogously, $next : \mathbb{T} \to \mathbb{T}$ returns the next time-stamp in the trace. Since the set of time-stamps is non-Zeno it is always possible to compute these functions.[1]

$\mathcal{KBL}_{\mathcal{RT}}$ formulae are very similar to $\mathcal{L}_n$ from epistemic logic [17]. There are two standard ways to define semantics of epistemic logics. First, one can define for every agent an undistinguishability relation between the *worlds* that the agent considers possible [17]. When considering traces of events, the framework

---

[1] We can assume that the predecessor of the initial time-stamp is the initial state itself, and similarly the next of the end of the trace returns the equal to itself.

typically used is *interpreted systems*. An alternative encoding, proposed by Fagin *et al.* [17, Sect. 7.3] consists in encoding the answer of epistemic queries from knowledge bases of accumulated facts. We follow this way of modelling knowledge here by equipping each agent with a knowledge base and defining the semantics of $\mathcal{KBL}_{\mathcal{RT}}$ formulae based on answers by these knowledge bases.

Extended Knowledge Bases. An *Extended Knowledge Base* consists of a collection of $\mathcal{KBL}_{\mathcal{RT}}$ formulae, which represents the basic knowledge of the agent at a point in time. Epistemic derivations allow to answer whether a formula follows from the information stored in a knowledge base.

Derivations in EKBs. The EKB of an agent contains the explicit knowledge she acquired previously. Additional knowledge can be derived from the explicit pieces of information stored in these EKBs. Derivations can use formulae at a given point in time and at older times. We introduce the notion of *time window* (or simply, *window*) to determine how knowledge from the past can be used in a derivation. We write $\Gamma \vdash (\varphi, w)$ to denote that φ can be derived from Γ given a window w. We provide a set of deduction rules, DR, of the form given on the right meaning that, given the set of premises Γ, ψ can be derived with a window w from φ with a window w'.

$$\frac{\Gamma \vdash (\varphi, w')}{\Gamma \vdash (\psi, w)}$$

Definition 3. *A* timed derivation *of a formula φ with a window w, is a finite sequence of pairs* $(\varphi_1, w_1), (\varphi_2, w_2), \ldots, (\varphi_n, w_n) = (\varphi, w)$ *such that each φ_i, for $1 \le i \le n$, φ_i follows by an application of a deduction rule of DR whose premises φ_j, with $j < i$, have already been derived, and $w_j \le w_i$.*

We now present the concrete derivation rules that allow to derive knowledge from the facts stored in EKBs. These rules extend axiomatizations of knowledge and belief with rules to deal with knowledge propagation through time.

Knowledge and Belief in EKBs. In our EKBs knowledge and belief can coexist. The common axiomatization of knowledge is **S5**. In [17], Fagin *et al.* provided an axiomatization for belief known as **KD45**, which includes the same set of axioms as **S5** —replacing K_i by B_i—except for the axiom $K_i\varphi \implies \varphi$ (A3). The reason is that beliefs do not need to be true—as required by A3 for knowledge. The requirement for beliefs is that an agent must have *consistent* beliefs, which is captured by $\neg B_i \bot$ (axiom D). To derive new knowledge, axioms from **S5** can be applied to formulas of the form $K_i\varphi$ and axioms from **KD45** for formulas of the form $B_i\varphi$. Additionally, derivations can also relate knowledge and beliefs, for which we use two axioms proposed by Halpern *et al.* in [12]: (L1) $K_i\varphi \implies B_i\varphi$ and (L2) $B_i\varphi \implies K_i B_i\varphi$. L1 states that when agents know a fact they also believe it, which is sound with respect to the definition of both modalities, since knowledge is required to be true (A3). Axiom L1 provides a way to convert knowledge to belief. L2 encodes that when agents believe a fact φ they know that they believe φ.

Table 1. EKB axioms for a trace σ for each $t \in \mathbb{T}_\sigma$.

Knowledge axioms		Belief axioms		Knowledge-Belief axioms	
A1	All tautologies of first-order logic	K	$(B_i^t\varphi \wedge B_i^t(\varphi \implies \psi))$	L1	$K_i^t\varphi \implies B_i^t\varphi$
A2	$(K_i^t\varphi \wedge K_i^t(\varphi \implies \psi))$		$\implies B_i^t\psi$	L2	$B_i^t\varphi \implies K_i^tB_i^t\varphi$
	$\implies K_i^t\psi$	D	$\neg B_i^t\bot$		
A3	$K_i^t\varphi \implies \varphi$	B4	$B_i^t\varphi \implies B_i^tB_i^t\varphi$		
A4	$K_i^t\varphi \implies K_i^tK_i^t\varphi$	B5	$\neg B_i^t\varphi \implies B_i^t\neg B_i^t\varphi$		
A5	$\neg K_i^t\varphi \implies K_i^t\neg K_i^t\varphi$				

The previous axiomatizations are restricted to reasoning about a concrete time (or to timeless information), but we are interested in reasoning about the dynamic acquisition of knowledge in the changing world of online social networks. Consequently, we decorate all modalities with a time-stamp t, to explicitly capture the time at which an agent knows something and the time of occurrence of events and relations. Table 1 shows the complete list of axioms for a given $t \in \mathbb{T}_\sigma$.

To use these axioms in timed derivations we express them as deduction rules in Table 2. Note that all derivations that use these axioms use the same t and w. We add an explicit K_i^t to every formula in a user's EKB so that we can syntactically determine when some knowledge enters an EKB. Formally, we say that users in a trace σ are *self-aware* whenever for all $t \in \mathbb{T}_\sigma$ if $\varphi \in EKB_i^{\sigma[t]}$ then $\varphi = K_i^t\varphi'$. In what follows, we always assume that agents are self-aware.

Example 1. Consider the following EKB from a trace σ of an agent i at time t.

$$EKB_i^{\sigma[t]} \quad \boxed{\begin{array}{c} K_i^t(\forall t' \cdot \forall j : Ag^{t'} \cdot event^{t'}(j, pub) \implies loc^{t'}(j, pub)) \\ K_i^t event^t(Alice, pub) \end{array}}$$

In this EKB i can derive, using the axioms in Table 1, that Alice's location at time t is a pub, i.e., $loc^t(Alice, pub)$. Here we show the steps to derive this piece of information. We recall that quantifiers are unfolded when added to the knowledge base. For example, given formula $\varphi(x) : K_i^t\forall j : Ag^x \cdot event^x(j, pub) \implies loc^x(j, pub)$ and $\mathbb{T}_\sigma = \{t_0, t_1, \ldots, t\}$, the EKB contains $\varphi(t_0) \wedge \varphi(t_1) \wedge \ldots \wedge \varphi(t)$. The predicate $event^t(j, pub)$ means that j attended an event at time t in a *pub*. The predicate $loc^t(j, pub)$ means that j's location is a *pub*. Thus, the implication above encodes that: if i knows at t that an agent is attending an event in a pub at time t', then her location will be a pub. In this example, i knows at time t that Alice is attending an event at the pub, $event^t(Alice, pub)$. Since knowledge is required to be true, $event^t(Alice, pub)$ must be a true predicate. Hence, $K_i^t event^t(Alice, pub) \implies loc^t(Alice, pub)$ must also be present in $EKB_i^{\sigma[t]}$. Applying A2 to $K_i^t event^t(Alice, pub)$ and the previous implication we can derive $K_i^t loc^t(Alice, pub)$. $\qquad\square$

Table 2. EKB deduction rules for a trace σ for each $t \in \mathbb{T}_\sigma$.

Knowledge deduction rules axioms		
$\dfrac{\varphi \text{ is a first-order tautology}}{\Gamma \vdash (\varphi, w)}$ (A1)	$\dfrac{\Gamma \vdash (K_i^t \varphi, w) \quad \Gamma \vdash (K_i^t(\varphi \implies \psi), w)}{\Gamma \vdash (K_i^t \psi, w)}$ (A2)	
$\dfrac{\Gamma \vdash (K_i^t \varphi, w)}{\Gamma \vdash (\varphi, w)}$ (A3)	$\dfrac{\Gamma \vdash (K_i^t \varphi, w)}{\Gamma \vdash (K_i^t K_i^t \varphi, w)}$ (A4)	$\dfrac{\Gamma \vdash (\neg K_i^t \varphi, w)}{\Gamma \vdash (K_i^t \neg K_i^t \varphi, w)}$ (A5)

Belief deduction rules			
$\dfrac{\begin{array}{c}\Gamma \vdash (B_i^t \varphi, w) \\ \Gamma \vdash (B_i^t(\varphi \implies \psi), w)\end{array}}{\Gamma \vdash (B_i^t \psi, w)}$ (K)	$\dfrac{}{\Gamma \vdash (\neg B_i^t \bot, w)}$ (D)	$\dfrac{\Gamma \vdash (B_i^t \varphi, w)}{\Gamma \vdash (B_i^t B_i^t \varphi, w)}$ (B4)	$\dfrac{\Gamma \vdash (\neg B_i^t \varphi, w)}{\Gamma \vdash (B_i^t \neg B_i^t \varphi, w)}$ (B5)

Premise deduction rule	Knowledge-Belief deduction rules	
$\dfrac{\varphi \in \Gamma}{\Gamma \vdash (\varphi, w)}$ (PREMISE)	$\dfrac{\Gamma \vdash (K_i^t \varphi, w)}{\Gamma \vdash (B_i^t \varphi, w)}$ (L1)	$\dfrac{\Gamma \vdash (B_i^t \varphi, w)}{\Gamma \vdash (K_i^t B_i^t \varphi, w)}$ (L2)

Handling Time-Stamps. Users can also use EKBs to reason about time. For instance, if Alice learns Bob's birthday she will remember this piece of information, possibly forever. Some other times information is transient and changes over time. Consider Alice, who shares with Bob a post including her location. Right after posting, Bob will know Alice's location—assuming she said the truth. However, after a few hours, Bob will not be certain about whether Alice remains in the same location. We denote the period of time in which some piece of information remains true as its *duration*.

Different pieces of information might have different durations. Duration also depends on the OSN, which can be designed in such a way that the effect of events disappears after some time. For example, in Snapchat messages last 10 s; in Whatsapp status messages last 24 h; and in Facebook posts remain forever unless a user removes them. We introduce the parameter w (see Sect. 1) to model the duration of the information. Using w we define the following deduction rule, which encodes a notion of duration-aware propagation of knowledge. Given $t, t' \in \mathbb{T}_\sigma$ where $t < t'$, the axiom (KR1) is shown on the right. The intuition behind KR1 is that some time in w is consumed every time knowledge is propagated. Consider that Alice knows at time 1 the formula φ, that is, $K_{Alice}^1 \varphi$. Using KR1 in a derivation allows to derive that she knows φ at a later time, e.g., $K_{Alice}^5 \varphi$. Note that this derivation requires w to be at least 4. The following example explains why.

$$\dfrac{\Gamma \vdash (K_i^t \varphi, w - (t' - t))}{\Gamma \vdash (K_i^{t'} \varphi, w)} \text{ (KR1)}$$

Example 2. Consider the following sequence of EKBs of an agent i from a trace σ where $\mathbb{T}_\sigma = \{0, \ldots, 4\}$.

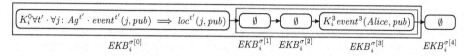

$$EKB_i^{\sigma[0]} \qquad\qquad EKB_i^{\sigma[1]} \quad EKB_i^{\sigma[2]} \qquad EKB_i^{\sigma[3]} \qquad EKB_i^{\sigma[4]}$$

Note that deriving Alice's location requires to combine knowledge from different knowledge bases at different times. This derivations use the knowledge recall rule KR1 with a large enough window. In the figure, the inner (red) rectangle marks the accessible knowledge for $w = 2$ and the outer (blue) rectangle for $w = 3$. In order for i to derive $loc^3(Alice, pub)$ she needs to combine knowledge from $EKB_i^{\sigma[0]}$ and $EKB_i^{\sigma[3]}$. Let $EKB_i^\sigma = \bigcup_{t \in \mathbb{T}_\sigma} EKB_i^{\sigma[t]}$. We first show how to construct a proof forwards, starting from the premises and a window of 0, and move forward increasing w until the inference can be performed. In particular, we show that $EKB_i^\sigma \vdash (K_i^3 loc^3(Alice, pub), w)$ for $w \in \mathbb{N}$. Applying the rule PREMISE with $w = 0$, we derive $EKB_i^\sigma \vdash (K_i^0 event^3(Alice, pub) \implies loc^3(Alice, pub), 0)$. Now we use KR1 to combine this knowledge with knowledge at time 3:

$$(\text{KR1}) \quad \frac{EKB_i^\sigma \vdash (K_i^0 event^3(Alice, pub) \implies loc^3(Alice, pub), 0)}{EKB_i^\sigma \vdash (K_i^3 event^3(Alice, pub) \implies loc^3(Alice, pub), 3)}$$

This inference requires the window to be increased to 3. We apply PREMISE again to obtain $(EKB_i^\sigma \vdash K_i^3 event^3(Alice, pub), 3)$, which allows A2 to derive $(EKB_i^\sigma \vdash K_i^3 loc^3(Alice, pub), 3)$. This proof shows that i knows Alice's location provided that agents remember information for at least 3 units of time.

A window smaller than 3 makes this derivation impossible. We now construct the proof backwards, considering $w = 2$ to show that the derivation is impossible. We try to show that $EKB_i^\sigma \vdash (K_i^3 loc^3(Alice, pub), 2)$, which requires:

$$(\text{A2}) \quad \frac{(EKB_i^\sigma \vdash K_i^3 event^3(Alice, pub), 2)}{EKB_i^\sigma \vdash (K_i^3 event^3(Alice, pub) \implies loc^3(Alice, pub), 2)} \over EKB_i^\sigma \vdash (K_i^3 loc^3(Alice, pub), 2)$$

The first premise, $(EKB_i^\sigma \vdash K_i^3 event^3(Alice, pub), 2)$, trivially follows by PREMISE. To prove the second premise we first try move one step back using KR1: $EKB_i^\sigma \vdash (K_i^2 event^3(Alice, pub) \implies loc^3(Alice, pub), 1)$, but since there is no knowledge at time 2, the previous statement cannot be proven. We apply again KR1 obtaining $EKB_i^\sigma \vdash (K_i^1 event^3(Alice, pub) \implies loc^3(Alice, pub), 0)$, which cannot be proven. Since the remaining window is 0, we have already accessed all knowledge that i remembers, and older EKBs cannot be accessed. This closes the proof. □

Belief Propagation. Beliefs cannot be propagated as easily as knowledge because new beliefs may contradict current knowledge or beliefs of an agent. Instead of using timed derivations, we model agents that try to propagate beliefs if these beliefs are consistent, and discard them otherwise. We describe two kinds of agents: *conservative* and *susceptible*, but other criteria for choosing between incompatible beliefs are possible. We use the parameter β in the framework to denote the kind of agent. Conservative agents reject any new belief that contradicts their current set of beliefs, while susceptible agents always accept new beliefs that replace old believes if necessary to guarantee a consistent set of beliefs. Here we present a belief propagation algorithm which describes how agents behave when faced with a new belief.

Consider a trace σ with $\mathbb{T}_\sigma = \{t_0, \ldots, t_{n-1}, t_n\}$. We use the following notation $EKB_i^{\sigma[t_j, t_k]} = \bigcup_{t \in \{t_j, \ldots, t_k\}} EKB_i^{\sigma[t]}$. Also, we introduce the event $\mathsf{enter}(B_i^t \varphi)$ meaning that *belief φ enters i's knowledge base at time t*. The moment at which this event occurs identifies the moment when a belief is inserted in an agent's knowledge base, which is crucial to propagate beliefs. Given a belief $B_i^{t_n} \varphi$ that is about to enter $EKB_i^{\sigma[t_n]}$, i.e., $SN_{t_{n-1}} \xrightarrow{\mathsf{enter}(B_i^{t_n} \varphi), t_n} SN_{t_n}$, Algorithm 1 propagates the accumulated set of beliefs as long as they are inside the window w, and resolves conflicts according to β.

Lines 2–3 of Algorithm 1 construct a set Ψ of candidate beliefs to be propagated—according to w—together with the new belief that tries to enter i's EKB. The if block (lines 4–6) sorts Ψ according to β. In the foreach block (lines 7–11), we iterate over the sorted list of beliefs and add them to $EKB_i^{\sigma[t_n]}$ if they are consistent with the rest of knowledge and beliefs. It is easy to see that traversing beliefs from newest to oldest gives preference to newer beliefs in entering $EKB_i^{\sigma[t_n]}$, which corresponds to susceptible agents. In particular, $B_i^{t_n} \varphi$—the newest belief—will always enter the $EKB_i^{\sigma[t_n]}$ unless this belief contradicts actual knowledge. On the contrary, when sorting from oldest to newest, the older beliefs will have preference to enter $EKB_i^{\sigma[t_n]}$, thus, preventing new inconsistent beliefs to enter $EKB_i^{\sigma[t_n]}$, as required for conservative agents. In particular, $B_i^{t_n} \varphi$ will not be added to $EKB_i^{\sigma[t_n]}$ unless it is consistent with all the previous beliefs and knowledge. Finally, we always include the predicate $occurred^{t_n}(\mathsf{enter}(B_i^{t_n} \varphi))$ (line 12) so that the agent remembers that she was told $B_i^{t_n} \varphi$ —independently on whether she started to believe it. Note that consistency of $EKB_i^{\sigma[t_n]}$ in both cases is directly guaranteed by the inclusion condition in line 8.

Example 3. At 20:00 Alice sends a message to Bob indicating that she is at work, so $EKB_{Bob}^{\sigma[20:00]}$ contains $occurred^{20:00}$ ($\mathsf{enter}(B_{Bob}^{20:00} loc^{20:00}(Alice, work))$) and also $K_{Bob}^{20:00} B_{Bob}^{20:00} loc^{20:00}(Alice, work)$. At 22:00 Bob checks his Facebook timeline, and he sees a post of Charlie—who is a coworker of Alice—at 20:00 saying that he is with all his coworkers in a pub having a beer. Assuming that at 22:00 Bob still remembers his belief from 20:00 this new information creates a conflict with Bob's beliefs. Note that information from Charlie's post is also taken as a belief since there is no way for Bob to validate it. If Bob is a conservative agent, then $EKB_{Bob}^{\sigma[22:00]} = \{K_{Bob}^{22:00} B_{Bob}^{22:00} loc^{20:00}(Alice, work)\} \cup \{occurred^{22:00}(\mathsf{enter}(B_{Bob}^{22:00} loc^{20:00}(Alice, pub)))\}$, meaning that the new belief

---

Algorithm 1. Belief propagation

1: **procedure** BELIEF-PROPAGATION($EKB_i^{\sigma[t_n]}$, $B_i^{t_n}\varphi$, w, β)
2:     $\Psi \leftarrow \{K_i^{t_n} B_i^{t_n}\psi | occurred^t(\text{enter}(B_i^t\varphi)) \in EKB_i^{\sigma[t_n-w,t_n]}$ where $t \in [t_n - w, t_n]\}$
3:     $\Psi \leftarrow \Psi \cup \{K_i^{t_n} B_i^{t_n}\varphi\}$
4:     **if** $\beta = susceptible$ **then** $[b_0, b_1, \ldots, b_n] \leftarrow sortNewestOldest(\Psi)$
5:     **else if** $\beta = conservative$ **then** $[b_0, b_1, \ldots, b_n] \leftarrow sortOldestNewest(\Psi)$
6:     **end if**
7:     **foreach** b in $[b_0, b_1, \ldots, b_n]$ **do**
8:         **if** $EKB_i^{\sigma[t_0,t_n]} \cup \{b\} \not\vdash B_i^{t_n}\bot$ **then**
9:             $EKB_i^{\sigma[t_n]} \leftarrow EKB_i^{\sigma[t_n]} \cup \{b\}$
10:        **end if**
11:    **end foreach**
12:    $EKB_i^{\sigma[t_n]} \leftarrow EKB_i^{\sigma[t_n]} \cup \{occurred^{t_n}(\text{enter}(B_i^{t_n}\varphi))\}$
13:    **return** $EKB_i^{\sigma[t_n]}$
14: **end procedure**

---

is rejected. If Bob is a susceptible agent: $EKB_{Bob}^{\sigma[22:00]} = \{K_{Bob}^{22:00} B_{Bob}^{22:00} loc^{20:00}$ $(Alice, pub)\} \cup \{occurred^{22:00}(\text{enter}(B_{Bob}^{22:00} loc^{20:00}(Alice, pub)))\}$. Bob believes that Alice's location at time t ($20:00 \leq t < 22:00$) is work—due to belief propagation. After 22:00, this belief does not propagate to avoid contradictions with the new belief $B_{Bob}^{22:00} loc^{20:00}(Alice, pub)$. □

Semantics of $\mathcal{KBL_{RT}}$. The semantics of $\mathcal{KBL_{RT}}$ formulae is given by the satisfaction relation $\models$. Given a well-formed trace $\sigma \in \mathcal{WFT}$, a window $w \in \mathbb{N}$, a time-stamp $t \in \mathbb{T}_\sigma$, agents $i, j \in Ag$, a finite set of agents $G \subseteq Ag$, formulae $\varphi, \psi \in \mathcal{F_{KBL_{RT}}}$, predicate symbols $c^t(i,j), a^t(i,j), p^t(\vec{s})$ where $c \in \mathcal{C}$ and $a \in \Sigma$, a domain $D \in \mathcal{D}$, an event $e \in EVT$, and a variable x, the *satisfaction relation* $\models \subseteq \mathcal{WFT} \times \mathcal{F_{KBL_{RT}}}$ is defined as follows:

$$\sigma \models occurred^t(e) \quad \text{iff} \quad (SN, E, t) \in \sigma \text{ such that } e \in E$$
$$\sigma \models \neg\varphi \quad \text{iff} \quad \sigma \not\models \varphi$$
$$\sigma \models \varphi \wedge \psi \quad \text{iff} \quad \sigma \models \varphi \text{ and } \sigma \models \psi$$
$$\sigma \models \forall t \cdot \varphi \quad \text{iff} \quad \text{for all } v \in \mathbb{T}_\sigma, \sigma \models \varphi[v/t]$$
$$\sigma \models \forall x : D^t \cdot \varphi \quad \text{iff} \quad \text{for all } v \in D^{\sigma[t]}, \sigma \models \varphi[v/x]$$
$$\sigma \models c^t(i,j) \quad \text{iff} \quad (i,j) \in C_c^{\sigma[t]}$$
$$\sigma \models a^t(i,j) \quad \text{iff} \quad (i,j) \in A_a^{\sigma[t]}$$
$$\sigma \models p^t(\vec{s}) \quad \text{iff} \quad p^t(\vec{s}) \in KB_e^{\sigma[t]}$$
$$\sigma \models K_i^t\varphi \quad \text{iff} \quad \bigcup_{\{t'|t'<t,t'\in\mathbb{T}_\sigma\}} KB_i^{\sigma[t']} \vdash (\varphi, w)$$
$$\sigma \models B_i^t\varphi \quad \text{iff} \quad \bigcup_{\{t'|t'<t,t'\in\mathbb{T}_\sigma\}} KB_i^{\sigma[t']} \vdash (B_i^t\varphi, w)$$

Predicates of type $occurred^t(e)$ are true if the event e is part of the events that occurred at time t in the trace. $\forall t$ quantifies over all the time-stamps in the trace $\mathbb{T}_\sigma$, which is a finite set. For the remaining domains, $\forall x : D^t$, the substitution is carried out over the elements of the domain at a concrete time t. Remember that each individual domain D^t always contains a finite set of elements. However, the same domain at different points in time, e.g., D^t and $D^{t'}$, for any $t \neq t'$ might contain different number of elements. When checking connections $c^t(i,j)$ and actions $a^t(i,j)$ at time t, we check whether the corresponding relation— $C_c^{\sigma[t]}$ and $A_a^{\sigma[t]}$, respectively—of the SNM at time t contains the pair of users in question. Checking whether a predicate of type $p^t(\vec{s})$ holds is equivalent to looking into the knowledge base of the environment at time t. The environment's knowledge base contains all predicates that are true in the real world at a given moment in time. For example, "it is raining in Gothenburg at 19:00" $rain^{19:00}(Gothenburg)$ or "Alice's location at 20:00 is Madrid" $loc^{20:00}(Alice, Madrid)$. Determining whether an agent knows or believes a fact at a certain moment in time—i.e., $K_i^t \varphi$ or $B_i^t \varphi$—boils down to derivability from the union of all her EKBs for the given window w. This way of defining belief is based on the fact that agents are aware of their beliefs, recall axiom (L2) in Table 1.

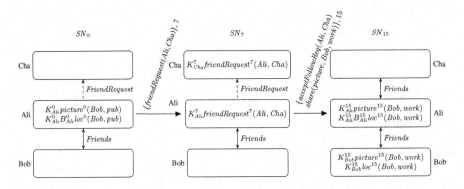

Fig. 1. Example of a Snapchat trace

Example 4 (Snapchat). In Snapchat users can perform two main events: (1) Connect through a friend relation; (2) share timed messages, which last up to 10 seconds with their friends. Figure 1 shows an example trace for Snapchat with three agents $Ag = \{Alice, Bob, Charlie\}$. Since Ag does not change we avoid using the superindex indicating the time-stamp of the domain. The trace consists of three SNMs SN_0, SN_7 and SN_{15}, where the subindex indicates the time-stamp.

At time 0, Alice and Bob are friends, $friends^0(Alice, Bob)$, which is represented by including the pair $(Alice, Bob)$ in the relation $Friends^{\sigma[0]}$ in SN_0. Alice and Bob's friendship does not change along σ. Also, Alice is permitted to send a friend request to Charlie—depicted as an outgoing dashed arrow. Thus, $\sigma \models P_{Alice}^{Charlie} friendRequest^0$ holds. Finally, Alice knows that there is a picture of Bob at the pub, $picture^0(Bob, pub)$, and she *believes* that Bob is at the pub, $loc^0(Bob, pub)$. This is a belief because she cannot verify that the picture has not been modified or she cannot precisely identify the location. However, the existence of $picture^0(Bob, pub)$ can be verified since it is a picture that Alice can see in the OSN. At time 7, Alice sends a friend request to Charlie. After the execution of the event both agents know $friendRequest^7(Alice, Charlie)$. Note that this event produces knowledge, because the agents can verify that the friend request has occurred. Finally, at time 15, Charlie accepts Alice's request and Bob shares a picture at work. Note that these two events are independent. After Bob accepts Alice's request $(Alice, Charlie) \notin FriendRequest^{\sigma[15]}$, and $(Alice, Charlie) \in Friends^{\sigma[15]}$. That is, Alice cannot send more friend requests to Charlie, and now they have become friends. Furthermore, both, Alice and Bob know that Bob shared a picture at work. In this case, Bob also knows that his location is work, but Alice only believes it.[2] The reason is that, unlikely Bob, Alice cannot confirm that Bob's location is work.

As on Snapchat messages last for up to 10 seconds, we can assume w.l.o.g. that all messages last 10 seconds, i.e., $w = 10$. Consequently, in σ, Alice remembers Bob picture from 0 to 10: $\sigma \models \forall t \cdot 0 \leq t \leq 10 \implies K_{Alice}^{t} picture^{0}(Bob, pub)$. Similarly, her belief about Bob location, $picture^{0}(Bob, pub)$, vanishes at time 10. Note also that, when Charlie accepts Alice's friend request, he still knows (or remembers) that Alice sent it. In Snapchat friend requests are permanent, but in our framework we can choose whether friend requests disappear after a few seconds. This can be done by requiring that the agent knows that a friend request occurred in order to accept it. In such a case, in σ, after time 18 Charlie would not be able to accept Alice's request. □

2.3 Model Checking $\mathcal{KBL}_{\mathcal{RT}}$

In this section, we show that the model checking problem for $\mathcal{KBL}_{\mathcal{RT}}$ is decidable.

Theorem 1. *The model checking problem for $\mathcal{KBL}_{\mathcal{RT}}$ is decidable.*

Proof. Let σ be a trace, φ a formula and w a window. Since all domains are finite, we unfold universal quantifiers $\forall x: D \cdot \varphi'$ and $\forall t \cdot \varphi'$ into a conjunction of formulas $\varphi'[v/x]$ for each element v in the domain D or in $\mathbb{T}_\sigma$. The resulting formula is quantifier free and has size $O(|\varphi| \times d^q)$ where d is a bound on the size of the domain and q is the maximum nested stack of quantifiers. Let $\varphi_1, \ldots, \varphi_m$ be the subformulas of the resulting formula, ordered respecting the subformula relation. An easy induction on $k < m$ shows that we can label every agent and at every step of the trace with either φ_k or $\neg \varphi_k$. The labelling proceeds from the earliest time-stamp on. We show only the epistemic operators here (see [22] for the complete proof):

- Checking $\psi_k = \neg \psi_j$ and $\psi_k = \psi_j \wedge \psi_i$ can be done in constant time for each instant t and agent i, using the induction hypothesis.
- First, we construct a set Δ where we instantiate all the axioms in Table 1 for each $t \in \mathbb{T}_\sigma$. The resulting set has size $|\Delta| = |\mathbb{T}_\sigma| \times 11$ (number of axioms in Table 1). Secondly, we instantiate KR1 (cf. Table 1), for w and for

---

[2] For readability we omit $occurred^{15}(\text{enter}(B_{Alice}^{15} loc^{15}(Bob, work)))$ in Fig. 1 which is included in $EKB_{Alice}^{\sigma[15]}$.

all $t, t' \in \mathbb{T}_\sigma$ such that $t > t'$ and $t - t' < w$. The resulting set of axioms has size $O(\sum_{n=1}^{|\mathbb{T}_\sigma|-1} n \times w)$. That is, all legal combinations of timestamps (n) times the window size (w). These axioms are also included in Δ, which, consequently, contains a finite set of axioms. Finally, checking $K_i^t \psi_j$ and $B_i^t \psi_j$ requires one query to the epistemic engine for $\Delta, \bigcup_{\{t'|t'<t\in\mathbb{T}_\sigma\}} EKB_i^{\sigma[t]} \vdash \psi_j$. The previous query is equivalent to model checking a Kripke structure where relations are labelled with triples (i, t, w). Solving this problem is known to be decidable in PSPACE [17].

It is easy to see that the semantics of $\mathcal{KBL_{RT}}$ is captured by this algorithm. $\square$

2.4   Properties of the Framework

Here we present a set of novel derived operators not present in traditional epistemic logics and we prove some properties of the framework (see [22] for the proofs).

To learn or not to learn — To believe or not to believe. In [6] we introduced a primitive modality $L_i \varphi$, to capture that i learns φ at the first moment at which $K_i \varphi$ becomes true. Here $L_i^t \varphi$ becomes a derived operator defined formally as: $L_i^t \varphi \triangleq \neg K_i^{pred(t)} \varphi \wedge K_i^t \varphi$. We can also model when users start to believe something, or *accept* a belief, as follows, $A_i^t \varphi \triangleq \neg B_i^{pred(t)} \varphi \wedge B_i^t \varphi$. Analogously we can express when users *forget* some knowledge or when they *reject* a belief. Intuitively, an agent forgets φ at time t if she knew it in the previous timestamp and in t she does not know φ, and, analogously, for reject. Formally, $F_i^t \varphi \triangleq K_i^{pred(t)} \varphi \wedge \neg K_i^t \varphi$, and $R_i^t \varphi \triangleq B_i^{pred(t)} \varphi \wedge \neg B_i^t \varphi$.

Temporal modalities. The traditional temporal modalities $\square$ and $\diamond$ can easily be defined using quantification over timestamps as follows: $\square \varphi(t) \triangleq \forall t \cdot \varphi(t)$, and $\diamond \varphi(t) \triangleq \exists t \cdot \varphi(t)$, where $\varphi(t)$ is a formula φ which depends on t.

How long do agents remember? Agents remember according to the length of the parameter w, which can be seen as the size of their memory. Increasing agents memory could only increase their knowledge as stated in the following lemma.

Lemma 1 (Increasing window and Knowledge). *Given* σ, $t \in \mathbb{T}_\sigma$ *and* $w, w' \in \mathbb{N}$ *where* $w \leq w'$, *we have that: If* $EKB_i^{\sigma[t]} \vdash (K_i^t \varphi, w)$, *then* $EKB_i^{\sigma[t]} \vdash (K_i^t \varphi, w')$.

We can characterise how long agents remember information depending on w and β.

Lemma 2 (w knowledge monotonicity). *Given* σ *and* $t \in \mathbb{T}_\sigma$. *If* $K_i^t \varphi \in EKB_i^{\sigma[t]}$ *then for all* $t' \in \mathbb{T}_\sigma$ *such that* $t \leq t' \leq t + w$ *it holds* $\sigma \models K_i^{t'} \varphi$.

Perfect recall is obtained by choosing $w = \infty$ so agents never forget. Dualy, $w = 0$ models agents who do not remember anything. The parameter β also influences how beliefs are preserved in time. When $\beta = conservative$, memories about beliefs behave in the same way as knowledge. Similarly monotonicity results can be proven for beliefs as the lemmas above. For example, if $\beta = conservative$ then beliefs are preserved until these beliefs are forgotten—due to w—or contradict knowledge. Similarly, an agent with $\beta = susceptible$ rejects a belief when exposed to new contradictory beliefs. Therefore, the duration of their beliefs can be limited by an event introducing new beliefs in the EKBs. Other versions of β are possible, for example based on the reputation of the agent that emits the information. It is also possible to consider different w for different pieces of information. However, these extensions are out of the scope of this paper.

3 Writing Privacy Policies

We introduce here the language $\mathcal{PPL_{RT}}$ for writing privacy polices: a restricted version of $\mathcal{KBL_{RT}}$ wrapped with $[\![\ ]\!]_i^s$ (i is the owner of the policy, and s its starting time).

Definition 4 (Syntax of $\mathcal{PPL_{RT}}$). *Given agents $i, j \in Ag$, a nonempty set of agents $G \subseteq Ag$, timestamps $s, t \in \mathbb{T}$, a domain $D \in \mathcal{D}$, a variable x, predicate symbols $c^t(i, j), a^t(i, j), p^t(\vec{s})$ where $c \in \mathcal{C}$ and $a \in \Sigma$, and a formula $\varphi \in \mathcal{F}_{KBL_{RT}}$, the syntax of the real-time privacy policy language $\mathcal{PPL_{RT}}$ is inductively defined as:*

$$\delta ::= \delta \wedge \delta \mid \forall x \cdot \delta \mid [\![\neg\alpha]\!]_i^s \mid [\![\varphi \implies \neg\alpha]\!]_i^s \qquad \gamma' ::= K_i^t \gamma \mid B_i^t \gamma$$
$$\alpha ::= \alpha \wedge \alpha \mid \forall x : D \cdot \alpha \mid \exists x : D \cdot \alpha \mid \psi \mid \gamma' \qquad \psi ::= c^t(i, j) \mid a^t(i, j) \mid occurred^t(e)$$
$$\gamma ::= \gamma \wedge \gamma \mid \neg\gamma \mid p^t(\vec{s}) \mid \gamma' \mid \psi \mid \forall x \cdot \gamma$$

We use $\mathcal{F}_{\mathcal{PPL_{RT}}}$ to denote the set of all privacy policies according to δ, and $\mathcal{F}_{\mathcal{PPL_{RT}}}^{\mathcal{R}}$ the set positive formulae according to α, which we refer to as *restrictions*. As we show below restrictions appear always preceded by $\neg$. To determine whether a policy is violated in an evolving social network, we formalise the notion of conformance.

Definition 5 (Conformance Relation). *Given a trace $\sigma \in \mathcal{WFT}$, timestamp $s \in \mathbb{T}_\sigma$, formulae $\delta \in \mathcal{F}_{\mathcal{PPL_{RT}}}$ and $\alpha \in \mathcal{F}_{\mathcal{PPL_{RT}}}^{\mathcal{R}}$, agent $i \in Ag$, domain $D \in \mathcal{D}$, and variable x, the conformance relation $\models_C$ is defined as follows:*

$$\sigma \models_C \forall x \cdot \delta \qquad \text{iff } \text{for all } v \in D, \ \sigma \models_C \delta[v/x]$$
$$\sigma \models_C [\![\neg\alpha]\!]_i^s \qquad \text{iff } \sigma \models \neg\alpha$$
$$\sigma \models_C [\![\varphi \implies \neg\alpha]\!]_i^s \text{ iff } s\sigma \models (\varphi \implies \neg\alpha)$$

The definition is quite simple, especially compared to that of conformance of $\mathcal{PPL_T}$ [6]. If the policy is quantified, we substitute in the usual way. The main body of the policy in double brackets is dealt with by simply delegating to the satisfaction relation.

Example 5. Alice decides to hide all her weekend locations from her supervisor Bob. She has a number of options how to achieve this using $\mathcal{PPL_{RT}}$. If she wants to restrict Bob learning her weekend location directly when she posts it, she can define a policy stating that "if x is a time instant during a weekend, then Bob is not allowed to learn at x Alice's location from time x": $\delta_1 = \forall t \cdot [\![weekend(t) \implies \neg K^t_{Bob} loc^t(Alice)]\!]^{2017\text{-}10\text{-}20}_{Alice}$, where *weekend* is true if t represents a time during a weekend. This, however, is a very specialized scenario that captures only a small number of situations. Bob is, for example, free to learn Alice's location at any point not during the weekend, or at any point during the weekend when Alice's location is no longer up-to-date. We can consider a more precise policy concerning the learning of one's location: $\delta_2 = \forall t \cdot [\![weekend(t) \implies \neg \exists t' \cdot (K^{t'}_{Bob} loc^t(Alice))]\!]^{2017\text{-}10\text{-}20}_{Alice}$. Here, Bob is not allowed to learn Alice's location from a weekend, no matter when this information is learnt. □

Since checking conformance of $\mathcal{PPL_{RT}}$ privacy policies reduces to model checking the given trace the following corollary follows directly from Theorem 1.

Corollary 1. *Checking conformance of $\mathcal{PPL_{RT}}$ policies is decidable.*

4 Related Work and Concluding Remarks

Related Work. Combining epistemic and timed reasoning has been previously studied. For example, [10] presents a logic for reasoning about actions and time. The logic includes a belief modality, actions, as well as time-stamps for atoms, modalities and actions. In our work we do not focus on reasoning about action and time but on defining dynamic privacy policies for OSNs. Also, [10] cannot reason about knowledge. Moses *et al.* [17] extends interpreted systems to reason about past and future knowledge. In [23] they extend K with a time-stamp $K_{i,t}$ allowing for reasoning about knowledge at different times, also having a similar predicate to our $occurred^t(e)$. However, our logic (unlike [23]) includes beliefs and associates time-stamps with both modalities and predicates, whereas [17] only uses time-stamps for knowledge. Additionally, [23] aims at modeling delays in protocols, whereas we want to express dynamic privacy policies for OSNs. Recently, Xiong *et al.* [11] presented a logic to reason about belief propagation in Twitter. The logic includes an (untimed) belief modality and actions, which are used in a dynamic logic fashion. Their models are similar to our untimed SNMs [15,24]. Even though we do not include actions, we use time-stamps and knowledge modalities. Also, one of the main contributions of our paper is solving inconsistent beliefs.

Concluding Remarks. We have presented a novel privacy policy framework based on a logic with time-stamps in events and epistemic operators. This framework extends [15,24], which did not offer any support for time, and [6] which only had limited support due to the implicit treatment of time. A query in our framework starts by instantiating a number of epistemic axioms that handle knowledge, belief and time. Our proof system gives an algorithm to deduce the knowledge of agents acquired at each instant, and a model checking algorithm which can be used to check violations of privacy policies. The explicit time-stamps allow to derive learning and forget operators for knowledge, and accept and reject operators for beliefs. In our new framework we can define eternal OSNs like Facebook and ephemeral OSNs like Snapchat.

Two important avenues for future research are the following. First, the algorithm presented in this paper is not efficient enough for practical purposes, but serves as a formal foundation to develop provably correct efficient privacy violation detectors and enforcers, which can exploit specific details of each social network about how actions affect the knowledge of the agents involved. For instance, once the effect of the actions is fixed one can develop distributed algorithms that guarantee the same outcome as the direct algorithm proposed here. For example, tweets can only affect the knowledge of subscribers so all other users are unaffected. Second, once an effective system to check policy violations is in place, there are different possibilities that the OSN can offer. One is to enforce the policy by forbidding the action that the last agent executed (the action that leads to the violation). Another can be the analysis of the trace to assign blame (and affect the reputation) to the agents involved in the chain of actions. For example, the creator of a gossip or fake news may be held more responsible than users forwarding the gossip. A finer analysis of controllability allow more powerful algorithms that detecting which agents could have prevented the information flow that lead to the violation. Yet another possibility is to remove past events from the history trace of the OSN creating a pruned trace with no violation.

References

1. Lenhart, A., Purcell, K., Smith, A., Zickuhr, K.: Social media & mobile internet use among teens and young adults. Millennials. Pew Internet & American Life Project (2010)
2. Madejski, M., Johnson, M., Bellovin, S.: A study of privacy settings errors in an online social network. In: PERCOM Workshops 2012, pp. 340–345. IEEE (2012)
3. Johnson, M., Egelman, S., Bellovin, S.M.: Facebook and privacy: it's complicated. In: SOUPS 2012, pp. 9:1–9:15. ACM (2012)
4. Liu, Y., Gummadi, K.P., Krishnamurthy, B., Mislove, A.: Analyzing facebook privacy settings: user expectations vs. reality. In: IMC 2011, pp. 61–70. ACM (2011)
5. Madejski, M., Johnson, M.L., Bellovin, S.M.: The failure of online social network privacy settings. Technical report, Columbia University (2011)
6. Pardo, R., Kellyérová, I., Sánchez, C., Schneider, G.: Specification of evolving privacy policies for online social networks. In: TIME 2016, pp. 70–79. IEEE (2016)
7. The Guardian: As fake news takes over Facebook feeds, many are taking satire as fact. www.theguardian.com/media/2016/nov/17/facebook-fake-news-satire. Accessed 20 Oct 2017
8. The Guardian: How to solve Facebook's fake news problem: experts pitch their ideas. www.theguardian.com/technology/2016/nov/29/facebook-fake-news-problem-experts-pitch-ideas-algorithms. Accessed 20 Oct 2017

9. The Guardian: Obama is worried about fake news on social media-and we should be too. www.theguardian.com/media/2016/nov/20/barack-obama-facebook-fake-news-problem. Accessed 20 Oct 2017
10. van Zee, M., Doder, D., Dastani, M., van der Torre, L.W.N.: AGM revision of beliefs about action and time. In: IJCAI 2015, pp. 3250–3256. AAAI Press (2015)
11. Xiong, Z., Ågotnes, T., Seligman, J., Zhu, R.: Towards a logic of tweeting. In: Baltag, A., Seligman, J., Yamada, T. (eds.) LORI 2017. LNCS, vol. 10455, pp. 49–64. Springer, Heidelberg (2017). https://doi.org/10.1007/978-3-662-55665-8_4
12. Halpern, J.Y., Samet, D., Segev, E.: Defining knowledge in terms of belief: the modal logic perspective. Rev. Symbolic Logic 2, 469–487 (2009)
13. Fong, P.W.: Relationship-based access control: Protection model and policy language. In: CODASPY 2011, pp. 191–202. ACM (2011)
14. Bruns, G., Fong, P.W., Siahaan, I., Huth, M.: Relationship-based access control: its expression and enforcement through hybrid logic. In: CODASPY 2012, pp. 117–124. ACM (2012)
15. Pardo, R., Balliu, M., Schneider, G.: Formalising privacy policies in social networks. J. Logical Algebraic Methods Program. 90, 125–157 (2017)
16. Snodgrass, R., Ahn, I.: Temporal databases. Computer 19(9), 35–42 (1986)
17. Fagin, R., Halpern, J.Y., Moses, Y., Vardi, M.Y.: Reasoning About Knowledge, vol. 4. MIT press Cambridge, Cambridge (2003)
18. Erciyes, K.: Complex Networks: An Algorithmic Perspective, 1st edn. CRC Press Inc., Boca Raton (2014)
19. FlockDB: A distributed fault-tolerant graph database. github.com/twitter/flockdb. Accessed 20 Oct 2017
20. Bronson, N., Amsden, Z., Cabrera, G., Chakka, P., Dimov, P., Ding, H., Ferris, J., Giardullo, A., Kulkarni, S., Li, H., Marchukov, M., Petrov, D., Puzar, L., Song, Y.J., Venkataramani, V.: Tao: Facebook's distributed data store for the social graph. In: ATC 2013, pp. 49–60 (2013)
21. Neo4j decreases development time-to-market for LinkedIn's Chitu App. neo4j.com/case-studies/linkedin-china/. Accessed 20 Oct 2017
22. Pardo, R., Sánchez, C., Schneider, G.: Timed Epistemic Knowledge Bases for Social Networks (Extended Version). ArXiv e-prints (2017)
23. Ben-Zvi, I., Moses, Y.: Agent-time epistemics and coordination. In: Lodaya, K. (ed.) ICLA 2013. LNCS, vol. 7750, pp. 97–108. Springer, Heidelberg (2013). https://doi.org/10.1007/978-3-642-36039-8_9
24. Pardo, R., Schneider, G.: A formal privacy policy framework for social networks. In: Giannakopoulou, D., Salaün, G. (eds.) SEFM 2014. LNCS, vol. 8702, pp. 378–392. Springer, Cham (2014). https://doi.org/10.1007/978-3-319-10431-7_30

Optimal and Robust Controller Synthesis
Using Energy Timed Automata with Uncertainty

Giovanni Bacci[1(✉)], Patricia Bouyer[2], Uli Fahrenberg[3],
Kim Guldstrand Larsen[1], Nicolas Markey[4], and Pierre-Alain Reynier[5]

[1] Department of Computer Science, Aalborg University, Aalborg, Denmark
`giovbacci@cs.aau.dk`
[2] LSV, CNRS & ENS Cachan, Université Paris-Saclay, Cachan, France
[3] École Polytechnique, Palaiseau, France
[4] Univ. Rennes, IRISA, CNRS & INRIA, Rennes, France
[5] Aix Marseille Univ., Université de Toulon, CNRS, LIS, Marseille, France

Abstract. In this paper, we propose a novel framework for the synthesis of robust and optimal energy-aware controllers. The framework is based on energy timed automata, allowing for easy expression of timing constraints and variable energy rates. We prove decidability of the energy-constrained infinite-run problem in settings with both certainty and uncertainty of the energy rates. We also consider the optimization problem of identifying the minimal upper bound that will permit existence of energy-constrained infinite runs. Our algorithms are based on quantifier elimination for linear real arithmetic. Using Mathematica and Mjollnir, we illustrate our framework through a real industrial example of a hydraulic oil pump. Compared with previous approaches our method is completely automated and provides improved results.

1 Introduction

Design of controllers for embedded systems is a difficult engineering task. Controllers must ensure a variety of safety properties as well as optimality with respect to given perprocessformance properties. Also, for several systems, e.g. [8,25,27], the properties involve non-functional aspects such as time and energy.

We provide a novel framework for automatic synthesis of safe and optimal controllers for resource-aware systems based on *energy timed automata*. Synthesis of controllers is obtained by solving time- and energy-constrained infinite run problems. Energy timed automata [12] extend timed automata [2] with a continuous *energy* variable that evolves with varying rates and discrete updates during the behaviour of the model. Closing an open problem from [12], we prove decidability of the infinite run problem in settings, where rates and updates may be both positive and negative and possibly subject to uncertainty. Additionally, the accumulated energy may be subject to lower and upper bounds reflecting constraints on capacity. Also we consider the optimization problems of identifying minimal

Work supported by ERC projects Lasso and EQualIS.

upper bounds that will permit the existence of infinite energy-constrained runs. Our decision and optimization algorithms for the energy-constrained infinite run problems are based on reductions to quantifier elimination (QE) for linear real arithmetic, for which we combine Mathematica [28] and Mjollnir [24] into a tool chain.

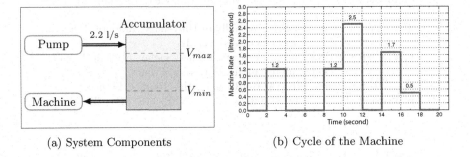

(a) System Components   (b) Cycle of the Machine

Fig. 1. Overview of the HYDAC system

To demonstrate the applicability of our framework, we revisit an industrial case study provided by the HYDAC company in the context of the European project Quasimodo [26]. It consists in an on/off control system (see Fig. 1a) composed of (i) a machine that consumes oil according to a cyclic pattern of 20 s (see Fig. 1b), (ii) an accumulator containing oil and a fixed amount of gas in order to put the oil under pressure, and (iii) a controllable pump which can pump oil into the accumulator with rate 2.2 l/s. The control objective for switching the pump on and off is twofold: first the level of oil in the accumulator (and so the gas pressure) shall be maintained within a safe interval; second, the controller should try to minimize the (maximum and average) level of oil such that the pressure in the system is kept minimal. We show how to model this system, with varying constraints on pump operation, as energy timed automata. Thus our tool chain may automatically synthesize guaranteed safe and optimal control strategies.

The HYDAC case was first considered in [16] as a timed game using the tool UPPAAL-TIGA [5,15] for synthesis. Discretization of oil-level (and time) was used to make synthesis feasible. Besides limiting the opportunity of optimality, the discretization also necessitated posterior verification using PHAVER [20] to rule out possible resulting incorrectness. Also, identification of safety and minimal oil levels were done by manual and laborious search. In [23] the timed game models of [16] (rephrased as Timed Discrete Event Systems) are reused, but BDDs are applied for compact representation of the discrete oil-levels and time-points encountered during synthesis. [21] provides a framework for learning optimal switching strategies by a combination of off-the-shelf numerical optimization and generalization by learning. The HYDAC case is one of the considered cases. The method offers no absolute guarantees of hard constraints on energy-level, but rather attempts to enforce these through the use of high penalties. [29] focuses exclusively on the HYDAC case using a direct encoding of the safety- and optimality-constraints as QE problems. This gives—like in our case—absolute guarantees. However, we are additionally offering a complete and decidable framework based on energy timed automata, which extends to several other systems. Moreover, the controllers we obtain perform significantly better than those of [16] and [29] (respectively up to 22% and 16% better) and are obtained automatically by our tool chain combining Mjollnir and Mathematica. This combination permits quantifier elimination and formula simplification to be done in a compositional manner, resulting in performance surpassing each tool individually. We believe that this shows that our framework has a level of maturity that meets the complexity of several relevant industrial control problems.

Our work is related to controllability of (constrained) piecewise affine (PWA) [7] and hybrid systems [1]. In particular, the energy-constrained infinite-run problem is related to the so called *stability problem* for PWAs. Blondel and Tsitsiklis [10] have shown that verifying stability of autonomous piecewise-linear (PWL) systems is NP-hard, even in the simple case of two-component subsystems; several global properties (e.g. global convergence, asymptotic stability and mortality) of PWA systems have been shown undecidable in [9].

2   Energy Timed Automata

Definitions. Given a finite set X of clocks, the set of *closed clock constraints* over X, denoted $C(X)$, is the set of formulas built using $g ::= x \sim n \mid g \wedge g$, where x ranges over X, $\sim$ ranges over $\{\leq, \geq\}$ and n ranges over $\mathbb{Q}_{\geq 0}$. That a clock valuation $v \colon X \to \mathbb{R}_{\geq 0}$ satisfies a clock constraint g, denoted $v \models g$, is defined in the natural way. For a clock valuation v, a real $t \in \mathbb{R}_{\geq 0}$, and a subset $R \subseteq X$, we write $v + t$ for the valuation mapping each clock $x \in X$ to $v(x) + t$, and $v[R \to 0]$ for the valuation mapping clocks in R to zero and clocks not in R to their value in v. Finally we write $\mathbf{0}_X$ (or simply $\mathbf{0}$) for the clock valuation assigning 0 to every $x \in X$.

For $E \subseteq \mathbb{R}$, we let $\mathcal{I}(E)$ be the set of closed intervals of $\mathbb{R}$ with bounds in $E \cap \mathbb{Q}$. Notice that any interval in $\mathcal{I}(E)$ is bounded, for any $E \subseteq \mathbb{R}$.

Definition 1. *An* energy timed automaton *(ETA for short; a.k.a.* priced *or* weighted timed automaton *[3, 6]) is a tuple* $\mathcal{A} = (S, S_0, X, I, r, T)$ *where* S *is a finite set of states,* $S_0 \subseteq S$ *is the set of initial states,* X *is a finite set of clocks,* $I \colon S \to C(X)$ *assigns invariants to states,* $r \colon S \to \mathbb{Q}$ *assigns rates to states, and* $T \subseteq S \times C(X) \times \mathbb{Q} \times 2^X \times S$ *is a finite set of transitions.*

An energy timed path *(ETP, a.k.a. linear energy timed automaton) is an energy timed automaton for which* S *can be written as* $\{s_i \mid 0 \leq i \leq n\}$ *in such a way that* $S_0 = \{s_0\}$, *and* $T = \{(s_i, g_i, u_i, z_i, s_{i+1}) \mid 0 \leq i < n\}$. *We additionally require that all clocks are reset on the last transition, i.e.,* $z_{n-1} = X$.

Let $\mathcal{A} = (S, S_0, X, I, r, T)$ be an ETA. A *configuration* of $\mathcal{A}$ is a triple $(\ell, v, w) \in S \times (\mathbb{R}_{\geq 0})^X \times \mathbb{R}$, where v is a clock valuation, and w is the energy level. Let $\tau = (t_i)_{0 \leq i < n}$ be a finite sequence of transitions, with $t_i = (s_i, g_i, u_i, z_i, s_{i+1})$ for every i. A finite *run* in $\mathcal{A}$ on τ is a sequence of configurations $\rho = (\ell_j, v_j, w_j)_{0 \leq j \leq 2n}$ such that there exists a sequence of delays $(d_i)_{0 \leq i < n}$ for which the following requirements hold:

- for all $0 \leq j < n$, $\ell_{2j} = \ell_{2j+1} = s_j$, and $\ell_{2n} = s_n$;
- for all $0 \leq j < n$, $v_{2j+1} = v_{2j} + d_j$ and $v_{2j+2} = v_{2j+1}[z_j \to 0]$;
- for all $0 \leq j < n$, $v_{2j} \models I(s_j)$ and $v_{2j+1} \models I(s_j) \wedge g_j$;
- for all $0 \leq j < n$, $w_{2j+1} = w_{2j} + d_j \cdot r(s_j)$ and $w_{2j+2} = w_{2j+1} + u_j$.

We will by extension speak of runs read on ETPs (those runs will then end with clock valuation $\mathbf{0}$). The notion of infinite run is defined similarly. Given $E \in \mathcal{I}(\mathbb{Q})$, such a run is said to satisfy energy constraint E if $w_j \in E$ for all j.

Example 1. Figure 2 displays an example of an ETP $\mathcal{P}$ and one of its runs ρ. Since no time will be spent in s_2, we did not indicate the invariant and rate of that state. The sequence ρ is a run of $\mathcal{P}$. Spending 0.6 time units in s_0, the value of clock x reaches 0.6, and the energy level grows to $3 + 0.6 \times 2 = 4.2$; it equals $4.2 - 3 = 1.2$ when entering s_1. Then ρ satisfies energy constraint $[0; 5]$.   ◁

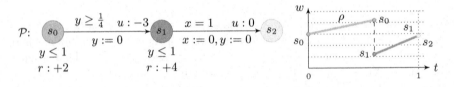

Fig. 2. An energy timed path $\mathcal{P}$, and a run ρ of $\mathcal{P}$ with initial energy level 3.

Definition 2. *A* segmented energy timed automaton *(SETA for short) is a tuple $\mathcal{A} = (S, T, P)$ where (S, T) is a finite graph (whose states and transitions are called* macro-states *and* macro-transitions*), S_0 is a set of initial macro-states, and P associates with each macro-transition $t = (s, s')$ of $\mathcal{A}$ an ETP with initial state s and final state s'. We require that for any two different transitions t and t' of $\mathcal{A}$, the state spaces of $P(t)$ and $P(t')$ are disjoint and contain no macro-states, except (for both conditions) for their first and last states.*

A SETA is flat *if the underlying graph (S, T) is (i.e., for any $s \in S$, there is at most one non-empty path in the graph (S, T) from s to itself [14, 17]). It is called* depth-1 *whenever the graph (S, T) is tree-like, with only loops at leaves.*

A (finite or infinite) execution of a SETA is a (finite or infinite) sequence of runs $\rho = (\rho^i)_i$ such that for all i, writing $\rho^i = (\ell^i_j, v^i_j, w^i_j)_{0 \le j \le 2n_i}$, it holds:

- ℓ^i_0 and $\ell^i_{2n_i}$ are macro-states of $\mathcal{A}$, and ρ^i is a run of the ETP $P(\ell^i_0, \ell^i_{2n_i})$;
- $\ell^{i+1}_0 = \ell^i_{2n_i}$ and $w^{i+1}_0 = w^i_{2n_i}$.

Hence a run in a SETA should be seen as the concatenation of paths ρ^i between macro-states. Notice also that each ρ^i starts and ends with all clock values zero, since all clocks are reset at the end of each ETP, when a main state is entered. Finally, given an interval $E \in \mathcal{I}(\mathbb{Q})$, an execution $(\rho^i)_i$ satisfies energy constraint E whenever all individual runs ρ^i do.

Remark 1. In contrast with ETAs, the class of SETAs is not closed under parallel composition. Intuitively, the ETA resulting from the parallel composition of two SETAs may not be "segmented" into a graph of energy timed-paths because the requirement that all clocks are reset on the last transition may not be satisfied. Furthermore, parallel composition does not preserve flatness because it may introduce nested loops.

Example 2. Figure 3 displays a SETA $\mathcal{A}$ with two macro-states s_0 and s_2, and two macro-transitions. The macro-self-loop on s_2 is associated with the energy timed path of Fig. 2. The execution $\rho = \rho^1 \cdot (\rho^2 \cdot \rho^3)^\omega$ is an ultimately-periodic execution of $\mathcal{A}$. This infinite execution satisfies the energy constraint $E = [0; 5]$ (as well as the (tight) energy constraint $[1; 4.6]$). $\quad\lhd$

In this paper, we consider the following *energy-constrained infinite-run problem* [12]: given an energy timed automaton $\mathcal{A}$ and a designated state s_0, an energy constraint $E \in \mathcal{I}(\mathbb{Q})$ and an initial energy level $w_0 \in E$, does there exist an infinite execution in $\mathcal{A}$ starting from $(s_0, \mathbf{0}, w_0)$ that satisfies E?

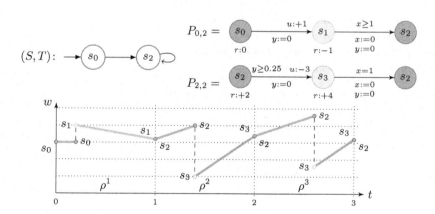

Fig. 3. A SETA $\mathcal{A} = (S, T, P)$ with implicit global invariant $y \le 1$; omitted discrete updates are assumed to be zero. The map P associates with each $(s_i, s_j) \in T$ the ETP $P_{i,j}$. The infinite sequence $\rho^1 \cdot (\rho^2 \cdot \rho^3)^\omega$ is an infinite execution of $\mathcal{A}$ with initial energy level 3 satisfying the energy constraint $E = [0; 5]$.

In the general case, the energy-constrained infinite-run problem is undecidable, even when considering ETA with only two clocks [22]. In this paper, we prove:

Theorem 3. *The energy-constrained infinite-run problem is decidable for flat SETA.*

Theorem 4. *Given a fixed lower bound L, the existence of an upper bound U, such that there is a solution to the energy-constrained infinite-run problem for energy constraint $E = [L; U]$, is decidable for flat SETA. If such a U exists, then for depth-1 flat SETA, we can compute the least one.*

We only sketch a proof of the former result, and refer to [4] for the full proof.

Binary Energy Relations. Let $\mathcal{P} = (\{s_i \mid 0 \leq i \leq n\}, \{s_0\}, X, I, r, T)$ be an ETP from s_0 to s_n. Let $E \subseteq \mathcal{I}(\mathbb{Q})$ be an energy constraint. The *binary energy relation* $\mathcal{R}_{\mathcal{P}}^E \subseteq E \times E$ for $\mathcal{P}$ under energy constraint E relates all pairs (w_0, w_1) for which there is a finite run of $\mathcal{P}$ from $(s_0, \mathbf{0}, w_0)$ to $(s_n, \mathbf{0}, w_1)$ satisfying energy constraint E. This relation is characterized by the following first-order formula:

$$\mathcal{R}_{\mathcal{P}}^E(w_0, w_1) \iff \exists (d_i)_{0 \leq i < n}.\Phi_{\text{timing}} \wedge \Phi_{\text{energy}} \wedge w_1 = w_0 + \sum_{k=0}^{n-1}(d_k \cdot r(s_k) + u_k)$$

where Φ_{timing} encodes all the timing constraints that the sequence $(d_i)_{0 \leq i < n}$ has to fulfill (derived from guards and invariants, by expressing the values of the clocks in terms of $(d_i)_{0 \leq i < n}$), while Φ_{energy} encodes the energy constraints (in each state, the accumulated energy must be in E).

It is easily shown that $\mathcal{R}_{\mathcal{P}}^E$ is a closed, convex subset of $E \times E$ (remember that we consider closed clock constraints); thus it can be described as a conjunction of a finite set of linear constraints over w_0 and w_1 (with non-strict inequalities), using quantifier elimination of variables $(d_i)_{0 \leq i < n}$.

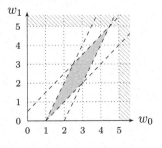

Example 3. We illustrate this computation on the ETP of Fig. 2. For energy constraint $[0; 5]$, the energy relation (after removing redundant constraints) reads as

$$\mathcal{R}_{\mathcal{P}}^E(w_0, w_1) \iff \exists d_0, d_1.d_0 \in [0.25; 1] \wedge d_1 \in [0; 1] \wedge d_0 + d_1 = 1 \wedge$$
$$w_0 \in [0; 5] \wedge w_0 + 2d_0 \in [0; 5] \wedge w_0 + 2d_0 - 3 \in [0; 5] \wedge$$
$$w_1 = w_0 + 2d_0 + 4d_1 - 3 \wedge w_1 \in [0; 5].$$

This simplifies to $(w_1 + 2 \leq 2w_0 \leq w_1 + 4) \wedge (w_1 - 0.5 \leq w_0 \leq w_1 + 1)$. The corresponding polyhedron is depicted above.   ◁

Energy Functions. We now focus on properties of energy relations. First notice that for any interval $E \in \mathcal{I}(\mathbb{Q})$, the partially-ordered set $(\mathcal{I}(E), \supseteq)$ is ω-complete, meaning that for any chain $(I_j)_{j \in \mathbb{N}}$, with $I_j \supseteq I_{j+1}$ for all j, the limit $\bigcap_{j \in \mathbb{N}} I_j$ also belongs to $\mathcal{I}(E)$. By Cantor's Intersection Theorem, if additionally each interval I_j is non-empty, then so is the limit $\bigcap_{j \in \mathbb{N}} I_j$.

With an energy relation $\mathcal{R}_\mathcal{P}^E$, we associate an *energy function* (also denoted with $\mathcal{R}_\mathcal{P}^E$, or simply $\mathcal{R}$, as long as no ambiguity may arise), defined for any closed sub-interval $I \in \mathcal{I}(E)$ as $\mathcal{R}(I) = \{w_1 \in E \mid \exists w_0 \in I.\ \mathcal{R}(w_0, w_1)\}$. Symmetrically:

$$\mathcal{R}^{-1}(I) = \{w_0 \in E \mid \exists w_1 \in I.\ \mathcal{R}(w_0, w_1)\}.$$

Observe that $\mathcal{R}(I)$ and $\mathcal{R}^{-1}(I)$ also belong to $\mathcal{I}(E)$ (because the relation $\mathcal{R}$ is closed and convex). Moreover, $\mathcal{R}$ and $\mathcal{R}^{-1}$ are non-decreasing: for any two intervals I and J in $\mathcal{I}(E)$ such that $I \subseteq J$, it holds $\mathcal{R}(I) \subseteq \mathcal{R}(J)$ and $\mathcal{R}^{-1}(I) \subseteq \mathcal{R}^{-1}(J)$. Energy function $\mathcal{R}^{-1}$ also satisfies the following continuity property:

Lemma 5. *Let $(I_j)_{j \in \mathbb{N}}$ be a chain of intervals of $\mathcal{I}(E)$, such that $I_j \supseteq I_{j+1}$ for all $j \in \mathbb{N}$. Then $\mathcal{R}^{-1}(\bigcap_{j \in \mathbb{N}} I_j) = \bigcap_{j \in \mathbb{N}} \mathcal{R}^{-1}(I_j)$.*

Composition and Fixpoints of Energy Functions. Consider a finite sequence of paths $(\mathcal{P}_i)_{1 \leq i \leq k}$. Clearly, the energy relation for this sequence can be obtained as the composition of the individual energy relations $\mathcal{R}_{\mathcal{P}_k}^E \circ \cdots \circ \mathcal{R}_{\mathcal{P}_1}^E$; the resulting energy relation still is a closed convex subset of $E \times E$ that can be described as the conjunction of finitely many linear constraints over w_0 and w_1. As a special case, we write $(\mathcal{R}_\mathcal{P}^E)^k$ for the composition of k copies of the same relations $\mathcal{R}_\mathcal{P}^E$.

Now, using Lemma 5, we easily prove that the greatest fixpoint $\nu \mathcal{R}^{-1}$ of $\mathcal{R}^{-1}$ in the complete lattice $(\mathcal{I}(E), \supseteq)$ exists and equals:

$$\nu \mathcal{R}^{-1} = \bigcap_{i \in \mathbb{N}} (\mathcal{R}^{-1})^i(E).$$

Moreover $\nu \mathcal{R}^{-1}$ is a closed (possibly empty) interval. Note that $\nu \mathcal{R}^{-1}$ is the maximum subset $S_\mathcal{R}$ of E such that, starting with any $w_0 \in S_\mathcal{R}$, it is possible to iterate $\mathcal{R}$ infinitely many times (that is, for any $w_0 \in S_\mathcal{R}$, there exists $w_1 \in S_\mathcal{R}$ such that $\mathcal{R}(w_0, w_1)$—any such set S is a post-fixpoint of $\mathcal{R}^{-1}$, i.e. $S \subseteq \mathcal{R}^{-1}(S)$).

If $\mathcal{R}$ is the energy relation of a cycle $\mathcal{C}$ in the flat SETA, then $\nu \mathcal{R}^{-1}$ precisely describes the set of initial energy levels allowing infinite runs through $\mathcal{C}$ satisfying the energy constraint E. If $\mathcal{R}$ is described as the conjunction $\phi_\mathcal{C}$ of a finite set of linear constraints, then we can characterize those intervals $[a, b] \subseteq E$ that constitute a post-fixpoint for $\mathcal{R}^{-1}$ by the following first-order formula:

$$a \leq b \wedge a \in E \wedge b \in E \wedge \forall w_0 \in [a; b].\ \exists w_1 \in [a; b].\ \phi_\mathcal{C}(w_0, w_1). \tag{1}$$

Applying quantifier elimination (to w_0 and w_1), the above formula may be transformed into a direct constraint on a and b, characterizing all post-fixpoints of $\mathcal{R}^{-1}$. We get a characterization of $\nu \mathcal{R}^{-1}$ by computing the values of a and b that satisfy these constraint and maximize $b - a$.

Example 4. We again consider the flat SETA of Fig. 3, and consider the energy constraint $E = [0; 5]$. We first focus on the cycle $\mathcal{C}$ on the macro-state s_2: using the energy relation computed in Example 3, our first-order formula for the fix-point then reads as follows:

$$0 \le a \le b \le 5 \wedge \forall w_0 \in [a; b]. \ \exists w_1 \in [a; b].$$
$$\big((w_1 + 2 \le 2w_0 \le w_1 + 4) \wedge (w_1 - 0.5 \le w_0 \le w_1 + 1)\big).$$

Applying quantifier elimination, we end up with $2 \le a \le b \le 4$. The maximal fixpoint then is $[2; 4]$. Similarly, for the path $\mathcal{P}$ from s_0 to s_2:

$$\mathcal{R}_{\mathcal{P}}^E(w_0, w_1) \iff \exists d_0, d_1. \ 0 \le d_0 \le 1 \wedge 0 \le d_1 \le 1 \wedge d_0 + d_1 \ge 1 \wedge$$
$$0 \le w_0 \le 5 \wedge 0 \le w_0 + 1 \le 5 \wedge w_1 = w_1 + 1 - d_1 \wedge 0 \le w_1 \le 5$$

which reduces to $0 \le w_0 \le 4 \wedge w_0 \le w_1 \le w_0 + 1$. Finally, the initial energy levels w_0 for which there is an infinite-run in the whole SETA are characterized by $\exists w_1. \ (0 \le w_0 \le 4 \wedge w_0 \le w_1 \le w_0 + 1) \wedge (2 \le w_1 \le 4)$, which reduces to $1 \le w_0 \le 4$.

Algorithm for Flat Segmented Energy Timed Automata. Following Example 4, we now prove that we can solve the energy-constrained infinite-run problem for any flat SETA. The next theorem is crucial for our algorithm:

Theorem 6. *Let $\mathcal{R}$ be the energy relation of an ETP $\mathcal{P}$ with energy constraint E, and let $I \in \mathcal{I}(E)$. Then either $I \cap \nu\mathcal{R}^{-1} \ne \emptyset$ or $\mathcal{R}^n(I) = \emptyset$ for some n.*

It follows that the energy-constrained infinite-run problem is decidable for flat SETAs. The decision procedure traverses the underlying graph of $\mathcal{A}$, forward propagating an initial energy interval $I_0 \subseteq E$ looking for a simple cycle C such that $\nu\mathcal{R}_C^{-1} \cap I \ne \emptyset$, where $I \subseteq E$ is the energy interval forward-propagated until reaching the cycle. Algorithm 1 gives a detailed description of the decision procedure. It traverses the underlying graph (S, T) of the flat SETA $\mathcal{A}$, using a waiting list W to keep track of the macro-states that need to be further explored. The list W contains tasks of the form $(m, I, flag)$ where $m \in S$ is the current macro-state, $I \in \mathcal{I}(E)$ is the current energy interval, and $flag \in \{c, \bar{c}\}$ is a flag indicating if m shall be explored by following a cycle it belongs to $(flag = c)$, or proceed by exiting that cycle $(flag = \bar{c})$. Theorem 6 ensures termination of the **while** loop of lines 17–21, whereas flatness ensures the correctness of Algorithm 1.

It is worth noting that the flatness assumption for the SETA $\mathcal{A}$ implies that the graph (S, T) has finitely many cycles (each macro-state belongs to at most one simple cycle of (S, T), therefore the number of cycles is bounded by the number of macro-states). As a consequence, Algorithm 1 performs in the worst case an exhaustive search of all cycles in $\mathcal{A}$. The technique does not trivially extend to SETAs with nested cycles, because they may have infinitely many cycles.

Input: A *flat SETA* $\mathcal{A} = (S, T, P)$; initial state $m_0 \in S$; energy interval I_0
1. $W \leftarrow \{(m_0, I_0, c)\}$ ◁ initialize the waiting list
2. **while** $W \neq \emptyset$ **do**
3.   pick $(m, I, flag) \in W$ ◁ pick an element from the waiting list
4. $W \leftarrow W \setminus (m, I, flag)$ ◁ remove the element from the waiting list
5.   **if** $flag = \bar{c}$ **then**   ◁ the node m shall be explored without following a cycle
6.   **for each** $(m, m') \in T$ that is not part of a simple cycle of (S, T) **do**
7. $W \leftarrow W \cup \{(m', \mathcal{R}^E_{P(m, m')}(I), c)\}$ ◁ add this new task to the waiting list
8.   **else**   ◁ the node m shall be explored by following a cycle
9.   **if** m belongs to a cycle of (S, T) **then**
10.   let $\mathcal{C} = (m_1, m_2) \cdots (m_k, m_{k+1})$ be the simple cycle s.t. $m = m_1 = m_{k+1}$
11.   let $\mathcal{R}_\mathcal{C} = \mathcal{R}_{P(m_k, m_{k+1})} \circ \cdots \circ \mathcal{R}_{P(m_1, m_2)}$ ◁ energy relation of the cycle
12.   **if** $I \cap \nu \mathcal{R}_\mathcal{C}^{-1} \neq \emptyset$ **then**   ◁ check if there is an infinite run via the cycle C
13.   **return tt**
14.   **else**   ◁ the cycle can be executed only finitely many times
15. $W \leftarrow W \cup \{(m, I, \bar{c})\}$ ◁ add a new task to the waiting list
16. $i \leftarrow 0$ ◁ initialize the number of cycle executions
17.   **while** $\mathcal{R}_\mathcal{C}^i(I) \neq \emptyset$ **do**   ◁ while i-th energy relation is satisfied
18.   **for** $1 \leq j < k$ **do**
19.   let $\mathcal{R}_{\mathcal{P}_j} = \mathcal{R}_{P(m_j, m_{j+1})} \circ \cdots \circ \mathcal{R}_{P(m_1, m_2)}$ ◁ unfold C up to m_{j+1}
20. $W \leftarrow W \cup \{(m_{j+1}, \mathcal{R}_{\mathcal{P}_j}(\mathcal{R}_\mathcal{C}^i(I)), \bar{c})\}$ ◁ add a task to the waiting list
21. $i \leftarrow i + 1$ ◁ increment the number of cycle executions
22.   **else**   ◁ m doesn't belong to a cycle
23. $W \leftarrow W \cup \{(m, I, \bar{c})\}$ ◁ add a new task to the waiting list
24. **return ff**   ◁ no infinite run could be found

Algorithm 1: Existence of energy-constrained infinite runs in flat SETA

3   Energy Timed Automata with Uncertainties

The assumptions of perfect knowledge of energy-rates and energy-updates are often unrealistic, as is the case in the HYDAC oil-pump control problem (see Sect. 4). Rather, the knowledge of energy-rates and energy-updates comes with a certain imprecision, and the existence of energy-constrained infinite runs must take these into account in order to be robust. In this section, we revisit the energy-constrained infinite-run problem in the setting of imprecisions, by viewing it as a two-player game problem.

Adding Uncertainty to ETA. An *energy timed automaton with uncertainty* (ETAu for short) is a tuple $\mathcal{A} = (S, S_0, X, I, r, T, \epsilon, \Delta)$, where (S, S_0, X, I, r, T) is an energy timed automaton, with $\epsilon \colon S \to \mathbb{Q}_{>0}$ assigning imprecisions to rates of states and $\Delta \colon T \to \mathbb{Q}_{>0}$ assigning imprecisions to updates of transitions. This notion of uncertainty extends to *energy timed path with uncertainty* (ETPu) and to *segmented energy timed automaton with uncertainty* (SETAu).

Let $\mathcal{A} = (S, S_0, X, I, r, T, \epsilon, \Delta)$ be an ETAu, and let $\tau = (t_i)_{0 \leq i < n}$ be a finite sequence of transitions, with $t_i = (s_i, g_i, u_i, z_i, s_{i+1})$ for every i. A finite *run* in $\mathcal{A}$

on τ is a sequence of configurations $\rho = (\ell_j, v_j, w_j)_{0 \le j \le 2n}$ such that there exist a sequence of delays $d = (d_i)_{0 \le i < n}$ for which the following requirements hold:

- for all $0 \le j < n$, $\ell_{2j} = \ell_{2j+1} = s_j$, and $\ell_{2n} = s_n$;
- for all $0 \le j < n$, $v_{2j+1} = v_{2j} + d_j$ and $v_{2j+2} = v_{2j+1}[z_j \to 0]$;
- for all $0 \le j < n$, $v_{2j} \models I(s_j)$ and $v_{2j+1} \models I(s_j) \wedge g_j$;
- for all $0 \le j < n$, it holds that $w_{2j+1} = w_{2j} + d_j \cdot \alpha_j$ and $w_{2j+2} = w_{2j+1} + \beta_j$, where $\alpha_j \in [r(s_j) - \epsilon(s_j), r(s_j) + \epsilon(s_j)]$ and $\beta_j \in [u_j - \Delta(t_j), u_j + \Delta(t_j)]$.

We say that ρ is a possible outcome of d along τ, and that w_{2n} is a possible final energy level for d along τ, given initial energy level w_0. Note that due to uncertainty, a given delay sequence d may have several possible outcomes (and corresponding energy levels) along a given transition sequence τ. In particular, we say that τ together with d and initial energy level w_0 satisfy an energy constraint $E \in \mathcal{I}(\mathbb{Q})$ if any possible outcome run ρ for t and d starting with w_0 satisfies E. All these notions are formally extended to ETPu.

Given an ETPu $\mathcal{P}$, and a delay sequence d for $\mathcal{P}$ satisfying a given energy constraint E from initial level w_0, we denote by $\mathcal{E}^E_{\mathcal{P},d}(w_0)$ the set of possible final energy levels. It may be seen that $\mathcal{E}^E_{\mathcal{P},d}(w_0)$ is a closed subset of E.

Example 5. Figure 4 is the energy timed path $\mathcal{P}$ of Fig. 2 extended with uncertainties of ± 0.1 on all rates and updates. The runs associated with path $\mathcal{P}$, delay sequence $d = (0.6, 0.4)$ and initial energy level $w_0 = 3$ satisfy the energy constraint $E = [0; 5]$. The set $\mathcal{E}^E_{\mathcal{P},d}(w_0)$ then is $[2.5; 3.1]$.

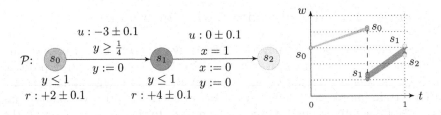

Fig. 4. An energy timed path $\mathcal{P}$ with uncertainty, and a representation of the runs corresponding to the delay sequence $(0.6, 0.4)$ with initial energy level 3.

Now let $\mathcal{A} = (S, T, P)$ be an SETAu and let E be an energy constraint. A (memoryless[1]) *strategy* σ returns for any macro-configuration (s, w) ($s \in S$ and $w \in E$) a pair (t, d), where $t = (s, s')$ is a successor edge in T and $d \in \mathbb{R}^n_{\ge 0}$ is a delay sequence for the corresponding energy timed path, i.e. $n = |P(\bar{t})|$. A (finite or infinite) execution of $(\rho^i)_i$ writing $\rho^i = (\ell^i_j, x^i_j, w^i_j)_{0 \le j \le 2n_i}$, is an outcome of σ if the following conditions hold:

---

[1] For the infinite-run problem, it can be shown that memoryless strategies suffice.

- s_0^i and $s_{2n_i}^i$ are macro-states of $\mathcal{A}$, and ρ^i is a possible outcome of $P(s_0^i, s_{2n_i}^i)$ for d where $\sigma(s_0^i, w_0^i) = ((s_0^i, s_{2n_i}^i), d)$;
- $s_0^{i+1} = s_{2n_i}^i$ and $w_0^{i+1} = w_{2n_i}^i$.

Now we may formulate the infinite-run problem in the setting of uncertainty: for a SETAu $\mathcal{A}$, an energy constraint $E \in \mathcal{I}(\mathbb{Q})$, and a macro-state s_0 and an initial energy level w_0 the *energy-constrained infinite-run problem* is to decide the existence of a strategy σ for $\mathcal{A}$ such that all runs $(\rho^i)_i$ that are outcome of σ starting from configuration (s_0, w_0) satisfy E?

Ternary Energy Relations. Let $\mathcal{P} = (\{s_i \mid 0 \le i \le n\}, \{s_0\}, X, I, r, T, \epsilon, \Delta)$ be an ETPu and let $E \in \mathcal{I}(\mathbb{Q})$ be an energy constraint. The ternary energy relation $\mathcal{U}_\mathcal{P}^E \subseteq E \times E \times E$ relates all triples (w_0, a, b) for which there is a strategy σ such that any outcome of ρ from $(s_0, \mathbf{0}, w_0)$ satisfies E and ends in a configuration $(s_n, \mathbf{0}, w_1)$ where $w_1 \in [a; b]$. This relation can be characterized by the following first-order formula:

$$\mathcal{U}_\mathcal{P}^E(w_0, a, b) \iff \exists (d_i)_{0 \le i < n}. \; \Phi_{\text{timing}} \wedge \Phi_{\text{energy}}^i \wedge$$
$$w_0 + \sum_{k=0}^{n-1}(r(s_k) \cdot d_k + u_k) + \sum_{k=0}^{n-1}([-\epsilon(s_k); \epsilon(s_k)] \cdot d_k + [-\Delta(t_k); \Delta(t_k)]) \subseteq [a; b]$$

where Φ_{energy}^i encodes the energy constraints as the inclusion of the interval of reachable energy levels in the energy constraint (in the same way as we do on the second line of the formula). Interval inclusion can then be expressed as constraints on the bounds of the intervals. It is clear that $\mathcal{U}_\mathcal{P}^E$ is a closed, convex subset of $E \times E \times E$ and can be described as a finite conjunction of linear constraints over w_0, a and b using quantifier elimination.

Example 6. We illustrate the above translation on the ETPu of Fig. 4. For energy constraint $[0; 5]$, the energy relation can be written as:

$$\mathcal{U}_\mathcal{P}^E(w_0, a, b) \iff \exists d_0, d_1. \; d_0 \in [0.25; 1] \wedge d_1 \in [0; 1] \wedge d_0 + d_1 = 1 \wedge w_0 \in [0; 5] \wedge$$
$$w_0 + [1.9; 2.1] \cdot d_0 \subseteq [0; 5] \wedge$$
$$w_0 + [1.9; 2.1] \cdot d_0 + [-3.1; -2.9] \subseteq [0; 5] \wedge$$
$$w_0 + [1.9; 2.1] \cdot d_0 + [-3.1; -2.9] + [3.9; 4.1] \cdot d_1 \subseteq [0; 5] \wedge$$
$$w_0 + [1.9; 2.1] \cdot d_0 + [-3.1; -2.9] + [3.9; 4.1] \cdot d_1 + [-0.1; 0.1] \subseteq [a; b] \subseteq [0; 5]]$$

Applying quantifier elimination, we end up with:

$$\mathcal{U}_\mathcal{P}^E(w_0, a, b) \iff 0 \le a \le b \le 5 \wedge b \ge a + 0.6 \wedge a - 0.2 \le w_0 \le b + 0.7 \wedge$$
$$(4.87 + 1.9 \cdot a)/3.9 \le w_0 \le (7.27 + 2.1 \cdot b)/4.1$$

We can use this relation in order to compute the set of initial energy levels from which there is a strategy to end up in $[2.5; 3.1]$ (which was the set of possible final energy levels in the example of Fig. 4). We get $w_0 \in [37/15; 689/205]$, which is (under-)approximately $w_0 \in [2.467; 3.360]$.   ◁

Algorithm for SETAu. Let $\mathcal{A} = (S, T, P)$ be a SETAu and let $E \in \mathcal{I}(\mathbb{Q})$ be an energy constraint. Let $\mathcal{W} \subseteq S \times E$ be the maximal set of configurations satisfying the following:

$$(s, w) \in \mathcal{W} \Rightarrow \exists t = (s, s') \in T. \exists a, b \in E.$$
$$\mathcal{U}_{P(t)}^E(w, a, b) \wedge \forall w' \in [a; b].(s', w') \in \mathcal{W} \tag{2}$$

Now $\mathcal{W}$ is easily shown to characterize the set of configurations (s, w) that satisfy the energy-constrained infinite-run problem. Unfortunately this characterization does not readily provide an algorithm. We thus make the following restriction and show that it leads to decidability of the energy-constrained infinite-run problem:

(R) in any of the ETPu $P(t)$ of $\mathcal{A}$, on at least one of its transitions, some clock x is compared with a positive lower bound. Thus, there is an (overall minimal) positive time-duration D to complete any $P(t)$ of $\mathcal{A}$.

Theorem 7. *The energy-constrained infinite-run problem is decidable for SETAu satisfying* **(R)**.

It is worth noticing that we do **not** assume flatness of the model for proving the above theorem. Instead, the minimal-delay assumption **(R)** has to be made: it entails that any stable set is made of intervals whose size is bounded below, which provides an upper bound on the number of such intervals. We can then rewrite the right-hand-size expression of (2) as:

$$\bigwedge_{s \in S} \bigwedge_{1 \le j \le N} [a_{s,j}; b_{s,j}] \subseteq E \wedge w_0 \in \bigvee_{1 \le j \le N} [a_{s_0,j}; b_{s_0,j}] \wedge \forall w \in [a_{s,j}; b_{s,j}].$$
$$\bigvee_{(s,s') \in T} [\exists a, b \in E. \mathcal{U}_{P(s,s')}^E(w, a, b) \wedge \bigvee_{1 \le k \le N} ([a; b] \subseteq [a_{s',k}; b_{s',k}])] \tag{3}$$

Example 7. We pursue on Example 6. If ETPu $\mathcal{P}$ is iterated (as on the loop on state s_2 of Fig. 3, but now with uncertainty), the set $\mathcal{W}$ (there is a single macro-state) can be captured with a single interval $[a, b]$. We characterize the set of energy levels from which the path $\mathcal{P}$ can be iterated infinitely often while satisfying the energy constraint $E = [0; 5]$ using Eq. (3), as follows:

$$0 \le a \le b \le 5 \wedge \forall w_0 \in [a; b]. \mathcal{U}_{\mathcal{P}}^E(w_0, a, b).$$

We end up with $2.435 \le a \wedge b \le 3.635 \wedge b \ge a + 0.6$, so that the largest interval is $[2.435; 3.635]$ (which can be compared to the maximal fixpoint $[2; 4]$ that we obtained in Example 4 for the same cycle without uncertainty).

As in the setting without uncertainties, we can also synthesize an (optimal) upper-bound for the energy constraint:

Theorem 8. *Let $\mathcal{A} = (S, T, P)$ be a depth-1 flat SETAu satisfying* **(R)**. *Let $L \in \mathbb{Q}$ be an energy lower bound, and let (s_0, w_0) be an initial macro-configuration. Then the existence of an upper energy bound U, such that the energy-constrained infinite-run problem is satisfied for the energy constraint $[L; U]$ is decidable. Furthermore, one can compute the least upper bound, if there is one.*

4   Case Study

Modelling the Oil Pump System. In this section we describe the character-istics of each component of the HYDAC case, which we then model as a SETA. *The Machine.* The oil consumption of the machine is cyclic. One cycle of con-sumptions, as given by HYDAC, consists of 10 periods of consumption, each having a duration of two seconds, as depicted in Fig. 1b. Each period is described by a rate of consumption m_r (expressed in litres per second). The consumption rate is subject to noise: if the mean consumption for a period is c l/s (with $c \geq 0$) its actual value lies within $[\max(0, c - \epsilon); c + \epsilon]$, where ϵ is fixed to 0.1 l/s.

The Pump. The pump is either On or Off, and we assume it is initially Off at the beginning of a cycle. While it is On, it pumps oil into the accumulator with a rate $p_r = 2.2$ l/s. The pump is also subject to timing constraints, which prevent switching it on and off too often.

The Accumulator. The volume of oil within the accumulator will be modelled by means of an energy variable v. Its evolution is given by the differential inclusion $dv/dt - u \cdot p_r \in -[m_r + \epsilon; m_r - \epsilon]$ (or $-[m_r + \epsilon; 0]$ if $m_r - \epsilon < 0$), where $u \in \{0, 1\}$ is the state of the pump.

The controller must operate the pump (switch it on and off) to ensure the following requirements: (R1) the level of oil in the accumulator must always stay within the safety bounds $E = [V_{\min}; V_{\max}] = [4.9; 25.1]$ l (R2) the average level of oil in the accumulator is kept as low as possible.

By modelling the oil pump system as a SETA $\mathcal{H}$, the above control problem can be reduced to finding a deterministic schedule that results in a safe infinite run in $\mathcal{H}$. Furthermore, we are also interested in determining the minimal safety interval E, i.e., finding interval bounds that minimize $V_{\max} - V_{\min}$, while ensuring the existence of a valid controller for $\mathcal{H}$.

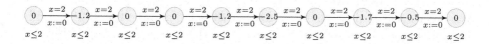

Fig. 5. The ETP representing the oil consumption of the machine.

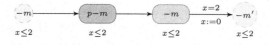

Fig. 6. An ETP for modelling the pump

As a first step in the definition of $\mathcal{H}$, we build an ETP representing the behaviour of the machine, depicted on Fig. 5. In order to fully model the behaviour of our oil-pump system, one would require the parallel composition of this ETP with another ETP representing the pump. The resulting ETA would not be a flat SETA, and is too large to be handled by our algorithm with uncertainty. Since it still provides interesting results, we develop this (incomplete) approach in the long version of this article [4].

Instead, we consider an alternative model of the pump, which only allows to switch it on and off once during each 2-second slot. This is modelled by inserting, between any two states of the model of Fig. 5, a copy of the ETP depicted on Fig. 6. In that ETP, the state with rate $p - m$ models the situation when the pump is on. Keeping the pump off for the whole slot can be achieved by spending delay zero in that state. We name $\mathcal{H}_1 = (M, T, P_1)$ the SETA made of a single macro-state equipped with a self-loop labelled with the ETP above.

In order to represent the timing constraints of the pump switches, we also consider a second SETA model $\mathcal{H}_2 = (M, T, P_2)$ where the pump can be operated only during every other time slot. This amounts to inserting the ETP of Fig. 6 only after the first, third, fifth, seventh and ninth states of the ETP of Fig. 5.

We also consider extensions of both models with uncertainty $\epsilon = 0.1\,\text{l/s}$ (changing any negative rate $-m$ into rate interval $[-m-\epsilon; -m+\epsilon]$, but changing rate 0 into $[-\epsilon; 0]$). We write $\mathcal{H}_1(\epsilon)$ and $\mathcal{H}_2(\epsilon)$ for the corresponding models.

Synthesizing Controllers. For each model, we synthesize minimal upper bounds U (within the interval $[V_{\min}; V_{\max}]$) that admit a solution to the energy-constrained infinite-run problem for the energy constraint $E = [V_{\min}; U]$. Then, we compute the greatest stable interval $[a; b] \subseteq [L; U]$ of the cycle witnessing the existence of an E-constrained infinite-run. This is done by following the methods described in Sects. 2 and 3 where quantifier elimination is performed using Mjollnir [24].

Finally for each model we synthesise *optimal* strategies that, given an initial volume $w_0 \in [a, b]$ of the accumulator, return a sequence of pump activation times t_i^{on} and t_i^{off} to be performed during the cycle. This is performed in two steps: first we encode the set of safe *permissive strategies* as a quantifier-free first-order linear formula having as free variables w_0, and the times t_i^{on} and t_i^{off}. The formula is obtained by relating w_0, and the times t_i^{on} and t_i^{off} with the intervals $[L; U]$ and $[a; b]$ and delays d_i as prescribed by the energy relations presented in Sects. 2 and 3. We use Mjollnir [24] to eliminate the existential quantifiers on the delays d_i. Then, given an energy value w_0 we determine an optimal safe strategy for it (i.e., some timing values when the pump is turned on and off) as the solution of the optimization problem that minimizes the average oil volume in the tank during one consumption cycle subject to the *permissive strategies* constraints. To this end, we use the function FindMinimum of Mathematica [28] to minimize the non-linear cost function expressing the average oil volume subject to the linear constraints obtained above. Figure 7 shows the resulting strategies: there, each horizontal line at a given initial oil level indicates the delays (green intervals) where the pump will be running.

Table 1 summarizes the results obtained for our models. It gives the optimal volume constraints, the greatest stable intervals, and the values of the

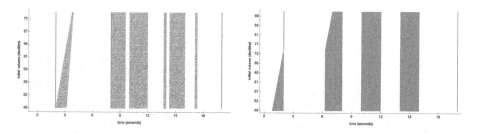

Fig. 7. Local strategies for $\mathcal{H}_1(\epsilon)$ (left) and $\mathcal{H}_2(\epsilon)$ (right) for a single cycle of the HYDAC system.

Table 1. Characteristics of the synthesized strategies, compared with the strategies proposed in [16, 29].

Controller	$[L; U]$	$[a; b]$	Mean vol. (l)
$\mathcal{H}_1$	$[4.9; 5.84]$	$[4.9; 5.84]$	5.43
$\mathcal{H}_1(\epsilon)$	$[4.9; 7.16]$	$[5.1; 7.16]$	6.15
$\mathcal{H}_2$	$[4.9; 7.9]$	$[4.9; 7.9]$	6.12
$\mathcal{H}_2(\epsilon)$	$[4.9; 9.1]$	$[5.1; 9.1]$	7.24
G1M1 [16]	$[4.9; 25.1]^a$	$[5.1; 9.4]$	8.2
G2M1 [16]	$[4.9; 25.1]^a$	$[5.1; 8.3]$	7.95
[29]	$[4.9; 25.1]^a$	$[5.2; 8.1]$	7.35

^{a}Safety interval given by the HYDAC company.

worst-case (over all initial oil levels in $[a; b]$) mean volume. It is worth noting that the models without uncertainty outperform the respective version with uncertainty. Moreover, the worst-case mean volume obtained both for $\mathcal{H}_1(\epsilon)$ and $\mathcal{H}_2(\epsilon)$ are significantly better than the optimal strategies synthesized both in [16, 29].

The reason for this may be that (i) our models relax the latency requirement for the pump, (ii) the strategies of [16] are obtained using a discretization of the dynamics within the system, and (iii) the strategies of [16, 29] were allowed to activate the pump respectively two and three times during each cycle.

We proceed by comparing the performances of our strategies in terms of accumulated oil volume. Figure 8 shows the result of simulating our strategies for a duration of 100 s. The plots illustrate in blue (resp. red) the dynamics of the mean (resp. min/max) oil level in the accumulator as well as the state of the pump. The initial volume used for the simulations is 8.3 l, as done in [16] for evaluating respectively the Bang-Bang controller, the Smart Controller developed by HYDAC, and the controllers G1M1 and G2M1 synthesized with UPPAAL-TIGA.

Table 2 presents, for each of the strategies, the resulting accumulated volume of oil, and the corresponding mean volume. There is a clear evidence that the strategies for $\mathcal{H}_1$ and $\mathcal{H}_2$ outperform all the other strategies. Clearly, this is due to the fact that they assume full precision in the rates, and allow for more

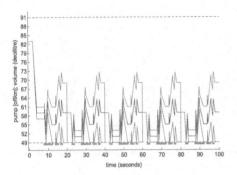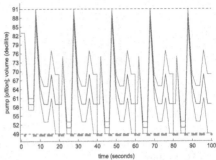

Fig. 8. Simulations of 5 consecutive machine cycles for $\mathcal{H}_1(\epsilon)$ and $\mathcal{H}_2(\epsilon)$.

Table 2. Performance based on simulations of 200 s starting with 8.3 l.

Controller	Acc. vol. (l)	Mean vol. (l)	Controller	Acc. vol. (l)	Mean vol. (l)
$\mathcal{H}_1$	1081.77	5.41	Bang-Bang	2689	13.45
$\mathcal{H}_2$	1158.90	5.79	HYDAC	2232	11.60
$\mathcal{H}_1(\epsilon)$	1200.21	6.00	G1M1	1518	7.59
$\mathcal{H}_2(\epsilon)$	1323.42	6.62	G2M1	1489	7.44

switches of the pump. However, these results shall be read as what one could achieve by investing in more precise equipment. The results also confirm that both our strategies outperform those presented in [16]. In particular the strategy for $\mathcal{H}_1(\epsilon)$ provides an improvement of 55%, 46%, 20%, and 19% respectively for the Bang-Bang controller, the Smart Controller of HYDAC, and the two strategies synthesized with UPPAAL-TIGA.

Tool Chain[2]. Our results have been obtained using Mathematica and Mjollnir. Specifically, Mathematica was used to construct the formulas modelling the post-fixpoint of the energy functions, calling Mjollnir for performing quantifier elimination on them. The combination of both tools allowed us to solve one of our formulas with 27 variables in a compositional manner in ca. 20 ms, while Mjollnir alone would take more than 20 min. Mjollnir was preferred to Mathematica's built-in support for quantifier elimination because the latter does not scale.

5   Conclusion

We developed a novel framework allowing for the synthesis of safe and optimal controllers, based on energy timed automata. Our approach consists in a translation to first-order linear arithmetic expressions representing our control problem, and solving these using quantifier elimination and simplification.

---

[2] More details on our scripts are available at http://people.cs.aau.dk/~giovbacci/tools. html, together with the models we used for our examples and case study.

We demonstrated the applicability and performance of our approach by revisiting the HYDAC case study and improving its best-known solutions.

Future works include extending our results to non-flat and non-segmented energy timed automata. However, existing results [22] indicate that we are close to the boundary of decidability. Another interesting continuation of this work would be to add UPPAAL STRATEGO [18,19] to our tool chain. This would allow to optimize the permissive strategies that we compute with quantifier elimination in the setting of probabilistic uncertainty, thus obtaining controllers that are optimal with respect to expected accumulated oil volume.

References

1. Alur, R., Courcoubetis, C., Henzinger, T.A., Ho, P.-H.: Hybrid automata: an algorithmic approach to the specification and verification of hybrid systems. In: Grossman, R.L., Nerode, A., Ravn, A.P., Rischel, H. (eds.) HS 1991-1992. LNCS, vol. 736, pp. 209–229. Springer, Heidelberg (1993). https://doi.org/10.1007/3-540-57318-6_30

2. Alur, R., Dill, D.L.: A theory of timed automata. Theor. Comput. Sci. **126**(2), 183–235 (1994)

3. Alur, R., La Torre, S., Pappas, G.J.: Optimal paths in weighted timed automata. In: Di Benedetto, M.D., Sangiovanni-Vincentelli, A. (eds.) HSCC 2001. LNCS, vol. 2034, pp. 49–62. Springer, Heidelberg (2001). https://doi.org/10.1007/3-540-45351-2_8

4. Bacci, G., Bouyer, P., Fahrenberg, U., Larsen, K.G., Markey, N., Reynier, P.-A.: Optimal and robust controller synthesis: using energy timed automata with uncertainty (2018). arXiv:1805.00847 [cs.FL]

5. Behrmann, G., Cougnard, A., David, A., Fleury, E., Larsen, K.G., Lime, D.: UPPAAL-Tiga: time for playing games!. In: Damm, W., Hermanns, H. (eds.) CAV 2007. LNCS, vol. 4590, pp. 121–125. Springer, Heidelberg (2007). https://doi.org/10.1007/978-3-540-73368-3_14

6. Behrmann, G., et al.: Minimum-cost reachability for priced time automata. In: Di Benedetto, M.D., Sangiovanni-Vincentelli, A. (eds.) HSCC 2001. LNCS, vol. 2034, pp. 147–161. Springer, Heidelberg (2001). https://doi.org/10.1007/3-540-45351-2_15

7. Bemporad, A., Ferrari-Trecate, G., Morari, M.: Observability and controllability of piecewise affine and hybrid systems. IEEE Trans. Autom. Control **45**(10), 1864–1876 (2000)

8. Bisgaard, M.: Battery-aware scheduling in low orbit: the GoMX–3 case. In: Fitzgerald, J., Heitmeyer, C., Gnesi, S., Philippou, A. (eds.) FM 2016. LNCS, vol. 9995, pp. 559–576. Springer, Cham (2016). https://doi.org/10.1007/978-3-319-48989-6_34

9. Blondel, V.D., Bournez, O., Koiran, P., Tsitsiklis, J.N.: The stability of saturated linear dynamical systems is undecidable. J. Comput. Syst. Sci. **62**(3), 442–462 (2001)

10. Blondel, V.D., Tsitsiklis, J.N.: Complexity of stability and controllability of elementary hybrid systems. Automatica **35**(3), 479–489 (1999)

11. Bouyer, P., Fahrenberg, U., Larsen, K.G., Markey, N.: Timed automata with observers under energy constraints. In: Johansson, K.H., Yi, W. (eds.) Proceedings of the 13th International Workshop on Hybrid Systems: Computation and Control (HSCC 2010), pp. 61–70. ACM Press, April 2010
12. Bouyer, P., Fahrenberg, U., Larsen, K.G., Markey, N., Srba, J.: Infinite runs in weighted timed automata with energy constraints. In: Cassez, F., Jard, C. (eds.) FORMATS 2008. LNCS, vol. 5215, pp. 33–47. Springer, Heidelberg (2008). https://doi.org/10.1007/978-3-540-85778-5_4
13. Bouyer, P., Larsen, K.G., Markey, N.: Lower-bound constrained runs in weighted timed automata. Perform. Eval. **73**, 91–109 (2014)
14. Bozga, M., Iosif, R., Lakhnech, Y.: Flat parametric counter automata. In: Bugliesi, M., Preneel, B., Sassone, V., Wegener, I. (eds.) ICALP 2006. LNCS, vol. 4052, pp. 577–588. Springer, Heidelberg (2006). https://doi.org/10.1007/11787006_49
15. Cassez, F., David, A., Fleury, E., Larsen, K.G., Lime, D.: Efficient on-the-fly algorithms for the analysis of timed games. In: Abadi, M., de Alfaro, L. (eds.) CONCUR 2005. LNCS, vol. 3653, pp. 66–80. Springer, Heidelberg (2005). https://doi.org/10.1007/11539452_9
16. Cassez, F., Jessen, J.J., Larsen, K.G., Raskin, J.-F., Reynier, P.-A.: Automatic synthesis of robust and optimal controllers – an industrial case study. In: Majumdar, R., Tabuada, P. (eds.) HSCC 2009. LNCS, vol. 5469, pp. 90–104. Springer, Heidelberg (2009). https://doi.org/10.1007/978-3-642-00602-9_7
17. Comon, H., Jurski, Y.: Multiple counters automata, safety analysis and presburger arithmetic. In: Hu, A.J., Vardi, M.Y. (eds.) CAV 1998. LNCS, vol. 1427, pp. 268–279. Springer, Heidelberg (1998). https://doi.org/10.1007/BFb0028751
18. David, A., et al.: On time with minimal expected cost!. In: Cassez, F., Raskin, J.-F. (eds.) ATVA 2014. LNCS, vol. 8837, pp. 129–145. Springer, Cham (2014). https://doi.org/10.1007/978-3-319-11936-6_10
19. David, A., Jensen, P.G., Larsen, K.G., Mikučionis, M., Taankvist, J.H.: UPPAAL STRATEGO. In: Baier, C., Tinelli, C. (eds.) TACAS 2015. LNCS, vol. 9035, pp. 206–211. Springer, Heidelberg (2015). https://doi.org/10.1007/978-3-662-46681-0_16
20. Frehse, G.: Phaver: algorithmic verification of hybrid systems past hytech. STTT **10**(3), 263–279 (2008)
21. Jha, S., Seshia, S.A., Tiwari, A.: Synthesis of optimal switching logic for hybrid systems. In: Chakraborty, S., Jerraya, A., Baruah, S.K., Fischmeister, S. (eds.) Proceedings of the 11th International Conference on Embedded Software, EMSOFT 2011, Part of the Seventh Embedded Systems Week, ESWeek 2011, Taipei, Taiwan, 9–14 October 2011, pp. 107–116. ACM (2011)
22. Markey, N.: Verification of Embedded Systems - Algorithms and Complexity. Mémoire d'habilitation, École Normale Supérieure de Cachan, France (2011)
23. Miremadi, S., Fei, Z., Åkesson, K., Lennartson, B.: Symbolic supervisory control of timed discrete event systems. IEEE Trans. Contr. Syst. Technol. **23**(2), 584–597 (2015)
24. Monniaux, D.: Quantifier elimination by lazy model enumeration. In: Touili, T., Cook, B., Jackson, P. (eds.) CAV 2010. LNCS, vol. 6174, pp. 585–599. Springer, Heidelberg (2010). https://doi.org/10.1007/978-3-642-14295-6_51
25. Phan, A.-D., Hansen, M.R., Madsen, J.: EHRA: specification and analysis of energy-harvesting wireless sensor networks. In: Iida, S., Meseguer, J., Ogata, K. (eds.) Specification, Algebra, and Software. LNCS, vol. 8373, pp. 520–540. Springer, Heidelberg (2014). https://doi.org/10.1007/978-3-642-54624-2_26
26. Quasimodo: Quantitative system properties in model-driven design of embedded systems. http://www.quasimodo.aau.dk/

27. von Bochmann, G., Hilscher, M., Linker, S., Olderog, E.: Synthesizing and verifying controllers for multi-lane traffic maneuvers. Formal Asp. Comput. **29**(4), 583–600 (2017)

28. Wolfram Research, Inc.: Mathematica, Version 11.2. Champaign (2017)

29. Zhao, H., Zhan, N., Kapur, D., Larsen, K.G.: A "hybrid" approach for synthesizing optimal controllers of hybrid systems: a case study of the oil pump industrial example. In: Giannakopoulou, D., Méry, D. (eds.) FM 2012. LNCS, vol. 7436, pp. 471–485. Springer, Heidelberg (2012). https://doi.org/10.1007/978-3-642-32759-9_38

Encoding Fairness in a Synchronous Concurrent Program Algebra

Ian J. Hayes[(⊠)] and Larissa A. Meinicke

The University of Queensland, Brisbane, Queensland, Australia
ian.hayes@itee.uq.edu.au

Abstract. Concurrent program refinement algebra provides a suitable basis for supporting mechanised reasoning about shared-memory concurrent programs in a compositional manner, for example, it supports the rely/guarantee approach of Jones. The algebra makes use of a synchronous parallel operator motivated by Aczel's trace model of concurrency and with similarities to Milner's SCCS. This paper looks at defining a form of fairness within the program algebra. The encoding allows one to reason about the fair execution of a single process in isolation as well as define fair-parallel in terms of a base parallel operator, of which no fairness properties are assumed. An algebraic theory to support fairness and fair-parallel is developed.

1 Introduction

In shared memory concurrency, standard approaches to handling fairness [13,16] focus on defining a fair parallel operator, $c \parallel_f d$, that ensures each process gets its fair share of processor cycles. That complicates reasoning about a single process running as part of a parallel composition because its progress is determined in part by the fair parallel operator. In this paper we first focus on a single process that is run fairly with respect to its environment. That allows one to reason about its progress properties in relative isolation, although one does need to rely on its environment (i.e. all processes running in parallel with it) satisfying assumptions the single process makes about its environment. Fair parallel composition of processes can then be formulated as (unfair) parallel composition of fair executions of each of the individual processes (i.e. fair-execution(c) $\parallel$ fair-execution(d)), where fair-execution of a command is defined below.

Unfair Parallel. For a parallel composition, $c \parallel d$, the execution of c may be pre-empted forever by the execution of d, or vice versa. For example, execution of

$$x := 1 \parallel \mathbf{do}\, x \neq 1 \rightarrow y := y + 1 \,\mathbf{od} \tag{1}$$

with x initially zero may not terminate if the right side loop pre-empts the left side assignment forever [17]. A minimal fairness assumption is that neither process of a parallel composition can be pre-empted by the other process indefinitely.

This work was supported by Australian Research Council (ARC) Discovery Project DP130102901.

K. Havelund et al. (Eds.): FM 2018, LNCS 10951, pp. 222–239, 2018.
https://doi.org/10.1007/978-3-319-95582-7_13

Aczel Traces. The denotational semantics that we use for concurrency [3] is based on Aczel's model [2,4,5], in which the possible behaviours of a process, specified by *Aczel traces*, describe both the steps taken by the process itself as well as the steps taken by its environment. An Aczel trace is a sequence of atomic steps from one state σ to the next σ', in which each atomic step is either a *program step* of the form $\Pi(\sigma, \sigma')$ or an *environment step* of the form $\mathcal{E}(\sigma, \sigma')$. Parallel composition has an interleaving interpretation and so program and environment steps are disjoint. Infinite atomic-step sequences denote non-terminating executions, and finite sequences are labeled to differentiate those that (i) *terminate*, (ii) *abort* or (iii) become *infeasible* after the last atomic step in the sequence. Abortion represents failure (e.g. failure caused by a violation of environment assumptions), that may be *refined* (i.e. implemented) by any subsequent behaviour. Infeasibility may arise due to conflicting constraints in specifications, and is a refinement of any subsequent behaviours. Because each Aczel trace of a process defines both its behaviour as well as the behaviour of its environment, it is possible to include assumptions and constraints (including fairness) on the environment of a process in its denotation – the set of Aczel traces that it (or any valid implementation of it) may perform.

When two processes are combined in parallel, each must respect the environmental constraints placed upon it by the other process – unless either fails, in which case the parallel composition also fails. For example, assuming neither process has failed, one process may only take a program step $\Pi(\sigma, \sigma')$ if its parallel process may perform a step $\mathcal{E}(\sigma, \sigma')$, which permits its environment to take that program step at that point of execution. This is achieved by requiring parallel processes to synchronise on every atomic step they take: a program step $\Pi(\sigma, \sigma')$ of one process matches the corresponding environment step $\mathcal{E}(\sigma, \sigma')$ of the other to give a program step $\Pi(\sigma, \sigma')$ of the parallel composition, and identical environment steps of both processes match to give that environment step for the parallel composition. Attempting to synchronise other steps is infeasible.

Let π specify the nondeterministic command that executes a single atomic program step and then terminates, but does not constrain the state-transition made by that step, that is, π could take $\Pi(\sigma, \sigma')$ for any possible states σ and σ'. Similarly, let ϵ represent the non-deterministic command that executes any single atomic environment step and then terminates [3,8,9]. Neither π nor ϵ is allowed to fail: they do not contain aborting behaviour.

The command $c^\star$ represents finite iteration of command c, zero or more times, and c^ω represents finite or infinite iteration of c, zero of more times. The command c^∞ is the infinite iteration of c. Note that c^ω splits into finite and infinite iteration of c, where $\sqcap$ represents (demonic) nondeterministic choice.

$$c^\omega = c^\star \sqcap c^\infty \tag{2}$$

Imposing Fairness. If a process is pre-empted forever its behaviour becomes an infinite execution of any environment steps, i.e. ϵ^∞. The process **fair** that allows any behaviour, except abortion and pre-emption by its environment forever, can be defined by

$$\textbf{fair} \mathbin{\widehat{=}} \epsilon^\star\ (\pi\ \epsilon^\star)^\omega \tag{3}$$

where juxtaposition represents sequential composition. The process **fair** requires all contiguous subsequences of environment steps to be finite. A process representing *fair execution* of a process c is represented by

$$c \mathbin{\text{\reflectbox{$\mathbb{m}$}}} \textbf{fair}$$

where the *weak conjunction*, $c \mathbin{\text{\reflectbox{$\mathbb{m}$}}} d$, of c and d behaves as both c and d unless one of them aborts, in which case $c \mathbin{\text{\reflectbox{$\mathbb{m}$}}} d$ aborts [3,6]. Because **fair** never aborts, any aborting behaviour of $c \mathbin{\text{\reflectbox{$\mathbb{m}$}}} \textbf{fair}$ arises solely from c. In this way, c is constrained to be fair until it fails, if ever. Weak conjunction is associative, commutative and idempotent; it has identity **chaos** defined in terms of iteration of any number of atomic steps, where α represents a single atomic step, either program or environment.

$$\alpha = \pi \sqcap \epsilon \tag{4}$$

$$\textbf{chaos} \mathbin{\widehat{=}} \alpha^\omega \tag{5}$$

Because program and environment steps are disjoint, the conjunction of these commands is the infeasible command $\top$, i.e. $\pi \mathbin{\text{\reflectbox{$\mathbb{m}$}}} \epsilon = \top$.

Our interpretation of the execution of the process,

$$\textbf{do}\, \text{true} \rightarrow y := y + 1 \ \textbf{od}, \tag{6}$$

from an initial state in which y is zero allows the loop to be pre-empted forever by its environment and thus does not guarantee that y is ever set to, say, 7. In contrast, the fair execution of (6),

$$\textbf{do}\, \text{true} \rightarrow y := y + 1 \ \textbf{od} \mathbin{\text{\reflectbox{$\mathbb{m}$}}} \textbf{fair}, \tag{7}$$

rules out pre-emption by its environment forever and hence ensures that eventually y becomes 7 (or any other natural number).

Fair Termination. The command **term** allows only a finite number of program steps but does not rule out infinite pre-emption by its environment. It is defined as follows [3,6], recalling that $\alpha = \pi \sqcap \epsilon$.

$$\textbf{term} \mathbin{\widehat{=}} \alpha^\star\ \epsilon^\omega \tag{8}$$

If **term** is combined with **fair**, pre-emption by the environment forever is eliminated giving a stronger termination property that allows only a finite number of both program and environment steps, see Lemma 14 (term-fair).

$$\textbf{term} \mathbin{\text{\reflectbox{$\mathbb{m}$}}} \textbf{fair} = \alpha^\star$$

The notation $c \sqsubseteq d$ means c is refined (or implemented) by d and is defined by,

$$c \sqsubseteq d \mathbin{\widehat{=}} ((c \sqcap d) = c). \tag{9}$$

Hence if $\textbf{term} \sqsubseteq c$, then $\textbf{term} \mathbin{\text{\reflectbox{$\mathbb{m}$}}} \textbf{fair} \sqsubseteq c \mathbin{\text{\reflectbox{$\mathbb{m}$}}} \textbf{fair}$, i.e. fair execution of c gives strong termination, meaning that there are only a finite number of steps overall, both program and environment.

Fairness and Concurrency. Consider the following variation of example (1).

$$((x := 1) \cap \mathbf{fair}) \parallel (\mathbf{do}\, x \neq 1 \to y := y + 1 \,\mathbf{od} \cap \mathbf{fair}) \qquad (10)$$

The fair execution of $x := 1$ rules out infinite pre-emption by the right side and hence x is eventually set to one, and hence the right side also terminates thus ensuring termination of the parallel composition. Note that

$$(c \parallel d) \cap \mathbf{fair} \sqsubseteq (c \cap \mathbf{fair}) \parallel (d \cap \mathbf{fair})$$

but the reverse refinement does not hold in general because $(c \parallel d) \cap \mathbf{fair}$ does not rule out c being pre-empted forever by d (or vice versa) within the parallel; it only rules out the whole of the parallel composition from being preempted by its environment forever.

Parallel with Synchronised Termination. The parallel operator $\parallel$ is interpreted as synchronous parallel for which every step of the parallel (until failure of either process) must be a synchronisation of steps of its component processes: a program and environment step synchronise to give a program step, $\pi \parallel \epsilon = \pi$, two environment steps synchronise to give an environment step, $\epsilon \parallel \epsilon = \epsilon$ and both the processes must terminate together, $\mathbf{nil} \parallel \mathbf{nil} = \mathbf{nil}$. This is in contrast to the *early-termination* interpretation of parallel in which, if one process terminates the parallel composition reduces to the other process. The command ϵ^ω, referred to as **skip**,

$$\mathbf{skip} \mathrel{\widehat{=}} \epsilon^\omega \qquad (11)$$

is the identity of parallel composition, meaning that it permits any possible environment behaviour when executed in parallel with any other command, e.g. $c \parallel \mathbf{skip} = c$. A command c for which

$$c = c\,\mathbf{skip} \qquad (12)$$

is said to be *unconstrained after program termination*. When it is executed in parallel with another command, then after termination of c, the parallel composition $c \parallel d$ does reduce to the other command, d. If d is also unconstrained after program termination, then $c \parallel d$ corresponds to the early-termination interpretation of parallel. Moreover, $c \parallel d$ is then also unconstrained after program termination, e.g. $c \parallel d = (c \parallel d)\,\mathbf{skip}$, see Lemma 8 (par-skip). In this way (12) can be perceived as a healthiness condition, that is preserved by parallel composition of healthy commands.

The fair execution of any process c constrains the environment, even after the termination of the program steps in c, so that it cannot execute an infinite number of steps in a row, e.g. $\mathbf{term} \cap \mathbf{fair} = \alpha^\star$. This means that it is not healthy (12), and so for parallel with synchronised termination, simply conjoining $\mathbf{fair}$ to both sides of a synchronous parallel can lead to infeasibility. Consider another of Van Glabbeek's examples [17]:

$$(x := 1 \cap \mathbf{fair}) \parallel (\mathbf{do}\,\mathrm{true} \to y := y + 1 \,\mathbf{od} \cap \mathbf{fair}). \qquad (13)$$

The fair execution of $x := 1$ rules out infinite pre-emption by the right side loop, ensuring x is assigned one, but fair execution of $x := 1$ forces termination of the left side, including environment steps, which as the right side is non-terminating leads to an infeasible parallel composition. To remedy this one needs to allow infinite pre-emption of a branch in a fair parallel *once the command in the branch has terminated*. For a command c satisfying (12) we have that

$$(c \mmop \mathbf{fair})\ \mathbf{skip} \tag{14}$$

represents fair execution of c *until program termination*. Like the original command c, it remains unconstrained after program termination (i.e. healthy). For the example above, we have implicitly that $x := 1$ and the loop (**do** true $\rightarrow$ $y := y + 1$ **od**) are unconstrained after program termination, and so only requiring both branches to execute fairly until program termination we get

$$(x := 1 \mmop \mathbf{fair})\ \mathbf{skip}\ \|\ (\mathbf{do}\ \mathrm{true} \rightarrow y := y + 1\ \mathbf{od} \mmop \mathbf{fair})\ \mathbf{skip} \tag{15}$$

which is no longer infeasible, since the second process is allowed to execute forever after termination of the program steps in the first.

That leads to the following definition for fair parallel,

$$c \parallel_f d \mathrel{\widehat{=}} (c \mmop \mathbf{fair})\ \mathbf{skip}\ \|\ (d \mmop \mathbf{fair})\ \mathbf{skip} \tag{16}$$

which imposes fairness on c until it terminates, and similarly for d.

Our theory of fairness is based on the synchronous concurrent refinement algebra, which is summarised in Sect. 2, and Sect. 3 gives a set of lemmas about iterations in the algebra. Section 4 gives basic properties of the command **fair**, while Sect. 5 gives properties of **fair** combined with (unfair) concurrency and Sect. 6 uses these to derive properties of the fair-parallel operator which is defined in terms of (unfair) parallel (16).

2   Synchronous Concurrent Refinement Algebra

The synchronous concurrent refinement algebra is defined in [8,9]. In this section we introduce the aspects that are used to define and reason about fairness in this paper. A model for the algebra based on Aczel traces, as discussed in the introduction, can be found in [3].

A concurrent refinement algebra with atomic steps ($\mathcal{A}$), and synchronisation operators parallel ($\|$) and weak conjunction ($\mmop$) is a two-sorted algebra

$$(\mathcal{C}, \mathcal{A}, \bigsqcap, \bigsqcup, \,\mathbf{;}, \|, \mmop, !\,, \mathbf{nil}, \alpha, \mathbf{skip}, \mathbf{chaos}, \epsilon)$$

where the carrier set $\mathcal{C}$ is interpreted as the set of *commands* and forms a complete distributive lattice with meet ($\bigsqcap$), referred to as *choice*, and join ($\bigsqcup$), referred to as *conjunction*, and refinement ordering given by (9), where we use $c \sqcap d \mathrel{\widehat{=}} \bigsqcap\{c, d\}$, and $c \sqcup d \mathrel{\widehat{=}} \bigsqcup\{c, d\}$ to represent the meet and join over pairs of elements. The least and greatest elements in the lattice are the aborting command $\bot \mathbin{\hat{=}} \sqcap \mathcal{C}$, and the infeasible command $\top \mathbin{\hat{=}} \bigsqcup \mathcal{C}$, respectively. The binary operator ";", with identity element **nil**, represents *sequential* composition (and satisfies the axioms listed in Fig. 1), however we abbreviate $c;d$ to $c\,d$ throughout this paper.

For $i \in \mathbb{N}$, we use c^i to represent the fixed-iteration of the command c, i times. It is inductively defined by $c^0 \mathbin{\hat{=}} \mathbf{nil}$, $c^{i+1} \mathbin{\hat{=}} c\,c^i$. More generally, fixed-point operators finite iteration (*), finite or infinite iteration ($^\omega$), and infinite iteration ($^\infty$) are defined using the least (μ) and greatest (ν) fixed-point operators of the complete distributive lattice of commands,

$$c^\star \mathbin{\hat{=}} (\nu x.\mathbf{nil} \sqcap c\,x) \qquad (17) \qquad\qquad c^\infty \mathbin{\hat{=}} c^\omega \top \qquad (19)$$

$$c^\omega \mathbin{\hat{=}} (\mu x.\mathbf{nil} \sqcap c\,x) \qquad (18)$$

and satisfy the properties outlined in Sect. 3.

The second carrier set $\mathcal{A} \subseteq \mathcal{C}$ is a sub-algebra of *atomic step commands*, defined so that $(\mathcal{A}, \sqcap, \sqcup, !, \top, \alpha)$ forms a Boolean algebra with greatest element $\top$ (also the greatest command), which can be thought of the atomic step that is disabled from all initial states, the least element α, the command that can perform any possible atomic step. The negation of an atomic step $a \in \mathcal{A}$, written $!\,a$, represents all of the atomic steps that are not in a. Distinguished atomic step $\epsilon \in \mathcal{A}$ is used to stand for any possible environment step, and its complement, $\pi \mathbin{\hat{=}} !\,\epsilon$, is then the set of all possible program steps, giving us that $\alpha = \pi \sqcap \epsilon$.

Both *parallel* composition ($\|$) and *weak conjunction* ($\Cap$) are instances of the synchronisation operator ($\otimes$), in which parallel has command identity $\mathbf{skip} = \epsilon^\omega$, and atomic-step identity ϵ; and weak conjunction has command identity $\mathbf{chaos} = \alpha^\omega$, and atomic-step identity α. As well as satisfying the synchronisation axioms from Fig. 1, a number of additional axioms, also listed in the figure, are assumed. These include, for example, that both operators are abort-strict, (36) and (37), weak conjunction is idempotent (38), and they include assumptions about the synchronisation of atomic steps, e.g. (39) and (40).

We follow the convention that c and d stands for arbitrary commands, and a and b for atomic step commands. Further, subscripted versions of these stand for entities of the same kind. We also assume that choice ($\sqcap$) has the lowest precedence, and sequential composition has the highest; and we use parentheses to disambiguate other cases.

3   Properties of Iterations

In this section we outline the iteration properties required in this paper. Omitted or abbreviated proofs can be found in [7].

First, from [8,9], we have that the iteration operators satisfy the basic properties listed in Fig. 2. The following lemma (also from [8]), captures that prefixes of finite iterations of atomic steps $a^\star\,c$ and $b^\star\,d$ combine in parallel until either $a^\star$ or $b^\star$ or both complete. If both $a^\star$ and $b^\star$ complete together, the remaining commands after the prefixes run in parallel: $c \parallel d$. If the first completes before the second, c runs in parallel with at least one b followed by d, and symmetrically if the second completes before the first.

Lemma 1 (finite-finite-prefix)

$$a^\star\, c \parallel b^\star\, d = (a \parallel b)^\star\, ((c \parallel d) \sqcap (c \parallel b\, b^\star\, d) \sqcap (a\, a^\star\, c \parallel d)).$$

The next lemma is similar to Lemma 1, except one of the prefixes is finite and the other is possibly infinite.

Sequential

$$c_0\, (c_1\, c_2) = (c_0\, c_1)\, c_2 \quad (20)$$
$$c\, \text{nil} = c = \text{nil}\, c \quad (21)$$
$$\bot\, c = \bot \quad (22)$$

$$\left(\textstyle\bigsqcap C\right) d = \bigsqcap_{c \in C} (c\, d) \quad (23)$$
$$D \neq \emptyset \;\Rightarrow\; c\left(\textstyle\bigsqcap D\right) = \bigsqcap_{d \in D} (c\, d) \quad (24)$$

Synchronisation operators parallel and weak conjunction Both parallel ($\parallel$) and weak conjunction ($\Cap$) are instances of the synchronisation operator ($\otimes$). For parallel we take the identity command $\mathcal{I}d$ to be **skip**, and atomic-step identity **1** to be ϵ, and for weak conjunction we take $\mathcal{I}d$ to be **chaos** and **1** to be α.

$$c_0 \otimes (c_1 \otimes c_2) = (c_0 \otimes c_1) \otimes c_2 \quad (25)$$
$$c \otimes d = d \otimes c \quad (26)$$
$$c \otimes \mathcal{I}d = c \quad (27)$$
$$D \neq \emptyset \;\Rightarrow\; c \otimes \left(\textstyle\bigsqcap D\right) = \bigsqcap_{d \in D} (c \otimes d) \quad (28)$$

$$a \otimes 1 = a \quad (29)$$
$$\text{nil} \otimes \text{nil} = \text{nil} \quad (30)$$
$$\text{nil} \otimes a\, c = \top \quad (31)$$
$$a \otimes b \in \mathcal{A} \quad (32)$$

$$(a\, c) \otimes (b\, d) = (a \otimes b)\, (c \otimes d) \quad (33)$$
$$a^\infty \otimes b^\infty = (a \otimes b)^\infty \quad (34)$$
$$(c_0\, d_0) \otimes (c_1\, d_1) \sqsubseteq (c_0 \otimes c_1)\, (d_0 \otimes d_1) \quad (35)$$

Additional parallel and weak conjunction axioms As well as satisfying the synchronisation axioms the following axioms of parallel and weak conjunction are assumed to hold.

$$c \parallel \bot = \bot \quad (36)$$
$$c \Cap \bot = \bot \quad (37)$$
$$c \Cap c = c \quad (38)$$

$$\pi \parallel \pi = \top \quad (39)$$
$$\pi \Cap \epsilon = \top \quad (40)$$
$$c \Cap \alpha^i = c \parallel \epsilon^i \quad (41)$$
$$c \Cap \alpha^\infty = c \parallel \epsilon^\infty \quad (42)$$

$$(c_0 \Cap \alpha^i)\, d_0 \parallel (c_1 \Cap \alpha^i)\, d_1 = ((c_0 \Cap \alpha^i) \parallel (c_1 \Cap \alpha^i))\, (d_0 \parallel d_1) \quad (43)$$
$$(c_0 \Cap \alpha^i)\, d_0 \Cap (c_1 \Cap \alpha^i)\, d_1 = (c_0 \Cap c_1 \Cap \alpha^i)\, (d_0 \Cap d_1) \quad (44)$$
$$(c_0 \parallel d_0) \Cap (c_1 \parallel d_1) \sqsubseteq (c_0 \Cap c_1) \parallel (d_0 \Cap d_1) \quad (45)$$

Fig. 1. Axioms for the synchronous concurrent refinement algebra. We let $c, d \in \mathcal{C}$ be commands, $C, D \in \mathbb{P}\,\mathcal{C}$ be sets of commands, $a, b \in \mathcal{A}$ be atomic steps, and $i \in \mathbb{N}$ be a natural number.

$$c^* = \mathbf{nil} \sqcap c\, c^* \qquad (46)$$

$$c^\omega = \mathbf{nil} \sqcap c\, c^\omega \qquad (47)$$

$$c^\omega = c^* \sqcap c^\infty \qquad (48)$$

$$c^* = \textstyle\bigsqcap_{i \in \mathbb{N}} c^i \qquad (49)$$

$$d \sqcap c\, x \sqsubseteq x \implies c^\omega\, d \sqsubseteq x \qquad (50)$$

$$x \sqsubseteq d \sqcap c\, x \implies x \sqsubseteq c^*\, d \qquad (51)$$

$$c\, (d\, c)^* = (c\, d)^*\, c \qquad (52)$$

$$c\, (d\, c)^\omega = (c\, d)^\omega\, c \qquad (53)$$

$$(c \sqcap d)^\omega = c^\omega\, (d\, c^\omega)^\omega \qquad (54)$$

Fig. 2. Basic properties of iteration operators for commands $c, d, x \in \mathcal{C}$.

Lemma 2 (finite-omega-prefix)

$$a^*\, c \parallel b^\omega\, d = (a \parallel b)^*\, ((c \parallel d) \sqcap (c \parallel b\, b^\omega\, d) \sqcap (a\, a^*\, c \parallel d)).$$

The following lemma uses the fact that program steps do not synchronise with other program steps in parallel (39), to simplify the parallel composition of two iterations.

Lemma 3 (iterate-pi-par-pi). $(\pi\, c)^\omega \parallel (\pi\, d)^\omega = \mathbf{nil}.$

Proof. The proof uses (47), distribution and then (30), (31) twice, (33), and (39). □

Lemma 4 (iterate-pi-sync-atomic). *For either synchronisation operator,* $\parallel$ *or* ⓜ, *and atomic step command* a,

$$(\pi\, c)^\omega \otimes a\, d = (\pi \otimes a)\, (c\, (\pi\, c)^\omega \otimes d).$$

Proof. The proof uses (47), distribution and then (31) and (33). □

Lemma 5 (distribute-infeasible-suffix). *For any synchronisation operator* $(\otimes)$ *that is abort strict, i.e.* $(c \otimes \bot) = \bot$ *for all* c, *then we have that for any commands* c, d,

$$c \otimes d\, \top = (c \otimes d)\, \top.$$

Lemma 6 (infinite-annihilates). $(c \text{ ⓜ } \alpha^\infty)\, d_1 = (c \text{ ⓜ } \alpha^\infty)\, d_2.$

Proof. The result follows straightforwardly from the fact that weak conjunction is abort strict (37), $\alpha^\infty = \alpha^\infty\, \top$ from (19) and Lemma 5 (distribute-infeasible-suffix), together with the fact that $\top\, d_1 = \top = \top\, d_2$ from (23) by taking C in (23) to be empty. □

Taking d_2 to be **nil** in the above lemma gives $(c \text{ ⓜ } \alpha^\infty)\, d = c \text{ ⓜ } \alpha^\infty$, for any d.

Lemma 7 (sync-termination). *For commands* c *and* d *such that* $c = c \text{ ⓜ } \alpha^*$ *and* $d = d \text{ ⓜ } \alpha^*$,

$$(c\, a^* \parallel d\, b^*)\, (a^\omega \parallel b^\omega) = c\, a^\omega \parallel d\, b^\omega$$

The following lemma gives us that parallel composition preserves the healthiness property (12).

Lemma 8 (par-skip). $(c \text{ skip} \parallel d \text{ skip}) \text{ skip} = c \text{ skip} \parallel d \text{ skip}$

Proof. Refinement from left to right is straightforward because $\text{skip} \sqsubseteq \text{nil}$:

$$(c \text{ skip} \parallel d \text{ skip}) \text{ skip} \sqsubseteq (c \text{ skip} \parallel d \text{ skip}) \text{ nil} = c \text{ skip} \parallel d \text{ skip}.$$

Refinement from right to left can be shown as follows.

$$
\begin{aligned}
& c \text{ skip} \parallel d \text{ skip} \\
= \quad & \text{as } \text{skip} = \text{skip skip} \\
& c \text{ skip skip} \parallel d \text{ skip skip} \\
\sqsubseteq \quad & \text{by sync-interchange-seq (35)} \\
& (c \text{ skip} \parallel d \text{ skip}) (\text{skip} \parallel \text{skip}) \\
= \quad & \text{skip is the identity of parallel composition} \\
& (c \text{ skip} \parallel d \text{ skip}) \text{ skip}
\end{aligned}
$$

$\square$

4   Properties of fair

This section provides a set of properties of the command **fair** culminating with Theorem 1 (fair-termination), which allows termination arguments to be decoupled from fairness. The command **chaos** allows any non-aborting behaviour. If a command refines **chaos**, that command is therefore non-aborting. The command **fair** is non-aborting.

Lemma 9 (chaos-fair). $\text{chaos} \sqsubseteq \text{fair}$

Proof. The proof uses the definition of **chaos** (5), (54), the property that $c^\omega \sqsubseteq c^*$, for any command c, and the definition of **fair** (3).

$$\text{chaos} = (\epsilon \sqcap \pi)^\omega = \epsilon^\omega (\pi \epsilon^\omega)^\omega \sqsubseteq \epsilon^* (\pi \epsilon^*)^\omega = \text{fair} \qquad \square$$

Fair execution of a command is always a refinement of the command.

Lemma 10 (introduce-fair). $c \sqsubseteq c \cap \text{fair}$

Proof. The lemma holds because **chaos** is the identity of $\cap$ and Lemma 9 (chaos-fair):

$$c = c \cap \text{chaos} \sqsubseteq c \cap \text{fair}. \qquad \square$$

Fair execution followed by fair execution is equivalent to fair execution.

Lemma 11 (fair-fair). $\textbf{fair } \textbf{fair} = \textbf{fair}$

Proof

fair fair
$=$ by definition of **fair** (3) $=$ by (53)
$\epsilon^{\star} (\pi \ \epsilon^{\star})^{\omega} \ \epsilon^{\star} (\pi \ \epsilon^{\star})^{\omega}$ $\epsilon^{\star} (\pi \ \epsilon^{\star})^{\omega} \ (\pi \ \epsilon^{\star})^{\omega}$
$=$ by (53) $=$ as $c^{\omega} \ c^{\omega} = c^{\omega}$, for any c
$(\epsilon^{\star} \ \pi)^{\omega} \ \epsilon^{\star} \ \epsilon^{\star} (\pi \ \epsilon^{\star})^{\omega}$ $\epsilon^{\star} (\pi \ \epsilon^{\star})^{\omega}$
$=$ as $c^{\star} \ c^{\star} = c^{\star}$, for any c $=$ by definition of **fair** (3)
$(\epsilon^{\star} \ \pi)^{\omega} \ \epsilon^{\star} (\pi \ \epsilon^{\star})^{\omega}$ **fair**   □

Fair execution of a sequential composition is implemented by fair execution of each command in sequence.

Lemma 12 (fair-distrib-seq). $(c \ d) \pitchfork \textbf{fair} \sqsubseteq (c \pitchfork \textbf{fair}) \ (d \pitchfork \textbf{fair})$

Proof. The proof uses Lemma 11 (fair-fair) and then interchanges weak conjunction with sequential (35).

$$(c \ d) \pitchfork \textbf{fair} = (c \ d) \pitchfork (\textbf{fair } \textbf{fair}) \sqsubseteq (c \pitchfork \textbf{fair}) \ (d \pitchfork \textbf{fair})$$

□

The command **skip** $(= \epsilon^{\omega})$ is the identity of parallel composition. It allows any sequence of environment steps, including ϵ^{∞}, but fair execution of **skip** excludes ϵ^{∞}, leaving only a finite sequence of environment steps: $\epsilon^{\star}$.

Lemma 13 (skip-fair). $\textbf{skip} \pitchfork \textbf{fair} = \epsilon^{\star}$

Proof. Expanding the definitions of **skip** (11) and **fair** (3) in the left side to start.

$\epsilon^{\omega} \pitchfork \epsilon^{\star} (\pi \ \epsilon^{\star})^{\omega}$
$=$ by Lemma 2 (finite-omega-prefix)
$\epsilon^{\star} ((\textbf{nil} \pitchfork (\pi \ \epsilon^{\star})^{\omega}) \sqcap (\textbf{nil} \pitchfork \epsilon \ \epsilon^{\star} (\pi \ \epsilon^{\star})^{\omega}) \sqcap (\epsilon \ \epsilon^{\omega} \pitchfork (\pi \ \epsilon^{\star})^{\omega}))$
$=$ by (31) and Lemma 4 (iterate-pi-sync-atomic) and (40)
$\epsilon^{\star} (\textbf{nil} \sqcap \top \sqcap \top)$
$= \epsilon^{\star}$ □

The command **term** (8) allows only a finite number of program steps but does not exclude an infinite sequence of environment steps, whereas **fair** excludes an infinite sequence of environment steps. When **term** and **fair** are conjoined, only a finite number of steps is allowed overall.

Lemma 14 (term-fair). term ⋒ fair = α^*

Proof. Note that $\alpha^* = \alpha^* \, \alpha^* \sqsubseteq \alpha^* \, \epsilon^* \sqsubseteq \alpha^* \, \textbf{nil} = \alpha^*$, and hence $\alpha^* = \alpha^* \, \epsilon^*$.

$$\text{term} \Cap \textbf{fair} = \alpha^*$$
$$\Leftrightarrow \quad \text{by the definition of } \textbf{term} \text{ (8) and } \alpha^* = \alpha^* \, \epsilon^*$$
$$\alpha^* \, \epsilon^\omega \Cap \textbf{fair} = \alpha^* \, \epsilon^*$$

The fixed point fusion theorem [1] is applied with $F \mathrel{\widehat{=}} \lambda x \cdot x \Cap \textbf{fair}$, $G \mathrel{\widehat{=}} \lambda x \cdot \epsilon^\omega \sqcap \alpha \, x$ and $H \mathrel{\widehat{=}} \lambda x \cdot \epsilon^* \sqcap \alpha \, x$. The lemma corresponds to $F(\nu G) = \nu H$, which holds by the fusion theorem if $F \circ G = H \circ F$ and F distributes arbitrary nondeterministic choices.

$$(F \circ G)(x)$$
$$= \quad \text{by the definitions of } F \text{ and } G$$
$$(\epsilon^\omega \sqcap \alpha \, x) \Cap \textbf{fair}$$
$$= \quad \text{distributing}$$
$$(\epsilon^\omega \Cap \textbf{fair}) \sqcap (\alpha \, x \Cap \textbf{fair})$$
$$= \quad \text{by Lemma 13 (skip-fair) and expanding the definition of } \textbf{fair} \text{ (3)}$$
$$\epsilon^* \sqcap (\alpha \, x \Cap \epsilon^* \, (\pi \, \epsilon^*)^\omega)$$
$$= \quad \text{by unfolding (46) on } \epsilon^* \text{ and distribute}$$
$$\epsilon^* \sqcap (\alpha \, x \Cap (\pi \, \epsilon^*)^\omega) \sqcap (\alpha \, x \Cap \epsilon \, \epsilon^* \, (\pi \, \epsilon^*)^\omega)$$
$$= \quad \text{by Lemma 4 (iterate-pi-sync-atomic) and } \alpha \Cap \pi = \pi \text{ and (33)}$$
$$\epsilon^* \sqcap \pi \, (x \Cap \epsilon^* \, (\pi \, \epsilon^*)^\omega) \sqcap \epsilon \, (x \Cap \epsilon^* \, (\pi \, \epsilon^*)^\omega)$$
$$= \quad \text{distribute and use definition of } \textbf{fair} \text{ (3)}$$
$$\epsilon^* \sqcap \alpha \, (x \Cap \textbf{fair})$$
$$= \quad \text{by the definitions of } H \text{ and } F$$
$$(H \circ F)(x)$$

Finally F distributes arbitrary nondeterministic choices because for nonempty C,

$$F(\textstyle\bigsqcap C) = (\textstyle\bigsqcap C) \Cap \textbf{fair} = \bigsqcap_{c \in C} (c \Cap \textbf{fair}) = \bigsqcap_{c \in C} F(c),$$

and for C empty, $F(\bigsqcap \emptyset) = \top \Cap \textbf{fair} = \top = \bigsqcap_{c \in \emptyset} (c \Cap \textbf{fair}) = \bigsqcap_{c \in \emptyset} F(c)$ because **chaos** $\sqsubseteq$ **fair**. ∎

We do not build fairness into our definitions of standard sequential programming constructs such as assignment, conditionals and loops [3], rather their definitions allow preemption by their environment forever. Hence any executable sequential program code may be preempted forever. The command **term** allows only a finite number of program steps but also allows preemption by the environment forever. If a command c refines **term** it will terminate in a finite number of steps provided it is not preempted by its environment forever, and hence fair execution of c only allows a finite number of steps because preemption by the environment forever is precluded by fair execution. That allows one to show termination by showing the simpler property, **term** $\sqsubseteq c$, which does not need to consider fairness. Existing methods for proving termination can then be used in the context of fair parallel.

Theorem 1 (fair-termination). *If* **term** $\sqsubseteq c$, *then* $\alpha^\star \sqsubseteq c \pitchfork$ **fair**.

Proof. If **term** $\sqsubseteq c$, by Lemma 14 (term-fair) $\alpha^\star =$ **term** $\pitchfork$ **fair** $\sqsubseteq c \pitchfork$ **fair**.   □

5   Properties of Fair and Concurrency

This section provides a set of properties for combining **fair** with (unfair) concurrency, in particular it provides lemmas for distributing fairness over a parallel composition. Details of abbreviated proofs can be found in [7]. The following is a helper lemma for Lemma 16 (fair-par-fair).

Lemma 15 (fair-par-fair-expand). **fair** $\|$ **fair** $= \epsilon^\star (\mathbf{nil} \sqcap \pi \, (\mathbf{fair} \| \mathbf{fair}))$

Proof. The proof begins by expanding the definition of **fair** (3), then uses Lemma 1 (finite-finite-prefix) and (29), then Lemma 3 (iterate-pi-par-pi), Lemma 4 (iterate-pi-sync-atomic) and (29) and finally the definition of **fair** once more.   □

Fair execution is implemented by fair execution of two parallel processes.

Lemma 16 (fair-par-fair). **fair** $\sqsubseteq$ **fair** $\|$ **fair**

Proof

$$\mathbf{fair} \sqsubseteq \mathbf{fair} \| \mathbf{fair}$$
$\Leftrightarrow$ by the definition of **fair** (3) and (53)
$$(\epsilon^\star \, \pi)^\omega \, \epsilon^\star \sqsubseteq \mathbf{fair} \| \mathbf{fair}$$
$\Leftarrow$ by (50)
$$\epsilon^\star \sqcap \epsilon^\star \, \pi \, (\mathbf{fair} \| \mathbf{fair}) \sqsubseteq \mathbf{fair} \| \mathbf{fair}$$

The above follows by Lemma 15 (fair-par-fair-expand) by distributing.   □

Fair execution of $c \| d$ can be implemented by fair execution of each of c and d but the reverse does not hold in general.

Lemma 17 (fair-distrib-par-both). $(c \| d) \pitchfork \mathbf{fair} \sqsubseteq (c \pitchfork \mathbf{fair}) \| (d \pitchfork \mathbf{fair})$

Proof. The proof uses Lemma 16 (fair-par-fair) and then interchanges weak conjunction and parallel (45).

$$(c \| d) \pitchfork \mathbf{fair} \sqsubseteq (c \| d) \pitchfork (\mathbf{fair} \| \mathbf{fair}) \sqsubseteq (c \pitchfork \mathbf{fair}) \| (d \pitchfork \mathbf{fair})$$ □

The following is a helper lemma for Lemma 19 (fair-par-chaos).

Lemma 18 (fair-par-chaos-expand). **fair** $\|$ **chaos** $= \epsilon^\star(\mathbf{nil} \sqcap \pi \, (\mathbf{fair} \| \mathbf{chaos}))$

Proof. The proof uses the definitions of **fair** (3) and **chaos** (5) and (54), then Lemma 2 (finite-omega-prefix) and (29), then Lemma 3 (iterate-pi-par-pi) and Lemma 4 (iterate-pi-sync-atomic) and (29), and finally (54) and definitions (3) and (5).   □

Fair execution in parallel with **chaos** gives a fair execution because **chaos** never aborts.

Lemma 19 (fair-par-chaos). fair $\|$ chaos $=$ fair

Proof. The refinement from left to right is straightforward as **chaos** $\sqsubseteq$ **skip** and **skip** is the identity of parallel: **fair** $\|$ **chaos** $\sqsubseteq$ **fair** $\|$ **skip** $=$ **fair**. The refinement from right to left uses the definition of **fair**.

$$\textbf{fair} \sqsubseteq \textbf{fair} \parallel \textbf{chaos}$$
$$\Leftrightarrow \quad \text{by the definition of \textbf{fair} (3) and (53)}$$
$$(\epsilon^* \; \pi)^\omega \; \epsilon^* \sqsubseteq \textbf{fair} \parallel \textbf{chaos}$$
$$\Leftarrow \quad \text{by (50)}$$
$$\epsilon^* \sqcap \epsilon^* \; \pi \; (\textbf{fair} \parallel \textbf{chaos}) \sqsubseteq \textbf{fair} \parallel \textbf{chaos}$$

The above follows by Lemma 18 (fair-par-chaos-expand) and distributing. $\square$

Fair execution of one process of a parallel composition eliminates behaviour ϵ^∞ for that process and hence because parallel compositions synchronise on ϵ (29), that eliminates behaviour ϵ^∞ from the parallel composition as a whole, provided the parallel process does not abort. Aborting behaviour of one process of a parallel aborts the whole parallel (36) and aborting behaviour allows any behaviour, including ϵ^∞. Fair execution of $c \parallel d$ can be implemented by fair execution of c (or by symmetry d).

Lemma 20 (fair-distrib-par-one). $(c \parallel d) \Cap \textbf{fair} \sqsubseteq (c \Cap \textbf{fair}) \parallel d$

Proof. The proof uses Lemma 19 (fair-par-chaos), then interchanges weak conjunction and parallel (45) and finally uses the fact that **chaos** is the identity of weak conjunction.

$$(c \parallel d) \Cap (\textbf{fair} \parallel \textbf{chaos}) \sqsubseteq (c \Cap \textbf{fair}) \parallel (d \Cap \textbf{chaos}) = (c \Cap \textbf{fair}) \parallel d \qquad \square$$

6   Properties of Fair Parallel

This section examines the properties of the fair-parallel operator (16), such as commutativity, distribution over nondeterministic choice and associativity. The first three results derive readily from the equivalent properties for parallel.

Theorem 2 (fair-parallel-commutes). $c \parallel_f d = d \parallel_f c$

Proof. The proof is straightforward from definition (16) of fair-parallel because (unfair) parallel is commutative. $\square$

Theorem 3 (fair-parallel-distrib). $D \neq \emptyset \Rightarrow c \parallel_f (\sqcap D) = \sqcap_{d \in D} (c \parallel_f d)$

Proof. Let D be non-empty.

$c \|_f (\sqcap D)$
$=$ by the definition of $\|_f$ (16)
$\quad (c \cap \textbf{fair}) \, \textbf{skip} \, \| \, ((\sqcap D) \cap \textbf{fair}) \, \textbf{skip}$
$=$ as non-empty choice distributes over $\cap$, sequential composition and $\|$
$\quad \sqcap_{d \in D} (c \cap \textbf{fair}) \, \textbf{skip} \, \| \, (d \cap \textbf{fair}) \, \textbf{skip}$
$=$ by the definition of $\|_f$ (16)
$\quad \sqcap_{d \in D} (c \|_f d)$ □

Theorem 4 (fair-par-monotonic). *If* $d_1 \sqsubseteq d_2$, *then* $c \|_f d_1 \sqsubseteq c \|_f d_2$.

Proof. The refinement $d_1 \sqsubseteq d_2$ holds if and only if $d_1 \sqcap d_2 = d_1$ and hence, by Theorem 3 (fair-parallel-distrib),

$$c \|_f d_1 \sqsubseteq c \|_f d_2$$
$$\Leftrightarrow c \|_f d_1 \sqcap c \|_f d_2 = c \|_f d_1$$
$$\Leftrightarrow c \|_f (d_1 \sqcap d_2) = c \|_f d_1$$

because $d_1 \sqcap d_2 = d_1$ follows from the assumption.   □

Fair-parallel retains fairness for its component processes with respect to the overall environment even when one component process terminates.

Theorem 5 (fair-parallel-nil). $c \|_f \textbf{nil} = (c \cap \textbf{fair}) \, \textbf{skip}$

Proof. The proof uses the definition of fair parallel (16), the facts that **skip** is the identity of parallel composition and $\textbf{nil} \cap \textbf{fair} = \textbf{nil}$.

$(c \cap \textbf{fair}) \, \textbf{skip} \, \| \, (\textbf{nil} \cap \textbf{fair}) \, \textbf{skip} = (c \cap \textbf{fair}) \, \textbf{skip} \, \| \, \textbf{skip} = (c \cap \textbf{fair}) \, \textbf{skip}$ □

While properties such as commutativity and distributivity are relatively straightforward to verify, associativity of fair-parallel is more involved. A property that is essential to the associativity proof is that fair-parallel execution of two commands not only ensures that each of its commands are executed fairly until program termination, but also that the whole parallel composition is executed fairly until program termination; this is encapsulated in Theorem 6 (absorb-fair-skip), but first we show the easy direction of this proof in Lemma 21 (introduce-fair-skip) and then give lemmas for the finite and infinite cases for Theorem 6 (absorb-fair-skip).

Lemma 21 (introduce-fair-skip). $c \|_f d \sqsubseteq ((c \|_f d) \cap \textbf{fair}) \, \textbf{skip}$

Proof

$c \|_f d$
$=$ by Lemma 8 (par-skip) using the definition of fair parallel (16)
$\quad (c \|_f d) \, \textbf{skip}$
$\sqsubseteq$ by Lemma 10 (introduce-fair)
$\quad ((c \|_f d) \cap \textbf{fair}) \, \textbf{skip}$ □

Lemma 22 (finite-absorb-fair-skip)

$$(((c \cap \alpha^\star) \|_f (d \cap \alpha^\star)) \cap \mathbf{fair}) \; \mathbf{skip} = (c \cap \alpha^\star) \|_f (d \cap \alpha^\star)$$

Proof. The refinement from right to left follows by Lemma 21 (introduce-fair-skip). The refinement from left to right follows.

$\quad (((c \cap \alpha^\star) \|_f (d \cap \alpha^\star)) \cap \mathbf{fair}) \; \mathbf{skip}$

$=\quad$ by the definition of $\|_f$ (16)

$\quad (((c \cap \alpha^\star \cap \mathbf{fair}) \; \mathbf{skip} \| (d \cap \alpha^\star \cap \mathbf{fair}) \; \mathbf{skip}) \cap \mathbf{fair}) \; \mathbf{skip}$

$\sqsubseteq\quad$ by Lemma 17 (fair-distrib-par-both)

$\quad ((((c \cap \alpha^\star \cap \mathbf{fair}) \; \mathbf{skip}) \cap \mathbf{fair}) \| (((d \cap \alpha^\star \cap \mathbf{fair}) \; \mathbf{skip}) \cap \mathbf{fair})) \; \mathbf{skip}$

$\sqsubseteq\quad$ by Lemma 12 (fair-distrib-seq) and $\cap$ idempotent (38)

$\quad ((c \cap \alpha^\star \cap \mathbf{fair}) \; (\mathbf{skip} \cap \mathbf{fair}) \| (d \cap \alpha^\star \cap \mathbf{fair}) \; (\mathbf{skip} \cap \mathbf{fair})) \; \mathbf{skip}$

$\sqsubseteq\quad$ as $\mathbf{skip} \cap \mathbf{fair} = \epsilon^\star$ by Lemma 13 (skip-fair)

$\quad ((c \cap \alpha^\star \cap \mathbf{fair}) \; \epsilon^\star \| (d \cap \alpha^\star \cap \mathbf{fair}) \; \epsilon^\star) \; \mathbf{skip}$

$\sqsubseteq\quad$ by Lemma 7 (sync-termination) as $\mathbf{skip} \| \mathbf{skip} = \mathbf{skip}$ and $\mathbf{skip} = \epsilon^\omega$

$\quad (c \cap \alpha^\star \cap \mathbf{fair}) \; \mathbf{skip} \| (d \cap \alpha^\star \cap \mathbf{fair}) \; \mathbf{skip}$

$=\quad$ by the definition of $\|_f$ (16)

$\quad (c \cap \alpha^\star) \|_f (d \cap \alpha^\star)$ $\hfill\square$

Lemma 23 (infinite-absorb-fair-skip).

$$(((c \cap \alpha^\infty) \|_f d) \cap \mathbf{fair}) \; \mathbf{skip} = (c \cap \alpha^\infty) \|_f d$$

Proof. The refinement from right to left follows by Lemma 21 (introduce-fair-skip). The refinement from left to right follows.

$\quad (((c \cap \alpha^\infty) \|_f d) \cap \mathbf{fair}) \; \mathbf{skip}$

$=\quad$ by the definition of $\|_f$ (16)

$\quad (((c \cap \alpha^\infty \cap \mathbf{fair}) \; \mathbf{skip} \| (d \cap \mathbf{fair}) \; \mathbf{skip}) \cap \mathbf{fair}) \; \mathbf{skip}$

$=\quad$ by Lemma 6 (infinite-annihilates)

$\quad (((c \cap \alpha^\infty \cap \mathbf{fair}) \| (d \cap \mathbf{fair}) \; \mathbf{skip}) \cap \mathbf{fair}) \; \mathbf{skip}$

$\sqsubseteq\quad$ by Lemma 20 (fair-distrib-par-one) and $\cap$ is idempotent (38)

$\quad ((c \cap \alpha^\infty \cap \mathbf{fair}) \| (d \cap \mathbf{fair}) \; \mathbf{skip}) \; \mathbf{skip}$

$=\quad$ by Lemma 6 (infinite-annihilates)

$\quad ((c \cap \alpha^\infty \cap \mathbf{fair}) \; \mathbf{skip} \| (d \cap \mathbf{fair}) \; \mathbf{skip}) \; \mathbf{skip}$

$=\quad$ by Lemma 8 (par-skip)

$\quad (c \cap \alpha^\infty \cap \mathbf{fair}) \; \mathbf{skip} \| (d \cap \mathbf{fair}) \; \mathbf{skip}$

$=\quad$ by the definition of $\|_f$ (16)

$\quad (c \cap \alpha^\infty) \|_f d$ $\hfill\square$

Theorem 6 (absorb-fair-skip). $((c \parallel_f d) \Cap \mathbf{fair}) \; \mathbf{skip} = c \parallel_f d$

Proof. The proof decomposes c and d into their finite and infinite components based on the observation that the identity of "$\Cap$" is **chaos**, which equals $\alpha^* \sqcap \alpha^\infty$.

$$
\begin{aligned}
& ((c \parallel_f d) \Cap \mathbf{fair}) \; \mathbf{skip} \\
=\quad & \text{combine } \alpha^* \sqcap \alpha^\infty \text{ with each of } c \text{ and } d \text{ and distribute} \\
& ((((c \Cap \alpha^*) \sqcap (c \Cap \alpha^\infty)) \parallel_f ((d \Cap \alpha^*) \sqcap (d \Cap \alpha^\infty))) \Cap \mathbf{fair}) \; \mathbf{skip} \\
=\quad & \text{by repeated application of Theorem 3 (fair-parallel-distrib)} \\
& (((c \Cap \alpha^*) \parallel_f (d \Cap \alpha^*)) \Cap \mathbf{fair}) \; \mathbf{skip} \sqcap (((c \Cap \alpha^*) \parallel_f (d \Cap \alpha^\infty)) \Cap \mathbf{fair}) \; \mathbf{skip} \sqcap \\
& (((c \Cap \alpha^\infty) \parallel_f (d \Cap \alpha^*)) \Cap \mathbf{fair}) \; \mathbf{skip} \sqcap (((c \Cap \alpha^\infty) \parallel_f (d \Cap \alpha^\infty)) \Cap \mathbf{fair}) \; \mathbf{skip} \\
=\quad & \text{by Lemma 22 (finite-absorb-fair-skip) and Lemma 23 (infinite-absorb-fair-skip)} \\
& (c \Cap \alpha^*) \parallel_f (d \Cap \alpha^*) \sqcap (c \Cap \alpha^*) \parallel_f (d \Cap \alpha^\infty) \sqcap \\
& (c \Cap \alpha^\infty) \parallel_f (d \Cap \alpha^*) \sqcap (c \Cap \alpha^\infty) \parallel_f (d \Cap \alpha^\infty) \\
=\quad & \text{by Theorem 3 (fair-parallel-distrib)} \\
& ((c \Cap \alpha^*) \sqcap (c \Cap \alpha^\infty)) \parallel_f ((d \Cap \alpha^*) \sqcap (d \Cap \alpha^\infty)) \\
=\quad & \text{distributing} \\
& (c \Cap (\alpha^* \sqcap \alpha^\infty)) \parallel_f (d \Cap (\alpha^* \sqcap \alpha^\infty)) \\
=\quad & \text{as } \alpha^* \sqcap \alpha^\infty = \mathbf{chaos}, \text{ the identity of } \Cap \\
& c \parallel_f d \qquad\qquad\qquad\qquad\qquad\qquad\qquad \square
\end{aligned}
$$

With these results we can now verify associativity of fair parallel.

Theorem 7 (fair-parallel-associative). $(c \parallel_f d) \parallel_f e = c \parallel_f (d \parallel_f e)$

Proof

$$
\begin{aligned}
& (c \parallel_f d) \parallel_f e \\
=\quad & \text{by definition of } \parallel_f \; (16) \\
& ((c \parallel_f d) \Cap \mathbf{fair}) \; \mathbf{skip} \parallel (e \Cap \mathbf{fair}) \; \mathbf{skip} \\
=\quad & \text{by Theorem 6 (absorb-fair-skip)} \\
& (c \parallel_f d) \parallel (e \Cap \mathbf{fair}) \; \mathbf{skip} \\
=\quad & \text{by definition of } \parallel_f \; (16) \\
& ((c \Cap \mathbf{fair}) \; \mathbf{skip} \parallel (d \Cap \mathbf{fair}) \; \mathbf{skip}) \parallel (e \Cap \mathbf{fair}) \; \mathbf{skip} \\
=\quad & \text{by associativity of parallel} \\
& (c \Cap \mathbf{fair}) \; \mathbf{skip} \parallel ((d \Cap \mathbf{fair}) \; \mathbf{skip} \parallel (e \Cap \mathbf{fair}) \; \mathbf{skip}) \\
=\quad & \text{by definition of } \parallel_f \; (16) \\
& (c \Cap \mathbf{fair}) \; \mathbf{skip} \parallel (d \parallel_f e) \\
=\quad & \text{by Theorem 6 (absorb-fair-skip)} \\
& (c \Cap \mathbf{fair}) \; \mathbf{skip} \parallel ((d \parallel_f e) \Cap \mathbf{fair}) \; \mathbf{skip} \\
=\quad & \text{by definition of } \parallel_f \; (16) \\
& c \parallel_f (d \parallel_f e) \qquad\qquad\qquad\qquad\qquad\qquad \square
\end{aligned}
$$

Other properties of fair parallel can be proven in a similar manner, for example, the equivalent of the interchange law (45) with parallel replaced by fair parallel.

7   Conclusions

Earlier work on fairness [13,16] focused on defining fairness as part of a fair-parallel operator. The main contribution of this paper is to separate the concerns of fairness and the parallel operator. That allows us to (i) reason about the fair execution of a single process in isolation, for example, via Theorem 1 (fair-termination); (ii) start from a basis of the (unfair) parallel operator, which has simpler algebraic properties; and (iii) define the fair-parallel operator in terms of the more basic (unfair) parallel operator and hence prove properties of the fair-parallel operator in terms of its definition.

The first point is important for devising a compositional approach to reasoning about the fairness properties of concurrent systems in terms of the fairness properties of their components. The second point allows us to utilise the synchronous concurrent refinement algebra [3,8,9] (which has similarities to Milner's SCCS [14,15]) to encode fairness in an existing theory with no built-in fair-parallel operator. The third point shows that no expressive power is lost compared to starting with a fair-parallel operator, in fact, there is a gain in expressiveness as one can define a parallel composition which imposes fairness on only one of its components: $((c \pitchfork \textbf{fair})\ \textbf{skip}) \parallel d$.

Overall, these results indicate that a suitable foundation of handling concurrency and fairness can start from a theory in which the parallel operator has no built-in fairness assumptions. The ability to do this derives from the use of a synchronous parallel operator motivated by the rely/guarantee approach of Jones [10–12] and Aczel's trace model for that approach [2–5], in which environment steps are made explicit.

Acknowledgements. This research was supported Australian Research Council Discovery Grant DP130102901. Thanks are due to Robert Colvin, Rob Van Glabbeek, Peter Höfner, Cliff Jones, and Kirsten Winter, for feedback on ideas presented here. This research has benefited greatly from feedback members of IFIP Working Group 2.3 on Programming Methodology, in particular, at the meeting in Villebrumier.

References

1. Aarts, C., Backhouse, R., Boiten, E., Doombos, H., van Gasteren, N., van Geldrop, R., Hoogendijk, P., Voermans, E., van der Woude, J.: Fixed-point calculus. Inf. Process. Lett. **53**, 131–136 (1995)
2. Aczel, P.H.G.: On an inference rule for parallel composition (1983). Private communication to Cliff Jones. http://homepages.cs.ncl.ac.uk/cliff.jones/publications/MSs/PHGA-traces.pdf
3. Colvin, R.J., Hayes, I.J., Meinicke, L.A.: Designing a semantic model for a wide-spectrum language with concurrency. Formal Aspects Comput. **29**, 853–875 (2016)
4. de Boer, F.S., Hannemann, U., de Roever, W.-P.: Formal justification of the rely-guarantee paradigm for shared-variable concurrency: a semantic approach. In: Wing, J.M., Woodcock, J., Davies, J. (eds.) FM 1999. LNCS, vol. 1709, pp. 1245–1265. Springer, Heidelberg (1999). https://doi.org/10.1007/3-540-48118-4_16

5. de Roever, W.-P.: Concurrency Verification: Introduction to Compositional and Noncompositional Methods. Cambridge University Press, Cambridge (2001)
6. Hayes, I.J.: Generalised rely-guarantee concurrency: an algebraic foundation. Formal Aspects Comput. **28**(6), 1057–1078 (2016)
7. Hayes, I.J., Meinicke, L.A.: Encoding fairness in a synchronous concurrent program algebra: extended version with proofs. arXiv:1805.01681 [cs.LO] (2018)
8. Hayes, I.J., Colvin, R.J., Meinicke, L.A., Winter, K., Velykis, A.: An algebra of synchronous atomic steps. In: Fitzgerald, J., Heitmeyer, C., Gnesi, S., Philippou, A. (eds.) FM 2016. LNCS, vol. 9995, pp. 352–369. Springer, Cham (2016). https://doi.org/10.1007/978-3-319-48989-6_22
9. Hayes, I.J., Meinicke, L.A., Winter, K., Colvin, R.J.: A synchronous program algebra: a basis for reasoning about shared-memory and event-based concurrency. Accepted for publication in Formal Aspects of Computing (2018)
10. Jones, C.B.: Development methods for computer programs including a notion of interference. Ph.D. thesis, Oxford University, June 1981. Available as: Oxford University Computing Laboratory (now Computer Science) Technical Monograph PRG-25
11. Jones, C.B.: Specification and design of (parallel) programs. In: Proceedings of IFIP 1983, pp. 321–332. North-Holland (1983)
12. Jones, C.B.: Tentative steps toward a development method for interfering programs. ACM ToPLaS **5**(4), 596–619 (1983)
13. Lehmann, D., Pnueli, A., Stavi, J.: Impartiality, justice and fairness: the ethics of concurrent termination. In: Even, S., Kariv, O. (eds.) ICALP 1981. LNCS, vol. 115, pp. 264–277. Springer, Heidelberg (1981). https://doi.org/10.1007/3-540-10843-2_22
14. Milner, A.J.R.G.: Communication and Concurrency. Prentice-Hall, Upper Saddle River (1989)
15. Milner, R.: Calculi for synchrony and asynchrony. Theor. Comput. Sci. **25**(3), 267–310 (1983)
16. Park, D.: On the semantics of fair parallelism. In: Bjøorner, D. (ed.) Abstract Software Specifications. LNCS, vol. 86, pp. 504–526. Springer, Heidelberg (1980). https://doi.org/10.1007/3-540-10007-5_47
17. van Glabbeek, R.J.: Ensuring liveness properties of distributed systems (a research agenda). Technical report, NICTA, March 2016. Position paper

A Wide-Spectrum Language for Verification of Programs on Weak Memory Models

Robert J. Colvin and Graeme Smith[✉]

School of Information Technology and Electrical Engineering,
The University of Queensland, Brisbane, Australia
r.colvin@uq.edu.au, smith@itee.uq.edu.au

Abstract. Modern processors deploy a variety of weak memory models, which for efficiency reasons may (appear to) execute instructions in an order different to that specified by the program text. The consequences of instruction reordering can be complex and subtle, and can impact on ensuring correctness. Previous work on the semantics of weak memory models has focussed on the behaviour of assembler-level programs. In this paper we utilise that work to extract some general principles underlying instruction reordering, and apply those principles to a wide-spectrum language encompassing abstract data types as well as low-level assembler code. The goal is to support reasoning about implementations of data structures for modern processors with respect to an abstract specification.

Specifically, we encode a weak memory model in a pair-wise reordering relation on instructions. Some architectures require an additional definition of the behaviour of the global storage system if it does not provide multi-copy atomicity. In this paper we use the reordering relation in an operational semantics. We derive some properties of program refinement under weak memory models, and encode the semantics in the rewriting engine Maude as a model-checking tool. The tool is used to validate the semantics against the behaviour of a set of litmus tests (small assembler programs) run on hardware, and also to model check implementations of data structures from the literature against their abstract specifications.

1 Introduction

Modern processor architectures provide a challenge for developing efficient and correct software. Performance can be improved by parallelising computation to utilise multiple cores, but communication between threads is notoriously error-prone. Weak memory models go further and improve overall system efficiency through sophisticated techniques for batching reads and writes to the same variables and to and from the same processors. However, code that is run on such memory models is not guaranteed to take effect in the order specified in the program code, creating unexpected behaviours for those who are not forewarned [1]. For instance, the instructions $x := 1;\ y := 1$ may, from the perspective of

© Springer International Publishing AG, part of Springer Nature 2018
K. Havelund et al. (Eds.): FM 2018, LNCS 10951, pp. 240–257, 2018.
https://doi.org/10.1007/978-3-319-95582-7_14

another process, taken effect in the order $y := 1$; $x := 1$. Architectures typically provide *memory barrier/fence* instructions which can enforce ordering – so that $x := 1$; **fence**; $y := 1$ can not be reordered – but reduce performance improvements (and so should not be overused).

Previous work on formalising weak memory models has resulted in abstract formalisations which were developed incrementally through communication with processor vendors and rigorous testing on real machines [2–4]. A large collection of "litmus tests" have been developed [5,6] which demonstrate the sometimes confusing behaviour of hardware. We utilise this existing work to provide a wide-spectrum programming language and semantics that runs on the same relaxed principles that apply to assembler instructions. When these principles are specialised to the assembler of ARM and POWER processors our semantics gives behaviour consistent with existing litmus tests. Our language and semantics, therefore, connect instruction reordering to higher-level notions of correctness. This enables verification of low-level code targeting specific processors against abstract specifications.

We begin in Sect. 2 with the basis of an operational semantics that allows reordering of instructions according to pair-wise relationships between instructions. In Sect. 3 we describe the semantics in more detail, focussing on its instantiation for the widely used ARM and POWER processors. In Sect. 4 we give a summary of the encoding of the semantics in Maude and its application to model-checking concurrent data structures. We discuss related work in Sect. 5 before concluding in Sect. 6.

2   Instruction Reordering in Weak Memory Models

2.1   Thread-Local Reorderings

It is typically assumed processes are executed in a fixed sequential order (as given by sequential composition – the "program order"). However program order may be inefficient, e.g., when retrieving the value of a variable from main memory after setting its value, as in $x := 1$; $r := x$, and hence weak memory models sometimes allow execution out of program order to improve overall system efficiency. While many reorderings can seem surprising, there are basic principles at play which limit the number of possible permutations, the key being that the new ordering of instructions preserves the original sequential intention.

A classic example of weak memory models producing unexpected behaviour is the "store buffer" pattern below [5]. Assume that all variables are initially 0, and that thread-local variables (registers) are named r, r_1, r_2, etc., and that x and y are shared variables.

$$(x := 1;\ r_1 := y) \parallel (y := 1;\ r_2 := x) \tag{1}$$

It is possible to reach a final state in which $r_1 = r_2 = 0$ in several weak memory models: the two assignments in each process are independent (they reference different variables), and hence can be reordered. From a sequential semantics perspective, reordering the assignments in process 1, for example, preserves the final values for r_1 and x.

Assume that c and c' are programs represented as sequences of atomic actions α; β; ..., as in a sequence of instructions in a processor or more abstractly a semantic trace. Program c may be reordered to c', written $c \rightsquigarrow c'$, if the following holds:

1. c' is a permutation of the actions of c, possibly with some modifications due to *forwarding* (see below).
2. c' preserves the sequential semantics of c. For example, in a weakest preconditions semantics [7], for all predicates P, $wp(c, P) \Rightarrow wp(c', P)$.
3. c' preserves *coherence-per-location* with respect to c (cf. po-loc in [3]). This means that the order of updates and accesses of each shared variable, considered individually, is maintained.

We formalise these constraints in the context of pair-wise reordering of instructions below. The key challenge for reasoning about programs executed on a weak memory model is that the behaviour of $c \parallel d$ is in general quite different to the behaviour of $c' \parallel d$, even if $c \rightsquigarrow c'$. We focus in this paper on the principles for ARM and POWER processors; for space reasons we do not address TSO [8], which has fewer relevant instruction types (e.g., only one type of fence) and stricter conditions on reordering.

2.2   Reordering and Forwarding Instructions

We write $\alpha \overset{R}{\Leftarrow} \beta$ if instruction β may be reordered before instruction α. It is relatively straightforward to define when two assignment instructions (encompassing stores, loads, and register operations at the assembler level) may be reordered. Below let x nfi f mean that x does not appear free in the expression f, and say expressions e and f are *load-distinct* if they do not reference any common shared variables.

$$x := e \overset{R}{\Leftarrow} y := f \quad if \quad \begin{array}{l} (1)\ x,\ y \text{ are distinct;} \quad (2)\ x \text{ nfi } f; \quad (3)\ y \text{ nfi } e; \text{ and} \\ (4)\ e,\ f \text{ are load-distinct;} \end{array} \qquad (2)$$

Note that $\overset{R}{\Leftarrow}$ as defined above is symmetric, however when calculated after the effect of forwarding is applied (as described below) there are instructions that may be reordered in one direction but not the other. The relation is neither reflexive nor transitive. In TSO processors a load may be reordered before a store, but not vice versa [8], and hence the general condition for TSO is stronger and not reflexive.

Provisos (1), (2) and (3) ensure executing the two assignments in either order results in the same final values for x and y, and proviso (4) maintains order on accesses of the shared state. If two updates do not refer to any common variables they may be reordered. The provisos allow some reordering when they share common variables. Proviso (1) eliminates reorderings such as $(x := 1;\ x := 2) \rightsquigarrow (x := 2;\ x := 1)$ which would violate the sequential semantics (the final value of

x). Proviso (2) eliminates reorderings such as $(x := 1;\ r := x) \rightsquigarrow (r := x;\ x := 1)$ which again would violate the sequential semantics (the final value of r). Proviso (3) eliminates reorderings such as $(r := y;\ y := 1) \rightsquigarrow (y := 1;\ r := y)$ which again would violate the sequential semantics (the final value of r). Proviso (4), requiring the update expressions to be load-distinct, preserves coherence-per-location, eliminating reorderings such as $(r_1 := x;\ r_2 := x) \rightsquigarrow (r_2 := x;\ r_1 := x)$, where r_2 may receive an earlier value of x than r_1 in an environment which modifies x.

The instructions used in the above examples, where each instruction references at most one global variable and uses simple integer values, correspond to the basic load and store instruction types of ARM and POWER processors. We may instantiate (2) to such instructions, giving reordering rules such as the following, which states that a store may be reordered before a load if they are to different locations $(r_1 := y \overset{R}{\Leftarrow} x := r_2)$. We use ARM syntax to emphasise the application to a real architecture.

$$\text{LDR } r_1, y \overset{R}{\Leftarrow} \text{STR } r_2, x \tag{3}$$

In practice, proviso (2) may be circumvented by *forwarding*[1]. This refers to taking into account the effect of the earlier update on the expression of the latter. We write $\beta_{[\alpha]}$ to represent the effect of forwarding the (assignment) instruction α to the instruction β. For assignments we define

$$(y := f)_{[x := e]} \;=\; y := (f_{[x \backslash e]}) \quad if \quad e \text{ does not refer to global variables} \tag{4}$$

where the term $f_{[x \backslash e]}$ stands for the syntactic replacement in expression f of references to x with e. The proviso of (4) prevents additional loads of globals being introduced by forwarding.

We specify the reordering and forwarding relationships with other instructions such as branches and fences in Sect. 3.3.

2.3   General Operational Rules for Reordering

The key operational principle allowing reordering is given by the following transition rules for a program $(\alpha;\ c)$, i.e., a program with initial instruction α.

$$(\alpha;\ c) \xrightarrow{\alpha} c \quad (a) \qquad \frac{c \xrightarrow{\beta} c' \quad \alpha \overset{R}{\Leftarrow} \beta_{[\alpha]}}{(\alpha;\ c) \xrightarrow{\beta_{[\alpha]}} (\alpha;\ c')} \quad (b) \tag{5}$$

Rule (5a) is the straightforward promotion of the first instruction into a step in a trace, similar to the basic prefixing rules of CCS [9] and CSP [10]. Rule (5b), however, states that, unique to weak memory models, an instruction of c, say β, can happen before α, provided that $\beta_{[\alpha]}$ can be reordered before α according

---

[1] We adopt the term "forwarding" from ARM and POWER [3]. The equivalent effect is referred to as *bypassing* on TSO [8].

244 R. J. Colvin and G. Smith

to the rules of the architecture. Note that we forward the effect of α to β before deciding if the reordering is possible.

Applying Rule (5b) then (5a) gives the following reordered behaviour of two assignments.

$$(r := 1;\ x := r;\ \mathbf{nil}) \xrightarrow{x := 1} (r := 1;\ \mathbf{nil}) \xrightarrow{r := 1} \mathbf{nil} \tag{6}$$

We use the command **nil** to denote termination. The first transition above is possible because we calculate the effect of $r := 1$ on the update of x before executing that update, i.e., $x := r_{[r := 1]} = x := 1$.

The definitions of instruction reordering, $\alpha \overset{R}{\Leftarrow} \beta$, and instruction forwarding, $\beta_{[\alpha]}$ are architecture-specific, and are the only definitions required to specify an architecture's instruction ordering.[2] The instantiations for *sequentially consistent* processors (i.e., those which do not have a weak memory model) are trivial: $\alpha \overset{R}{\nLeftarrow} \beta$ for all α, β, and there is no forwarding. Since reordering is not possible Rule (5b) never applies and hence the standard prefixing semantics is maintained. TSO is relatively straightforward: loads may be reordered before stores (provided they reference different shared variables). In our framework there is no need to explicitly model local buffers, as the forwarding (bypassing) mechanism ensures that only the most recently stored value for a global x is used locally (or x's value is retrieved from the storage system). In this paper we focus on the more complex ARM and POWER memory models. These memory models are very similar, the notable difference being the inclusion of the *lightweight fence* instruction in POWER. Due to space limitations, we omit lightweight fences in this paper but see the appendix of [11] for a full definition.

2.4 Reasoning About Reorderings

The operational rules allow a standard trace model of correctness to be adopted, that is, we say program c *refines to* program d, written $c \sqsubseteq d$, iff every trace of d is a trace of c. Let the program $\alpha \cdot c$ have the standard semantics of prefixing, that is, the action α always occurs before any action in c (Rule (5a)). Then we can derive the following laws that show the interplay of reordering and true prefixing.

$$\alpha;\ c \sqsubseteq \alpha \cdot c \tag{7}$$

$$\alpha;\ (\beta \cdot c) \sqsubseteq \beta_{[\alpha]} \cdot (\alpha;\ c) \qquad \text{if } \alpha \overset{R}{\Leftarrow} \beta_{[\alpha]} \tag{8}$$

Note that in Law (8) α may be further reordered with instructions in c. A typical interleaving law is the following.

$$(\alpha \cdot c) \parallel d \sqsubseteq \alpha \cdot (c \parallel d) \tag{9}$$

---

[2] Different architectures may have different storage subsystems, however, and these need to be separately defined (see Sect. 3.2).

We may use these laws to show how the "surprise" behaviour of the store buffer pattern above arises.[3] In derivations such as the following, to save space, we abbreviate a thread α; **nil** or α . **nil** to α, that is, we omit the trailing **nil**.

$$(x := 1;\ r_1 := y)\ \|\ (y := 1;\ r_2 := x)$$
$\sqsubseteq$ From Law (8) (twice), since $x := 1 \overset{R}{\Leftarrow} r_1 := y$ from (2).
$$(r_1 := y\ .\ x := 1)\ \|\ (r_2 := x\ .\ y := 1)$$
$\sqsubseteq$ Law (9) (four times) and commutativity of $\|$.
$$r_1 := y\ .\ r_2 := x\ .\ x := 1\ .\ y := 1$$

If initially $x = y = 0$, a standard sequential semantics shows that $r_1 = r_2 = 0$ is a possible final state in this behaviour.

3 Semantics

3.1 Formal Language

The elements of our wide-spectrum language are actions (instructions) α, commands (programs) c, processes (local state and a command) p, and the top level system s, encompassing a shared state and all processes. Below x is a variable (shared or local) and e an expression.

$$
\begin{aligned}
\alpha &::= x := e \ \mid\ [e] \ \mid\ \textbf{fence} \ \mid\ \textbf{cfence} \ \mid\ \alpha^* \\
c &::= \textbf{nil} \ \mid\ \alpha;\ c \ \mid\ c_1 \sqcap c_2 \ \mid\ \textbf{while } b \textbf{ do } c \\
p &::= (\textbf{lcl } \sigma \bullet c) \ \mid\ (\textbf{tid}_N\ p) \ \mid\ p_1 \| p_2 \\
s &::= (\textbf{glb } \sigma \bullet p) \ \mid\ (\textbf{stg } W \bullet p)
\end{aligned}
\tag{10}
$$

An action may be an update $x := e$, a guard $[e]$, a (full) fence, a control fence (see Sect. 3.3), or a finite sequence of actions, α^*, executed atomically. Throughout the paper we denote an empty sequence by $\langle\rangle$, and construct a non-empty sequence as $\langle \alpha_1,\ \alpha_2 \ldots \rangle$.

A command may be the empty command **nil**, which is already terminated, a command prefixed by some action α, a choice between two commands, or an iteration (for brevity we consider only one type of iteration, the while loop). Conditionals are modelled using guards and choice.

$$\textbf{if } b \textbf{ then } c_1 \textbf{ else } c_2 \ \hat{=}\ ([b];\ c_1) \sqcap ([\neg b];\ c_2) \tag{11}$$

A well-formed process is structured as a process id $N \in$ PID encompassing a (possibly empty) local state σ and command c, i.e., a term $(\textbf{tid}_N \textbf{ lcl } \sigma \bullet c)$. We assume that all local variables referenced in c are contained in the domain of σ.

A system is structured as the parallel composition of processes within the global storage system, which may be either a typical global state, σ, that maps all global variables to their values (modelling the storage systems of TSO, the

---

[3] To focus on instruction reorderings we leave local variable declarations and process ids implicit, and assume a multi-copy atomic storage system (see Sect. 3.2).

$$(\text{glb } \sigma \bullet (\text{tid}_1 \text{ lcl } \sigma_1 \bullet c_1) \parallel (\text{tid}_2 \text{ lcl } \sigma_2 \bullet c_2) \parallel \ldots)$$
$$(\text{stg } W \bullet (\text{tid}_1 \text{ lcl } \sigma_1 \bullet c_1) \parallel (\text{tid}_2 \text{ lcl } \sigma_2 \bullet c_2) \parallel \ldots) \tag{12}$$

$$(\alpha \,;\, c) \xrightarrow{\alpha} c \quad (a) \qquad \frac{c \xrightarrow{\beta} c' \quad \alpha \overset{R}{\Leftarrow} \beta_{[\alpha]}}{(\alpha \,;\, c) \xrightarrow{\beta_{[\alpha]}} (\alpha \,;\, c')} \quad (b) \quad (13) \qquad \frac{}{c \sqcap d \xrightarrow{\tau} c} \atop \frac{}{c \sqcap d \xrightarrow{\tau} d} \quad (14)$$

$$\textbf{while } b \textbf{ do } c \xrightarrow{\tau} ([b] \,;\, c \,;\, \textbf{while } b \textbf{ do } c) \sqcap ([\neg b] \,;\, \textbf{nil}) \tag{15}$$

$$\frac{c \xrightarrow{r := v} c'}{(\text{lcl } \sigma \bullet c) \xrightarrow{\tau} (\text{lcl } \sigma_{[r := v]} \bullet c')} \quad (16) \qquad \frac{c \xrightarrow{x := r} c' \quad \sigma(r) = v}{(\text{lcl } \sigma \bullet c) \xrightarrow{x := v} (\text{lcl } \sigma \bullet c')} \quad (17)$$

$$\frac{c \xrightarrow{r := x} c'}{(\text{lcl } \sigma \bullet c) \xrightarrow{[x = v]} (\text{lcl } \sigma_{[r := v]} \bullet c')} \quad (18) \qquad \frac{c \xrightarrow{[e]} c'}{(\text{lcl } \sigma \bullet c) \xrightarrow{[e_\sigma]} (\text{lcl } \sigma \bullet c')} \quad (19)$$

$$\frac{p \xrightarrow{\alpha} p'}{(\text{tid}_N \, p) \xrightarrow{N:\alpha} (\text{tid}_N \, p')} \quad (20) \qquad \frac{p_1 \xrightarrow{\alpha} p_1'}{p_1 \parallel p_2 \xrightarrow{\alpha} p_1' \parallel p_2} \quad \frac{p_2 \xrightarrow{\alpha} p_2'}{p_1 \parallel p_2 \xrightarrow{\alpha} p_1 \parallel p_2'} \quad (21)$$

$$\frac{p \xrightarrow{N:x := e} p'}{(\text{glb } \sigma \bullet p) \xrightarrow{\tau} (\text{glb } \sigma_{[x := e_\sigma]} \bullet p')} \quad (22) \qquad \frac{p \xrightarrow{N:[e]} p' \quad e_\sigma \equiv true}{(\text{glb } \sigma \bullet p) \xrightarrow{\tau} (\text{glb } \sigma \bullet p')} \quad (23)$$

Fig. 1. Semantics of the language

most recent version of ARM, and abstract specifications), or a storage system, W, formed from a list of "writes" to the global variables (modelling the storage systems of older versions of ARM and POWER). The storage W injects more nondeterminism into the system than the typical global state approach. A top-level system is in one of the two following forms.

3.2   Operational Semantics

The meaning of our language is formalised using an operational semantics, summarised in Fig. 1. Given a program c the operational semantics generates a *trace*, i.e., a possibly infinite sequence of steps $c_0 \xrightarrow{\alpha_1} c_1 \xrightarrow{\alpha_2} \ldots$ where the labels in the trace are actions, or a special label τ representing a silent or internal step that has no observable effect.

The terminated command **nil** has no behaviour; a trace that ends with this command is assumed to have completed. The effect of instruction prefixing in Rule (13) is discussed in Sect. 2.3. Note that actions become part of the trace. We describe an instantiation for reordering and forwarding corresponding to the semantics of ARM and POWER in Sect. 3.3.

A nondeterministic choice (the *internal choice* of CSP [10]) can choose either branch, as given by Rule (14). The semantics of loops is given by unfolding, e.g., Rule (15) for a 'while' loop. Note that *speculative execution*, i.e., early execution of instructions which occur after a branch point [12], is theoretically unbounded, and loads from inside later iterations of the loop could occur in earlier iterations.

For ease of presentation in defining the semantics for local states, we give rules for specific forms of actions, i.e., assuming that r is a local variable in the domain of σ, and that x is a global (not in the domain of σ). The more general version can be straightforwardly constructed from the principles below.

Rule (16) states that an action updating variable r to value v results in a change to the local state (denoted $\sigma_{[r := v]}$). Since this is a purely local operation there is no interaction with the storage subsystem and hence the transition is promoted as a silent step τ. Rule (17) states that a *store* of the value in variable r to global x is promoted as an instruction $x := v$ where v is the local value for r. Rule (18) covers the case of a *load* of x into r. The value of x is not known locally. The promoted label is a guard requiring that the value read for x is v. This transition is possible for any value of v, but the correct value will be resolved when the label is promoted to the storage level. Rule (19) states that a guard is partially evaluated with respect to the local state before it is promoted to the global level. The notation e_σ replaces x with v in e for all $(x \mapsto v) \in \sigma$.

Rule (20) simply tags the process id to an instruction, to assist in the interaction with the storage system, and otherwise has no effect. Instructions of concurrent processes are interleaved in the usual way as described by Rule (21).

Other straightforward rules which we have omitted above include the promotion of fences through a local state, and that atomic sequences of actions are handled inductively by the above rules.

Multi-copy Atomic Storage Subsystem. Traditionally, changes to shared variables occur on a shared global state, and when written to the global state are seen instantaneously by all processes in the system. This is referred to as *multi-copy atomicity* and is a feature of TSO and the most recent version of ARM [13]. Older versions of ARM and POWER, however, lack such multi-copy atomicity and require a more complex semantics. We give the simpler case (covered in Fig. 1) first.[4]

Recall that at the global level the process id N has been tagged to the actions by Rule (20). Rule (22) covers a store of some expression e to x. Since all local variable references have been replaced by their values at the process level due to Rules (16)–(19), expression e must refer only to shared variables in σ. The value of x is updated to the fully evaluated value, e_σ.

Rule (23) states that a guard transition $[e]$ is possible exactly when e evaluates to true in the global state. If it does not, no transition is possible; this is how incorrect branches are eliminated from the traces. If a guard does not evaluate to *true*, execution stops in the sense that no transition is possible.

---

[4] In this straightforward model of shared state there is no global effect of fences, and we omit the straightforward promotion rule.

This corresponds to a false guard, i.e., **magic** [14,15], and such behaviours do not terminate and are ignored for the purposes of determining behaviour of a real system. Interestingly, this straightforward concept from standard refinement theory allows us to handle speculative execution straightforwardly. In existing approaches, the semantics is complicated by needing to restart reads if speculation proceeds down the wrong path. Treating branch points as guards works because speculation should have no effect if the wrong branch was chosen.

To understand how this approach to speculative execution works, consider the following derivation. Assume that (a) loads may be reordered before guards if they reference independent variables, and (b) loads may be reordered if they reference different variables. Recall that we omit trailing **nil** commands to save space.

$$r_1 := x; \; (\textbf{if } r_1 = 0 \textbf{ then } \underline{r_2 := y})$$
$=$ Definition of **if** (11)
$$r_1 := x; \; ((\underline{[r_1 = 0]; \; r_2 := y}) \sqcap [r_1 \neq 0])$$
$\sqsubseteq$ Resolve to the first branch, since $(c \sqcap d) \sqsubseteq c$
$$r_1 := x; \; [r_1 = 0]; \; \underline{r_2 := y}$$
$\sqsubseteq$ From Law (8) and assumption (a)
$$r_1 := x; \; \underline{r_2 := y} \bullet [r_1 = 0]$$
$\sqsubseteq$ From Law (8) and assumption (b)
$$\underline{r_2 := y} \bullet r_1 := x; \; [r_1 = 0]$$

This shows that the inner load (underlined) may be reordered before the branch point, and subsequently before an earlier load. Note that this behaviour results in a terminating trace only if $r_1 = 0$ holds when the guard is evaluated, and otherwise becomes **magic** (speculation down an incorrect path). On ARM processors, placing a control fence (**cfence**) instruction inside the branch, before the inner load, prevents this reordering (see Sect. 3.3).

Non-multi-copy Atomic Storage Subsystem. Some versions of ARM and POWER allow processes to communicate values to each other without accessing the heap. That is, if process p_1 is storing v to x, and process p_2 wants to load x into r, p_2 may preemptively load the value v into r, before p_1's store hits the global shared storage. Therefore different processes may have different views of the values of global variables; see litmus tests such as the WRC family [3].

Our approach to modelling this is based on that of the operational model of [2]. However, that model maintains several partial orders on operations reflecting the nondeterminism in the system, whereas we let the nondeterminism be represented by choices in the operational rules. This means we maintain a simpler data structure, a single global list of writes. The shared state from the perspective of a given process is a particular view of this list. There is no single definitive shared state. In addition, viewing a value in the list causes the list to be updated and this affects later views. To obtain the value of a variable this list is searched starting with the most recent write first. A process p_1 that has already seen the latter of two updates to a variable x may not subsequently then see the earlier

$$\frac{p \xrightarrow{\text{N}:[x=v]} p' \qquad \forall\, w \in \text{ran}(W_1) \bullet x = w.var \Rightarrow \text{N} \notin w.seen}{(\textbf{stg } W_1 \frown (x \mapsto v)_{\mathcal{S}}^{\text{M}} \frown W_2 \bullet p) \xrightarrow{\text{N}:[x=v]} (\textbf{stg } W_1 \frown (x \mapsto v)_{\mathcal{S} \cup \{\text{N}\}}^{\text{M}} \frown W_2 \bullet p')} \tag{24}$$

$$\frac{p \xrightarrow{\text{N}:x\,:=\,v} p' \qquad \forall\, w \in \text{ran}(W_1) \bullet \text{N} \neq w.thread \wedge (x = w.var \Rightarrow \text{N} \notin w.seen)}{(\textbf{stg } W_1 \frown W_2 \bullet p) \xrightarrow{\text{N}:x\,:=\,v} (\textbf{stg } W_1 \frown (x \mapsto v)_{\{\text{N}\}}^{\text{N}} \frown W_2 \bullet p')} \tag{25}$$

$$\frac{p \xrightarrow{\text{N}:\textbf{fence}} p'}{(\textbf{stg } W \bullet p) \xrightarrow{\text{N}:\textbf{fence}} (\textbf{stg } \mathit{flush}_{\text{N}}(W) \bullet p')} \tag{26}$$

where

$$\mathit{flush}_{\text{N}}(\langle\rangle) = \langle\rangle \qquad \mathit{flush}_{\text{N}}(w \frown W) = \begin{cases} w_{[seen\,:=\,\text{PID}]} \frown \mathit{flush}_{\text{N}}(W) & \text{if } \text{N} \in w.seen \\ w \frown \mathit{flush}_{\text{N}}(W) & \text{otherwise} \end{cases}$$

Fig. 2. Rules for the non-multi-copy atomic subsystem of ARM and POWER

update. Hence the list keeps track of which processes have seen which stores. Accesses of the storage subsystem are also influenced by fences.

A write w has the syntactic form $(x \mapsto v)_{\mathcal{S}}^{\text{N}}$, where x is a global variable being updated to value v, N is the process id of the process from which the store originated, and $\mathcal{S}$ is the set of process ids that have "seen" the write. For such a w, we let $w.var = x$, $w.thread = \text{N}$ and $w.seen = \mathcal{S}$. For a write $(x \mapsto v)_{\mathcal{S}}^{\text{N}}$ it is always the case that $\text{N} \in \mathcal{S}$. The storage W is a list of writes, initially populated with writes for the initial values of global variables, which all processes have "seen".

We give two specialised rules (for a load and store) in Fig. 2.[5] Rule (24) states that a previous write to x may be seen by process N if there are no more recent writes to x that it has already seen. Its id is added to the set of processes that have seen that write. Rule (25) states that a write to x may be added to the system by process N, *appearing earlier than existing writes in the system*, if the following two conditions hold for each of those existing writes w: they are not by N ($\text{N} \neq w.thread$, local coherence), and $x = w.var \Rightarrow \text{N} \notin w.seen$, i.e., writes to the same variable are seen in a consistent order (although not all writes need be seen). A **fence** action by process N 'flushes' all previous writes by and seen by N. The *flush* function modifies W so that all processes can see all writes by N, effectively overwriting earlier writes. This is achieved by updating the write so that all processes have seen it, written as $w_{[seen\,:=\,\text{PID}]}$.

---

[5] To handle the general case of an assignment $x := e$, where e may contain more than one shared variable, the antecedents of the rules are combined, retrieving the value of each variable referenced in e individually and accumulating the changes to W.

$$\alpha \not\overset{R}{\Leftarrow} \textbf{fence} \qquad (27)$$

$$\textbf{fence} \not\overset{R}{\Leftarrow} \alpha \qquad (28)$$

$$[b] \not\overset{R}{\Leftarrow} \textbf{cfence} \qquad (29)$$

$$\textbf{cfence} \not\overset{R}{\Leftarrow} r := e \qquad (30)$$

$$[b_1] \overset{R}{\Leftarrow} [b_2] \qquad (31)$$

$$[b] \not\overset{R}{\Leftarrow} \varphi := e \qquad (32)$$

$$[b] \overset{R}{\Leftarrow} r := e \quad \text{iff } r \text{ nfi } b \qquad (33)$$

$$x := e \overset{R}{\Leftarrow} [b] \quad \text{iff } x \text{ nfi } b \qquad (34)$$

$$\alpha \overset{R}{\Leftarrow} \beta \quad \text{in all other cases}$$

$$x := e \overset{R}{\Leftarrow} y := f \text{ iff} \qquad (35)$$
$$x \neq y, \ x \text{ nfi } f, \ y \text{ nfi } e, \text{ and}$$
$$e, f \text{ are load-distinct}$$

$$x := e_{[y := f]} = x := e_{[y \backslash f]} \text{ if} \qquad (36)$$
$$e \text{ has no shared variables}$$

$$[e]_{[y := f]} = [e_{[y \backslash f]}] \text{ if} \qquad (37)$$
$$e \text{ has no shared variables}$$

$$\beta_{[\alpha]} = \beta \quad \text{otherwise}$$

Fig. 3. Reordering and forwarding following ARM assembler semantics. Let x, y denote any variable, r a local variable, and φ a global variable.

3.3 Reordering and Forwarding for ARM and POWER

Our general semantics is instantiated for ARM and POWER processors in Fig. 3 which provides particular definitions for the reordering relation and forwarding that are generalised from the orderings on stores and loads in these processors.[6]

Fences prevent all reorderings (27, 28). Control fences prevent speculative loads when placed between a guard and a load (29, 30). Guards may be reordered with other guards (31), but stores to shared variables may not come before a guard evaluation (32). This prevents speculative execution from modifying the global state, in the event that the speculation was down the wrong branch. An update of a local variable may be reordered before a guard provided it does not affect the guard expression (33). Guards may be reordered before updates if those updates do not affect the guard expression (34).

Assignments may be reordered as shown in (35) and discussed in Sect. 2.2. Forwarding is defined straightforwardly so that an earlier update modifies the expression of a later update or guard (36, 37), provided it references no shared variables.

4 Model Checking Concurrent Data Structures

Our semantics has been encoded in the Maude rewriting system [16]. We have used the resulting prototype tool to validate the semantics against litmus tests which have been used in other work on ARM (348 tests) [4] and POWER (758 tests) [2]. As that research was developed through testing on hardware and in consultation with the processor vendors themselves we consider compliance with

---

[6] We have excluded address shifting, which creates *address dependencies* [3], as this does not affect the majority of high-level algorithms in which we are interested. However, address dependencies are accounted for in our tool as discussed in [11].

those litmus tests to be sufficient validation. With two exceptions, as discussed in Sect. 5, our semantics agrees with those results.

We have employed Maude as a model checker to verify that a (test-and-set) lock provides mutual exclusion on ARM and POWER, and that a lock-free stack algorithm, and a deque (double-ended queue) algorithm, satisfy their abstract specifications on ARM and POWER. We describe the verification of the deque below, in which we found a bug in the published algorithm.

4.1   Chase-Lev Deque

Lê et. al [17] present a version of the Chase-Lev deque [18] adapted for ARM and POWER. The deque is implemented as an array, where elements may be *put* on or *taken* from the tail, and additionally, processes may *steal* an element from the head of the deque. The *put* and *take* operations may be executed by a single process only, hence there is no interference between these two operations (although instruction reordering could cause consecutive invocations to overlap). The *steal* operation can be executed by multiple processes concurrently.

The code we tested is given in Fig. 4 where L is the maximum size of the deque which is implemented as a cyclic array, with all elements initialised to some irrelevant value. The original code includes handling array resizing, but here we focus on the insert/delete logic. For brevity we omit trailing **nils**. We have used a local variable *return* to model the return value, and correspondingly have refactored the algorithm to eliminate returns from within a branch. A $CAS(x, r, e)$ (compare-and-swap) instruction atomically compares the value of global x with the value r and if the same updates x to e. We model a conditional statement with a CAS as follows.

$$\textbf{if } CAS(x, r, e) \textbf{ then } c_1 \textbf{ else } c_2 \mathrel{\widehat{=}} (\langle [x = r] \,,\, x := e \rangle; \, c_1) \sqcap ([x \neq r]; \, c_2) \quad (38)$$

The *put* operation straightforwardly adds an element to the end of the deque, incrementing the *tail* index. It includes a full fence so that the tail pointer is not incremented before the element is placed in the array. The *take* operation uses a CAS operation to atomically increment the head index. Interference can occur if there is a concurrent *steal* operation in progress, which also uses CAS to increment *head* to remove an element from the head of the deque. The *take* and *steal* operation return empty if they observe an empty deque. In addition the *steal* operation may return the special value *fail* if interference on *head* occurs. Complexity arises if the deque has one element and there are concurrent processes trying to both *take* and *steal* that element at the same time.

Operations *take* and *steal* use a **fence** operation to ensure they have consistent readings for the head and tail indexes, and later use CAS to atomically update the head pointer (only if necessary, in the case of *take*). Additionally, the *steal* operation contains two **cfence** barriers (`ctrl_isync` in ARM).

Verification. We use an abstract model of the deque and its operations to specify the allowed final values of the deque and return values. The function

$$put(v) \;\hat{=}\; q := q \frown \langle v \rangle$$

$$take \;\hat{=}\; \textbf{lcl } return := none \; \bullet$$

$$\langle [q = \langle \rangle] \;,\; return := empty \rangle \; \sqcap$$

$$\langle [q \neq \langle \rangle] \;,\; return := last(q) \;,\; q := front(q) \rangle$$

$Initial\ state: \{ head \mapsto 0, tail \mapsto 0, tasks \mapsto \langle \_, \_, \ldots \rangle \}$

$put(v) \;\hat{=}$
  lcl $t \mapsto \_ \; \bullet$
  $t := tail;$
  $tasks[t \bmod L] := v;$
  fence;
  $tail := t + 1$

$take \;\hat{=}$	$steal \;\hat{=}$
lcl $h \mapsto \_, t \mapsto \_, return \mapsto \_ \; \bullet$	**lcl** $h \mapsto \_, t \mapsto \_, return \mapsto \_ \; \bullet$
$t := tail - 1\;;$	$h := head\;;$
$tail := t\;;$	**fence**;
fence;	$t := tail\;;$
$h := head\;;$	**cfence**; $//\; unnecessary$
if $h \leq t$ **then**	**if** $h < t$ **then**
$return := tasks[t \bmod L]\;;$	$return := tasks[h \bmod L]\;;$
if $h = t$ **then**	**cfence**; $//\; incorrectly\ placed$
if $\neg CAS(head, h, h+1)$ **then**	**if** $\neg CAS(head, h, h+1)$ **then**
$return := empty$	$return := fail$
$tail := t + 1$	**else**
else	$return := empty$
$return := empty\;;$	
$tail := t + 1$	

Fig. 4. A version of Lê et. al's work-stealing deque algorithm for ARM [17]

$last(q)$ returns the last element in q and $front(q)$ returns q excluding its last element.

$$steal \;\hat{=}\; \textbf{lcl } return := none$$

$$\langle [q = \langle \rangle] \;,\; return := empty \rangle \; \sqcap$$

$$\langle [q \neq \langle \rangle] \;,\; return := head(q) \;,\; q := tail(q) \rangle$$

For simplicity the abstract specification for *steal* does not attempt to detect interference and return *fail*, and as such we exclude corresponding behaviours of the concrete code from the analysis. We could encode this special failure case for *steal*, requiring additional data to track which processes are active.

We ran several contextual programs calling the abstract model alongside the same programs calling the concrete model, comparing final states after applying a straightforward simulation relation between abstract and concrete states. The contextual programs were combinations of concurrent processes – 1, 2 or 3 – each sequentially making one or two calls to the three operations. This exposed a bug in the code which may occur when a *put* and *steal* operation execute in parallel on an empty deque. The load $return := tasks[h \bmod L]$ can be speculatively executed before the guard $h < t$ is evaluated, and hence also before the load of *tail*. Thus the steal process may load *head*, load an irrelevant *return* value, at which point a *put* operation may complete, storing a value and incrementing *tail*. The *steal* operation resumes, loading the new value for *tail* and observing a non-empty deque, succeeding with its *CAS* and returning the irrelevant value, which was loaded before the *put* operation had begun.

Swapping the order of the second **cfence** with the load of $tasks[h \bmod L]$ eliminates this bug, and our analysis did not reveal any other problems. In addition, eliminating the first **cfence** does not change the possible outcomes.

5   Related Work

This work makes use of an extensive suite of tests elucidating the behaviour of weak memory models in ARM and POWER via both operational and axiomatic semantics [2–4, 19]. Those semantics were developed and validated through testing on real hardware and in consultation with processor vendors themselves. Our model is validated against their results, in the form of the results of litmus tests. The hardware vendor does not provide a formal specification of the assembler language, and hence the results of the litmus tests and their abstraction to axiomatic relations in the above work is the most reliable validation benchmark. However, as identified by Alglave et al. [3], some chips have different behaviour to others, contain bugs, and do not implement certain features; in addition given that instructions sets and definitions may change over time it is difficult to achieve a single canonical specification.

Excluding two tests involving "shadow registers", which appear to be processor-specific facilities which are not intended to conform to sequential semantics (they do not correspond to higher-level code), all of the 348 ARM litmus tests run on our model agreed with the results in [4], and all of the 758 POWER litmus tests run on our model agreed with the results in [2], which the exception of litmus test PP0015, which we give below, translated into our formal language.[7]

---

[7] We simplified some of the syntax for clarity, in particular introducing a higher-level **if** statement to model a jump command and implicit register (referenced by the compare (CMP) and branch-not-equal (BNE) instructions). We have also combined some commands, retaining dependencies, in a way that is not possible in the assembler language. The xor operator is exclusive-or; its use here artificially creates a *data dependency* [3] between the updates to r_0 and z.

$$x := 1; \textbf{ fence}; \ y := 1 \quad \|$$
$$r_0 := y; \ z := (r_0 \text{ xor } r_0) + 1; \ z := 2; \ r_3 := z; \quad\quad (39)$$
$$(\textbf{if } r_3 = r_3 \textbf{ then nil else nil}) \ ; \textbf{ cfence}; \ r_4 := x$$

The tested condition is $z = 2 \wedge r_0 = 1 \wedge r_4 = 0$, which asks whether it is possible to load x (the last statement of process 2) before loading y (the first statement of process 2). At a first glance the control fence prevents the load of x happening before the branch. However, as indicated by litmus tests such as MP+dmb.sy+fri-rfi-ctrisb, [4, Sect. 3, *Out of order execution*], under some circumstances the branch condition can be evaluated early, as discussed in the speculative execution example. We expand on this below by manipulating the second process, taking the case where the success branch of the **if** statement is chosen. To aid clarity we underline the instruction that is the target of the (next) refinement step.

$r_0 := y; \ z := (r_0 \text{ xor } r_0) + 1; \ z := 2; \ \underline{r_3 := z}; \ [r_3 = r_3]; \ \textbf{cfence}; \ r_4 := x$

$\sqsubseteq$ Promote load with forwarding (from $z := 2$), from Laws (7) and (8)

$r_3 := 2 \ \textbf{.} \ r_0 := y; \ z := (r_0 \text{ xor } r_0) + 1; \ z := 2; \ \underline{[r_3 = r_3]}; \ \textbf{cfence}; \ r_4 := x$

$\sqsubseteq$ Promote guard by Laws (7) and (8) (from (34))

$r_3 := 2 \ \textbf{.} \ [r_3 = r_3] \ \textbf{.} \ r_0 := y; \ z := (r_0 \text{ xor } r_0) + 1; \ z := 2; \ \underline{\textbf{cfence}}; \ r_4 := x$

$\sqsubseteq$ Promote control fence by Laws (7) and (8) ((29) does not now apply)

$r_3 := 2 \ \textbf{.} \ [r_3 = r_3] \ \textbf{.} \ \textbf{cfence} \ \textbf{.} \ r_0 := y; \ z := (r_0 \text{ xor } r_0) + 1; \ z := 2; \ \underline{r_4 := x}$

$\sqsubseteq$ Promote load by Laws (7) and (8)

$r_3 := 2 \ \textbf{.} \ [r_3 = r_3] \ \textbf{.} \ \textbf{cfence} \ \textbf{.} \ r_4 := x \ \textbf{.} \ r_0 := y; \ z := (r_0 \text{ xor } r_0) + 1; \ z := 2$

The load $r_4 := x$ has been reordered before the load $r_0 := y$, and hence when interleaved with the first process from (39) it is straightforward that the condition may be satisfied.

In the Flowing/POP model of [4], this behaviour is forbidden because there is a data dependency from the load of y into r_0 to r_3, via z. This appears to be because of the consecutive stores to z, one of which depends on r_0. In the testing of real processors reported in [4], the behaviour that we allow was never observed, but is allowed by the model in [3]. As such we deem this discrepancy to be a minor issue in Flowing/POP (preservation of transitive dependencies) rather than a fault in our model.

Our model of the storage subsystem is similar to that of the operational models of [2,4]. However our thread model is quite different, being defined in terms of relationships between actions. The key difference is how we handle branching and the effects of speculative execution. The earlier models are complicated in the sense that they are closer to the real execution of instructions, involving restarting reads if an earlier read invalidates the choice taken at a branch point.

The axiomatic models, as exemplified by Alglave et al. [3], define relationships between instructions in a whole-system way, including relationships between instructions in concurrent processes. This gives a global view of how an architecture's reordering rules (and storage system) interact to reorder instructions in a system. Such global orderings are not immediately obvious from our pair-wise orderings on instructions. On the other hand, those globals orderings become quite complex and obscure some details, and it is unclear how to extract some of the generic principles such as (2).

6   Conclusion

We have utilised earlier work to devise a wide-spectrum language and semantics for weak memory models which is relatively straightforward to define and extend, and which lends itself to verifying low-level code against abstract specifications. While abstracting away from the details of the architecture, we believe it provides a complementary insight into why some reorderings are allowed, requiring a pairwise relationship between instructions rather than one that is system-wide.

A model-checking approach based on our semantics exposed a bug in an algorithm in [17] in relation to the placement of a control fence. The original paper includes a hand-written proof of the correctness of the algorithm based on the axiomatic model of [19]. The possible traces of the code were enumerated and validated against a set of conditions on adding and removing elements from the deque (rather than with respect to an abstract specification of the deque). The conditions being checked are non-trivial to express using final state analysis only. An advantage of having a semantics that can apply straightforwardly to abstract specifications, rather than a proof technique that analyses behaviours of the concrete code only, is that we may reason at a more abstract level.

We have described the ordering condition as syntactic constraints on atomic actions, which fits with the low level decisions of hardware processors. However our main reordering principle (2) is based on semantic concerns, and as such may be applicable as a basis for understanding the interplay of software memory models, compiler optimisations and hardware memory models [20].

Future Work. A feature of our framework is that we can potentially reason about reordering of abstract instructions (i.e., those working with abstract data types), and not only low-level assembler instructions. This allows the potential for stepwise verification techniques to be applied, in particular potentially capturing the complex interaction of the environment using rely-guarantee reasoning [21–24]. In this paper we consider assignments as the fundamental command, which is sufficient for specifying many concurrent programs. However we hope to extend the language to encompass more general constructs such as the specification command [25], which may modify and access multiple global variables. Refinement laws for decomposing a (non-atomic) rely-guarantee specification into a sequence of atomic steps will have proof obligations referencing the reordering relation to ensure that any reordering of the actions does not affect the guarantee; alternatively, where reordering would affect the guarantee, the law could specify one or more fences in the implementation sequence.

Acknowledgements. We thank Kirsten Winter, Ian Hayes, and the anonymous reviewers for feedback on this work. It was supported by Australian Research Council Discovery Grant DP160102457.

References

1. Adve, S.V., Boehm, H.J.: Memory models: a case for rethinking parallel languages and hardware. Commun. ACM **53**(8), 90–101 (2010)
2. Sarkar, S., Sewell, P., Alglave, J., Maranget, L., Williams, D.: Understanding POWER multiprocessors. SIGPLAN Not. **46**(6), 175–186 (2011)
3. Alglave, J., Maranget, L., Tautschnig, M.: Herding cats: modelling, simulation, testing, and data mining for weak memory. ACM Trans. Program. Lang. Syst. **36**(2), 701–774 (2014)
4. Flur, S., Gray, K.E., Pulte, C., Sarkar, S., Sezgin, A., Maranget, L., Deacon, W., Sewell, P.: Modelling the ARMv8 architecture, operationally: concurrency and ISA. In: Proceedings of the 43rd Annual ACM SIGPLAN-SIGACT Symposium on Principles of Programming Languages, POPL 2016, pp. 608–621. ACM, New York (2016)
5. Alglave, J., Maranget, L., Sarkar, S., Sewell, P.: Litmus: running tests against hardware. In: Abdulla, P.A., Leino, K.R.M. (eds.) TACAS 2011. LNCS, vol. 6605, pp. 41–44. Springer, Heidelberg (2011). https://doi.org/10.1007/978-3-642-19835-9_5
6. Mador-Haim, S., Alur, R., Martin, M.M.K.: Generating litmus tests for contrasting memory consistency models. In: Touili, T., Cook, B., Jackson, P. (eds.) CAV 2010. LNCS, vol. 6174, pp. 273–287. Springer, Heidelberg (2010). https://doi.org/10.1007/978-3-642-14295-6_26
7. Dijkstra, E.W.: Guarded commands, nondeterminacy and formal derivation of programs. Commun. ACM **18**(8), 453–457 (1975)
8. Sewell, P., Sarkar, S., Owens, S., Nardelli, F.Z., Myreen, M.O.: X86-TSO: a rigorous and usable programmer's model for x86 multiprocessors. Commun. ACM **53**(7), 89–97 (2010)
9. Milner, R.: A Calculus of Communicating Systems. Springer, New York (1982). https://doi.org/10.1007/3-540-10235-3
10. Hoare, C.A.R.: Communicating Sequential Processes. Prentice-Hall Inc., Upper Saddle River (1985)
11. Colvin, R.J., Smith, G.: A wide-spectrum language for verification of programs on weak memory models. CoRR abs/1802.04406 (2018)
12. Sorin, D.J., Hill, M.D., Wood, D.A.: A Primer on Memory Consistency and Cache Coherence, 1st edn. Morgan & Claypool Publishers, San Francisco (2011)
13. Pulte, C., Flur, S., Deacon, W., French, J., Sarkar, S., Sewell, P.: Simplifying ARM concurrency: multicopy-atomic axiomatic and operational models for ARMv8. In: Proceedings of the ACM SIGPLAN-SIGACT Symposium on Principles of Programming Languages (POPL). ACM Press (2018, to appear)
14. Morgan, C.: Programming from Specifications, 2nd edn. Prentice Hall, New York (1994)
15. Back, R.J., von Wright, J.: Refinement Calculus: A Systematic Introduction. Springer, New York (1998). https://doi.org/10.1007/978-1-4612-1674-2
16. Clavel, M., Duran, F., Eker, S., Lincoln, P., Marti-Oliet, N., Meseguer, J., Quesada, J.F.: Maude: specification and programming in rewriting logic. Theor. Comput. Sci. **285**(2), 187–243 (2002)
17. Lê, N.M., Pop, A., Cohen, A., Nardelli, F.Z.: Correct and efficient work-stealing for weak memory models. In: Proceedings of the 18th ACM SIGPLAN Symposium on Principles and Practice of Parallel Programming, PPoPP 2013, pp. 69–80. ACM, New York (2013)

18. Chase, D., Lev, Y.: Dynamic circular work-stealing deque. In: SPAA 2005: Proceedings of the 17th Annual ACM Symposium on Parallelism in Algorithms and Architectures, pp. 21–28. ACM Press, New York (2005)
19. Mador-Haim, S., et al.: An axiomatic memory model for POWER multiprocessors. In: Madhusudan, P., Seshia, S.A. (eds.) CAV 2012. LNCS, vol. 7358, pp. 495–512. Springer, Heidelberg (2012). https://doi.org/10.1007/978-3-642-31424-7_36
20. Kang, J., Hur, C.K., Lahav, O., Vafeiadis, V., Dreyer, D.: A promising semantics for relaxed-memory concurrency. In: Proceedings of the 44th ACM SIGPLAN Symposium on Principles of Programming Languages, POPL 2017, pp. 175–189. ACM, New York (2017)
21. Jones, C.B.: Specification and design of (parallel) programs. In: IFIP Congress, pp. 321–332 (1983)
22. Jones, C.B.: Tentative steps toward a development method for interfering programs. ACM Trans. Program. Lang. Syst. 5, 596–619 (1983)
23. Hayes, I.J., Colvin, R.J., Meinicke, L.A., Winter, K., Velykis, A.: An algebra of synchronous atomic steps. In: Fitzgerald, J., Heitmeyer, C., Gnesi, S., Philippou, A. (eds.) FM 2016. LNCS, vol. 9995, pp. 352–369. Springer, Cham (2016). https://doi.org/10.1007/978-3-319-48989-6_22
24. Colvin, R.J., Hayes, I.J., Meinicke, L.A.: Designing a semantic model for a wide-spectrum language with concurrency. Formal Aspects Comput. 29(5), 853–875 (2017)
25. Morgan, C.: The specification statement. ACM Trans. Program. Lang. Syst. 10, 403–419 (1988)

Operational Semantics of a Weak Memory Model with Channel Synchronization

Daniel Schnetzer Fava[1(✉)], Martin Steffen[1(✉)], and Volker Stolz[1,2]

[1] Department of Informatics, University of Oslo, Oslo, Norway
{danielsf,msteffen}@ifi.uio.no
[2] Western Norway University of Applied Sciences, Bergen, Norway

Abstract. A multitude of weak memory models exists supporting various types of relaxations and different synchronization primitives. On one hand, such models must be lax enough to account for hardware and compiler optimizations; on the other, the more lax the model, the harder it is to understand and program for. Though the right balance is up for debate, a memory model should provide what is known as the *SC-DRF guarantee*, meaning that data-race free programs behave in a sequentially consistent manner.

We present a weak memory model for a calculus inspired by the Go programming language. Thus, different from previous approaches, we focus on a memory model with buffered channel communication as the sole synchronization primitive. We formalize our model via an operational semantics, which allows us to prove the SC-DRF guarantee using a standard simulation technique. Contrasting against an axiomatic semantics, where the notion of a program is abstracted away as a graph with memory events as nodes, we believe our semantics and simulation proof can be clearer and easier to understand. Finally, we provide a concrete implementation in $\mathbb{K}$, a rewrite-based executable semantic framework, and derive an interpreter for the proposed language.

1 Introduction

A *memory model* dictates which values may be observed when reading from memory, thereby affecting how concurrent processes communicate through shared memory. One of the simplest memory models, called *sequentially consistent*, stipulates that operations must appear to execute one at a time and in program order [25]. SC was one of the first formalizations to be proposed and, to this day, constitutes a baseline for well-behaved memory. However, for efficiency reasons, modern hardware architectures do not guarantee sequential consistency. SC is also considered much too strong to serve as the underlying memory semantics of programming languages; the reason being that sequential consistency prevents many established compiler optimizations and robs from the compiler writer the chance to exploit the underlying hardware for efficient parallel execution. The research community, however, has not been able to agree on exactly what a proper memory model should offer. Consequently, a bewildering

K. Havelund et al. (Eds.): FM 2018, LNCS 10951, pp. 258–276, 2018.
https://doi.org/10.1007/978-3-319-95582-7_15

array of *weak* or *relaxed memory models* have been proposed, investigated, and implemented. Different taxonomies and catalogs of so-called *litmus tests*, which highlight specific aspects of memory models, have also been researched [1].

Memory models are often defined axiomatically, meaning via a set of rules that constrain the order in which memory events are allowed to occur. The *candidate execution* approach falls in this category [6]. These formalizations are not without controversy. For example, despite many attempts, there does not exist an well-accepted comprehensive specification of the $C^{++}11$ [7,8] or Java memory models [5,27,34]. Luckily, more recently, one fundamental principle of relaxed memory has emerged, namely: no matter how much relaxation is permitted by a memory model, if a program is *data-race free* or *properly synchronized*, then the program must behave in a sequentially consistent manner [2,27]. This is known as the *SC-DRF* guarantee.

We present an *operational* semantics for a weak memory. Similar to Boudol and Petri [10], we favor an operational semantics because it allows us to prove the SC-DRF guarantee using a standard simulation technique. Compared to axiomatic semantics in which the notion of a program is abstracted away (often in the form of a graph with nodes as memory events), we think that our formalism leads to an easier to understand proof of the SC-DRF guarantee. The lemmas we build up in the process of constructing the proof highlight meaningful invariants and give insight into the workings of the memory model.

Our calculus is inspired by the Go programming language: similar to Go, our model focuses on channel communication as the main synchronization primitive. Go's memory model, however, is described, albeit succinctly and precisely, in prose [18]. we provide a formal semantics instead.

The main contributions of our work are:

- There are few studies on channel communication as synchronization primitive for weak memory. We give an operational theory for a weak memory with bounded channel communication by leveraging thread-local happens-before information.
- We prove that the proposed memory upholds the *sequential consistency guarantee for data-race free* programs using a standard conditional simulation proof.
- We implement the operational semantics in the $\mathbb{K}$ executable semantics framework [22,35] and make the source code publicly available via a git-repository [14].

The remaining of the paper is organized as follows. Section 2 presents background information directly related to the formalization of our memory model. Sections 3 and 4 provide the syntax and the semantics of the calculus with relaxed memory and channel communication. Section 6 establishes the SC-DRF guarantee. Sections 7 and 8 conclude with related and future work.

2   Background

Go's Memory Model. The Go language [13,17] recently gained traction in networking applications, web servers, distributed software and the like. It prominently features goroutines, that is, asynchronous execution of function calls resembling lightweight threads, and buffered channel communication in the tradition of CSP [20] (resp. the π-calculus [30]) or Occam [21]. While encouraging message passing as the prime mechanism for communication and synchronization, threads can still exchange data via shared variables. Consequently, Go's specification includes a memory model which spells out, in precise but informal English, the few rules governing memory interaction at the language level [18].

Concerning synchronization primitives, the model covers goroutine creation and destruction, channel communication, locks, and the **once**-statement. Our semantics will concentrate on thread creation and channel communication because lock-handling and the **once** statement are *not* language primitives but part of the **sync**-library. Thread destruction, i.e. termination, comes with *no* guarantees concerning visibility: it involves no synchronization and thus the semantics does not treat thread termination in any special way. In that sense, our semantics treats all of the *primitives* covered by Go's memory model specification. As will become clear in the next sections, our semantics does not, however, relax read events. Therefore, our memory model is stronger than Go's. On the plus side, this prevents a class of undesirable behavior called *out-of-thin-air* [9]. On the negative, the absence of relaxed reads comes at the expense of some forms of compiler optimizations.

Languages like Java and C++ go to great lengths not only to offer the crucial SC-DRF guarantee for well-synchronized programs, but beyond that, strive to clarify the resulting non-SC behavior when the program is *ill*-synchronized. This involves ruling out definitely unwelcome behavior. Doing this precisely, however, is far from trivial. One class of unwanted behavior that is particularly troublesome is the so called *out-of-thin-air* behavior [9]. In contrast, Go's memory model is rather "laid back." Its specification [18] does not even mention "out-of-thin-air" behavior.

Happens-Before Relation and Observability. Like Java's [27,34], C++11's [7,8], and many other memory models, ours centers around the definition of a *happens-before* relation. The concept dates back to 1978 [24] and was introduced in a pure *message-passing* setting, i.e., without shared variables. The relation is a technical vehicle for defining the semantics of memory models. It is important to note that just because an instruction or event is in a *happens-before* relation with a second one, it does not necessarily mean that the first instruction *actually* "happens" before the second in the operational semantics. Consider the sequence of assignments $x := 1; y := 2$ as an example. The first assignment "happens-before" the second as they are in program order, but it does not mean the first instruction is actually "done" before the second,[1] and especially, it does not mean that

---

[1] Assuming that x and y are not aliases in the sense that they refer to the same or "overlapping" memory locations.

the effect of the two writes become observable in the given order. For example, a compiler might choose to change the order of the two instructions. Alternatively, a processor may rearrange memory instructions so that their effect may not be visible in program order. Conversely, the fact that two events happen to occur one after the other in a particular schedule does not imply that they are in happens-before relationship, as the order may be coincidental. To avoid confusion between the technical happens-before relation and our understanding of what happens when the programs runs, we speak of event e_1 "happens-before" e_2 in reference to the technical definition (also abbreviated as $e_1 \rightarrow_{hb} e_2$ in this section) as opposed to its natural language interpretation. Also, when speaking about steps and events in the operational semantics, we avoid talking about something happening before something else, and rather say that a step or transition "occurs" in a particular order.

The happens-before relation regulates observability, and it does so very liberally. It allows a read r from a shared variable to *possibly observe* a particular write w to said variable *unless* one of the following two conditions hold:

$$r \rightarrow_{hb} w \quad \text{or} \tag{1}$$
$$w \rightarrow_{hb} w' \rightarrow_{hb} r \quad \text{for some other write } w' \text{ to the same variable.} \tag{2}$$

For the sake of discussion, let's concentrate on the following two constituents for the happens-before relation: (1) *program order* and (2) the order stemming from channel communication. According to the Go memory model [18], we have the following constraints related to a channel c with capacity k:

$$\text{A send on } c \text{ happens-before the corresponding receive from } c \text{ completes.} \tag{3}$$
$$\text{The } i^{th} \text{ receive from } c \text{ happens-before the } (i+k)^{th} \text{ send on } c. \tag{4}$$

To illustrate, consider the example on Listing 1.1. The main function spawns an asynchronous execution of setup, at which point main and setup can run concurrently. In the thread or goroutine executing setup, the write to variable a happens-before the write to done, as they are in program order. For the same reason, the read(s) of done happen-before the read of a in the main thread. Without synchronization, the variable accesses are ordered locally *per thread* but not across threads. Since neither condition (1) or (2) applies, the main procedure may or may not observe writes performed by setup; it is possible for main to observe the initial value of a instead. This makes the writes to a and done performed by setup to potentially appear out-of-order from the main thread's perspective.

Replacing the use of done by channel synchronization properly synchronizes the two functions (cf. Listing 1.2). As the receive happens-after the send, an order is established between events belonging to the two threads. One can think of the main thread as receiving not only a value but also the knowledge that the write event to a in setup has taken place. With condition (3), channels implicitly communicate the happens-before relation from the sender to the receiver. Then, with condition (2), we can conclude that once main receives a message from setup, the initial value of a is no longer observable from main's perspective.

Listing (1.1) Erroneous synchronization   Listing (1.2) Channel synchronization

```
1    var a string                              var a string
2    var done bool                             var c = make(chan int , 10)
3
4    func setup() {                            func setup() {
5       a = "hello ,_world"                      a = "hello ,_world"
6       done = true                             c <- 0   // send
7    }                                         }
8
9    func main() {                             func main() {
10      go setup()                              go setup()
11      for !done { } // try waiting            <-c       // receive
12      print(a)                                print(a)
13   }                                         }
```

Fig. 1. Synchronization via channel communication [18]

Condition (4) is not shown in the example. This condition accounts for the boundedness of channels by transmitting happens-before information in the backward direction for some receiver to some sender. For *synchronous* channels, where $k = 0$, the two threads participating in the rendezvous symmetrically exchange their happens-before information.

In summary, the operational semantics captures the following principles:

Immediate positive information: a *write* is globally observable instantaneously.

Delayed negative information: in contrast, negative information overwriting previously observable *writes* is *not* immediately effective. Referring back to the example of Fig. 1, the fact that **setup** has overwritten the initial value of variable a is not immediately available to other threads. Instead, the information is spread via message passing in the following way:

    Causality: information regarding condition (3) travels with data through channels.

    Channel capacity: *backward channels* are used to account for condition (4).

Local view: Each thread maintains a local view on the happens-before relationship of past write events, i.e. which events are unobservable. Thus, the semantics does not offer multi-copy atomicity.

3   Abstract Syntax

The abstract syntax of the calculus is given in Table 1. *Values v* can be of two forms: r is used to denote the value of local variables or registers, while n in used to denote references or names in general and, in specific, c for channel names. We do not explicitly list values such as the unit value, booleans, integers, etc. We also omit compound local expressions like $r_1 + r_2$. Shared variables are denoted by x, z etc., **load** z represents the reading the shared variable z into the thread, and $z := v$ denotes writing to z.

References are dynamically created and are, therefore, part of the *run-time* syntax. Run-time syntax is highlighted with an underline as $\underline{n}$ in the grammar.

Table 1. Abstract syntax

$v ::= r \mid \underline{n}$	values
$e ::= t \mid v \mid \mathtt{load}\, z \mid z := v \mid \mathtt{if}\, v\, \mathtt{then}\, t\, \mathtt{else}\, t \mid \mathtt{go}\, t$	expressions
$\quad\mid\ \mathtt{make}\,(\mathtt{chan}\, T, v) \mid\ \leftarrow v \mid v \leftarrow v \mid \mathtt{close}\, v$	
$g ::= v \leftarrow v \mid\ \leftarrow v \mid \mathtt{default}$	guards
$t ::= \mathtt{let}\, r = e\, \mathtt{in}\, t \mid \sum_i \mathtt{let}\, r_i = g_i\, \mathtt{in}\, t_i$	threads

A new channel is created by $\mathtt{make}$ ($\mathtt{chan}\ T, v$) where T represents the type
of values carried by the channel and v a non-negative integer specifying the
channel's capacity. Sending a value over a channel and receiving a value as input
from a channel are written respectively as $v_1 \leftarrow v_2$ and $\leftarrow v$. After the operation
$\mathtt{close}$, no further values can be sent on the specified channel. Attempting to
send values on a closed channel leads to a panic.

Starting a new asynchronous activity, called goroutine in Go, is done using
the $\mathtt{go}$-keyword. In Go, the $\mathtt{go}$-statement is applied to function calls only. We
omit function calls, asynchronous or otherwise, since they are orthogonal to the
memory model's formalization. See Steffen [36] for an operational semantics dealing with goroutines and closures in a purely functional setting, that is, without
shared memory.

The select-statement, here written using the $\sum$-symbol, consists of a finite set
of branches which are called communication clauses by the Go specification [17].
These branches act as guarded threads. General expressions in Go can serve as
guards. Our calculus, however, imposes the restriction that only communication
statements (i.e., channel sending and receiving) and the $\mathtt{default}$-keyword can
serve as guards. This restriction is in line with the A-normal form representation
and does not impose any actual reduction in expressivity. Both in Go and in our
formalization, there is at most one branch guarded by $\mathtt{default}$ in each select-
statement. The same channel can be mentioned in more than one guard. "Mixed
choices" [31,32] are also allowed, meaning that sending and receiving guards can
both be used in the same select-statement. We use $\mathtt{stop}$ as syntactic sugar for
the empty select statement; it represents a permanently blocked thread. The
$\mathtt{stop}$-thread is also the only way to syntactically "terminate" a thread, meaning
that it is the only element of t without syntactic sub-terms.

The $\mathtt{let}$-construct $\mathtt{let}\ r = e$ in t combines sequential composition and the
use of scopes for local variables r: after evaluating e, the rest t is evaluated where
the resulting value of e is handed over using r. The let-construct is seen as a
binder for variable r in t. When r does not occur free in t, $\mathtt{let}$ then boils down
to *sequential composition* and, therefore, is replaced by a semicolon.

4   Operational Semantics

In this section we define the operational semantics of the calculus. We fix the runtime configurations of a program before giving the operational rules in Sect. 4.2.

4.1   Local States, Events, and Configurations

Let X represent a set of shared variables such as x, $z \ldots$ and let N represent an infinite set of names or identifiers with typical elements n, $n'_2 \ldots$ As mentioned earlier, for readability, we will use names like c, $c_1, \ldots$ for channels, and p, p'_1 ... for goroutines or processes. A run-time configuration is then given by the following syntax:

$$P ::= n\langle \sigma, t \rangle \mid n(\!|z{:=}v|\!) \mid n[q] \mid \bullet \mid P \parallel P \mid \nu n \, P. \qquad (5)$$

Configurations consist of the parallel composition of goroutines $p\langle \sigma, t \rangle$, write events $n(\!|z{:=}v|\!)$, and channels $c[q]$; $\bullet$ represents the empty configuration. The ν-binder, known from the π-calculus, indicates dynamic scoping [30]. Goroutines or processes $p\langle \sigma, t \rangle$ contain, besides the code t to be executed, a local view $\sigma = (E_{hb}, E_s)$ detailing the observability of write events from the perspective of p. Local observability is formulated "negatively," meaning that all write events are observable by default. It is possible for an event to no longer be visible from a thread's perspective; such events are called *shadowed* and are tracked in σ, specifically in E_s. Note that, in order to properly update the list of shadowed events, σ must also contain thread-local information about the "happens-before" relationship between write events. This information is kept in E_{hb}.

Definition 1 (Local state). *A local state σ is a tuple of type $2^{(N \times X)} \times 2^N$. We use the notation (E_{hb}, E_s) to refer to the tuples and abbreviate their type by Σ. Let's furthermore denote by $E_{hb}(z)$ the set $\{n \mid (n, z) \in E_{hb}\}$. We write $\sigma_\perp$ for the local state $(\emptyset, \emptyset)$ containing neither happens-before nor shadow information.*

4.2   Reduction Steps

The operational semantics is given in several stages. We start with local steps, that is, steps not involving shared variables.

4.2.1   Local Steps

The reduction steps are given modulo structural congruence $\equiv$ on configurations. The congruence rules are standard and thus omitted here (see the report [15] for details). Local steps $\rightsquigarrow$ (cf. Table 2) reduce a thread t without touching shared variables, and $t_1 \rightsquigarrow t_2$ implies $\langle \sigma, t_1 \rangle \rightarrow \langle \sigma, t_2 \rangle$.

4.2.2   Global Steps

Writing a value records the corresponding event $n(\!|z{:=}v|\!)$ in the global configuration, with n freshly generated (cf. rule R-WRITE). The write events are remembered without keeping track of the order of their issuance. Therefore, as far as the global configuration is concerned, no write event ever invalidates an "earlier" write event or overwrites a previous value in a shared variable. Instead, the

Table 2. Operational semantics: local steps

$\mathtt{let}\ x = v\ \mathtt{in}\ t \rightsquigarrow t[v/x]$ R-RED

$\mathtt{let}\ x_1 = (\mathtt{let}\ x_2 = e\ \mathtt{in}\ t_1)\ \mathtt{in}\ t_2 \rightsquigarrow \mathtt{let}\ x_2 = e\ \mathtt{in}\ (\mathtt{let}\ x_1 = t_1\ \mathtt{in}\ t_2)$ R-LET

$\mathtt{if\ true\ then}\ t_1\ \mathtt{else}\ t_2 \rightsquigarrow t_1$ R-COND$_1$ $\mathtt{if\ false\ then}\ t_1\ \mathtt{else}\ t_2 \rightsquigarrow t_2$ R-COND$_2$

---

global configuration accumulates the "positive" information about all available write events which potentially can be observed by reading from shared memory.

The *local* state σ of a goroutine captures which events are actually observable from a thread-local perspective. Its primary function is to contain "negative" information: A read can observe all write events *except* for those shadowed, that is, write events whose identifiers are contained in E_s (see rule R-READ). In addition, the local state keeps track of write events that are thread-locally known to have *happened-before*. These are stored in E_{hb}. So, issuing a write command (rule R-WRITE on Table 3) with a write event labeled n updates the local E_{hb} by adding (n, z). Additionally, it marks all previous writes to the variable z as shadowed, thus enlarging E_s.

Channels in Go are the primary mechanism for communication and synchronization. They are typed and assure FIFO communication from a sender to a receiver sharing a channel. Channels can be dynamically created and closed. Channels are *bounded*, i.e., each channel has a finite capacity fixed upon creation. Channels of capacity 0 are called *synchronous*. Our semantics largely ignores that channel values are typed and that only values of an appropriate type can be communicated over a given channel.

Definition 2 (Channels). *A channel is of the form $c[q_1, q_2]$, where c is a name and (q_1, q_2) a pair of queues. The first queue, q_1, contains elements of type $(Val \times \Sigma) + (\{\perp\} \times \Sigma)$, where $\perp$ is a distinct, separate value representing the "end-of-transmission"; the second queue, q_2, contains elements of type Σ. We write (v, σ), $(\perp, \sigma)$ resp. (σ) for the respective queue values. The queues are also referred to as* forward *resp.* backward *queue. Furthermore, we use the following notational convention: We write $c_f[q]$ to refer to the forward queue of the channel and $c_b[q]$ to the backward queue. We also speak of the forward channel and the backward channel. We write $[]$ for an empty queue, $e :: q$ for a queue with e as the element most recently added into q, and $q :: e$ for the queue where e is the element to be dequeued next. We denote with $|q|$ the number of elements in q. A channel is closed, written $closed(c[q])$, if q is of the form $\perp :: q'$. Note that it is possible for a non-empty queue to be closed.*

When creating a channel (cf. rule R-MAKE) the forward direction is initially empty but the backward is not: it is initialized to a queue of length v corresponding to the channel's capacity. The backward queue contains *empty* happens-before and shadow information, represented by the elements $\sigma_\perp$. The

Table 3. Operational semantics: global steps

$$\dfrac{\sigma = (E_{hb}, E_s) \qquad \sigma' = (E_{hb} + (n,z), E_s + E_{hb}(z)) \qquad fresh(n)}{p\langle \sigma, z := v; t\rangle \;\to\; \nu n\, (p\langle \sigma', t\rangle \parallel n\langle\!\langle z := v\rangle\!\rangle)} \text{ R-WRITE}$$

$$\dfrac{\sigma = (\_, E_s) \qquad n \notin E_s}{p\langle \sigma, \texttt{let } r = \texttt{load } z \texttt{ in } t\rangle \parallel n\langle\!\langle z := v\rangle\!\rangle \;\to\; p\langle \sigma, \texttt{let } r = v \texttt{ in } t\rangle \parallel n\langle\!\langle z := v\rangle\!\rangle} \text{ R-READ}$$

$$\dfrac{q = [\sigma_\perp, \ldots, \sigma_\perp] \qquad |q| = v \qquad fresh(c)}{p\langle \sigma, \texttt{let } r = \texttt{make (chan } T, v) \texttt{ in } t\rangle \;\to\; \nu c\, (p\langle \sigma, \texttt{let } r = c \texttt{ in } t\rangle \parallel c_f[] \parallel c_b[q])} \text{ R-MAKE}$$

$$\dfrac{\neg closed(c_f[q_2]) \qquad \sigma' = \sigma + \sigma''}{c_b[q_1 :: \sigma''] \parallel p\langle \sigma, c \leftarrow v; t\rangle \parallel c_f[q_2] \;\to\; c_b[q_1] \parallel p\langle \sigma', t\rangle \parallel c_f[(v, \sigma) :: q_2]} \text{ R-SEND}$$

$$\dfrac{v \neq \perp \qquad \sigma' = \sigma + \sigma''}{c_b[q_1] \parallel p\langle \sigma, \texttt{let } r = \leftarrow c \texttt{ in } t\rangle \parallel c_f[q_2 :: (v, \sigma'')] \;\to\; c_b[\sigma :: q_1] \parallel p\langle \sigma', \texttt{let } r = v \texttt{ in } t\rangle \parallel c_f[q_2]} \text{ R-REC}$$

$$\dfrac{\sigma' = \sigma + \sigma''}{p\langle \sigma, \texttt{let } r = \leftarrow c \texttt{ in } t\rangle \parallel c_f[(\perp, \sigma'')] \;\to\; p\langle \sigma', \texttt{let } r = \perp \texttt{ in } t\rangle \parallel c_f[(\perp, \sigma'')]} \text{ R-REC}_\perp$$

$$\dfrac{\sigma' = \sigma_1 + \sigma_2}{c_b[] \parallel p_1\langle \sigma_1, c \leftarrow v; t\rangle \parallel p_2\langle \sigma_2, \texttt{let } r = \leftarrow c \texttt{ in } t_2\rangle \parallel c_f[] \;\to\; c_b[] \parallel p_1\langle \sigma', t\rangle \parallel p_2\langle \sigma', \texttt{let } r = v \texttt{ in } t_2\rangle \parallel c_f[]} \text{ R-SEND-REC}$$

$$\dfrac{\neg closed(c_f[q])}{p\langle \sigma, \texttt{close } (c); t\rangle \parallel c_f[q] \;\to\; p\langle \sigma, t\rangle \parallel c_f[(\perp, \sigma) :: q]} \text{ R-CLOSE}$$

$$\dfrac{fresh(p_2)}{p_1\langle \sigma, \texttt{go } t'; t\rangle \;\to\; \nu p_2\, (p_1\langle \sigma, t\rangle \parallel p_2\langle \sigma, t'\rangle)} \text{ R-GO}$$

---

rule R-MAKE covers both synchronous and asynchronous channels. An asynchronous channel is created with empty forward $c_f[]$ and backward queue $c_b[]$.

Channels can be closed, after which no new values can be sent Values "on transit" in a channel when it is being closed are *not* discarded and can be received as normal. The special value $\perp$ indicates the end-of-transmission. Note that there is a difference between an empty open channel $c[]$ and an empty closed one $c[\perp]$. The value $\perp$ is relevant to the forward channel only. Rules R-SEND and R-REC govern asynchronous channel communication while R-SEND-REC implements synchronous communication. In an asynchronous send, a process places a value on the forward channel along with its local state (provided the channel is not full, i.e., the backward queue is non-empty). In the process of sending, the sender's local state is updated with the knowledge that the previous k^{th} receive has completed; this is captured by $\sigma' = \sigma + \sigma''$ in the R-SEND rule. To receive a value from a (non-empty) asynchronous channel (cf. rule R-REC), the communicated value v is stored locally (in the rule, ultimately in variable r). Additionally, the local state of the receiver is updated by adding the previously sent local-state information. Furthermore, the state of the receiver before the update is sent back via the backward channel. In synchronous communication, the receiver obtains a value from the sender and together they exchange local state information. The R-CLOSE rule closes both sync and async channels. Executing a receive on a *closed* channel results in receiving the end-of-transmission marker $\perp$ (cf. rule R-REC$_\perp$) and updating the local state σ in the same way as when receiving a properly sent value. The "value" $\perp$ is not removed from the queue, so that all clients attempting to receive from the closed channel obtain the communicated happens-before synchronization information. Furthermore, there is no need to communicate happens-before constraints from the receiver to a potential future sender on the closed channel: after all, the channel is closed. Closing a channel resembles sending the special end-of-transmission value $\perp$ (cf. rule R-CLOSE). An already closed channel cannot be closed again. In Go, such an attempt would raise a panic. Here, this is captured by the absence of enabled transitions.

Thread creation leads to a form of a synchronization where the spawned goroutine inherits the local state of the parent (cf. rule R-GO). Finally, rules dealing with the select statement are given in the accompanying report [15].

Starting from an *initial weak configuration*, as far as the sizes of the queues of a channel in connection with the channel's capacity are concerned, the semantics assures the following invariant.

Definition 3 (Initial weak configuration). *An* initial *weak configuration is of the form* $\nu \boldsymbol{n}\ (\langle \sigma_0, t_0 \rangle \parallel n_0 (\!|z_0 := v_1|\!) \parallel \dots \parallel n_k (\!|z_k := v_k|\!))$ *where* $z_0, \dots z_k$ *are all shared variables of the program,* $\boldsymbol{n}$ *represents* $n_0, \dots, n_k$*, and* $\sigma_0 = (E_{hb}^0, E_s^0)$ *where* $E_{hb}^0 = \{(n_0, z_0), \dots, (n_k, z_k)\}$ *and* $E_s^0 = \emptyset$*.*

Lemma 4 (Invariant for channel queues). *The following global invariant holds for a channel* c *created with capacity* k*:* $|q_f| + |q_b| - p = k$*.*

$\square$

5   Strong Semantics

The strong semantics can be seen as a simpler version of the weak one. It represents a standard interleaving semantics, i.e., write and reads immediately interact with a shared global state. Therefore, there is no need for local thread information σ.

$$S ::= p\langle t \rangle \ \mid \ (\!|z := v|\!) \ \mid \ \bullet \ \mid \ S \parallel S \ \mid \ n[q] \ \mid \ \nu n \ P. \tag{6}$$

Structural congruence $\equiv$ and the local transition steps $\rightsquigarrow$ remain unchanged (cf. Table 2). Apart from leaving out the events and other information, the only

Table 4. Strong operational semantics: read and write steps

$$\frac{}{p\langle z := v; t\rangle \parallel (\!|z := v'|\!) \to p\langle t\rangle \parallel (\!|z := v|\!)} \text{ R-WRITE}$$

$$\frac{}{p\langle \texttt{let } r = \texttt{load } z \texttt{ in } t\rangle \parallel (\!|z := v|\!) \to p\langle \texttt{let } r = v \texttt{ in } t\rangle \parallel (\!|z := v|\!)} \text{ R-READ}$$

---

rules that conceptually change are the ones for read and write. These are included on Table 4.

Definition 5 (Initial configuration). *Initially, a strong configuration is of the form* $p\langle t_0\rangle \parallel (\!|z_0 := v_1|\!) \parallel \ldots \parallel (\!|z_k := v_k|\!)$, *where* $z_0, \ldots z_k$ *are all shared variables of the program and* t_0 *contains no run-time syntax.*

Cf. also the "weak" version from Definition 3.

Definition 6 (Well-formed strong configuration). *An strong configuration* S *is* well-formed *if, for every variable* $z \in V_s$, *there exists exactly one write event* $(\!|z := v|\!)$ *in* S. *We write* $\vdash_s S : ok$ *for such well-formed configurations.*

6 Relating the Strong and the Weak Semantics

Let's recall the definition of simulation [29] relating states of labeled transition systems. The set of transition labels and the information carried by the labels may depend on the specific steps or transitions done by a program and/or the observations one wishes to attach to those steps. This leads to a distinction between internally and externally visible steps. Let's write α for arbitrary transition labels. Later we will use a for visible labels and τ as the label of invisible or internal steps.

Definition 7 (Simulation). *Assume two labeled transition systems over the same set of labels and with state sets* S *and* T. *A binary relation* $\mathcal{R} \subseteq S \times T$ *is a* simulation relation *between the two transition systems if* $s_1 \xrightarrow{\alpha} s_2$ *and* $s_1 \mathcal{R} t_1$ *implies* $t_1 \xrightarrow{\alpha} t_2$ *for some state* t_2. *A state* t simulates s, *written* $t \gtrsim s$, *if there exists a simulation relation* $\mathcal{R}$ *such that* $s\mathcal{R}t$.

We use formulations like "s is simulated by t" interchangeably, and $\lesssim$ as the corresponding symbol. Also, we subscript the operational rules for disambiguation; for example, R-READ$_s$ refers to the strong version of the read while R-WRITE$_w$ to the weak version of the write operation. The rules of the strong semantics are simplifications of the weak rules given in Sect. 4.

The operational semantics is given as unlabeled global transitions $\to$. To establish the relationship between the strong and the weak semantics, we make the steps of the operational semantics more "informative" by labeling them appropriately: For read steps by rule R-READ$_s$ and R-READ$_w$, when reading a value v from a variable z, the corresponding step takes the form $\xrightarrow{(z?v)}$. All other steps, $\rightarrow$ as well as $\rightsquigarrow$ steps, are treated as invisible and noted as $\xrightarrow{\tau}$ in the simulation proofs. We make use of the following "alternative" labeling for the purpose of defining races and for some of the technical lemmas: we label write and read steps with the identity of the goroutine responsible for the action and the affected shared variable, i.e. $\xrightarrow{p_2(z!)}$ and $\xrightarrow{p_2(z?)}$. Note that the identity of the write event is omitted as well as the value exchanged; they will not be needed in the proofs. We often use subscripts when distinguishing the strong from the weak semantics; e.g. $\xrightarrow{p(z!)}_w$ and $\xrightarrow{p(z!)}_s$.

6.1   The Strong Semantics Conditionally Simulates the Weak One

That the weak semantics "contains" the sequentially consistent strong one as special case, i.e., the weak semantics simulates the strong one, should be intuitively clear and expected. Equally clear is that the opposite direction —the strong semantics simulates the weak— does *not* hold in general. If a simulation relation would hold in both directions, the two semantics would be equivalent, thus obviating the whole point of a weak or relaxed memory model.

Simulation of the weak semantics by the strong one can only be guaranteed "conditionally." The standard condition is that the program is "well-synchronized." We take that notion to represent the absence of data races, where a data race is a situation in which two different threads have access to the same shared variable "simultaneously," with at least one of the accesses being a write.

Definition 8 (Data race). *A well-formed configuration S_i contains a* manifest data race *if $S_i \xrightarrow{p_1(z!)}_s$ and $S_i \xrightarrow{p_2(z!)}_s$ for some $p_1 \neq p_2$ (a manifest write-write race on z), or if $S_i \xrightarrow{p_1(z?)}_s$ and $S_i \xrightarrow{p_2(z!)}_s$ (a manifest read-write race on z). We say a program S has a data race if a manifest data race is reachable from the initial configuration S_0.*

Definition 9 (Data race). *A well-formed configuration S_i contains a manifest data race if either hold:*

$$S_i \xrightarrow{p_1(z!)}_s \text{ and } S_i \xrightarrow{p_2(z!)}_s \text{ for some } p_1 \neq p_2 \qquad (manifest\ write - write\ race\ on\ z)$$
$$S_i \xrightarrow{p_1(z?)}_s \text{ and } S_i \xrightarrow{p_2(z!)}_s \qquad\qquad (manifest\ read - write\ race\ on\ z)$$

We say a program S has a data race if a manifest data race is reachable from the initial configuration S_0.

The definition is used analogously for the weak semantics. We also say a program is data-race free or *properly synchronized* if it does not have a data race.

Definition 10 (Observable and concurrent writes). *Let W_P stand for the set of all write events $n(z:=v)$ in a weak configuration P and let $W_P(z)$ stand for the set of identifiers of writes events to the variable z, i.e. $W_P(z) = \{n\ |$*

$n(\!|z:=v|\!) \in W_P\}$. *Given a well-formed configuration P, the sets of writes that* happens-before, *that are* concurrent, *and that are* observable *by process p for a variable z are defined as follows:*

$$W_P^{\mathsf{hb}}(z@p) = E_{hb}(z@p) \tag{7}$$

$$W_P^{\parallel}(z@p) = W_P(z) \setminus E_{hb}(z@p) \tag{8}$$

$$W_P^{\mathsf{o}}(z@p) = W_P(z) \setminus E_s(z@p). \tag{9}$$

We also use notations like $W_P^{\mathsf{o}}(\_@p)$ to denote the set of observable write events in P for any shared variable.

6.1.1 General Invariant Properties

Lemma 11 (Invariants about write events). *The weak semantics has the following invariants.*

1. *For all local states (E_{hb}, E_s) of all processes, $E_s \subset E_{hb}(z)$.*
2. $W_P^{\parallel}(z@p) \subseteq W_P^{\mathsf{o}}(z@p)$.
3. $W_P^{\parallel}(z@p) \neq W_P^{\mathsf{o}}(z@p)$.
4. $W_P^{\mathsf{hb}}(z@p) \cap W_P^{\mathsf{o}}(z@p) \neq \emptyset$.

As $W_P^{\mathsf{o}}(z@p)$ is a proper superset of $W_P^{\parallel}(z@p)$ (by part (2) and (3)), each thread can observe at least one value held by a variable. This means, unsurprisingly, that no thread will encounter an "undefined" variable. More interesting is the following generalization, namely that at each point and for each variable, some value is *jointly* observable by all processes. The property holds for arbitrary programs, race-free or not. Under the assumption of race-freedom, we will later obtain a stronger "consensus" result: not only is a consensus possible, but there is *exactly one* possible observable write, not more.

Lemma 12 (Consensus possible). *Weak configurations obey the following invariant*

$$\bigcap_{p \in P} W_P^{\mathsf{o}}(z@p) \neq \emptyset. \tag{10}$$

6.1.2 Race-Free Reductions

Next, we present invariants that hold specifically for race-free programs but not generally. They will be needed to define the relationship between the strong and weak semantics via a bisimulation relation. More concretely, the following properties are ultimately needed to establish that the relationship connecting the strong and the weak behavior of a program is well-defined.

Lemma 13 (No concurrent writes when it counts). *Assume $P_0 \rightarrow_w^* P$ where P_0 is the initial configuration derived from program P.*

1. *Assume P has no read-write race. If $P \xrightarrow{p(z?)}_w$, then $W_P^{\parallel}(z@p) = \emptyset$.*
2. *Assume P has no write-write race. If $P \xrightarrow{p(z!)}_w$, then $W_P^{\parallel}(z@p) = \emptyset$.*

Lemma 14 (Race-free consensus when it counts). *Assume $P_0 \to_w^* P$ with P_0 race-free. If $P \xrightarrow{p(z?)}_w$ or $P \xrightarrow{p(z!)}_w$, then*

$$\bigcap_{p_i} W_P^{\mathrm{o}}(z@p_i) = \{n\}, \tag{11}$$

where the intersection ranges over an arbitrary set of processes which includes p.

Lemma 15 (Race-free consensus). *Weak configurations for race-free programs obey the following invariant*

$$\bigcap_{p_i \in P} W_P^{\mathrm{o}}(z@p_i) = \{n\}. \tag{12}$$

Definition 16 (Well-formedness for race-free programs). *A weak configuration P is* well-formed *if*

1. *write-event references and channel references are unique, and*
2. *equation (12) from Lemma 15 holds.*

We write $\vdash_w^{rf} P : ok$ for well-formed configurations P.

We need to relate the weak and strong configurations via a simulation relation in order to establish the connection between the race-free behaviors of the weak and strong semantics. We will do so by the means of an erasure function from the weak to the strong semantics.

Definition 17 (Erasure). *The erasure of a well-formed weak configuration P, written $\lfloor P \rfloor$, is defined as $\lfloor P \rfloor^{\emptyset}$ where $\lfloor P \rfloor^R$ is given on Table 5 and R is a set of write event identifiers. On the queues q_1 and q_2 in the last case, the function simply jettisons the σ-component in the queue elements.*

Table 5. Definition of the erasure function $\lfloor P \rfloor^R$

$\lfloor \bullet \rfloor^R = \bullet$	(13)
$\lfloor p\langle \sigma, t \rangle \rfloor^R = \langle t \rangle$	(14)
$\lfloor n(\!\lvert z := v \rvert\!)\rfloor^R = \begin{cases} \bullet & \text{if } n \in R \\ (\!\lvert z := v \rvert\!) & \text{otherwise} \end{cases}$	(15)
$\lfloor P_1 \parallel P_2 \rfloor^R = \lfloor P_1 \rfloor^R \parallel \lfloor P_2 \rfloor^R$	(16)
$\lfloor \nu n\ P \rfloor^R = \begin{cases} \lfloor P \rfloor^R & \text{if } \forall p \in P.\ n \in W_P^{\mathrm{o}}(\_@p) \\ \lfloor P \rfloor^{R \cup \{n\}} & \text{otherwise} \end{cases}$	(17)
$\lfloor c[q_1, q_2] \rfloor^R = c[\lfloor q_1 \rfloor^R, \lfloor q_2 \rfloor^R]$	(18)

Note that $\lfloor P \rfloor$ is not necessarily a well-formed strong configuration. In particular, $\lfloor P \rfloor$ may contain two different write events $(\!\lvert z := v_1 \rvert\!)$ and $(\!\lvert z := v_2 \rvert\!)$ for the same variable. Besides, it is not *a priori* clear whether $\lfloor P \rfloor$ could remove all write events for a given variable (thus leaving its value undefined) and the configuration ill-formed.

Lemma 18 (Erasure and congruence). $P_1 \equiv P_2$ *implies* $\lfloor P_1 \rfloor \equiv \lfloor P_2 \rfloor$.

Lemma 19 (Erasure preserves well-formedness). *Let P be a race-free reachable weak configuration. If $\vdash_w P : ok$ then $\vdash_s \lfloor P \rfloor : ok$.*

Theorem 20 (Race-free simulation). *Let S_0 and P_0 be a strong, resp. a weak initial configuration for the same thread t and representing the same values for the global variables. If S_0 is data-race free, then $S_0 \gtrsim P_0$.*

Proof. Assume two initial race-free configurations P_0 and S_0 from the same program and the same initial values for the shared variables. To prove the $\gtrsim$-relationship between the respective initial configurations we need to establish a simulation relation, say $\mathcal{R}$, between well-formed strong and weak configurations such that P_0 and S_0 are in that relation.

Let P and S be well-formed configurations reachable (race-free) from P_0 resp. S_0. Define $\mathcal{R}$ as relation between race-free reachable configurations as

$$P \, \mathcal{R} \, S \quad \text{if} \quad S \equiv \lfloor P \rfloor \tag{19}$$

using the erasure from Definition 17. Note that by Lemma 18, $P_1 \, \mathcal{R} \, S$ and $P_1 \equiv P_2$ implies $P_2 \, \mathcal{R} \, S$.

Case: R-WRITE$_w$: $p\langle \sigma, z := v; t \rangle \rightarrow_w \nu n \ (p\langle \sigma', t \rangle \ \| \ n(\!| z{:=}v |\!))$, where $\sigma = (E_{hb}, E_s)$ and $\sigma' = (E'_{hb}, E'_s) = (E_{hb} + (n, z), E_s + E_{hb}(z))$. By the concurrent-writes Lemma 13(2), $W_P^{\|\|}(z@p) = \emptyset$, i.e., there are no concurrent write events from the perspective of p. This implies that for all write events $n'(\!| z{:=}v' |\!)$ in P, we have $n' \in E_{hb}$. If $n' \in E_s$, then $n \in E'_s$ as well. If $n' \in E_{hb} \setminus E_s$, then $n' \in E'_s$ as well. Either way, *all* write events to z contained in P prior to the step are shadowed in p after the step.

Now for the new write event n in P': clearly $n \in W_{P'}^o(z@p_i)$, i.e., the event is observable for all threads. By the race-free consensus Lemma 15, we have that this is the only event that is observable by all threads, i.e.

$$\bigcap_{p_i} W_{P'}^o(z@p_i) = \{n\}. \tag{20}$$

That means for the erasure of P' that $\lfloor P' \rfloor \equiv \ldots \ \| \ p\langle t \rangle \ \| \ (\!| z{:=}v |\!)$ where $(\!| z{:=}v |\!)$ is the result of applying $\lfloor \_ \rfloor$ to the write event $n(\!| z{:=}v |\!)$ of P. In particular, equation (20) shows that the write event n is not "filtered out" (cf. the cases of equation (15) and (17) in Definition 17) and furthermore that all other write events for z in P' are filtered out.[2] It is then easy to see that by R-WRITE$_s$, $\lfloor P \rfloor \rightarrow_s \lfloor P' \rfloor$.

The remaining cases are similar.   □

---

[2] The latter is indirectly clear already as we have established that $\lfloor \rfloor$ preserves well-formedness under the assumption of race-freedom (Lemma 19).

7 Related Work

There are numerous proposals for and investigations of weak and relaxed memory models [1,3,28]. One widely followed approach, called *axiomatic*, specifies allowed behavior by defining various ordering relations on memory accesses and synchronizing events. Go's memory model [18] gives an informal impression of that style of specification. Less frequent are *operational* formalizations.

Boudol and Petri [10] investigate a relaxed memory model for a calculus with locks relying on concepts of rewriting theory. Unlike the presentation here, writes are buffered in a hierarchy of fifo-buffers reflecting the syntactic tree structure of configurations: immediately neighboring processors share one write buffer, neighbors syntactically further apart share a write buffer closer to the shared global memory located at the root. The position of a redex in the configuration is used as thread identifier and determines which buffers are shared. Consequently, parallel composition cannot be commutative and, therefore, terms cannot be interpreted up-to congruence $\equiv$ as in our case.

Flanagan and Freund [16] give an operational semantics of a weak memory model ("adversarial" memory) used as the basis for a race checker. The model is not as weak as the official JMM but weaker than standard JVM implementations.

Zhang and Feng [37] use an abstract machine to operationally describe a happens-before memory model. Different from us, they make use of event *buffers*. Similar to us, they keep "older" write events to account for more than one observable variable value. The paper does not, however, deal with channel communication. Another operational semantics that uses histories of time-stamped, past read/write events is given by Kang et al. [23]. In this semantics, threads can promise future writes, and a reader acquires information on the writer's view of memory. Fences then synchronize global time-stamps on memory with thread-local information. Bi-simulation proofs mechanized in Coq show correctness of compilation to various architectures.

Demange et al. [12] formalize a weak semantics for Java using buffers. The semantics is quite less relaxed than the official JMM specification, the goal being to avoid the intricacies of the happens-before JMM and offer a firmer ground for reasoning. The model is defined axiomatically and operationally and the equivalence of the two formalizations is established.

Pichon-Pharabod and Sewell [33] investigate an operational representation of a weak memory model that avoids problems of the axiomatic candidate-execution approach in addressing out-of-thin-air behavior. The semantics is studied in a calculus featuring locks as well as relaxed atomic and non-atomic memory accesses.

Guerraoui et al. [19] introduce a "relaxed memory language" with an operational semantics to enable reasoning about various relaxed memory models. Their aim is to allow correctness arguments for software transactional memories implemented on weak-memory hardware.

Alrahman et al. [4] formalize a relaxed total-store order memory model with fence and wait operations. They provide an implementation in Maude, a rewriting-based executable framework that precedes $\mathbb{K}$, and explore ways to mitigate state-space explosion.

Lange et al. [26] define a small calculus, dubbed MiGo or mini-Go, featuring channels and thread creation. The formalization does not cover weak memory. Instead, the paper uses a behavioral effect type system to analyze channel communication.

8   Conclusion

We present an *operational* specification for a weak memory model with channel communication as the prime means of synchronization. We prove a central guarantee, namely that race-free programs behave sequentially consistently. The our semantics is accompanied by an implementation in the $\mathbb{K}$ framework and by several examples and test cases [14]. We plan to use the implementation towards the verification of program properties such as data-race freedom.

The current weak semantics remembers past write events as part of the run-time configuration, but does not remember read events. We are working on further relaxing the model by treating read events similar to the representation of writes. This will allow us to accommodate load buffering behavior common to relaxed memory models, including that of Go.

References

1. Adve, S.V., Gharachorloo, K.: Shared memory consistency models: A tutorial. Research Report 95/7, Digital WRL (1995)
2. Adve, S.V., Hill, M.D.: Weak ordering—a new definition. SIGARCH Comput. Archit. News **18**(3a), 2–14 (1990)
3. Alglave, J., Maranget, L., Tautschnig, M.: Herding cats: modelling, simulation, testing, and data-mining for weak memory. ACM Trans. Program. Lang. Syst. **36**(2), 7 (2014)
4. Abd Alrahman, Y., Andric, M., Beggiato, A., Lafuente, A.L.: Can we efficiently check concurrent programs under relaxed memory models in Maude? In: Escobar, S. (ed.) WRLA 2014. LNCS, vol. 8663, pp. 21–41. Springer, Cham (2014). https://doi.org/10.1007/978-3-319-12904-4_2
5. Aspinall, D., Ševčík, J.: Java memory model examples: good, bad and ugly. In: Proceedings of VAMP, vol. 7 (2007)
6. Batty, M., Memarian, K., Nienhuis, K., Pichon-Pharabod, J., Sewell, P.: The problem of programming language concurrency semantics. In: Vitek, J. (ed.) ESOP 2015. LNCS, vol. 9032, pp. 283–307. Springer, Heidelberg (2015). https://doi.org/10.1007/978-3-662-46669-8_12
7. Becker: Programming languages — C++. ISO/IEC 14882:2001 (2011)
8. Boehm, H.-J., Adve, S.V.: Foundations of the C++ concurrency memory model. In: ACM SIGPLAN Conference on Programming Language Design and Implementation (PLDI). ACM (2008)

9. Boehm, H.-J., Demsky, B.: Outlawing ghosts: avoiding out-of-thin-air results. In: Proceedings of the Workshop on Memory Systems Performance and Correctness, MSPC 2014, pp. 7:1–7:6. ACM, New York (2014)
10. Boudol, G., Petri, G.: Relaxed memory models: an operational approach. In: Proceedings of POPL 2009, pp. 392–403. ACM (2009)
11. Castagna, G., Gordon, A.D. (eds.): 44th Symposium on Principles of Programming Languages (POPL). ACM (2017)
12. Demange, D., Laporte, V., Zhao, L., Jagannathan, S., Pichardie, D., Vitek, J.: Plan B: a buffered memory model for Java. In: Proceedings of POPL 2013, pp. 329–342. ACM (2013)
13. Donovan, A.A.A., Kernighan, B.W.: The Go Programming Language. Addison-Wesley, Boston (2015)
14. Fava, D.: Operational semantics of a weak memory model with channel synchronization (2017). https://github.com/dfava/mmgo
15. Fava, D., Steffen, M., Stolz, V.: Operational semantics of a weak memory model with channel synchronization: proof of sequential consistency for race-free programs. Technical report 477, University of Oslo, Faculty of Mathematics and Natural Sciences, Department of Informatics (2018). http://www.ifi.uio.no/~msteffen/download/18/oswmm-chan-rep.pdf
16. Flanagan, C., Freund, S.N.: Adversarial memory for detecting destructive races. In: Zorn, B., Aiken, A. (eds.) ACM SIGPLAN Conference on Programming Language Design and Implementation (PLDI). ACM (2010)
17. The Go programming language specification (2016). https://golang.org/ref/spec
18. The Go memory model (2014). https://golang.org/ref/mem. Version of 31 May 2014, covering Go version 1.9.1
19. Guerraoui, R., Henzinger, T.A., Singh, V.: Software transactional memory on relaxed memory models. In: Bouajjani, A., Maler, O. (eds.) CAV 2009. LNCS, vol. 5643, pp. 321–336. Springer, Heidelberg (2009). https://doi.org/10.1007/978-3-642-02658-4_26
20. Hoare, C.A.R.: Communicating sequential processes. Commun. ACM **21**(8), 666–677 (1978)
21. Jones, G., Goldsmith, M.: Programming in Occam2. Prentice-Hall International, Hemel Hampstead (1988)
22. The K framework (2017). http://www.kframework.org/
23. Kang, J., Hur, C., Lahav, O., Vafeiadis, V., and Dreyer, D.: A promising semantics for relaxed-memory concurrency. In: [11], pp. 175–189 (2017)
24. Lamport, L.: Time, clocks, and the ordering of events in a distributed system. Commun. ACM **21**(7), 558–565 (1978)
25. Lamport, L.: How to make a multiprocessor computer that correctly executes multiprocess programs. IEEE Trans. Comput. **C−28**(9), 690–691 (1979)
26. Lange, J., Ng, N., Toninho, B., and Yoshida, N.: Fencing off Go: liveness and safety for channel-based programming. In: [11] (2017)
27. Manson, J., Pugh, W., Adve, S.V.: The Java memory model. In: Proceedings of POPL 2005. ACM (2005)
28. Maranget, L., Sarkar, S., Sewell, P.: A tutorial introduction to the ARM and POWER relaxed memory models (version 120) (2012)
29. Milner, R.: An algebraic definition of simulation between programs. In: Proceedings of the Second International Joint Conference on Artificial Intelligence, pp. 481–489. William Kaufmann, London (1971)
30. Milner, R., Parrow, J., Walker, D.: A calculus of mobile processes, part I/II. Inf. Comput. **100**, 1–77 (1992)

31. Palamidessi, C.: Comparing the expressive power of the synchronous and the asynchronous π-calculus. In: Proceedings of POPL 1997, pp. 256–265. ACM (1997)
32. Peters, K., Nestmann, U.: Is it a "good" encoding of mixed choice? In: Birkedal, L. (ed.) FoSSaCS 2012. LNCS, vol. 7213, pp. 210–224. Springer, Heidelberg (2012). https://doi.org/10.1007/978-3-642-28729-9_14
33. Pichon-Pharabod, J., Sewell, P.: A concurrency-semantics for relaxed atomics that permits optimisation and avoids out-of-thin-air executions. In: Proceedings of POPL 2016. ACM (2016)
34. Pugh, W.: Fixing the Java memory model. In: Proceedings of the ACM Java Grande Conference (1999)
35. Roşu, G., Şerbănuţă, T.F.: An overview of the K semantic framework. J. Logic Algebraic Methods Program. **79**(6), 397–434 (2010)
36. Steffen, M.: A small-step semantics of a concurrent calculus with goroutines and deferred functions. In: Ábrahám, E., Bonsangue, M., Johnsen, E.B. (eds.) Theory and Practice of Formal Methods. LNCS, vol. 9660, pp. 393–406. Springer, Cham (2016). https://doi.org/10.1007/978-3-319-30734-3_26
37. Zhang, Y., Feng, X.: An operational happens-before memory model. Front. Comput. Sci. **10**(1), 54–81 (2016)

Stepwise Development and Model Checking of a Distributed Interlocking System - Using RAISE

Signe Geisler$^{(\boxtimes)}$ and Anne E. Haxthausen

DTU Compute, Technical University of Denmark, Kongens Lyngby, Denmark
signe.geisler@gmail.com, aeha@dtu.dk

Abstract. This paper considers the challenge of designing and verifying control protocols for geographically distributed railway interlocking systems. It describes for a real-world case study how this can be tackled by stepwise development and model checking of state transition models in an extension of the RAISE Specification Language (RSL). This method also allows different variants of the control protocols to be explored.

Keywords: Stepwise development · Model checking
RAISE · Railway interlocking systems · Distributed systems

1 Introduction

This paper considers the challenge of formally modelling and verifying the real-world geographically distributed railway interlocking system presented in [8]. The engineering concept of this was originally developed by INSY GmbH Berlin for their railway control system RELIS 2000 designed for local railway networks.

1.1 Background

A railway *interlocking system* is a safety-critical system controlling the track side equipment and movement of trains in a railway network such that train collisions and derailments are avoided. Current computer-based interlocking systems usually have a *centralised* design, but in a few cases, as for instance described in [8], the control has been *geographically distributed* to processors deployed at the sensors and actuators (e.g. points) along the track layout and to onboard train control computers. One of the motivating factors for this is the lower cost, making it available as a solution for small, local railway networks, cf. the discussion in [3,8].

To verify the safety of *distributed* railway interlocking systems is even more challenging than for centralised systems. For centralised interlocking systems, there is a global notion of the state of the system, which can be observed by the control computer to make interlocking decisions. In contrast to this, in the

© Springer International Publishing AG, part of Springer Nature 2018
K. Havelund et al. (Eds.): FM 2018, LNCS 10951, pp. 277–293, 2018.
https://doi.org/10.1007/978-3-319-95582-7_16

geographically distributed approach, where each train is equipped with a train control computer, and additional control components are distributed throughout the railway network, the interlocking data must be distributed (but also duplicated to some extent) in the different control components. Furthermore, the control components must collaborate in order to take safe decisions, so communication between the control computers must be introduced. This adds additional threads which would not be present in a centralised system. Hence, the distribution of control gives new challenges for the safety verification.

Using formal methods for the verification of distributed interlocking systems is a natural choice, as formal methods are strongly recommended by the CENELEC standard EN 50128 [2] for safety-critical railway control components and have proved useful for many applications. For instance, Haxthausen and Peleska demonstrated this in [8], where they modelled and verified the distributed interlocking system considered in this paper. For this they used the RAISE Specification Language, RSL [11], and the RAISE theorem prover, respectively.

Theorem proving, as used in [8], handles complex systems very well, but the proof derivation process is very time consuming, as it must be directed by a human. Furthermore, theorem provers are often unable to give counter-examples when a proof fails. With model checking, the verification process is fully automated, and if some asserted property is not satisfied in some state of the system, the model checking tool will produce a counter-example, usually showing the path to that state. The path can then be investigated in order to discover the unintended behaviour. Therefore, in this paper, we will investigate the use of *model checking* for verifying the considered interlocking system.

1.2   Contribution

The main contribution of the paper is a method for modelling and verifying a distributed system by stepwise specification and model checking, and the application of this method to a distributed railway interlocking system.

For the system specification the method uses an extension of RSL, called RSL-SAL [10], which allows to specify systems by state transition system models. In contrast to this, the work in [8] used the RSL process algebra to specify the final model of the system. The formal verification is now performed using the SAL symbolic model checker which is a backend to RSL-SAL. The challenge of capturing the system behaviour in appropriate detail was tackled by using *stepwise development* of state transition system models. This approach is novel in the context of RAISE.

1.3   Related Work

Formal verification of interlocking systems via *model checking* is an active research topic, investigated by several research groups, see e.g., [5,9,13,14] mostly focusing on *centralised* interlocking. In [6,7] RSL-SAL and SAL was also used for modelling and verifying an interlocking system, but this was a centralised (relay) interlocking system, and in that work no stepwise development was used.

In [4], a geographically distributed railway interlocking system was formally modelled and verified using UMC instead of RSL-SAL and SAL. The control protocol presented in [4] radically differs from the one considered in our case study: in [4], full train routes are allocated before trains start moving. This is done using a two-phase commit protocol for determining agreement between the control components. The control protocol in our case study allows trains to allocate each section of their routes separately, which allows for greater flexibility, since train routes can be interleaved to a greater extent.

1.4   Paper Overview

First Sect. 2 gives a brief introduction to the case study: the engineering concept of the considered distributed interlocking system and an overview of the formal development. Then, the following sections (Sects. 3, 4 and 5) give an overview of the generic model specifications and the development steps between them. The verification of model instances is described in Sect. 6. Finally, Sect. 7 gives a conclusion and states ideas for future work.

2   Case Study

2.1   Engineering Concept

The *control strategy* of the system must ensure the safety of the system by preventing the derailment and collision of trains. In this engineering concept, safety is achieved by only allowing one train on each track segment at the same time and ensuring that points are locked in correct position while trains are passing them. To this end, trains must *reserve* track segments before entering them and *lock* points in correct position before passing them.

The *control components* of the system are responsible for implementing the control strategy. Each train is equipped with a *train control computer*. In the railway network, several *switchboxes* are distributed, each controlling a single point or an end point of the network. These components communicate with each other in order to collaboratively control the system. Each control component has its own, local state space for keeping track of the relevant information. As can be seen from Fig. 1, each of the train control computers has information about the train's route (a list of track segments) with its switch boxes, the train position, and the reservations and locks it has achieved. Each switchbox has information about its associated sensor (used to detect whether a train is passing the critical area close to the point), which segments are connected at its associated point (if any), for which train the point is locked (if any), and for which train each of the associated segments is reserved (if any).

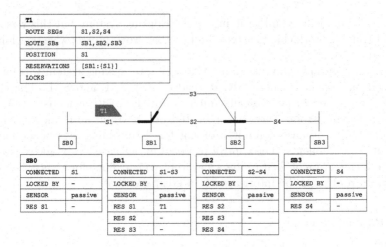

Fig. 1. An example system.

The basic idea of the control strategy is as follows:

1. *Permisson to enter a segment:* For a train control computer (TCC) to decide whether it is legal to enter the next segment of its route, the TCC must observe its local state space and check whether it has the needed reservations and locks. More precisely, the following must hold:
   - the next segment must have been reserved for the train at the two upcoming switchboxes, and
   - the point must have been switched in the direction for the train route and locked for the train at the next switchbox.

   In the scenario shown in Fig. 1, for the train $T1$, this means that it must have reservations for segment $s2$ at both the switchboxes $SB1$ and $SB2$, and a lock for the point at $SB1$, before it can be allowed to enter $s2$.

2. *Making reservations and locks:* Reservations and locks are made by the trains by issuing requests to the relevant switchboxes. Depending on its local state, a switchbox may or may not comply with a request from a train. The switchbox can only fulfil a segment reservation request if the segment is not already reserved at the switchbox. Similarly, a switchbox can only lock a point (after potentially having switched the point in the direction for the train route), if the point is not already locked. Additionally, a request for locking a point can only be made if the train has reservations for the two segments in its route on either side of the point to be locked. In the scenario shown in Fig. 1, for the train $T1$, this means that it must have a reservation for segments $s1$ and $s2$ at the switchbox $SB1$, before it can request to lock the point at $SB1$.

   If a switchbox can meet a request, it will update its state space accordingly. In any case, the switchbox will send a response to the train, based on which the train can determine whether the request has been met and, thereby, whether the train should update its state space as well.

3. *Release of reservations and locks:* When a train has passed the critical area of a switchbox, both the lock and reservations for that train at that switchbox are *released* in the state space of the train as well as in the state space of the switchbox.

2.2   Overview of Formal Development

The modelling process follows a *stepwise development* paradigm, where several different models are developed, going from a very abstract view of the real-world system to a more concrete view. In this way, three specifications of generic state transition system models were developed.

The first is an abstract model capturing the system behaviour, but abstracting away from the explicit communication between the control components. Hence, e.g. a *reservation* event is treated as an atomic event, abstracting away from the intermediate steps issuing requests and acknowledgements. However, it was known from the start that these intermediate steps should later be explicitly modelled. The starting point is thus a stage where there is already an idea of needing *event decomposition*. This affects the specification of the first model, where the auxiliary functions for checking and updating the state spaces of the control components are divided into functionality for train control computers and switchboxes, respectively.

The second model is developed using event decomposition for collaborative events (i.e. events involving communication between control components) of the first model in order to model the steps of the communication protocols for such events. At this modelling level, the transition rules are specified in a property-oriented manner, resulting in the least restrictive possible behaviour of the system. This allows for several different legal orders of events.

The third model is an example of restricting the second model to a more specific control protocol for each collaborative event inducing a specific order of events. This is achieved by restricting the guards of relevant transition rules, such that the corresponding transitions can only be executed in fewer cases. Thus the set of paths of the state transition system of the third model is a subset of that of the second model.

The specified system models are generic, i.e. without any configuration data describing the railway network and the control components with their data. To verify the models by model checking, they must be instantiated with configuration data. The instantiation and verification will be described in Sect. 6, while the generic models will be explained in Sects. 3, 4, and 5.

3   First Model

The specification of the first (generic) model can be divided into several different parts:

- Types and values for the static configuration data and dynamic data.
- Functions describing wellformedness and consistency of configuration data.

- Functions describing the safety of the system.
- Guard and state updater functions.
- State variables.
- Transition system rules.

Static Configuration Data. The static configuration data consist of the data for the railway network, which includes information about which segments and switchboxes are in the network, and data about which trains are in the network.

Unique identifiers for segments, switchboxes, and trains of the system are given by types. These are not further specified in the generic model, but are intended to be defined by variant types enumerating the concrete identifiers when the model is instantiated. Train identifiers must at least include the special value *t_none*.

type
  Segment,
  TrainID == t_none | _,
  SwitchboxID

The network layout describing how the segments of the system are connected is given by a value *network* of an explicitly defined type *Network*. The *network* value is not specified further in the generic model, but is intended to be explicitly defined by a constant when the model is instantiated.

type Network = ...
value
  network : Network

Types for Dynamic Data. Besides configuring the system with static configuration data, the system must also be configured with initial values for dynamic data which changes e.g. when trains move. The types specified are the ones needed for each of the fields in the state spaces of the control components. For example, the type for the reservations of a switchbox is called *SbResMap* and is a mapping from segment identifiers to train identifiers:

type SbResMap = Segment $\overrightarrow{m}$ TrainID

There is a similar map for reservations stored in a train:

type TResMap = SwitchboxID $\overrightarrow{m}$ Segment-**set**

For modelling the *state spaces* of each control component, types of the form *TrainID* $\overrightarrow{m}$ [*value type*] and *SwitchboxID* $\overrightarrow{m}$ [*value type*] have been defined. For example, the reservations for each of the switchboxes are saved in a variable of the type

type SbResState = SwitchboxID $\overrightarrow{m}$ SbResMap,

and the reservations for the trains are saved in a variable of the type

type TResState = TrainID $\overrightarrow{m}$ TResMap

Using maps from component identifiers to state values allows for the specification of the local state of each component.[1]

Wellformedness, Consistency and Safety Functions. The functions describing wellformedness and consistency of configuration data and the functions describing the safety of the system are used when formulating the transition system assertions, i.e. the properties which the instantiations of the models are checked against.

Guard and State Updater Functions. The guard and state updater functions are also used when formulating the transition system. They are used in the transition system rules, where each rule consists of a guard and a collection of effects, i.e. state updates. An example of a guard function is the following, *sb_can_reserve*, which is used to determine, from the point of view of a switchbox, whether a reservation can be made. This should be the case if the switchbox is associated with the segment to be reserved and the segment is not reserved already by any train at the switchbox.

sb_can_reserve : SbResMap × Segment → **Bool**
sb_can_reserve (res ,seg) ≡ seg ∈ **dom**(res) ∧ res(seg) = t_none

The parameters of the guard function are the segment which should be reserved (*seg*) and the reservations of the switchbox itself (*res*).

An example of an updater function is the following *sb_res*, which updates the reservations of a switchbox:

sb_res : SbResMap × TrainID × Segment → SbResMap
sb_res (res , tid ,seg) ≡ res † [seg ↦ tid]

The parameters for the updater function consist of the data component, i.e. the reservations of the switchbox, (*res*) to which changes should be made, and the data necessary for the change, i.e. the train (*tid*) for which the segment (*seg*) should be reserved.

For the reservation event, there is a similar guard function *t_can_reserve* which is used to determine, from the point of view of a train control computer, whether a reservation can be made and there is an updater function *t_res* to be used to update the train state.

For other events *e* there are similar guard functions and updater functions.

State Variables. Several local variables are declared in the transition system. The initial values of these determine the initial state of the transition system. In the generic model, the variables are uninitialised, so they must be given values when the model is instantiated for model checking.

The variables are specified using the types for dynamic data mentioned earlier. There is a variable for each field of the control component state spaces. For

---

[1] As the model is generic, the number of components is not yet known, so we can't specify a variable for each component holding its local state. Instead we use maps as shown above.

example, the variables for the switchbox reservations and for the train reservations are specified as follows:

local sbRes : SbResState, tRes : TResState

Transition System Rules. The rules of the transition system define the possible events (state transitions) of the system. A transition rule consists of a guard and an effect, where the guard is a predicate over the state variables determining for which states the effect of the rule can be applied, and the effect of the rule is a collection of state variable updates. In the state variable updates, primed versions of the variables refer to the variables in the resulting post state. Transition rules can be combined by non-deterministic choice ($\Box$). Furthermore, a non-deterministic choice over a set of rules of the same form, only differing by a parameter x of finite type T, can be expressed as ($\Box\ x : T \bullet rule$), where x occurs in the rule *rule*. It is a shorthand for writing a non-deterministic choice between all rules that can be obtained by substituting a value $v : T$ for x in *rule*.

In this first model, for each event e, there is a rule of the following form:

($\Box$ sbid : SwitchboxID, tid : TrainID, ... $\bullet$
  [rule_name]
  t_can_e (...) $\wedge$ sb_can_e (...) ==>
    tData$'$(tid) = t_e (...), sbData$'$(sbid) = sb_e (...))

the ellipsis in the first line represents any extra values needed for that particular event; *tData* and *sbData* are place-holders for variables in the train control computer state space and the switchbox state space, respectively, changed by the transition (multiple variables from each state space may be changed by one transition); *t_e* and *sb_e* are place-holders for updater functions returning the new value for the variables.

In case an event is not collaborative, but e.g. a pure train event like *move*, the format of the rule is reduced by removing the quantification over *tid* or *sbid*, respectively, and the guard and updates for the *tid* or *sbid* component, respectively.

As an example of a transition system rule, the rule for the *reservation* event is specified as follows:

($\Box$ sbid : SwitchboxID, tid : TrainID, seg : Segment $\bullet$
  [res]
  t_can_reserve (tSboxes(tid),sbid,seg,tRoute(tid),tRes(tid)) $\wedge$
  sb_can_reserve (sbRes(sbid),seg) ==>
    tRes$'$(tid) = t_res(tRes(tid),sbid,seg),
    sbRes$'$(sbid) = sb_res(sbRes(sbid),tid,seg))

where *tRoute(tid)* and *tSboxes(tid)* give the segments and switchboxes of the route of train *tid*, respectively, and *tRes(tid)* and *sbRes(sbid)* give the reservations of train *tid* and switchbox *sbid*, respectively.

As can be seen, two guard functions are used to determine whether the reservation can be made: only if both the train and the switchbox agree, the event can take place. The effect of the rule is specified using two updater functions to update the reservations of both the train and the switchbox in question.

4   Second Model

In the second step, the model has been refined to explicitly model a communication scheme between the control components of the system. The collaborative events of the system are decomposed into multiple sub-events, such that a simple request-acknowledge protocol scheme is modelled. The event refinement has been chosen to be atomic (i.e. all the sub-events of an event have to be completed before a new event can happen) in order to keep the state space as small as possible. It can be shown that removing the atomicity requirements from the resulting model M_2 leads to a model M_2' which is behaviourally equivalent to M_2 with respect to the externally (physical) observable state, i.e. train positions and point positions. This is because the internal protocol states of different communication events are disjoint, so that every set of interleaved communication transactions has an outcome which is equivalent to that of a serialised execution of the same transactions in some specific order. Hence, any safety conditions proved for M_2 will also hold for M_2'.

In the communication protocols, the train control computers are the initiating party, issuing requests to the switchboxes. When a switchbox receives a request, it decides whether it is able to comply with the request and, depending on this, sends either a positive or negative acknowledgement to the train. If the switchbox can comply with the request, it will also update its state space accordingly. Similarly, when a train control computer receives a positive acknowledgement, it will update its state space accordingly. If the switchbox cannot comply with the request, neither the state space of the switchbox nor of the train control computer will be updated.

To model the communication between the control components, the collaborative events of the system have been decomposed in the following manner. For each collaborative event e, the single transition rule in the first model is now replaced with several separate sub-rules:

- req_e, which is the initiation of the event. This corresponds to a train control computer issuing a request to a specific switchbox with any relevant information for the event in question.
- ack_e, which is the positive acknowledgement rule for the switchbox. This corresponds to the switchbox accepting the request, changing its own state space accordingly and issuing the positive acknowledgement to the train control computer in question.
- end_e, which concludes the event. This corresponds to the train control computer receiving the positive acknowledgement signal from the switchbox and updating its own state space accordingly.
- $nack\_e$, which is the negative acknowledgement rule for the switchbox. This corresponds to the switchbox not being able to comply with the request, and therefore issuing a negative acknowledgement to the train control computer in question.

– *end_nack_e* is an auxiliary action for "consuming" the negative acknowledgement from a switchbox and not changing the state space of the train control computer.

To keep track of the messages sent between the control components, several variables have been added to the model:

Interface variables are used to record whether a message is a *request*, an *acknowledgement* or a *negative acknowledgement*, and to record who the sender and receiver are:

req : TrainID $\xrightarrow{m}$ SwitchboxID, −− *request variable*
ack : SwitchboxID $\xrightarrow{m}$ TrainID, −− *positive acknowledge variable*
nack : SwitchboxID $\xrightarrow{m}$ TrainID, −− *negative acknowledge variable*

For instance, *ack(sb)* = *t* models a *positive acknowlegment* from a switchbox *sb* to a train *t*.

Data variables are used for storing data sent as part of a request. For example, for a *reservation* request, the following variable[2] is used to store the segment to be reserved:

tmpSeg : Segment

Event variables are used to keep track of which type of the collaborative events is currently ongoing (if any). There is a Boolean variable for each kind of collaborative event. For example, for the *reservation* event, the following variable is used:[3]

resEvent : **Bool**

The variable is set to true whenever a train control computer requests a reservation of a segment at some switchbox, and set to false when the train control computer has received an acknowledgement (either positive or negative).

As an example of how the new rules of the transition system are specified and how the additional variables are used, consider the rules for requesting, (positive) acknowledging and concluding the *reservation* event:

($\Box$ sbid : SwitchboxID, tid : TrainID, seg : Segment •
[req_res]
  ¬resEvent ∧ ¬switchLockEvent ∧
  t_can_reserve (tSboxes(tid),sbid,seg,tRoute(tid),tRes(tid)) ∧
  tid ∉ **dom**(req) ==>
    req$'$ = req † [tid ↦ sbid],
        resEvent$'$ = **true**,

---

[2] Since only one event should be allowed at the same time in this model, it is sufficient to store a segment rather than a map from trains to segments, where for each train *t*, *tmpSeg(t)* could hold data sent by *t*.
[3] For this variable there is a similar comment as for *tmpSeg*.

$$tmpSeg' = seg)$$

⫿
(⫿ sbid : SwitchboxID, tid : TrainID •
[ack_res]
  tid ∈ **dom**(req) ∧ req(tid) = sbid ∧ resEvent ∧
  sb_can_reserve(sbRes(sbid),tmpSeg) ==>
    req' = req \ {tid},
    ack' = ack † [sbid ↦ tid],
    sbRes'(sbid) = sb_res(sbRes(sbid),tid,tmpSeg))

⫿
(⫿ sbid : SwitchboxID, tid : TrainID •
[end_res]
  sbid ∈ **dom**(ack) ∧ ack(sbid) = tid ∧ resEvent ==>
    tRes'(tid) = t_res(tRes(tid),sbid,tmpSeg),
    ack' = ack \ {sbid},
    resEvent' = **false**)

The *req_res* rule can be applied when the system is idle, i.e. when no events
are ongoing[4], when the reservation is legal from the train control computer's
point of view and the train control computer has not already sent a request. As
its effect, the rule sets the request variable for the train identifier and switchbox
identifier in question, enables the *reservation event variable* and sets a data
variable to the segment to be reserved.

The *ack_res* rule can be applied when a request has been issued, the reservation event variable is enabled and the *reservation* event is legal from the point
of view of the switchbox. As its effect, the rule removes the issued request, issues
a positive acknowledgement and updates the state space of the switchbox with
the reservation (here, the segment data variable from before is used).

Finally, the *end_res* rule can be applied when a positive acknowledgement has
been received and the *reservation event variable* is enabled. As its effect, the rule
updates the state space of the train control computer (and again uses the segment
data variable), removes the acknowledgement and disables the *reservation event
variable*.

There are two additional rules (not shown here) for expressing the sending
of a negative acknowledgement from a switchbox to a train and for the train
receiving it, respectively.

Relation to the First Model. Instances of this model are clearly able to
simulate all possible events of the corresponding instances of the first generic
model, which was the intention with this step in which no behaviour should be
lost. Furthermore, instances of the first model are able to simulate all atomic
events of the corresponding instances of this second generic model.

---

[4] It is this condition which enforces the atomic event refinement.

5   Third Model

The third model has been restricted to model a *just-in-time* allocation principle. In the previous models, any order of legal events was possible. This means, for example, that nothing was preventing a train from reserving the last segment of its route as the first event (other than if the segment was already reserved, of course). This third model should now specify a control strategy, stating that a train must only make reservations of the next upcoming segment in its route (at the two upcoming switchboxes of its route), and must only lock the point at the next upcoming switchbox. This strategy is just one of many choices, and is used to demonstrate the possibility and technique of restricting the protocol of the second model to enforce events to happen in a more specific order.

As mentioned, the train control computers are the initiating party for collaborative events. Therefore, the desired restriction can be achieved by strengthening the guard functions used by the train control computers. This limits the amount of possible events such that they match the steps of the control strategy.

The restriction of the guard functions is accomplished by using the following pattern. If the guard function was previously of the form

t_can_e : ... → **Bool**
t_can_e (...) ≡ ...

then the new, restricted guard function is of the form

restricted_t_can_e : ... → **Bool**
restricted_t_can_e (...) ≡
    t_can_e (...) ∧ new_restriction_1 ∧ ... ∧ new_restriction_n

The extra conjunct(s) can, in some cases, lead to the possibility of the properties of *t_can_e* to be reduced. This is the case when one of the new restrictions implies (parts of) the properties found in the *can_e* guard function.

For the *reservation* event, the restrictions to be included in the updated guard function consist of only allowing a train t to reserve a segment *seg* at a switchbox *sb*, if (1) *sb* is one of the two upcoming switchboxes of the route of t and (2) the segment *seg* is the next segment with respect to the train's position and route.

Hence, the restricted guard function is specified as follows:

restricted_t_can_reserve : SboxMap × SwitchboxID × SwitchboxID × Segment ×
    Route × Position × ResMap → **Bool**
restricted_t_can_reserve (sboxes,sbid,nextsb,segment,route,pos,res) ≡
    t_can_reserve (sboxes,sbid,segment,route,res) ∧
    (sbid = nextsb ∨ (nextsb ∈ **dom**(sboxes) ∧ sbid = sboxes(nextsb))) ∧
    is_single_pos (pos) ∧ seg(pos) ∈ **dom**(route) ∧ segment = route(seg(pos))

In this case it turned out that some of the added sub-properties imply some of the sub-properties in *t_can_reserve(sboxes,sbid,segment,route,res)*, so we simplified the conjunction.

The transition rule for *req_res* is obtained from the second model by replacing *t_can_reserve(tSboxes(tid),sbid,seg,tRoute(tid),tRes(tid))* with *restricted_t_can_reserve(tSboxes(tid),sbid,tNextsb(tid),seg,tRoute(tid), tPos(tid),tRes(tid))*.

Relation to Second Model. Instances of the second model can clearly simulate all possible behaviours of the corresponding instances of this third generic model.

6 Verification

At each of the three specification steps, model instances of the generic model at that level have been verified and tested in several different ways, as explained below, in order to get confidence in the correctness of the generic models. Later, if new network and train configurations are considered, the idea is that the final generic model should be instantiated with that data and model checked.

Note that we have not formally verified a formal refinement/simulation relation between the models, which would require considerably higher verification effort, but only discussed this informally in the previous sections.

6.1 Model Checking

Each of the three generic models have been instantiated with several typical network layouts and a collection of trains. The network layouts and train routes should be chosen such that they include cases where trains need access to the same shared resources (e.g. track segments). In this paper we consider the configuration shown in Fig. 2. In this network two trains are shown in their initial position and the coloured lines show their routes. As it can be seen, the two trains have routes passing the same station in opposite direction. Another typical case we have considered is one, where two trains have routes passing the same line between two stations in opposite direction.

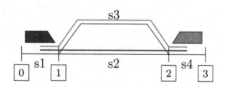

Fig. 2. An example system configuration with two trains and their routes.

After having instantiated the three generic models with configuration data for our example, the three resulting model instances were model checked against several assertions expressed in Linear Temporal Logic (LTL) using the symbolic model checking tool of *Symbolic Analysis Laboratory* (SAL) [1]. The properties asserted were as follows.

- *Safety* properties, stating the absence of derailments and collisions of trains in all reachable states. The absence of collisions is stated as follows, using an auxiliary function named *no_collide*:

[no_collide]   TS ⊢ (∀tid1,tid2 : TrainID •
    G(tid1 ≠ tid2 ∧ tid1 ≠ t_none ∧ tid2 ≠ t_none ⇒ no_collide(tid1,tid2,tPos)))

where *no_collide*(*tid1, tid2, tPos*) expresses that the intersection of the segments of the positions of *tid1* and *tid2* is empty, i.e. the trains are not both occupying the same section. *tPos* is a state variable storing the positions of all the trains. Similarly, the absence of derailments is stated as follows:

[no_derail] TS ⊢ (∀tid : TrainID •
    G(¬is_single_pos(tPos(tid)) ⇒ no_derail(tPos(tid),sbConn))),

where ¬ *is_single_pos*(*tPos*(*tid*)) expresses that the train is passing a point (is not on a single segment) and *no_derail*(*tPos*(*tid*), *sbConn*) expresses that the train's position *tPos*(*tid*) fits the position of the point. *sbConn* is a state variable storing the point positions at all the switchboxes.
- *Consistency* properties, stating the consistency of distributed data, e.g. that reservations saved in the train control computer state spaces are in agreement with those from the switchbox state spaces, in all reachable states.
- *Wellformedness* properties, stating the wellformedness of configuration data wrt. the static configuration data in all reachable states.
- *Liveness* properties, stating that events are always completed. This only applies to the second and third model. For example, the fact that the reservation event is always completed is stated as follows:

[finish_res]   TS ⊢ G(resEvent ⇒ F(¬resEvent))

Note that the result for such properties is only sound if there are no deadlocks.
- *Reachability* properties, expressing that there is at least one possible schedule where all trains reach their destination. These have been verified by contradiction: by model checking properties stating that the trains do *not* all eventually arrive at their destination:

[not_all_trains_arrive]   TS ⊢ G(¬(∀tid : TrainID •tPos(tid) = dest(tid)))

where *dest*(*tid*) is the destination position of train *tid*. This property is expected to be false and should generate a counter example showing a trace where all trains arrive at their destination.

All the desired properties were successfully verified for the three model instances. (In particular, the property [*not_all_trains_arrive*] gave in each case, as desired, rise to a counter example demonstrating that there exists at least one schedule, where all trains arrive at their destination.)

Furthermore, we applied successfully the SAL deadlock checker to the three model instances to ensure *absence of deadlocks*.

Note that even if invariant properties for a model instance of the first generic model has been model checked, we need to model check them again for the corresponding instance of the second generic model as there are new intermediate states we want to be sure are safe.

Note also that in principle, the model checking of invariant properties for a model instance of the third generic model should not be necessary when they have been model checked for the corresponding instance of the second generic model (as all behaviours of the third model are simulated by behaviours in the second model), but since we made some simplifications of the guards in the third generic model, we also model checked the properties for the model instance of the third model.

6.2   Other Verification Activities

Before beginning the process of symbolic model checking different model instances against the desired properties, other tools were used to gain confidence in the correctness of the function and transition system rule specifications.

– *Testing of functions:* Important functions (e.g. for expressing safety and consistency properties, which are used in the transition system assertions) were tested using the RSL test case construct. The functions were validated to ensure that the assertions to be verified in the model checking process are correct. This testing activity was only needed in the first specification step, as no new functions were used in the later steps.
– *Bounded model checking:* The transition rules of the model instances were tested using the SAL bounded model checker, which only explores the paths in the transition system to a certain, given depth. Therefore, attempting to verify the properties stated above with the bounded model checker reveals bugs much faster.

7   Conclusion and Future Work

In this paper we have shown a method to stepwise develop a generic state transition system model of a real-world distributed railway interlocking system and verify safety and consistency properties of instances of these models by model checking. This method could also carry over to other, similar applications.

The models are expressed in an extension to RSL: RSL-SAL [10]. Although stepwise development of state transition systems is well known from other languages, it is novel for RSL. The stepwise development has shown to be very useful: Firstly, it allows the initial specification to abstract away from details and complexity which can be added later in a development step. This means that a simpler model expressing essential system behaviour can be developed first without worrying about concrete details. This eases the modelling process. It also has the advantage that essential system behaviour can be verified already at this stage, allowing the developer to gain confidence in the specification, before adding details that would most likely increase the time and memory usage of the verification. Secondly, the idea of letting the second model be so general (e.g. without having a restriction on the ordering of reservations that a train should send) that it can be refined to several different concrete behaviours (e.g. with specific orderings of reservations) by restricting the guards is useful as the invariant properties which are shown to be satisfied by the general model will also be satisfied by any restrictions. In this way one can create a *library* of different families of models, and variants of different control protocols can be explored and compared.

For the model checking, the SAL symbolic model checker was used, just for a proof of concept of our method, but other back-ends can be used as well.

In future work we plan to experiment with other model checking techniques, e.g. SAT-based k-induction, and other back-ends, e.g. RT-Tester [12], in order to find the most efficient verification technique and apply these also to larger networks. In another case study [13], RT-Tester was used to perform k-induction in order to prove a centralised interlocking system and turned out to be very efficient and scale up to big networks. We also plan to extend the models with additional operations for cancelling reservations and for changing the direction of a train.

Acknowledgements. The authors would like to express their gratitude to Jan Peleska from whom the case study originates and together with whom the second author had the great pleasure to verify the same case study by theorem proving [8]. We would also like to thank him and the reviewers for very useful comments to drafts of this paper.

References

1. Symbolic Analysis Laboratory, SAL (2001). http://sal.csl.sri.com
2. CENELEC European Committee for Electrotechnical Standardization. EN 50128:2011 - Railway applications - Communications, signalling and processing systems - Software for railway control and protection systems (2011)
3. Fantechi, A., Gnesi, S., Haxthausen, A., van de Pol, J., Roveri, M., Treharne, H.: SaRDIn - a safe reconfigurable distributed interlocking. In: Proceedings 11th World Congress on Railway Research (WCRR 2016). Ferrovie dello Stato Italiane, Milano (2016)
4. Fantechi, A., Haxthausen, A.E., Nielsen, M.B.R.: Model checking geographically distributed interlocking systems using UMC. In: 2017 25th Euromicro International Conference on Parallel, Distributed and Network-based Processing (PDP), pp. 278–286 (2017)
5. Ferrari, A., Magnani, G., Grasso, D., Fantechi, A.: Model checking interlocking control tables. In: Schnieder, E., Tarnai, G. (eds.) FORMS/FORMAT 2010, pp. 107–115. Springer, Heidelberg (2010). https://doi.org/10.1007/978-3-642-14261-1_11
6. Haxthausen, A.E., Automated generation of formal safety conditions from railway interlocking tables. Int. J. Softw. Tools Technol. Transf. (STTT) **16**(6), 713–726 (2014). Special Issue on Formal Methods for Railway Control Systems
7. Haxthausen, A.E., Le Bliguet, M., Kjær, A.A.: Modelling and verification of relay interlocking systems. In: Choppy, C., Sokolsky, O. (eds.) Monterey Workshop 2008. LNCS, vol. 6028, pp. 141–153. Springer, Heidelberg (2010). https://doi.org/10.1007/978-3-642-12566-9_8

8. Haxthausen, A.E., Peleska, J.: Formal development and verification of a distributed railway control system. IEEE Trans. Softw. Eng. **26**, 687–701 (2000)
9. James, P., et al.: Verification of scheme plans using CSP||B. In: Counsell, Steve, Núñez, Manuel (eds.) SEFM 2013. LNCS, vol. 8368, pp. 189–204. Springer, Cham (2014). https://doi.org/10.1007/978-3-319-05032-4_15
10. Perna, J.I., George, C.: Model checking RAISE applicative specifications. In: Proceedings of the Fifth IEEE International Conference on Software Engineering and Formal Methods, pp. 257–268. IEEE Computer Society Press (2007)
11. The RAISE Language Group: George, C., Haff, P., Havelund, K., Haxthausen, A.E., Milne, R., Nielsen, C.B., Prehn, S., Wagner, K.R.: The RAISE Specification Language. The BCS Practitioners Series. Prentice Hall Int., Englewood Cliffs (1992)
12. Verified Systems International GmbH. RT-Tester Model-Based Test Case and Test Data Generator - RTT-MBT - User Manual (2013). http://www.verified.de
13. Vu, L.H., Haxthausen, A.E., Peleska, J.: Formal modelling and verification of interlocking systems featuring sequential release. Sci. Comput. Programm. **133**(2), 91–115 (2017). https://doi.org/10.1016/j.scico.2016.05.010
14. Winter, K.: Model checking railway interlocking systems. In: Proceedings of Twenty-Fifth Australasian Computer Science Conference (ACSC 2002), pp. 303–310 (2002)

Resource-Aware Design for Reliable Autonomous Applications with Multiple Periods

Rongjie Yan[1], Di Zhu[3,4], Fan Zhang[1,2], Yiqi Lv[1,2], Junjie Yang[3,4], and Kai Huang[3,4(✉)]

[1] State Key Laboratory of Computer Science, ISCAS, Beijing, China
{yrj,zhangf,lvyq}@ios.ac.cn
[2] University of Chinese Academy of Sciences, Beijing, China
[3] Key Laboratory of Machine Intelligence and Advanced Computing, Sun Yat-sen University, Ministry of Education, Guangzhou, China
{zhud5,yangjj27}@mail2.sysu.edu.cn, huangk36@mail.sysu.edu.cn
[4] School of Data and Computer Science, Sun Yat-sen University, Guangzhou, China

Abstract. Reliability is the most important design issue for current autonomous vehicles. How to guarantee reliability and reduce hardware cost is key for the design of such complex control systems intertwined with scenario-related multi-period timing behaviors. The paper presents a reliability and resource-aware design framework for embedded implementation of such autonomous applications, where each scenario may have its own timing constraints. The constraints are formalized with the consideration of different redundancy based fault-tolerant techniques and software to hardware allocation choices, which capture the static and various causality relations of such systems. Both exact and heuristic-based methods have been implemented to derive the lower bound of hardware usage, in terms of processor, for the given reliability requirement. The case study on a realistic autonomous vehicle controller demonstrates the effectiveness and feasibility of the framework.

1 Introduction

As the automotive industry is striving for autonomous vehicles through intensive sensing, computation, and communication, a larger number of more complex control applications with guaranteed performances are expected to be on board. Such complex control applications are usually composed of a set of functions that are characterized by various timing behaviors, e.g., environment constraints, sensing/acting frequencies, or various worst case execution times of

This work has been partly funded by the National Key Basic Research (973) Program of China under Grant No. 2014CB340701, Key Research Program of Frontier Sciences, CAS, under Grant No. QYZDJ-SSW-JSC036, the CAS-INRIA major project under No. GJHZ1844, the National Science Foundation of China under Grant No. U1435220, No. U1711265, and the Fundamental Research Funds for the Central Universities under grant No. 17lgjc40.

© Springer International Publishing AG, part of Springer Nature 2018
K. Havelund et al. (Eds.): FM 2018, LNCS 10951, pp. 294–311, 2018.
https://doi.org/10.1007/978-3-319-95582-7_17

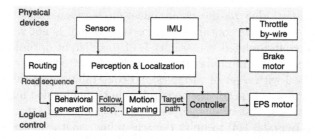

Fig. 1. Functionality of an autonomous controller

software components. For these kinds of on-board control applications, reliability is the most critical design issue, as any failure will incur catastrophes. Since algorithm development for these control applications is well-established, system-level mechanisms are mandatory to mitigate the impact of transient faults to ensure system reliability, even though hardware becomes more reliable.

Reliability, however, comes with costs. In principle, system-level mechanisms always adopt active or passive redundancy based fault-tolerant techniques [10]. We consider active redundancy as the major technique to guarantee system reliability, which replicates software tasks into multiple copies. Those copies can be executed on the same processor (temporal redundancy), or distributed to multiple processors (spatial redundancy). In the case of temporal redundancy, additional latency will be introduced which may hamper the response time of the applications. In the case of spatial redundancy techniques, additional hardware is needed to accommodate the replicas. The additionally imposed hardware has to be minimal as automotive industry is particularly sensitive in terms of hardware costs [13]. Therefore, safety-critical control components in automobiles have to be carefully designed, to deploy control components and their redundancy into a given hardware architecture by considering all the constraints.

To motivate our work, let us consider an autonomous automobile controller shown in Fig. 1, whose role is to extract the target path derived from motion planning according to collected information from physical devices, and to control low level actuators to track the path. The frequency of path tracking is usually higher to follow environment updating. Meanwhile, the frequencies of every functionality in different scenarios, such as going straight and making u-turns, are also different. Since, for example, making a u-turn is generally harder than going straight, a higher frequency is required to minimize the tracking error. We expect to adopt minimal number of homogeneous processors for its embedded implementation, to meet reliability guarantees and all timing constraints.

To guarantee reliability and reduce hardware cost at the same time is not easy for such complex control systems intertwined with scenario-related multi-period timing behaviors as well as fault-tolerant mechanisms. The reason is multifold. First, scenario-related multi-period timing behaviors incur more design and implementation considerations: (1) timing constraints are scenario-related, and the implementation should accommodate all scenarios; (2) various data dependencies exist, due to the communication between tasks with different periods. Second, hardware optimization for such design is not straightforward: (1) different scenario-related constraints lead to different optimization results; (2) the goal of processor minimization cannot be formatted as an expression that can be calculated with a set of variables and constraints, because it is regarded as a fixed parameter to encode the constraints in the embedded implementation.

To deal with the first challenge, we adopt *hyper period* (the least common multiple of all periods) [14] to unify the scheduling length (makespan) for software to hardware deployment consideration. Meanwhile, we adopt data refreshing technique for communication between tasks with different periods to avoid accessing to empty buffer, where buffered data will not be removed until new data comes and overwrites the old. For the second challenge, to reduce the cost for hardware and the latency for fault tolerance, as well as guaranteeing reliability, we introduce both spatial and temporal redundancy of tasks. Majority fault-free voters are applied to choose the result in majority from multiple replicas, to simplify the implementation. To calculate the least number of required processors, the hardware optimization problem is translated into a satisfiability problem [3], i.e., whether a scheduler satisfying all the constraints exists, with the given number of processors. Then we could provide the result by repeatedly checking the satisfiability problem with various numbers of processors. The method can be employed in various scenarios, and we take the maximum number among the minimized number of processors in various scenarios, such that the implementation is capable of serving all scenarios.

The contributions of the paper are as follows. First, we provide a framework for reliable and resource-aware design of autonomous applications with scenario-related multi-period behaviors, where reducing processor usage is the basis of other resource optimization. Second, we propose an effective method for processor optimization to derive the solution for scenario-related applications. Meanwhile, we present a rule to infer processor usage among various scenarios. We also employ various techniques for solution calculation, such as model checking, constraint solving and heuristic-based methods. The case study on realistic autonomous automobile control systems has demonstrated the feasibility and the effectiveness of our method.

The organization of paper is as follows. Section 2 discusses the related work. Section 3 concretizes the motivating example. We present the related concepts in Sect. 4. Section 5 formalizes the constraints for scenario-related multi-period behaviors and fault-tolerant techniques, and proposes the detailed implementation. Section 6 provides the experimental results on the case study, and Sect. 7 concludes.

2   Related Work

Automotives are classical instances of mixed-critical systems [5]. We concentrate on reliability and resource-aware design for safety-critical parts of these mixed-critical systems.

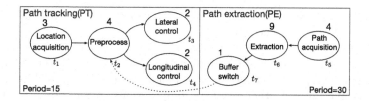

Fig. 2. Task graph of the autonomous controller.

Reliability-aware design is widely acknowledged for safety-critical systems [2,8,9], which is always regarded as an optimization goal in design space exploration. For example, the work in [9] applies temporal and spatial redundancy and optimize the amount of redundancy with genetic algorithms. For automotive systems, a model based strategy is introduced for soft error tolerance techniques under real-time constraints [16]. The work in [12] analyzes transient errors for automotive safety-critical applications. We consider transient faults caused by hardware and regard reliability as the fundamental requirement. Once the reliability can be guaranteed, we try to minimize hardware resources, which is a hot topic for embedded systems [6,15]. The work in [6] considers the optimization of hardware resources for multi-rate automotive control systems on single-processor platforms. Zhao et al. concentrates on stack usage minimization for AUTOSAR models [15]. Our concern is the minimization of processors, which is also the basis of other resource optimizations.

To deal with data communication in multi-period systems, various techniques, such as communication protocols [11] and *lossless buffering* [14], have been introduced. In [14], base period (the *greatest common divisor* of all task periods) is adopted as the length of the scheduling. We apply hyper period of all tasks, and the communication is implemented with data refreshing technique.

3   The Motivating Example

We present in Fig. 2 the structure of the controller[1] mentioned in Sect. 1, whose role is to receive a target path and control low level actuators to track the path. It consists of two components: (1) Path tracking (PT), to track the path according to the input from IMU (Inertial Measurement Unit); (2) Path extraction (PE), to process the target path calculated from a motion planning module.

PT consists of three processes: location acquisition, preprocessing and control instruction output. Once data from IMU is available (t_1), tracking error will be calculated in the preprocessing step (t_2). This step also considers the output from the buffer switch task (t_7) in PE when it is available. Next, lateral control (t_3) and longitudinal control (t_4) run in parallel. In the former, steering angle is calculated by a structure with both feedforward controller and feedback controller,

---

[1] To ease the description, periods, computation costs (labelled on tasks) presented here are simplified.

and supplemented by yaw damping. The latter includes two PID controllers for
throttle and brake, respectively.

PE involves three steps: path acquisition (t_5), extraction (t_6) and buffer
switch (t_7). Once a path is acquired in the first step, it will be delivered to
the extraction step. The extraction step mainly targets for spline interpolation,
radius calculation and other relevant computations. After the extraction, the
double buffer implemented for parallel writing and reading will be updated.

Difference in sampling rates makes the periods of PT and PE different. And
the periods of PT (or PE) are different in various scenarios, such as making a
u-turn, or going straight, though the worst case execution time (WCET) of every
task in all scenarios is the same.

4   Preliminaries

To globally consider multi-period timing behaviors among various subsystems
in a scenario and optimize hardware resources, we first propose the concept of
atypical task graph. Then we present the communication model for multi-period
behaviors. Finally, the fault-tolerant techniques applied here are recapped.

4.1   Atypical Task Graph

Every task can be encoded as a tuple with $t = (id, \delta, w)$, where id is the identity
of the task, δ indicates the cost of worst case execution, and w shows the degree
of importance. A subsystem can be described with an acyclic directed graph
$G_i = \langle T_i, E_i \rangle$ and period of occurrence $\mathcal{P}_i$, where T_i is a finite set of tasks, and
$E_i \subseteq T_i \times T_i$ is a set of precedence relations with $c_e : E_i \to \mathbb{N}$ to indicate the
cost of data transferred between each pair of tasks. A system is composed of a
set of subsystems and the connection maintained by data transfer between these
subsystems. Due to the difference in periods, a task in a subsystem may ignore
the unavailable resource from another subsystem. Consequently, we introduce
strong and weak dependency for the relations of tasks in a global system and
formalize them in the model of *atypical task graph*.

Definition 1. *An atypical task graph is a tuple $\mathcal{G} = \langle T, E \rangle$, where $T = \bigcup_{i=1}^{n} T_i$,*
and $E \subseteq \{T_i \times T_j \mid 1 \leq i, j \leq n\}$, with $G_i = \langle T_i, E_i \rangle \in \mathcal{G}$. For $t_i, t_j \in T$, we have
– strong dependency: if $t_i \to t_j \in E_i$, t_j has to wait for the output of t_i,
– weak dependency: if $t_i \rightsquigarrow t_j \in E \setminus (\bigcup_{i=1}^{n} E_i)$, t_j can ignore the output of t_i.

In the model of Fig. 2, we have $t_7 \rightsquigarrow t_2$ (which is connected with dashed line).
Other precedence relations are strong.

4.2   Communication Model

Communication for weak dependency relation is implemented with buffer refresh
semantics, i.e., the sink task reads the old data in the buffer until it is refreshed.

Given two tasks t_i and t_j from two subsystems with periods $\mathcal{P}_i$ and $\mathcal{P}_j$, respectively, if $t_j \rightsquigarrow t_i$, their communication scenario can be described as the case in Fig. 3, where the arrow shows the direction of data transfer for the weak dependency relation. In the scheduling of Fig. 3, though t_j finishes its execution at time point σ_1, t_i has to wait for additional σ_2 time units to use the refreshed data. Intuitively, the number of iterations for t_i to obtain the refreshed data is in the range of $[\lceil \sigma_1/\mathcal{P}_i \rceil, \lceil \mathcal{P}_j/\mathcal{P}_i \rceil + 1]$, where in the worst case t_j is scheduled in the end of its subsystem.

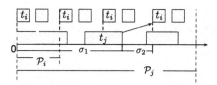

Fig. 3. Communication model for weak dependency relation.

For safety-critical systems, we may expect to reduce the time that one has to wait for the other, i.e., minimize σ_1 in the scheduling of Fig. 3. The optimization is a local scheduling for the corresponding subsystem.

4.3 Active Redundancy Based Fault Tolerance

We consider spatial redundancy, and spatial and temporal mixed redundancy in the paper. Intuitively, temporal redundancy will prolong the execution of tasks, and spatial redundancy will require more hardware resources. The mixture of the two may reduce these disadvantages. Consider the model given in Fig. 2. When three replicas exist for t_2 and t_6, respectively, we present two schedulers in Fig. 4 with two redundancy strategies, where applying pure temporal redundancy violates timing constraints and is ignored. In the case of spatial redundancy shown in Fig. 4(a), four processors are required to satisfy timing requirements. However, the case of mixed redundancy in Fig. 4(b) only needs three processors, though data update for t_2 from t_7 is delayed by one period of PT.

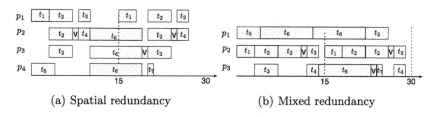

(a) Spatial redundancy   (b) Mixed redundancy

Fig. 4. Two schedulers for the model in Fig. 2.

5   Reliable and Resource-Aware Design

Two design objectives, i.e., reliability guarantee and processor minimization, introduce two optimization steps: (1) calculate the redundancy degree of every task for system reliability, by assuming that communication between tasks is reliable; (2) find the minimal number of processors such that all the constraints can be satisfied. We first present restrictions on satisfying reliability requirements, and constraints on adopting various fault-tolerant techniques with multi-period timing behaviors. Then we discuss the implementation for optimizing two goals.

5.1   Redundancy Optimization

We adopt the Poisson fault model [2] to compute the success/failure probability of tasks. Given task t_i and processor p with failure rate λ_p, the probability for t_i executing correctly on processor p is $\mathscr{P}_i = e^{-\lambda_p \delta_i}$. Then the probability of t_i encountering a transient fault is $1 - \mathscr{P}_i$. We employ $\mathscr{P}_i$ as the reliability of t_i.

Given a system depicted with an atypical task graph $\mathcal{G}$, we first evaluate the reliability of its subsystems. For the task graph G_k of a subsystem, if one of the tasks fails, it is not reliable. Therefore, for the task graph with $|T_k|$ tasks, where the reliability of every task is $\mathscr{P}_i$, the reliability of its subsystem is

$$R_k = \prod_{i=1}^{|T_k|} \mathscr{P}_i. \tag{1}$$

If a task contains r replicas, its reliability becomes $1 - (1 - \mathscr{P}_i)^r$, which is greater or equal to $\mathscr{P}_i$. As redundancy can increase reliability, the subsystem reliability can be enhanced with replicas of its tasks. Let r_i be the number of replicas for task t_i with reliability $\mathscr{P}_i$, we have

$$R_k = \prod_{i=1}^{|T_k|} (1 - (1 - \mathscr{P}_i)^{r_i}). \tag{2}$$

Given a requirement that the system reliability should be at least $\mathcal{R}$, we can calculate the minimal number of replicas for all the tasks in a system, such that all the subsystems satisfy the reliability requirement, i.e.,

$$\begin{aligned}
&minimize(\textstyle\sum_{T_k \subseteq T} \sum_{i=1}^{|T_k|} r_i \cdot w_i)\\
&\text{subject to:}\\
&\quad \text{forall } k, \ \textstyle\prod_{i=1}^{|T_k|}(1 - (1 - \mathscr{P}_i)^{r_i}) \geq \mathcal{R}
\end{aligned} \tag{3}$$

where w_i is the weight of task t_i, and $|T_k|$ is the number of tasks in T_k.

We consider a majority voter, to generate an output if and only if more than half of the inputs have the same value. And the reliability of a voter is assumed to be 1. A voter can be regarded as a task by inserting it into the task graph, according to the dependency relation of its predecessor.

5.2   Constraint Formalization and Resource Optimization

To formalize the mapping and scheduling constraints for the corresponding embedded implementation, we assume that the number of replicas for every task has been calculated, and all the necessary voters are converted into tasks. The necessary notations for constants and variables are listed in Table 1. For multiple periods, we first compute the least common multiple M of these periods. Then the number of iterations of every task in a hyper period is $N_i = M/\mathcal{P}_i$. We introduce d_{ij} to record the precedence relation between pairs of tasks, where $d_{ij} = 0$ stands for the non-existence of dependency relation, $d_{ij} = 1$ is for the strong dependency relation, and $d_{ij} = -1$ is for the weak dependency relation.

Table 1. Constraints and variables

Const.	Explanation	Var.	Explanation
N_i	The number of iterations for task t_i	o_{ij}	Indicating the existence of communication
r_i	The number of replicas for task t_i	m_{ijk}^u	The jth replica of task t_i is mapped to p_k in iteration u
$\mathcal{P}_i$	The period of task t_i	s_{il}^u	Start time of executing the lth replica of t_i in iteration u
δ_i	The cost of executing task t_i	f_{il}^u	End time of executing the lth replica of t_i in iteration u
d_{ij}	Dependency relation for t_i and t_j	se_{ij}^u	Time for starting data transfer from t_i to t_j in iteration u
c_{ij}	Cost of data transfer from t_i to t_j	fe_{ij}^u	Time for finishing data transfer from t_i to t_j in iteration u
		α_i^u	Arrival time for t_i in iteration u

Mapping and Scheduling Constraints. The constraints presented here mainly involve the mapping of tasks and replicas, the behaviors between strong and weak dependent tasks, and the causality between various actions. For the type of redundancy, we consider the cases of spatial, spatial and temporal mixed redundancy. For the mapping relation between tasks and processors, it can be fixed (the mapping will not change in various iterations) or flexible (the mapping can change among various iterations).

The constraints in Table 2 depict the mapping restriction in various cases. For spatial redundancy, every processor $p \in P$ can only accommodate one replica of a task. However, in the mixed case, such limitation does not exist. If the mapping is fixed, the allocation relations of tasks to processors keep the same in all the iterations, and we ignore the iteration index.

Table 2. Case-specified mapping constraints

Type	Fixed mapping		Flexible mapping	
Spatial	$\sum_{j=1}^{r_i}\sum_{k=1}^{\|P\|} m_{ijk}=r_i,$	$\sum_{j=1}^{r_i} m_{ijk}\le 1$ (4)	$\sum_{j=1}^{r_i}\sum_{k=1}^{\|P\|} m_{ijk}^{u}=r_i,$	$\sum_{j=1}^{r_i} m_{ijk}^{u}\le 1$ (5)
Mixed	$\sum_{j=1}^{r_i}\sum_{k=1}^{\|P\|} m_{ijk}=r_i$	(6)	$\sum_{j=1}^{r_i}\sum_{k=1}^{\|P\|} m_{ijk}^{u}=r_i$	(7)

Equation 8 requires that in spatial redundancy, all replicas of a task should be executed at the same time, which is not involved in mixed redundancy.

$$\forall 1 \le l, l' \le r_i, s_{il}^{u} = s_{il'}^{u} \tag{8}$$

The general causality constraints on scheduling are depicted in Table 3.

Table 3. General constraints

Explanation	Constraints
For any two dependent tasks, if they are not allocated to the same processor, communication exists	$(d_{ij}\neq 0)\wedge(\exists k,k'.(m_{ilk}^{u}\wedge m_{jl'k'}^{u}))\to o_{ij}$ (9)
The quantitive relation exists between task execution and data transformation	$f_{il}^{u}=s_{il}^{u}+\delta_i,\ fe_{ij}^{u}\ge se_{ij}^{u}+o_{ij}\cdot c_{ij}$ (10)
Causality exists between data transfer and subsequent tasks	$se_{ij}^{u}\ge f_{il}^{u},\ (d_{ij}=1)\to s_{jl}^{u}\ge fe_{ij}^{u}$ (11)
Tasks executing on the same processor cannot overlap	$m_{ilk}^{u}\wedge m_{jl'k}^{u}\to s_{il}^{u}\ge f_{jl'}^{v}\vee s_{jl'}^{v}\ge f_{il}^{u}$ (12)
The arrival of tasks is periodic	$\alpha_i^{u+1}-\alpha_i^{u}=\mathcal{P}_i\wedge s_{il}^{u}\ge\alpha_i^{u}\wedge u+1\le N_i$ (13)

Objectives. The reliability requirement demands sufficient number of processors to accommodate redundancy and to satisfy the timing requirements. Meanwhile, we also expect to reduce the adopted hardware resources for cost consideration. Therefore, we expect to minimize the number of allocated processors without sacrificing system reliability.

Let T be a set of tasks with $|T|=n$, S be a set of scenarios of a system with $|S|=m$, and $\mathcal{P}_{ij}$ be the period of task t_i in scenario s_j. The minimum number of processors we need is

$$max\{minimize(|P_j|) \mid 1\le j\le m\} \tag{14}$$

where $minimize(|P_j|)$ is the minimum number of processors used in scenario s_j to satisfy time constraints in the hyper period by considering the set of periods

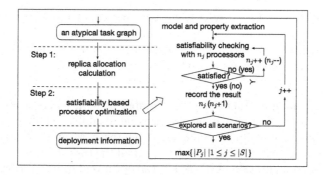

Fig. 5. Optimization steps

$\{\mathcal{P}_{ij}\}_{1 \le i \le n}$. To satisfying the constraints of all the scenarios, we need to select the maximum among all the results.

Theorem 1. *Given a system with a set of tasks T and a set of applied scenarios S, where $\mathcal{P}_{ij}$ is the period of task $t_i \in T$ in scenario $s_j \in S$, let M_j be the least common multiple of all tasks T in scenario s_j, and $|P_j|$ be the minimal number of required processors for a satisfiable scheduler in scenario s_j. If there exists $s_{j'} \in S$ such that*

$$(M_j \le M_{j'}) \wedge \bigwedge_{i=1}^{|T|} (\frac{M_j}{\mathcal{P}_{ij}} \ge \frac{M_{j'}}{\mathcal{P}_{ij'}}),$$

the tasks in s'_j is schedulable with $|P_j|$ processors.

Proof. If $|P_j|$ is the number of required processors for scenario s_j, we have

$$\sum_{i=1}^{|T|} \frac{M_j}{\mathcal{P}_{ij}} \cdot \delta_i \le M_j \cdot |P_j|.$$

Then we have

$$\sum_{i=1}^{|T|} \frac{M_{j'}}{\mathcal{P}_{ij'}} \cdot \delta_i \le \sum_{i=1}^{|T|} \frac{M_j}{\mathcal{P}_{ij}} \cdot \delta_i \le M_j \cdot |P_j| \le M_{j'} \cdot |P_j|.$$

Therefore, the tasks in $s_{j'}$ is schedulable with $|P_j|$ processors.

Informally speaking, with Theorem 1, we could save the effort of optimization by ignoring the scenarios that the hardware resource usage can be inferred. The reason is that we need to satisfy the requirements of all scenarios.

5.3 Implementation

We adopt a stepwise strategy for the optimization of the goals, as shown in Fig. 5. First, we introduce a greedy algorithm to calculate the allocation of replicas, where every subsystem should satisfy the reliability requirement. Then, the optimization for the minimal number of processors is translated into a satisfiability problem, such that the existence of a deployment strategy satisfying all the constraints can be checked.

Replica Calculation. Increasing the number of replicas for tasks with lower reliabilities is more effective in enhancing system reliability. Therefore, the greedy algorithm tends to assign more replicas to such tasks. Meanwhile, the number of replicas is set to be odd for majority voting. If all the tasks have the same weight, the calculated configuration of replicas is the optimized solution. However, when the weights are different, there may exist many solutions for a given expected system reliability. The algorithm just outputs one replica configuration.

Hardware Resource Minimization. It is difficult to directly apply constraint-based or meta-heuristic based optimization techniques to minimize the number of adopted processors. The reason is that an optimization objective is usually encoded as an expression that can be calculated with a set of variables and constraints. However, the number of processors is regarded as a fixed parameter to encode the constraints in the design for an embedded implementation. The intuition of the problem is to find a minimal number of processors, such that the system is schedulable with the constraints. When the number is given, checking whether there exists a scheduler meeting the constraints is a satisfiability problem. Then we can use various techniques, such as model checking, constraint solving or heuristic-based methods, for satisfiability analysis. Therefore, we could keep on checking the satisfiability of the constraints mentioned in Sect. 5.2 with various numbers of processors, until we reach the minimum such that all the constraints in a certain scenario are satisfied.

We have encoded the constraints in various cases (the product between mapping and redundancy choices) with model checking, constraint solving and heuristic-based methods. As illustrated in the right-side of Fig. 5, the method implemented with model checking works as follows:

1. we build a formal model to depict the constraints for tasks (replicas) being executed on processors, such that the minimal number of required processors to satisfy the constraints in the model can be checked.
2. the property we check is whether all the tasks can be done within a specified deadline (hyper period) of scenario s_j.
3. for a given number of processors n_j,
   - if the property is satisfied, reduce n_j by one and check the satisfiability of the property until it is not satisfied. Then $n_j + 1$ is the result in s_j.
   - if the property is not satisfied, increase n_j by one and check the satisfiability of the property until it is satisfied. Then n_j is the result.

The condition marked with $\succ$ in Fig. 5 must be explored at least once. Steps 2 and 3 are repeated until all necessary scenarios have been checked. Then the maximal number among all the scenarios is the expected result.

The model mainly contains templates for tasks and processors, which are formalized with timed automata [1]. The execution of tasks on processors is encoded as the coordination between the corresponding components.

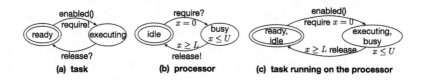

Fig. 6. Models in timed automata

We provide the templates for flexible mapping and mixed redundancy in Fig. 6(a) and (b) with two timed automata for tasks (replicas) and processors, respectively, where the nodes with double cycles are initial locations. The condition labelled on edges between two locations describes the constraints for the transition. There is a clock variable x in the processor model. When a task starts execution on a processor, x is reset to zero to record time elapse. When x reaches L, the task can release the occupation of the processor. The constraint $x \leq U$ requires that the execution of a task should not exceed U (the WCET of a task). The two timed automata coordinate via the message marked with ! and ?. The composition of task and processor via message synchronization is shown in Fig. 6(c). Additional to the constraint of deadline, we could also encode the timing requirements between weak dependent tasks that the scheduler should satisfy. The templates can be instantiated with multiple tasks and processors. Then we can check whether a scheduler satisfying all the timing constraints exists.

We employ model checker UPPAAL [4] to deal with the checking process. Once we fix the minimal number of processors, a counter-example showing the configuration and scheduling strategy can be given. If the given number of processors cannot guarantee to satisfy all the constraints, the whole state space will be explored by using model checking techniques. Then the model checker may not present an answer due to state space explosion for large scale systems. With this consideration, we also apply SMT solver Yices [7] to encode and solve the constraints. Additionally, a heuristic-based method is implemented with some greedy strategies, which is sound but not complete. That is, if the algorithm can find a scheduler, adopting the given number of processors can satisfy the constraints. However, if the algorithm fails to find a scheduler within finite number of iterations, we cannot say that the system is not schedulable with the given number of processors.

6   Case Study

We conduct experiments on the autonomous vehicle controller depicted in Fig. 1. The autonomous vehicle is modified from Dongfeng Fengshen AX7 SUV

(Fig. 7(a)) with drive-by-wire ability. The vehicle is equipped with a variety of sensors and low-level actuators. The actuators, e.g., electronic power steering motor, brake motor, and throttle by-wire, receive and actuate commands from the controller. Vehicle data such as current steering angle is sensed by on-board sensors and obtained through a CAN bus. The IMU used for localization is an Inertial Navigation System (INS) aided by external Differential Global Positioning System (DGPS). Other sensors, e.g., LiDAR, Radar and camera, provide data for the centre computer. Then the centre computer delivers environment perception and generates a target path that is a sequence of position points with maximum speed information. Next, the controller keeps the vehicle tracking this path.

(a) Dongfeng Fengshen AX7   (b) Autonomous control systems

Fig. 7. Our autonomous vehicle

In the autonomous control system (Fig. 7(b)), the controller is a real-time application running under a Linux kernel with PREEMPT_RT patch. The type of processors for controller execution is Raspberry Pi 3, namely a 1.2 GHz quad-core ARM Cortex A53 cluster. The communication between various processors is via Ethernet. We conduct real urban road tests as well as simulation tests with scenarios covering straight, curve, lane change, and u-turns. The frequencies of PE and PT among various scenarios of the vehicle are listed in Table 4, where "NA" means not available. The execution times of the tasks are recorded when the controller runs on one processor. Their worst case execution times are analyzed based on the collected data, as presented in Table 5.

Table 4. Various frequencies (Hz) of PE and PT in different scenarios

Speed	Path tracking (PT)			Path extraction (PE)		
	Straight	Turn	U-turn	Straight	Turn	U-turn
10 km/h	100	100	120	10	10	12
20 km/h	100	100	181	10	10	19
30 km/h	100	107	NA	10	11	NA
40 km/h	120	NA	NA	12	NA	NA
60 km/h	197	NA	NA	20	NA	NA

Table 5. Worst case execution time of the tasks

Type	Path tracking (PT)				Path extraction (PE)		
Tasks	t_1	t_2	t_3	t_4	t_5	t_6	t_7
WCET(ms)	0.2842	0.0820	0.6674	0.5932	0.1306	6.7042	0.0868

6.1 Redundancy Degree for Various Reliability Requirements

The numbers of required replicas with respect to various system reliabilities, the reliabilities of tasks and the weights of the tasks are listed in Table 6. Totally, we consider four tasks in PT and present two groups of weights $w_1 = (0.25, 0.25, 0.25, 0.25)$, and $w_2 = (0.33, 0.01, 0.33, 0.33)^2$, and four groups of task reliabilities, to compare the number of required replicas with various system reliability requirements. The four groups of task reliability distributions in ascending order are:

$$D_1 = (0.96, 0.99, 0.94, 0.94), \qquad D_2 = (0.996, 0.999, 0.994, 0.994)$$
$$D_3 = (0.9996, 0.9999, 0.9994, 0.9994), \quad D_4 = (0.99996, 0.99999, 0.99994, 0.99994)$$

The legends in Table 6 are as follows. The first column lists various reliability requirements. The second column presents different weights explained above. The other four columns provide the number of required replicas for the four tasks in PT, respectively, with respect to various distributions of reliabilities and weights of the tasks.

Table 6. The number of replicas for various reliability requirements

Reliability	Weight	D_1	D_2	D_3	D_4
$1 - 10^{-6}$	w_1	(5,5,7,5)	(3,3,3,3)	(3,3,3,3)	(3,3,3,3)
	w_2	(5,5,7,5)	(3,3,3,3)	(3,3,3,3)	(3,3,3,3)
$1 - 10^{-9}$	w_1	(7,5,9,9)	(5,5,5,5)	(3,3,3,3)	(3,3,3,3)
	w_2	(7,7,9,9)	(5,5,5,5)	(3,3,3,3)	(3,3,3,3)
$1 - 10^{-12}$	w_1	(9,7,11,11)	(7,5,7,7)	(5,5,5,5)	(3,3,3,3)
	w_2	(9,7,11,11)	(7,5,7,7)	(5,5,5,5)	(3,3,3,3)

According to the results presented in Table 6, when the reliabilities of tasks are lower, more replicas are required to meet system reliability requirements. However, the allocation of replicas is less sensitive to weights, except for the case with the lowest task reliabilities.

The total numbers of replicas in various reliability requirements and weights with respect to more distributions of task reliabilities are illustrated in Fig. 8

---

[2] The smaller the value is, the more important the task is.

(i in D_i stands for the degree of reliabilities, i.e., the bigger the number is, the more reliable the tasks are). In every reliability requirement, the numbers of required replicas in two sets of weights are similar, except for the case already shown in Table 6. When task reliabilities are higher, the change in the number of required replicas is not so obvious as the change in reliability requirements.

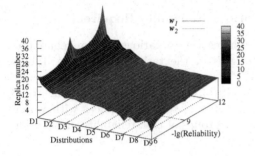

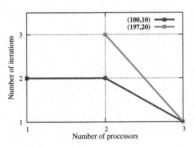

Fig. 8. Replicas distribution.   Fig. 9. PT's iteration for fresh data.

6.2 Resource Optimization Within Various Scenarios

Hardware resource is sensitive to the number of replicas and the corresponding timing requirements. We take two sets of experimentation to compare the usage of hardware resource with respect to various scenarios, and different fault-tolerant strategies, i.e., spatial redundancy, spatial and temporal mixed redundancy, respectively. The experiments are conducted with the three methods mentioned in Sect. 5.3, to compare the performance of various techniques in the satisfiability-based optimization.

In Table 7, we present the number of required processors by considering spatial redundancy, with different mapping strategies and various numbers of task replicas in various scenarios. In the table, the first column presents the frequencies of various scenarios. The second lists the number of replicas for various tasks, where $t_i \times r$ stands for the existence of r replicas for all the tasks. The third presents the number of used processors. Then the rest of columns provide the satisfiability of the problem (the existence of a scheduler), and the cost of the computation in seconds, with constraint solving, model checking and greedy algorithm.

Experimental results show that the performance of constraint solving is better than the other two methods. When the total number of replicas is small, the method of model checking may find a solution very quickly. However, with the increasing scalability, the performance of model checking degrades rapidly. For the case of heuristic-based method, the heuristic used here is not always effective, which may fail to find a solution, though it exists. Among the results of fixed mapping and flexible mapping, the model checking cost of the latter is

Resource-Aware Design for Reliable Autonomous Applications 309

Table 7. Optimization with spatial redundancy

Frequency (Hz)	Replica	$\|P\|$	Constraint solving				Model checking				Greedy algorithm			
			Fixed map.		Flexible map.		Fixed map.		Flexible map.		Fixed map.		Flexible map.	
			sat.	cost	sat.	cost	sat.	cost	sat.	cost	sat.	cost	sat.	cost
(100, 10)	$t_i \times 1$	1	Y	0.041	Y	0.037	Y	0.010	Y	0.010	Y	0.003	Y	0.003
	$t_i \times 3$	3	Y	0.161	Y	0.189	Y	7148.820	Y	7218.180	Y	0.003	Y	0.004
(120, 12)	$t_i \times 1$	1	Y	0.036	Y	0.035	Y	0.010	Y	0.010	Y	0.003	Y	0.003
	$t_i \times 3$	3	Y	0.095	Y	0.090	Y	5464.940	Y	6714.620	Y	0.003	Y	0.004
(107, 11)	$t_i \times 1$	1	Y	0.040	Y	0.039	Y	0.010	Y	0.010	Y	3.579	Y	3.073
	$t_i \times 3$	3	Y	0.098	Y	0.103	Y	7083.540	Y	8520.740	N	32.574	N	32.251
(197, 20)	$t_i \times 1$	1	Y	0.070	Y	0.073	Y	0.020	Y	0.010	Y	0.003	Y	0.004
	$t_i \times 3$	3	Y	0.198	Y	0.189	Y	7183.370	Y	8494.460	N	30.043	N	30.681

almost always higher than that of the former, due to the increased complexity for the allowed flexibility. For these scenarios, it is enough to use three processors to accommodate the spatial redundancy of three replicas for each task to satisfy reliability requirements.

We present the experimental results with spatial and temporal mixed redundancy in Table 8. In the table, "-" means out of memory. The underlined results in model checking are obtained by applying under approximation to relieve state space explosion, which is sound for satisfiability problem if the result is positive[3]. Intuitively, the delay of mixed redundancy is larger than the case with only spatial redundancy, which is a trade-off between time and space. However, for the first three scenarios, only one processor is enough to accommodate three replicas for all the tasks, which is benefited from the small portion of task execution with respect to the periods of the two subsystems. When we allow two processors (the

Table 8. Optimization with spatial and temporal mixed redundancy

Frequency (Hz)	Replica	$\|P\|$	Constraint solving				Model checking				Greedy algorithm			
			Fixed map.		Flexible map.		Fixed map.		Flexible map.		Fixed map.		Flexible map.	
			sat.	cost	sat.	cost	sat.	cost	sat.	cost	sat.	cost	sat.	cost
(100, 10)	$t_i \times 3$	1	Y	189.207	Y	228.648	Y	4.790	Y	2.650	N	106.903	N	110.818
		2	Y	0.472	Y	1.127	Y	_0.012_	Y	_0.013_	Y	0.003	Y	0.006
(120, 12)	$t_i \times 3$	1	Y	152.501	Y	150.642	Y	3.510	Y	2.540	N	132.833	N	117.347
		2	Y	1.140	Y	1.235	Y	_0.014_	Y	_0.013_	Y	0.004	Y	0.004
(107, 11)	$t_i \times 3$	1	Y	102.439	Y	101.999	Y	3.500	Y	2.560	N	119.581	N	142.081
		2	Y	1.167	Y	1.088	Y	_0.011_	Y	_0.012_	Y	0.004	Y	0.004
(197, 20)	$t_i \times 3$	1	N	5708.326	N	4232.964	N	3.180	N	2.370	N	75.561	N	75.964
		2	Y	4.506	Y	3.564	Y	_0.014_	-	-	Y	0.004	Y	0.003

---

[3] We can also run the method to check the results in Table 7.

number of solutions is larger), these methods can find a solution more quickly, except for the fourth scenario with the model checking method.

According to the results presented in Tables 7 and 8, in fact we could just calculate the number of required processors for the last scenario, where others can be inferred according to Theorem 1.

6.3 Timing Constraint on Weak Dependency

For the weak dependency between two tasks, we have presented the upper and lower bounds of iterations that the successor should wait in Sect. 4.2. In our case study, we expect that data can be refreshed as early as possible in every hyper period. Therefore, we have encoded the constraints such that the property can be checked. Experimental results show that in the first iteration of PT, data from PE cannot be refreshed with the existing scenarios, for the mixed redundancy with one or two processors. Only using three processors can meet such constraint. In Fig. 9, we present the number of minimal iterations for PT to acquire the updated data from PE with various numbers of processors and various scenarios[4], where the horizontal shows the number of processors, and the vertical stands for the number of iterations. It is obvious that data can be refreshed earlier for PT with more processors. And when the frequencies are lower, it takes fewer iterations to be refreshed.

Concluded from the experimental results, we could adopt three processors in the implementation to accommodate various design considerations.

7 Conclusion

The paper presents an embedded design framework for safety-critical systems with scenario-related multi-period timing behaviors in autonomous vehicles. The main technical challenge is to guarantee system reliability and minimize processor usage, with various timing constraints and design choices. We have formalized the constraints and employed both exact (model checking and constraint solving) and heuristic-based (greedy algorithm) methods for solution calculation. The realistic case study for the controller of an autonomous vehicle has demonstrated the applicability and flexibility of our framework. As the future work, we are interested in considering the reliability issues in mixed-critical systems of autonomous vehicles.

Acknowledgments. The authors would like to thank Jian Zhang and Feifei Ma for their assistance with the work and valuable comments on this paper.

---

[4] As the cases of (120,12) and (107,11) coincidence with the case of (100,10), we ignore them in the figure.

References

1. Alur, R., Dill, D.L.: A theory of timed automata. Theor. Comput. Sci. **126**(2), 183–235 (1994)
2. Axer, P., Sebastian, M., Ernst, R.: Reliability analysis for MPSoCs with mixed-critical, hard real-time constraints. In: CODES+ISSS, pp. 149–158. IEEE/ACM/IFIP (2011)
3. Baier, C., Katoen, J.-P., Larsen, K.G.: Principles of Model Checking. MIT Press, Cambridge (2008)
4. Behrmann, G., David, A., Larsen, K.G.: A tutorial on Uppaal. In: Formal Methodsfor the Design of Real-Time Systems, pp. 33–35 (2004)
5. Burns, A., Davis, R.: Mixed criticality systems-a review. Department of Computer Science, University of York, Technical report (2013)
6. Chang, W., Chakraborty, S., et al.: Resource-aware automotive control systems design: a cyber-physical systems approach. Found. Trends® Electr. Des. Autom. **10**(4), 249–369 (2016)
7. Dutertre, B.: Yices 2.2. In: Biere, A., Bloem, R. (eds.) CAV 2014. LNCS, vol. 8559, pp. 737–744. Springer, Cham (2014). https://doi.org/10.1007/978-3-319-08867-9_49
8. Glaß, M., Lukasiewycz, M., Streichert, T., Haubelt, C., Teich, J.: Reliability-aware system synthesis. In: DATE, pp. 1–6 (2007)
9. Huang, J., Barner, S., Raabe, A., Buckl, C., Knoll, A.: A framework for reliability-aware embedded system design on multiprocessor platforms. Microprocess. Microsyst. **38**(6), 539–551 (2014)
10. Jiang, J., Yu, X.: Fault-tolerant control systems: a comparative study between active and passive approaches. Ann. Rev. Control **36**(1), 60–72 (2012)
11. Pagetti, C., Forget, J., Boniol, F., Cordovilla, M., Lesens, D.: Multi-task implementation of multi-periodic synchronous programs. Discrete Event Dyn. Syst. **21**(3), 307–338 (2011)
12. Pandey, S., Vermeulen, B.: Transient errors resiliency analysis technique for automotive safety critical applications. In: DATE, p. 9 (2014)
13. Sangiovanni-Vincentelli, A., Di Natale, M.: Embedded system design for automotive applications. Computer **40**(10), 42–51 (2007)
14. Yip, E., Kuo, M.M., Roop, P.S., Broman, D.: Relaxing the synchronous approach for mixed-criticality systems. In: RTAS, pp. 89–100. IEEE (2014)
15. Zhao, Q., Gu, Z., Zeng, H.: Design optimization for AUTOSAR models with preemption thresholds and mixed-criticality scheduling. J. Syst. Architect. **72**, 61–68 (2017)
16. Zheng, B., Liang, H., Zhu, Q., Yu, H., Lin, C.-W.: Next generation automotive architecture modeling and exploration for autonomous driving. In: VLSI (ISVLSI), pp. 53–58. IEEE (2016)

Verifying Auto-generated C Code from Simulink
An Experience Report in the Automotive Domain

Philipp Berger[1]([✉]), Joost-Pieter Katoen[1], Erika Ábrahám[1],
Md Tawhid Bin Waez[2], and Thomas Rambow[3]

[1] RWTH Aachen University, Aachen, Germany
{berger,katoen,abraham}@cs.rwth-aachen.de
[2] Ford Motor Company, Dearborn, USA
mwaez@ford.com
[3] Ford Werke GmbH, Cologne, Germany
trambow@ford.com

Abstract. This paper presents our experience with formal verification
of C code that is automatically generated from Simulink open-loop controller models. We apply the state-of-the-art commercial model checker
BTC EmbeddedPlatform to two Ford R&D prototype case studies: a
next-gen Driveline State Request and a next-gen E-Clutch Control.
These case studies contain various features (decision logic, floating-point
arithmetic, rate limiters and state-flow systems) implemented in discrete-
time logic. The diverse features and the extensive use of floating-point
variables make the formal code verification highly challenging. The paper
reports our findings, identifies shortcomings and strengths of formal
verification when adopted in an automotive setting. We also provide
recommendations to tool developers and requirement engineers so as
to integrate formal code verification into the automotive mass product
development.

1 Introduction

The Need for Formal Verification in Automotive. In the automotive industry
an increasing number of features are implemented in software. As a result the
complexity and dependence on produced artefacts is on the rise. Additionally,
customers demand more flexibility in selecting features leading to an ever increasing number of feature flags and build configurations. The automotive functional
safety standard ISO 26262 defines a ASIL (Automotive Safety Integrity Level)
classification scheme and recommends appropriate verification techniques for
each ASIL level such as testing and *formal verification.* Testing focuses on showing the presence of bugs, whereas the rigorous state exploration provided by
formal verification aims to show the absence of bugs. Although testing nowadays is commonplace, the application of formal verification to software artefacts
in the industry is in its infancy.

© Springer International Publishing AG, part of Springer Nature 2018
K. Havelund et al. (Eds.): FM 2018, LNCS 10951, pp. 312–328, 2018.
https://doi.org/10.1007/978-3-319-95582-7_18

Verifying Simulink Models. This paper considers the use of formal verification in a model-based system development process in the automotive domain. We concentrate on Simulink, a popular model-based software development tool that is widely used in the automotive industry. Simulink is developed by MathWorks and provides a graphical environment for modeling, simulating and analyzing dynamical systems. Formal verification of Simulink so far has primarily concentrated on the model level verification, which has been done with the first generation of model checkers, i.e., verification tools that focus on verifying models of real artefacts. Experiences using the commercial Simulink Design Verifier (SLDV) [1] as well as using model checkers such as NuSMV, SPIN and Uppaal [2–4] have been reported.

Verifying C Code. In contrast, this paper considers the *formal verification of C code* that is automatically generated from Simulink models. More precisely, we aim at checking whether the requirements imposed on Simulink models are satisfied by the C code that is obtained by push-button technology from these models. Formal verification of auto-generated code is of interest as automotive companies such as Ford Motor Company have been deploying more and more auto-generated code to reduce development time and lower the risk of introducing errors by manual coding. The auto-generated C code may differ from the behavior of the Simulink model due to the lack of formal semantics, or potential bugs in the translation procedure. Program code verification is supported by second-generation model checkers such as CBMC [5], Ultimate Automizer [6], and CPA Checker [7], to mention a few. As our aim is to integrate formal code verification into Ford's mass product development, we focus on a *commercial verification tool for code verification.* We selected the BTC EmbeddedPlatform[1] (BTC, for short) as developed by BTC Embedded Systems AG. This tool includes amongst others CBMC. It has been developed for industrial use and a dedicated support team is available.

Approach. This paper reports on our findings by applying BTC on two R&D prototype case studies: a next-gen *Driveline State Request* and a next-gen *E-Clutch Control.* Their Simulink models consist of a few thousand blocks, and their C code is about 2,000 and 5,000 lines of code, respectively. The formal verification of industrial-scale open-loop[2] controller models is challenging especially due to the diverse feature-set and the extensive use of floating-point variables, see also [8]. We checked these models against 42 and 70 requirements, respectively, which were made available to us in textual form as Microsoft Word documents.

Our Findings. The formal verification—including the formalization of the requirements and running the verification tool—was carried out by researchers having knowledge in model checking. Issues were found in 43% of the 112 requirements. 35 requirements were either ambiguous, incomplete or inconsistent, nine

---

[1] https://www.btc-es.de/en/products/btc-embeddedplatform/.

[2] Open-loop means that the model does not include the controlled environment.

requirements could not be taken into account due to restrictions of the verifier while four requirements were missing details about the exact algorithm to be implemented. The formal verification revealed 20 code implementations that are inconsistent with the requirements of the prototype features. These errors could all be traced back to the Simulink models. All detected issues were communicated with Ford Motor Company and subsequently resolved. For 29 requirements, only a bounded proof of correctness could be derived. These findings stress the importance of formal verification for automotive software.

Our Recommendations. This paper reports on our findings, identifies shortcomings and strengths of formal verification when adopted in an automotive setting. Our focus points were automation, scalability and usability, that are necessary for an integration into a large-scale automotive development process. Though the verification of both models was successful, we encountered different technical challenges with respect to requirement formalization, tool usage and model structures. Integrating formal verification into mass automotive product development is not easy: engineers are not familiar with formal methods, and are not trained in writing formal requirements. We provide a detailed set of recommendations to ease the requirement formalization, most notably by using specification patterns and the use of pre-defined requirement blocks. We also present some ideas for new features in verification tools that can further support the integration of formal verification into C code targeted development in the automotive sector: The mitigation of spurious counterexamples, enabling batch processing, and support for automated "continuous" verification, i.e., when parts of the Simulink model, the requirement or the tools change.

Main Contributions. To summarize, our main contributions are:

- a detailed report on experiences with using a modern commercial verification tool to formally verify C code automatically generated from Simulink models,
- a detailed set of recommendations for engineers in the automotive domain to enable the use of formal code verification in the design process, and
- a detailed list of recommendations for verification tool builders to integrate their tools into the automotive mass product development.

Organization of the Paper. Section 2 introduces the two R&D prototype case studies. Section 3 briefly introduces the BTC verification tool and its features. Section 4 presents our findings concerning requirement formalization and formal code verification. Section 5 presents our observations and recommendations for enabling and integrating formal verification into the automotive development process. Section 6 concludes the paper.

2   The Case Studies

The aim of this joint project between Ford Motor Company and RWTH Aachen University is the feasibility analysis of discrete-time verification of industrial-scale C code controllers for mass production. The aim includes assessing the current state of requirement specification within Ford, check the quality of generated C code from Simulink models by a commercial verification tool and identify possible solutions for a highly-automated verification tool-chain that can be integrated into an automotive development process. This section presents the two R&D prototype case studies from Ford. Due to confidentiality reasons, we cannot provide access to model files, source code or requirements.

Table 1. The variables and calibration parameters of the Simulink models.

		Scalar			Array/Matrix		
		bool	int	float	bool	int	float
DSR	I/O Vars	7	16	8	0	1 (1×10)	1 (1×10)
	Calibration Pars	15	3	24	1 (1×12)	1 (1×32)	9 (1×6...12)
ECC	I/O Vars	3	4	29	0	0	0
	Calibration Pars	7	1	71	0	0	72 (1×2...11×11)

R&D Prototype Features. Our case study was conducted using the auto-generated code of two R&D prototype Simulink models: a model of the next-gen *Driveline State Request* (DSR) feature and of the next-gen *E-Clutch Control* (ECC) feature. None of these features are safety-critical. Let us describe the role and importance of these two features. Energy saving, exhaust emission reduction, and exhaust noise reduction are among the main objectives in the development of modern vehicles. On flat roads, the engine drag torque typically slows down the vehicle when the driver takes his foot from the accelerator pedal. A vehicle with a combustion engine can be operated in Sailing Mode when the vehicle is rolling without engine drag torque in order to maintain its speed and to save fuel in certain driving situations and where the driver is not actively accelerating or braking the vehicle. In Sailing Mode, the driveline[3] is opened automatically when the driver releases the accelerator pedal. When the driveline is open, the engine can be shut off or run at idle speed without introducing drag torque in order to reduce fuel consumption. Different system- or driver-interactions, such as pressing the brake or accelerator pedal, will result in closing the driveline again. The DSR feature implements the decision logic to open or close the driveline. This feature takes driver interactions and vehicle status information to decide in which situations the driveline should be opened and closed again. The ECC feature calculates the desired clutch torque capacity and corresponding engine control torques or speeds for opening and closing the driveline.

Model Characteristics. The aim of this study is to investigate how C code formal verification performs when applied to the auto-generated code of Simulink models having decision logic, state-charts, filters, rate limiters, look-up tables and

---

[3] A motor vehicle's driveline consists of the parts of the powertrain excluding the engine. It is the portion of a vehicle, after the prime mover, that changes depending on whether a vehicle is front-wheel, rear-wheel, or four-wheel drive.

feedback control. Therefore, we selected two features that contain mixtures of these different kinds of functionalities. The Simulink model for the DSR feature has 42 functional requirements, 28 inputs, six outputs, 53 calibration parameters and 1149 blocks. Calibratable parameters remain constant during software execution but can be adjusted before the execution for tuning or selecting the possible functionalities. Calibration is the adjustment of calibratable parameters of software functions realizing the control functionalities. This model contains several variables as summarized in the first two rows of Table 1. The C code comprises about 2100 lines. The next-gen DSR feature has several calibration parameters, amongst others 42 scalar parameters and nine array parameters of six to 12 single-precision floating-point elements, one Boolean array with 12 elements and one unsigned 8-bit integer array with 32 elements.

The Simulink model for the next-gen ECC feature has 70 functional requirements, 27 inputs, nine outputs, 151 calibration parameters and 2098 blocks. In total, it comprises about 4900 lines of C code. This model contains Boolean, integer and a huge number of floating-point variables, see Table 1. The calibration parameters include 79 scalar parameters and 13 arrays of single-precision floats.

Requirement Characteristics. For the DSR case study, from 42 functional requirements we extracted 54 properties, consisting of 50 invariants and four bounded-response properties. Invariant properties are assertions that are supposed to hold for all reachable states. Bounded-response properties request that a certain assertion holds within a given number of computational steps whenever a given, second assertion holds. For the ECC case study, from 70 functional requirements we extracted 82 invariants and two bounded-response properties.

3   The BTC Tool

We exploited BTC, a commercial tool for formal specification and verification.

3.1   The BTC EmbeddedPlatform

BTC is an integrated development environment featuring requirements-based testing, back-to-back testing and a formal verification suite with an integrated graphical user interface aiding the formal specification. The user interface aims to support industry software engineers without much knowledge in formal methods. An overview of the formal verification portion is illustrated in Fig. 1.

The initial architectural set-up of a new BTC project requires in-depth knowledge of the C code to be verified, its structure and variables.

A BTC Project Setup. Our imported C code defines the architecture of a project, including available functions, variables, entry points and initialization routines. Auto-generated C code for automotive controllers usually consists of an *initialization* and a *step* routine. After selecting a (sub-)set of available functions to instrument, global and local variables are collected and categorized as "input", "output", "local", "parameter" or "ignore" through manual user input and simple heuristics. The range of input variables and parameters can be restricted by specifying minimal and maximal values. The execution time per step, i.e., the amount of time that passes between two consecutive executions of the main step method, can be configured as a constant when creating the project. The user interface is divided into views, each focusing on different aspects of testing and formal verification. Here, we only consider the latter view.

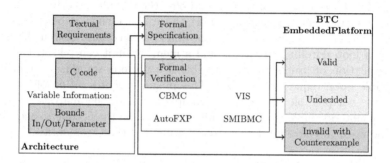

Fig. 1. Overview of the ins and outs of the BTC.

Formal Specification. The requirements of the two case studies are textual, i.e., use natural language (English) for describing functional feature behavior. BTC supports importing textual requirements from various sources, such as Microsoft Excel, allowing engineers to develop the formal (requirement) specification directly on the requirement text.

Pattern-Based Specification. Whereas most model checkers use some form of temporal logic for the property specification, BTC supports safety as well as liveness properties through *pattern-based specification* [9]. These patterns are a kind of template and are based on an intuitive and graphical representation of the formal semantics. The patterns enable the usage of BTC without being an expert in temporal logic. In its most basic form, a BTC pattern-based specification represents an invariant together with start-up delays, or models Trigger/Action conditions with timing information. The BTC user goes through the textual requirement (template), selects and maps parts of the text to macros, place-holders for logical formulas. Take e.g., the expression "When *in reverse*, [...]", containing a high-level description of an external input state condition, namely the gear selection. By creating a macro mapping the term *in reverse* to a formal definition in terms of variables and values like "selectedGear $== -1$", the textual requirement is enriched with the information necessary for formalization. Macros can be shared between multiple requirements in the same project/architecture and may contain other macros, but do not support parameters.

Operators. The specification language used for defining triggers, actions and invariant conditions contains all basic boolean operators (NOT, logical OR and AND, $\Rightarrow$, $=$, $\neq$), bitwise operators ($\gg$, $\&$, $|$, $\oplus$) as well as basic math operators ($+$, $-$, $\cdot$, $/$, $<$ and $>$). Additionally, floating-point operators (`fabs`, `feq`, `min`, `max`) and temporal operators for step-based timing information are available.

Verification. After formalizing the requirements, the *Formal Verification* view allows for creating a *proof* for the requirements. For model-checking purposes, BTC uses four back-end verification engines: CBMC [5], SMIBMC, VIS [10] and AUTOFXP. These can be turned on and off—the default, used by us, is to use all four. We treat the verification engine and its back-ends as black box as no further information is available. A time limit, a maximum search depth, the number of loop unrolling iterations and a memory limit can be set. Currently, batch execution of proofs is only possible using a non-standard plugin which is available upon request from BTC. This plugin executes all proofs; selecting a subset is not possible. If a counterexample is found, the analysis terminates and the counterexample is automatically simulated on the C code to account for errors between the internal data representation and the C semantics.

4   Experience Report

This section reports our experiences with the formal verification (using BTC) of the two R&D prototype case studies focusing on verifying the auto-generated C code of a few thousand lines from Simulink models.

4.1   Formalizing the Requirements

For a formal verification, formally specified requirements are indispensable. At the start of this work, the requirements were available in the form of textual phrases formulated in natural language. This section reports the issues that were encountered when formalizing these requirements for subsequent use by the C code verification by BTC. These issues range from incomprehensibility of some of the requirements to incomplete requirements, ambiguities and inconsistencies.

Requirement Formalization. We incrementally formalized the Ford requirements given to us in textual form and turned them into BTC formal requirements. Unclarities or other issues were discussed with the Ford engineers. Small issues involving missing domain knowledge were often solved by looking at the corresponding code implementation. *The process of requirement formalization took most of the total project time of about 900 man hours and involved frequent meetings between the researchers conducting the verification and the Ford engineers.*
   While reviewing and formalizing the 112 requirements, we identified 35 issues that can be categorized into ambiguous wording, inconsistencies and underspecification. Without a background in automotive engineering, the learning curve for

formalization, especially regarding domain knowledge, was steep, further indicating issues of underspecification.

Each formalized requirement resulted in one or more *Formal Requirements* for BTC. If a requirement contains multiple cases or can be easily split into distinct logical blocks, we did so. Splitting eases verification by the model checker. *Nine requirements could not be formalized* due to the fact that *BTC does not support the use of array access with variables as index nor the use of lookup tables with pointers in the formal specification. Four requirements have not been considered as they use underspecified complex operators* such as rate limiters and filters.

Table 2. Identified requirement issues.

Case study	Incomplete	Ambiguous	Inconsistent
DSR	12	5	1
ECC	11	3	3

If varA is set to [TRUE] and varB is above a threshold with hysteresis (calVarBThres, calVarBHyst), OR (varA is set to false and varC is above a threshold with hysteresis (calVarCThres, calVarCHyst) AND (varC - varD) is above a threshold with hysteresis (calVarCThres, calVarCHyst)), then varE shall be set to true, and to false otherwise.

Fig. 2. Example of an incomplete requirement involving hysteresis.

Incomplete Requirements. We encountered 23 *incomplete requirements* (Table 2). Typical examples of incompleteness are preconditions like "when no preprocessing feature is active" where no information on signals related to the status of preprocessing features is given, and declarations like "variable A shall be input B with hysteresis (lower threshold calibratable C and upper threshold calibratable D)"; see also Fig. 2. Hysteresis is often used to prevent rapid toggling when observing an input signal against some threshold and can be implemented using a set-reset flip-flop.

Other encountered issues are whether the thresholds are strict (e.g., <10) or non-strict (e.g., ≤ 10), and what the initial output state should be. The analyzed requirements include several such abstract high-level descriptions of functionality. In these complex cases, e.g., when using hysteresis, saturation or rate limiting, the requirements are often lacking necessary information for accurately specifying function behavior. Several of these issues could not be resolved without consulting the code. Typical omitted information in the requirements includes the initial configuration, exact (formal) state change conditions including a priority ordering of the signals, and complete documentation of state variables.

For the successful verification of a stateful system, access to all state variables is required. These are usually not visible in the global interface as they are unnecessary for using and embedding the system. Therefore, *we manually adapted the Simulink model by adding necessary variables to the global interfaces.*

Ambiguous Requirements. We identified *eight cases of ambiguity in the prototype features, mostly related to cases of missing parentheses.* We identified cases where in chains of AND- and OR-conditions either applying the mathematical operator precedence did not make sense when considering the condition content or where there were an uneven number of opening and closing parentheses present.

Inconsistencies. Another group of issues focuses on inconsistencies between requirements. We found *four issues in the prototype features where a commonality shared between several requirements is invalidated by another one.* Take, e.g., *n* requirements of the form "When in state X, do..." among which a single requirement specifying similar behavior, is missing the "When in state X" scope. It is unclear whether this omission is intentional or not. While this inconsistency is not a problem of the formalization per se, these discrepancies are often closely related to incompleteness issues in requirements, e.g., when "boilerplate" information is omitted because preconditions like being in a specific state are made implicit by a chapter heading or a requirement name. While implicit preconditions may be acceptable for textual requirements, it hampers formal verification.

Table 3. Verification results on the case studies using BTC.

Case study	Calibration type	Valid	Unknown	Invalid
DSR	Fixed	24 (Bounded: 7)	8	10
	Varying	23 (Bounded: 8)	12	7
ECC	Fixed	44 (Bounded: 22)	16	10
	Varying	36 (Bounded: 24)	20	14

4.2 Formal Verification of Auto-generated Code

We now report our findings when applying BTC to the C code of the two R&D prototype features. All verification experiments were carried out on a Intel Core i7-6700HQ machine with 16 GB RAM, running Windows 7 (64-bit), BTC v2.0.3[4] and Matlab R2015b. The maximal verification time was set to 7200 s.

Verification Results. Each formalized requirement was formally verified on the C code of the entire respective feature with fixed calibration parameters. To ease the verification, we fixed the time bounds in the Ford requirements to five simulation steps (50 ms). Typical time bounds in the model vary between 50 ms and 5 s.

---

[4] The most recent version of BTC as of submission is v2.1.0.

For three requirements involving direct lookup tables (i.e., no interpolation)—not natively supported by BTC—we embedded their data directly into the formal specification. Table 3 summarizes our verification results. We consider the fixed calibration parameters unless stated otherwise; we will discuss the varying calibration parameters later on. In our experience, model checking is performed by BTC in three phases:

1. CBMC runs for a number of iterations, in many cases returning counterexamples (if any) in a matter of seconds.
2. If CBMC is not able to refute the property, a combination of AUTOFXP and SMIBMC is used.
3. If the combination is not successful, i.e., results in an unbounded proof, the tool switches back to CBMC, providing a bounded result.

Most of our results seem to be mostly a result of CBMC as we did not observe termination during the AutoFXP/SMIBMC phase. Runtime data like memory consumption or CPU time is only shown while the tools are actively running and can unfortunately not be obtained once model checking has terminated.

Implementation Flaws. In total, BTC found 20 *cases of invalid code implementations* against the formal requirement specification with fixed calibration parameters of the R&D prototype features. These include:

- Four instances of *incorrect relational operators* (e.g., < instead of ≤).
- Four instances of *incorrect variables* used in comparisons. As inputs are processed, for many there are secondary variables available containing derived versions of the input, for example with rate-limiting applied. When comparing inputs, it is important to select the right variant.
- 12 cases where *variables were named differently* than in the specification.
- One instance where the implementation contained a fix for a logical error in the specification which was not passed back and reflected in the requirements.
- One instance where an *output signal was unexpectedly delayed* by one time step even though the delay was not apparent from the requirement specification.
- Two instances of *incorrect use of negations.*
- Various instances of the *incorrect use of chained if-statements*. When a requirement contains several consecutive if-statements followed by a final else-statement, the activation condition for the else section is comprised of the negation of the disjunction over all preceding if-conditions. When changing the else if blocks, correcting all dependents is easily forgotten.
- One instance where *an initialization step was not implemented*. This omission leads to minor initial differences.
- Two instances where *part of a comparison was omitted*.
- An *offset* mentioned in a requirement that was *not used* in the code.
- One case where an *activation/deactivation was unintentionally implemented* using a state toggle such that no signal has precedence over the other.

All detected issues are also present in the respective Simulink models and thus not the result of incorrect C code generation.

Undecided. A total of 24 requirements of the R&D prototype features are undecided, i.e., we were unable to determine whether the implementation and specification match. More precisely:

- Nine requirements contain *properties unsupported* (lookup tables containing pointers, array access with variables as index) by BTC.
- For three requirements we encountered *spurious counterexamples* which were automatically detected as spurious by BTC. Whenever a counterexample for a property is detected, there is a chance that this counterexample exists only due to imprecision introduced by abstraction, for example when approximating floating-point numbers. Thus, each counterexample is simulated on the C code to ensure it is a valid counterexample under the C semantics. Currently, spurious counterexamples prevent further analysis with this combination of formal specification and C code in BTC.
- For two requirements, the tool reported that the verification *unexpectedly terminated*. We are working with BTC to fix these issues.
- For six requirements, structural properties of the implementation prevent formal verification as *necessary outputs are overridden before they can be captured*. Note that in these cases while formalization was seemingly successful, we discovered during the analysis of counterexamples that because of how outputs are stored or combined formalization does not work.
- Four requirements were not formalized, mainly due to the mixture of underspecification and the use of complex operators (low-pass filter, first-order lead filter, second-order notch filter and rate-limiting) made the *formalization process too time-consuming*.

Fixed and Varying Calibration Parameters. We also analyzed the features with *varying calibrations*. Where model checking with fixed calibrations only checks conformance to the specification in one specific calibration setting, with varying calibrations conformance is checked for all possible calibration valuations allowed by the configured calibration bounds. With 53 calibration parameters in the DSR feature and 151 in the ECC feature, we expected the number of undecided results to go up significantly, but out of 42 requirements (DSR) and 70 requirements (ECC) *only the result of five (DSR) and nine (ECC) requirements changed*. We are unable to fully explain the overall lack of impact. We did notice a significant change of depth reached in bounded model checking, with differences being as high as depth 151 in fixed calibration versus a depth of 8 in varying calibration within the same time bound. With DSR, for one requirement the result changed from unbounded satisfied to bounded satisfied, two requirements changed to undecided because of a detected spurious counterexample and two more resulted in time-outs during preprocessing (also now undecided). With ECC, for five requirements the result changed from valid to invalid, three requirements changed from valid to undecided, one requirement changed from invalid to undecided and two requirements changed from unbounded satisfied to bounded satisfied. We found *no cases where a requirement was inconsistent with its implementation while analyzing with fixed calibrations but satisfied with varying calibrations*. During this analysis we uncovered several issues in the implementation that were not visible during analysis with fixed calibrations.

Bounded and Unbounded Results. *BTC was not able to derive an unbounded proof of correctness for a total of 29 requirements.* Whereas a bounded proof for depth n only guarantees a safety property to hold for the first n steps, an unbounded proof (if successful) proves such a property for any depth. In the bounded case [11], correctness is up to depth n and no guarantees are given for depths beyond n. An unbounded proof of correctness usually includes deriving loop invariants for all included loops in the C code, a hard problem that is undecidable in general. Heuristics for generating these loop invariants often only work on small and simple (e.g., linear) loops with few variables and even fewer floating-point operations [12].

Subsystem Verification. With subsystem verification the goal is to reduce model checking complexity by reducing C code size. When a formalized property is handled entirely within some distinct part of the C code, all surrounding and unrelated code can be removed, replacing the original interface with one only containing inputs, parameters and outputs relevant to the selected property. We picked a set of ten requirements from the DSR case study specifying the behavior of a stateflow chart to compare formal verification on controller level with that on subsystem level. We extracted the subsystem from the Simulink model by hand and generated code from the reduced model. While BTC supports subsystem verification using a hierarchical architecture representation, the auto-generated C code in our use case was not in suitable form, making manual preparation necessary. Using the subsystem significantly shrunk the overall complexity of the analyzed model ($\approx$ 350 lines of code) and reduced the number of variables and calibration parameters. The reduced system has six inputs (four Boolean, one (1×16) array of Boolean, one unsigned 8-bit integer), two outputs and one parameter (one (1×32) array of unsigned 8-bit integer). However, the input variable domains might grow since values are no longer restricted by other upstream parts of the model. In the full feature, the inputs of this subsystem are derived from external inputs and may be between tight bounds that are not apparent nor documented explicitly because of implemented behavior. Therefore, subsystem verification over-approximates correctness with respect to the correctness within the entire system. A specific input valuation leading to a property violation might be caught and avoided beforehand in the upstream components of the entire system, but this input restriction is not apparent anymore in the subsystem. While BTC was not able to produce unbounded correctness proofs for the ten requirements when verifying the code of the complete feature, using subsystem verification it was able to do so.

Invalid Verification Results. While investigating issues with NaN (not a number) values on some floating-point variables, we discovered conflicting results for properties with comparisons involving floating-point variables that can become

NaN where an incorrect simplification step potentially leads to invalid results. The issue has been fixed in a new version of BTC.

5 Reflections and Recommendations

This section reflects on our findings and presents our recommendations towards requirement engineers, verification tool developers as well as tool users.

5.1 Requirements

Requirement Completeness. A big hurdle during this work was domain knowledge implicitly required to understand the textual requirements of Ford. This domain knowledge ranges from simple things such as unknown abbreviations to structural details like how the data flow influences delays on certain variables (breaking circular dependencies requires using one-step delays). Certain information is ubiquitous in the Ford development process and not re-iterating every detail makes requirements short and concise. For the same reason, some requirements do not state their full preconditions but instead rely on their positioning inside the requirement catalogue, e.g., in a chapter containing all requirements related to being in a certain state, the subsidiary requirements do not state explicitly that being in that state is a precondition. Four of the requirement violations were due to unexpected delays introduced to break circular dependencies in the model. In practice, certain bounded and small deviations like one- or two-step delays are acceptable while basic behavior is correctly implemented, it highlights *the conflict between the ease-of-use of textual requirements and the degree of precision which is required for formal verification.*

Requirement Interdependencies and Priorities. We found several instances where two requirements could apply simultaneously to the same output variable. In these cases, a priority chain needs to be in place for *defining precedence*. It is also advisable to reorder requirements such that *conditions are grouped per output variable* so that analyzing a single requirement should be sufficient to determine all pre- and postconditions for any given output variable.

Environmental Assumptions. While performing verification with varying calibrations, we encountered situations where the upper bound of a hysteresis block was calibrated below its lower bound. *Calibration parameters should therefore be clearly documented including side conditions and interdependencies,* such that appropriate assertions can be added for verification.

Specification Patterns. For effectively applying formal verification, we recommend engineers switching from textual requirement specifications to an approach that guarantees unambiguous requirements like a *pattern-based approach* [13]. These use specification patterns—templates phrased in natural language with holes that need to be completed by the verification engineers with conditions on code variables. Tools tailored to the knowledge of the engineers should be provided in order to help and enforce writing clear, unambiguous and complete specifications in a format that is agnostic of verification tools and can be automatically transformed for any chosen tool. Specification patterns have been used in automotive [14], aerospace [15] and service-oriented computing [16].

Tool Support and Automation. We believe that while enforcing completeness, verification tools need to provide the engineers with the *ability of building a library of more complex pre-defined formal requirement specification blocks.* Specification blocks enable more consistent requirements presented at a high level of abstraction while still supporting a formal semantics. *We found several instances of complex behavior requiring large and equally complex formalizations that are ideal for attracting small mistakes during formalization.*

5.2 Code Verification

Code Complexity and Subsystem Verification. We found that BTC works *extremely well on invariant properties with no or very few floating-point variables involved.* Counterexamples are typically found within seconds and even unbounded proofs are mostly found in less than a minute. Floating-point numbers are ubiquitous in the automotive domain and pose a challenge to most, if not all, verification tools, see also a discussion on the results in the latest software verification competition [8]. While BTC scales well with the number of parameters, we found that *subsystem verification is a necessity for tackling more complex properties.* In a proof-of-concept of subsystem verification, we achieved unbounded (rather than bounded) verification results for all requirements.

Requirement Robustness. While experimenting with scalability we discovered that even small changes to the requirements can have great impact on the verification times. Take, e.g., a requirement describing that event A implies that event B occurs exactly one time step later. This requirement can be modeled using a Trigger/Action (response) pattern or using an Invariant pattern. While these specifications are semantically equivalent, the corresponding verification times are not. In some instances, the Invariant approach took seconds to verify whereas the Trigger/Response variant took several hours. We recommend tool vendors to adapt *internal optimization routines* such that, by default, the simplest requirement representation is used.

Counterexample Verification. During verification, we encountered several instances where BTC concluded after internal simulations that a discovered counterexample was in fact spurious, i.e., the counterexample was introduced due to used approximations. Verification tools should *automatically mitigate spurious counterexamples* whenever possible.

326   P. Berger et al.

Verification Times. In our experiments, we noticed that generally an unbounded result is obtained within the first minute or no such result is obtained at all. Outliers are obtained for *temporal* properties that usually include a timer that has to expire. We encoded these properties using a Trigger/Action pattern where the delay between the two is given by a calibration parameter. As BTC does not offer *access to verification timing data*, a more detailed analysis of verification times is not possible. In academia, CPU time and memory consumption are common practice [8] and *the* means to compare verification algorithms and tools. This comparison is useful for industrial applications too as it enables comparing different verification engines (even within a single tool) and provides a means to study scalability.

Tool Automation. Repetitive verification tasks are prone to human errors. Hence we envision a fully automated *continuous integration pipeline for mass product development where model checking is performed whenever the specification, the code or the tools change.* Similar approaches—referred to as continuous verification—have been advocated for adaptive software [17]. Therefore, verification tools should support batch processing of verification tasks, provide a better automation interface and a structured output of all relevant result data. A new version of BTC released after conducting our study comes with an automation API and Jenkins integration, enabling continuous verification.

Bug Reporting. Because source code, models and requirement documents usually are confidential, reporting bugs and spurious counterexamples is difficult and time consuming, usually involving an engineer shrinking and anonymizing the code by hand. Automated tools for this purpose such as CReduce [18] require an adequate automation interface. We recommend to include the *automated generation of minimal anonymized examples of bug triggers* in verification tools.

Counterexample Representation. Currently counterexamples can be either viewed as charts showing variable values in each time step or by exporting a stimulation vector containing the generated sequence of input values as a Microsoft Visual Studio C code project. It would be very helpful to *see what part of a requirement is inconsistent with its implementation*, especially when dealing with large conjunctions. Going through a huge number of variables, comparing them to other variables or constants and evaluating the boolean expressions one by one on a sheet of paper is very time consuming and error prone. A graphical tree representation of the formal specification could be beneficial.

6   Conclusion

In this paper, we reported our experiences and presented our recommendations concerning applying formal verification with BTC on two case studies provided by Ford Motor Company. We performed formal verification of 7000 lines of code generated from two Simulink models implementing 112 textual requirements. We identified 35 requirements of the R&D prototype features which are either ambiguous, incomplete or inconsistent; nine cannot be verified due to restrictions of the verifier; while four could not be formalized. Formal verification revealed 20 code implementations that were inconsistent with the requirements.

We spent more than 70% of the project time on requirement analysis and formalization. The overhead should be much larger if performed by automotive engineers whom do not have experience in formal methods. In the automotive industry, both the software-requirements and their implementations change rapidly within strict deadlines. Natural languages, hence, are preferred over formal notations to write requirements in the practice although natural languages often lead to ambiguity, incompleteness and inconsistency. Moreover, we experienced that not all open-loop requirements can be formalized and are supported by the formal verification tools. We also observed spurious counterexamples and unexpected terminations. Recently formal verification tools matured a lot but have yet to provide unbounded and decisive results for most industrial cases.

Our case studies show the benefits that formal verification can add into the automotive development process. We, therefore, believe the use of formal verification will increase slowly but surely in this domain. For this progress, we recommend to develop a technique—such as automated conversion of textual requirements into formal requirements—that will allow engineers to use formal specifications for a fast pace industry without introducing much overhead. Tool vendors need to increase the percentages of unbounded and conclusive results. Additionally, to enable an easier integration of verification tools into the (automotive) industrial design process, we also recommend improving the usability of these tools such as automated mitigation of spurious counterexamples and better diagnostic feedback for the refuted properties.

Acknowledgments. We thank BTC Embedded Systems AG for their continuing support and helpful advice. We are grateful to Johanna Nellen, William Milam and Cem Mengi for fruitful discussions on formal verification and Simulink.

References

1. Nellen, J., Rambow, T., Waez, M.T.B., Ábrahám, E., Katoen, J.P.: Formal verification of automotive Simulink controller models: empirical technical challenges, evaluation and recommendations. In: Havelund, K., Peleska, J., Roscoe, B., de Vink, E. (eds.) FM 2018. LNCS, vol. 10951, pp. 382–398. Springer, Cham (2018)
2. Meenakshi, B., Bhatnagar, A., Roy, S.: Tool for translating simulink models into input language of a model checker. In: Liu, Z., He, J. (eds.) ICFEM 2006. LNCS, vol. 4260, pp. 606–620. Springer, Heidelberg (2006). https://doi.org/10.1007/11901433_33
3. Barnat, J., Beran, J., Brim, L., Kratochvíla, T., Ročkai, P.: Tool chain to support automated formal verification of avionics simulink designs. In: Stoelinga, M., Pinger, R. (eds.) FMICS 2012. LNCS, vol. 7437, pp. 78–92. Springer, Heidelberg (2012). https://doi.org/10.1007/978-3-642-32469-7_6

328 P. Berger et al.

4. Filipovikj, P., Mahmud, N., Marinescu, R., Seceleanu, C., Ljungkrantz, O., Lönn, H.: Simulink to UPPAAL statistical model checker: analyzing automotive industrial systems. In: Fitzgerald, J., Heitmeyer, C., Gnesi, S., Philippou, A. (eds.) FM 2016. LNCS, vol. 9995, pp. 748–756. Springer, Cham (2016). https://doi.org/10.1007/978-3-319-48989-6_46

5. Kroening, D., Tautschnig, M.: CBMC – C bounded model checker. In: Ábrahám, E., Havelund, K. (eds.) TACAS 2014. LNCS, vol. 8413, pp. 389–391. Springer, Heidelberg (2014). https://doi.org/10.1007/978-3-642-54862-8_26

6. Heizmann, M., Hoenicke, J., Podelski, A.: Software model checking for people who love automata. In: Sharygina, N., Veith, H. (eds.) CAV 2013. LNCS, vol. 8044, pp. 36–52. Springer, Heidelberg (2013). https://doi.org/10.1007/978-3-642-39799-8_2

7. Beyer, D., Keremoglu, M.E.: CPACHECKER: a tool for configurable software verification. In: Gopalakrishnan, G., Qadeer, S. (eds.) CAV 2011. LNCS, vol. 6806, pp. 184–190. Springer, Heidelberg (2011). https://doi.org/10.1007/978-3-642-22110-1_16

8. Beyer, D.: Software verification with validation of results. In: Legay, A., Margaria, T. (eds.) TACAS 2017. LNCS, vol. 10206, pp. 331–349. Springer, Heidelberg (2017). https://doi.org/10.1007/978-3-662-54580-5_20

9. Bienmüller, T., Teige, T., Eggers, A., Stasch, M.: Modeling requirements for quantitative consistency analysis and automatic test case generation

10. Brayton, R.K., et al.: VIS: a system for verification and synthesis. In: Alur, R., Henzinger, T.A. (eds.) CAV 1996. LNCS, vol. 1102, pp. 428–432. Springer, Heidelberg (1996). https://doi.org/10.1007/3-540-61474-5_95

11. Biere, A., Cimatti, A., Clarke, E.M., Strichman, O., Zhu, Y.: Bounded model checking. Adv. Comput. **58**, 117–148 (2003)

12. Bagnara, R., Mesnard, F., Pescetti, A., Zaffanella, E.: The automatic synthesis of linear ranking functions: the complete unabridged version. CoRR abs/1004.0944 (2010)

13. Autili, M., Grunske, L., Lumpe, M., Pelliccione, P., Tang, A.: Aligning qualitative, real-time, and probabilistic property specification patterns using a structured english grammar. IEEE Trans. Softw. Eng. **41**(7), 620–638 (2015)

14. Filipovikj, P., Nyberg, M., Rodríguez-Navas, G.: Reassessing the pattern-based approach for formalizing requirements in the automotive domain. In: RE, pp. 444–450. IEEE Computer Society (2014)

15. Bozzano, M., Cimatti, A., Katoen, J.P., Nguyen, V.Y., Noll, T., Roveri, M.: Safety, dependability and performance analysis of extended AADL models. Comput. J. **54**(5), 754–775 (2011)

16. Bianculli, D., Ghezzi, C., Pautasso, C., Senti, P.: Specification patterns from research to industry: a case study in service-based applications. In: Software Engineering. LNI, vol. 227, pp. 51–52. GI (2014)

17. Calinescu, R., Ghezzi, C., Kwiatkowska, M.Z., Mirandola, R.: Self-adaptive software needs quantitative verification at runtime. Commun. ACM **55**(9), 69–77 (2012)

18. Regehr, J., Chen, Y., Cuoq, P., Eide, E., Ellison, C., Yang, X.: Test-case reduction for C compiler bugs. In: PLDI, pp. 335–346. ACM (2012)

QFLan: A Tool for the Quantitative Analysis of Highly Reconfigurable Systems

Andrea Vandin[1]([✉]), Maurice H. ter Beek[2], Axel Legay[3],
and Alberto Lluch Lafuente[1]

[1] DTU, Lyngby, Denmark
{anvan,albl}@dtu.dk
[2] ISTI–CNR, Pisa, Italy
maurice.terbeek@isti.cnr.it
[3] Inria, Rennes, France
axel.legay@inria.fr

Abstract. QFLAN offers modeling and analysis of highly reconfigurable systems, like product lines, which are characterized by combinatorially many system variants (or products) that can be obtained via different combinations of installed features. The tool offers a modern integrated development environment for the homonym probabilistic feature-oriented language. QFLAN allows the specification of a family of products in terms of a feature model with quantitative attributes, which defines the valid feature combinations, and probabilistic behavior subject to quantitative constraints. The language's behavioral part enables dynamic installation, removal and replacement of features. QFLAN has a discrete-time Markov chain semantics, permitting quantitative analyses. Thanks to a seamless integration with the statistical model checker MultiVeStA, it allows for analyses like the likelihood of specific behavior or the expected average value of non-functional aspects related to feature attributes.

1 Introduction

Product line engineering is a methodology that aims to develop and manage, in a cost-effective and time-efficient manner, a family of products or (re)configurable system variants, to allow the mass customization of individual variants. Their variability is captured by feature models, whose features represent stakeholder-relevant functionalities or system aspects [1]. The challenge when lifting successful modeling and analysis techniques for single systems to families of products or configurable systems, is to handle their variability, due to which the number of possible variants may be exponential in the number of features. This led to so-called *family-based* analyses [32]: analyse properties on an entire product line and use variability knowledge about valid feature configurations to deduce results for individual products. This is applied in, e.g., [8,10,11,15,19–23,28,30].

In [2–4], we presented various facets of the probabilistic modeling language QFLAN, capable of describing a wide spectrum of aspects of (software) product

© Springer International Publishing AG, part of Springer Nature 2018
K. Havelund et al. (Eds.): FM 2018, LNCS 10951, pp. 329–337, 2018.
https://doi.org/10.1007/978-3-319-95582-7_19

lines (SPL). The type of quantitative constraints that are supported by QFLAN are significantly more complex than those commonly associated to attributed feature models [9,18,26]. This paper presents the QFLAN tool, a multi-platform tool for the specification and analysis of QFLAN models, which has been implemented in the Eclipse environment using XTEXT technology, thus obtaining a state-of-the-art integrated development environment (IDE). The tool is available, together with installation and usage instructions, from http://github.com/qflanTeam/QFLan.

Related Work. The QFLAN prototypes from [2,3] were the first tools that offered statistical model checking tailored for SPL, generating approximately correct results via sampling, which is particularly useful on very large models when exact model checking is infeasible [25]. Next to dedicated exact model checkers such as VMC [6] and the tool suite ProVeLines [17], which offers the best known SPL-specific model checker, SNIP [12], also popular model checkers like mCRL2 and SPIN have been made amenable to SPL model checking [7,8,19–21]. Furthermore, the tool ProFeat [11] extends the probabilistic model checker PRISM [24] with feature-oriented concepts to be able to model families of stochastic systems and to analyze them through probabilistic model checking. QFLAN scales to larger models with respect to precise probabilistic analysis techniques. In fact, we can handle (cf. http://github.com/qflanTeam/QFLan and [5]) significantly larger instances of the Elevator case study. Originally introduced in [29], this case study is now a benchmark for SPL analysis known to be very demanding in terms of scalability when large sizes of Elevator systems are considered (cf., e.g., [5,10,11,13,14,18,19]).

Outline. Section 2 describes the tool's architecture, while Sect. 3 applies the tool to a simple family of coffee vending machines. Section 4 concludes the paper.

2   QFLan Architecture

The architecture of QFLAN is sketched in Fig. 1. It consists of a GUI layer and a core layer, devoted to modeling and analysis tasks, respectively.

GUI Layer. The components of the GUI layer are depicted in Fig. 2. The QFLAN editor provides state-of-the-art editing support, including auto-completion, syntax and error highlighting, and fix suggestions. This was obtained using XTEXT technology. For instance, the editor does on-the-fly error-detection on the structure of the feature model. The editor also offers

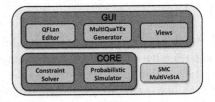

Fig. 1. QFLAN's architecture

support for MultiQuaTEx, the query language of the statistical model checker MultiVeStA [31] integrated in the tool. In particular, the user can specify properties to be analyzed with a high-level language consisting of QFLAN ingredients only, from which MultiQuaTEx queries are automatically generated. In addition, the GUI layer offers a number of views, including the *project explorer* to navigate across different QFLAN models, the tree-like *outline* to navigate in the elements

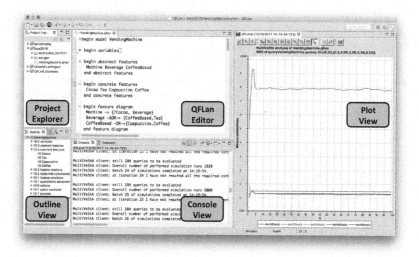

Fig. 2. A screenshot of the QFLAN tool

of QFLAN model, the *console view* to display diagnostic information, and the *plot view* to display analysis results.

Core Layer. The main component of the core layer is a probabilistic simulator. According to QFLAN's semantics, each state can have a set of outgoing admissible transitions, each labeled with a weight to compute the probability distribution of the transitions outgoing from each state. This leads to a discrete-time Markov chain semantics. Starting from the initial configuration specified by the modeler, the simulator iteratively computes all one-step transitions allowed in the state, and probabilistically selects one according to the probability distribution that results from normalizing the rates of the generated transitions. In particular, to check whether a transition is admissible the tool uses an ad-hoc constraint solver to guarantee that the transition does not violate any of the constraints specified by the modeler.

In [3,4], we presented a prototypical implementation of a QFLAN simulator based on the Maude toolkit [16] and Microsoft's SMT solver Z3 [27], integrated with MultiVeStA. The mature QFLAN tool presented in this paper has been redeveloped from scratch using Java-based technologies in order to obtain a multi-platform modern IDE for QFLAN instead of a command-line prototype. Furthermore, this led to an analysis speedup of several orders of magnitude.

3   QFLan at Work: Coffee Vending Machine

We consider a family of vending machines inspired by examples from the literature (e.g., [2,6–8,15,28]). For illustration purposes, we consider a simple version. Larger case studies can be found at http://github.com/qflanTeam/QFLan, including the bike-sharing case study used as running example in [2–4], the above mentioned SPL benchmark Elevator case study used in [5] to evaluate QFLAN's scalability, and a case study concerning risk analysis of a safe lock system with variability used in [5] to illustrate QFLAN's applicability in a non-SPL setting.

This family of vending machines sells either tea, or the coffee-based beverages coffee, cappuccino, and cappuccino with cocoa (chocaccino). Its feature model is depicted in Fig. 3. Listing 1 shows its QFLAN specification in 1:1 correspondence.

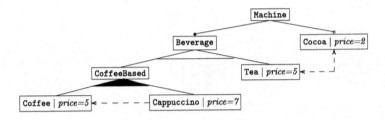

Fig. 3. Feature model of vending machine product line

Each node is a feature, while edges denote constraints defining admissible combinations of installed features. As is common in feature models, we distinguish between *concrete* and *abstract* features. The former are the tree's leaves, and can be explicitly (un)installed, whereas the latter are internal nodes, used mainly to group features. The root denotes a product, i.e. a specific vending machine. To instantiate a machine, one may install the *optional* feature Cocoa (its optionality is denoted by a circle in Fig. 3 and with a ? in Listing 1), while it must contain the *mandatory* feature Beverage (as denoted by a filled circle in Fig. 3 and by the absence of a ? in Listing 1). Finer constraints on the presence of

```
begin abstract features                        1
  Machine Beverage Coffee-based                2
end abstract features                          3
                                               4
begin concrete features                        5
  Cocoa Tea Cappuccino Coffee                  6
end concrete features                          7
                                               8
begin feature diagram                          9
  Machine -> {?Cocoa,Beverage}                10
  Beverage -XOR> {CoffeeBased,Tea}            11
  CoffeeBased -OR> {Cappuccino,Coffee}        12
end feature diagram                           13
                                               14
begin cross-tree constraints                  15
  Cappuccino requires Coffee                  16
  Tea excludes Cocoa                          17
end cross-tree constraints                    18
                                               19
begin feature predicates                      20
  price = {Cocoa=2,Tea=5,Cappuccino=7,       21
    Coffee=5}
end feature predicates                        22
                                               23
begin quantitative constraints                24
  price(Machine) <= 10                        25
end quantitative constraints                  26
```

Listing 1. QFLAN encoding of feature model displayed in Fig. 3

features other than mandatory or optional also can be imposed. The machine may come equipped with either a Tea dispenser or with one for CoffeeBased beverages. This is specified by the XOR edges connecting Beverage to Tea and to CoffeeBased. The CoffeeBased dispenser can be used to pour Coffee, Cappuccino, or both, as denoted by the OR edges.

Features can also be subject to *cross-tree constraints*. The arrow from Cappuccino to Coffee denotes that the former *requires* the latter, the rationale being that coffee is a prerequisite for preparing cappuccino. Instead, the double-headed arrow connecting Cocoa and Tea denotes that they *exclude* each other, since cocoa only serves to prepare chocaccino. Such constraints are specified in QFLAN as shown in Lines 15–18 of Listing 1. Finally, features can have quantitative predicates as attributes. In the example, all concrete features have *price* as attribute (Lines 20–22 of Listing 1). Abstract features implicitly inherit all predicates from concrete ones, with the cumulative value of all descendant concrete features actually installed.

Lines 24–26 of Listing 1 show that QFLAN supports another family of constraints regarding feature predicates, the *quantitative constraints*, used in this case study to exclude machines with a cumulative *price* that is superior to 10.

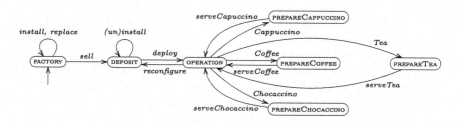

Fig. 4. Sketch of vending machine behavior

```
1   begin variables
2     sold = 0 deploys = 0
3   end variables
4
5   begin actions
6     sell deploy reconfigure chocaccino serveTea
7     serveCoffee serveCappuccino serveChocaccino
8   end actions
9
10  begin action constraints
11    do(chocaccino) -> (has(cappuccino) and has(cocoa))
12  end action constraints
13
14  begin process dynamics
15    states = factory,deposit,operation,prepareCoffee,
              prepareCappuccino,prepareTea,prepareChocaccino
16    transitions =
17    //Factory
18    factory -(replace(coffee,tea),20)-> factory,
19    factory -(install(cocoa),10)-> factory,
20    factory -(install(cappuccino),10)-> factory,
21  factory -(sell,1,{sold=1})-> deposit,
```

```
//Deposit                                          23
deposit -(install(cappuccino),2)->                 24
        deposit,
deposit -(uninstall(cappuccino),2)->               25
        deposit,
deposit -(install(cocoa),2)->                      26
        deposit,
deposit -(uninstall(cocoa),2)->                    27
        deposit,
deposit -(deploy,2,{deploys+=1})->                 28
        operation,
//Operation                                        29
operation -(coffee,3)->                            30
        prepareCoffee,
prepareCoffee -(serveCoffee,1)->                   31
        operation,
//Tea, Cappuccino & Chocaccino are                 32
        similar...
operation -(reconfigure,1)-> deposit               33

end process                                        34
                                                   35
begin init                                         36
  installedFeatures = { coffee }                   37
  initialProcesses = dynamics                      38
end init                                           39
```

Listing 2. QFLAN encoding of vending machine behavior sketched in Fig. 4

The dynamics of our example family is sketched in Fig. 4, while Listing 2 shows a textual QFLAN specification in close correspondence. The machine, initialized with a `Coffee` dispenser only, is pre-configured in the FACTORY by possibly *installing* any admissible feature configuration. After this, one can *sell* the machine to a company, in whose DEPOSIT minor customizations can be done before *deployment*. Once in OPERATION, the machine can *serve* customer requests, depending on the installed features, or be *reconfigured* in the DEPOSIT.

In QFLAN, one first specifies real-valued *variables* (Lines 1–3 of Listing 2) that can be used in the guards of constraints or to facilitate the analysis phase. Variables can be updated as side effects of the execution of *actions*, defined in the `actions` block (Lines 5–8). In addition, also installed concrete features can be executed as actions, meaning a user is using them. Note that `Chocaccino` is not a feature (like `Cappuccino` or `Coffee`) but an action. The rationale is that any machine provided with `Cappuccino` and `Cocoa` dispensers can serve `Chocaccino`. This is expressed in QFLAN using yet another family of constraints, the *action constraints* (Lines 10–12). Finally, Lines 14–32 specify the actual behavior in terms of a process named `dynamics` with sets of states (Line 15) and transitions (Lines 16–31), corresponding to the nodes and edges, respectively, of Fig. 4. Each transition is labeled with an action, including the (un)installation or replacement of features, and its weight, used to calculate the probability that it is executed.

The model is completed by specifying an initial configuration (Lines 34–37).

Note that, as side-effect of executing an action (`sell`), the transition in Line 20 sets the variable `sold` to 1 when a machine is sold. Pinpointing this precise moment allows to study, e.g., the average price of sold machines, or the probability that they have dispensers for `Coffee`, `Tea`, `Cappuccino`, and `Cocoa`.

These five properties (average price and four distinct probabilities) can be expressed as in Listing 3. The `query` specifies the properties to evaluate in the first state that satisfies `sold == 1`. The expected value x of each property is estimated by MultiVeStA as the mean value $\overline{x}$

```
begin analysis                                    1
query = eval when {sold == 1 } :                  2
    { price(Machine) [delta = 0.5],               3
      Coffee,Tea,Cappuccino,Cocoa }               4
default delta = 0.05 alpha = 0.05                  5
    parallelism = 1                               6
end analysis                                       7
```

Listing 3. QFLAN properties

of n samples (obtained from n independent simulations), with n large enough such that with probability $(1-\alpha)$ we have $x \in [\overline{x} - \delta/2, \overline{x} + \delta/2]$. Default values of α and δ are provided by the user via the keywords `alpha` and `delta` (these can be overruled for a specific property by providing its new value in square brackets, cf. Line 3). Finally, keyword `parallelism = p` allows to distribute simulations across `p` processes to be allocated on different cores. The analysis of the five properties in Listing 3 with QFLAN required ± 2000 simulations, for which it ran in under a second on a laptop with a 2.4 GHz Intel Core i5 processor and 4 GB of RAM.

The probability of having `Cappuccino` dispensers in machines sold is zero: any machine always has at least either a `Tea` or `Coffee` dispenser, with `price 5`, so installing `Cappuccino` would violate the constraint `price(Machine) <= 10` because `Cappuccino` has `price 7`. For the same reason, the probability to have `Coffee` installed is 0.33, which is roughly $\frac{1+10}{1+10+20}$, since in Lines 18–20 of Listing 2 we see that 1, 10, and 20 are the weights assigned to `sell`, `install(Cocoa)`, and `replace(Coffee,Tea)`, respectively (the weight of installing `Cappuccino` is ignored as it is not allowed). Note that `Coffee` is installed in machines sold if `replace(Coffee,Tea)` is not executed, which happens if `sell` is executed first, or if `Cocoa` gets installed, which prevents the execution of `replace(Coffee,Tea)` due to constraint `Tea excludes Cocoa`. The probability of installing `Cappuccino` becomes 0.46 if we use the more permissive constraint `price(Machine) <= 15`.

QFLAN also allows to study parametric properties as time progresses. For example, by replacing "`when {sold == 1.0}`" with "`from 0 to 100 by 1`" in Listing 3, we study the five properties at each of the first 100 simulation steps, for a total of 500 properties. Analysis results of parametric properties are visualized in interactive plots, in this case the one in Fig. 2, computed in a few seconds.

4   Outlook

We presented QFLAN, a quantitative modeling and verification environment for highly (re)configurable systems, like SPL, including Eclipse-based tool support. QFLAN offers an IDE for specifying system configurations and their probabilistic behavior in a high-level language as well as advanced statistical analyses of non-functional properties based on a discrete-time Markov chain semantics.

In the future, we envision a stochastic semantics based on continuous-time Markov chains for the analysis of time-related properties and a semantics based on featured transition systems to interface with the ProVeLines tool suite [17].

References

1. Apel, S., Batory, D.S., Kästner, C., Saake, G.: Feature-Oriented Software Product Lines: Concepts and Implementation. Springer, Heidelberg (2013). https://doi.org/10.1007/978-3-642-37521-7

2. ter Beek, M.H., Legay, A., Lluch Lafuente, A., Vandin, A.: Quantitative analysis of probabilistic models of software product lines with statistical model checking. In: FMSPLE 2015. EPTCS, vol. 182, pp. 56–70 (2015). https://doi.org/10.4204/EPTCS.182.5

3. ter Beek, M.H., Legay, A., Lluch Lafuente, A., Vandin, A.: Statistical analysis of probabilistic models of software product lines with quantitative constraints. In: SPLC 2015, pp. 11–15. ACM (2015). https://doi.org/10.1145/2791060.2791087

4. ter Beek, M.H., Legay, A., Lluch Lafuente, A., Vandin, A.: Statistical model checking for product lines. In: Margaria, T., Steffen, B. (eds.) ISoLA 2016. LNCS, vol. 9952, pp. 114–133. Springer, Cham (2016). https://doi.org/10.1007/978-3-319-47166-2_8

5. ter Beek, M.H., Legay, A., Lluch Lafuente, A., Vandin, A.: A framework for quantitative modeling and analysis of highly (re)configurable systems. IEEE Transactions in Software Engineering (2018). http://arxiv.org/abs/1707.08411

6. ter Beek, M.H., Mazzanti, F., Sulova, A.: VMC: a tool for product variability analysis. In: Giannakopoulou, D., Méry, D. (eds.) FM 2012. LNCS, vol. 7436, pp. 450–454. Springer, Heidelberg (2012). https://doi.org/10.1007/978-3-642-32759-9_36

7. ter Beek, M.H., de Vink, E.P.: Using mCRL2 for the analysis of software product lines. In: FormaliSE 2014, pp. 31–37. ACM (2014). https://doi.org/10.1145/2593489.2593493

8. ter Beek, M.H., de Vink, E.P., Willemse, T.A.C.: Family-based model checking with mCRL2. In: Huisman, M., Rubin, J. (eds.) FASE 2017. LNCS, vol. 10202, pp. 387–405. Springer, Heidelberg (2017). https://doi.org/10.1007/978-3-662-54494-5_23

9. Benavides, D., Segura, S., Ruiz-Cortés, A.: Automated analysis of feature models 20 years later: a literature review. Inf. Syst. **35**(6), 615–636 (2010). https://doi.org/10.1016/j.is.2010.01.001

10. Chrszon, P., Dubslaff, C., Klüppelholz, S., Baier, C.: Family-based modeling and analysis for probabilistic systems – featuring PROFEAT. In: Stevens, P., Wąsowski, A. (eds.) FASE 2016. LNCS, vol. 9633, pp. 287–304. Springer, Heidelberg (2016). https://doi.org/10.1007/978-3-662-49665-7_17

11. Chrszon, P., Dubslaff, C., Klüppelholz, S., Baier, C.: ProFeat: feature-oriented engineering for family-based probabilistic model checking. Formal Asp. Comput. **30**(1), 45–75 (2018). https://doi.org/10.1007/s00165-017-0432-4

12. Classen, A., Cordy, M., Heymans, P., Legay, A., Schobbens, P.Y.: Model checking software product lines with SNIP. Int. J. Softw. Tools Technol. Transf. **14**(5), 589–612 (2012). https://doi.org/10.1007/s10009-012-0234-1

13. Classen, A., Cordy, M., Heymans, P., Legay, A., Schobbens, P.Y.: Formal semantics, modular specification, and symbolic verification of product-line behaviour. Sci. Comput. Program. **80**(B), 416–439 (2014). https://doi.org/10.1145/2499777.2499781

14. Classen, A., Heymans, P., Schobbens, P.Y., Legay, A.: Symbolic model checking of software product lines. In: ICSE 2011, pp. 321–330. ACM (2011). https://doi.org/10.1145/1985793.1985838

15. Classen, A., Heymans, P., Schobbens, P.Y., Legay, A., Raskin, J.F.: Model checking lots of systems: efficient verification of temporal properties in software product lines. In: ICSE 2010, pp. 335–344. ACM (2010). https://doi.org/10.1145/1806799.1806850

16. Clavel, M., et al.: All About Maude - A High-Performance Logical Framework. LNCS, vol. 4350. Springer, Heidelberg (2007). https://doi.org/10.1007/978-3-540-71999-1

17. Cordy, M., Classen, A., Heymans, P., Schobbens, P.Y., Legay, A.: ProVeLines: a product line of verifiers for software product lines. In: SPLC 2013, pp. 141–146. ACM (2013). https://doi.org/10.1145/2499777.2499781

18. Cordy, M., Schobbens, P.Y., Heymans, P., Legay, A.: Beyond Boolean product-line model checking: dealing with feature attributes and multi-features. In: ICSE 2013, pp. 472–481. IEEE (2013). https://doi.org/10.1109/ICSE.2013.6606593

19. Dimovski, A.S., Al-Sibahi, A.S., Brabrand, C., Wąsowski, A.: Efficient family-based model checking via variability abstractions. Int. J. Softw. Tools Technol. Transf. **19**(5), 585–603 (2017). https://doi.org/10.1007/s10009-016-0425-2

20. Dimovski, A.S., Al-Sibahi, A.S., Brabrand, C., Wąsowski, A.: Family-based model checking without a family-based model checker. In: Fischer, B., Geldenhuys, J. (eds.) SPIN 2015. LNCS, vol. 9232, pp. 282–299. Springer, Cham (2015). https://doi.org/10.1007/978-3-319-23404-5_18

21. Dimovski, A.S., Wąsowski, A.: Variability-specific abstraction refinement for family-based model checking. In: Huisman, M., Rubin, J. (eds.) FASE 2017. LNCS, vol. 10202, pp. 406–423. Springer, Heidelberg (2017). https://doi.org/10.1007/978-3-662-54494-5_24

22. Gruler, A., Leucker, M., Scheidemann, K.: Modeling and model checking software product lines. In: Barthe, G., de Boer, F.S. (eds.) FMOODS 2008. LNCS, vol. 5051, pp. 113–131. Springer, Heidelberg (2008). https://doi.org/10.1007/978-3-540-68863-1_8

23. Kowal, M., Schaefer, I., Tribastone, M.: Family-based performance analysis of variant-rich software systems. In: Gnesi, S., Rensink, A. (eds.) FASE 2014. LNCS, vol. 8411, pp. 94–108. Springer, Heidelberg (2014). https://doi.org/10.1007/978-3-642-54804-8_7

24. Kwiatkowska, M., Norman, G., Parker, D.: PRISM 4.0: verification of probabilistic real-time systems. In: Gopalakrishnan, G., Qadeer, S. (eds.) CAV 2011. LNCS, vol. 6806, pp. 585–591. Springer, Heidelberg (2011). https://doi.org/10.1007/978-3-642-22110-1_47

25. Legay, A., Delahaye, B., Bensalem, S.: Statistical model checking: an overview. In: Barringer, H., et al. (eds.) RV 2010. LNCS, vol. 6418, pp. 122–135. Springer, Heidelberg (2010). https://doi.org/10.1007/978-3-642-16612-9_11

26. Mauro, J., Nieke, M., Seidl, C., Yu, I.C.: Context aware reconfiguration in software product lines. In: VaMoS 2016, pp. 41–48. ACM (2016). https://doi.org/10.1145/2866614.2866620

27. de Moura, L., Bjørner, N.: Z3: an efficient SMT solver. In: Ramakrishnan, C.R., Rehof, J. (eds.) TACAS 2008. LNCS, vol. 4963, pp. 337–340. Springer, Heidelberg (2008). https://doi.org/10.1007/978-3-540-78800-3_24

28. Muschevici, R., Proença, J., Clarke, D.: Feature nets: behavioural modelling of software product lines. Softw. Syst. Model. **15**(4), 1181–1206 (2016). https://doi.org/10.1007/s10270-015-0475-z

29. Plath, M., Ryan, M.: Feature integration using a feature construct. Sci. Comput. Program. **41**(1), 53–84 (2001). https://doi.org/10.1016/S0167-6423(00)00018-6

30. Salay, R., Famelis, M., Rubin, J., Sandro, A.D., Chechik, M.: Lifting model transformations to product lines. In: ICSE 2014, pp. 117–128. ACM (2014). https://doi.org/10.1145/2568225.2568267

31. Sebastio, S., Vandin, A.: MultiVeStA: statistical model checking for discrete event simulators. In: ValueTools 2013, pp. 310–315. ACM (2013) https://doi.org/10.4108/icst.valuetools.2013.254377

32. Thüm, T., Apel, S., Kästner, C., Schaefer, I., Saake, G.: A classification and survey of analysis strategies for software product lines. ACM Comput. Surv. **47**(1), 6:1–6:45 (2014). https://doi.org/10.1145/2580950

Modular Verification of Programs
with Effects and Effect Handlers in Coq

Thomas Letan[1,2(✉)], Yann Régis-Gianas[3,4], Pierre Chifflier[1],
and Guillaume Hiet[2]

[1] French Network Information Security Agency (ANSSI), Paris, France
thomas.letan@ssi.gouv.fr
[2] CentraleSupélec, Inria Rennes – Bretagne Atlantique, IRISA-D1, Rennes, France
[3] Univ Paris Diderot, Sorbonne Paris Cité, IRIF/PPS,
UMR 8243 CNRS, Paris, France
[4] PiR2, Inria Paris-Rocquencourt, Paris, France

Abstract. Modern computing systems have grown in complexity, and
the attack surface has increased accordingly. Even though system components are generally carefully designed and even verified by different
groups of people, the *composition* of these components is often regarded
with less attention. This paves the way for "architectural attacks", a
class of security vulnerabilities where the attacker is able to threaten the
security of the system even if each of its components continues to act as
expected. In this article, we introduce FreeSpec, a formalism built upon
the key idea that components can be modelled as programs with algebraic effects to be realized by other components. FreeSpec allows for the
modular modelling of a complex system, by defining idealized components connected together, and the modular verification of the properties
of their composition. In addition, we have implemented a framework for
the Coq proof assistant based on FreeSpec.

1   Introduction

A typical computing platform is made of dozens of hardware components, and
some of them execute complex software stacks. In this context, building a secure
computing system with respect to a given security policy remains challenging,
because attackers will leverage any vulnerability they can find. Both local component flaws and components composition inconsistencies, that is, a mismatch
between requirements assumed by some client components and the actual guarantees provided by others, can be used by attackers.

The latter scenario may lead to a situation where every component seems
to be working as expected, but their composition creates an attack path. We
name this class of security vulnerabilities "architectural attacks" [1]. Over the
past decade, many critical vulnerabilities affecting computing systems, in particular those relying on the x86 architecture, have raised awareness about the
threat posed by architectural attacks. Figure 1 summarizes several significant

© Springer International Publishing AG, part of Springer Nature 2018
K. Havelund et al. (Eds.): FM 2018, LNCS 10951, pp. 338–354, 2018.
https://doi.org/10.1007/978-3-319-95582-7_20

attacks [2–7] inside an idealized view of an x86 computing platform. In all cases, the vulnerability was rooted in an inconsistency in the components' composition.

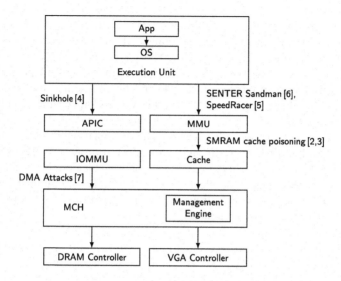

Fig. 1. Idealized x86 computing platform

The isolation of the System Management Mode (SMM) code by the hardware architecture is a good example to illustrate the threat posed by architectural attacks. The SMM is the most privileged execution mode of x86 CPU. Its purpose is to provide an "isolated processor environment that operates transparently to the operating system" [8] to execute so-called SMM code provided by the computer manufacturer. Since the SMM code is the most privileged software component executed by an x86 CPU, it is a desirable target for an attacker. The SMM code is stored in a dedicated memory region within the system memory, called the SMRAM; it is expected that only a CPU in SMM can access the SMRAM. In particular, the Memory Controller Hub (MCH) [9] provides a security mechanism to that end. In 2009, Duflot *et al.* [3] and Wojtczuk *et al.* [2] have independently shown that the cache could be used to circumvent this protection. The countermeasure required adding a new security mechanism to the CPU, meaning only computers produced after 2009 are protected against this particular vulnerability.

For many years, industrial manufacturers [10, 11] and researchers [12, 13] have aimed to formally specify and verify hardware architectures. However, verifying properties of existing computing platforms poses significant challenges, because they tend to be both complex and under-specified; we are not aware of any model of an existing and broadly used computing system that is comprehensive in terms of its hardware and software components. Unfortunately, such a model is a prerequisite to verify a computing platform in terms of architectural attacks.

The Coq proof assistant [14] has proven to be effective to model specific hardware components [13,15–17]. It provides a rich specification language, tools to write machine-checked proofs and a mechanism to derive executable programs to experimentally validate models. The scale of the task dictates several requirements regarding the formalism to adopt in this particular case. It must allow for considering independently each component of our system, before composing them to conclude about the properties of the system as a whole.

This objective is reminiscent of the programming language problematic to model and verify large programs with side effects. Reasoning about side effects in purely functional languages such as GALLINA, the Coq specification language, is difficult, firstly because they require somehow taking into account an outer *stateful* environment and secondly, because the composition of stateful computations is not well-handled by traditional (monadic) approaches. Algebraic effects and handlers [18] are a generic approach overcoming this double challenge. They allow modelling large classes of effects (e.g., exception, state, non-determinism) and to compose effects within purely functional programs, while deferring the realizations of these effects to dedicated handlers.

In this paper, we aim to show how a variant of algebraic effects based on Free monads can be used to reason about large systems, by modelling their components as effect handlers. Our contribution is threefold:

- We propose an approach which leverages the key concepts of algebraic effects and handlers to model and to verify each component of a computing system independently, while providing the necessary abstractions to compose these components in order to verify the properties of the resulting system.
- We have implemented FreeSpec[1], a framework for the Coq proof assistant to *modularly* verify programs with effects and effects handlers with our approach.
- We have modelled and verified a simplified MCH with FreeSpec, in a first step towards illustrating how our formalism can be leveraged to tackle our initial objective, that is modelling and verifying computing platforms.

The rest of the paper proceeds as follows. We describe how we model components in terms of programs with effects and effect handlers (Sect. 2) and we introduce so-called abstract specifications to verify their respective properties (Sect. 3). We also discuss the current limitations of our approach in terms of components connection; FreeSpec works well with tree of components, when more complex connection patterns require more investigation. To illustrate our definitions, we use a running example in the form of the specification and verification of a simplified MCH. Then, we discuss how the different levels of composition of FreeSpec can be leveraged to scale the modelling and verification work for larger systems (Sect. 4). Finally, we detail how FreeSpec is in line with an ongoing effort to modularly verify both large systems and programs with effects (Sect. 5).

---

[1] FreeSpec has been released as a free software, under the terms of the GPLv3. https:// github.com/ANSSI-FR/FreeSpec.

2   Modelling Programs with Effects

The first objective of FreeSpec is to incrementally model a complex system, one component at a time. To do so, we use the key concepts of algebraic effects and effect handlers, implemented with a variant of the Free monad called the Program monad as defined in the `operational` package of Haskell [19].

This section and the one afterwards proceed through a running example: a minimalist Memory Controller Hub (MCH) of the x86 hardware architecture. The MCH acts as a dispatcher for the CPU memory accesses; in our case, to the VGA controller or the DRAM controller. The MCH takes part in the isolation of the SMRAM, that is the special-purpose memory region inside the system memory which contains the SMM code. If correctly configured, the MCH will reroute any memory access which targets the SMRAM to the VGA controller, if this access is done by a CPU in another execution mode than SMM.

2.1   Interface of Effects

Within a computing system, interconnected components communicate through interfaces. A component which exhibits an interface receives computational requests from other components; it handles these requests by computing their results and sending the latter back to the client component. In FreeSpec, a computational request is modelled with an effect, that is a symbolic value which represents the request and its potential result.

Thereafter, we often define sets of values, and interfaces in particular, in terms of functions to construct these values. These functions are called "constructors"[2], and they have mutually exclusive images, i.e. it is not possible to construct the same value with two different constructors. For $\mathcal{I}$ an interface, we denote by $\mathcal{I}|_{\mathcal{A}} \subseteq \mathcal{I}$ the subset of effects whose results belong to a set $\mathcal{A}$.

Example 1 (MCH Interfaces). *The VGA and the DRAM controllers exhibit a similar interface which allows reading and writing into a memory region. Their interfaces are denoted by $\mathcal{I}_{\text{VGA}}$ and $\mathcal{I}_{\text{DRAM}}$ respectively. Let Loc be the set of memory locations and Val the set of values stored inside the memory region. We use the value () to model effects without results (similarly to the* `void` *keyword in an imperative language). We define $\mathcal{I}_{\text{DRAM}}$ (respectively $\mathcal{I}_{\text{VGA}}$) with two constructors:*

- **Read**$_{\text{DRAM}}$: *Loc* $\rightarrow \mathcal{I}_{\text{DRAM}}|_{Val}$
- **Write**$_{\text{DRAM}}$: *Loc* $\rightarrow Val \rightarrow \mathcal{I}_{\text{DRAM}}|_{\{()\}}$

Then, $\mathcal{I}_{\text{DRAM}} = \mathcal{I}_{\text{DRAM}}|_{\{()\}} \cup \mathcal{I}_{\text{DRAM}}|_{Val}$, and **Read**$_{\text{DRAM}}(l) \in \mathcal{I}_{\text{DRAM}}|_{Val}$ *is an effect that describes a memory access to read the value $v \in Val$ stored at the location $l \in Loc$.*

The MCH interface is similar, but it distinguishes between privileged and unprivileged accesses. It also provides one effect to lock the SMRAM protection

---

[2] In this article, functions are written in bold. In addition, constructors begin with a capital letter.

mechanism, i.e. it enables the SMRAM isolation until the next hardware reset. We define the set $\mathcal{P}riv \triangleq \{\,\mathtt{smm}, \mathtt{unprivileged}\,\}$ to distinguish between privileged memory accesses made by a CPU in SMM and unprivileged accesses made the rest of the time. The MCH interface, denoted by $\mathcal{I}_{\mathrm{MCH}}$, is defined with three constructors:

- $\mathbf{Read}_{\mathrm{MCH}} : \mathcal{L}oc \rightarrow \mathcal{P}riv \rightarrow \mathcal{I}_{\mathrm{MCH}}|_{\mathcal{V}al}$
- $\mathbf{Write}_{\mathrm{MCH}} : \mathcal{L}oc \rightarrow \mathcal{V}al \rightarrow \mathcal{P}riv \rightarrow \mathcal{I}_{\mathrm{MCH}}|_{\{()\}}$
- $\mathbf{Lock} : \mathcal{I}_{\mathrm{MCH}}|_{\{()\}}$

2.2 Operational Semantics for Effects

An effect corresponds to a computational request made to an implementation of a given interface. For a given computational request, we define its *operational semantics* to compute its result. Ultimately, we will model a component as an operational semantics for all the effects of its interface. Since operational semantics are defined using a purely functional language, they always compute the same result for a given effect, which is inconsistent with the stateful aspect of hardware components. Thus, an operational semantics produces not only a result, but also a new operational semantics, which encapsulates the new state of the component.

Definition 1 (Operational Semantics). *We write $\Sigma_{\mathcal{I}}$ for the set of operational semantics for a given interface $\mathcal{I}$, defined co-inductively as*

$$\Sigma_{\mathcal{I}} \triangleq \{\sigma \mid \sigma : \forall \mathcal{A}, \mathcal{I}|_{\mathcal{A}} \rightarrow \mathcal{A} \times \Sigma_{\mathcal{I}}\}.$$

An operational semantics $\sigma \in \Sigma_{\mathcal{I}}$ is a function which, given any effect of $\mathcal{I}$, produces both a result which belongs to the expected set and a new operational semantics to use afterwards.

A component may use more than one interface. For instance, the MCH of our running example can access the system memory and the memory shared by the VGA controller. But an operational semantics is defined for only one interface. In FreeSpec, we solve this issue by composing interfaces together to create new ones.

Definition 2 (Interfaces Composition). *Let $\mathcal{I}$ and $\mathcal{J}$ be two interfaces. $\oplus$ is the interface composition operator, defined with two constructors:*

- $\mathbf{InL} : \forall \mathcal{A}, \mathcal{I}|_{\mathcal{A}} \rightarrow (\mathcal{I} \oplus \mathcal{J})|_{\mathcal{A}}$
- $\mathbf{InR} : \forall \mathcal{A}, \mathcal{J}|_{\mathcal{A}} \rightarrow (\mathcal{I} \oplus \mathcal{J})|_{\mathcal{A}}$

The resulting interface $\mathcal{I} \oplus \mathcal{J}$ contains the effects of both $\mathcal{I}$ and $\mathcal{J}$, wrapped into either $\mathbf{InL}$ or $\mathbf{InR}$ constructors, defined to preserve the effects results sets.

Example 2 (VGA and DRAM Composition). *We consider $\mathcal{I}_{\mathrm{DRAM}} \oplus \mathcal{I}_{\mathrm{VGA}}$. Then, $\mathbf{InL}(\mathbf{Read}_{\mathrm{DRAM}}(l)) \in (\mathcal{I}_{\mathrm{DRAM}} \oplus \mathcal{I}_{\mathrm{VGA}})|_{\mathcal{V}al}$ is an effect that describes a read access targeting the DRAM controller, whereas $\mathbf{InR}(\mathbf{Write}_{\mathrm{VGA}}(l,c)) \in (\mathcal{I}_{\mathrm{DRAM}} \oplus \mathcal{I}_{\mathrm{VGA}})|_{\{()\}}$ is an effect that describes a write access targeting the VGA controller.*

Using ⊕, we can compose several interfaces together. We then need another composition operator, this time for operational semantics. We compose operational semantics together to construct a new operational semantics for the composed interface.

Definition 3 (Operational Semantics Composition). *Let $\mathcal{I}$ and $\mathcal{J}$ be two interfaces, $\sigma_i \in \Sigma_{\mathcal{I}}$ and $\sigma_j \in \Sigma_{\mathcal{J}}$ be two operational semantics dedicated to these interfaces. In this article, we use the λ-calculus abstraction notation for functions. $\otimes$ is the composition operator for operational semantics, defined as*

$$\sigma_i \otimes \sigma_j \triangleq \lambda e. \begin{cases} (x, \sigma_i' \otimes \sigma_j) \ when \ e = \mathbf{InL}(e_i) \, and \, \sigma_i(e_i) = (x, \sigma_i') \\ (x, \sigma_i \otimes \sigma_j') \ when \ e = \mathbf{InR}(e_j) \, and \, \sigma_j(e_j) = (x, \sigma_j') \end{cases}$$

The definition of $\otimes$ has an important impact over what we can specify in FreeSpec. Handling an effect of $\mathcal{I}$ (respectively $\mathcal{J}$) does not interfere with σ_j (respectively σ_i). As a consequence, *we can only specify as-is trees of components*, while graphs with, for instance, cycles or forward edges are still out of scope. This is the main limitation of FreeSpec, but its incidence is abated because computing platforms are often designed as a hierarchical succession of layers.

2.3   The Program Monad

Modelling programs with side effects in purely functional languages such as GAL-LINA (the Coq specification language) or Haskell is usually achieved thanks to monads [20]. FreeSpec leverages a variant of the Free monad called the Program monad [19] to model programs with effects. Operational semantics play the role of `operational` [19] interpreters. We write $P_{\mathcal{I}}(\mathcal{A})$ for the set of programs with effects which belongs to $\mathcal{I}$, modelled thanks to the Program monad, and whose result belongs to a set $\mathcal{A}$.

Definition 4 (Program Monad). $P_{\mathcal{I}}(\mathcal{A})$ *is defined with three constructors:*

– **Pure** : $\mathcal{A} \to P_{\mathcal{I}}(\mathcal{A})$
– **Bind** : $\forall \mathcal{B}, P_{\mathcal{I}}(\mathcal{B}) \to (\mathcal{B} \to P_{\mathcal{I}}(\mathcal{A})) \to P_{\mathcal{I}}(\mathcal{A})$
– **Request** : $\mathcal{I}|_{\mathcal{A}} \to P_{\mathcal{I}}(\mathcal{A})$

These constructors allow for the construction of values which act similarly to abstract syntax trees to model programs with effects. On the one hand, **Pure** and **Request** are comparable to the leaves of a syntax tree and model atomic computations; **Pure** models local computations, whereas **Request** models deferring a computational request to a handler and waiting for its result. On the other hand, **Bind** (denoted by the infix operator $\ggg$ afterwards) models the control flow of a program with effects, like the abstract syntax tree nodes would. It defines how the result of one computation determines the following ones.

Example 3 (Copy). *We define* **copy** : $Loc \to Loc \to P_{\mathcal{I}_{\mathrm{DRAM}}}(\{()\})$ *such that* **copy**(l, l') *models a program with effects that returns no result, but copies the value v stored at the memory location l inside the memory location l'.*

$$\mathbf{copy}(l, l') \triangleq \mathbf{Request}(\mathbf{Read}_{\mathrm{DRAM}}(l)) \ggg \lambda v.\mathbf{Request}(\mathbf{Write}_{\mathrm{DRAM}}(l', v))$$

Given $l \in \mathit{Loc}$ and $l' \in \mathit{Loc}$, $\mathbf{copy}(l, l')$ symbolically models a program with effects. To assign an interpretation of this program, it must be completed with an operational semantics which realizes the interface $\mathcal{I}_{\mathrm{DRAM}}$.

Definition 5 (Program with Effects Realization). *Let $\mathcal{I}$ be an interface, $\sigma \in \Sigma_{\mathcal{I}}$ an operational semantics for this interface and $\rho \in P_{\mathcal{I}}(\mathcal{A})$ a program with effects which belong to this interface. $\sigma[\rho] \in \mathcal{A} \times \Sigma_{\mathcal{I}}$ denotes the realization of this program by σ, defined as:*

$$\sigma[\rho] \triangleq \begin{cases} (x, \sigma) & \text{if } \rho = \mathbf{Pure}(x) \\ \sigma(e) & \text{if } \rho = \mathbf{Request}(e) \\ \sigma'[f(y)] & \text{if } \rho = q \ggg f \text{ and } (y, \sigma') = \sigma[q] \end{cases}$$

2.4 Components as Programs with Effects

With the interfaces, their operational semantics, the $\oplus$ and $\otimes$ operators to compose them and the Program monad to model programs with effects which belong to these interfaces, we now have all we need to model a given component which exposes an interface $\mathcal{I}$ and uses another interface $\mathcal{J}$. We proceed with the following steps: modelling the component in terms of programs with effects, then deriving one operational semantics for $\mathcal{I}$ from these programs, assuming provided an operational semantics for $\mathcal{J}$.

The behaviour of a component is often determined by a local, mutable state. When it computes the result of a computational request, not only a component may read its current state; but it can also modify it, for instance to handle the next computational request differently. This means we have to model the state of a component with a set $\mathcal{S}$ of symbolic state representations. We map the current state of the component and effects of $\mathcal{I}$ to a program with effects of $\mathcal{J}$. These programs must compute the effect result and the new state of the component.

Definition 6 (Component). *Let $\mathcal{I}$ be the interface exhibited by a component and $\mathcal{J}$ the interface it uses. Let $\mathcal{S}$ be the set of its states. The component C, defined in terms of programs with effects of $\mathcal{J}$, is of the form*

$$\forall \mathcal{A}, \mathcal{I}|_{\mathcal{A}} \to \mathcal{S} \to P_{\mathcal{J}}(\mathcal{A} \times \mathcal{S})$$

Hence, C specifies how the component handles computational requests, both in terms of computation results and state changes.

Example 4 (Minimal MCH Model). *Let C_{MCH} be the MCH defined in terms of programs with effects of $\mathcal{I}_{\mathrm{DRAM}} \oplus \mathcal{I}_{\mathrm{VGA}}$, then C_{MCH} is of the form*

$$\forall \mathcal{A}, \mathcal{I}_{\mathrm{MCH}}|_{\mathcal{A}} \to \mathcal{S}_{\mathrm{MCH}} \to P_{\mathcal{I}_{\mathrm{DRAM}} \oplus \mathcal{I}_{\mathrm{VGA}}}(\mathcal{A} \times \mathcal{S}_{\mathrm{MCH}})$$

where $\mathcal{S}_{\mathrm{MCH}} \triangleq \{\mathtt{on}, \mathtt{off}\}$ means the SMRAM protection is either activated (on) or deactivated (off).

*One the one hand, the **Lock** effect will activate the isolation mechanism of the MCH, setting its state to on. On the other hand, the effects constructed with*

Read$_{\text{MCH}}$ *and* **Write**$_{\text{MCH}}$ *will use the current state of the MCH, the privileged parameter of the effect and the memory location to lookup to determine if it uses the DRAM or the VGA controller. By default, it fetches the memory of the DRAM controller, except if the isolation mechanism is activated, the access is unprivileged and the targeted memory location belongs to the SMRAM. In such a case, it reroutes access to the VGA controller.*

A component C defined in terms of programs with effects cannot be used as-is to compute the result of a given effect. To do that, we need to derive an operational semantics for $\mathcal{I}$ from C.

Definition 7 (Deriving Operational Semantics). *Let C be a component which exhibits an interface $\mathcal{I}$, uses an interface $\mathcal{J}$ and whose states belong to $\mathcal{S}$. Let $s \in \mathcal{S}$ be the current state of the component and $\sigma_j \in \Sigma_{\mathcal{J}}$ be an operational semantics for $\mathcal{J}$. We can derive an operational semantics for $\mathcal{I}$, denoted by $\langle C, s, \sigma_j \rangle$, defined as*

$$\langle C, s, \sigma_j \rangle \triangleq \lambda i.(x, \langle C, s', \sigma_j' \rangle) \text{ where } ((x, s'), \sigma_j') = \sigma_j[C(i, s)]$$

The resulting operational semantics models a system made of interconnected components, and can then be used to derive another component model into an operational semantics which models a larger system. For instance, we can proceed with the following steps to comprehensively model our running example: (i) defining the operational semantics for the DRAM and VGA controllers; (ii) using these operational semantics to derive an operational semantics from C_{MCH}. The resulting operational semantics can take part in the derivation of a cache defined in terms of programs with effects of $\mathcal{I}_{\text{MCH}}$, to model a larger part of the system pictured in the Fig. 1.

3 Modular Verification of Programs with Effects

The first objective of FreeSpec is to provide the required tools to model each component of a system independently, and to compose these components to model the whole system. Its second objective is to verify that the composition of several components satisfies a set of properties. To achieve that, we introduce the so-called abstract specifications, which allows for specifying, for each interface, expected properties for the effect results, independently of any underlying handler. Abstract specifications can be used to emphasize the responsibility of each component of a system regarding the enforcement of a given security policy. Verifying a component is done against abstract specifications of the interfaces it directly uses, even if it relies on a security property enforced by a deeper component in the components graph. In this case, we have to verify that every single component which separate them preserve this property. This procedure can help to prevent or uncover architectural attacks.

In this section, we proceed with our running example by verifying that the MCH correctly isolates the SMRAM. In order to do that, we define an abstract specification which states that privileged reads targeting the SMRAM returns the value which has previously been stored by a privileged write. It models the SMRAM isolation: unprivileged writes cannot tamper with the content of the SMRAM, as read by a privileged CPU.

3.1   Definition

In FreeSpec, an abstract specification dedicated to an interface $\mathcal{I}$ is twofold. It defines a precondition over the effects that a caller must satisfy; and, in return, it specifies a postcondition over the effects results that an operational semantics must enforce. Since both the precondition and the postcondition may vary in time, we parameterize an abstraction specification with an abstract state and a step function to update this state after each effect realization.

Definition 8 (Abstract Specification). *We write A for an abstract specification dedicated to an interface $\mathcal{I}$, defined as a tuple $\langle \Omega, \mathbf{step}, \mathbf{pre}, \mathbf{post} \rangle$ where*

- *Ω is a set of abstract states*
- *$\mathbf{step} : \forall \mathcal{A}, \mathcal{I}|_{\mathcal{A}} \to \mathcal{A} \to \Omega \to \Omega$ is a transition function for the abstract state.*
- *$\mathbf{pre} \subseteq \mathcal{I} \times \Omega$ is the precondition over effects, such that $(e, \omega) \in \mathbf{pre}$ if and only if the effect e satisfies the precondition parameterized with the abstract state ω (denoted by $\mathbf{pre}(e, \omega)$).*
- *$\mathbf{post} \subseteq \bigcup_{\mathcal{A}} (\mathcal{I}|_{\mathcal{A}} \times \mathcal{A} \times \Omega)$ is the postcondition over effects results, such that $(e, x, \omega) \in \mathbf{post}$ if and only if the results x computed for the effects e satisfies the postcondition parameterized with the abstract state ω (denoted by $\mathbf{post}(e, x, \omega)$).*

By defining an abstract specification of an interface $\mathcal{I}$, it becomes possible to abstract away the effect handler, i.e. the underlying component. As a consequence, reasoning about a program with effects can be achieved without the need to look at the effect handlers. An abstract specification is dedicated to one verification problem (in our context, one security property), and it is possible to define as many abstraction specifications as required.

We write $\mathbf{run_{step}} : \forall \mathcal{A}, \Sigma_{\mathcal{I}} \to P_{\mathcal{I}}(\mathcal{A}) \to \Omega \to (\mathcal{A} \times \Sigma_{\mathcal{I}} \times \Omega)$ for the function which, in addition to realize a program with effects, updates an abstract state after each effect. Using $\mathbf{run_{step}}$, we can determine both the precondition over effects and the postcondition over effects results while an operational semantics realizes a program with effects.

Example 5 (MCH Abstract Specification). *Let A_{MCH} be the abstract specification such that $A_{\mathrm{MCH}} = \langle \Omega_{\mathrm{MCH}}, \mathbf{step}_{\mathrm{MCH}}, \mathbf{pre}_{\mathrm{MCH}}, \mathbf{post}_{\mathrm{MCH}} \rangle$. A_{MCH} models the following property: "privileged reads targeting the SMRAM return the value which has been previously stored by a privileged write":*

- *Let Smram $\subseteq$ Loc be the set of memory locations which belong to the SMRAM. We define $\Omega_{\mathrm{MCH}} \triangleq Smram \to Val$, such that $\omega \in \Omega_{\mathrm{MCH}}$ models a view of the SMRAM as exposed by the MCH for privileged reads.*

– *We define* $\textbf{step}_{\text{MCH}}$ *which updates the view of the MCH (modelled as a function) after each privileged write access targeting any SMRAM location l, that is*

$$\textbf{step}_{\text{MCH}}(e, x, \omega) \triangleq \begin{cases} \lambda l'.\ (\textit{if } l = l' \textit{ then } v \textit{ else } \omega(l')) \\ \qquad \textit{if } e = \textbf{Write}_{\text{MCH}}(l, v, \text{smm}) \textit{ and } l \in \textit{Smram} \\ \omega \qquad \textit{otherwise} \end{cases}$$

– *There is no precondition to the use of the MCH effects, so*

$$\forall e \in \mathcal{I}, \forall \omega \in \Omega_{\text{MCH}}, \textbf{pre}_{\text{MCH}}(e, \omega)$$

– *The postcondition enforces that the result x of a privileged read targeting the SMRAM (*$\textbf{Read}(l, \text{smm})$*) has to match the value stored in* A_{MCH} *abstract state, i.e. the expected content for this memory location* $\omega(l)$.

$$\textbf{post}_{\text{MCH}}(e, x, \omega) \triangleq \forall l \in \textit{Loc}, e = \textbf{Read}_{\text{MCH}}(l, \text{smm}) \wedge l \in \textit{Smram} \Rightarrow x = \omega(l)$$

3.2   Compliance and Correctness

The verification of a component C, which exhibits $\mathcal{I}$ and uses $\mathcal{J}$, consists in proving we can derive an operational semantics σ_i for $\mathcal{I}$ from an operational semantics σ_j for $\mathcal{J}$. This semantics σ_i enforces the postcondition of an abstract specification $A_{\mathcal{I}}$ dedicated to $\mathcal{I}$ (compliance). As C is defined in terms of programs with effects of $\mathcal{J}$, the latter needs to make a legitimate usage of $\mathcal{J}$ with respect to an abstract specification $A_{\mathcal{J}}$ dedicated to $\mathcal{J}$ (correctness).

First, σ_i complies with $A_{\mathcal{I}}$ if, (1) given any effect which satisfies $A_{\mathcal{I}}$ precondition, σ_i produces a result which satisfies its postcondition, and if (2) the new operational semantics σ_i' also complies with $A_{\mathcal{I}}$. The precondition and the postcondition are parameterized by an abstract state, so is the compliance property.

Definition 9 (Operational Semantics Compliance). *Let A be an abstract specification for an interface* $\mathcal{I}$, *defined as* $\langle \Omega, \textbf{step}, \textbf{pre}, \textbf{post} \rangle$, $\omega \in \Omega$, *then* $\sigma \in \Sigma_{\mathcal{I}}$ *complies with A in accordance with* ω *(denoted by* $\sigma \models A[\omega]$*) iff.*

$$\forall e \in \mathcal{I}, \textbf{pre}(e, \omega) \Rightarrow \textbf{post}(e, x, \omega) \wedge \sigma' \models A[\textbf{step}(e, x, \omega)] \textit{ where } (x, \sigma') = \sigma(e)$$

Secondly, programs with effects of C make a legitimate usage of an operational semantics $\sigma_j \in \Sigma_{\mathcal{J}}$ which complies with $A_{\mathcal{J}}$ if they only use effects which satisfy $A_{\mathcal{J}}$ precondition. As for the compliance property, correctness is parameterized with an abstract state.

Definition 10 (Program with Effects Correctness). *Let A be an abstract specification for an interface* $\mathcal{I}$, *defined as* $\langle \Omega, \textbf{step}, \textbf{pre}, \textbf{post} \rangle$, $\omega \in \Omega$, *and* $\rho \in P_{\mathcal{I}}(\mathcal{A})$, *then* ρ *is correct with respect to A in accordance with* ω *(denoted by* $A[\omega] \dashv \rho$*), iff.*

$$A[\omega] \models\!\mid \rho \triangleq \begin{cases} \textit{True} & \textit{if } \rho = \mathbf{Pure}(x) \\ \mathbf{pre}(e, \omega) & \textit{if } \rho = \mathbf{Request}(e) \\ \forall \sigma \in \Sigma_{\mathcal{I}} \textit{ such that } \sigma \models A[\omega], & \\ \quad A[\omega] \models\!\mid q \wedge A[\omega'] \models\!\mid f(x) & \textit{if } \rho = q \ggg f \\ \textit{where } (x, \_, \omega') = \mathbf{run_{step}}_{\mathcal{J}}(\sigma, q, \omega) & \end{cases}$$

Every local computation (**Pure**) is correct with respect to A in accordance with ω. A computation which uses an effect $e \in \mathcal{I}$ (**Request**) is correct with respect to A in accordance with ω if and only if e satisfies the precondition of A for the abstract state ω. Finally, the chaining of two programs with effects (**Bind**) is correct with A in accordance with ω if the first program is correct with A in accordance with ω, and the second program is correct in accordance with the abstract state reached after the realization of the first program.

Properties, inferred from an abstract specification, of a correct program with effects only hold if it is realized by a compliant operational semantics. Besides, we prove that correct programs preserve operational semantics compliance.

Theorem 1 (Compliance Preservation). *Let A be an abstract specification dedicated to an interface $\mathcal{I}$. σ a compliant operational semantics for $\mathcal{I}$ produces a compliant operational semantics σ' if it realizes a correct program ρ, that is*

$$\sigma \models A[\omega] \wedge A[\omega] \models\!\mid \rho \Rightarrow \sigma' \models A[\omega'] \textit{ where } \mathbf{run_{step}}(\sigma, \rho, \omega) = (x, \sigma', \omega')$$

As for interfaces (with $\oplus$) and operational semantics (with $\otimes$), we have also defined an abstract specification composition operator $\odot$. We do not detail its definition in this article, but it has the significant property of allowing for reasoning about the composition of interfaces and composition of operational semantics.

Theorem 2 (Congruent Composition). *Let $\mathcal{I}$ (respectively $\mathcal{J}$) be an interface. Let $A_{\mathcal{I}}$ (respectively $A_{\mathcal{J}}$) be an abstract specification and $\sigma_i \in \Sigma_{\mathcal{I}}$ (respectively $\sigma_j \in \Sigma_{\mathcal{J}}$) be an operational semantics for this interface.*

$$\sigma_i \models A_{\mathcal{I}}[\omega_i] \wedge \sigma_j \models A_{\mathcal{J}}[\omega_j] \Rightarrow \sigma_i \otimes \sigma_j \models (A_{\mathcal{I}} \odot A_{\mathcal{J}})[\omega_i, \omega_j]$$

With the Compliance Preservation, we know that as long as we follow the abstract specification precondition related to the effects we use, compliant operational semantics keep enforcing the postcondition. With the Compliance Preservation and Congruent Composition, we know we can reason locally, that is component by component.

3.3   Proofs Techniques to Show Compliance for Components

We have dived into the mechanisms which allow for composing together compliant operational semantics, but little has been said about how to prove the compliance property to begin with. In a typical FreeSpec use case, operational semantics are not built as-is, but rather derived from a component model (Definition 7). How to prove the resulting operational semantics complies with an abstract specification depends on how the component is connected to the rest of the system. We have already discussed the consequences of the operational semantics composition operator $\otimes$ (Definition 3). Notably, a graph of components which connects two nodes with more than one path cannot be easily modelled and verified in FreeSpec. In its current state, FreeSpec provides some theorems to verify the properties of a component model in terms of an abstract specification, depending on the composition pattern.

The most composition connection pattern consists of one component which uses many components, and is only used by one other component. Let $\mathcal{I}$ and $\mathcal{J}$ be two interfaces and let C, a component with a set of possible states $\mathcal{S}$, which exhibits $\mathcal{I}$ and uses $\mathcal{J}$. Let $A_{\mathcal{I}}$ be an abstract specification dedicated to $\mathcal{I}$. Deriving an operational semantics from C which complies with $A_{\mathcal{I}}$ in accordance with $\omega_i \in \Omega_I$ requires to show the existence of $s \in \mathcal{S}$ and $\sigma_j \in \Sigma_{\mathcal{J}}$ such that

$$\langle C, s, \sigma_j \rangle \models A_{\mathcal{I}}[\omega_i].$$

However, proving this statement would not be very satisfying, as it ties our verification results to one specific operational semantics σ_j, and by extension one specific component. As a consequence, we define an abstract specification $A_{\mathcal{J}}$ to generalize our statement and abstracting away σ_j. We now need to prove it exists $\omega_j \in \Omega_{\mathcal{J}}$ such that given an operational semantics σ_j which complies with $A_{\mathcal{J}}$ in accordance with ω_j, the operational semantics derived from C, s and σ_j complies with $A_{\mathcal{I}}$ in accordance with ω_i, that is

$$\forall \sigma_j \in \Sigma_{\mathcal{J}}, \sigma_j \models A_{\mathcal{J}}[\omega_j] \Rightarrow \langle C, s, \sigma_j \rangle \models A_{\mathcal{I}}[\omega_i]$$

The combinatorial explosion of cases introduced by ω_i, s and ω_j, modified as the component handles effects, makes inductive reasoning challenging. The FreeSpec framework provides a useful theorem to address these challenges, which leverages a so-called predicate of synchronization. The latter is defined by the user on a case-by-case basis, to act as an invariant for the induction, and a sufficient condition to enforce compliance.

Theorem 3 (Derivation Compliance). *Let* **sync**, *a relation between abstract states of $\Omega_{\mathcal{I}}$ and $\Omega_{\mathcal{J}}$, states of $\mathcal{S}$, be a predicate of synchronization. Then, it is expected that, $\forall \omega_i \in \Omega_{\mathcal{I}}$, $s \in \mathcal{S}$ and $\omega_j \in \Omega_{\mathcal{J}}$ such that* **sync**(ω_i, s, ω_j) *holds, then $\forall \sigma_j \in \Sigma_{\mathcal{J}}$ such that $\sigma_j \models A_{\mathcal{J}}[\omega_j]$ and $\forall e \in \mathcal{I}$ such that* **pre**$_{\mathcal{I}}(e, \omega_i)$,

1. *C preserves the synchronization of states, that is* **sync**$(\omega_i', s', \omega_j')$
2. *C is defined in terms of programs with effects which are correct with respect to $A_{\mathcal{J}}$ in accordance with ω_j, that is $A_{\mathcal{J}}[\omega_j] \models C(e, s)$*
3. *C computes a result for e which satisfies $A_{\mathcal{I}}$ postcondition, that is* **post**$_{\mathcal{I}}(e, x, \omega_i)$

*where $((x, s'), \sigma_j', \omega_j') = $* **run**$_{\text{step}_{\mathcal{J}}}(\sigma_j, C(e, s), \omega_j)$ *and $\omega_i' = $* **step**$_{\mathcal{I}}(e, x, \omega_i)$. *Should these three properties be verified, then we show that*

$$\textbf{sync}(\omega_i, s, \omega_j) \wedge \sigma_j \models A_{\mathcal{J}}[\omega_j] \Rightarrow \langle C, s, \sigma_j \rangle \models A_{\mathcal{I}}[\omega_i].$$

Example 6 (MCH Compliance). *We want to prove we can derive an operational semantics from C_{MCH} (Example 4) which complies with A_{MCH} (Example 5).*

We define $A_{\mathrm{DRAM}} \triangleq \langle \Omega_{\mathrm{DRAM}}, \mathbf{step}_{\mathrm{DRAM}}, \mathbf{pre}_{\mathrm{DRAM}}, \mathbf{post}_{\mathrm{DRAM}} \rangle$ an abstract specification dedicated to $\mathcal{I}_{\mathrm{DRAM}}$ to express the following property: "a read access to a memory location which belongs to the SMRAM return the value which have been previously written at this memory location." In particular, $\Omega_{\mathrm{DRAM}} = \Omega_{\mathrm{MCH}}$, i.e. they are two views of the SMRAM, as exposed by the DRAM controller or by the MCH. In this context, the behaviour of VGA is not relevant. Let $\top$ be the abstract specification which has no state and such that its precondition and postcondition are always satisfied (meaning every operational semantics always complies with it). Therefore, the abstract specifications dedicated to the interface used by C_{MCH}, that is $\mathcal{I}_{\mathrm{DRAM}} \oplus \mathcal{I}_{\mathrm{VGA}}$, is $A_{\mathrm{DRAM}} \odot \top$ whose abstract state is Ω_{DRAM}.

We define the predicate of synchronization $\mathbf{sync}_{\mathrm{MCH}}$ such that

$$\mathbf{sync}_{\mathrm{MCH}}(\omega_i, s, \omega_j) \triangleq s = \mathbf{on} \wedge \forall l \in Smram, \omega_i(l) = \omega_j(l)$$

Hence, we start our reasoning from a situation where the SMRAM isolation is already activated and the states of the two abstract specifications are the same, meaning the two views of the SMRAM (as stored in the DRAM, and as exposed by the MCH) coincide. We prove $\mathbf{sync}_{\mathrm{MCH}}$ satisfies the three premises of the Theorem 3. We conclude we can derive an operational semantics from C_{MCH} which complies with A_{MCH}.

Another common composition pattern consists of a component which is used by more than one other component. FreeSpec provides a theorem which allows for extending the result obtained with the Theorem 3, in the specific case where concurrent accesses do not lead to any change of the abstract state.

4   Discussion

For two sections, we have introduced the FreeSpec key definitions and theorems so that we could model a minimal MCH component and verify its properties in the presence of a well-behaving DRAM controller. This example has been driven by a real mechanism commonly found inside x86-based computing platforms. We now discuss how FreeSpec can be leveraged to model and verify larger systems.

4.1   FreeSpec as a Methodology

The typical workflow of FreeSpec can be summarized as follows: specifying the interfaces of a system; modelling the components of the system in terms of programs with effects of these interfaces; identifying the abstract specifications which express the requirements over each interface; verifying each component in terms of compliance with these abstract specifications.

Independent groups of people can use FreeSpec to modularly model and verify a system, as long as they agree on the interfaces and abstract specifications. If, during the verification process, one group finds out a given interface or abstract specification needs to be updated, the required modifications may impact its neighbours. For instance, modelling a x86-based computing system, as pictured in Fig. 1, using FreeSpec requires to take into account the CPU cache, and to verify it complies with an abstract specification similar to the one defined in Example 5. Thus, FreeSpec could have helped uncover the attack mentioned in Sect. 1 [2,3], and other similar architectural attacks.

The abstract specifications are defined in terms of interfaces, i.e. independently from components. It has two advantages. First, for a given verification problem modelled with a set of abstract specifications, two components which exhibit the same interface can be proven to comply with the same abstract specification. In such a case, we can freely interchange these components, and the verification results remain true. This is useful to consider the challenge posed by components versioning, i.e. a new version of a component brings new features which could be leveraged by an attacker. Then, it is possible to verify a given component in terms of several abstract specifications. This means we can independently conduct several verification works against the same component.

4.2   FreeSpec as a Framework

FreeSpec includes about 8,000 lines of code: 6,000 for its core, 2,000 for the experiments. It has been built upon three objectives: readability of models, automation of proofs, opportunity to extract these models for experimental validation.

To achieve readability, FreeSpec borrows several popular concepts to modern functional programming language, such as Haskell. We have used the `Notation` feature of Coq to add the do-notation of Haskell to GALLINA. This allows for writing monadic functions that can be read as if it were pseudo-code. The readers familiar with the monad transformers mechanism [21] may also have recognized the definition of the transformer variant of the State monad in the Definition 6. FreeSpec takes advantage of the State monad mechanism to seamlessly handle the local state of the component.

To achieve automation of proofs, we have developed specific Coq tactics. Some definitions of FreeSpec can be pretty verbose, and the proofs quickly become difficult to manage as the program grows in complexity. FreeSpec provides two tactics to explore the control flow of programs with effects.

Finally, to achieve model extraction, we have defined the key concepts of FreeSpec so that they remain compatible with the extraction mechanism of Coq. As a consequence, component models can be derived into executable programs. For a hardware component, it means we could, for instance, compare its behaviour with its concrete counterpart. For a software component, it means we can fill the gap between the model and the implementation.

5   Related Work

FreeSpec falls within two domains of research: the verification of large systems made of components, and the modular verification of programs with effects.

FreeSpec follows our previous work named SpecCert [1], whose lack of modularity complexified scalability. KAMI [13] shares many concepts with FreeSpec, but implements them in a totally different manner: components are defined as labelled transition systems and can be extracted into FPGA bitstreams. KAMI is hardware-specific, thus is not suitable to reason about systems which also include software components. However, it allows for expressing more composition pattern than FreeSpec (e.g. components cycle). Thomas Heyman *et al.* [22] have proposed a component-based modelling technique for Alloy [23], where components are primarily defined as semantics for a set of operations; a component is connected to another when it leverages its operations. Alloy leverages a model finder to verify a composition of these components against known security patterns, and to assume or verify facts about operations semantics; however, it lacks an extraction mechanism, which makes it harder to validate the model.

Algebraic effects and effect handlers led to a lot of research about verification of programs with side effects [18,24], but to our surprise, we did not find any approach to write and verify programs with effects and effect handlers written for GALLINA. However, other approaches exist. Ynot [25] is a framework for the Coq proof assistant to write, reason with and extract GALLINA programs with side effects. Ynot side effects are specified in terms of Hoare preconditions and postconditions parameterized by the program heap, and does not dissociate the definition of an effect and properties over its realization. To that extent, FreeSpec abstract specification is more expressive (thanks to the abstract state) and flexible (we can define more than one abstract specification for a given interface). Claret *et al.* have proposed Coq.io, a framework to specify and verify interactive programs in terms of use cases [26]. The proofs rely on *scenarios* which determine how an environment would react to the program requests. These scenarios are less generic and expressive than FreeSpec abstract specifications, but they are declarative and match a widely adopted software development process. As a consequence, they may be easier to read and understand for software developers.

Previous approaches from the Haskell community to model programs with effects using Free monads [19,27] are the main source of inspiration for FreeSpec. In comparison, we provide a novel method to verify these programs, inspired by the interface refinement of the B-method [28]. It also had some similiraties with FoCaLiZe [29], a proof environment where proofs are attached to components.

6   Conclusion and Future Work

We have proposed an approach to model and verify each component of a computing system independently, while providing the necessary abstractions to compose these components together in order to verify the properties of the resulting system. We have implemented FreeSpec, an open-source framework for the Coq proof assistant which implements our approach. Finally, we applied our approach to a simplified x86-based computing platform in terms of programs.

We would like to consider more composition patterns. We also anticipate abstract specifications may become harder to understand as their complexity grows. We want to make them more declarative, so they could be more easily understood by software developers who are less familiar with functional programming and formal verification.

References

1. Letan, T., Chifflier, P., Hiet, G., Néron, P., Morin, B.: SpecCert: specifying and verifying hardware-based security enforcement. In: Fitzgerald, J., Heitmeyer, C., Gnesi, S., Philippou, A. (eds.) FM 2016. LNCS, vol. 9995, pp. 496–512. Springer, Cham (2016). https://doi.org/10.1007/978-3-319-48989-6_30
2. Wojtczuk, R., Rutkowska, J.: Attacking SMM memory via Intel CPU cache poisoning. Invisible Things Lab (2009)
3. Duflot, L., Levillain, O., Morin, B., Grumelard, O.: Getting into the SMRAM: SMM Reloaded. CanSecWest, Vancouver (2009)
4. Domas, C.: The memory sinkhole. In: BlackHat USA, July 2015
5. Kallenberg, C., Wojtczuk, R.: Speed racer: exploiting an intel flash protection race condition. Bromium Labs, January 2015
6. Kovah, X., Kallenberg, C., Butterworth, J., Cornwell, S.: SENTER Sandman: using Intel TXT to attack BIOSes. Hack in the Box (2015)
7. Stewin, P., Bystrov, I.: Understanding DMA malware. In: Flegel, U., Markatos, E., Robertson, W. (eds.) DIMVA 2012. LNCS, vol. 7591, pp. 21–41. Springer, Heidelberg (2013). https://doi.org/10.1007/978-3-642-37300-8_2
8. Manual I.P.: Intel IA-64 Architecture Software Developer's Manual. Itanium Processor Microarchitecture Reference for Software Optimization, August 2000
9. Intel: Intel 5100 Memory Controller Hub Chipset
10. Reid, A.: Who guards the guards? Formal validation of the Arm v8-M architecture specification. In: Proceedings of the ACM on Programming Languages, vol. 1(OOPSLA), p. 88 (2017)
11. Leslie-Hurd, R., Caspi, D., Fernandez, M.: Verifying linearizability of Intel® software guard extensions. In: Kroening, D., Păsăreanu, C.S. (eds.) CAV 2015. LNCS, vol. 9207, pp. 144–160. Springer, Cham (2015). https://doi.org/10.1007/978-3-319-21668-3_9
12. Chong, S., Guttman, J., Datta, A., Myers, A., Pierce, B., Schaumont, P., Sherwood, T., Zeldovich, N.: Report on the NSF Workshop on Formal Methods for Security. ArXiv preprint arXiv:1608.00678 (2016)
13. Choi, J., Vijayaraghavan, M., Sherman, B., Chlipala, A., et al.: Kami: a platform for high-level parametric hardware specification and its modular verification. In: Proceedings of the ACM on Programming Languages, vol. 1(ICFP), p. 24 (2017)
14. Inria: The Coq Proof Assistant. https://coq.inria.fr/
15. Braibant, T.: Coquet: a coq library for verifying hardware. In: Jouannaud, J.-P., Shao, Z. (eds.) CPP 2011. LNCS, vol. 7086, pp. 330–345. Springer, Heidelberg (2011). https://doi.org/10.1007/978-3-642-25379-9_24
16. Morrisett, G., Tan, G., Tassarotti, J., Tristan, J.B., Gan, E.: RockSalt: better, faster, stronger SFI for the x86. In: ACM SIGPLAN Notices, vol. 47, pp. 395–404. ACM (2012)

17. Jomaa, N., Nowak, D., Grimaud, G., Hym, S.: Formal proof of dynamic memory isolation based on MMU. In: 2016 10th International Symposium on Theoretical Aspects of Software Engineering (TASE), pp. 73–80. IEEE (2016)
18. Bauer, A., Pretnar, M.: Programming with algebraic effects and handlers. J. Log. Algebraic Methods Program. **84**(1), 108–123 (2015)
19. Apfelmus, H.: The `operational` package. https://hackage.haskell.org/package/operational
20. Hoareetal, C.: Tackling the awkward squad: monadic input/output, concurrency, exceptions, and foreign-language calls in Haskell. Engineering Theories of Software Construction (2001)
21. Liang, S., Hudak, P., Jones, M.: Monad transformers and modular interpreters. In: Proceedings of the 22nd ACM SIGPLAN-SIGACT Symposium on Principles of Programming Languages, pp. 333–343. ACM (1995)
22. Heyman, T., Scandariato, R., Joosen, W.: Reusable formal models for secure software architectures. In: 2012 Joint Working IEEE/IFIP Conference on Software Architecture and European Conference on Software Architecture, WICSA/ECSA 2012, Helsinki, Finland, 20–24 August 2012, pp. 41–50 (2012)
23. Jackson, D.: Software Abstractions: Logic, Language and Analysis. MIT Press, Cambridge (2012)
24. Brady, E.: Resource-dependent algebraic effects. In: Hage, J., McCarthy, J. (eds.) TFP 2014. LNCS, vol. 8843, pp. 18–33. Springer, Cham (2015). https://doi.org/10.1007/978-3-319-14675-1_2
25. Nanevski, A., Morrisett, G., Shinnar, A., Govereau, P., Birkedal, L.: Ynot: dependent types for imperative programs. In: ACM Sigplan Notices, vol. 43, pp. 229–240. ACM (2008)
26. Claret, G., Régis-Gianas, Y.: Mechanical verification of interactive programs specified by use cases. In: Proceedings of the Third FME Workshop on Formal Methods in Software Engineering, pp. 61–67. IEEE Press (2015)
27. Kiselyov, O., Ishii, H.: Freer monads, more extensible effects. In: ACM SIGPLAN Notices, vol. 50, pp. 94–105. ACM (2015)
28. Abrial, J.R., Abrial, J.R.: The B-Book: Assigning Programs to Meanings. Cambridge University Press, Cambridge (2005)
29. Pessaux, F.: FoCaLiZe: inside an F-IDE. ArXiv preprint arXiv:1404.6607 (2014)

Combining Tools for Optimization and Analysis of Floating-Point Computations

Heiko Becker[1], Pavel Panchekha[2], Eva Darulova[1(✉)], and Zachary Tatlock[2]

[1] MPI-SWS, Saarbrücken, Germany
{hbecker,eva}@mpi-sws.org
[2] University of Washington, Seattle, USA
{pavpan,ztatlock}@cs.washington.edu

Abstract. Recent renewed interest in optimizing and analyzing floating-point programs has lead to a diverse array of new tools for numerical programs. These tools are often complementary, each focusing on a distinct aspect of numerical programming. Building reliable floating point applications typically requires addressing several of these aspects, which makes easy composition essential. This paper describes the composition of two recent floating-point tools: Herbie, which performs accuracy optimization, and Daisy, which performs accuracy verification. We find that the combination provides numerous benefits to users, such as being able to use Daisy to check whether Herbie's unsound optimizations improved the worst-case roundoff error, as well as benefits to tool authors, including uncovering a number of bugs in both tools. The combination also allowed us to compare the different program rewriting techniques implemented by these tools for the first time. The paper lays out a road map for combining other floating-point tools and for surmounting common challenges.

1 Introduction

Across many domains, numerical computations specified over the reals are actually implemented using floating-point arithmetic. Due to their finite nature, operations on floating-point numbers cannot be calculated exactly and accumulate roundoff errors. In addition, real-valued identities such as associativity no longer hold, making manual reasoning and optimization challenging. To address these challenges, new automated tools have recently been developed which build on advances in program rewriting and verification techniques to enable even non-experts to analyze and optimize their floating point code.

Some of these tools use sound techniques to statically bound roundoff errors of straight-line floating-point programs [8,9,12,15,16,22] and partially automate complex analysis tasks [10,18]. Other such tools use dynamic techniques to find inputs that suffer from large rounding errors [4,23]. Yet other tools perform rewriting-based optimization [5,8,17,20] and mixed-precision tuning [3,7] to improve the accuracy and performance of floating-point programs.

© Springer International Publishing AG, part of Springer Nature 2018
K. Havelund et al. (Eds.): FM 2018, LNCS 10951, pp. 355–363, 2018.
https://doi.org/10.1007/978-3-319-95582-7_21

Since these tools are typically complementary, each focusing on a distinct aspect of numerical reliability, users will need to compose several to meet their development needs. This makes ease of composition essential, and some first steps in this regard have been taken by the FPBench project [6], which provides a common specification language for inputs to floating-point analysis tools similar to the one provided by the SMT-LIB standard [1]. However, no literature yet exists on the actual use of FPBench to compose tools and on the challenges that stand in the way of combining different floating-point tools, such as differing notions of error and different sets of supported functions.

In this paper we report on our experience implementing the first combination of two complementary floating-point analysis tools using FPBench: Herbie [17] and Daisy [8]. Herbie optimizes the accuracy of straight-line floating-point expressions, but employs a dynamic roundoff error analysis and thus cannot provide sound guarantees on the results. In contrast, Daisy performs static analysis of straight-line expressions, which is sound w.r.t. IEEE754 floating-point semantics [13]. Our combination of the tools is implemented as a script in the FPBench repository (https://github.com/FPBench/FPBench).

We see this combination of a heuristic and a sound technique as particularly interesting; Daisy can act as a backend for validating Herbie's optimizations. Daisy computes improved worst-case roundoff error bounds for many (but not all) expressions optimized by Herbie. On others it raises an alarm, discovering division-by-zero errors introduced by Herbie. We also improved the precision of Daisy's analysis of special functions as we found that some were sound but not accurate enough. Thus, the combination was also useful in uncovering limitations of both tools.

Daisy additionally implements a sound genetic programming-based accuracy optimization procedure. Our combination of Daisy and Herbie allows us to compare it to Herbie's unsound procedure based on greedy search. We discover important differences between the two procedures, suggesting that the techniques are not competitive but in fact complementary and best used in combination.

Some of the challenges we encountered, such as differing supported functions and different error measures, are likely to be encountered by other researchers or even end users combining floating-point tools, and our experience shows how these challenges can be surmounted. Our evaluation on benchmarks from the FPBench suite also shows that tool composition can provide end-to-end results not achievable by either tool in isolation and suggests that further connections with other tools should be investigated.

2   Implementation

The high-level goal of our combination is to use Daisy as a verification backend to Herbie to obtain a sound upper bound on the roundoff error of the expression returned by Herbie. By also evaluating the roundoff error of Herbie's output and of the input expression, we can obtain additional validation of the improvement. It should be noted, however, that Daisy cannot verify whether the actual worst-case or average roundoff error has decreased—a decrease in the computed upper bound can be due to an actual decrease or simply due to a stronger static bound. In many cases, however, such as in safety-critical systems, just *proving* a smaller static bound is already useful.

We have implemented the combination in a script, which we sketch in Fig. 1. For each straight-line input program f_{src}, we first run Herbie to compute an optimized version f_{res}. Both the optimized and unoptimized version are translated into Daisy's input format (using FPCore2Scala), and Daisy is run on both versions to compute error bounds.

```
f_res = Herbie(f_src)
err_src = min{ Daisy(A, FPCore2Scala(f_src)) | A <- AnalysisTypes }
err_res = min{ Daisy(A, FPCore2Scala(f_res)) | A <- AnalysisTypes }
```

Fig. 1. Pseudocode of the script used to compose Herbie and Daisy into a single tool; AnalysisTypes contains different modes Daisy can be run in.

Daisy supports several different types of error analysis, and we run Daisy in a portfolio style, where the tightest bound computed by any of the analyses is used. In particular, we use the interval analysis with subdivisions mode and the SMT solver mode (with Z3 [11] as the solver).[1] Since each analysis is sound, this provides the tightest error bound that Daisy can prove.

When implementing the script that runs Herbie and Daisy together we had to address two major differences between the two tools: Herbie and Daisy use different input (and output) formats, and Daisy requires domain bounds on all input variables, whereas Herbie allows unbounded inputs. While the implemented script is simple, it took several iterations to implement. The most time consuming part was the improvements that only became apparent after running the tools together. We will first explain how we solved the two differences between Daisy and Herbie and then give an overview on the improvements in both tools.

Formats. To avoid having to add new frontends, we implemented a translator from FPBench's FPCore format to Daisy's Scala-based input language. As Herbie produces optimized expressions in FPCore, this translator allows us to run Daisy on both the benchmarks and on Herbie's optimized expressions. This translator is now part of the FPBench toolchain and can be used by other researchers and by users to integrate Daisy with other tools developed as part of the FPBench project.

Preconditions. Both Daisy and Herbie allow preconditions for restricting the valid inputs to a floating-point computation. For Herbie, these preconditions are optional. In contrast, Daisy requires input ranges for performing a forward dataflow analysis to compute sound absolute roundoff error bounds. Several of

---

[1] We found that neither interval analysis without subdivision nor alternate SMT solvers provided tighter bounds.

the benchmarks in FPBench did not have a specified precondition. For our experiments, we manually added a meaningful precondition to these programs, with preconditions chosen to focus on input values with significant rounding errors. To avoid biasing the results, the preconditions were simple order-of magnitude ranges for each variable, with the endpoints of these ranges chosen from 1, 10^{10}, or 10^{20} and their inverses and negations.

Improvements in Daisy and Herbie. Connecting Daisy and Herbie and running each on several previously unseen benchmarks uncovered numerous possibilities for improvements in Herbie and Daisy.

In Herbie, several bugs were discovered by our efforts: an incorrect type-checking rule for let statements (which would reject some valid programs); incorrect handling of duplicate fields (which allowed one field to improperly override another); and an infinite loop in the sampling code (triggered by some preconditions). Real users running older versions of Herbie have since also reported these bugs, suggesting that issues addressed during tool composition helped improve user experience generally.

In Daisy, we discovered that the analysis of elementary functions was unnecessarily conservative and improved the rational approximations used. Error handling in both tools was also improved such that issues like (potential) divisions by zero or timeouts are now accurately reported. This more precise feedback significantly improves user friendliness and reduces debugging time.

3 Experimental Results

We perform two evaluations of our combination of Daisy and Herbie: we first use Daisy as a verification backend for Herbie and then we compare Daisy's and Herbie's rewriting algorithms. Both experiments use all supported benchmarks from the FPBench suite. We give the full table with all the evaluation data in our technical report [2]. The experiments were run on a machine with an i7-4790K CPU and 32 GB of memory. For each benchmark we give both Daisy and Herbie a timeout of 10 min.

Composing Daisy and Herbie. Our first experiment considers Daisy solely as a tool for computing floating-point error bounds. Herbie is then used to attempt to improve the benchmark's accuracy.

Of the 103 benchmarks, Herbie times out on 31 of them. Of the remaining 72 benchmarks, Daisy raises an alarm[2] on 24 and can prove a bound on 48. Of the 48 benchmarks where Daisy can prove an error bound, Daisy's roundoff error analysis can prove a tighter worst-case error bound for 22 of Herbie's outputs, an equal bound for 18, and a looser bound for 8. These results are summarized in the left-most graph in Fig. 2.

---

[2] Indicating that it could not prove the absence of invalid operations, such as divisions by zero.

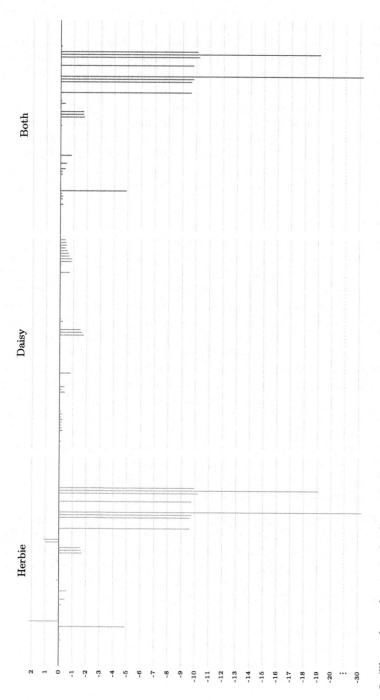

Fig. 2. The orders of magnitude change in Daisy's worst case error estimate after rewriting with Herbie, Daisy, and both Herbie and Daisy (left to right). Note that combining both rewriting algorithms keeps the large beneficial changes introduced by Herbie but avoids its detrimental changes.

Of the 24 benchmarks where Daisy raises an alarm, for 13 Daisy raises an alarm on the original input program and for 16 the alarm is raised on the output program Herbie produced. Some of these alarms are true positives while others are spurious. For example, in some benchmarks Herbie had introduced a possible division by 0, which Daisy was able to detect. In others, the output contained expressions like $1/(x(1 + x))$, with $10^{10} < x < 10^{20}$, where Daisy is unable to prove that no division by zero occurs.

We see this as good evidence that Daisy can be used as a verification back-end for Herbie. One challenge is that Daisy's error analysis can only show that Herbie's output has a smaller error *bound*, not that it is more accurate at any particular point on the original program. Additionally, it is difficult to determine which of Daisy's alarms are spurious. Despite these challenges, the combination of Daisy and Herbie was able to produce large, verified improvements in rounding error in many benchmarks.

Comparing Daisy's and Herbie's Error Measures. One topic of particular interest in combining Daisy and Herbie is their different measures of floating-point error. Herbie measures the error in terms *units in the last place*, or ULPs. To compute this error, Herbie randomly samples input values and takes the average of error across those inputs. It thus provides a *dynamic, unsound measure of average ULPs* of error. Daisy, meanwhile, uses a mathematical abstraction based on the definition of rounding and IEEE754 operator semantics to provide *static, sound bounds on the maximum absolute error*. The relationship between these two measures of error is central to using Herbie and Daisy together.

Despite these stark differences between Herbie's and Daisy's error measures, our evaluation data shows that Daisy and Herbie can be fruitfully used together: Daisy verifies that Herbie's improved program is no less accurate for 40/48 of the benchmarks. This suggests that, though Daisy and Herbie use very different means to measure error, both are successfully measuring the same underlying notion of error. The fact that Daisy's and Herbie's error measures are suited to their particular approaches (static analysis and program search) suggests that future tools should focus not on measuring error "correctly" but on finding an error measure well suited to their technical approach.

Comparing Daisy and Herbie. Our second experiment compares Daisy's and Herbie's rewriting algorithms. Daisy uses genetic programming to search for a program with a tighter bound. Herbie, by contrast, uses a greedy search over a suite of different rewriting steps. We compare Herbie's rewriting algorithm, Daisy's rewriting algorithm, and Daisy's rewriting algorithm applied to the results of Herbie's rewriting algorithm. Figure 2 summarizes the accuracy improvements.

Of the 103 benchmarks, at least one of the rewriting algorithms succeeds on 71. Of the 71, Daisy's rewriting algorithm tightens the worst-case bound for 42 benchmarks; Herbie's for 22 benchmarks; and the combination for 34 benchmarks. Furthermore, Herbie's rewriting algorithm loosens the worst-case bound for 8 benchmarks, a consequence of its unsound error measurement technique or differing notion of error, while the combination does so for only 2.

Not only the number but also size of the error improvement matters. Daisy's rewriting algorithm was able to reduce the error bound by a factor of 1.39 (0.14 orders of magnitude) on average; Herbie's by a factor of 13.07 (1.12 orders of magnitude); and the combination by a factor of 15.3 (1.18 orders of magnitude). The combination clearly provided the greatest reduction in error bounds; furthermore, Daisy's algorithm provides larger benefits when applied to Herbie's optimized program than when applied to the benchmark directly.

It seems that Daisy's rewriting algorithm provides a fairly consistent but small tightening of error bounds, while Herbie's algorithm can suggest dramatic and unexpected changes in the expression. However, these large changes sometimes have significantly *looser* error bounds. In those cases, combining Herbie's and Daisy's rewriting algorithms provides a tighter error bound, reaping the benefits of Herbie's rewriting algorithm without the large increases in error bounds that it sometimes causes.

4   Discussion

This paper reports on the combination of Daisy and Herbie and illustrates the benefits of composing complementary floating-point tools to achieve results neither tool provides in isolation. This case study serves as a representative example: similar combinations could be constructed for other tools using this paper's approach. Combinations of Gappa [10], Fluctuat [12], FPTaylor [22], or other verification tools [9,15,16] with Herbie could also allow validating Herbie's optimizations. Verification tools could also be used to validate the output of other unsound tools, such as Precimonious [19] and STOKE [21]. Comparisons with sound optimization tools such as Salsa [5] and FPTuner [3] could also be explored.

Ultimately, we envision using the combination of Daisy and Herbie within larger developments such as VCFloat [18]. VCFloat provides partial automation for reasoning about floating-point computations in CompCert C-light [14] programs. In this context, our toolchain could provide an optimization tactic, that could be applied to (provably) increase accuracy for floating-point segments of C-light programs.

References

1. Barrett, C., Stump, A., Tinelli, C.: The SMT-LIB standard: version 2.0. In: Gupta, A., Kroening, D. (eds.) International Workshop on Satisfiability Modulo Theories, Edinburgh, UK (2010)
2. Becker, H., Panchekha, P., Darulova, E., Tatlock, Z.: Combining tools for optimization and analysis of floating-point computations. arXiv preprint arXiv:1805.02436 (2018)
3. Chiang, W.F., Baranowski, M., Briggs, I., Solovyev, A., Gopalakrishnan, G., Rakamarić, Z.: Rigorous floating-point mixed-precision tuning. In: Symposium on Principles of Programming Languages (POPL), pp. 300–315. ACM (2017)

4. Chiang, W.F., Gopalakrishnan, G., Rakamaric, Z., Solovyev, A.: Efficient search for inputs causing high floating-point errors. In: Symposium on Principles and Practice of Parallel Programming (PPoPP), vol. 49, pp. 43–52. ACM (2014)
5. Damouche, N., Martel, M., Chapoutot, A.: Intra-procedural optimization of the numerical accuracy of programs. In: Núñez, M., Güdemann, M. (eds.) FMICS 2015. LNCS, vol. 9128, pp. 31–46. Springer, Cham (2015). https://doi.org/10.1007/978-3-319-19458-5_3
6. Damouche, N., et al.: Toward a standard benchmark format and suite for floating-point analysis. In: Bogomolov, S., Martel, M., Prabhakar, P. (eds.) NSV 2016. LNCS, vol. 10152, pp. 63–77. Springer, Cham (2017). https://doi.org/10.1007/978-3-319-54292-8_6
7. Darulova, E., Horn, E., Sharma, S.: Sound mixed-precision optimization with rewriting. In: International Conference on Cyber-Physical Systems (ICCPS) (2018)
8. Darulova, E., et al.: Daisy - framework for analysis and optimization of numerical programs (tool paper). In: Beyer, D., Huisman, M. (eds.) TACAS 2018. LNCS, vol. 10805, pp. 270–287. Springer, Cham (2018). https://doi.org/10.1007/978-3-319-89960-2_15
9. Darulova, E., Kuncak, V.: Towards a compiler for reals. ACM Trans. Program. Lang. Syst. (TOPLAS) 39(2), 8 (2017)
10. De Dinechin, F., Lauter, C.Q., Melquiond, G.: Assisted verification of elementary functions using Gappa. In: ACM Symposium on Applied Computing, pp. 1318–1322. ACM (2006)
11. de Moura, L., Bjørner, N.: Z3: an efficient SMT solver. In: Ramakrishnan, C.R., Rehof, J. (eds.) TACAS 2008. LNCS, vol. 4963, pp. 337–340. Springer, Heidelberg (2008). https://doi.org/10.1007/978-3-540-78800-3_24. http://dl.acm.org/citation.cfm?id=1792734.1792766
12. Goubault, E., Putot, S.: Robustness analysis of finite precision implementations. In: Shan, C. (ed.) APLAS 2013. LNCS, vol. 8301, pp. 50–57. Springer, Cham (2013). https://doi.org/10.1007/978-3-319-03542-0_4
13. IEEE Computer Society: IEEE standard for floating-point arithmetic. IEEE Std 754–2008 (2008)
14. Leroy, X.: Formal verification of a realistic compiler. Commun. ACM 52(7), 107–115 (2009)
15. Magron, V., Constantinides, G., Donaldson, A.: Certified roundoff error bounds using semidefinite programming. ACM Trans. Math. Softw. 43(4), 1–34 (2017)
16. Moscato, M., Titolo, L., Dutle, A., Muñoz, C.A.: Automatic estimation of verified floating-point round-off errors via static analysis. In: Tonetta, S., Schoitsch, E., Bitsch, F. (eds.) SAFECOMP 2017. LNCS, vol. 10488, pp. 213–229. Springer, Cham (2017). https://doi.org/10.1007/978-3-319-66266-4_14
17. Panchekha, P., Sanchez-Stern, A., Wilcox, J.R., Tatlock, Z.: Automatically improving accuracy for floating point expressions. In: Conference on Programming Language Design and Implementation (PLDI) (2015)
18. Ramananandro, T., Mountcastle, P., Meister, B., Lethin, R.: A unified Coq framework for verifying C programs with floating-point computations. In: Certified Programs and Proofs (CPP), pp. 15–26. ACM (2016)
19. Rubio-González, C., Nguyen, C., Nguyen, H.D., Demmel, J., Kahan, W., Sen, K., Bailey, D.H., Iancu, C., Hough, D.: Precimonious: tuning assistant for floating-point precision. In: Proceedings of the International Conference on High Performance Computing, Networking, Storage and Analysis, SC 2013, pp. 27:1–27:12. ACM (2013)

20. Sanchez-Stern, A., Panchekha, P., Lerner, S., Tatlock, Z.: Finding root causes of floating point error with herbgrind. arXiv preprint arXiv:1705.10416 (2017)

21. Schkufza, E., Sharma, R., Aiken, A.: Stochastic optimization of floating-point programs with tunable precision. In: Proceedings of the 35th ACM SIGPLAN Conference on Programming Language Design and Implementation, PLDI 2014, pp. 53–64. ACM (2014)

22. Solovyev, A., Jacobsen, C., Rakamarić, Z., Gopalakrishnan, G.: Rigorous estimation of floating-point round-off errors with symbolic Taylor expansions. In: Bjørner, N., de Boer, F. (eds.) FM 2015. LNCS, vol. 9109, pp. 532–550. Springer, Cham (2015). https://doi.org/10.1007/978-3-319-19249-9_33

23. Zou, D., Wang, R., Xiong, Y., Zhang, L., Su, Z., Mei, H.: A genetic algorithm for detecting significant floating-point inaccuracies. In: IEEE International Conference on Software Engineering (ICSE), vol. 1, pp. 529–539. IEEE (2015)

A Formally Verified Floating-Point Implementation of the Compact Position Reporting Algorithm

Laura Titolo[1]([✉]), Mariano M. Moscato[1]([✉]), César A. Muñoz[2]([✉]),
Aaron Dutle[2], and François Bobot[3]

[1] National Institute of Aerospace, Hampton, VA, USA
{laura.titolo,mariano.moscato}@nianet.org
[2] NASA, Hampton, VA, USA
{cesar.a.munoz,aaron.dutle}@nasa.gov
[3] CEA LIST, Software Security Lab, Gif-sur-Yvette, France
francois.bobot@cea.fr

Abstract. The Automatic Dependent Surveillance-Broadcast (ADS-B) system allows aircraft to communicate their current state, including position and velocity information, to other aircraft in their vicinity and to ground stations. The Compact Position Reporting (CPR) algorithm is the ADS-B module responsible for the encoding and decoding of aircraft positions. CPR is highly sensitive to computer arithmetic since it heavily relies on functions that are intrinsically unstable such as floor and modulo. In this paper, a formally-verified double-precision floating-point implementation of the CPR algorithm is presented. The verification proceeds in three steps. First, an alternative version of CPR, which reduces the floating-point rounding error is proposed. Then, the Prototype Verification System (PVS) is used to formally prove that the ideal real-number counterpart of the improved algorithm is mathematically equivalent to the standard CPR definition. Finally, the static analyzer Frama-C is used to verify that the double-precision implementation of the improved algorithm is correct with respect to its operational requirement. The alternative algorithm is currently being considered for inclusion in the revised version of the ADS-B standards document as the reference implementation of the CPR algorithm.

The authors are thankful to Guillaume Melquiond for his help and useful insights on the tool Gappa.

Research by the first two authors was supported by the National Aeronautics and Space Administration under NASA/NIA Cooperative Agreement NNL09AA00A.

The work by the fifth author was partially funded by the National Aeronautics and Space Administration under NASA/NIA Cooperative Agreement NNL09AA00A and the grant ANR-14-CE28-0020.

K. Havelund et al. (Eds.): FM 2018, LNCS 10951, pp. 364–381, 2018.
https://doi.org/10.1007/978-3-319-95582-7_22

1   Introduction

The Automatic Dependent Surveillance-Broadcast (ADS-B) protocol [27] is a fundamental component of the next generation of air transportation systems. It is intended to augment or replace ground-based surveillance systems such as radar by providing real-time accurate surveillance information based on global positioning systems. Aircraft equipped with ADS-B services broadcast a variety of information related to the current state of the aircraft, such as position and velocity, to other traffic aircraft and to ground stations. The use of ADS-B transponders is required to fly in some regions and, by 2020, it will become mandatory for most commercial aircraft in the US [11] and Europe [17]. Thousands of aircraft are currently equipped with ADS-B.[1]

The ADS-B broadcast message is defined to be 112 bits long. Its data frame takes 56 bits, while the rest is used to transmit aircraft identification, message type, and parity check information. When the data frame contains a position, 21 bits are devoted to the status information and altitude, leaving 35 bits in total for latitude and longitude. If raw latitude and longitude data were expressed as numbers of 17 bits each, the resulting position accuracy would be worse than 300 m, which is inadequate for safe navigation. For this reason, the ADS-B protocol uses an algorithm called Compact Position Reporting (CPR) to encode/decode the aircraft position in 35 bits in a way that, for airborne applications, is intended to guarantee a position accuracy of approximately 5 meters. Unfortunately, pilots and manufacturers have reported errors in the positions obtained by encoding and decoding with the CPR algorithm.

In [16], it was formally proven that the original operational requirements of the CPR algorithm are not enough to guarantee the intended precision, even when computations are assumed to be performed using exact arithmetic. Additionally, the ideal real number implementation of CPR has been formally proven correct for a slightly tightened set of requirements [16]. Nevertheless, even assuming these more restrictive requirements, a straight-forward floating-point implementation of the CPR algorithm may still be unsound and produce incorrect results due to round-off error. For instance, using a standard single-precision floating-point implementation of CPR on a position whose latitude is $-77.368°$ and longitude is $180°$, the recovered position differs from the original one by approximately 1500 nautical miles.

In this paper, an alternative implementation of the CPR algorithm is presented. This version includes simplifications that decrease the numerical complexity of the expressions with respect to the original version presented in the ADS-B standard. In this way, the accumulated round-off error is reduced. Frama-C [21] is used to prove that the double-precision floating-point implementation of the proposed CPR algorithm is correct in the sense that the encoding has no rounding error and the decoded position satisfies the required operational accuracy of the algorithm. The Frama-C WP (Weakest Precondition) plug-in

---

[1] https://generalaviationnews.com/2017/09/18/more-than-40000-aircraft-now-equipped-with-ads-b/.

is used to generate verification conditions ultimately discharged with the aid of the automatic solvers Gappa [15] and Alt-Ergo [12]. In addition, the interactive theorem prover PVS [26] is used to formally prove that the real counterpart of the proposed alternative CPR algorithm is mathematically equivalent to the one defined in the standard [27]. It follows that the correctness results presented in [16] also hold for the proposed version of CPR. The PVS formalization of this equivalence is available at https://shemesh.larc.nasa.gov/fm/CPR/.

The remainder of the paper is organized as follows. In Sect. 2, the original definition of the CPR algorithm and the correctness of its real-valued version [16] are summarized. The alternative version of CPR is presented in Sect. 3 along with the results ensuring its mathematical equivalence with respect to the original algorithm. In Sect. 4, the verification approach used to prove the correctness of the double-precision implementation of the alternative algorithm is explained. Related work is discussed in Sect. 5. Finally, Sect. 6 concludes the paper.

2   The Compact Position Reporting Algorithm

In this section, the CPR algorithm is introduced, summarizing its definition in the ADS-B standard [27]. The CPR goal is to encode latitude and longitude in 17 bits while keeping a position resolution of approximately 5 meters. CPR is based on the fact that transmitting the entire latitude and longitude at each broadcasted message is inefficient since the higher order bits are very unlikely to change over a short period of time. In order to overcome this inefficiency, only an encoding of the least significant bits of the position is transmitted and two different techniques are used to recover the higher order bits.

CPR uses a special coordinate system where each direction (latitude and longitude) is divided into zones of approximately 360 nautical miles. There are two different subdivisions of the space in zones, based on the *format* of the message, either *even* or *odd*. The number of zones depends on the format and, in the case of the longitude, also on the current latitude of the target. Each zone is itself divided into 2^{17} parts, called *bins*. Figure 1 shows how the latitude is divided into 60 zones (for the even subdivision) or into 59 zones (for the odd subdivision) and how each zone is then divided into 2^{17} bins. The CPR encoding procedure transforms degree coordinates into CPR coordinates and is parametric with respect to the chosen subdivision (even or odd). The decoding procedure recovers the position of the aircraft from the CPR coordinates. A CPR message coordinate is exactly the number corresponding to the bin where the target is located. The correct zone can be recovered from either a previously known position (for *local decoding*) or from a matched pair of even and odd messages (for *global decoding*). The decoding procedures return a coordinate which corresponds to the centerline of the bin where the target is located (see Fig. 1). In a latitude zone (respectively longitude zone), all the latitudes (respectively longitudes) inside a *bin* have the same encoding. This means that the recovered latitude (respectively longitude) corresponds to the *bin centerline*. Therefore, the difference between a given position and the result of encoding and decoding should be less than or equal to the size of half of a bin.

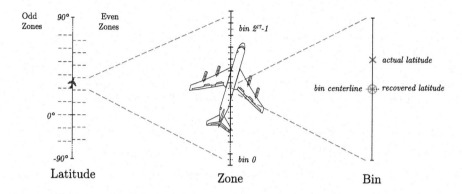

Fig. 1. CPR latitude coordinate system.

The modulo function is assumed to be computed as $\mathsf{mod}\,(x, y) = x - y\,\lfloor x/y \rfloor$. In this section, all computations are assumed to be performed in real arithmetic. Therefore, no rounding error occurs. All the results presented in this section have been formally proven in a previous work [16].

2.1 Encoding

The CPR encoding translates latitude and longitude coordinates, expressed in degrees, into a pair of CPR coordinates, i.e., bin indices. Each CPR message is transmitted inside the data frame of an ADS-B message. The 35 bits composing the CPR message are grouped into three parts. One bit determines the format (0 for even and 1 for odd), 17 bits are devoted to the bin number for the latitude, and the other 17 bits to the bin number for the longitude.

Let $i \in \{0, 1\}$ be the format of the message to be sent, the size of a latitude zone is defined as $dlat_i = 360/(60 - i)$. Given a latitude in degrees $lat \in [-90, 90]$, the *latitude encoding* is defined as follows:

$$latEnc(i, lat) = \mathsf{mod}\left(\left\lfloor 2^{17} \frac{\mathsf{mod}\,(lat, dlat_i)}{dlat_i} + \frac{1}{2} \right\rfloor, 2^{17}\right). \qquad (2.1)$$

In (2.1), $\mathsf{mod}\,(lat, dlat_i)$ is the distance between lat and the bottom of a zone edge. Thus, $\frac{\mathsf{mod}(lat, dlat_i)}{dlat_i}$ is the zone fraction of lat. Multiplying by 2^{17} gives a value between 0 and 2^{17}, while $\lfloor x + \frac{1}{2} \rfloor$ rounds a number x to the nearest integer. The external modulo ensures that the encoded latitude fits in 17 bits. It may appear that this final truncation can discard some useful information. However, it only affects half of a bin at the top of a zone, which is accounted for by the adjacent zone. For longitude, the CPR coordinate system keeps the size of zones approximately constant by reducing the number of longitude zones as the latitude increases. As a consequence, the number of longitude zones circling the globe is a function of the latitude. The function that determines the number of longitude zones is called *NL*. While its value can be calculated directly from a given latitude, in practice, it is determined from a pre-calculated lookup table. Since the construction of this table occurs off-line it can be computed with enough precision to ensure its correctness during the encoding stage. Note that the latitude used to compute NL for encoding is actually the *recovered latitude*, which is the centerline of the bin containing the location. This ensures that the broadcaster and receiver can calculate the same value of NL for use in longitude decoding.

Given a latitude value $lat \in [-90, 90]$, the NL value is used to compute the longitude zone size as follows.

$$dlon_i(lat) = 360/ \max\{1, NL(rlat(lat)) - i\}. \tag{2.2}$$

Note that the denominator in the above expression uses the max operator when NL is 1, which occurs for latitudes beyond ± 87 degrees. In this case, there is only one longitude zone and even and odd longitude encodings coincide.

Given a longitude value $lon \in [0, 360]$ and a latitude value $lat \in [-90, 90]$, the *longitude encoding* is defined similarly to latitude encoding:

$$lonEnc(i, lat, lon) = \mathsf{mod} \left(\left\lfloor 2^{17} \frac{\mathsf{mod}\,(lon, dlon_i(lat))}{dlon_i(lat)} + \frac{1}{2} \right\rfloor, 2^{17} \right). \tag{2.3}$$

Let $\mathcal{BN}$ denote the domain of bin numbers which is composed by the integers in the interval $[0, 2^{17} - 1]$. The following lemma ensures the message is of the proper length.

Lemma 1. *Given* $i \in \{0, 1\}$, *lat* $\in [-90, 90]$, *and lon* $\in [0, 360]$, *then latEnc$(i, lat) \in \mathcal{BN}$ and lonEnc$(i, lat, lon) \in \mathcal{BN}$.*

2.2   Local Decoding

Each encoded coordinate broadcast in a CPR message identifies exactly one bin inside each zone. In order to unambiguously compute the decoded position, it suffices to determine the zone. To this end, the CPR *local decoding* uses a reference position that is known to be near the broadcast one. This reference position can be a previously decoded position or can be obtained by other means. The idea behind local decoding is simple. Observe that a one zone wide interval centered around a given reference position does not contain more than one occurrence of the same bin number. Therefore, as long as the target is close enough to the reference position (slightly less than half a zone), decoding can be performed correctly.

Given a format $i \in \{0, 1\}$, the encoded latitude $YZ_i \in \mathcal{BN}$, and a reference latitude $lat_{ref} \in [-90, 90]$, the local decoding uses the following formula to calculate the *zone index number* (zin).

$$latZin_{\mathsf{L}}(i, YZ_i, lat_{ref}) = \left\lfloor \frac{lat_{ref}}{dlat_i} \right\rfloor + \left\lfloor \frac{1}{2} + \frac{\mathsf{mod}\,(lat_{ref}, dlat_i)}{dlat_i} - \frac{YZ_i}{2^{17}} \right\rfloor. \tag{2.4}$$

The first term in this sum calculates which zone the reference latitude lies in, while the second term adjusts it by -1, 0, or 1 based on the difference between the reference latitude and the received encoded latitude. The zone index number is then used to compute the recovered latitude using the following function.

$$rlat_L(i, YZ_i, lat_{ref}) = dlat_i \left(latZin_L(i, YZ_i, lat_{ref}) + \frac{YZ_i}{2^{17}} \right).$$ (2.5)

This recovered latitude is used to determine the NL value for computing the value of $dlon_i$ by Formula (2.2). Given a reference longitude $lon_{ref} \in [0, 360]$, the recovered latitude $rlat \in [-90, 90]$, and the encoded longitude $XZ_i \in \mathcal{BN}$, the longitude zone index and recovered longitude are computed similarly to the case of the latitude. In the following formulas, $dlon_i$ is used as an abbreviation for $dlon_i(rlat_L(i, YZ_i, lat_{ref}))$.

$$lonZin_L(i, XZ_i, lon_{ref}, rlat) = \left\lfloor \frac{lon_{ref}}{dlon_i} \right\rfloor + \left\lfloor \frac{1}{2} + \frac{\mod(lon_{ref}, dlon_i)}{dlon_i} - \frac{XZ_i}{2^{17}} \right\rfloor.$$ (2.6)

$$rlon_L(i, XZ_i, lon_{ref}, rlat) = dlon_i \left(lonZin_L(i, XZ_i, lon_{ref}, rlat) + \frac{XZ_i}{2^{17}} \right).$$ (2.7)

When the difference between original and reference latitude (respectively longitude) is less than half zone size minus half bin size, local decoding is correct. This means that the difference between the original and recovered latitude (respectively longitude) is at most half of a bin size.

Theorem 1 (Local Decoding Correctness). *Given a format $i \in \{0, 1\}$, a latitude lat $\in [-90, 90]$, and a reference latitude $lat_{ref} \in [-90, 90]$ such that $|lat - lat_{ref}| < \frac{dlat_i}{2} - \frac{dlat_i}{2^{18}}$,*

$$|lat - rlat_L(i, latEnc(i, lat), lat_{ref})| \leq \frac{dlat_i}{2^{18}}.$$

Furthermore, given a recovered latitude rlat $\in [-90, 90]$, a longitude lon $\in [0, 360]$, and a reference longitude $lon_{ref} \in [0, 360]$ such that $|lon - lon_{ref}| < \frac{dlon_i(rlat)}{2} - \frac{dlon_i(rlat)}{2^{18}}$,

$$|lon - rlon_L(i, lonEnc(i, rlat, lon), lon_{ref}, rlat)| \leq \frac{dlon_i(rlat)}{2^{18}}.$$

2.3   Global Decoding

Global decoding is used when a valid reference position is unknown. This can occur when a target is first encountered, or when messages have not been received for a significant amount of time. Similarly to the local decoding case, the correct zone in which the encoded position lies has to be determined. To accomplish this, the global decoding uses a pair of messages of different formats, one even and one odd. The algorithm computes the number of *zone offsets* (the difference between an odd zone length and an even zone length) from the origin (either equator or prime meridian) to the encoded position. This can be used to establish the zone for either message type, and hence used to decode the position.

The first step in global decoding is to determine the number of zone offsets between the southern boundaries of the two encoded latitudes. Given two integers $YZ_0, YZ_1 \in \mathcal{BN}$, the zone index number for the latitude is computed as follows.

$$latZin_G(YZ_0, YZ_1) = \left\lfloor \frac{59\, YZ_0 - 60\, YZ_1}{2^{17}} + \frac{1}{2} \right\rfloor. \qquad (2.8)$$

Note that $YZ_0/2^{17}$ is the fraction into the even zone that the encoded latitude lies in. Since exactly 59 zone offsets fit into each even zone, $59\, YZ_0/2^{17}$ is the number of zone offsets from the southern boundary of an even zone. Similarly, $60\, YZ_1/2^{17}$ is the number of zone offsets from the southern boundary of an odd zone. The difference between these gives the number of zone offsets between southern boundaries of the respective zones, which corresponds to the correct zone. For example, if both are in zone 0, the southern boundaries coincide. If both are in zone 1, the southern boundaries differ by 1 zone offset. The case when encoding zones differ is accounted for by the modulo operation.

Given $i \in \{0, 1\}$, the recovered latitude is calculated as shown below.

$$rlat_G(i, YZ_0, YZ_1) = dlat_i \left(\mathsf{mod}\,(latZin_G(YZ_0, YZ_1), 60 - i) + \frac{YZ_i}{2^{17}} \right). \quad (2.9)$$

For the global decoding of a longitude, it is essential to check that the even and odd messages being used were calculated with the same NL value. To this end, both even and odd latitude messages are decoded, and their NL values are calculated. If they differ, the messages are discarded, otherwise, the longitude decoding can proceed using the common NL value. Given $i \in \{0, 1\}$ and $XZ_0, XZ_1 \in \mathcal{BN}$, if $NL(rlat_G(0, YZ_0, YZ_1)) = NL(rlat_G(1, YZ_0, YZ_1))$ the zone index number is computed as follows, where NL denotes $NL(rlat_G(i, YZ_0, YZ_1))$ for $i = 0, 1$.

$$lonZin_G(XZ_0, XZ_1) = \left\lfloor \frac{(NL - 1)XZ_0 - (NL)XZ_1}{2^{17}} + \frac{1}{2} \right\rfloor. \qquad (2.10)$$

Using $rlat_G(i, YZ_0, YZ_1)$ to compute $dlon_i$ and NL, and letting nl_i stand for $\max(NL - i, 1)$, the recovered longitude is computed as follows.

$$rlon_G(i, XZ_0, XZ_1) = dlon_i \left(\mathsf{mod}\,(latZin_G(XZ_0, XZ_1), nl_i) + \frac{XZ_i}{2^{17}} \right). \quad (2.11)$$

The zone offset represents the difference between an even and an odd zone. For the latitude it is defined as $ZO_{lat} = dlat_1 - dlat_0$, while for the longitude, given a latitude $rlat$, is defined as $ZO_{lon} = dlon_1(rlat) - dlon_0(rlat)$. When the difference between the original coordinates is less than half zone offset minus the size of one odd bin, global decoding is correct. This means that the difference between the original and recovered latitude and longitude is at most the size of half bin.

Theorem 2 (Global Decoding Correctness). *Given* $i \in \{0, 1\}$, *for all* lat_0, $lat_1 \in [-90, 90]$ *such that* $|lat_0 - lat_1| < \frac{ZO_{lat}}{2} - \frac{dlat_1}{2^{17}}$,

$$|lat_i - rlat_G(i, latEnc(0, lat_0), latEnc(1, lat_1))| \leq \frac{dlat_i}{2^{18}}.$$

Furthermore, let $rlat_0 = rlat_G(0, latEnc(0, lat_0), latEnc(1, lat_1))$ *and* $rlat_1 = rlat_G(1, latEnc(0, lat_0), latEnc(1, lat_1))$ *be even and odd recovered latitudes, respectively. If* $NL(rlat_0) = NL(rlat_1)$, *then for all* $lon_0, lon_1 \in [0, 360]$ *such that* $|lon_0 - lon_1| < \frac{ZO_{lon}}{2} - \frac{dlon_1(rlat_i)}{2^{17}}$,

$$|lon_i - rlon_G(i, lonEnc(0, rlat_0, lon_0), lonEnc(1, rlat_1, lon_1))| \leq \frac{dlon_i(rlat_i)}{2^{18}}$$

3   An Alternative Implementation of CPR

In this section, an alternative implementation of CPR is presented. This version uses mathematical simplifications that decrease the numerical complexity of the expressions with respect to the original implementation presented in the ADS-B standard. The alternative version is designed to be more numerically stable and to minimize the accumulated floating-point round-off error. Whenever possible, the formulas are transformed in order to perform multiplications and divisions by a power of 2, which are known to produce no round-off error as long as no over or under-flow occurs. Other simplifications are applied to reduce the number of operations, especially the modulo and floor. These operations are particularly problematic because a small difference in the arguments can lead to a significant difference in the result. For instance, consider a variable x that has an ideal real value of 1, while its floating-point version $\tilde{x}$ has value 0.999999. The round-off error associated to x is $|x - \tilde{x}| = 0.000001$, but the error associated to the application of the floor operation is $|\lfloor x \rfloor - \lfloor \tilde{x} \rfloor| = 1$.

Assuming real arithmetic, the proposed implementation is shown to be equivalent to the original one. All the results presented in this section have been formally verified using the PVS theorem prover. The input coordinates for this CPR algorithm are assumed to be given in a format called *32 bit angular weighted binary* (AWB), a standard format for expressing geographical positions used by GPS manufacturers and many others. An AWB coordinate is a 32 bit integer in the interval $[0, 2^{32} - 1]$, where the value x corresponds to $\frac{360x}{2^{32}}$ degrees (negative latitudes are identified with their value modulo 360). In the following, $\mathcal{AWB}$ denotes the domain of AWB numbers and a hat is used to emphasize that a given variable denotes an AWB value.

3.1   Alternative Encoding

Given a latitude $\widehat{lat} \in \mathcal{AWB}$, Algorithm 1 encodes it in a bin index number. The encoding is slightly different for AWB latitudes greater than 2^{30} because the input latitude range for the original encoding is $[-90, 90]$ and the AWB interval from 2^{30} to 2^{32} corresponds to the range $[90, 360]$. Therefore, a shift must be performed to put the range $[270, 360]$ in the expected input format $[-90, 0]$.

Algorithm 2 implements the longitude encoding similarly to Algorithm 1. In this case, no shift is needed since the input longitude range is $[0, 360]$. The variable nz denotes the number of longitude zones, which is 1 when $NL = 1$ and $NL-i$ otherwise. This is equivalent to taking the maximum between 1 and $NL-i$ as done in the original version of the algorithm (see Formula (2.2)). The following theorem states the mathematical equivalence of the proposed alternative encoding with respect to the one described in Subsect. 2.1 assuming ideal real-valued arithmetic.

Algorithm 1. $latEnc'(i, \widehat{lat})$

$nz \leftarrow 60 - i$
if $\widehat{lat} \leq 2^{30}$ **then**
$\quad tmp_1 = (\widehat{lat} * nz + 2^{14}) * 2^{-15}$
$\quad tmp_2 = (\widehat{lat} * nz + 2^{14}) * 2^{-32}$
else
$\quad tmp_1 = ((\widehat{lat} - 2^{32}) * nz + 2^{14}) * 2^{-15}$
$\quad tmp_2 = ((\widehat{lat} - 2^{32}) * nz + 2^{14}) * 2^{-32}$
end if
return $\lfloor tmp_1 \rfloor - 2^{17} * \lfloor tmp_2 \rfloor$

Algorithm 2. $lonEnc'(i, NL, \widehat{lon})$

if $NL = 1$ **then**
$\quad nz \leftarrow 1$
else
$\quad nz \leftarrow NL - i$
end if
$tmp_1 = (\widehat{lon} * nz + 2^{14}) * 2^{-15}$
$tmp_2 = (\widehat{lon} * nz + 2^{14}) * 2^{-32}$
return $\lfloor tmp_1 \rfloor - 2^{17} * \lfloor tmp_2 \rfloor$

Theorem 3. Let $lat \in [-90, 90]$, $lon \in [0, 360]$, $\widehat{lat}, \widehat{lon} \in \mathcal{AWB}$, and $i \in \{0, 1\}$, if $lat = \frac{360\widehat{lat}}{2^{32}}$, $lon = \frac{360\widehat{lon}}{2^{32}}$, and $NL = NL(rlat'(lat))$, then

$$latEnc'(i, \widehat{lat}) = latEnc(i, lat)$$
$$lonEnc'(i, NL, \widehat{lon}) = lonEnc(i, lat, lon).$$

To prove this lemma, it is necessary to use the following intermediate results. First, the following alternative formula for encoding is used, which avoids the external modulo of 2^{17} used in Equations (2.1) and (2.3).

Lemma 2. Let $lat \in [-90, 90]$, $lon \in [0, 360]$, and $i \in \{0, 1\}$,

$$latEnc(i, lat) = \left\lfloor 2^{17} \frac{\mathsf{mod}\left(lat + 2^{-18} dlat_i, dlat_i\right)}{dlat_i} \right\rfloor$$

$$lonEnc(i, lat, lon) = \left\lfloor 2^{17} \frac{\mathsf{mod}\left(lon + 2^{-18} dlon_i(lat), dlon_i(lat)\right)}{dlon_i(lat)} \right\rfloor.$$

The following two results, which have been formally proven correct in [16], are also used. When the modulo operator is divided by its second argument, the following simplification can be applied.

$$\frac{\mathsf{mod}(a, b)}{b} = \frac{a}{b} - \left\lfloor \frac{a}{b} \right\rfloor. \tag{3.1}$$

Additionally, given any number x and any integer n, the floor function and the addition of integers is commutative.

$$\lfloor x + n \rfloor = \lfloor x \rfloor + n. \tag{3.2}$$

Given l denoting either a latitude or a longitude and dl representing $dlat$ or $dlon$ respectively, the following equality holds.

$$\left\lfloor 2^{17} \frac{\mathrm{mod}\left(l + 2^{-18}dl, dl\right)}{dl} \right\rfloor = \left\lfloor 2^{17} \frac{l}{dl} + \frac{1}{2} \right\rfloor - 2^{17} \left\lfloor \frac{l}{dl} + \frac{1}{2^{18}} \right\rfloor. \tag{3.3}$$

Since the input coordinate l is assumed to correspond to an AWB, there exists $\hat{l} \in \mathcal{AWB}$ such that $l = \frac{360\hat{l}}{2^{32}}$. By replacing l, after some basic arithmetic simplifications, the formula used in Algorithms 1 and 2 is obtained as follows.

$$\left\lfloor 2^{17} \frac{l}{dl} + \frac{1}{2} \right\rfloor - 2^{17} \left\lfloor \frac{l}{dl} + \frac{1}{2^{18}} \right\rfloor = \left\lfloor (\hat{l} \cdot nz + 2^{14})2^{-15} \right\rfloor - 2^{17} \left\lfloor (\hat{l} \cdot nz + 2^{14})2^{-32} \right\rfloor. \tag{3.4}$$

3.2   Alternative Local Decoding

Given an encoded latitude YZ and a reference latitude in AWB format, Algorithm 3 recovers the latitude corresponding to the centerline of the bin where the original latitude was located. Similarly to the encoding algorithm, it is necessary to shift the AWB to correctly represent the latitudes between -90 and 0 degrees. Correspondingly, Algorithm 4 recovers the longitude centerline bin. Note that the two algorithms differ only in the computation of the zone index number (zin). Let ref be the reference latitude (respectively longitude) in degrees, dl be the zone size, and enc the 17-bit encoding. By applying Equations (3.1) and (3.2), the latitude (respectively longitude) zone index number Formulas (2.4) and (2.6) can be rewritten in the form

$$\left\lfloor \frac{1}{2} + \frac{ref}{dl} - \frac{enc}{2^{17}} \right\rfloor.$$

Algorithm 3. $rlat'_L(i, \widehat{lat}, YZ)$

$nz \leftarrow 60 - i$
$dlat \leftarrow 360/nz$
if $\widehat{lat} \leq 2^{30}$ **then**
    $zin \leftarrow \left\lfloor (\widehat{lat} * nz - (YZ - 2^{16}) * 2^{15}) * 2^{-32} \right\rfloor$
else
    $zin \leftarrow \left\lfloor ((\widehat{lat} - 2^{32}) * nz - (YZ - 2^{16}) * 2^{15}) * 2^{-32} \right\rfloor$
end if
return $dlat * (YZ * 2^{-17} + zin)$

Algorithm 4. $rlon'_\mathsf{L}(i, NL, \widehat{lon}, XZ)$

---

if $NL = 1$ **then**
    $nz \leftarrow 1$
else
    $nz \leftarrow NL - i$
end if
$dlon \leftarrow 360/nz$
$zin \leftarrow \left\lfloor (\widehat{lon} * nz - (XZ - 2^{16}) * 2^{15}) * 2^{-32} \right\rfloor$
return $dlon * (XZ * 2^{-17} + zin)$

Since the reference coordinate ref is assumed to represent an AWB, there exists $\widehat{ref} \in \mathcal{AWB}$ such that $ref = \frac{360\widehat{ref}}{2^{32}}$. After some simple algebraic simplification, Theorem 4 directly follows.

Theorem 4. Let $i \in \{0,1\}$, $YZ_i, XZ_i \in \mathcal{BN}$, if $lat_{ref} = \frac{360\widehat{lat_{ref}}}{2^{32}}$ and $lon_{ref} = \frac{360\widehat{lon_{ref}}}{2^{32}}$, then

$$rlat_\mathsf{L}(i, YZ_i, lat_{ref}) = rlat'_\mathsf{L}(i, YZ_i, \widehat{lat}_{ref})$$

$$rlon_\mathsf{L}(i, XZ_i, lon_{ref}, lat_{ref}) = rlon'_\mathsf{L}(i, NL(rlat'_\mathsf{L}(i, YZ_i, \widehat{lat}_{ref})), \widehat{lon}_{ref}, XZ_i).$$

3.3 Alternative Global Decoding

Algorithms 5 and 6 perform the global decoding for latitude and longitude, respectively. Variable i represents the format of the most recent message received, which is used to determine the aircraft position. In Algorithm 6, NL is the common value computed using both latitudes recovered by Algorithm 5. When $NL = 1$, the computation is significantly simplified due to having only one zone. Otherwise, the recovered longitude is computed similarly to the latitude. Theorem 5 directly follows from simple algebraic manipulations. The sum of the two fractions inside the floor in Formula (2.8) is explicitly calculated and the modulo in Formulas (2.9) and (2.11) is expanded.

Algorithm 5. $rlat'_\mathsf{G}(i, YZ_0, YZ_1)$

$dlat \leftarrow 360/(60 - i)$
$zin = \lfloor (59 * YZ_0 - 60 * YZ_1 + 2^{16}) * 2^{-17} \rfloor$
if $i = 0$ **then**
    return $dlat * ((zin - 60 * \lfloor zin/60 \rfloor) + YZ_0 * 2^{-17})$
else
    return $dlat * ((zin - 59 * \lfloor zin/59 \rfloor) + YZ_1 * 2^{-17})$
end if

Algorithm 6. $rlon'_{\mathsf{G}}(i, NL, XZ_0, XZ_1)$

---

if $NL = 1$ then
  if $i = 0$ then
    return $360 * XZ_0 * 2^{-17}$
  else
    return $360 * XZ_1 * 2^{-17}$
  end if
else
  $dlon \leftarrow 360/(NL-i)$
  $zin \leftarrow \lfloor ((NL-1) * XZ_0 - NL * XZ_1 + 2^{16}) * 2^{-17} \rfloor$
  $zin' \leftarrow zin/(NL-i)$
  if $i = 0$ then
    return $dlon * ((zin - (NL-i) * \lfloor zin' \rfloor) + XZ_0 * 2^{-17})$
  else
    return $dlon * ((zin - (NL-i) * \lfloor zin' \rfloor) + XZ_1 * 2^{-17})$
  end if
end if

Theorem 5. *Let* $i \in \{0,1\}$, $YZ_i, XZ_i \in \mathcal{BN}$, *and* $NL = NL(rlat'_{\mathsf{G}}(i, YZ_0, YZ_1))$,

$$rlat_{\mathsf{G}}(i, YZ_0, YZ_1) = rlat'_{\mathsf{G}}(i, YZ_0, YZ_1)$$
$$rlon_{\mathsf{G}}(i, XZ_0, XZ_1) = rlon'_{\mathsf{G}}(i, NL, XZ_0, XZ_1).$$

4 Verification Approach

This section presents the verification approach used to prove that double precision floating-point arithmetic is enough to obtain a correct implementation of the CPR algorithm. In the following, the double-precision floating-point counterpart of a real-valued function f will be represented with a tilde, as $\tilde{f}$. In the floating-point version, every mathematical operator on real numbers is replaced by the corresponding double-precision floating-point operator.

The floating-point encoding of CPR is considered correct if it returns exactly the same value of the real number implementation. This means that no round-off error affects the final outcome. The double precision implementation of encoding achieves this, as indicated by the following theorem.

Theorem 6 (Correctness Double-precision Encoding). *Let* $\widehat{lat} \in \mathcal{AWB}$, $\widehat{lon} \in \mathcal{AWB}$, *NL be an integer in the range* $[1, 59]$, *and* $i \in \{0, 1\}$,

$$latEnc'(i, \widehat{lat}) = \widetilde{latEnc'}(i, \widehat{lat})$$

$$lonEnc'(i, NL, \widehat{lon}) = \widetilde{lonEnc'}(i, NL, \widehat{lon}).$$

For decoding, note that Theorems 1 and 2 state that the original coordinate and the bin centerline differs by at most half the size of a bin. If the recovered coordinate computed with floating-point decoding differs from the bin-centerline computed with real numbers by at most half the size of a bin, then the original coordinate, the bin-centerline, and the recovered coordinate are all located in the same bin. Hence, a floating-point decoding function can be considered correct when the recovered coordinate differs from the bin-centerline by at most half the size of a bin. From the previous observation, it follows that a new table $\widetilde{NL}$, which takes as input the floating-point latitude resulting from $\widehat{rlat}'_L$, can be computed off-line with sufficient precision. For each transition latitude l in the original NL table the floating-point representation of the closest bin centerlines enclosing l are used to decide the corresponding NL value. Recall from Sect. 2 that the bin size for the even configuration is approximatively 4.578×10^{-5} degrees, and for the odd one is 4.655×10^{-5} degrees. In the following theorems, the lower bound for half the bin size of 2.2888×10^{-5} degrees is used.

Theorem 7 (Correctness Double-precision Local Decoding). *Let $i \in \{0,1\}$, $YZ_i, XZ_i \in \mathcal{BN}$, and $\widehat{lat}_{ref}, \widehat{lon}_{ref} \in \mathcal{AWB}$,*

$$|rlat'_L(i, \widehat{lat}_{ref}, YZ_i) - \widehat{rlat}'_L(i, \widehat{lat}_{ref}, YZ_i)| \leq 2.2888 \times 10^{-5}$$

$$|rlon'_L(i, NL, \widehat{lon}_{ref}, XZ_i) - \widehat{rlon}'_L(i, \widetilde{NL}, \widehat{lon}_{ref}, XZ_i)| \leq 2.2888 \times 10^{-5}$$

where $NL = NL(rlat'_L(i, YZ_i, \widehat{lat}_{ref}))$ and $\widetilde{NL} = \widetilde{NL}(\widehat{rlat}'_L(i, YZ_i, \widehat{lat}_{ref}))$.

Theorem 8 (Correctness Double-precision Global Decoding). *Let $i \in \{0,1\}$ and $YZ_i, XZ_i \in \mathcal{BN}$, if $NL(rlat'_G(0, YZ_0, yz1)) = NL(rlat_G'(1, YZ_0, YZ_1))$,*

$$|rlat'_G(i, YZ_0, YZ_1) - \widehat{rlat}'_G(i, YZ_0, YZ_1)| \leq 2.2888 \times 10^{-5}$$

$$|rlon'_G(i, NL, YZ_0, YZ_1) - \widehat{rlon}'_G(i, NL, YZ_0, YZ_1)| \leq 2.2888 \times 10^{-5}$$

where $NL = NL(rlat'_G(j, YZ_0, YZ_1))$ and $\widetilde{NL} = \widetilde{NL}(\widehat{rlat}_G'(j, YZ_0, YZ_1))$ for $j = 0, 1$.

Figure 2 depicts the verification approach followed in this work. Frama-C was used to formally verify that Theorems 6, 7, and 8 hold. Frama-C is a tool suite that collects several static analyzers for the C language. C programs can be annotated with ACSL [2] annotations that state function contracts, pre and post conditions, assertions, and invariants. The Frama-C WP plug-in implements a weakest precondition calculus for ACSL annotations through C programs. For each ACSL annotation, this plug-in generates a set of verification conditions (VCs) that can be discharged by external provers. In the analysis presented in this paper, the SMT solver Alt-Ergo and the prover Gappa are used.

Gappa [15] is a tool able to formally verify properties on finite precision computations and to bound the associated round-off error. Additionally, it generates a formal proof of the results that can be checked independently by an external proof assistant. This feature provides a higher degree of confidence in the analysis of the numerical code. Gappa models the propagation of the round-off error by using interval arithmetic and a battery of theorems on real and floating-point numbers. The main drawback of interval arithmetic is that it does not keep track of the correlation between expressions sharing subterms, which may lead to imprecise over-approximations. To improve precision, Gappa accepts hints from the user. These hints can be used to perform a bisection on the domain of an expression, or to propose rewriting rules that appear as hypotheses in the generated formal proof. Gappa is very efficient and precise for checking enclosures for floating-point rounding errors, but it is not always suited to tackle other types of verification conditions generated by Frama-C. For this reason, the SMT solver Alt-Ergo is used in combination with Gappa.

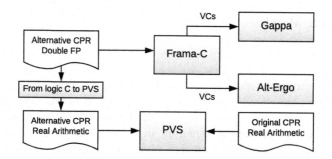

Fig. 2. Verification approach.

The real counterpart of each C function implementing the alternative version of CPR is expressed as an ACSL logic function. As mentioned in Sect. 3, PVS is used to formally verify the mathematical equivalence of these logic functions with respect to the PVS formalization of the original CPR definition. Pre and post-conditions are added to relate logic real-valued functions with the corresponding C double-precision floating-point implementation and to model Theorems 6, 7, and 8. Also, additional intermediate assertions are added after specific instructions to help the WP reasoning.

Algorithms 1 and 2 are annotated with assertions stating that tmp_1 and tmp_2 do not introduce rounding error. This generates VCs that are easily proved by Gappa because the computation just involves operations between integers and multiplications by powers of 2. Since the floor operation is applied to expressions that do not carry a round-off error, the computation of the floor is also exact and, therefore, Theorem 6 holds.

Algorithms 3 and 4 are annotated with assertions stating that the computation of the zone index number zin has no round-off error. This holds and can be easily discharged in Gappa since the computation of zin involves just integer sums and multiplications, and multiplications by powers of 2. The only calculation that carries a round-off error different from 0 is the one of the zone size ($dlat$ and $dlon$) that involves a division. However, Gappa is able to prove that the propagation of this error in the result is bounded by half bin size (Theorem 7).

The verification of the global decoding procedures involves more complex reasoning. Similarly to the local decoding case, the code is annotated to explicitly state that the zone index number is not subject to rounding errors, and that its value is between -59 and 60. These two assertions are easily proved by Gappa. With nz denoting the number of zones (60 or 59 for latitude, and the maximum of $NL-1$ and 1 for longitude), an annotation is added to assert that the real-valued and double-precision computation of $\lfloor zin/nz \rfloor$ coincide. In order to prove the verification conditions generated by this assertion, Gappa was provided with a hint on how to perform the bisection. It is important to remark that this hint does not add any hypothesis to the verification process. Given these intermediate assertions, Gappa is able to verify Theorem 8 as well.

5   Related Work

Besides Frama-C, other tools are available to formally verify and analyze numerical properties of C code. Fluctuat [20] is a commercial static analyzer that, given a C program with annotations about input bounds and uncertainties on its arguments, produces bounds for the round-off error of the program decomposed with respect to its provenance. Caduceus [18] produces verification conditions from annotated C code and discharges them in an independent theorem prover. In [7], the Caduceus tool is extended to reason about floating-point arithmetics. Here, Why [5] is used to generate verification conditions that are manually proven in the Coq proof assistant [3]. The static analyzer Astrée [13] detects the presence of run-time exceptions such as division by zero and under and over-flows by means of sound floating-point abstract domains [10,24].

The verification approach used in this work is similar to the analysis of numerical programs described in [8], where a chain of tools composed of Frama-C, the Jessie plug-in [23], and Why is used. The verification conditions obtained from the ACSL annotated C programs are checked by several external provers including Coq, Gappa, Z3 [25], CVC3 [1], and Alt-Ergo.

Recently, much work has been done on the verification of numerical properties for industrial and safety-critical C code, including aerospace software. The approach presented in [8] was applied to the formal verification of wave propagation differential equations [6] and to the verification of numerical properties of a pairwise state-based conflict detection algorithm [19]. A similar verification approach was employed to verify numerical properties of industrial software related to inertial navigation [22]. Astrée has been successfully applied to automatically check the absence of runtime errors associated with floating-point computations in aerospace control software [4]. More specifically, in [14] the fly-by-wire primary software of commercial airplanes is verified. Additionally, Astrée and Fluctuat were combined to analyze on-board software acting in the Monitoring and Safing Unit of the Automated Transfer Vehicle (ATV) [9].

6   Conclusion

In this paper, an alternative version of the CPR algorithm is proposed. This algorithm is an essential component of the ADS-B protocol which will soon be required in nearly all commercial aircraft in Europe and the USA. This alternative algorithm includes several simplifications aimed to reduce its numerical complexity. The equivalence between this version and the original algorithm in the ADS-B standard is formally proven in PVS. Additionally, it is shown that double-precision floating-point computation guarantees the correct operation of the alternative algorithm when implemented in C.

The verification approach applied in this work requires some level of expertise. A background in floating-point arithmetic is needed to express the properties to be verified and to properly annotate for the weakest precondition deductive reasoning. Deep understanding of the features of each tool is essential for the analysis. Careful choice of types in the C implementation leads to fewer and simpler verification conditions. Also, Gappa requires user input to identify critical subexpressions when performing bisection.

The work presented here relies on several tools: the PVS interactive prover, the Frama-C analyzer, and the automatic provers AltErgo and Gappa. These tools are based on rigorous mathematical foundations and have been used in the verification of several industrial and safety-critical systems. In addition, proof certificates for significant parts of the analysis were generated (PVS and Gappa). However, the overall proof chain must be trusted. For instance, AltErgo does not generate any proof certificate that can be checked externally. Furthermore, though some effort has been made to formalize and verify the Frama-C WP plug-in, this endeavor is still incomplete. Nevertheless, the CPR algorithm is relatively simple, containing no complex features such as pointers or loops, and so the generation of verification conditions for CPR can be allegedly trusted.

References

1. Barrett, C., Tinelli, C.: CVC3. In: Damm, W., Hermanns, H. (eds.) CAV 2007. LNCS, vol. 4590, pp. 298–302. Springer, Heidelberg (2007). https://doi.org/10.1007/978-3-540-73368-3_34
2. Baudin, P., Cuoq, P., Filliâtre, J.C., Marché, C., Monate, B., Moy, Y., Prevosto, V.: ACSL: ANSI/ISO C Specification Language, version 1.12 (2016)
3. Bertot, Y., Castéran, P.: Interactive Theorem Proving and Program Development - Coq'Art: The Calculus of Inductive Constructions. Texts in Theoretical Computer Science. An EATCS Series. Springer, Heidelberg (2004). https://doi.org/10.1007/978-3-662-07964-5
4. Bertrane, J., Cousot, P., Cousot, R., Feret, J., Mauborgne, L., Miné, A., Rival, X.: Static analysis and verification of aerospace software by abstract interpretation. Found. Trends Program. Lang. 2(2–3), 71–190 (2015)
5. Bobot, F., Filliâtre, J.C., Marché, C., Paskevich, A.: Let's verify this with Why3. Int. J. Softw. Tools Technol. Transfer 17(6), 709–727 (2015)

6. Boldo, S., Clément, F., Filliâtre, J.C., Mayero, M., Melquiond, G., Weis, P.: Wave equation numerical resolution: a comprehensive mechanized proof of a C program. J. Autom. Reasoning **50**(4), 423–456 (2013)

7. Boldo, S., Filliâtre, J.C.: Formal verification of floating-point programs. In: Proceedings of ARITH18 2007, pp. 187–194. IEEE Computer Society (2007)

8. Boldo, S., Marché, C.: Formal verification of numerical programs: from C annotated programs to mechanical proofs. Math. Comput. Sci. **5**(4), 377–393 (2011)

9. Bouissou, O., Conquet, E., Cousot, P., Cousot, R., Feret, J., Goubault, E., Ghorbal, K., Lesens, D., Mauborgne, L., Miné, A., Putot, S., Rival, X., Turin, M.: Space software validation using abstract interpretation. In: Proceedings of the International Space System Engineering Conference, Data Systems in Aerospace (DASIA 2009), pp. 1–7. ESA publications (2009)

10. Chen, L., Miné, A., Cousot, P.: A sound floating-point polyhedra abstract domain. In: Ramalingam, G. (ed.) APLAS 2008. LNCS, vol. 5356, pp. 3–18. Springer, Heidelberg (2008). https://doi.org/10.1007/978-3-540-89330-1_2

11. Code of Federal Regulations: Automatic Dependent Surveillance-Broadcast (ADS-B) Out, 91 c.f.r., section 225 (2015)

12. Conchon, S., Contejean, E., Kanig, J., Lescuyer, S.: CC(X): semantic combination of congruence closure with solvable theories. Electron. Notes Theor. Comput. Sci. **198**(2), 51–69 (2008)

13. Cousot, P., Cousot, R., Feret, J., Mauborgne, L., Miné, A., Monniaux, D., Rival, X.: The ASTRÉE analyzer. In: Sagiv, M. (ed.) ESOP 2005. LNCS, vol. 3444, pp. 21–30. Springer, Heidelberg (2005). https://doi.org/10.1007/978-3-540-31987-0_3

14. Delmas, D., Souyris, J.: Astrée: from research to industry. In: Nielson, H.R., Filé, G. (eds.) SAS 2007. LNCS, vol. 4634, pp. 437–451. Springer, Heidelberg (2007). https://doi.org/10.1007/978-3-540-74061-2_27

15. de Dinechin, F., Lauter, C., Melquiond, G.: Certifying the floating-point implementation of an elementary function using Gappa. IEEE Trans. Comput. **60**(2), 242–253 (2011)

16. Dutle, A., Moscato, M., Titolo, L., Muñoz, C.: A formal analysis of the compact position reporting algorithm. In: Paskevich, A., Wies, T. (eds.) VSTTE 2017. LNCS, vol. 10712, pp. 19–34. Springer, Cham (2017). https://doi.org/10.1007/978-3-319-72308-2_2

17. European Commission: Commission Implementing Regulation (EU) 2017/386 of 6 March 2017 amending Implementing Regulation (EU) No 1207/2011, C/2017/1426 (2017)

18. Filliâtre, J.-C., Marché, C.: Multi-prover verification of C programs. In: Davies, J., Schulte, W., Barnett, M. (eds.) ICFEM 2004. LNCS, vol. 3308, pp. 15–29. Springer, Heidelberg (2004). https://doi.org/10.1007/978-3-540-30482-1_10

19. Goodloe, A.E., Muñoz, C., Kirchner, F., Correnson, L.: Verification of numerical programs: from real numbers to floating point numbers. In: Brat, G., Rungta, N., Venet, A. (eds.) NFM 2013. LNCS, vol. 7871, pp. 441–446. Springer, Heidelberg (2013). https://doi.org/10.1007/978-3-642-38088-4_31

20. Goubault, E., Putot, S.: Static analysis of numerical algorithms. In: Yi, K. (ed.) SAS 2006. LNCS, vol. 4134, pp. 18–34. Springer, Heidelberg (2006). https://doi.org/10.1007/11823230_3

21. Kirchner, F., Kosmatov, N., Prevosto, V., Signoles, J., Yakobowski, B.: Frama-C: a software analysis perspective. Formal Aspects Comput. **27**(3), 573–609 (2015)

22. Marché, C.: Verification of the functional behavior of a floating-point program: an industrial case study. Sci. Comput. Program. **96**, 279–296 (2014)

23. Marché, C., Moy, Y.: The Jessie Plugin for Deductive Verification in Frama-C (2017)
24. Miné, A.: Relational abstract domains for the detection of floating-point run-time errors. In: Schmidt, D. (ed.) ESOP 2004. LNCS, vol. 2986, pp. 3–17. Springer, Heidelberg (2004). https://doi.org/10.1007/978-3-540-24725-8_2
25. de Moura, L., Bjørner, N.: Z3: an efficient SMT solver. In: Ramakrishnan, C.R., Rehof, J. (eds.) TACAS 2008. LNCS, vol. 4963, pp. 337–340. Springer, Heidelberg (2008). https://doi.org/10.1007/978-3-540-78800-3_24
26. Owre, S., Rushby, J.M., Shankar, N.: PVS: a prototype verification system. In: Kapur, D. (ed.) CADE 1992. LNCS, vol. 607, pp. 748–752. Springer, Heidelberg (1992). https://doi.org/10.1007/3-540-55602-8_217
27. RTCA SC-186: Minimum Operational Performance Standards for 1090 MHz extended squitter Automatic Dependent Surveillance - Broadcast (ADS-B) and Traffic Information Services - Broadcast (TIS-B) (2009)

Formal Verification of Automotive Simulink Controller Models: Empirical Technical Challenges, Evaluation and Recommendations

Johanna Nellen[1]([✉]), Thomas Rambow[2], Md Tawhid Bin Waez[3], Erika Ábrahám[1], and Joost-Pieter Katoen[1]

[1] RWTH Aachen University, Aachen, Germany
{johanna.nellen,abraham,katoen}@cs.rwth-aachen.de
[2] Ford Werke GmbH, Cologne, Germany
[3] Ford Motor Company, Dearborn, USA
{trambow,mwaez}@ford.com

Abstract. The automotive industry makes increasing usage of Simulink-based software development. Typically, automotive Simulink designs are analyzed using non-formal test methods, which do not guarantee the absence of errors. In contrast, formal verification techniques aim at providing formal guarantees or counterexamples that the analyzed designs fulfill their requirements for all possible inputs and parameters. Therefore, the automotive safety standard ISO 26262 recommends the usage of formal methods in safety-critical software development.

In this paper, we report on the application of formal verification to check discrete-time properties of a Simulink model for a park assistant R&D prototype feature using the commercial *Simulink Design Verifier* tool. During our evaluation, we experienced a gap between the offered functionalities and typical industrial needs, which hindered the successful application of this tool in the context of model-based development. We discuss these issues and propose solutions related to system development, requirements specification and verification tools, in order to prepare the ground for the effective integration of computer-assisted formal verification in automotive Simulink-based development.

1 Introduction

In modern cars a huge number of embedded software components support the vehicle control. These software components are usually developed in a model-based approach with a graphical modeling language like Simulink/Stateflow that allows automatic code generation for the deployment of the controller. Though the safe operation of a software component is rigorously tested in offline simulations, the absence of errors cannot be guaranteed by testing.

The automotive safety standard ISO 26262 recommends to integrate — besides other approaches — also *formal verification* in the development process of safety-critical software. Formal verification either guarantees that the

© Springer International Publishing AG, part of Springer Nature 2018
K. Havelund et al. (Eds.): FM 2018, LNCS 10951, pp. 382–398, 2018.
https://doi.org/10.1007/978-3-319-95582-7_23

property holds for *all* possible input and parameter combinations, or it provides a counterexample (i.e., a system run that violates the property) which can be used to identify the error and to re-design the controller.

In this paper we present an industrial case study from the automotive sector with the aim to *empirically identify and solve technical problems that might arise during the integration of discrete-time formal verification in Simulink-based mass production* of safety-critical systems by engineers who are not formal methods experts. These problems might not be obvious or seem pressing but they become prominent and relevant for large-scale development, a development process with much legacy, or a development without a strong dedicated formal methods team.

We decided to rely on the commercial verification tool *Simulink Design Verifier (SLDV)* [1], which is developed by the vendors of Simulink and backed by a dedicated support team. We applied SLDV to analyze a Simulink controller model for a park assistant R&D prototype feature against 41 functional requirements, which were given informally in textual form as a Microsoft Word document. The model is open-loop, as the controlled environment is not included, and contains no continuous-time blocks, such that we could use SLDV's discrete-time verification functionalities. Using formal verification we detected inconsistencies between requirements and their implementations in our model, which demonstrates the importance of formal verification for safety-critical software components.

Besides the verification results, we report on the strengths of SLDV, identify its limitations and collect important general observations.

Though the verification of our model was successful, we encountered different technical challenges. Introducing formal verification into fast pace mass automotive product development by engineers who are not familiar with formal methods is not at all straightforward and needs a high level of automation. We give recommendations to support requirement engineers to build complete, unambiguous and consistent requirements and to help system engineers to develop "verification-friendlier" models. We also give some ideas for new features in verification tools that can support the integration of formal verification into Simulink-based development in the utomotive sector.

Related Work. Techniques and tools for formal discrete-time verification of Simulink models has been widely studied. Regarding applications, a medical case study using SLDV is presented in [2]. In [3] the authors apply the SMT-based static verification tool *VerSAA* to a Simulink model and also provide a comparison to SLDV. In [4] an SMT-based approach for explicit LTL model checking of Simulink models is presented. A tool chain for the formal verification of Simulink models in the avionics industry using the LTL model checker *DiVinE* and a proprietary verification tool *HiLiTE* is presented in [5,6].

Some other approaches transform Simulink models into the input modeling language of different verification tools. The authors of [7] transformed Simulink models into the modeling language *Boogie* and compare the performance of the Boogie verification framework with SLDV on an automotive case study. The work [8] translates Simulink to *UCLID* and applies SMT-based bounded model checking to an automotive case study. The works [9,10] and the Simulink toolbox *cocoSim* [11] offer translations of Simulink resp. SCADE models to the intermediate language Lustre in order to enable the application of different verification tools. Additionally, [9,10] report on the experiences with the integration of formal verification in an avionics model-based development process. The *RCRS* project [12,13] formalizes Simulink models in Isabelle and uses the Isabelle theorem prover for formal analysis. SLDV and UPPAAL were used for the formal verification of an automotive case study in [14].

A project to establish formal verification in the development process in automotive industry is presented in [15]. The work [16] presents a study that explores the extent to which model checking can be performed *usefully* in an industrial environment, where usefully means that model checking is cheaper, faster, more thorough than conventional testing or review or able to find more subtle errors.

A complementary automotive case study on C code verification using BTC is presented in [17].

Contributions. Although a lot of research has been done on the verification of Simulink models, we are not aware of an *exhaustive analysis of SLDV where different verification approaches and the scalability are evaluated*. Moreover, our aim is to *investigate the gap that still exists to integrate formal verification into Simulink-based development*, even if a verification tool like SLDV is used, that is tightly integrated into Simulink. We present our observations and ideas to *improve the level of automation for the preprocessing of the model, the formalization of a specification, and the feature set of a verification tool*.

Outline. In Sect. 2 we describe our case study, the SLDV verification tool and specify the project goals. The verification process and the results are presented in Sect. 3. In Sect. 4 we list our observations and formalize some recommendations for computer-assisted solutions to integrate formal verification into Simulink-based development. We conclude the paper in Sect. 5.

2   The Case Study

First, we present our case study, the SLDV verification tool and our project goals. Due to confidentiality reasons, we cannot provide access to the concrete model and requirements, but we provide high-level insight into issues that are relevant for understanding the aims and results of this work.

2.1   Controller Model

Simulink. Simulink is an extension of Matlab which allows to build and simulate complex system models. Simulink (SL) models are block diagrams. Stateflow (SF) charts, that are based on finite-state machines and flow diagrams, can be embedded into Simulink models. Blocks and charts can be nested to create a hierarchical structure. For Simulink models which might contain Stateflow charts, in the following we use the abbreviation *SLSF model*.

Besides internal variables, Simulink models define a set of signals, (calibration) parameters and constants whose properties are fixed by attributes like, e.g. the data type, the dimensions, lower and/or upper bounds and initial values. *Signals* can take any value from their data type domain during a simulation while *constants* have a fixed value. *Calibration parameters* allow to define abstract models and specifications, which can be concretized by assigning concrete values to the parameters. E.g. a specification $x = c \cdot y$ parameterized in c can be concretized to $x = 2 \cdot y$ by fixing $c = 2$.

Controller Model. Our case study models the R&D prototype feature Low Speed Control for a next-gen Park Assist. The Park Assist allows the vehicle to park automatically and operates at relatively low speeds compared to other driving situations. During assisted parking maneuvers, the vehicle speed has to be controlled at low vehicle speed targets and scenarios like climbing on a curb during parking have to be supported. The selected R&D prototype feature Low Speed Control takes the vehicle speed set point from Park Assist and controls the combustion engine speed and the brakes during automated parking.

We want to investigate how well Simulink formal verification performs for decision logic, state charts, filters, rate limiters, look-up tables and feedback control. Therefore, we selected our case study such that it contains a mixture of these different kinds of functionalities. The model has 41 open-loop functional requirements, 26 inputs, 5 outputs, 69 calibration parameters and 1095 blocks ($\approx$ 1500 lines of C code). The model contains Boolean, integer and floating-point variables: All input and output signals are scalar with the following data type distribution: 5 Boolean, 12 unsigned 8-bit integer and 14 single-precision floating point. Among the calibration parameters we have 52 scalar parameters (2 Boolean and 50 single-precision floating-point) and 17 parameters are arrays with 7 to 14 single-precision floating-point elements.

Requirements. The 41 textual requirements of the R&D prototype feature Low Speed Control describe the functional behavior of the controller and are used to develop the Simulink model. A single requirement typically describes only a part of the model that is implemented in a subsystem.

We classified 39 requirements as safety properties which follow the pattern "*Always* P". In 30 of these safety requirements P is an invariant without any temporal operators. For the remaining 9 safety properties, P describes time-bounded temporal properties. The two remaining requirements are liveness properties which claim that something good eventually happens. They follow the pattern "*The value of x is eventually equal to c*" and express unbounded temporal properties.

Since 30 of the 41 requirements contain floating-point variables, the state space is relatively large in most cases. Only 11 requirements are restricted to Boolean and integer data types, which reduces the verification effort.

Most of the requirements can be specified using the following common operators: $+, -, *, /, \min, \max, \text{if}, \text{abs}$. Twelve requirements make use of special operators such as saturation, rate limiters, filters, PID controllers, or lookup tables.

2.2 Simulink Design Verifier

For our case study we used the commercial verification tool *Simulink Design Verifier (SLDV)* [1,18]. Due to the tight integration into Simulink, the support team and detailed documentation we expect to minimize problems with embedding formal verification in an automotive development process. SLDV is a toolbox that offers the following analysis methods for SLSF models: Automatic test case generation, static analysis and *discrete-time formal verification*.

The SLDV tool uses software from *Polyspace* [19] and *Prover Technology AB* [20]. The latter offers (un)bounded model checking and test case generation. Unfortunately, the translation of the SLSF model and the specification into the formal input language of the verification engine, the verification engine itself and the generation of counterexamples remains a black box to the user. For `Property Proving` (formal verification) SLDV offers the following options: `FindViolation` checks if a property can be violated within a bounded number of steps, while `Prove` performs an unbounded analysis. `ProveWithViolationDetection` is a combination of `FindViolation` and `Prove` and performs a bounded analysis.

Properties that describe a *subsystem* of the model, i.e. properties that are restricted to the input and output signals of a subsystem, can be verified either on the complete model or on a subsystem (bottom-up approach). Subsystem verification is over-approximative because it considers arbitrary input for the subsystem instead of the values which it might receive as input signals in the complete model. As a consequence, properties that could be verified with subsystem verification hold also at the complete model level, but counterexamples on subsystem level might be spurious, i.e. not realizable in the complete model.

If the model includes *calibration parameters*, the verification can be performed either for a fixed model and specification (a concrete calibration parameter valuation is considered) or in one shot for all model and specification instances (all possible calibration parameter values are considered). For historic reasons, we speak of *fixed* or *varying* calibration parameters.

SLDV does not use a formal specification language with a formal semantics. Instead, an SLDV specification is an SLSF model which forms a *verification subsystem* (cf. Fig. 1). This specification language allows the flexibility to use complex operators and it is easy to use for engineers, but there is no formal semantics for Simulink blocks.

Each verification subsystem should contain at least one *proof objective* that outputs `true` as long as its input is constantly `true`. The input of a proof objective is typically the result of an implication or a comparison between the specification and an output of the model. SLDV is shipped with a library that contains — among others — verification subsystems, proof objectives and temporal operators.

The verification result of a requirement is *valid* if the corresponding proof objective returns `true` for all possible input combinations of the model. Otherwise, the verification tool cannot decide if the requirement is valid in the model or not and returns *undecided* or the requirement is *violated* and a counterexample is generated. The counterexample is given on the level of the SLSF model in

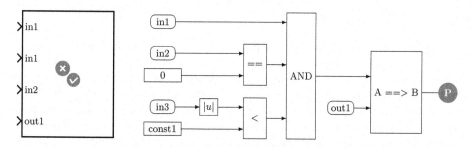

Fig. 1. A verification subsystem (left) and the specification (right) of the requirement: "If all of the following conditions are true: in1 is TRUE; in2 is zero; the absolute value of in3 is below a threshold (const1); then out1 shall be set."

form of a *harness model*. This harness model can be used to simulate the execution path that violates the specification. An HTML or PDF report can be generated that contains the verification results, the analysis options and approximations SLDV applied to the model. An example for an approximation is floating-point arithmetic that is approximated by rational arithmetic.

In this paper, we primarily use the Property Proving feature of SLDV with the Prove option for an unbounded analysis.

2.3 Goals

Our project goal is to evaluate formal verification of Simulink controller models using SLDV, to identify empirical technical challenges for a tight integration of formal verification into Simulink-based development in the automotive industry and to propose solutions for a higher level of automation and a better support of engineers without expert knowledge in formal methods. We are especially interested in a clear separation of the controller model from the specification, the speed and scalability of the verification tool, the usefulness, generality and reliability of the analysis results and automated batch processing.

We assume that problems with the specification of complex operators like filters, feedback control and lookup tables might occur. Expected challenges for the verification tool are temporal requirements, the high proportion of floating-point variables and the complexity of the model.

3 Feasibility Analysis

In this section, we report on our experiences with formal verification of our SLSF model using SLDV and present the verification results. We performed our experiments using Matlab R2014b on a 2.5 GHz Intel Core i5 machine with 8 GB RAM running Windows 7 (64-bit).

3.1 Preparation

Requirement Issues. We were not surprised to find incomplete, ambiguous and inconsistent formulations in 20 of the 41 textual requirements. Incomplete specifications have been found in 15 requirements, eight ambiguity issues have been detected, and two requirement pairs were inconsistent with each other. Causes for incompleteness were missing declaration of values for discrete signals (e.g., certain gear lever positions), missing information for complex operators like filters or hysteresis functions, or no mentioning of the output signal whose computation is described in the requirement. Reasons for the detected ambiguity in the requirements are imprecise formulations (e.g. to distinguish between the status or the event of status change), formulations that need further explanations and different textual descriptions for the same signal name. An example for inconsistency is two requirements that allow activation and deactivation of a signal to occur simultaneously.

Discussions with the requirement and feature engineers and reviewing the model implementation helped to resolve the issues.

SLDV Specification. Finally, we could manually transform all textual requirements to an SLDV specification in form of new verification subsystems.

For each requirement a separate verification subsystem was created and added to the model to have the flexibility to add/remove certain blocks and to copy them for verification on model- or subsystem-level. Some requirements have been easy to handle while for roughly half of the requirements discussions with the requirement and control engineers and/or information from the controller model were needed to clarify all issues. Finally, all 41 requirements could be specified for SLDV, although twelve requirements make use of *complex operators* like feedback control, rate limiters, filters and lookup tables, which might be difficult to express in a common specification language like formal logics.

Block Replacement. A compatibility check of SLDV on our model revealed a set of *custom blocks* that are not supported by SLDV. These blocks include additional functionality for code generation but can be replaced by blocks from the standard library with equivalent functionality. We used the block replacement feature of SLDV to automate the replacement. This feature allows to continue the iterative development with the original model but to generate a model with replaced blocks for formal verification.

3.2 Verification

We analyzed each of the 41 requirements, specified as 41 independent verification subsystems, separately on model- and subsystem-level using either fixed or varying calibration parameters. To do so, we temporarily removed the other 40 verification subsystems that contain the specification of the other requirements. To analyze the impact of bounded temporal operators in the specification on the running time of the verification, we use fixed time bounds (five simulation steps) as an upper limit. This reduces the number of calibration parameters in our model. We also fix the lookup-table data for the verification. Thus, for our analysis we consider only 47 out of 69 varying calibration parameters. An overview of the verification results is given in Table 1. For a majority of requirements we got conclusive results. However, the analysis revealed inconclusive results for up to 31% (resp. 12%) of the requirements on model- (resp. subsystem-)level. Reasons for inconclusive results are nonlinear behavior in the model and timeouts (running times > 7200s) for temporal requirements.

Table 1. Verification results and accumulated running times for model and subsystem verification using varying and fixed calibration parameters.

	Model verification		Subsystem verification	
	Varying	Fixed	Varying	Fixed
Valid	24	26	25	26
Unknown	13	10	5	4
Invalid	4	5	11	11
Running time > 300s	7	7	2	2
Running time > 7200s (TO)	1	1	1	1
Acc. running times [s]	22062	21465	7672	7783

Invalid Verification Results. Simulink Design Verifier detected eleven instances of invalid implementation against the specifications. Most of them were implementation flaws like missing or wrong operators. In other cases, implementation details were omitted in the textual requirements, parameters have been incorrectly calibrated, or the initialization causes requirement violations.

Analysis Time. We did not notice a significant difference in the analysis time for valid, unknown and invalid verification results on subsystem-level: 39 verification results were delivered within four seconds. An exception are two *temporal properties* for which we observed running times above 300 s. On model level, 22 verification results are available within four seconds, 12 results have running times between 11 and 133 s and the running times of the remaining 7 requirements are above 300 s. Further investigations revealed that all running times above 300 s can be explained by temporal behavior either in the analyzed requirement or in a subsystem that delivers an input for the analyzed subsystem.

Model- vs. Subsystem-level. We compare the results for verification on model- and subsystem-level: The number of *inconclusive verification results* can be reduced from 10 for fixed (respectively, 13 for varying) calibration parameters on model-level to 4 for fixed (resp. 5 for varying) calibration parameters on subsystem-level. Also the *analysis time* can be reduced by almost four hours if the verification is applied on subsystem-level. An explanation for both observations can be that on model-level nonlinear and/or temporal behavior in other parts of the model is propagated.

On subsystem-level we revealed two requirement violations for requirements that were proven valid on model-level. A missing minimum operator and time delays in the implementation that are not reflected in the textual requirement are the reasons for the invalid results on subsystem-level. These conflicting results were either caused by considering arbitrary inputs on subsystem-level, leading to spurious counterexamples in which some subsystem inputs are not realizable at the model-level. An alternative explanation can be a bug that produces false *valid* verification results in the verification on model-level.

Varying vs. Fixed Calibration Parameters. Using subsystem verification, the running time could be decreased if we defined fixed (instead of varying) values for 47 calibration parameters, while for model verification the running time increased, both differences being within 3%.

Based on the experience with our model, we believe *SLDV to scale well with increasing state space size.* Although on subsystem-level only a few of the calibration parameters influence the verification, on model-level the effect on the state space is much stronger. Thus, we have the impression that SLDV can handle a large number of input signals and parameters with large data type domains quite well. To our surprise, *the number of inconclusive verification results does not change much with increasing state space*: For verification on model-level three and on subsystem-level one additional requirements could be decided using fixed calibration parameters.

Simultaneous Execution on Model-Level. We found a serious tool issue in SLDV (R2014b – R2017a): When running the formal verification on model-level simultaneously for all 41 requirements, we detected *conflicting analysis results*, i.e. a valid and an invalid result for the same requirement. We observed a conflict for two different verification runs using simultaneous execution of all requirements. Another conflict occurred between a verification run using simultaneous execution (valid) and a verification run analyzing only the respective requirement either on model- or subsystem-level (invalid). We could confirm the requirement violations, i.e. the valid results are caused by a bug. Another finding using R2016b were verification runs using simultaneous execution of all requirements where *all requirements were reported as violated and no counterexamples were generated*. However, MathWorks assured that these problems are resolved in release R2017b. Note that these bugs in SLDV can also be an explanation for the conflicting results of a single requirement on model- and subsystem-level.

We also detected nondeterminism in the results (the order and number of counterexamples changes). This results from the fact that SLDV implements a portfolio solution where different counterexample search strategies are applied.

3.3   Scalability

For a better understanding of the scalability of SLDV with respect to temporal requirements on our model we analyzed the following property from the set of requirements for an increasing time duration d and fixed calibration parameter values on both model- and subsystem-level: "*If a Boolean signal in1 is true for* *longer than a time duration d then the Boolean output signal **out1** shall be set; it shall be cleared otherwise."* The Boolean signal in1 is computed using four floating-point signals in2, in3, in4 and in5 with single precision: *"The Boolean signal **in1** is **true** if any of the following conditions is **true**: The signal **in2** is above 4000.0 with offset −100.0, (the signal **in3** is above 2000.0 with offset −30.0 and the absolute value of the signal **in5** is below 0.2,), or the signal **in3** is not increasing and the signal **in4** is below the signal **in3** with offset −30.0".*

We considered time durations d between 0.05 and 1 s and a fixed simulation step size of 0.01 s. Note that the temporal operators of SLDV only support simulation steps as the unit for time bounds, we converted the time durations. The results are presented in Fig. 2.

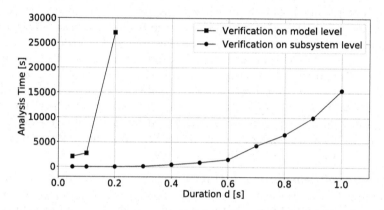

Fig. 2. The analysis time needed to prove a temporal property with increasing time duration d on model- and subsystem-level with fixed calibration parameters.

The running time grows exponentially in the time duration d. The results show that on subsystem-level up to 80 simulation steps can be handled with a time out of 7200 s. More than four hours are needed to complete the analysis for 100 simulation steps. The results for model verification are much worse due to the complexity of the model. Already for 20 simulation steps more than seven hours were needed for the analysis.

For a more general result on the scalability of SLDV, a more rigorous analysis on a larger benchmark set would be needed.

4 Lessons Learned

In this section, we report our observations and recommendations for formal verification of SLSF models using SLDV.

4.1 Specification

Interferences. We encountered several examples with different requirements for the same output signal. These interferences may lead to inconsistencies. Proper specification of priorities can be applied to solve this kind of inconsistency. Requirement engineers may also follow the defensive approach to use exactly one requirement for each disjunctive part of the model.

Specification Language. The Simulink Design Verifier uses Simulink as specification language. On the one hand, Simulink offers a rich set of operators that are often not available in other specification languages. To speed up the specification work, *a custom library with efficient implementations of commonly used operators might be helpful.* For example, a hysteresis function and customized lookup tables can be provided. This approach also ensures that the same block parameters (e.g. interpolation and extrapolation methods) are used for each occurrence of an operator. On the other hand, we are not aware of a formal semantics for Simulink, and using the same language for modeling and specification can easily lead to false-positive verification results. *A formal specification language may assist the requirement engineers to avoid incompleteness and ambiguity* [21]. This language should be easy to understand for engineers without expert knowledge in formal methods. We propose a pattern-based textual language as in [22,23]. This formal specification language would also help to separate the formalization of a property from its Simulink implementation.

Compositional Reasoning. All 41 requirements have been formulated on subsystem level. Thus, verification on subsystem-level and bottom-up compositional reasoning can be applied to verify the complete model. The main benefits of this approach are shorter analysis time and stronger verification results.

4.2 Model

Floating-Point Numbers. A big challenge for the formal verification are the *floating-point numbers*, which are approximated by SLDV. Although it is not possible to eliminate all floating-point signals, we encourage to search for integer implementations with equivalent functionality. The R&D prototype `Low Speed Control` contains timers with floating-point arithmetic, which often leads to undecided results or to spurious counterexamples, the latter because floating-point approximation leads to property violation but the provided counterexample cannot be confirmed by simulation, where the approximation is not applied.

Consider a timer using floating-point arithmetic and a counter using integer arithmetic, that are both initialized with 0. In each simulation step, the timer is updated according to `timer := timer + timestep` while the counter is increased by one: `counter := counter + 1`. The timer is reset if the upper bound `ub` is reached (`timer` $\geq$ `ub`). The counter restarts if an upper limit `c := `$\lfloor \frac{ub}{timeStep} \rfloor$ is reached (`counter` $\geq$ `c`). Because controller models use fixed-step solvers, the bound c can always be computed. Using such transformations, *we recommend to replace floating-point timers by equivalent integer counters* in Simulink models.

We also found another example in the model where the number of operations on floating-point variables could be reduced by an alternative implementation.

Value Domains. To keep the state space as small as possible and the analysis time low, a system engineer should specify lower and upper bounds for all input, output and calibration parameters reducing the admissible valuations as much as possible. E.g., the data type domain of a floating-point signal representing the vehicle speed can be restricted to values between 0 and 320 km/h.

Stateflow Models. Special attention is needed for Stateflow implementations. We observed time delays, that are not reflected in the textual requirements. For example, moving from one state to another takes a simulation step, and outgoing transitions of the new state are not evaluated immediately. The engineer should be aware of the time delays he/she introduces in the model and the textual requirements should be updated. To facilitate the specification for a Stateflow chart, *a variable storing the active state of the chart should be introduced.*

Calibration Parameters. A special class of calibration parameters are time bounds. Our case study includes such a calibration parameter whose value should be set to the simulation step size before each simulation run. To verify such models for all possible step sizes, we propose to automatically replace all occurrences of such calibration parameters by `Weighted Sample Time` blocks or to add an assertion stating the equality between the calibration parameter and the output of a `Weighted Sample Time` block, before formal verification is started.

4.3   Verification Tool

Usability. Simulink Design Verifier is intuitive to use and easy to integrate in Simulink. Although no expert knowledge is necessary to apply formal verification on a Simulink model, finding explanations for certain verification results and the development of workarounds are hardly possible without special expertise. The black box implementation of SLDV hinders even experts to exploit the strengths of the underlying verification techniques and to avoid their weaknesses.

Inconclusive Results. We encountered a lot of inconclusive verification results. Most of them occurred due to nonlinear behavior in the model. Often the issues could be resolved by verification on subsystem level, which indicates that the nonlinear behavior on model-level is propagated from other parts of the model. However, it is hard to identify the block causing the nonlinear behavior. It would be very helpful to have tool support. We also suspect that sometimes issues with floating-point arithmetic are reported as inconclusive due to nonlinear behavior in the model.

Floating-Point Variables. SLDV approximates floating-point arithmetic by rational arithmetic. This approximation often results in inconclusive verification results or spurious counterexamples, which cannot be confirmed by simulation where the approximation is not applied. Even more dangerous are results reporting correctness, because they are not reliable: the generated C-code of a successfully verified Simulink model might violate its requirements. We would appreciate to get more information how the approximation is done, how it affects the verification outcome, whether the analysis tool uses exact or inexact computations and an explanation for non-expert users that counterexamples might not be reproducible via simulation.

Specification Implementation. To analyze whether the model is initialized correctly, we compared two different implementations of a correct-initialization requirement for an unsigned integer variable: the first one uses an `Extender` block (a temporal operator provided by SLDV) and the second one a `Delay` and an `Implication` block. To our surprise, the running times were quite different: while the verification result was available in less than a second for the first approach, the analysis time was 23 s for the second one. This example demonstrates once more that for an *efficient* implementation sometimes knowledge of the verification techniques or even implementation details are necessary.

Model- vs. Subsystem-level Verification. The strengths of model-level verification are the clear separation between specification and implementation and the possibility to analyze all enabled proof objectives simultaneously. Drawbacks are longer analysis times and more inconclusive results. Verification on subsystem level is faster and independent of other parts of the model, yielding conclusive results in more cases. Verification results on subsystem-level can be reused if a subsystem is embedded into another model, while results on model-level cannot be transferred. However, the user needs to know the model well to be able to identify a subsystem that assures the validity of a requirement, independently of its context. Moreover, for subsystem-verification the chosen subsystem must be modified to be an *atomic unit*. Though this modification does not change the behavior of the subsystem, it affects the processing order of blocks in the model. Therefore, these modifications must be undone after verification. An automated solution would be helpful that temporarily treats the subsystem as atomic during verification while the original model remains unaffected.

Recommended Tool-Chain. A first verification run should be performed on model-level using varying calibration with all proof objectives enabled and with a short running time e.g., 100 s. If verification on model-level yields inconclusive results, the analysis of the corresponding requirement should be repeated on subsystem-level with a larger running time for temporal requirements. Since the analysis time of SLDV for temporal requirements can increase exponentially in the number of simulation steps, we recommend to start with a small number of time steps (e.g. 5), which can slowly be increased to more realistic values as long as the analysis time remains acceptable. It might also be possible to include a different verification tool that scales better for temporal properties in the tool chain. Note that if any parameter value or data type domain is changed in the model, e.g. if lookup table data is replaced, former verification results cannot be trusted anymore for all analyses on model-level and for those task on subsystem-level, where the changed parameter is used in the subsystem.

Counterexamples. If verification on model-level verification reports a counterexample we recommend to simulate it to strengthen its reliability. Subsystem verification assumes arbitrary subsystem-inputs and may therefore produce spurious counterexamples, but these subsystem-counterexamples cannot be easily simulated at model level because the inputs for the subsystem's environment are not fixed. If the user can argue that the inputs in the subsystem-counterexample are not possible in the full model, we recommend to limit the domains for the subsystem's inputs by adding assumptions and re-check the limited subsystem. Otherwise, if a subsystem-counterexample seems plausible, we propose to add assumptions to restrict the subsystem's behavior to the counterexample and apply model-level verification to this restricted model to search for an extension at the model level. Restricting the subsystem's behavior to the counterexample is doable, however, it is a non-trivial and tedious task. Furthermore, we observed one case where subsystem verification returned a counterexample but at model-level the requirement could be proven, indicating the spuriousness of the subsystem counterexample. However, we found strong indications that instead a software bug produced a false *valid* verification result on model-level.

Batch Verification. For large-scale applications, formal verification with a higher level of automation is needed that offers one-click solutions for the sequential verification of a set of requirements both on model- and on subsystem-level. Currently, the simultaneous verification of a set of requirements is possible on model level, but we have the impression that this mode does not process the requirements sequentially one after the other, but it rather uses an incremental verification technique (possibly incremental SMT-solving) that considers all requirements simultaneously. Although we are aware that using the provided API, it is possible to develop a custom solution for batch processing on model- and subsystem-level, a built-in solution would be appreciated.

Temporal Requirements. One weakness of SLDV is the verification of temporal requirements. In some cases, checking temporal requirements over just 5 simulation steps took more than two hours. For the temporal operators provided by SLDV, numerical values are needed to specify upper bounds for the time steps. The support of constants or calibration parameters would offer much more flexibility, e.g. if different bounds need to be checked. We also noticed that the upper bounds are restricted to values of ≈ 128 simulation steps (depending on the temporal operator), while in practice larger time bounds might be needed.

Calibration Parameters. We like the automated solution to verify models for all calibration parameter values from some user-defined intervals, which is of high relevance in the automotive sector. However, it is not clear what such an interval domain means for, e.g., lookup tables data. We encountered a bug in R2014b where calibration parameters of data type *Boolean* were not supported. An available bug-fix for R2015b could be adapted to R2014b. Furthermore, calibration parameter values can be restricted to intervals but we have found no ways to restrict such hyperrectangle-domains further by putting restrictions on the relation of different parameters, e.g. assuming that the value of one parameter is not larger than the value of another one. As some blocks work correctly only for certain calibration parameter combinations, it was sometimes necessary to add assumptions to such blocks when verifying over calibration parameter domains. For example, a saturation block expects an upper-bound value to be larger or equal to a lower-bound value; if the definition of these bounds involve some calibration parameters then we need to add such assertions to the model.

Reliability. During our experiments we detected (and reported) some bugs in SLDV. We are aware that software for formal verification is quite complex and that bugs in the code are likely. Thus, our recommendation is to use more than one analysis tool for a better reliability on the verification results (though, for Simulink unfortunately the number of available tools is quite small). It would also be helpful to have open-source tools, which offer the possibility for temporary patches by the user, such that he/she can proceed and does not need to wait for the next release. Furthermore, we strongly recommend to use the latest tool release if possible to avoid resolved bugs.

Verification Report. SLDV generates a report containing information like verification results, analysis times and applied approximations. Counterexamples can be simulated which is very helpful for the detection of property violations. Unfortunately, the time that is needed for translation and compilation of the model to create the input for the verification engine is not listed in the report.

5   Conclusions and Discussion

In this paper, we shared our experiences with the application of formal verification to an automotive controller model using the commercial verification tool SLDV. Despite the mixture of different functionalities in the model and all requirement issues, we achieved verification results for all 41 functional requirements of the R&D prototype feature `Low Speed Control`.

SLDV is easy to use, well integrated into Simulink and provides features for a high degree of automation like block replacement and support for calibration parameters. Still, the level of automation could be further improved, e.g. by one-click solutions for batch processing. All in all, we experienced SLDV to be scalable for open-loop controller models, especially using subsystem-level verification, but temporal properties bring SLDV to its limits. Closed-loop models that contain plant models with continuous time and varying-step solvers are currently not supported. A serious concern is the missing formal semantics for Simulink and the black box implementation of the verification tool. We further discovered a serious tool issue that leads to contradicting verification results. We recommend to use SLDV release R2017b, where the bug is supposedly resolved.

We strongly suggest to not only apply verification on the Simulink model where counterexamples can be analyzed relatively easy and comfortable in the high-level, hierarchical, graphical simulation environment. Additionally, verification on generated C code [17] can be beneficial since data types like floating-points and data type domains can be handled exactly.

Although SLDV is quite comfortable to use, there is still a gap which needs to be closed for a smooth integration in the industrial Simulink-based development. For future work, we want to put further effort into closing this gap and developing computer-assisted methods for complete, unambiguous and consistent requirement writing and for verification into Simulink-based development.

Acknowledgments. The authors want to thank Petter Nilsson, Philipp Berger, William Milam and Cem Mengi for numerous fruitful discussions on Simulink verification. We also express our appreciation to the MathWorks support team for their fast response and helpful advice.

References

1. MathWorks: Simulink Design Verifier. https://de.mathworks.com/products/sldesignverifier.html
2. Gholami, M.-R., Boucheneb, H.: Applying formal methods into safety-critical health applications. In: Ortmeier, F., Rauzy, A. (eds.) IMBSA 2014. LNCS, vol. 8822, pp. 195–208. Springer, Cham (2014). https://doi.org/10.1007/978-3-319-12214-4_15
3. Boström, P., Heikkilä, M., Huova, M., Waldén, M., Linjama, M.: Verification and validation of a pressure control unit for hydraulic systems. In: Majzik, I., Vieira, M. (eds.) SERENE 2014. LNCS, vol. 8785, pp. 101–115. Springer, Cham (2014). https://doi.org/10.1007/978-3-319-12241-0_8
4. Barnat, J., Bauch, P., Havel, V.: Temporal verification of Simulink diagrams. In: Proceedings of HASE 2014, pp. 81–88. IEEE (2014)
5. Barnat, J., Beran, J., Brim, L., Kratochvíla, T., Ročkai, P.: Tool chain to support automated formal verification of avionics simulink designs. In: Stoelinga, M., Pinger, R. (eds.) FMICS 2012. LNCS, vol. 7437, pp. 78–92. Springer, Heidelberg (2012). https://doi.org/10.1007/978-3-642-32469-7_6
6. Barnat, J., Brim, L., Beran, J.: Executing model checking counterexamples in Simulink. In: Proceedings of TASE 2012, pp. 245–248. IEEE (2012)
7. Reicherdt, R., Glesner, S.: Formal verification of discrete-time MATLAB/simulink models using boogie. In: Giannakopoulou, D., Salaün, G. (eds.) SEFM 2014. LNCS, vol. 8702, pp. 190–204. Springer, Cham (2014). https://doi.org/10.1007/978-3-319-10431-7_14
8. Herber, P., Reicherdt, R., Bittner, P.: Bit-precise formal verification of discrete-time MATLAB/Simulink models using SMT solving. In: Proceedings of EMSOFT 2013, pp. 1–10. IEEE (2013)
9. Cofer, D.: Model checking: cleared for take off. In: van de Pol, J., Weber, M. (eds.) SPIN 2010. LNCS, vol. 6349, pp. 76–87. Springer, Heidelberg (2010). https://doi.org/10.1007/978-3-642-16164-3_6
10. Whalen, M., Cofer, D., Miller, S., Krogh, B.H., Storm, W.: Integration of formal analysis into a model-based software development process. In: Leue, S., Merino, P. (eds.) FMICS 2007. LNCS, vol. 4916, pp. 68–84. Springer, Heidelberg (2008). https://doi.org/10.1007/978-3-540-79707-4_7
11. Bourbouh, H., Garoche, P.L., Garion, C., Gurfinkel, A., Kahsai, T., Thirioux, X.: Automated analysis of Stateflow models. In: Proceedings of LPAR 2017. EPiC Series in Computing, vol. 46, pp. 144–161. EasyChair (2017)

12. Dragomir, I., Preoteasa, V., Tripakis, S.: Compositional semantics and analysis of hierarchical block diagrams. In: Bošnački, D., Wijs, A. (eds.) SPIN 2016. LNCS, vol. 9641, pp. 38–56. Springer, Cham (2016). https://doi.org/10.1007/978-3-319-32582-8_3

13. Preoteasa, V., Dragomir, I., Tripakis, S.: Type inference of simulink hierarchical block diagrams in Isabelle. In: Bouajjani, A., Silva, A. (eds.) FORTE 2017. LNCS, vol. 10321, pp. 194–209. Springer, Cham (2017). https://doi.org/10.1007/978-3-319-60225-7_14

14. Ali, S., Sulyman, M.: Applying model checking for verifying the functional requirements of a Scania's vehicle control system. Master's thesis, Mälardalen University (2012)

15. Botham, J., Dhadyalla, G., Powell, A., Miller, P., Haas, O., McGeoch, D., Rao, A.C., O'Halloran, C., Kiec, J., Farooq, A., Poushpas, S., Tudor, N.: PICASSOS - Practical applications of automated formal methods to safety related automotive systems. In: SAE Technical Paper, SAE International (2017)

16. Bennion, M., Habli, I.: A candid industrial evaluation of formal software verification using model checking. In: Proceedings of ICSE Companion 2014, pp. 175–184. ACM (2014)

17. Berger, P., Katoen, J.P., Ábrahám, E., Waez, M.T.B., Rambow, T.: Verifiying auto-generated C code from Simulink – an experience report in the automotive domain. In: Havelund, K., Peleska, J., Roscoe, B., de Vink, E. (eds.) FM 2018. LNCS, vol. 10951, pp. 312–328. Springer, Cham (2018)

18. MathWorks: Simulink Design Verifier - User's guide. https://de.mathworks.com/help/pdf_doc/sldv/sldv_ug.pdf

19. MathWorks: Polyspace. http://www.mathworks.com/products/polyspace/

20. Prover Technology AB: Prover Plug-In. http://www.prover.com

21. Bozzano, M., Bruintjes, H., Cimatti, A., Katoen, J.P., Noll, T., Tonetta, S.: The compass 3.0 toolset (short paper). In: Proceedings of IMBSA 2017 (2017)

22. Dwyer, M.B., Avrunin, G.S., Corbett, J.C.: Patterns in property specifications for finite-state verification. In: Proceedings of ICSE 1999, pp. 411–420. ACM (1999)

23. Autili, M., Grunske, L., Lumpe, M., Pelliccione, P., Tang, A.: Aligning qualitative, real-time, and probabilistic property specification patterns using a structured english grammar. IEEE Trans. Softw. Eng. **41**(7), 620–638 (2015)

Multi-robot LTL Planning Under Uncertainty

Claudio Menghi[1](✉)(iD), Sergio Garcia[1](iD), Patrizio Pelliccione[1](iD),
and Jana Tumova[2](iD)

[1] Chalmers – University of Gothenburg, Gothenburg, Sweden
{claudio.menghi,sergio.garcia,patrizio.pelliccione}@gu.se
[2] Royal Institute of Technology (KTH), Stockholm, Sweden
tumova@kth.se

Abstract. Robot applications are increasingly based on teams of robots that collaborate to perform a desired mission. Such applications ask for *decentralized* techniques that allow for tractable automated planning. Another aspect that current robot applications must consider is *partial knowledge* about the environment in which the robots are operating and the uncertainty associated with the outcome of the robots' actions.

Current planning techniques used for teams of robots that perform complex missions do not systematically address these challenges: (1) they are either based on centralized solutions and hence not scalable, (2) they consider rather simple missions, such as A-to-B travel, (3) they do not work in partially known environments. We present a planning solution that decomposes the team of robots into subclasses, considers missions given in temporal logic, and at the same time works when only partial knowledge of the environment is available. We prove the correctness of the solution and evaluate its effectiveness on a set of realistic examples.

1 Introduction

A *planner* is a software component that receives as input a model of the robotic application and computes a *plan* that, if performed, allows the achievement of a desired mission [26]. As done in some recent works in robotics (e.g., [3,4]), we assume that a robot application is defined using finite transition systems and each robot has to achieve a mission, indicated as *local mission*, specified as an LTL property. As opposed to more traditional specification means, such as consensus or trajectory tracking in robot control, A-to-B travel in robot motion planning, or STRIPS or PDDL in robot task planning, LTL allows the specification of a rich class of temporal goals that include surveillance, sequencing, safety, or reachability [8]. LTL has also been recently considered as a reference logic for the specification of patterns for robotic mission, in which LTL template solutions are provided to recurrent specification problems [33].

Several works studied centralized planners that are able to manage *teams* of robots that collaborate to achieve a global mission (e.g., [20,28,34]), and how

© Springer International Publishing AG, part of Springer Nature 2018
K. Havelund et al. (Eds.): FM 2018, LNCS 10951, pp. 399–417, 2018.
https://doi.org/10.1007/978-3-319-95582-7_24

to decompose a global mission into a set of local missions (e.g., [16,16,36,38]). Local missions have been recently exploited by *decentralized* planners [38], which avoid the expensive centralized planning by analyzing the satisfaction of local missions inside subsets of the robots.

Another aspect that current planners must consider is partial knowledge about the environment in which the robots operate. Partial knowledge has been strongly studied by the software engineering and formal methods communities. Partial models have been used to support requirement analysis and elicitation [27,31,32], to help designers in producing a model of the system that satisfies a set of desired properties [29,39,40], and to verify whether already designed models possess some properties of interest [2,5,7,30]. However, most of the existing planners assume that the environment in which the robots are deployed is known [9]. Literature considering planners that work in partially specified environments is more limited and usually rely on techniques based on probabilistic models (e.g., [10,12,35]). Furthermore, decentralized planners are rarely applied when partial knowledge about the robot application is present [16].

Contribution. This work presents MAPmAKER (Multi-robot plAnner for PArtially Known EnviRonments), a *novel decentralized* planner for *partially* known robotic applications. Given a team of robots and a local mission for each robot, MAPmAKER partitions the set of robots into classes based on dependencies dictated by the local missions of each robot. For each of these classes, it explores the state space of the environment and the models of the robot searching for definitive and possible plans. Definitive plans ensure the satisfaction of the local mission for each robot. Possible plans may satisfy the local mission due to some unknown information in the robotic application. MAPmAKER chooses the plan to be executed among definitive and possible plans that allow the achievement of the mission.

Specific Novel Contributions. The specific contributions are:

(1) We define the concept of *partial robot model*. This definition customizes partial models (e.g., PKS [5] and MTS [24]) in a robotic domain context [38] allowing the description of the robots and their environments when partial information is available. A partial robot model allows considering three types of partial information: partial knowledge about the execution of transitions (possibility of changing the robot location), the service provision (whether the execution of an action succeed in providing a service) and the meeting capabilities (whether a robot can meet with another).

(2) We define the concept of local mission satisfaction for partial robot models and the thorough LTL *word* semantics. This semantics extends the well known thorough LTL semantics [6] for partial models and allows the thorough evaluation of an LTL formula over words. This definition is needed to define when an LTL formula is satisfied or possibly satisfied on a given plan.

(3) We define the distributed planning problem for partially specified robots.

(4) We prove that under certain assumptions the planning problem can be solved by relying on two calls of a "classical" planner.

(5) We propose a distributed planning algorithm and we prove its correctness. The distributed algorithm enables a tractable planning.

(6) We evaluate the proposed algorithm on a robot application obtained from the RoboCup Logistics League competition [18] and on a robotic application working in an apartment which is part of a large residential facility for senior citizens [1]. The results show the effectiveness of MAPmAKER.

Organization. Section 2 presents our running example. Section 3 describes the problem and Sect. 4 describes how MAPmAKER supports partial models. Section 5 presents the proposed planning algorithm. Section 6 evaluates the approach. Section 7 presents related work. Section 8 concludes with final remarks and future research directions.

2 Running Example

Robots r_1, r_2, and r_3 are deployed in the environment graphically described in Fig. 1. This environment represents a building made up of rooms l_1, l_2, l_3, and l_4. The environment is partitioned in cells, each labeled with an identifier in $c_1, c_2, \ldots, c_{30}$. Robots r_1, r_2, and r_3 are placed in their initial locations. Each robot is able to move from one cell to another, by performing action mov. The robots are also able to perform the following actions. Robot r_1 is able to load debris of the building by performing action ld. Given a robot r and a generic action α, in Fig. 1 the cells in which r can perform α are marked with the label $r(\alpha)$. Robot r_2 can wait until another robot loads debris on it by performing action rd and can unload debris by performing one of the two actions $ud1$ and $ud2$. Actions $ud1$ and $ud2$ use different actuators. Specifically, action $ud1$ uses a gripper while action $ud2$ exploits a dump mechanism. Robot r_3 is able to take pictures by performing action tp and send them using a communication network through the execution of action sp. Symbols $r_1(ld)$, $r_2(rd)$, $r_2(ud1)$, $r_2(ud2)$, $r_3(tp)$, and $r_3(sp)$ mark the regions where actions can be executed by the robots, while movement actions are not reported for graphical reasons. Actions ld, rd, tp, and sp are associated with the services *load_carrier*, *detect_load*, *take_snapshot*, and *send_info*, respectively, which are high-level functionalities provided by the robot when actions are performed. Actions $ud1$ and $ud2$ are associated with service *unload*. The labels $L(\pi, \alpha) = \top$ below Fig. 1 are used to indicate that a service π is associated with action α. Robots must meet and synchronously execute actions. Robots r_1 and r_2 must meet in cell c_7 and synchronously execute actions ld and rd, respectively. Rotating arrows marked with robots identifiers, are used to indicate where robots must meet.

The *global mission* the team of robots has to achieve is to check whether toxic chemicals have been released by the container located in l_4. We assume that the mission is specified through a set of *local missions* assigned to each robot of the team and described in LTL as in Fig. 2. Informally, while r_3 continuously takes pictures and sends them using the communication network, r_1 and r_2 remove debris to allow r_3 having a better view on the container. The pictures allow verifying whether toxic chemicals have been released.

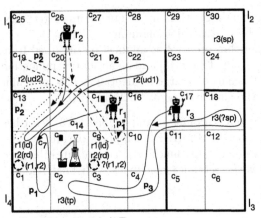

r1: L(ld,load_carrier)=T
r2: L(rd,detect_load)=T, L(ud2,unload)=?,
    L(ud1,unload)=T
r3: L(sp,send_info)=T, L(tp,take_snapshot)=T

$\phi_1 = $ G(F(*load_carrier*)): periodically robot r_1 loads debris on r_2 (by providing service *load_carrier*).

$\phi_2 = $ G(F(*detect_load*∧F(*unload*))): robot r_2 receives debris (service *detect_ load*) and brings them to an appropriate unload area (service *unload*).

$\phi_3 = $ G(F(*take_snapshot*∧F(*send_info*))): robot r_3 repeatedly takes pictures (service *take_snapshot*) and sends them using the communication network (service *send_info*).

Fig. 1. An example showing the model of the robots and their environment. Plans are represented by trajectories marked with arrows.

Fig. 2. The local missions assigned to each robot.

Partial Knowledge About the Actions Execution. The robots can move between cells separated by grey lines, while they cannot cross black bold lines. It is unknown whether it is possible to move between cells c_{14} and c_{20} since the structure may have been affected by collapses. This is indicated using a dashed black bold line. It is also unknown whether robot r_3 can send pictures using a communication network, performing action s_p in location l_3 and specifically in cell c_{18}. Locations of the environment where it is unknown if an action can be executed are marked with the name of the action preceded by symbol ?.

Unknown Service Provisioning. There are cases in which actions can be executed but there is uncertainty about service provisions. For example, actions $ud1$ and $ud2$ of robot r_2 unload the robot. Action $ud1$ will always be able to provide the *unload* service, while it is unknown whether $ud2$ provides this service since its effectiveness depends on the size of the collected debris. In Fig. 1, the label $L(ud2, unload) =?$ indicates that there is partial knowledge about the provision of the *unload* service when action $ud2$ is performed.

Unknown Meeting Capabilities. It is unknown whether robots r_1 and r_2 can meet in one cell of the environment. For example, a collapse in the roof of the building may forbid the two robots to concurrently execute actions ld and rd, e.g., there is not enough space for $r1$ to load $r2$. Unknown meeting capabilities are indicated with rotating arrows labeled with the symbol ?. For example, in Fig. 1, it is unknown whether robots r_1 and r_2 are able to meet in cell c_9.

3   Modeling Partial Knowledge in a Robotic Application

We extend the model of a robotic application [38] with partial knowledge.

Definition 1. *Consider a set of robots* $\mathcal{R}$. *A partial robot model of a single robot* $r \in \mathcal{R}$ *is a tuple* $r = (S, init, A, \Pi, T, T_p, Meet, Meet_p, L)$, *where* S *is a finite set of states; init* $\in S$ *is the initial state;* A *is a finite set of actions;* Π *is a set of services;* $T, T_p : S \times A \rightarrow S$ *are partial deterministic transition functions such that for all* $s, s' \in S$ *and* $\alpha \in A$, *if* $T(s, \alpha) = s'$ *then* $T_p(s, \alpha) = s'$; $L : A \times \Pi \rightarrow \{\top, \bot, ?\}$ *is the service labeling;* $Meet, Meet_p : S \rightarrow (\wp(\mathcal{R}) \cup \{\#\})$ *are functions ensuring:*

(1) for all $s \in S$ *either* $Meet(s) \subseteq \wp(\mathcal{R})$ *or* $Meet(s) = \{\#\}$;
(2) for all $s \in S$ *such that* $Meet(s) \neq \emptyset$, $Meet_p(s) = Meet(s)$.

A partial robot model has three sources of partial knowledge:

Partial knowledge about the action execution. A transition $T_p(s, \alpha) = s'$ is called *possible transition* and is indicated as $s \xrightarrow{\alpha} s'$. Given two states s and s' and an action α, if $T_p(s, \alpha) = s'$ and $T(s, \alpha) \neq s'$ (i.e., it is undefined) it is uncertain whether the robot moves from s to s' by performing α. A transition $T_p(s, \alpha) = s'$, such that $T(s, \alpha) \neq s'$ is called *maybe transition*. A transition $T_p(s, \alpha) = s'$, such that $T(s, \alpha) = s'$, is a *definitive transition* and is indicated as $s \xrightarrow{\alpha} s'$.

Partial knowledge about the service provisioning. The service labeling specifies whether a service $\pi \in \Pi$ is provided when an action $\alpha \in A$ is performed. If $L(\alpha, \pi) = \top$, then the service π is provided by the action α, if $L(\alpha, \pi) = \bot$, then the service π is not provided by the action α, and, finally, if $L(\alpha, \pi) =?$, then it is uncertain whether service π is provided when the action α is executed.

Partial knowledge about robot meeting capabilities. Function $Meet_p$ labels a state s with a set of robots that must meet with r in s. If $Meet(s) = \emptyset$ and $Meet_p(s) \neq \emptyset$, it is uncertain whether the robots in $Meet_p(s)$ can meet. Otherwise $Meet(s) = Meet_p(s)$, i.e., the meeting capabilities are definitive. When $Meet(s) = \{\#\} = Meet_p(s)$ the meeting is not possible.

A definitive robot model is a partial robot model that does not contain partial information about the action execution, the service provisioning, and the meeting capabilities.

Variations of finite state machines are strongly used by planning algorithms in the robotic community (e.g. [16,17,38]). They can be directly computed by abstracting maps of real environments (e.g. [21]) or generated for other types of specifications such as Ambient Calculus (e.g., [37]). Within the context of this work we assume the model of the robotic application is given. Note that the notion of partial robot model does not extends PKS [5] and MTS [24] in terms of expressive power, but allows handling explicitly partial knowledge about the execution of transitions, the service provision, and the meeting capabilities, which are key aspects to be considered in robotic applications [38].

A plan describes the states and actions a robot has to traverse and perform.

Definition 2. *Given a partial robot model $r = (S, init, A, \Pi, T, T_p, Meet, Meet_p, L)$, a definitive plan of r is an infinite alternating sequence of states and actions $\beta = s_1, \alpha_1, s_2, \alpha_2, \ldots$, such that $s_1 = init$, for all $i \geq 1$ and $\pi \in \Pi$, $s_i \xrightarrow{\alpha_i} s_{i+1}$, $Meet(s_i) = Meet_p(s_i)$, $Meet(s_i) \neq \{\#\} \neq Meet_p(s_i)$ and $L(\alpha_i, \pi) \neq ?$. A possible plan of r is infinite alternating sequence of states and actions $\beta = s_1, \alpha_1, s_2, \alpha_2, \ldots$, such that $s_1 = init$, and for all $i \geq 1$, $s_i \dashrightarrow^{\alpha_i} s_{i+1}$ and $Meet(s_i) \neq \{\#\} \neq Meet_p(s_i)$.*

The plan $c_{17}, mov, c_{23}, mov, c_{29}, mov, c_{30}, (sp, c_{30})^\omega$ is a definitive plan for robot r_3 since all the transitions, service provisioning and meeting capabilities are definitive. The plan $c_{26}, mov, c_{20}, mov, c_{14}, (mov, c_{14})^\omega$ for robot r_1 is a possible plan since the transition from cell c_{20} to c_{14} executed by performing action mov is a maybe transition.

Definition 3. *A partial robot application $\mathcal{H}$ is a set of partial robot models $\{r_1, r_2, \ldots, r_N\}$ such that for every couple of partial robot models $r_n, r_m \in \mathcal{H}$, where $r_n = (S_n, init_n, A_n, \Pi_n, T_n, T_{p,n}, Meet_n, Meet_{p,n}, L_n)$ and $r_m = (S_m, init_m, A_m, \Pi_m, T_m, T_{p,m}, Meet_m, Meet_{p,m}, L_m)$, the following is satisfied $\Pi_n \cap \Pi_m = \emptyset$ and $A_n \cap A_m = \emptyset$.*

In Definition 3 and in the rest of the paper we will assume that the sets of services and actions of different robots are disjoint. This is not a strong limitation for usage in real applications, where an action α (resp. service π) shared among two robots r_1 and r_2 can be mapped in two actions α_1 and α_2 (resp. π_1 and π_2) to be used in robots r_1 and r_2. The local mission should then be changed accordingly, i.e., occurrences of service π must be replaced with the formula $\pi_1 \vee \pi_2$.

Let us consider a partial robot application $\mathcal{H}$. We use $\mathcal{B}_d$ to indicate a set $\{\beta_1^d, \beta_2^d, \ldots, \beta_N^d\}$ of definitive plans, where β_n^d is a definitive plan for the partial robot r_n in $\mathcal{H}$. We use $\mathcal{B}_p$ to indicate a set $\{\beta_1^p, \beta_2^p, \ldots, \beta_N^p\}$ of possible plans, where β_n^p is the possible plan for the partial robot r_n in $\mathcal{H}$.

The notion of plan should reflect the meeting scheme, meaning that robots should enter and leave locations of the environment depending on the functions $Meet$ and $Meet_p$. Consider a partial robot application $\mathcal{H}$ and a set $\mathcal{B} = \{\beta_1, \beta_2, \ldots, \beta_N\}$ of definitive or possible plans, where β_n is the plan for the robot r_n in $\mathcal{H}$. We indicate as *compatible plans* the plans in $\mathcal{B}$ that ensure a meeting scheme.

Definition 4. *Given a set of definitive (possible) plans $\mathcal{B}_d$ ($\mathcal{B}_p$), the set $\mathcal{B}_d$ ($\mathcal{B}_p$) is compatible if the following holds for all $r_n \in \mathcal{H}$, and $j \geq 1$. For each plan $\beta_n = s_{n,1}, \alpha_{n,1}, s_{n,2}, \alpha_{n,2}, \ldots$ of each robot r_n if $s_{n,j-1} \neq s_{n,j}$ and $Meet(s_{n,j}) \neq \emptyset$ then*

(1) $s_{n,j} = s_{n,j+1}$;
(2) for all $r_m \in Meet_n(s_{n,j})$, it holds that $s_{m,j} = s_{n,j}$ and $s_{n,j} = s_{m,j+1}$.

The condition enforces the constraint dictated by the $Meet$ function when state $s_{n,j}$ is entered. Specifically, (1) ensures that after a robot r_n meets another in a state $s_{n,j}$, it proceeds with the execution of a transition that has state $s_{n,j}$

as a source and destination and (2) ensures that each robot r_m that belongs to $Meet_n(s_{n,j})$ reaches state $s_{n,j}$ at step j and remains in $s_{n,j}$ at step $j+1$. Note that, compatible plans force the robots r_n and r_m to synchronously perform and action among steps j and $j+1$.

A plan is *executed* by a robot, by performing the actions and transitions specified in the plan. Executing plans allows discovering information about action execution, service provisioning, and meeting capabilities. Every time a transition that is associated with partial information about its action is executed, an action associated with uncertainty in the service provisioning is performed and a state with unknown meeting capabilities is reached, new information is detected. If a transition is detected to be executable, a service to be provided, or a meeting to be possible, we say that a *true evidence* about the partial information is detected. In the opposite case, we say that *false evidence* is detected.

Given a *robot application* $\mathcal{H} = \{r_1, r_2, \ldots, r_N\}$, such that $r_n = (S_n, init_n, A_n, \Pi_n, T_n, T_{p,n}, Meet_n, Meet_{p,n}, L_n)$ we define $\Pi = \Pi_1 \cup \Pi_2 \cup \ldots \cup \Pi_N$. We assume that the mission assigned to the team of robots is made by a set $\Phi = \{\phi_1, \phi_2, \ldots, \phi_N\}$ of local missions such that each mission $\phi_n \in \Phi$ is assigned to the robot r_n of $\mathcal{H}$. Each local mission ϕ_n is specified as an LTL formula defined over the set of atomic propositions $\Pi_{\phi,n} \subseteq \Pi$, i.e., the mission can also involve services that are not provided by robot r_n, but are provided by other robots of $\mathcal{H}$.

A dependency class $dp_n = r_1, r_2, \ldots, r_n$ is a subset of robots that depends on each other for achieving their missions. Two robots $r_n = (S_n, init_n, A_n, \Pi_n, T_n, T_{p,n}, Meet_n, Meet_{p,n}, L_n)$ and $r_m = (S_m, init_m, A_m, \Pi_m, T_m, T_{p,m}, Meet_m, Meet_{p,m}, L_m)$ with missions defined over $\Pi_{\phi,n}$ and $\Pi_{\phi,m}$, are in dp_n if $\Pi_{\phi,n} \cap \Pi_m \neq \emptyset$, or there exists a state s of r_n such that $r_m \in Meet_n(s) \cup Meet_{p,n}(s)$. In the first case, one of the services of the mission of robot r_n is provided by robot r_m; in the second, robot r_m must meet robot r_n.

The definitions of a definitive robot model, refinement and completion of partial robot models and execution of possible and definitive plans are in Appendix A1, available at goo.gl/Hp33j2.

4   Planning with Partial Knowledge

Solving the planning problem requires defining what it means that a plan satisfies a mission. This section provides two different definitions of this concept through the three-valued and the thorough LTL semantics. The first allows implementing an efficient procedure to check whether a plan satisfies a mission. However, the obtained result does not always reflect the natural intuition. The second allows returning a precise result but requires implementing a checking procedure that is more computationally expensive.

Consider for a moment a definitive (possible) plan $\beta = s_1 \alpha_1 s_2 \alpha_2 \ldots$. The *definitive (possible) word* associated with β is $w_\tau = \varpi_1 \varpi_2 \ldots$, such that for each $i > 1$ and $\pi \in \Pi$, $\varpi_i(\pi) = L_n(\alpha_i, \pi)$. Intuitively, each element ϖ_i of w_τ maps a service π with the value of function $L_n(\alpha_i, \pi)$. Note that definitive words associate services with values in the set $\{\top, \bot\}$, while possible words w_τ associate services with values in the set $\{\top, ?, \bot\}$.

The three-valued LTL semantics $\overset{3}{=}$ allows efficiently checking a property ϕ and a word w_τ. This can be done at the same computational cost as regular two-valued semantics [5]. While a formula is evaluated as $\top$ and $\bot$ reflecting the natural intuition, it has been shown [6] that the three-valued semantics returns a ? value more often than expected. Specifically, it is desirable that a property ϕ is evaluated to ? when there are two words w_τ' and w_τ'' that can be obtained by replacing ? values of w_τ with $\top$ and $\bot$, such that w_τ' satisfies ϕ and w_τ'' does not satisfy ϕ. For this reason, the thorough LTL semantics has been proposed [6].

The thorough LTL semantics is usually defined considering partial models [6]. Given a partial model M and a formula ϕ, the thorough LTL semantics assigns the value ? if there exist two completions M' and M'' of M, obtained by assigning $\top$ and $\bot$ to proposition with value ?, such that M' satisfies ϕ and M'' violates ϕ. However, since our goal is to evaluate the satisfaction of a formula on plans we define a notion of thorough LTL semantics based on words. Given a word w_τ a completion w_τ' of w_τ is obtained from w_τ by assigning $\top$ and $\bot$ values to $\varpi_i(\pi)$ for each $i > 1$ and π such that $\varpi_i(\pi) =?$

Definition 5. *Given a word w_τ and a property ϕ, the* thorough *LTL semantics $\overset{T}{=}$ associates the word w_τ with a value in the set $\{\top, ?, \bot\}$ as follows*

(1) $[w_\tau \models \phi] \overset{T}{=} \top$ iff all the completions w_τ' of w_τ are such that $[w_\tau' \models \phi] = \top$;
(2) $[w_\tau \models \phi] \overset{T}{=} \bot$ iff all the completions w_τ' of w_τ are such that $[w_\tau' \models \phi] = \bot$;
(3) $[w_\tau \models \phi] \overset{T}{=}?$ otherwise.

Since a word is a simple linear model (a sequence of states connected by transitions), the properties that hold for the thorough LTL semantics for partial models also hold for the thorough LTL word semantics.

Lemma 1. *Given two words w_τ and w_τ', such that $w_\tau \preceq w_\tau'$, and an LTL formula ϕ the following are satisfied: (1) $[w_\tau \models \phi] \overset{3}{=} \top \Rightarrow [w_\tau' \models \phi] \overset{T}{=} \top$; (2) $[w_\tau \models \phi] \overset{3}{=} \bot \Rightarrow [w_\tau' \models \phi] \overset{T}{=} \bot$.*

Checking whether a word w_τ and a property ϕ in the sense of the thorough LTL word semantics levies performance penalties: it can be done in polynomial time in the length of w_τ and double exponential time in the size of ϕ [15].

There exists a subset of LTL formulae, known in literature as *self-minimizing* formulae, such that the three valued and the thorough semantics coincide [14]. This result can also be applied on words. Given a word w_τ and a self-minimizing LTL property ϕ, then $[w_\tau \models \phi] \overset{T}{=} x \overset{3}{=} [w_\tau \models \phi]$ where $x \in \{\bot, \top, ?\}$. It has been observed that most practically useful LTL formulae, such as absence, universality, existence, response and response chain, are self-minimizing [14]. Furthermore, since for this set the two semantics coincide, the more efficient procedure for checking a property w.r.t. the three-valued semantics can be used [6].

Local definitive and possible LTL satisfaction can be then defined as follows.

Definition 6. *Let $\overset{X}{=}$ be a semantics in $\{\overset{3}{=}, \overset{T}{=}\}$. Let r_n and D be a robot and a set of robots, such that $\{r_n\} \subseteq D \subseteq \mathcal{H}$. Let us consider a set of compatible plans $\mathcal{B}$ such that each word w_m of robot r_m is infinite and defined as $w_m = \varpi_{m,1}\varpi_{m,2}\ldots$. The word produced by a set of definitive (resp. possible) compatible plans $\mathfrak{B} = \{\beta_m \mid r_m \in D\}$ is $w_{\mathfrak{B}} = \omega_1\omega_2\ldots$, where for all $j \geq 1$ and for all $\pi \in \Pi$, $\omega_j(\pi) = \max\{\varpi_{m,j}(\pi) \mid r_m \in D\}$. The set of definitive (resp. possible) compatible plans $\mathfrak{B}$ locally definitively (resp. possibly) satisfies ϕ_n for the agent n, i.e., $\mathfrak{B} \models \phi_n$, iff $\mathfrak{B}$ is valid and $[w_{\mathfrak{B}} \models \phi_n] \overset{X}{=} \top$ ($[w_{\mathfrak{B}} \models \phi_n] \overset{X}{=} ?$).*

The thorough semantics ensures that when the word associated with the plan possibly satisfies a mission ϕ, there exists a way to assign $\top$ and $\bot$ to ? such that it is possible to obtain a word that satisfies ϕ and another that does not satisfy ϕ. Thus, there is a chance that, if executed, the plan satisfies a mission ϕ. This is not true for the three-valued semantics since it can be the case that a plan possibly satisfies a mission ϕ, but the mission is trivially unsatisfiable. Note that since a plan $w_{\mathfrak{B}}$ is such that $w_{\mathfrak{B}} \models \phi_n$, it can be rewritten using an ω-word notation as $w_{\mathfrak{B}} = \omega_1\omega_2\ldots\omega_{n-1}(\omega_n\omega_{n+1}\ldots\omega_m)^\omega$ [41], where m is the length of the plan. We use the notation $\mathcal{L}(w_{\mathfrak{B}})$ to indicate length m of the ω-word associated with plan $w_{\mathfrak{B}}$ with minimum length.

In this work we assume local missions are given. We also assume that all the local missions must be satisfied for achieving the global mission. Formally, given a global mission ϕ, the corresponding set of the local missions $\{\phi_1, \phi_2, \ldots, \phi_N\}$ (one for each robot in $\mathcal{H}$) and the *word* $\mathfrak{B}$ produced by a set of definitive (resp. possible) compatible plans, $[\mathfrak{B} \models \phi] \overset{X}{=} \top$ if for all $1 \leq n \leq N$, $[\mathfrak{B} \models \phi_n] \overset{X}{=} \top$; $[\mathfrak{B} \models \phi] \overset{X}{=} ?$ if for all $1 \leq n \leq N$, $[\mathfrak{B} \models \phi_n] \overset{X}{>} \bot$, where $\geq$ is defined such as $\top > ? > \bot$; $[\mathfrak{B} \models \phi] \overset{X}{=} \bot$ otherwise.

Based on these definitions, the planning problem is formulated as follows:

Problem 1 (Planning). Consider a partial robot application $\mathcal{H}$ defined over the set of partial robot models $\{r'_1, r'_2, \ldots, r'_N\}$ and a semantics $\overset{X}{=}$ in $\{\overset{3}{=}, \overset{T}{=}\}$. Given a set of local missions $\{\phi_1, \phi_2, \ldots, \phi_n\}$, one for each robot $r_n \in \mathcal{H}$ find a set of plans $\mathfrak{B} = \{\beta_1, \beta_2, \ldots, \beta_N\}$ that

(1) are compatible and
(2) $\mathfrak{B}$ *locally definitively (resp. possibly) satisfies* each ϕ_n w.r.t. the given semantics.

Appendix A2, available at goo.gl/Hp33j2, contains the proof of Lemma 1 and additional theorems and proofs.

5 Algorithms

MAPmAKER solves Problem 1 by implementing a decentralized planning with partial knowledge. First, we discuss how robots are partitioned into dependency classes; then, we discuss how planning is performed within each of these classes.

Compute the Dependency Classes. To compute dependency classes the following rule [16] is iteratively applied: a robot r_n assigned to a local mission ϕ_n defined over the services $\Pi_{\phi,n}$ is in the same dependency class D_i of r_m if and only if (1) the local mission predicates on a service π provided by robot r_m, i.e., $\pi \in \Pi_{\phi,n} \cap \Pi_m$, or (2) r_n and r_m must meet.

In the running example, one dependency class contains robots r_1 and r_2 since these robots must meet in cell c_7, the other contains robot r_3.

Planning with Partial Knowledge. Algorithm 1 receives a partial robot application and a set of local missions and computes a set of definitive (or possible) plans that ensures the mission satisfaction. We discuss how the different types of partial information are handled by Algorithm 1 by incrementally enabling Algorithm 1 to handle types of partial information. Identifiers A1, A2, and A3 mark lines that enable handling different types of partial information. *Managing Partial Information in the Transition Relation.* Let us first assume that we have a partial robot application $\mathcal{H} = \{r_1, r_2, \ldots, r_N\}$ where each robot r_n is such that $Meet_n = Meet_{p,n}$ and for each service $\pi \in \Pi_n$ and action $\alpha \in A_n$, $L_n(\alpha, \pi) \in \{\top, \bot\}$. In this case, partial information only refers to the presence of maybe transitions, i.e., transitions $s_n \dashrightarrow^{\alpha} s'_n$ such that $s_n \xrightarrow{\alpha} s'_n \notin T_n$. Lines marked with the identifier A1 allow Algorithm 1 to handle this case.

The algorithm works in three steps.

Step 1. For each robot $r_n \in \mathcal{H}$ it removes the transitions $s_n \dashrightarrow^{\alpha} s'_n$ such that $s_n \xrightarrow{\alpha} s'_n \notin T_n$ (Line 3) and applies a classical decentralized planning algorithm (Line 8). Variable pd contains whether the planner had found a plan, $\{pd_1, pd_2, \ldots, pd_N\}$ contains the plans if they are found. If a plan is found, pd is assigned to *true* and the definitive plans for each of the robots are stored in variables $\{pd_1, pd_2, \ldots, pd_N\}$. Otherwise, pd is assigned to *false*.

Step 2. It considers the original partial robot application (Line 9) and it applies the decentralized planning algorithm (Line 12). If a set of possible plans is found, pp is equal to *true* and the possible plans (one for each robot) are stored in $\{pp_1, pp_2, \ldots, pp_N\}$.

Step 3. It analyzes the results contained in pd and pp. If both pd and pp are equal to *false* then no plans are synthesizable (Line 13). If pd is *false* while pp is not, only possible plans are available and they are returned as output (Line 14). Otherwise, a policy is used to choose between $\{pd_1, pd_2, \ldots, pd_N\}$ and $\{pp_1, pp_2, \ldots, pp_N\}$ (Line 15).

If no meeting primitives are specified in cell c_9, actions ld and rd cannot be performed by robots r_1 and r_2 in c_9 and ud_2 does not provide service *unload*, plans p_1, p_2, and p_3 are returned from robots r_1, r_2, and r_3. Plan p_2 is possible since it is not known whether robot r_1 can move from cell c_8 to c_{14}. Plan p_3 is possible since it is unknown whether robot r_3 can perform action sp in cell c_{18}.

Managing Uncertainties in the Service Provision. Let us assume that we have a partial robot application $\mathcal{H}$ where each robot r_n is such that $Meet_n = Meet_{p,n}$, i.e., there is no partial information about meeting capabilities. We designed an algorithm similar to [5], specified by Lines marked with the identifier A2.

Algorithm 1. The *PARTIAL_PLAN* function.

1: **Input** a partial robot application $\mathcal{H}$ and a set of missions Φ
2: **Output** a definitive or a possible plan (if they exist)
3: **For each** robot $r_n \in \mathcal{H}$ **remove** transitions $s_n \overset{\alpha}{\dashrightarrow} s'_n$ s.t. $s_n \overset{\alpha}{\rightarrow} s'_n \notin T_n$ **(A1)**
4: **Put** each formula $\phi_n \in \Phi$ in its negation normal form and rename the negated propositions as in [5] **(A2)**
5: **Compute** the complement closed model r'_n of each $r_n \in \mathcal{H}$ **(A2)**
6: **For each** r'_n and $s \in S_n$ if $Meet_{n,p}(s) \neq Meet_n(s)$ **then** $Meet_{n,p}(s) = \{\#\}$**(A3)**
7: **For each** model r'_n **construct** the pessimistic approximation $r'_{p,n}$ **(A2)**
8: $[pd, \{pd_1, pd_2, \ldots, pd_N\}]$=DEC_PLANNER $(\{r'_{p,1}, r'_{p,2}, \ldots, r'_{p,N}\}, \Phi)$
9: **For each** robot r_n **insert** the transitions $s_n \overset{\alpha}{\dashrightarrow} s'_n$ s.t. $s_n \overset{\alpha}{\rightarrow} s'_n \notin T_n$ **(A1)**
10: **For each** model r'_n **construct** the optimistic approximation $r'_{o,n}$ **(A2)**
11: **For each** r'_n **insert** all the meeting requests in $Meet_{n,p}$ **(A3)**
12: $[pp, \{pp_1, pp_2, \ldots, pp_N\}]$=DEC_PLANNER $(\{r'_{o,1}, r'_{o,2} \ldots, r'_{o,N}\}, \Phi)$
13: **if** $pd = false$ **and** $pp = false$ **then return** NO_PLAN_AVAILABLE
14: **if** $pd = false$ **then return** $\{pp_1, pp_2, \ldots, pp_N\}$;
15: **else return** choose($\{pd_1, pd_2, \ldots, pd_N\}, \{pp_1, pp_2, \ldots, pp_N\}$)

Step 1. For each r_n, remove all the transitions $s_n \overset{\alpha}{\dashrightarrow} s'_n$ such that $s_n \overset{\alpha}{\rightarrow} s'_n \notin T_n$ (Line 3).

Step 2. Put each formula $\phi_n \in \Phi$ in its negation normal form (Line 4).

Step 3. For each r_n, construct a model r'_n called complement-closed, in which for action $\alpha \in A$ and service $\pi \in AP$, there exists a new service $\overline{\pi}$, called complement-closed service, such that $L_n(\alpha, \overline{\pi}) = comp(L_n(\alpha, \pi))$ (Line 5).

Step 4. Substitute function L_n of each r'_n with its pessimistic approximation $L_{n,pes}$. Specifically, $L_{n,pes}$ is constructed as follows: for each action α and π such that $L_n(\alpha, \pi) =?$, $L_{n,pes}(\alpha, \pi) = \bot$ otherwise $L_{n,pes}(\alpha, \pi) = L_n(\alpha, \pi)$ (Line 7).

Step 5. Apply the decentralized planning algorithm (Line 8). If a set of plans is found they are definitive plans and stored in $\{pd_1, pd_2, \ldots, pd_N\}$ otherwise a *false* value is associated to pd.

Step 6. For each r_n insert all the transitions $s_n \overset{\alpha}{\dashrightarrow} s'_n$ such that $s_n \overset{\alpha}{\rightarrow} s'_n \notin T_n$ (Line 9).

Step 7. Construct the optimistic approximation function $L_{n,opt}$ by associating the value $\top$ to each atomic proposition of the complement-closure of r' with value ? (Line 10).

Step 8. Apply the decentralized planning algorithm (Line 12). If a set of plans are found they are possible plans and stored in $\{pp_1, pp_2, \ldots, pp_N\}$ otherwise a *false* value is associated to pp.

Step 9. Analyzes the results. If both pd and pp are assigned with the *false* value (Line 13), neither a possible nor a definitive plan can be synthesized. If pd is *false* while pp is not (Line 14), then no definitive plans are available while a possible plan has been found. Otherwise (Line 15), an appropriate policy is used to choose between $\{pp_1, pp_2, \ldots, pp_N\}$ and $\{pd_1, pd_2, \ldots, pd_N\}$.

If no meeting is required in cell c_9, actions ld and rd cannot be performed by robots r_1 and r_2 in c_9 and it is not known whether ud_2 provides service $unload$, plans p_1, p_2', and p_3 are returned for r_1, r_2, and r_3. Plan p_2' is possible since it is unknown whether the execution of action ud_2 provides the service $unload$.

Managing Uncertainties in the Meeting Capabilities. Partial knowledge in the meeting capabilities is handled considering lines marked with A3. These lines ensure that before searching for a definitive plan, the meeting requests that are possible in the partial model of each robot of the robot application are removed (Line 6). These requests are added (Line 11) before searching for possible plans.

If meeting in cell c_{21} is considered, and actions ld and rd can be performed by robots r_1 and r_2 in c_9, plans p_1'', p_2'', and p_3 are returned from robot r_1, r_2, and r_3, respectively. Plans p_1'' and p_2'' are shorter plans than p_2' and p_1.

Algorithm 1 calls a classical decentralized planning algorithm twice. This algorithm is also re-executed every time during that the plan execution a *false* evidence about partial information is detected.

Theorem 1. *Consider a partial robot application $\mathcal{H}$, a set of missions Φ (one for each robot) and the three-valued LTL semantics ($\stackrel{3}{=}$). A set of plans $\mathfrak{B}$ that (1) are compatible and (2) $\mathfrak{B}$ locally definitively (resp. possibly) satisfies each ϕ_n w.r.t. the three-valued semantics. is returned from Algorithm 1 if and only if they exist in $\mathcal{H}$. If formulae are self-minimizing this theorem also applies to the thorough LTL semantics ($\stackrel{T}{=}$).*

Proof of Theorem 1 and additional details of the algorithm are in Appendix A3, available at goo.gl/Hp33j2.

6   Evaluation

This section reports on our experience evaluating MAPmAKER. We considered the following research questions: **RQ1:** *How does MAPmAKER help planning in partially known environments?* **RQ2:** *How does the employed decentralized algorithm help in planning computation?*

Implementation. As a proof of concepts we implemented MAPmAKER as a Matlab application, based on the planner proposed in [38]. The source code, a complete replication package and a set of videos showing MAPmAKER in action can be found at https://github.com/claudiomenghi/MAPmAKER/.

RQ1. We analyzed MAPmAKER on a set of *simulated* models.

Methodology. We considered two existing examples proposed in literature.

Example 1. The model of the robot application of the RoboCup Logistics League competition [18] which has a map made by 169 cells and 4 rooms.

Example 2. The model of a robot application deployed in an apartment of about $80\,\mathrm{m}^2$, which is part of a large residential facility for senior citizens [1]. The map had originally been used to evaluate a planning algorithm for a single robot based on information contained in RFID tags present in the environment [19].

In both the examples, we considered a team of 2 robots (r_1 and r_2), which is the same number of robots used in the RoboCup competition. However, we considered a higher number of services. Specifically, we considered 5 services: services s_1, s_2, and s_3 for robot r_1 and services s_4 and s_5 for robot r_2.

We simulated the presence of partial knowledge about the robot application to evaluated the impact of partial information about the execution of transitions (*Exp 1*), services provisioning (*Exp 2*) and meeting capabilities (*Exp 3*) on the planning procedure. To simulate the presence of partial information we constructed a partial robot application that conforms with Definition 1. To analyze partial information in the execution of transitions (*Exp 1*) we considered 2 rooms (that had multiple exits) and for each of these we added two unknown transitions. Both of these transitions allow leaving the room and are placed in correspondence with an exit and a wall. Thus, they will turn into a *true* and *false* evidence about the partial information when reached by the robot, respectively. To simulate partial information about the service provisioning (*Exp 2*) we assumed that service s_2 is associated with actions a_1 and a_2. However, there is partial information on whether the execution of a_1 and a_2 actually provides service s_2. In one case, when action a_1 is executed a *true* evidence on the provision of s_2 is returned. Contrariwise, when action a_2 is executed, a *false* evidence is returned by the dynamic discovering procedure. To simulate partial information about the meeting capabilities (*Exp 3*) we assumed that it is unknown whether robots r_1 and r_2 can meet in two cells when service s_1 is provided. In one of the cells, when meeting is performed, a *true* evidence is returned while in the other case *false* evidence is returned.

We consider different missions since in the RoboCup competition each mission was supposed to be performed in isolation by a single robot, while we aim to evaluate the behavior of the overall team. Our missions were inspired by the one used in the RoboCup competition and formalized as self-minimizing LTL properties and based on well known properties patterns [21,43]. The following missions were considered: (1) robot r_1 must achieve the mission $\mathsf{F}(s_1 \wedge (\mathsf{F}(s_2 \vee s_3)))$. It had to reach a predefined destination where service s_1 is provided, and then perform either service s_2 or service s_3. (2) robot r_2 must achieve the following mission $\mathsf{G}(\mathsf{F}(s_4 \vee s_5))$. Furthermore, it aims at helping r_1 in providing service s_1, i.e., robots r_1 and r_2 must meet in cells where service s_1 is provided.

Our simulation scenarios were obtained by considering different initial conditions (indicated as I_1, I_2, and I_3), where robots were initially located in different cells, and models of the partial robot application (indicated as C_1, C_2, and C_3), obtained by making different choices about partial information. Each simulation scenario is associated with an identifier (ID) and is obtained by considering a model of the partial robot application in one of the initial conditions.

Then, we performed the two following steps.

Step 1. We run MAPmAKER by considering the partial model of the robot application. The algorithm iteratively computes possible plans that are executed by the robots. As the robots explore their environment, *true* or *false* evidence about partial information is detected meaning that a transition, service, and meeting capability is detected to be firable, provided, and possible, respectively. If a *false* evidence about a partial information is detected, e.g., a transition of the plan is not executable, MAPmAKER is re-executed to recompute a new possible plan. As all the partial information needed to achieve the mission is turned into a *true* or a *false* evidence, the produced plan is actually *definitive.*

Step 2. We run MAPmAKER on a model of the robotic application obtained by assuming that unknown transitions, services, and meeting capabilities are not executable, not provided, and not possible, respectively. Thus, MAPmAKER returns a *definitive* plan (if present). This model is not the real model of the robot application since some transitions, services, and meeting capabilities may be turned into not firable, not provided and not possible, when they can actually be fired, are provided, and are possible in the real model, respectively.

We measured (1) the *time* T_1 and T_2 spent by MAPmAKER in Steps 1 and 2 in computing possible and definitive plans. For Step 1 it also includes the time necessary for synthesizing new plans where a *false* evidence about a partial information is detected. For Step 2 it only includes the time spent by MAPmAKER in computing the definitive plan. (2) the *length* L_1 and L_2 of the plans computed by MAPmAKER, in Steps 1 and 2. For Step 1 it is obtained by computing the sum of the length of the portions of the possible plans performed before a *false* evidence about a partial information is detected and the length of the final definitive plan (more details are provided in Appendix A4, available at goo.gl/Hp33j2). For Step 2 it corresponds to the length of the definitive plan. We compared the time spent by MAPmAKER in Steps 1 and 2 and the length of the computed plans.

Table 1. Results of Experiments 1, 2, and 3 for Examples 1 and 2.

| | | | Example 1 | | | | | | | | | | | | | Example 2 | | | | | | | | | | | | |
| | | | Exp 1 | | | | Exp 2 | | | | Exp 3 | | | | Exp 1 | | | | Exp 2 | | | | Exp 3 | | | |
ID	I	C	F	T	T_r	L_r	F	T	T_r	L_r	F	T	T_r	L_r	F	T	T_r	L_r	F	T	T_r	L_r	F	T	T_r	L_r
1	I_1	C_1	1	1	4.9	1.3	0	1	1.4	0.6	0	0	2.3	1.0	0	1	-	-	1	1	3.2	1.1	1	0	3.5	1.4
2	I_1	C_2	0	1	3.6	0.9	0	0	2.1	1.0	0	1	2.3	0.7	0	0	3.4	1.0	0	0	2.0	1.0	0	0	2.0	1.0
3	I_1	C_3	1	1	5.2	1.3	1	1	3.3	1.1	1	0	4.0	1.4	1	0	6.3	1.9	0	1	1.2	0.6	0	0	2.1	1.0
4	I_2	C_2	1	1	5.2	1.4	0	1	2.0	0.9	0	0	2.1	1.0	0	2	-	-	0	1	1.8	0.8	1	0	3.0	1.0
5	I_2	C_2	1	2	-	-	0	1	1.5	0.6	0	1	1.8	0.9	0	1	-	-	0	0	2.0	1.0	0	0	2.0	1.0
6	I_2	C_2	1	2	7.6	1.1	0	1	1.9	0.9	1	1	3.1	0.8	1	0	3.0	1.2	1	1	3.8	1.3	0	0	2.0	1.0
7	I_3	C_3	0	0	3.9	1.0	0	0	2.0	1.0	0	0	2.0	1.0	0	1	-	-	1	0	3.6	1.6	0	0	2.0	1.0
8	I_3	C_3	0	1	-	-	1	0	2.1	1.0	0	1	1.8	0.8	0	2	-	-	0	1	1.8	0.8	0	1	1.5	0.8
9	I_3	C_3	0	0	3.5	1.0	0	0	1.9	1.0	1	1	3.4	0.9	0	1	1.9	0.8	0	1	1.9	0.9	0	1	1.5	0.8

Results. Table 1 shows the obtained results. Column $\mathcal{T}_r$ contains the ratio between $\mathcal{T}_1$ and $\mathcal{T}_2$, column $\mathcal{L}_r$ contains the ratio between $\mathcal{L}_1$ and $\mathcal{L}_2$. Columns F and T contain the number of times *true* or *false* evidence about partial information about a transition, service and meeting capability was detected while the plans were executed.

Example 1. Four cases are identified. In ID 2 for Exp 1, IDs $1, 4, 5, 6$ for Exp 2 and IDs $2, 5, 6, 8, 9$ for Exp 3 the plans computed in Step 1 were shorter than the one computed in Step 2 (Case 1). In IDs $1, 3, 4, 6$ for Exp 1, IDs 3 for Exp 2 and ID 3 for Exp 3 the plans computed in Step 1 were longer than the one computed in Step 2 (Case 2). In IDs $7, 9$ for Exp 1, IDs $2, 7, 8$ for Exp 2 and IDs $1, 4, 7, 9$ for Exp 3 the plans computed in Step 1 correspond with the one computed in Step 2 (Case 3). In IDs $5, 8$ for Exp 1 plans were found in Step 1, while no plans were obtained in Step 2 (Case 4). Thus, they are marked with a $-$ since no comparison was possible.

Example 2. In ID 9 for Exp 1, IDs $3, 4, 8, 9$ for Exp 2 and IDs $8, 9$ for Exp 3 the plans computed in Step 1 were shorter than the one computed in Step 2 (Case 1). In IDs $3, 6$ for Exp 1, IDs $1, 6, 7$ for Exp 2 and IDs 1 for Exp 3 the plans computed in Step 1 were longer than the one computed in Step 2 (Case 2). In ID 2 for Exp 1, IDs $2, 5$ for Exp 2 and IDs $2, 3, 4, 5, 6, 7$ for Exp 3 the plans computed in Step 1 correspond with the one computed in Step 2 (Case 3). In IDs $1, 4, 5, 7, 8$ for Exp 1 plans were found in Step 1, while no plans were obtained in Step 2 (Case 4).

Discussion. MAPmAKER is effective whenever it computes a possible plan, and during its execution a *true* evidence about partial information is detected (Case 1). When no partial information was involved in the plans computed by MAPmAKER, the generated plans had the same length than a classical planner (Case 3). In several configurations MAPmAKER allows the achievement of the mission while a classical procedure is not able to do so (Case 4). Indeed, MAPmAKER computes a possible plan when no definitive plan is available and *true* evidence about partial information is detected during the plan execution. Finally, the detection of a *false* evidence decreases the effectiveness of MAPmAKER (Case 2). It happens due to the need of recomputing the plans to be followed by the robots.

MAPmAKER introduced an overhead in plan computation since it runs two times the decentralized planner. The average, median, minimum, and maximum time required to compute the plans for Step 1 considering all the examples of the previous experiments are 1982.28, 2371.38, 990.76, and 2972.64 s respectively; while for Step 2 are 400.24, 387.34, 277.85 and 533,8 s respectively. The high computation time is due to the planner on top of which MAPmAKER is developed, which uses an explicit representation of the state space of the robotic application. However, MAPmAKER simply relies on two invocations of a general planner to compute plans, thus more efficient planners can be used.

RQ2. We analyzed the behavior of the decentralized procedure.

Methodology. We considered the set of partial models previously described. We added an additional robot r_3 which must achieve the mission $G(F(s_6 \lor s_7))$ and does not meet neither with robot r_1 nor with robot r_2. We then perform the following steps: Step 1 we run MAPmAKER with the decentralized procedure enabled; Step 2 we run MAPmAKER without the decentralized procedure enabled. For each of the steps, we set a timeout of 1 hour. We recorded the time T_1 and T_2 required in Steps 1 and 2.

Results and Discussion. In Step 1 MAPmAKER computes two dependency classes; one containing robots r_1 and r_2 and one containing robot r_3. In Step 2 the team containing robots r_1, r_2, and r_3 is analyzed. For all the configurations and experiments, MAPmAKER ends within the timeout for Step 1, while MAPmAKER was not able to find a solution for Step 2.

Threats to Validity. The random identification of elements that are considered uncertain is a threat to *construct validity* since it may generate not realistic models. To mitigate this threat we ensured that partial information about transitions is added in correspondence with an exit and a wall. This ensures that both true and false evidence for transition executions can occur while the computed plans are executed. Biases in the creation of models is a threat to *internal validity* and is mitigated by considering real models. The limited number of examples is a threat to *external validity*. To mitigate this threat, we verified that as possible plans were executed, both true and false evidence about partial information were detected.

7   Related Work

Decentralized Solutions. The decentralized planning problem has been studied for known environments [16,36,38]. However, planners for partially known environments do not usually employ decentralized solutions [10,12,35].

Dealing with Partial Knowledge in Planning. Most of the works proposed in literature to plan in partially known environments (see for example [11,13,22, 42]) treat partial information by modeling the robotic application using some form of Markov decision processes (MDP). In MDPs, transitions are associated with probabilities indicating the likelihood of reaching the destination state when an action is performed [13]. The planning problem usually requires the actions the robots must perform to reach a set of goal states. In our work, the planning goal is specified in a richer language, i.e., LTL. Planning with LTL specifications has been considered in MDPs (e.g., [11,23,25]). However, in MDPs the developer knows the probabilities associated with transitions, while in the formulation proposed in this work this information is not available. Encoding a partial robot model into a MDP by associating a probability of 0.5 to maybe transitions is not correct. Indeed, the obtained MDP would not correctly represent the current scenario in which the probability of firing transitions is unknown.

8 Conclusions

This work presented MAPmAKER, a novel decentralized planner for partially known environments. MAPmAKER solves the decentralized planning problem when partial robot applications made by multiple robots are analyzed and missions are provided through a set of LTL specifications that are assigned to the different robots. The results showed that MAPmAKER was effective in dealing with partially known environments. They evidenced that the number of actions performed by the robots was lower when the computed possible plans were actually executable in the real model of the robotic application. Furthermore, they highlight that MAPmAKER outperformed classical planners by achieving the desired mission when only possible plans were available. Finally, the show that decentralization allows considering partial models of the robotic applications that can not be handled with a classical centralized approaches.

Future work and research directions include (1) studying techniques to support developers in the automatic or manual development of the (partial) model of a robotic application; (2) evaluation of the proposed procedure using robots deployed in real environments; (3) the study of appropriate policies to select between definitive and possible plans; (4) the use of more efficient planners to speed up plan computation. These may be based for example on symbolic techniques.

References

1. The Angen Research and Innovation Apartment (2014). http://angeninnovation.se
2. Bernasconi, A., Menghi, C., Spoletini, P., Zuck, L.D., Ghezzi, C.: From model checking to a temporal proof for partial models. In: Cimatti, A., Sirjani, M. (eds.) SEFM 2017. LNCS, vol. 10469, pp. 54–69. Springer, Cham (2017). https://doi.org/10.1007/978-3-319-66197-1_4
3. Bhatia, A., Kavraki, L.E., Vardi, M.Y.: Motion planning with hybrid dynamics and temporal goals. In: Conference on Decision and Control (CDC), pp. 1108–1115. IEEE (2010)
4. Bhatia, A., Kavraki, L.E., Vardi, M.Y.: Sampling-based motion planning with temporal goals. In: International Conference on Robotics and Automation (ICRA), pp. 2689–2696. IEEE (2010)
5. Bruns, G., Godefroid, P.: Model checking partial state spaces with 3-valued temporal logics. In: Halbwachs, N., Peled, D. (eds.) CAV 1999. LNCS, vol. 1633, pp. 274–287. Springer, Heidelberg (1999). https://doi.org/10.1007/3-540-48683-6_25
6. Bruns, G., Godefroid, P.: Generalized model checking: reasoning about partial state spaces. In: Palamidessi, C. (ed.) CONCUR 2000. LNCS, vol. 1877, pp. 168–182. Springer, Heidelberg (2000). https://doi.org/10.1007/3-540-44618-4_14
7. Chechik, M., Devereux, B., Easterbrook, S., Gurfinkel, A.: Multi-valued symbolic model-checking. ACM Trans. Softw. Eng. Methodol. **12**(4), 1–38 (2004)
8. Chen, Y., Tůmová, J., Ulusoy, A., Belta, C.: Temporal logic robot control based on automata learning of environmental dynamics. Int. J. Robot. Res. **32**(5), 547–565 (2013)
9. Cunningham, A.G., Galceran, E., Eustice, R.M., Olson, E.: MPDM: multipolicy decision-making in dynamic, uncertain environments for autonomous driving. In: International Conference on Robotics and Automation (ICRA), pp. 1670–1677 (2015)

10. Diaz, J.F., Stoytchev, A., Arkin, R.C.: Exploring unknown structured environments. In: FLAIRS Conference, pp. 145–149. AAAI Press (2001)
11. Ding, X.C.D., Smith, S.L., Belta, C., Rus, D.: LTL control in uncertain environments with probabilistic satisfaction guarantees*. IFAC Proc. Vol. **44**(1), 3515–3520 (2011)
12. Du Toit, N.E., Burdick, J.W.: Robot motion planning in dynamic, uncertain environments. IEEE Trans. Robot. **28**(1), 101–115 (2012)
13. Ghallab, M., Nau, D., Traverso, P.: Automated Planning and Acting, 1st edn. Cambridge University Press, New York (2016)
14. Godefroid, P., Huth, M.: Model checking vs. generalized model checking: semantic minimizations for temporal logics. In: Logic in Computer Science, pp. 158–167. IEEE Computer Society (2005)
15. Godefroid, P., Piterman, N.: LTL generalized model checking revisited. Int. J. Softw. Tools Technol. Transf. **13**(6), 571–584 (2011)
16. Guo, M., Dimarogonas, D.V.: Multi-agent plan reconfiguration under local LTL specifications. Int. J. Robot. Res. **34**(2), 218–235 (2015)
17. Guo, M., Johansson, K.H., Dimarogonas, D.V.: Revising motion planning under linear temporal logic specifications in partially known workspaces. In: International Conference on Robotics and Automation (ICRA), pp. 5025–5032. IEEE (2013)
18. Karras, C.D.U., Neumann, T., Rohr, T.N.A., Uemura, W., Ewert, D., Harder, N., Jentzsch, S., Meier, N., Reuter, S.: RoboCup logistics league rules and regulations (2016)
19. Khaliq, A.A., Saffiotti, A.: Stigmergy at work: planning and navigation for a service robot on an RFID floor. In: International Conference on Robotics and Automation (ICRA), pp. 1085–1092. IEEE (2015)
20. Kloetzer, M., Ding, X.C., Belta, C.: Multi-robot deployment from LTL specifications with reduced communication. In: Conference on Decision and Control and European Control Conference (CDC-ECC), pp. 4867–4872. IEEE (2011)
21. Kress-Gazit, H., Fainekos, G.E., Pappas, G.J.: Temporal-logic-based reactive mission and motion planning. IEEE Trans. Robot. **25**(6), 1370–1381 (2009)
22. Kurniawati, H., Du, Y., Hsu, D., Lee, W.S.: Motion planning under uncertainty for robotic tasks with long time horizons. Int. J. Robot. Res. **30**(3), 308–323 (2011)
23. Lacerda, B., Parker, D., Hawes, N.: Optimal and dynamic planning for Markov decision processes with co-safe LTL specifications. In: 2014 IEEE/RSJ International Conference on Intelligent Robots and Systems, pp. 1511–1516 (2014)
24. Larsen, K.G., Thomsen, B.: A modal process logic. In: Logic in Computer Science, pp. 203–210. IEEE (1988)
25. Lassaigne, R., Peyronnet, S.: Approximate planning and verification for large markov decision processes. Int. J. Softw. Tools Technol. Transf. **17**(4), 457–467 (2015)
26. Latombe, J.C.: Robot Motion Planning, vol. 124. Springer, New York (2012). https://doi.org/10.1007/978-1-4615-4022-9
27. Letier, E., Kramer, J., Magee, J., Uchitel, S.: Deriving event-based transition systems from goal-oriented requirements models. Autom. Softw. Eng. **15**, 175–206 (2008)
28. Loizou, S.G., Kyriakopoulos, K.J.: Automated planning of motion tasks for multi-robot systems. In: Conference on Decision and Control and European Control Conference (CDC-ECC), pp. 78–83. IEEE (2005)

29. Menghi, C., Spoletini, P., Chechik, M., Ghezzi, C.: Supporting verification-driven incremental distributed design of components. In: Russo, A., Schürr, A. (eds.) FASE 2018. LNCS, vol. 10802, pp. 169–188. Springer, Cham (2018). https://doi.org/10.1007/978-3-319-89363-1_10

30. Menghi, C., Spoletini, P., Ghezzi, C.: Dealing with incompleteness in automata-based model checking. In: Fitzgerald, J., Heitmeyer, C., Gnesi, S., Philippou, A. (eds.) FM 2016. LNCS, vol. 9995, pp. 531–550. Springer, Cham (2016). https://doi.org/10.1007/978-3-319-48989-6_32

31. Menghi, C., Spoletini, P., Ghezzi, C.: COVER: Change-based goal verifier and reasoner. In: Knauss, E., et al. (eds.) Proceedings of the 22nd International Conference on Requirements Engineering: Foundation for Software Quality: Companion Proceeedings, REFSQ 2017, Essen, Germany, February 27, 2017, pp. 434–435, vol. 1796. CEUR-WS.org (2017). http://ceur-ws.org/Vol-1796

32. Menghi, C., Spoletini, P., Ghezzi, C.: Integrating goal model analysis with iterative design. In: Grünbacher, P., Perini, A. (eds.) REFSQ 2017. LNCS, vol. 10153, pp. 112–128. Springer, Cham (2017). https://doi.org/10.1007/978-3-319-54045-0_9

33. Menghi, C., Tsigkanos, C., Berger, T., Pelliccione, P., Ghezzi, C.: Property specification patterns for robotic missions. In: Proceedings of the 40th International Conference on Software Engineering: Companion Proceeedings, ICSE 2018, Gothenburg, Sweden, May 27–June 03, pp. 434–435. ACM (2018). https://doi.org/10.1145/3183440.3195044

34. Quottrup, M.M., Bak, T., Zamanabadi, R.: Multi-robot planning: a timed automata approach. In: International Conference on Robotics and Automation, vol. 5, pp. 4417–4422. IEEE (2004)

35. Roy, N., Gordon, G., Thrun, S.: Planning under uncertainty for reliable health care robotics. In: Yuta, S., Asama, H., Prassler, E., Tsubouchi, T., Thrun, S. (eds.) Field and Service Robotics, pp. 417–426. Springer, Heidelberg (2006). https://doi.org/10.1007/10991459_40

36. Schillinger, P., Bürger, M., Dimarogonas, D.: Decomposition of finite LTL specifications for efficient multi-agent planning. In: International Symposium on Distributed Autonomous Robotic Systems (2016)

37. Tsigkanos, C., Pasquale, L., Menghi, C., Ghezzi, C., Nuseibeh, B.: Engineering topology aware adaptive security: preventing requirements violations at runtime. In: International Requirements Engineering Conference (RE), pp. 203–212 (2014)

38. Tumova, J., Dimarogonas, D.V.: Multi-agent planning under local LTL specifications and event-based synchronization. Automatica **70**, 239–248 (2016)

39. Uchitel, S., Alrajeh, D., Ben-David, S., Braberman, V., Chechik, M., De Caso, G., D'Ippolito, N., Fischbein, D., Garbervetsky, D., Kramer, J., et al.: Supporting incremental behaviour model elaboration. Comput. Sci. Res. Dev. **28**(4), 279–293 (2013)

40. Uchitel, S., Brunet, G., Chechik, M.: Synthesis of partial behavior models from properties and scenarios. IEEE Trans. Softw. Eng. **35**(3), 384–406 (2009)

41. Vardi, M., Wolper, P.: Reasoning about infinite computations. Inf. Comput. **115**(1), 1–37 (1994)

42. Wolff, E.M., Topcu, U., Murray, R.M.: Robust control of uncertain markov decision processes with temporal logic specifications. In: Annual Conference on Decision and Control (CDC), pp. 3372–3379. IEEE (2012)

43. Yoo, C., Fitch, R., Sukkarieh, S.: Online task planning and control for fuel-constrained aerial robots in wind fields. Int. J. Robot. Res. **35**(5), 438–453 (2016)

Vector Barrier Certificates
and Comparison Systems

Andrew Sogokon[1]([✉]) [ID], Khalil Ghorbal[2]([✉]) [ID], Yong Kiam Tan[1] [ID],
and André Platzer[1] [ID]

[1] Computer Science Department, Carnegie Mellon University, Pittsburgh, USA
{asogokon,yongkiat,aplatzer}@cs.cmu.edu
[2] Inria, Rennes, France
khalil.ghorbal@inria.fr

Abstract. Vector Lyapunov functions are a multi-dimensional extension of the more familiar (scalar) Lyapunov functions, commonly used to prove stability properties in systems of non-linear ordinary differential equations (ODEs). This paper explores an analogous vector extension for so-called *barrier certificates* used in safety verification. As with vector Lyapunov functions, the approach hinges on constructing appropriate *comparison systems*, i.e., related differential equation systems from which properties of the original system may be inferred. The paper presents an accessible development of the approach, demonstrates that most previous notions of barrier certificate are special cases of comparison systems, and discusses the potential applications of vector barrier certificates in safety verification and invariant synthesis.

Keywords: Ordinary differential equations · Safety verification
Vector barrier certificates · Comparison systems

1 Introduction

Over the past decade, *barrier certificates* have emerged as a rather popular Lyapunov-like technique for proving safety properties of continuous systems governed by ODEs, as well as hybrid dynamical systems, which combine continuous and discrete dynamics and provide models for modern control and embedded systems. Since the original formulation of barrier certificates [37], significant efforts have been directed at the problem of generalizing and relaxing the conditions that are required under this approach, so as to broaden its scope and applicability. A number of generalizations have been reported in the verification community (e.g. [11,22]). We demonstrate in this paper how *comparison systems* (a well-established concept in the theory of ODEs) fundamentally underlie these developments and provide a clean conceptual basis for understanding

This work was supported by the National Science Foundation under NSF CPS Award CNS-1739629 and by the AFOSR under grant number FA9550-16-1-0288; the third author was supported by the National Science Scholarship from A*STAR, Singapore.

and further developing the method of barrier certificates. Following the seminal work of R. E. Bellman, who first introduced *vector Lyapunov functions* [2] as a way of relaxing the standard (scalar) Lyapunov conditions for proving stability in ODEs, we will explore an extension of barrier certificates based on multi-dimensional (i.e. vector) comparison systems.

Structure of this Paper. Mathematical preliminaries are reviewed in Sect. 2. Thereafter, the paper consists of two technical parts. The first part, in Sect. 3, reviews the method of barrier certificates and demonstrates how *convex* [37], *exponential-type* [22] and the more recent *general barrier certificates* [11] effectively amount to a straightforward application of the *comparison principle* and can be interpreted as special cases of this more general framework. The second part, in Sect. 4, uses multi-dimensional comparison systems to extend existing (scalar) notions of barrier certificates to what we term *vector barrier certificates*, analogously to vector Lyapunov functions known from control theory. Section 6 discusses related work and Sect. 7 concludes with a short summary.

2   Fundamental Definitions

We begin with an overview of some important concepts and definitions. In this paper we are concerned with studying systems of polynomial ODEs and will work under the assumption that functions are polynomials, unless stated otherwise.

2.1   Systems of Ordinary Differential Equations

An autonomous n-dimensional system of ODEs is of the form:

$$x_1' = f_1(x_1, x_2, \ldots, x_n),$$
$$\vdots$$
$$x_n' = f_n(x_1, x_2, \ldots, x_n),$$

where $f_i : \mathbb{R}^n \to \mathbb{R}$ is a real-valued (typically continuous) function for each $i \in \{1, \ldots, n\}$, and x_i' denotes the time derivative of x_i, i.e. $\frac{dx_i}{dt}$. In applications, constraints are often used to specify the states where the system is allowed to evolve, i.e. the system may only be allowed to evolve inside some given set $Q \subseteq \mathbb{R}^n$, which is known as the *evolution constraint* (or a *mode invariant* of some mode q in the context of hybrid automata). We can write down systems of constrained ODEs concisely by using vector notation, i.e. by writing $\boldsymbol{x}' = \boldsymbol{f}(\boldsymbol{x})$, $\boldsymbol{x} \in Q$. Here we have $\boldsymbol{x}' = (x_1', \ldots, x_n')$ and $\boldsymbol{f} : \mathbb{R}^n \to \mathbb{R}^n$ is a *vector field* generated by the system, i.e. $\boldsymbol{f}(\boldsymbol{x}) = (f_1(\boldsymbol{x}), \ldots, f_n(\boldsymbol{x}))$ for all $\boldsymbol{x} \in \mathbb{R}^n$. If no evolution constraint is given, Q is assumed to be the Euclidean space $\mathbb{R}^n$. The Lie derivative of a differentiable scalar function $g : \mathbb{R}^n \to \mathbb{R}$ in the state variables of such a system is denoted by g' and given by $\sum_{i=1}^{n} \frac{\partial g}{\partial x_i} f_i$.

   A *solution* to the initial value problem (IVP) for the system of ODEs $\boldsymbol{x}' = \boldsymbol{f}(\boldsymbol{x})$ with initial value $\boldsymbol{x}_0 \in \mathbb{R}^n$ is a (differentiable) function $\boldsymbol{x} : (a, b) \to \mathbb{R}^n$

defined for all t in some open interval including zero, i.e. $t \in (a, b)$, where $a, b \in \mathbb{R} \cup \{\infty, -\infty\}$, $a < 0 < b$, and such that $\boldsymbol{x}(0) = \boldsymbol{x}_0$ and $\frac{d}{dt}\boldsymbol{x}(t) = \boldsymbol{f}(\boldsymbol{x}(t))$ for all $t \in (a, b)$. At time t, for solutions to IVPs with initial value $\boldsymbol{x}_0$, we shall write $\boldsymbol{x}(\boldsymbol{x}_0, t)$, or simply $\boldsymbol{x}(t)$ if the initial condition is understood from context. If the solution $\boldsymbol{x}(\boldsymbol{x}_0, t)$ is available in closed-form,[1] then one can study properties such as safety and liveness by analysing the closed-form expression. However, in non-linear ODEs it is in practice highly uncommon for solutions to exist explicitly in closed-form [3,20], and even if closed-form solutions can be found, transcendental functions in these expressions lead to undecidable arithmetic [41].

Remark 1. In this paper we employ a slight abuse of notation for sets and formulas characterizing those sets, i.e. Q denotes both a set $Q \subseteq \mathbb{R}^n$ and a formula Q of real arithmetic with free variables $x_1, \ldots, x_n$ which characterizes this set. In the case of sub-level sets, i.e. sets characterized by predicates of the form $B \leq 0$ where B is a real valued function in the (dependent) variables $x_1, \ldots, x_n$, we will write $B(\boldsymbol{x}) \leq 0$ to mean $B \leq 0$ is true in state $\boldsymbol{x} \in \mathbb{R}^n$, and will explicitly use the independent time variable t to write $B(\boldsymbol{x}(t)) \leq 0$ when we are interested in evaluating the predicate along a solution $\boldsymbol{x}(t)$ of a differential equation.

2.2   Safety Verification and Direct Methods

In continuous systems governed by ODEs, a common verification challenge lies in establishing *safety* in a given system, which requires showing that no state in some designated set of *unsafe* states is reachable by following the solutions to the system from some given set of initial configurations. More precisely:

Definition 1 (Safety in ODEs). *Given a system of ODEs $\boldsymbol{x}' = \boldsymbol{f}(\boldsymbol{x})$ with evolution constraint $Q \subseteq \mathbb{R}^n$, and the sets $\mathrm{Init} \subseteq \mathbb{R}^n$, $\mathrm{Unsafe} \subseteq \mathbb{R}^n$ of initial and unsafe states, respectively, the system is said to be* safe *if and only if:* $\forall \boldsymbol{x}_0 \in \mathrm{Init}. \ \forall t \geq 0. \Big((\ \forall \tau \in [0, t]. \ \boldsymbol{x}(\boldsymbol{x}_0, \tau) \ \in Q) \Rightarrow \boldsymbol{x}(\boldsymbol{x}_0, t) \notin \mathrm{Unsafe} \Big).$

The above is a *semantic* definition, since it explicitly involves the solutions $\boldsymbol{x}(t)$ of the system. The fact that exact solutions to non-linear ODEs are rarely available is a significant limitation, and was historically the principal driving force behind the development of the so-called *qualitative theory* of differential equations, which is concerned with proving properties about differential equations *directly*, i.e. without explicitly computing their solutions. Powerful methods, such as Lyapunov's *direct method* [26] for proving stability in ODEs, emerged out of this theory and have become standard tools in the field of dynamical systems and control (see e.g. [19,42,51]). The next section will give a comprehensive review of direct methods for solving the safety verification problem for continuous systems using existing notions of barrier certificates.

---

[1] i.e. As a *finite* expression in terms of polynomials and *elementary functions* that can be constructed using the usual arithmetic operations $+, -, \times, \div$, from $\exp, \sin, \cos$, and their inverses; this includes natural logarithms, nth roots, etc. (see [3, Chap. 4]).

3   Barrier Certificates

First introduced by Prajna and Jadbabaie [37], the method of barrier certificates works by exhibiting a real-valued *barrier* function B which serves to partition the state space into two disjoint regions, respectively containing the initial and the unsafe states of the system, and such that the trajectories of the system cannot leave the initial states into the region containing unsafe states. The most general principle was not elaborated explicitly in the original work [37], but is stated, e.g., in [11, Sect. 3] as the *principle of barrier certificates*. The semantic statement of this principle (reproduced below) is not in itself useful for verifying safety properties because it explicitly involves the solutions to the system of ODEs.

Lemma 1 (Safety with semantic barrier certificates). *Given a system of ODEs $x' = f(x)$, possibly with an evolution constraint $Q \subseteq \mathbb{R}^n$, a set of initial states Init $\subseteq \mathbb{R}^n$, and a set of unsafe states Unsafe $\subseteq \mathbb{R}^n$, if a differentiable (barrier) function $B : \mathbb{R}^n \to \mathbb{R}$ satisfies the following conditions, then safety of the system in the sense of Definition 1 follows trivially:*

1. $\forall x \in$ Unsafe. $B(x) > 0$,
2. $\forall x_0 \in$ Init. $\forall t \geq 0. \Big((\forall \tau \in [0, t]. \, x(x_0, \tau) \in Q) \Rightarrow B(x(x_0, t)) \leq 0 \Big)$.

Fortunately, there are a number of ways in which one can establish whether or not a given function B has the properties required by the semantic principle stated in Lemma 1 *without* having to compute solutions. There are at present a number of different kinds of barrier certificates in the literature, which differ in the kinds of conditions they employ for ensuring the second requirement of the general principle in Lemma 1. We can broadly separate these into two classes: (**i**) those which essentially reduce to an application of the so-called *comparison principle*, and (**ii**) those explicitly based on reasoning about (positive) *invariant sets* [2]. In what follows, it is important to recall that *semi-definite programming* (SDP) and *sum-of-squares* (SOS) decomposition techniques (whose use to search for Lyapunov functions was pioneered by Parrilo [31]) provide a tractable search procedure only for certain kinds of barrier certificates.

3.1   Comparison System-Based Barrier Certificates

Convex/Weak. The original formulation in [37] is known as a *convex* [36,38] (also *weak* [45]) barrier certificate and imposes the following three formal requirements, which are sufficient to satisfy the conditions in Lemma 1 (we elide the x-dependency in Unsafe, Init, Q, and B):

CBC 1. $\forall x \in \mathbb{R}^n. (\text{Unsafe} \to B > 0)$,
CBC 2. $\forall x \in \mathbb{R}^n. (\text{Init} \to B \leq 0)$,
CBC 3. $\forall x \in \mathbb{R}^n. (Q \to B' \leq 0)$.

---

[2] i.e. Sets of states that remain invariant under the flow of the system as time advances.

The above conditions ensure that the sub-level set $B \leq 0$ is a sound over-approximation of the set of states reachable from Init. If the evolution constraint Q, as well as Init and Unsafe, are all given by conjunctions of polynomial inequalities, one can formulate a search for polynomial $B \in \mathbb{R}[x]$ as a semi-definite program by fixing some maximum degree for a symbolic polynomial *template* of B and using an SDP solver to obtain its monomial coefficients [37]. The convexity in the name refers to the set of functions B, since for any two functions $B, \tilde{B}$ that satisfy the requirements **CBC 1–3**, any convex combination $\alpha B + (1 - \alpha)\tilde{B}$, where $\alpha \in [0, 1]$, will also be a convex/weak barrier certificate satisfying the same requirements. It is precisely this convexity property which enables the use of SDP from convex optimization and makes barrier certificates of this kind interesting from a practical standpoint.

Exponential-Type. So-called *exponential-type* barrier certificates [22] extend weak barrier certificates by generalizing the condition on the derivative of B in a way that maintains the convexity of the search space. These conditions are:

ETBC 1. $\forall x \in \mathbb{R}^n. (\text{Unsafe} \to B > 0)$,
ETBC 2. $\forall x \in \mathbb{R}^n. (\text{Init} \to B \leq 0)$,
ETBC 3. $\forall x \in \mathbb{R}^n. (Q \to B' \leq \lambda B)$, for some fixed $\lambda \in \mathbb{R}$.

Since these conditions also define a convex set, one can search for barrier certificates of this kind using semi-definite programming for fixed $\lambda \in \mathbb{R}$ and bounded degree polynomial templates of B, analogously to the weak/convex barrier certificates. To use this method, one is required to supply a value for λ: with $\lambda = 0$ one recovers the conditions for convex barrier certificates; the choice of $\lambda > 0$ or $\lambda < 0$ was observed to have significant practical impact on the barrier functions that one can generate using semi-definite programming [22, Sect. 3.1].

General. More recently, so-called *general* barrier certificates were reported in [11] and generalize the condition used in exponential-type barrier certificates yet further by allowing the right-hand side of the differential inequality to be a (potentially non-linear) univariate *function* of the barrier function itself. The conditions are as follows:

GBC 1. $\forall x \in \mathbb{R}^n. (\text{Unsafe} \to B > 0)$,
GBC 2. $\forall x \in \mathbb{R}^n. (\text{Init} \to B \leq 0)$,
GBC 3. $\forall x \in \mathbb{R}^n. (Q \to B' \leq \omega(B))$,
GBC 4. $\forall t \geq 0. \ b(x(t)) \leq 0$, where $b(x(t)) : \mathbb{R} \to \mathbb{R}$ is some continuously differentiable function such that: (i) $b(x(0)) \leq 0$, and (ii) $b' = \omega(b)$.

Barrier certificates satisfying the above requirements will *not* form a convex set. To use this method of verification in practice, one is first required to supply some *fixed* univariate function ω, e.g. one could take $\omega(b) = -b + b^2$, and make sure that the solutions $b(t)$ to the differential equation $b' = \omega(b)$ exist and remain non-positive for all time, i.e. $\forall t \geq 0. \ b(t) \leq 0$, from the initial conditions (at which b is required to be non-positive). One may be forgiven for thinking these conditions obscure and unmotivated at first; in the next section we will elucidate how these conditions in fact amount to a simple exercise in applying the comparison principle in the theory of ODEs to safety verification.

3.2   Comparison Systems

Informally, one may think of a *comparison system* for a given system of ODEs as being another system of ODEs that (i) is in some sense simpler to analyse and (ii) enables one to establish properties of the original system of ODEs. The idea behind the *comparison principle* is that by establishing some desired property of the comparison system (which is hopefully not as difficult), one is able to draw the conclusion that this property also holds in the original system.

Remark 2. A comparison system may be described as a certain *abstraction* of a system of ODEs by another system.

The comparison principle emerged as a coherent technique in the theory of ODEs and applied mathematics in the middle of the twentieth century. It was employed by numerous authors, e.g. by Conti [10] to study existence of solutions of ODEs, and by Brauer [6] to study stability using comparison systems as a way of generalizing the classic requirement $V' \leq 0$ on the derivative of Lyapunov functions V. For demonstrating stability of some n-dimensional system of ODEs $\boldsymbol{x}' = \boldsymbol{f}(\boldsymbol{x})$, if one has a *positive definite* function $V : \mathbb{R}^n \to \mathbb{R}$ that satisfies a more general differential inequality

$$V' \leq \omega(V)\,,$$

where $\omega : \mathbb{R} \to \mathbb{R}$ is an appropriately chosen scalar function, one can construct a (scalar) comparison system by introducing a fresh variable (e.g. v; really a function of time $v(t)$) and replacing the inequality by an equality, thus obtaining a *one-dimensional* first order system of ODEs, i.e. the differential *equation*

$$v' = \omega(v)\,.$$

The comparison principle relates properties of the solutions $v(t)$ of this one-dimensional system to properties of the solutions $\boldsymbol{x}(t)$ of the original n-dimensional system $\boldsymbol{x}' = \boldsymbol{f}(\boldsymbol{x})$ by using solutions $V(t)$, i.e. $V(\boldsymbol{x}(t))$, to the differential inequality. For example, one use of the comparison principle in the theory of ODEs is to infer stability of the original system by establishing stability of the one-dimensional comparison system (see e.g. Brauer [7], Habets and Peiffer [18, Sect. 2]).[3] The comparison principle hinges on an appropriate *comparison theorem*, which establishes the relationship between the solutions of the one-dimensional system to the solutions of the differential inequality. Below we state a particularly useful comparison theorem (a corollary to the comparison theorem in Walter [49, Chap. II, Sect. IX]) which we shall use in later sections.

---

[3] The comparison principle is described in some detail in [48], and also in a number of textbooks, e.g. in [42, Chap. II Sect. 3, Chap. IX], [51, Sect. 1.4], [19, Theorem 4.16].

Theorem 1 (Scalar comparison theorem). *Let $B(t)$ and $b(t)$ be real val-ued functions differentiable on some real interval $[0,T]$. If $B' \leq \omega(B)$ and $b' = \omega(b)$ holds on $[0,T]$ for some locally Lipschitz continuous function ω and if $B(0) = b(0)$, then for all $t \in [0,T]$ one has $B(t) \leq b(t)$.*

The comparison theorem above ensures that the solutions $b(t)$ to the comparison system of *ODEs* act as upper bounds on the solutions $B(t)$ to the corresponding system of differential *inequalities*. We note in passing that the above theorem also holds more generally for ω with explicit time-dependence, i.e. $\omega(t, B)$.

3.3 Comparison Principle Interpretation of Barrier Certificates

The original formulation of convex barrier certificates in [37] can be interpreted using the comparison principle viewpoint as the trivial case in which the differential inequality $B' \leq 0$ (i.e. ω being the constant function 0) leads to the comparison system given by $b' = 0$, in which there is no motion. The initial states in the comparison system are defined as $b_{\mathrm{Init}} = \{k \in \mathbb{R} \mid B(\boldsymbol{x}) = k, \boldsymbol{x} \in \mathrm{Init}\}$; analogously, the unsafe states are $b_{\mathrm{Unsafe}} = \{k \in \mathbb{R} \mid B(\boldsymbol{x}) = k, \boldsymbol{x} \in \mathrm{Unsafe}\}$. Since the value of B at unsafe states is required to be greater than its values at initial states by conditions **CBC 1–2**, the safety property follows because the solutions of the comparison system $b(t)$ bound the solutions $B(t)$ from above and cannot increase. Figure 1a illustrates this comparison system. Since every point is an equilibrium and $b(0) \leq 0$ is required for all initial states in b_{Init}, and $b(t) = b(0) \leq 0$ will hold for all $t \geq 0$, the comparison system cannot evolve into a potentially unsafe state $b(\tau) > 0$ (i.e. $b(\tau) \in b_{\mathrm{Unsafe}}$) for any $\tau > 0$. As a consequence, $B(\boldsymbol{x}(t)) \leq 0$ will hold for all $\boldsymbol{x}(0) \in \mathrm{Init}$ for *as long as solutions are defined in the original system*, by Theorem 1, satisfying the requirements in Lemma 1.

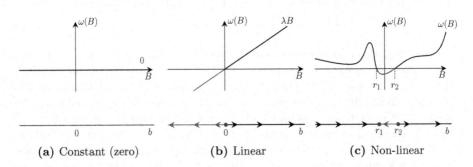

(a) Constant (zero)   (b) Linear   (c) Non-linear

Fig. 1. Right-hand sides of differential inequalities $B' \leq \omega(B)$ shown above. Their corresponding scalar comparison systems $b' = \omega(b)$ are shown below as vector fields on the real line. The motion in these comparison systems is directed "to the right" whenever ω is above zero, and "to the left" when it is below; equilibria are those points where ω evaluates to zero, i.e. the real roots of ω.

The *exponential-type* [22] and *general* [11] barrier certificates can also be easily understood as special instances of applying the comparison principle. With the former, one has a *linear* differential inequality $B' \leq \lambda B$, for some $\lambda \in \mathbb{R}$, which leads to the simple linear comparison system $b' = \lambda b$ (i.e. $\omega(b) = \lambda b$) defined on the real line (illustrated in Fig. 1b). As before, by showing unreachability of unsafe states b_{Unsafe} from the initial states b_{Init} in the comparison system, Theorem 1 allows one to soundly conclude the safety property in the original system provided that $B(\boldsymbol{x}) \leq 0$ for all initial states and $B(\boldsymbol{x}) > 0$ for all unsafe states, as required by **ETBC 1–2** (cf. Sect. 3.1). We note also that the solutions $b(t)$ in the comparison system are defined for all $t \geq 0$, since the system is linear, and the bounding property stated in the comparison theorem will hold for as long as solutions are defined in the original system.

The general barrier certificates reported in [11] simply allow for a *non-linear* function ω of B in the right-hand side of the differential inequality, i.e. $B' \leq \omega(B)$. This leads to a non-linear scalar comparison system $b' = \omega(b)$ which can exhibit more interesting flows on the real line (as shown in Fig. 1c). The principle, however, is exactly the same: the unreachability of the unsafe states from the initial states *in the comparison system* (e.g. the one-dimensional flow shown in Fig. 1c) implies the safety property in the original system. However, since ω can be non-linear, it also becomes important to ensure that solutions from the initial states in the comparison systems do not escape to infinity before they do in the original system. Thus, the last requirement of general barrier certificates **GBC 4** is essentially requiring one to explicitly supply an appropriate comparison system.[4]

3.4   Invariant Set-Based Barrier Certificates

An alternative way of ensuring condition (2.) in Lemma 1 is by directly requiring the *continuous invariance* property of the entire sub-level set of the barrier function, i.e. $B \leq 0$, and explicitly requiring that all initial states lie inside this sub-level set, i.e. $\forall \boldsymbol{x} \in \text{Init}. B(\boldsymbol{x}) \leq 0$. The set $\{\boldsymbol{x} \in \mathbb{R}^n \mid B(\boldsymbol{x}) \leq 0\}$ is a *continuous invariant* under constraint Q if the system cannot continuously evolve from a state $\boldsymbol{x} \in \mathbb{R}^n$ satisfying $B(\boldsymbol{x}) \leq 0$ into a state $\boldsymbol{x}(t)$ satisfying $B(\boldsymbol{x}(t)) > 0$, while respecting the constraint Q. Semantically, this amounts to showing that the following holds:

$$\forall \boldsymbol{x}_0 \in \mathbb{R}^n. (B(\boldsymbol{x}_0) \leq 0 \Rightarrow (\forall t \geq 0. (\forall \tau \in [0, t].\boldsymbol{x}(\boldsymbol{x}_0, \tau) \in Q) \Rightarrow B(\boldsymbol{x}(\boldsymbol{x}_0, t)) \leq 0))$$

Notice the subtle difference of this requirement to that in Lemma 1, which does *not* require the sub-level set $B \leq 0$ to be a continuous invariant.

---

[4] For the interested reader, we note that in [11, Theorem 1], the barrier function B is denoted by φ, the function ω is denoted ψ, and the variable b of the comparison system denoted by θ. Indeed, the final condition (5) in [11, Theorem 1] simply requires that the solution of the comparison system $b' = \omega(b)$ (i.e. $\theta' = \psi(\theta)$ using notation employed in the article) does not become positive as time (denoted by ξ) advances. No reference to the comparison principle is made in that work.

Remark 3. Continuous invariance is a generalization of the notion of *positive invariance* used in control (e.g. see [4]); its greater generality is due to an appropriate handling of evolution constraints. We note that the problem of checking whether a given *semi-algebraic set* (i.e. a set described by a finite Boolean combination of polynomial equations and inequalities) defines a continuous invariant under the flow of a polynomial first-order system of ODEs is decidable (a remarkable result due to Liu, Zhan and Zhao [25]).

However, *searching* for continuous invariants – even those of restricted form, such as sub-level sets of polynomial functions – using tools such as real quantifier elimination is impractical due to the time complexity of existing algorithms (e.g. partial CAD [9]).

An example of barrier certificate conditions based on continuous invariance is the so-called *strict* [45] (also known as *non-convex* [36,38]) barrier certificate, which imposes the following formal requirements:

SBC 1. $\forall x \in \mathbb{R}^n.\,(\text{Unsafe} \to B > 0)$,
SBC 2. $\forall x \in \mathbb{R}^n.\,(\text{Init} \to B \leq 0)$,
SBC 3. $\forall x \in \mathbb{R}^n.\,(Q \wedge B = 0 \to B' < 0)$.

In the last condition, the strict inequality $B'(x) < 0$ is only required to hold at the roots of the function B, i.e. for all $x \in Q$ such that $B(x) = 0$. This condition[5] is in practice less conservative than that used in convex barrier certificates, since it does not impose a requirement on the derivative everywhere in the evolution constraint Q. However, the set of functions B satisfying this condition is no longer convex and as a result one may no longer directly apply semi-definite programming to search for this type of barrier functions. An alternative *iterative* search method for strict barrier certificates was explored in [36,37] and was also used to search for (likewise non-convex) general barrier certificates [11, Sect. 4].

We note that continuous invariance is the main principle underlying safety verification problems. In fact, scalar comparison systems are essentially means of generating sufficient continuous invariants to solve the problem at hand. For example, in a one-dimensional comparison system $b' = \omega(b)$, obtained from the differential inequality $B' \leq \omega(B)$, for any $k \in \mathbb{R}$ such that $\omega(k) < 0$ it is guaranteed that $B'(x) < 0$ holds at all states x satisfying $B(x) = k$.[6] This property is sufficient to conclude that the sub-level set $B \leq k$ is a continuous invariant in the original n-dimensional system. For example, in the non-linear system $b' = \omega(b)$ illustrated in Fig. 1c, any $k \in (r_1, r_2)$ can be used to extract such an invariant; for the linear example in Fig. 1b one may take any $k < 0$.

---

[5] Note that the inequality needs to be *strict*; the original formulation of non-convex barrier certificates in [37] featured a non-strict inequality $B' \leq 0$, which leads to *unsoundness* in certain degenerate cases. A finite number of inequalities involving higher-order derivatives of B can be used instead to soundly establish continuous invariance of the sub-level set $B \leq 0$, following the result reported in [25].

[6] Each point k on the real line in a scalar comparison system $b' = \omega(b)$ corresponds to $\{x \in \mathbb{R}^n \mid B(x) = k\}$ in the original state space.

4   From Scalar to Vector Comparison Systems

A multi-dimensional version of Lyapunov functions, known as vector Lyapunov functions, was first introduced in 1962 by Bellman [2], using the more general *vector* comparison principle. [7] Below we briefly review this development.

4.1   Vector Lyapunov Functions

The main idea behind vector Lyapunov functions is as follows: instead of searching for a single Lyapunov function $V : \mathbb{R}^n \to \mathbb{R}$, one searches for a *vector* function $\boldsymbol{V} : \mathbb{R}^n \to \mathbb{R}^m$, where $\boldsymbol{V}(\boldsymbol{x})$ is a vector $(V_1(\boldsymbol{x}), \ldots, V_m(\boldsymbol{x}))$ and $V_1, \ldots, V_m$ are scalar functions, such that for each $i = 1, \ldots, m$ one has $V_i' \leq \omega_i(V_1, \ldots, V_m)$, where $\omega_i : \mathbb{R}^m \to \mathbb{R}$. In the classic (scalar) Lyapunov case, i.e. the special case where $m = 1$, if one had $V' \leq \omega(V)$, with positive definite V and some appropriate scalar function ω, one could use the comparison principle to infer stability by showing this property in the scalar comparison system $v' = \omega(v)$ (e.g. see Brauer [7]). With vector Lyapunov functions one is instead interested in analysing the *vector* comparison system $\boldsymbol{v}' = \boldsymbol{\omega}(\boldsymbol{v})$, obtained from a *system* of differential inequalities $\boldsymbol{V}' \leq \boldsymbol{\omega}(\boldsymbol{V})$, where $\boldsymbol{\omega} : \mathbb{R}^m \to \mathbb{R}^m$. There is, however, an (unpleasant) extra requirement: in order to conclude stability of the original system from the stability of the vector comparison system, the vector function $\boldsymbol{\omega}$ needs to be *quasi-monotone increasing*.

Definition 2. *A function $\boldsymbol{\omega} : \mathbb{R}^m \to \mathbb{R}^m$ is said to be* quasi-monotone increasing *on a set $U \subseteq \mathbb{R}^m$ if $\omega_i(\boldsymbol{x}) \leq \omega_i(\boldsymbol{y})$ for all $i = 1, \ldots, m$ and all $\boldsymbol{x}, \boldsymbol{y} \in U$ such that $x_i = y_i$, and $x_k \leq y_k$ for all $k \neq i$.*

In particular, univariate functions (case $m = 1$) are always quasi-monotone increasing by definition since the required inequality holds trivially ($x = y$ implies $\omega(x) \leq \omega(y)$). In the vector case, a linear multivariate function $\boldsymbol{\omega}(\boldsymbol{x}) = A\boldsymbol{x}$ is quasi-monotone increasing if and only if all the off-diagonal entries of the $m \times m$ real matrix A are non-negative (e.g. see [48]). Such a matrix is said to be *essentially non-negative*, *quasi-positive*, or a *Metzler matrix*.

Remark 4. Clearly, vector comparison systems are only interesting in practice insofar as they are easier to analyse than the original system. For stability analysis with vector Lyapunov functions, linear vector comparison systems of the form $\boldsymbol{v}' = \omega(\boldsymbol{v}) = A\boldsymbol{v}$, where A is an appropriate essentially non-negative $m \times m$ real matrix, are easier to work with than non-linear vector comparison systems. One may easily create linear quasi-monotone increasing vector comparison systems $\boldsymbol{v}' = A\boldsymbol{v}$ that are stable *a priori* and then search for vector Lyapunov functions that satisfy the corresponding system of differential inequalities $\boldsymbol{V}' \leq A\boldsymbol{V}$; see [17]. Indeed, Bellman's approach [2] only focused on linear vector comparison systems. The general method of vector Lyapunov functions has been applied extensively to study stability of non-linear systems; the interested reader is invited to consult [24,28], and [19, Sect. 4.11] for a more thorough overview.

---

[7] The technique itself was also independently developed by Matrosov [27], who also published his research in 1962, shortly after Bellman.

4.2   Vector Comparison Principle

Quasi-monotonicity of the right-hand side in the comparison system $b' = \omega(b)$ ensures that its solutions $b(t)$ majorize (bound above component-by-component) the solutions $B(t)$ to the system of differential inequalities $B' \leq \omega(B)$, analogously to the scalar comparison case in Theorem 1. Following [2], we state (in Theorem 2) a vector comparison theorem which enables one to employ the *vector comparison principle* for the practically interesting case where ω is *linear* (for a proof, see e.g. [1, Chap. 4, Sect. 6, Theorem 4]).

Theorem 2 (Linear vector comparison theorem). *For a given system of ODEs $x' = f(x)$ and an essentially non-negative matrix, $A \in \mathbb{R}^{m \times m}$, if $B = (B_1, B_2, \ldots, B_m)$ satisfies the system of differential inequalities $B' \leq AB$, then for all $t \geq 0$ the inequality $B(t) \leq b(t)$ holds component-wise, where $b(t)$ is the solution to the comparison system $b' = Ab$, $B(t)$ is any solution to the system of differential inequalities, and $b(0) = B(0)$.*

The above vector comparison theorem can be generalized to the non-linear case where $B' \leq \omega(B)$ and $b' = \omega(b)$, provided that the non-linear vector function $\omega : \mathbb{R}^m \to \mathbb{R}^m$ is quasi-monotone increasing. For a precise statement and proof see e.g. [19, Sect. 4.13], [49, Chap. III, Sect. XII], [23, Sect. 4.1].

4.3   Safety with Vector Barrier Certificates

The main interest in pursuing the vector comparison approach is to relax the conditions on each individual function component of the vector. The hope is that it is easier to search for functions that satisfy less rigid criteria. It is natural to ask whether one might profitably apply vector comparison systems to safety verification. We begin by stating a useful lemma.

Lemma 2. *If $A \in \mathbb{R}^{m \times m}$ is an essentially non-negative matrix, then for any initial value $b_0 \leq 0$, the solution $b(t)$ to the linear system $b' = Ab$ is such that $b(t) \leq 0$ for all $t \geq 0$.*

Proof. This follows from the fact that solutions to the linear system $b' = Ab$ from an initial value $b_0 \leq 0$ are given by $b(t) = e^{At}b_0$, and all the elements of the matrix exponential e^{At} are non-negative for all $t \geq 0$ if and only if A is essentially non-negative (e.g. see proof of Theorem 4 in [1, Chap. 4, Sect. 6]). □

Theorem 3. *Given $x' = f(x)$, Q, Init, and Unsafe as before, an m-vector of continuously differentiable functions $B = (B_1, B_2, \ldots, B_m)$ and some essentially non-negative $m \times m$ matrix A, if the following conditions hold, then the safety property of the system is guaranteed:*

$VBC_{\wedge}1.$ $\forall x \in \mathbb{R}^n. (\text{Init} \to \bigwedge_{i=1}^{m} B_i \leq 0),$

$VBC_{\wedge}2.$ $\forall x \in \mathbb{R}^n. (\text{Unsafe} \to \bigvee_{i=1}^{m} B_i > 0),$

$VBC_{\wedge}3.$ $\forall x \in \mathbb{R}^n. (Q \to B' \leq AB).$

Proof. Elementary, since the states satisfying $\bigwedge_{i=1}^{m} B_i(\boldsymbol{x}) \leq 0$ include all the initial states, no unsafe states, and majorizing solutions $\boldsymbol{b}(t)$ of the comparison system $\boldsymbol{b}' = A\boldsymbol{b}$ cannot take on positive values in any component for any time $t \geq 0$ (by Lemma 2). Thus, $\boldsymbol{B}(t) \leq \boldsymbol{0}$ for all $t \geq 0$ (by Theorem 2). $\qquad\square$

For any given matrix $A \in \mathbb{R}^{m \times m}$ if the m-vectors $\boldsymbol{B} = (B_1, B_2, \ldots, B_m)$ and $\tilde{\boldsymbol{B}} = (\tilde{B}_1, \tilde{B}_2, \ldots, \tilde{B}_m)$ satisfy conditions $\mathbf{VBC}_\wedge 1$ and $\mathbf{VBC}_\wedge 3$, then so does their convex combination $\widehat{\boldsymbol{B}} = \alpha\boldsymbol{B} + (1 - \alpha)\tilde{\boldsymbol{B}}$, where $\alpha \in [0, 1]$. The latter holds since $\widehat{\boldsymbol{B}}' = \alpha\boldsymbol{B}' + (1 - \alpha)\tilde{\boldsymbol{B}}' \leq \alpha A\boldsymbol{B} + (1 - \alpha)A\tilde{\boldsymbol{B}} = A\widehat{\boldsymbol{B}}$. Unfortunately, the condition $\mathbf{VBC}_\wedge 2$, while intuitive and desirable, leads to non-convexity. To recover convexity one may write down a stronger condition as follows.[8]

Corollary 1. *Given $\boldsymbol{x}' = f(\boldsymbol{x})$, Q, Init, Unsafe, $\boldsymbol{B}$ and A as before, if for some $i^* \in \{1, \ldots, m\}$ the following conditions hold, then the safety property of the system is guaranteed:*

VBC 1. $\forall \boldsymbol{x} \in \mathbb{R}^n. (\text{Init} \rightarrow \bigwedge_{i=1}^{m} B_i \leq 0)$,
VBC 2. $\forall \boldsymbol{x} \in \mathbb{R}^n. (\text{Unsafe} \rightarrow B_{i^*} > 0)$,
VBC 3. $\forall \boldsymbol{x} \in \mathbb{R}^n. (Q \rightarrow \boldsymbol{B}' \leq A\boldsymbol{B})$.

Notice that a barrier function B_{i^*} satisfying the conditions **VBC 1–3** satisfies the requirement of the semantic principle in Lemma 1, but its sub-level set $B_{i^*} \leq 0$ need *not* be a continuous invariant (unlike in scalar barrier certificates).

Remark 5. Vector barrier certificates can also be defined using a non-linear vector differential inequality $\boldsymbol{B}' \leq \boldsymbol{\omega}(\boldsymbol{B})$, where $\boldsymbol{\omega}$ is some non-linear quasi-monotone increasing function. This, however, would lead to the convexity property being lost and would also require the solutions to the comparison system to be of sufficient duration in order to ensure soundness. This approach does not appear to be at all promising from a practical standpoint, but provides the most general notion for vector barrier certificates.

Theorem 4 (Deductive power). *Every polynomial convex or 'exponential-type' barrier certificate is (trivially) a vector barrier certificate satisfying the conditions $\mathbf{VBC}_\wedge 1$–3 (or $\mathbf{VBC}$ 1–3). The converse is false, i.e. there exist polynomial vector barrier certificates sufficient for proving certain safety properties where a scalar barrier certificate does not exist.*

Proof. For the non-trivial part, consider the system $x_1' = x_2$, $x_2' = x_1$. Suppose that the initial states in this system satisfy the formula $x_1 \leq 0 \wedge x_2 \leq 0$ and the unsafe states satisfy $x_1 > 0$. If we take $B_1 = x_1$ and $B_2 = x_2$ then, since $B_1' = x_1'$ and $B_2' = x_2'$, the following system of differential inequalities is satisfied: $B_1' \leq B_2$, $B_2' \leq B_1$, which is equivalently written down as a linear system of differential inequalities with an essentially non-negative matrix:

---

[8] Naturally, for the vectorial formulation to be interesting, *none* of the functions $B_1, \ldots, B_m$ should be (scalar) barrier certificates in their own right.

430   A. Sogokon et al.

$\begin{pmatrix} B_1' \\ B_2' \end{pmatrix} \leq \begin{pmatrix} 0 & 1 \\ 1 & 0 \end{pmatrix} \begin{pmatrix} B_1 \\ B_2 \end{pmatrix}$. The vector (B_1, B_2) satisfies all the conditions in Theorem 3 and Corollary 1 with $i^* = 1$ (note that the comparison system is in this case equivalent to the original essentially non-negative system in the new variables b_1, b_2). However, there is *no* polynomial function B that can act as a scalar barrier certificate. For contradiction, assume there is such a (continuous) B. The verification problem requires that $B(x_1, x_2)$ evaluates to 0 whenever $x_1 = 0 \wedge x_2 \leq 0$ holds, therefore the univariate polynomial $B(0, x_2)$ has infinitely many real roots and is therefore the zero polynomial, from which we conclude that $B(x_1, x_2)$ has real roots on the entire line $x_1 = 0$. The set $B(x_1, x_2) \leq 0$ thus cannot be a continuous invariant (and B is therefore not a convex or an 'exponential-type' barrier certificate) because any trajectory initialized from $x_1 = 0 \wedge x_2 > 0$ enters the unsafe set where the function B is required to be positive.   □

Vector barrier certificates can also exist with lower polynomial degrees than is possible with scalar barrier certificates. To take an example, consider the verification problem (with $x_1' = x_2, x_2' = x_1$, as that in the above proof) illustrated in Fig. 2, where the initial states are represented by the green rectangle $[-7, -\frac{1}{2}] \times [-4, -\frac{3}{2}]$ and the unsafe states by the red circle of radius $\sqrt{2}$ centred at $(-3, 2)$. The vector barrier certificate $(B_1, B_2) = (x_1, x_2)$ is *linear* in each component (i.e. has polynomial degree 1) and satisfies all the conditions required by Theorem 3 and Corollary 1. However, there is no *linear/affine* function that is a *scalar* barrier certificate for this problem because

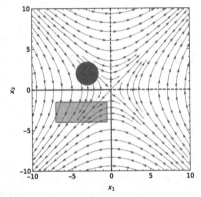

Fig. 2. Vector barrier certificate $(B_1, B_2) = (x_1, x_2)$. (Colour figure online)

there is no half-plane that includes all the initial states, no unsafe states, and is invariant under the dynamics (i.e. such that trajectories cannot escape). This holds because any line separating the two sets cannot have slope 1 or -1, which are the only possible values for slope of a linear function defining an invariant half-plane in this system.

As with barrier certificates based on scalar comparison systems, one is able to extract invariant sets from the vector generalization; the class of invariants one can extract is, in fact, richer. For example, given a vector differential inequality $B' \leq AB$, where A is essentially non-negative, one may extract a *conjunctive* invariant $\bigwedge_{i=1}^{m} B_i \leq 0$. Furthermore, the constituent conjuncts $B_i \leq 0$ of such a conjunction need not define invariant sets in their own right.

4.4   Generating Vector Barrier Certificates Using SDP

Generation of vector barrier certificates based on Corollary 1 using sum-of-squares optimization can be performed with a straightforward generalization of corresponding techniques for scalar barrier certificates [37]. Let us assume that the sets Init, Unsafe, Q are characterized by the conjunctions: $\bigwedge_{i=1}^{a} I_i \geq 0$, $\bigwedge_{i=1}^{b} U_i \geq 0$, and $\bigwedge_{i=1}^{c} Q_i \geq 0$ respectively, where I_i, U_i, Q_i are polynomials. Fix a small, positive constant $\epsilon > 0$, and fix an essentially non-negative $m \times m$ matrix A. Let B_i be template polynomials, and $\sigma_{I_{i,j}}, \sigma_{U_j}, \sigma_{Q_{i,j}}$ be sum-of-squares template polynomials.[9] The following is a sum-of-squares optimization problem for size m vector barrier certificates $B_1, B_2, \ldots, B_m$, with $i^* \in \{1, \ldots, m\}$:

$$-B_i - \Sigma_{j=1}^{a}\sigma_{I_{i,j}}I_j \geq 0 \text{ for all } i = 1, 2, \ldots, m \qquad \textbf{(VBC 1)}$$

$$B_{i^*} - \Sigma_{j=1}^{b}\sigma_{U_j}U_j - \epsilon \geq 0 \qquad \textbf{(VBC 2)}$$

$$\Sigma_{j=1}^{m} A_{ij}B_j - B_i' - \Sigma_{j=1}^{c}\sigma_{Q_{i,j}}Q_j \geq 0 \text{ for all } i = 1, 2, \ldots, m \qquad \textbf{(VBC 3)}$$

The three optimization constraints ensure that the corresponding **VBC** condition holds for the resulting B_i. We show an example of barrier certificates that can be generated by this method.

Example 1 (Linear barriers). Consider the following 3-dimensional system:

$$x_1' = 2x_1 + x_2 + 2x_3 - x_1^2 + x_1x_3 - x_3^2,$$
$$x_2' = -2 + x_1 - x_2 - x_2^2,$$
$$x_3' = -2 - x_2 - x_3 + x_1^2 - x_1x_3,$$

where Init is defined by $\bigwedge_{i=1}^{3} -x_i \geq 0$, Unsafe by $x_1 + x_2 + x_3 \geq 1$, and there is no evolution constraint. Using the matrix $A = \begin{pmatrix} 0 & 1 & 2 \\ 1 & -1 & 0 \\ 1 & 0 & 1 \end{pmatrix}$, $i^* = 1$, and the sum-of-squares solver SOSTOOLS [30], we obtain the following *true* vector barrier certificate by manually tweaking the floating-point coefficients returned by the solver.[10] Observe that neither $B_1 \leq 0$ nor $B_2 \leq 0$ define invariant sets.

$$B_1 = (365x_1 + 365x_2 + 365x_3 - 60)/100,$$
$$B_2 = (175x_1 + 180x_2 + 100x_3 - 160)/100,$$
$$B_3 = (460x_1 + 155x_2 + 270x_3 - 250)/100.$$

Alternatives to SDP. There exist a number of alternatives to semi-definite programming which can be employed to generate vector barrier certificates. For example, constraint programming techniques for solving inequality constraints over the reals were studied by Ratschan [39] and applied to search for Lyapunov-like functions [40]. Computation of strict barrier certificates using interval constraint satisfaction techniques was later investigated by

---

[9] Template polynomials are polynomials of fixed degree, but with symbolic coefficients. Sum-of-squares optimization searches for appropriate values for these coefficients.

[10] Numerical inaccuracies plague SOS-based approaches to generating all types of barrier certificates and render most generated barrier certificates subtly incorrect. Mitigating this issue is an important, but orthogonal, question that has been investigated elsewhere [32,43].

Bouissou [5], Djaballah et al. [12]. Another intriguing alternative studied by Sankaranarayanan et al. [44] (and later Yang et al. [50]) is the linear relaxation approach based on so-called Handelman representations [21] (which allow the use of linear programming to establish the positive semi-definite property of a polynomial over a compact convex polyhedron); this technique was observed to be much less prone to numerical errors than methods based on interior-point solvers. These approaches, however, are limited to problems with bounded domains.

5   Limitations and Outlook

The trade-off in employing the vector comparison principle comes down to the following: the relaxation of requirements on each individual component of the vector function comes at the price of increased complexity (due to increased dimension) of the comparison system. Already in the scalar ($m = 1$) special case corresponding to the 'exponential-type' barrier certificate, the choice of the single coefficient λ in the comparison system $b' = \lambda b$ was observed to impact the results [22]. Our approach provides more flexibility but also requires more choices in the essentially non-negative matrix A. While we do not yet have general heuristics, a possible strategy for picking alternative matrices A when the initial choice fails is to change the values of the matrix in a way that changes the qualitative behaviour of the trajectories of the comparison system $b' = Ab$ (i.e. changes the structure of the *phase portrait*; see e.g. [3, Chap. 5, pp. 147–149]). It is clear that in practice one should always attempt to find a scalar barrier certificate ($m = 1$) first and proceed to increase the dimension m of the comparison system if the search was unsuccessful (for example due to numerical inaccuracies when polynomials of high degree are involved [11]). Vector barrier certificates could alleviate some of these problems because they allow us to reduce the polynomial degree of the barriers. An empirical study of this trade-off (and indeed of existing scalar notions of barrier certificates) falls outside of the scope of this work and would require a large set of verification benchmarks to be objective, but presents an interesting direction for further investigation.

   We remark, however, that scalar comparison systems, even when they are insufficient to prove the safety property at hand, may reveal structure in the dynamics which could help in constructing an appropriate comparison system for vector barrier certificates. The proposition below is a direct consequence of a property of essentially non-negative (Metzler) matrices, akin to the Perron-Frobenius theorem for non-negative matrices which establishes the existence of an eigenvector in the non-negative orthant (e.g. see [46, Proposition 1]).

Proposition 1. *For a given system of ODEs $x' = f(x)$ and an essentially non-negative matrix, $A \in \mathbb{R}^{m \times m}$, if $B = (B_1, B_2, \ldots, B_m)$ satisfies the system of differential inequalities $B' \leq AB$, then there exists a scalar function g and a scalar μ such that $g' \leq \mu g$.*

Proof. Since A is Metzler, then its transpose, A^T, is also a Metzler matrix. Let $\boldsymbol{u}$ be an eigenvector of A^T in the non-negative orthant with eigenvalue μ, i.e. $A^T\boldsymbol{u} = \mu\boldsymbol{u}$. Then, the scalar product $g := \boldsymbol{u} \cdot \boldsymbol{B}$ satisfies the scalar comparison inequality: $g' = \boldsymbol{u} \cdot \boldsymbol{B}' \leq \boldsymbol{u} \cdot (A\boldsymbol{B}) = (A^T\boldsymbol{u}) \cdot \boldsymbol{B} = (\mu\boldsymbol{u}) \cdot \boldsymbol{B} = \mu g$. The inequality is justified since all the components of the vector $\boldsymbol{u}$ are non-negative. □

The (real) eigenvalue μ is in fact the *dominant eigenvalue* (also called the *spectral abscissa*) of A: it is the maximum of the real parts of all the eigenvalues of A which coincides with the Perron-Frobenius root of A if A is non-negative. As a consequence, if a linear scalar comparison system cannot be found for a given scalar λ, one can rule out Metzler matrices with dominant eigenvalue below λ.

6 Related Work

In [11], Dai *et al.* explored an approach for combining more than one barrier certificate in order to prove safety in examples where a single barrier certificate could not be found (see [11, Lemmas 3 and 4]). However, these so-called *combined barrier certificates* only use the scalar variant of the comparison principle, i.e. for each barrier function B_i, a differential inequality of the form $B_i' \leq \omega_i(B_i)$ is considered, where $\omega_i : \mathbb{R} \to \mathbb{R}$ is a *univariate* analytic function, rather than a *multivariate* quasi-monotone increasing function, as we do in the vector barrier certificate framework. The way combined barrier certificates are constructed in [11] is closely related to the principle of *differential cuts* (DC), which was explored previously [15,33]. Platzer and Clarke [34] investigated ways of automatically generating *differential invariants*, which lift convex/weak barrier certificates from defining invariant sub-level sets of differentiable functions to formulas which can feature Boolean combinations of equalities and inequalities and thus describe a richer class of continuous invariants. In this paper we pursued a fundamentally different generalization; however, we remark that purely conjunctive differential invariants (of the form $\bigwedge_{i=1}^{m} B_i \leq 0$) in [34] reduce to the special case of vector barrier certificates where the matrix A is the zero matrix. Besides the method of barrier certificates, a number of other complementary methods are available for safety verification of continuous and hybrid systems, e.g. [8,13,14,29,35,47] (an overview of some techniques may be found in [16]).[11]

7 Conclusion

The comparison principle used in control theory and applied mathematics offers a powerful mechanism for creating abstractions of ODEs. In the domain of safety verification this principle can – in a very natural way – provide a theoretically

---

[11] Note, however, that the article [16] reproduces the unsound version of non-convex barrier certificates from [37], i.e. using the condition $\forall \boldsymbol{x} \in \mathbb{R}^n.(Q \wedge B = 0 \to B' \leq 0)$.

satisfying foundation for understanding existing (scalar) notions of barrier certificates reported in [11,22,37]. Adopting the comparison principle viewpoint leads naturally to consider existing generalizations of this principle. In this vein, a multi-dimensional generalization of the method of barrier certificates (vector barrier certificates) has been formulated, in which the conditions on the derivative of barrier functions are relaxed in a way analogous to vector Lyapunov functions [2]. In the linear special case of this multidimensional extension (Corollary 1), the convexity of the search space can be preserved, allowing the use of tractable semi-definite programming techniques to search for more general classes of barrier certificates satisfying the semantic principle (Lemma 1) than was previously possible.

Acknowledgements. The authors would like to thank the FM 2018 reviewers for their feedback, constructive criticisms and suggestions, and extend special thanks to Dr. Stefan Mitsch and Brandon Bohrer at Carnegie Mellon University for their detailed comments and scrutiny.

References

1. Beckenbach, E.F.: Inequalities. Ergebnisse der Mathematik und ihrer Grenzgebiete, vol. 30. Springer, New York (1961). https://doi.org/10.1007/978-3-642-64971-4
2. Bellman, R.: Vector Lyapunov functions. SIAM J. Control Optim. **1**(1), 32–34 (1962)
3. Birkhoff, G., Rota, G.C.: Ordinary Differential Equations. Wiley, New York (1989)
4. Blanchini, F.: Set invariance in control. Automatica **35**(11), 1747–1767 (1999)
5. Bouissou, O., Chapoutot, A., Djaballah, A., Kieffer, M.: Computation of parametric barrier functions for dynamical systems using interval analysis. In: 53rd IEEE Conference on Decision and Control, CDC 2014, Los Angeles, CA, USA, 15–17 December 2014, pp. 753–758. IEEE (2014)
6. Brauer, F.: Global behavior of solutions of ordinary differential equations. J. Math. Anal. Appl. **2**(1), 145–158 (1961)
7. Brauer, F.: Some refinements of Lyapunov's second method. Canad. J. Math. **17**, 811–819 (1965)
8. Chen, X., Ábrahám, E., Sankaranarayanan, S.: Taylor model flowpipe construction for non-linear hybrid systems. In: Proceedings of the 33rd IEEE Real-Time Systems Symposium, RTSS 2012, San Juan, PR, USA, 4–7 December 2012, pp. 183–192. IEEE Computer Society (2012)
9. Collins, G.E., Hong, H.: Partial cylindrical algebraic decomposition for quantifier elimination. J. Symb. Comput. **12**(3), 299–328 (1991)
10. Conti, R.: Sulla prolungabilità delle soluzioni di un sistema di equazioni differenziali ordinarie. Bollettino dell'Unione Matematica Italiana **11**(4), 510–514 (1956)
11. Dai, L., Gan, T., Xia, B., Zhan, N.: Barrier certificates revisited. J. Symb. Comput. **80**(1), 62–86 (2017)
12. Djaballah, A., Chapoutot, A., Kieffer, M., Bouissou, O.: Construction of parametric barrier functions for dynamical systems using interval analysis. Automatica **78**, 287–296 (2017)

13. Fan, C., Kapinski, J., Jin, X., Mitra, S.: Locally optimal reach set over-approximation for nonlinear systems. In: 2016 International Conference on Embedded Software, EMSOFT 2016, Pittsburgh, Pennsylvania, USA, 1–7 October 2016, pp. 6:1–6:10. ACM (2016)
14. Frehse, G., et al.: SpaceEx: scalable verification of hybrid systems. In: Gopalakrishnan, G., Qadeer, S. (eds.) CAV 2011. LNCS, vol. 6806, pp. 379–395. Springer, Heidelberg (2011). https://doi.org/10.1007/978-3-642-22110-1_30
15. Ghorbal, K., Sogokon, A., Platzer, A.: A hierarchy of proof rules for checking positive invariance of algebraic and semi-algebraic sets. Comput. Lang. Syst. Struct. **47**, 19–43 (2017)
16. Guéguen, H., Lefebvre, M., Zaytoon, J., Nasri, O.: Safety verification and reachability analysis for hybrid systems. Ann. Rev. Control **33**(1), 25–36 (2009)
17. Gunderson, R.W.: A stability condition for linear comparison systems. Quart. Appl. Math. **29**(2), 327–328 (1971)
18. Habets, P., Peiffer, K.: Classification of stability-like concepts and their study using vector Lyapunov functions. J. Math. Anal. Appl. **43**(2), 537–570 (1973)
19. Haddad, W.M., Chellaboina, V.: Nonlinear Dynamical Systems and Control, A Lyapunov-Based Approach. Princeton University Press, Princeton (2008)
20. Hale, J.K., LaSalle, J.P.: Differential equations: linearity vs. nonlinearity. SIAM Rev. **5**(3), 249–272 (1963)
21. Handelman, D.: Representing polynomials by positive linear functions on compact convex polyhedra. Pac. J. Math. **132**(1), 35–62 (1988)
22. Kong, H., He, F., Song, X., Hung, W.N.N., Gu, M.: Exponential-condition-based barrier certificate generation for safety verification of hybrid systems. In: Sharygina, N., Veith, H. (eds.) CAV 2013. LNCS, vol. 8044, pp. 242–257. Springer, Heidelberg (2013). https://doi.org/10.1007/978-3-642-39799-8_17
23. Lakshmikantham, V., Leela, S.: Differential and Integral Inequalities: Theory and Applications. Volume I: Ordinary Differential Equations. Academic Press, New York (1969)
24. Lakshmikantham, V., Matrosov, V.M., Sivasundaram, S.: Vector Lyapunov Functions and Stability Analysis of Nonlinear Systems. Mathematics and Its Applications, vol. 63. Springer, Dordrecht (1991). https://doi.org/10.1007/978-94-015-7939-1
25. Liu, J., Zhan, N., Zhao, H.: Computing semi-algebraic invariants for polynomial dynamical systems. In: Chakraborty, S., Jerraya, A., Baruah, S.K., Fischmeister, S. (eds.) Proceedings of Ninth ACM International Conference on Embedded Software, EMSOFT 2011, 9–14 October 2011, pp. 97–106. ACM (2011)
26. Lyapunov, A.M.: The general problem of stability of motion. Int. J. Control **55**, 531–773 (1992). Comm. Math. Soc. Kharkov (1892), English translation
27. Matrosov, V.M.: On the theory of stability of motion. Prikl. Mat. Mekh. **26**(6), 1506–1522 (1962). English translation (1962)
28. Michel, A.N., Miller, R.K.: Qualitative Analysis of Large Scale Dynamical Systems. Mathematics in Science and Engineering, vol. 134. Academic Press, New York (1977)
29. Mitchell, I., Tomlin, C.J.: Level set methods for computation in hybrid systems. In: Lynch, N., Krogh, B.H. (eds.) HSCC 2000. LNCS, vol. 1790, pp. 310–323. Springer, Heidelberg (2000). https://doi.org/10.1007/3-540-46430-1_27
30. Papachristodoulou, A., Anderson, J., Valmorbida, G., Prajna, S., Seiler, P., Parrilo, P.A.: SOSTOOLS version 3.00 sum of squares optimization toolbox for MATLAB. CoRR abs/1310.4716 (2013)

31. Parrilo, P.A.: Structured semidefinite programs and semialgebraic geometry methods in robustness and optimization. Ph.D. thesis, California Institute of Technology, May 2000
32. Peyrl, H., Parrilo, P.A.: Computing sum of squares decompositions with rational coefficients. Theor. Comput. Sci. **409**(2), 269–281 (2008)
33. Platzer, A.: The structure of differential invariants and differential cut elimination. Log. Meth. Comput. Sci. **8**(4), 1–38 (2012)
34. Platzer, A., Clarke, E.M.: Computing differential invariants of hybrid systems as fixedpoints. Formal Meth. Syst. Des. **35**(1), 98–120 (2009)
35. Platzer, A., Tan, Y.K.: Differential equation axiomatization: the impressive power of differential ghosts. In: Dawar, A., Grädel, E. (eds.) LICS. ACM, New York (2018)
36. Prajna, S.: Optimization-based methods for nonlinear and hybrid systems verification. Ph.D. thesis, California Institute of Technology, January 2005
37. Prajna, S., Jadbabaie, A.: Safety verification of hybrid systems using barrier certificates. In: Alur, R., Pappas, G.J. (eds.) HSCC 2004. LNCS, vol. 2993, pp. 477–492. Springer, Heidelberg (2004). https://doi.org/10.1007/978-3-540-24743-2_32
38. Prajna, S., Jadbabaie, A., Pappas, G.J.: A framework for worst-case and stochastic safety verification using barrier certificates. IEEE Trans. Autom. Control **52**(8), 1415–1428 (2007)
39. Ratschan, S.: Efficient solving of quantified inequality constraints over the real numbers. ACM Trans. Comput. Log. **7**(4), 723–748 (2006)
40. Ratschan, S., She, Z.: Providing a basin of attraction to a target region of polynomial systems by computation of Lyapunov-like functions. SIAM J. Control Optim. **48**(7), 4377–4394 (2010)
41. Richardson, D.: Some undecidable problems involving elementary functions of a real variable. J. Symb. Log. **33**(4), 514–520 (1968)
42. Rouche, N., Habets, P., Laloy, M.: Stability Theory by Liapunov's Direct Method. Applied Mathematical Sciences, vol. 22. Springer, New York (1977). https://doi.org/10.1007/978-1-4684-9362-7
43. Roux, P., Voronin, Y.-L., Sankaranarayanan, S.: Validating numerical semidefinite programming solvers for polynomial invariants. In: Rival, X. (ed.) SAS 2016. LNCS, vol. 9837, pp. 424–446. Springer, Heidelberg (2016). https://doi.org/10.1007/978-3-662-53413-7_21
44. Sankaranarayanan, S., Chen, X., Ábrahám, E.: Lyapunov function synthesis using Handelman representations. In: Tarbouriech, S., Krstic, M. (eds.) 9th IFAC Symposium on Nonlinear Control Systems, NOLCOS 2013, Toulouse, France, 4–6 September 2013, pp. 576–581. International Federation of Automatic Control (2013)
45. Sloth, C., Pappas, G.J., Wiśniewski, R.: Compositional safety analysis using barrier certificates. In: Dang, T., Mitchell, I.M. (eds.) Proceedings of Hybrid Systems: Computation and Control, HSCC 2012, 17–19 April 2012, pp. 15–24. ACM (2012)
46. Son, N.K., Hinrichsen, D.: Robust stability of positive continuous time systems. Numer. Funct. Anal. Optim. **17**(5–6), 649–659 (1996)
47. Tiwari, A.: Abstractions for hybrid systems. Formal Meth. Syst. Des. **32**(1), 57–83 (2008)
48. Walter, W.: Differential inequalities and maximum principles: theory, new methods and applications. Nonlinear Anal. Theor. Meth. Appl. **30**(8), 4695–4711 (1997). Proceedings of the Second World Congress of Nonlinear Analysts
49. Walter, W.: Ordinary Differential Equations. Undergraduate Texts in Mathematics. Springer, New York (1998)

50. Yang, Z., Huang, C., Chen, X., Lin, W., Liu, Z.: A linear programming relaxation based approach for generating barrier certificates of hybrid systems. In: Fitzgerald, J., Heitmeyer, C., Gnesi, S., Philippou, A. (eds.) FM 2016. LNCS, vol. 9995, pp. 721–738. Springer, Cham (2016). https://doi.org/10.1007/978-3-319-48989-6_44
51. Yoshizawa, T.: Stability Theory by Liapunov's Second Method. Publications of the Mathematical Society of Japan, vol. 9. The Mathematical Society of Japan, Tokyo (1966)

Timed Vacuity

Hana Chockler[1], Shibashis Guha[2(✉)], and Orna Kupferman[3]

[1] King's College London, London, UK
[2] Université Libre de Bruxelles, Brussels, Belgium
shibashis.guha@ulb.ac.be
[3] The Hebrew University, Jerusalem, Israel

Abstract. Vacuity is a leading sanity check in model-checking, applied when the system is found to satisfy the specification. The check detects situations where the specification passes in a trivial way, say when a specification that requires every request to be followed by a grant is satisfied in a system with no requests. Such situations typically reveal problems in the modelling of the system or the specification, and indeed vacuity detection is a part of most industrial model-checking tools.

Existing research and tools for vacuity concern discrete-time systems and specification formalisms. We introduce *real-time vacuity*, which aims to detect problems with real-time modelling. Real-time logics are used for the specification and verification of systems with a continuous-time behavior. We study vacuity for the branching real-time logic TCTL, and focus on vacuity with respect to the time constraints in the specification. Specifically, the logic TCTL includes the temporal operator U^J, which specifies real-time eventualities in real-time systems: the parameter $J \subseteq \mathbb{R}_{\geq 0}$ is an interval with integral boundaries that bounds the time in which the eventuality should hold. We define several tightenings for the U^J operator. These tightenings require the eventuality to hold within a strict subset of J. We prove that vacuity detection for TCTL is PSPACE-complete, thus it does not increase the complexity of model-checking of TCTL. Our contribution involves an extension, termed TCTL$^+$, of TCTL, which allows the interval J not to be continuous, and for which model checking stays in PSPACE. Finally, we describe a method for ranking vacuity results according to their significance.

1 Introduction

In temporal logic model-checking, we verify the correctness of a system with respect to a desired behavior by checking whether a mathematical model of the system satisfies a temporal-logic formula that specifies this behavior [12]. When the formula fails to hold in the model, the model checker returns a counterexample — some erroneous execution of the system [13]. In the last years there has been a growing awareness of the need of suspecting positive results of the model-checking process, as errors may hide in the modelling of the system or the behavior [22]. As an example, consider the property $G(req \rightarrow F\,grant)$ ("every request is eventually granted"). This property is clearly satisfied in a system in

© Springer International Publishing AG, part of Springer Nature 2018
K. Havelund et al. (Eds.): FM 2018, LNCS 10951, pp. 438–455, 2018.
https://doi.org/10.1007/978-3-319-95582-7_26

which requests are never sent. It does so, however, in a *vacuous* (non-interesting) way, suggesting a suspicious behavior of the system.

In [6], Beer et al. suggested a first formal treatment of vacuity. As described there, vacuity is a serious problem: "our experience has shown that typically 20% of specifications pass vacuously during the first formal-verification runs of a new hardware design, and that vacuous passes always point to a real problem in either the design or its specification or environment" [6]. In the last decade, the challenge of detecting vacuous satisfaction has attracted significant attention (c.f., [5, 7–9, 11, 18–20, 23, 25–27]).

Different definitions for vacuity exist in the literature and are used in practice. The most commonly used ones are based on the "mutation approach" of [6] and its generalization, as defined in [24]. Consider a model M satisfying a specification Φ. A subformula ψ of Φ *does not affect* (the satisfaction of) Φ in M if M satisfies also the (stronger) formula $\Phi[\psi \leftarrow \bot]$, obtained from Φ by changing ψ in the most challenging way. Thus, if ψ appears positively in Φ, the symbol $\bot$ stands for *false*, and if ψ is negative, then $\bot$ is *true*[1]. We say that M satisfies Φ vacuously if Φ has a subformula that does not affect Φ in M. Consider for example the formula $\Phi = G(req \rightarrow F grant)$ described above. In order to check whether the subformula *grant* affects the satisfaction of Φ, we model check $\Phi[grant \leftarrow false]$, which is equivalent to $G \neg req$. That is, a model with no requests satisfies Φ vacuously. In order to check whether the subformula *req* affects the satisfaction of Φ, we model check $\Phi[req \leftarrow true]$. This is equivalent to $GF grant$, thus a model with infinitely many *grant* signals satisfies Φ vacuously.

So far, research on vacuity has been chiefly limited to systems with a *discrete-time* behavior, modeled by means of labeled finite state-transition graphs. More and more systems nowadays have a *continuous-time* behavior. This includes embedded systems, mixed-signal circuits, general software-controlled physical systems, and cyber-physical systems. Such systems are modeled by *timed transition systems* [2], and their behaviors are specified by *real-time logics* [4]. Some preliminary study of vacuity for the linear real-time logic MITL [3] has been done in [16]. The framework there, however, considers only mutations that change literals in the formula to *true* or *false*. Thus, it adapts the propositional approach of [6,24] and does not involve mutations applied to the real-time aspects of the specifications.

In this paper, we extend the general notion of vacuity to the satisfaction of real-time properties. We focus on the temporal logic *Timed Computation Tree Logic* (TCTL, for short) [1]. The logic TCTL has a single temporal operator U^J, where $J \subseteq \mathbb{R}_{\geq 0}$ is an interval with integer bounds. The semantics of TCTL is defined over *Timed Transition Systems* (TTSs, for short). A TTS is typically generated by a timed automaton (TA) [2], which is an automaton equipped with a finite set of clocks, and whose transitions are guarded by clock constraints.

---

[1] The above definition assumes that ψ appears once in Φ, or at least that all its occurrences are of the same polarity; a definition that is independent of this assumption replaces ψ by a universally quantified proposition [5]. Alternatively, one could focus on a single occurrence of ψ.

The mutations we apply to TCTL formulas in order to examine real-time vacuity concern the U^J operator. Unlike the approach in [6,16,24], our mutations are applied to the real-time parameter, namely the interval J. The semantics of timed eventualities suggests two conceptually different types of strengthening for the U^J operator. First, we may tighten the upper bound for the satisfaction of the eventuality; that is, reduce the right boundary of J. Such a mutation corresponds to a check whether the specification could have actually required the eventuality to be satisfied more quickly. Second, we may reduce the span of J, namely replace it by a strict subset. Such a mutation corresponds to a check whether the specification could have been more precise about the time in which the eventuality has to be satisfied. From a technical point of view, when replacing the interval J by a strict subset J' (that is, $J' \subset J \subseteq \mathbb{R}_{\geq 0}$), we distinguish between cases where J' is continuous (that is, J' is an interval of the form $[m_1, m_2]$, $(m_1, m_2]$, $[m_1, m_2)$, or (m_1, m_2), for $m_1, m_2 \in \mathbb{N}$), and cases where J' is not continuous; that is, J' is a union of intervals. Dually, a specification may be weakened, again by two types of mutations, which replace J by an interval or a union of intervals J' such that $J \subset J'$.

Given a TTS M and a TCTL formula Φ, we say that a subformula ψ with a U^J operator (that is, ψ is $A\Phi_1 U^J \Phi_2$ or $E\Phi_1 U^J \Phi_2$) is not tight in Φ with respect to M if J can be strengthened to J' and still M satisfies Φ with the tighter eventuality. For example, if $\psi = A\Phi_1 U^J \Phi_2$, then M satisfies $\Phi[\psi \leftarrow A\Phi_1 U^{J'} \Phi_2]$. We say that Φ is *timed-vacuous* in M if $M \models \Phi$ and has a subformula ψ that is not tight in Φ. Note that timed vacuity is interesting only in cases ψ affects the satisfaction of Φ in M in the untimed case. In other words, if we could have mutated ψ to *true* or *false* without affecting the satisfaction of Φ in M, then clearly mutating J is not interesting. Thus, while we focus in this paper on timed vacuity, it is important to combine it with traditional vacuity checks. Consider for example the formula $\Phi = G(req \rightarrow F^{[0,4]} grant)$, asking each request to be satisfied within 4 time units. In order to check whether the subformula $F^{[0,4]} grant$ is tight, we can model check $\Phi[F^{[0,4]} grant \leftarrow F^{[0,1]} grant]$, where requests are asked to be satisfied within 1 time unit. A model that satisfies the stronger specification then satisfies Φ timed vacuously.

The need to consider mutations in which J' is not continuous results in formulas that are not in TCTL. Indeed, in the U^J operator in TCTL, the interval J is continuous, and we would like to examine mutations that replace, for example, the interval $[0, 4]$ by the union of the intervals $[0, 1] \cup [3, 4]$. We introduce an extension TCTL$^+$ of TCTL that allows to express eventualities that occurs in a union of a constant number of intervals with integral boundaries. We prove that the complexity of TCTL$^+$ model-checking is PSPACE-complete, thus it is not more complex than TCTL model checking. The PSPACE model-checking procedure for TCTL$^+$ leads to a PSPACE algorithm for timed vacuity, and we provide a matching lower bound.

In the case of traditional vacuity, it has been recognized that vacuity results differ in their significance. While in many cases vacuity results are valued as highly informative, there are also cases in which the results are viewed as meaningless by users. Typically, a user gets a long list of mutations that are satisfied, each pointing to a different cause for vacuous satisfaction. In [15], the authors suggest a framework for *ranking of vacuity results* for LTL formulas. The framework is based on the *probability* of the mutated specification to hold in a random computation: the lower the probability of the mutation to hold is, the more alarming the vacuity information is. For example, the probability of $G\neg req$ to hold in a random computation is low, hence if the system satisfies it, this probably needs to be examined. We suggest an extension of the framework to TCTL. The extension involves two technical challenges. First, moving to a branching-time setting requires the development of a probabilistic space for trees (rather than computations). Second, the timed setting requires the probabilistic space to capture continuous time. We argue that once we move to an approximated reasoning about the probability of the mutations, the framework in [15] can be easily extended to TCTL, thus vacuity results can be ranked efficiently.

2   Preliminaries

2.1   TCTL, Timed Automata, and Timed Transition Systems

We assume that the reader is familiar with the branching time temporal logic CTL. We consider the logic Timed CTL (TCTL) [1], which is a real time extension of CTL. Formulas in TCTL are defined over a set AP of atomic propositions and use two path quantifiers A (for all paths) and E (exists a path), and one temporal operator U^J. A TCTL path formula is defined by the syntax $\varphi ::= \Phi_1 U^J \Phi_2$, where $J \subseteq \mathbb{R}_{\geq 0}$ is an interval whose bounds are natural numbers. Thus, the interval J is of the form $[m_1, m_2], (m_1, m_2], [m_1, m_2),$ or (m_1, m_2), for $m_1, m_2 \in \mathbb{N}$ and $m_1 \leq m_2$. For right-open intervals, we have $m_2 = \infty$. We refer to the quantity $m_2 - m_1$ as the *span* of J. Note that the next-step X operator of CTL is absent in TCTL, as time is considered to be continuous.

A timed automaton (TA, for short) is a non-deterministic finite state automaton that allows modelling of actions or events to take place at specific time instants or within a time interval. A TA expresses timed behaviours using a finite number of clock variables. All the clocks increase at the same rate. We use lower case letters x, y, z to denote clock variables and C to denote the set of clock variables. Clock variables take non-negative real values.

A *guard* is a conjunction of assertions of the form $x \sim k$ where $x \in C$, $k \in \mathbb{N}$ and $\sim \in \{\leq, <, =, >, \geq\}$. We use $\mathcal{B}(C)$ to denote the set of guards. A *clock valuation* or a valuation for short is a point $v \in \mathbb{R}_{\geq 0}^C$. For a clock $x \in C$, we use $v(x)$ to denote the value of clock x in v. We use $\lfloor v(x) \rfloor$ to denote the integer part of $v(x)$ while $frac(v(x))$ is used to denote the fractional part of $v(x)$. We define $\lceil v(x) \rceil$ as $\lfloor v(x) \rfloor + 1$ if $frac(v(x)) \neq 0$, else $\lceil v(x) \rceil = \lfloor v(x) \rfloor$. Along with other propositions, we will also use propositions of the form $v(x) \in J$, where $v(x)$ is the valuation of clock x and J is an interval with integer boundaries.

For a clock valuation v and $d \in \mathbb{R}_{\geq 0}$, we use $v + d$ to denote the clock valuation where every clock is being increased by d. Formally, for each $d \in \mathbb{R}_{\geq 0}$, the valuation $v + d$ is such that for every $x \in C$, we have $(v + d)(x) = v(x) + d$.

For a clock valuation v and a set $R \subseteq C$, we use $v_{[R \leftarrow \overline{0}]}$ to denote the clock valuation in which every clock in R is set to zero, while the value of the clocks in $C \backslash R$ remains the same as in v. Formally, for each $R \subseteq C$, the valuation $v_{[R \leftarrow \overline{0}]}$ is such that for every $x \in C$, we have

$$
v_{[R \leftarrow \overline{0}]}(x) = \begin{cases} 0 & \text{if } x \in R \\ v(x) & \text{otherwise} \end{cases}
$$

A timed automaton is defined by the tuple $\langle AP, \mathcal{L}, l_0, C, E, L \rangle$, where AP is a set of atomic propositions, $\mathcal{L}$ is a finite set of locations, $l_0 \in L$ is an initial location, C is a finite set of clocks, $E \subseteq \mathcal{L} \times \mathcal{B}(C) \times 2^C \times \mathcal{L}$ is a finite set of edges, and $L : \mathcal{L} \mapsto 2^{AP}$ is a labeling function.

A timed transition system, (TTS for short) [21], is $S = \langle AP, Q, q_0, \rightarrow, \hookrightarrow, L \rangle$, where AP is a set of atomic propositions, Q is a set of states, $q_0 \in Q$ is an initial state, $\rightarrow \subseteq Q \times \mathbb{R}_{\geq 0} \times Q$ is a set of delay transitions, $\hookrightarrow \subseteq Q \times Q$ is a set of discrete transitions, and $L : Q \mapsto 2^{AP}$ is a labelling function. We write $q \xrightarrow{d} q'$ if $(q, d, q') \in \rightarrow$ and write $q \hookrightarrow q'$ if $(q, q') \in \hookrightarrow$.

Let $\mathcal{A} = \langle AP, \mathcal{L}, l_0, C, E, L \rangle$ be a timed automaton. The semantics of a timed automaton is described by a TTS. The timed transition system $T(\mathcal{A})$ generated by $\mathcal{A}$ is defined as $T(\mathcal{A}) = (AP, Q, q_0, \rightarrow, \hookrightarrow, L)$, where

- $Q = \{(l, v) \mid l \in \mathcal{L}, v \in \mathbb{R}_{\geq 0}{}^C\}$. Intuitively, a state (l, v) corresponds to A being in location l and the clock valuation is v. Note that due to the real nature of time, this set is generally uncountable.
- Let v_{init} denote the valuation such that $v_{init}(x) = 0$ for all $x \in C$. Then $q_0 = (l_0, v_{init})$.
- $\rightarrow = \cup_{l \in \mathcal{L}} \cup_{v \in \mathbb{R}_{\geq 0}^C} \cup_{d \in \mathbb{R}_{\geq 0}} \{(l, v), d, (l, v + d)\}$.
- $\hookrightarrow = \{((l, v), (l', v')) \mid (l, v), (l', v') \in Q$ and there is an edge $e = (l, g, R, l') \in E$ and $v \models g$ and $v' = v_{[R \leftarrow \overline{0}]}\}$. That is, if there exists a discrete transition from l that is guarded by g and leads to l' while resetting the clocks in R, then if $v \models g$, the TTS can move from (l, v) to $(l, v_{[R \leftarrow \overline{0}]})$.

A run of a timed automaton is a sequence of the form $\pi = (l_0, v_0), (l_0, v_0'), (l_1, v_1),$ $(l_1, v_1'), (l_2, v_2), \ldots$ where for all $i \geq 0$, we have $(l_i, v_i) \xrightarrow{d_i} (l_i, v_i')$, i.e., $v_i' = v_i + d_i$ and $((l_i, v_i'), (l_i, v_{i+1})) \in \hookrightarrow$. Note that π is a continuous run in the sense that for a delay transition $(l_i, v_i) \xrightarrow{d_i} (l_i, v_i')$, the run also includes all states $(l_i, v_i + d)$ for all $0 \leq d \leq d_i$, where $v_i' = v_i + d_i$. For a time $t_{\geq 0}$, we denote by $\pi[t]$ the state in π that is reached after elapsing time t.

Given a state $s \in Q$ of a TTS, we denote by $Paths(s)$, the set of all runs starting at s. Let AP be a set of action propositions. The satisfaction relation for TCTL formulas is as follows.

- $s \models p$, for $p \in AP$, iff $p \in L(s)$.
- $s \models \neg \Phi$ iff $s \not\models \Phi$.
- $s \models \Phi_1 \wedge \Phi_2$ iff $s \models \Phi_1$ and $s \models \Phi_2$.

- $s \models A\Phi_1 U^J \Phi_2$ iff for all paths $\pi \in Paths(s)$, there exists a time $t \in J$ such that $\pi[t] \models \Phi_2$ and for all $t' < t$, we have $\pi[t'] \models \Phi_1$.
- $s \models E\Phi_1 U^J \Phi_2$ iff there exists a path $\pi \in Paths(s)$ and a time $t \in J$ such that $\pi[t] \models \Phi_2$ and for all $t' < t$, we have $\pi[t'] \models \Phi_1$.

We say that a timed automaton $\mathcal{A}$ satisfies a TCTL formula Φ if the initial state (l_0, v_0) of $T(\mathcal{A})$ satisfies Φ.

Consider a timed automaton $A = \langle AP, \mathcal{L}, l_0, C, E, L \rangle$. For each clock $x \in C$, let M_x be the maximum constant that appears in A. We say that two valuations, v and v', are *region equivalent* with respect to A, denoted $v \equiv v'$, iff the following conditions are satisfied.

1. $\forall x \in C$, we have that $v(x) > M_x$ iff $v'(x) > M_x$, and
2. $\forall x \in C$, if $v(x) \leq M_x$, then $\lfloor v(x) \rfloor = \lfloor v'(x) \rfloor$ and $\lceil v(x) \rceil = \lceil v'(x) \rceil$, and
3. for each pair of clocks $x, y \in C$, if $v(x) \leq M_x$ and $v(y) \leq M_y$, we have $v(x) < v(y)$ iff $v'(x) < v'(y)$.

For a given valuation v, let $[v] = \{v' | v' \equiv v\}$. Note that the region equivalence is actually an equivalence relation. Every such equivalence class is called a *region*. Note that the number of regions is exponential in the number of clocks of a timed automaton. A tuple of the form $\langle l, [v] \rangle$, where $l \in \mathcal{L}$ is a location and $[v]$ is a region is called a *symbolic state* of A. Two valuations v and v' of a symbolic state $\langle l, [v] \rangle$ satisfy the same set of TCTL formulas [1].

A *region graph* is defined using the transition relation $\rightsquigarrow$ between symbolic states which is as follows:

- $(l, [v]) \rightsquigarrow (l, [v'])$ if there exists a $d \in \mathbb{R}_{\geq 0}$ such that $(l, v) \xrightarrow{d} (l, v')$ and
- $(l, [v]) \rightsquigarrow (l', [v'])$ if $(l, v) \hookrightarrow (l', v')$.

We note that the transition relation is finite since there are finitely many symbolic states. The *size of a region graph* equals the sum of the number of regions and the number of transitions in it. The region equivalence relation partitions the uncountably many states into a finite number of symbolic states.

2.2 Timed Vacuity

Consider a TCTL formulas Φ. Let ψ be a subformula of Φ, and let ξ be a TCTL formula. We use $\Phi[\psi \leftarrow \xi]$ to denote the TCTL formula obtained from Φ by replacing ψ by ξ.[2] Consider a TA $\mathcal{A}$ such that $\mathcal{A}$ satisfies Φ. We say that a subformula ψ of Φ *does not affect the satisfaction* of Φ in $\mathcal{A}$ (ψ does not affect Φ in $\mathcal{A}$, for short) if $\mathcal{A}$ satisfies $\Phi[\psi \leftarrow \xi]$ for every formula ξ. The above definition adapts the propositional approach of [6,24] to TCTL, and as we show in Lemma 2, checking this type of vacuity is easy and does not add challenges that are unique to the real-time setting. We thus focus on mutations applied to the real-time operator of TCTL.

---

[2] As discussed on Sect. 1, we assumes that ψ appears once in Φ or focus on a single occurrence of ψ in Φ.

Consider two intervals $J, J' \subseteq \mathbb{R}_{\geq 0}$ such that $J' \subset J$. Clearly, the TCTL formula $Q\Phi_1 U^J \Phi_2$, for $Q \in \{A, E\}$, is weaker than the formula $Q\Phi_1 U^{J'} \Phi_2$. In timed vacuity, we are interested in formulas of the form $Q\Phi_1 U^J \Phi_2$ in which the interval J can be mutated. Rather than considering all subsets of J, we restrict attention to subsets that are intervals or the union of two intervals where the interval boundaries are integers. Formally, we say that J' is a *strengthening* of J if $J' \subset J$ and either J' is an interval or $J' = J_1 \cup J_2$ for intervals J_1 and J_2. For example, $(2, 5]$ and $[2, 3) \cup (4, 5]$ are both strengthenings of $[2, 6)$. Dually, J' is a *weakening* of J if $J \subset J'$ and either J' is an interval or $J' = J_1 \cup J_2$ for continuous J_1 and J_2. We note here that dividing J into more than two intervals might not capture the user's intent.

A subformula ψ of Φ may have either *positive polarity* in Φ, namely be in the scope of an even number of negations, or a *negative polarity* in Φ, namely be in the scope of an odd number of negations (note that an antecedent of an implication is considered to be under negation).

Consider a TA $\mathcal{A}$ and a TCTL formula Φ such that $\mathcal{A} \models \Phi$. Let $\psi = Q\Phi_1 U^J \Phi_2$ be a subformula of Φ. We say that the ψ *is not tight in* Φ with respect to $\mathcal{A}$ if ψ is in a positive polarity and J can be strengthened to J' or ψ is in a negative polarity and J can be weakened to J' and we have that $\mathcal{A} \models \Phi[\psi \leftarrow Q\Phi_1 U^{J'} \Phi_2]$. We say that Φ is *timed-vacuous* in $\mathcal{A}$ if $\mathcal{A} \models \Phi$ and has a subformula ψ that is not tight in Φ.

3   TCTL$^+$ and Its Model Checking

Recall that in the definition of strengthening and weakening, we allowed the replacement of an interval J by the union of intervals. In order to handle such tightenings, we introduce an extension of TCTL, called TCTL$^+$, where path formulas may be a disjunction of formulas of the form $\Phi_1 U^J \Phi_2$. The semantics is extended in the expected way. That is, $s \models A \bigvee_{1 \leq i \leq k} \Phi_1^i U^{J_i} \Phi_2^i$ iff for all paths $\pi \in Paths(s)$ and for every $1 \leq i \leq k$, there exists a time $t_i \in J_i$ such that $\pi[t_i] \models \Phi_2^i$ and for all $t_i' < t_i$, we have $\pi[t_i'] \models \Phi_1^i$. The definition for the existential case is similar.

Remark 1. In CTL, allowing Boolean operations within the path formulas does not extend the expressive power [17]. In particular, the formula $A(Fp \vee Fq)$, for $p, q \in AP$, is equivalent to the CTL formula $AF(p \vee q)$. We conjecture that in the timed setting, Boolean operations within the path formulas do extend the expressive power. In particular, we conjecture that the TCTL$^+$ formula $A(F^{[1,2]}p \vee F^{[3,4]}q)$, does not have an equivalent TCTL formula. We also think that a technical proof for the above statement is highly non-trivial.

In this section we show that model-checking of TCTL$^+$ formulas is PSPACE-complete. First, recall that TCTL model-checking is PSPACE-complete [1]. TCTL model-checking is done by reducing it to CTL model-checking over region graph. Let $\mathcal{A} = \langle AP, \mathcal{L}, l_0, C, E, L \rangle$ be a TA and Φ be a TCTL formula and we want to check if $\mathcal{A} \models \Phi$. Let z be a clock that is not in the set C of clocks of the

TA $\mathcal{A}$. Consider the TTS $T(\mathcal{A})$ generated by $\mathcal{A}$. For a state $s = (l, v)$ in $T(\mathcal{A})$, we denote by $s[z = 0]$, the state (l, v') such that $v' \in \mathbb{R}_{\geq 0}^{C \cup \{z\}}$ and $v'(z) = 0$ and for all clocks $x \in C$, we have $v'(x) = v(x)$. We construct the region graph of $\mathcal{A}$ with this additional clock z such that z is never reset. Now for every state s in the TTS, we say that $s \models E(\Phi_1 U^J \Phi_2)$ iff $s[z = 0] \models E(\Phi_1 U(z \in J \wedge \Phi_2))$ and $s \models A(\Phi_1 U^J \Phi_2)$ iff $s[z = 0] \models A(\Phi_1 U(z \in J \wedge \Phi_2))$.

Algorithm 1. Computation of satisfaction set of TCTL$^+$ formula $\Phi = A(\Phi_1 U^{J_1} \Phi_2 \vee \Phi_3 U^{J_2} \Phi_4)$

Require: Region graph $R_{\mathcal{A}}$ of TA $\mathcal{A}$ extended with a fresh clock z that is never reset and a TCTL$^+$ formula Φ

Ensure: Compute $Sat(\Phi)$

1: $T_1 \leftarrow Sat(z \in J_1) \cap Sat(\Phi_2)$ $\triangleright$ T_1 is the set of vertices (regions) all whose
2:   successors are in $\Phi_1 U^{J_1} \Phi_2$
3: $T_2 \leftarrow Sat(z \in J_2) \cap Sat(\Phi_4)$ $\triangleright$ T_2 is the set of vertices (regions) all whose
4:   successors are in $\Phi_3 U^{J_2} \Phi_4$
5: $T_3 \leftarrow \emptyset$ $\triangleright$ T_3 is the set of vertices (regions) from which some paths satisfy
6:                    $\Phi_1 U^{J_1} \Phi_2$ while the other paths satisfy $\Phi_3 U^{J_2} \Phi_4$
7: $T \leftarrow T_1 \cup T_2$ $\triangleright$ The satisfaction set of Φ, finally also includes T_3
8: $T_4 \leftarrow \emptyset$ $\triangleright$ T_4 is the set of regions r for which all successor regions
9:                              are in T but r itself is not in the satisfaction set T
10: **while** $\{r \in Sat(\Phi_1) \cup Sat(\Phi_3) - (T \cup T_4) \mid Post(r) \subseteq T\} \neq \emptyset$ **do**
11:      Let $r \in Sat(\Phi_1) \cup Sat(\Phi_3) - (T \cup T_4) \mid Post(r) \subseteq T$
12:      **if** $r \in Sat(\Phi_1) - T$ **then**
13:          **if** $Post(r) \subseteq T_1$ **then**
14:              $T_1 \leftarrow T_1 \cup \{r\}$
15:              $T \leftarrow T \cup \{r\}$
16:          **end if**
17:      **end if**
18:      **if** $r \in Sat(\Phi_2) - T$ **then**
19:          **if** $Post(r) \subseteq T_2$ **then**
20:              $T_2 \leftarrow T_2 \cup \{r\}$
21:              $T \leftarrow T \cup \{r\}$
22:          **end if**
23:      **end if**
24:      **if** $r \in Sat(\Phi_1) \cap Sat(\Phi_3) - T$ and $Post(r) \subseteq T$ **then**
25:          **if** there exist two distinct successors r_1 and r_2 of r such that $r_1 \in T1 - T2$ and $r2 \in T2 - T1$ or there exists a successor r' of r such that $r' \in T_3$ **then**
26:              $T_3 \leftarrow T_3 \cup \{r\}$
27:              $T \leftarrow T \cup \{r\}$
28:          **end if**
29:      **end if**
30:      **if** $r \notin T$ **then** $T_4 = T_4 \cup \{r\}$
31:      **end if**
32: **end while**
33: **return** T

Let R_A be the region graph of TA $\mathcal{A}$. The model-checking procedure involves CTL model-checking $(l_0, v_{init})[z = 0] \models \Phi'$, over a region graph over the set $C \cup \{z\}$ of clocks such that clock z is never reset. The formula Φ' is obtained from Φ by modifying the path formulas by introducing subformulas of the form $z \in J$ as mentioned above.

For a TCTL$^+$ formula Φ, the set of regions in the region graph of $\mathcal{A}$ that satisfy Φ is denoted by $Sat(\Phi)$. In Algorithm 1, we give a method to compute the satisfaction set for the TCTL$^+$ formula $\Phi = A(\Phi_1 U^{J_1} \Phi_2 \vee \Phi_3 U^{J_2} \Phi_4)$. Given a region r in a region graph, we denote by $Post(r)$, the set of regions that can be reached from r in a single step, i.e. using the transition $\rightsquigarrow$ once.

The running time of Algorithm 1 is proportional to the size of the region graph and the size of the TCTL$^+$ formula. It is easy to see that it runs in PSPACE. We note here that given a TA and a TCTL formula, model-checking of TCTL also takes time that is proportional to the size of the region graph of the TA and the size of the TCTL formula.

Lemma 1. *Algorithm 1 runs in PSPACE.*

In a TCTL$^+$ formula Φ, if we have arbitrary number of disjunctions of the form $\Phi_{1_1} U^J \Phi_{1_2}, \Phi_{2_1} U^J \Phi_{2_2}, \ldots, \Phi_{n_1} U^J \Phi_{n_2}$, then we need to maintain different subsets of the set $\mathcal{I} = \{J_1, \ldots, J_n\}$ of intervals. For each subset I of $\mathcal{I}$, we have the set of vertices (regions) from which for every member $J \in I$, there exists a path satisfying the disjunct $\Phi_1 U^J \Phi_2$. Hence with arbitrary number of intervals, the algorithm is also exponential in the size of the formula, but is still in PSPACE.

Showing PSPACE-hardness for TCTL$^+$ model-checking follows directly from the complexity of TCTL model-checking, since the syntax of TCTL is a proper subset of the syntax of TCTL$^+$. Thus we have the following theorem.

Theorem 1. *The model-checking problem for TCTL$^+$ is PSPACE-complete.*

4   Satisfying a TCTL Formula Timed Vacuously

In this section, we study the complexity of checking vacuity and timed vacuity in TCTL. We describe algorithms for strengthening an interval J in formulas of the form $Q\Phi_1 U^J \Phi_2$ and algorithms for checking timed vacuity.

4.1   Complexity Results

We start with the propositional approach, where a subformula ψ of Φ does not affect the satisfaction of Φ in a TA $\mathcal{A}$ iff $\mathcal{A}$ satisfies $\Phi[\psi \leftarrow \xi]$ for all formulas ξ. This definition is not effective, as it requires evaluating $\Phi[\psi \leftarrow \xi]$ for all formulas ξ. We first prove that as in the case of CTL [24], also in TCTL it is possible to check only the replacements of ψ by *true* and *false*.

Lemma 2. *For every subformula ψ of a TCTL formula Φ and for every TA $\mathcal{A}$ such that $\mathcal{A} \models \Phi$, if $\mathcal{A} \models \Phi[\psi \leftarrow \bot]$, then for every formula ξ, we have $\mathcal{A} \models \Phi[\psi \leftarrow \xi]$.*

Proof. We prove that for every formula ξ, the implications $\mathcal{A} \models \Phi[\psi \leftarrow \bot] \rightarrow \mathcal{A} \models \Phi[\psi \leftarrow \xi]$. This can be shown by proving $\Phi[\psi \leftarrow \bot] \rightarrow \Phi[\psi \leftarrow \xi]$. The proof is by structural induction on the syntax of TCTL formulas.

We only need to prove the induction step for the subformulas with a timed component, as the other cases are proved in [24].

Let $\Phi = E(\Phi_1 U^J \Phi_2)$. Thus we want to prove that for every formula ξ, we have $E(\Phi_1[\psi \leftarrow \bot] U^J \Phi_2[\psi \leftarrow \bot]) \rightarrow E(\Phi_1[\psi \leftarrow \xi] U^J \Phi_2[\psi \leftarrow \xi])$.

By induction hypothesis, we have that $E(\Phi_1[\psi \leftarrow \bot]) \rightarrow E(\Phi_1[\psi \leftarrow \xi])$ and $E(\Phi_2[\psi \leftarrow \bot]) \rightarrow E(\Phi_2[\psi \leftarrow \xi])$.

Suppose $\mathcal{A} \models E(\Phi[\psi \leftarrow \bot])$. Hence we have a time $t \in J$ and a run $\rho = (l_0, v_0) \xrightarrow{d_0} (l_0, v_0 + d) \xrightarrow{\tau} (l_1, v_1) \xrightarrow{d_1} \ldots \xrightarrow{d_i} (l_i, v_i) \ldots$ such that $t = \sum_{j=0}^{i} d_j$, and $s_i = (l_i, v_i) \models E(\Phi_2[\psi \leftarrow \bot])$. By the induction hypothesis, $(l_i, v_i) \models E(\Phi_2[\psi \leftarrow \xi])$. Also since $\mathcal{A} \models E(\Phi[\psi \leftarrow \bot])$, we have that over all the intermediate (possibly uncountably many) states s in ρ from (l_0, v_0) to s_i and possibly excluding s_i, we have $s \models E(\Phi_1[\psi \leftarrow \bot])$. Again, from the induction hypothesis, we have that $s \models E(\Phi_1[\psi \leftarrow \xi])$. Hence $\mathcal{A} \models E(\Phi_1[\psi \leftarrow \xi] U^J \Phi_2[\psi \leftarrow \xi])$, i.e., $\mathcal{A} \models \Phi[\psi \leftarrow \xi]$.

The proof for $A(\Phi_1 U^J \Phi_2)$ is similar. $\qquad\square$

Theorem 2. *Given a TA $\mathcal{A}$, a TCTL formula Φ and a subformula ψ of Φ such that $\mathcal{A} \models \Phi$, the problem of checking whether ψ does not affect Φ in $\mathcal{A}$ is PSPACE-complete.*

Proof. We prove that the complementary problem, of deciding whether ψ affects Φ in $\mathcal{A}$ is PSPACE-complete. Since PSPACE is closed under complementation, the result follows. The membership follows from the fact that whether ψ affects the satisfaction of Φ in $\mathcal{A}$ can be decided by checking whether $\mathcal{A} \models \Phi[\psi \leftarrow \bot]$ and that TCTL model-checking is PSPACE-complete [1].

We prove PSPACE-hardness using a reduction from TCTL model checking. We construct a formula $\neg \Phi'$, a subformula ψ of $\neg \Phi'$ and a TA $\mathcal{A}'$ such that $\mathcal{A} \models \Phi$ iff ψ affects the satisfaction of $\neg \Phi'$ in $\mathcal{A}'$. Let $\mathcal{A} = \langle AP, \mathcal{L}, l_0, E, C, L \rangle$. We define $\mathcal{A}' = \langle AP', \mathcal{L}, l_0, E, C, L' \rangle$, such that $AP' = AP \cup \{q, r\}$ and $q, r \notin AP$ and $L'(l_0) = L(l_0) \cup \{r\}$ and $L'(l) = L(l)$ for $l \neq l_0 \in \mathcal{L}$. Let $\Phi' = q \wedge \Phi$. Clearly $\mathcal{A}' \not\models \Phi'$ and hence $\mathcal{A}' \models \neg \Phi'$. If $\mathcal{A} \models \Phi$, then considering $\psi = q$ and $\xi = r$, we have that $\mathcal{A}' \models \Phi'[\psi \leftarrow \xi]$, and hence $\mathcal{A}' \not\models \neg \Phi'[\psi \leftarrow \xi]$, i.e., q affects the satisfaction of Φ' in $\mathcal{A}'$. Now consider the case $\mathcal{A} \not\models \Phi$. Then also $\mathcal{A}' \models \Phi$ and hence $\mathcal{A}' \not\models q \wedge \Phi = \Phi'$. Thus if $\mathcal{A} \not\models \Phi$, we still have $\mathcal{A}' \models \neg \Phi'$. For all ξ, we have $\mathcal{A}' \not\models \Phi'[\psi \leftarrow \xi]$, and hence $\mathcal{A}' \models \neg \Phi'[\psi \leftarrow \xi]$, i.e. q does not affect the satisfaction of Φ' in $\mathcal{A}'$. $\qquad\square$

We now proceed to timed vacuity. In Theorem 3 below, we use a reduction from the set consisting of the true quantified boolean formulas (TQBF) which is a canonical PSPACE-complete problem.

Theorem 3. *Given a TA $\mathcal{A}$, a formula Φ such that $\mathcal{A} \models \Phi$ and a subformula $\psi = Q\Phi_1 U^J \Phi_2$ of Φ (where Q stands for a path quantifier A or E), the problem of checking whether ψ is not tight in Φ with respect to $\mathcal{A}$ is PSPACE-complete.*

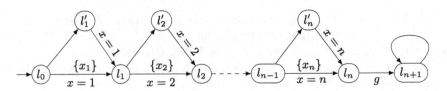

Fig. 1. Timed Automata encoding QBF in the proof of Theorem 3

Proof. We show that the complementary problem, of deciding whether ψ is tight in Φ with respect to $\mathcal{A}$ is PSPACE-complete. Since PSPACE is closed under complementation, the result follows. The membership follows from the fact that whether ψ is tight in Φ with respect to $\mathcal{A}$ can be decided by checking whether $\mathcal{A} \models \Phi[\psi \leftarrow Q\Phi_1 U^{J'}\Phi_2]$ where J' is a largest proper subset of J when ψ has a positive polarity and J' is a smallest proper superset of J when ψ has a negative polarity and this can be done in PSPACE. For example, if J is of the form $[m_1, m_2]$ and ψ has a positive polarity, then we consider replacing J with both $(m_1, m_2]$ and $[m_1, m_2)$, while if ψ has a negative polarity, then we consider replacing J with both $(m_1 - 1, m_2]$ and $[m_1, m_2 + 1)$.

For the lower bound, we show a reduction from TQBF[3], which is known to be PSPACE-complete [28]. Let $\alpha = Q_1 p_1.Q_2 p_2 \ldots Q_n p_n.\beta(p_1, \ldots, p_n)$ be a quantified boolean formula (QBF), such that β is a propositional formula over the propositions $p_1, \ldots, p_n$, and each $Q_i \in \{\exists, \forall\}$ is an existential or a universal quantifier.

Consider the timed automaton $\mathcal{A} = \langle \{p\}, \{l_0, \ldots, l_n\}, l_0, C, E, L \rangle$ shown in Fig. 1. The set of clocks C is $\{x, x_1, \ldots, x_n\}$, i.e., we have a clock x and for each proposition p_i, with $1 \leq i \leq n$, we have a clock x_i. The guard g is obtained from β by replacing each p_i in β with the atomic formula $x_i = n + 1$. For example, considering $n = 3$, if $\beta(p_1, p_2, p_3) = (p_1 \vee \neg p_2) \wedge (\neg p_1 \vee p_3)$, then $g = (x_1 = 4 \vee x_2 \neq 4) \wedge (x_1 \neq 4 \vee x_3 = 4)$. We have $L(l_{n+1}) = \{p\}$, and for all $0 \leq i \leq n$, we have $L(l_i) = \emptyset$.

For every run of $\mathcal{A}$, for every $1 \leq i \leq n$, the location l_i is reached at time i. Let v be the clock valuation at time n when location l_n is reached. Note that $v(x) = n$, and for every $1 \leq i \leq n$, we have that $v(x_i)$ equals n if at location l_{i-1}, the edge (l_{i-1}, l'_i) is taken and equals $n - i$, if at location l_{i-1}, the edge (l_{i-1}, l_i) is taken. There are 2^n different paths from l_0 to l_n, and each can be viewed as encoding a different truth assignment for the n propositions $p_1, \ldots, p_n$. Location l_{n+1} is reached at time $n + 1$ with clock valuation $v + 1$. Let Φ be the TCTL formula $Q'_1 F^{[0,1)}(Q'_2 F^{[1,1]}(Q'_3 F^{[1,1]} \ldots Q'_n F^{[1,1]}(EF^{[1,1]}p)) \ldots)$ with $Q'_i = A$ if $Q_i = \forall$ and $Q'_i = E$ if $Q_i = \exists$ for all $1 \leq i \leq n$. Note that $\mathcal{A} \not\models \Phi$ since location l_1 is reached only after 1 unit of time elapses and we have $Q'_1 F^{[0,1)}$. Thus $\mathcal{A} \models \neg\Phi$. We claim that if α is satisfiable, then the subformula $\psi = \Phi$ of $\neg\Phi$ is tight in Φ with respect to $\mathcal{A}$. Note that ψ has a negative polarity in $\neg\Phi$,

---

[3] A similar construction has been used in [1] for showing the lower bound of model-checking TCTL formulas, but the proof we have here is different and more involved.

and hence we consider weakening the interval $[0,1)$ in $Q'_1 F^{[0,1)}$. We consider the minimum possible weakening of $[0,1)$ which gives us the interval $[0,1]$. Let Φ' be the formula obtained from Φ by replacing $Q'_1 F^{[0,1)}$ with $Q'_1 F^{[0,1]}$. Note that $\mathcal{A} \models \Phi'$ and hence $\mathcal{A} \not\models \neg\Phi'$. Thus the formula $\psi = \Phi$ is tight in $\neg\Phi$ w.r.t. $\mathcal{A}$.

On the other hand, if α is not satisfiable, then also $\mathcal{A} \not\models \Phi$ and hence $\mathcal{A} \models \neg\Phi$, and no matter how we weaken the interval $F^{[0,1)}$ in $Q'_1 F^{[0,1)}$ in $\neg\Phi$, we have that $\mathcal{A}$ satisfies the resultant formula. Thus if α is not satisfiable, then ψ is not tight in Φ with respect to $\mathcal{A}$, and we are done. □

Theorem 4. *Given a TA $\mathcal{A}$ and a TCTL formula Φ, checking whether Φ is timed vacuous in $\mathcal{A}$ is in PSPACE.*

Proof. By Theorem 3, for a given ψ, the problem of checking whether ψ is not tight is in PSPACE. Since there are there are $|\Phi|$ subformulas, we are done. □

4.2   Algorithms for Tightening TCTL Formulas

In this section we propose some algorithms for tightening TCTL formulas of the form $Q\Phi_1 U^J \Phi_2$, for $Q \in \{A, E\}$. We consider two types of tightening that are the most interesting ones from a user's perspective: One in which the interval J is strengthened to an interval that ends at the earliest possible time, and the other one in which J is strengthened to the smallest possible span.

Given a TA $\mathcal{A}$, a TCTL formula Φ and a subformula ψ of Φ, we propose an algorithm that strengthens J so that it ends at the earliest possible time. The algorithm proceeds as follows. Consider a path formula $\psi = \Phi_1^{\prec l, r \succ} \Phi_2$, where $\prec l \in \{[l, (l\}$ and $r \succ \in \{r), r]\}$, and assume that ψ appears in a positive polarity. Then, ψ is tightened to $\psi' = \Phi_1 U^{\prec l', r' \succ} \Phi_2$ if there is no $\psi'' = \Phi_1 U^{\prec l'', r'' \succ} \Phi_2$ such that $\mathcal{A} \models \Phi[\psi \leftarrow \psi'']$ and one of the following holds:

1. $r'' < r'$.
2. $r'' = r'$, $\psi'' = \Phi_1 U^{\prec l'', r')} \Phi_2$, and $\psi' = \Phi_1 U^{\prec l', r']} \Phi_2$.
3. $r'' \succ= r' \succ$ and $l' < l''$.
4. $r'' \succ= r' \succ$, $l' = l''$, $\psi'' = \Phi_1 U^{(l', r' \succ} \Phi_2$, and $\psi' = \Phi_1 U^{[l', r' \succ} \Phi_2$.

Given a TA $\mathcal{A}$, a TCTL formula Φ such that $\mathcal{A} \models \Phi$, and a subformula $\psi = \Phi_1 U^{\prec l, r \succ} \Phi_2$ of Φ, we first fix the right boundary, i.e. change $r \succ$ to $r' \succ'$ and get a formula $\psi' = \Phi_1 U^{\prec l, r' \succ'} \Phi_2$. The bound is found by a binary search on the right boundary, while keeping $\prec l$ fixed and each time dividing the current interval in two. Once the right boundary is fixed in the subformula, the left boundary is tightened in a similar way.

The algorithm makes $\mathcal{O}(\log(n))$ calls to TCTL model-checking procedure where $n = r - l$.

With inputs from a user, we can further tighten TCTL formulas is to split the interval, resulting in a TCTL$^+$ formula. As the split might result in a pair of intervals such that their union is smaller than the original interval, the user might choose this tightening option. The split and tightening algorithm proceeds as follows. For a formula $\psi = \Phi_1 U^J \Phi_2$, let $J = \prec l, r \succ$. The user can specify how to split the J, i.e. remove an interval I from J and check if $\mathcal{A}$ satisfies the formula $\Phi[\psi \leftarrow (\Phi_1 U^{\prec l, \inf(I)]}\Phi_2) \vee (\Phi_1 U^{[\sup(I), r \succ]}\Phi_2)]$. If $\mathcal{A}$ satisfies the formula, then the intervals in each of the disjunct can be strengthened subsequently. A user can actually use the algorithm to strengthen an interval J to J' and then split J' leading to a TCTL$^+$ formula.

The second interesting algorithm tightens a subformula $\Phi_1 U^J \Phi_2$ by strengthening J to the smallest possible single interval $J' \subseteq J$. This algorithm performs a binary search on the length of J' and makes $\mathcal{O}(n \log(n))$ calls to TCTL model-checking procedure (compared with the naive approach that tries all possibilities, hence making $\mathcal{O}(n^2)$ calls).

If ψ has a negative polarity then we weaken J to get the largest possible interval. We argue below that the weakening too can be done in PSPACE. If $\psi = \Phi_1 U^J \Phi_2$ has a negative polarity then we weaken J to J'. Suppose $J =\prec m_1, m_2 \succ$, where $\prec m_1 \in \{[, (\}$ and $m_2 \succ \in \{],)\}$. We reduce the left boundary of the interval, i.e. replace $\prec m_1$ with $[0, (0, [1, (1, \ldots, [m_1$ one after another when $\prec m_1 = (m_1$ and replace $\prec m_1$ with $[0, (0, [1, (1, \ldots, (m_1 - 1$ when $\prec m_1 = [m_1$ one after another and for each replacement check whether $\mathcal{A}$ still satisfies the formula obtained after the replacement.

Once we fix the left boundary to $\prec l$, we check how far the right boundary can be increased. Finding this maximum right boundary is tricky. We first replace $m_2 \succ$ with $\infty)$ and check if the formula obtained by replacing J with $J' =\prec l, \infty)$ in ψ is satisfied by $\mathcal{A}$. If $\mathcal{A}$ satisfies the formula obtained by replacing J with J', we are done. Otherwise, Let R be the number of regions in the region graph of $\mathcal{A}$. All valuations of a region satisfy the same set of TCTL formulas [1] and the amount by which the right boundary of J can be increased is related to the number of regions in the region graph of $\mathcal{A}$. We note that from any region r, a given region r' can be reached within a maximum time of R time units. If $\mathcal{A}$ does not satisfy the formula obtained by replacing J with J', then we find the maximal weakening of the right interval by replacing $m_2 \succ$ with $m_2 + R], m_2 + R), m_2 + R - 1], \ldots, m_2]$ one after another when $m_2 \succ$ is $m_2)$ and by replacing $m_2 \succ$ with $m_2 + R], m_2 + R), m_2 + R - 1], \ldots, m_2 + 1)$ one after another when $m_2 \succ$ is $m_2]$ and checking if $\mathcal{A}$ satisfies the formula obtained after the replacement.

5   Ranking Vacuity Results

In [15], the authors suggest to rank vacuity results for LTL according to their significance, where significance is defined using probability. The probabilistic model in [15] is that for each atomic proposition p and for each state in a random computation π, the probability of p to hold in the state is $\frac{1}{2}$. Then, $pr(\Psi)$, namely the probability of an LTL formula Ψ, is defined as the probability of Ψ to hold in a random infinite computation. To see the idea behind the framework, consider the LTL specification $G(req \rightarrow F grant)$ and its mutations $G(\neg req)$ and $GF grant$. It not hard to see that in the probabilistic model above, the probability of $G(\neg req)$ to hold in a random infinite computation is 0, whereas the probability of *GF grant* to hold is 1. It is argued in [15] that the lower is the probability of the mutation to hold in a random computation, the higher the vacuity rank should be. In particular, vacuities in which the probability of the mutation is 0, as is the case with $G(\neg req)$, should get the highest rank and vacuities in which the probability is 1, as is the case with $GF(grant)$, should get the lowest rank. Intuitively, when a mutation with a low probability holds, essentially against all chances, then the user should be more alarmed than when a mutation with a high probability holds, essentially as expected.

Since the problem of calculating $pr(\Psi)$ is PSPACE-complete [14,15], an efficient way to obtain an *estimated* probability of satisfaction in random computations has been proposed in [15]. Rather than a probability in $[0, 1]$, the estimation is *three valued*, returning 0, 1, or $\frac{1}{2}$, with $\frac{1}{2}$ indicating that the estimated probability is in $(0, 1)$. Extending the framework to TCTL involves two technical challenges: a transition to a branching-time setting, and a transition to a timed setting. As we show below, once we compensate on an estimated reasoning, the transitions do not require new techniques.

Let us start with the transition to the branching setting. Recall that the probabilistic model in [15] defines $pr(\Psi)$ as the probability of Ψ to hold in a random infinite computation. Thus, [15] ignores the structure of the analyzed system, in particular the fact that infinite computations are generated by finitely many states. This makes a difference, as, for example, the probability of Gp to hold in a computation generated by n states is $\frac{1}{2^n}$, whereas $pr(Gp) = 0$. In the branching setting, ignoring the structure of the analyzed system plays an additional role, as it abstracts the branching degree. For example, the probability of a CTL formula AXp to hold in a state with n successors is $\frac{1}{2^n}$ (see also [10]). Note, however, that once we move to a three-valued approximation, the approximated probability of $AX\Phi$ to hold in a state agrees with the approximated probability of Φ to hold in a state, and is independent of the number of successors! Moreover, the same holds for existential path quantification: the approximation probability of $EX\Phi$ agrees with that of Φ. It follows that the calculation of the estimated probability of a CTL formula can ignore path quantification and proceeds as the one for LTL described in [15].

We continue to the timed setting and TCTL formulas. Our probabilistic model is based on random region graphs. Indeed, as the truth value of a TCTL formula in a TTS is defined with respect to the induced region graph, we define the probability of a TCTL formula as its probability to hold in a random region graph. It is easy to see that for TCTL formulas of the form *true*, *false*, p, $\neg\Phi$, and $\Phi \vee \Psi$, the estimated probability defined for CTL is valid also for TCTL. We continue to formulas of the form $A\Phi U^J \Psi$ and $E\Phi U^J \Psi$. Here too, we can ignore path quantification and observe that if the estimated probability of Ψ is 0, then so is the estimated probability of $\Phi U^J \Psi$, and similarly for 1. Another way for $\Phi U^J \Psi$ to have estimated probability 1 is when the estimated probabilities of Φ is 1, that of Ψ is in $(0, 1)$, and $J = [0, \infty)$. In all other cases, the estimated probability of $\Phi U^J \Psi$ is in $(0, 1)$.

By the above, the three-valued estimated probability of a TCTL formula Φ, denoted $Epr(\Phi)$, is defined by induction on the structure of the formula as follows (with $Q \in \{A, E\}$).

- $Epr(false) = 0$.
- $Epr(true) = 1$.
- $Epr(p) = \frac{1}{2}$.
- $Epr(\neg\Phi) = 1 - Epr(\Phi)$.
- $Epr(\Phi \wedge \Psi) = \begin{cases} 1 & \text{if } Epr(\Phi) = 1 \text{ and } Epr(\Psi) = 1 \\ 04 & \text{if } Epr(\Phi) = 0 \text{ or } Epr(\Psi) = 0 \\ \frac{1}{2} & \text{otherwise.} \end{cases}$
- $Epr(Q\Phi U^J\Psi) = \begin{cases} 0 & \text{if } Epr(\Psi) = 0 \\ 1 & \text{if } (Epr(\Psi) = 1) \text{ or} \\ & (Epr(\Phi) = 1, Epr(\Psi) = \frac{1}{2}, \text{ and } J = [0, \infty)) \\ \frac{1}{2} & \text{otherwise.} \end{cases}$

Recall that we calculate the three-valued estimated probability for the mutations of a given TCTL specification. Thus, the calculation may also be applied for TCTL$^+$ formulas. Fortunately, the estimated probability of a disjunction $\bigvee_{1 \leq i \leq k} \Phi^i U^{J_i}\Psi^i$ follows the same lines as these in which $k = 1$. In particular, for the purpose of calculating the estimated probability of mutations, we know that the formula at hand is obtained by strengthening $Q\Phi U^J\Psi$ by splitting J to intervals that form a strict subset of it. Hence, we can assume that the formula is of the form $Q \bigvee_{1 \leq i \leq k} \Phi U^{J_i}\Psi$ (that is, same Φ^i and Ψ^i in all disjuncts), and the union of the intervals J_i is a strict subset of $[0, \infty)$. Accordingly, we have the following.

- $Epr(Q \bigvee_{1 \leq i \leq k} \Phi U^{J_i}\Psi) = \begin{cases} 0 & \text{if } Epr(\Psi) = 0 \\ 1 & \text{if } Epr(\Psi) = 1 \\ \frac{1}{2} & \text{otherwise.} \end{cases}$

Note that the estimation not only loses preciseness when the probability is in $(0, 1)$ but also ignores semantic relations among subformulas. For example, $Epr(p \wedge \neg p) = \frac{1}{2}$, whereas $pr(p \wedge \neg p) = 0$. Such relations, however, are the reasons to the PSPACE-hardness of calculating $pr(\varphi)$ precisely, and the estimation in Epr is satisfactory, in the following sense:

Theorem 5. *For every TCTL$^+$ formula Φ, the following hold.*

- *If $pr(\Phi) = 1$, then $Epr(\Phi) \in \{1, \frac{1}{2}\}$, if $pr(\Phi) = 0$, then $Epr(\Phi) \in \{0, \frac{1}{2}\}$, and if $pr(\Phi) \in (0, 1)$, then $Epr(\Phi) = \frac{1}{2}$.*
- *$Epr(\Phi)$ be calculated in linear time.*

By Theorem 5, ranking of mutations for TCTL formulas by estimated probability of their mutations can be done in linear time. Now, one can ask how helpful the estimation is. As demonstrated in [15], the estimation agrees with the intuition of designers about the importance of vacuity information. In fact, when $Epr(\Phi)$ does not agree with $pr(\Phi)$, the reason is often *inherent vacuity* in the specification [18], as in the example of $p \wedge \neg p$ above, where we want the formula to be ranked as alarming.

6   Conclusions

Vacuity detection is a widely researched problem, with most commercial model-checking tools including an automated vacuity check. In this paper, we extended the definition of vacuity to the timed logic TCTL and demonstrated that vacuous satisfaction can indicate problems in the timing aspects of the modelling or the specification. We considered strengthening of TCTL properties resulting from tightening the interval J in the operator U^J. While we can tighten the interval in many different ways, we considered only the tightenings that preserve the user's intent: tightening the right bound (forcing the eventuality to happen as early as possible), shortening the interval (forcing it to be tighter), and replacing the interval J with a strictly smaller union of its two sub-intervals J_1 and J_2 (allowing the tightening be more precise). We note that, in principle, it is possible to examine a replacement of J by a union of a larger number of sub-intervals, incurring only a polynomial increase in runtime. Replacing an interval J with $J_1 \cup J_2$ results in a formula that is not in TCTL. We introduced an extension TCTL$^+$ of TCTL, which includes eventualities occurring in a union of a constant number of intervals and proved that TCTL$^+$ model-checking is PSPACE-complete, thus it is not higher than that of TCTL. We also proved that the vacuity problem for TCTL is in PSPACE, hence it is not harder than model checking. Finally, as extending vacuity to consider real-time leads to a high number of vacuity results, we observed that the framework for ranking of LTL vacuity results by their approximated importance can be applied to TCTL as well.

References

1. Alur, R., Courcoubetis, C., Dill, D.: Model-checking in dense real-time. Inf. Comput. **104**(1), 2–34 (1993)
2. Alur, R., Dill, D.: A theory of timed automata. Theoret. Comput. Sci. **126**(2), 183–236 (1994)
3. Alur, R., Feder, T., Henzinger, T.A.: The benefits of relaxing punctuality. J. ACM **43**(1), 116–146 (1996)
4. Alur, R., Henzinger, T.A.: Logics and models of real time: a survey. In: de Bakker, J.W., Huizing, C., de Roever, W.P., Rozenberg, G. (eds.) REX 1991. LNCS, vol. 600, pp. 74–106. Springer, Heidelberg (1992). https://doi.org/10.1007/BFb0031988
5. Armoni, R., et al.: Enhanced vacuity detection in linear temporal logic. In: Hunt, W.A., Somenzi, F. (eds.) CAV 2003. LNCS, vol. 2725, pp. 368–380. Springer, Heidelberg (2003). https://doi.org/10.1007/978-3-540-45069-6_35
6. Beer, I., Ben-David, S., Eisner, C., Rodeh, Y.: Efficient detection of vacuity in ACTL formulas. Formal Methods Syst. Des. **18**(2), 141–162 (2001)
7. Bustan, D., Flaisher, A., Grumberg, O., Kupferman, O., Vardi, M.Y.: Regular vacuity. In: Borrione, D., Paul, W. (eds.) CHARME 2005. LNCS, vol. 3725, pp. 191–206. Springer, Heidelberg (2005). https://doi.org/10.1007/11560548_16
8. Chechik, M., Gheorghiu, M., Gurfinkel, A.: Finding environment guarantees. In: Dwyer, M.B., Lopes, A. (eds.) FASE 2007. LNCS, vol. 4422, pp. 352–367. Springer, Heidelberg (2007). https://doi.org/10.1007/978-3-540-71289-3_27

9. Chockler, H., Gurfinkel, A., Strichman, O.: Beyond vacuity: towards the strongest passing formula. In: Proceedings of the 8th International Conference on Formal Methods in Computer-Aided Design, pp. 1–8 (2008)
10. Chockler, H., Halpern, J.Y.: Responsibility and blame: a structural-model approach. In: Proceedings of the 19th International Joint Conference on Artificial Intelligence, pp. 147–153 (2003)
11. Chockler, H., Strichman, O.: Before and after vacuity. Formal Methods Syst. Des. **34**(1), 37–58 (2009)
12. Clarke, E., Grumberg, O., Long, D.: Verification tools for finite-state concurrent systems. In: de Bakker, J.W., de Roever, W.-P., Rozenberg, G. (eds.) REX 1993. LNCS, vol. 803, pp. 124–175. Springer, Heidelberg (1994). https://doi.org/10.1007/3-540-58043-3_19
13. Clarke, E.M., Grumberg, O., McMillan, K.L., Zhao, X.: Efficient generation of counterexamples and witnesses in symbolic model checking. In: Proceedings of the 32st Design Automation Conference, pp. 427–432. IEEE Computer Society (1995)
14. Courcoubetis, C., Yannakakis, M.: The complexity of probabilistic verification. J. ACM **42**, 857–907 (1995)
15. Ben-David, S., Kupferman, O.: A framework for ranking vacuity results. In: Van Hung, D., Ogawa, M. (eds.) ATVA 2013. LNCS, vol. 8172, pp. 148–162. Springer, Cham (2013). https://doi.org/10.1007/978-3-319-02444-8_12
16. Dokhanchi, A., Hoxha, B., Fainekos, G.E.: Formal requirement elicitation and debugging for testing and verification of cyber-physical systems. CoRR, abs/1607.02549 (2016)
17. Emerson, E.A., Halpern, J.Y.: Sometimes and not never revisited: on branching versus linear time. J. ACM **33**(1), 151–178 (1986)
18. Fisman, D., Kupferman, O., Sheinvald-Faragy, S., Vardi, M.Y.: A framework for inherent vacuity. In: Chockler, H., Hu, A.J. (eds.) HVC 2008. LNCS, vol. 5394, pp. 7–22. Springer, Heidelberg (2009). https://doi.org/10.1007/978-3-642-01702-5_7
19. Gurfinkel, A., Chechik, M.: Extending extended vacuity. In: Hu, A.J., Martin, A.K. (eds.) FMCAD 2004. LNCS, vol. 3312, pp. 306–321. Springer, Heidelberg (2004). https://doi.org/10.1007/978-3-540-30494-4_22
20. Gurfinkel, A., Chechik, M.: How vacuous is vacuous? In: Jensen, K., Podelski, A. (eds.) TACAS 2004. LNCS, vol. 2988, pp. 451–466. Springer, Heidelberg (2004). https://doi.org/10.1007/978-3-540-24730-2_34
21. Henzinger, T.A., Manna, Z., Pnueli, A.: Timed transition systems. In: de Bakker, J.W., Huizing, C., de Roever, W.P., Rozenberg, G. (eds.) REX 1991. LNCS, vol. 600, pp. 226–251. Springer, Heidelberg (1992). https://doi.org/10.1007/BFb0031995
22. Kupferman, O.: Sanity checks in formal verification. In: Baier, C., Hermanns, H. (eds.) CONCUR 2006. LNCS, vol. 4137, pp. 37–51. Springer, Heidelberg (2006). https://doi.org/10.1007/11817949_3
23. Kupferman, O., Li, W., Seshia, S.A.: A theory of mutations with applications to vacuity, coverage, and fault tolerance. In: Proceedings of the 8th International Conference on Formal Methods in Computer-Aided Design, pp. 1–9 (2008)
24. Kupferman, O., Vardi, M.Y.: Vacuity detection in temporal model checking. Softw. Tools Technol. Transf. **4**(2), 224–233 (2003)
25. Namjoshi, K.S.: An efficiently checkable, proof-based formulation of vacuity in model checking. In: Alur, R., Peled, D.A. (eds.) CAV 2004. LNCS, vol. 3114, pp. 57–69. Springer, Heidelberg (2004). https://doi.org/10.1007/978-3-540-27813-9_5

26. Purandare, M., Somenzi, F.: Vacuum cleaning CTL formulae. In: Brinksma, E., Larsen, K.G. (eds.) CAV 2002. LNCS, vol. 2404, pp. 485–499. Springer, Heidelberg (2002). https://doi.org/10.1007/3-540-45657-0_39

27. Purandare, M., Wahl, T., Kroening, D.: Strengthening properties using abstraction refinement. In: Proceedings of Design, Automation and Test in Europe (DATE), pp. 1692–1697. IEEE (2009)

28. Stockmeyer, L.J.: On the combinational complexity of certain symmetric boolean functions. Math. Syst. Theory **10**, 323–336 (1977)

Falsification of Cyber-Physical Systems Using Deep Reinforcement Learning

Takumi Akazaki[1,2(✉)], Shuang Liu[3], Yoriyuki Yamagata[4], Yihai Duan[3], and Jianye Hao[3]

[1] The University of Tokyo, Tokyo, Japan
akazaki@ms.k.u-tokyo.ac.jp
[2] Japan Society for the Promotion of Science, Tokyo, Japan
[3] School of Software, Tianjin University, Tianjin, China
[4] National Institute of Advanced Industrial Science and Technology (AIST), Tokyo, Japan

Abstract. With the rapid development of software and distributed computing, *Cyber-Physical Systems* (CPS) are widely adopted in many application areas, e.g., smart grid, autonomous automobile. It is difficult to detect defects in CPS models due to the complexities involved in the software and physical systems. To find defects in CPS models efficiently, robustness guided falsification of CPS is introduced. Existing methods use several optimization techniques to generate counterexamples, which falsify the given properties of a CPS. However those methods may require a large number of simulation runs to find the counterexample and are far from practical. In this work, we explore state-of-the-art *Deep Reinforcement Learning (DRL)* techniques to reduce the number of simulation runs required to find such counterexamples. We report our method and the preliminary evaluation results.

1 Introduction

Cyber-Physical Systems (CPS) are more and more widely adopted in safety-critical domains, which makes it extremely important to guarantee the correctness of CPS systems. Testing and verification on *models* of CPS are common methods to guarantee the correctness. However, it is hard for testing to achieve a high coverage; verification techniques are usually expensive and undecidable [3] due to the infinite state space of CPS models. Therefore, robustness guided falsification [2,5] method is introduced to detect defects efficiently. In robustness guided falsification, *Signal Temporal Logic* (STL) [9] formulas are usually used to specify properties which must be satisfied by a CPS model. Robustness of an STL formula, which is a numeric measure of how "robust" a property holds in the given CPS model, is defined. The state space of the CPS model is explored and a trajectory which minimizes the robustness value is identified as a good candidate for testing. In this way, robustness guided falsification aids to generate defect-leading inputs (counterexamples), which enables more efficient, yet automatic detection of defects. Although non-termination of robustness guided falsification

K. Havelund et al. (Eds.): FM 2018, LNCS 10951, pp. 456–465, 2018.
https://doi.org/10.1007/978-3-319-95582-7_27

does not mean the absence of counterexamples, it suggests the correctness of the CPS model to some extent.

Existing approaches adopt various kinds of stochastic global optimization algorithms e.g., simulated annealing [3] and cross-entropy [27], to minimize robustness. These methods take a full trajectory (a sequence of actions) as input, and adjusting input during the simulation is not supported. As a result, a large number of simulation runs are required in the falsification process. Existing methods cannot guarantee finding a counterexample of practical CPS models in a limited time window because the simulation would then be tremendous.

In this paper, we adopt *deep reinforcement learning* (DRL) [25] algorithms to solve the problem of falsification of STL properties for CPS models. Reinforcement learning techniques can observe feedbacks from the environment, and adjust the input action immediately. In this way, we are able to converge faster towards minimum robustness value. In particular, we adopt two state-of-the-art DRL techniques, i.e., *Asynchronous Advanced Actor Critic* (A3C) and Double *Deep-Q Network* (DDQN). Our contributions are two folds: (1) we show how to transform the problem of falsifying CPS models into a reinforcement learning problem; and (2) we implement our method and conduct preliminary evaluations to show DRL technology can help reduce the number of simulation runs required to find a falsifying input for CPS models. Reducing the number of simulation runs is important because during falsification, the majority of execution time is spent for simulation runs if CPS models are complex.

Related Work. There are two kinds of works, i.e., robustness guided falsification and controller synthesis, which are most related to our approach.

In robustness guided falsification methods, quantitative semantics over *Metric Interval Temporal Logic* (MITL) and its variants STL [16,23] are employed. Then the fault detection problem is translated into the numerical minimization problem. Several tools e.g., S-TaLiRo [5,19] and Breach [15] are developed to realize this approach. Moreover, various kind of numerical optimization techniques, e.g., simulated annealing [3], cross-entropy [27], and Gaussian process optimization [4,7,8,28], are studied to solve the falsification problem efficiently. All these methods optimize the whole output trajectory of a CPS by changing the whole input trajectory. As stated above, we use reinforcement learning which can observe feedbacks from a CPS and adjust the input immediately. Thus, our method can be expected to arrive the falsifying input faster.

In contrast to robustness guided falsification, controller synthesis techniques enable choosing the input signal at a certain step based on observations of output signals. There are works that synthesize the controller to enforce the *Markov decision process* to satisfy a given LTL formula [13,14,22,26,29]. The most closely related works [20,21] apply reinforcement learning techniques to enforce the small robotic system to satisfy the given LTL formula. Our work is different from those works in two aspects: (1) we falsify the properties while the control synthesis methods try to satisfy the properties; and (2) with DRL, we could employ complex non-linear functions to learn and model the environment, which is suitable to analyze the complex dynamics of CPS.

2 Preliminary

Robustness Guided Falsification. In this paper, we employ a variant of *Signal Temporal Logic* (STL) defined in [9]. The syntax is defined in the Eq. (1),

$$\varphi ::= v \sim c \mid p \mid \neg\varphi \mid \varphi_1 \vee \varphi_2 \mid \varphi_1 \mathcal{U}_I \varphi_2 \mid \varphi_1 \mathcal{S}_I \varphi_2 \qquad (1)$$

where v is *real* variable, c is a rational number, p is atomic formula, $\sim \in \{<, \le\}$ and I is an interval over non-negative real numbers. If I is $[0, \infty]$, I is omitted. We also use other common abbreviations, e.g., $\Box_I \varphi \equiv \mathsf{True}\,\mathcal{U}_I\,\varphi$ and $\boxminus_I \varphi \equiv \mathsf{True}\,\mathcal{S}_I\,\varphi$.

For a given formula φ, an output signal $\mathbf{x}$ and time t, we adopt the notation of work [9] and denote the *robustness degree* of output signal $\mathbf{x}$ satisfying φ at time t by $\rho(\varphi, \mathbf{x}, t)$. It takes a real value such that (1) its sign stands for the formula φ is satisfied or not by $\mathbf{x}$ at t (positive is true), and (2) its absolute value stands for how "robustly" the formula is satisfied or not.

We also adopt the notion of *future-reach* $\mathsf{fr}(\varphi)$ and *past-reach* $\mathsf{pr}(\varphi)$ following [18]. Intuitively, $\mathsf{fr}(\varphi)$ is the time in future which is required to determine the truth value of formula φ, and $\mathsf{pr}(\varphi)$ is the time in past. For example, $\mathsf{fr}(p) = 0$, $\mathsf{fr}(\Box_{[0,3]}p) = 3$ and $\mathsf{fr}(\boxminus_{[0,3]}p) = 0$. Similarly, for past-reach, $\mathsf{pr}(p) = 0$, $\mathsf{pr}(\Box_{[0,3]}p) = 0$, $\mathsf{pr}(\boxminus_{[0,3]}p) = 3$.

In this paper, we focus on a specific class of the formula called *life-long property*.

Definition 1 (life-long property). *A* life-long property *is an STL formula* $\psi \equiv \Box\varphi$ *where* $\mathsf{fr}(\varphi), \mathsf{pr}(\varphi)$ *are finite. If* $\mathsf{fr}(\varphi) = 0$, *we call* ψ past-dependent life-long property.

Let us consider the life-long property $\psi \equiv \Box\varphi$. Intuitive meaning of this formula is that whenever the property φ must hold. In falsification scenario, to observe the violation of φ, output signals obtained by simulations should be long enough with respect to both $\mathsf{pr}(\varphi)$ and $\mathsf{fr}(\varphi)$. If the output signal is infinitely long to past and future directions, ψ is logically equivalent to a past-dependent life-long property $\Box\boxminus_{[\mathsf{fr}(\varphi),\mathsf{fr}(\varphi)]}\varphi$. In general, the output signal is not infinitely long but using this conversion we convert all life-long properties to past-dependent life-long properties. Our evaluation in Sect. 4 suggests that this approximation does not adversely affect the performance.

Reinforcement Learning. Reinforcement learning is one of machine learning techniques in which an agent learns the structure of the environment based on observations, and maximizes the rewards by acting according to the learnt knowledge. The standard setting of a reinforcement learning problem consists of an agent and an environment. The agent observes the current state and reward from the environment, and returns the next action to the environment. The goal of reinforcement learning is for each step n, given the sequence of previous states $x_0, \ldots, x_{n-1}$, rewards $r_1, \ldots, r_n$ and actions $a_0, \ldots, a_{n-1}$, generate an action a_n, which maximizes expected value of the sum of rewards: $r = \sum_{k=n}^{\infty} \gamma^k r_{k+1}$, where $0 < \gamma \leq 1$ is a discount factor. Deep reinforcement learning is a reinforcement learning technique which uses a *deep neural network* for learning. In this work, we particularly adopted two state-of-the-art deep reinforcement learning algorithms, i.e., *Asynchronous Advantage Actor-Critic* (A3C) [24] and *Double Deep Q Network* (DDQN) [17].

3   Our Approach

3.1   Overview of Our Algorithm

Let us consider the falsification problem to find a counterexample of the life-long property $\psi \equiv \Box \varphi$. As we mentioned in Sect. 2, we can assume that ψ is past-dependent. Our mission is to generate an input signal $\mathbf{u}$ for system $\mathcal{M}$, such that the corresponding output signal $\mathcal{M}(\mathbf{u})$ does not satisfy ψ.

In our algorithm, we fix the simulation time to be T_{end} and call one simulation until time T_{end} an *episode* in conformance with the reinforcement learning terminology. We fix the discretization of time to a positive real number Δ_T. The agent $\mathcal{A}$ generates the piecewise-constant input signal $\mathbf{u} = \big[(0, u_0), (\Delta_T, u_1), (2\Delta_T, u_2), \ldots \big]$ by iterating the following steps:

(1) At time $i\Delta_T$ ($i = 0, 1, \ldots$), the agent $\mathcal{A}$ chooses the next input value u_i. The generated input signal is extended to $\mathbf{u} = \big[(0, u_0), \ldots, (i\Delta_T, u_i)\big]$.
(2) Our algorithm obtains the corresponding output signal $\mathbf{x} = \mathcal{M}(\mathbf{u})$ by stepping forward one simulation on the model $\mathcal{M}$ from time $i\Delta_T$ to $(i+1)\Delta_T$ with input u_i.
(3) Let $x_{i+1} = \mathbf{x}((i+1)\Delta_T)$ be the new state (i.e., output) of the system.
(4) We compute reward r_{i+1} by $\mathsf{reward}(\varphi, \mathbf{x})$ (defined in Sect. 3.2).
(5) The agent $\mathcal{A}$ updates its action based on the new state x_{i+1} and reward r_{i+1}.

At the end of each episode, we obtain the output signal trajectory $\mathbf{x}$, and check whether it satisfies the property $\psi = \Box\varphi$ or not. If it is falsified, return the current input signal $\mathbf{u}$ as a counterexample. Otherwise, we discard the current generated signal input and restart the episode from the beginning.

The complete algorithm of our approach is shown in Algorithm 1. The method call $\mathcal{A}.\mathsf{step}(x, r)$ represents the agent $\mathcal{A}$ push the current state reward pair (x, r) into its memory and returns the next action u (the input signal in the next step). The method call $\mathcal{A}.\mathsf{reset}(x, r)$ notifies the agent that the current episode is completed, and returns the current state and reward. Function $\mathsf{reward}(\mathbf{x}, \psi)$ calculates the reward based on Definition 2.

Algorithm 1. Falsification for $\psi = \Box\varphi$ by reinforcement learning

---

input: A past-dependent life-long property $\psi = \Box\varphi$, a system $\mathcal{M}$, an agent $\mathcal{A}$
output: A counterexample input signal **u** if exists
parameters: A step time Δ_T, the end time T_{end}, the maximum number of the episode N
1: **for** numEpisode $\leftarrow 1$ to N **do**
2:     $i \leftarrow 0$, $r \leftarrow 0$, x be the initial (output) state of $\mathcal{M}$
3:     **u** be the empty input signal sequence
4:     **while** $i\Delta_T < T_{\text{end}}$ **do**
5:         $u \leftarrow \mathcal{A}.\text{step}(x, r)$, $\mathbf{u} \leftarrow \text{append}(\mathbf{u}, (i\Delta_T, u))$ ▷ choose the next input by the agent
6:         $\mathbf{x} \leftarrow \mathcal{M}(\mathbf{u})$, $x \leftarrow \mathbf{x}((i+1)\Delta_T)$ ▷ simulate, observe the new output state
7:         $r \leftarrow \text{reward}(\mathbf{x}, \psi)$
8:         $i \leftarrow i + 1$ ▷ calculate the reward by following eq. (2)
9:     **end while**
10:     **if** $\mathbf{x} \not\models \psi$ **then return u** as a falsifying input
11:     **end if**
12:     $\mathcal{A}.\text{reset}(x, r)$
13: **end for**

3.2 Reward Definition for Life-Long Property Falsification

Our goal is to find the input signal **u** to the system $\mathcal{M}$ which minimizes $\rho(\psi, \mathcal{M}(\mathbf{u}), 0)$ where $\psi = \Box\varphi$ and ρ is a robustness. We determine $u_0, u_1, \ldots$ in a greedy way.

Assume that $u_0, \ldots, u_i$ are determined. u_{i+1} can be determined by

$$u_{i+1} = \arg\min_{u_{i+1}} \min_{u_{i+2}, \ldots} \rho(\Box\varphi, \mathcal{M}([(0, u_0), (\Delta_T, u_1), \ldots]), 0) \tag{2}$$

$$= \arg\min_{u_{i+1}} \min_{u_{i+2}, \ldots} \min_{t \in \mathbb{R}} \rho(\varphi, \mathcal{M}([(0, u_0), (\Delta_T, u_1), \ldots]), t) \tag{3}$$

$$\sim \arg\min_{u_{i+1}} \min_{u_{i+2}, \ldots} \min_{k=i+1, i+2, \ldots} \rho(\varphi, \mathcal{M}([(0, u_0), \ldots, (k\Delta_T, u_k)]), k\Delta_T) \tag{4}$$

$$\sim \arg\min_{u_{i+1}} \min_{u_{i+2}, \ldots} \left[-\log\left\{ 1 + \sum_{k=i+1}^{\infty} \left\{ e^{-\rho(\varphi, \mathcal{M}([(0, u_0), \ldots, (k\Delta_T, u_k)]), k\Delta_T)} - 1 \right\} \right\} \right] \tag{5}$$

$$= \arg\max_{u_{i+1}} \max_{u_{i+2}, \ldots} \sum_{k=i+1}^{\infty} \left\{ e^{-\rho(\varphi, \mathcal{M}([(0, u_0), \ldots, (k\Delta_T, u_k)]), k\Delta_T)} - 1 \right\}. \tag{6}$$

Here the Eq. (4) uses the fact φ is past-dependent and (5) uses an approximation of minimum by the log-sum-exp function [11].

In our reinforcement learning base approach, we use discounting factor $\gamma = 1$ and reward $r_i = e^{-\rho(\varphi, \mathcal{M}([(0, u_0), \ldots, (i\Delta_T, u_i)]), i\Delta_T)} - 1$ to approximately compute action u_{i+1}, from $u_0, \ldots, u_i$, $\mathcal{M}([(0, u_0), \ldots, (i\Delta_T, u_i)])$ and $r_1, \ldots, r_i$.

Definition 2 (reward). *Let $\psi \equiv \Box\varphi$ be a past-dependent formula and $\mathbf{x} = \mathcal{M}(\mathbf{u})$ be a finite length signal until the time t. We define the reward* $\text{reward}(\psi, \mathbf{x})$ *as*

$$\text{reward}(\psi, \mathbf{x}) = \exp(-\rho(\varphi, \mathbf{x}, t)) - 1 \tag{7}$$

4   Preliminary Results

Implementation. The overall architecture of our system is shown in Fig. 1. Our implementation consists of three components, i.e., input generation, output handling and simulation. The input generation component adopts reinforcement learning techniques and is implemented based on the ChainerRL library [1]. We use default hyper-parameters in the library or sample programs without change. The output handling component conducts reward calculation using dp-TaliRo [5]. The simulation is conducted with Matlab/Simulink models, which are encapsulated by the openAI gym library [10].

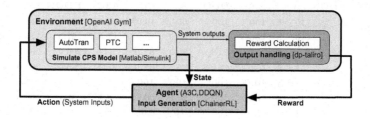

Fig. 1. Architecture of our system

Evaluation Settings. We use a widely adopted CPS model, automatic transmission control system (**AT**) [6], to evaluate our method. **AT** has throttle and brake as input ports, and the output ports are the vehicle velocity v, the engine rotation speed ω and the current gear state g. We conduct our evaluation with the formulas in Table 1. Formulas φ_1–φ_6 are rewriting of φ_1^{AT}–φ_6^{AT} in benchmark [6] into life-long properties in our approach. In addition, we propose three new formulas φ_7–φ_9. For each formula φ_1–φ_9, we compare the performance of our approaches (A3C, DDQN), with the baseline algorithms, i.e., simulated annealing (SA) and cross entropy (CE). For each property, we run the falsification procedure 20 times. For each falsification procedure, we execute simulation episodes up to 200 times and measure the number of simulation episodes required to falsify the property. If the property cannot be falsified within 200 episodes, the procedure fails. We observe that Δ_T may strongly affect the performance of each algorithm. Therefore, we vary Δ_T (among $\{1, 5, 10\}$ except for the cases of **A3C** and **DDQN** for φ_7–φ_9 among we use $\{5, 10\}^1$) and report the setting (of Δ_T) which leads to the best performance (the least episode number and highest success rate) for each algorithm.

Evaluation Results. The preliminary results are presented in Table 2. The Δ_T columns indicate the best performing Δ_T for each algorithm. The "Success rate" columns indicate the percentage that the falsification procedure could find a counterexample within the maximum allowed simulation episodes (200). The

---

[1] These methods with $\Delta_T = 1$ for φ_7–φ_9 shows bad performance and did not terminate in 5 days.

Table 1. The list of the evaluated properties on **AT**.

id	Formula
φ_1	$\Box \omega \leq \overline{\omega}$
φ_2	$\Box(v \leq \overline{v} \wedge \omega \leq \overline{\omega})$
φ_3	$\Box((g_2 \wedge \Diamond_{[0,0.1]} g_1) \rightarrow \Box_{[0.1,1.0]} \neg g_2)$
φ_4	$\Box((\neg g_1 \wedge \Diamond_{[0,0.1]} g_1) \rightarrow \Box_{[0.1,1.0]} g_1)$
φ_5	$\Box \bigwedge_{i=1}^{4} ((\neg g_i \wedge \Diamond_{[0,0.1]} g_i) \rightarrow \Box_{[0.1,1.0]} g_i)$

id	Formula
φ_6	$\Box(\Box_{[0,t_1]} \omega \leq \overline{\omega} \rightarrow \Box_{[t_1,t_2]} v \leq \overline{v})$
φ_7	$\Box v \leq \overline{v}$
φ_8	$\Box \Diamond_{[0,25]} \neg(\underline{v} \leq v \leq \overline{v})$
φ_9	$\Box \neg \Box_{[0,20]} (\neg g_4 \wedge \omega \geq \overline{\omega})$

Table 2. The experimental result on **AT**.

id	Δ_T				Success rate				numEpisode			
	A3C	DDQN	SA	CE	A3C	DDQN	SA	CE	A3C	DDQN	SA	CE
φ_1	5	1	10	5	100%*	100%*	65.0%	10.0%	**16.5****	24.5	118.5	200.0
φ_2	5	1	10	5	100%*	100%*	65.0%	10.0%	**11.5****	27.5	118.5	200.0
φ_3	1	1	1	1	75.0	5.0%	20.0%	**85.0%**	44.0	200.0	200.0	**26.5**
φ_4	1	1	1	1	75.0	10.0%	20.0%	**85.0%**	67.5	200.0	200.0	**26.5***
φ_5	1	1	1	1	100%	100%	100%	100%	**1.0**	2.0	**1.0**	**1.0**
φ_6	10	10	10	10	100%*	100%*	70.0%	50.0%	**3.5****	**3.5****	160.5	119.0
φ_7	5	5	1	1	65.0%	100%**	0.0%	0.0%	125.0	**63.0****	200.0	200.0
φ_8	10	10	10	1	80.0%	**95.0%**	90.0%	75.0%	72.0	52.0	83.0	**21.0**
φ_9	10	10	10	10	95.0%	100%**	15.0%	5.0%	46.0	**12.0****	200.0	200.0

"numEpisode" columns show the median (among the 20 procedures) of the number of simulation episodes required to falsify the formula. We use median since the distribution of the number of simulation episodes tends to be skewed.

The best results (success rate and numEpisode) of each formula are highlighted in bold. If the difference between the best entry of our methods and the best entry of the baseline methods is statistically significant by Fisher's exact test and the Mann Whitney U-test [12], we mark the best entry with $*$ ($p < 0.05$) or $**$ ($p < 0.001$), respectively.

As shown in Table 2, RL based methods almost always outperforms baseline methods on success rate, which means RL based methods are more likely to find the falsified inputs with a limited number of episodes. This is because RL based methods learn knowledge from the environment and generate input signals adaptively during the simulations. Among the statistically significant results of numEpisode, our methods are best for five cases ($\varphi_1, \varphi_2, \varphi_6, \varphi_7, \varphi_9$), while the baseline methods are best for one case (φ_4). For the case of φ_4, it is likely because that all variables in this formula take discrete values, thus, reinforcement learning is less effective. Further, DDQN tends to return extreme values as actions, which are not solutions to falsify φ_3 and φ_4. This explains poor performance of DDQN for the case of φ_3 and φ_4.

Unfortunately, our current implementation has a disadvantage of large computational time due to the overhead caused by wrapping a simulation in openAI gym API. We believe that the performance for time would be much better with proper implementation.

5   Conclusion and Future Work

In this paper, we report an approach which adopts reinforcement learning algorithms to solve the problem of robustness-guided falsification of CPS systems. We implement our approach in a prototype tool and conduct preliminary evaluations with a widely adopted CPS system. The evaluation results show that our method can reduce the number of episodes to find the falsifying input. As a future work, we plan to extend the current work to explore more reinforcement learning algorithms and evaluate our methods on more CPS benchmarks.

References

1. The ChainerRL Library. https://github.com/chainer/chainerrl
2. Abbas, H., Fainekos, G., Sankaranarayanan, S., Ivančić, F., Gupta, A.: Probabilistic temporal logic falsification of cyber-physical systems. ACM Trans. Embed. Comput. Syst. **12**(2s), 95:1–95:30 (2013)
3. Abbas, H., Fainekos, G.E.: Convergence proofs for simulated annealing falsification of safety properties. In: 50th Annual Allerton Conference on Communication, Control, and Computing, Allerton 2012, Allerton Park & Retreat Center, Monticello, IL, USA, 1–5 October 2012, pp. 1594–1601. IEEE (2012)
4. Akazaki, T.: Falsification of conditional safety properties for cyber-physical systems with gaussian process regression. In: Falcone, Y., Sánchez, C. (eds.) RV 2016. LNCS, vol. 10012, pp. 439–446. Springer, Cham (2016). https://doi.org/10.1007/978-3-319-46982-9_27
5. Annpureddy, Y., Liu, C., Fainekos, G., Sankaranarayanan, S.: S-TaLiRo: a tool for temporal logic falsification for hybrid systems. In: Abdulla, P.A., Leino, K.R.M. (eds.) TACAS 2011. LNCS, vol. 6605, pp. 254–257. Springer, Heidelberg (2011). https://doi.org/10.1007/978-3-642-19835-9_21
6. Bardh Hoxha, H.A., Fainekos, G.: Benchmarks for temporal logic requirements for automotive systems. In: Proceedings of Applied Verification for Continuous and Hybrid Systems (2014)
7. Bartocci, E., Bortolussi, L., Nenzi, L., Sanguinetti, G.: On the robustness of temporal properties for stochastic models. In: Dang, T., Piazza, C. (eds.) Proceedings Second International Workshop on Hybrid Systems and Biology, HSB 2013. EPTCS, Taormina, Italy, 2nd September 2013, vol. 125, pp. 3–19 (2013)
8. Bartocci, E., Bortolussi, L., Nenzi, L., Sanguinetti, G.: System design of stochastic models using robustness of temporal properties. Theor. Comput. Sci. **587**, 3–25 (2015)
9. Bartocci, E., et al.: Specification-based monitoring of cyber-physical systems: a survey on theory, tools and applications. In: Bartocci, E., Falcone, Y. (eds.) Lectures on Runtime Verification. LNCS, vol. 10457, pp. 135–175. Springer, Cham (2018). https://doi.org/10.1007/978-3-319-75632-5_5
10. Brockman, G., Cheung, V., Pettersson, L., Schneider, J., Schulman, J., Tang, J., Zaremba, W.: OpenAI gym (2016)
11. Cook, J.D.: Basic properties of the soft maximum (2011)
12. Corder, G.W., Foreman, D.I.: Nonparametric Statistics: A Step-by-Step Approach. Wiley, Hoboken (2014)

13. Ding, X.C., Smith, S.L., Belta, C., Rus, D.: MDP optimal control under temporal logic constraints. In: Proceedings of the 50th IEEE Conference on Decision and Control and European Control Conference, CDC-ECC 2011, Orlando, FL, USA, 12–15 December 2011, pp. 532–538. IEEE (2011)

14. Ding, X.C., Smith, S.L., Belta, C., Rus, D.: Optimal control of markov decision processes with linear temporal logic constraints. IEEE Trans. Autom. Control **59**(5), 1244–1257 (2014)

15. Donzé, A.: Breach, a toolbox for verification and parameter synthesis of hybrid systems. In: Touili, T., Cook, B., Jackson, P. (eds.) CAV 2010. LNCS, vol. 6174, pp. 167–170. Springer, Heidelberg (2010). https://doi.org/10.1007/978-3-642-14295-6_17

16. Donzé, A., Maler, O.: Robust satisfaction of temporal logic over real-valued signals. In: Chatterjee, K., Henzinger, T.A. (eds.) FORMATS 2010. LNCS, vol. 6246, pp. 92–106. Springer, Heidelberg (2010). https://doi.org/10.1007/978-3-642-15297-9_9

17. Gu, S., Lillicrap, T., Sutskever, I., Levine, S.: Continuous deep q-learning with model-based acceleration. In: Balcan, M.F., Weinberger, K.Q. (eds.) Proceedings of The 33rd International Conference on Machine Learning, Proceedings of Machine Learning Research, PMLR, New York, USA, 20–22 June 2016, vol. 48, pp. 2829–2838 (2016)

18. Ho, H.-M., Ouaknine, J., Worrell, J.: Online monitoring of metric temporal logic. In: Bonakdarpour, B., Smolka, S.A. (eds.) RV 2014. LNCS, vol. 8734, pp. 178–192. Springer, Cham (2014). https://doi.org/10.1007/978-3-319-11164-3_15

19. Hoxha, B., Abbas, H., Fainekos, G.E.: Using S-TaLiRo on industrial size auimmlertomotive models. In: Frehse, G., Althoff, M. (eds.) 1st and 2nd International Workshop on Applied Verification for Continuous and Hybrid Systems, ARCH@CPSWeek 2014.EPiC Series in Computing, Berlin, Germany, 14 April 2014/ARCH@CPSWeek 2015, Seattle, WA, USA, 13 April 2015, vol. 34, pp. 113–119. EasyChair (2014)

20. Li, X., Ma, Y., Belta, C.: A policy search method for temporal logic specified reinforcement learning tasks. CoRR, abs/1709.09611 (2017)

21. Li, X., Vasile, C.I., Belta, C.: Reinforcement learning with temporal logic rewards. In: 2017 IEEE/RSJ International Conference on Intelligent Robots and Systems, IROS 2017, Vancouver, BC, Canada, 24–28 September 2017, pp. 3834–3839. IEEE (2017)

22. Luna, R., Lahijanian, M., Moll, M., Kavraki, L.E.: Asymptotically optimal stochastic motion planning with temporal goals. In: Akin, H.L., Amato, N.M., Isler, V., van der Stappen, A.F. (eds.) Algorithmic Foundations of Robotics XI. STAR, vol. 107, pp. 335–352. Springer, Cham (2015). https://doi.org/10.1007/978-3-319-16595-0_20

23. Maler, O., Nickovic, D.: Monitoring temporal properties of continuous signals. In: Lakhnech, Y., Yovine, S. (eds.) FORMATS/FTRTFT -2004. LNCS, vol. 3253, pp. 152–166. Springer, Heidelberg (2004). https://doi.org/10.1007/978-3-540-30206-3_12

24. Mnih, V., Badia, A.P., Mirza, M., Graves, A., Lillicrap, T.P., Harley, T., Silver, D., Kavukcuoglu, K.: Asynchronous methods for deep reinforcement learning, vol. 48 (2016)

25. Mnih, V., Kavukcuoglu, K., Silver, D., Rusu, A.A., Veness, J., Bellemare, M.G., Graves, A., Riedmiller, M., Fidjeland, A.K., Ostrovski, G., et al.: Human-level control through deep reinforcement learning. Nature **518**(7540), 529–533 (2015)

26. Sadigh, D., Kim, E.S., Coogan, S., Sastry, S.S., Seshia, S.A.: A learning based approach to control synthesis of Markov decision processes for linear temporal logic specifications. In: 53rd IEEE Conference on Decision and Control, CDC 2014, Los Angeles, CA, USA, 15–17 December 2014, pp. 1091–1096. IEEE (2014)

27. Sankaranarayanan, S., Fainekos, G.E.: Falsification of temporal properties of hybrid systems using the cross-entropy method. In: Dang, T., Mitchell, I.M. (eds.) Hybrid Systems: Computation and Control (part of CPS Week 2012), HSCC 2012, Beijing, China, 17–19 April 2012, pp. 125–134. ACM (2012)

28. Silvetti, S., Policriti, A., Bortolussi, L.: An active learning approach to the falsification of black box cyber-physical systems. In: Polikarpova, N., Schneider, S. (eds.) IFM 2017. LNCS, vol. 10510, pp. 3–17. Springer, Cham (2017). https://doi.org/10.1007/978-3-319-66845-1_1

29. Soudjani, S.E.Z., Majumdar, R.: Controller synthesis for reward collecting Markov processes in continuous space. In: Frehse, G., Mitra, S. (eds.) Proceedings of the 20th International Conference on Hybrid Systems: Computation and Control, HSCC 2017, Pittsburgh, PA, USA, 18–20 April 2017, pp. 45–54. ACM (2017)

Dynamic Symbolic Verification of MPI Programs

Dhriti Khanna[1], Subodh Sharma[2(✉)], César Rodríguez[3],
and Rahul Purandare[1]

[1] IIIT Delhi, New Delhi, India
dhritik@iiitd.ac.in
[2] IIT Delhi, New Delhi, India
svs@cse.iitd.ac.in
[3] Université Paris 13, Sorbonne-Paris-Cité, LIPN, CNRS, Villetaneuse, France

Abstract. The success of dynamic verification techniques for Message Passing Interface (MPI) programs rests on their ability to address *communication nondeterminism*. As the number of processes in the program grows, the dynamic verification techniques suffer from the problem of exponential growth in the size of the reachable state space. In this work, we provide a hybrid verification technique for message passing programs that combines explicit-state dynamic verification with symbolic analysis. The dynamic verification component deterministically replays the execution runs of the program, while the symbolic component encodes a set of interleavings of the observed run of the program in a quantifier-free first order logic formula and verifies it for communication deadlocks. In the absence of property violations, it performs analysis to generate a different run of the program that does not fall in the set of already verified runs. We demonstrate the effectiveness of our approach, which is sound and complete, using our prototype tool HERMES. Our evaluation indicates that HERMES performs significantly better than the state-of-the-art verification tools for *multi-path* MPI programs.

Keywords: Dynamic verification · Message passing interface
Deadlock detection · Symbolic analysis

1 Introduction

Message passing (MP) is a prominent paradigm via which nodes of the distributed systems can communicate. Typically, the MP programs are run on large computer clusters and are developed not only by career computer professionals but also by unconventional programmers affiliated to other disciplines of science. However, designing MP programs is known to be a challenging exercise. Programmers have to anticipate the messaging patterns, perform data marshaling and compute the locations for coordination in order to design correct and efficient programs. Unsurprisingly, this design complexity lends itself to the verification complexity of MP programs. The problem of communication races, which

© Springer International Publishing AG, part of Springer Nature 2018
K. Havelund et al. (Eds.): FM 2018, LNCS 10951, pp. 466–484, 2018.
https://doi.org/10.1007/978-3-319-95582-7_28

leads to data corruption or communication deadlocks, plays a central role in the verification complexity of MP programs.

In the context of discovering communication deadlocks, the problem has been studied extensively over the years [2,11,14,17,19,20,23,25,28]. However, a scalable solution remains elusive; this is primarily due to the nondeterminism in the semantics of MP primitives. For instance, in MPI (Message Passing Interface [21], a popular standard for writing parallel programs in C/Fortran) use of the *wildcard receive* call can lead to nondeterministic matching with potential senders at runtime [30]. Presence (or absence) of buffering in MPI nodes can also contribute to nondeterminism; for instance, standard blocking sends semantics are dependent on the presence of system buffering – under no system buffering the send calls behave as synchronous calls while under infinite buffering the same send calls complete immediately without even requiring a matching receive call. MPI implementations allow nodes to provide buffering in order to improve the performance, however, the nondeterminism resulting from buffering can potentially introduce additional deadlocks [31].

It is worthwhile to note that nondeterministic communication of data can affect the control-flow of the program (*e.g.*, when the communicated data to a wildcard receive is used in a subsequent branch instruction of the program). Programs with the pattern mentioned above are termed as *multi-path* programs [9], and they significantly affect the scalability of existing verification techniques. Correspondingly, *single-path* programs are those (paraphrasing from [9]) where the program executes irrespective of the data communicated to a receive call, the same sequence of instructions, *i.e.*, the control-flow of the program remains unaffected by the communication actions in the program.

Explicit-state runtime model checkers of MPI programs, such as ISP [30] and DAMPI [33], can analyse multi-path (and single-path) MPI programs for the absence of communication deadlocks and assertion violations. However, they require the programs to be repeatedly run such that in each run a distinct communication pattern (such as a send-receive match) is explored. Though the said model checkers are exhaustive in their exploration under a fixed input and a buffering mode (viz. *zero* and *infinite* [31]), they suffer from a possible requirement of a considerable number of program re-runs. It is often the case that much of the time is spent in verifying the loops of the program containing only computation code that is of little relevance to establish the correctness of the communication structure of the program.

Recently, symbolic analysis techniques for MP program executions have been proposed. Although they do address the problem of program re-runs by symbolically encoding the interleavings to explore, they can only be applied to single-path programs [10,15,22]. These techniques are classified as *trace verification* techniques and the tools as *trace verifiers*.

Techniques which perform full-blown symbolic execution of a program can discover deadlocks and other assertion violations in multi-path programs [3,11, 28]. While they cover both the input space and communication nondeterminism, they are known to not scale beyond a relatively small size of the program and a few processes.

We present a sound and complete technique to verify multi-path MPI that is complementary to the above-mentioned techniques. Our technique combines the strengths of trace verification and symbolic execution techniques, which, respectively, provide scalability and multi-path coverage. Furthermore, our technique is able to verify programs with not only zero- or infinite-buffering, but also with nondeterministic buffering decisions up to a bound k. While we present the technique in the context of verifying MPI programs for the absence of deadlocks, it can be applied to other properties, such as assertion violations. We demonstrate the effectiveness of the technique by implementing it as a prototype tool HERMES and comparing it with state-of-the-art tools.

2 Overview

In this section, we present an overview of our hybrid method which discovers deadlocks in multi-path MPI programs. The technique exhaustively explores the executions of the program under a fixed input as follows: (i) it obtains a concrete run ρ of the program via dynamic analysis (via a scheduler that orchestrates a run); (ii) encodes symbolically the set of *feasible runs* obtained from the same set of events as observed in ρ such that each process triggers the same control-flow decisions and executes the same sequence of communication calls as in ρ (note that the encoding captures the entire set of runtime matches of communication events from ρ); (iii) check for violations of any property (in our case, communication deadlocks); and (iv) if no property is violated, then alter the symbolic encoding to explore the feasibility of taking an alternate control flow behavior which is different from ρ. In case of such a feasibility, initiate a different concrete run.

Consider the program shown in Fig. 1(a). It is a nondeterministic, multi-path, and deadlock-free program. The non-colored lines illustrate the pseudo-code of the program. It is worthy to note that *trace verifiers* will fail to verify the program since the program has multiple control flow branches and the nondeterministic matching choice of $R1$ governs the execution of these branches.

Our approach statically discovers the code locations where the received data or message tags (a field in MPI send and receive calls that serve as a unique marker for messages) are used to branch at conditional statements. At these locations, we instrument certain calls to a *scheduler*. The *scheduler* schedules the MPI calls of the program according to the MPI semantics and drives the execution. The scheduler is also responsible for building a partially ordered *happens-before* relation between these calls (refer Sect. 3). At runtime, the instrumented code communicates the predicate expression in the branching instruction to the scheduler. The instrumented code is shown in blue color in Fig. 1(a).

Based on a trace ρ the symbolic encoding is generated from the execution of the program with instrumented code. The communication events and the branching decisions made in this trace are modeled as an SMT formula. This formula encodes all the semantically possible schedules of events observed in ρ, which follow the same control-flow decisions as made in ρ.

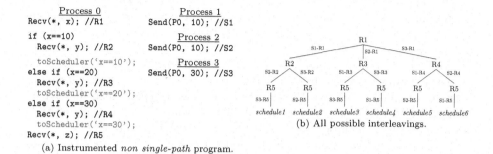

```
       Process 0                 Process 1
Recv(*, x); //R1          Send(P0, 10); //S1

if (x==10)                       Process 2
  Recv(*, y); //R2        Send(P0, 10); //S2

  toScheduler('x==10');          Process 3
else if (x==20)           Send(P0, 30); //S3
  Recv(*, y); //R3
  toScheduler('x==20');
else if (x==30)
  Recv(*, y); //R4
  toScheduler('x==30');
Recv(*, z); //R5
```

(a) Instrumented *non single-path* program.

(b) All possible interleavings.

Fig. 1. Multi-path program and its interleavings. (Color figure online)

In the example shown in Fig. 1(a), **Process** 0 executes the first control flow branch if $R1$ matches with either $S1$ or $S2$. If $R1$ matches $S1$, the SMT formula will encode the interleavings 1 and 2 as shown in Fig. 1(b). An SMT solver is used to solve this formula, which checks for the violation of the safety property. This verifies two interleavings. If there is no property violation, we verify another control flow path that may have been taken if $R1$ had matched with some other send. To this effect, we want to change the path condition obtained from the trace to reschedule another execution through an unvisited control-flow. Hence, we alter the path condition (in a typical symbolic execution style) and execute the program again, so that it follows the path corresponding to the altered path condition. To force the scheduler to follow a different control-flow branch, we may also have to force a wildcard receive call to match with a send call that sends data different from the send call that matched before. We repeat this process until all the paths in the program are exhausted. In the context of the above example, in the second execution, $R1$ must match $S3$, and it must avoid matching $S2$ because $S2$ is sending the same data as $S1$ ($S1$ had already matched with $R1$ in the first execution). The encoding resulting from this run will cover schedules 3 to 6.

The example program has six possible interleavings across multiple control flow paths. Our technique executes the program only twice to cover all of them and thus shows the contrasting difference from trace verification which does not provide full path coverage and from dynamic verification which executes the program as many times as there are possible interleavings.

3   MPI Model and Execution Semantics

In this section we formalize the execution of an MPI program. The MPI runtime often provides buffers to store the data of issued but unfinished calls. The presence of buffers can introduce subtle behaviors in a program [26,31]. Due to space limitations we present a zero-buffer semantics, but our results hold for *zero-*, *infinite-*, and κ-buffer modes, with $\kappa \in \mathbb{N}$.

We consider *MPI programs* consisting of $n \in \mathbb{N}$ processes $P_1, \cdots, P_n$ in a single communication group. Each process P_i manipulates a set of *process-local variables* Var_i. Let $Var = \bigcup_i Var_i$. We model the execution of the program as a sequence of events, one for each executed MPI call. An event of process P_i is a tuple $e := \langle c, a, d \rangle$, where c is a *path constraint* over Var_i (describing the conditional branches taken by P_i to produce the event, the constraint language is left unspecified), a is an *MPI call*, and $d \in \mathbb{N}$ is a *depth* which increments monotonically with the events of P_i. We let E denote the set of all possible events, $p(e) := P_i$ the process of e, and $l(e) := a$ the MPI call of e.

Without loss of generality, we only model nonblocking MPI operations and MPI_Wait. Nonblocking calls return immediately with a handle that can later be passed to MPI_Wait for the process to block until the operation completes. An MPI call is either a nonblocking *send* (resp. *receive*) issued by process P_i to send data to (resp. receive from) process P_j with tag t, denoted by $S_{i,j,t}$ (resp. $R_{i,j,t}$); or a nonblocking *barrier* issued by process P_i, denoted by B_i; or a (blocking) *wait* issued by process P_i in order to wait for the completion of the so-called corresponding event at depth h, denoted by $W_{i,h}$. For a wait event $e := \langle c, W_{i,h}, d \rangle$ the *corresponding event*, *corr(e)*, is the only event of P_i whose depth is h.

The MPI runtime matches send and receive operations (among others) using the well-defined semantics. Given events $e := \langle c, a, d \rangle$ and $e' := \langle c', b, d' \rangle$, we say that e *matches before* e', denoted by $e_1 \prec_{mo} e_2$, iff $p(e) = p(e')$, and $d \le d'$, and one of the following is satisfied: (i) a and b are send calls (resp. receive calls) to the same destination (resp. from the same source) with the same tags; (ii) a is a wildcard receive call and b is a receive call sourcing from the same process, or a wildcard receive and the tags of calls a and b are the same, or the tag of call a is a wildcard; (iii) a is a nonblocking call and b is an associated wait call.

We view the execution of an MPI program as a sequence of events in E^*, but not all sequences correspond to executions. We now define a Labeled Transition System (LTS) $\langle Q, \to, q_0 \rangle$ whose runs capture the valid executions. The *states* in Q are tuples of the form $\langle I, M, z \rangle$ where $I \subseteq E$ is the set of *issued* events, $M \subseteq E$ is the set of *matched* events, and $z \colon \mathbb{N} \to \mathbb{N}$ maps every process to the depth of the next event expected from that process. The *initial state* q_0 is $\langle \emptyset, \emptyset, z_o \rangle$, where z_0 maps all processes to 0.

The $\prec_{mo}$ order captures matching constraints that exclusively depend on the types of the calls involved in the check. However, matching $R_{i,*,t}$ calls requires information about the state. Given a state $s := \langle I, M, z \rangle$ and events $e := \langle c, R_{i,j,t}, d \rangle$ and $e' := \langle c', R_{i,*,t}, d' \rangle$, we say that e *conditionally matches before* e', denoted by $e \prec_{co} e'$, iff $d \le d'$ and $\exists \hat{e} \in I$ such that $l(\hat{e}) = S_{j,i,t}$.

The transitions in $\to \in Q \times 2^E \times Q$ are labeled by sets of events representing either the issuing or completion of MPI calls to the runtime or the matching of communication calls by the runtime. Thus, we have three classes of transitions: Issue, Match, and Complete transitions.

Issue transitions capture the call to a nonblocking MPI primitive represented by event $e := \langle c, a, d \rangle$. Formally, $\langle I, M, z \rangle \xrightarrow{\{e\}} \langle I \cup \{e\}, M, z' \rangle$ iff $d = z(p(e))$, and z' is equal to z except for $z'(p(e))$ which is $z(p(e)) + 1$, and I does not contain any event whose action is a wait from process $p(e)$.

Match transitions correspond to the MPI runtime matching a set of issued events (e.g., a send with a receive). Formally, $\langle I, M, z \rangle \xrightarrow{m} \langle I \setminus m, M \cup m, z \rangle$ exactly when there is some $m \subseteq I$ such that either of the three conditions hold: (i) $m := \{e, e'\}$ with $l(\langle e, e' \rangle) = \langle S_{i,j,t}, R_{j,i,t'} \rangle$ and $\nexists \hat{e} \in I, (\hat{e} \prec_{mo} e \vee \hat{e} \prec_{mo} e')$, and $t' \in \{t, *\}$; or (ii) $m := \{e, e'\}$ with $l(\langle e, e' \rangle) = \langle S_{i,j,t}, R_{j,*,t'} \rangle$ and $\nexists \hat{e} \in I, (\hat{e} \prec_{mo} e \vee \hat{e} \prec_{mo} e' \vee \hat{e} \prec_{co} e')$, and $t' \in \{t, *\}$; or (iii) $m := \{e_1, \ldots, e_n\}$ with $l(e_i) = B_i$ for all $i \in \{1, \ldots, n\}$ and $\nexists \hat{e} \in I, (\hat{e} \prec_{mo} e_1 \vee \ldots \vee \hat{e} \prec_{mo} e_n)$.

Finally, *complete transitions* correspond to calls to MPI_wait returning the control to the process because the corresponding event has already been matched. Formally, $\langle I, M, z \rangle \xrightarrow{\{e\}} \langle I \setminus \{e\}, M \setminus \{corr(e)\}, z \rangle$ iff $l(e) := W_{i,d}$ and $corr(e) \in M$.

An *execution trace* (or just *trace*) $\rho \in E^*$ is any sequence formed by the events contained in the singletons that label a run of the LTS which only uses *issue* transitions. An MPI program P has a *deadlock* if it can generate a trace ρ that ends in a *deadlocking state*, i.e., one with no successors in the LTS. Deciding whether a single-path program has a deadlock is an NP-complete problem [10], under finite and infinite system buffering. Note that our events are guarded MPI calls and thus each trace of P is essentially a single-path program. Since, P has a finite number of single-path programs, it follows that the deadlock detection problem under κ-buffering for P is also NP-complete.

4   Encoding Rules

In this section we define SMT encoding rules such that for a deadlocking execution trace ρ, the variables of the encoding get satisfied and the generated model provides information about the calls that remained unmatched in ρ. The first step is defining an (over-approximated) set of sets of events, $\mathbb{M}^+ \in 2^E$, consisting of all possible sets that the LTS could make using the *match transition* using the same events as in ρ but possibly issued in a different order.

Definition 1. $\mathbb{M}^+$: *The $\mathbb{M}^+$ set is an over-approximate set of the matching calls in a trace [10]:*

$$\mathbb{M}^+ = \{\{a, b\} \subseteq E \mid a = \langle -, S_{i,j,-}, - \rangle, b = \langle -, R_{j,i/*,-}, - \rangle,$$
$$\forall a' \prec_{mo} a \, \exists b' \nprec_{mo} b : \{ a', b' \} \in \mathbb{M}^+,$$
$$\forall b' \prec_{mo} b \, \exists a' \nprec_{mo} a : \{ a', b' \} \in \mathbb{M}^+\}$$
$$\cup \{\{a\} \subseteq E \mid a = \langle -, W_{i,h}, - \rangle\}$$
$$\cup \{\{a_1, \cdots, a_N\} \subseteq E \mid \forall i \in \{1, \ldots, n\}, a_i = \langle -, B_i, - \rangle\} .$$

Let $\mathbb{M}^+(a) = \bigcup\{b|\exists\alpha \in \mathbb{M}^+ : a,b \in \alpha\}$ be the set of all potential matching calls for the operation a. Let $Imm(a)$ be the set of all immediate ancestors of event a. We define it by $Imm(a) = \{x|x \prec a, \forall z : x \preceq z \preceq a \implies z \in \{x,a\}\}$. Note that $\prec = (\prec_{mo} \cup \prec_{co})$ (resp. for $\preceq$).

Following [10], we restrict our presentation to problems without barriers without introducing spurious models. In Fig. 2, we provide the list of rules that encode all feasible interleavings of a given ρ. First, we explain the meaning and purpose of each variable used in the encoding. We use *tag, src (resp. dest)*, and *val* as integer variables to encode MPI call operands such as message tag, sender's (resp. receiver's) identity, and the data payload, respectively. Note that for simplicity we assume the data payload to be of primitive types (such as Integer). In order to model an interleaved run, we use an integer variable *clk* for each call in ρ. Variables m and r are boolean variables which signify the matching and the *readiness* (all $\prec_{mo}$ ancestors of the event are matched) of an event, respectively. A boolean variable *bufferUsed* is used when an event uses the buffer provided by the MPI runtime. We refer the above mentioned variables corresponding to an event a by the variable name sub-scripted with event symbol, for instance, clock variable for event a is denoted by clk_a.

Corresponding to every $\alpha \in \mathbb{M}^+$ we have a boolean variable s_α which we set to true when the events in α occur as a match in ρ. We further define $\mathcal{I} \subseteq E_\rho$ to be the set of event pairs (a,b) such that a and b are consecutive sends from one process but with different destinations. Buffering a can potentially impact the $\prec_{mo}$ relation with respect to call b. When both a and b are send calls targeting the same destination, then, despite buffering, the $\prec_{mo}$ relation between a and b stands unmodified. This is because the FIFO matching guarantee provided by the MPI standard is impervious to the underlying system buffering.

In Fig. 2, most SMT rules are similar to the propositional rules from [10], except Rules 2, 5, 10, 11 and 14. Rule 1 encodes the $\prec_{mo}$ relation with an exception – the order between a pair of send calls $(a,b) \in \mathcal{I}$ is encoded in Rule 10. Rule 5 encodes the semantics of $\prec_{co}$ ordering. We start with an over-approximate set $\mathcal{E}$ that has pairs of receive calls (deterministic receive call, a, followed by a wildcard receive call b). An order is established between such a pair only when there is a *ready* send call that can match a but no send call that can match b. To record the notion of time at which calls become ready, we use the variable r_{clk}. Rules 12 and 13 encode the deadlock detection constraints.

Encoding for κ-Buffer Mode Semantics: Rules 10 and 11 encode the behavior of a program with κ-buffer semantics. The maximum number of buffer slots, κ, available with the program is provided by the user. If a buffer slot is available, the partial order relation between some of the send calls can be relaxed (as explained before).

Encoding for Path Condition: Rule 14 encodes the guards of each event in E_ρ. The guards are the path constraints obtained from the expressions of conditional statements encountered along the program execution.

1. Partial Order: $\bigwedge_{b \in E_\rho} \bigwedge_{a \in Imm(b):(a,b) \notin \mathcal{I}} clk_a < clk_b$

2. Match Pair: $\bigwedge_{a:(s,r) \in M^+} s_a \rightarrow (clk_s = clk_r) \wedge (data_s = data_r) \wedge (tag_s = tag_r)$

3. Unique Match for Send: $\bigwedge_{(a,b) \in M^+} \bigwedge_{(a,c) \in M^+} s_{ab} \rightarrow !s_{ac}$

4. Unique Match for Receive: $\bigwedge_{(a,b) \in M^+} \bigwedge_{(c,b) \in M^+} s_{ab} \rightarrow !s_{cb}$

5. Conditional Partial Order:

    (a) $\bigwedge_{a \in E_\rho} r_a \rightarrow r\_clk_a = clk_{Imm(a)} + 1$

    (b) $\bigwedge_{(a,b) \in \mathcal{E}} \bigwedge_{c \in M^+(b)} (r\_clk_c > r\_clk_a \wedge \bigwedge_{d \in M^+(a)} r\_clk_c > r\_clk_d) \rightarrow clk_a < clk_b$

6. Match Correct: $\bigwedge_{a \in r} (m_a \rightarrow \bigvee_{(b,a) \in M^+} (s_{ba})) \wedge \bigwedge_{a \in s} (m_a \rightarrow \bigvee_{(a,b) \in M^+} (s_{ab}))$

7. Matched only: $\bigwedge_{a:(a_1,a_2,\ldots,a_n) \in M^+} s_a \rightarrow \bigwedge_{a_i \in a} m_{a_i}$

8. All Ancestors Matched: $\bigwedge_{b \in E_\rho} (r_b \leftrightarrow \bigwedge_{a = Imm(b)} m_a)$

9. Match Only Issued: $\bigwedge_{a \in E_\rho} (m_a \rightarrow r_a)$

10. Use Buffer: $\bigwedge_{(a,b) \in \mathcal{I}} (r_a \wedge k > 0 \rightarrow (bufferUsed_a \wedge dec(k))) \wedge (k = 0 \rightarrow !bufferUsed_a \wedge clk_a < clk_b)$

11. Free buffer: $\bigwedge_{a \in E_\rho} k = ite(m_a \wedge bufferUsed_a, inc(k), k)$

12. No Match Possible: $\bigwedge_{a \in M^+} (\bigvee_{t \in a} (m_t \vee !r_t))$

13. Not All Matched: $\bigvee_{a \in E_\rho} !m_a$

14. Path Condition: π_ρ

Fig. 2. SMT rules.

Theorem 1. *Given a trace ρ of program P, ρ ends in a deadlocking state iff there is a satisfying assignment of the variables to values in the SMT encoding of the deadlock detection problem.*

The proof of this theorem is similar to the one used in [10]. It suffices to show that (i) for every deadlocking trace of the program, the encoding rules are satisfied, and (ii) whenever the rules are satisfied, the trace deadlocks. For this, we construct a trace corresponding to the model generated by the solver (which conforms to the MPI semantics) and prove that it is deadlocking. Theorem 1 formally establishes the correctness of our SMT encoding.

5   Design

HERMES comprises of three components: program instrumenter, constraint generator and solver, and instruction rescheduler. In this section, we describe the functionality of these components and present the algorithm that HERMES implements. Figure 3 gives an architectural overview of HERMES.

5.1 Components

Program Instrumenter: The instrumenter is developed using Clang [5]. Clang is the front-end for the LLVM compiler and provides features to analyse, optimize, and instrument C/C++ source code. It targets the locations in the code where the data or the tag received in a wildcard `receive` is decoded in the predicate expression of a conditional construct, the body of which issues an MPI call. It instruments these locations with TCP calls to the scheduler which is responsible for driving the execution of the program. The instrumented calls are used to communicate the predicate expressions to the scheduler at runtime. We use ISP's dynamic verification engine as the scheduler.

Constraint Generator and Solver: The instrumented program is input to the ISP scheduler which executes it. The execution of the program drives the instrumentation to generate a path condition π which corresponds to the expressions of the conditional constructs encountered at target locations during the run. We also generate a set of potential matches, M^+, and a sequence of MPI events, ρ, from the run. M^+, π, and ρ are used to encode the trace of the program in the form of SMT rules given in Sect. 4, which conform to the MPI semantics. The satisfiability of the rules signifies the presence of a deadlock. Please note that the technique presented in this paper is a general verification technique to cover all possible schedules for a given input. The encoding rules provided in Sect. 4, however, are targeted for deadlock detection.

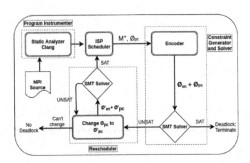

Fig. 3. Architecture of the approach.

Instruction Rescheduler: If the SMT solver cannot generate a model (UNSAT query), we modify π in a way similar to the concolic execution to try and infer the existence of another executable control flow path. In a non-chronological order, we perform a depth-first search over a tree of control flow paths where the branching points in the tree map to the conditional constructs in the target program. The resulting formula is denoted by ϕ. Although we modify the path condition in a fashion similar to concolic execution, we do not inherit its legacy problem of path complexity. This is because (i) unlike concolic execution, we do not symbolically interpret the entire program, and (ii) in our experience, the conditional expressions in multi-path MPI programs are simple equality checks (we have not come across benchmark programs where the relevant conditional expressions were complex).

Algorithm 1. Deadlock Detection.

Data: Instrumented Program: P
Result:
1. Guarantee that a deadlock does not occur
2. Model of the MPI calls if a deadlock is present

1 <Path Condition: π; Trace: ρ; Potential Matches: $\mathbb{M}^+$ > = execute P
2 **while** *true* **do**
3   ϕ_{en} = encode($\mathbb{M}^+$, ρ)
4   res = solver($\phi_{en} \cup \phi_\pi$)
5   **if** *res* == *SAT* **then**
6   report 'Deadlock'; exit
7   **else**
8   ϕ = SearchDifferentPath(ρ, π, $\mathbb{M}^+$)
9   **if** $\phi = \emptyset$ **then**
10   report 'No Deadlock'; exit
11   **else**
12             $< \pi, \rho, \mathbb{M}^+ >$ = execute P conforming to ϕ

5.2   Deadlock Detection

Algorithm 1 formally presents the functionality of the components described in
Sect. 5.1. The input to the algorithm is an instrumented MPI program. Execution
of the program at line 1 generates a program trace: ρ, a path condition: π, and
the potential send-receive match set generated from ρ: $\mathbb{M}^+$. The while loop at
line 2 executes the program repeatedly until either all of the possible control
flow paths are explored or a deadlock is reported. In every iteration of the loop,
we encode the trace ρ into a set of SMT rules and check their satisfiability. If
we get a model from the SMT solver, then we report the deadlock as the output
and exit as shown in lines 3–7. Otherwise, we search for a different control flow
path by calling the procedure SearchDifferentPath at line 9. If that procedure
is unable to find any other feasible path, we report an absence of the deadlock
at line 11 and exit. Otherwise, we repeat the entire process.

We describe in Algorithm 2 the procedure SearchDifferentPath, to change
the path condition and to generate constraints ϕ. The input to the algorithm is
π, ρ, $\mathbb{M}^+$. Incrementally, we start negating the expressions in π from last to first
in the loop starting at line 2. In line 3, we remove the expressions in the path
condition from $(i+1)^{th}$ position until the end and invert the ith last conditional in
π to get the altered conditional expression c at line 5. This c is clubbed with the
already present constraints in a maintained constraint stack to get ϕ at line 7.

We check if it is possible to drive the execution through the altered path in
lines 8–11. For this, we issue a query to the solver with constraints formed from
the rules given in Sect. 4 (ϕ'_{en}) and the constraints accumulated in the constraint
stack (ϕ).

In order to compute ϕ'_{en}, we require (i) a subset of $\mathbb{M}^+$ which we denote by
$\mathbb{M}^+_{clip}$, and (ii) a subsequence of the execution trace which is denoted by ρ_{clip}.

Algorithm 2. Searching different control flow path.

> **Data:** ρ, π, $\mathbb{M}^+$
> **Result:** ϕ

1 size = length(π)-1
2 **forall** $i \in size : 0$ **do**
3   remove($\pi[i + 1] : \pi[size]$)
4      $\pi' = $ negate($\pi[i]$)
5   c = $\pi'[i]$
6   add c in constraintStack
7      $\phi = \bigcup\limits_{j=1}^{j=top} constraintStack[j]$
8      $\phi'_{en} = $ encode($\mathbb{M}^+_{clip}$, σ_{clip}) - ϕ_{safety}
9   res = solver($\phi'_{en} \cup \phi$)
10   **if** $res == SAT$ **then**
11   return ϕ
12 return $\emptyset$

Both $\mathbb{M}^+_{clip}$ and ρ_{clip}, are formed over the set of ordered MPI calls until the point of the conditional block whose predicate is negated in $\pi'(c)$. For brevity, we have only shown the details for chronological backtracking without any optimizations. An optimization strategy is presented in Sect. 6.1.

5.3   Correctness and Termination

The encoding presented in [10] is shown to be sound and complete. The encoding in Algorithm 1 is similar to the encoding from [10], hence the proof of soundness and completeness is also similar. We omit the proof here due to space consideration, but it can be found at HERMES's site.[1] The procedure SearchDifferentPath (shown in Algorithm 2) is sound and complete since we assume the traces are of finite length and the number of distinct control-flow paths in a program is bounded. Thus, by composition, HERMES is sound and complete for a single input.

Algorithm 2 returns $\emptyset$ and terminates at line 12 when it finishes its exhaustive search corresponding to the complete tree of possible control-flow execution paths. Note that the tree of possible control-flow paths is of finite height and width. Algorithm 1's termination is either contingent on the termination of Algorithm 2 or when a deadlock is found at line 6. We conclude that the analysis performed by HERMES terminates.

6   Implementation

We have implemented the proposed technique in a prototype tool called HERMES. We used Clang [5] to instrument the program, ISP [30] as the execution engine or

---

[1] https://github.com/DhritiKhanna/Hermes.

the scheduler, and Z3 [6] as the constraint solver. In the following subsections, we describe the optimizations that we have implemented to limit infeasible control flow paths. These optimizations are conservative and do not affect the soundness and completeness of the approach.

6.1 Non-chronological Backtracking

P_i	P_j
$R_{i,1}$(from $*, x$)	$R_{j,1}$(from $*, y$)
$if(x == 10)$	$if(y == 5)$
$R_{i,2}$(from P_k)	$S_{j,2}$(to $P_i, 10$)

Performing chronological backtracking to alter the path condition π may result in generating queries that cannot be satisfied by the solver. Consider the call $R_{i,1}$ in the adjoining example matches with $S_{j,2}$. π will contain the constraint assume($x == 10$) which, at some point during backtracking, will be inverted. However, inverting this condition alone will generate no new feasible control-flow path unless $R_{i,1}$ matches with a send other than $S_{j,2}$. Thus, inverting the constraint assume($x == 10$) will require the inversion of assume($y == 5$). These two conditions can be a part of a chain of dependencies that form an *unsat-core* of the unsatisfied formula. Hence, instead of chronological backtracking, we find the culpable conflict and backjump directly to the root of this dependency chain and negate the expression of the root node. The static analysis component of the program instrumentation block identifies the conditional expressions which introduce these dependencies.

In a tree of control flow paths, let there be a dependency chain of size d on path p. After verifying p, the number of SAT queries required (in the worst case) to find another feasible control-flow path in chronological backtracking is d. However, with non-chronological backtracking, only one SAT query should suffice.

6.2 Terminated Interleavings

Discovering a new control-flow path in Algorithm 2 requires a change of received data of the wildcard receive corresponding to the negated assume expression. In order to ascertain whether such an execution exists SMT solver is invoked with the modified path condition along with the other constraints. The constraints of the modified path condition depend on the over-approximate match-set $\mathbb{M}^+$, but the program actually runs with ISP's scheduler which makes the matches based on the ample-set. Since $|ample\text{-}set| \leq |\mathbb{M}^+|$, there may be cases when the SMT solver returns a model from line 10 in Algorithm 2, but an actual run satisfying ϕ may not be possible. We handle these scenarios in our implementation by terminating such runs and restoring the state of the previous correct run. We provide an example of a terminated interleaving at our tool's site.[2]

---

[2] https://github.com/DhritiKhanna/Hermes.

7 Evaluation

The purpose of evaluating HERMES is to assess its efficiency and effectiveness in verifying message passing programs. We set this evaluation in the context of C/C++ MPI programs (see footnote 2) and compare HERMES against the state-of-the-art verification tools. To guide the evaluation, we ask the following research questions: [RQ1] How well does the proposed approach fair against state-of-the-art techniques for single-path and multi-path programs? [RQ2] Is the proposed approach effective in discovering deadlocks exposed under finite buffer mode?

Artifacts and Runtime Environment: We used the FEVS test-suite [27] and benchmarks from prior research papers [2,13,29,36]. The multi-path benchmarks include Matrix Multiply, Integrate, Workers, and Monte Carlo for *pi* calculation. A majority of the benchmarks are based on the client-server architecture. The experiments were performed on a 64 bit, Intel quad-core machine with 1.7 GHz processors, 4 GB of RAM, and Ubuntu version 14.04. We used ISP version 3.1 and Z3 version 4.4.2. All timings reported are in seconds and are averaged over 20 runs. TO signifies the time-out after 30 min. Note that the number of executions of HERMES also include the runs which were terminated.

[RQ1] We compared HERMES against the state-of-the-art tools - Mopper (a trace verifier), Aislinn and ISP (dynamic verifiers), and CIVL (a stateful symbolic model checker). We summarize the results in Table 1. On most single-path

Table 1. Performance comparison for single-path MPI programs.

B'mark	#P	B	D	ISP Detect	Runs	Time	Mopper Detect	Time	Aislinn Detect	Time	CIVL Detect	Time	HERMES Detect	Time
DTG	5	0	✔	Yes	3	2.135	Yes	0.007	Yes	0.830	Yes	8.72	Yes	0.0365
	5	∞			3	2.257		0.043		0.815				0.077
	8	0	✔	Yes	3	2.220	Yes	0.011	Yes	1.135	Yes	8.78	Yes	0.040
	8	∞			3	2.307		0.044		1.139				0.080
Gauss Elim	4	0			1	0.529		0.210		8.936		TO		0.300
	8	0			1	0.371		0.295		14.322		TO		0.423
	16	0			1	2.041		0.408		TO		TO		0.659
	32	0			1	5.457		0.856		TO		TO		1.163
Heat	4	0	✔	Yes	7	8.572	Yes	0.365		★		★	Yes	0.389
	8	0	✔	-	>1K	TO	Yes	0.593		★		★	Yes	0.660
	16	0	✔	-	>1K	TO	Yes	0.927		★		★	Yes	1.063
	32	0	✔	-	>1K	TO	Yes	1.709		★		★	Yes	2.036
2D Diffusion	4	0	✔	Yes	1	0.008		NI			Yes	8.523		NI
	4	∞			90	123.733		0.388		0.908				0.451
	8	0	✔	Yes	1	0.05		NI			Yes	12.461		NI
	8	∞			>1.1K	TO		TO		16.020				TO
Floyd (5)	4	0			1	0.005		0.020		0.640		TO		0.078
	8	0			>1.6K	TO		0.116		1.391		TO		0.218
	16	0			>1.6K	TO		0.128		2.998		TO		0.540
	32	0			>1.6K	TO		3.836		6.424		TO		2.829

B'mark: Benchmark; #P: Number of Processes, B: Buffering Mode; D: Deadlock Exists
★: Benchmark not supported; NI: Not Invoked

Table 2. Performance comparison for multi-path MPI programs.

B'mark	#P	B	D	ISP		Aislinn	CIVL	HERMES	
				Runs	Time	Time	Time	Runs	Time
Monte (0.15)	4	0		6	6.025	0.971	⋆	3	2.326
	5	0		24	28.346	1.668	⋆	4	3.472
	6	0		120	151.598	5.028	⋆	5	4.819
	8	0		>1.2K	TO	10.173	⋆	7	7.434
MatrixMul (2 × 2 matrices)	4	∞		36	39.669	0.866	17.93	1	7.252
	5	∞		144	163.277	1.101	25.307	1	9.993
	6	∞		720	837.633	1.334	48.068	1	12.925
	8	∞		~1.5K	TO	2.206	258.86	1	19.670
Integrate	4	0		27	32.755	0.858	910.36◇	1	0.206
	5	0		256	332.362	3.030	156.82◇	1	0.302
	6	0		3125	TO	27.839	157.63◇	1	0.497
	8	0		>1.5K	TO	TO	173.27◇	1	0.852
Workers (8 jobs; size of job = 2)	4	0		18	20.975	1.549	37.76	1	0.360
	5	0		24	28.433	1.368	72.333	1	0.384
	6	0		120	151.525	2.286	1027.31	1	0.510
	8	0		~1.3K	TO	9.113	TO	1	1.021

B'mark: Benchmark; #P: Number of Processes, B: Buffer Mode; D: Deadlock Exists
⋆: Benchmark not supported; ◇: Result = null (probably an internal CIVL error: the theorem prover has not said anything)

benchmarks the performance of HERMES is comparable to Mopper and considerably better than the other state-of-the-art explicit-state model checkers without compromising on error-reporting. Benchmark 2D Diffusion exhibits a complex communication pattern and a high degree of nondeterminism which leads to a huge M^+. Hence, symbolic analysis tools do not perform well for such benchmarks. We use --potential-deadlock option of CIVL which verifies the program irrespective of the buffering mode.

Evaluation with multi-path programs required us to compare HERMES with all tools except Mopper, since Mopper is constrained to work with only single-path programs. The basis for comparing against ISP is the number of times a program is executed while the basis for comparing with other tools is the time taken to complete the verification. The results of our comparison are summarized in Table 2. On all benchmarks ISP times out for as few as 8 processes. Aislinn on most benchmarks (barring MatrixMul) either takes longer execution time in comparison with HERMES or times out. The results indicate that when the number of processes increases, the growth in execution time is relatively reasonable in HERMES in comparison with ISP and Aislinn. The scalability of HERMES regarding number of processes comes from the fact that it prunes out the redundant paths and explores only the feasible ones. CIVL is a powerful and a heavy stateful model checker that can backtrack as soon as it witnesses a visited state. An advantage of CIVL over the other tools is that it can verify programs on complex correctness properties over a wide range of inputs. However, CIVL was consistently slower than HERMES on all benchmarks barring Heat. The Heat benchmark contained MPI calls that are not supported by CIVL yet.

[RQ2] MPI standard allows flexibility in the ways send calls are buffered. Aislinn buffers send calls if the size of the sent message is not greater than a parameter provided by the user. On the other hand, we follow the approach taken by Siegel et al. [26] and model the buffer as a limited resource. In other words, send calls use the buffer if it is available. Due to these differences, we cannot compare HERMES with Aislinn in the context of κ-buffer mode.

To demonstrate the importance of κ-buffer mode, we ran HERMES on the benchmarks used in [2,31]. HERMES detected the deadlocks when a buffer of size one was provided. The deadlock in the program disappears under zero-buffer and infinite-buffer modes.

8   Related Work

Deadlock detection in message passing programs is an active research domain with a rich body of literature. There are numerous popular debuggers or program correctness checkers which provide features such as monitoring the program run [16,18,32]. However, they fall short to verify the space of communication non-determinism.

Predictive trace analysis for multi-threaded C programs is another popular area of work. The central idea in these techniques is to encode the thread interleavings of a program execution [34,35]. These techniques rely on the computation of a symbolic causal relation in the form of a partial order. The work in [34] motivated the predictive trace analysis work for MPI, MCAPI, and CSP/CCS programs [7,9,14,15,22]. The encoding presented by Forejt et al. [9] is similar to the encoding for a static bounded model checking approach to analyse shared memory programs [1] but is restricted to *single-path* programs.

HERMES's contribution on selective program instrumentation is motivated by the work in [12], which identified, using taint analysis, the relevant input sources and shared accesses that influence control-flow decisions. The use of taint analysis to extract input sources and shared accesses is an important step for covering relevant program behaviors.

Marques et al. developed a type-based strategy to statically verify MPI programs [17,20]. They verify the annotated MPI program against the protocol specifications capturing the behavior of the program using session types. Unlike model checking, their approach is not influenced by the number of processes and problem size and is insensitive to scalability issues. But they consider only deterministic and loop-free programs.

Concolic Testing (Dynamic Symbolic Execution) combines concrete execution and symbolic execution [4,24] to overcome the limitation of SAT/SMT solvers when faced with nonlinear constraints. Sherlock [8] is a deadlock detector for Java concurrent programs which combines concolic execution with constraint solving. While we use SMT encoding to scan through all permissible schedules of a path, Sherlock instead permutes the instructions of one schedule to get another schedule. A fair comparison of HERMES with concolic execution techniques cannot be performed since HERMES does not consider every conditional statement to be included in the path condition.

CIVL [19] is an intermediate language to capture concurrency semantics of a set of concurrency dialects such as OpenMP, Pthreads, CUDA, and MPI. The back-end verifier can statically check properties such as functional correctness, deadlocks, and adherence to the rules of the MPI standard. CIVL creates a model of the program using symbolic execution and then uses model checking. HERMES creates a model of a single path of the program and uses symbolic encoding to verify that path of the program. It also uses data-aware analysis to prune irrelevant control-flow branches of the program. CIVL does not handle non-blocking MPI operations.

Vakkalanka et al. proposed POE_{MSE} algorithm [31] to dynamically verify MPI programs under a varying buffer capacity of MPI nodes. To this effect they employ an enumerative strategy to find a minimal set of culprit sends which, if buffered, can cause deadlocks. Siegel had proposed a model checking approach where the availability of buffers is encoded in the states of model itself [26].

Aislinn [2] is an explicit-state model checker which verifies MPI programs with arbitrary-sized system buffers and uses POR to prune the redundant state space. Aislinn models the buffer as an unlimited entity and the send calls use the buffers when their message size is bigger than a user provided value.

9   Conclusion and Future Work

We combined constraint solving with dynamic verification to discover communication deadlocks in *multi-path* MPI programs. For C/C++ MPI programs, the technique is concretized in a tool HERMES. It formulates an SMT query from the program's trace by conforming to the MPI runtime semantics and the non-deterministic buffer modes provided by MPI implementations. By capturing the flow of data values through communication calls, HERMES restricts the dynamic scheduler to explore a significantly fewer number of traces as compared to the explorations performed by a dynamic verifier. We tested our proposed technique on FEVS test suite and other benchmarks used in past research and found that our technique compares favorably with the state-of-the-art dynamic verification tools.

In the future, we plan to focus on ensuring the correctness of MPI programs with collective operations. Currently, we have implemented our tool with the assumption that the data which is received in a wildcard `receive` call and used in a conditional statement is only an integer variable or tag. This is a limitation of the implementation, which we plan to address in future work. However, a more subtle limitation that we impose is that the received data is not modified between the point from where it is received to the point where it is used (in the conditional statement). The constraint was motivated by analysing a large number of benchmarks. We, in our experience, did not find that the received data underwent a transformation before it was decoded in a control statement. Note, however, that this limitation can be relaxed by allowing assignment statement in the trace language that we defined in Sect. 3. Extending the technique on these lines will possibly allow us to analyse a larger and more complex set of MPI programs.

Acknowledgements. This work is partly supported by the Tata Consultancy Services grant and Infosys Centre for Artificial Intelligence at IIIT Delhi. The authors thank the anonymous reviewers for their valuable feedback.

References

1. Alglave, J., Kroening, D., Tautschnig, M.: Partial orders for efficient bounded model checking of concurrent software. In: Sharygina, N., Veith, H. (eds.) CAV 2013. LNCS, vol. 8044, pp. 141–157. Springer, Heidelberg (2013). https://doi.org/10.1007/978-3-642-39799-8_9
2. Böhm, S., Meca, O., Jančar, P.: State-space reduction of non-deterministically synchronizing systems applicable to deadlock detection in MPI. In: Fitzgerald, J., Heitmeyer, C., Gnesi, S., Philippou, A. (eds.) FM 2016. LNCS, vol. 9995, pp. 102–118. Springer, Cham (2016). https://doi.org/10.1007/978-3-319-48989-6_7
3. Bucur, S., Ureche, V., Zamfir, C., Candea, G.: Parallel symbolic execution for automated real-world software testing. In: Proceedings of the Sixth Conference on Computer Systems. EuroSys 2011, pp. 183–198. ACM (2011)
4. Cadar, C., Dunbar, D., Engler, D.: Klee: unassisted and automatic generation of high-coverage tests for complex systems programs. In: Proceedings of the 8th USENIX Conference on Operating Systems Design and Implementation. OSDI 2008, pp. 209–224. USENIX Association (2008)
5. Clang: A C language family frontend for LLVM. http://clang.llvm.org/
6. de Moura, L., Bjørner, N.: Z3: an efficient SMT solver. In: Ramakrishnan, C.R., Rehof, J. (eds.) TACAS 2008. LNCS, vol. 4963, pp. 337–340. Springer, Heidelberg (2008). https://doi.org/10.1007/978-3-540-78800-3_24
7. Elwakil, Mohamed, Yang, Zijiang, Wang, Liqiang: CRI: symbolic debugger for MCAPI applications. In: Bouajjani, Ahmed, Chin, Wei-Ngan (eds.) ATVA 2010. LNCS, vol. 6252, pp. 353–358. Springer, Heidelberg (2010). https://doi.org/10.1007/978-3-642-15643-4_27
8. Eslamimehr, M., Palsberg, J.: Sherlock: scalable deadlock detection for concurrent programs. In: Proceedings of the 22nd ACM SIGSOFT International Symposium on Foundations of Software Engineering. FSE 2014, pp. 353–365. ACM (2014)
9. Forejt, V., Joshi, S., Kroening, D., Narayanaswamy, G., Sharma, S.: Precise predictive analysis for discovering communication deadlocks in MPI programs. ACM Trans. Program. Lang. Syst. **39**(4), 15:1–15:27 (2017)
10. Forejt, V., Kroening, D., Narayanaswamy, G., Sharma, S.: Precise predictive analysis for discovering communication deadlocks in MPI programs. In: Jones, C., Pihlajasaari, P., Sun, J. (eds.) FM 2014. LNCS, vol. 8442, pp. 263–278. Springer, Cham (2014). https://doi.org/10.1007/978-3-319-06410-9_19
11. Fu, X., Chen, Z., Yu, H., Huang, C., Dong, W., Wang, J.: Symbolic execution of MPI programs. In: Proceedings of the 37th International Conference on Software Engineering, vol. 2. ICSE 2015, pp. 809–810. IEEE Press (2015)

12. Ganai, M., Lee, D., Gupta, A.: DTAM: dynamic taint analysis of multi-threaded programs for relevancy. In: Proceedings of the ACM SIGSOFT 20th International Symposium on the Foundations of Software Engineering. FSE 2012, pp. 46:1–46:11 (2012)
13. Gropp, W., Lusk, E., Skjellum, A.: Using MPI: Portable Parallel Programming with the Message-passing Interface, 2nd edn. MIT Press, Cambridge (1999)
14. Huang, Y., Mercer, E.: Detecting MPI zero buffer incompatibility by SMT encoding. In: Havelund, K., Holzmann, G., Joshi, R. (eds.) NFM 2015. LNCS, vol. 9058, pp. 219–233. Springer, Cham (2015). https://doi.org/10.1007/978-3-319-17524-9_16
15. Huang, Y., Mercer, E., McCarthy, J.: Proving MCAPI executions are correct using SMT. In: Proceedings of the 28th IEEE/ACM International Conference on Automated Software Engineering, pp. 26–36. IEEE (2013)
16. Krammer, B., Bidmon, K., Müller, M.S., Resch, M.M.: MARMOT: an MPI analysis and checking tool. In: PARCO. Advances in Parallel Computing. Elsevier (2003)
17. López, H.A., Marques, E.R.B., Martins, F., Ng, N., Santos, C., Vasconcelos, V.T., Yoshida, N.: Protocol-based verification of message-passing parallel programs. In: Proceedings of the 2015 ACM SIGPLAN International Conference on Object-Oriented Programming, Systems, Languages, and Applications. OOPSLA 2015, pp. 280–298. ACM (2015)
18. Luecke, G.R., Zou, Y., Coyle, J., Hoekstra, J., Kraeva, M.: Deadlock detection in MPI programs. Concurrency Comput. Pract. Experience 14(11), 911–932 (2002)
19. Luo, Z., Zheng, M., Siegel, S.F.: Verification of MPI programs using CIVL. In: Proceedings of the 24th European MPI Users' Group Meeting. EuroMPI 2017, pp. 6:1–6:11. ACM (2017)
20. Marques, E.R.B., Martins, F., Vasconcelos, V.T., Ng, N., Martins, N.: Towards deductive verification of MPI programs against session types. In: Proceedings 6th Workshop on Programming Language Approaches to Concurrency and Communication-cEntric Software. PLACES 2013, pp. 103–113 (2013)
21. MPI: A message-passing interface standard version 3.1. http://mpi-forum.org/docs/mpi-3.1/
22. Narayanaswamy, G.: When truth is efficient: analysing concurrency. In: Proceedings of the 2015 International Symposium on Software Testing and Analysis. ISSTA 2015, pp. 141–152. ACM (2015)
23. Sato, K., Ahn, D.H., Laguna, I., Lee, G.L., Schulz, M., Chambreau, C.M.: Noise injection techniques to expose subtle and unintended message races. In: Proceedings of the 22Nd ACM SIGPLAN Symposium on Principles and Practice of Parallel Programming. PPoPP 2017, pp. 89–101 (2017)
24. Sen, K., Marinov, D., Agha, G.: Cute: a concolic unit testing engine for c. In: Proceedings of the 10th European Software Engineering Conference Held Jointly with 13th ACM SIGSOFT International Symposium on Foundations of Software Engineering. ESEC/FSE 2013, pp. 263–272 (2005)
25. Sharma, S.V., Gopalakrishnan, G., Kirby, R.M.: A survey of MPI related debuggers and tools. Technical Report UUCS-07-015, University of Utah, School of Computing (2007). http://www.cs.utah.edu/research/techreports.shtml
26. Siegel, S.F.: Efficient verification of halting properties for MPI programs with wildcard receives. In: Cousot, R. (ed.) VMCAI 2005. LNCS, vol. 3385, pp. 413–429. Springer, Heidelberg (2005). https://doi.org/10.1007/978-3-540-30579-8_27
27. Siegel, S.F., Zirkel, T.K.: Fevs: a functional equivalence verification suite for high-performance scientific computing. Math. Comput. Sci. 5, 427–435 (2011)

28. Siegel, S.F., Zirkel, T.K.: TASS: the toolkit for accurate scientific software. Math. Comput. Sci. 5(4), 395–426 (2011)
29. Vakkalanka, S.: Efficient Dynamic Verification Algorithms for MPI Applications. Ph.D thesis (2010)
30. Vakkalanka, S., Gopalakrishnan, G., Kirby, R.M.: Dynamic verification of MPI programs with reductions in presence of split operations and relaxed orderings. In: Gupta, A., Malik, S. (eds.) CAV 2008. LNCS, vol. 5123, pp. 66–79. Springer, Heidelberg (2008). https://doi.org/10.1007/978-3-540-70545-1_9
31. Vakkalanka, S., Vo, A., Gopalakrishnan, G., Kirby, R.M.: Precise dynamic analysis for slack elasticity: adding buffering without adding bugs. In: Keller, R., Gabriel, E., Resch, M., Dongarra, J. (eds.) EuroMPI 2010. LNCS, vol. 6305, pp. 152–159. Springer, Heidelberg (2010). https://doi.org/10.1007/978-3-642-15646-5_16
32. Vetter, J.S., de Supinski, B.R.: Dynamic software testing of MPI applications with umpire. In: Proceedings of the 2000 ACM/IEEE Conference on Supercomputing. SC 2000. IEEE Computer Society (2000)
33. Vo, A., Aananthakrishnan, S., Gopalakrishnan, G., Supinski, B.R.D., Schulz, M., Bronevetsky, G.: A scalable and distributed dynamic formal verifier for MPI programs. In: Proceedings of the 2010 ACM/IEEE International Conference for High Performance Computing, Networking, Storage and Analysis. SC 2010, pp. 1–10. IEEE Computer Society (2010)
34. Wang, C., Kundu, S., Ganai, M., Gupta, A.: Symbolic predictive analysis for concurrent programs. In: Cavalcanti, A., Dams, D.R. (eds.) FM 2009. LNCS, vol. 5850, pp. 256–272. Springer, Heidelberg (2009). https://doi.org/10.1007/978-3-642-05089-3_17
35. Wang, C., Limaye, R., Ganai, M., Gupta, A.: Trace-based symbolic analysis for atomicity violations. In: Proceedings of the 16th International Conference on Tools and Algorithms for the Construction and Analysis of Systems. TACAS 2010, pp. 328–342 (2010)
36. Xue, R., Liu, X., Wu, M., Guo, Z., Chen, W., Zheng, W., Zhang, Z., Voelker, G.: Mpiwiz: subgroup reproducible replay of mpi applications. In: Proceedings of the 14th ACM SIGPLAN Symposium on Principles and Practice of Parallel Programming. PPoPP 2009, pp. 251–260 (2009)

To Compose, or Not to Compose, That Is the Question: An Analysis of Compositional State Space Generation

Sander de Putter$^{(\boxtimes)}$ (ID) and Anton Wijs$^{(\boxtimes)}$ (ID)

Eindhoven University of Technology,
PO Box 513, 5600 MB Eindhoven, The Netherlands
{s.m.j.d.putter,a.j.wijs}@tue.nl

Abstract. To combat state space explosion several compositional verification approaches have been proposed. One such approach is compositional aggregation, where a given system consisting of a number of parallel components is iteratively composed and minimised. Compositional aggregation has shown to perform better (in the size of the largest state space in memory at one time) than classical monolithic composition in a number of cases. However, there are also cases in which compositional aggregation performs much worse.

It is unclear when one should apply compositional aggregation in favor of other techniques and how it is affected by action hiding and the scale of the model.

This paper presents a descriptive analysis following the quantitiative experimental approach. The experiments were conducted in a controlled test bed setup in a computer laboratory environment. A total of eight scalable models with different network topologies considering a number of varying properties were investigated comprising 119 subjects. This makes it the most comprehensive study done so far on the topic. We investigate whether there is any systematic difference in the success of compositional aggregation based on the model, scaling, and action hiding. Our results indicate that both scaling up the model and hiding more behaviour has a positive influence on compositional aggregation.

1 Introduction

Although model checking [5] is one of the most successful approaches for the analysis and verification of the behaviour of concurrent systems, it is plagued with the so-called *state space explosion problem*: the state space of a concurrent system tends to increase exponentially as the number of parallel processes increases linearly.

To combat state space explosion several compositional approaches have been proposed such as assume-guarantee reasoning [19,29] and partial model checking [2]. An evaluation of assume-guarantee reasoning was recently

S. de Putter—This work is supported by ARTEMIS Joint Undertaking project EMC2 (grant nr. 621429).

conducted [7]. The study raises doubt whether it is an effective alternative to classical, monolithic model checking.

A prominent alternative approach is compositional aggregation [9,10] (also known as compositional state space generation [36], incremental composition and reduction [33], incremental reachability analysis [34,35], and inductive compression [32]). Given a system consisting of a number of parallel components the *compositional aggregation* approach iteratively composes the components and minimises the result. *Action abstraction* or *hiding* [24] may be applied to abstract away all actions irrelevant for the property being verified such that minimisation is more effective. The idea of compositional aggregation is that incremental minimisation should warrant a lower maximum memory use than composing the system monolithicly. Compositional aggregation has shown to perform better (in the size of the largest state space in memory) than monolithic composition in a number of cases [8,9,11,30,34]. However, sometimes the former is not effective, even producing a (much) larger state space than the monolithic approach [11].

The aggregation order of a composition can be understood as a tree, where leaves are the parallel components and the nodes represent an operation that constructs a composite Labelled Transition System (LTS) from the children nodes and minimises the result. As such the number of possible aggregation orders is exponential in the number of parallel components. The selection of an efficient order, i.e., that results in compositional aggregation being as memory efficient as possible is still an unsolved issue [9].

To automate the selection of the aggregation order several heuristics have been proposed [8,9,34]. However, it is unpredictable whether aggregation orders selected by the heuristics are an improvement over the monolithic approach. Insights in the conditions in which compositional aggregation is expected to perform well are vital for successful application of the techniques, but these insights are currently limited. Evaluation of compositional aggregation and heuristics is, to the best of our knowledge, only limited to small benchmarks with no control on aggregation order, model scale, and action hiding. To gain understanding on how these variables influence the effectiveness of compositional aggregation, this paper presents a *characterisation* of the compositional aggregation method. The *objective* of this study is as follows:

> Analyse *compositional aggregation* for the purpose of *characterisation* of the *maximum memory use of the generated state space* in the context of *aggregation orderings of concurrent models with different scaling and action hiding*.

The goal is to find guidelines that help deciding whether to apply compositional aggregation. To this end we address the following main research question.

> **RQ main:** *When can compositional aggregation be expected to be more (memory) efficient than monolithic minimisation?*

To answer this question we first answer a number of smaller questions. First, we investigate the effect of three specific aspects of the application of compositional aggregation: the aggregation order, the amount of action hiding, and the number of parallel processes in the model that compositional aggregation is applied on.

RQ 1: *How do action hiding, number of parallel processes, and aggregation order affect the memory consumption of compositional aggregation?*

As stated earlier, some aggregation orders are better than others. Heuristics are employed in an attempt to find the well performing aggregation orders. Therefore, to determine whether or not it is wise to apply compositional aggregation the performance of the heuristics must be kept in mind.

RQ 2: *How effective are the aggregation orders chosen by current heuristics?*

Having established what minimisation approach is most efficient on which variants of the models, we finally investigate the relation between subjects within these two groups (compositional aggregation and monolithic minimisation). Answering this research question provides insights into which structural properties of models are indicative for the success or failure of compositional aggregation.

RQ 3: *How can the success or failure of compositional aggregation be explained?*

In terms of scaling, due to the exponential growth of aggregation orders, we limit the number of analysed aggregation orders to 2,647, this is precisely the number of aggregation orders for a model consisting of six parallel components, hence, an optimum can be found for subjects up to a scale of six. The action hiding sets are derived from properties formulated for the corresponding models using the *maximal hiding* technique [24]. Finally, for minimisation we use branching bisimulation with explicit divergence [15] as it supports a broad range of safety and liveness properties.

Contributions. We present our findings after having conducted a thorough experiment to study the effectiveness of compositional aggregation when applied on models with varying network topologies. Having exhaustively analysed a significant number of possible aggregation orders, we are able to compare several heuristics proposed in the literature with the optimal composition results. In total, we have selected 119 subjects for the analysis, making this the most comprehensive study performed on the topic so far. Our main conclusion is that the amount of internal behaviour of individual processes in the model, and the amount of synchronisation between those processes, seem to be the two main factors influencing the success of compositional aggregation. Furthermore, our results suggest that there is real potential to construct better heuristics in the near future.

Note that the study was conducted on networks of LTSs and, therefore, the results are possibly limited to models represented as networks of LTSs.

Structure of the Paper. In Sect. 2, we discuss related work. Preliminaries are given in Sect. 3. The methodology used in our experiment is discussed in Sect. 4. Section 5 presents our results, and finally, conclusions and future work are discussed in Sect. 6.

2   Related Work

Compositional Aggregation. In the past, compositional aggregation has been applied in a number of experiments [8,11,35]. In [35], the experiments do not involve the optimal aggregation order for each considered case, and they target a set of models mostly consisting of randomly generated models and variations of only one or two real use cases. Not involving the optimal order means that it is impossible to indicate the quality of the considered heuristics, i.e., how well they perform compared to how well they *could* potentially perform. The usefulness of insights gained by analysing randomly generated models heavily depends on how similar the models are to real models, in terms of their structural characteristics.

In [8], two of the three heuristics proposed in [35] are further developed and combined into what the authors call *smart reduction*. They consider a benchmark set of 28 models that are variants of 13 models. This is a relatively high number of subjects, but unfortunately, discussion of the results is very limited, and the differences between subjects based on the same model are not explained. Due to this, the effect of these differences between the subjects cannot be correlated to the presented performance.

In [11] the combined heuristic is subjected to another experiment to show the effect of action hiding, i.e., abstraction of behaviour irrelevant for the considered functional property. The experiment measures the largest number of states generated during aggregation with and without action hiding. The experiment considers 90 subjects; a single (industrial) use case consisting of 5 scenarios, each considering a subset of 25 properties. They report that action hiding improves the performance of the heuristic. It is not reported whether there is a correlation between the amount of reduction and the properties.

Other Compositional Approaches. A method for automatically generating context constraints for compositional aggregation methods is proposed in [6]. It consists of generating an interface LTS representing the communicating behaviour of a set of components, and then composing this interface with the remainder of the components. The resulting state space is observably equivalent to the monolithicly generated state space. To evaluate the approach the authors perform several experiments with client/server models that are scaled by adding clients to the model. In each experiment the aggregation order was fixed. In contrast, we both scale the models and vary the aggregation orders to see how they affect the effectiveness of the technique.

An evaluation of automated assume-guarantee reasoning was conducted in [7]. The authors study whether assume-guarantee reasoning provides an advantage over monolithic verification. They conclude by raising doubts whether assume-guarantee reasoning is an effective compositional verification approach. However, no attempts were made to investigate the effects of combining multiple components in one step, i.e., n-way decomposition, and action hiding. Assume-guarantee reasoning may be more effective when these approaches are involved.

Assume-guarantee reasoning by abstraction refinement [14] improves upon the approach. The technique is inspired by the experience that small interfaces between components positively affect compositional reasoning. The study considers four cases with a total of twelve subjects. The improved approach uses less memory than the original one in seven of the twelve subjects. However, it is not reported how the memory consumption is measured (i.e., of what the memory consumption is measured exactly), and furthermore, the results are not compared to monolithic verification.

An n-way decomposition with alphabet refinement is proposed in [1]. A benchmark consisting of three cases with a total of fifteen subjects is performed, but memory consumption is not reported. In eight of the fifteen subjects, the approach turned out to be faster than monolithic verification.

Other contributions to assume-guarantee reasoning [16,26] present similarly small benchmarks with the number of cases not exceeding four and the number of subjects not exceeding seventeen. In [16] memory consumption is reported as the number of states in an assumption LTS, however, no correlation with actual memory consumption is discussed. In [26] the memory consumption of the tools used is reported. Still, all these benchmarks suffer from the problem of repeated measures.

Concluding, compared to our study, none of the related studies consider (non-random) models of varying network topologies, and take those topologies explicitly into account. We also study in detail the effect of action hiding. Furthermore, in none of the studies the results are corrected for repeated measures, which occur when you obtain results from variations of test cases. Finally, it should be noted that most studies consider to few cases and subjects to extract general conclusions.

3   Background

Our experiments are performed using the CADP toolbox [11]. In this section, we explain the computational model behind compositional aggregation as offered by CADP.

Vectors. A vector $\bar{v}$ of size n contains n elements indexed from 1 to n. We write $1..n$ for the set of integers ranging from 1 to n. For all $i \in 1..n$, $\bar{v}_i$ represents the ith element of $\bar{v}$. Given a vector of indices $I \subseteq 1..n$, the *projection* of a vector $\bar{v}$ on to I is defined as the vector $\bar{v}^I = \langle \bar{v}_{I_1}, \ldots, \bar{v}_{I_{|I|}} \rangle$ of length $|I|$.

Labelled Transition System (LTS). The semantics of a process, or a composition of several processes, can be formally expressed by an LTS as presented in Definition 1.

490   S. de Putter and A. Wijs

Definition 1 (Labelled Transition System). *An LTS $\mathcal{G}$ is a tuple $(\mathcal{S}_\mathcal{G}, \mathcal{A}_\mathcal{G}, \mathcal{T}_\mathcal{G}, \mathcal{I}_\mathcal{G})$, with*

- $\mathcal{S}_\mathcal{G}$ *a finite set of states;*
- $\mathcal{A}_\mathcal{G}$ *a set of action labels;*
- $\mathcal{T}_\mathcal{G} \subseteq \mathcal{S}_\mathcal{G} \times \mathcal{A}_\mathcal{G} \times \mathcal{S}_\mathcal{G}$ *a transition relation;*
- $\mathcal{I}_\mathcal{G} \subseteq \mathcal{S}_\mathcal{G}$ *a (non-empty) set of initial states.*

Internal, or hidden, system steps are represented by the special action label $\tau \in \mathcal{A}_\mathcal{G}$. A transition $(s, a, s') \in \mathcal{T}_\mathcal{G}$, or $s \xrightarrow{a}_\mathcal{G} s'$ for short, denotes that LTS $\mathcal{G}$ can move from state s to state s' by performing the a-action. A sequence consisting of at least one τ-transition is denoted by $\xrightarrow{\tau}{}^+_\mathcal{G}$.

An equivalence relation between two LTSs relates states that have equivalent behaviour. We use *divergence-preserving branching Bisimulation*, also called *branching bisimulation with explicit divergence* [15]. It supports action hiding and preserves both safety and liveness properties, due to the fact that it is sensitive to cycles of τ-transitions, i.e., inifinite internal behaviour. The smallest infinite ordinal is denoted by ω.

Definition 2 (Divergence-Preserving Branching bisimulation). *A binary relation B between two LTSs $\mathcal{G}_1$ and $\mathcal{G}_2$ is a divergence-preserving branching bisimulation iff it is symmetric and for all $s \in \mathcal{S}_{\mathcal{G}_1}$ and $t \in \mathcal{S}_{\mathcal{G}_2}$, $s\ B\ t$ implies:*

1. *if $s \xrightarrow{a}_{\mathcal{G}_1} s'$ then*
   (a) *either $a = \tau$ with $s'\ B\ t$;*
   (b) *or $t \xrightarrow{\tau}{}^*_{\mathcal{G}_2} \hat{t} \xrightarrow{a}_{\mathcal{G}_2} t'$ with $s\ B\ \hat{t}$ and $s'\ B\ t'$.*
2. *if there is an infinite sequence of states $(s^k)_{k\in\omega}$ such that $s = s^0$, $s^k \xrightarrow{\tau}_{\mathcal{G}_1} s^{k+1}$ and $s^k\ B\ t$ for all $k \in \omega$, then there exists a state t' such that $t \xrightarrow{\tau}{}^+_{\mathcal{G}_2} t'$ and $s^k\ B\ t'$ for some $k \in \omega$.*

The *minimisation* of an LTS consists of the merging of all states that are related by a divergence-preserving branching bisimulation relation. To maximise the potential for minimisation, *maximal hiding* [24] can be applied, which identifies exactly which actions are essential to correctly determine whether an LTS satisfies a given functional property or not. This roughly corresponds to hiding all actions except those occurring in the formula. For this to work correctly, the property needs to be specified in a fragment of the modal μ-calculus, which is expressive enough to express most properties. When combined with compositional model checking, actions of one process that require synchronisation with those of another cannot be abstracted away prematurely.

LTS Network. An *LTS network* $\mathcal{M}$ is a tuple $(\Pi, \mathcal{V})$, with Π a vector of *process* LTSs and $\mathcal{V}$ a set of synchronisation laws that define by means of vectors of actions which actions of the corresponding LTSs can synchronise with each other. For example, a law $(\langle a, b\rangle, c)$ defines that in a network consisting of two LTSs, a transition labelled a of LTS Π_1 can synchronise with a b-transition of LTS Π_2, resulting in a c-transition in the resulting LTS, called the *system*

LTS. This system LTS is the result of first combining the initial states of the individual process LTSs into state vectors, together defining the set of initial states, and then repeatedly combining process transitions according to the laws, and combining the target states of those transitions into vectors of process LTS states. This LTS can by obtained through monolithic state space construction.

In line with the notion of projection for vectors, an LTS network $\mathcal{M}$ can be projected onto a vector of indices, by projecting both Π and $\mathcal{V}$ onto I. The result is an LTS network that can be considered as a subsystem or component of $\mathcal{M}$ consisting of the processes originally indexed in Π at the positions indicated by I.

Minimisation of processes in an LTS network (such as in compositional aggregation) is possible if the used equivalence relation is a congruence for LTS networks. Branching bisimulation, branching bisimulation with explicit divergence, observational equivalence, safety equivalence and weak trace equivalence, are congruences for *admissible* LTS networks [11,30]. An LTS network is called *admissible* if the synchronisation laws of the network do not synchronise, rename, or cut τ-transitions [22]. The intuition behind this is that internal behaviour, i.e., τ-transitions. should not be restricted by any operation.

Compositional order. The compositional aggregation of an LTS network $\mathcal{M} = (\Pi, \mathcal{V})$ is the incremental composition and minimisation of subsets of processes in Π. More specifically, the composition of a set of LTSs followed by a minimisation of the result is called an *aggregation*. The *compositional aggregation* modulo R of an LTS network $\mathcal{M}$ is the incremental aggregation of the processes in Π subject to $\mathcal{V}$ such that the result LTS is R-equivalent to the system LTS. Before we formally define compositional aggregation, we must first introduce aggregation orders.

The *aggregation order* organises the processes of an LTS network in a tree-structure as presented in Definition 3. The leaves represent the individual process LTSs in Π, and the nodes represent subsets of Π. The root represents all the processes in Π. For the sake of simplicity, the processes are represented by their index in the process vector Π. An example of an aggregation order is presented in Fig. 1.

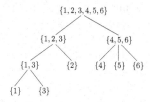

Fig. 1. Aggregation order; leaves are minimised first, then the tree is aggregated following an post-order walk of the tree

Definition 3 (Aggregation Order). *Given an LTS network* $\mathcal{M} = (\Pi, \mathcal{V})$ *of size* n*, an aggregation order of* $\mathcal{M}$ *is a tree* $T_{\mathcal{M}} = (V, E)$ *where* $\emptyset \subset V \subset 2^{1..n}$ *such that*

- *1..n is the root of the tree,*
- *The singleton sets* $\{i\} \in V$ *with* $i \in 1..n$ *are the leaves of the tree, and*
- *For every non-leaf node* $t \in V$*, the children of* t *must form a partition of* t*.*

The *compositional aggregation* of a network $\mathcal{M}$ proceeds as follows. Let t be the root of aggregation order tree T. Compositional aggregation decomposes $\mathcal{M}$ by projecting $\mathcal{M}$ *on the sets* of the nodes in T and *by pre-order walk* of the aggregation order. That is, each component represented by a child of t is aggregated, i.e., the LTSs of its children are combined after which the result is minimised, before finally constructing and minimising the state space corresponding to t. Minimisation starts at the leaves. Aggregation is performed in a post-order walk of the aggregation tree (i.e., children are processed before their parents). At each non-leaf node t the state space of component t is constructed by concatenating the process vectors of the child networks and restoring synchronisations according to the sychronisation laws of the complete model $\mathcal{M}$.

The CADP toolbox offers several minimisation generation strategies.

- The monolithic approach, referred to as *root reduction*, directly computes the system LTS of an LTS network and then applies minimisation.
- *Root leaf reduction* applies minimisation on the process LTSs of a network and then applies root reduction on the resulting network.
- *Smart reduction* [8] is a heuristic that attempts to find an efficient aggregation order. First, all the process LTSs are minimised. Then, recursively, a set I of process LTSs is selected and the LTS in I are replaced by their aggregation.

4   Methodology

Setup. Our experiments were conducted in a controlled test bed comprising a set of homogeneous machines from the DAS-4 [4] cluster. Each machine has a dual quad-core INTEL XEON E5620 2.4 GHz CPU, 24 GB memory, and runs CENTOS LINUX 6. We used CADP version 2017-e "Sophia Antipolis" as implementation for the monolithic and compositional aggregation approaches.

The monolithic approach has been used as the control group. For compositional aggregation, all possible aggregation orders were computed using REFINER [37] in combination with the `decomposition.brute_force` plugin. The minimisation strategies were coded in the Script Verification Language (SVL) [13] of CADP. Given a property the hiding set was calculated using the maximal hiding technique [24]. This technique produces a set of property relevant actions that may not be hidden in the system. All other actions can be safely hidden without affecting the verification result.

As *cases* we consider LTS network models in CADP's EXP format. As *subjects* we consider case instances with a particular scale and hiding set. We use *minimisation strategy* to refer to both aggregation according to some order, and monolithic minimisation.

Research Questions. The variable of interest, i.e., the response variable, is the maximum memory cost of the state spaces produced by compositional aggregation. However, CADP reports the disk space cost of their LTS storage format, i.e., Binary Code Graphs (BCG), rather than the internal memory cost. As an alternative we use the *maximum number of transitions* generated as a measure for memory cost. The maximum number of transitions of an LTS has a strong and highly significant correlation with the disk space cost reported by CADP, i.e., they have a Kendall's τ_b coefficient [21] of 0.91 with a p-value of $2.2 \cdot 10^{-16}$. An additional advantage is that the metric is tool agnostic.

To answer RQ 1 (see Sect. 1) we measured the *maximum number of transitions* among the state spaces produced by compositional aggregation for *all possible* aggregation orders on a set of subjects. The effect of scaling and action hiding were investigating by controlling, respectively, the number of parallel processes and the property.

Next, *the performance of current heuristics are compared to that of other aggregation orders* in RQ 2. The *smart reduction* and *root leaf reduction* heuristics were applied on the subjects. Both heuristics are supported by CADP and have shown to be competitive w.r.t. other heuristics [8]. Again we measured the *maximum number of transitions* among the state spaces processed by compositional aggregation.

The intention of RQ 3 is to *explain the success or failure of composition aggregation.* Observed difference in performance between the subjects of the cases were investigated closer by inspecting the effect of action hiding, number of parallel processes, and aggregation order. Findings were verified with adjusted models fixing one or more aspects, therefore, obtaining more controlled measurements.

There are numerous variables that may affect the performance of compositional aggregation w.r.t. monolithic minimisation. Variables of interest are typically related to the size of a process LTS, or the reduction or interleaving that a process LTS or the composition of process LTSs may introduce.

Case and Subject Selection. The cases were sampled using *quota sampling* [25], i.e., cases with various characteristics were selected. To avoid source bias the cases were selected from four different sources, and where needed, converted to LTS networks.

Source 1. The BEnchmark for Explicit Model checkers (BEEM) database [27]. The benchmark includes 57 parameterised models with corresponding properties.[1]

Source 2. The demos of the CADP distribution. The CADP distribution contains a set of 42 demos. Many of the demos were extracted from the numerous real world verification case studies performed with CADP.

Source 3. The cases considered in an evaluation of automated assume-guarantee reasoning [7]. This set contains 6 scalable cases with corresponding properties.[2]

---

[1] paradise.fi.muni.cz/beem.

[2] http://laser.cs.umass.edu/breakingup-examples.

Source 4. The cases considered in our previous work [31]. In previous work we experimented with a set of 10 cases of which some are scalable.[3]

As mentioned by Cobleigh et al. [7] the generality of their work is threatened by the limited variety in network topology. To avoid this, we selected cases with a variety of network topologies. In addition, we took the following considerations into account:

1. The effect of action hiding was considered by selecting for each case various relevant safety and liveness properties.
2. To investigate the effect of the number of parallel LTSs on compositional aggregation we selected scalable cases. Each scalable case has one or more repeatable LTSs with which the model was scaled up; e.g., a model consisting of single server LTS and two client LTSs was scaled up by adding copies of the client LTSs.
3. The number of possible aggregation orders and the time required to construct state spaces grow exponentially with scale. Due to time considerations we limited each compositional aggregation to two hours. In addition, we prematurely terminated a compositional aggregation procedure as soon as it required more than the available (physical) memory, i.e., 24 GB. Any subjects violating the time or memory criteria were discarded from the experiment.
4. It is infeasible to calculate all 34,588 possible aggregation orders at seven parallel LTSs within reasonable time. For six parallel LTSs, this number is 2,647. To still find best and worst aggregation orders for up to six parallel LTS we limit the number of considered aggregation orders to 2,647.

Initially the sources above provided 115 models. We selected a number of scalable cases with a variety of network topologies. We discarded the cases for which it was infeasible to compute 2,647 aggregation orders for less than two scaled up version of the case. Finally, *eight* cases were selected covering *five* different network topologies. *Six* out of the *eight* cases were able scale to a size of six parallel LTSs while satisfying the time and memory criteria. The other two cases were scaled to *four* and *seven* parallel LTSs, respectively.

Next, we selected a range of properties relevant for the cases and modeled several scaled-up LTS networks. This finally resulted in a total of 129 subjects. The experiments were run on these 129 subjects. In total 117,879 decompositions were considered costing a total of 2.5 CPU-years. Finally, for 119 subjects all the run aggregation orders satisfied the time and memory criteria.

5   Results

5.1   Case and Subject Descriptions

Network Topologies. The selected cases are characterised by the network topologies depicted in Fig. 2. Dots indicate parallel processes and lines indicate synchronisation relations. Dashed lines show the synchronisation relations that are introduced by adding a repeatable process p.

---

[3] http://www.win.tue.nl/mdse/property_preservation/FAC2017_experiments.zip.

Table 1. Selected cases and their characteristics; with $p \geq 1$ the # of repeated LTSs

Case ID	Case description	Topology	Scaling	Source
1	The gas station problem [17]	a (3 servers)	$3 + p \geq 4$	1,3
2	Chiron user interface (single dispatcher) [20]	a (2 servers)	$3 + p \geq 4$	3
3	Eratosthenes' Sieve (distributed calculation of primes)	b	$1 + p \geq 3$	2
4	Le Lann leader election protocol [23]	c	$2 \cdot p \geq 4$	1
5	A simple token ring	c	$1 + p \geq 3$	4
6	Peterson's mutual exclusion protocol [28]	d	$2 \cdot p \geq 4$	1,2,3
7	Anderson's mutual exclusion protocol [3]	d	$1 + 2 \cdot p \geq 5$	1
8	Open Distributed Processing trader (ODP) [12]	e	$1 + p \geq 3$	2

Figure 2a shows a *client-server* topology. Such a network contains one or more servers and one or more clients.

In Fig. 2b a *pipes and filter* topology is presented. The first process p_1 produces data and each process p_i $(i \in 1..n)$ in the sequence processes the data and filters before forwarding the filtered data to the next process p_{i+1}.

A *ring* network topology is shown in Fig. 2c. Communication between processes is organised as a ring structure. Often a token is passed along the edges that grants special privileges to the process holding the token.

Figure 2d depicts communication via a number of *shared variables*. In the selected cases, for each repeatable process p_i there is a repeatable variable v_i.

In Fig. 2e a *peer-to-peer* network topology is shown. Addresses and services of the peers p_i $(i \in 1..n)$ are published via the tracker-server s after which the offered services can be employed on a peer-to-peer basis.

Case Descriptions. We have selected *eight* scalable models as cases. An overview of these cases is given in Table 1. We identify the cases by their case number indicated in the *Case ID* column. The *Scaling* column shows the scaling of the cases in the number of repeated LTSs p and, on the right-hand side of the inequality, the minimum number of parallel LTSs; e.g., ODP's scaling $1 + p \geq 3$ states that there is one non-repeated LTSs (the trader) and one repeated LTS (the client), but the number of processes

(a) Clients p_i $(i \in 1..n)$ and server s

(b) Pipes and filters with processing nodes p_i $(i \in 1..n)$

(c) Ring with processing nodes p_i $(i \in 1..n)$

(d) Processes p_i sharing variables v_i $(i \in 1..n)$

(e) Peer-to-peer network with peers p_i $(i \in 1..n)$ and tracker-server s

Fig. 2. Network topologies

must be at least 3. Finally, in the *Source* column the sources of the cases are given, these correspond to the list of sources (Sect. 4).[4]

Subject Descriptions. Subjects correspond to instances of cases with a particular scale and hiding set, i.e., property. Subjects are identified by three alphanumeric characters: the first indicating the number of the case ID, the second indicating the letter of a corresponding case property, and the third indicating the scale of the case model. With "_", we denote the absence of a property, i.e., no hiding is applied. For instance, 1e5 is the case 1 model where actions not relevant to property e (of case 1) have been hidden and the subject has a total of 5 parallel LTSs. For each model, we identified between two and eight relevant properties.

The selected *scaling* is from the minimum scale of the case up to the possible scale nearest to six; e.g., for case 1 with property a the set of subjects is 1a4, 1a5, 1a6 and for case 6 with no property the set of subjects is 6_4, 6_6.

5.2   Analysis

Figure 3 shows the distribution of the normalised maximum number of transitions of the generated state spaces for all possible aggregation orders of each subject, in the form of violin plots [18].[5] The black horizontal lines within each plot connected by a black vertical line indicate the first, second, and third quartiles. On the x-axis the subjects are displayed, grouped by case ID and scale. The y-axis displays the largest number of transitions the state space contained during compositioning on a $\log_{10}$-scale. Furthermore, the dashed horizontal line indicates the performance of monolithic construction. Finally, the normalised maximum number of transitions in memory during *smart reduction* and *root leaf reduction* are indicated by a red dot and blue diamond, respectively. It should be noted that the repeating of LTSs have a noticeable effect on the distribution of aggregation orders. Some peaks arise due to accumulation of sets of symmetric aggregation orders measuring the same normalized maximum number of transitions. However, as can be seen in the plots, in most cases this effect does not change significantly as more repeated LTSs are added.

RQ 1. How do action hiding, number of parallel processes, and aggregation order affect the memory consumption of compositional aggregation? We answer this research question using Fig. 3. The chosen *aggregation order* has a major impact on the maximum number of transitions residing in memory. Two aggregation orders may differ up to several orders of magnitude depending on the subject.

In general we observe that the range covered by the distribution of aggregation orders increases as the *number of parallel processes* increases. In all cases scaling up results in a better performance of the best aggregation orders w.r.t.

---

[4] The models are available at http://www.win.tue.nl/mdse/composition/test_cases. zip.

[5] All generated data is available at http://www.win.tue.nl/mdse/composition/test_cases_data.zip.

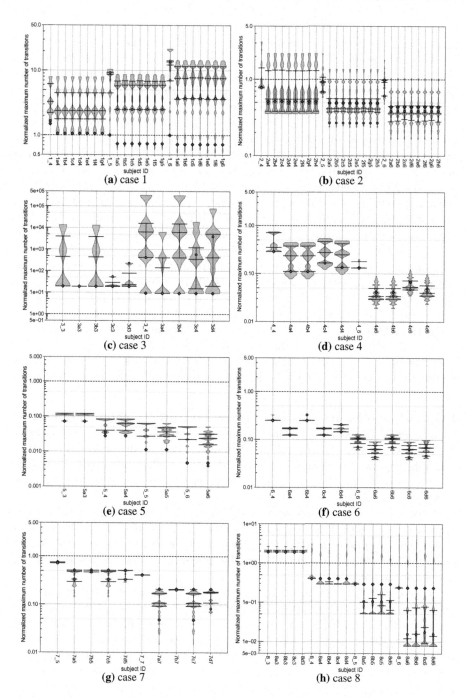

Fig. 3. Distribution of the *normalised maximum number of transitions* generated by the aggregation orders per subject (violin plots) and case (sub-figures). (Color figure online)

monolithic verification, i.e., as the subjects increase in size, compositional aggregation becomes increasingly viable. In cases 1, 3, and 8 the range extends both upwards and downwards as the scale is increased; compared to the smaller subjects (in scale) the bad aggregation orders become worse and the good aggregation orders better. In the remaining cases the whole range shifts downwards as the number of parallel processes increases.

The shape of the distributions tends to change as the number of parallel processes increases. One of the factors contributing to this phenomenon is the increasing number of data points in the distributions as the scale increases; there are 4, 26, 236, and 2,647 distinct aggregation orders at 3, 4, 5, and 6 parallel processes, respectively. At larger scales a sample of 2,647 orders was taken. This effect is particularly visible in case 3, where the model at scales 3 and 4 are compared. However, most likely the changes are due to the number of repeated processes. Due to this the balance of constituents of the model changes causing the high density areas to change accordingly.

Applying action hiding practically always results in an improvement, the only exception being subjects 5a3 and 8a3 to 8d3. In cases 1 and 2 practically no distinction in performance is observed between the applied hiding sets. Cases 3, 4, 6, 7, and 8 show moderate to significant variation in performance depending on the applied hiding set. For those subjects where the hiding sets have a noticeable impact, also the shape of the distribution is affected. For instance, subject 7c5 has a higher density around the optimal, forming a vase shape between the minimum and the first quartile, than 7d5, which has a short tail in the same area.

RQ 2. How effective are the aggregation orders chosen by current heuristics? Fig. 3 shows how smart reduction (indicated by a red dot) and root leaf reduction (indicated by a blue diamond) relate to the other orders. Both action hiding and the scaling can have a significant effect on their performance. However, there is no clear relation between these variables and the performance, which is particularly visible for case 3.

Smart reduction requires fewer transitions in memory than the monolithic approach in 80 out of 119 subjects. Root leaf reduction performs better than monolithic minimisation in 94 out of 119 subjects. Furthermore, smart reduction and root leaf reduction find an optimal aggregation order for, respectively, 29 and 40 of the subjects.

Since our data is obtained from repeated measurements over eight cases, to make a fair and meaningful comparison we select cases under related conditions. We select the *"smallest"* and *"largest"* *subjects* in the number of parallel processes from the subjects in Fig. 3. From the properties we select the only two property IDs that all cases have in common; "_" (no property) and "a" (no deadlock). The intersection of these two pairs of selections yields four sets of subjects within which a comparison is made. First a comparison between the performance of the smart reduction and root leaf reduction is made, after which their performances are compared with the performance of optimal aggregation orders.

Table 2. Normalised (w.r.t. monolithic) max. transitions descriptive statistics; with "Smallest" and "Largest" indicating, respectively, the smallest and largest number of parallel processes of subjects shown in Fig. 3

Size	Prop. ID	Mean		Median		# cases < monolithic		# cases < other heuristic	
		smart	root leaf	smart	root leaf	smart	root leaf	smart	root leaf
Smallest	–	3.12	3.10	0.74	0.77	5	5	3	1
Smallest	a	2.89	2.91	0.41	0.51	5	5	2	1
Largest	–	54.65	1.53	0.32	0.32	6	6	4	2
Largest	a	1.68	1.36	0.05	0.22	6	7	6	1

Table 2 compares the normalised maximum number of transitions of smart reduction and root leaf reduction. The first two columns indicate the selection criteria for the number of parallel processes. A comparison is made between smart reduction and root leaf reduction indicated by the *smart* and *root leaf* columns. The *Mean, Median* columns show the mean and median normalised maximum transitions. The final two columns, *# cases < monolithic* and *# cases < other heuristic*, indicate in how many cases the heuristics perform better than monolithic and the other heuristics, respectively.

In the groups of *"smallest"* subjects there is little difference between the means of smart reduction and root leaf reduction. For both heuristics the mean performance is around 3 times that of the monolithic approach. On a positive note, the median is much lower than the mean for both heuristics. Smart reduction has a slightly better median performance. Both heuristics perform better than the monolithic approach in 5 out of 8 cases in both property ID groups. The remaining three cases being 1, 3, and 8 for both heuristics and property ID groups.

In the groups of *"largest"* subjects there is signification difference between the means of smart reduction and root leaf reduction in group *"–"*. In group *"a"* this difference is only 0.32 in favor of root leaf reduction. The high mean value for smart reduction is caused by its poor performance at cases 1 and 3. Again the median performance is much better than the mean performance for both heuristics. The median performance of root leaf reduction is over four times that of smart reduction. Both heuristics perform better than the monolithic approach in 6 out of 8 cases in property ID group *"–"*, while root leaf reduction performs better in one additional case in group *"a"*. The two remaining cases being 1 and 3, excluding case 1 in group *"a"* for root leaf reduction.

Table 3 compares the maximum number of transitions of the smart reduction and root leaf reduction heuristics normalised w.r.t. the optimum performance of compositional aggregation. The final columns, *# opt. found*, indicate how many times an optimal aggregation order was found.

If we compare the groups *"smallest"* and *"largest"* both the means and medians increase, and the number of optimums found decrease. This may indicate that it becomes harder for the heuristics to find (near-)optimal aggregation orders as

Table 3. Normalised (w.r.t opt. aggregation order) max. transitions descriptive statistics

Size	Prop. ID	Mean		Median		# opt. found	
		smart	root leaf	smart	root leaf	smart	root leaf
Smallest	_	1.02	1.02	1.00	1.00	5	5
Smallest	a	1.31	1.44	1.18	1.00	4	5
Largest	_	8.14	1.24	1.07	1.01	2	4
Largest	a	2.43	6.78	1.90	1.89	2	1

the number of parallel processes increases, however, this should be confirmed by further experiments.

RQ 3. How can the success or failure of compositional aggregation be explained? Although our experiment involves a large number of subjects, the number of different cases per topology is still rather limited. However, based on this data, we make the following observations, backed up by results obtained for additional models with the same topology that we constructed to focus on specific key aspects of the cases.

Two factors seem to be most influential regarding the effectiveness of compositional aggregation: the amount of internal behaviour within single process LTSs, and the amount of synchronisation among the process LTSs. In the latter case, the involvement of data has a noticeable effect, in particular the size of the data domain; for instance, when synchronisation on a Boolean value is specified, the receiver only needs to be able to synchronise on **true** and **false**, while the synchronisation on a Byte value already requires 256 transitions, many of which may be unnecessary in the complete model, since they handle values on which synchronisation actually never happens. However, if in an aggregation order, this receiver is selected before the corresponding sender, then in each step before selecting the sender, all 256 transitions of the receiver will remain, and interleave with the transitions of all LTSs that *are* added to the composition.

Among the subjects, case 3 demonstrates best that the involvement of a lot of (to be synchronised) data has a negative effect on compositional aggregation. Additional experiments with a simple pipes and filters model, one with a data domain ranging from 1 to 2 and the other from 1 to 100, underline this observation, the latter performing an order of magnitude worse than the former. Furthermore, the former performs very well compared to monolithic verification, demonstrating that the bad performance of compositional aggregation is not inherent to the pipes and filters topology.

The positive effect of involving a property to be checked, and therefore action hiding, demonstrates the importance of internal behaviour in the process LTSs, as action hiding adds internal behaviour. It seems of little importance which property is actually added, i.e., whether it allows abstraction from all actions in the case of deadlock detection, or only a subset. This is best demonstrated by the token ring cases, i.e., cases 4 and 5. We manipulated case 5 in two different ways: increasing the amount of synchronisation, and increasing the amount of process-local (but not hidden) behaviour. The results clearly show that the former has a negative impact on performance, while the latter results in much better performance (by two orders of magnitude) iff a property is involved that allows the additional behaviour to be abstracted away, such as deadlock freedom.

The mutual exclusion algorithms, i.e., cases 6 and 7, have exactly the same set of properties. Those results demonstrate that the effect of adding a property is not always the same for all models of the same topology; adding a property seems to have a bigger effect on case 7 than case 6, resulting in a bigger range between the worst and best performing aggregation orders.

In a follow-up experiment, we will extend the number of cases and/or subjects per topology, to achieve conclusive evidence that could generalise these observations.

5.3   Threats to Validity

When interpreting the results of this study consider the following threats to validity:

- Only one tool has been involved to conduct the experiment, hence the results may be implementation specific. On the other hand, involving multiple tools introduces the problem that differences in implementations may affect the outcome.
- The scope of this study is limited to models that are represented as networks of LTSs. Therefore, the results of this study are possibly only applicable to models represented as networks of LTSs. As the compositional aggregation method is limited to these kind of models we have not considered alternative model representations.
- The study only considers the DPBB equivalence as aggregation relation. Results may vary depending on the chosen equivalence relation. The DPBB equivalence is the strongest aggregation order offered by CADP that still allows abstraction. Hence, other relations are expected to show better performance improvements.
- The scaled up models make use of a repeatable LTSs. It may be possible that the results are skewed due to lack of heterogeneous components. However, the used compositional aggregation methods do not take advantage of the symmetry in the model.
  The repeating of LTSs is noticeable in the violin plots (Fig. 3) as accumulation of sets of symmetric aggregation orders measuring the same normalized maximum number of transitions. Nevertheless, in most cases this effect does not change significantly as more repeated LTSs are added.
- A relatively small set of different cases has been studied, even though this experiment is the most comprehensive one performed thus far. In the future, we plan to extend this set considerably, but obtaining such a large set is very

time-consuming. The lack of a (publicly available) set of nicely scalable models is a problem in general when analysing and designing formal verification techniques.

– Models with a relatively small number of parallel processes were considered. Beyond models with six parallel LTSs the experiments quickly become unfeasible. Extrapolation of the results presented in this work to models with more parallel LTSs should be done with caution. In the future, we plan to extend our analysis to subjects with more processes.

6   Conclusions

Our thorough analysis of compositional aggregation when applied on 119 subjects with varying topology, scale, and hiding set provides the following insights:

1. The amount of internal behaviour in process LTSs and the amount of synchronisation between process LTSs have the biggest impact on the performance, in terms of the largest number of generated transitions in memory.
2. The involvement of a functional property, and therefore a hiding set, is significant. The size of this hiding set is of less importance. For typical properties, maximal hiding already allows the hiding of a relatively large amount of behaviour.
3. Among the five network topologies we considered, none of them fundamentally rule out compositional aggregation as an effective technique.
4. As the number of processes in a model is increased, the effectiveness of compositional aggregation tends to increase as well.

It should be noted that we only considered a few cases per topology. To generalise our conclusions, we will have to work on extending our benchmark set. The first two conclusions underline observations made in earlier work [8]. Since they worked with a set of subjects of less variety, we can make these observations with more confidence.

Future Work. In the near future, we will extend the current analysis to further explain the success and failure of compositional aggregation for the different subjects, and based on this, work on the construction of a new heuristic. For this to be successful, we will have to involve many more cases. As scalable models have now been thoroughly investigated, we can next focus on non-scalable models, of which many are publicly available.

Acknowledgements. The authors would like to thank Vrije Universiteit Amsterdam for their generosity in supplying the computing resources for the experiments.

References

1. Abd Elkader, K., Grumberg, O., Păsăreanu, C.S., Shoham, S.: Automated circular assume-guarantee reasoning with N-way decomposition and alphabet refinement. In: Chaudhuri, S., Farzan, A. (eds.) CAV 2016. LNCS, vol. 9779, pp. 329–351. Springer, Cham (2016). https://doi.org/10.1007/978-3-319-41528-4_18

2. Andersen, H.: Partial model checking. In: LICS, pp. 398–407. IEEE Computer Society Press (1995)
3. Anderson, J.H., Kim, Y.J., Herman, T.: Shared-memory mutual exclusion: major research trends since 1986. Distrib. Comput. **16**(2–3), 75–110 (2003)
4. ASCI: The Distributed ASCI Supercomputer DAS4. http://www.cs.vu.nl/das4/. Accessed 09-08-2017
5. Baier, C., Katoen, J.P.: Principles of Model Checking. MIT Press, Cambridge (2008)
6. Cheung, S.C., Kramer, J.: Context constraints for compositional reachability analysis. ACM Trans. Softw. Eng. Methodol. **5**(4), 334–377 (1996)
7. Cobleigh, J.M., Avrunin, G.S., Clarke, L.A.: Breaking up is hard to do: an evaluation of automated assume-guarantee reasoning. ACM Trans. Softw. Eng. Methodol. **17**(2), 7:1–7:52 (2008)
8. Crouzen, P., Lang, F.: Smart reduction. In: Giannakopoulou, D., Orejas, F. (eds.) FASE 2011. LNCS, vol. 6603, pp. 111–126. Springer, Heidelberg (2011). https://doi.org/10.1007/978-3-642-19811-3_9
9. Crouzen, P., Hermanns, H.: Aggregation ordering for massively compositional models. In: 10th International Conference on Application of Concurrency to System Design, pp. 171–180. IEEE (2010)
10. Fernandez, J.: ALDEBARAN: un système de vérification par réduction de processus communicants. (Aldebaran : a system of verification of communicating processes by using reduction). Ph.D. thesis, Joseph Fourier University, Grenoble, France (1988)
11. Garavel, H., Lang, F., Mateescu, R.: Compositional Verification of Asynchronous Concurrent Systems using CADP (extended version). Research Report RR-8708, INRIA Grenoble - Rhône-Alpes, Apr 2015. https://hal.inria.fr/hal-01138749
12. Garavel, H., Sighireanu, M.: A graphical parallel composition operator for process algebras. In: FORTE/PSTV 1999. IFIP Conference Proceedings, vol. 156, pp. 185–202. Kluwer (1999)
13. Garavel, H., Lang, F.: SVL: a scripting language for compositional verification. In: 21st International Conference on Formal Techniques for Networked and Distributed Systems, pp. 377–392. Kluwer, Boston, MA (2002)
14. Gheorghiu Bobaru, M., Păsăreanu, C.S., Giannakopoulou, D.: Automated assume-guarantee reasoning by abstraction refinement. In: Gupta, A., Malik, S. (eds.) CAV 2008. LNCS, vol. 5123, pp. 135–148. Springer, Heidelberg (2008). https://doi.org/10.1007/978-3-540-70545-1_14
15. Glabbeek, R.V., Luttik, S., Trčka, N.: Branching bisimilarity with explicit divergence. Fundam. Inform. **93**(4), 371–392 (2009)
16. Gupta, A., McMillan, K.L., Fu, Z.: Automated assumption generation for compositional verification. In: Damm, W., Hermanns, H. (eds.) CAV 2007. LNCS, vol. 4590, pp. 420–432. Springer, Heidelberg (2007). https://doi.org/10.1007/978-3-540-73368-3_45
17. Heimbold, D., Luckham, D.: Debugging ada tasking programs. IEEE Softw. **2**, 47–57 (1985)
18. Hintze, J., Nelson, R.: Violin plots: a box plot-density trace synergism. Am. Stat. **52**(2), 181–184 (1998)
19. Jones, C.B.: Specification and design of (parallel) programs. In: IFIP Congress, vol. 83, pp. 321–332 (1983)
20. Keller, R.K., Cameron, M., Taylor, R.N., Troup, D.B.: User interface development and software environments: the Chiron-1 system. In: Proceedings of the 13th International Conference on Software Engineering, pp. 208–218. IEEE (1991)

21. Kendall, M., Gibbons, J.: Rank correlation methods, chap. 3, 5th edn. Oxford University Press, Oxford (1990)
22. Lang, F.: Refined interfaces for compositional verification. In: Najm, E., Pradat-Peyre, J.-F., Donzeau-Gouge, V.V. (eds.) FORTE 2006. LNCS, vol. 4229, pp. 159–174. Springer, Heidelberg (2006). https://doi.org/10.1007/11888116_13
23. Le Lann, G.: Distributed systems - towards a formal approach. In: IFIP Congress, pp. 155–160 (1977)
24. Mateescu, R., Wijs, A.: Property-dependent reductions adequate with divergence-sensitive branching bisimilarity. Sci. Comput. Program. **96**(3), 354–376 (2014)
25. O'Leary, Z.: The Essential Guide to Doing Research. SAGE Publications, Thousand Oaks (2004)
26. Păsăreanu, C.S., Giannakopoulou, D., Bobaru, M.G., Cobleigh, J.M., Barringer, H.: Learning to divide and conquer: applying the l* algorithm to automate assume-guarantee reasoning. Form. Methods Syst. Des. **32**(3), 175–205 (2008)
27. Pelánek, R.: BEEM: benchmarks for explicit model checkers. In: Bošnački, D., Edelkamp, S. (eds.) SPIN 2007. LNCS, vol. 4595, pp. 263–267. Springer, Heidelberg (2007). https://doi.org/10.1007/978-3-540-73370-6_17
28. Peterson, G.L.: Myths about the mutual exclusion problem. IPL **12**, 115–116 (1981)
29. Pnueli, A.: In transition from global to modular temporal reasoning about programs. Logics and Models of Concurrent Systems. NATO ASI, vol. 13, pp. 123–144. Springer, Berlin (1985). https://doi.org/10.1007/978-3-642-82453-1_5
30. de Putter, S., Wijs, A.: Compositional model checking is lively. In: Proença, J., Lumpe, M. (eds.) FACS 2017. LNCS, vol. 10487, pp. 117–136. Springer, Cham (2017). https://doi.org/10.1007/978-3-319-68034-7_7
31. de Putter, S., Wijs, A.: A formal verification technique for behavioural model-to-model transformations. Form. Asp. Comput. **30**, 3–43 (2017). https://doi.org/10.1007/s00165-017-0437-z
32. Roscoe, A.W.: The Theory and Practice of Concurrency. Prentice Hall PTR, Upper Saddle River (1997)
33. Sabnani, K.K., Lapone, A.M., Uyar, M.U.: An algorithmic procedure for checking safety properties of protocols. IEEE Trans. Commun. **37**(9), 940–948 (1989)
34. Tai, K.C., Koppol, P.V.: Hierarchy-based incremental analysis of communication protocols. In: 1993 International Conference on Network Protocols, pp. 318–325. IEEE (1993)
35. Tai, K.C., Koppol, P.V.: An incremental approach to reachability analysis of distributed programs. In: Proceedings of the 7th International Workshop on Software Specification and Design, pp. 141–150. IEEE Computer Society Press (1993)
36. Valmari, A.: Compositional state space generation. In: Rozenberg, G. (ed.) ICATPN 1991. LNCS, vol. 674, pp. 427–457. Springer, Heidelberg (1993). https://doi.org/10.1007/3-540-56689-9_54
37. Wijs, A., Engelen, L.: REFINER: towards formal verification of model transformations. In: Badger, J.M., Rozier, K.Y. (eds.) NFM 2014. LNCS, vol. 8430, pp. 258–263. Springer, Cham (2014). https://doi.org/10.1007/978-3-319-06200-6_21

View Abstraction for Systems with Component Identities

Gavin Lowe[✉]

Department of Computer Science, University of Oxford, Oxford, UK
gavin.lowe@cs.ox.ac.uk

Abstract. The *parameterised verification problem* seeks to verify all members of some family of systems. We consider the following instance: each system is composed of an arbitrary number of similar *component processes*, together with a fixed number of *server* processes; processes communicate via synchronous message passing; in particular, each component process has an *identity*, which may be included in messages, and passed to third parties. We extend Abdulla et al.'s technique of *view abstraction*, together with techniques based on symmetry reduction, to this setting. We give an algorithm and implementation that allows such systems to be verified for an arbitrary number of components. We show how this technique can be applied to a concurrent datatype built from reference-linked nodes, such as a linked list. Further, we show how to capture the specification of a queue or of a stack.

1 Introduction

The *parameterised verification problem* considers a family of systems $P(x)$ where the parameter x ranges over a potentially infinite set, and asks whether such systems are correct for all values of x. In this paper we consider the following instance of the parameterised verification problem. Each system is built from some number of similar *replicated component processes*, together with a fixed number of *server processes*; the parameter is the number of component processes. The components and servers communicate via (CSP-style) synchronous message passing; we call each message an *event*. In particular each component has an *identity*, drawn from some potentially infinite set. These identities can be included in events; thus a process can obtain the identity of a component process, and possibly pass it on to a third process. This means that each process has a potentially infinite state space (a finite control state combined with data from a potentially infinite set). We describe the setting for our work more formally in the next section. The problem is undecidable in general [5,23]; however, verification techniques prove effective on a number of specific problems.

We adapt the technique of *view abstraction* of Abdulla et al. [1] to this setting. The idea of view abstraction is that we abstract each system state to its *views* of some size k, recording the states of just k of the replicated component processes. We can (with a finite amount of work) calculate an over-estimate of all views of

© Springer International Publishing AG, part of Springer Nature 2018
K. Havelund et al. (Eds.): FM 2018, LNCS 10951, pp. 505–522, 2018.
https://doi.org/10.1007/978-3-319-95582-7_30

size k of the system; this gives us an over-estimate of the states of the system. We then check that all states of this over-estimate satisfy our correctness condition: if so, we can deduce that *all* systems of size k or larger are correct (systems of smaller sizes can be checked directly). We present our use of view abstraction in Sects. 3 and 4.

Our setting is made more complicated by the presence of the identities of the components. These mean that the set of views (for some fixed k) is potentially infinite. However, in Sect. 5 we use techniques from *symmetry reduction* [8–10,14,17,19,28] to reduce the views that need to be considered to a finite set.

We present the main algorithm in Sect. 6, and prove its correctness. We then present our prototype implementation: this is based upon the process algebra CSP [26], and builds on the model checker FDR [16], so as to support all of machine-readable CSP. We stress, though, that the main ideas of this paper are not CSP-specific: they apply to any formalism with a similar computational model, and, we believe, could be adapted to other computational models.

A major advantage of this use of identities is that it allows us to model and analyse reference-linked data structures, such as linked lists. Each node in the data structure is modelled by a replicated component process; such a process can hold the identity of another such process, modelling a reference to that node. We illustrate this technique in Sect. 7 by modelling and analysing a simple lock-based concurrent queue and stack, each based on a linked list; in particular, we show how to capture the specifications of these datatypes in a finite-state way, using techniques from data independence [30]. Our longer-term aim is to extend these techniques to more interesting, lock-free concurrent datatypes.

We see our main contributions as follows.

- An adaptation of view abstraction to synchronous message passing (this is mostly a straightforward adaptation of the techniques of [1]);
- An extension of view abstraction to include systems where components have identities, and these identities can be passed around, using techniques based on symmetry reduction to produce a finite-state abstraction;
- The implementation of these ideas, using FDR so as to support all of machine-readable CSP;
- The application to reference-linked concurrent datatypes;
- The finite-state specification of a queue and a stack.

1.1   Related Work

There have been many approaches to the parameterised model checking problem.

Much recent work has been based on *regular model checking*, e.g. [7,12,20,31]. Here, the state of each individual process is from some finite set, and each system state is considered as a word over this finite set; the set of initial states is a regular set; and the transition relation is a regular relation, normally defined by a transducer. An excellent survey is in [3]. Techniques include widening [29], acceleration [2] and abstraction [6].

The work [1] that the current paper builds on falls within this class. However, our setting is outside this class: the presence of component identities means that each individual process has a potentially infinite state space.

Other approaches include induction [13,15,27], network invariants [32], and counter abstraction [11,22,23,25]. In particular, [23] applied counter abstraction to systems, like in the current paper, where components had identities which could be passed from one process to another: some number B of the identities were treated faithfully, and the remainder were abstracted; the approach of the current paper seems better able to capture relationships between components, as required for the analysis of reference-linked data structures.

The work [4] tackles a similar problem to this paper. It captures the specification of a queue or a stack using an automaton that, informally, guesses the data value that will be treated incorrectly. The authors use shape analysis to finitely analyse data structures built on linked lists. They are able to prove linearizability of concurrent datatypes assuming explicit linearization points are given.

Most approaches to symmetry reduction in model checking [8,10,14,17,19] work by identifying symmetric states, and, during exploration, replace each state encountered with a *representative member* of its symmetry-equivalence class: if several states map to the same representative, this reduces the work to be done. This representative might not be unique, since finding unique representatives is hard, in general; however, such approaches work well in most cases. Our approach is closer to that of [28]: we test whether a state encountered during exploration is equivalent to a state previously encountered, and if so do not explore it further.

2   The Framework

In this section, we introduce more formally the class of systems that we consider, and our framework.

We introduce a toy example to illustrate the ideas. The replicated components run a simple token-based mutual exclusion protocol. Component j can receive the token from component i via a transition with event $pass.i.j$; it can then enter and leave the critical section, before passing the token to another component. In the initial state, a single component holds the token.

A *watchdog* server process observes components entering and leaving the critical section, and signals with event *error* if mutual exclusion is violated. Our correctness condition will be that the event *error* does not occur. (In larger examples, we might have additional servers, playing some part in the protocol, in addition to a watchdog that checks the correctness condition.) Fig. 1 illustrates state machines for these processes.

Each process's state can be thought of as the combination of a *control state* and a vector of zero or more *parameters*, each of which is a *component identity*, either its own identity or that of another component. In more interesting examples, these parameters can be passed on to a third party. Processes synchronise on some common events, with at most two components synchronising on each event. We want to verify such systems for an arbitrary number of replicated components.

Formally, each process is represented by a parameterised state machine.

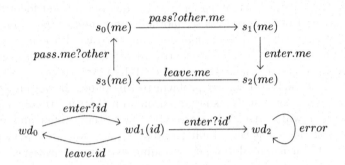

Fig. 1. Illustration of the state machines for the toy example. The diagrams are symbolic, and parameterised by the set of component identities. For example, the latter state diagram has a state $wd_1(id)$ for each identity id; there is a transition labelled $enter.id$ from wd_0 to $wd_1(id)$ for each identity id.

Definition 1. A *state machine* is a tuple (Q, Σ, δ), where: Q is a set of *states*; Σ is a set of *visible events* with $\tau \notin \Sigma$ (τ represents an internal event); and $\delta \subseteq Q \times (\Sigma \cup \{\tau\}) \times Q$ is a transition relation.

A *parameterised state machine* is a state machine where: (1) the states Q are a subset of $S \times T^*$, for some finite set S of *control states* and some potentially infinite set T of *component identities*; and (2) the events Σ are a subset of $Chan \times T^*$, for some finite set $Chan$ of *channels*.

We sometimes write a state $(s, \mathbf{x})$ as $s(\mathbf{x})$: s is a control state, and $\mathbf{x}$ records the values of its parameters (cf. Fig. 1). Similarly, we write an event $(c, \mathbf{y})$ as $c.\mathbf{y}$, and write $s(\mathbf{x}) \xrightarrow{c.\mathbf{y}} s'(\mathbf{z})$ to denote $((s, \mathbf{x}), (c, \mathbf{y}), (s', \mathbf{z})) \in \delta$.

We assume that the component identities are treated polymorphically: they can be received, stored, sent, and tested for equality; but no other operations, such as arithmetic operations, can be performed on them. Processes defined in this way are naturally symmetric. Let π be a permutation on T; we write $Sym(T)$ for the set of all such permutations. We lift π to vectors from T^* by point-wise application; we then lift it to states and events by $\pi(s(\mathbf{x})) = s(\pi(\mathbf{x}))$ and $\pi(c.\mathbf{x}) = c.\pi(\mathbf{x})$. We require each state $s(\pi(\mathbf{x}))$ to be equivalent to $s(\mathbf{x})$ but with all events renamed by π: formally the states are π-bisimilar.

Definition 2. Let $M = (Q, \Sigma, \delta)$ be a state machine, and let $\pi \in Sym(T)$. We say that $\sim \subseteq Q \times Q$ is a π-*bisimulation* iff whenever $(q_1, q_2) \in \sim$ and $a \in \Sigma \cup \{\tau\}$:

- If $q_1 \xrightarrow{a} q_1'$ then $\exists q_2' \in Q \cdot q_2 \xrightarrow{\pi(a)} q_2' \wedge q_1' \sim q_2'$;
- If $q_2 \xrightarrow{a} q_2'$ then $\exists q_1' \in Q \cdot q_1 \xrightarrow{\pi^{-1}(a)} q_1' \wedge q_1' \sim q_2'$.

Definition 3. A parameterised state machine (Q, Σ, δ) is *symmetric* if for every $\pi \in Sym(T)$, $\{(s(\mathbf{x}), s(\pi(\mathbf{x}))) \mid s(\mathbf{x}) \in Q\}$ is a π-bisimulation.

This is a natural condition. In [17], we proved that under rather mild syntactic conditions, an *arbitrary* process defined using machine-readable CSP will be symmetric in this sense. The conditions are that the definition of the process contains no constant from the type T, and that it does not use certain FDR built-in functions over sets and maps, or certain compression functions.

2.1 Systems

Each system will contain a server and some number of replicated components. We assume a *single* server here, for simplicity: a system with multiple servers can be modelled by considering the parallel composition of the servers as a single server.

Each system state contains a state for the server, and a finite multiset containing the state for each component.[1] For example, one state of the toy example is $(wd_1(T_0), \{s_2(T_0), s_0(T_1), s_0(T_2)\})$, where $\{T_0, T_1, T_2\} \subseteq T$.

Definition 4. A *system* is a tuple $(Server, Cpts, Sync, Init)$ where

1. $Server = (Q_s, \Sigma_s, \delta_s)$ is a symmetric parameterised state machine representing the server;
2. $Cpts = (Q_c, \Sigma_c, \delta_c)$ is a symmetric parameterised state machine representing each replicated component;
3. $Sync \subseteq \Sigma_c$ is a set of events that require the synchronisation of two replicated components; we require $\pi(Sync) = Sync$ for each $\pi \in Sym(T)$;
4. $Init \subseteq SS$ is a set of initial states, where $SS = Q_s \times \mathbb{M}(Q_c)$ denotes all possible system states.

Given such a system, a *system state* is a pair $(q_s, m) \in SS$, where $q_s \in Q_s$ gives the state of the server, and $m \in \mathbb{M}(Q_c)$ gives the states of the components.

A system defines a state machine $(SS, \Sigma_s \cup \Sigma_c, \delta)$, where δ is defined by the following five rules (where $\rightarrow_s$ and $\rightarrow_c$ correspond to δ_s and δ_c, respectively). The rules represent, respectively: events of just the server; events of just one component; synchronisations between the server and a single component; synchronisations between two components; and synchronisations between the server and two components.

---

[1] We write $\mathbb{M}$ for a finite multiset type constructor. We mostly use set notation for multisets, but write "$\uplus$" for a multiset union.

$$\frac{q_s \xrightarrow{a}_s q'_s \quad a \in (\Sigma_s - \Sigma_c) \cup \{\tau\}}{(q_s, m) \xrightarrow{a} (q'_s, m)} \qquad \frac{q_c \xrightarrow{a}_c q'_c \quad a \in (\Sigma_c - Sync - \Sigma_s) \cup \{\tau\}}{(q_s, m \uplus \{q_c\}) \xrightarrow{a} (q_s, m \uplus \{q'_c\})}$$

$$\frac{q_s \xrightarrow{a}_s q'_s \quad q_c \xrightarrow{a}_c q'_c \quad a \in (\Sigma_c - Sync) \cap \Sigma_s}{(q_s, m \uplus \{q_c\}) \xrightarrow{a} (q'_s, m \uplus \{q'_c\})}$$

$$\frac{q_{c,1} \xrightarrow{a}_c q'_{c,1} \quad q_{c,2} \xrightarrow{a}_c q'_{c,2} \quad a \in Sync - \Sigma_s}{(q_s, m \uplus \{q_{c,1}, q_{c,2}\}) \xrightarrow{a} (q_s, m \uplus \{q'_{c,1}, q'_{c,2}\})}$$

$$\frac{q_s \xrightarrow{a}_s q'_s \quad q_{c,1} \xrightarrow{a}_c q'_{c,1} \quad q_{c,2} \xrightarrow{a}_c q'_{c,2} \quad a \in Sync \cap \Sigma_s}{(q_s, m \uplus \{q_{c,1}, q_{c,2}\}) \xrightarrow{a} (q'_s, m \uplus \{q'_{c,1}, q'_{c,2}\})}$$

For example, in the toy example, we can take *Cpts* and *Server* to be the state machines illustrated in Fig. 1; *Sync* is the set of all events on channel *pass*; *Init* is all states with the watchdog in state wd_0, a single replicated component in state s_1, and the remaining components in state s_0 (and with components having distinct identities).

Definition 5. We define the *reachable states* $\mathcal{R}$ of a system to be those system states reachable from an initial state by zero or more transitions.

Our normal correctness condition will be that the distinguished event *error* cannot occur.

Definition 6. A system is *error-free* if there are no reachable states ss and ss' such that $ss \xrightarrow{error} ss'$.

Our normal style will be to include a *watchdog* server, that observes (some) events by other processes, and performs the event *error* after an erroneous trace. In [18] it is shown that an arbitrary CSP traces refinement can be encoded in this way. Hence this technique can capture an arbitrary finite-state safety property.

3 Using View Abstraction

In this section we describe our application of view abstraction, adapting the techniques from [1] to our synchronous message-passing setting. Fix a system $(Server, Cpts, Sync, Init)$, and let Q_s and Q_c be the states of *Server* and *Cpts*, respectively. Let $k \in \mathbb{Z}^+$.

A *view* of size k over Q_c is a multiset $v \in \mathbb{M}(Q_c)$ of size k. A *system view* of size k is a pair (q, v) with $q \in Q_s$ and v a view of size k. We write $\mathcal{SV}_k$ for the set of all system views of size k. Note that system states and systems views have the same type: however, the latter record only part of the full system state.

Let $\mathcal{SS}_{\geq k}$ be all system states with at least k replicated components. We define the following abstraction relation, for $(q, m) \in \mathcal{SS}_{\geq k}$ and $(q, v) \in \mathcal{SV}_k$:

$$(q, v) \sqsubseteq_k (q, m) \text{ iff } v \subseteq m.$$

The system view (q, v) records the states of just k of the components of (q, m).

The abstraction function $\alpha_k : \mathcal{SS}_{\geq k} \rightarrow \mathbb{P}(\mathcal{SV}_k)$ abstracts a system state by its system views of size k:

$$\alpha_k(q,m) = \{(q,v) \in \mathcal{SV}_k \mid (q,v) \sqsubseteq_k (q,m)\}.$$

We lift α_k to sets of system states by pointwise application.

The concretization function $\gamma_k : \mathbb{P}(\mathcal{SV}_k) \rightarrow \mathcal{SS}_{\geq k}$ takes a set SV of system views, and produces those system states that are consistent with SV, i.e. such that all views of the state of size k are in SV.

$$\gamma_k(SV) = \{(q,m) \in \mathcal{SS}_{\geq k} \mid \alpha_k(q,m) \subseteq SV\}.$$

The following lemma is proved as in [1].

Lemma 7. (α_k, γ_k) *forms a Galois connection: if* $A \subseteq \mathcal{SS}_{\geq k}$ *and* $B \subseteq \mathcal{SV}_k$, *then* $\alpha_k(A) \subseteq B \Leftrightarrow A \subseteq \gamma_k(B)$.

We define an abstract transition relation. If $SV \subseteq \mathcal{SV}_k$ and $sv' \in \mathcal{SV}_k$ then define

$$SV \xrightarrow{a}_k sv' \Leftrightarrow \exists\, ss \in \gamma_k(SV)\,;\, ss' \in \mathcal{SS} \bullet ss \xrightarrow{a} ss' \wedge sv' \sqsubseteq_k ss'.$$

For example, in the running example we have the transition

$$\{\,(wd_0, \{s_3(T_0), s_0(T_1)\}),\ (wd_0, \{s_3(T_0), s_0(T_2)\}),\ (wd_0, \{s_0(T_1), s_0(T_2)\})\,\}$$
$$\xrightarrow{pass.T_0,T_1}_2 (wd_0, \{s_0(T_0), s_1(T_1)\})$$

corresponding to the concrete transition

$$(wd_0, \{s_3(T_0), s_0(T_1), s_0(T_2)\}) \xrightarrow{pass.T_0,T_1} (wd_0, \{s_0(T_0), s_1(T_1), s_0(T_2)\}).$$

We then define the abstract post-image of a set of system views $SV \subseteq \mathcal{SV}_k$ by

$$aPost_k(SV) = \{sv' \mid \exists\, a \bullet SV \xrightarrow{a}_k sv'\} = \alpha_k(post(\gamma_k(SV))),$$

where *post* gives the concrete post-image of a set $X \subseteq \mathcal{SS}$:

$$post(X) = \{(s',m') \mid \exists\, a, (s,m) \in X \bullet (s,m) \xrightarrow{a} (s',m')\}.$$

The following lemma relates abstract and concrete post-images; it is easily proved using Lemma 7.

Lemma 8. *If* $SV \subseteq \mathcal{SV}_k$ *and* $X \subseteq \gamma_k(SV)$, *then* $post(X) \subseteq \gamma_k(aPost_k(SV))$.

Let $Init_{\geq k}$ and $\mathcal{R}_{\geq k}$ be, respectively, those initial states from $Init$, and those reachable states from $\mathcal{R}$, with at least k replicated components. The following theorem shows how $\mathcal{R}_{\geq k}$ can be over-approximated by iterating the abstract post-image. We write $f^*(X)$ for $\bigcup_{i=0}^{\infty} f^i(X)$.

Theorem 9. *If $AInit \subseteq SV_k$ is such that $\alpha_k(Init_{\geq k}) \subseteq AInit$ then*

$$\mathcal{R}_{\geq k} \subseteq \gamma_k(aPost_k^*(AInit)).$$

Proof: The assumption implies $Init_{\geq k} \subseteq \gamma_k(AInit)$, from Lemma 7. Then Lemma 8 implies $post^n(Init_{\geq k}) \subseteq \gamma_k(aPost^n(AInit))$ via a trivial induction. The result then follows from the fact that $\mathcal{R}_{\geq k} = post^*(Init_{\geq k})$. □

Hence, if we can show that all states in $\gamma_k(aPost_k^*(AInit))$ are error-free, then we will be able to deduce that all systems with k or more components are error-free; systems with fewer than k components can be checked directly (for a fixed set of parameters, and appealing to symmetry).

In the running example, we can take $AInit$ to contain all system views of size k with the watchdog in state wd_0, zero or one components in state s_1, and the remaining components in state s_0 (and with components having distinct identities). Then, for $k \geq 2$, $\gamma_k(aPost_k^*(AInit))$ contains all system views as follows: (1) at most one component is in state s_1, s_2 or s_3, and the remainder are in s_0; and (2) if component id is in s_2 then the watchdog is in $wd_1(id)$; if every component is in s_0 then the watchdog is in either wd_0 or $wd_1(id)$ where component id is not in the view; and otherwise the watchdog is in wd_0. This approximates the invariant that a single component holds the token, and the watchdog records the component in the critical region. In particular, the event *error* is not available from any such state. The above theorem then shows that all systems of size at least two are error-free.

However, the above theorem does not immediately give an algorithm. The application of γ_k within $aPost$ can produce an infinite set, for two reasons:

- It can give system states with an arbitrary number of components;
- The parameters of type T within system states can range over a potentially infinite set.

We tackle the former problem in Sect. 4, by showing that it is enough to build concretizations of size at most $k + 2$. We tackle the latter problem in Sect. 5, using symmetry.

4   Bounding the Number of Components

We now show that, when calculating $aPost_k$, it is enough to consider concretizations with at most two additional component states.

For $k \leq l$ and $SV \subseteq SV_k$, define

$$\gamma_k^l(SV) = \{(q, m_c) \in SS \mid \alpha_k(q, m_c) \subseteq SV \wedge k \leq \#m_c \leq l\},$$

i.e., those concretizations with between k and l component states. For $k \leq l$, $SV \subseteq SV_k$ and $sv' \in SV_k$, define the abstract transitions involving such concretizations as follows:

$$SV \xrightarrow{a}{}_k^l sv' \Leftrightarrow \exists ss \in \gamma_k^l(SV) ; ss' \in SS \bullet ss \xrightarrow{a} ss' \wedge sv' \sqsubseteq_k ss'.$$

Lemma 10. *Suppose $SV \subseteq \mathcal{SV}_k$, $sv' \in \mathcal{SV}_k$, $k \geq 1$, and $SV \xrightarrow{a}_k sv'$. Then $SV \xrightarrow{a}_k^{k+2} sv'$.*

Proof: If $SV \xrightarrow{a}_k sv' = (q_s', v')$ then for some $(q_s, m) \in \gamma_k(SV)$ and some (q_s', m') we have $(q_s, m) \xrightarrow{a} (q_s', m')$ and $sv' \sqsubseteq_k (q_s', m')$. Let $\hat{m}'$ be the smallest subset of m' that includes v' and each of the (at most two) replicated components that change state in the transition; and let $\hat{m} \subseteq m$ be the pre-transition states of the components in $\hat{m}'$. For example, suppose the transition corresponds to the fourth rule in Definition 4, so, for some m_0, $m = m_0 \uplus \{q_{c,1}, q_{c,2}\}$ and $m' = m_0 \uplus \{q_{c,1}', q_{c,2}'\}$; and suppose v' contains $q_{c,1}'$ but not $q_{c,2}'$; then $\hat{m}' = v' \uplus \{q_{c,2}'\} \subseteq m'$; and $\hat{m} \subseteq m$ is the same as $\hat{m}'$ but with $q_{c,1}$ and $q_{c,2}$ in place of $q_{c,1}'$ and $q_{c,2}'$.

In each case, it is easy to see that $(q_s, \hat{m}) \xrightarrow{a} (q_s', \hat{m}')$, via the same transition rule that produced the original transition. Also $sv' = (q_s', v') \sqsubseteq_k (q_s', \hat{m}')$. And $k \leq \#\hat{m} = \#\hat{m}' \leq k + 2$, since we have added at most two components to v'. Finally, $\hat{m} \subseteq m$, so $\alpha_k(q_s, \hat{m}) \subseteq \alpha_k(q_s, m) \subseteq SV$, so $(q_s, \hat{m}) \in \gamma_k^{k+2}(SV)$. Hence $SV \xrightarrow{a}_k^{k+2} sv'$. □

Abdulla et al. [1] prove a similar result in their setting, although using concretizations of size at most $k + 1$. We require concretizations of size $k + 2$, essentially because of the possibility of a three-way synchronisation between the server and two component states (corresponding to the fifth transition rule in Definition 4). The following lemma shows that when we remove the possibility of such synchronisations, we also obtain a limit of $k + 1$. However, the result is weakened to include the possibility that the system view produced was in the initial set of system views.

Lemma 11. *Suppose $Sync \cap \Sigma_s = \{\}$. Suppose further that $SV \subseteq \mathcal{SV}_k$, $sv' \in \mathcal{SV}_k$, $k \geq 1$, and $SV \xrightarrow{a}_k sv'$. Then either $sv' \in SV$ or $SV \xrightarrow{a}_k^{k+1} sv'$.*

Proof: The only cases in the proof of Lemma 10 where concretizations of size $k + 2$ were required were transitions involving *two* replicated components—so via the fourth and fifth transition rules—where neither component state was included in sv'. The case of the fifth rule is prevented by the assumption of this lemma. In the remaining case, we have (using identifiers as in the proof of Lemma 10): $a \in Sync$, $q_s = q_s'$, $m = m_0 \uplus \{q_{c,1}, q_{c,2}\}$, $m' = m_0 \uplus \{q_{c,1}', q_{c,2}'\}$, $v' \subseteq m_0$, $q_{c,1} \xrightarrow{a}_c q_{c,1}'$, and $q_{c,2} \xrightarrow{a}_c q_{c,2}'$. But then $sv' = (q_s, v') \sqsubseteq_k (q_s, m)$ so $sv' \in SV$. □

The above lemmas show that, in order to calculate $aPost_k$ (as required for Theorem 9) it is enough to calculate either $aPost_k^{k+2}$ or (if $Sync \cap \Sigma_s = \{\}$) $aPostId_k^{k+1}$ where

$$aPost_k^l(SV) = \alpha_k(post(\gamma_k^l(SV))),$$
$$aPostId_k^l(SV) = \alpha_k(post(\gamma_k^l(SV))) \cup SV.$$

The result below follows easily from Lemmas 10 and 11.

Corollary 12. *Let* $SV \subseteq \mathcal{SV}_k$ *and* $k \geq 1$. *Then*

1. $aPost_k^*(SV) = (aPost_k^{k+2})^*(SV);$
2. *If* $Sync \cap \Sigma_s = \{\}$ *then* $aPost_k^*(SV) \subseteq (aPostId_k^{k+1})^*(SV).$

5 Using Symmetry

The abstract transition relation from the previous section still produces a potentially infinite state space, because of the potentially unbounded set of component identities. In this section, we use techniques based on symmetry reduction to reduce this to a finite state space. We fix a system, as in Definition 4.

Recall (Definitions 3 and 4) that we assume that the server and each replicated component is symmetric. We show that this implies that the system as a whole is symmetric. We lift permutations to system states by point-wise application: $\pi(q, m) = (\pi(q), \{\pi(q_c) \mid q_c \in m\})$.

Lemma 13. *The state machine defined by a system is symmetric: if* $(q, m) \in \mathcal{SS}$ *and* $\pi \in Sym(T)$, *then* $(q, m) \sim_\pi \pi(q, m)$.

Proof: We show that the relation $\{((q, m), \pi(q, m)) \mid (q, m) \in \mathcal{SS}\}$ is a π-bisimulation. Suppose $(q, m) \xrightarrow{a} (q', m')$. We show that $\pi(q, m) \xrightarrow{\pi(a)} \pi(q', m')$ by a case analysis on the rule used to produce the former transition. For example, suppose the transition is produced by the third rule, so is of the form

$$(q, m_1 \uplus \{q_c\}) \xrightarrow{a} (q', m_1 \uplus \{q_c'\}),$$

such that $q \xrightarrow{a}_s q'$, $q_c \xrightarrow{a}_c q_c'$ and $a \in (\Sigma_c - Sync) \cap \Sigma_s$. Then since *Server* and *Cpts* are symmetric, and $\pi(Sync) = Sync$, we have $\pi(q) \xrightarrow{\pi(a)}_s \pi(q')$, $\pi(q_c) \xrightarrow{\pi(a)}_c \pi(q_c')$ and $\pi(a) \in (\Sigma_c - Sync) \cap \Sigma_s$. But then

$$\pi(q, m_1 \uplus \{q_c\}) \xrightarrow{\pi(a)} \pi(q', m_1 \uplus \{q_c'\}),$$

using the same rule. The cases for other rules are similar. And conversely, we can check that each transition of $\pi(q, m)$ is matched by a transition of (q, m). □

We now show a similar result for the abstract transition relation. We lift π to system views and sets of system views by point-wise application. The following lemma shows that abstract transitions from π-related sets are related in the obvious way; it is proven using Lemma 13 and straightforward properties of permutations.

Lemma 14. *If* $SV \xrightarrow{a}{}^l_k sv'$ *then* $\pi(SV) \xrightarrow{\pi(a)}{}^l_k \pi(sv')$.

Our approach will be to treat symmetric system views as equivalent, requiring the exploration of only one system view in each equivalence class. We will need the following definition and lemma.

Definition 15. Let $sv_1, sv_2 \in \mathcal{SV}_k$. We write $sv_1 \approx sv_2$ if $sv_1 = \pi(sv_2)$ for some $\pi \in Sym(T)$. Note that this is an equivalence relation. We say that sv_1 and sv_2 are *equivalent* in this case.

Let $SV_1, SV_2 \subseteq \mathcal{SV}_k$. We write $SV_1 \lesssim SV_2$ if

$$\forall\, sv_1 \in SV_1 \cdot \exists\, sv_2 \in SV_2 \cdot sv_1 \approx sv_2.$$

We write $SV_1 \approx SV_2$, and say that SV_1 and SV_2 are *equivalent*, if $SV_1 \lesssim SV_2$ and $SV_2 \lesssim SV_1$. This is again an equivalence relation.

Lemma 16. *Suppose $SV_1, SV_2 \subseteq \mathcal{SV}_k$ with $SV_1 \approx SV_2$. Then $aPost_k^l(SV_1) \approx aPost_k^l(SV_2)$.*

Proof: This follows directly from Lemma 14. □

6   The Algorithm and Implementation

We now present our algorithm, and prove its correctness. The algorithm takes as inputs a system, a positive integer k, and a set $AInit$ of initial system views such that $\alpha_k(Init_{\geq k}) \subseteq AInit$. If $Sync \cap \Sigma_s = \{\}$ then let $l = k + 1$; otherwise let $l = k + 2$. The algorithm iterates $aPost_k^l$, maintaining a set $SV \subseteq \mathcal{SV}_k$, which stores the system views encountered so far, up to equivalence.

$SV := AInit$

while$(true)\{$

    if $SV \xrightarrow{error\ l}_k$ then return $failure$

    for$(sv' \in aPost_k^l(SV))$ if $\nexists\, sv \in SV \cdot sv \approx sv'$ then $SV := SV \cup \{sv'\}$

    if no new view was added to SV then return $success$

$\}$

When this algorithm is run on the toy example with $k = 2$, it encounters just five system views:

$$(wd_0, \{s_1(T_0), s_0(T_1)\}), \ (wd_0, \{s_0(T_0), s_0(T_1)\}),$$
$$(wd_1(T_0), \{s_2(T_0), s_0(T_1)\}), \ (wd_1(T_0), \{s_0(T_1), s_0(T_2)\}), \ (wd_0, \{s_3(T_0), s_0(T_2)\})$$

(or equivalent system views), the former two being the initial system views.

Lemma 17. *If the algorithm does not return $failure$ then the final value of SV is such that $\mathcal{R}_{\geq k} \lesssim \gamma_k(SV)$.*

Proof: We show that after n iterations, $SV \approx (aPostId_k^l)^n(AInit)$, by induction on n. The base case is trivial. For the inductive case, suppose, at the start of an iteration, $SV \approx (aPostId_k^l)^n(AInit)$. Each element sv' of $aPost_k^l(SV)$ is added to SV, unless SV already contains an equivalent system view. Hence the subsequent value of SV is equivalent to the value of $SV \cup aPost_k^l(SV)$ at the beginning of the iteration. But

$$SV \cup aPost_k^l(SV) \approx (aPostId_k^l)^n(AInit) \cup aPost_k^l((aPostId_k^l)^n(AInit))$$
$$= (aPostId_k^l)^{n+1}(AInit),$$

using the inductive hypothesis and Lemma 16, as required.

SV_k contains a finite number of equivalence classes. Hence the iteration must reach a fixed point such that SV is equivalent to $(aPostId_k^l)^*(AInit) = \bigcup_{n=0}^{\infty}(aPostId_k^l)^n(AInit)$. By Corollary 12, this contains $aPost_k^*(AInit)$. And by Theorem 9, $\mathcal{R}_{\geq k} \subseteq \gamma_k(aPost_k^*(AInit))$. $\qquad \square$

Theorem 18. *If the algorithm returns success, then the system is error-free for systems of size at least k.*

Proof: We prove the contra-positive: suppose there is some system state $ss \in \mathcal{R}_{\geq k}$ such that $ss \xrightarrow{error}$; we show that the algorithm returns *failure*. From Lemma 17, for the fixed point of SV, we have $ss \in \gamma_k(SV)$, and so $SV \xrightarrow{error}_k$. Then by Lemmas 10 and 11, $SV \xrightarrow{error\ l}_k$. Hence the algorithm returns *failure*. $\qquad \square$

Of course, the algorithm may sometimes return *failure* when, in fact, all systems are error-free: a *spurious counterexample*. This might just mean that it is necessary to re-run the algorithm with a larger value of k: the current value of k is not large enough to capture relevant properties of the system. Or it might be that the algorithm would fail for all values of k. This should not be surprising, since the problem is undecidable in general.

6.1   Prototype Implementation

We have created a prototype implementation, in Scala, following the above algorithm[2]. Unlike the model in earlier sections, the implementation allows multiple servers: the parallel composition of these can be considered as a single server, for compatibility with the model. The current implementation supports only the conditions of Lemma 11, corresponding to $l = k+1$; in practice, nearly all examples fit within this setting.

The implementation takes as input a value for k, and a description of the system modelled in machine-readable CSP (CSP_M): more precisely, it takes a standard CSP_M script, suitable for model checking using FDR [16], augmented with annotations to identify the processes representing the replicated components and the servers (with their initial states), their alphabets, and the type T of components' identities. CSP_M is a very expressive language, which makes it convenient for defining systems. The script must contain a concrete definition for T that is big enough, in a sense that we make clear below.

---

[2] The implementation and the scripts for the examples in the next section are available from www.cs.ox.ac.uk/people/gavin.lowe/ViewAbstraction/index.html.

The initial state $aInit$ of the components and servers should be such that $\alpha_k(Init_{\geq k}) \subsetneq \{aInit\}$. A common case is that each initial state in $Init_{\geq k}$ contains some small number n of components in distinguished states (in the toy example, a single component in state s_1, holding the token), and all other components in some default state (in the toy example, state s_0, not holding the token), possibly with servers holding the identities of components in distinguished states. In this case, it is enough for the initial state to include the n components in distinguished states (with servers holding their identities, if appropriate), plus k components in the default state.

The program interrogates FDR to obtain state machines for the servers and components (based upon the concrete definition for T), and to check that they are symmetric in T. Using the implementation of symmetry reduction from [17], each state is represented by a control state (an integer) and a list of parameters (each an integer). From these, the program can calculate transitions from concrete system states.

The program then follows the algorithm from Sect. 6 quite closely. When a concretization of size l is produced, it is possible that the concretization contains more identities than were included in the concrete definition of T; in this case, the program gives an error, and the user must provide a larger type.

Internally, a view (a multiset of states) is represented by a list; a system view is then represented by a list of the states of the servers (in some standard order) and this view. Hence testing whether two system views are equivalent corresponds to testing whether there is some way of permuting the view list and uniformly replacing component identities so as to make the system views equal. To make this efficient, each system view is replaced by an equivalent system view where the control states of components are in non-decreasing order, the identities are an initial segment of the natural numbers, and their first occurrences in the representation are in increasing order. The set of system views (the set SV of Sect. 6) is then stored as a mapping, with each system view keyed against its control states; to test whether a particular system view is equivalent to an existing one, it is enough to compare against those with the same key.

7 Analysing Reference-Linked Data Structures

We now show how our technique can be used to analyse a reference-linked data structure, such as a linked list. We illustrate our technique be verifying a lock-based concurrent queue, that uses an unbounded linked list, and that is used by two threads. We outline possible extensions to this setting in the conclusions. The queue contains data taken from the set $\{A, B, C\}$; we justify this choice below.

Each node in the linked list is modelled by a component process, and can be defined using CSP notation as follows.

$$FreeNode(me) = initNode?t!me?d \rightarrow Node_d(me, null),$$
$$Node_d(me, next) = getDatum?t!me!d \rightarrow Node_d(me, next)$$
$$\square\ getNext?t!me!next \rightarrow Node_d(me, next)$$
$$\square\ setNext?t!me?newNext \rightarrow Node_d(me, newNext)$$
$$\square\ freeNode?t!me \rightarrow FreeNode(me).$$

The state $FreeNode(me)$ represents a free node with identity me: it can be initialised by any thread t to store datum d and to have next reference to a distinguished value $null$. The state $Node_d(me, next)$ represents a node with identity me holding datum d and with next reference $next$ (we write d as a subscript, since this is not from the type of node identities, so not a parameter in the sense of the model). In this state, a thread t may: get the datum d; get the next reference $next$; set the next reference to a new value $newNext$; or free the node. Thus, nodes may be joined together to form a linked list.

In the initial state, a single node is initialised as a dummy header node in the state $Node_A(N_0, null)$, and the remaining nodes are initialised in the $FreeNode$ state.

The system contains three server processes representing part of the datatype: a lock process, that allows a thread to lock the queue; and two processes representing shared variables referencing the dummy header node, and the last node in the list, respectively, each initially holding N_0. Further, the system contains two server processes representing threads operating on the queue, enqueueing and dequeueing values (a dequeue on an empty queue returns a special value). These processes are defined as expected.

In order to verify that the system forms a queue, we adapt ideas from Wolper [30]. A process is *data independent* in a particular type D if the only operations it can perform on values of that type are to input them, store them, and output them. This means that for each trace tr of the process, uniformly replacing values from D within tr will give another trace of the process.

Lemma 19. *Suppose a process is data independent in a type D. Suppose further that whenever a sequence of data values from the language A^*BC^* is enqueued, then a sequence from $A^*BC^* + A^*$ is dequeued, and no dequeue operation finds the queue empty between the enqueue and dequeue of B. Then it is a queue.*

Proof (sketch). Consider a behaviour of such a process that violates the property of being a queue, by either losing, duplicating or reordering a particular piece of data. Then, by data independence, a similar behaviour would occur on an input from A^*BC^*, losing, duplicating or reordering B. But this would produce an output not from this language, or a dequeue would find the queue empty between the enqueue and dequeue of B. $\square$

We add two servers so as to exploit this idea:

- A regulator process, that synchronises with the threads, to force them to enqueue a sequence from A^*BC^*;
- A watchdog process, that observes the values dequeued, and performs *error* if the sequence is not from $A^*BC^* + A^*$, or if a dequeue finds the queue empty between the enqueue and dequeue of B.

The prototype implementation can be used to explore this system: the test succeeds in the case $k = 2$, and completes in about 12 s. Hence, by Theorem 18, all systems with at least two nodes implement a queue (for two threads). It is necessary to include at least nine values in the type of node identities: when considering transitions from states of size $k + 1 = 3$ (cf. Lemma 11), system states are encountered with three nodes, each holding their own identity and one other; the *Header* and *Tail* processes can each hold one other identity; and the thread holding the lock can hold one of these and one other identity.

We have used similar ideas to analyse a lock-based stack that uses a linked list. The modelling is very similar to as for the queue. For verification, we ensure that the values pushed onto the stack form a sequence from A^*BC^*; we then check (using a watchdog) that (1) before B is pushed, only A can be popped; (2) after B is pushed, the sequence of values popped is from $C^*B(A + C)^*$; and (3) a pop does not find the stack empty between the B being pushed and popped. An argument similar to Lemma 19 justifies the correctness of this test. The analysis, with $k = 2$, takes about 10 s in this case.

8   Conclusions

In this paper we have tackled a particular instance of the parameterised model checking problem, where replicated component processes have identities that may be passed between processes. We have adapted the technique of view abstraction, which records, for each system state, the states of just some small number k of replicated components. We have used techniques from symmetry reduction, to bound the number of identities of components that are stored. We have provided an implementation based on systems defined in CSP (although the underlying ideas are not CSP-specific). We have shown that the framework allows us to analyse unbounded reference-linked datatypes.

Roughly speaking, our technique, with a particular value of k, succeeds for systems whose invariant can be described in terms of the states of servers and at most k replicated components. For example, with the queue of Sect. 7, when a sequence from A^*BC^* is enqueued, each pair of adjacent nodes in the linked list hold data values (A, A), (A, B), (B, C) or (C, C), which implies that the sequence held is from $A^* + A^*BC^* + C^*$: this invariant talks about the states of just two components, so taking $k = 2$ succeeds.

Wolper [30] uses a technique similar to ours for characterising queues, but based on enqueueing a sequence from $A^*BA^*CA^*$. Curiously, our approach will not work with such a sequence, and gives a spurious error. This is because the corresponding invariant cannot be described in terms of the states of a bounded number of components, because a node holding A can be followed by a node holding any datum. This suggests that when trying to characterise a particular datatype based on chosen input sequences, those sequences should not contain the same data value in two different "chunks".

In this paper we have assumed a *single* family of replicated components. We intend to extend this to multiple such families. For example, in Sect. 7, we could have considered a family of processes representing the threads that interact with the queue, to allow us to verify that the datatype is correct when used by an arbitrary number of threads.

Our main motivating domain for this work is the study of concurrent datatypes, particularly lock-free datatypes. In [21] we used CSP and FDR to analyse a lock-free queue based on a linked list [24] for a *fixed* number of nodes and threads. We would like to use the techniques from this paper to consider an *arbitrary* number of nodes and threads. The main challenge here is capturing the correctness condition of linearizability: we believe this will be straightforward when explicit linearization points are given, but harder otherwise.

We have assumed a fully connected topology, where each replicated component can communicate with each other. We intend to also consider more restrictive topologies, such as a ring, following [1, Sect. 3.4].

In this paper we have considered only safety properties, corresponding to traces of the system. We would like to be able to consider also liveness properties, such as deadlock-freedom. One can adapt the algorithm from Sect. 6 to test whether any concretization of the set of system views deadlocks; one can then prove a variant of Theorem 18 that shows that if no such deadlock is found, then no system of size at least k deadlocks. However, this does not work in practice, since the abstraction introduces too many spurious deadlocks that do not occur in the unabstracted system. We intend to investigate whether other abstractions work better for this purpose.

Acknowledgements. I would like to thank Tom Gibson-Robinson for useful discussions concerning this work, and for extending the FDR4 API to support various functions necessary for the implementation from Sect. 6.1.

References

1. Abdulla, P., Haziza, F., Holík, L.: Parameterized verification through view abstraction. Int. J. Softw. Tools Technol. Transf. **18**, 495–516 (2016)
2. Abdulla, P.A., Jonsson, B., Nilsson, M., d'Orso, J.: Regular model checking made simple and effcient*. In: Brim, L., Křetínský, M., Kučera, A., Jančar, P. (eds.) CONCUR 2002. LNCS, vol. 2421, pp. 116–131. Springer, Heidelberg (2002). https://doi.org/10.1007/3-540-45694-5_9
3. Abdulla, P.A., Jonsson, B., Nilsson, M., Saksena, M.: A survey of regular model checking. In: Gardner, P., Yoshida, N. (eds.) CONCUR 2004. LNCS, vol. 3170, pp. 35–48. Springer, Heidelberg (2004). https://doi.org/10.1007/978-3-540-28644-8_3

4. Abdullah, P., Haziza, F., Holík, L., Jonsson, B., Rezine, A.: An integrated specification and verification technique for highly concurrent data structures. Int. J. Softw. Tools Technol. Transf. **19**, 549–563 (2017)
5. Apt, K.R., Kozen, D.C.: Limits for automatic verification of finite-state concurrent systems. Inf. Process. Lett. **22**(6), 307–309 (1986)
6. Bouajjani, A., Habermehl, P., Vojnar, T.: Abstract regular model checking. In: Alur, R., Peled, D.A. (eds.) CAV 2004. LNCS, vol. 3114, pp. 372–386. Springer, Heidelberg (2004). https://doi.org/10.1007/978-3-540-27813-9_29
7. Bouajjani, A., Jonsson, B., Nilsson, M., Touili, T.: Regular model checking. In: Emerson, E.A., Sistla, A.P. (eds.) CAV 2000. LNCS, vol. 1855, pp. 403–418. Springer, Heidelberg (2000). https://doi.org/10.1007/10722167_31
8. Bošnački, D., Dams, D., Holenderski, L.: Symmetric spin. Int. J. Softw. Tools Technol. Transf. **4**, 92–106 (2002)
9. Clarke, E.M., Emerson, E.A., Jha, S., Sistla, A.P.: Symmetry reductions in model checking. In: Hu, A.J., Vardi, M.Y. (eds.) CAV 1998. LNCS, vol. 1427, pp. 147–158. Springer, Heidelberg (1998). https://doi.org/10.1007/BFb0028741
10. Clarke, E.M., Enders, R., Filkorn, T., Jha, S.: Exploiting symmetry in temporal logic model checking. Formal Methods Syst. Des. **9**, 77–104 (1996)
11. Clarke, E.M., Grumberg, O.: Avoiding the state explosion problem in temporal logic model checking. In: Proceedings of the 6th Annual Association for Computing Machinery Symposium on Principles of Distributed Computing, pp. 294–303 (1987)
12. Dams, D., Lakhnech, Y., Steffen, M.: Iterating transducers. J. Logic Algebraic Program. **52–53**, 109–127 (2002)
13. Emerson, E.A., Namjoshi, K.S.: Reasoning about rings. In: Proceedings of the Symposium on Principles of Programming Languages (POPL 1995) (1995)
14. Emerson, E.A., Sistla, A.P.: Symmetry and model checking. Formal Methods Syst. Des. **9**, 105–131 (1996)
15. German, S.M., Sistla, A.P.: Reasoning about systems with many processes. J. ACM **39**(3), 675–735 (1992)
16. Gibson-Robinson, T., Armstrong, P., Boulgakov, A., Roscoe, A.W.: FDR3: a parallel refinement checker for CSP. Int. J. Softw. Tools Technol. Transf. **18**(2), 149–167 (2015)
17. Gibson-Robinson, T., Lowe, G.: Symmetry Reduction in CSP Model Checking (2017, Submitted for publication). http://www.cs.ox.ac.uk/people/gavin.lowe/SymmetryReduction/
18. Goldsmith, M., Moffat, N., Roscoe, B., Whitworth, T., Zakiuddin, I.: Watchdog transformations for property-oriented model-checking. In: Araki, K., Gnesi, S., Mandrioli, D. (eds.) FME 2003. LNCS, vol. 2805, pp. 600–616. Springer, Heidelberg (2003). https://doi.org/10.1007/978-3-540-45236-2_33
19. Ip, C.N., Dill, D.L.: Better verification through symmetry. Formal Methods Syst. Des. **9**, 41–75 (1996)
20. Kesten, Y., Maler, O., Marcus, M., Pnueli, A., Shahar, E.: Symbolic model checking with rich assertional languages. Theoret. Comput. Sci. **256**, 93–112 (2001)
21. Lowe, G.: Analysing lock-free linearizable datatypes using CSP. In: Gibson-Robinson, T., Hopcroft, P., Lazić, R. (eds.) Concurrency, Security, and Puzzles. LNCS, vol. 10160, pp. 162–184. Springer, Cham (2017). https://doi.org/10.1007/978-3-319-51046-0_9
22. Lubachevsky, B.: An approach to automating the verification of compact parallel coordination programs. Acta Inform. **21**(2), 125–169 (1984)
23. Mazur, T., Lowe, G.: CSP-based counter abstraction for systems with node identifiers. Sci. Comput. Program. **81**, 3–52 (2014)

24. Michael, M., Scott, M.: Simple, fast, and practical non-blocking and blocking concurrent queue algorithms. In: Proceedings of the Fifteenth Annual ACM Symposium on Principles of Distributed Computing, pp. 267–275 (1996)

25. Pnueli, A., Xu, J., Zuck, L.: Liveness with $(0, 1, \infty)$-counter abstraction. In: Brinksma, E., Larsen, K.G. (eds.) CAV 2002. LNCS, vol. 2404, pp. 107–122. Springer, Heidelberg (2002). https://doi.org/10.1007/3-540-45657-0_9

26. Roscoe, A.W.: Understanding Concurrent Systems. Springer, London (2010). https://doi.org/10.1007/978-1-84882-258-0

27. Roscoe, A.W., Creese, S.: Data independent induction over structured networks. In: Proceedings of PDPTA 2000 (2000)

28. Sistla, A.P., Gyuris, V., Emerson, E.A.: SMC: a symmetry-based model checker for verification of safety and linveness properties. ACM Trans. Softw. Eng. Methodol. **9**(2), 133–166 (2000)

29. Touili, T.: Regular model checking using widening techniques. Electr. Notes Theoret. Comput. Sci. **50**(4), 342–356 (2001). Proceedings of VEPAS 2001

30. Wolper, P.: Expressing interesting properties of programs in propositional temporal logic. In: Thirteenth Annual ACM Symposium on Principles of Programming Languages, pp. 184–193 (1986)

31. Wolper, P., Boigelot, B.: Verifying systems with infinite but regular state spaces. In: Hu, A.J., Vardi, M.Y. (eds.) CAV 1998. LNCS, vol. 1427, pp. 88–97. Springer, Heidelberg (1998). https://doi.org/10.1007/BFb0028736

32. Wolper, P., Lovinfosse, V.: Verifying properties of large sets of processes with network invariants. In: Sifakis, J. (ed.) Automatic Verification Methods for Finite State Systems. LNCS, vol. 407, pp. 68–80. Springer, Heidelberg (1989). https://doi.org/10.1007/3-540-52148-8

Compositional Reasoning
for Shared-Variable Concurrent Programs

Fuyuan Zhang[1]([✉]), Yongwang Zhao[3], David Sanán[1], Yang Liu[1], Alwen Tiu[2], Shang-Wei Lin[1], and Jun Sun[4]

[1] School of Computer Science and Engineering,
Nanyang Technological University, Singapore, Singapore
fuyuanzhang@163.com
[2] Research School of Computer Science,
Australian National University, Canberra, Australia
[3] School of Computer Science and Engineering, Beihang University, Beijing, China
[4] Singapore University of Technology and Design, Singapore, Singapore

Abstract. Scalable and automatic formal verification for concurrent systems is always demanding. In this paper, we propose a verification framework to support automated compositional reasoning for concurrent programs with shared variables. Our framework models concurrent programs as succinct automata and supports the verification of multiple important properties. Safety verification and simulations of succinct automata are parallel compositional, and safety properties of succinct automata are preserved under refinements. We generate succinct automata from infinite state concurrent programs in an automated manner. Furthermore, we propose the first automated approach to checking rely-guarantee based simulations between infinite state concurrent programs. We have prototyped our algorithms and applied our tool to the verification of multiple refinements.

1 Introduction

Automatic verification of concurrent programs is a challenging task. Due to interleaving, the state space of a concurrent program could grow exponentially, which makes it infeasible to directly reason about the global state space. A promising way of conquering the state explosion problem is compositional reasoning [18,25,26,33,36], which aims at breaking the global verification problems into small localized problems. Extensive research [10,14,15,19,22,23] has been conducted on developing rely-guarantee based automatic verification techniques for safety properties of concurrent programs. However, to ensure that safety properties of concurrent programs are preserved after compilation, it is also necessary to show that the checked programs are refined correctly. To the best of our knowledge, all existing approaches to checking rely-guarantee based simulations of concurrent programs [28] are manual.

In this paper, we propose a framework of automated compositional reasoning for shared-variable concurrent programs, which supports both safety verification and refinement checking. In our framework, concurrent programs are modelled as succinct automata, which can be viewed as an extension of program graphs [2]. A succinct automaton consists of both component transitions, specifying behaviors of a local program, and environment transitions, which overapproximate behaviors of other programs in the environment. The idea of integrating these two types of transitions is the key to ensure parallel compositionality. The development of our framework proceeds in the following two directions.

The first direction focuses on parallel compositionalities of safety and simulations of succinct automata, which are very useful in developing compositional proof of global properties. For example, our definition of weak simulations between succinct automata allows compositional reasoning through establishing a local refinement relationship. Let SA_1 (resp. $\widehat{SA_1}$) and SA_2 (resp. $\widehat{SA_2}$) be two succinct automata and $SA_1 \| SA_2$ (resp. $\widehat{SA_1} \| \widehat{SA_2}$) be their parallel composition. Since our notion of weak simulation is compositional, we can prove that $SA_1 \| SA_2$ weakly refines $\widehat{SA_1} \| \widehat{SA_2}$ by proving that SA_1 (resp. SA_2) weakly refines $\widehat{SA_1}$ (resp. $\widehat{SA_2}$). As safety properties of succinct automata are preserved under refinements, parallel compositionalities of safety and simulations allow us to extend safety properties of high level concurrent programs to low level concurrent programs in compositional ways.

The second direction aims at automating our compositional reasoning techniques. One difficulty of modelling concurrent programs as succinct automata is to find appropriate environment transitions that overapproximate the interleavings between concurrent programs. We show that such environment transitions can be inferred automatically for succinct automata with infinite domains. Moreover, we have developed an SMT-based approach to checking weak simulations between infinite state succinct automata. To the best of our knowledge, we are the first to propose automatic verification of rely-guarantee based simulations for infinite state shared-variable concurrent programs. We have prototyped our tool in F# and verified multiple refinements in automated manner.

Our contributions are fourfold. First, we propose a new formalism, succinct automata, that facilitates automatic verification of multiple properties of shared-variable concurrent programs. Second, we show compositionality results on safety properties and simulations in our framework. Third, we show that succinct automata can be generated automatically from infinite state concurrent programs. Fourth, we provide an SMT-based approach to verifying simulations for infinite state succinct automata.

2 Related Work

Extensive research has been conducted on the verification of concurrent programs. Basic approaches to conquering the state explosion problem of concurrent systems include (but not limited to) symbolic model checking [4], partial order reduction [16,32,35], abstraction [8,9,11,17], compositional reasoning [18,25,26,31,33] and symmetry reduction [7,13,24]. The formalism of succinct automata is inspired by rely-guarantee style reasoning [25,26]. We mainly discuss related work on the compositional reasoning of properties considered in this paper.

Safety Verification. Our approach to safety verification is closest to thread-modular verification [15], where safety properties are characterized by a set of unsafe states and a global system is safe iff unsafe states are not reachable. In this paper, we focus on invariance properties of succinct automata. Checking strong invariants of succinct automata is dual to verifying whether corresponding sets of unsafe states are reachable. Hence, the approach in [15] can be applied to verify strong invariants of (parallel) succinct automata with finite domains. Work in [10,19,22,23] combined compositional reasoning with abstraction refinement [8]. Moreover, [10,19] allow local variables of different threads to be correlated, which makes their proof rules complete.

Simulations. Our work on checking weak simulations is related to previous approaches [3,5,28,29] on compositional reasoning of concurrent programs refinement. In [3,5,29], parallel compositionality is achieved by allowing the environments to have arbitrary behaviors, which is considered too strong in general. Our definition of weak simulations for succinct automata is closely related to and inspired by [28], where a rely-guarantee based simulation, called RGSim, for concurrent programs is proposed. Their compositionality rules for RGSim form the basis of a relational proof method for concurrent programs transformations. Our work differs with theirs mainly in that we aim at developing automatic verification of weak simulations between succinct automata. Also, instead of treating all variables as global variables, we distinguish between local variables and global variables. This greatly reduces the state space of local succinct automata. Compared to [21], which has proposed the first automated proof system for refinement verification of concurrent programs, our approach to refinement checking is more general and is not limited to any specific rules of refinement. Work in [27] proposed an automated refinement checking technique for infinite state CSP programs. Their approach is not developed for shared-variable concurrent programs.

3   Succinct Automata

Succinct automata aim to model both local behaviors of a program and its environment in a unified way, and to provide a convenient way to specify useful properties of programs and to support compositional reasoning over them. We distinguish between global variables and local variables when modeling concurrent programs.

3.1   Syntax and Semantics

Let Dom be a finite or infinite (numeric) domain and $V = \{v_1, ..., v_n\}$ be a finite set of variables ranging over Dom. An *atomic predicate* over V is of the form $f(v_1, ..., v_n) \sim b$, where $f : Dom^n \to Dom$ is a function, $\sim \in \{=, <, \leq, >, \geq\}$ and

$b \in Dom$. A *predicate* over V is a Boolean combination of atomic predicates over V. We write V' for $\{v'_1, ..., v'_n\}$ that refers to variables in V after transitions. Let $\mathcal{F}(V)$ (resp. $\mathcal{F}(V \cup V')$) denote the set of predicates over V (resp. $V \cup V'$). A *valuation* is a function from variables to a domain. Given a valuation $\mathbf{v} : V \to Dom$, we define $n(\mathbf{v}) : V' \to Dom$ as $n(\mathbf{v})(v'_i) = \mathbf{v}(v_i)$ for $v_i \in V$. Given a predicate $\psi \in \mathcal{F}(V_1)$ and a valuation $\mathbf{v} : V_2 \to Dom$, where $V_1 \subseteq V_2$, we write $\psi(\mathbf{v})$ to denote that ψ evaluates to true under the valuation $\mathbf{v}$. We write $\mathbf{Val}_V$ to denote the set of all valuations for variables in V.

Definition 1. *A Succinct Automaton is a tuple* $SA = (Q, q_0, V, Init, Inv, Env, \Sigma, Edge)$, *where*

- Q *is a finite set of locations and* $q_0 \in Q$ *is an initial location.*
- $V = V_G \cup V_L$ *and* V_G *(resp.* V_L*) is a finite set of global (resp. local) variables ranging over Dom, where* $V_G \cap V_L = \emptyset$.
- $Init \in \mathcal{F}(V)$ *defines initial values of variables at* q_0.
- $Inv : Q \to \mathcal{F}(V)$ *constrains the values of variables at each location.*
- $Env : Q \to \mathbf{Val}_{V_G} \times \mathbf{Val}_{V_G}$ *specifies environment transitions at each location.*
- Σ *is a finite set of action labels which includes the silent action* τ.
- $Edge \subseteq Q \times \Sigma \times \mathcal{F}(V \cup V') \times Q$ *is a finite set of edges specifying component transitions.*

For each location $q \in Q$, transitions specified by $Env(q)$ are made by the environment when SA stays at q. In the rest of the paper, we also use predicates or first order formulas to specify $Env(q)$ for convenience. For example, when using $\phi \in \mathcal{F}(V_G \cup V'_G)$ to specify $Env(q)$, $Env(q)$ is defined by $Env(q) = \{(\mathbf{v}_G, \mathbf{v}'_G) \mid \phi(\mathbf{v}_G, n(\mathbf{v}'_G)) \text{ holds}\}$. An edge is of the form $e = (q, \sigma, \mu, q')$, where μ defines the transition condition and is of the form $\mu := G(V) \wedge \bigwedge_{v'_i \in V'} v'_i = f_i(V)$, where $G(V)$ is a guard for e and f_i is a function $f_i : Dom^n \to Dom$ for $1 \leq i \leq n$. Action labels in Σ are used when we check weak simulations of succinct automata. The main purpose of Inv is to overapproximate reachable states at each control location of a concurrent program. This also facilitates the formalization of the compatibility condition on succinct automata (introduced later). A succinct automaton is *closed* if its environment cannot modify its global variables.

The semantics of succinct automata is defined as a labeled transition system. A *state* of a succinct automaton is a pair $s = (q, \mathbf{v})$ of location q and valuation $\mathbf{v} : V \to Dom$. We denote with S_{SA} the state space of SA. A state $(q, \mathbf{v})$ is an initial state iff $q = q_0$ and $Init(\mathbf{v})$ holds. We say that a predicate ψ is satisfied on $(q, \mathbf{v})$ iff $\psi(\mathbf{v})$ holds.

Let $\mathbf{v}_1 : V_1 \to Dom$ and $\mathbf{v}_2 : V_2 \to Dom$ be two valuations such that $V_1 \cap V_2 = \emptyset$. We define $\mathbf{v}_1 \oplus \mathbf{v}_2 : V_1 \cup V_2 \to Dom$ by $\mathbf{v}_1 \oplus \mathbf{v}_2(v) = \mathbf{v}_1(v)$ for $v \in V_1$ and $\mathbf{v}_1 \oplus \mathbf{v}_2(v) = \mathbf{v}_2(v)$ for $v \in V_2$. Let $\mathbf{v}_G : V_G \to Dom$ (resp. $\mathbf{v}_L : V_L \to Dom$) be valuations over global (resp. local) variables. In the rest of the paper, we also use $(q, \mathbf{v}_G \oplus \mathbf{v}_L)$ to represent a state for convenience.

We define two types of transitions, namely *component transitions* and *environment transitions*, for succinct automata. There is a component transition between two states $(q, \mathbf{v}) \xrightarrow{\sigma} (q', \mathbf{v}')$ iff there exists an edge of the form $(q, \sigma, \mu, q') \in Edge$ and $Inv(q)(\mathbf{v}) \wedge \mu(\mathbf{v} \oplus n(\mathbf{v}')) \wedge Inv(q')(\mathbf{v}')$ holds. There is an environment transition between two states $(q, \mathbf{v}) \xrightarrow{env} (q', \mathbf{v}')$ iff $q = q'$, $Inv(q)(\mathbf{v}) \wedge Inv(q)(\mathbf{v}')$ holds, $(\mathbf{v}_G, \mathbf{v}'_G) \in Env(q)$ and $\mathbf{v}_L = \mathbf{v}'_L$, where $\mathbf{v} = \mathbf{v}_G \oplus \mathbf{v}_L$ and $\mathbf{v}' = \mathbf{v}'_G \oplus \mathbf{v}'_L$. Notice that in an environment transition, only values of global variables can be modified and values of local variables remain unchanged.

A *run* of SA is a finite or infinite sequence of environment and component transitions starting from an initial state $(q_0, \mathbf{v}_0)$:

$$(q_0, \mathbf{v}_0) \xrightarrow{env} (q_0, \mathbf{v}'_0) \xrightarrow{\sigma_1} (q_1, \mathbf{v}_1) \xrightarrow{env} (q_1, \mathbf{v}'_1) \xrightarrow{\sigma_2} (q_2, \mathbf{v}_2) \cdots$$

We say that a predicate ψ is satisfied on a run iff it is satisfied on all states on that run.

A finite *local path* of SA is a sequence of edges $\pi = e_1, ..., e_n$, where $e_i = (q_i, \sigma_i, \mu_i, q'_i)$, $e_n = (q_n, \sigma_n, \mu_n, q'_n)$ and $q'_i = q_{i+1}$ for $1 \le i < n$.

We write $(q, \mathbf{v}) \to^* (q', \mathbf{v}')$ if there exists a finite run of SA, (consisting of zero or more transitions), from $(q, \mathbf{v})$ to $(q', \mathbf{v}')$ and say that $(q', \mathbf{v}')$ is *reachable* from $(q, \mathbf{v})$. The set of reachable states of SA is the set of states reachable from initial states of SA. Regarding environment transitions, we write $(q, \mathbf{v}) \xrightarrow{env^*} (q, \mathbf{v}')$ to denote a finite sequence of environment transitions of SA starting from $(q, \mathbf{v})$ to $(q, \mathbf{v}')$. For component transitions, we write $(q, \mathbf{v}) \xrightarrow{\tau^* \sigma \tau^*} (q', \mathbf{v}')$ to mean that SA has first taken a finite number of silent actions τ, followed by a component transition labelled by an action σ, and then made another finite number of silent actions.

Example 1. We model a simplified Peterson's algorithm using succinct automata as an example. The pseudo code in Fig. 1 shows a simplified version of Peterson's algorithm with two processes P_1 and P_2.

```
P1:                              P2:
while (true) {                   while (true) {
  flag1:=1;                        flag2:=1;
  turn:=2;                         turn:=1;
  await(flag2=0∨turn=1){          await(flag1=0∨turn=2){
    Critical Section;                Critical Section;
  }                                }
  flag1:=0;                        flag2:=0;
}                                }
```

Fig. 1. A simplified Peterson's algorithm

In Fig. 2, we model the above two processes as $SA_1 = (Q_1, q_0, V, Init_1, Inv_1, Env_1, \Sigma_1, Edge_1)$ and $SA_2 = (Q_2, p_0, V, Init_2, Inv_2, Env_2, \Sigma_2, Edge_2)$ respectively, where $V = \{flag_1, flag_2, critical_1, critical_2, turn\}$,

528   F. Zhang et al.

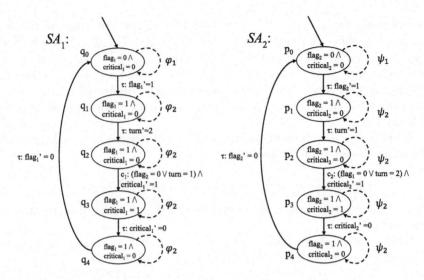

Fig. 2. Succinct automata for the simplified Peterson's algorithm

$\Sigma_1 = \{\tau, c_1\}$ and $\Sigma_2 = \{\tau, c_2\}$. Here, we treat all variables as global variables. The automaton SA_1 (resp. SA_2) starts at location q_0 (resp. p_0), where each variable has an initial value of 0, and has five locations q_0, q_1, q_2, q_3 and q_4 (resp. p_0, p_1, p_2, p_3 and p_4). Invariants for locations are presented in ovals. Component transitions are represented by solid line arrows, together with the action labels and predicates on them. We omitted the predicates specifying the variables whose values remain unchanged in component transitions. Environment transitions are represented by dashed line arrows and predicates on these arrows specify the binary relations that define environment transitions.

We now briefly explain SA_1. At location q_0, the environment transition is specified by $\varphi_1 = (flag'_1 = flag_1 \wedge critical'_1 = critical_1) \wedge (critical'_2 = 1 \Rightarrow flag'_2 = 1)$, meaning that SA_2 never modifies the values of $flag_1$ and $critical_1$ and that if SA_2 enters the critical section after the transition, denoted by $critical'_2 = 1$, we have $flag'_2 = 1$. Then, SA_1 takes a silent action to set $flag_1$ to 1, meaning that it wants to enter the critical section, and enters q_1. At location q_1, the environment transition is specified by $\varphi_2 = (flag'_1 = flag_1 \wedge critical'_1 = critical_1) \wedge (critical'_2 = 1 \Rightarrow (flag'_2 = 1 \wedge turn' = 2))$. Compared with φ_1, we see that if SA_2 enters the critical section when SA_1 is at q_1, $flag'_2$ (resp. $turn'$) must be 1 (resp. 2). This is because SA_2 must wait until its turn, denoted by $turn = 2$, to enter the critical section once SA_1 has set $flag_1$ to 1. After taking another silent action, SA_1 arrives at q_2. At location q_2, if $flag_2 = 0 \vee turn = 1$, SA_1 takes the action c_1 and enters the critical section. By entering q_4, SA_1 leaves the critical section. Finally, SA_1 resets $flag_1$ to 0 and comes back to q_0.

The environment transitions of SA_2 are defined by $\psi_1 = (flag'_2 = flag_2 \wedge critical'_2 = critical_2) \wedge (critical'_1 = 1 \Rightarrow flag'_1 = 1)$ and $\psi_2 = (flag'_2 = flag_2 \wedge critical'_2 = critical_2) \wedge (critical'_1 = 1 \Rightarrow (flag'_1 = 1 \wedge turn' = 1))$.

3.2 Parallel Composition

In rely-guarantee reasoning, the guarantee of one thread should imply the rely conditions of other threads. Similarly, we impose a compatibility condition on succinct automata running in parallel. Let q_1 (resp. q_2) be an arbitrary location in SA_1 (resp. SA_2). Informally, the compatibility condition guarantees that if SA_1 (resp. SA_2) makes a component transition from q_1 (resp. q_2) to q_1' (resp. q_2'), SA_2 (resp. SA_1) can mimic this transition by its environment transitions at q_2 (resp. q_1). We formalize the *compatibility* condition as follows.

Definition 2. SA_1 and SA_2 are compatible iff for all $(q_1, v_G \oplus v_{L_1}) \in S_{SA_1}, (q_2, v_G \oplus v_{L_2}) \in S_{SA_2}$ such that $Inv_1(q_1)(v_G \oplus v_{L_1})$ and $Inv_2(q_2)(v_G \oplus v_{L_2})$, we have

1. If $(q_1, v_G \oplus v_{L_1}) \xrightarrow{\sigma_1} (q_1', v_G' \oplus v_{L_1}')$, then $(q_2, v_G \oplus v_{L_2}) \xrightarrow{env} (q_2, v_G' \oplus v_{L_2})$.
2. If $(q_2, v_G \oplus v_{L_2}) \xrightarrow{\sigma_2} (q_2', v_G' \oplus v_{L_2}')$, then $(q_1, v_G \oplus v_{L_1}) \xrightarrow{env} (q_1, v_G' \oplus v_{L_1})$.

Succinct automata running in parallel execute their component transitions in an interleaved manner. The formal definition of parallel composition of compatible succinct automata is defined as follows.

Definition 3. Let $SA_1 = (Q_1, q_0^1, V_G \cup V_{L_1}, Init_1, Inv_1, Env_1, \Sigma_1, Edge_1)$ and $SA_2 = (Q_2, q_0^2, V_G \cup V_{L_2}, Init_2, Inv_2, Env_2, \Sigma_2, Edge_2)$ be two compatible succinct automata. The parallel composition of SA_1 and SA_2 is a succinct automaton $SA_1 \parallel SA_2 = (Q, q_0, V_G \cup V_L, Init, Inv, Env, \Sigma, Edge)$, where

- $Q = Q_1 \times Q_2$, $q_0 = (q_0^1, q_0^2)$, $V_L = V_{L_1} \cup V_{L_2}$ and $\Sigma = \Sigma_1 \cup \Sigma_2$.
- $Init = Init_1 \wedge Init_2$.
- $Inv((q_1, q_2)) = Inv_1(q_1) \wedge Inv_2(q_2)$ for each $q_1 \in Q_1$ and $q_2 \in Q_2$.
- $Env((q_1, q_2)) = Env_1(q_1) \cap Env_2(q_2)$ for each $q_1 \in Q_1$ and $q_2 \in Q_2$.
- $((q_1, q_2), \sigma, \mu, (q_1', q_2')) \in Edge$ iff either:
    1. there exists an edge $(q_1, \sigma, \mu, q_1') \in Edge_1$ and $q_2 = q_2'$, or
    2. there exists an edge $(q_2, \sigma, \mu, q_2') \in Edge_2$ and $q_1 = q_1'$.

After parallel composition, SA_1 and SA_2 share a common environment. The environment of $SA_1 \parallel SA_2$ for location (q_1, q_2) is the intersection of the environments of SA_1 and SA_2 for location q_1 and q_2 respectively. Intuitively, for each finite run of the parallel composition of two compatible succinct automata, there is a corresponding finite run in each of its components.

4 Compositional Reasoning for Succinct Automata

4.1 Safety Verification of Succinct Automata

Safety properties require that bad things should not happen. Invariants are a particular kind of safety properties that are useful in specifications. For example, the mutual exclusion property is an invariant which specifies that no more than one thread is in its critical section at any time. We introduce compositional reasoning methods for invariant verification of succinct automata and checking other safety properties can be reduced to invariant verification.

Recall that a predicate $\lambda \in \mathcal{F}(V)$ is an invariant of a transition system TS if λ is satisfied on all reachable states of TS. Unlike in a transition system, we have two kinds of transitions, local and environment. The way we treat them leads us to define two types of invariants of succinct automata, strong and weak. When treating both kinds of transitions equally, we reach the notion of strong invariants.

Definition 4. *A predicate $\lambda \in \mathcal{F}(V)$ is a strong invariant of SA if λ is satisfied on all reachable states of SA.*

When focusing on runs of succinct automata where environment transitions preserve λ, we reach the notion of weak invariants. Here, we say that an environment (resp. a component) transition $(q, \mathbf{v}) \xrightarrow{env} (q, \mathbf{v}')$ (resp. $(q, \mathbf{v}) \xrightarrow{\sigma} (q', \mathbf{v}')$) preserves λ if $\lambda(\mathbf{v})$ implies $\lambda(\mathbf{v}')$. The intention of weak invariants is as follows: For a program T modelled as SA, if λ is a weak invariant of SA, then, running in any environment that preserves λ, T can guarantee that λ is preserved in all its local transitions.

Definition 5. *A predicate $\lambda \in \mathcal{F}(V)$ is a weak invariant of SA if λ is satisfied on all runs of SA where environment transitions preserve λ.*

The notion of weak invariants is more general than strong invariants. In the following, we focus on compositionality of weak invariants. We first impose a noninterference condition on local weak invariants. This condition is to guarantee that local transitions of any component that preserve its own local weak invariant cannot invalidate local weak invariants of other components. Let λ_1 (resp. λ_2) be a weak invariant of SA_1 (resp. SA_2). Formally, we use $noninterfere(\lambda_1, \lambda_2)$ to mean the following condition: $((\lambda_1 \wedge \lambda_2 \wedge \lambda_1') \Rightarrow \lambda_2[V_G'/V_G]) \wedge ((\lambda_1 \wedge \lambda_2 \wedge \lambda_2') \Rightarrow \lambda_1[V_G'/V_G])$, where λ_i' is derived from λ_i by substituting all its variables with corresponding primed variables and $\lambda_i[V_G'/V_G]$ is derived by substituting all global variables in V_G with corresponding primed variables in V_G' for $i = 1, 2$. The parallel compositionality of weak invariants of succinct automata are formalized in the following theorem, which says that local weak invariants satisfied by all the components of the parallel composition of succinct automata guarantee a global weak invariant satisfied by the entire system as long as local weak invariants satisfy the noninterference condition.

Theorem 1. *Let SA_1 and SA_2 be compatible. Assume that $noninterfere(\lambda_1, \lambda_2)$ and λ_1 (resp. λ_2) is a weak invariant of SA_1 (resp. SA_2). We have that $\lambda_1 \wedge \lambda_2$ is a weak invariant of $SA_1 \| SA_2$.*

Example 2. To show that the simplified Peterson's algorithm in Fig. 1 guarantees mutual exclusion, we check whether $critical_1 = 0 \vee critical_2 = 0$ is a weak invariant of $SA_1 \| SA_2$ in Fig. 2. We define λ_1 and λ_2 by $\lambda_1 = \lambda_2 = (critical_1 = 0 \vee critical_2 = 0)$. It is easy to verify that λ_1 (resp. λ_2) is a weak invariant of SA_1 (resp. SA_2). Also, it is easy to see that $noninterfere(\lambda_1, \lambda_2)$ holds trivially as $\lambda_1 = \lambda_2$. According to Theorem 1, we know that $critical_1 = 0 \vee critical_2 = 0$ is a weak invariant of $SA_1 \| SA_2$, which implies that P_1 and P_2 in Fig. 1 cannot be in the critical section at the same time.

Example 3. We show the correctness of the abstract concurrent GCD programs (T_1 and T_2) in Fig. 3(a). (The code is taken from [28].) To check that $T_1 \| T_2$ really compute the greatest common divisor (gcd) of variables a and b, we first model T_1 (resp. T_2) as SA_1 (resp. SA_2). The construction of SA_1 is shown in Fig. 4 (left), where $\varphi = (a' = a) \wedge (a < b \vee b' = b)$. We omit the construction of SA_2 due to space limitation.

For convenience, we introduce two auxiliary variables A and B to SA_1 and SA_2. The value of A (resp. B) equals to the initial value of the input variable a (resp. b) and remain unchanged. Let $\lambda_1 = \lambda_2 = (\mathbf{gcd}(a, b) = \mathbf{gcd}(A, B))$, where **gcd** is a function that returns the gcd of its input. It is easy to verify that λ_1 (resp. λ_2) is a weak invariant of SA_1 (resp. SA_2). Also, it is easy to see that $noninterfere(\lambda_1, \lambda_2)$ holds. According to Theorem 1, we know that $\mathbf{gcd}(a, b) = \mathbf{gcd}(A, B)$ is a weak invariant of $SA_1 \| SA_2$, which implies that $T_1 \| T_2$ really compute the gcd of the input values of a and b.

4.2 Simulations of Succinct Automata

We define weak simulations between succinct automata as follows.

Definition 6. *A binary relation $\theta \subseteq S_{SA_1} \times S_{SA_2}$ is a weak simulation for (SA_1, SA_2) w.r.t. a precondition $\kappa \in \mathcal{F}(V_1 \cup V_2)$ and an invariant $\iota \in \mathcal{F}(V_1 \cup V_2)$, denoted by $SA_1 \preceq_\theta^{(\kappa, \iota)} SA_2$, iff we have the following:*

1. *$\kappa(\boldsymbol{v}_1, \boldsymbol{v}_2)$ implies $((q_1, \boldsymbol{v}_1), (q_2, \boldsymbol{v}_2)) \in \theta$, where both q_1 and q_2 are initial.*
2. *$((q_1, \boldsymbol{v}_1), (q_2, \boldsymbol{v}_2)) \in \theta$ implies $\iota(\boldsymbol{v}_1, \boldsymbol{v}_2)$, $Inv_1(q_1)(\boldsymbol{v}_1)$, $Inv_2(q_2)(\boldsymbol{v}_2)$ and the following:*

   a. *if $(q_1, \boldsymbol{v}_1) \xrightarrow{env} (q_1, \boldsymbol{v}_1')$ and $(q_2, \boldsymbol{v}_2) \xrightarrow{env^*} (q_2, \boldsymbol{v}_2')$ and $\iota(\boldsymbol{v}_1', \boldsymbol{v}_2')$, then we have that $((q_1, \boldsymbol{v}_1'), (q_2, \boldsymbol{v}_2')) \in \theta$.*

   b. *if $(q_1, \boldsymbol{v}_1) \xrightarrow{\sigma_1} (q_1', \boldsymbol{v}_1')$ and $\sigma_1 \neq \tau$, then there exist $(q_2', \boldsymbol{v}_2') \in S_{SA_2}$ and $\sigma_2 \in \Sigma_2$ such that $\sigma_2 = \sigma_1$, $(q_2, \boldsymbol{v}_2) \xrightarrow{\tau^* \sigma_2 \tau^*} (q_2', \boldsymbol{v}_2')$ and $((q_1', \boldsymbol{v}_1'), (q_2', \boldsymbol{v}_2')) \in \theta$.*

   c. *if $(q_1, \boldsymbol{v}_1) \xrightarrow{\tau} (q_1', \boldsymbol{v}_1')$, then there exists $(q_2', \boldsymbol{v}_2') \in S_{SA_2}$ such that $(q_2, \boldsymbol{v}_2) \xrightarrow{\tau^*} (q_2', \boldsymbol{v}_2')$ and $((q_1', \boldsymbol{v}_1'), (q_2', \boldsymbol{v}_2')) \in \theta$.*

Conditions 2.b and 2.c constrain local behaviors of SA_1 and SA_2 and are similar to standard notions of weak simulations [30]. Condition 2.a constrains the environments of the two succinct automata and requires that the weak simulation should not be affected by the environments as long as the valuations of variables in V_1 and V_2 are related by ι. Note that if merely we were to require that an environment transition from q_1 is simulated by zero or more environment transitions from q_2, the resulting simulation relation would not be compositional under parallel composition. Our way of dealing with environments in defining simulation or bi-simulation relations is not without precedent. For example, in process calculi, e.g., higher-order calculi [34] or cryptographic calculi [1], environments are treated separately from local transitions, and one typically requires certain relations to hold between the environments, e.g., as in the relation ι we have above. Condition 2.a is the key for compositionality in our notion of weak simulation.

T_1:
```
m:=0;
while (m=0) {
   atomic {
      if (a=b)
         m:=1;
      if (a>b)
         a:=a-b;
   }
}
```

T_2:
```
n:=0;
while (n=0) {
   atomic {
      if (a=b)
         n:=1;
      if (a<b)
         b:=b-a;
   }
}
```

T_1':
```
m:=0;
while (m=0) {
   x1:=a;
   x2:=b;
   if (x1=x2)
      m:=1;
   if (x1>x2)
      a:=x1-x2;
}
```

T_2':
```
n:=0;
while (n=0) {
   y1:=a;
   y2:=b;
   if (y1=y2)
      n:=1;
   if (y1<y2)
      b:=y2-y1;
}
```

(a) Abstract GCD Programs   (b) Concrete GCD Programs

Fig. 3. Concurrent GCD programs

Given κ and ι, we say that SA_1 is *weakly simulated by* SA_2 (or SA_1 *weakly refines* SA_2) *with respect to* κ *and* ι, denoted by $SA_1 \preceq^{(\kappa,\iota)} SA_2$, if there exists a weak simulation θ such that $SA_1 \preceq_\theta^{(\kappa,\iota)} SA_2$. We say that SA_1 is *weakly simulated by* SA_2, denoted by $SA_1 \preceq SA_2$, if there exist κ and ι such that $SA_1 \preceq^{(\kappa,\iota)} SA_2$. The relation $\preceq$ on succinct automata is reflexive but not transitive. However, the relation $\preceq$ on closed succinct automata is transitive. This allows us to chain together two refinement steps when reasoning about simulations between closed succinct automata.

Theorem 2. *The relation $\preceq$ on closed succinct automata forms a pre-order.*

For succinct automata that are not closed, we can still chain together successive refinement steps if the environment transitions of related succinct automata satisfy a certain condition. We formalize this in the following theorem.

Theorem 3. *Assume that $SA_1 \preceq_{\theta_1}^{(\kappa_1,\iota_1)} SA_2$ and $SA_2 \preceq_{\theta_2}^{(\kappa_2,\iota_2)} SA_3$. Let $\kappa, \iota \in \mathcal{F}(V_1 \cup V_3)$ be predicates such that $\kappa(v_1, v_3)$ (resp. $\iota(v_1, v_3)$) holds iff there exists v_2 such that $\kappa_1(v_1, v_2) \wedge \kappa_2(v_2, v_3)$ (resp. $\iota_1(v_1, v_2) \wedge \iota_2(v_2, v_3)$) holds. We have that $SA_1 \preceq_{\theta_2 \circ \theta_1}^{(\kappa,\iota)} SA_3$ if the following holds: Assume that $(q_1, v_1) \xrightarrow{env} (q_1, v_1')$, $(q_3, v_3) \xrightarrow{env} (q_3, v_3')$, $\iota(v_1, v_3)$ and $\iota(v_1', v_3')$. For any v_2 such that $\iota_1(v_1, v_2) \wedge \iota_2(v_2, v_3)$ and for all $q_2 \in Q_2$, there exists v_2' such that $(q_2, v_2) \xrightarrow{env} (q_2, v_2')$ and $\iota_1(v_1', v_2') \wedge \iota_2(v_2', v_3')$.*

Given $\theta_1 \subseteq S_{SA_1} \times S_{\widehat{SA_1}}$ and $\theta_2 \subseteq S_{SA_2} \times S_{\widehat{SA_2}}$, we define $\theta_1 \otimes \theta_2 \subseteq S_{SA_1 \| SA_2} \times S_{\widehat{SA_1} \| \widehat{SA_2}}$ as follows: $(((q_1, q_2), \mathbf{v}), ((\widehat{q_1}, \widehat{q_2}), \widehat{\mathbf{v}})) \in \theta_1 \otimes \theta_2$ iff $((q_1, \mathbf{v}_G \oplus$

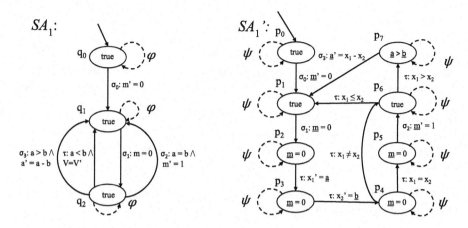

Fig. 4. Succinct automata for concurrent GCD

$\mathbf{v}_{L_1}), (\widehat{q_1}, \widehat{\mathbf{v}_G} \oplus \widehat{\mathbf{v}_{L_1}})) \in \theta_1$ and $((q_2, \mathbf{v}_G \oplus \mathbf{v}_{L_2}), (\widehat{q_2}, \widehat{\mathbf{v}_G} \oplus \widehat{\mathbf{v}_{L_2}})) \in \theta_2$, where $\mathbf{v} = \mathbf{v}_G \oplus \mathbf{v}_{L_1} \oplus \mathbf{v}_{L_2}$ and $\widehat{\mathbf{v}} = \widehat{\mathbf{v}_G} \oplus \widehat{\mathbf{v}_{L_1}} \oplus \widehat{\mathbf{v}_{L_2}}$.

To ensure compositionality of weak simulations, we also impose a noninterference condition on ι_1 and ι_2 here. We reuse $noninterfere(\iota_1, \iota_2)$ to denote the following condition: $((\iota_1 \wedge \iota_2 \wedge \iota_1') \Rightarrow \iota_2[V_G'/V_G][\widehat{V_G}'/\widehat{V_G}]) \wedge ((\iota_1 \wedge \iota_2 \wedge \iota_2') \Rightarrow \iota_1[V_G'/V_G][\widehat{V_G}'/\widehat{V_G}])$. The following theorem shows that weak simulations of succinct automata are preserved under parallel composition.

Theorem 4. *Assume that SA_1 (resp. $\widehat{SA_1}$) and SA_2 (resp. $\widehat{SA_2}$) are compatible and that $noninterfere(\iota_1, \iota_2)$. We have that $SA_1 \preceq_{\theta_1}^{(\kappa_1, \iota_1)} \widehat{SA_1}$ and $SA_2 \preceq_{\theta_2}^{(\kappa_2, \iota_2)} \widehat{SA_2}$ implies $SA_1 \| SA_2 \preceq_{\theta_1 \otimes \theta_2}^{(\kappa_1 \wedge \kappa_2, \iota_1 \wedge \iota_2)} \widehat{SA_1} \| \widehat{SA_2}$.*

Example 4. We show that the abstract concurrent GCD programs (T_1 and T_2) in Fig. 3(a) are refined by the concrete GCD programs (T_1' and T_2') in Fig. 3(b). The bodies of the while loops in T_1 and T_2 are executed atomically and are refined to corresponding code in T_1' and T_2' to allow interleaving.

In Fig. 4, we model thread T_1 (resp. T_1') as SA_1 (resp. SA_1'), where $\varphi = (a' = a) \wedge (a < b \vee b' = b)$ and $\psi = (\underline{a}' = \underline{a}) \wedge (\underline{a} < \underline{b} \vee \underline{b}' = \underline{b})$. Let κ_1 and ι_1 be defined by $\kappa_1 = (\underline{a} = a \wedge \underline{b} = b \wedge \underline{m} = m)$ and $\iota_1 = (\underline{a} = a \wedge \underline{b} = b \wedge \underline{m} = m)$. In our experiment, using the verification tool we have implemented, we have verified that $SA_1' \preceq_{\theta_1}^{(\kappa_1, \iota_1)} SA_1$ holds for some θ_1. Similarly, we have modeled T_2 (resp. T_2') as SA_2 (resp. SA_2') and checked in our experiment that $SA_2' \preceq_{\theta_2}^{(\kappa_2, \iota_2)} SA_2$ holds for some θ_2. By Theorem 4, we have that $SA_1' \| SA_2' \preceq_{\theta_1 \otimes \theta_2}^{(\kappa_1 \wedge \kappa_2, \iota_1 \wedge \iota_2)} SA_1 \| SA_2$.

4.3   Safety Property Preservation Under Refinement

It is obvious that strong invariants are preserved under refinements. We show in the following that weak invariants of succinct automata are also preserved under refinements.

We write $\mathcal{WS}(\theta, Env_1, Env_2)$ to mean that: if $((q_1, \mathbf{v}_1), (q_2, \mathbf{v}_2)) \in \theta$ and $(q_1, \mathbf{v}_1) \xrightarrow{env} (q_1, \mathbf{v}_1')$, there exists $(q_2, \mathbf{v}_2') \in S_{SA_2}$ such that $(q_2, \mathbf{v}_2) \xrightarrow{env^*} (q_2, \mathbf{v}_2')$ and $((q_1, \mathbf{v}_1'), (q_2, \mathbf{v}_2')) \in \theta$. If $\mathcal{WS}(\theta, Env_1, Env_2)$ holds, for each run in SA_1, we can construct a corresponding run in SA_2 such that the two runs are related by θ. Thus, we have the following lemma that links reachability and weak simulations.

Lemma 1. *Assume that* $SA_1 \preceq_\theta^{(\kappa,\iota)} SA_2$ *holds for some* θ, κ *and* ι, *where* $\mathcal{WS}(\theta, Env_1, Env_2)$ *holds. For all states* $(q_1, \mathbf{v}_1) \in S_{SA_1}$ *and* $(q_2, \mathbf{v}_2) \in S_{SA_2}$ *such that* $((q_1, \mathbf{v}_1), (q_2, \mathbf{v}_2)) \in \theta$, *if* $(q_1, \mathbf{v}_1) \rightarrow^* (q_1', \mathbf{v}_1')$ *for some* $(q_1', \mathbf{v}_1') \in S_{SA_1}$, *there exists* $(q_2', \mathbf{v}_2') \in S_{SA_2}$ *such that* $(q_2, \mathbf{v}_2) \rightarrow^* (q_2', \mathbf{v}_2')$ *and* $((q_1', \mathbf{v}_1'), (q_2', \mathbf{v}_2')) \in \theta$.

As invariants verification can be reduced to reachability problems, we can prove by contradiction that the following theorem holds.

Theorem 5. *Assume that* $SA_1 \preceq_\theta^{(\kappa,\iota)} SA_2$ *holds for some* θ, κ *and* ι, *where* $\mathcal{WS}(\theta, Env_1, Env_2)$ *holds, and for each initial state* $(q_1, \mathbf{v}_1) \in S_{SA_1}$, *there exists an initial state* $(q_2, \mathbf{v}_2) \in S_{SA_2}$ *such that* $\kappa(\mathbf{v}_1, \mathbf{v}_2)$. *Let* $\lambda_1 \in \mathcal{F}(V_1)$ *and* $\lambda_2 \in \mathcal{F}(V_2)$ *be two predicates such that* $\neg\lambda_1(\mathbf{v}_1) \wedge \iota(\mathbf{v}_1, \mathbf{v}_2)$ *implies* $\neg\lambda_2(\mathbf{v}_2)$. *If* λ_2 *is a weak invariant of* SA_2, *then* λ_1 *is a weak invariant of* SA_1.

Example 5. We give a short example to show that $\mathbf{gcd}(a, b) = \mathbf{gcd}(A, B)$ is a weak invariant of the concrete GCD programs, which implies that the concrete GCD programs also compute the gcd of the input variables. First, we know from Example 3 that $\mathbf{gcd}(a, b) = \mathbf{gcd}(A, B)$ is a weak invariant of the abstract GCD programs. Second, we know from Example 4 that the concrete GCD programs refine the abstract GCD programs. Hence, from Theorem 5, we can prove that $\mathbf{gcd}(a, b) = \mathbf{gcd}(A, B)$ is also a weak invariant of the concrete GCD programs.

5   Automatic Verification of Succinct Automata

We focus on two aspects of automated verification of succinct automata: generation of succinct automata from infinite state concurrent programs and refinement checking between infinite state succinct automata. We prototyped our tool in the functional programming language F# in over 3700 lines of code and used Z3 [12] in our implementation. We applied our tool to check multiple weak simulations between concurrent C programs. Experimental results are included in the appendix of [37].

5.1   Generation of Succinct Automata

The hardest part of generating succinct automata from infinite state concurrent programs is to construct their invariant components and environment components. Intuitively, invariant components overapproximate reachable states at control locations of concurrent programs and environment components abstract the transitions of other programs in the environment. To construct these components, we perform separate forward reachability analysis for each concurrent program on abstract domains, and for component transitions of a concurrent program that modify global variables, corresponding environment transitions are generated for other concurrent programs in the environment. We present our algorithm for generating succinct automata in Algorithm 1.

The main function in Algorithm 1 is *Generate-SAs*. Given two concurrent programs T_1 and T_2, it first constructs two intermediate automata SA_1 and SA_2, where Inv_1, Env_1, Inv_2 and Env_2 are not specified. At this step, SA_1 and SA_2 are essentially the program graphs of T_1 and T_2. Then, it initializes Inv_i and $EnvSet_i$. Here, $EnvSet_i$ is used to keep track of changes of global variables made by SA_j, where $i \neq j$ and $i, j = 1, 2$. After that, it starts fixed-point iterations (Line 21–26) to overapproximate reachable states at each location by calling function *Reach* and generate corresponding environment transitions by calling function *GenEnvTrans*. After the least fixed points are reached, it constructs Env_i from $EnvSet_i$. If the relation specified by $EnvSet_i$ is not reflexive, we explicitly add $V_G = V_G'$ to make Env_i reflexive.

Function *Reach* performs the forward reachability analysis for SA_i, where $EnvSet_i$ specifies the environment transitions of SA_i. Function $Post_{Comp}(Inv_i(q), \mu)$ (Line 4) calculates a predicate that overapproximates states reachable from $Inv_i(q)$ by executing a component transition whose transition condition is μ. Function $Post_{Env}(Inv_i(q), EnvSet_i)$ (Line 6) calculates a predicate that overapproximates states reachable from $Inv_i(q)$ by executing environment transitions specified by $EnvSet_i$.

Function *GenEnvTrans* takes Inv_i and $Edge_i$ of SA_i and generates environment transitions for SA_j, where $i \neq j$ and $i, j = 1, 2$. For each edge $(q, \sigma, \mu, q') \in Edge_i$ that modifies global variables, we generate a corresponding pair $(Inv_i(q), \mu)$ (Line 14) to be used to specify environment transitions of SA_j. Function *GenEnvTrans* is the key to guarantee the compatibility of SA_1 and SA_2.

We have the following theorem that guarantees the compatibility of SA_1 and SA_2.

Theorem 6. *SA_1 and SA_2 generated by Algorithm 1 are compatible.*

From Theorem 6, it's easy to prove by contradiction that $SA_1 \| SA_2$ overapproximates $T_1 \| T_2$, which means for each execution trace of $T_1 \| T_2$, there is a corresponding run of $SA_1 \| SA_2$.

In our prototype, the abstract domain we use is Boxes [20] and an element on the Boxes domain is implemented as a corresponding Linear Decision Diagram (LDD) [6]. To guarantee the termination of the iteration in *Reach*, we used widening techniques [11] for the Boxes domain, which is not listed in Algorithm 1 due to space limitation. On the other hand, we point out here that Algorithm 1 is a general algorithm that can be implemented on top of other abstract domains and the correctness of Theorem 6 is independent of the abstract domains underlying Algorithm 1.

Algorithm 1. Generating Succinct Automata from Concurrent Programs

---

Input: Concurrent programs T_1 and T_2.
Output: Compatible SA_1 and SA_2 that models T_1 and T_2.

1   **Function** $Reach(SA_i, EnvSet_i)$ **is**
2   **repeat**
3   **foreach** $(q, \sigma, \mu, q') \in Edge_i$ **do**
4         $Inv_i(q') := Inv_i(q') \vee Post_{Comp}(Inv_i(q), \mu)$
5   **foreach** $q \in Q_i$ **do**
6         $Inv_i(q) := Inv_i(q) \vee Post_{Env}(Inv_i(q), EnvSet_i)$
7   **until** *No more reachable states are added to $Inv_i(q)$ for all $q \in Q_i$*
8   **return** Inv_i

9
10 **Function** $GenEnvTrans(Inv_i, Edge_i, j)$ **is**
11    $EnvSet_j := \emptyset$
12   **foreach** $(q, \sigma, \mu, q') \in Edge_i$ **do**
13   **if** *μ modifies global variables* **then**
14        $EnvSet_j := EnvSet_j \cup (Inv_i(q), \mu)$
15   **return** $EnvSet_j$

16
17 **Function** Generate-SAs(T_1, T_2) **is**
18   Construct intermediate succinct automata SA_1 and SA_2
19    $Inv_i(q) := false$ for all $q \in Q_i$ and $i = 1, 2$
20    $EnvSet_i = \emptyset$ for $i = 1, 2$
21   **repeat**
22      $Inv_1 := Reach(SA_1, EnvSet_1)$
23      $Inv_2 := Reach(SA_2, EnvSet_2)$
24      $EnvSet_1 := GenEnvTrans(Inv_2, Edge_2, 1)$
25      $EnvSet_2 := GenEnvTrans(Inv_1, Edge_1, 2)$
26   **until** *Least Fixed Points are Reached*
27   Construct Env_i from $EnvSet_i$ and make Env_i reflexive for $i = 1, 2$
28   **return** SA_1 *and* SA_2

5.2   Refinement Checking Between Succinct Automata

We propose an SMT-based approach (Algorithm 2) to checking weak simulations between infinite state succinct automata. One difficulty in developing an SMT-based approach here comes from Condition 2.a in Definition 6, because environment transitions of the abstract succinct automata can be executed arbitrary finite number of times. However, we have noticed in practice that the length of local paths of succinct automata whose action labels are of the form $\tau^* \sigma \tau^*$ or τ^* are usually bounded. Hence, in Algorithm 2, we only specify the execution of environment transitions of the abstract succinct automata up to a bound k, which is precalculated by our prototyped tool.

Algorithm 2. An Algorithm to Check Weak Simulations of Succinct Automata

Input: SA_1 and SA_2 and parameters κ and ι.
Output: If the algorithm return *Yes*, $SA_1 \preceq^{(\kappa,\iota)} SA_2$ holds. If the algorithm returns *No*, $SA_1 \preceq^{(\kappa,\iota)} SA_2$ does not hold.

```
 1  Function GenConstraints(SA₁, SA₂, Θ, ι) is
 2      foreach (q₁, q₂) ∈ Θ do
 3          C₁ := Ψ_(q₁,q₂) ⇒ ((Φ_Env₁(q₁) ∧ ι[V'₁/V₁]) ⇒ Ψ_(q₁,q₂)[V'₁/V₁])
 4          constraints := constraints ∪ {¬C₁}
 5          foreach 1 ≤ j ≤ k do
 6              C₂ʲ := Ψ_(q₁,q₂) ⇒ ((Φ_Env₁(q₁) ∧ Φ_Env₂(q₂))ʲ ∧
 7                     ι[V'₁/V₁][V₂ʲ/V₂]) ⇒ Ψ_(q₁,q₂)[V'₁/V₁][V₂ʲ/V₂])
 8              constraints := constraints ∪ {¬C₂ʲ}
 9          foreach e = (q₁, σ, μ, q'₁) ∈ Edge₁ do
10              C₃ := Ψ_(q₁,q₂) ⇒ (G ⇒ (WP(e', ⋁_{π∈Πσ(q₂)} WP(π, Ψ_(q'₁,q'₂)))))
11                  where G is the guard of e, e' is derived from e by substituting its guard
12                  with True, and π ends at location q'₂
13              constraints := constraints ∪ {¬C₃}

14      return constraints

15
16  Function UpdatePsi(constraints, V₁, V₂, Θ) is
17      foreach (q₁, q₂) ∈ Θ do
18          Ψ'_(q₁,q₂) := Ψ_(q₁,q₂)

19      foreach ¬(Ψ_(q₁,q₂) ⇒ Φ) ∈ constraints do
20          if ¬(Ψ_(q₁,q₂) ⇒ Φ) is satisfiable then
21              if ¬(Ψ_(q₁,q₂) ⇒ Φ) is a type 1 constraint then
22                  Ψ'_(q₁,q₂) := Ψ'_(q₁,q₂) ∧ ∀V Φ
23                  where V = FreeVar(Φ)\(V₁ ∪ V₂)
24              if ¬(Ψ_(q₁,q₂) ⇒ Φ) is a type 2 constraint then
25                  Ψ'_(q₁,q₂) := Ψ'_(q₁,q₂) ∧ Φ

26      foreach (q₁, q₂) ∈ Θ do
27          Ψ_(q₁,q₂) := Ψ'_(q₁,q₂)

28      if none of the constraints are satisfiable then
29          return Fixed Point Reached
30      else
31          return Continue Iteration

32
33  Function Check-Weak-Simulation(SA₁, SA₂, κ, ι) is
34      Θ := GenPairs({(q_init₁, q_init₂)})
35      foreach (q₁, q₂) ∈ Θ do
36          Ψ_(q₁,q₂) := ι ∧ Inv₁(q₁) ∧ Inv₂(q₂)

37      constraints := ∅
38      repeat
39          constraints := GenConstraints(SA₁, SA₂, Θ, ι)
40          result := UpdatePsi(constraints, V₁, V₂, Θ)
41      until result = Fixed Point Reached
42      if κ ⇒ Ψ_(q_init1,q_init2) is valid then
43          return Yes
44      else
45          return No
```

Proving $SA_1 \preceq^{(\kappa, \iota)} SA_2$ amounts to showing the existence of a simulation relation θ such that $SA_1 \preceq_\theta^{(\kappa, \iota)} SA_2$. We define first order formulas $\Psi_{(q_1, q_2)}$ over $V_1 \cup V_2$ for a set of pairs of locations $(q_1, q_2) \in Q_1 \times Q_2$. The intention is that when our algorithm terminates, we can construct a relation $\theta = \{((q_1, \mathbf{v}_1), (q_2, \mathbf{v}_2)) \mid \Psi_{(q_1, q_2)}(\mathbf{v}_1, \mathbf{v}_2) \text{ holds}\}$ such that θ satisfies Condition 2 in Definition 6.

Our algorithm follows the basic fixed point iteration method. The main function in Algorithm 2 is $Check\text{-}Weak\text{-}Simulation$. It first computes a set Θ that contains all the pairs (q_1, q_2) for which we need to define constraints. Then, it defines the initial value of $\Psi_{(q_1, q_2)}$ for each $(q_1, q_2) \in \Theta$. In each fixed point iteration (Line 38-41), we first generate constraints for each $(q_1, q_2) \in \Theta$ that specify Condition 2 of Definition 6 by calling function $GenConstraints$. Then, we refine the value of $\Psi_{(q_1, q_2)}$ through function $UpdatePsi$ according to the satisfiability of the constraints generated for (q_1, q_2). When the greatest fixed point is reached, it is guaranteed that Condition 2 of Definition 6 is satisfied. Finally, we check whether Condition 1 of Definition 6 is also satisfied (Line 42).

Due to space limitation, we omit the pseudo code for the function $GenPairs$ (called in Line 34) and explain it briefly as follows. Let $\Pi_\sigma(q)$ denote the set of finite local paths π such that π starts from q and the action labels along π are of the form $\tau^* \sigma \tau^*$ (resp. τ^*), when $\sigma \neq \tau$ (resp. $\sigma = \tau$). $GenPairs$ is a recursive function which takes a set Θ of pairs of locations as input and returns another set of pairs of locations. Let Θ' be an empty set. First, for each $(q_1, q_2) \in \Theta$, it adds to Θ' the set of (q_1', q_2') such that there exists an edge (q_1, σ, μ, q_1') and a path $\pi \in \Pi_\sigma(q_2)$ that ends in q_2'. Then, $GenPairs$ makes a recursive call $GenPairs(\Theta' \backslash \Theta)$ and returns $\Theta \cup GenPairs(\Theta' \backslash \Theta)$.

Function $GenConstraints$ generates following constraints $\neg C_1, \neg C_2^1, ..., \neg C_2^k$ and $\neg C_3$ for each $(q_1, q_2) \in \Theta$. Formulas C_1 and C_2^j (Line 3 and 6–7) are used to specify Condition 2.a in Definition 6, where $\Phi_{Env_1(q_1)}$ is a predicate that specifies the execution of environment transitions $Env_1(q_1)$ once and $\Phi_{Env_2(q_2)^j}$ is a predicate specifying the execution of environment transitions $Env_2(q_2)$ for j steps. In Line 7, we write V_2^j to mean $\{v_1^j, ..., v_n^j\}$ for $V_2 = \{v_1, ..., v_n\}$. Formula C_3 (Line 10) specifies Condition 2.b and 2.c. We use $WP(e, \Psi)$ (resp. $WP(\pi, \Psi)$) to denote the weakest precondition such that Ψ holds after taking a component transition (resp. a sequence of component transitions) by executing e (resp. π).

Function $UpdatePsi$ checks the satisfiability of all the constraints generated by $GenConstraints$. If a constraint $\neg(\Psi_{(q_1, q_2)} \Rightarrow \Phi)$ is satisfiable, $\Psi_{(q_1, q_2)}$ fails to satisfy Condition 2 in Definition 6. In this case, we strengthen $\Psi_{(q_1, q_2)}$ in Line 21–25 depending on the type of the constraint. Here, type 1 (resp. type 2) constraints refer to those of the form $\neg C_1$ and $\neg C_2^j$ (resp. $\neg C_3$) generated by $GenConstraints$.

6   Conclusions and Future Work

In this paper, we have laid the theoretical underpinning for succinct automata, which is a formalism for formal verification of shared-variable concurrent programs. In our framework, safety verification and simulations of concurrent programs are parallel compositional and algorithmic. Succinct automata-based approaches can be applied to extend safety verification of concurrent programs from the source code level down to the binary level in a compositional way.

At the current stage, our prototype is able to verify refinements between concurrent C programs. Compared with manual proofs, our automated verification technique saves considerable time. In our future work, we will study how to generate succinct automata from assembly code and further develop our tool so that it can verify refinements between concurrent C programs and assembly code.

Acknowledgement. This research is supported (in part) by the National Research Foundation, Prime Ministers Office, Singapore under its National Cybersecurity R&D Program (Award No. NRF2014NCR-NCR001-30) and administered by the National Cybersecurity R&D Directorate.

References

1. Abadi, M., Gordon, A.D.: A calculus for cryptographic protocols: the spi calculus. Inf. Comput. **148**(1), 1–70 (1999)
2. Baier, C., Katoen, J.: Principles of Model Checking. MIT Press, New York (2008)
3. Brookes, S.D.: Full abstraction for a shared variable parallel language. In: Proceedings of the 8th Annual Symposium on Logic in Computer Science (LICS 1993), Montreal, Canada, pp. 98–109 (1993)
4. Burch, J.R., Clarke, E.M., McMillan, K.L., Dill, D.L., Hwang, L.J.: Symbolic model checking: 10^20 states and beyond. Inf. Comput. **98**(2), 142–170 (1992)
5. Burckhardt, S., Musuvathi, M., Singh, V.: Verifying local transformations on relaxed memory models. In: Gupta, R. (ed.) CC 2010. LNCS, vol. 6011, pp. 104–123. Springer, Heidelberg (2010). https://doi.org/10.1007/978-3-642-11970-5_7
6. Chaki, S., Gurfinkel, A., Strichman, O.: Decision diagrams for linear arithmetic. In: Proceedings of the 9th International Conference on Formal Methods in Computer-Aided Design (FMCAD 2009), Austin, Texas, USA, pp. 53–60 (2009)
7. Clarke, E.M., Filkorn, T., Jha, S.: Exploiting symmetry in temporal logic model checking. In: Courcoubetis, C. (ed.) CAV 1993. LNCS, vol. 697, pp. 450–462. Springer, Heidelberg (1993). https://doi.org/10.1007/3-540-56922-7_37
8. Clarke, E.M., Grumberg, O., Jha, S., Lu, Y., Veith, H.: Counterexample-guided abstraction refinement for symbolic model checking. J. ACM **50**(5), 752–794 (2003)
9. Clarke, E.M., Grumberg, O., Long, D.E.: Model checking and abstraction. ACM Trans. Program. Lang. Syst. **16**(5), 1512–1542 (1994)
10. Cohen, A., Namjoshi, K.S.: Local proofs for global safety properties. Formal Methods Syst. Des. **34**(2), 104–125 (2009)
11. Cousot, P., Cousot, R.: Abstract interpretation: a unified lattice model for static analysis of programs by construction or approximation of fixpoints. In: Proceedings of the 4th Symposium on Principles of Programming Languages (POPL 1977), Los Angeles, California, USA, pp. 238–252 (1977)
12. de Moura, L., Bjørner, N.: Z3: an efficient SMT solver. In: Ramakrishnan, C.R., Rehof, J. (eds.) TACAS 2008. LNCS, vol. 4963, pp. 337–340. Springer, Heidelberg (2008). https://doi.org/10.1007/978-3-540-78800-3_24

13. Emerson, E.A., Sistla, A.P.: Symmetry and model checking. In: Courcoubetis, C. (ed.) CAV 1993. LNCS, vol. 697, pp. 463–478. Springer, Heidelberg (1993). https://doi.org/10.1007/3-540-56922-7_38

14. Flanagan, C., Freund, S.N., Qadeer, S.: Thread-modular verification for shared-memory programs. In: Le Métayer, D. (ed.) ESOP 2002. LNCS, vol. 2305, pp. 262–277. Springer, Heidelberg (2002). https://doi.org/10.1007/3-540-45927-8_19

15. Flanagan, C., Qadeer, S.: Thread-modular model checking. In: Ball, T., Rajamani, S.K. (eds.) SPIN 2003. LNCS, vol. 2648, pp. 213–224. Springer, Heidelberg (2003). https://doi.org/10.1007/3-540-44829-2_14

16. Godefroid, P.: Using partial orders to improve automatic verification methods. In: Clarke, E.M., Kurshan, R.P. (eds.) CAV 1990. LNCS, vol. 531, pp. 176–185. Springer, Heidelberg (1991). https://doi.org/10.1007/BFb0023731

17. Graf, S., Saidi, H.: Construction of abstract state graphs with PVS. In: Grumberg, O. (ed.) CAV 1997. LNCS, vol. 1254, pp. 72–83. Springer, Heidelberg (1997). https://doi.org/10.1007/3-540-63166-6_10

18. Grumberg, O., Long, D.E.: Model checking and modular verification. ACM Trans. Program. Lang. Syst. 16(3), 843–871 (1994)

19. Gupta, A., Popeea, C., Rybalchenko, A.: Predicate abstraction and refinement for verifying multi-threaded programs. In: Proceedings of the 38th Symposium on Principles of Programming Languages (POPL 2011), Austin, TX, USA, pp. 331–344 (2011)

20. Gurfinkel, A., Chaki, S.: BOXES: a symbolic abstract domain of boxes. In: Cousot, R., Martel, M. (eds.) SAS 2010. LNCS, vol. 6337, pp. 287–303. Springer, Heidelberg (2010). https://doi.org/10.1007/978-3-642-15769-1_18

21. Hawblitzel, C., Petrank, E., Qadeer, S., Tasiran, S.: Automated and modular refinement reasoning for concurrent programs. In: Kroening, D., Păsăreanu, C.S. (eds.) CAV 2015. LNCS, vol. 9207, pp. 449–465. Springer, Cham (2015). https://doi.org/10.1007/978-3-319-21668-3_26

22. Henzinger, T.A., Jhala, R., Majumdar, R.: Race checking by context inference. In: Proceedings of the 2004 Conference on Programming Language Design and Implementation (PLDI 2004), Washington, DC, USA, pp. 1–13 (2004)

23. Henzinger, T.A., Jhala, R., Majumdar, R., Qadeer, S.: Thread-modular abstraction refinement. In: Hunt, W.A., Somenzi, F. (eds.) CAV 2003. LNCS, vol. 2725, pp. 262–274. Springer, Heidelberg (2003). https://doi.org/10.1007/978-3-540-45069-6_27

24. Ip, C.N., Dill, D.L.: Better verification through symmetry. In: Proceedings of the 11th International Conference on Computer Hardware Description Languages and their Applications (CHDL 1993), Ontario, Canada, pp. 97–111 (1993)

25. Jones, C.B.: Specification and design of (parallel) programs. In: IFIP Congress, pp. 321–332 (1983)

26. Jones, C.B.: Tentative steps toward a development method for interfering programs. ACM Trans. Program. Lang. Syst. 5(4), 596–619 (1983)

27. Kundu, S., Lerner, S., Gupta, R.: Automated refinement checking of concurrent systems. In: Proceedings of the 2007 International Conference on Computer-Aided Design (ICCAD 2007), San Jose, CA, USA, pp. 318–325 (2007)

28. Liang, H., Feng, X., Fu, M.: Rely-guarantee-based simulation for compositional verification of concurrent program transformations. ACM Trans. Program. Lang. Syst. 36(1), 3 (2014)

29. Lochbihler, A.: Verifying a compiler for Java threads. In: Gordon, A.D. (ed.) ESOP 2010. LNCS, vol. 6012, pp. 427–447. Springer, Heidelberg (2010). https://doi.org/10.1007/978-3-642-11957-6_23

30. Milner, R.: Communication and Concurrency. PHI Series in Computer Science. Prentice Hall, Upper Saddle River (1989)
31. Misra, J., Chandy, K.M.: Proofs of networks of processes. IEEE Trans. Softw. Eng. **7**(4), 417–426 (1981)
32. Peled, D.: Combining partial order reductions with on-the-fly model-checking. In: Dill, D.L. (ed.) CAV 1994. LNCS, vol. 818, pp. 377–390. Springer, Heidelberg (1994). https://doi.org/10.1007/3-540-58179-0_69
33. Pnueli, A.: In transition from global to modular temporal reasoning about programs. In: Apt, K.R. (ed.) Logics and Models of Concurrent Systems, pp. 123–144. Springer, New York (1985). https://doi.org/10.1007/978-3-642-82453-1_5
34. Sangiorgi, D., Kobayashi, N., Sumii, E.: Environmental bisimulations for higher-order languages. In: Proceedings of the 22nd IEEE Symposium on Logic in Computer Science (LICS 2007), Wroclaw, Poland, pp. 293–302 (2007)
35. Valmari, A.: A stubborn attack on state explosion. In: Clarke, E.M., Kurshan, R.P. (eds.) CAV 1990. LNCS, vol. 531, pp. 156–165. Springer, Heidelberg (1991). https://doi.org/10.1007/BFb0023729
36. Xu, Q., de Roever, W.P., He, J.: The rely-guarantee method for verifying shared variable concurrent programs. Formal Asp. Comput. **9**(2), 149–174 (1997)
37. Zhang, F., Zhao, Y., Sanán, D., Liu, Y., Tiu, A., Lin, S.-W., Sun, J.: Compositional Reasoning for Shared-Variable Concurrent Programs. CoRR arXiv:1611.00574v2 (2018)

Statistical Model Checking of LLVM Code

Axel Legay[1], Dirk Nowotka[2], Danny Bøgsted Poulsen[2(✉)],
and Louis-Marie Tranouez[1]

[1] Inria, Rennes, France
[2] Kiel University, Kiel, Germany
dbp@informatik.uni-kiel.de

Abstract. We present the new tool LODIN for statistical model checking of LLVM-bitcode. LODIN implements a simulation engine for LLVM-
bitcode and implements classic statistical model checking algorithms on
top of it. The simulation engine implements only the core of LLVM but
supports extending this core through a plugin-architecture. Besides the
statistical model checking algorithms LODIN also provides an interactive simulation front-end. The simulator front-end was integral for our
second contribution - an integration of LODIN into PLASMA-LAB. The
integration with PLASMA-LAB is integral to allow reasoning about rare
properties of programs.

1 Introduction

Statistical Model Checking (SMC) [17] is an approximate verification technique that has attained a high interest from the formal methods community
in recent years - evidenced by statistical model checking tools being developed [1,2,13,15,16] and by classical model checking tools implementing statistical methods [6,11]. The reason for this interest is two-fold: firstly SMC is
simulation-based and can therefore be applied to models for which the model
checking problem [7] is undecidable, secondly SMC scales better with increased
state spaces. Another interest of the formal verification community is applying
formal methods to the analysis of real-life code [3,4,18]. These works are mainly
focused on applying an exhaustive state space exploration of the source language.
In this paper we present a tool, LODIN, that permits applying SMC-based techniques to programs. LODIN relies on a pre-compilation of the program with clang
to produce a LLVM-bitcode [12] file used as the input model of LODIN. Functions
defined externally of the program itself (e.g. system calls) are given semantics
in LODIN through platform plugins. In this way LODIN is configurable to analyse embedded programs for various execution environments. Simulation-based
techniques have the major downfall of rare properties requiring an infeasible
number of samples to locate one with the property. To manage this, we seamlessly integrate LODIN with PLASMA-LAB and get access to their implementation

This work has been partially supported by the BMBF through the ARAMiS2
(01IS160253) project.

of importance splitting. Importance splitting is an efficient rare event simulation technique where a property is decomposed into several sub-properties that must be satisfied before the main property is satisfied.

2   LODIN

LODIN[1] is a fairly new software analysis tool with the goal of analysing programs without modelling the program in an analysis-specific modelling language. LODIN achieves this ability by using LLVM bitcode [12] as its model language - thereby making LODIN available to any source language translatable to LLVM. The analysis techniques available in LODIN is currently explicit-state model checking and statistical model checking [17]. In this paper we focus on the latter.

Architecture. LODIN consists of a user interface, algorithms or a simulator, state generators and a system model (Fig. 1). The system model is a state and transition representation of the program under analysis. The system exposes a successor generation interface for higher architectural levels. During the generation of successor states, the system calls an interpreter module responsible for implementing the semantics of LLVM instructions. In between the algorithms and system level is a state generator level. This is mostly relevant for the explicit-state model checking part of LODIN. It allows for selecting various techniques to reduce the searched state space. For statistical model checking there is only a

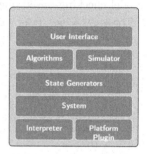

Fig. 1.   Architecture of LODIN

probabilistic state generator that selects what transition to perform according to probabilities obtained from the system. Real-life programs are developed to run under some execution environment providing core functionality to the program. To make LODIN as oblivious to the specific execution environment as possible, the core interpreter of LODIN has no built-in semantics for these. Instead it is possible to extend LODIN with platform plugins providing support for an execution environment. A platform plugin registers all the functions implemented by it when loaded by LODIN and the interpreter lets the plugin handle calls to one of these functions. In addition to implementing these external functions, platform plugins also have an interface to do their own transitions. This is useful for mimicking an interrupt system / signalling system.

Preparing Files. LODIN requires input in LLVM bitcode. We achieve this by compiling the program with `clang -emit-llvm -S -c file.c -o file.ll`. This is sufficient for programs without external dependencies. Properties are specified as expressions over LLVM registers thus we run `opt -instnamer file.ll -S -o fileN.ll` to generate the file `fileN.ll` in which registers have been given names. When a program has external dependencies and verification therefore requires the use of a platform

---

[1] available at https://spark.informatik.uni-kiel.de/data/lodin/FM18/Lodin-FM.zip.

plugin, the program must be compiled with headers specific for that plugin. If the header files are located in /path/to/includes then programs should be compiled with the command

```
clang -nodefaultlibs -ffreestanding -fno-builtin -emit-llvm -S -c -I/path/
   to/includes file.c -o file.ll
```

ensuring clang compiles the program without using any of its built-in libraries and only rely on the header files included on the command line.

How to Use. LODIN is a command line tool and is invoked by

```
./Lodin [options] file.ll query.q
```

where [options] includes options for selecting a platform plugin, setting a random seed and so on. The query.q file contains a one line query. The possible statistical model checking-based queries are generated by the below EBNF:

⟨Query⟩ ::= 'Pr' '[' '<=' ⟨integer⟩ ']' '(' '<>' ⟨bool⟩ ')'
    | 'Estimate' '[' '<=' ⟨integer⟩ ',' ⟨integer⟩ ']' '{' 'max' ⟨arith⟩ '}'
    | 'EnumStatesSMC' '<=' ⟨integer⟩ ⟨integer⟩

⟨bool⟩ :== 'DataRace'
    | '[' ⟨processid⟩'.'⟨string⟩ ']'
    | ⟨arith⟩ ⟨comp⟩ ⟨arith⟩
    | '('⟨bool⟩ '&&' ⟨bool⟩ '&&' ... '&&' ⟨bool⟩ ')'
    | '(' ⟨bool⟩ '||' ⟨bool⟩ ... '||' ⟨bool⟩ ')'
    | 'Exists' '('⟨char⟩ ')' '(⟨bool⟩')'
    | 'Forall' '('⟨char⟩ ')' '(⟨bool⟩')'
    |

⟨comp⟩ ::= '<' | '<=' | '==' | '>=' | '>' | '!='

where <arith> is an arithmetic expression over LLVM registers. LODIN also has limited support for using source variables in arithmetic expressions - this is how-ever dependent on the debugging symbols contained in the input file. An expression [0.func] is true if the zero[th] process can call the function func. The expression Exists (p)(<bool>) is true if for some process the Boolean expression is true. Any occurrence of p is replaced by an actual process during the evaluation. On the query side, Pr[<=500] (<> <bool>) estimates the probability of the Boolean expression being true within 500 steps. The number of samples needed is automatically adjusted using the Clopper-Pearson interval [8]. A query Estimate [<=500,5000] {max < arith>} generates 5000 runs each of 500 steps and estimates the expected maximal value of the expression. Finally, EnumStatesSMC <=500 5000 generates 5000 runs each of 500 steps and counts the number of different states encountered during those simulations.

Listing 1.1. Calculating the Fibonacci Numbers. A main function initialising t1 and t2 is omitted.

```
1  #include <pthread.h>
2
3  int i=1, j=1;
4
5  #define NUM 16
6  #define NULL 0
7
8
9  void *
10 t1(void* arg)
11 {
12     int k = 0;
13
14     for (k = 0; k < NUM; k++)
15         i+=j;
16
17     pthread_exit(NULL);
```

```
18 | }
19 |
20 | void *
21 | t2(void* arg)
22 | {
23 |   int k = 0;
24 |
```

```
25 |   for (k = 0; k < NUM; k++)
26 |     j+=i;
27 |
28 |   pthread_exit(NULL);
29 | }
```

Example 1. Consider the program in Listing 1.1 where two threads cooperatively attempt to calculate the 32nd Fibonacci number. With LODIN we estimate the expected number of i at termination of the program with `Estimate [<=5000,5000] {max@0.main.%tmp11}`, where `main.%tmp11` is a register in the compiled LLVM containing the value of the i variable. The result of this query is 438037. In addition to estimating the value, the query also outputs the values of the runs to a file. That file can the be used to generate a histogram.

Example 2. The Fibonacci program considered in Example 1 is only correct if it at termination has found the 32nd Fibonacci number (2178309). Using LODIN we estimate the probability of having either $i = 2178309$ or $j = 2178309$ using `Pr [<=5000] (<> [0.VERIFIERError])` which asks for the probability that a state is reached where the 0th process can call `VERIFIERError` - a call the main function does if either $i = 2178309$ or $j = 2178309$. Verifying the query with LODIN results in the probability being in the range $[0, 0.01]$ with confidence 0.95 and no satisfying traces found.

In Table 1 we show results for a range of programs we have applied LODIN to. For space limitations we omit descriptions of the programs and instead refer

Table 1. LODIN results. The Runs columns is total number of generated runs, Satisfying is the number of satisfying runs while the CI column is a 95% confidence interval.

Program	Runs	Satisfying	CI	Time (s)
fib/fib_4.ll	19242	2789	[0.14, 0.15]	3.80
fib/fib_8.ll	7453	370	[0.04, 0.05]	2.26
fib/fib_16.ll	299	0	[0.00, 0.01]	0.16
fib/fib_32.ll	299	0	[0.00, 0.01]	0.28
ptrace/ptrace.ll	33249	10412	[0.31, 0.32]	22.82
gossip/gossip_2.ll	34470	11575	[0.33, 0.34]	219.68
gossip/gossip_3.ll	13187	1229	[0.09, 0.10]	94.41
gossip/gossip_4.ll	8450	481	[0.05, 0.06]	66.30
petersons/petersonsBug.ll	10870	816	[0.07, 0.08]	1.64
petersons/petersons.ll	299	0	[0.00, 0.01]	0.05
robot/robot.ll	2507	38	[0.01, 0.02]	109.65
stack/stack.ll	299	0	[0.00, 0.01]	7.16

the reader to [14] which contains both the source code and descriptions of the programs. We will note though, that the verification queries are all of the form `Pr[<=N] (<> ... )`.

3   PLASMA-LAB

In Example 2 we saw that simulation-based techniques may fail to find traces satisfying rare events - in the particular example the event is rare because it requires a very specific interleaving of the two threads. In the following we integrate LODIN with PLASMA-LAB and see how importance splitting can help guiding the simulation to one of these rare interleavings.

PLASMA-LAB [5] is a modular platform for statistical model-checking[2]. The tool offers a series of SMC algorithms, including advanced techniques for rare event simulation, distributed SMC, non-determinism, and optimization. They are used with several modeling formalisms and simulators. The main difference between PLASMA-LAB and other SMC tools is that PLASMA-LAB proposes an API abstraction of the concepts of stochastic model simulator, property checker (monitoring) and SMC algorithm. In other words, the tool has been designed to use external simulators, input languages, or SMC algorithms. This also allows us to create direct plug-in interfaces with external specification tools, without using extra compilers.

PLASMA-LAB architecture is illustrated in Fig. 2. The core of PLASMA-LAB is a light-weight controller managing the experiments and the distribution mechanism. It implements an API that allows controlling the experiments either through user interfaces or through external tools. It loads three types of plugins: 1. algorithms, 2. checkers, and 3. simulators. These plugins

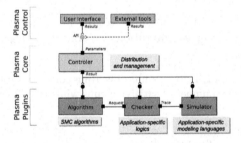

Fig. 2. PLASMA-LAB architecture.

communicate with each other and with the controller through the API.

In PLASMA-LAB rare properties are decomposed into intermediate properties using a notion of score function over the model-property product automaton. Intuitively, a score function discriminates good paths from bad, assigning higher scores to paths that are "closer" to satisfy the overall property. The model-property product automaton is usually hidden in the implementation of the checker plugin. Therefore Plasma Lab includes a specific checker plugin for importance splitting that facilitates the construction of score functions. The plugin allows writing small observer automata checking properties over traces and compute the score function. These observers implement a subset of the Bounded Linear Temporal Logic presented in [10].

---

[2] Available for download at https://project.inria.fr/plasma-lab/.

PLASMA-LAB implements two rare event algorithms based on the importance splitting technique, a fixed level algorithm and an adaptive level algorithm [9]. The fixed level algorithm requires the user to define a monotonically increasing sequence of score values whose last value corresponds to satisfying the property. The adaptive algorithm finds optimal levels automatically and requires only the maximum score to be specified. Both algorithms estimate the probability of passing from one level to the next by the proportion of a constant number of simulations reaching the upper level from the lower. New simulations to replace those that failed to reach the upper level are started from states chosen uniformly from the terminal states of successful simulations. The overall estimate is the product of the estimates of going from one level to the next.

LLVM Simulator Plugin. We have developed a simulator plugin for PLASMA-LAB that interfaces with LODIN. This plugin is a pure wrapper around the simulator interface of LODIN. It communicates with the LODIN simulator via standard input and standard output. LODIN exposes the registers of all functions of the program to PLASMA-LAB, and exposes Boolean variables corresponding to the [0.func] style propositions of LODIN. The registers are named in the style Pn_funcname_registerName where Pn designates a variable belonging to the nth process. If the program has been compiled with debug symbols and without optimisations, LODIN also exposes the original C-source primitive type variables to PLASMA-LAB. For supporting the importance splitting algorithm of PLASMA-LAB, LODIN provides a *State-Tag* that PLASMA-LAB uses to restart a simulation from that given state. In Table 2 we have applied the LODIN PLASMA-LAB integration to the models for which LODIN previously failed in finding a satisfying trace for.

Example 3. Consider again Example 2 and recall we want to reach a state where the 0th process can call VERIFIERError. In order to reach a state where the 32nd Fibonacci number is found, all previous Fibonacci numbers must be found first. In Listing 1.2 we show an excerpt of the observer we use. First the score variable is defined

Table 2. PLASMA-LAB Importance Splitting Results. The algorithm was run with a budget of 1000 runs per level.

Program	Levels	Probability	Time (s)
fib/fib_16.ll	7	1.5e−3	18.20
fib/fib_32.ll	14	4.0e−6	51.66
stack/stack.ll	13	3.86e−15	530.58

as required by PLASMA-LAB. PLASMA-LAB also requires a decided variable. The observer should set this to true if it is no longer possible to satisfy a trace. An auxilliary variable, steps, is used by the observer to count the steps in the trace. After these variable declarations follows a series of update transitions in the style of reactive modules. Basically these transitions state that, if the sum of i and j is equal to a given Fibonacci number, and t1 and t2 are in the same iteration of their loop then update the score variable to a given value (t1_tmp9, t1_tmp9 and ti_tmp4 correspond to i, j and k respectively). The last two rules update the steps variable and terminate the trace when exceeding 5000 steps.

Listing 1.2. The observer used by PLASMA-LAB for Fibonacci example.

```
 1  observer rareObserver
 2       score : int init 0;
 3       decided : bool init false;
 4       steps : int init 0;
 5       [] (P1_t1_tmp9 + P2_t2_tmp9 = 5)& (P1_t1_tmp4=P2_t2_tmp4)-> (score
              '= 1);
 6       [] P1_t1_tmp9 + P2_t2_tmp9 = 13 & (P1_t1_tmp4=P2_t2_tmp4) -> (
              score '= 2);
 7       ...
 8       [] P0_Call_VERIFIERError=1 -> (score'=14);
 9       [] steps<5000 ->(steps'=steps+1);
10       [] steps>=5000 ->(decided'=true);
11  endobserver
```

4 Conclusion

In this paper we presented LODIN   a tool implementing SMC of LLVM code. The tool provides a plugin-architecture making it extendable to many execution environments. The tool also includes a simulation-component that is used to connect LODIN to PLASMA-LAB and thereby provide the first importance splitting implementation for LLVM.

References

1. AlTurki, M., Meseguer, J.: PVESTA: a parallel statistical model checking and quantitative analysis tool. In: Corradini, A., Klin, B., Cîrstea, C. (eds.) CALCO 2011. LNCS, vol. 6859, pp. 386–392. Springer, Heidelberg (2011). https://doi.org/10.1007/978-3-642-22944-2_28

2. Ballarini, P., Djafri, H., Duflot, M., Haddad, S., Pekergin, N.: COSMOS: a statistical model checker for the hybrid automata stochastic logic. In: QEST, pp. 143–144. IEEE Computer Society (2011). https://doi.org/10.1109/QEST.2011.24. ISBN 978-1-4577-0973-9

3. Barnat, J., Brim, L., Rockai, P.: Towards LTL model checking of unmodified thread-based C & C++ programs. In: Goodloe, A., Person, S. (eds.) NFM 2012. LNCS, vol. 7226, pp. 252–266. Springer, Heidelberg (2012). https://doi.org/10.1007/978-3-642-28891-3_25

4. Beyer, D., Keremoglu, M.E.: CPACHECKER: a tool for configurable software verification. In: Gopalakrishnan, G., Qadeer, S. (eds.) CAV 2011. LNCS, vol. 6806, pp. 184–190. Springer, Heidelberg (2011). https://doi.org/10.1007/978-3-642-22110-1_16

5. Boyer, B., Corre, K., Legay, A., Sedwards, S.: PLASMA-lab: a flexible, distributable statistical model checking library. In: Joshi, K., Siegle, M., D'Argenio, P.R. (eds.) QEST 2013. LNCS, vol. 8054, pp. 160–164. Springer, Heidelberg (2013)

6. Bulychev, P.E., David, A., Larsen, K.G., Mikucionis, M., Poulsen, D.B., Legay, A., Wang, Z.: UPPAAL-SMC: statistical model checking for priced timed automata. In: Wiklicky, H., Massink, M. (eds.) QAPL. EPTCS, vol. 85, pp. 1–16 (2012). https://doi.org/10.4204/EPTCS.85.1

7. Clarke, E., Grumberg, O., Peled, D.: Model Checking. MIT Press, Cambridge (1999)

8. Clopper, C.J., Pearson, E.S.: The use of confidence or fiducial limits illustrated in the case of the binomial. Biometrika **26**(4), 404–413 (1934)
9. Jegourel, C., Legay, A., Sedwards, S.: An effective heuristic for adaptive importance splitting in statistical model checking. In: Margaria, T., Steffen, B. (eds.) ISoLA 2014. LNCS, vol. 8803, pp. 143–159. Springer, Heidelberg (2014). https://doi.org/10.1007/978-3-662-45231-8_11
10. Jegourel, C., Legay, A., Sedwards, S., Traonouez, L.-M.: Distributed verification of rare properties using importance splitting observers. In: ECEASST, vol. 72 (2015)
11. Kwiatkowska, M.Z., Norman, G., Parker, D.: PRISM 4.0: verification of probabilistic real-time systems. In: Gopalakrishnan, G., Qadeer, S. (eds.) CAV 2011. LNCS, vol. 6806, pp. 585–591. Springer, Heidelberg (2011). https://doi.org/10.1007/978-3-642-22110-1_47
12. Lattner, C., Adve, V.: LLVM: a compilation framework for lifelong program analysis & transformation. In: Proceedings of the 2004 International Symposium on Code Generation and Optimization (CGO 2004), Palo Alto, California, March 2004
13. Legay, A., Sedwards, S., Traonouez, L.M.: Plasma lab: a modular statistical model checking platform. In: Margaria, T., Steffen, B. (eds.) ISoLA 2016. LNCS, vol. 9952, pp. 77–93. Springer, Cham (2016). https://doi.org/10.1007/978-3-319-47166-2_6
14. Legay, A., Nowotka, D., Tranoues, L.-M., Poulsen, D.B.: Lodin and Plasma-Lab examples (2018). https://spark.informatik.uni-kiel.de/data/lodin/FM18/LodinExamples.zip. Accessed 08 May 2018
15. Sen, K., Viswanathan, M., Agha, G.A.: VESTA: a statistical model-checker and analyzer for probabilistic systems. In: QEST, pp. 251–252. IEEE Computer Society (2005). https://doi.org/10.1109/QEST.2005.42. ISBN 0-7695-2427-3
16. Younes, H.L.S.: Ymer: a statistical model checker. In: Etessami, K., Rajamani, S.K. (eds.) CAV 2005. LNCS, vol. 3576, pp. 429–433. Springer, Heidelberg (2005). https://doi.org/10.1007/11513988_43
17. Younes, H.L.S., Kwiatkowska, M.Z., Norman, G., Parker, D.: Numerical vs. statistical probabilistic model checking. STTT **8**(3), 216–228 (2006)
18. Zaks, A., Joshi, R.: Verifying multi-threaded C programs with SPIN. In: Havelund, K., Majumdar, R., Palsberg, J. (eds.) Model Checking Software SPIN 2008. LNCS, vol. 5156, pp. 325–342. Springer, Heidelberg (2008). https://doi.org/10.1007/978-3-540-85114-1_22

SDN-Actors: Modeling and Verification of SDN Programs

Elvira Albert[1], Miguel Gómez-Zamalloa[1(✉)], Albert Rubio[2],
Matteo Sammartino[3], and Alexandra Silva[3]

[1] Complutense University of Madrid, Madrid, Spain
mzamalloa@fdi.ucm.es
[2] Universitat Politècnica de Catalunya, Barcelona, Spain
[3] University College London, London, UK

Abstract. Software-Defined Networking (SDN) is a recent networking paradigm that has become increasingly popular in the last decade. It gives unprecedented control over the global behavior of the network and provides a new opportunity for formal methods. Much work has appeared in the last few years on providing bridges between SDN and verification. This paper advances this research line and provides a link between SDN and traditional work on formal methods for verification of distributed software—actor-based modelling. We show how SDN programs can be seamlessly modelled using *actors*, and thus existing advanced model checking techniques developed for actors can be directly applied to verify a range of properties of SDN networks, including consistency of flow tables, violation of safety policies, and forwarding loops.

1 Introduction

SDN is a novel networking architecture which is now widely used in industry, with many companies –such as Google and Facebook– using SDN to control their backbone networks and datacenters. The core principle in SDN is the separation of the control and data planes –there is a centralized *controller* which operates a collection of distributed interconnected switches. The controller can dynamically update switches' policies depending on the observed flow of packets, which is a simple but powerful way to react to unexpected events in the network. Network verification has become increasingly popular since SDN was introduced, because in this new paradigm the amount of detailed information available about network events is rich enough and can be centrally gathered to check for properties, both statically and dynamically, of the network behavior. Moreover, the controller itself is a program which can be analyzed. The distributed and concurrent nature

This work was partially funded by the Spanish MECD Salvador de Madariaga Mobility Grants PRX17/00297 and PRX17/00303, the Spanish MINECO projects TIN2015–69175-C4-2-R, TIN2015-69175-C4-3-R, and he CM project S2013/ICE-3006, the ERC starting grant Profoundnet (679127) and a Leverhulme Prize (PLP-2016-129).

© Springer International Publishing AG, part of Springer Nature 2018
K. Havelund et al. (Eds.): FM 2018, LNCS 10951, pp. 550–567, 2018.
https://doi.org/10.1007/978-3-319-95582-7_33

of network behavior makes the verification tasks challenging and has inspired much research in the verification and formal methods communities.

This paper provides a new bridge between SDN and a strand of formal methods –actor-based modeling [2], which is a framework that was developed to analyze concurrent systems. Actors form the basic unit of computation in such framework, are equipped with a private memory, and can interact with others through *asynchronous* messages. This setup enables reasoning about local properties without knowledge of the whole program, which gives rise to more compositional and thus scalable methods. Actors provide the foundations for the concurrency model of languages used in industry, e.g., *Erlang* and *Scala*, and libraries used in mainstream languages, e.g., *Akka*.

Contributions. The main contributions of this paper are:

1. SDN-Actors: An encoding of all components of a SDN network into the actor-based language ABS [14]. One of the most challenging aspects to encode were the OpenFlow *barrier* messages, special instructions that the controller can use to force switches to execute all their queued tasks.
2. A soundness proof of the encoding (and implementation) of *barriers* (Theorem 2).
3. Application of (context-sensitive) dynamic partial-order reduction (DPOR) techniques to model check SDN programs. We have implemented this model checker on top of the SYCO tool [4] for actors.
4. Several case studies of SDN and properties to illustrate the versatility and potential of the approach. We were able to find bugs related to programming errors in the controller, forwarding loops, and violation of safety policies.

Though we did not explore it in this paper, the encoding we provide opens the door to apply a range of techniques other than model checking. For instance, static analysis, runtime monitoring or simulation of network behavior can be done now using the ABS toolsuite [1]. Other tools and methods for verification of message-passing and concurrent-object systems could be also easily adapted [7, 9,16,17]. In addition, because the encoding is not very far from the original flow tables, both model extraction from existing network code and code generation from an actor model should be achievable with a small extension of the tool.

2 Overview

This section provides an overview of the contents of the paper through an extended example, that we also use to introduce some basic concepts and notations.

2.1 Concurrency Errors in SDN Networks

SDN is a networking architecture where a central software *controller* can dynamically change how network switches forward packets by monitoring the traffic. Switches can be connected to hosts and to other switches via bidirectional channels that may reorder packets. Each switch has a *flow table*, that is a collection of

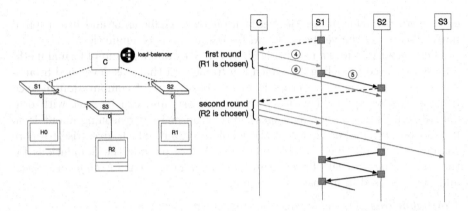

Fig. 1. Example SDN load-balancer. On the left: structure of the SDN. On the right: messages exchanged in a possible execution of a naive controller program. Coloured arrows stand for control messages to switches, indicating which flow rule to install (colours specify the link to be used for the forwarding). Grey boxes and arrows among them represent packet forwardings. Dashed arrows indicate messages to the controller. (Color figure online)

guarded forwarding rules to determine the route of incoming packets. Whenever a switch receives a packet, it checks if one of the flow table rules applies. If no rule applies, the switch sends a message to the controller via a dedicated link, and the packet is buffered until instructions arrive. Depending on its policy, the controller instructs the switch, and possibly other switches in the network, on how to update their flow tables. Such control messages between the controller and the switches can be processed in arbitrary order.

We now show how a simple load-balancer can be implemented in SDN (example taken from [12]) and how potential bugs can easily arise due to the concurrent behavior and asynchrony of message passing. Suppose we want to balance the traffic to a server by using two replicas R1 and R2 to which the controller alternates the traffic in a round-robin fashion. The structure of the SDN is shown in Fig. 1, on the left: H0 is any host that wants to communicate with the server and S1, S2 and S3 are switches (numbers on endpoints stand for port numbers).

Even in this simple network, an incorrect implementation of the controller can lead to serious problems. In Fig. 1, on the right, we show an execution of a naive controller, which simply instructs switches to forward packets along the shortest path to the chosen replica. This implementation ignores the potential concurrency in actions taken by switches and controller, leading to a forwarding loop between S1 and S2. In the first round, when S1 queries the controller, R1 is chosen. The figure shows S1 forwarding the packet to S2 before the end of the first round, i.e., before a rule is installed on S2 (green arrow). This causes S2 to query the controller, which triggers the second round in which the controller chooses R2. Thus, it sends instructions to install rules on S2, S1 and S3 to forward the packet to S1, S3 and R2, resp. When the controller rules arrive at S1, it will have two contradictory instructions, telling to forward the packet either to S2 or to S3. In the former, the loop at the bottom of the figure occurs. This issue can be avoided if the implementation uses barriers –the controller will then guarantee that S2 receives and processes control messages before taking any other action.

2.2   Actor-Based Modeling of SDN Networks

We now explain how we can automatically detect the above problem using actors and model checking. We use the object-oriented actor language ABS [1,14], where each actor type is specified as a class, consisting of a set of fields and methods. Actors are instances of actor classes. For instance, the instructions: Controller ctrl = new Controller(); Switch s1 = new Switch("S1",ctrl); Host h0 = new Host("H0",s1,0); create three actors: a controller ctrl; a switch s1 with name "S1" and a reference to ctrl; a host h0, with name "H0", connected to the switch s1 via the port 0. The SDN in Fig. 1 can be modeled using one actor per component (additional data structures for network links will be shown later).

The execution model of actors is *asynchronous*. Each actor can be thought of as a processor, with a queue of pending tasks and a local memory. Actors are executed in parallel and, at each actor, one task is *nondeterministically* selected among all the pending ones and executed. The syntax Fut<type> f=a!m($\overline{x}$) spawns an asynchronous task m($\overline{x}$), that is added to the queue of pending tasks of a, type is the type of the data returned by m or Unit if no data is returned. This task consists in executing the method m of a with arguments $\overline{x}$. The variable f is a *future variable* [10] that will allow us to check if such task has been completed. *Synchronous* calls are written a.m($\overline{x}$), we omit a if the target actor is this.

A partial trace of execution of our SDN actor model computed by the model checker is (the code that the tasks below execute will be given in Sect. 3):

$$\boxed{1: \text{h0!sendIn}} \xrightarrow{1} \boxed{2: \text{s1!switchHandlePacket}} \xrightarrow{2} \boxed{3: \text{ctrl!controlHandleMessage}}$$

$$\xrightarrow{3} \boxed{4: \text{s1!switchHandleMessage(s2)}, 5: \text{s1!sendOut}, 6: \text{s2!switchHandleMessage(r1)}}$$

Intuitively, a packet sending (sendIn) is executed on h0 (label 1), which causes the packet to be forwarded to the switch s1 (2), then s1 sends a control message to the controller (3). Finally, the controller spawns the three tasks in the last state (parameters tell where to forward the packet). When executed, these tasks will produce the messages in Fig. 1 with the same numbers. Their execution order is arbitrary: if it is the one shown in Fig. 1, the execution trace may lead to a state exhibiting a forwarding cycle between s1 and s2. As we will show later, this situation can be easily detected by our model checker via an exploration of a *reduced* execution tree, which avoids equivalent executions (Sect. 4).

The ABS language provides a convenient await primitive that will be used to model barriers and to rule out the behavior described above. The instruction await f? can be used to synchronize with the termination of the task associated to the future variable f, by releasing the processor (so that another task can be scheduled) if the task is not finished. Once the awaited task is finished, the suspended task can resume. The await can be used also with boolean conditions await b? to suspend the execution of the current active task until condition b holds. The formal semantics of the language can be found in the appendix of [5].

3   SDN-Actors: An Actor Based Encoding of SDN Programs

We present the concept of *SDN-Actor* in four steps: Sect. 3.1 describes the creation and initialization of the actors according to the topology. Section 3.2 provides the encoding of the operations and communication for Switch and Host actors. Section 3.3 proposes the encoding of the controller, and Sect. 3.4 the extension to implement barriers. Altogether, our encoding provides an actor-based semantics foundation of SDN networks that follow the OpenFlow specification [19].

3.1   Network Topology

The topology can be given as a relation with two types of links:

- *SHlink(s,h,o)*: switch s is connected to host h through the port o
- *SSlink(s$_1$,i$_1$,s$_2$,i$_2$)*: switch s_1 is connected via port i_1 to port i_2 of switch s_2

from which we automatically generate the initial configuration as follows.

Definition 1 (initial configuration). *Let S and H be, respectively, the set of different switch and host identifiers available in the* link *relations that define the network topology. The initial configuration (method main) is defined as:*

- *We create a controller actor* Controller ctrl=**new** Controller()
- *For each* sid∈*S, we create an actor* Switch s=**new** Switch(sid,ctrl)
- *For each* hid∈*H, we create an actor* Host h=**new** Host(hid,s,o) *where* s *is the reference to the switch actor,* o *the port identifier, that* hid *is connected to.*
- *The data structures* srefs *and* hrefs *store, resp., the relations between identifier in the topology and reference in the program, for all switches in S and hosts in H.*
- *The data structure* ntw *contains the link relations in the network topology.*
- *The synchronous call* ctrl.addConfig(srefs,hrefs,ntw) *initializes in the controller the topology relations and the references to switches and hosts s.t. the controller can send control messages to redirect the traffic to the involved links.*

Example 1. By applying Definition 1 to the topology in Fig. 1, given as the relation: $SHlink(S1, H0, 0)$, $SHlink(S2, R1, 0)$, $SHlink(S3, R2, 0)$, $SSlink(S1, 1, S2, 1)$, $SSlink(S1, 2, S3, 1)$, we obtain the following initial configuration which constitutes the main method from which the execution starts:

```
1 main() { Controller ctrl = new Controller(); Switch s1 = new Switch("S1",ctrl);
2          Switch s2 = new Switch("S2",ctrl); Switch s3 = new Switch("S3",ctrl);
3          Host h0 = new Host("H0",s1,0); Host r1 = new Host("R1",s2,0);
4          Host r2 = new Host("R2",s3,0);
5          Map<SwitchId,Switch> srefs = {"S1":s1, "S2":s2, "S3":s3};
6          Map<HostId,Host> hrefs = {"H0":h0, "R1":r1, "R2":r2};
7          List<Link> ntw = [SHLink("S1","H0",0), SSLink("S1","S2",1),..];
8          ctrl.addConfig(srefs,hrefs,ntw); }
```

The data structures srefs and hrefs are implemented using maps, and the network ntw as a heterogeneous list. The use of data structures is nevertheless orthogonal to the encoding as actors. We just assume standard functions to create, initialize, access them (like getters, put, lookup, etc.) that will appear in italics in the code.

```
 9 type SwitchId=... type HostId=... type PortId=... type PacketId=...
10 type PacketH=... type Packet=... type Action=... type Link=...
11 type MatchF=(PacketH,PortId);

12 class Host(HostId hid, Switch s, PortId o) {
13    Unit sendIn(Packet p){ s!switchHandlePacket(p,o);}
14    Unit hostHandlePacket(Packet p){ /* output packet */}
15 }
16 class Switch(SwitchId sid, Controller ctrl) {
17    Map<MatchF,Action> flowT={};
18    Map<PacketId,(Packet,PortId)> buffer={};
19 Unit switchHandlePacket(Packet p, PortId o){
20    Action l=lookup(flowT,(getHeader(p),o));
21    if (isSwitch(l)) getSwitch(l)!switchHandlePacket(p,getPort(l));
22    else if (isHost(l)) getHost(l)!hostHandlePacket(p);
23    else { buffer=put(buffer,getId(p),(p,o));
24          ctrl!controlHandleMessage(sid,o,getId(p),getHeader(p)); }}
25 Unit sendOut(PacketId pi){
26    Packet p; PortId o; (p,o)=lookup(buffer,pi);
27    Action l=lookup(flowT,(getHeader(p),o));
28    if (isSwitch(l)) getSwitch(l)!switchHandlePacket(p,getPort(l));
29    else if (isHost(l)) getHost(l)!hostHandlePacket(p);
30    /* else packet is dropped */}
31 Unit switchHandleMessage(MatchF m, Action a){ flowT=put(flowT,m,a);}
32 }
```

Fig. 2. Type declarations (top) and actor-based host and switch classes (bottom)

3.2   The Switch and Host Classes

Figure 2 presents the actor-based Switch and Host classes. We include at the top some **type** declarations that are assumed and must be implemented (such as identifiers, packets and their headers, etc.). There are two main data structures that are implemented in more detail to make explicit the information they contain:

– the buffer at Line 18 (L18 for short) is a *map* that must contain pairs of packet and input port indexed by their PacketId.
– the flow table flowT (L17) is implemented as a *map* indexed by the so-called *match field* [19] represented by type MatchF in Fig. 2. The match field is composed by information stored in the header of a Packet (retrieved by function *getHeader*) and the input port. For a given matching, the flow table contains the Action the switch has to perform upon the reception of the Packet. An action l can be of three types: (i) send the packet to a host h, (ii) send the packet to the port o of a switch s, (iii) drop the packet. Given an action l, function *isSwitch* resp. *isHost* succeeds if the action is of type (ii) resp. (i), and functions *getSwitch*, *getHost* and *getPort* return the s, h and o resp. The full implementation must allow duplicate entries (non-deterministically selected), and the use of wildcards in the match fields, but these aspects are unrelated to the encoding of SDN actors, and skipped for simplicity.

Upon creation, hosts receive their identifier and a reference to the switch and the port identifier they are connected to (defined as class parameters that are initialized at the actor creation). Their method sendIn is used to send a packet to the switch, and method hostHandlePacket to receive a packet from the switch. Switches receive upon creation their identifier and a reference to the controller. They have as additional fields: (a) the flow table flowT (as described above) in which they store the actions to take upon receiving each kind of package, and (b) a buffer in which they store packets that are waiting for a response from the controller. Switches can perform three operations: (1) switchHandlePacket receives a packet, looks up in the flow table the action to be made L20, and, if there is an entry for the packet in the table, it asynchronously makes the corresponding action (either send it to a host L22 or to a switch L21). Otherwise, it sends a controlHandleMessage request and puts the packet and input port in the buffer (L23 and L24) until it can be handled later upon receipt of a sendOut; (2) sendOut receives a packet identifier that corresponds to a waiting packet, retrieves it from the buffer (L26), looks up the action l to be performed in the flow table, and makes the corresponding asynchronous call (as in switchHandlePacket); (3) switchHandleMessage corresponds to a message received from the controller with an instruction to update the flow table. Other switch operations like *forward packet*, that is similar to sendOut but directly tells the switch the action to be performed, or *flood*, that sends a packet through all ports except the input port, can be encoded similarly and are used in the experiments in Sect. 5.

Example 2. In main, after L8, we add h0!sendIn(p), where p is a packet to be sent to the IP address of the replica servers (the information on the destination is part of the packet header). This is the only asynchronous task that main spawns. Its execution in turn spawns a new task s1!switchHandlePacket(p,0) at L13, that does not find an entry in flowT at L20 and spawns a controlHandleMessage task on the controller at L24, whose code is presented in the next section.

3.3 The Controller

After creating the controller actor, the method addConfig is invoked synchronously to initialize the references to switches and hosts and set up the initial network topology (see L8). A simple controller is presented in Fig. 3, removing the blue lines 35, 36, 41, 44, 46, 48, 49 which provide the implementation of barriers. When a switch asynchronously invokes controlHandleMessage, the controller applies the current policy—applyPolicy must be implemented for each different type of controller. The implementation of the policy typically requires the definition of new data structures in the controller to store additional information (see Sect. 5). When applying the policy, we obtain a list of switch identifiers and corresponding actions to be applied to them. The while loop at L42 in controlHandleMessage asynchronously invokes switchHandleMessage at L45 on each

```
33 class Controller() {
34    Map<SwitchId,Switch> srefs={}; Map<HostId,Host> href={}; List<Link> ntw=[];
35    Map<SwitchId,List<Fut<Unit>> barrierMap={};
36    Set<SwitchId> barrierOn = ∅;
37    Unit addConfig(Map<SwitchId,Switch> sr, Map<HostId,Host> hr, List<Link> n){
38        / * references to switches and hosts and network topology initialized * / }
39    Unit controlHandleMessage(SwitchId sid, PortId o, PacketId p, PacketH h){
40        List<(SwitchId,MatchF,Action)> l=applyPolicy(sid,o,h);
41        List<SwitchId> ls = [];
42        while (not(isEmpty(l))) {
43            SwitchId s1; Action a1; MatchF m1; (s1,m1,a1)=head(l);
44            barrierWait(s1);
45            Fut<Unit> f=lookup(srefs,s1)!switchHandleMessage(m1,a1);
46            barrierMap=putAdd(barrierMap,s1,f); ls = add(ls,s1);
47            l=tail(l);}
48        while (not(isEmpty(ls))) {barrierRequest(head(ls)); ls=tail(ls);}
49        barrierWait(sid);
50        lookup(srefs,sid)!sendOut(p);
51    }
52    List<(SwitchId,MatchF,Action)> applyPolicy(SwitchId sid, PortId o, PacketH h) {
53        / * implementation of specific policy * /}
54    }
```

Fig. 3. Controller class w/o barriers in black (w/barriers extended in blue) (Color figure online)

of the switches in the list, and passes as parameter the corresponding action to be applied for the given match entry. Finally, it notifies at L50 the switch from which the packet came that the packet can already be sent out. More sophisticated controllers that build upon this encoding are described in Sect. 5.

Example 3. In the example, applyPolicy corresponds to the load-balancer described in Sect. 2, which directs external requests to a chosen replica in a round-robin fashion. For the call applyPolicy(s1,0,h), it chooses r1 and thus, it returns in L40 two actions: (s1→s2), (s2→r1), i.e., one action to install in s1 the rule to send the packet to s2, and the second to install in s2 the rule to send it to r1. For simplicity, we assume that the Action just contains the location to which the packet has to be sent (without including the port). The while loop thus spawns two asynchronous calls, s1!switchHandleMessage(m1,s2) and s2!switchHandleMessage(m1,r1). Besides, it sends a s1!sendOut(p) in L50. Several problems may arise in this implementation. One problem, as explained in Sect. 2, is that the packet is sent from s1 to s2 before the control message is processed by s2. Then, s2 gets the packet and it does not find any matching rule, thus it sends a controlHandleMessage to the controller. Applying the above policy, the controller chooses now as replica r2 and returns the actions: (s2→s1), (s1→s3), (s3→r2), i.e., the packet should be sent to r2 by first sending from s2 to s1 (first action), and so on. This might create the circularity depicted in Fig. 1.

The following theorem ensures the soundness of our modeling. Essentially we guarantee that, for a given SDN network that follows the OpenFlow specification, any execution in the network has an equivalent execution in the SDN-Actor model. An execution in the network is characterized by the messages in the queues of the switches, hosts, and controller and the state of their data structures. An *equivalent* execution in the model will thus ensure the same messages in the actors queues and the same state in actors data structures.

```
55  Unit barrierWait (SwitchId sid){
56      await not(contains(barrierOn,sid))?;
57  }
58  Unit barrierRequest (SwitchId sid){
59      barrierOn=add(barrierOn,sid);
60      List<Fut<Unit>> futSid=lookup(barrierMap,sid);
61      while (not(isEmpty(futSid)) {
62          Fut<Unit> fi=head(futSid);
63          await fi?;
64          futSid=tail(futSid); }
65      barrierOn=delete(barrierOn,sid);
66  }
```

Fig. 4. Implementation of barriers (part of class Controller)

Theorem 1 (soundness). *Given a SDN network N, consider its SDN-Actor model N^a with an initial configuration* main *obtained by Definition 1, and the* Switch, Host *and* Controller *classes in Figs. 2 and 3. Then, for each execution in N, there exists an equivalent execution trace in N^a using the semantics in the appendix of [5].*

3.4   Barriers

Barriers [19] have been designed to force a switch to handle previous control messages, and thus avoid problems such as the one described above.

Definition 2 (OF barrier). *Following OpenFlow [19], upon receipt of a barrier message, the switch must finish processing all previously-received controller messages, before executing any messages beyond the barrier message.*

Figures 3 and 4 show our modeling that intuitively consists in the controller not sending further messages to any switch on which a barrier has been activated, until this switch acknowledges that all previous control messages have been already processed. The main points in the implementation are: (1) the controller creates a future variable at L45 for every asynchronous task that it posts on all switches; (2) it keeps in barrierMap the list of future variables (not yet acknowledged) for each of the switches (putAdd in L46 adds the future variable to the list indexed by s1 in the map); (3) it keeps in barrierOn the set of switches with an active barrier; (4) a barrier on a switch consists in the controller awaiting on the list of future variables that the switch needs to acknowledge to ensure that its control messages have already been processed (method barrierRequest); (5) all control messages must be now preceded by an invocation to barrierWait that checks if the corresponding switch has an active barrier, L56. This is because while suspended in a barrier, the controller can start to process another controlHandleMessage unrelated to the previous one, but which affects (some of) the same switches for which a barrier was set. So, we cannot send messages to them until their barriers are set to off. Note that this is not a restriction on the type of controllers we model, but rather an effective way to encode barriers using actors and **await** instructions that ensures the behaviour of OpenFlow barriers.

Theorem 2 (soundness of barriers). *Methods* barrierRequest *and* barrierWait *provide a sound encoding of the OF* barrier *messages in Definition 2.*

4   DPOR-Based Model Checking of SDN-Actors

Model checking tools deal with a combinatorial blow-up of the state space (a.k.a. the state space problem) that must be faced to solve real-world problems. As for model checking SDN programs, the problem is exacerbated because of the concurrent and distributed nature of networks: all network components (switches, hosts, controllers) are distributed nodes that run in parallel and whose concurrent tasks can interact. As we have seen, a controller message sent from a switch can change the state of another switch, and affect the route of an incoming packet. Thus, a model checker needs to explore all possible reorderings of *dependent* tasks (i.e., those whose execution might interfere with each other) leading to a huge number of possible executions even for networks with few nodes and few packets. Besides, the space is unbounded because hosts may generate unboundedly many packets that could be simultaneously traversing the network.

There are two *incomplete* approaches to handle unbounded inputs: one is to impose a bound k on the number of packets of each type (as e.g. in [8]) and the other one is to use abstraction (as e.g. in [18]). In the former, the search space is exhausted for the considered input, but there could be bugs that only show up when more packets are considered. In the latter, abstraction requires to lose information and bugs may only show up when the omitted information is considered. Therefore, the sources of incompleteness are different, and the approaches can complement each other. Our implementation uses the former, e.g., in Example 2 we have considered one packet (limit $k = 1$). The rest of the section presents the key features of our approach assuming such a k bound.

4.1   DPOR-Based Model Checking in Actors

DPOR [13] is able to dynamically identify and avoid the exploration of redundant executions and prune the search space exponentially. It is based on the idea of initially exploring an arbitrary interleaving of the various concurrent tasks, and *dynamically* tracking dependent interactions between them to identify backtracking points where alternative paths in the state space need to be explored. Two tasks are *independent* when changing their order of execution will not affect their combined effect. When DPOR is applied to actor systems, there are inherent reductions [23] because: (i) we can atomically execute each task (without re-orderings) until a return or an **await** instruction are found, because concurrency is non-preemptive and the active task cannot be interrupted. This avoids having to consider the reorderings at the level of instructions (as one must do in thread-based concurrency), and allows us to work at the level of tasks. (ii) Besides that, two tasks can have a dependency only if they belong to the same actor. This is because only the actor itself can modify its private memory.

Example 4. Figure 5 shows the search tree computed by DPOR for our SDN-Actor program without barriers. It has no redundancy, i.e., each execution corresponds to a different behavior on the packet arrival and/or the actions installed in the flow tables (see top right descriptions). At each node (i.e., state), we show the available tasks. A task is given an identifier the first time it appears, and afterwards only its identifier is shown. Method names are abbreviated as shown in the top left, and parameters are omitted except in tasks executing switchHandleMessage, for which we only include the switch identifier that is part of the Action to be installed. For instance, 4:s1!shm(s2) is a task with identifier 4, that will execute method switchHandleMessage on s1 and will add to its flow table the information that the packet must be sent to s2. Labels on the edges

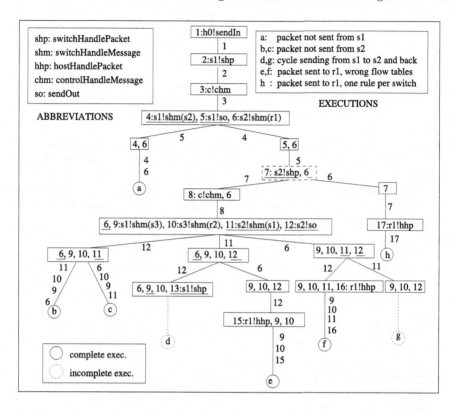

Fig. 5. Search tree for running example w/o barriers (rightmost branch w/barriers)

show the task(s) that have been executed. At each state, we underline the tasks which have an interacting dependency. The execution starts by executing the main method in Example 1 with the instruction sendIn added in Example 2 which appears in the root. The next two steps have one task available, but in the fourth state we have tasks 4 and 5, belonging to the same actor, whose reordering needs to be considered (leading to branching), while 6 is independent of them. Out of the 8 branches of the tree, only the rightmost execution (h) corresponds to the correct behavior in which the packet is actually sent to r1 and the actions are installed in the flow tables in the expected order. In execution (a) the packet does not arrive at the destination because the sendOut is executed before the action has been installed. Executions (d) and (g) correspond to the cycle described in Sect. 2, each of them with different installations of actions.

Importantly, we do not need specific optimizations to use the DPOR algorithm in [3] to model check SDN-Actors. The use of **await** (is already covered by DPOR and) does not require any change either and, as expected, the search tree for the implementation with barriers only contains branch (h). The difference arises from task 3 in the tree: in the presence of barriers, this leads to a state in which we have the asynchronous calls 4 and 6 and task 3 suspended at the **await** in L63 (awaiting first the termination of 4 and then that of 6). Therefore, the dependent tasks 4 and 5 will not coexist because 5 is not spawned until 4 and 6 terminate.

4.2   Entry-Level and Context-Sensitive Independence

When two tasks that belong to the same actor are found, in the context of DPOR techniques independence is commonly over-approximated by requiring that actor fields accessed by one task are not modified by the other. In our model, all tasks posted on a given switch access its flow table, namely sendOut and switchHandlePacket read it and switchHandleMessage writes it. Thus, in principle, any task executing switchHandleMessage is considered dependent on the other two. This explains the tasks underlinings in the figure and the branching in the tree. When there are multiple packets traversing the network it is usually the case that the different packets access distinct entries in the flow table. This results in the inaccurate detection of many dependencies hence producing redundant executions. Using Context-sensitive DPOR [3], we alleviate this state explosion:

1. *Entry-level independence.* We adopt a finer-grained notion of *entry-level independence* for which an access to entry i is independent from an access to j if $i \neq j$. This aspect is not visible when considering a single packet as in the example, as all accesses to the flow table refer to the same entry. However, by simply adding another packet to the erroneous program, the state explosion is huge and the system times out if entry-level independence is not implemented, while it computes 92 executions (exploring 761 states) with entry-level independence.

2. *Context-sensitiveness.* Even when two tasks t and p access the same entry, Context-sensitive DPOR introduces some further checks that execute the considered tasks from the current state S in the two orders $t \cdot p$ and $p \cdot t$. If they lead to the same state, one of the derivations is pruned and further exploration from it is thus avoided. For instance, executing two consecutive switchHandleMessage on the same entry might lead to the same state if the flow table may contain duplicate entries, as our implementation allows.

4.3   Comparison of DPOR Reductions with Related Work

Other model checkers for SDN programs have used DPOR-based algorithms before [8,18]. According to the experiments in the NICE tool, DPOR only achieves a 20% reduction of the search space because even the finest granularity does not distinguish independent flows. The reason for this modest reduction might be that it does not take advantage of the inherent independence of the code executed by the distributed elements of the network (switches, host, clients), nor to the fact that barriers allow removing dependencies, as our actor-based SDN model does. In Kuai [18], a number of optimizations are defined to take advantage of these aspects. Such optimizations must be (1) identified and formalized in the semantics, (2) proven correct and, (3) implemented in the model checker. Instead, due to our formalization using actors, the optimizations are already implicit in the model and handled by the model checker without requiring any extension. Another main difference with Kuai is that they make two important simplifications to the kind of SDNs they can handle: (i) they assume a simplified model of switches in which a switch gets suspended (i.e., does not process further packets nor controller messages) while awaiting a controller request. The error showed in Example 1 would thus not be captured. We do not make any simplification and thus a switch can start to process a new packet while awaiting the controller and can also receive other controller actions (triggered by other switches). (ii) It works on a class of SDNs in which the size of the controller queue is one. Therefore, it will not capture potential errors that arise due to the reordering of messages by the controller. In contrast, our model checker works on the general model of SDN networks.

5   Checking SDN Properties in Case Studies

We have built the extension for property checking on top of SYCO [4], a system that implements context-sensitive DPOR exploration. To evaluate our approach, we have implemented a series of standard SDN benchmarks used in previous work [6,12,18]. In order to check property P we add to the controller a new method called error_message and encode P as a Boolean function F_p using the programming language itself. Then, in all places where the property has to hold, we add an if statement checking the negation of F_p and if it holds we call asynchronously to error_message on the controller. Then property holds for the given input if and only if there is no trace in the execution tree including a call to error_message.

Our goal is on the one hand to show the versatility of our approach to check properties that are handled using different approaches in the literature (e.g., programming errors in the controller as in [6], safety policy violations as in [6,18], or loop detection as in [12]). And, on the other hand, to show that we are able to handle networks at least as large as (and sometimes larger than) in related systems [18], but without requiring simplifications to the SDN models, nor extensions for DPOR reduction, and in spite of using a non-distributed model checker. We should note that a precise comparison of figures is not possible due to the differences described in Sect. 4.3 and the use of different implementations of controllers. Our system can be used online at http://costa.ls.fi.upm.es/syco using the POR algorithm CDPOR and disabling the automatic generation of independence constraints. The benchmarks can be found in the folder FM18.

Table 1 shows a summary of the experimental results. Times are obtained on an Intel Core i7 at 3.4 Ghz with 8 GB of RAM (Linux Kernel 3.2). For each benchmark, we show in the second column the number of switches, hosts and packets, **Execs** corresponds to the number of different executions (i.e., branches in the search tree), **States** to the number of nodes in the search tree, and **Time** is the time taken by the analysis in ms. Although entry-level independence can be proved automatically, this is not yet implemented in SYCO and we have used annotations to declare it. As an example, in method switchHandleMsg, the annotation: [indep(switchHandlePacket(pin,pkt),!matchHeaderAndPort(getHeader(pkt),pin,m))] states that tasks executing switchHandleMessage(m,a) are independent of those executing switchHandlePacket(pin,pkt) if the match field of the message does not match the header and the input port of the packet (the condition is checked by the auxiliary function matchHeaderAndPort).

Table 1. Experimental evaluation

Name	Switch x Host x Packet	Execs	States	Time
LB	3x3x1/3x4x2	8/92	64/761	15/263
LBB	3x4x2/3x7x5/3x10x8/3x12x10	3/21/171/683	48/482/3996/16028	13/212/3542/22941
SSHE	2x2x(1ssh/1oth/2each/2cor)	9/21/2648/1201	56/135/24116/9406	14/37/12308/3276
SSHB	2x2x/2x2x3	27/2013	318/23643	119/13261
MI	1x5x(8/10/11)	122/753/1506	2710/17613/35870	1003/11800/34894
MIB	1x5x(8/10/11)	138/831/1653	3215/20640/41512	1668/18591/53349
LE	3x3x(2/5)/6x3x2	10/46/40	178/1269/1239	59/467/649
	6x3x5/9x2x2	132/944	5765/12339	3798/12230

Controller with Load Balancer [12] (LB/LBB). This corresponds to the controller of [12], similar to our running example. It performs stateless load balancing among a set of replica identified by a virtual IP (VIP) address. When receiving packets destined to a VIP, the controller selects a particular host and installs flow rules along the entire path. For a buggy controller without barriers (LB) and a network with 3 switches and 3 hosts, we detect that there is a forwarding loop (i.e., that a packet reaches a switch more than once) in 15 ms. For this, we have added to the switches a field to store the packet identifiers that they have already received, and when the same packet reaches it, it sends an error message, which is observable from the final state. When we add a second packet with the same header and another host, as expected, the number of dependencies increases and, many reorderings need to be tried, leading to 92 different executions and 761 states. Once we check the correct version with barriers (LBB), we are able to scale up to 12 hosts and 10 packets. As it can be observed, for the largest network, 16028 states are explored and in all cases we verify that the traffic is balanced. The experiments in [12] do not specify the time to detect the bug for this controller (they only mentioned that their analysis finishes in less than 32s in the vast majority of cases). Nevertheless, the underlying techniques to find the bugs are unrelated (see Sect. 6), and thus time comparison is not meaningful.

SSH Controller [18] (SSHE/SSHB). This is based on a controller that dynamically modifies the behaviors of the switches as follows: it can update the switches with a rule that states that no SSH packets are forwarded, and another that states that all non-SSH packets are forwarded. We have two versions of the SSH controller. In the row SSHE, the first three evaluations correspond to an erroneous SSH controller that installs the rule to forward packets and the rule to drop SSH packets with the same priority, and thus the safety policy can be violated. As in [18], we evaluate a network with 2 switches and 2 hosts. As for packets, we write 1ssh, 1other, and 2each to indicate that we send one SSH packet, one non-SSH packet and one of each type. We detect the error by checking in the switch if two contradictory drop and forward packet actions are received for the same entry. The results that we obtain for 1 packet are in the same order of magnitude as [18]: they produce 13 executions, while we produce 9 or 21, depending on the type of packet. Analysis times are also similar: 0.1 s in their case versus 0.014 s or 0.037 s in our case. This is as expected because there is almost no redundancy using plain DPOR, thus no need for our entry-independence or context-sensitiveness. When we add more packets, the number of dependencies grows exponentially. This is because the controller receives 2 requests from the 2 messages, and sends dependent control messages to all switches. Therefore, all reorderings must be tried and the state explosion is huge. The last evaluation 2cor corresponds to the correct SSH controller for which we achieve a notable improvement as we have now less tasks that match the same entry (as priority is different). The row SSHB is a correct implementation with barriers that reduces the number of executions for 2 packets notably because it guarantees that forward rules are installed and thus switches will not send further requests.

Firewall with Migration [6] **(MI/MIB).** MI is the implementation of a firewall that supports migration of trusted hosts. A host is trusted if it either sent/received (on some switch) a message through/from port 1. Thus, when a trusted host migrates to a new switch, the controller will remember it was trusted before and will allow communication from either port. For the same network 1×5 as [6], we can scale the number of packets up to 11 packets that actually modify the data base for trusted hosts. We can keep on adding more packets if those do not affect the shared data base. In MIB, we introduce the same bug in the controller as [6], which forgets to check if trusted on events from port 2. We detect the error by checking in the final state of the derivations that a packet arrives to a host that is not in the trusted data base. The scalability of MI and MIB are rather similar. Both [6] and us find the bug in a negligible time.

Network Authentication with Learning [6,18] **(LE).** This implements a composition of a learning switch with authentication in [6]. Also, [18] evaluates a MAC learning controller but using a different implementation. LE implements a controller with barriers for which we can verify that the packet flows satisfy the intended policy and that the flow tables are consistent. We have considered configurations of 3×3, 6×3 and 9×2. When compared to [18], we handle similar sizes for networks but we explore less **States** in less **Time**. We note that this might be due to different implementations of the controller and the differences pointed out in Sect. 4.3.

6 Conclusions and Related Work

We have proposed an actor-based framework to model and verify SDN programs. A unique feature of our approach is that we can use existing advanced verification algorithms without requiring any specific extension to handle SDN features. The last years have witnessed the development of many static and dynamic techniques for verification that are closely related to our approach. Using static approaches, one has the main advantage that, when the property can be proved, it is ensured for any possible execution, while using dynamic analysis only guarantees the property for the considered inputs. As a counterpart, in order to cover all possible behaviors, static analysis needs to perform abstraction, that can give a don't-know answer, and, possibly, false positives. In [6], the work on Horn-based verification is lifted to the SDN programming paradigm, but excluding barriers. Using this kind of verification, one can prove safety invariants on the program. Using our framework, we can furthermore check liveness invariants (e.g., loop detection) by inspecting the traces computed by the model checker. In [20], a particular type of attacks in the context of SDN networks has been modeled in Maude using the so-called hierachically structured composite actor systems described in [11]. This work does not provide a general model for SDN networks and, besides, barriers are not considered. On the other hand, it applies a statistical model checker, which requires to have a given scheduler for the messages. Such scheduler determines the exact order in which messages are handled while our framework captures all possible behaviours. Hence, both their aim and their SDN model are radically different from ours. As regards dynamic techniques, our work is mostly related to the model checkers NICE and Kuai for SDN programs, which have been compared in detail in Sect. 4.3. Our approach could be adapted to apply abstractions that bound the size of buffers [18] and to consider environment messages [22]. The approach of [12,15] is fundamentally different from ours because it is based on analyzing dynamically given snapshots of the network from real executions. Instead, our approach tries to find programming errors by inspecting only the SDN program and considering all possible execution traces, thus enabling verification at system design time.

References

1. The ABS tool suite. http://abs-models.org
2. Agha, G.: Actors: A Model of Concurrent Computation in Distributed Systems. MIT Press, Cambridge (1986)
3. Albert, E., Arenas, P., de la Banda, M.G., Gómez-Zamalloa, M., Stuckey, P.J.: Context-sensitive dynamic partial order reduction. In: Majumdar, R., Kunčak, V. (eds.) CAV 2017. LNCS, vol. 10426, pp. 526–543. Springer, Cham (2017). https://doi.org/10.1007/978-3-319-63387-9_26
4. Albert, E., Gómez-Zamalloa, M., Isabel, M.: SYCO: a systematic testing tool for concurrent objects. In: CC, pp. 269–270 (2016)
5. Albert, E., Gómez-Zamalloa, M., Rubio, A., Sammartino, M., Silva, A.: SDN-Actors: Modeling and Verification of SDN Programs. Technical report (2018). http://costa.ls.fi.upm.es/papers/costa/AlbertGRSS18TR.pdf
6. Ball, T., Bjørner, N., Gember, A., Itzhaky, S., Karbyshev, A., Sagiv, M., Schapira, M., Valadarsky, A.: VeriCon: towards verifying controller programs in software-defined networks. In: PLDI, pp. 282–293 (2014)
7. Bouajjani, A., Emmi, M., Enea, C., Hamza, J.: Tractable refinement checking for concurrent objects. In: POPL, pp. 651–662 (2015)

8. Canini, M., Venzano, D., Peresíni, P., Kostic, D., Rexford, J.: A NICE way to test OpenFlow applications. In: NSDI, pp. 127–140 (2012)
9. Christakis, M., Gotovos, A., Sagonas, K.F.: Systematic testing for detecting concurrency errors in Erlang programs. In: ICST, pp. 154–163 (2013)
10. de Boer, F.S., Clarke, D., Johnsen, E.B.: A complete guide to the future. In: De Nicola, R. (ed.) ESOP 2007. LNCS, vol. 4421, pp. 316–330. Springer, Heidelberg (2007). https://doi.org/10.1007/978-3-540-71316-6_22
11. Eckhardt, J., Mühlbauer, T., Meseguer, J., Wirsing, M.: Statistical model checking for composite actor systems. In: Martí-Oliet, N., Palomino, M. (eds.) WADT 2012. LNCS, vol. 7841, pp. 143–160. Springer, Heidelberg (2013). https://doi.org/10.1007/978-3-642-37635-1_9
12. El-Hassany, A., Miserez, J., Bielik, P., Vanbever, L., Vechev, M.T.: SDNRacer: concurrency analysis for software-defined networks. In: POPL, pp. 402–415 (2016)
13. Flanagan, C., Godefroid, P.: Dynamic partial-order reduction for model checking software. In: POPL, pp. 110–121 (2005)
14. Johnsen, E.B., Hähnle, R., Schäfer, J., Schlatte, R., Steffen, M.: ABS: a core language for abstract behavioral specification. In: Aichernig, B.K., de Boer, F.S., Bonsangue, M.M. (eds.) FMCO 2010. LNCS, vol. 6957, pp. 142–164. Springer, Heidelberg (2011). https://doi.org/10.1007/978-3-642-25271-6_8
15. Kazemian, P., Varghese, G., McKeown, N.: Header space analysis: static checking for networks. In: NSDI, pp. 113–126 (2012)
16. Lauterburg, S., Karmani, R.K., Marinov, D., Agha, G.: Basset: a tool for systematic testing of actor programs. In: SIGSOFT FSE, pp. 363–364 (2010)
17. Liang, H., Feng, X.: A program logic for concurrent objects under fair scheduling. In: POPL, pp. 385–399 (2016)
18. Majumdar, R., Tetali, S.D., Wang, Z.: Kuai: a model checker for software-defined networks. In: FMCAD, pp. 163–170 (2014)
19. Openflow switch specification, October 2013. Version 1.4.0. http://www.opennetworking.org/software-defined-standards/specifications
20. Pascoal, T.A., Dantas, Y.G., Fonseca, I.E., Nigam, V.: Slow TCAM exhaustion DDoS attack. In: De Capitani di Vimercati, S., Martinelli, F. (eds.) SEC 2017. IAICT, vol. 502, pp. 17–31. Springer, Cham (2017). https://doi.org/10.1007/978-3-319-58469-0_2
21. Sen, K., Agha, G.: Automated systematic testing of open distributed programs. In: Baresi, L., Heckel, R. (eds.) FASE 2006. LNCS, vol. 3922, pp. 339–356. Springer, Heidelberg (2006). https://doi.org/10.1007/11693017_25
22. Sethi, D., Narayana, S., Malik, S.: Abstractions for model checking SDN controllers. In: FMCAD, pp. 145–148 (2013)
23. Tasharofi, S., et al.: TransDPOR: a novel dynamic partial-order reduction technique for testing actor programs. In: Giese, H., Rosu, G. (eds.) FMOODS/FORTE-2012. LNCS, vol. 7273, pp. 219–234. Springer, Heidelberg (2012). https://doi.org/10.1007/978-3-642-30793-5_14

CompoSAT: Specification-Guided Coverage for Model Finding

Sorawee Porncharoenwase$^{(\boxtimes)}$, Tim Nelson, and Shriram Krishnamurthi

Brown University, Providence, USA
tn@cs.brown.edu

Abstract. Model-finding tools like the Alloy Analyzer produce concrete examples of how a declarative specification can be satisfied. These formal tools are useful in a wide range of domains: software design, security, networking, and more. By producing concrete examples, they assist in exploring system behavior and can help find surprising faults.

Specifications usually have many potential candidate solutions, but model-finders tend to leave the choice of which examples to present entirely to the underlying solver. This paper closes that gap by exploring notions of coverage for the model-finding domain, yielding a novel, rigorous metric for output quality. These ideas are realized in the tool CompoSAT, which interposes itself between Alloy's constraint-solving and presentation stages to produce ensembles of examples that maximize coverage.

We show that high-coverage ensembles like CompoSAT produces are useful for, among other things, detecting overconstraint—a particularly insidious form of specification error. We detail the underlying theory and implementation of CompoSAT and evaluate it on numerous specifications.

1 Introduction

Model-finding tools, like the popular Alloy Analyzer [1], find concrete examples of how a set of declarative constraints can be satisfied. These tools have found application in a wide range of domains because of their power and generality. Specifying a network configuration may yield examples of packets traversing a firewall [2]. A UML class diagram may yield corresponding object diagrams [3,4]. Other applications abound in security [5,6], protocol design [7], network switch programming [8,9] and more. Output models can either act as counterexamples to expected properties or more generally improve intuition and aid understanding of a system. However, specifications define a (frequently large) *set* of models, each of which is useful to differing degrees (e.g., some showing a bug, some not). The choice of *which models to present* and in *what order* is usually left entirely to the underlying solvers, which are performance-focused and unconcerned with the quality of each model found.

Some have proposed more rigorous notions of model quality. For instance, *minimal* models [10–12] discard extraneous information that may clutter the

K. Havelund et al. (Eds.): FM 2018, LNCS 10951, pp. 568–587, 2018.
https://doi.org/10.1007/978-3-319-95582-7_34

model and hamper comprehension. Although it is appealing in broad strokes, minimality falls short when it comes to showing what is merely possible or contingent—negating one of the chief strengths of model finding. Indeed, recent studies [13] suggest that purely-minimal output does not suffice. Most current model-quality notions are also defined only in terms of the content of the models themselves—i.e., they are purely *semantic*—rather than what models can reveal about the specification, making them ill-suited to debugging.

In this work, we break with this trend to explore *syntax-guided* notions of which models are best. For any specification, we extract a maximally representative *ensemble* (i.e., set) of models from the considerably larger stream provided by the solver. To do so, we draw inspiration from test-suite coverage [14] but, as we will show, doing so is subtle in this domain. One complication lies in the fact that, with traditional coverage, code and tests are in principle written independently. In contrast, the solver generates models directly from the specification. Thus, using the specification to dictate whether a model is "good" may appear circular. However, the essence of our work consists in filtering the generation process itself. We detect how a specification constrains portions of a model in context, effectively showing the "weight" of individual constraints in the specification. Where the default enumeration may produce bad coverage, ours does far better—with relatively few models. We demonstrate this in Sect. 2.

Our theory and algorithms are realized in CompoSAT, a new extension to the Alloy Analyzer ecosystem. CompoSAT directs users to high-coverage models that exercise contingencies in the specification, rather than ignoring contingent behavior (like a minimal model-finder) or potentially concealing them in a stream of mediocrity (like Alloy's default enumeration). Similarly to classical coverage, this approach can also reveal when portions of the specification are never exercised by any output model. Finally, as we will show, coverage is particularly suited to detecting overconstraint bugs, which the online Alloy tutorial [15] goes so far as to call the "bane of declarative modeling".

2 Motivation and Example

We first show a small running example: an address book for email contacts. (Sect. 8 examines more substantial, real-world specifications.) This example is similar to others in Jackson [1, Chap. 2] but, for brevity, is less complete.

```
1   abstract sig Target {}
2   abstract sig Name extends Target {}
3   sig Alias , Group extends Name {}
4   sig Addr extends Target {}
5   one sig Book {
6     entries: Name -> Target
7   } {
8     all n: Name | n not in n.^entries  -- No cycles
9     all a: Name | some a.entries  -- Names denote
10  }
11  run {}
```

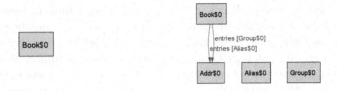

Fig. 1. The two-model ensemble produced for the specification of Sect. 2.

Lines 1–4 declare types (called `sigs` in Alloy). The **abstract** keyword says that a type is equal to the union of its subtypes. `Addrs` are meant to denote actual email addresses; `Names` denote `Aliases` or `Groups` that address books will translate. At this stage, only one `Book` (lines 5–10) is allowed in each model. Books have an **entries** field—a relation between `Names` and `Targets`. Line 8 says that no `Name` atom is self-reachable via **entries** (^ denotes transitive closure and -> means product). Line 9 says that the book contains entries for all `Names`.

The final line tells Alloy to run the specification and produce models up to the default size bound: 3 of each top-level **sig**. At this bound, Alloy produces 21 non-isomorphic models—daunting to page through, even at this small scale. On the other hand, a *minimal* model finder would produce only one: the leftmost model in Fig. 1, which contains nothing but an empty `Book`. This is because no constraint forces `Names` to exist, in spite of the fact that lines 9 and 10 apply if any do. Neither solution is ideal: one risks overloading the user with a huge example set, but the other hides important insight into how constraints behave.

CompoSAT stakes out a position between these two extreme approaches. The high-coverage ensemble it generates contains *two* models (both shown in Fig. 1). These are not chosen arbitrarily: they together demonstrate—in a way we will make precise in the next sections—*all possible ways* the constraints force truth or falsity in models of the specification.

3   Adapting Coverage to Model Finding

Coverage for *software* [14] measures test-suite quality in terms of the statements or branches of the program it exercises. Obtaining a similar definition for model finding is subtle. We might start by defining the coverage of a model analogously to *line coverage* in software by saying that a top-level constraint (e.g., line 8 in Sect. 2) is covered by a model if it is true in that model. But this is unhelpful since *all* models found must make every such constraint true!

The difficulty is that, even if a constraint is true in a model, it does not *directly determine* the contents of that model in the same way that executing a program statement determines that program's behavior. We would nevertheless like to capture an analogous intuition. Our solution has two components.

First, we focus on the non-determinism in constraints that comes from disjunction, implication, existential quantifiers, etc. Each disjunctive choice is analogous to a branch-point in a program, so we might imagine defining a coverage metric that captures the different ways that models satisfy constraints. Unfortunately, this approach is computationally infeasible: if a specification has 100 possible branches—a modest number compared to many—there are up to $2^{100}-1$ paths to cover, and in the worst case just as many models to present! Moreover, the fact that a constraint was satisfied does not imply that it actually had *impact in the model*. For instance, consider the constraint-set (A or B) and (A and B). The first conjunct is satisfied in the model { A, B } but without the second conjunct, either literal could be consistently negated.

We therefore restrict our attention to branches that force what we call *local necessity* in the model (we make this precise in Sect. 4). Informally, a portion of a model is locally necessary if altering it would violate the specification in context of the rest of the model. For instance, in the right model of Fig. 1, the address-book entries are locally necessary because (1) a constraint said every Name must have an entry and (2) there were no other entries for that Name already present. CompoSAT takes the view that a model is "good" to the extent that it provides new demonstrations of local necessity.

Note that a granularity of top level constraints (rather than branches) is too broad for even the simple example in Sect. 2. CompoSAT must be able to distinguish different ways that constraints apply—some, but not all, of which may be unexpected or otherwise useful to show. Because branches often involve expansion and instantiation of high-level constraints, *we cannot define coverage only in terms of source locations* and must instead work with logical formulas.

4   Foundations

Formally, Alloy specifications are theories of relational logic with transitive closure. Their syntax includes the usual Boolean connectives (conjunction, negation, etc.) along with first-order quantification (all, some) and relational operators (product, join, transpose, transitive closure, etc.). Readers interested in the full grammar of Alloy are encouraged to peruse Jackson [1] or the Alloy documentation [16].

Given a specification $\mathcal{T}$, its *satisfying models*, denoted $Mod(\mathcal{T})$, are the set of finite first-order models[1] M that satisfy it, i.e., in which it evaluates to true. Truth in a model is defined in the usual, recursive manner [18], e.g. the constraint $\alpha \wedge \beta$ is true in model M if and only if both α and β are true in M.

4.1   Bounded Model Finding

These definitions mean that the model-finding is just the (finite) satisfiability problem for first-order logic with transitive closure. Unfortunately, this is well-known to be undecidable [19] in general. In order to render satisfiability checking feasible, Alloy performs *bounded* model-finding. In addition to a specification and

---

[1] We use the term *model* in its mathematical sense: a relational structure over a set. We follow Milicevic [17] and others in referring to the constraint-set as the *specification*.

the name of a predicate to run (essentially just an additional constraint in the specification), users must provide an explicit bound B be given on all top-level sigs to check up to. Once given these numeric bounds, Alloy creates concrete atoms (like `Alias$1, Book$0`, etc.) that populate the potential universe of models within the bounds given. This yields a finite search space.

We will implicitly enrich the language with a distinct constant for every element in the generated bounds and abuse notation somewhat to write formulas involving these constants, e.g., "`Alias$1 -> Addr$2 in entries`". When a formula only expresses whether a product of atoms is in some `sig` or field name, we will refer to it as *atomic*. A *literal* is either an atomic formula or its negation. The vital intuition here is that each atomic formula is essentially bound to a Boolean variable in each model, since under a bound every specification is a propositional theory—which is what enables Alloy's use of SAT-solving technology. Finally, the *diagram* of a model $\mathbb{M}$, which we denote as $\Delta(\mathbb{M})$, is the set of literals true in $\mathbb{M}$.

4.2   Local Necessity and Provenance

Our goal is to identify when constraints have direct impact upon model contents. To make this intuition precise, we need to define what it means to have "impact". We introduce the following helpful definitions from prior work [20].

Definition 1 (L-alternate model). *Let T be a specification and $\mathbb{M}$ a model satisfying it. Let L be a literal true in $\mathbb{M}$. The L-alternate of $\mathbb{M}$, $\mathbb{M}^L$, is the model with the same universe as $\mathbb{M}$ but with $\Delta(\mathbb{M}^L) = (\Delta(\mathbb{M}) \setminus \{L\}) \cup \{\neg L\}$.*

Definition 2 (Local Necessity.) *L is said to be* locally necessary *for T in $\mathbb{M}$ if and if only if $\mathbb{M}$ makes T true but $\mathbb{M}^L$ does not.*

That is, a literal is locally necessary if changing its value from positive to negative (or vice versa) would necessitate other changes in the model. This means that whenever a literal is locally necessary, some constraint forces it to hold in the context of the larger model. Local necessity is far weaker than entailment: T may have models whose diagram contains L's negation, but L cannot be consistently changed *in this particular model* without other concurrent changes.

Constraints may act to force L in different ways. We make this precise by defining *provenances* as particular conditions that satisfy constraint branches and cause L to be locally necessary:

Definition 3 (Provenance). *A provenance for L in $\mathbb{M}$ with respect to T is a set of sentences $\alpha_1, ..., \alpha_n$ where each α_i is true in both $\mathbb{M}$ and $\mathbb{M}^L$ such that $T \wedge \alpha_1 \wedge ... \wedge \alpha_n$ entails L under the user-provided bounds B.*

For instance, the constraint on line 9 of Sect. 2's example, under the rightmost model in Fig. 1, induces the provenance { `Group$0 in Name` } for the local necessity of the book entry `Group$0->Addr$0`—because the element `Group$0` is a valid instantiation of the quantifier.

$$\mathbb{E}_+(\beta \vee \gamma) = \begin{cases} \mathbb{E}_+(\beta) \vee \mathbb{E}_+(\gamma) & \text{if } M \models \beta \text{ and } M \models \gamma \\ \mathbb{E}_+(\beta) & \text{if } M \models \beta \text{ and } M \not\models \gamma \\ \mathbb{E}_+(\gamma) & \text{if } M \not\models \beta \text{ and } M \models \gamma \end{cases}$$

$$\mathbb{E}_+(\beta \wedge \gamma) = \mathbb{E}_+(\beta) \wedge \mathbb{E}_+(\gamma)$$

$$\mathbb{E}_+(\neg\beta) = \neg\mathbb{E}_-(\beta)$$

$$\mathbb{E}_+(L) = L \text{ where } L \text{ is a literal}$$

Fig. 2. Expansion function $\mathbb{E}_+$ for expanding provenance formulas in a positive context. For brevity, we omit the symmetric negative-context $\mathbb{E}_-$, as well as cases for routine syntactic sugar like bi-implication. Quantifiers are eliminated by instantiation up to the (always finite) pertinent upper bound.

We restrict our attention to provenances that are partial instantiations and expansions of original constraints. Although in principle we could consider provinances that are fully expanded into conjunctions of literals, this would result in a plethora of provenances, many of which would imply each other modulo $\mathcal{T}$.

5   Algorithmics of Coverage

We might stop with the definitions in Sect. 4 and define the provenance-coverage of a model M, denoted *Provs*(M), to be the set of provenances that it induces across all literals. However, this definition proves to be unsatisfying. We discuss and address three improvements that make it more practicable.

5.1   Expansion

Consider the constraint all a: Name | some a.entries in Sect. 2's example, along with the rightmost model in Fig. 1. Why is it locally necessary that the Book's entries contain the tuple Alias$0 -> Addr$0? Because: **(1)** Alias$0 is a Name and thus the variable a can be bound to it, and **(2)** there are no other extant entries for Alias$0. Without some means of telling the two cases apart, the provenance for the Group$0 entry is identical. That is, a model with (say) only Groups would cover the constraint applying to an Alias.

To account for this and other (possibly nested) disjunction[2] in provenance formulas, we expand each formula to reflect which disjunctive branches satisfy it in M. In the above example, then, the first formula becomes either Alias$0 in Alias or Group$0 in Group, depending on context. This difference reflects the different insight these two provenances bring. Figure 2 gives the expansion function $\mathbb{E}_+$, which maps formulas to expanded formulas, in more detail. The input formula must be an α from some provenance (and thus true in both M and $M^{\mathbb{L}}$). The output formula is fully desugared and instantiated, in that it will only contain the operators $\wedge$, $\vee$, $\neg$, and literals.

---

[2] The original constraint is equivalent to all a: Alias+Group | some a.entries.

5.2   Canonicalization

While expansion makes provenance-coverage more fine-grained, there are cases in which we need to do the opposite and gloss over differences. For instance, two models that are identical except for atom names will have differing provenance sets, yet their provenances give the same information. To eliminate this and other similar issues caused by atom names, we *canonicalize* provenances (post-expansion) to eliminate variation in atom name. This amounts to simple substitution: replacing atom names and integer constants with canonical representatives. A provenance that has undergone both expansion and canonicalization is called a *provenance skeleton*.

5.3   Coverage and Subsumption

The *provenance coverage* of a model $\mathbb{M}$, $Provs(\mathbb{M})$, is a set of provenance skeletons:

$$\{p \mid p \text{ is a provenance skeleton for some literal } L \text{ in } \mathbb{M} \text{ with respect to } \mathcal{T}\}$$

We lift this to a *set E* of models: $Provs(E) \triangleq \bigcup_{\mathbb{M} \in E} Provs(\mathbb{M})$. It is now reasonable to speak of one set (i.e., ensemble) of models providing more provenance information than another. Naturally, $Mod(\mathcal{T})$ has the largest provenance coverage for $\mathcal{T}$. As user time and attention is precious, the ideal goal is thus to find a *minimal* set of models E with the same coverage.

While attempting to cover a set of skeletons, we observe that some contain strictly more information than others. By not attempting to cover superfluous skeletons, we can reduce the runtime and memory requirements of coverage computation (Sect. 6), and even the eventual ensemble size.

Consider the (propositional) constraint (q or r) implies s and three models that satisfy it: $\mathbb{M}_1$, $\mathbb{M}_2$, and $\mathbb{M}_3$ with diagrams $\Delta(\mathbb{M}_1) = \{q, \neg r, s\}$, $\Delta(\mathbb{M}_2) = \{\neg q, r, s\}$, and $\Delta(\mathbb{M}_3) = \{q, r, s\}$. The literal s is locally necessary in all three. Let p_1, p_2, p_3 be provenance skeletons for s from $\mathbb{M}_1$, $\mathbb{M}_2$, and $\mathbb{M}_3$ respectively. In explaining why s holds, p_3 gives q and r as a reason, while p_1 and p_2 give either q or r but not both. Because p_3 blames a strict superset of branches that p_1 and p_2 do, we say that p_3 *subsumes* p_1 and p_2. Formally, the provenance subsumption relation $\leq$ is a preorder on provenance skeletons. Given two provenance skeletons for the same literal $P_1 = \{\alpha_1, ..., \alpha_n\}$ and $P_2 = \{\beta_1, ..., \beta_m\}$, $P_1 \leq P_2$ iff $\forall \alpha_i, \exists \beta_j, \alpha_i \leq \beta_j$, where the subsumption relation on subformulas is

$$L_1 \leq L_2 \triangleq L_1 = L_2 \text{ for literals } L_1, L_2$$

$$\bigvee_i^n A_i \leq \bigvee_j^m B_j \triangleq \forall A_i, \exists B_j, A_i \leq B_j$$

$$\neg A \leq \neg B \triangleq A \leq B$$

Fig. 3. Subformula subsumption relation $\leq$. (The conjunction case is defined similarly.)

given in Fig. 3. If $p_i \leq p_j$ and $p_j \not\leq p_i$, then p_i strictly contains information less than p_j, so we can safely remove p_i from consideration.

6   Implementation

CompoSAT is implemented as an extension to Alloy, leveraging our Amalgam [20] provenance-generation toolkit. High-coverage ensembles are enabled via menu options. We made this design choice so that users can seamlessly transition from default Alloy to CompoSAT and back again without disruption—or even exiting the tool. CompoSAT supports the same rich subset of Alloy that Amalgam does, namely relational and boolean operators, transitive closure, set cardinality and numeric inequalities without arithmetic.

Given a (user-defined) time budget, the tool first enumerates as many models as possible, behind the scenes, via the underlying solver. As each model arrives, CompoSAT generates all provenances via Amalgam, then performs expansion and canonicalization to produce a skeleton set for each model. A subsumption check then removes extraneous skeletons. Once the time limit or the supply of models has expired, CompoSAT solves the set-cover problem to produce the optimal ensemble. We use the Z3 [21] solver for this purpose.

In principle, a specification may have far more models than can feasibly be enumerated. In such cases, CompoSAT reports that its enumeration was incomplete: enumeration has produced only a subset of $Mod(\mathcal{T})$. Thus, the provenances obtained form a subset of $Provs(Mod(\mathcal{T}))$. However, even when the provenances obtained are a *strict* subset of $Provs(Mod(\mathcal{T}))$, our evaluation (Sect. 8) shows that the tool still often produces an ensemble that is demonstrably better than what Alloy's enumeration would provide, skipping over dozens or hundreds of models that give no new provenance information. Moreover, as we will discuss in Sect. 7, even an incomplete high-coverage enumeration can be useful in revealing errors and giving modelers new insight.

7   Qualitative Use Case: Overconstraint

We now discuss two key qualitative advantages of high-coverage ensembles. Both are related to a class of specification bug called overconstraint. A specification is said to be *under*constrained if it is satisfied by unintended models and *over*constrained if some intended models do not satisfy it. One of the advantages of model finding is that underconstraint can be discovered by simply viewing surprising models. Overconstraint, however, is more challenging: *missing* models cannot be discovered without iterating through all of them and then remembering what was never seen. For specifications with many models, this is impractical.

Both of these issues are easy to accidentally introduce when refining constraints. To mitigate this risk, experienced Alloy users often run testing predicates that characterize models that should or should not satisfy the specification. Surprising results then indicate over- and underconstraint respectively. But this technique requires anticipating potential problems in advance; unexpected bugs and failures of intuition can still occur. Moreover, one of the strengths of Alloy is that it facilitates both in-depth, detailed analysis and lightweight experimentation. In the latter case, codifying detailed expectations can be premature.

7.1 Detecting Overconstraint via Local Necessity

Overconstraint can often appear as unexpected local necessity. In such cases, showing the user which portions of their models are locally necessary can lead to surprise and insight. For example, suppose that the constraint on line 9 in Sect. 2 overconstrains: it was meant to say that the book must contain an entry for all Aliases, but empty Groups should be permitted. Unfortunately, the user has committed a common error and quantified over a too-general type: Name. Alloy will never produce an unexpected model due to this error, but it will neglect models that the author expected to see—those with empty Groups.

Showing the rightmost model in Fig. 1 along with the information that Group$0's entry is forced by the constraint on line 9 points immediately to the issue and suggests possible sites to implement a fix. Amalgam, which CompoSAT invokes for provenance generation, does exactly this. However, Amalgam's feedback is per-model, and so this useful information will *never appear* if suspect models come late. (We have observed empirically that most users rarely view more than the first few models *unless they have reason to believe they have made an error.* This is especially true for more complex specifications where models may require time and effort to understand.)

In this case, the first suspect model Alloy, and therefore Amalgam, produces is the sixth—i.e., the user must click "Next" five times to have any chance of discovering the bug, even with local-necessity highlighting.[3] But as mentioned in Sect. 2, CompoSAT produces an ensemble of only *two* models, one of which contains the suspect necessity. Coverage thus enables far superior model enumeration in this context.

7.2 Highlighting Uncovered Constraints

High-coverage ensembles have power even without displaying local necessity. If a constraint can never contribute to a provenance, it may indicate either that the uncovered constraint is too weak or that some other constraint overshadows it. Space limitations preclude a full example, but consider again the propositional constraint-set (A or B) and (A and B). The first conjunct can never contribute to a provenance since the second conjunct only admits the model { A, B }. This benefit is similar to that observed by Torlak [23], except that we consider highlighting induced by constraint coverage rather than unsatisfiable cores.

---

[3] Model-ordering is dependent on solver engine and other settings. Here, we use Minisat [22] with unsatisfiable cores and symmetry-breaking enabled.

8   Evaluation

We evaluate CompoSAT with a variety of metrics in order to answer 3 research questions. Namely: **(RQ1)** Can a relatively small ensemble of models cover a large quantity of total provenances? **(RQ2)** Can model enumeration reasonably be used to discover the provenances of a specification? **(RQ3)** How much coverage does enumerating only *minimal* models achieve? Together, these questions evaluate the practicality of high-coverage ensembles as well as comparing them against the two extremes discussed in Sect. 2: *all* models and *minimal* models.

8.1   Experimental Setup

We evaluate on a wide variety of specifications that exercise different Alloy operations and represent multiple domains. When examples came with only unsatisfiable commands (e.g., properties without counterexamples) we added a command `run {}` to enumerate all models to the default bound.

Paper is the example from Sect. 2. From the Amalgam suite, we include colored, undirected trees (**ctrees**), directed graph (**digraph**), directed tree (**dtree**, **dtbug**), a logic puzzle (**abc**), trees without a vertex of degree 2 (**gwh**), and two labs from an Alloy course: transitive closure and garbage collection (**tclab** and **gclab**). Bad employee (**bempl**), grade book (**grade**), and other groups (**other**) originally come from Saghafi, et al. [11]. Address book (**addr**), geneology (**gene**) and own-grandpa (**grand**) come from the basic examples in the Alloy distribution. Hotel-locking (**hl4**), ring election (**elect**), media asset management (**media**), and memory (**simplem, fixedm, cachem**) come from the longer case-studies in Jackson [1]. Flowlog [9] (**flow**) specifies a program written in Flowlog, a software-defined network programming language. Model finding reveals a bug in the program. Our UML diagram specifications (**uml1, uml2**) come from Maoz, et al. [3], and the semantic differences between those diagrams (**cddiff1, cddiff2**) likewise come from Maoz, et al.'s CDDiff [4].

Various tools perform automatic compilation to Alloy from other input languages—the UML, Semantic Differences, and Flowlog specifications were all machine generated in this way. Since specification errors can be introduced by these compilers, improved model output benefits not only end-users but also compiler authors, who must have high confidence in their translation.

All experiments were performed on a Xeon E3-1240 v5 CPU at 3.50 GHz running Debian 9.1. No experiment but **media** consumed more than 4 GB of memory; for uniformity, we terminated **media** when recording its many large provenances exceeded 4 GB. Figure 4 summarizes the results.

8.2   RQ1: Do Small Ensembles Suffice?

For each experiment, column 5 (*Ensm size*) shows the ensemble sizes needed to achieve 50%, 70%, 90%, and 100% coverage discovered of provenance skeletons. To compute these, we enumerate models and find the optimal 100% ensemble as specified in Sect. 6. We then order each model in the ensemble by number of

Spec	Command and Max bound	# skels.	All?	Time (s) [# mdls] to get 50%	70%	90%	100%	Ensm size 50%	70%	90%	100%	Total enum	Total time (s)	# mdls	Minimal skels	[missed]
paper	{} 3	5		<1 [4]	<1 [4]	<1 [4]	<1 [6]	1	1	1	2	21	<1	1	1	4
ctrees	{} 3	17		<1 [2]	<1 [4]	<1 [4]	<1 [5]	1	2	2	2	12	<1	1	3	14
ctreesb	{} 3	16		<1 [1]	<1 [6]	<1 [6]	<1 [6]	1	2	2	2	14	<1	1	3	13
digraph	test 4	5		<1 [1]	<1 [1]	<1 [5]	<1 [5]	1	1	1	2	6343	19	1	3	2
dtree	partialTree 7	6		<1 [2]	<1 [2]	<1 [2]	<1 [2]	1	1	1	1	2	<1	1	3	5
dtbug	isDTBug 4	10		<1 [1]	<1 [1]	<1 [2]	<1 [2]	1	1	1	1	15	<1	1	2	10
tclab	connectedK 3	28		<1 [1]	<1 [1]	<1 [3]	<1 [5]	1	2	2	3	55	2	3	23	5
gclab	completeness 6	34	X	<1 [1]	1 [1]	4 [36]	338 [2092]	1	1	1	2	21904	3600	>3000	34	2
abc	{} 3	13		<1 [1]	<1 [1]	<1 [1]	<1 [1]	1	1	1	1	2	<1	2	12	1
gwh	{} 6	10		<1 [1]	<1 [1]	<1 [1]	<1 [1]	1	1	1	1	2	<1	2	10	0
grade	noGradeOwn 3	25		<1 [1]	<1 [1]	<1 [1]	<1 [1]	1	1	1	1	2428	41	1	25	0
bempl	noThief 3	21		<1 [1]	<1 [1]	<1 [2]	<1 [6]	1	1	1	1	33283	432	3	18	5
other	noThief 3	10		<1 [1]	<1 [2]	5 [581]	6 [682]	1	1	1	1	1620	10	1	9	3
ring	{} 6	7		<1 [1]	<1 [1]	<1 [1]	<1 [1]	1	1	1	2	52	4	9	7	0
addr	inAddr 4	16	X	<1 [7]	2 [37]	39 [820]	495 [7700]	1	1	1	2	47339	3600	1	8	11
grand	ownGrandpa 4	36		<1 [1]	<1 [1]	1 [1]	1 [4]	1	1	1	2	768	5	36	36	0
gene	Show 6	37		1 [1]	1 [1]	1 [1]	1 [1]	2	3	3	6	768	321	768	37	0
hl4	{} 3	245		1 [1]	3 [3]	34 [38]	67 [70]	2	3	7	13	168	166	3	182	66
elect-1	AtLeastOne 7	193	X	15 [6]	24 [10]	437 [225]	1304 [619]	2	4	7	13	1568	3600	184	193	0
elect-2	looplessPath 12	179		11 [1]	11 [1]	21 [2]	31 [3]	2	3	3	3	3	31	3	179	0
media	CutPaste 3	674	M	754 [15]	1652 [33]	1899 [38]	2076 [41]	5	8	10	16	41	2077	6	150	640
media	PasteCut 3	639	M	626 [11]	1184 [22]	3013 [64]	3582 [75]	5	7	9	19	75	3583	14	221	535
simplem	{} 3	13		<1 [9]	<1 [18]	<1 [29]	1 [68]	1	1	1	2	5732	139	1	0	13
fixedm	{} 3	13		<1 [1]	<1 [1]	<1 [6]	<1 [22]	1	1	1	2	769	24	1	0	13
cachem	{} 3	12	X	<1 [1]	<1 [1]	1 [13]	1 [13]	1	1	1	2	86035	3600	1	0	12
uml1	cd 10	79	X	7 [1]	7 [1]	11 [2]	530 [104]	1	1	1	3	457	3600	2	40	39
uml2	cd 10	48	X	2 [2]	19 [18]	19 [18]	786 [659]	1	2	3	3	1829	3600	3	39	9
cddiff1	M1minusM2 6	80		4 [2]	4 [2]	4 [2]	181 [86]	1	1	1	4	385	827	5	74	6
cddiff2	M2minusM1 6	63		14 [5]	42 [14]	42 [14]	188 [64]	2	2	2	6	70	211	1	26	38
flow	isTCReallyTC 4	223	X	18 [2]	43 [5]	115 [13]	1345 [144]	1	2	5	12	383	3600	12	170	58

Fig. 4. Summary of results. Each row describes a separate experiment on a distinct specification, predicate (or assertion) and bounds. *Max bound* denotes the highest bound used. We report the *maximum* because model-generation time tends to be exponential in the bounds. We stop enumeration when either all models have been processed or after *one hour* has passed. Column 3 (**All?**) is blank if all models were enumerated (i.e., the true set of provenances is known). It contains a **X** if enumeration (for that experiment) terminated after one hour and an **M** if enumeration is incomplete due to the 4 GB memory limit.

new skeletons and report how far into the ensemble the pertinent coverage level is reached. This is a conservative metric, as a better ensemble might exist for, say, 50% coverage than a 50% subset of the optimal 100% ensemble. Low sizes may therefore be especially encouraging.

The largest 100% ensembles by far belong to incompletely enumerated experiments: **media** (16 and 19) being the highest. It is possible that high-coverage models (which would reduce the ensemble size) remain undiscovered, but this will not always be true. These specifications are complex, with many skeletons up to subsumption. We thus conclude that 100%-coverage ensembles are necessarily large for some specifications. However, we temper this with two observations.

When we compare even these relatively high ensemble sizes with the total number of models enumerated in the experiment, we see significant reduction in the number of models shown. Even in **media**, the worst case, we see a 3-fold reduction, and in **flow** a 10-fold reduction. Oftentimes, we see a 100x (**fixedm**), 1000x (**digraph**) or even 10000x (**gclab**) reduction. We also observe that ensemble sizes at the 70% and 90% coverage levels are far more manageable. With the exception of **media**, the 90% coverage ensembles are all under 10 models and 70% coverage ensembles are no larger than 4—for most, only 1 or 2.

Finally, we see in Column 4 that some experiments find relatively high-coverage models within the first few enumerated. However, the lion's share of these occur in specifications with relatively few total models (**gwh** with 2 total or **elect-2** with 3). To achieve 90% coverage almost invariably requires a large number of models be enumerated. This demonstrates the truth of our hypothesis that automatic enumeration can filter valuable models from the chaff. We defer questions of *time to generate* ensembles to the next section, as it separately evaluates the viability of model-enumeration.

8.3   RQ2: Is Enumeration Effective?

For each experiment, column 4 reports the time taken and number of models enumerated before reaching 50%, 70%, 90%, and 100% coverage. This is subtle since subsumption reduces the number of overall skeletons during enumeration.

If we reported percentages *without subsumption*, the number of skeletons shown would not reflect our actual coverage computation and inaccurately inflate ensemble size. Yet if we reported percentages of the total up to subsumption *by all skeletons found*, it would introduce a pro-CompoSAT bias into these results. To see why, suppose **(A)** the first model contained provenances $\{p_1, p_2\}$ and the thousandth model contained p_3 which subsumed p_1 and p_2. Then there would be only one skeleton up to subsumption, not seen until the thousandth model— but two of the three skeletons in total manifest in the first model. Now consider **(B)** the opposite case: the first model contains p_3 and the thousandth contains $\{p_1, p_2\}$, which are both subsumed by p_3. Our evaluation should make clear that the first model achieves 100% coverage, not merely 33%.

Our measurements therefore take subsumption into account only up to the current model M; skeletons enumerated later will contribute to the denominator (reducing the coverage of M) but no skeleton will be subsumed by one as-yet-unseen. This means that in **(A)**, the first model reaches 66% coverage and in **(B)** the first model achieves 100%—as expected. This approach ensures that early models receive "credit" for skeletons they exhibit even if these are later subsumed.

Columns 6 and 7 report the number of models enumerated and the total time spent. These numbers are often different from the 100% sub-column in column 4 because there we are measuring only how long it takes to reach full coverage. Even if all skeletons are seen early, our experiments still run to completion.

The results here somewhat echo Sect. 8.2 above. For completely enumerated experiments, with one exception (**cddiff** at roughly 3 min) enumeration produces 100% coverage ensembles in under 70 seconds. We also see many incomplete experiments (e.g., **gclab**) reaching full coverage (relative to skeletons discovered) far quicker than their duration. A small, truly high-coverage ensemble may be worth the wait. Even if not, the time to achieve 70% and 90% coverage is far more modest across the board, with 27 of 29 experiments reaching 70% in under one minute. **Media** remains an outlier, with new skeletons appearing up until the very end of the enumeration process. This happens because, in **media**, most models only contain a small handful of skeletons. We observe that this case is not common.

In incomplete cases, it is possible that new skeletons (or superior models) could be discovered with further enumeration. This is quite likely for **media**. In others, such as **uml1** (457 enumerated, last skeleton at 104) we see a long trail of enumeration after a relatively early final skeleton discovery—making it more likely, although not certain, that few skeletons remain undiscovered.

Overall, although enumeration has its weaknesses, it appears to be effective for producing high-coverage ensembles in practice. Indeed, as *the only other available option* in Alloy at present is *manual* enumeration, CompoSAT's approach is, at worst, automating that process to produce optimal coverage.

8.4   RQ3: Minimal Model Coverage

Column 8 reports the number of *minimal* models for each experiment, collected via the Aluminum [10] model-finder. It also gives the total provenance skeletons found in these. The bracketed number says how many skeletons (column 2) were *not subsumed* by any skeleton in a minimal model. Because these numbers are computed up to subsumption, the found and unfound skeletons need not always total the value in column 2. Where minimal models do well, it is for one of two reasons. Some specifications (e.g., **gene**) are so constrained that all satisfying models are minimal. Others (e.g., **grade**) contain no implications with unnecessary antecedents; here, minimality covers all possible provenances.

For the remaining 23 experiments, minimal models omit swathes of provenance skeletons. Minimal-model enumeration was complete for all except **gclab**. Thus, the bracketed numbers are a strict *lower* bound on the amount of coverage neglected in all other incomplete cases; minimal models can do no better than we report here. Finally, we note that the number of minimal models is often far larger than the 100% ensemble, and when there are fewer minimal models (as in Sect. 2), their coverage is under 100% in every case.

9 Related Work

Model finders fall into two classes: SEM-style [24], which reasons about a surface logic directly, and MACE-style [25], which compiles to Boolean logic and applies a SAT solver. Alloy and its internal engine, Kodkod [26], take the latter approach. Our work is not SAT-specific and could apply to either group.

Model Quality. Some effort has been applied to improving output-model quality. Aluminum [10] and Razor [11] present only *minimal* models in an attempt to reduce distracting example bloat. The Cryptographic Protocol Shapes Analyzer [27] is a domain-specific model-finder that produces minimal illustrative protocol runs. Minimal models only contain locally-necessary *positive* literals—everything present has a provenance, but negative literals may not be locally necessary. CompoSAT is more general, and can detect when the specification disallows either adding or removing elements. Target-Oriented Model Finding [12,28] (TOMF) minimizes distance from user-defined targets, enabling, e.g., maximal models. Bordeaux [29] uses relative minimization to find near-miss models that fail to satisfy the specification but nearly do so in terms of edit distance. Our approach differs starkly from all these as it is *syntax-guided* rather than purely semantic.

Alloy and other model-finders endeavor to suppress models that are *isomorphic* to one already presented. Such symmetry-breaking [30,31] increases the quality of the stream of models shown, but in a way orthogonal to ours.

Coverage in Other Settings. Coverage [14] has been a valued metric for test suites since at least the 1960s [32]. While coverage is not without its weaknesses [33], some of which we share (Sect. 10), it provides powerful insight. Our work is the first to explore what it means for *models* to cover *constraints*.

Concolic testing [34–36] is a coverage-driven technique close to ours in spirit. It marries *concrete* test generation and symb*olic* execution [37] to generate high-coverage test suites for programs. CompoSAT operates on declarative constraints rather than code: there may be no "execution" due to often-deliberate underconstraint and the fact that not all specifications are temporal.

Coverage has also been applied (e.g., by Hoskote, et al. [38]) to model-checking to measure how much of a system is exercised by properties. This improves the set of properties to check, not counterexample quality or overconstraint detection. Others [39–42] use declarative specifications to aid in testing *programs*, whereas we are concerned with helping modelers debug the specification itself. As these approaches rely on a correct specification, CompoSAT is not only orthogonal, but also potentially *complementary* to specification-aided test generation.

Coverage for Declarative Specifications. Detecting vacuity [43,44], which can cause constraints to never apply or properties to be unhelpfully true, can be seen as another coverage analysis. Heaven and Russo [45] detect vacuity and other bug-prone patterns in specifications. However, their work is focused on detecting patterns, not optimizing output. Torlak, et al. [23] improve Alloy's unsat-core highlighting, which can be viewed as a coverage metric that applies only to unsatisfiabile specifications. They observe that a suspiciously small core suggests a problem with the property or the bounds given. This insight is useful to debug unsatisfiable results but does not apply to improving models.

AUnit [46,47] also takes inspiration from code coverage, but differs in foundation and execution. In AUnit, coverage atoms correspond to truth of subformulas and cardinality of subexpressions. In our analogy, this is a refinement of statement coverage. CompoSAT considers sets of subexpressions that capture unique ways in which models are constrained, analogously to path coverage. Moreover, AUnit enumerates models via SAT invocations until all coverage atoms are seen; CompoSAT post-filters Alloy's default enumeration process. Scenario Tour [48] generates models using a combinatorial test-generation strategy. Combinations comprise a pair of relations having specific cardinalities (empty, singleton, and higher) in models found. This interesting approach is nevertheless more related to pairwise test generation than statement or path coverage.

Provenance. Provenance for databases was introduced by Cui and Widom [49] as the set of tuples in a source database that contribute to a tuple's presence in a query answer. Variations exist, e.g., Buneman et al. [50] and others distinguish between tuples that bear responsibility from tuples that provide data in the query answer. Meliou, et al. [51,52] find provenance for *negative* answers to conjunctive queries. One key difference between this work and CompoSAT is that specifications are strictly more expressive than conjunctive queries.

Provenance is also useful in other settings. Vermeer [53], for instance, explains assertion violations in C programs via causal traces. WhyLine [54,55] "Why..." and "Why not..." queries about Java program behavior. Y! [56,57] finds and presents both positive and negative provenance for network events. These tools all extract provenance from deterministic runtime logs, which possess temporal structure that models need not possess—and are not available to a model finder.

In addition to minimal model output, Razor [11] is also able to give provenance for every piece of a model. To do so, it draws on constructive model-finding ideas (the Chase [58] algorithm) while still leveraging SAT. Amalgam [20] gives provenance in arbitrary, rather than just minimal, models. Although CompoSAT uses Amalgam as an engine to generate provenances, the core topic of this work— syntax-guided model-quality criteria—is separate from provenance generation.

10   Conclusion and Discussion

We have introduced specification-guided coverage as a new metric for producing high-quality model output. We now conclude with discussion.

Coverage vs. Increased Bounds. Alloy searches for models of size *up to* to given bounds. E.g, we write "`for 4 Name`" to search for models with *up to* 4 `Name`s. Because of this, increasing bounds will never lose provenances. Moreover, as bounds increase, models can contain more skeletons; a higher bound often means that a smaller ensemble is possible (at the cost of more models to enumerate). In Sect. 2's specification, for instance, raising the bound to 4 reveals a single-model optimal ensemble. However, if we permit `exact` rather than upper bounds, this property fails since exact bounds omit models of smaller size.

Weaknesses of Coverage. High-coverage ensembles have one significant weakness: they are entirely syntax-guided. CompoSAT may thus do poorly at revealing *under*constraint bugs: e.g., if a relation is left completely unconstrained, CompoSAT may not demonstrate this. This is analogous to program coverage's blindness to missing complexity [59] in code, and is thus not unique to this work. We see CompoSAT as a new and powerful option in what must become a more diverse toolbox of output strategies, each focusing on a particular set of user needs.

Alternatives to Post-Processing. One might wonder why CompoSAT filters Alloy's default output, rather than directly interfacing with SAT. For instance, one could add SAT clauses to find as-yet-unseen locally-necessary literals. Suppose that T is our specification, and we are interested in enumerating models wherein some literal L is locally necessary. We could reflect this goal by temporarily adding the constraint $L \land \neg T[L \mapsto \bot]$ to the specification. That is, requiring L to be true in any model found, and moreover that if L were false, the specification would not be satisfied.

Example 1. Consider the propositional formula $T \equiv (1 \lor 2) \land (\neg 1 \lor 3) \land (4 \lor 5)$. Suppose $L = \neg 1$. Then $\neg T[L \mapsto \bot] \equiv \neg((1 \lor 2) \land (\bot \lor 3) \land (4 \lor 5))$ which is equivalent to $(\neg 1 \land \neg 2) \lor (\top \land \neg 3) \lor (\neg 4 \land \neg 5))$. The left and right disjuncts can be discarded since they contradict the original specification when L holds. The resulting addition forces the solver to find models where $\neg 3$ holds, which is enough to render L locally necessary.

Via this technique, CompoSAT could proceed to query SAT for locally-necessary literals in round-robin fashion, ensuring at least one provenance for each local necessity early in enumeration. Unfortunately, one literal may be locally necessary for many different reasons, so this approach, alone, would greatly reduce the granularity of coverage. CompoSAT distinguishes between different *causes* of necessity, which would be challenging to encode in SAT up to subsumption. Post-processing also allows CompoSAT to act as a modular extension to other enumeration strategies, such as TOMF [12].

Acknowlegements. We are grateful to the developers of Alloy and Kodkod, as well as Natasha Danas and Daniel J. Dougherty for useful discussions and their work on the Amalgam tool. We also thank the anonymous reviewers for their helpful remarks. This work is partially supported by the U.S. National Science Foundation.

References

1. Jackson, D.: Software Abstractions: Logic, Language, and Analysis, 2nd edn. MIT Press, Cambridge (2012)
2. Nelson, T., Barratt, C., Dougherty, D.J., Fisler, K., Krishnamurthi, S.: The Margrave tool for firewall analysis. In: USENIX Large Installation System Administration Conference (2010)
3. Maoz, S., Ringert, J.O., Rumpe, B.: CD2Alloy: class diagrams analysis using alloy revisited. In: Whittle, J., Clark, T., Kühne, T. (eds.) MODELS 2011. LNCS, vol. 6981, pp. 592–607. Springer, Heidelberg (2011). https://doi.org/10.1007/978-3-642-24485-8_44
4. Maoz, S., Ringert, J.O., Rumpe, B.: CDDiff: semantic differencing for class diagrams. In: Mezini, M. (ed.) ECOOP 2011. LNCS, vol. 6813, pp. 230–254. Springer, Heidelberg (2011). https://doi.org/10.1007/978-3-642-22655-7_12
5. Akhawe, D., Barth, A., Lam, P., Mitchell, J., Song, D.: Towards a formal foundation of web security. In: IEEE Computer Security Foundations Symposium (2010)
6. Maldonado-Lopez, F.A., Chavarriaga, J., Donoso, Y.: Detecting network policy conflicts using alloy. In: Ait Ameur, Y., Schewe, K.D. (eds.) Abstract State Machines, Alloy, B, TLA, VDM, and Z. ABZ 2014. LNCS, vol. 8477, pp. 314–317. Springer, Heidelberg (2014). https://doi.org/10.1007/978-3-662-43652-3_31
7. Zave, P.: Using lightweight modeling to understand Chord. ACM Comput. Commun. Rev. **42**(2), 49–57 (2012)
8. Ruchansky, N., Proserpio, D.: A (not) NICE way to verify the OpenFlow switch specification: formal modelling of the OpenFlow switch using Alloy. ACM Comput. Commun. Rev. **43**(4), 527–528 (2013)
9. Nelson, T., Ferguson, A.D., Scheer, M.J.G., Krishnamurthi, S.: Tierless programming and reasoning for software-defined networks. In: Networked Systems Design and Implementation (2014)
10. Nelson, T., Saghafi, S., Dougherty, D.J., Fisler, K., Krishnamurthi, S.: Aluminum: Principled scenario exploration through minimality. In: International Conference on Software Engineering (2013)
11. Saghafi, S., Danas, R., Dougherty, D.J.: Exploring theories with a model-finding assistant. In: Felty, A.P., Middeldorp, A. (eds.) CADE 2015. LNCS (LNAI), vol. 9195, pp. 434–449. Springer, Cham (2015). https://doi.org/10.1007/978-3-319-21401-6_30
12. Cunha, A., Macedo, N., Guimarães, T.: Target oriented relational model finding. In: Gnesi, S., Rensink, A. (eds.) FASE 2014. LNCS, vol. 8411, pp. 17–31. Springer, Heidelberg (2014). https://doi.org/10.1007/978-3-642-54804-8_2
13. Danas, N., Nelson, T., Harrison, L., Krishnamurthi, S., Dougherty, D.J.: User studies of principled model finder output. In: Cimatti, A., Sirjani, M. (eds.) SEFM 2017. LNCS, vol. 10469, pp. 168–184. Springer, Cham (2017). https://doi.org/10.1007/978-3-319-66197-1_11
14. Zhu, H., Hall, P.A.V., May, J.H.R.: Software unit test coverage and adequacy. ACM Comput. Surv. **29**(4), 366–427 (1997)
15. Alloy Team: Overconstraint–the bane of declarative modeling. http://alloy.mit.edu/alloy/tutorials/online/sidenote-overconstraint.html. Accessed 14 Aug 2017
16. Jackson, D.: Alloy: a language & tool for relational models. http://alloy.mit.edu/alloy/ (2016). Accessed 1 Nov 2016
17. Milicevic, A., Near, J.P., Kang, E., Jackson, D.: Alloy*: a general-purpose higher-order relational constraint solver. In: International Conference on Software Engineering (2015)

18. Enderton, H.B.: A Mathematical Introduction to Logic. Academic Press, New York (1972)
19. Libkin, L.: Elements of Finite Model Theory. Texts in Theoretical Computer Science. An EATCS Series. Springer, Heidelberg (2004). https://doi.org/10.1007/978-3-662-07003-1
20. Nelson, T., Danas, N., Dougherty, D.J., Krishnamurthi, S.: The power of "why" and "why not": Enriching scenario exploration with provenance. In: Foundations of Software Engineering (2017)
21. de Moura, L., Bjørner, N.: Z3: an efficient SMT solver. In: Ramakrishnan, C.R., Rehof, J. (eds.) TACAS 2008. LNCS, vol. 4963, pp. 337–340. Springer, Heidelberg (2008). https://doi.org/10.1007/978-3-540-78800-3_24
22. Eén, N., Sörensson, N.: An extensible SAT-solver. In: Giunchiglia, E., Tacchella, A. (eds.) SAT 2003. LNCS, vol. 2919, pp. 502–518. Springer, Heidelberg (2004). https://doi.org/10.1007/978-3-540-24605-3_37
23. Torlak, E., Chang, F.S.-H., Jackson, D.: Finding minimal unsatisfiable cores of declarative specifications. In: Cuellar, J., Maibaum, T., Sere, K. (eds.) FM 2008. LNCS, vol. 5014, pp. 326–341. Springer, Heidelberg (2008). https://doi.org/10.1007/978-3-540-68237-0_23
24. Zhang, J., Zhang, H.: SEM: a system for enumerating models. In: International Joint Conference On Artificial Intelligence (1995)
25. McCune, W.: Mace4 reference manual and guide. CoRR cs.SC/0310055 (2003)
26. Torlak, E., Jackson, D.: Kodkod: a relational model finder. In: Grumberg, O., Huth, M. (eds.) TACAS 2007. LNCS, vol. 4424, pp. 632–647. Springer, Heidelberg (2007). https://doi.org/10.1007/978-3-540-71209-1_49
27. Doghmi, S.F., Guttman, J.D., Thayer, F.J.: Searching for shapes in cryptographic protocols. In: Grumberg, O., Huth, M. (eds.) TACAS 2007. LNCS, vol. 4424, pp. 523–537. Springer, Heidelberg (2007). https://doi.org/10.1007/978-3-540-71209-1_41
28. Macedo, N., Cunha, A., Guimarães, T.: Exploring scenario exploration. In: Egyed, A., Schaefer, I. (eds.) FASE 2015. LNCS, vol. 9033, pp. 301–315. Springer, Heidelberg (2015). https://doi.org/10.1007/978-3-662-46675-9_20
29. Montaghami, V., Rayside, D.: Bordeaux: a tool for thinking outside the box. In: Huisman, M., Rubin, J. (eds.) FASE 2017. LNCS, vol. 10202, pp. 22–39. Springer, Heidelberg (2017). https://doi.org/10.1007/978-3-662-54494-5_2
30. Crawford, J.M., Ginsberg, M.L., Luks, E.M., Roy, A.: Symmetry-breaking predicates for search problems. In: Principles of Knowledge Representation and Reasoning (1996)
31. Shlyakhter, I.: Generating effective symmetry-breaking predicates for search problems. Disc. Appl. Math. (2007)
32. Miller, J.C., Maloney, C.J.: Systematic mistake analysis of digital computer programs. Commun. ACM 6(2), 58–63 (1963)
33. Inozemtseva, L., Holmes, R.: Coverage is not strongly correlated with test suite effectiveness. In: International Conference on Software Engineering (2014)
34. Godefroid, P., Klarlund, N., Sen, K.: DART: directed automated random testing. In: Programming Language Design and Implementation (PLDI) (2005)
35. Larson, E., Austin, T.: High coverage detection of input-related security faults. In: USENIX Security Symposium (2003)
36. Sen, K., Marinov, D., Agha, G.: CUTE: a concolic unit testing engine for C. In: Foundations of Software Engineering (2005)
37. King, J.C.: Symbolic execution and program testing. Commun. ACM 19(7), 385–394 (1976)

38. Hoskote, Y., Kam, T., Ho, P.H., Zhao, X.: Coverage estimation for symbolic model checking. In: Design Automation Conference (1999)
39. Gopinath, D., Zaeem, R.N., Khurshid, S.: Improving the effectiveness of spectra-based fault localization using specifications. In: Automated Software Engineering (2012)
40. Marinov, D., Khurshid, S.: TestEra: A novel framework for automated testing of Java programs. In: Automated Software Engineering (2001)
41. Milicevic, A., Misailovic, S., Marinov, D., Khurshid, S.: Korat: A tool for generating structurally complex test inputs. In: International Conference on Software Engineering (2007)
42. Shao, D., Khurshid, S., Perry, D.E.: Whispec: White-box testing of libraries using declarative specifications. In: Symposium on Library-Centric Software Design (2007)
43. Beatty, D.L., Bryant, R.E.: Formally verifying a microprocessor using a simulation methodology. In: Design Automation Conference (1994)
44. Beer, I., Ben-David, S., Eisner, C., Rodeh, Y.: Efficient detection of vacuity in actl formulas. In: International Conference on Computer Aided Verification, pp. 279–290 (1997)
45. Heaven, W., Russo, A.: Enhancing the Alloy analyzer with patterns of analysis. In: Workshop on Logic-based Methods in Programming Environments (2005)
46. Sullivan, A., Zaeem, R.N., Khurshid, S., Marinov, D.: Towards a test automation framework for Alloy. In: Symposium on Model Checking of Software (SPIN), pp. 113–116 (2014)
47. Sullivan, A., Wang, K., Zaeem, R.N., Khurshid, S.: Automated test generation and mutation testing for Alloy. In: Software Testing, Verification and Validation (ICST) (2017)
48. Saeki, T., Ishikawa, F., Honiden, S.: Automatic generation of potentially pathological instances for validating Alloy models. In: International Conference on Formal Engineering Methods (ICFEM), pp. 41–56 (2016)
49. Cui, Y., Widom, J.: Practical lineage tracing in data warehouses. In: International Conference on Data Engineering (2000)
50. Buneman, P., Khanna, S., Wang-Chiew, T.: Why and where: a characterization of data provenance. In: Van den Bussche, J., Vianu, V. (eds.) ICDT 2001. LNCS, vol. 1973, pp. 316–330. Springer, Heidelberg (2001). https://doi.org/10.1007/3-540-44503-X_20
51. Meliou, A., Gatterbauer, W., Moore, K.F., Suciu, D.: The complexity of causality and responsibility for query answers and non-answers. Proc. VLDB Endow. 4(1), 34–45 (2010)
52. Meliou, A., Gatterbauer, W., Moore, K.F., Suciu, D.: WHY SO? or WHY NO? functional causality for explaining query answers. In: VLDB workshop on Management of Uncertain Data (MUD), pp. 3–17 (2010)
53. Schwartz-Narbonne, D., Oh, C., Schäf, M., Wies, T.: VERMEER: a tool for tracing and explaining faulty C programs. In: International Conference on Software Engineering, pp. 737–740 (2015)
54. Ko, A.J., Myers, B.A.: Designing the WhyLine: a debugging interface for asking questions about program behavior. In: Proceedings of the SIGCHI Conference on Human Factors in Computing Systems, pp. 151–158. ACM (2004)
55. Ko, A.J., Myers, B.A.: Finding causes of program output with the Java Whyline. In: Proceedings of the SIGCHI Conference on Human Factors in Computing Systems, pp. 1569–1578. ACM (2009)

56. Wu, Y., Zhao, M., Haeberlen, A., Zhou, W., Loo, B.T.: Diagnosing missing events in distributed systems with negative provenance. In: Conference on Communications Architectures, Protocols and Applications (SIGCOMM), pp. 383–394. ACM (2014)
57. Chen, A., Wu, Y., Haeberlen, A., Zhou, W., Loo, B.T.: Differential provenance: better network diagnostics with reference events. In: Workshop on Hot Topics in Networks, vol. 25. ACM (2015)
58. Maier, D., Mendelzon, A.O., Sagiv, Y.: Testing implications of data dependencies. ACM Trans. Database Syst. **4**(4), 455–469 (1979)
59. Glass, R.L.: Persistent software errors. IEEE Trans. Softw. Eng. **7**(2), 162–168 (1981)

Approximate Partial Order Reduction

Chuchu Fan$^{(\boxtimes)}$, Zhenqi Huang, and Sayan Mitra

ECE Department, University of Illinois at Urbana-Champaign, Champaign, USA
{cfan10,zhuang25,mitras}@illinois.edu

Abstract. We present a new partial order reduction method for
reachability analysis of nondeterministic labeled transition systems over
metric spaces. Nondeterminism arises from both the choice of the initial state and the choice of actions, and the number of executions
to be explored grows exponentially with their length. We introduce a
notion of ε-independence relation over actions that relates approximately
commutative actions; ε-equivalent action sequences are obtained by
swapping ε-independent consecutive action pairs. Our reachability algorithm generalizes individual executions to cover sets of executions that
start from different, but δ-close initial states, and follow different, but
ε-independent, action sequences. The constructed over-approximations
can be made arbitrarily precise by reducing the δ, ε parameters. Exploiting both the continuity of actions and their approximate independence,
the algorithm can yield an exponential reduction in the number of
executions explored. We illustrate this with experiments on consensus,
platooning, and distributed control examples.

1 Introduction

Actions of different computing nodes interleave arbitrarily in distributed
systems. The number of action sequences that have to be examined for state-
space exploration grows exponentially with the number of nodes. Partial order
reduction methods tackle this combinatorial explosion by eliminating executions that are *equivalent*, i.e., do not provide new information about reachable
states (see [20, 23, 28] and the references therein). This equivalence is based on
independence of actions: a pair of actions are independent if they commute, i.e.,
applying them in any order results in the same state. Thus, of all execution
branches that start and end at the same state, but perform commuting actions
in different order, only one has to be explored. Partial order reduction methods have become standard tools for practical software verification. They have
been successfully applied to election protocols [2], indexers [19], file systems [9],
security protocol [8], distributed schedulers [3], among many others.

Current partial order methods are limited when it comes to computation with
numerical data and physical quantities (e.g., sensor networks, vehicle platoons,

---

This work is supported by the grants CAREER 1054247 and CCF 1422798 from the
National Science Foundation.

K. Havelund et al. (Eds.): FM 2018, LNCS 10951, pp. 588–607, 2018.
https://doi.org/10.1007/978-3-319-95582-7_35

IoT applications, and distributed control and monitoring systems). First, a pair of actions are considered independent only if they commute exactly; actions that nearly commute—as are common in these applications—cannot be exploited for pruning the exploration. Second, conventional partial order methods do not eliminate executions that start from nearly similar states and experience equivalent action sequences.

We address these limitations and propose a state space exploration method for nondeterministic, infinite state transition systems based on *approximate partial order reduction*. Our setup has two mild assumptions: (i) the state space of the transition system has a discrete part L and a continuous part X and the latter is equipped with a metric; (ii) the actions on X are continuous functions. Nondeterminism arises from both the choice of the initial state and the choice of actions. Fixing an initial state q_0 and a sequence of actions τ (also called a *trace*), uniquely defines an execution of the system which we denote by $\xi_{q_0,\tau}$. For a given approximation parameter $\varepsilon \geq 0$, we define two actions a and b to be ε-independent if from any state q, the continuous parts of states resulting from applying action sequences ab and ba are ε-close. Two *traces* of $\mathcal{A}$ are ε-equivalent if they result from permuting ε-independent actions. To compute the reachable states of $\mathcal{A}$ using a finite (small) number of executions, the key is to generalize or expand an execution $\xi_{q_0,\tau}$ by a factor $r \geq 0$, so that, this expanded set contains all executions that start δ-close to q_0 and experience action sequences that are ε-equivalent to τ. We call this r a (δ, ε)-*trace equivalent discrepancy factor (ted)* for ξ.

For a fixed trace τ, the only source of nondeterminism is the choice of the initial state. The reachable states from $B_\delta(q_0)$—a δ-ball around q_0—can be over-approximated by expanding $\xi_{q_0,\tau}$ by a $(\delta, 0)$-*ted*. This is essentially the sensitivity of $\xi_{q_0,\tau}$ to q_0. Techniques for computing it are now well-developed for a broad class of models [11,13,14,16].

Fixing q_0, the only source of nondeterminism is the possible sequence of actions in τ. The reachable states from q_0 following all possible valid traces can be over-approximated by expanding $\xi_{q_0,\tau}$ by a $(0, \varepsilon)$-*ted*, which includes states reachable by all ε-equivalent action sequences. Computing $(0, \varepsilon)$-*ted* uses the principles of partial order reduction. However, unlike exact equivalence, here, starting from the same state, the states reached at the end of executing two ε-equivalent traces are not necessarily identical. This breaks a key assumption necessary for conventional partial order algorithms: here, an action enabled after ab may not be enabled after ba. Of course, considering disabled actions can still give over-approximation of reachable states, but, we show that the precision of approximation can be improved arbitrarily by shrinking δ and ε.

Thus, the reachability analysis in this paper brings together two different ideas for handling nondeterminism: it combines sensitivity analysis with respect to initial state and ε-independence of actions in computing (δ, ε)-*ted*, i.e., upper-bounds on the distance between executions starting from initial states that are δ-close to each other and follow ε-equivalent action sequences (Theorem 1). As a matter of theoretical interest, we show that the approximation error can be made arbitrarily small by choosing sufficiently small δ and ε (Theorem 2). We validate the correctness and effectiveness of the algorithm with three case studies where conventional partial order reduction would not help: an iterative consensus protocol, a simple vehicle platoon control system, and a distributed building heating system. In most cases, our reachability algorithm reduces the number of explored executions by a factor of $O(n!)$, for a time horizon of n, compared with exhaustive enumeration. Using these over-approximations, we could quickly decide safety verification questions. These examples illustrate that our method has the potential to improve verification of a broader range of distributed systems for consensus [5,17,26,27], synchronization [29,31] and control [18,25].

Related Work. There are two main classes of partial order reduction methods. The *persistent/ample set* methods compute a subset of enabled transitions –the persistent set (or ample set)– such that the omitted transitions are independent to those selected [2,10]. The reduced system which only considers the transitions in the persistent set is guaranteed to represent all behaviors of the original system. The persistent sets and the reduced systems are often derived by static analysis of the code. More recently, researchers have developed dynamic partial order reduction methods using the *sleep set* to avoid the static analysis [1,19,32]. These methods examine the history of actions taken by an execution and decide a set of actions that need to be explored in the future. The set of omitted actions is the sleep set. In [6], Cassez and Ziegler introduce a method to apply symbolic partial order reduction to infinite state discrete systems.

Analysis of sensitivity and the related notion of robustness analysis functions, automata, and executions has recently received significant attention [7,11,30]. Majumdar and Saha [24] present an algorithm to compute the output deviation with bounded disturbance combining symbolic execution and optimization. In [7,30], Chaudhuri etc., present algorithms for robustness analysis of programs and networked systems. Automatic techniques for local sensitivity analysis combining simulations and static analysis and their applications to verification of hybrid systems have been presented in [11,14,16].

In this paper, instead of conducting conventional partial order reduction, we propose a novel method of approximate partial order reduction, and combine it with sensitivity analysis for reachability analysis and safety verification for a broader class of systems.

2   Preliminaries

Notations. The state of our labeled transition system is defined by the valuations of a set of variables. Each variable v has a type, $type(v)$, which is either the set of reals or some finite set. For a set of variables V, a valuation $\mathbf{v}$ maps each $v \in V$ to a point in $type(v)$. The set of all valuations of V is $Val(V)$. $\mathbb{R}$ denotes the set of reals, $\mathbb{R}_{\geq 0}$ the set of non-negative reals, and $\mathbb{N}$ the set of natural numbers. For $n \in \mathbb{N}$, $[n] = \{0, \ldots, n-1\}$. The spectral radius $\rho(A)$ of a square matrix $A \in \mathbb{R}^{n \times n}$ is the largest absolute value of its eigenvalues. A square matrix A is *stable* if its spectral radius $\rho(A) < 1$. For a set of tuples $S = \{\langle s_{j1}, \ldots, s_{jn} \rangle_j\}$, $S \lceil i$ denotes the set $\{s_{ji}\}$ which is the set obtained by taking the ith component of each tuple in S.

2.1   Transition Systems

Definition 1. *A labeled transition system $\mathcal{A}$ is a tuple $\langle X \cup L, \Theta, A, \rightarrow \rangle$ where (i) X is a set of* real-valued variables *and L is a set of* finite-valued variables. *$Q = Val(X \cup L)$ is the* set of states, *(ii) $\Theta \subseteq Q$ is a set of* initial states *such that the sets of real-valued variables are compact, (iii) A is a finite set of* actions, *and (iv) $\rightarrow \subseteq Q \times A \times Q$ is a* transition relation.

A state $q \in Q$ is a valuation of the real-valued and finite-valued variables. We denote by $q.X$ and $q.L$, respectively, the real-valued and discrete (finite-valued) parts of the state q. We will view the continuous part $q.X$ as a vector in $\mathbb{R}^{|X|}$ by fixing an arbitrary ordering of X. The norm $|\cdot|$ on $q.X$ is an arbitrary norm unless stated otherwise. For $\delta \geq 0$, the δ-*neighborhood* of q is denoted by $\mathcal{B}_\delta(q) \triangleq \{q' \in Q : q'.L = q.L \wedge |q'.X - q.X| \leq \delta\}$. For any $(q, a, q') \in \rightarrow$, we write $q \xrightarrow{a} q'$. For any action $a \in A$, its guard is the set $guard(a) = \{q \in Q \mid \exists q' \in Q, q \xrightarrow{a} q'\}$. We assume that guards are closed sets. An action a is *deterministic* if for any state $q \in Q$, if there exists $q_1, q_2 \in Q$ with $q \xrightarrow{a} q_1$ and $q \xrightarrow{a} q_2$, then $q_1 = q_2$.

Assumption 1. *(i) Actions are deterministic. For notational convenience, the name of an action a is identified with its transition function, i.e., for each $q \in guard(a)$, $q \xrightarrow{a} a(q)$. We extend this notation to all states, i.e., even those outside $guard(a)$. (ii) For any state pair q, q', if $q.L = q'.L$ then $a(q).L = a(q').L$.*

Executions and Traces. For a deterministic transition system, a state $q_0 \in Q$ and a finite action sequence (also called a *trace*) $\tau = a_0 a_1 \ldots a_{n-1}$ uniquely specifies a *potential execution* $\xi_{q_0, \tau} = q_0, a_0, q_1, a_1, \ldots, a_{n-1}, q_n$ where for each $i \in [n]$, $a_i(q_i) = q_{i+1}$. A *valid execution* (also called execution for brevity) is a potential execution with (i) $q_0 \in \Theta$ and (ii) for each $i \in [n]$, $q_i \in guard(a_i)$. That is, a valid execution is a potential execution starting from the initial set with each action a_i enabled at state q_i. For any potential execution $\xi_{q_0, \tau}$, its *trace* is the action sequence τ, i.e., $trace(\xi_{q_0, \tau}) = \tau \in A^*$. We denote by $len(\tau)$ the length of τ. For any for $i \in [len(\tau)]$, $\tau(i)$ is the i-th action in τ. The length of $\xi_{q_0, \tau}$ is the length of its trace and $\xi_{q_0, \tau}(i) = q_i$ is the state visited after the i-th transition. The first and last state on a execution ξ are denoted as $\xi.\mathsf{fstate} = \xi(0)$ and $\xi.\mathsf{lstate} = \xi(len(\xi))$.

For a subset of initial states $S \subseteq \Theta$ and a time bound $T \geq 0$, $\mathsf{Execs}(S, T)$ is the set of length T executions starting from S. We denote the *reach set at time T* by $\mathsf{Reach}(S, T) \triangleq \{\xi.\mathsf{lstate} \mid \xi \in \mathsf{Execs}(S, T)\}$. Our goal is to precisely over-approximate $\mathsf{Reach}(\Theta, T)$ exploiting partial order reduction.

592   C. Fan et al.

```
1 automaton Consensus(n ∈ N, N ∈ N)        transitions                                    1
    variables                                  aᵢ for each i ∈ [N]
3      x : ℝⁿ                                    pre ¬dᵢ                                     3
       d : 𝔹ᴺ                                     eff x := Aᵢx ∧ d[i] := true
5   initially                                   a⊥                                           5
       x[i] ∈ [−4, 4] for each i ∈ [n]           pre ∧ᵢ∈[N]d[i]
7      d[i] := false for each i ∈ [n]            eff d[i] := false for each i ∈ [N]           7
```

Fig. 1. Labeled transition system model of iterative consensus.

Example 1 (Iterative consensus). An n-dimensional iterative consensus protocol with N processes is shown in Fig. 1. The real-valued part of state is a vector x in $\mathbb{R}^n$ and each process i changes the state by the linear transformation $x \leftarrow A_i x$. The system evolves in rounds: in each round, each process i updates the state exactly once but in arbitrary order. The boolean vector d marks the processes that have acted in a round. The set of actions is $\{a_i\}_{i \in [N]} \cup \{a_\perp\}$. For each $i \in [N]$, the action a_i is enabled when $d[i]$ is *false* and when it occurs x is updated as $A_i x$, where A_i is an $n \times n$ matrix. The action $a_\perp$ can occur only when all $d[i]$'s are set to *true* and it resets all the $d[i]$'s to *false*. For an instance with $N = 3$, a valid execution could have the trace $\tau = a_0 a_2 a_1 a_\perp a_1 a_0 a_2 a_\perp$. It can be checked that Assumption 1 holds. In fact, the assumption will continue to hold if $A_i x$ is replaced by a nonlinear transition function $a_i : \mathbb{R}^n \to \mathbb{R}^n$.

2.2 Discrepancy Functions

A discrepancy function bounds the changes in a system's executions as a continuous function of the changes in its inputs. Methods for computing discrepancy of dynamical and hybrid systems are now well-developed [12,14,22]. We extend the notion naturally to labeled transition systems: a discrepancy for an action bounds the changes in the continuous state brought about by its transition function.

Definition 2. *For an action* $a \in A$, *a continuous function* $\beta_a : \mathbb{R}_{\geq 0} \to \mathbb{R}_{\geq 0}$ *is a* discrepancy function *if for any pair of states* $q, q' \in Q$ *with* $q.L = q'.L$, *(i)* $|a(q).X - a(q').X| \leq \beta_a(|q.X - q'.X|)$, *and (ii)* $\beta_a(\cdot) \to 0$ *as* $|q.X - q'.X| \to 0$.

Property (i) gives an upper-bound on the changes brought about by action a and (ii) ensures that the bound given by β_a can be made arbitrarily precise. If the action a is Lipschitz continuous with Lipschitz constant L_a, then $\beta_a(|q.X - q'.X|) = L_a(|q.X - q'.X|)$ can be used as a discrepancy function. Note that we do not assume the system is stable. As the following proposition states, given discrepancy functions for actions, we can reason about distance between executions that share the same trace but have different initial states.

Proposition 1. *Suppose each action $a \in A$ has a discrepancy function β_a. For any $T \geq 0$ and action sequence $\tau = a_0 a_1 a_2 \ldots a_T$, and for any pair of states $q, q' \in Q$ with $q.L = q'.L$, the last states of the pair of potential executions satisfy:*

$$\xi_{q,\tau}.\mathsf{lstate}.L = \xi_{q',\tau}.\mathsf{lstate}.L, \tag{1}$$

$$|\xi_{q,\tau}.\mathsf{lstate}.X - \xi_{q',\tau}.\mathsf{lstate}.X| \leq \beta_{a_T}\beta_{a_{T-1}}\ldots\beta_{a_0}(|q.X - q'.X|). \tag{2}$$

Example 2. Consider an instance of Consensus of Example 1 with $n = 3$ and $N = 3$ with the standard 2-norm on $\mathbb{R}^3$. Let the matrices A_i be

$$A_0 = \begin{bmatrix} 0.2 & -0.2 & -0.3 \\ -0.2 & 0.2 & -0.1 \\ -0.3 & -0.1 & 0.3 \end{bmatrix}, A_1 = \begin{bmatrix} 0.2 & 0.3 & 0.2 \\ 0.3 & -0.2 & 0.3 \\ 0.2 & 0.3 & 0 \end{bmatrix}, A_2 = \begin{bmatrix} -0.1 & 0 & 0.4 \\ 0 & 0.4 & -0.2 \\ 0.4 & -0.2 & -0.1 \end{bmatrix}.$$

It can be checked that for any pair $q, q' \in Q$ with $q.L = q'.L$, $|a_i(q).X - a_i(q').X|_2 \leq |A_i|_2 |q.X - q'.X|_2$. Where the induced 2-norms of the matrices are $|A_0|_2 = 0.57, |A_1|_2 = 0.56, |A_2|_2 = 0.53$. Thus, for any $v \in \mathbb{R}_{\geq 0}$, we can use discrepancy functions for a_0, a_1, a_2: $\beta_{a_0}(v) = 0.57v, \beta_{a_1}(v) = 0.56v$, and $\beta_{a_2}(v) = 0.53v$.

For actions with nonlinear transition functions, computing global discrepancy functions is difficult in general but local approaches using the eigenvalues of the Jacobian matrices are adequate for computing reachable sets from compact initial sets [16,21].

2.3   Combining Sets of Discrepancy Functions

For a finite set of discrepancy functions $\{\beta_a\}_{a \in A'}$ corresponding to a set of actions $A' \subseteq A$, we define $\beta_{max} = \max_{a \in A'}\{\beta_a\}$ as $\beta_{max}(v) = \max_{a \in A'}\beta_a(v)$, for each $v \geq 0$. From Definition 2, for each $a \in S$, $\beta_a(|q.X - q'.X|) \to 0$ as $|q.X - q'.X| \to 0$. Hence, as the maximum of β_a, we have $\beta_{max}(|q.X - q'.X|) \to 0$ as $|q.X - q'.X| \to 0$. It can be checked that β_{max} is a discrepancy function of each $a \in S$.

For $n \geq 0$ and a function β_{max} defined as above, we define a function $\gamma_n = \sum_{i=0}^{n} \beta_{max}^i$; here $\beta^i = \beta \circ \beta^{i-1}$ for $i \geq 1$ and β^0 is the identity mapping. Using the properties of discrepancy functions as in Definition 2, we can show the following properties of $\{\gamma_n\}_{n \in \mathbb{N}}$.

Proposition 2. *Fix a finite set of discrepancy functions $\{\beta_a\}_{a \in A'}$ with $A' \subseteq A$. Let $\beta_{max} = \max_{a \in A'}\{\beta_a\}$. For any $n \geq 0$, $\gamma_n = \sum_{i=0}^{n} \beta_{max}^i$ satisfies (i) $\forall \varepsilon \in \mathbb{R}_{\geq 0}$ and any $n \geq n' \geq 0$, $\gamma_n(\varepsilon) \geq \gamma_{n'}(\varepsilon)$, and (ii) $\lim_{\varepsilon \to 0} \gamma_n(\varepsilon) = 0$.*

Proof. (i) For any $n \geq 1$, we have $\gamma_n - \gamma_{n-1} = \beta_{max}^n$. Since $\beta_{max}^n = \max_{a \in S}\{\beta_a\}$ for some finite S, using Definition 2, β_{max}^n takes only non-negative values. Hence, the sequence of functions $\{\gamma_n\}_{n \in \mathbb{R}_{\geq 0}}$ is non-decreasing.

(ii) Using the property of discrepancy functions, we have $\lim_{\varepsilon \to 0} \beta_{max}(\varepsilon) = 0$. By induction on the nested functions, we have $\lim_{\varepsilon \to 0} \beta_{max}^i(0)$ for any $i \geq 0$. Hence for any $n \in \mathbb{R}_{\geq 0}$, $\lim_{\varepsilon \to 0} \gamma_n(\varepsilon) = \lim_{\varepsilon \to 0} \sum_{i=0}^{n} \beta_{max}^i(\varepsilon) = 0$.

The function γ_n depends on the set of $\{\beta_a\}_{a \in A'}$, but as the βs will be fixed and clear from context, we write γ_n for brevity.

3 Independent Actions and Neighboring Executions

Central to partial order methods is the notion of independent actions. A pair of actions are independent if from any state, the occurrence of the two actions, in either order, results in the same state. We extend this notion and define a pair of actions to be ε-independent (Definition 3), for some $\varepsilon > 0$, if the continuous states resulting from swapped action sequences are within ε distance.

3.1 Approximately Independent Actions

Definition 3. *For $\varepsilon \geq 0$, two distinct actions $a, b \in A$ are ε-independent, denoted by $a \overset{\varepsilon}{\sim} b$, if for any state $q \in Q$ (i) (Commutativity) $ab(q).L = ba(q).L$, and (ii) (Closeness) $|ab(q).X - ba(q).X| \leq \varepsilon$.*

The parameter ε captures the degree of the approximation. Smaller the value of ε, more restrictive the independent relation. If a and b are ε-independent with $\varepsilon = 0$, then $ab(q) = ba(q)$ and the actions are independent in the standard sense (see e.g. Definition 8.3 of [4]). Definition 3 extends the standard definition in two ways. First, b need not be enabled at state $a(q)$, and vice versa. That is, if $\xi_{q_0,ab}$ is an execution, we can only infer that $\xi_{q_0,ba}$ is a potential execution and not necessarily an execution. Secondly, with $\varepsilon > 0$, the continuous states can mismatch by ε when ε-independent actions are swapped. Consequently, an action c may be enabled at $ab(q)$ but not at $ba(q)$. If $\xi_{q_0,abc}$ is a valid execution, we can only infer that $\xi_{q_0,bac}$ is a potential execution and not necessarily an execution.

We assume that the parameter ε does not depend on the state q. When computing the value of ε for concrete systems, we could first find an invariant for the state's real-valued variable $q.X$ such that $q.X$ is bounded, then find an upper-bound of $|ab(q).X - ba(q).X|$ as ε. For example, if a and b are both linear mappings with $a(q).X = A_1 q.X + b_1$ and $b(q).X = A_2 q.X + b_2$ and there is an invariant for $q.X$ is such that $|q.X| \leq r$, then it can be checked that $|ab(q).X - ba(q).X| = |(A_2 A_1 - A_1 A_2)q.X + (A_2 b_1 - A_1 b_2 + b_2 - b_1)| \leq |A_2 A_1 - A_1 A_2| r + |A_2 b_1 - A_1 b_2 + b_2 - b_1|$.

For a trace $\tau \in A^*$ and an action $a \in A$, τ is ε-independent to a, written as $\tau \overset{\varepsilon}{\sim} a$, if τ is empty string or for every $i \in [len(\tau)]$, $\tau(i) \overset{\varepsilon}{\sim} a$. It is clear that the approximate independence relation over A is symmetric, but not necessarily transitive.

Example 3. Consider approximate independence of actions in Consensus. Fix any $i, j \in [N]$ such that $i \neq j$ and any state $q \in Q$. It can be checked that: $a_i a_j(q).d[k] = a_j a_i(q).d[k] = true$ if $k \in \{i, j\}$, otherwise it is $q.d[k]$. Hence, we have $a_i a_j(q).d = a_j a_i(q).d$ and the commutativity condition of Definition 3 holds. For the closeness condition, we have $|a_i a_j(q).x - a_j a_i(q).x|_2 = |(A_i A_j - A_j A_i).q.x|_2 \le |A_i A_j - A_j A_i|_2 |q.x|_2$. If the matrices A_i and A_j commute, then a_i and a_j are ε-approximately independent with $\varepsilon = 0$.

Suppose initially $x \in [-4, 4]^3$ then the 2-norm of the initial state is bounded by the value $4\sqrt{3}$. The specific matrices $A_i, i \in [3]$ presented in Example 2 are all stable, so $|a_i(q).x|_2 \le |q.x|_2$, for each $i \in [3]$ and the norm of state is non-increasing in any transitions. Therefore, $Inv = \{x \in \mathbb{R}^3 : |x|_2 \le 4\sqrt{3}\}$ is an invariant of the system. Together, we have $|a_0 a_1(q).x - a_1 a_0(q).x|_2 \le 0.1$, $|a_0 a_2(q).x - a_2 a_0(q).x|_2 \le 0.07$, and $|a_1 a_2(q).x - a_2 a_1(q).x|_2 \le 0.17$. Thus, with $\varepsilon = 0.1$, it follows that $a_0 \overset{\varepsilon}{\sim} a_1$ and $a_0 \overset{\varepsilon}{\sim} a_2$ and $\overset{\varepsilon}{\sim}$ is not transitive, but with $\varepsilon = 0.2$, $\overset{\varepsilon}{\sim}$ is transitive.

3.2 (δ, ε)-trace Equivalent Discrepancy for Action Pairs

Definition 3 implies that from a single state q, executing two ε-independent actions in either order, we end up in states that are within ε distance. The following proposition uses discrepancy to bound the distance between states reached after performing ε-independent actions starting from *different* initial states q and q'.

Proposition 3. *If a pair of actions $a, b \in A$ are ε-independent, and the two states $q, q' \in Q$ satisfy $q.L = q'.L$, then we have (i)$ba(q).L = ab(q').L$, and (ii) $|ba(q).X - ab(q').X| \le \beta_b \circ \beta_a(|q.X - q'.X|) + \varepsilon$, where β_a, β_b are discrepancy functions of a, b respectively.*

Proof. Fix a pair of states $q, q' \in Q$ with $q.L = q'.L$. Since $a \overset{\varepsilon}{\sim} b$, we have $ba(q).L = ab(q).L$. Using the Assumption, we have $ab(q).L = ab(q').L$. Using triangular inequality, we have $|ba(q).X - ab(q').X| \le |ba(q).X - ba(q').X| + |ba(q').X - ab(q').X|$. The first term is bounded by $\beta_b \circ \beta_a(|q.X - q'.X|)$ using Proposition 1 and the second is bounded by ε by Definition 3, and hence, the result follows.

4 Effect of ε-independent Traces

In this section, we will develop an analog of Proposition 3 for ε-independent traces (action sequences) acting on neighboring states.

4.1 ε-equivalent Traces

First, we define what it means for two finite traces in A^* to be ε-equivalent.

Definition 4. *For any $\varepsilon \ge 0$, we define a relation $R \subseteq A^* \times A^*$ such that $\tau R \tau'$ iff there exists $\sigma, \eta \in A^*$ and $a, b \in A$ such that $a \overset{\varepsilon}{\sim} b$, $\tau = \sigma a b \eta$, and $\tau' = \sigma b a \eta$. We define an equivalence relation $\overset{\varepsilon}{\equiv} \subseteq A^* \times A^*$ called ε-equivalence, as the reflexive and transitive closure of R.*

That is, two traces $\tau, \tau' \in A^*$ are ε-equivalent if we can construct τ' from τ by performing a sequence of swaps of consecutive ε-independent actions.

In the following proposition, states that the last states of two potential executions starting from the same initial discrete state (location) and resulting from equivalent traces have identical locations.

Proposition 4. *Fix potential executions* $\xi = \xi_{q_0,\tau}$ *and* $\xi' = \xi_{q_0',\tau'}$. *If* $q_0.L = q_0'.L$ *and* $\tau \stackrel{\varepsilon}{\equiv} \tau'$, *then* ξ. Istate$.L = \xi'$. Istate$.L$.

Proof. If $\tau = \tau'$, then the proposition follows from the Assumption. Suppose $\tau \neq \tau'$, from Definition 4, there exists a sequence of action sequences $\tau_0, \tau_1, \ldots, \tau_k$ to join τ and τ' by swapping neighboring approximately independent actions. Precisely the sequence $\{\tau_i\}_{i=0}^k$ satisfies: (i) $\tau_0 = \tau$ and $\tau_k = \tau'$, and (ii) for each pair τ_i and τ_{i+1}, there exists $\sigma, \eta \in A^*$ and $a, b \in A$ such that $a \stackrel{\varepsilon}{\sim} b$, $\tau_i = \sigma a b \eta$, and $\tau_{i+1} = \sigma b a \eta$. From Definition 3, swapping approximately independent actions preserves the value of the discrete part of the final state. Hence for any $i \in [k]$, ξ_{q_0,τ_i}. Istate$.L = \xi_{q_0,\tau_{i+1}}$. Istate$.L$. Therefore, ξ. Istate$.L = \xi'$. Istate$.L$.

Next, we relate pairs of potential executions that result from ε-equivalent traces and initial states that are δ-close.

Definition 5. *Given* $\delta, \varepsilon \geq 0$, *a pair of initial states* q_0, q_0', *and a pair traces* $\tau, \tau' \in A^*$, *the corresponding potential executions* $\xi = \xi_{q_0,\tau}$ *and* $\xi' = \xi_{q_0',\tau'}$ *are* (δ, ε)-*related, denoted by* $\xi \stackrel{\delta,\varepsilon}{\approx} \xi'$, *if* $q_0.L = q_0'.L$, $|q_0.X - q_0'.X| \leq \delta$, *and* $\tau \stackrel{\varepsilon}{\equiv} \tau'$.

Example 4. In Example 3, we show that $a_0 \stackrel{\varepsilon}{\sim} a_1$ and $a_0 \stackrel{\varepsilon}{\sim} a_2$ with $\varepsilon = 0.1$. Consider the executions $\xi = q_0, a_0, q_1, a_1, q_2, a_2, q_3, a_\perp, q_4$ and $\xi' = q_0', a_1, q_1', a_2, q_2', a_0, q_3', a_\perp, q_4'$. with traces $trace(\xi) = a_0 a_1 a_2 a_\perp$ and $trace(\xi') = a_1 a_2 a_0 a_\perp$. For $\varepsilon = 0.1$, we have $a_0 a_1 a_2 a_\perp \stackrel{\varepsilon}{\equiv} a_1 a_0 a_2 a_\perp$ and $a_1 a_0 a_2 a_\perp \stackrel{\varepsilon}{\equiv} a_1 a_2 a_0 a_\perp$. Since the equivalence relation $\stackrel{\varepsilon}{\equiv}$ is transitive, we have $trace(\xi) \stackrel{\varepsilon}{\equiv} trace(\xi')$. Suppose $q_0 \in \mathcal{B}_\delta(q_0')$, then ξ and ξ' are (δ, ε)-related executions with $\varepsilon = 0.1$.

It follows from Proposition 4 that the discrete state (locations) reached by any pair of (δ, ε)-related potential executions are the same. At the end of this section, in Lemma 2, we will bound the distance between the continuous state reached by (δ, ε)-related potential executions. We define in the following this bound as what we call *trace equivalent discrepancy factor (ted)*, which is a constant number that works for all possible values of the variables starting from the initial set. Looking ahead, by bloating a single potential execution by the corresponding *ted*, we can over-approximate the reachset of all related potential executions. This will be the basis for the reachability analysis in Sect. 5.

Definition 6. *For any potential execution* ξ *and constants* $\delta, \varepsilon \geq 0$, *a* (δ, ε)-*trace equivalent discrepancy factor (ted) is a nonnegative constant* $r \geq 0$, *such that for any* (δ, ε)-*related potential finite execution* ξ',

$$|\xi'. \text{Istate}.X - \xi. \text{Istate}.X| \leq r.$$

That is, if r is a (δ, ε)-*ted*, then the r-neighborhood of ξ's last state $\mathcal{B}_r(\xi.\mathsf{lstate})$ contains the last states of all other (δ, ε)-related potential executions.

4.2 $(0, \varepsilon)$-trace Equivalent Discrepancy for Traces (on the Same Initial States)

In this section, we will develop an inductive method for computing (δ, ε)-*ted*. We begin by bounding the distance between potential executions that differ only in the position of a single action.

Lemma 1. *Consider any $\varepsilon \geq 0$, an initial state $q_0 \in Q$, an action $a \in A$ and a trace $\tau \in A^*$ with $len(\tau) \geq 1$. If $\tau \overset{\varepsilon}{\sim} a$, then the potential executions $\xi = \xi_{q_0, \tau a}$ and $\xi' = \xi_{q_0, a\tau}$ satisfy*

(i) $\xi'.\mathsf{lstate}.L = \xi.\mathsf{lstate}.L$ and
(ii) $|\xi'.\mathsf{lstate}.X - \xi.\mathsf{lstate}.X| \leq \gamma_{n-1}(\varepsilon)$, where γ_n corresponds to the set of discrepancy functions $\{\beta_c\}_{c \in \tau}$ for the actions in τ.

Proof. Part (i) directly follows from Proposition 4. We will prove part (ii) by induction on the length of τ.

Base: For any trace τ of length 1, ξ and ξ' are of the form $\xi = q_0, b_0, q_1, a, q_2$ and $\xi' = q_0, a, q_1', b_0, q_2'$. Since $a \overset{\varepsilon}{\sim} b_0$ and the two executions start from the same state, it follows from Definition 3 that $|q_2'.X - q_2.X| \leq \varepsilon$. Recall from the preliminary that $\gamma_0(\varepsilon) = \beta^0(\varepsilon) = \varepsilon$. Hence $|q_2'.X - q_2.X| \leq \gamma_0(\varepsilon)$ holds for trace τ with $len(\tau) = 1$.

Induction: Suppose the lemma holds for any τ with length at most $n-1$. Fixed any $\tau = b_0 b_1 \ldots b_{n-1}$ of length n, we will show the lemma holds for τ. Let the potential executions $\xi = \xi_{q_0, \tau a}$ and $\xi' = \xi_{q_0, a\tau}$ be the form

$\xi = q_0, b_0, q_1, b_1, \ldots, b_{n-1}, q_n, a, q_{n+1},$

$\xi' = q_0, a, q_1', b_0, q_2', b_1, \ldots, b_{n-1}, q_{n+1}'.$

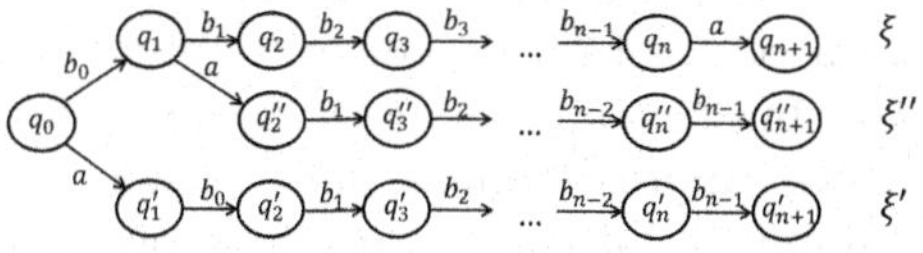

Fig. 2. Potential executions ξ, ξ', and ξ''.

It suffices to prove that $|\xi.\mathsf{lstate}.X - \xi'.\mathsf{lstate}.X| = |q_{n+1}.X - q_{n+1}'.X| \leq \gamma_{n-1}(\varepsilon)$. We first construct a potential execution $\xi'' = \xi_{q_0, b_0 a b_1 \ldots b_{n-1}}$ by swapping the first two actions of ξ'. Then, ξ'' is of the form: $\xi'' = q_0, b_0, q_1, a, q_2'', b_1, \ldots, b_{n-1}, q_{n+1}''$. The potential executions ξ, ξ' and ξ'' are shown in Fig. 2. We first compare the potential executions ξ and ξ''. Notice that, ξ and ξ'' share a common prefix q_0, b_0, q_1. Starting from q_1, the action sequence of ξ'' is derived from $trace(\xi)$ by inserting action a in front of the action sequence $\tau' = b_1 b_2 \ldots b_{n-1}$.

Since $\tau' \overset{\varepsilon}{\sim} a$, applying the induction hypothesis on the length $n-1$ action sequence τ', we get $|q_{n+1}.X - q_{n+1}''.X| \leq \gamma_{n-2}(\varepsilon)$. Then, we compare the potential executions ξ' and ξ''. Since $b_0 \overset{\varepsilon}{\sim} a$, by applying the property of Definition 3 to the first two actions of ξ' and ξ'', we have $|q_2'.X - q_2''.X| \leq \varepsilon$. We note that ξ' and

ξ'' have the same suffix of action sequence from q_2' and q_2''. Using Proposition 1 from states q_2' and q_2'', we have

$$|q_{n+1}'.X - q_{n+1}''.X| \le \beta_{b_1}\beta_{b_2}\ldots\beta_{b_{n-1}}(|q_2'.X - q_2''.X|) \le \beta^{n-1}(\varepsilon). \qquad (3)$$

Combining the bound on $|q_2'.X - q_2''.X|$ and (3) with triangular inequality, we have $|q_{n+1}.X - q_{n+1}'.X| \le |q_{n+1}.X - q_{n+1}''.X| + |q_{n+1}'.X - q_{n+1}''.X| \le \gamma_{n-2}(\varepsilon) + \beta^{n-1}(\varepsilon) = \gamma_{n-1}(\varepsilon)$.

4.3 (δ, ε)-trace Equivalent Discrepancy for Traces

Lemma 1 gives a way to compute $(0, \varepsilon)$-*ted*. Now, we generalize this to compute (δ, ε)-*ted*, for (δ, ε)-related potential executions, with any $\delta \ge 0$. The following lemma gives an inductive way of constructing *ted* as an action a is appended to a trace τ. The proof is analog to the proof of Lemma 1 and is provided in the full version of this paper [15].

Lemma 2. *For any potential execution* $\xi = \xi_{q_0,\tau}$ *and constants* $\delta, \varepsilon \ge 0$, *if* r *is a* (δ, ε)-*ted for* ξ, *and the action* $a \in A$ *satisfies* $\tau \stackrel{\varepsilon}{\sim} a$, *then* $r' = \beta_a(r) + \gamma_{len(\tau)-1}(\varepsilon)$ *is a* (δ, ε)-*ted for* $\xi_{q_0,\tau a}$.

5   Reachability with Approximate Partial Order Reduction

We will present our main algorithm (Algorithm 2) for reachability analysis with approximate partial order reduction in this section. The core idea is to over-approximate $\mathsf{Reach}(B_\delta(q_0), T)$ by (a) computing the actual execution $\xi_{q_0,\tau}$ and (b) expanding this $\xi_{q_0,\tau}$ by a (δ, ε)-*ted* to cover all the states reachable from any other (δ_0, ε)-related potential execution. Combining such over-approximations from a cover of Θ, we get over-approximations of $\mathsf{Reach}(\Theta, T)$, and therefore, Algorithm 2 can be used to soundly check for bounded safety or invariance. The over-approximations can be made arbitrarily precise by shrinking δ_0 and ε (Theorem 2). Of course, at $\varepsilon = 0$ only traces that are exactly equivalent to τ will be covered, and nothing else. Algorithm 2 avoids computing (δ_0, ε)-related executions, and therefore, gains (possibly exponential) speedup.

The key subroutine in Algorithm 2 is *CompTed* which computes the *ted* by adding one more action to the traces. It turns out that, the *ted* is independent of q_0, but only depends on the sequence of actions in τ. *CompTed* is used to compute δ_t from δ_{t-1}, such that, δ_t is the *ted* for the length t prefix of ξ. Let action a be the tth action and $\xi = \xi_{q_0,\tau a}$. If a is ε-independent to τ, then the *ted* δ_t can be computed from δ_{t-1} just using Lemma 2. For the case where a is not ε-independent to the whole sequence τ, we would still want to compute a set of executions that $\xi_{q_0,\tau a}$ can cover. We observe that, with appropriate computation of *ted*, $\xi_{q_0,\tau a}$ can cover all executions of the form $\xi_{q_0,\phi a\eta}$, where $\phi a\eta$ is ε-equivalent to τa and $a \notin \eta$. In what follows, we introduce this notion of *earliest equivalent position of* a *in* τ (Definition 7), which is the basis for the *CompTed* subroutine, which in turn is then used in the main reachability Algorithm 2.

5.1   Earliest Equivalent Position of an Action in a Trace

For any trace $\tau \in A^*$ and action $a \in \tau$, we define $lastPos(\tau, a)$ as the largest index k such that $\tau(k) = a$. The earliest equivalent position, $eep(\tau, a, \varepsilon)$ is the minimum of $lastPos(\tau', a)$ in any τ' that is ε-equivalent to τa.

Definition 7. *For any trace $\tau \in A^*$, $a \in A$, and $\varepsilon > 0$, the* earliest equivalent position *of a on τ is* $eep(\tau, a, \varepsilon) \triangleq \min_{\tau' \stackrel{\varepsilon}{=} \tau a} lastPos(\tau', a)$.

For any trace τa, its ε-equivalent traces can be derived by swapping consecutive ε-independent action pairs. Hence, the eep of a is the leftmost position it can be swapped to, starting from the end. Any equivalent trace of τa is of the form $\phi a \eta$ where ϕ and η are the prefix and suffix of the last occurrence of action a. Hence, equivalently: $eep(\tau, a, \epsilon) = \min_{\phi a \eta \stackrel{\varepsilon}{=} \tau a, \ a \notin \eta} len(\phi)$. In the full version of this paper [15] we give a simple $O(len(\tau)^2)$ algorithm for computing $eep()$. If the ε-independence relation is symmetric, then it eep can be computed in $O(len(\tau))$ time.

Example 5. In Example 3, we showed that $a_0 \stackrel{\varepsilon}{\sim} a_1$ and $a_0 \stackrel{\varepsilon}{\sim} a_2$ with $\varepsilon = 0.1$; $a_\perp$ is not ε-independent to any actions. What is $eep(a_\perp a_0 a_1, a_2, \varepsilon)$? We can swap a_2 ahead following the sequence $\tau a_2 = a_\perp a_0 a_1 a_2 \stackrel{\varepsilon}{=} a_\perp a_1 a_0 a_2 \stackrel{\varepsilon}{=} a_\perp a_1 a_2 a_0$. As $a_\perp$ and a_1 are not independent of a_2, it cannot occur earlier. $eep(a_\perp a_0 a_1, a_2, \varepsilon) = 2$.

5.2   Reachability Using (δ, ε)-trace Equivalent Discrepancy

CompTed (Algorithm 1) takes inputs of trace τ, a new action to be added a, a parameter $r \geq 0$ such that r is a (δ_0, ε)-ted for the potential execution $\xi_{q_0, \tau}$ for some initial state q_0, initial set radius δ_0, approximation parameter $\varepsilon \geq 0$, and a set of discrepancy functions $\{\beta_a\}_{a \in A}$. It returns a (δ_0, ε)-ted r' for the potential execution $\xi_{q_0, \tau a}$.

Algorithm 1. $CompTed(\tau, a, r, \varepsilon, \{\beta_a\}_{a \in A})$

1: $\beta \leftarrow \max_{b \in \tau}\{\beta_b\}$; $k \leftarrow eep(\tau, a, \epsilon)$; $t \leftarrow len(\tau)$;
2: **if** $k = t$ **then** $r' \leftarrow \beta_a(r)$ **else** $r' \leftarrow \beta_a(r) + \gamma_{t-k-1}(\varepsilon)$
3: **return** r';

Lemma 3. *For some initial state q_0 and initial set size δ_0, if r is a (δ_0, ε)-ted for $\xi_{q_0, \tau}$ then value returned by CompTed() is a (δ_0, ε)-ted for $\xi_{q_0, \tau a}$.*

Proof. Let us fix some initial state q_0 and initial set size δ_0.

Let $\xi_t = \xi_{q_0,\tau}$ be the potential execution starting from q_0 by taking the trace
τ, and $\xi_{t+1} = \xi_{q_0,\tau a}$. Fix any ξ' that
is (δ_0, ε)-related to ξ_{t+1}. From Proposition 4,
$\xi'.\mathsf{lstate}.L = \xi_{t+1}.\mathsf{lstate}.L$. It suffice to prove
that $|\xi'.\mathsf{lstate}.X - \xi_{t+1}.\mathsf{lstate}.X| \le r'$.

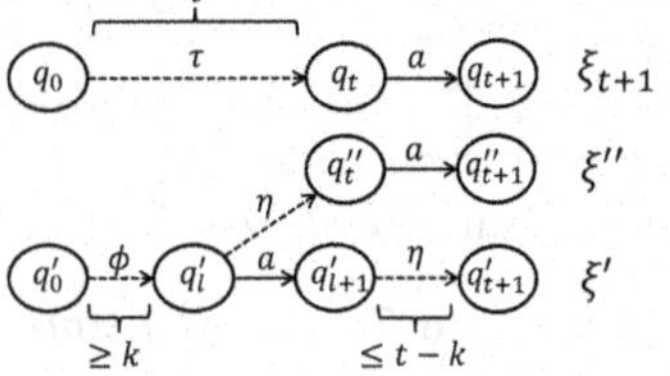

Since $trace(\xi') \overset{\varepsilon}{\equiv} \tau a$, action a is in the
sequence $trace(\xi')$. Partitioning $trace(\xi')$ on the

Fig. 3. Potential executions

last occurrence of a, we get $trace(\xi') = \phi a \eta$ for
ξ_{t+1}, ξ', ξ''

some $\phi, \eta \in A^*$ with $a \notin \eta$. Since k is the *eep*, from Definition 7, the position
of the last occurrence of a on $trace(\xi')$ is at least k. Hence we have $len(\phi) \ge k$
and $len(\eta) = t - len(\phi) \le t - k$. We construct another potential execution
$\xi'' = \xi_{q'_0, \phi \eta a}$ with the same initial state as ξ'. The executions ξ_{t+1}, ξ' and ξ'' are
illustrated in Fig. 3.

q_t is the last state of the execution ξ_t. From the assumption, $\mathcal{B}_r(q_t)$ is an
over-approximation of the reachset at step t. We note that the length t prefix
ξ'' is (δ_0, ε)-related to ξ_t. Therefore, $|q_t.X - q''_t.X| \le r$. Using the discrepancy
function of action a, we have

$$|q_{t+1}.X - q''_{t+1}.X| \le \beta_a(|q_t.X - q''_t.X|) \le \beta_a(r). \tag{4}$$

We will quantify the distance between ξ' and ξ''. There are two cases:
(i) If $k = t$ then, $len(\eta) \le t - k = 0$, that is, η is an empty string.
Hence, ξ' and ξ'' are indeed identical and $q'_{t+1} = q''_{t+1}$. Thus from (4),
$|q_{t+1}.X - q'_{t+1}.X| = |q_{t+1}.X - q''_{t+1}.X| \le \beta_a(r)$, and the lemma holds. (ii) Otherwise $k < t$ and from Lemma 1, we can bound the distance between ξ' and ξ''
as $|q'_{t+1}.X - q''_{t+1}.X| \le \gamma_{len(\eta)-1}(\varepsilon) \le \gamma_{t-k-1}(\varepsilon)$. Combining with (4), we get
$|q_{t+1}.X - q'_{t+1}.X| \le |q_{t+1}.X - q''_{t+1}.X| + |q'_{t+1}.X - q''_{t+1}.X| \le \beta_a(r) + \gamma_{t-k-1}(\varepsilon)$.

Next, we present the main reachability algorithm which uses *CompTed*.
Algorithm 2 takes inputs of an initial set Θ, time horizon T, two parameters
$\delta_0, \varepsilon \ge 0$, and a set of discrepancy functions $\{\beta_a\}_{a \in A}$. It returns the over-
approximation of the reach set for each time step.

The algorithm first computes a δ_0-cover Q_0 of the initial set Θ such that
$\Theta \subseteq \cup_{q_0 \in Q_0} \mathcal{B}_\delta(q_0)$ (Line 2). The **for**-loop from Line 3 to Line 14 will compute the
over-approximation of the reachset from each initial cover $\mathsf{Reach}(\mathcal{B}_{\delta_0}(q_0), t)$. The
over-approximation from each cover is represented as a collection $\langle R_0, \ldots, R_T \rangle$,
where each R_t is a set of tuples $\langle \tau_t, q_t, \delta_t \rangle$ such that (i) the traces $R_t \restriction 1$ and
their ε-equivalent traces contain the traces of all valid executions of length t, (ii)
the traces in $R_t \restriction 1$ are mutually non-ε-equivalent, (iii) for each tuple δ_t is the
(δ_0, ε)-*ted* for ξ_{q_0,τ_t},

For each initial cover $\mathcal{B}_{\delta_0}(q_0)$, R_0 is initialized as the tuple of empty string,
the initial state q_0 and size δ_0 (Line 4). Then the reachset over-approximation
is computed recursively for each time step by checking for the maximum set
of enabled actions EA for the set of states $\mathcal{B}_{\delta_t}(q_t)$ (Line 8), and try to attach
each enabled action $a \in EA$ to τ_t unless $\tau_t a$ is ε-equivalent to some length $t+1$
trace that is already in $R_{t+1} \restriction 1$. This is where the major reduction happens

using approximate partial order reduction. If not, the (δ_0, ε)-*ted* for $\xi_{q_0, \tau_t a}$ will be computed using *CompTed*, and new tuple $\langle \tau_t a, q_{t+1}, \delta_{t+1} \rangle$ will be added to R_{t+1} (Line 13).

If there are k actions in total and they are mutually ε-independent, then as long as the numbers of each action in τ_t and τ_t' are the same, $\tau_t \stackrel{\varepsilon}{=} \tau_t'$. Therefore, in this case, R_t contains at most $\binom{t+k-1}{k-1}$ tuples. Furthermore, for any length t trace τ_t, if all actions in τ_t are mutually ε-independent, the algorithm can reduce the number of executions explored by $O(t!)$. Essentially, each $\tau_t \in R_t \lceil 1$ is a representative trace for the length t ε-equivalence class.

Algorithm 2. Reachability algorithm to over-approximate $\mathsf{Reach}(\Theta, T)$

1: **Input**: $\Theta, T, \varepsilon, \delta_0, \{\beta_a\}$;
2: $Q_0 \leftarrow \delta_0\text{-}cover(\Theta)$; $\mathcal{R} \leftarrow \emptyset$
3: **for** $q_0 \in Q_0$ **do**
4:     $R_0 \leftarrow \{\langle '', q_0, \delta_0\rangle\}$;
5:     **for** $t = [T]$ **do**
6:         $R_T \leftarrow \emptyset$;
7:         **for** each $\langle \tau_t, q_t, \delta_t \rangle \in R_t$ **do**
8:             $EA \leftarrow enabledactions(\mathcal{B}_{\delta_t}(q_t))$;
9:             **for** $a \in EA$ **do**
10:                 **if** $\forall \tau_{t+1} \in R_{t+1} \lceil 1, \neg\left(\tau_t a \stackrel{\varepsilon}{=} \tau_{t+1}\right)$ **then**;
11:                     $q_{t+1} \leftarrow a(q_t)$
12:                     $\delta_{t+1} \leftarrow CompTed(\tau_t, a, \delta_t, \varepsilon, \{\beta_a\}_{a \in A})$
13:                     $R_{t+1} \leftarrow R_{t+1} \cup \langle \tau_t a, q_{t+1}, \delta_{t+1}\rangle$
14:     $\mathcal{R} \leftarrow \mathcal{R} \cup \langle R_0, \ldots, R_T\rangle$
15: **return** $\mathcal{R}$;

Theorem 1 shows that Algorithm 1 indeed computes an over-approximation for the reachsets, and Theorem 2 states that the over-approximation can be made arbitrarily precise by reducing the size of δ_0, ε.

Theorem 1 (Soundness). *Set $\mathcal{R}$ returned by Algorithm 2, satisfies* $\forall t = 0, \ldots, T$,

$$\mathsf{Reach}(\Theta, t) \subseteq \bigcup_{R_t \in \mathcal{R} \lceil t} \bigcup_{\langle \tau, q, \delta\rangle \in R_t} \mathcal{B}_\delta(q). \tag{5}$$

Proof. Since $\cup_{q_0 \in Q_0} \mathcal{B}_\delta(q_0) \supseteq \Theta$, it suffices to show that at each time step $t = 0, \ldots, T$, the R_t computed in the **for**-loop from Line 4 to Line 13 satisfy $\mathsf{Reach}(\mathcal{B}_{\delta_0}(q_0), t) \subseteq \cup_{\langle \tau, q, \delta\rangle \in R_t} \mathcal{B}_\delta(q)$. Fix any $q_0 \in Q_0$, we will prove by induction.

Base case: initially before any action happens, the only valid trace is the empty string $''$ and the initial set is indeed $\mathcal{B}_{\delta_0}(q_0)$.

Induction step: assume that at time step $t < T$, the union of all the traces $R_t \lceil 1$ and their ε-equivalent traces contain the traces of all length t valid executions, and for each tuple $\langle \tau_t, q_t, \delta_t \rangle \in R_t$, δ_t is a (δ_0, ε)-*ted* for ξ_{q_0,τ_t}. That is, $\mathcal{B}_{\delta_t}(q_t)$ contains the final states of all (δ_0, ε)-related executions to ξ_{q_0,τ_t}. This is sufficient for showing that $\mathsf{Reach}(\mathcal{B}_{\delta_0}(q_0), t) \subseteq \cup_{\langle \tau, q, \delta \rangle \in R_t} \mathcal{B}_\delta(q)$.

Since for each tuple contained in R_t, we will consider the maximum possible set of actions enabled at Line 8 and attempts to compute the (δ_0, ε)-*ted* for $\xi_{q_0,\tau_t a}$. If $\tau_t a$ is not ε-equivalent to any of the length $t+1$ traces that has already been added to R_{t+1}, then Lemma 3 guarantees that the q_{t+1} and δ_{t+1} computed at Line 11 and 12 satisfy that δ_{t+1} is the (δ_0, ε)-*ted* for $\xi_{q_0,\tau_t a}$. Otherwise, $\tau_t a$ is ε-equivalent to some trace τ_{t+1} that has already been added to R_{t+1}, then for any initial state q_0' that is δ_0-close to q_0, $\xi_{q_0',\tau_t a}$ and $\xi_{q_0,\tau_{t+1}}$ are (δ_0, ε)-related and the final state of $\xi_{q_0',\tau_t a}$ is already contained in $\mathcal{B}_{\delta_{t+1}}(q_{t+1})$. Therefore, the union of all the traces $R_{t+1} \lceil 1$ and their ε-equivalent traces contain the traces of all length $t+1$ valid executions, and for each tuple $\langle \tau_{t+1}, q_{t+1}, \delta_{t+1} \rangle \in R_{t+1}$, δ_{t+1} is a (δ_0, ε)-*ted* for $\xi_{q_0,\tau_{t+1}}$, which means $\mathsf{Reach}(\mathcal{B}_{\delta_0}(q_0), t+1) \subseteq \cup_{\langle \tau, q, \delta \rangle \in R_{t+1}} \mathcal{B}_\delta(q)$. So the theorem holds.

Theorem 2 (Precision). *For any $r > 0$, there exist $\delta_0, \varepsilon > 0$ such that, the reachset over-approximation $\mathcal{R}$ computed by Algorithm 2 satisfies $\forall t = 0, \ldots, T$,*

$$\bigcup_{R_t \in \mathcal{R} \lceil t} \bigcup_{\langle \tau, q, \delta \rangle \in R_t} \mathcal{B}_\delta(q) \subseteq \mathcal{B}_r(\mathsf{Reach}(\Theta, t)). \tag{6}$$

The proof is based on the fact that δ_t computed in Algorithm 2 converges to zero as $\delta_0 \to 0$ and $\varepsilon \to 0$, and the details are given in the full version of the paper [15]. Notice that as δ_0 and ε go to 0, the Algorithm 2 actually converges to a simulation algorithm which simulates every valid execution from a single initial state.

6   Experimental Evaluation of Effectiveness

We discuss the results from evaluating Algorithm 2 in three case studies. Our Python implementation runs on a standard laptop (Intel Core™ i7-7600 U CPU, 16G RAM).

Iterative Consensus. This is an instance of Consensus (Example 1) with 3 continuous variables and 3 actions a_0, a_1, a_2. We want to check if the continuous states converge to $[-0.4, 0.4]^3$ in 3 rounds starting from a radius 0.5 ball around $[2.5, 0.5, -3]$. Figure 4 (Left) shows reachset over-approximation computed and projected on $x[0]$. The blue and red curves give the bounds. As the figure shows, $x[0]$ converges to $[-0.4, 0.4]$ at round 3; and so do $x[1]$ and $x[2]$ (not shown). We also simulated 100 random valid executions (yellow curves) from the initial set and validate that indeed the over-approximation is sound.

Recall, three actions can occur in any order in each round, i.e., $3! = 6$ traces per round, and $6^3 = 216$ executions from a single initial state up to 3 rounds. We showed in Example 3 that $a_0 \overset{\varepsilon}{\sim} a_1$ and $a_0 \overset{\varepsilon}{\sim} a_2$ with $\varepsilon = 0.1$. Therefore, $a_0 a_1 a_2 \overset{\varepsilon}{\equiv} a_1 a_0 a_2 \overset{\varepsilon}{\equiv} a_1 a_2 a_0$ and $a_0 a_2 a_1 \overset{\varepsilon}{\equiv} a_2 a_0 a_1 \overset{\varepsilon}{\equiv} a_2 a_1 a_0$, and Algorithm 2

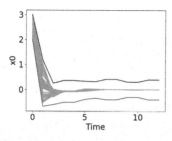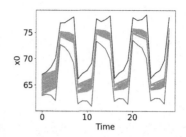

Fig. 4. Reachset computations. The blue curves are the upper bound of the reachsets and the red curves are the lower bound of the reachsets. Between the blue and red curves, the yellow curves are 100 random simulations of valid executions. *Left:* Linear transition system. *Right:* Room heating system. (Color figure online)

explored only 2 (length 12) executions from a set of initial states for computing the bounds. The running time for Algorithm 2 is 1 ms while exploring all valid executions from even only a single state took 20 ms.

Platoon. Consider an N car platoon on a single lane (see Fig. 7 in the full version of the paper [15] for the pseudocode and details). Each car can choose one of three actions at each time step: a (accelerate), b (brake), or c (cruise). Car 0 can choose any action at each time step; remaining cars try to keep safe distance with predecessor by choosing accelerate (a) if the distance is more than 50, brake (b) if the distance is less than 30, and cruise (c) otherwise.

Consider a 2-car platoon and a time horizon of $T = 10$. We want to verify that the cars maintain safe separation. Reachset over-approximations projected on the position variables are shown in Fig. 5, with 100 random simulations of valid executions as a sanity check. Car 0 has lots of choices and it's position over-approximation diverges (Fig. 5). Car 1's position depends on its initial relative distance with Car 0. It is also easy to conclude from Fig. 5 that two cars maintain safe relative distance for these different initial states.

From a single initial state, in every step, Car 0 has 3 choices, and therefore there are 3^{10} possible executions. Considering a range of initial positions for two cars, there are infinitely many execution, and 9^{10} (around 206 trillion) possible traces. With $\epsilon = 0.282$, Algorithm 2 explored a maximum of $\binom{18}{8} = 43758$ traces; the concrete number varies for different initial sets. The running time for Algorithm 2 is 5.1 ms while exploring all valid executions from even only a single state took 2.9 s.

For a 4-car platoon and a time horizon of $T = 10$, there are 81^{10} possible traces considering a range of initial positions. With $\varepsilon = 0.282$, Algorithm 2 explored 7986 traces to conclude that all cars maintain safe separation for the setting where all cars are initially separated by a distance of 40 and has an initial set radius of 4. The running time for Algorithm 2 is 62.3 ms, while exploring all valid executions from even only a single state took 6.2 s.

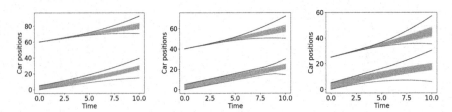

Fig. 5. Position over-approximations for 2 cars. The blue curves are the upper bound of the reachsets and the red curves are the lower bound of the reachsets. Between the blue and red curves, the yellow curves are 100 random simulations of valid executions. Car1's initial position is in the range [0, 5], Car2's initial position is 60 (Left), 40 (Center) and 25 (Right). (Color figure online)

Building Heating System. Consider a building with N rooms, each with a heater (see the full version of the paper [15] for pseudocode and details). For $i \in [N]$, $x[i] \in \mathbb{R}$ is the temperature of room i and $m[i] \in \{0, 1\}$ captures the off/on state of it's heater. The controller measures the temperature of rooms periodically; based on these measurements ($y[i]$) heaters turn on or off. These decisions are made asynchronously across rooms in arbitrary order. The room temperature $x[i]$ changes linearly according to the heater input $m[i]$, the thermal capacity of the room, and the thermal coupling across adjacent rooms as given in the benchmark problem of [18]. For $i \in [N]$, actions $\mathsf{on}_i, \mathsf{off}_i$ capture the decision making process of room i on whether or not to turn on the heater. Time elapse is captured by a flow action that updates the temperatures. We want to verify that the room temperatures remain in the [60, 79] range.

Consider a building with $N = 3$ rooms. In the full version of the paper [15], we provide computation details to show that for any $i, j \in [3]$ with $i \neq j$, $a \in \{\mathsf{on}_i, \mathsf{off}_i\}$ and $b \in \{\mathsf{on}_j, \mathsf{off}_j\}$, $a \overset{\varepsilon}{\sim} b$ with $\varepsilon = 0.6$; but, flow is not independent with any other actions. Computed reachset over-approximation for 8 rounds and projected on the temperature of Room 0 is shown in Fig. 4 (*Right*). Indeed, temperature of Room 0 is contained within the range.

For a round, where each room makes a decision once in arbitrary order, there are $3! = 6$ ε-equivalent action sequences. Therefore, from a single initial state, there are 6^8 (1.6 million) valid executions. Algorithm 2, in this case explore only one (length 32) execution with $\varepsilon = 0.6$ to approximate all executions starting from an initial set with radius $\delta = 2$. The running time for Algorithm 2 is 1 ms while exploring all valid executions from even only a single state took 434 s.

7   Conclusion

We proposed a partial order reduction technique for reachability analysis of infinite state transition systems that exploits approximate independence and bounded sensitivity of actions to reduce the number of executions explored. This relies on a novel notion of ε-independence that generalizes the traditional notion of independence by allowing approximate commutation of actions. With this ε-independence relation, we have developed an algorithm for soundly over-approximating reachsets of all executions using only ε-equivalent traces. The over-approximation can also be made arbitrarily precise by reducing the size of δ, ε. In experimental evaluation with three case studies we observe that it can reduce the number of executions explored exponentially compared to explicit computation of all executions.

The results suggest several future research directions. In Definition 3, ε-independent actions are required to be approximately commutative globally. For reachability analysis, this definition could be relaxed to actions that approximately commute locally over parts of the state space. An orthogonal direction is to apply this reduction technique to verify temporal logic properties and extend it to hybrid models.

References

1. Abdulla, P., Aronis, S., Jonsson, B., Sagonas, K.: Optimal dynamic partial order reduction. In: ACM SIGPLAN Notices, vol. 49, pp. 373–384. ACM (2014)
2. Alur, R., Brayton, R.K., Henzinger, T.A., Qadeer, S., Rajamani, S.K.: Partial-order reduction in symbolic state space exploration. In: Grumberg, O. (ed.) CAV 1997. LNCS, vol. 1254, pp. 340–351. Springer, Heidelberg (1997). https://doi.org/10.1007/3-540-63166-6_34
3. Baier, C., Größer, M., Ciesinski, F.: Partial order reduction for probabilistic systems. QEST **4**, 230–239 (2004)
4. Baier, C., Katoen, J.P., Larsen, K.G.: Principles of Model Checking. MIT press, Cambridge (2008)
5. Blondel, V., Hendrickx, J.M., Olshevsky, A., Tsitsiklis, J., et al.: Convergence in multiagent coordination, consensus, and flocking. In: IEEE Conference on Decision and Control, vol. 44, p. 2996. IEEE; 1998 (2005)
6. Cassez, F., Ziegler, F.: Verification of concurrent programs using trace abstraction refinement. In: Davis, M., Fehnker, A., McIver, A., Voronkov, A. (eds.) LPAR 2015. LNCS, vol. 9450, pp. 233–248. Springer, Heidelberg (2015). https://doi.org/10.1007/978-3-662-48899-7_17
7. Chaudhuri, S., Gulwani, S., Lublinerman, R.: Continuity and robustness of programs. Commun. ACM **55**(8), 107–115 (2012)
8. Clarke, E., Jha, S., Marrero, W.: Partial order reductions for security protocol verification. In: Graf, S., Schwartzbach, M. (eds.) TACAS 2000. LNCS, vol. 1785, pp. 503–518. Springer, Heidelberg (2000). https://doi.org/10.1007/3-540-46419-0_34
9. Clarke, E.M., Grumberg, O., Minea, M., Peled, D.: State space reduction using partial order techniques. Int. J. Softw. Tools Technol. Transfer **2**(3), 279–287 (1999)
10. Clarke, E.M., Grumberg, O., Peled, D.: Model Checking. MIT press, Cambridge (1999)
11. Donzé, A.: Breach, a toolbox for verification and parameter synthesis of hybrid systems. In: Computer Aided Verification (CAV) (2010)
12. Donzé, A., Maler, O.: Systematic simulation using sensitivity analysis. In: Bemporad, A., Bicchi, A., Buttazzo, G. (eds.) HSCC 2007. LNCS, vol. 4416, pp. 174–189. Springer, Heidelberg (2007). https://doi.org/10.1007/978-3-540-71493-4_16

13. Duggirala, P.S., Mitra, S., Viswanathan, M.: Verification of annotated models from executions. In: EMSOFT (2013)
14. Duggirala, P.S., Mitra, S., Viswanathan, M., Potok, M.: C2E2: a verification tool for stateflow models. In: Baier, C., Tinelli, C. (eds.) TACAS 2015. LNCS, vol. 9035, pp. 68–82. Springer, Heidelberg (2015). https://doi.org/10.1007/978-3-662-46681-0_5
15. Fan, C., Huang, Z., Mitra, S.: Approximate partial order reduction (full version), May 2018. https://arxiv.org/abs/1610.06317
16. Fan, C., Mitra, S.: Bounded verification with on-the-fly discrepancy computation. In: Finkbeiner, B., Pu, G., Zhang, L. (eds.) ATVA 2015. LNCS, vol. 9364, pp. 446–463. Springer, Cham (2015). https://doi.org/10.1007/978-3-319-24953-7_32
17. Fang, L., Antsaklis, P.J.: Information consensus of asynchronous discrete-time multi-agent systems. In: Proceedings of the 2005, American Control Conference, pp. 1883–1888. IEEE (2005)
18. Fehnker, A., Ivančić, F.: Benchmarks for hybrid systems verification. In: Alur, R., Pappas, G.J. (eds.) HSCC 2004. LNCS, vol. 2993, pp. 326–341. Springer, Heidelberg (2004). https://doi.org/10.1007/978-3-540-24743-2_22
19. Flanagan, C., Godefroid, P.: Dynamic partial-order reduction for model checking software. In: ACM Sigplan Notices, vol. 40, pp. 110–121. ACM (2005)
20. Godefroid, P. (ed.): Partial-Order Methods for the Verification of Concurrent Systems: An Approach to the State-Explosion Problem. LNCS, vol. 1032. Springer, Heidelberg (1996). https://doi.org/10.1007/3-540-60761-7
21. Huang, Z., Fan, C., Mereacre, A., Mitra, S., Kwiatkowska, M.: Simulation-based verification of cardiac pacemakers with guaranteed coverage. IEEE Des. Test 32(5), 27–34 (2015)
22. Huang, Z., Mitra, S.: Proofs from simulations and modular annotations. In: Proceedings of the 17th International Conference on Hybrid systems: Computation and Control, pp. 183–192. ACM (2014)
23. Kurshan, R., Levin, V., Minea, M., Peled, D., Yenigün, H.: Static partial order reduction. In: Steffen, B. (ed.) TACAS 1998. LNCS, vol. 1384, pp. 345–357. Springer, Heidelberg (1998). https://doi.org/10.1007/BFb0054182
24. Majumdar, R., Saha, I.: Symbolic robustness analysis. In: 30th IEEE Real-Time Systems Symposium, RTSS 2009, pp. 355–363. IEEE (2009)
25. Mitra, D.: An asynchronous distributed algorithm for power control in cellular radio systems. In: Holtzman, J.M., Goodman, D.J. (eds.) Wireless and Mobile Communications, pp. 177–186. Springer, Boston (1994)
26. Mitra, S., Chandy, K.M.: A formalized theory for verifying stability and convergence of automata in PVS. In: Mohamed, O.A., Muñoz, C., Tahar, S. (eds.) TPHOLs 2008. LNCS, vol. 5170, pp. 230–245. Springer, Heidelberg (2008). https://doi.org/10.1007/978-3-540-71067-7_20
27. Olfati-Saber, R., Fax, J.A., Murray, R.M.: Consensus and cooperation in networked multi-agent systems. Proc. IEEE 95(1), 215–233 (2007)
28. Peled, D.: Ten years of partial order reduction. In: Hu, A.J., Vardi, M.Y. (eds.) CAV 1998. LNCS, vol. 1427, pp. 17–28. Springer, Heidelberg (1998). https://doi.org/10.1007/BFb0028727
29. Rhee, I.K., Lee, J., Kim, J., Serpedin, E., Wu, Y.C.: Clock synchronization in wireless sensor networks: an overview. Sensors 9(1), 56–85 (2009)
30. Samanta, R., Deshmukh, J.V., Chaudhuri, S.: Robustness analysis of networked systems. In: Giacobbazzi, R., Berdine, J., Mastroeni, I. (eds.) VMCAI 2013. LNCS, vol. 7737, pp. 229–247. Springer, Heidelberg (2013). https://doi.org/10.1007/978-3-642-35873-9_15

31. Welch, J.L., Lynch, N.: A new fault-tolerant algorithm for clock synchronization. Inf. Comput. **77**(1), 1–36 (1988)
32. Yang, Y., Chen, X., Gopalakrishnan, G., Kirby, R.M.: Efficient stateful dynamic partial order reduction. In: Havelund, K., Majumdar, R., Palsberg, J. (eds.) SPIN 2008. LNCS, vol. 5156, pp. 288–305. Springer, Heidelberg (2008). https://doi.org/10.1007/978-3-540-85114-1_20

A Lightweight Deadlock Analysis
for Programs with Threads
and Reentrant Locks

Cosimo Laneve[✉]

Department of Computer Science and Engineering,
University of Bologna – Inria Focus, Bologna, Italy
cosimo.laneve@unibo.it

Abstract. Deadlock analysis of multi-threaded programs with reentrant locks is complex because these programs may have infinitely many states. We define a simple calculus featuring recursion, threads and synchronizations that guarantee exclusive access to objects. We detect deadlocks by associating an abstract model to programs – the *extended lam model* – and we define an algorithm for verifying that a problematic object dependency (e.g. a *circularity*) between threads will not be manifested. The analysis is lightweight because the deadlock detection problem is fully reduced to the corresponding one in lams (without using other models). The technique is intended to be an effective tool for the deadlock analysis of programming languages by defining ad-hoc extraction processes.

1 Introduction

Threads and locks are a common model of concurrent programming that is nowadays widely used by the mainstream programming languages (Java, C#. C++, Objective C, etc.). Most of these languages feature thread creations and guarantee exclusive access to objects by means of synchronizations. In this model, deadlocks are flaws that occur when two or more threads are blocked because each one is attempting to acquire an object's lock held by another one. As an example, consider the following method

```
buildTable(x,y;n) = (newObject z)( if (n=0) then sync(y){ sync(x){ 0 } }
                                    else (newThread sync(x){ sync(z){ 0 } })
                                         buildTable(z,y;n-1)
                     )
```

where newObject z creates a new object (the class is omitted), (newThread P) Q creates a new thread whose body is P (the class is again omitted) and running it in parallel with the continuation Q, and sync(x){ P } is the operation locking the object x and performing P. This method creates a table of $n + 1$ threads – the *philosophers* – each one sharing an object – the *fork* – with the close one. Every philosopher, except one, grabs the fork on his left – the first

© Springer International Publishing AG, part of Springer Nature 2018
K. Havelund et al. (Eds.): FM 2018, LNCS 10951, pp. 608–624, 2018.
https://doi.org/10.1007/978-3-319-95582-7_36

argument – and on his right – the second argument – in this order and then release them. The exceptional case is the **then**-branch (n = 0) where the grabbing strategy is opposite. It is well-known that, when the method is invoked with *buildTable*(x,x;n), no deadlock will ever occur because at least one philosopher has a strategy that is different from the other ones. On the contrary, if we change the **then**-branch into sync(x){ sync(y){ 0 } } a deadlock may occur because philosophers' strategies are all symmetric. It is worth to notice that *buildTable*(x,x;0) is deadlock-free because it just locks twice the object x, which is admitted in the model with threads and locks – a thread may acquire a same lock several times (*lock-reentrancy*).

In order to ensure termination, current analysers [1,4,7,13,19,20] use finite approximate models representing the dependencies between object names. The corresponding algorithms usually return false positives with input *buildTable*(x,x;n) because they are not powerful enough to manage structures that are not statically bounded.

In [10,14] we solved this problem for value-passing CCS [16] and pi-calculus [17]. In that case, the technique used two formal models: Petri Nets and *deadLock Analysis Model* – lams, which are basic recursive models that collect dependencies and features recursion and dynamic name creation. In the pi-calculus analyser, Petri Nets were used to verify the consistency of the communication protocol of every channel, while lams were used for guaranteeing the correctness of the dependencies between different channels. In particular, the corresponding algorithm required a tool for verifying the reachability of Petri Nets that model channels' behaviours (which has exponential computational complexity with respect to the size of the net [12]) and a tool for analysing lams (which has exponential computational complexity with respect to the number of arguments of functions).

In this paper we demonstrate that it is possible to define a deadlock analyzer for programs with threads and (reentrant) locks by only using an extension of lams. For example, the lam function corresponding to *buildTable* is[1]

$$\texttt{buildTable}(t, x, y) = (\nu\, s, z)(\ (y, x)_t + (x, z)_s\ \&\ \texttt{buildTable}(t, z, y)\ ).$$

The term $(y, x)_t$, called *dependency*, indicates that the thread t, which owns the lock of y, is going to grab the lock of x. The operation "+" and "&" are disjunction and conjunctions of dependencies, respectively. The index t of $(y, x)_t$ was missing in [10,14]; it has been necessary for modelling reentrant locks. In particular, (x, x) is a circularity in the standard lam model, whilst $(x, x)_t$ is not a circularity in the *extended lam model* because it means that t is acquiring x *twice*. Therefore, $\texttt{buildTable}(t, x, x)$ manifests a circularity in the model of [10,14] and it does not in the extended model. A problematic lam in the extended model is $(y, x)_t \& (x, y)_s$, which denotes that two *different* threads are attempting to acquire two objects in different order. This lam gives $(x, x)_\checkmark$, which represents a circularity.

---

[1] Actually, the lam function associated to *buildTable* by the type system in Sect. 4 has an additional name that records the last name synchronized by the thread t.

Because of the foregoing extension, the algorithm for detecting circularities in extended lams is different than the one in [10,14]. In particular, while there is a *decision algorithm* for the presence/absence of circularities in standard lams, in Sect. 2 we define an algorithm that verifies the absence and is imprecise in some cases (it may return that a lam will manifest a circularity while it will not be the case – a false positive).

We also define a simple object-oriented calculus featuring recursion, threads and synchronizations that guarantee exclusive access to objects. (The method *buildTable* is written in our calculus.) The syntax, semantics, and examples of the object-oriented calculus are in Sect. 3. In Sect. 4 we define a type system that associates lams to processes. Using the type system, for example, the lam function buildTable can be extracted from the method *buildTable*. As a byproduct of the type system and the lams, our technique can detect deadlocks of programs like *buildTable*. For space constraints, the proof of soundness of the type system is omitted: is is reported in the full paper[2]. We discuss a few weaknesses of the techniques in Sect. 5 and we point to related works and deliver some concluding remark in Sect. 6.

Overall, the technicalities (the algorithm for lams, the syntax and semantics of the calculus, the typing rules, and the type safety) illustrate many interesting features of a deadlock analyser for a full object-oriented language, while remaining pleasingly compact. In fact, this paper also aims at presenting a handy tool for studying the consequences of extensions and variations of the constructs defined here.

2   Lams and the Algorithm for Detecting Circularities

This section extends the theory developed in [10,14] to cover thread reentrancy. In particular, the new definitions are those of transitive closure and Definition 3. Theorem 1 is new.

Preliminaries. We use an infinite set $\mathscr{A}$ of *names*, ranged over by x, y, t, s, $\cdots$. A relation on $\mathscr{A}$, denoted R, R', $\cdots$, is an element of $\mathscr{P}(\mathscr{A} \times \mathscr{A} \times \mathscr{A} \cup \{\checkmark, \bullet\})$, where $\mathscr{P}(\cdot)$ is the standard powerset operator, $\cdot \times \cdot$ is the cartesian product, and $\checkmark, \bullet \notin \mathscr{A}$ are two *special* names. The elements of R, called *dependencies*, are denoted by $(x, y)_t$, where t is called *thread*. The name $\checkmark$ indicates that the dependency is due to the contributions of two or more threads; $\bullet$ indicates that the dependency is due to a thread whose name is unknown.

Let

– R^+ be the least relation containing R and closed under the operations:
   1. if $(x, y)_t, (y, z)_{t'} \in \mathsf{R}^+$ and $t \neq t'$ then $(x, z)_{\checkmark} \in \mathsf{R}^+$;
   2. if $(x, y)_t, (y, z)_t \in \mathsf{R}^+$, $t \in \mathscr{A} \cup \{\checkmark\}$, then $(x, z)_t \in \mathsf{R}^+$;
   3. if $(x, y)_{\bullet}, (y, z)_{\bullet} \in \mathsf{R}^+$, $(x, y)_{\bullet} \neq (y, z)_{\bullet}$, then $(x, z)_{\checkmark} \in \mathsf{R}^+$.

---

[2] Available at http://cs.unibo.it/~laneve/papers/FM2018-full.pdf.

- $\{R_1, \cdots, R_m\} \Subset \{R'_1, \cdots, R'_n\}$ if and only if, for all R_i, there is R'_j such that
  1. if $(x,y)_t \in R_i$, $t \in \mathscr{A}$, then $(x,y)_t \in {R'_j}^+$
  2. if $(x,y)_\checkmark \in R_i$ then either $(x,y)_\checkmark \in {R'_j}^+$ or $(x,y)_t \in {R'_j}^+$ with $t \in \mathscr{A}$;
  3. if $(x,y)_\bullet \in R_i$ then either $(x,y)_\bullet \in {R'_j}^+$ or $(x,y)_t \in {R'_j}^+$ with $t \in \mathscr{A}$.

- $\{R_1, \cdots, R_m\} \& \{R'_1, \cdots, R'_n\} \stackrel{def}{=} \{R_i \cup R'_j \mid 1 \leqslant i \leqslant m \text{ and } 1 \leqslant j \leqslant n\}$.

We use $\mathscr{R}, \mathscr{R}', \cdots$ to range over $\{R_1, \cdots, R_m\}$, which are elements of $\mathscr{P}(\mathscr{P}(\mathscr{A} \times \mathscr{A} \times \mathscr{A} \cup \{\checkmark, \bullet\}))$.

The names $\checkmark$ and $\bullet$ are managed in an ad-hoc way in the transitive closure R^+ and in the relation $\Subset$. In particular, if $(x,y)_t$ and $(y,z)_{t'}$ belong to a relation and $t \neq t'$, the dependency obtained by transitivity, e.g. $(x,z)_\checkmark$, records that it has been produced by a contribution of two different threads – this is important for separating circularities, e.g. $(x,x)_\checkmark$, from lock reentrancy, e.g. $(x,x)_t$. The name $\bullet$ copes with another issue: it allows us to abstract out thread names that are created inside methods. For this reason the transitive dependency of $(x,y)_\bullet$ and $(y,z)_\bullet$ is $(x,z)_\checkmark$ because the threads producing $(x,y)_\bullet$ and $(y,z)_\bullet$ might be different. The meaning of $\mathscr{R} \Subset \mathscr{R}'$ is that $\mathscr{R}'$ is *"more precise"* with respect to pairs (x,y): if this pair is indexed with either $\checkmark$ or $\bullet$ in some $R \in \mathscr{R}$ then it may be indexed by a t ($t \neq \checkmark$) in the corresponding (transitive closure) relation of $\mathscr{R}'$. For example $\{\ \{(x,y)_\bullet, (y,z)_\bullet, (x,z)_\checkmark\}\ \} \Subset \{\ \{(x,y)_t, (y,z)_t\}\ \}$ and $\{\ \{(x,x)_\bullet\}\ \} \Subset \{\ \{(x,x)_t, (x,x)_{t'}\}\ \}$.

Definition 1. *A relation R has a circularity if $(x,x)_\checkmark \in R^+$ for some x. A set of relations $\mathscr{R}$ has a circularity if there is $R \in \mathscr{R}$ that has a circularity.*

Lams. In our technique, dependencies are expressed by means of *lams* [14], noted ℓ, whose syntax is

$$\ell ::= 0 \ \mid \ (x,y)_t \ \mid \ (\nu\, x)\, \ell \ \mid \ \ell \,\&\, \ell \ \mid \ \ell + \ell \ \mid \ \mathtt{f}(\overline{x})$$

The term 0 is the empty type; $(x,y)_t$ specifies a dependency between the name x and the name y that has been created by (the thread) t. The operation $(\nu\, x)\, \ell$ creates a new name x whose scope is the type ℓ; the operations $\ell \,\&\, \ell'$ and $\ell + \ell'$ define the conjunction and disjunction of the dependencies in ℓ and ℓ', respectively. The operators $+$ and $\&$ are associative and commutative. The term $\mathtt{f}(\overline{x})$ defines the invocation of $\mathtt{f}$ with arguments $\overline{x}$. The argument sequence $\overline{x}$ has always at least two elements in our case: the first element is the thread that performed the invocation, the second element is the last object whose lock has been acquired by it.

A *lam program* is a pair $(\mathscr{L}, \ell)$, where $\mathscr{L}$ is a *finite set* of *function definitions*

$$\mathtt{f}(\overline{x}) = \ell_\mathtt{f}$$

with $\ell_\mathtt{f}$ being the *body* of $\mathtt{f}$, and ℓ is the *main lam*. We always assume that $\ell_f = (\nu\, \overline{z})\, \ell'_\mathtt{f}$ where $\ell'_\mathtt{f}$ has no ν-binder. Similarly for ℓ. The function $\mathtt{buildTable}$ in the Introduction is an example of a lam function.

The semantics of lams is very simple: it amounts to unfolding function invocations. Let a *lam context*, noted L[ ], be a term derived by the following syntax:

$$\text{L}[\,] \ ::= \ [\,] \quad | \quad \ell\&\text{L}[\,] \quad | \quad \ell+\text{L}[\,]$$

As usual $\text{L}[\ell]$ is the lam where the hole of L[ ] is replaced by ℓ. We remark that, according to the syntax, lam contexts have no ν-binder. The operational semantics of a program $\big(\mathscr{L}, (\nu\,\overline{x})\,\ell\big)$ is a transition system where *states* are lams, the *transition relation* is the least one satisfying the rule

$$\text{(Red)}$$
$$\frac{\text{f}(\overline{x}) = (\nu\,\overline{z})\,\ell_{\text{f}} \in \mathscr{L} \qquad \overline{z}'\ \text{are fresh}}{\text{L}[\text{f}(\overline{u})] \longrightarrow \text{L}[\ell_{\text{f}}\{\overline{z}'/\overline{z}\}\{\overline{u}/\overline{x}\}]}$$

and the initial state is the lam ℓ. We write $\longrightarrow^*$ for the reflexive and transitive closure of $\longrightarrow$.

For example, if $\text{f}(t,x) = (\nu\ s,z)\ ((x,z)_t\&\text{f}(s,z))$ then $\text{f}(t,x) \longrightarrow (x,z')_t\&\text{f}(t',z')$, where t' and z' are fresh names. By continuing the evaluation of $\text{f}(t,x)$, the reader may observe that (i) every invocation creates new fresh names and (ii) the evaluation does not terminate because f is recursive. These two points imply that a lam model may have infinite states, which makes any analysis nontrivial.

Flattening and Circularities. Lams represent elements of the set $\mathscr{P}(\mathscr{P}(\mathscr{A} \times \mathscr{A} \times \mathscr{A} \cup \{\checkmark,\bullet\}))$. This property is displayed by the following flattening function. Let $\mathscr{L}$ be a set of function definitions and let $I(\cdot)$, called *flattening*, be a function on lams that (1) maps function name f defined in $\mathscr{L}$ to elements of $\mathscr{P}(\mathscr{P}(\mathscr{A} \times \mathscr{A} \times \mathscr{A} \cup \{\checkmark,\bullet\}))$ and (2) is defined on lams as follows

$$I(0) = \{\varnothing\}, \qquad I((x,y)_t) = \{\{(x,y)_t\}\}, \qquad I(\ell\&\ell') = I(\ell)\&I(\ell'),$$

$$I(\ell+\ell') = I(\ell)\cup I(\ell'), \qquad I((\nu\ x)\,\ell) = I(\ell)\{x'/x\}\ \text{with}\ x'\ \text{fresh},$$

$$I(\text{f}(\overline{u})) = I(\text{f})\{\overline{u}/\overline{x}\}\ (\text{where}\ \overline{x}\ \text{are the formal parameters of f}).$$

Let $I^\perp$ be the map such that, for every f defined in $\mathscr{L}$, $I^\perp(\text{f}) = \{\varnothing\}$. For example, let buildTable be the function in the Introduction and let

$$I(\text{buildTable}) = \{\{(y,x)_t\}\} \quad \ell = \text{buildTable}(t,x,y)\&(x,y)_s + (x,y)_s.$$

Then $I(\ell) = \big\{\{(y,x)_t, (x,y)_s\}, \{(x,y)_s\}\big\}$, $I^\perp(\ell) = \{\{(x,y)_s\}\}$.

Definition 2. *A lam ℓ has a circularity if $I^\perp(\ell)$ has a circularity. A lam program $(\mathscr{L},\ell)$ has a circularity if there is $\ell \longrightarrow^* \ell'$ and ℓ' has a circularity.*

For example the above lam ℓ has a circularity because

$$\text{buildTable}(t,x,y)\&(x,y)_s + (x,y)_s$$
$$\longrightarrow ((y,x)_t + (x,z)_s\&\text{buildTable}(t,z,y))\&(x,y)_s + (x,y)_s$$
$$= \ell'$$

and $I^\perp(\ell')$ has a circularity.

Fixpoint Definition of the Interpretation Function. Our algorithm relies on the computation of lam functions' interpretation, which is done by a standard fixpoint technique.

Let $\mathscr{L}$ be the set $\mathtt{f}_i(\overline{x}_i) = (\nu\ \overline{z_i})\ \ell_i$, with $i \in 1..n$. Let $A = \bigcup_{i \in 1..n} \overline{x}_i$ and $\varkappa$ be a special name that does not occur in $(\mathscr{L}, \ell)$. We use the domain $\Big(\mathscr{P}(\mathscr{P}(A \cup \{\varkappa\} \times A \cup \{\varkappa\} \times A \cup \{\checkmark, \bullet\})), \subseteq\Big)$ which is a *finite* lattice [5].

Definition 3. *Let* $\mathtt{f}_i(\overline{x}_i) = (\nu\ \overline{z_i})\ \ell_i$, *with* $i \in 1..n$, *be the function definitions in* $\mathscr{L}$. *The family of flattening functions* $I_{\mathscr{L}}^{(k)} : \{\mathtt{f}_1, \cdots, \mathtt{f}_n\} \to \mathscr{P}(\mathscr{P}(A \cup \{\varkappa\} \times A \cup \{\varkappa\} \times A \cup \{\checkmark, \bullet\}))$ *is defined as follows*

$$I_{\mathscr{L}}^{(0)}(\mathtt{f}_i) = \{\varnothing\} \qquad I_{\mathscr{L}}^{(k+1)}(\mathtt{f}_i) = \{\mathtt{proj}_{\overline{x}_i}^{\overline{z_i}}(\mathtt{R}^+) \mid \mathtt{R} \in I_{\mathscr{L}}^{(k)}(\ell_i)\}$$

where

$$
\begin{aligned}
\mathtt{proj}_{\overline{x}}^{\overline{z}}(\mathtt{R}) \stackrel{def}{=}\ & \{(u,v)_t \mid (u,v)_t \in \mathtt{R}\ and\ u,v \in \overline{x}\ and\ t \in \overline{x} \cup \{\checkmark\}\} \\
& \cup \{(\varkappa, \varkappa)_\checkmark \mid (u,u)_\checkmark \in \mathtt{R}\ and\ u \notin \overline{x}\} \\
& \cup \{(u,v)_\bullet \mid (u,v)_t \in \mathtt{R}\ and\ u,v \in \overline{x}\ and\ t \in \overline{z}\}
\end{aligned}
$$

We notice that $I_{\mathscr{L}}^{(0)}$ is the function $I^\perp$. Let us analyze the definition of $I_{\mathscr{L}}^{(k+1)}(\mathtt{f}_i)$ and, in particular, the function $\mathtt{proj}$:

- first of all, notice that $\mathtt{proj}$ applies to the transitive closures of relations, which may have names in A, $\overline{z}_i$, $\checkmark$, $\bullet$ and $\varkappa$;
- the transitive closure operation is crucial because a circularity may follow with the key contribution of fresh names. For instance the model of $\mathtt{f}(x) = (\nu\ t, t', z)\ (x, z)_t \,\&\, (z, x)_{t'}$ is $\{\{(x, x)_\checkmark\}\}$; the model of $\mathtt{g}() = (\nu\ t, t', x, y)\ (x, y)_t \,\&\, (y, x)_{t'}$ is $\{\{(\varkappa, \varkappa)_\checkmark\}\}$ (this is the reason why we use the name $\varkappa$);
- every dependency $(u, v)_t \in \mathtt{proj}_{\overline{x}}^{\overline{z}}(\mathtt{R})$ is such that $u, v \in \overline{x}$, except for $(\varkappa, \varkappa)_\checkmark$. For example, if $\mathtt{f}'(x, y) = (\nu\ s, z)\ ((x, y)_s \,\&\, (x, z)_s)$ then, if we invoke $\mathtt{f}'(u, v)$ we obtain $(u, v)_{t'} \,\&\, (u, z')_{t'}$, where t' and z' are fresh object names. This lam may be simplified because, being z' fresh and unknown elsewhere, the dependency $(u, z')_{t'}$ will never be involved in a circularity. For example, if we have $\ell = (v, u)_t \,\&\, \mathtt{f}'(u, v)$ then we may safely reason on ℓ'-simplified $(u, v)_t \,\&\, (u, v)_{t'}$. For this reason we drop the dependencies containing fresh names *after their contribution to the transitive closure has been computed*;
- the same argument does not apply to names used as threads. For example, in the above ℓ'-simplified lam we cannot drop $(u, v)_{t'}$ because t' is fresh. In fact, the context $(v, u)_t \,\&\, (u, v)_{t'}$ gives a circularity. Therefore, dependencies whose thread names are fresh must be handled in a different way. We take a simple solution: these dependencies all have $\bullet$ as thread name. That is, we assume that they are all generated by the contribution of different threads. For example, $\mathtt{g}'(x, y) = (\nu\ t)\ (x, y)_t$. Then, $I_{\mathscr{L}}^{(1)}(\mathtt{g}') = \{\{(x, y)_\bullet\}\}$.

Example 1. The flattening functions of `buildTable` are

$$I^{(0)}_{\mathscr{L}}(\texttt{buildTable}) = \{\varnothing\}$$
$$I^{(1)}_{\mathscr{L}}(\texttt{buildTable}) = \{\,\{(y, x)_t\}\,\}$$

As another example, consider the function $\mathbf{g}(x, y, z) = (\nu\, t, u)\,(x, y)_t\, \&\, \mathbf{g}(y, z, u)$. Then:

$$I^{(0)}_{\mathscr{L}}(\mathbf{g}) = \{\varnothing\}$$
$$I^{(1)}_{\mathscr{L}}(\mathbf{g}) = \{\,\{(x, y)_\bullet\}\,\}$$
$$I^{(2)}_{\mathscr{L}}(\mathbf{g}) = \{\,\{(x, y)_\bullet, (y, z)_\bullet, (x, z)_\checkmark\}\,\}$$

Proposition 1. *Let* $\mathbf{f}(\overline{x}) = (\nu\,\overline{z})\,\ell_{\mathbf{f}} \in \mathscr{L}$.

1. *For every* k, $I^{(k)}_{\mathscr{L}}(\mathbf{f}) \in \mathscr{P}(\mathscr{P}((\overline{x} \cup \{\varkappa\}) \times (\overline{x} \cup \{\varkappa\}) \times (\overline{x} \cup \{\checkmark, \bullet\})))$.
2. *For every* k, $I^{(k)}_{\mathscr{L}}(\mathbf{f}) \in I^{(k+1)}_{\mathscr{L}}(\mathbf{f})$, *where* $\overline{z'}$ *are fresh.*

Proof. (1) follows by definition. As regards (2), we observe that $I(\ell)$ is monotonic on I: for every $\mathbf{f}$, $I(\mathbf{f}) \in I'(\mathbf{f})$ implies $I(\ell) \in I'(\ell)$, which can be demonstrated by a standard structural induction on ℓ. Then, an induction on k gives $I^{(k)}_{\mathscr{L}}(\mathbf{f}) \in I^{(k+1)}_{\mathscr{L}}(\mathbf{f})$. □

Since, for every k, $I^{(k)}_{\mathscr{L}}(\mathbf{f}_i)$ ranges over a finite lattice, by the fixpoint theory [5], there exists m such that $I^{(m)}_{\mathscr{L}}$ is a fixpoint, namely $I^{(m)}_{\mathscr{L}} \approx I^{(m+1)}_{\mathscr{L}}$ where $\approx$ is the equivalence relation induced by $\in$. In the following, we let $I_{\mathscr{L}}$, called the *interpretation function* (of a lam), be the least fixpoint $I^{(m)}_{\mathscr{L}}$. In Example 1, $I^{(1)}_{\mathscr{L}}$ is the fixpoint of `buildTable` and $I^{(2)}_{\mathscr{L}}$ is the fixpoint of g.

Proposition 2. *Let* L *be a lam context,* ℓ *be a lam, and* $I(\cdot)$ *be a flattening. Then we have:*

1. $I(\mathrm{L}[\ell])$ *has a circularity if and only if* $I(\mathrm{L}[\mathrm{R}])$ *has a circularity for some* $\mathrm{R} \in I(\ell)$.
2. *Let* $(\mathscr{L}, \ell)$ *be a lam program,* $\mathbf{f}(\overline{x}) = (\nu\,\overline{z})\,\ell_f \in \mathscr{L}$ *and* $\mathrm{R} \in I(\ell_f\{\overline{z'}/\overline{z}\})$ *with* $\overline{z'}$ *fresh. If* $I(\mathrm{L}[\mathrm{R}\{\overline{u}/\overline{x}\}])$ *has a circularity then* $I(\mathrm{L}[(\mathrm{proj}^{\overline{z}}_{\overline{x}}(\mathrm{R}^+))\{\overline{u}/\overline{x}\}])$ *has a circularity.*

Proof. Property 1 follows from the definitions. To see 2, we use a straightforward induction on L. We analyze the basic case $\mathrm{L} = [\,]$: the general case follows by induction. Let $\mathrm{R} \in I(\ell_f\{\overline{z'}/\overline{z}\})$ such that $I(\mathrm{R}\{\overline{u}/\overline{x}\})$ has a circularity. There are two cases:

- $(v, v)_\checkmark \in \mathrm{R}^+$. By definition of $\mathrm{proj}^{\overline{z}}_{\overline{x}}(\mathrm{R}^+)$ either $(v, v)_\checkmark \in \mathrm{proj}^{\overline{z}}_{\overline{x}}(\mathrm{R}^+)$, when $v \notin \overline{z'}$, or $(\varkappa, \varkappa)_\checkmark \in \mathrm{proj}^{\overline{z}}_{\overline{x}}(\mathrm{R}^+)$, otherwise. In this case the statement 2 follows immediately.

– $(v,v)_{\checkmark} \in R\{\overline{u}/\overline{x}\}^+$. By definition of transitive closure $R\{\overline{u}/\overline{x}\}^+ = (R^+)\{\overline{u}/\overline{x}\}$. Then there is a dependency $(x_1,x_2)_{\checkmark} \in R^+$ such that $(x_1,x_2)_{\checkmark}\{\overline{u}/\overline{x}\} = (v,v)_{\checkmark}$. By definition of $\mathtt{proj}$, $(x_1,x_2)_{\checkmark} \in \mathtt{proj}_{\overline{x}}^{\overline{z}}(R^+)$. Therefore $\mathtt{proj}_{\overline{x}}^{\overline{z}}(R^+)\{\overline{u}/\overline{x}\}$ has also a circularity.   □

Lemma 1. *Let* $(\{f_1(\overline{x}_1) = (\nu\ \overline{z}_1)\ \ell_1, \cdots, f_n(\overline{x}_n) = (\nu\ \overline{z}_n)\ \ell_n\}, \ell)$ *be a lam program and let*

$$L[f_{i_1}(\overline{u}_1)] \cdots [f_{i_m}(\overline{u}_m)] \longrightarrow^m L[\ell_{i_1}\{\overline{z}'_1/\overline{z}_{i_1}\}\{\overline{u}_1/\overline{x}_{i_1}\}] \cdots [\ell_{i_m}\{\overline{z}'_m/\overline{z}_{i_m}\}\{\overline{u}_m/\overline{x}_{i_m}\}]$$

where $L[\cdot]\cdots[\cdot]$ *is a multiple context without function invocations.*

If $I_{\mathscr{L}}^{(k)}(L[\ell_{i_1}\{\overline{z}'_1/\overline{z}_{i_1}\}\{\overline{u}_1/\overline{x}_{i_1}\}] \cdots [\ell_{i_m}\{\overline{z}'_m/\overline{z}_{i_m}\}\{\overline{u}_m/\overline{x}_{i_m}\}])$ *has a circularity then* $I_{\mathscr{L}}^{(k+1)}(L[f_{i_1}(\overline{u}_1)] \cdots [f_{i_m}(\overline{u}_m)])$ *has also a circularity.*

Proof. To show the implication suppose that

$$I_{\mathscr{L}}^{(k)}(L[\ell_{i_1}\{\overline{z}'_1/\overline{z}_{i_1}\}\{\overline{u}_1/\overline{x}_{i_1}\}] \cdots [\ell_{i_m}\{\overline{z}'_m/\overline{z}_{i_m}\}\{\overline{u}_m/\overline{x}_{i_m}\}])$$

has a circularity. By repeated applications of Proposition 2(1), there exists $R_j \in I^{(k)}(\ell_{i_1}\{\overline{z}'_j/\overline{z}_{i_j}\}\{\overline{u}_j/\overline{x}_{i_j}\})$ with $1 \leqslant j \leqslant m$ such that $I^{(k)}(L[R_1]\cdots[R_m])$ has a circularity. It is easy to verify that every R_j may be written as $R'_j\{\overline{u}_j/\overline{x}_{i_j}\}$, for some R'_j. By repeated application of Proposition 2(2), we have that

$$I^{(k)}(L[\mathtt{proj}_{\overline{x}_{i_1}}^{\overline{z}_{i_1}}(R'_1{}^+)\{\overline{u}_1/\overline{x}_1\}] \cdots [\mathtt{proj}_{\overline{x}_{i_m}}^{\overline{z}_{i_m}}(R'_m{}^+)\{\overline{u}_m/\overline{x}_m\}])$$

has a circularity. Since, for every $1 \leqslant j \leqslant m$,

$$\mathtt{proj}_{\overline{x}_{i_j}}^{\overline{z}_{i_j}}(R'_j{}^+)\{\overline{u}_1/\overline{x}_1\} \in I^{(k+1)}(f_{i_j}(\overline{u}_j))$$

and since L has no function invocation, we derive that $I_{\mathscr{L}}^{(k+1)}(L[f_{i_1}(\overline{u}_1)] \cdots [f_{i_m}(\overline{u}_m)])$ has also a circularity.   □

Unlike [10,14], Lemma 1 is strict in our case, for every k. For example, consider

$$h(x,y,z) = (\nu\ t)\ (x,y)_t\ \&\ (y,z)_t.$$

Then, when $k \geqslant 1$, $I_{\mathscr{L}}^{(k)}(h) = \{\ \{(x,y)_{\bullet}, (y,z)_{\bullet}\}\ \}$. Notice that $I_{\mathscr{L}}^{(k)}(h(x,y,x)) = \{\ \{(x,y)_{\bullet}, (y,x)_{\bullet}\}\ \}$, which has a circularity – see Definition 1. However

$$I_{\mathscr{L}}^{(k)}((x,y)_t\ \&\ (y,x)_t) = \{\ \{(x,y)_t, (y,x)_t, (x,x)_t\}\ \}$$

has no circularity (this is a case of reentrant lock).

Theorem 1. *Let* $(\mathscr{L}, \ell)$ *be a lam program and* $\ell \longrightarrow^* \ell'$. *If* $I_{\mathscr{L}}(\ell')$ *has a circularity then* $I_{\mathscr{L}}(\ell)$ *has also a circularity. Therefore* $(\mathscr{L}, \ell)$ *has no circularity if* $I_{\mathscr{L}}(\ell)$ *has no circularity.*

Proof. Let ℓ' have a circularity. Hence, by definition, $I^{\perp}(\ell')$ has a circularity and, since $I^{\perp}(\ell') = I_{\mathscr{L}}^{(0)}(\ell')$, by Proposition 1(2) $I_{\mathscr{L}}^{(0)}(\ell') \in I_{\mathscr{L}}(\ell')$. Therefore $I_{\mathscr{L}}(\ell')$ has also a circularity. Then, by Lemma 1, since $I_{\mathscr{L}}$ is the fixpoint interpretation function, $I_{\mathscr{L}}(\ell)$ has also a circularity.   □

Our algorithm for verifying that a lam will never manifest a circularity consists of computing $I_{\mathscr{L}}(\mathtt{f})$, for every $\mathtt{f}$, and $I_{\mathscr{L}}(\ell)$, where ℓ is the main lam. As discussed in this section, $I_{\mathscr{L}}(\mathtt{f})$ uses a saturation technique on names based on a powerset construction. Hence it has a computational complexity that is *exponential* on the number of names. We remind that the names we consider are the *arguments* of lam functions (that corresponds to methods' arguments), which are usually not so many. In fact, this algorithm is quite efficient in practice [9].

3   The Language and Its Semantics

In the rest of the paper, we use lams to define an analysis technique for a simple programming model of concurrent object-oriented languages (the basic operations of thread creation and synchronization used in Java and C# may be easily recognized). In this section we first define the model, give a description of how deadlock may be identified, and discuss few examples. The next section defines the type system associating lams to the programs.

Our model has two disjoint countable sets of names: there are *integer and object names*, ranged over by $x, y, z, t, s, \cdots$, and *method names*, ranged over by A, B, $\cdots$. A *program* is a pair $(\mathscr{D}, P)$, where $\mathscr{D}$ is a *finite set* of *method name definitions* $A(\overline{x}; \overline{y}) = P_A$, with $\overline{x}; \overline{y}$ and P_A respectively being the *formal parameters* and the *body* of A, and P is the *main process*.

The syntax of processes P and expressions e is defined below

$$P ::= \quad 0 \quad | \quad (\nu\, x)\, P \quad | \quad (\nu\, P)\, P \quad | \quad \text{if } e \text{ then } P \text{ else } P \quad | \quad A(\overline{x}; \overline{y})$$
$$| \quad sync(x)\{\, P\, \}.\, P$$
$$e ::= \quad x \quad | \quad v \quad | \quad e\, \mathbf{op}\, e$$

A process can be the inert process 0, or a restriction $(\nu\, x)\, P$ that behaves like P except that the external environment cannot access to the object x, or the spawn $(\nu\, Q)\, P$ of a new thread Q by a process P, or a conditional if e then P else Q that evaluates e and behaves either like P or like Q depending on whether the value is $\neq 0$ (*true*) or $= 0$ (*false*), or an invocation $A(\overline{x}; \overline{y})$ of the process corresponding to A. In the invocation, a semicolon separates the arguments that are objects from those that are integers. The last process is $sync(x)\{\, P\, \}.\, Q$ that executes P with exclusive access to x and then performs Q. An expression e can be a name x, an integer value v, or a generic binary operation on integers $v\, \mathbf{op}\, v'$, where $\mathbf{op}$ ranges over a set including the usual operators like $+$, $\leqslant$, etc. Integer expressions without names (*constant expressions*) may be evaluated to an integer value (the definition of the evaluation of constant expressions is omitted). Let $[\![e]\!]$ be the evaluation of a constant expression e ($[\![e]\!]$ is undefined when the integer expression e contains integer names). Let also $[\![x]\!] = x$ when x is a non-integer name. We always shorten $sync(x)\{\ P\ \}.\ 0$ into $sync(x)\{\ P\ \}$.

In order to define the operational semantics, we use terms $\mathbb{P} ::= P \mid P \overset{x}{\bullet} \mathbb{P}$ that are called *threads*. The term $P \overset{x}{\bullet} \mathbb{P}$ corresponds to a thread that is performing P in a critical section for x; when P terminates, the lock of x must be released (if $\mathbb{P}$ does not contain $\overset{x}{\bullet}$) and the continuation $\mathbb{P}$ may start. The thread $\mathbb{P}$ is *reentrant* on x when $\overset{x}{\bullet}$ occurs at least twice in $\mathbb{P}$.

States, ranged over by $\mathscr{T}$, are multisets of threads, written $\mathbb{P}_1 \mid \cdots \mid \mathbb{P}_n$ and sometime shortened into $\prod_{i\in 1..n} \mathbb{P}_i$. We write $x \in \mathbb{P}$ if $\mathbb{P}$ contains $\overset{x}{\bullet}$; we write $x \in \mathscr{T}$ if there is $\mathbb{P} \in \mathscr{T}$ such that $x \in \mathbb{P}$.

Definition 4. *The* structural equivalence $\equiv$ *on threads is the least congruence containing alpha-conversion of bound names, commutativity and associativity of* $\mid$ *with identity* 0*, closed under the rule:*

$$((\nu\ x)\ \mathbb{P}) \mid \mathscr{T} \equiv (\nu\ x)\ (\mathbb{P} \mid \mathscr{T}) \qquad x \notin var(\mathscr{T}).$$

The operational semantics *of a program* $(\mathscr{D}, P)$ *is a transition system where the initial state is* P*, and the* transition relation $\longrightarrow_{\mathscr{D}}$ *is the least one closed under the rules (the notation* $P[\overset{x}{\bullet} \mathbb{P}]$ *stands for either* P *or* $P \overset{x}{\bullet} \mathbb{P}$*):*

$$\text{(ZERO)}$$
$$0 \overset{x}{\bullet} \mathbb{P} \mid \mathscr{T} \longrightarrow_{\mathscr{D}} \mathbb{P} \mid \mathscr{T}$$

$$\text{(NEWO)} \qquad \frac{z\ fresh}{(\nu\ x)\ \mathbb{P} \mid \mathscr{T} \longrightarrow_{\mathscr{D}} \mathbb{P}\{z/x\} \mid \mathscr{T}}$$

$$\text{(NEWT)} \qquad (\nu\ P)\ \mathbb{P} \mid \mathscr{T} \longrightarrow_{\mathscr{D}} P \mid \mathbb{P} \mid \mathscr{T}$$

$$\text{(IFT)} \qquad \frac{[\![e]\!] \neq 0}{\text{if } e \text{ then } P \text{ else } P'[\overset{x}{\bullet} \mathbb{P}] \mid \mathscr{T} \longrightarrow_{\mathscr{D}} P[\overset{x}{\bullet} \mathbb{P}] \mid \mathscr{T}}$$

$$\text{(IFF)} \qquad \frac{[\![e]\!] = 0}{\text{if } e \text{ then } P \text{ else } P'[\overset{x}{\bullet} \mathbb{P}] \mid \mathscr{T} \longrightarrow_{\mathscr{D}} P'[\overset{x}{\bullet} \mathbb{P}] \mid \mathscr{T}}$$

$$\text{(CALL)} \qquad \frac{[\![\overline{e}]\!] = \overline{v} \quad A(\overline{y}; \overline{z}) = P \in \mathscr{D}}{A(\overline{u}; \overline{e})[\overset{x}{\bullet} \mathbb{P}] \mid \mathscr{T} \longrightarrow_{\mathscr{D}} P\{\overline{u}; \overline{v}/\overline{y}, \overline{z}\}[\overset{x}{\bullet} \mathbb{P}] \mid \mathscr{T}}$$

$$\text{(SYNC)} \qquad \frac{x \notin \mathscr{T}}{sync(x)\{\ P\ \}.\ \mathbb{P} \mid \mathscr{T} \longrightarrow_{\mathscr{D}} P \overset{x}{\bullet} \mathbb{P} \mid \mathscr{T}}$$

$$\text{(CONG)} \qquad \frac{\mathscr{T}_1' \longrightarrow_{\mathscr{D}} \mathscr{T}_2'}{\mathscr{T}_1 \equiv (\nu\ x)\ \mathscr{T}_1' \quad (\nu\ x)\ \mathscr{T}_2' \equiv \mathscr{T}_2}{\mathscr{T}_1 \longrightarrow_{\mathscr{D}} \mathscr{T}_2}$$

We often omit the subscript of $\longrightarrow_{\mathscr{D}}$ *when it is clear from the context. We write* $\longrightarrow^*$ *for the reflexive and transitive closure of* $\longrightarrow$*.*

Definition 5 (deadlock-freedom). *A program* $(\mathscr{D}, P)$ *is deadlock-free if the following condition holds:*

whenever $P \longrightarrow^* \mathscr{T}$ *and* $\mathscr{T} \equiv (\nu\ x_1) \cdots (\nu\ x_n)\ (sync(x)\{\ P'\ \}.\ \mathbb{P} \mid \mathscr{T}')$
then there exists $\mathscr{T}''$ *such that* $\mathscr{T} \longrightarrow \mathscr{T}''$*.*

Example 2. We select three processes and discuss their behaviours, highlighting whether they deadlock or not:

- $(\nu \; sync(x)\{ \; sync(y)\{ \; 0 \; \} \; \})$ $sync(x)\{ \; sync(y)\{ \; 0 \; \} \; \}$. This process spawns a thread that acquire the locks of x and y in the *same order* of the main thread: no deadlock will ever occur.
- On the contrary, the process $(\nu \; sync(y)\{ \; sync(x)\{ \; 0 \; \} \; \})$ $sync(x)\{ \; sync(y) \{0\}\}$ spawns a thread acquiring the locks in reverse order. This is a computation giving a deadlock:

$$(\nu \; sync(y)\{ \; sync(x)\{ \; 0 \; \} \; \}) \; sync(x)\{ \; sync(y)\{ \; 0 \; \} \; \}$$
$$\longrightarrow \quad sync(y)\{ \; sync(x)\{ \; 0 \; \} \; \} \mid sync(x)\{ \; sync(y)\{ \; 0 \; \} \; \}$$
$$\longrightarrow \quad sync(x)\{ \; 0 \; \} \overset{y}{\bullet} 0 \mid sync(x)\{ \; sync(y)\{ \; 0 \; \} \; \}$$
$$\longrightarrow \quad sync(x)\{ \; 0 \; \} \overset{y}{\bullet} 0 \mid sync(y)\{ \; 0 \; \} \overset{x}{\bullet} 0$$

- The following method

$$A(x,y;n) = \texttt{if} \; (n = 0) \; \texttt{then} \; (\nu \; sync(y)\{ \; sync(x)\{ \; 0 \; \} \; \}) \; sync(y)\{ \; 0 \; \}$$
$$\texttt{else} \; sync(x)\{ \; A(x,y;n-1) \; \}$$

performs n-nested synchronizations on x (reentrancy) and then spawns a thread acquiring the locks y, x in this order, while the main thread acquire the lock y. This method deadlocks for every $n \geqslant 1$, however it never deadlocks when $n \leqslant 0$.

4   Static Semantics

Environments, ranged over by Γ, contain the types of objects, e.g. $x \; : \; \texttt{C}$ (we assume objects have all the same class $\texttt{C}$), the type of integer variables e.g. $x : \texttt{int}$, and the types of process names, e.g. $A : [\overline{C}; \overline{\texttt{int}}]$. Types $\texttt{C}$ and $\texttt{int}$ are ranged over by $\texttt{T}$. Let $dom(\Gamma)$ be the domain of Γ and let

- $\Gamma, x{:}\texttt{T}$, when $x \notin dom(\Gamma)$

$$(\Gamma, x{:}\texttt{T})(y) \overset{def}{=} \begin{cases} \texttt{T} & \text{if } y = x \\ \Gamma(x) & \text{otherwise} \end{cases}$$

- $\Gamma + \Gamma'$, when $x \in dom(\Gamma) \cap dom(\Gamma')$ implies $\Gamma(x) = \Gamma'(x)$:

$$(\Gamma + \Gamma')(x) \overset{def}{=} \begin{cases} \Gamma(x) & \text{if } x \in dom(\Gamma) \\ \Gamma'(x) & \text{if } x \in dom(\Gamma') \\ \text{undefined} & \text{otherwise} \end{cases}$$

We also use sequences σ of (object) names that record the nesting of synchronizations. Let $(x_1 \cdots x_n)^t \overset{def}{=} \&_{i \in 1..n-1}(x_i, x_{i+1})t$.

The static semantics has two judgments:

- $\Gamma \vdash e : \mathtt{T}$ – the expression e has type $\mathtt{T}$ in Γ;
- $\Gamma; \sigma \vdash_t P : \ell$ – the thread P with name t has lam ℓ in $\Gamma; \sigma$.

Processes:

$$(\text{T-Zero}) \quad \Gamma; \sigma \vdash_t 0 : (\sigma)^t$$

$$(\text{T-New}) \quad \frac{\Gamma, x{:}\mathtt{C}; \sigma \vdash_t P : \ell}{\Gamma \vdash_t (\nu\, x)\, P : (\nu\, x)\, \ell}$$

$$(\text{T-Sync}) \quad \frac{\Gamma; \sigma \cdot x \vdash_t P : \ell \quad \Gamma; \sigma \vdash_t P' : \ell'}{\Gamma; \sigma \vdash_t sync(x)\{\ P\ \}.\ P' : \ell + \ell'}$$

$$(\text{T-If}) \quad \frac{\Gamma \vdash_t e : \mathtt{int} \quad \Gamma; \sigma \vdash_t P : \ell \quad \Gamma; \sigma \vdash_t P' : \ell'}{\Gamma; \sigma \vdash_t \mathtt{if}\ e\ \mathtt{then}\ P\ \mathtt{else}\ P' : \ell + \ell'}$$

$$(\text{T-Par}) \quad \frac{\Gamma; \sigma \vdash_t P : \ell \quad \Gamma, t'{:}\mathtt{C}, z'{:}\mathtt{C}; z' \vdash_{t'} P' : \ell'}{\Gamma; \sigma \vdash_t (\nu\, P')\, P : \ell \& (\nu\, t', z')\, \ell'}$$

$$(\text{T-Call}) \quad \frac{\Gamma(A) = [\overline{\mathtt{C}}; \overline{\mathtt{int}}] \quad |\overline{u}| = |\overline{\mathtt{C}}| \quad \Gamma \vdash \overline{e} : \overline{\mathtt{int}}}{\Gamma; \sigma \cdot x \vdash_t A(\overline{u}; \overline{e}) : \mathtt{f}_A(t, x, \overline{u}) \& (\sigma \cdot x)^t}$$

Expressions:

$$(\text{T-Int}) \quad \Gamma \vdash n : \mathtt{int}$$

$$(\text{T-Var}) \quad \Gamma, x : \mathtt{T} \vdash x : \mathtt{T}$$

$$(\text{T-Op}) \quad \frac{\Gamma \vdash e : \mathtt{int} \quad \Gamma \vdash e' : \mathtt{int}}{\Gamma \vdash e\ op\ e' : \mathtt{int}}$$

$$(\text{T-Seq}) \quad \frac{(\Gamma \vdash e_i : \mathtt{T}_i)^{i \in 1..n}}{\Gamma \vdash e_1, \ldots, e_n : \mathtt{T}_1, \ldots, \mathtt{T}_n}$$

Programs:

$$(\text{T-Prog})$$
$$\mathscr{D} = \bigcup\nolimits_{i \in 1..n} \{A_i(\overline{x}_i; \overline{y}_i) = P_i\} \quad \Gamma = (A_i : [\overline{\mathtt{C}}; \overline{\mathtt{int}}])^{i \in 1..n}$$

$$(\Gamma, \overline{x}_i{:}\overline{\mathtt{C}}, \overline{y}_i{:}\overline{\mathtt{int}}, t_i{:}\mathtt{C}, z_i{:}\mathtt{C}; z_i \vdash_{t_i} P_i : \ell_i)^{i \in 1..n} \quad \Gamma, t{:}\mathtt{C}, z{:}\mathtt{C}; z \vdash_t P : \ell$$

$$\mathscr{L} = \bigcup\nolimits_{i \in 1..n} \{\mathtt{f}_{A_i}(t_i, z_i, \overline{x}_i) = \ell_i\}$$
$$\overline{\Gamma \vdash (\mathscr{D}, P) : (\mathscr{L}, \ell)}$$

Fig. 1. The type system (we assume a function name $\mathtt{f}_A$ for every process name A)

The type system is defined in Fig. 1. A few key rules are discussed. Rule (T-Zero) types the process 0 in a thread t that has locked the objects in σ in (inverse) order. The lam is the conjunction of dependencies in σ with thread t – c.f. notation $(\sigma)^t$. Rule (T-Sync) types the critical section P with a sequence of locks extended with x. The corresponding lam is in disjunction with the lam of the continuation P' because, in P' the lock on x has been released. Rule (T-Par) types a parallel composition of processes by collecting the lams of the components. Rule (T-Call) types a process name invocation in terms of a (lam) function invocation and constrains the sequences of object names in the two invocations to have equal lengths ($|\overline{u}| = |\overline{\mathtt{C}}|$) and the types of expressions to match with the types in the process declaration. The arguments of the lam function invocation are extended with the thread name of the caller and the name of the last object locked by it (and not yet released). In addition we also conjunct the dependencies $(\sigma \cdot x)^t$ created by the caller.

Example 3. Let us show the typing of the method `buildTable` in the Introduction (the keywords `newThread` and `newObject` are replaced by ν). Let

$$\Gamma = buildTable{:}[C,C,C,C;\text{int}], x{:}C, y{:}C, n{:}\text{int}, t{:}C, u{:}C$$
$$P = sync(y)\{sync(x)\{0\}\}$$
$$Q = (\nu\ sync(x)\{sync(z)\{0\}\})\ buildTable(t, u, z, y; n-1)$$

Then

$$\cfrac{\cfrac{\Gamma, z : C; u \cdot y \cdot x \vdash_t 0 : \ell_1 \quad \ell_1 = (u,y)_t \& (y,x)_t}{\cfrac{\Gamma, z : C; u \cdot y \vdash_t sync(x)\{0\} : \ell_1}{\Gamma, z : C; u \vdash_t P : \ell_1}} \quad \cfrac{(*)}{\Gamma, z : C; u \vdash_t Q : \ell_2}}{\cfrac{\Gamma, z : C; u \vdash_t \text{if } n = 0 \text{ then } P \text{ else } Q : \ell_1 + \ell_2}{\Gamma; u \vdash_t (\nu\ z)\ (\text{if } n = 0 \text{ then } P \text{ else } Q : (\nu\ z)\ \ell_1 + \ell_2)}}$$

where $\ell_2 = (\nu\ s, v)\ \ell'_2 + \ell''_2$ and $(*)$ are the two proof trees

$$\cfrac{\cdots}{\Gamma, z : C, s{:}C, v{:}C; v \vdash_t sync(x)\{sync(z)\{0\}\} : \ell'_2}$$

and

$$\cfrac{\cdots}{\Gamma, z : C; u \vdash_t buildTable(t, u, z, y; n-1) : \ell''_2}$$

(the reader may complete them). After completing the proof tree, one obtains the lam function

$$\text{buildTable}(t, u, x, y) = (\nu\ z, s, v)\ ((u,y)_t \& (y,x)_t$$
$$+ (v,x)_s \& (x,z)_s \& \text{buildTable}(t, u, z, y))$$

which has an additional argument with respect to the one in the Introduction.

The following theorem states the soundness of our type system.

Theorem 2. *Let* $\Gamma \vdash (\mathscr{D}, P) : (\mathscr{L}, \ell)$. *If* $(\mathscr{L}, \ell)$ *has no circularity then* $(\mathscr{D}, P)$ *is deadlock-free.*

Example 4. Let us verify whether the process $buildTable(x, x, n)$ is deadlock-free. The lam function associated by the type system is detailed in Example 3. The interpretation function $I_{\mathscr{L}}(\text{buildTable})$ is computed as follows:

$$I_{\mathscr{L}}^{(0)}(\text{buildTable}) = \{\varnothing\}$$
$$I_{\mathscr{L}}^{(1)}(\text{buildTable}) = \{\ \{(u,y)_t, (y,x)_t, (u,x)_t\}\ \}$$
$$I_{\mathscr{L}}^{(2)}(\text{buildTable}) = \{\ \{(u,y)_t, (y,x)_t, (u,x)_t\}, \{(u,y)_t\}\ \}.$$

Since $I_{\mathscr{L}}^{(2)} = I_{\mathscr{L}}$, we are reduced to compute $I_{\mathscr{L}}^{(2)}(\text{buildTable}(t,u,x,x))$. That is

$$\{\ \{(u,y)_t,(y,x)_t,(u,x)_t\},\ \{(u,y)_t\}\ \}\{^x/_y\} = \{\ \{(u,x)_t,(x,x)_t\},\ \{(u,x)_t\}\ \}$$

which has no circularity, therefore the process $\textit{buildTable}(x,x,n)$ is deadlock-free.

It is interesting to verify whether the process $\textit{buildTableD}(x,x,n)$ is deadlock-free, where $\textit{buildTableD}$ is the method having philosophers with symmetric strategies:

```
buildTableD(x,y;n) = (ν z)( if (n=0) then sync(x){ sync(y){ 0 } }
                           else (ν sync(x){ sync(z){ 0 } })
                                buildTableD(z,y;n-1)
                     )
```

In this case $I_{\mathscr{L}}(\text{buildTableD}) = \{\ \{(u,x)_t,(x,y)_t,(u,y)_t\},\ \{(x,y)_\checkmark,(u,y)_t\}\ \}$. It is easy to verify that $I_{\mathscr{L}}(\text{buildTableD}(t,x,x))$ has a circularity, therefore the process $\textit{buildTableD}(x,x,n)$ may have (and actually has) a deadlock.

5 Remarks About the Analysis Technique

The deadlock analysis technique presented in this paper is lightweight because it is compact, intelligible and theoretically manageable. The technique is also very powerful because we can successfully verify processes like buildTable and its variant where every philosopher has a symmetric strategy. However, there are processes for which our technique of collecting dependencies is too rough (and we get false positives).

One example is

$$(\nu\ \textit{sync}(x)\{\ \textit{sync}(z)\{\ \textit{sync}(y)\{\ 0\ \}\ \}\ \})\ \textit{sync}(x)\{\ \textit{sync}(y)\{\ \textit{sync}(z)\{\ 0\ \}\ \}\ \}.$$

This process has two threads: the first one locks x and then z and y in order; the second one locks x and then grabs y and z in order. Since the two threads initially compete on the object x, they will be executed *in sequence* and no deadlock will ever occur. However, if we compute the dependencies, we obtain

$$(x\cdot z\cdot y)^t\ \&\ (x\cdot y\cdot z)^s$$

that is equal to $((x,z)_t\&(z,y)_t)\ \&\ ((x,y)_s\&(y,z)_s)$ where the reader may easily recognize the circularity $(z,y)_t\&(y,z)_s$. This inaccuracy follows by the fact that our technique does not record the dependencies between threads and their state (of locks) when the spawns occur: this is the price we pay to simplicity. In [9] we overcome this issue by associating line codes to symbolic names and dependencies. Then, when a circularity is found, we can exhibit an abstract witness computation that, at least in the simple cases as the above one, can be used to manually verify whether the circularity is a false positive or not.

Another problematic process is $A(x, y, n)$ in Example 2(3). This process never deadlocks when $n \leqslant 0$. However, since our technique drops integer values, it always return a circularity (this is a correct result when $n > 0$ and it is false positive otherwise). To cope with these cases, it suffices to complement our analysis with standard techniques of data-flow analysis and abstract evaluation of expressions.

6   Related Works and Conclusions

In this paper we have defined a simple technique for detecting deadlocks in object-oriented programs. This technique uses an extension of the lam model in order to cope with reentrant locks, a standard feature of object-oriented programs. We have defined an algorithm for verifying the absence of circularities in lams and we have applied this model to a simple concurrent object-oriented calculus. This work is intended to serve as a core system for studying the consequences of extensions and variations.

The lam model has been introduced and studied for detecting deadlocks of an object-oriented language with futures (and no lock and lock reentrancy) [11], but the extension discussed in this paper is new as well as the algorithm for the circularity of lams. We have prototyped this algorithm in JaDA, where we use it for the deadlock analysis of Java bytecode [9]. The paper [15], reports an initial assessment of JaDA with respect to other tools (it also contains a (very) informal description of the algorithm). As we discussed in the Introduction, the model has been also applied to process calculi [10,14].

Several techniques have been developed for the deadlock detection of concurrent object-oriented languages. The technique [2] uses a data-flow analysis that constructs an execution flow graph and searches for cycles within this graph. Some heuristics are used to remove likely false positives. No alias analysis to resolve object identity across method calls is attempted. This analysis is performed in [6,18], which can detect reentrance on restricted cases, such as when lock expressions concern local variables (the reentrance of formal parameters, as in *buildTable*(x,x;0) is not detected). The technique in [3] and its refinement [6] use a theory that is based on monitors. Therefore the technique is a runtime technique that tags each segment of the program reached by the execution flow and specifies the exact order of lock acquisitions. Thereafter, these segments are analyzed for detecting potential deadlocks that might occur because of different scheduler choices (than the current one). This kind of technique is partial because one might overlook sensible patterns of methods' arguments (*cf. buildTable*, for instance). A powerful static techniques that is based on abstract interpretation is SACO [8]. SACO has been developed for ABS, an object-oriented language with a concurrent model different from Java. A comparison between SACO and a tool using a technique similar to the one in this paper can be found in [11].

Our future work includes the analysis of concurrent features of object-oriented calculi that have not been studied yet. A relevant one is thread coordination, which is usually expressed by the methods `wait` and `notify` (and `notifyAll`). These methods modify the scheduling of processes: the thread executing `wait`(x) is suspended, and the corresponding lock on x is released; the thread executing `notify`(x) wakes up one thread suspended on x, which will attempt again to grab x. A simple deadlock in programs with `wait` and `notify` is when the `wait` operation is either mismatched or *happens-after* the matching notification. For this reason we are currently analysing Petri Nets techniques that complement our extended lam model with *happen-before* informations, in the same way as we did for process calculi.

References

1. Abadi, M., Flanagan, C., Freund, S.N.: Types for safe locking: static race detection for java. ACM Trans. Program. Lang. Syst. **28**, 207–255 (2006)
2. Atkey, R., Sannella, D.: Threadsafe: static analysis for java concurrency. In: Electronic Communications of the ECEASST, vol. 72 (2015)
3. Bensalem, S., Havelund, K.: Dynamic deadlock analysis of multi-threaded programs. In: Ur, S., Bin, E., Wolfsthal, Y. (eds.) HVC 2005. LNCS, vol. 3875, pp. 208–223. Springer, Heidelberg (2006). https://doi.org/10.1007/11678779_15
4. Boyapati, C., Lee, R., Rinard, M.: Ownership types for safe program: preventing data races and deadlocks. In: OOPSLA, pp. 211–230. ACM (2002)
5. Davey, B.A., Priestley, H.A.: Introduction to Lattices and Order. Cambridge University Press, Cambridge (2002)
6. Eslamimehr, M., Palsberg, J.: Sherlock: scalable deadlock detection for concurrent programs. In: Proceedings of the 22nd International Symposium on Foundations of Software Engineering (FSE-22), pp. 353–365. ACM (2014)
7. Flanagan, C., Qadeer, S.: A type and effect system for atomicity. In: PLDI, pp. 338–349. ACM (2003)
8. Flores-Montoya, A.E., Albert, E., Genaim, S.: May-happen-in-parallel based deadlock analysis for concurrent objects. In: Beyer, D., Boreale, M. (eds.) FMOODS/-FORTE -2013. LNCS, vol. 7892, pp. 273–288. Springer, Heidelberg (2013). https://doi.org/10.1007/978-3-642-38592-6_19
9. Garcia, A., Laneve, C.: JaDA - the Java deadlock analyser. In: Behavioural Types: From Theories to Tools, pp. 169–192. River Publishers (2017)
10. Giachino, E., Kobayashi, N., Laneve, C.: Deadlock analysis of unbounded process networks. In: Baldan, P., Gorla, D. (eds.) CONCUR 2014. LNCS, vol. 8704, pp. 63–77. Springer, Heidelberg (2014). https://doi.org/10.1007/978-3-662-44584-6_6
11. Giachino, E., Laneve, C., Lienhardt, M.: A framework for deadlock detection in core ABS. Softw. Syst. Model. **15**(4), 1013–1048 (2016)
12. Jones, N.D., Landweber, L.H., Lien, Y.E.: Complexity of some problems in Petri nets. Theor. Comput. Sci. **4**(3), 277–299 (1977)
13. Kobayashi, N.: A new type system for deadlock-free processes. In: Baier, C., Hermanns, H. (eds.) CONCUR 2006. LNCS, vol. 4137, pp. 233–247. Springer, Heidelberg (2006). https://doi.org/10.1007/11817949_16
14. Kobayashi, N., Laneve, C.: Deadlock analysis of unbounded process networks. Inf. Comput. **252**, 48–70 (2017)

15. Laneve, C., Garcia, A.: Deadlock detection of java bytecode. In: LOPSTR 2017 Pre-proceedings (2017). http://arxiv.org/abs/1709.04152
16. Milner, R. (ed.): A Calculus of Communicating Systems. LNCS, vol. 92. Springer, Heidelberg (1980). https://doi.org/10.1007/3-540-10235-3
17. Milner, R., Parrow, J., Walker, D.: A calculus of mobile processes, ii. Inf. Comput. **100**, 41–77 (1992)
18. Naik, M., Park, C.-S., Sen, K., Gay, D.: Effective static deadlock detection. In: Proceedings of the 31st International Conference on Software Engineering (ICSE 2009), pp. 386–396. ACM (2009)
19. Suenaga, K.: Type-based deadlock-freedom verification for non-block-structured lock primitives and mutable references. In: Ramalingam, G. (ed.) APLAS 2008. LNCS, vol. 5356, pp. 155–170. Springer, Heidelberg (2008). https://doi.org/10.1007/978-3-540-89330-1_12
20. Vasconcelos, V.T., Martins, F., Cogumbreiro, T.: Type inference for deadlock detection in a multithreaded polymorphic typed assembly language. In: PLACES. EPTCS, vol. 17, pp. 95–109 (2009)

Formal Specification and Verification of Dynamic Parametrized Architectures

Alessandro Cimatti, Ivan Stojic$^{(\boxtimes)}$, and Stefano Tonetta

FBK-irst, Trento, Italy
{cimatti,stojic,tonettas}@fbk.eu

Abstract. We propose a novel approach to the formal specification and verification of dynamic architectures that are at the core of adaptive systems such as critical infrastructure protection. Key features include run-time reconfiguration based on adding and removing components and connections, resulting in systems with unbounded number of components. We provide a logic-based specification of a Dynamic Parametrized Architecture (DPA), where parameters represent the infinite-state space of possible configurations, and first-order formulas represent the sets of initial configurations and reconfiguration transitions. We encode information flow properties as reachability problems of such DPAs, define a translation into an array-based transition system, and use a Satisfiability Modulo Theories (SMT)-based model checker to tackle a number of case studies.

1 Introduction

In many applications, safety-critical systems are becoming more and more networked and open. For example, many critical infrastructures such as energy distribution, air traffic management, transport infrastructures, and industrial control nowadays employ remote communication and control. Critical infrastructure protection is becoming of paramount importance as witnessed for example by related European and US frameworks [1,2] which promote actions to make critical infrastructures more resilient.

In order to be resilient, a system must be adaptive, changing its architectural configuration at run-time, due to new requirements, component failures or attacks. A reconfiguration means adding and removing components and connections, so that the resulting system has an infinite state space where each state is an architectural configuration. In this context, simple reachability properties such as the existence of information flow paths become very challenging due to the interplay between communications and reconfigurations. The design, implementation, and certification of a system with such properties are the challenges of the European project CITADEL [3].

While the literature about the formal specification of dynamic software architectures is abundant [5,7–10,21,24–26,31–33], very few works consider their formal verification and none of them provided a concrete evaluation showing the feasibility of the proposed analysis.

© The Author(s) 2018
K. Havelund et al. (Eds.): FM 2018, LNCS 10951, pp. 625–644, 2018.
https://doi.org/10.1007/978-3-319-95582-7_37

If the number of components is bounded, formal verification can be reduced to static verification by encoding in the state if the component is active or not with possibly an additional component to control the (de)activation (see, for example, [9]). If, instead, new components can be added, the encoding is less trivial. In principle, parametrized verification, by verifying a system considering any number of replicas of components, seems a good candidate, but we need the capability to encode in the state the activation of an unbounded number of components.

In this paper, we propose Dynamic Parametrized Architectures (DPAs), which extend a standard architecture description of components and connections with (1) parameters and symbolic constraints to define a set of configurations, (2) symbolic constraints to define the sets of initial configurations and reconfigurations. In particular, the architectural topology is represented by indexed sets of components and symbolic variables that can enable/disable the connections, while the constraints are specified with first-order formulas with quantifiers over the set of indices.

We propose to use Satisfiability Modulo Theories (SMT)-based model checking for array-based transition systems [13,19], a syntactically restricted class of parametrized transition systems with states represented as arrays indexed by an arbitrary number of processes. We define carefully the fragment of first-order logic used in the architecture description so that we can provide a translation into array-based transition systems.

In this paper, we focus on simple information "can-flow" properties over DPAs: we check if information can pass from one component to another one through a sequence of communications between connected components and reconfigurations. We automatically translate the DPA and the properties into an array-based transition system and we verify the properties with Model Checker Modulo Theories (MCMT) [19].

Summarizing, the contributions of the paper are: (1) to define a new formal specification of dynamic architectures; (2) to translate the reachability problem of dynamic architectures into reachability problems for infinite-state array-based transition systems; (3) to provide a prototype implementation and an experimental evaluation of the feasibility of the approach.

The rest of the paper is structured as follows: Sect. 2 gives an account of related work; Sect. 3 exemplifies the problem using a concrete language; Sect. 4 defines the abstract syntax and semantics of DPAs; Sect. 5 describes array-based transition systems and the translation from DPAs; Sect. 6 presents some benchmarks and experimental results; and, finally, in Sect. 7, we draw some conclusions and directions for future works.

2   Related Work

The approach closest to the one presented below is proposed in [31] as extension of the BIP (Behavior, Interaction, Priority) framework [6]. BIP has been extended for dynamic and parametrized connections in [7,23], and to allow spawning new components and interactions in [9]. The work in [31] proposes a second-order logic to specify constraints on the evolution of the architecture including creation/removal of components. However, no model checking procedure is provided to verify such dynamic architectures. In this paper, we restrict the logic, for example avoiding second-order quantification, so that the language is still suitable to describe interesting dynamics but can be translated into array-based transition systems for model checking.

Since a system architecture can be seen as a graph of connections, graph grammars [29] are a good candidate for specification of dynamic architectures. In fact, in [21,26,32,33], the authors propose to model dynamic architectures in terms of graph transformation systems: the initial configuration is represented by a graph (or hypergraph) and reconfigurations as graph production rules, which are based on subgraph matching. In [21,26,32], there is no attempt at formal verification, while in [33] it is limited to finite-state model checking. Moreover, compared to our language, reconfigurations are limited to matching a finite subgraph which does not allow to express transition guards based on negation or updates that change sets of components. These limitations can be partly lifted considering infinite-state attributed graph grammars and related verification techniques [22]. After a first attempt to use these techniques as backends for DPAs, we concluded that in practice they do not scale very well on our benchmarks.

π-calculus [27] is another clear candidate to represent the semantics of dynamic architectures, since it has the ability to describe the creation of processes and their dynamic synchronizations. As is, it does not clearly define the topology of the network, but works such as [10,24] use it as underlying semantics for dynamic extensions of architecture specification languages. Also in this context, no previous work provided a concrete proposal for model checking showing the feasibility of the approach.

The analysis of how information can flow from one component to another is addressed in many contexts such as program analysis, process modeling, access control, and flow latency analysis. The novel challenge addressed by this paper is posed by the complexity of the adaptive systems' architectures, for which design and verification is an open problem. We propose a very rich system specification and we provide verification techniques for simple information flow properties formalized as reachability problems.

In this paper, we consider information flow as reachability, which is well studied for standard state machine models. More complex information flow properties extensively studied in the literature on security are related to the notion of *non-interference*. In the seminal work of Goguen and Meseguer [20], the simple information flow property is extended to make sure that components at different levels of security do not interfere. The verification of non-interference on DPAs is an open problem left for future work.

3   An Example of a Dynamic Parametrized Architecture

In this section, we describe an example of a dynamic architecture in an extended version of the Architecture Analysis and Design Language (AADL) [16], which is an industrial language standardized by SAE International [30]. The concrete language extension is under definition [12] within the CITADEL project, while in this paper we focus on the underlying formal specification and semantics of DPAs.

In AADL, the system is specified in terms of component types, defining the interfaces and thus the input/output ports, and component implementations, defining how composite components are built from other components, called subcomponents, composed by connecting their ports. An example of an AADL component implementation is shown in Fig. 1. The system represents a network of computers, in which one is a database server that contains sensitive data; three are application servers that provide services to the clients, with two of them connected to the database server; and the others are clients. Each client is connected to one server and may be connected to other clients. As can be seen, the number of components and that of their connections are finite and static. The specification represents a single static architecture.

We now extend the example to consider an arbitrary number of servers and clients and to consider changes in the configurations so that computers and connections can be added/removed and computers can be compromised becoming untrusted (due to a failure or attack).

```
system Implementation sys.impl
  subcomponents
    d:  system databaseServer;
    s1: system applicationServer;
    s2: system applicationServer;
    s3: system applicationServer;
    c1: system Client;
    c2: system Client;
    c3: system Client;
    c4: system Client;
    c5: system Client;

  connections
    con1: port d.output -> s1.input;
    con1: port d.output -> s2.input;
    con1: port s1.output -> c1.input;
    con1: port s1.output -> c2.input;
    con1: port s2.output -> c3.input;
    con1: port s3.output -> c4.input;
    con1: port s3.output -> c5.input;
    con1: port c4.output -> c1.input;
    con1: port c4.output -> c2.input;
    con1: port c4.output -> c3.input;
    con1: port c4.output -> c5.input;
    con1: port c5.output -> c1.input;
    con1: port c5.output -> c2.input;
    con1: port c5.output -> c3.input;
    con1: port c5.output -> c4.input;
  end sys.impl;
```

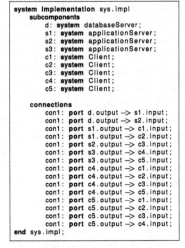

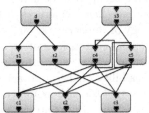

Fig. 1. Example of a component implementation in AADL

We consider the system to be *safe* if no information can flow from the database to the untrusted clients; otherwise the system is *unsafe*. This dynamic version of the system is specified in Fig. 2 (for the moment, ignore the highlighted parts of the code), in an extended version of AADL. In particular, the extension has two layers:

1. *Parametrized Architecture*: the subcomponents can now be indexed sets (e.g., clients is a set indexed by C) and connections are specified iterating over the indices (e.g., there is a connection from servers[s] to clients[c] for each s in S, c in C); besides the sets of indices, the architecture is parametrized by other parameters that can be used in expressions that guard the connections (e.g., there exists a connection from servers[s] to clients[c] only if s = connectedTo[c]); notice that also parameters may be indexed sets.

2. *Dynamic Parametrized Architecture*: an initial formula defines the set of initial configurations; a set of reconfigurations defines the possible changes in the values of the parameters.

Analyzing the reconfigurations of the example (still ignoring the highlighted parts), we can see that every time an untrusted client is connected to a server, the server becomes untrusted as well. Since the connection with the database is disabled when the server is not trusted, one may erroneously think that no information can flow from the database to an untrusted client. In fact, the information can flow to the server while it is trusted, a reconfiguration may happen making the server untrusted, and the information can then flow to an untrusted client, making the system unsafe.

```
system implementation sys.impl
  parameters
    C: set of indices;                      S: set of indices;
    trustedClients: set indexed by C of bool;   trustedServers: set indexed by S of bool;
    connectedTo: set indexed by C of index;     protected: bool;
  subcomponents
    d: system databaseServer;
    servers: set indexed by S of system applicationServer;
    clients: set indexed by C of system Client;
  connections
    con1: port d.output -> servers[s].input if protected and trustedServers[s] for s in S;
    con2: port servers[s].output -> clients[c].input if s = connectedTo[c] for s in S, c in C;
    con3: port clients[c].output -> clients[r].input if not trustedClients[c] for c in C, r in C;
  initial
    not protected and
    forall(c in C, forall (s in S, (not trustedClients[c] and s = connectedTo[c]) -> (not trustedServers[s]))) and
    forall(c in C, forall (s not in S, s != connectedTo[c]));
  reconfigurations
    next(protected) = true;
    exists(s not in S, next(S) = add(S, s) and next(trustedServers[s]) = true);
    exists(s in S, not protected and next(trustedServers[s]) = false);
    exists(s in S, exists (c not in C, not trustedServers[s] and next(C) = add(C, c)
                    and next(connectedTo[c]) = s and next(trustedClients[c]) = false));
    exists(s in S, exists (c not in C, trustedServers[s] and next(C) = add(C, c)
                    and next(connectedTo[c]) = s and next(trustedClients[c]) = true));
    exists(s in S, exists (c in C, not trustedClients[c] and not protected
                    and next(connectedTo[c]) = s and next(trustedServers[s]) = false));
    exists(s in S, exists (c in C, trustedClients[c] and s = connectedTo[c] and not protected
                    and next(trustedClients[c]) = false and next(trustedServers[s]) = false));
end sys.impl;
```

Fig. 2. Example of a DPA specified in an extension of AADL

The version of the example with the highlighted parts is safe because it introduces two phases (represented by the protected parameter) and it allows connection to the database only in the protected mode, while reconfigurations downgrading the servers are allowed only in the unprotected mode. Proving automatically that this system is safe is quite challenging.

4 Formal Specification of Dynamic Parametrized Architectures

4.1 Definitions

In the following, let N be a countable set of indexes (in practice, we set $N = \mathbb{Z}$). An *index set* is a finite subset of N. Given a set S and an index set I, S is indexed by I iff there exists a bijective mapping from I to S. If S is indexed by I, we write $S = \{s_i\}_{i \in I}$. An index set parameter is a variable whose domain is the set of finite subsets of N.

Definition 1. *An architectural* configuration *is a pair* (C, E), *where* C *is a set of* components *and* $E \subseteq C \times C$ *is a set of* connections *between components.*

We now define a more structured version of architecture, still flat but in which components are grouped into sets. We use indexed sets of components. For example, $I = \{1, 2, 3\}$ is a set of indexes and $C = \{c_1, c_2, c_3\}$ and $C' = \{c'_1, c'_2, c'_3\}$ are two sets of components indexed by I.

Definition 2. *An architectural* structured configuration *is a pair* $(\mathcal{C}, E)$, *where:*

- $\mathcal{C}$ *is a finite set of disjoint sets of* components *indexed by some index sets;*
- $E \subseteq \bigcup_{C \in \mathcal{C}} \times \bigcup_{C \in \mathcal{C}}$ *is a set of* connections *between components.*

If $c \in C$ *and* $C \in \mathcal{C}$ *we write simply (abusing notation)* $c \in \mathcal{C}$.

For example, consider index sets I_1, I_2, where $I_1 = \{1, 2, 3\}$, $I_2 = \{2\}$, $\mathcal{C} = \{C_1, C_2, C_3\}$, $C_1 = \{c_{1i}\}_{i \in I_1}$, $C_2 = \{c_{2i}\}_{i \in I_1}$, $C_3 = \{c_{3i}\}_{i \in I_2} = \{c_{32}\}$, $E = \{\langle c_{1i}, c_{2i} \rangle \mid i \in I_1\}$.

Definition 3. *A system of parameters is a pair* $(\mathcal{I}, \mathcal{V})$ *where* $\mathcal{I}$ *is a finite set of symbols for index set parameters and* $\mathcal{V}$ *is a finite set of symbols for indexed sets of parameters, where each* $V \in \mathcal{V}$ *is associated with an index set parameter symbol* $I_V \in \mathcal{I}$ *and with a sort* $\mathtt{sort}_V$ *(in practice,* $\mathtt{sort}_V \in \{\mathtt{bool}, \mathtt{int}\}$*).*

Definition 4. *An assignment to a system of parameters* $(\mathcal{I}, \mathcal{V})$ *is a tuple* $\mu = (\mu_{\mathcal{I}}, \{\mu_V\}_{V \in \mathcal{V}})$, *where*

- $\mu_{\mathcal{I}} : \mathcal{I} \to \{S \subset N : S \text{ finite}\}$;
- *For* $V \in \mathcal{V}$, $\mu_V : \mu_{\mathcal{I}}(I_V) \to R(\mathtt{sort}_V)$ *(in practice,* $R(\mathtt{bool}) = \mathbb{B} = \{\top, \bot\}$ *and* $R(\mathtt{int}) = \mathbb{Z}$*).*

The following definitions refer to formulas of the *logic for systems of parameters* and the evaluation (under an assignment μ) $\llbracket \cdot \rrbracket_\mu$ of its expressions and formulas. These are defined later in Sect. 4.2.

Definition 5. *A parametrized architecture is a tuple* $A = (\mathcal{I}, \mathcal{V}, \mathcal{P}, \Psi, \Phi)$ *where*

- $(\mathcal{I}, \mathcal{V})$ *is a system of parameters;*
- $\mathcal{P}$ *is a finite set of parametrized indexed sets of components; each set* $P \in \mathcal{P}$ *is associated with an index set* $I_P \in \mathcal{I}$;
- $\Psi = \{\psi_P(x)\}_{P \in \mathcal{P}}$ *is a set of formulas (*component guards*) over* $(\mathcal{I}, \mathcal{V})$ *and a free variable* x;
- $\Phi = \{\phi_{PQ}(x, y)\}_{P,Q \in \mathcal{P}}$ *is a set of formulas (*connection guards*) over* $(\mathcal{I}, \mathcal{V})$ *and free variables* x, y.

Given an assignment μ *to the system of parameters* $(\mathcal{I}, \mathcal{V})$, *the instantiated (structured architectural) configuration defined by the assignment* μ *is given by* $\mu(A) := (\mathcal{C}, E)$ *(we also write* $(\mathcal{C}_\mu, E_\mu)$*) where*

- $\mathcal{C} = \{C_{\mu P} : P \in \mathcal{P}\}$. *For all* $C_{\mu P} \in \mathcal{C}$, *for all indexes* i, $c_{Pi} \in C_{\mu P}$ *iff* $i \in \mu_{\mathcal{I}}(I_P)$ *and* $[\![\psi_P(i/x)]\!]_\mu = \top$.
- *for all* $C_{\mu P}, C_{\mu Q} \in \mathcal{C}$, *for all component instances* $c_{Pi} \in C_{\mu P}$, $c_{Qj} \in C_{\mu Q}$, $(c_{Pi}, c_{Qj}) \in E$ *iff* $[\![\phi_{PQ}(i/x, j/y)]\!]_\mu = \top$.

Syntactic restrictions: formulas in Ψ *and* Φ *are quantifier-free and do not contain index set predicates* $=$, $\subseteq$.

Example: For $\mathcal{I} = \{I_1, I_2\}$, $\mathcal{V} = \{V\}$, V a set of Boolean variables, with $I_V = I_1$, $\mathcal{P} = \{P_1, P_2, P_3\}$, $I_{P_1} = I_1$, $I_{P_2} = I_1$, $I_{P_3} = I_2$, $\psi_{P_1}(x) = \psi_{P_2}(x) = \psi_{P_3}(x) := \top$, $\phi_{P_1 P_2}(x, y) := x = y \wedge x \in I_V \wedge V[x]$, $\phi_{P_1 P_3}(x, y) := x \in I_V \wedge \neg V[x]$, $\phi_{P_2 P_3}(x, y) = \phi_{P_2 P_1}(x, y) = \phi_{P_3 P_1}(x, y) = \phi_{P_3 P_2}(x, y) := \bot$. By assigning $\mu_{\mathcal{I}}(I_1) = \{1, 2, 3\}$, $\mu_{\mathcal{I}}(I_2) = \{2\}$, $\mu_V(1) = \mu_V(2) = \mu_V(3) = \top$, we get the configuration in the previous example.

Definition 6. *A* dynamic parametrized architecture *is a tuple* (A, ι, κ, τ), *where*

- $A = (\mathcal{I}, \mathcal{V}, \mathcal{P}, \Psi, \Phi)$ *is a parametrized architecture;*
- ι *is a formula over* $(\mathcal{I}, \mathcal{V})$, *specifying the set of initial assignments;*
- κ *is a formula over* $(\mathcal{I}, \mathcal{V})$, *specifying the invariant;*
- τ *is a transition formula over* $(\mathcal{I}, \mathcal{V})$, *specifying the reconfiguration transitions.*

The dynamic parametrized architecture defines a dynamically changing architecture as a transition system over (structured architectural) configurations obtained by instantiation from A. *The set of initial configurations is given by*

$$\{\mu(A) : \mu \text{ is an assignment to } (\mathcal{I}, \mathcal{V}) \text{ such that } [\![\iota]\!]_\mu = \top \text{ and } [\![\kappa]\!]_\mu = \top\}.$$

A configuration $\mu'(A)$ *is directly reachable from a configuration* $\mu(A)$ *iff* $[\![\tau]\!]_{\mu\mu'} = \top$ *and* $[\![\kappa]\!]_{\mu'} = \top$.

Syntactic restrictions:

- ι *is of the form* $\forall_{\underline{I_1}} i_1 \forall_{\underline{I_2^C}} i_2 \, \alpha$, *where* α *is a quantifier-free formula in which index set predicates* $=$, $\subseteq$ *do not appear under negation.*
- κ *is a quantifier-free formula without index set predicates* $=$, $\subseteq$.
- τ *is a disjunction of transition formulas of the form* $\exists_{\underline{I_1}} i_1 \exists_{\underline{I_2^C}} i_2 \, (\alpha \wedge \beta \wedge \gamma_\beta)$ *where* $\underline{I_1}, \underline{I_2} \subseteq \mathcal{I}$, α *is a quantifier-free formula,* β *is a conjunction of transition formulas of the forms 1)* $I' = I \cup \{t_k\}_k$, *2)* $I' = I \setminus \{t_k\}_k$, *3)* $t \in I'$, *4)* $V'[t] = e$, *5)* $\forall_{I'_V} j \, V'[j] = e$, *where* $I \in \mathcal{I}$, $I' \in \mathcal{I}'$ *are variables of sort* is *(each variable* $I' \in \mathcal{I}'$ *may appear at most once),* t, t_k *are terms over* $(\mathcal{I}, \mathcal{V})$ *of sort* idx, $V' \in \mathcal{V}'$ *is a variable of one of the sorts* $\mathtt{vs}_k$ *(for each* V', *either atoms of the form 4 appear in* β, *or at most a single atom of the form 5 appears: atoms of forms 4, 5 never appear together),* e *are terms over* $(\mathcal{I}, \mathcal{V})$ *of sorts* $\mathtt{el}_k$, *and* j *is a variable of sort* idx; *furthermore, value* $V'[t_k]$ *of every introduced (by an atom of form 1, with* $I' = I'_V$, *and* $I = I_V$*) parameter must be set in* β *with an atom of form 4 or 5; finally, the frame condition* γ_β *is a conjunction of*

- *transition formulas* $\forall_{I'_V,j} \left(\left(\bigwedge_{t \in t_V}, (j \neq t) \right) \to V'[j] = V[j] \right)$ *for all* $V' \in \mathcal{V}$ *which do not appear in a conjunct of form 5 in* β, *where* $t_{V'}$ *is the (possibly empty) set of all terms which appear as indexes of* V' *in* β, *and*
- *transition formulas* $I' = I$ *for all* $I' \in \mathcal{I}'$ *which do not appear in conjuncts of forms 1, 2 in* β.

(In practice, when specifying the transition formulas, the frame condition γ_β *is generated automatically from* β, *instead of being specified directly by the user.)*

Example: Consider the parametrized architecture from the previous example, with $\iota := I_1 = \{1, 2, 3\} \wedge I_2 = \{2\} \wedge V[1] \wedge V[2] \wedge V[3]$; , $\kappa := \top$ and $\tau := \tau_1 \vee \tau_2$, where $\tau_1 := \exists_{I_1^C} i\, (I'_1 = I_1 \cup \{i\} \wedge V'[i])$ and $\tau_2 := \exists_{I_1} i\, (\neg V'[i])$. This defines the set of initial architectures which contains only the single architecture from the previous example and two transitions. The transition τ_1 adds a new index $i \in I_1^C$ into the index set I_1, adding two new components C_{1i} and C_{2i} and a new parameter $V[i]$ and sets the value of the newly added parameter $V[i]$ to $\top$, adding a connection between the two new components C_{1i} and C_{2i}. The transition τ_2 changes the value of some $V[i]$ to $\bot$, removing the connection between components C_{1i} and C_{2i} and adding connections between component C_{1i} and each of the components $C_{3j}, j \in I_2$.

Definition 7. *Given a dynamic parametrized architecture* (A, ι, κ, τ), *where* $A = (\mathcal{I}, \mathcal{V}, \mathcal{P}, \Psi, \Phi)$, *a* configuration *is an assignment to the system of parameters* $(\mathcal{I}, \mathcal{V})$. *For a configuration* $\mu(A) = (\mathcal{C}, E)$, *a* communication event *is a connection* $e \in E$.

Trace *of the dynamic parametrized architecture is a sequence* $e_1, e_2, \dots$ *of configurations and communication events, such that:*

- $e_1 = \mu_1$ *is a configuration such that* $\mu_1(A)$ *is in the set of initial configurations.*
- *The subsequence* $e_{k_1}, e_{k_2}, \dots$ *of all configurations in the trace is such that for all* k_i, $e_{k_{i+1}}(A)$ *(if it exists) is directly reachable from* $e_{k_i}(A)$.
- *For all communication events* $e_k = (c_k, c'_k)$ *in the trace,* $(c_k, c'_k) \in E_{e_{r(k)}}$, *where* $e_{r(k)}$, $r(k) := \max\{n \in \mathbb{N} : n < k, e_n \text{is a configuration}\}$, *is the last configuration prior to* e_k.

Definition 8. *An instance of the* dynamic information flow problem *is a tuple* $(D, P_{src}, \rho_{src}, P_{dst}, \rho_{dst})$ *where*

- $D = (A, \iota, \kappa, \tau)$ *is a dynamic parametrized architecture;*
- $P_{src} \in \mathcal{P}_A$ *and* $P_{dst} \in \mathcal{P}_A$ *are (source and destination) parametrized indexed sets of components;*
- $\rho_{src}(x)$ *and* $\rho_{dst}(x)$ *(source and destination guard) are formulas over* $(\mathcal{I}_A, \mathcal{V}_A)$.

The problem is to determine whether there exists a finite trace (called information flow witness trace*)* $e_1, e_2, \ldots, e_n$ *of* D *with a subtrace* $e_{k_1} = (c_{k_1}, c'_{k_1}), \ldots, e_{k_m} = (c_{k_m}, c'_{k_m})$ *of communication events such that:*

- $c_{k_1} = c_{P_{src}i_{src}} \in C_{e_{r(k_1)}P_{src}}$ *for some* i_{src}, *and* $\llbracket \rho_{src}(i_{src}/x) \rrbracket_{e_{r(k_1)}} = \top$ *(the information originates in a source component);*
- $c'_{k_m} = c_{P_{dst}i_{dst}} \in C_{e_{r(k_m)}P_{dst}}$ *for some* i_{dst}, *and* $\llbracket \rho_{dst}(i_{dst}/x) \rrbracket_{e_{r(k_m)}} = \top$ *(the information is received by a destination component);*
- *for all* n *such that* $1 \leq n < m$, $c'_{k_n} = c_{k_{n+1}}$ *(the intermediate components form a chain over which the information propagates);*
- *for all* n, $1 \leq n < m$, *for all configurations* $e_{k'}$ *such that* $k_n < k' < k_{n+1}$, $c_{k_{n+1}} \in C_{e_{k'}}$ *(after an intermediate component receives the information and before it passes it on, it is not replaced by a fresh component with the same index).*

If such a trace exists, we say that information may flow *from a source component which satisfies the source condition given by* P_{src}, ρ_{src} *to a destination component which satisfies the destination condition given by* P_{dst}, ρ_{dst}.

Syntactic restrictions: ρ_{src} *and* ρ_{dst} *are quantifier-free formulas, without index set predicates* $=, \subseteq$.

4.2 Logic for Systems of Parameters

In the following, we define a many-sorted first-order logic [15]. Signatures contain no quantifier symbols except those explicitly mentioned.

Syntax. Theory $T_{IDX} = (\Sigma_{IDX}, \mathcal{C}_{IDX})$ of indexes with a single sort idx (in practice, we are using the theory of integers with sort int and with standard operators).

A finite number K of theories $T_{EL_k} = (\Sigma_{EL_k}, \mathcal{C}_{EL_k})$ of elements, each with a single sort el_k with a distinguished constant symbol d_{el_k} (a *default value*) (in practice, we consider the theory of booleans with sort bool and the theory of integers, the same as the theory T_{IDX}).

The theory $SP_{IDX}^{EL_1,\ldots,EL_K}$ (or simply SP_{IDX}^{EL}) of systems of parameters with indexes in T_{IDX} and elements in $EL_1, \ldots, EL_K$ is a combination of the above theories. Its sort symbols are idx, is, $\text{el}_1, \ldots, \text{el}_K$, $\text{vs}_1, \ldots, \text{vs}_K$, where is is a sort for index sets and vs_k is a sort for indexed sets of parameters of sort el_k. The set of variable symbols for each sort vs_k contains a countable set of variables $\{V_{k,n}^I\}_{n \in \mathbb{N}}$ for each variable symbol I of sort is (we omit the superscript and subscripts when they are clear from the context). The signature is the union of the signatures of the above theories, $\Sigma_{IDX} \cup \bigcup_{k=1}^{K} \Sigma_{EL_k}$, with the addition of: for sort idx, quantifier symbols $\forall$, $\exists$, and $\forall_I$, $\forall_{I^c}$, $\exists_I$, $\exists_{I^c}$ for all variables I of the sort is; predicate symbol $\in$ of sort (idx, is); predicate symbols $=, \subseteq$ of sort (is, is); function symbols $\cup, \cap, \setminus$ of sort (is, is, is); for every $n \in \mathbb{N}$, n-ary function symbol $\{\cdot, \ldots, \cdot\}^{(n)}$ (we write simply $\{\cdot, \ldots, \cdot\}$) of sort (idx, $\ldots$, idx, is); function symbols $\cdot[\cdot]_k, k = 1, \ldots, K$ (we write simply $\cdot[\cdot]$) of sorts (vs_k, idx, el_k).

Semantics. A structure $\mathcal{M} = (\text{idx}^{\mathcal{M}}, \text{is}^{\mathcal{M}}, \text{el}_1^{\mathcal{M}}, \ldots, \text{el}_k^{\mathcal{M}}, \text{vs}_1^{\mathcal{M}}, \ldots, \text{vs}_k^{\mathcal{M}}, \mathcal{I}_{\mathcal{M}})$
for SP_{IDX}^{EL} is restricted in the following manner:

- $\text{is}^{\mathcal{M}}$ is the power set of $\text{idx}^{\mathcal{M}}$;
- each $\text{vs}_k^{\mathcal{M}}$ is the set of all (total and partial) functions from $\text{idx}^{\mathcal{M}}$ to $\text{el}_k^{\mathcal{M}}$;
- $\in$ is interpreted as the standard set membership predicate;
- $=, \subseteq$ are interpreted as the standard set equality and subset predicates;
- $\cup, \cap, \setminus$ are interpreted as the standard set union, intersection and difference on $\text{is}^{\mathcal{M}}$, respectively;
- for every $n \in \mathbb{N}$, $\mathcal{I}_{\mathcal{M}}(\{\cdot, \ldots, \cdot\}^{(n)})$ is the function that maps the n-tuple of its arguments to the set of indexes containing exactly the arguments, i.e. it maps every $(x_1, \ldots, x_n) \in (\text{idx}^{\mathcal{M}})^n$ to $\{x_1, \ldots, x_n\} \in \text{is}^{\mathcal{M}}$;
- $\cdot[\cdot]_k, k = 1, \ldots, K$ are interpreted as function applications: $(V[i])^{\mathcal{M}} := V^{\mathcal{M}}(i^{\mathcal{M}})$.

The structure $\mathcal{M}$ is a model of SP_{IDX}^{EL} iff it satisfies the above restrictions and $(\text{idx}^{\mathcal{M}}, \mathcal{I}_{\mathcal{M}}\restriction_{\Sigma_{IDX}})$, $(\text{el}_1^{\mathcal{M}}, \mathcal{I}_{\mathcal{M}}\restriction_{\Sigma_{EL_1}}), \ldots, (\text{el}_K^{\mathcal{M}}, \mathcal{I}_{\mathcal{M}}\restriction_{\Sigma_{EL_K}})$ are models of T_{IDX}, $T_{EL_1}, \ldots, T_{EL_K}$, respectively.

Definition 9. *A formula (resp. term) over a system of parameters $(\mathcal{I}, \mathcal{V})$ is a formula (resp. term) of the logic SP_{IDX}^{EL} in which the only occurring symbols of sort idx are from $\mathcal{I}$ and the only occurring symbols of sort vs_k are from the set $\{V \in \mathcal{V} : \text{sort}_V = \text{el}_k\}$, for $k = 1, \ldots, K$. Furthermore, in the formula all accesses $V[\cdot]$ to parameters $V \in \mathcal{V}$ are guarded parameter accesses, i.e. each atom $\alpha(V[t])$ that contains a term of the form $V[t]$ must occur in conjunction with a guard which ensures that index term t is present in the corresponding index set: $t \in I_V \wedge \alpha(V[t])$.*

Definition 10. *A transition formula over the system of parameters $(\mathcal{I}, \mathcal{V})$ is a formula of the logic SP_{IDX}^{EL} in which the only occurring symbols of sort idx are from $\mathcal{I} \cup \mathcal{I}'$ and the only occurring symbols of sort vs_k are from the set $\{W \in \mathcal{V} \cup \mathcal{V}' : \text{sort}_W = \text{el}_k\}$, for $k = 1, \ldots, K$. Furthermore, all accesses $W[\cdot]$ to parameters $W \in \mathcal{V} \cup \mathcal{V}'$ are guarded parameter accesses (as defined in Definition 9).*

The subscripted quantifier symbols are a syntactic sugar for quantification over index sets and their complements: all occurrences of the quantifiers $\forall_I i\ \phi$, $\forall_{I^c} i\ \phi$, $\exists_I i\ \phi$, $\exists_{I^c} i\ \phi$—where I is a variable of sort is, i is a variable of sort idx, and ϕ is a formula—are rewritten to $\forall i\ (i \in I \rightarrow \phi)$, $\forall i\ (i \notin I \rightarrow \phi)$, $\exists i\ (i \in I \wedge \phi)$, $\exists i\ (i \notin I \wedge \phi)$, respectively, after which the formula is evaluated in the standard manner.

Definition 11. *Evaluation $\llbracket \phi \rrbracket_\mu$ with respect to an assignment μ to a system of parameters $(\mathcal{I}, \mathcal{V})$, of a formula (or a term) ϕ over $(\mathcal{I}, \mathcal{V})$ is defined by interpreting I with $I^{\mathcal{M}} = \mu_{\mathcal{I}}(I)$ for every $I \in \mathcal{I}$ and interpreting $V[x]$ as follows for every $V \in \mathcal{V}$: $(V[x])^{\mathcal{M}} = \mu_V(x^{\mathcal{M}})$ if $x^{\mathcal{M}} \in \mu(I_V)$, and $(V[x])^{\mathcal{M}} = d_{\text{sort}_V}^{\mathcal{M}}$ otherwise. The evaluation $\llbracket \phi \rrbracket_{\mu\mu'}$ of a transition formula with respect to two assignments μ, μ' is defined by interpreting, in the above manner, $(\mathcal{I}, \mathcal{V})$ with μ and $(\mathcal{I}', \mathcal{V}')$ with μ'.*

5   Analysis with SMT-Based Model Checking

5.1   Background Notions on SMT-Based Model Checking

Many-sorted first-order logic of arrays. The target logic for the translation is the many-sorted first-order logic [15] with theories for indexes, elements and arrays as defined in [18]. Following that paper, we fix a theory $T_I = (\Sigma_I, \mathcal{C}_I)$ for indexes whose only sort symbol is **index** and we fix theories $T_{E_k} = (\Sigma_{E_k}, \mathcal{C}_{E_k}), k = 1, \ldots, K$ whose only sort symbols are $\mathtt{elem}_k$, respectively. The theory $A_I^{E_1, \ldots, E_K}$ (or simply A_I^E) of arrays with indexes in T_I and elements in $E_1, \ldots, E_K$ is defined as the combination of theories $T_I, T_{E_1}, \ldots, T_{E_K}$ as follows. The sort symbols of A_I^E are **index**, $\mathtt{elem}_1, \ldots, \mathtt{elem}_K$, $\mathtt{array}_1, \ldots, \mathtt{array}_K$, the signature is $\Sigma := \Sigma_I \cup \bigcup_{k=1}^K \Sigma_{E_i} \cup \bigcup_{k=1}^K \{\cdot[\cdot]_k\}$ where $\cdot[\cdot]_k$ are function symbols of sorts $(\mathtt{array}_k, \mathtt{index}, \mathtt{elem}_k)$. A structure $\mathcal{M} = (\mathtt{index}^{\mathcal{M}}, \mathtt{elem}_1^{\mathcal{M}}, \ldots, \mathtt{elem}_K^{\mathcal{M}}, \mathtt{array}_1^{\mathcal{M}}, \ldots, \mathtt{array}_K^{\mathcal{M}}, \mathcal{I})$ is a model of A_I^E iff $\mathtt{array}_k^{\mathcal{M}}$ are sets of all functions from $\mathtt{index}^{\mathcal{M}}$ to $\mathtt{elem}_k^{\mathcal{M}}$, respectively, the function symbols $\cdot[\cdot]_k$ are interpreted as function applications, and $\mathcal{M}_I = (\mathtt{index}^{\mathcal{M}}, \mathcal{I}\!\restriction_{\Sigma_I})$, $\mathcal{M}_{E_k} = (\mathtt{elem}_k^{\mathcal{M}}, \mathcal{I}\!\restriction_{\Sigma_{E_k}})$ are models of T_I, $T_{E_k}, k = 1, \ldots, K$, respectively.

Array-Based Transition Systems. In the following, i, j denote variables of the sort **index**, $\underline{i}$ denotes a set of such variables, a denotes a variable of one of the **array** sorts, $\underline{a}$ denotes a set of such variables, notation $\underline{a}[\underline{i}]$ denotes the set of terms $\{a[i] : a \in \underline{a}, i \in \underline{i}\}$, and $\phi(x), \psi(x)$ denote quantifier free $\Sigma(x)$ formulas.

As in [18], an *array-based (transition) system (for $(T_I, T_{E_1}, \ldots, T_{E_K})$)* is a triple $\mathcal{S} = (\underline{a}, Init, Tr)$ where

- $\underline{a} = \{a_1, \ldots, a_n\}$ is a set of state variables of the sorts $\mathtt{array}_1, \ldots, \mathtt{array}_K$.
- $Init(\underline{a})$ is the *initial* $\Sigma(\underline{a})$-formula of the form

$$\forall \underline{i}. \phi(\underline{i}, \underline{a}[\underline{i}]). \tag{1}$$

- $Tr(\underline{a}, \underline{a}')$ is the *transition* $\Sigma(\underline{a}, \underline{a}')$-formula and is a disjunction of formulas of the form

$$\exists \underline{i} \left(\psi(\underline{i}, \underline{a}[\underline{i}]) \wedge \bigwedge_{k=1}^n \forall j \; a_k'[j] = t_k(\underline{i}, \underline{a}[\underline{i}], j, \underline{a}[j]) \right) \tag{2}$$

where each t_k is a $\Sigma(\underline{a})$-term which may contain nested if-then-else operators.

Given an array-based system $\mathcal{S} = (\underline{a}, Init, Tr)$ and a $\Sigma(\underline{a})$-formula U (*unsafe* formula) of the form

$$\exists \underline{i}. \phi(\underline{i}, \underline{a}[\underline{i}]) \tag{3}$$

an instance of the *array-based safety problem* is to decide whether there exists $n \in \mathbb{N}$ such that the formula $Init(\underline{a}_0) \wedge Tr(\underline{a}_0, \underline{a}_1) \wedge \cdots \wedge Tr(\underline{a}_{n-1}, \underline{a}_n) \wedge U(\underline{a}_n)$ is A_I^E-satisfiable.

Decidability of the Array-Based Safety Problem. The array-based safety problem is in general undecidable (Thm. 4.1. in [18]), but it becomes decidable under 1) the following assumptions on the theory T_I of indexes: local finiteness, closedness under substructures, decidability of $\text{SMT}(T_I)$, 2) assumptions of local finiteness of T_E and of decidability of $\text{SMT}(T_E)$, and 3) further assumptions on the array-based transition system under analysis (for details see Theorem 3.3. and Theorem 4.6. in [18]).

5.2   Encoding into SMT-Based Model Checking

Translation of Formulas. We recursively define the translation $\cdot^{\mathcal{A}}$ of formulas and transition formulas of SP_{IDX}^{EL} to formulas of A_I^E. We set the index and element sorts to correspond, i.e. $\text{index} := \text{idx}$ and $\text{elem}_k := \text{el}_k, k = 1, \ldots, K$. In practice, we set T_I to be the theory of integers (with sort $\text{index} = \text{int}$), number of element theories to $K = 2$, and we set $E_1 = T_I$ and E_2 to be the theory of Booleans (with sort $\text{elem}_2 = \text{bool}$).

- Symbols of the sorts idx and $\text{el}_k, k = 1, \ldots, K$ are treated as symbols of the sorts $\text{index}, \text{elem}_k, k = 1, \ldots, K$, respectively.
- For a variable I of sort is, $I^{\mathcal{A}} := a_I$, where a_I is of the sort $\text{array}_{\text{bool}}$.
- For a variable V of sort vs_k, $V^{\mathcal{A}} := a_V$, where a_V is of the sort $\text{array}_{\text{elem}_k}$.
- For a term t of sort idx and term T of sort is, $(t \in T)^{\mathcal{A}} := T^{\mathcal{A}_t}$.
- For terms T_1, T_2 of sort is, $(T_1 \cap T_2)^{\mathcal{A}_t} := T_1^{\mathcal{A}_t} \wedge T_2^{\mathcal{A}_t}$; analogously for $\cup$ and $\backslash$.
- For a variable I of sort is, $I^{\mathcal{A}_t} := I^{\mathcal{A}}[t^{\mathcal{A}}]$.
- $(\{e_1, \ldots, e_n\})^{\mathcal{A}_t} := \bigvee_{k=1}^{n} (t^{\mathcal{A}} = e_k^{\mathcal{A}})$.
- For terms T_1, T_2 of sort is, $(T_1 = T_2)^{\mathcal{A}} := \forall i \, (T_1^{\mathcal{A}_i} = T_2^{\mathcal{A}_i})$, where i is a fresh variable of sort idx; analogously for $\subseteq$ which is translated using $\rightarrow$.
- For a variable V of sort vs_k and a term t of sort idx, $(V[t])^{\mathcal{A}} := V^{\mathcal{A}}[t^{\mathcal{A}}]$.
- Other logical connectives, quantifiers and operators are present in both logics and are translated directly, e.g. $(e_1 \leq e_2)^{\mathcal{A}} := e_1^{\mathcal{A}} \leq e_2^{\mathcal{A}}$ and $(\phi_1 \wedge \phi_2)^{\mathcal{A}} := \phi_1^{\mathcal{A}} \wedge \phi_2^{\mathcal{A}}$.

Translation of a Dynamic Information Flow Problem to an Array-Based Safety Problem. Given a dynamic parametrized architecture $D = (A, \iota, \kappa, \tau)$ where $A = (\mathcal{I}, \mathcal{V}, \mathcal{P}, \Psi, \Phi)$, and given an information flow problem instance $(D, P_{src}, \rho_{src}, P_{dst}, \rho_{dst})$, we generate a safety problem $(\mathcal{S}, U)$ where $\mathcal{S} = (\underline{a}, Init, Tr)$, as follows.

Given a system of parameters $(\mathcal{I}, \mathcal{V})$, we set $\underline{a}$ to be the (disjoint) union:

$$
\begin{aligned}
\underline{a} := \, & \{a_I : I \in \mathcal{I}, sort(a_I) = \text{array}_{\text{bool}}\} \\
& \cup \{a_V : V \in \mathcal{V}, sort(a_V) = \text{array}_{\text{sort}_V}\} \\
& \cup \{a_P : P \in \mathcal{P}, sort(a_P) = \text{array}_{\text{bool}}\},
\end{aligned}
\tag{4}
$$

of the set of boolean array symbols a_I which model index sets, the set of array symbols a_V which model sets of parameters, and the set of boolean array symbols a_P which model information taint of the component instances.

The initial formula $Init$ is set to

$$\iota^{\mathcal{A}} \wedge \kappa^{\mathcal{A}} \wedge \forall j \left(a_{P_{src}}[j] = \left(a_{I_{P_{src}}}[j] \wedge \psi_{P_{src}}(j/x)^{\mathcal{A}} \wedge \rho_{src}(j/x)^{\mathcal{A}} \right) \right)$$
$$\wedge \bigwedge_{P \in \mathcal{P} \setminus \{P_{src}\}} \forall j \ a_P[j] = \bot. \tag{5}$$

Here the third conjunct models the initial taint of the source components, by specifying that a source component with index j is tainted iff it is present in the system and satisfies the constraint ρ_{src}, and the last conjunct models the fact that initially all non-source components are not tainted.

Recall that $\tau = \bigvee_k \tau_k$, where τ_k are of the form $\exists_{I_1} i_1 \exists_{I_2^C} i_2 \left(\alpha_k \wedge \beta_k \wedge \gamma_{\beta_k} \right)$ (see Definition 6). The transition formula Tr is set to

$$\bigvee_{P,Q \in \mathcal{P}} Taint(P,Q) \vee \bigvee_k Reconf_k. \tag{6}$$

Here $Taint(P,Q)$ is the following formula that models taint propagation between two connected component instances of which the first one is tainted:

$$\exists i_1 \exists i_2 \left(\phi_{PQ}(i_1/x, i_2/y)^{\mathcal{A}} \wedge a_{I_P}[i_1] \wedge \psi_P(i_1/x)^{\mathcal{A}} \wedge a_{I_Q}[i_2] \wedge \psi_Q(i_2/x)^{\mathcal{A}} \right.$$
$$\left. \wedge \ a_P[i_1] \wedge \forall j \ (a_Q'[j] = (j = i_2 ? \top : a_Q[j])) \wedge \bigwedge_{a \neq a_Q} \forall j \ (a'[j] = a[j]) \right). \tag{7}$$

$Reconf_k$ is obtained from τ_k by the following steps.

Differentiation of Primed Parameter Accesses. We say that accesses to a primed parameter $V' \in \mathcal{V}'$ in τ_k are *differentiated* if for all pairs of conjuncts of form 4 in β_k as defined in Definition 6, $V'[t_1] = e_1$ and $V'[t_2] = e_2$, α_k contains a top-level conjunct $(t_1 \neq t_2)$, i.e., α_k is of the form $\alpha_k' \wedge (t_1 \neq t_2)$. We may assume that in τ_k, accesses to all primed parameters $V' \in \mathcal{V}'$ are differentiated. Note that if the accesses to some primed parameter $V' \in \mathcal{V}'$ in τ_k are not differentiated, then for a pair of undifferentiated accesses $V'[t_1] = e_1$ and $V'[t_2] = e_2$ formula τ_k can be rewritten as a disjunction of two formulas $\tau_k^=$ and $\tau_k^{\neq}$ which are of the same general form as τ_k and are defined by

- $\tau_k^= := \exists_{I_1} i_1 \exists_{I_2^C} i_2 \left(\alpha_k^= \wedge \beta_k^= \wedge \gamma_{\beta_k^=} \right)$ where $\alpha_k^= := \alpha_k \wedge (t_1 = t_2) \wedge (e_1 = e_2)$, and $\beta_k^=$ is obtained from β_k by removing the conjunct $V'[t_2] = e_2$;
- $\tau_k^{\neq} := \exists_{I_1} i_1 \exists_{I_2^C} i_2 \left(\alpha_k^{\neq} \wedge \beta_k \wedge \gamma_{\beta_k} \right)$ where $\alpha_k^{\neq} := \alpha_k \wedge (t_1 \neq t_2)$.

It is easy to verify that the formulas τ_k and $\tau_k^= \vee \tau_k^{\neq}$ are equivalent. By continuing the rewriting recursively, τ can be transformed into a disjunction of formulas with differentiated accesses to primed parameters.

For a symbol $I' \in \mathcal{I}'$, there is exactly one conjunct in τ_k in which I' appears in the equality, and it is one of $I' = I \cup \{t_k\}_k$, $I' = I \setminus \{t_k\}_k$, or $I' = I$. In all three cases, value of I' is a function of the value of I and some terms over $(\mathcal{I}, \mathcal{V})$, and therefore the conjunct can be rewritten as $\forall j \ (j \in I' \leftrightarrow Update_I(j))$ where $Update_I$ is a term of sort `bool` over $(\mathcal{I}, \mathcal{V})$ and a free variable. For example, for the first case we have $Update_I(j) = (j \in I \vee \bigvee_k (j = t_k))$. The conjuncts in τ_k of the form $t \in I'$ can be rewritten as $Update_I(t)$. From τ_k we obtain τ_k' by performing the above rewriting of conjuncts which contain I', for all $I' \in \mathcal{I}'$. It is easy to verify that τ'_k and τ_k are equivalent formulas.

For a symbol $V' \in \mathcal{V}'$, the set of conjuncts in the τ'_k in which V' occurs is either equal to $\{V'[t_k] = e_k : k = 1, \ldots, n\} \cup \{\forall_{I'_{V'}} j \, ((\bigwedge_{k=1}^{n} (j \neq t_k)) \rightarrow V'[j] = V[j])\}$ where t_k are differentiated, or to $\{\forall_{I'_{V'}} j \, V'[j] = e_j\}$. In both cases, the set of conjuncts can be rewritten as $\forall j \, (V'[j] = Update_V(j))$, where $Update_V$ is a term of sort $\text{sort}_{V'}$; in the first case,

$$Update_V(j) := \text{if } j = t_1 \text{ then } e_1 \text{ else if } \ldots \text{ else if } j = t_n \text{ then } e_n$$
$$\text{else if } Update_{I_V}(j) \text{ then } V[j] \text{ else } d_{\text{sort}_{V'}}$$

and in the second case $Update_V(j) := \text{if } Update_{I_V}(j) \text{ then } V[j] \text{ else } d_{\text{sort}_{V'}}$. Formula τ''_k is obtained from τ'_k by performing the above rewrites for every $V' \in \mathcal{V}'$. It is easy to verify that τ''_k and τ'_k are equivalent.

From the invariant formula κ we obtain the next-state invariant κ' by first distributing set membership operator over the set operations (e.g. transforming $t \in I \cup J$ to $t \in I \vee t \in J$), and then replacing, for all $I \in \mathcal{I}$, each term of the form $t \in I$ with the term $Update_I(t)$, and replacing, for all $V \in \mathcal{V}$, each term of the form $V[t]$ with the term $Update_V(t)$. Analogously, from the formula ρ_{src} and component guards $\psi_P, P \in \mathcal{P}$ we obtain their next-state versions ρ'_{src} and $\psi'_P, P \in \mathcal{P}$ by performing the same transformations. $Reconf_k$ is set to

$$\tau''^{\mathcal{A}}_k \wedge \kappa'^{\mathcal{A}} \wedge$$
$$\forall j \, (a'_{P_{src}}[j] = (Update_{I_{P_{src}}}(j)^{\mathcal{A}} \wedge \psi'_{P_{src}}(j/x)^{\mathcal{A}} \wedge (a_{P_{src}}[j] \vee \rho'_{src}(j/x)^{\mathcal{A}}))) \quad (8)$$
$$\wedge \bigwedge_{P \in \mathcal{P} \setminus \{P_{src}\}} \forall j \, (a'_P[j] = (Update_{I_P}(j)^{\mathcal{A}} \wedge \psi'_P(j/x)^{\mathcal{A}} \wedge a_P[j])) .$$

Here the last conjunct updates the information taint for all components, by setting it to true iff the component is present in the next state and it is currently tainted. The third conjunct performs the same update for source components, taking care to also taint the source components which satisfy the next-state source condition ρ'_{src}.

Finally, the unsafe formula U is set to

$$\exists i \, \left(a_{I_{P_{dst}}}[i] \wedge \psi_{P_{dst}}(i/x)^{\mathcal{A}} \wedge \rho_{dst}(i/x)^{\mathcal{A}} \wedge a_{P_{dst}}[i] \right), \quad (9)$$

modeling the set of states in which there exists a destination component with index i which satisfies the destination condition ρ_{dst} and is tainted.

The following theorems state that the information flow problem can be reduced to the array-based safety problem, using the above translation. The detailed proofs can be found in the extended version of the paper at https://es.fbk.eu/people/stojic/papers/fm18.

Theorem 1. *Problem $(\mathcal{S}, U)$, $\mathcal{S} = (\underline{a}, Init, Tr)$, which is obtained by translation from an arbitrary information flow problem, where $\underline{a}$ is given by (4), $Init$ is given by (5), Tr is given by (6), (7), (8), and U is given by (9), is an array-based safety problem.*

The proof amounts to the inspection of the obtained formulas, to confirm that they are indeed in the required fragment.

Theorem 2. *Let* $DIFP = (D, P_{src}, \rho_{src}, P_{dst}, \rho_{dst})$ *be an arbitrary instance of the dynamic information flow problem, and* $ASP = (\mathcal{S}, U)$ *the array-based safety problem obtained by translation from* $DIFP$. *There is an information flow witness trace for* $DIFP$ *if and only if* ASP *is unsafe.*

The proof involves constructing, for an information flow witness trace for $DIFP$, a counterexample (unsafe) trace of the problem ASP, and vice-versa.

Decidability. The dynamic information flow problem is undecidable in general (it is straightforward to model Minsky 2-counter machines [28]), but it is decidable under certain assumptions inherited from the array-based transition systems (see the remark on decidability at the end of Sect. 5.1).

6   Experimental Evaluation

6.1   Setup

Back-End Solver. We use MCMT [4] version 2.5.2 to solve array-based safety problems. MCMT is a model checker for array-based systems, based on the SMT solver Yices[1]. We run MCMT with the default settings. The time-out for testing is set to 1000 seconds.

Translation Implementation. We have implemented in C the translation from the extended version of AADL to the input language for MCMT using the parser generator GNU Bison. The input language of MCMT is low level and as such is not suitable for manual modeling of anything but the simplest examples, being instead intended as a target language for automatic generation from specifications written in a higher level language [17]. The translation follows the same outline as its theoretical description in Sect. 5.2, but is more complicated due to the specific features, limitations and idiosyncracies of the target MCMT input language. In particular, the more constraining limitations of MCMT, in addition to the theoretical restrictions on formulas from Sect. 5.1, are:

- The initial formula can contain at most two universally quantified variables.
- The transitions can contain at most two existentially quantified variables.
- The maximum number of transitions (the disjuncts in the transition formula) is 50.
- The unsafe formula can contain at most four existentially quantified variables.
- A term can contain at most ten index variables.

Our translator inherits the above restrictions on the formulas specified in the extended AADL model. While these restrictions do not severely limit the expressivity of the language, the limitation on the maximum number of transitions

---

[1] http://yices.csl.sri.com/.

limits the size of the examples that can be handled by the present version of the tool.

Hardware. We have used a desktop PC based on an Intel® Core™ i7 CPU 870 clocked at 2.93GHz, with 8 GB of main memory and running Ubuntu 14.04.5 LTS.

Distribution Tarball. The translator, tested models, scripts which automatically perform the translation from extended AADL to MCMT input language and run MCMT, as well as setup and usage instructions can be found at https://es.fbk.eu/people/stojic/papers/fm18/.

6.2 Benchmarks and Results

In the following diagrams, arrows between (sets of) components represent connections from all components in the source set to all components in the destination set, unless further restricted in the model description. All sets of components are dynamic, allowing addition/removal of components.

Converging Model. This model contains $2n + 1$ sets of components $a_0, \ldots, a_{n-1}, b_0, \ldots, b_{n-1}, c$, with the connections shown as black arrows in Fig. 3. There are also connections between all pairs of components in the same set. We test for information flow from the set $a_{\lfloor n/2 \rfloor}$ to the set b_0. The unsafe model in addition contains the connections shown as red arrows. Results for the model are in Fig. 7. We hit the MCMT limitation on the number of transitions (see Sect. 6.1) for $n = 7$ for the safe model, and for $n = 5$ for the unsafe model. Number of calls made by MCMT to the underlying SMT solver ranges from 211 (safe, $n = 1$) to 29907 (safe, $n = 6$).

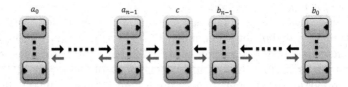

Fig. 3. Converging model (Color figure online)

Messenger Model. In this model, for $n = 1$ there are two sets of components, a and b, and a singleton component m_0. m_0 models a messenger which is intended to allow components within the same set to communicate; m_0 can connect in turn to any single component in a or in b, but not at the same time. We test for information flow from set a to set b. The system as described is unsafe because m_0

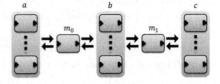

Fig. 4. Messenger model

can connect to some $a[i]$, disconnect, and then connect to some $b[j]$, therefore establishing a path for flow of information. The safe model removes such paths by using Boolean parameters to record whether m_0 has previously connected to components in a and b. If it has previously connected to one of these sets, then it is not allowed to connect to the other set before it is scrubbed (which is modeled by removing and re-adding it). For $n = 2$ (Fig. 4), the

Model	n	Time (s)	SMT calls
Messenger (safe)	1	1.894	9370
Messenger (safe)	2	TO	-
Messenger (unsafe)	1	0.240	1563
Messenger (unsafe)	2	24.639	82648
Messenger (unsafe)	3	TO	-
Network (safe)	-	0.875	3327
Network (unsafe)	-	0.171	1063

Fig. 5. Messenger and Network models results

system is extended with another set of components c and another messenger m_1 which is shared by b and c, and we check for information flow between a and c. Results are shown in Fig. 5.

Network Model. This is the model whose safe version is specified in Fig. 2, while the highlighted parts are omitted in the unsafe version. Results are shown in Fig. 5.

Sequence Model. This is a scalable example which models a sequence of n sets of components $a_0, \ldots, a_{n-1}$ (see Fig. 6 ignoring the dashed loop-back arrow). There is a connection from $a_x[i]$ to $a_y[j]$ iff $(x = y - 1 \lor x = y) \land i < j$. We check for information flow from $a_0[0]$ to $a_{n-1}[n-2]$ in the safe version and from $a_0[0]$ to $a_{n-1}[n-1]$ in the unsafe version. The results are shown in Fig. 8. The verification of this model times out for $n = 6$ (safe) and $n = 7$ (unsafe). Number of calls to the SMT solver ranges from 116 (unsafe, $n = 1$) to 60799 (unsafe, $n = 6$).

Ring Model. This model is the same as the Sequence model, but with additional connections from $a_{n-1}[i]$ to $a_0[j]$ (dashed loop-back arrow in Fig. 6) which are present only when $i < j+n$ in the safe version ($i < j + n + 1$ in the unsafe version), and we check for information flow from $a_0[0]$ to $a_{n-1}[n-2]$ in both the safe and unsafe versions. The results are shown

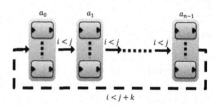

Fig. 6. Sequence and Ring models

in Fig. 9. The verification of this model times out for $n = 6$ (safe) and $n = 5$ (unsafe). Number of calls to the SMT solver ranges from 188 (unsafe, $n = 1$) to 130068 (unsafe, $n = 4$).

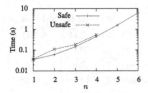
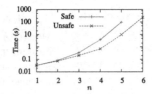
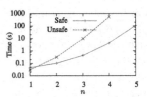

Fig. 7. Converging model results

Fig. 8. Sequence model results

Fig. 9. Ring model results

7   Conclusions and Future Work

We propose a new logic-based specification of dynamic architectures where the architectural topology is represented by a set of parameters, while first-order formulas over such parameters define the sets of initial configurations and reconfigurations. The Dynamic Parametrized Architectures so defined can be translated into array-based transition systems, which are amenable to SMT-based model checking. We provide an initial experimental evaluation of various DPAs proving safe and unsafe cases with the MCMT model checker. The results show that the approach is feasible and promising.

As future work, we aim at trying other SMT-based model checkers such as Cubicle [13] and nuXmv [11]. We will investigate new algorithms that directly exploit the topology of the architecture. We will extend the specification to incorporate component behavior and more complex interactions, as well as more general properties. Finally, we are interested in generating certifying proofs for the safe DPAs, possibly exploiting the existing automatic generation of proofs for array-based transition systems [14].

References

1. European Programme for Critical Infrastructure Protection (EPCIP). http://eur-lex.europa.eu/LexUriServ/LexUriServ.do?uri=COM:2006:0786:FIN:EN:PDF. Accessed 15 Jan 2018
2. NIST Cybersecurity Framework. http://www.nist.gov/cyberframework. Accessed 15 Jan 2018
3. The CITADEL Project (Critical Infrastructure Protection using Adaptive MILS). http://www.citadel-project.org/. Accessed 15 Jan 2018
4. Alberti, F., Ghilardi, S., Sharygina, N.: A framework for the verification of parameterized infinite-state systems. In: CEUR Workshop Proceedings, vol. 1195, pp. 302–308 (2014)
5. Allen, R., Douence, R., Garlan, D.: Specifying and analyzing dynamic software architectures. In: Astesiano, E. (ed.) FASE 1998. LNCS, vol. 1382, pp. 21–37. Springer, Heidelberg (1998). https://doi.org/10.1007/BFb0053581
6. Basu, A., Bozga, M., Sifakis, J.: Modeling heterogeneous real-time components in BIP. In: Fourth IEEE International Conference on Software Engineering and Formal Methods (SEFM 2006), Pune, India, pp. 3–12, 11–15 September 2006

7. Bozga, M., Jaber, M., Maris, N., Sifakis, J.: Modeling dynamic architectures using Dy-BIP. In: Gschwind, T., De Paoli, F., Gruhn, V., Book, M. (eds.) SC 2012. LNCS, vol. 7306, pp. 1–16. Springer, Heidelberg (2012). https://doi.org/10.1007/978-3-642-30564-1_1

8. Bradbury, J.S., Cordy, J.R., Dingel, J., Wermelinger, M.: A survey of self-management in dynamic software architecture specifications. In: Proceedings of the 1st ACM SIGSOFT Workshop on Self-Managed Systems WOSS 2004, Newport Beach, California, USA, pp. 28–33, 31 October - 1 November 2004

9. Bruni, R., Melgratti, H., Montanari, U.: Behaviour, interaction and dynamics. In: Iida, S., Meseguer, J., Ogata, K. (eds.) Specification, Algebra, and Software. LNCS, vol. 8373, pp. 382–401. Springer, Heidelberg (2014). https://doi.org/10.1007/978-3-642-54624-2_19

10. Canal, C., Pimentel, E., Troya, J.M.: Specification and refinement of dynamic software architectures. In: Donohoe, P. (ed.) Software Architecture. ITIFIP, vol. 12, pp. 107–125. Springer, Boston, MA (1999). https://doi.org/10.1007/978-0-387-35563-4_7

11. Cavada, R., Cimatti, A., Dorigatti, M., Griggio, A., Mariotti, A., Micheli, A., Mover, S., Roveri, M., Tonetta, S.: The NUXMV symbolic model checker. In: Biere, A., Bloem, R. (eds.) CAV 2014. LNCS, vol. 8559, pp. 334–342. Springer, Cham (2014). https://doi.org/10.1007/978-3-319-08867-9_22

12. CITADEL Modeling and Specification Languages. Technical report D3.1, Version 2.2, CITADEL Project, April 2018

13. Conchon, S., Goel, A., Krstić, S., Mebsout, A., Zaïdi, F.: Cubicle: a parallel SMT-based model checker for parameterized systems. In: Madhusudan, P., Seshia, S.A. (eds.) CAV 2012. LNCS, vol. 7358, pp. 718–724. Springer, Heidelberg (2012). https://doi.org/10.1007/978-3-642-31424-7_55

14. Conchon, S., Mebsout, A., Zaïdi, F.: Certificates for parameterized model checking. In: Bjørner, N., de Boer, F. (eds.) FM 2015. LNCS, vol. 9109, pp. 126–142. Springer, Cham (2015). https://doi.org/10.1007/978-3-319-19249-9_9

15. Enderton, H.B.: A Mathematical Introduction to Logic, 2nd edn. Academic Press, Boston (2001)

16. Feiler, P.H., Gluch, D.P.: Model-Based Engineering with AADL - An Introduction to the SAE Architecture Analysis and Design Language. Addison-Wesley, SEI series in software engineering (2012)

17. Ghilardi, S.: MCMT v2.5 - User Manual (2014). http://users.mat.unimi.it/users/ghilardi/mcmt/UM_MCMT_2.5.pdf. Accessed 15 Jan 2018

18. Ghilardi, S., Ranise, S.: Backward reachability of array-based systems by SMT solving: termination and invariant synthesis. Log. Meth. Comput. Sci. 6(4), 1–48 (2010)

19. Ghilardi, S., Ranise, S.: MCMT: a model checker modulo theories. In: Giesl, J., Hähnle, R. (eds.) IJCAR 2010. LNCS (LNAI), vol. 6173, pp. 22–29. Springer, Heidelberg (2010). https://doi.org/10.1007/978-3-642-14203-1_3

20. Goguen, J.A., Meseguer, J.: Security policies and security models. In: 1982 IEEE Symposium on Security and Privacy, Oakland, CA, USA, pp. 11–20, 26–28 April 1982

21. Hirsch, D., Inverardi, P., Montanari, U.: Reconfiguration of software architecture styles with name mobility. In: Porto, A., Roman, G.-C. (eds.) COORDINATION 2000. LNCS, vol. 1906, pp. 148–163. Springer, Heidelberg (2000). https://doi.org/10.1007/3-540-45263-X_10

22. König, B., Kozioura, V.: Towards the verification of attributed graph transformation systems. In: Ehrig, H., Heckel, R., Rozenberg, G., Taentzer, G. (eds.) ICGT 2008. LNCS, vol. 5214, pp. 305–320. Springer, Heidelberg (2008). https://doi.org/10.1007/978-3-540-87405-8_21

23. Konnov, I.V., Kotek, T., Wang, Q., Veith, H., Bliudze, S., Sifakis, J.: Parameterized systems in BIP: design and model checking. In: 27th International Conference on Concurrency Theory CONCUR 2016, Québec City, Canada, pp. 30:1–30:16, 23–26 August 2016

24. Magee, J., Kramer, J.: Dynamic structure in software architectures. In: SIGSOFT 1996 Proceedings of the Fourth ACM SIGSOFT Symposium on Foundations of Software Engineering, San Francisco, California, USA, pp. 3–14, 16–18 October 1996

25. Medvidovic, N., Taylor, R.N.: A classification and comparison framework for software architecture description languages. IEEE Trans. Softw. Eng. **26**(1), 70–93 (2000)

26. Métayer, D.L.: Describing software architecture styles using graph grammars. IEEE Trans. Softw. Eng. **24**(7), 521–533 (1998)

27. Milner, R., Parrow, J., Walker, D.: A Calculus of Mobile Processes I and II. Inf. Comput. **100**(1), 1–77 (1992)

28. Minsky, M.L.: Computation: Finite and Infinite Machines. Prentice-Hall Inc, Upper Saddle River (1967)

29. Rozenberg, G. (ed.): Handbook of Graph Grammars and Computing by Graph Transformations, Volume 1: Foundations. World Scientific, Singapore (1997)

30. Architecture Analysis & Design Language (AADL) (rev. B). SAE Standard AS5506B, International Society of Automotive Engineers, September 2012

31. Sifakis, J., Bensalem, S., Bliudze, S., Bozga, M.: A theory agenda for component-based design. In: De Nicola, R., Hennicker, R. (eds.) Software, Services, and Systems. LNCS, vol. 8950, pp. 409–439. Springer, Cham (2015). https://doi.org/10.1007/978-3-319-15545-6_24

32. Wermelinger, M., Fiadeiro, J.L.: Algebraic software architecture reconfiguration. In: Nierstrasz, O., Lemoine, M. (eds.) ESEC/SIGSOFT FSE -1999. LNCS, vol. 1687, pp. 393–409. Springer, Heidelberg (1999). https://doi.org/10.1007/3-540-48166-4_24

33. Xu, H., Zeng, G., Chen, B.: Description and verification of dynamic software architectures for distributed systems. JSW **5**(7), 721–728 (2010)

FM 2018 Industry Day

From Formal Requirements to Highly Assured Software for Unmanned Aircraft Systems

César Muñoz$^{(\boxtimes)}$, Anthony Narkawicz, and Aaron Dutle

NASA Langley Research Center, Hampton, VA 23681-2199, USA
{cesar.a.munoz,anthony.narkawicz,aaron.m.dutle}@nasa.gov

Abstract. Operational requirements of safety-critical systems are often written in restricted specification logics. These restricted logics are amenable to automated analysis techniques such as model-checking, but are not rich enough to express complex requirements of unmanned systems. This short paper advocates for the use of expressive logics, such as higher-order logic, to specify the complex operational requirements and safety properties of unmanned systems. These rich logics are less amenable to automation and, hence, require the use of interactive theorem proving techniques. However, these logics support the formal verification of complex requirements such as those involving the physical environment. Moreover, these logics enable validation techniques that increase confidence in the correctness of numerically intensive software. These features result in highly-assured software that may be easier to certify. The feasibility of this approach is illustrated with examples drawn for NASA's unmanned aircraft systems.

1 Introduction

Recent advances in theorem proving technology have prompted the development of environments such as ASSERT (Analysis of Semantic Specifications and Efficient generation of Requirements-based Test) [17] and SpeAR (Specification and Analysis of Requirements) [6] that provide English-like, but semantically rigorous, languages to capture requirements. These requirements are formally analyzed for consistency using automated theorem proving tools. Environments such as ASSERT and SpeAR are examples of the state-of-the-art in formal requirements design. Yet, the kinds of requirements that can be analyzed using these environments are those supported by automated verification techniques, which are typically limited to finite state machines and decidable theories supported by SMT solvers. These formalisms are not rich enough to allow for the specification of complex requirements of cyber-physical systems. This short paper reports work by the Formal Methods (FM) Team at NASA Langley

U.S. Government, as represented by the Administrator of the National Aeronautics and Space Administration. No copyright is claimed in the United States under Title 17, U.S. Code. All Other Rights Reserved. 2018
K. Havelund et al. (Eds.): FM 2018, LNCS 10951, pp. 647–652, 2018.
https://doi.org/10.1007/978-3-319-95582-7_38

Research Center (LaRC) on the use of higher-order logic and interactive the-orem proving for the specification, analysis, and implementation of operational and functional requirements of unmanned aircraft systems (UAS).

2   UAS Detect and Avoid

In 2011, the UAS Sense and Avoid Science and Research Panel (SARP) was tasked with making a recommendation to the FAA for a quantitative defini-tion of a concept for UAS called *well clear*. The origin of this concept is the see-and-avoid principle in manned aircraft operations that states that on-board pilots have, in part, the responsibility for not "operating an aircraft so close to another aircraft as to create a collision hazard", "to see and avoid other aircraft", and when complying with the particular rules addressing right-of-way, on-board pilots "may not pass over, under, or ahead [of the right-of-way aircraft] unless well clear" [7]. The lack of a similar principle for UAS was identified by the FAA as one of the main obstacles in the integration of UAS in the National Airspace System. Hence, the final report of the Federal Aviation Administration (FAA) Sense and Avoid (SAA) Workshop [5] defined the concept of *sense and avoid*, also called *detect and avoid* (DAA), as "the capability of a UAS to remain well clear from and avoid collisions with other airborne traffic."

Consiglio et al. proposed the following guiding principles for the definition of well clear and DAA requirements: (a) The well-clear concept should be geometri-cally represented by a time and distance volume in the airspace, (b) DAA should interoperate with existing collision avoidance systems, (c) DAA should avoid undue concern for traffic aircraft, and (d) DAA should enable self-separation capabilities [1]. Based on these guidelines, a family of well-clear volumes was formally specified in the Program Verification System (PVS) [14]. This family is defined by a Boolean predicate, representing a volume in the airspace, that depends on the position and velocity of the ownship and intruder aircraft at the current time. It was formally verified that volumes in this family satisfy several properties such as inclusion, symmetry, extensibility, local convexity, and conver-gence [8,10]. These properties were used by the UAS SARP to discard competing proposals for the well-clear volume. The volume ultimately recommended by the UAS SARP [3] is based on distance and time functions used in the detection logic of the second generation of the Traffic Alerting and Collision Avoidance System (TCAS II) Resolution Advisory (RA) detection logic [16]. Since this volume is a member of the family specified in PVS, it inherits the family's formally verified properties. For example, it has been formally verified that for a choice of thresh-old values, the well-clear volume is larger than the TCAS II RA volume [10] (inclusion) and that in pairwise encounter both aircraft simultaneously compute the same well-clear status (symmetry). The use of higher-order logic enabled the definition of this family of volumes that is not only parametric with respect to distance and time thresholds, but also with respect to continuous functions on positions and velocities.

The standards organization RTCA established Special Committee 228 (SC-228) to provide technical guidance to the FAA for defining minimum operational performance standards for a DAA concept based on the definition of well-clear recommended by the UAS SARP. This concept consists of three functional capabilities: detection logic, alerting logic, and maneuver guidance logic. The detection logic specifies a time interval where a well-clear violation occurs, within a lookhead time interval, assuming non-accelerating aircraft trajectories. A parametric algorithm that computes this time interval, for an arbitrary choice of the threshold values used in the definition of the well-clear volume, has been formally verified in PVS [9]. This parametric algorithm is key to the definition of the alerting logic, which is specified by a series of thresholds that yield volumes of decreasing size. Depending on the time to violation of these volumes, the alerting logic returns a numerical value representing the severity of a predicted conflict. The smaller the volume and the shorter the time to violation, the greater the severity. It has been formally verified that the alerting logic satisfies the following operational properties (assuming non-accelerating aircraft trajectories) [8,10]: (extensibility) alerts progress according to the severity level; (local convexity) once an alert is issued, it is continuously issued until threat disappears; and (convergence) once an alert is issued, it does not disappear before time of closest point of approach. Finally, the manuever guidance logic specifies ranges of one-dimensional maneuvers, i.e., change of horizontal direction, change of horizontal speed, change of vertical speed, or change of altitude, that lead to a well-clear violation within a lookahead time interval. In the case of a well-clear violation, the maneuver guidance logic specifies ranges of maneuvers that recover well-clear status. Assuming a kinematic model of the ownship trajectories, an algorithm that computes maneuver guidance for each dimension has been formally proved to be correct within a user specified granularity. This algorithm is parametric with respect to a detection algorithm for an arbitrary definition of the well-clear volume. These algorithms are collectively called DAIDALUS (Detect and Avoid Alerting Logic for Unmanned Systems) [11] and they are included in RTCA DO-365 [15].

3   From DAIDALUS to ICAROUS

Software implementations of DAIDALUS are available in Java and C++ and they are distributed under NASA's Open Source Agreement.[1] The PVS specifications and proofs are also available as part of the distribution. Except for language idiosyncrasies both implementations are identical and they closely follow the PVS algorithms. A formal verification of the software implementations is a major endeavor that has not been attempted. In particular, DAIDALUS algorithms are formally verified in PVS assuming real-number arithmetic, while the software implementations of DAIDALUS use floating-point arithmetic. However, the software implementations of DAIDALUS have been validated against the PVS algorithms using model animation [4] on a set of stressing cases. This

---

[1] https://github.com/nasa/wellclear.

validation improves the assurance that the hand translation from formal models to code is faithful and that floating point errors do not greatly affect correctness and safety properties that are formally verified in PVS.

The approach used in the development of DAIDALUS, from formal requirements to highly assured software, is called MINERVA [13] (Mirrored Implementation Numerically Evaluated against Rigorously Verified Algorithms). The MINERVA approach has been used in the development of other UAS applications. PolyCARP, a collection of algorithms for weather avoidance and geofencing has been formally developed in PVS [12]. Implementations of PolyCARP in Java, C++, and Python have been validated using model validation. This development, including software, specifications, and proofs, is available under NASA's Open Source Agreement.[2] DAIDALUS and PolyCARP are two of the algorithms included in ICAROUS (Independent Configurable Architecture for Reliable Operations of Unmanned Systems) [2]. ICAROUS is an open software architecture composed of mission specific software modules and highly assured core algorithms for building autonomous unmanned aircraft applications.[3]

4   Conclusion

The examples presented in this paper show that the use of expressive formalisms, such as PVS, for writing requirements and formally analyzing them is not only feasible but effective in the development of safety-critical systems. Higher-order logic enables, for example, the specification and formal analysis of generic models that can be instantiated and reused in multiple ways. DAIDALUS algorithms, for example, can be instantiated with different set of thresholds, different notions of well-clear, and different aircraft performance characteristics. The default configuration of DAIDALUS defined in DO-365 is appropriate for large fixed wing UAS. In ICAROUS, however, DAIDALUS is instantiated with the performance of a small rotorcraft and a smaller set of thresholds that define a cylindrical well-clear volume. The formal models are correct for both of any instantiation due to the parametric nature of the models.

However, rich formalisms such as higher-order logic are not the silver bullet. These expressive logics are typically undecidable and, in the case of PVS, even type-checking is undecidable. Interactive theorem proving is a human intensive activity and the tools are still difficult to use by system developers. Applications such as DAIDALUS, PolyCARP, and ICAROUS are possible because of years of fundamental developments in interactive theorem proving technology including formal libraries and proof strategies. The call in this paper is for the integration of this infrastructure, which is also available in other proofs assistants, in modern requirement engineering tools like ASSERT and SPEAR.

---

[2] https://github.com/nasa/PolyCARP.
[3] https://github.com/nasa/ICAROUS.

References

1. Consiglio, M., Chamberlain, J., Muñoz, C., Hoffler, K.: Concept of integration for UAS operations in the NAS. In: Proceedings of 28th International Congress of the Aeronautical Sciences, ICAS 2012, Brisbane, Australia (2012)
2. Consiglio, M., Muñoz, C., Hagen, G., Narkawicz, A., Balachandran, S.: ICAROUS: integrated configurable algorithms for reliable operations of unmanned systems. In: Proceedings of the 35th Digital Avionics Systems Conference (DASC 2016), Sacramento, California, US, September 2016
3. Cook, S.P., Brooks, D., Cole, R., Hackenberg, D., Raska, V.: Defining well clear for unmanned aircraft systems. In: Proceedings of the 2015 AIAA Infotech@ Aerospace Conference, Number AIAA-2015-0481, Kissimmee, Florida, January 2015
4. Dutle, A.M., Muñoz, C.A., Narkawicz, A.J., Butler, R.W.: Software validation via model animation. In: Blanchette, J.C., Kosmatov, N. (eds.) TAP 2015. LNCS, vol. 9154, pp. 92–108. Springer, Cham (2015). https://doi.org/10.1007/978-3-319-21215-9_6
5. FAA Sponsored Sense and Avoid Workshop. Sense and avoid (SAA) for Unmanned Aircraft Systems (UAS), October 2009
6. Fifarek, A.W., et al.: SpeAR v2.0: formalized past LTL specification and analysis of requirements. In: Barrett, C., Davies, M., Kahsai, T. (eds.) NFM 2017. LNCS, vol. 10227, pp. 420–426. Springer, Cham (2017). https://doi.org/10.1007/978-3-319-57288-8_30
7. International Civil Aviation Organization (ICAO): Annex 2 to the Convention on International Civil Aviation, July 2005
8. Muñoz, C., Narkawicz, A.: Formal analysis of extended well-clear boundaries for unmanned aircraft. In: Rayadurgam, S., Tkachuk, O. (eds.) NFM 2016. LNCS, vol. 9690, pp. 221–226. Springer, Cham (2016). https://doi.org/10.1007/978-3-319-40648-0_17
9. Muñoz, C., Narkawicz, A., Chamberlain, J.: A TCAS-II resolution advisory detection algorithm. In: Proceedings of the AIAA Guidance Navigation, and Control Conference and Exhibit 2013, Number AIAA-2013-4622, Boston, Massachusetts, August 2013
10. Muñoz, C., Narkawicz, A., Chamberlain, J., Consiglio, M., Upchurch, J.: A family of well-clear boundary models for the integration of UAS in the NAS. In: Proceedings of the 14th AIAA Aviation Technology, Integration, and Operations (ATIO) Conference, Number AIAA-2014-2412, Georgia, Atlanta, USA, June 2014
11. Muñoz, C., Narkawicz, A., Hagen, G., Upchurch, J., Dutle, A., Consiglio, M.: DAIDALUS: detect and avoid alerting logic for unmanned systems. In: Proceedings of the 34th Digital Avionics Systems Conference (DASC 2015), Prague, Czech Republic, September 2015
12. Narkawicz, A., Hagen, G.: Algorithms for collision detection between a point and a moving polygon, with applications to aircraft weather avoidance. In: 16th AIAA Aviation Technology, Integration, and Operations Conference, AIAA AVIATION Forum, Number AIAA-2016-3598, Washington, DC, USA, June 2016
13. Narkawicz, A., Muñoz, C., Dutle, A.: The MINERVA software development process. In: Proceedings of the Workshop on Automated Formal Methods 2017 (AFM 2017), Meno Park, California, USA (2017)

14. Owre, S., Rushby, J.M., Shankar, N.: PVS: a prototype verification system. In: Kapur, D. (ed.) CADE 1992. LNCS, vol. 607, pp. 748–752. Springer, Heidelberg (1992). https://doi.org/10.1007/3-540-55602-8_217
15. RTCA SC-1228. RTCA-DO-365, Minimum Operational Performance Standards for Detect and Avoid (DAA) Systems, May 2017
16. RTCA SC-147. RTCA-DO-185B, Minimum Operational Performance Standards for Traffic alert and Collision Avoidance System II (TCAS II), July 2009
17. Siu, K., Moitra, A., Durling, M., Crapo, A., Li, M., Yu, H., Herencia-Zapana, H., Castillo-Effen, M., Sen, S., McMillan, C., Russell, D., Roy, S., Manolios, P.: Flight critical software and systems development using ASSERT. In: 2017 IEEE/AIAA 36th Digital Avionics Systems Conference (DASC), Number 978-1-5386-0365-9/17, pp. 1–10, September 2017

Interlocking Design Automation Using Prover Trident

Arne Borälv[(✉)]

Prover Technology, Krukmakargatan 21, 118 51 Stockholm, Sweden
arne.boralv@prover.com

Abstract. This article presents the industrial-strength Prover Trident approach to develop and check safety-critical interlocking software for railway signaling systems. Prover Trident is developed by Prover Technology to meet industry needs for reduced cost and time-to-market, by capitalizing on the inherent repetitive nature of interlocking systems, in the sense that specific systems can be created and verified efficiently as specific instances of generic principles. This enables a high degree of automation in an industrial-strength toolkit for creation of design and code, with seamless integration of push-button tools for simulation and formal verification. Safety assessment relies on formal verification, performed on the design, the revenue service software code as well as the binary code, using an independent toolset for formal verification developed to meet the applicable certification requirements. Basic ideas of this approach have been around for some time [1, 2, 3], while methodology and tools have matured over many industrial application projects. The presentation highlights the main ingredients in this successful application of formal methods, as well as challenges in establishing this approach for production use in a conservative industry domain.

Keywords: Formal verification · Sign-off · Interlocking · Prover trident

1 Background

In railway signaling, interlocking systems control the signals, switches and other wayside objects to ensure railway operations are always safe. Interlocking systems used to be based on electro-mechanical relays, with most new systems being computerized. The interlocking principles vary considerably, in different countries and for different railway infrastructure managers, with high life-cycle cost (one of the costliest railway signaling components). The plethora of different signaling principles contributes to that development and checking is time-consuming and costly. The adoption of new technology such as automation tools is slow, due to the conservative nature of the industry, and the stringent safety integrity levels that pose a challenge of trust in automation tools. There is also resistance in terms of minds to change and win over.

This article presents Prover Trident, an industrial-strength approach based on formal methods to develop and check safety-critical interlocking software for railway signaling systems that is used in production.

© Springer International Publishing AG, part of Springer Nature 2018
K. Havelund et al. (Eds.): FM 2018, LNCS 10951, pp. 653–656, 2018.
https://doi.org/10.1007/978-3-319-95582-7_39

2 The Prover Trident Process

The Prover Trident process automates development and checking of interlocking software, leading to reduced effort and cost, and predictable schedules. This section outlines the main steps in configuring and using Prover Trident. Compared to "traditional" processes, more effort is spent on requirement specification, and a greater level of requirements precision is required. This extra effort is worthwhile, due to savings achieved from automated development of many systems, and the reduced long-term maintenance costs. Prover Trident is based on the following three main components:

- **PiSPEC IP:** A formal specification library of generic interlocking system requirements defined in PiSPEC, an object-oriented language supporting many-sorted first order logic and Boolean equations.
- **Prover iLock:** An Integrated Development Environment (IDE) that generates the design, test cases and safety requirements based on the PiSPEC IP and a system configuration, with push-button tools to automate simulation, formal verification and code generation.
- **Prover Certifier:** An independent sign-off verification tool that formally verifies that the revenue service code satisfies all safety requirements, using a process and tool chain designed to meet safety certification standards thanks to the use of diversified translation of input models, and proof logging and checking.

2.1 PiSPEC IP

The generic principles for a family of interlocking systems are determined by analyzing applicable standards, requirement specifications, interfaces, rules and regulations. To ensure good quality of results, with predictable development and maintenance, the principles are defined based on an *object model* (see Fig. 1). The object model defines the underlying ideas and objects, including both physical objects (e.g. signals, switches) and virtual objects (e.g. routes, protection areas), along with their properties and relations. The object model provides a common interface to ensure coherence and consistency in defining all interlocking software requirements, with clear separation of design, test and safety requirements. Configuration of individual interlocking systems populates the object model.

The object model and the generic design, test and safety requirements are defined in PiSPEC, using many-sorted first order logic. This enables to express requirements that are generic, using quantifiers over different sorts, corresponding to different types of objects in the object model. For example, to express a generic safety requirement that *a signal must display the stop aspect if it does not have control line safety* can be expressed as follows, where cl_safety() and stop() are predicates defined for signals:

$$\text{ALL si:SIGNAL (not cl\_safety(si)} \rightarrow \text{stop(si))} \tag{1}$$

A non-trivial task is to verify completeness of the safety requirements. This task is usually managed based on manual review by domain experts, and/or diversification.

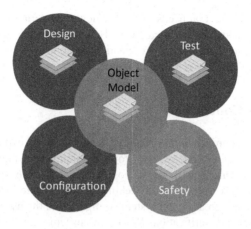

Fig. 1. Structure of generic principles (PiSPEC IP)

2.2 Prover iLock

Prover iLock is an Integrated Development Environment (IDE) for development of interlocking software. An individual system is created based on a high-level configuration of its track and signal arrangement that is created graphically (and other tabular data that can be imported). Prover iLock generates the design, test cases and safety requirements based on the PiSPEC IP and the system's configuration. Push-button tools can then be applied directly, for formal verification of design safety (Verifier), automated simulation of the design with its environment models using time-compression optimization techniques (Simulator), and generation of software code for revenue service (Coder).

Prover iLock supports animation in the graphical railyard configuration, providing visualization of state from interactive simulation or from counterexamples to safety requirements. This is useful for education purposes and during development of the PiSPEC IP. (In production use, simulation and verification are run in batch mode, normally not failing).

2.3 Prover Certifier

Using Prover Trident, safety verification of the revenue service code (target code) generated from Prover iLock is done using an independent sign-off verification tool. This step proves that the target code satisfies the same safety requirements that were verified against the design. This step also proves the equivalence of the design and the target code, or alternatively the equivalence of the target code and the resulting binary code.

A sign-off verification tool is based on Prover Certifier, which has been designed and developed as a reusable component that meets strict certification requirements. Prover Certifier uses techniques to reduce risks that errors go undetected, including diversified processing of input data using multiple implementation languages and using proof logging and proof checking. A sign-off verification tool extends Prover Certifier with diversified translators for the target code and the binary code.

The configuration data that needs manual review per interlocking system should be kept small. A dedicated format called LCF [4] is used for this purpose. This format provides easy-to-review, compact representation of configuration data, supported by diversified translation to Prover Certifier input.

3 Results and Conclusions

The Prover Trident approach is the result of many years of experience from formal verification of interlocking systems, and from development of high-integrity tools for formal verification. This has made it possible to automate repetitive and time-consuming tasks in development and checking of railway interlocking software, with manual tasks mainly for creating the system configuration, the use of push-button tools and running the sign-off verification. With new systems developed with much less effort, efficiency is increased, and time-to-market and cost are reduced. It also ensures that each system is developed and verified based on same (reusable) principles.

The Prover Trident approach is used for creating revenue service interlocking software for application in urban metro, mainline railway, light-rail and, in its core parts, even in freight railways. The process and tools used are essentially the same – the differences imposed for different target platforms and railway infrastructure managers are minor, with a variety of target platforms being supported. Generic tools can be extended by adding code generators and customizing the sign-off verification tool. This enables the support of any interlocking system type and any target, at least in principle.

The big difference lies in input data, in the form of different PiSPEC IP. Using the Prover Trident approach, the truly creative aspects lie in the specification work required for defining the generic interlocking software principles.

There are no real technical obstacles for using Prover Trident for interlocking software development. Rather, the main challenge lies in conversion from old habits and the many hearts and minds to win over in the conservative railway signaling domain. In addition, commercial aspects and job security are also real concerns.

References

1. Borälv, A.: Case study: formal verification of a computerized railway interlocking. Formal Aspects of Comput. **10**, 338 (1998). https://doi.org/10.1007/s001650050021
2. Borälv, A., Stålmarck, G.: Formal verification in railways. In: Hinchey, M.G., Bowen, J. P. (eds.) Industrial-Strength Formal Methods in Practice. Formal Approaches to Computing and Information Technology (FACIT), pp. 329–350. Springer, London (1999). https://doi.org/10.1007/978-1-4471-0523-7_15
3. Duggan (Siemens), P., Borälv, A.: Mathematical Proof in an Automated Environment for Railway Interlockings, Technical Paper in IRSE Presidential Programme, IRSE NEWS 217 (2015)
4. Layout Configuration Format (LCF) v1.1, Format Specification. PCERT-LCF-FMT, version 1.0, Prover Technology (2018)

Model-Based Testing for Avionics Systems

Jörg Brauer$^{(\boxtimes)}$ and Uwe Schulze

Verified Systems International GmbH, Bremen, Germany
{brauer,schulze}@verified.de

Abstract. Model-based testing is considered state-of-the-art in verification and validation of safety-critical systems. This paper discusses some experiences of applying the model-based testing tool RTT-MBT for the evacuation function of an aircraft cabin controller. One challenge of this project was the parametric design of the software, which allows to tailor the software to a certain aircraft configuration via application parameters. Further challenges consisted of connecting hardware signals of the system under test to abstract model variables, and handling incremental test model development during an ongoing test campaign. We discuss solutions that we developed to successfully conduct this test campaign.

1 Introduction

Over the past two decades, we have observed a wide-spread adoption of model-based development techniques in industry. In parallel, the scientific community has provided promising concepts and powerful solutions for the area of model-based testing, in particular with respect to the automation of the test case generation process. SMT solvers, to name just one example, have advanced to the state where they can easily solve problems involving thousands of variables, and thus support the automated generation of test data for large test models. This technological progress is a prerequisite for effective application of model-based testing in industry. In practise, however, there is often some mismatch between the scientific progress on the one hand and the industrial requirements on the other hand. In particular, we have observed that the successful and not so successful model-based testing projects often just differ in the supportive features offered by the model-based testing frameworks.

This paper is about effective model-based testing for the avionics domain, and the peculiarities that need to be taken care of, which in the end often make the difference between success and failure of a project. For the cabin control system of several Airbus aircrafts, our company has provided several hardware-in-the-loop (HIL) test benches which traditionally execute hand-written tests. More recently,

The work presented in this contribution has been partially funded by the German Federal Ministry for Economic Affairs and Energy (BMWi) in the context of project STEVE, grant application 20Y1301P.

the existing test infrastructure was extended by tests generated from test models using RTT-MBT [3], which is based on simulation and SMT solving [1,2]. Model-based testing for the cabin control system poses some interesting challenges that need to be taken care of:

- The runtime behavior of the system is highly configurable via application parameters that need to be selected by the test case generator with the test data. Trying out all admissible combinations of parameters is infeasible.
- The system uses numerous different I/O interfaces.
- The test case generator needs assistance for the creation of meaningful, descriptive test cases which not just cover the requirements using some arbitrary inputs, but also trigger the standard use cases of the system.

2   Core Challenges

The emergency evacuation function of the cabin controller has some interesting properties. First and foremost, the software is highly configurable at runtime, using a configuration file, which allows to adapt the software to the layout of and the devices installed in an aircraft. The logic implemented by the evacuation function itself strongly depends on these parameters. This characteristic has been investigated in recent years under the term product line testing. For instance, contemporary aircrafts have a set of attendant panels, the number of which is configurable. Attendant panels can be configured to indicate an evacuation situation differently: either a flashing light or a steady light can be used for this purpose. A test which examines the behavior of the evacuation function with respect to the attendant panels thus needs to be run with a configuration file that matches the prerequisites for the test. If the test objective is to examine whether the flashing behaviour is correctly implemented, a configuration needs to be created which (1) installs at least one attendant panel and (2) assigns the flashing mode to the panel indication lights used by the evacuation function. For testing the steady indication, another configuration and another test is needed.

2.1   Application Parameters

In our target system, the parameter configuration consists of roughly 100 C-structures. The parameters defined in the structures can themselves be structured and can define dependencies on other system parameters. This provides a very powerful way to customize the system, but also makes it virtually impossible to take all possible parameter settings into account when defining the test model. The complexity of the system parameters is also a serious challenge in manual test campaigns, because manually calculating suitable system parameters is complicated and error-prone. Normally only a small subset of the parameters is directly related to the functionality addressed by a test model. In case of the evacuation function, only 16 parameters defined in two of the structures directly affect the behavior of the function. These parameters must be adjusted to enable certain parts of the system behavior under consideration.

Other parameters are still relevant, but do not need to be changed to reach certain test goals. They do, however, define constraints to the system, and these must be taken into account when designing the test model. For these parameters, constants were defined in the model to represent the selected settings, and a fixed definition for this part of the parameter state space was used for all test generations of the test suite. The configuration parameters cannot be changed at runtime without restarting the system. This information is reflected in a model via a UML stereotype called "parameter", which is assigned to the respective model variables. The transition relation used by the test generator is augmented with constraints to ensure that the parameters do not change during a single test. This approach results in a significant improvement compared to manual test development with manual calculation of the configuration parameters.

2.2   Interface Modules

Despite the improvements on SMT solving, generating test cases may still be computationally infeasible on the concrete semantics of an application, which naturally leads to the question of abstraction. Modelling the application behavior on the granularity of hardware interfaces leads to state explosion, which entails that some kind of abstraction layer has to be introduced, which maps model inputs to concrete hardware signals and vice versa. For instance, it is not uncommon that some model input is represented by the conjunction of multiple concrete hardware signals. The mapping between model variables and hardware signals is implemented manually in a layer that resides between the device drivers and the test driver, and requires significant expertise of the test engineers.

2.3   Test Scenarios

Model-based test generation often produces tests that are semantically correct, but not very realistic, which may be an issue if the tests are used for certification purposes. RTT-MBT provides a mechanism to restrict the test generator by defining constraints for the test environment. Defining a complete test environment specification suitable for all tests generated from a model, however, can require a lot of effort or even be practically infeasible. Simple test goals with RTT-MBT can be defined as states or transitions to be covered, but complex test goals must be specified in LTL, which is not intuitive to most users. Both problems are addressed using additional state machines in the test models that define so-called *test scenarios*. A test scenario defines a complex test goal trough a sequence of sub-goals and excludes undesired behavior. An example of such a test scenario is given in Fig. 1. This way, a test scenario combines the partial definition of test environment restrictions that are tailored to a complex test goal together with the intuitive step by step definition of the goal itself. Note that the test generator is still used to calculate the concrete test data, but is restricted through the constraints imposed by the additional scenario state machine.

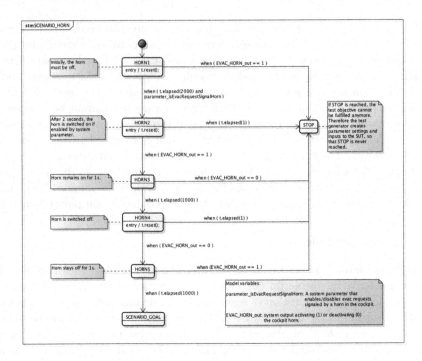

Fig. 1. A test scenario characterizes a family of stimulations

3   Conclusion

We have described an approach to model-based testing of highly configurable avionics control systems. To name one example, the approach has been used for the verification of sub-systems of the Airbus A350 aircraft. Our strategy relies on test models that describe the system behavior depending on application parameters, which are integrated as model constraints. An interesting aspect with respect to economic viability of model-based testing is the efficiency of test model development. Significant reductions in efforts can be achieved with regression campaigns, but the initial investment for the transition should not be underestimated, which may be explained by the fact that model development requires a different skill set than traditional test development. There are, of course, open issues to be addressed in the future. For instance, the question of sufficient configuration coverage needs to be answered. To this end, we currently adapt an input equivalence class testing strategy with guaranteed fault detection properties.

References

1. Lapschies, F.: SONOLAR homepage, June 2014. http://www.informatik.uni-bremen.de/agbs/florian/sonolar/
2. Peleska, J., Vorobev, E., Lapschies, F.: Automated test case generation with SMT-solving and abstract interpretation. In: Bobaru, M., Havelund, K., Holzmann, G.J., Joshi, R. (eds.) NFM 2011. LNCS, vol. 6617, pp. 298–312. Springer, Heidelberg (2011). https://doi.org/10.1007/978-3-642-20398-5_22
3. Verified Systems International GmbH: RTT-MBT: Model-Based Testing. https://www.verified.de/products/model-based-testing

On Software Safety, Security, and Abstract Interpretation

Daniel Kästner, Laurent Mauborgne, and Christian Ferdinand[✉]

AbsInt Angewandte Informatik GmbH, Saarbrücken, Germany
ferdinand@absint.com

Abstract. Static code analysis can be applied to show compliance to coding guidelines, and to demonstrate the absence of critical programming errors, including runtime errors and data races. In recent years, security concerns have become more and more relevant for safety-critical systems, not least due to the increasing importance of highly-automated driving and pervasive connectivity. While in the past, sound static analyzers have been primarily applied to demonstrate classical safety properties they are well suited also to address data safety, and to discover security vulnerabilities. This article gives an overview and discusses practical experience.

1 Introduction

In safety-critical systems, static analysis plays an important role. With the growing size of software-implemented functionality, preventing software-induced system failures becomes an increasingly important task. One particularly dangerous class of errors are runtime errors which include faulty pointer manipulations, numerical errors such as arithmetic overflows and division by zero, data races, and synchronization errors in concurrent software. Such errors can cause software crashes, invalidate separation mechanisms in mixed-criticality software, and are a frequent cause of errors in concurrent and multi-core applications. At the same time, these defects are also at the root of many security vulnerabilities, including exploits based on buffer overflows, dangling pointers, or integer errors.

In safety-critical software projects, obeying coding guidelines such as MISRA C is strongly recommended by safety standards like DO-178C, IEC-61508, ISO-26262, or EN-50128. In addition, all of them consider demonstrating the absence of runtime errors explicitly as a verification goal. This is often formulated indirectly by addressing runtime errors (e.g., division by zero, invalid pointer accesses, arithmetic overflows) in general, and additionally considering corruption of content, synchronization mechanisms, and freedom of interference in concurrent execution. Semantics-based static analysis has become the predominant technology to detect runtime errors and data races.

Abstract interpretation-based static analyzers provide full control and data coverage and allow conclusions to be drawn that are valid for all program runs with all inputs. Such conclusions may be that no timing or space constraints are

© Springer International Publishing AG, part of Springer Nature 2018
K. Havelund et al. (Eds.): FM 2018, LNCS 10951, pp. 662–665, 2018.
https://doi.org/10.1007/978-3-319-95582-7_41

violated, or that runtime errors or data races are absent: the absence of these errors can be guaranteed.

In the past, security properties have mostly been relevant for non-embedded and/or non-safety-critical programs. Recently due to increasing connectivity requirements (cloud-based services, car-to-car communication, over-the-air updates, etc.), more and more security issues are rising in safety-critical software as well.

Safety-critical software is developed according to strict guidelines which improve software verifiability. As an example dynamic memory allocation and recursion often are forbidden or used in a very limited way. Stronger code properties can be shown, so that also security vulnerabilities can be addressed in a more powerful way.

The topic of this article is to show that some classes of defects can be proven to be absent in the software so that exploits based on such defects can be excluded. Additional syntactic checks and semantical analyses become necessary to address security properties that are orthogonal to safety requirements.

2   Security in Safety-Critical Systems

MISRA C aims at avoiding programming errors and enforcing a programming style that enables the safest possible use of C. A particular focus is on dealing with undefined/unspecified behavior of C and on preventing runtime errors. As a consequence, it is also directly applicable to security-relevant code, which is explicitly addressed by Amendment 1 to MISRA C:2012. Other well-known coding guidelines are the ISO/IEC TS 17961, SEI CERT C, and the MITRE Common Weakness Enumeration CWE. The most prominent vulnerabilities at the C code level which are addressed in all coding guidelines are the following: Stack-based buffer overflows, heap-based buffer overflows, general invalid pointer accesses, uninitialized memory accesses, integer errors, format string vulnerabilities, and concurrency defects.

Most of these vulnerabilities are based on undefined behaviors, and among them buffer overflows seem to play the most prominent role. Most of them can be used for denial-of-service attacks by crashing the program or causing erroneous behavior. They can also be exploited to inject code and cause the program to execute it, and to extract confidential data from the system. It is worth noticing that from the perspective of a static analyzer most exploits are based on potential runtime errors: when using an unchecked value as an index in an array the error will only occur if the attacker manages to provide an invalid index value. The obvious conclusion is that safely eliminating all potential runtime errors due to undefined behaviors in the program significantly reduces the risk for security vulnerabilities.

From a semantical point of view, a safety property can always be expressed as a trace property. This means that to find all safety issues, it is enough to look at each trace of execution in isolation.

664   D. Kästner et al.

This is not possible any more for security properties. Most of them can only be expressed as set of traces properties, or hyperproperties [2]. A typical example is non-interference [7]: to express that the final value of a variable x can only be affected by the initial value of y and no other variable, one must consider each pair of possible execution traces with the same initial value for y, and check that the final value of x is the same for both executions. It was proven in [2] that any other definition (tracking assignments, etc) considering only one execution trace at a time would miss some cases or add false dependencies. This additional level of sets has direct consequences on the difficulty to track security properties soundly.

Finding expressive and efficient abstractions for such properties is a young research field (see [1]), which is the reason why no sound analysis of such properties appear in industrial static analyzers yet. The best solution using the current state of the art consists of using dedicated safety properties as an approximation of the security property in question, such as the taint propagation described below.

3   Proving the Absence of Defects

In the following we will concentrate on the sound static runtime error analyzer Astrée [3]. It reports program defects caused by unspecified and undefined behaviors and program defects caused by invalid concurrent behavior. Users are notified about: integer/floating-point division by zero, out-of-bounds array indexing, erroneous pointer manipulation and dereferencing (buffer overflows, null pointer dereferencing, dangling pointers, etc.), data races, lock/unlock problems, deadlocks, integer and floating-point arithmetic overflows, read accesses to uninitialized variables, unreachable code, non-terminating loops, and violations of coding rules (MISRA C, ISO/IEC TS 17961, CERT, CWE).

Astrée computes data and control flow reports containing a detailed listing of accesses to global and static variables sorted by functions, variables, and processes and containing a summary of caller/called relationships between functions. The analyzer can also report each effectively shared variable, the list of processes accessing it, and the types of the accesses (read, write, read/write).

To deal with concurrency defects, Astrée implements a sound low-level concurrent semantics [5] which provides a scalable sound abstraction covering all possible thread interleavings. In addition to the classes of runtime errors found in sequential programs, Astrée can report data races, and lock/unlock problems, i.e., inconsistent synchronization. After a data race, the analysis continues by considering the values stemming from all interleavings. Since Astrée is aware of all locks held for every program point in each concurrent thread, Astrée can also report all potential deadlocks. Practical experience on avionics and automotive industry applications are given in [3,6].

Sophisticated data and control flow information can be provided by two dedicated analysis methods: program slicing and taint analysis. Program slicing aims at identifying the part of the program that can influence a given set of variables at a given program point. Applied to a result value, e.g., it shows which functions, which statements, and which input variables contribute to its computation. Taint analysis tracks the propagation of specific data values through program execution. It can be used, e.g., to determine program parts affected by corrupted data from an insecure source. A sound taint analyzer will compute an over-approximation of the memory locations that may be mapped to a tainted value during program execution [4].

4 Conclusion

In this article, we have listed code-level defects and vulnerabilities relevant for functional safety and security. We have shown that many security attacks can be traced back to behaviors undefined or unspecified according to the C semantics. By applying sound static runtime error analyzers, a high degree of security can be achieved for safety-critical software. Security hyperproperties require additional analyses to be performed which, by nature, have a high complexity. We have given two examples of scalable dedicated analyses, program slicing and taint analysis. Applied as extensions of sound static analyzers, they allow to further increase confidence in the security of safety-critical embedded systems.

Acknowledgment. This work was funded within the project ARAMiS II by the German Federal Ministry for Education and Research with the funding ID 01—S16025. The responsibility for the content remains with the authors.

References

1. Assaf, M., Naumann, D.A., Signoles, J., Totel, E., Tronel, F.: Hypercollecting semantics and its application to static analysis of information flow. CoRR abs/1608.01654 (2016). http://arxiv.org/abs/1608.01654. Accessed Sep 2017
2. Clarkson, M.R., Schneider, F.B.: Hyperproperties. J. Comput. Secur. **18**, 1157–1210 (2010)
3. Kästner, D., Miné, A., Mauborgne, L., Rival, X., Feret, J., Cousot, P., Schmidt, A., Hille, H., Wilhelm, S., Ferdinand, C.: Finding all potential runtime errors and data races in automotive software. In: SAE World Congress 2017. SAE International (2017)
4. Kästner, D., Mauborgne, L., Ferdinand, C.: Detecting safety- and security-relevant programming defects by sound static analysis. In: Falk, R., Steve Chan, J.C.B. (eds.) The Second International Conference on Cyber-Technologies and Cyber-Systems (CYBER 2017). IARIA Conferences, vol. 2, pp. 26–31. IARIA XPS Press (2017)
5. Miné, A.: Static analysis of run-time errors in embedded real-time parallel C programs. Log. Methods Comput. Sci. (LMCS) **8**(26), 63 (2012)
6. Miné, A., Delmas, D.: Towards an industrial use of sound static analysis for the verification of concurrent embedded avionics software. In: Proceedings of the 15th International Conference on Embedded Software (EMSOFT 2015), pp. 65–74. IEEE CS Press, October 2015
7. Sabelfeld, A., Myers, A.C.: Language-based information-flow security. IEEE J. Sel. Areas Commun. **21**(1), 5–19 (2003)

Variant Analysis with QL

Pavel Avgustinov[(✉)], Kevin Backhouse, and Man Yue Mo

Semmle Ltd., Oxford, UK
{pavel,publications}@semmle.com

Abstract. As new security problems and innovative attacks continue to be discovered, program analysis remains a burgeoning area of research. QL builds on previous attempts to enable declarative program analysis through Datalog, but solves some of the traditional challenges: Its object-oriented nature enables the creation of extensive libraries, and the query optimizer minimizes the performance cost of the abstraction layers introduced in this way. QL enables agile security analysis, allowing security response teams to find all variants of a newly discovered vulnerability. Their work can then be leveraged to provide automated on-going checking, thus ensuring that the same mistake never makes it into the code base again. This paper demonstrates declarative variant analysis by example.

1 Introduction

QL is an object-oriented, declarative, logic language which has been successfully applied to the domain of program analysis. The idea is not new: Datalog-like formalisms are established as an effective way of implementing complex flow-sensitive analyses like points-to and dataflow [3,6]. However, the expressiveness and modularity of QL allows us to do something interesting and novel: Analysis building blocks are packaged up in reusable libraries, which can then be easily instantiated to particular problems encountered in the wild.

This process is known as *variant analysis*. Given a newly discovered bug or vulnerability, how can we find more instances (variants) of the same issue? Security research teams around the world currently do this by laborious manual search, but formally encoding the concern in QL can make the task significantly more achievable. The end result is a democratization of program analysis: Everyone is empowered to propose and implement new checks, or to proactively eradicate bugs of a certain class from the codebase they work on.

2 QL for Ad-hoc Variant Analysis

In order to make program analysis a standard part of the software developer's toolbox, we must make the barrier to getting started as low as possible. QL's approach of high-level, declarative queries, separate from the messy details of how to parse and compile the code, is a big step in that direction.

© Springer International Publishing AG, part of Springer Nature 2018
K. Havelund et al. (Eds.): FM 2018, LNCS 10951, pp. 666–670, 2018.
https://doi.org/10.1007/978-3-319-95582-7_42

We will use a recent example of this use case for a whirlwind tour of QL (for which [1] provides a full introduction). A vulnerability had been caused by an invalid overflow check in C++. The code looked something like this:

```
if (cur + offset < cur)
  return false;
use(cur + offset);
```

In the above, cur and offset were unsigned 16-bit values, and the check was intended to detect arithmetic overflow and wraparound. Unfortunately, it was flawed: The C/C++ standard specifies that 16-bit values are promoted to 32-bits for the purposes of arithmetic, and in this wider type the addition cannot possibly overflow. The comparison then has a 32-bit value on its left and a 16-bit value on its right, and will promote its right-hand side to 32 bits. Thus, a potential overflow in the 16-bit range would never be detected.

Here is the QL query we wrote as the customer was describing the issue:

```
from Variable v, RelationalOperation cmp, AddExpr add
where v.getAnAccess() = add.getAnOperand()
  and add = cmp.getAnOperand()
  and v.getAnAccess() = cmp.getAnOperand()
  and v.getType().getSize() < 4
  and not add.getExplictlyConverted().getType().getSize() < 4
select cmp, ''Bad overflow check.''
```

This directly encodes the verbal definition of the problem into machine-checkable QL. We are going to reason about a variable v, a relational operation cmp and an addition operation add, where: (a) an access to v figures as an operand of add, (b) the addition add is an operand of the comparison cmp, (c) another access to v is an operand of cmp, (d) the type of v is smaller than 4 bytes (*i.e.* subject to arithmetic promotion), and (e) the addition add is not explicitly truncated to a type smaller than 4 bytes.

This flagged the original problem and a few other variants in the same code base that had escaped manual detection. Indeed, the check is of general utility—there is nothing codebase-specific in it! In running it across other code bases, we have discovered numerous instances of incorrect overflow guards, and we are aware of several that turned out to be security vulnerabilities.

3   Variant Analysis from Building Blocks

Writing more sophisticated analyses is usually considered a highly specialist task. It is also extremely challenging to create general-purpose analyses that have high precision on arbitrary code bases. Both of these problems are addressed by creating easily reusable "analysis building blocks" in the standard QL libraries. We can provide a framework for doing dataflow analysis, or points-to analysis, or taint tracking, which encapsulates the complexities of the target language and allows end users to easily achieve remarkable bespoke results.

A recent spate of Java deserialization vulnerabilities suggests that numerous unknown variants might still be lurking in well-known code bases. The problem arises when untrusted (attacker-controlled) data is passed to some deserialization mechanism, which then creates attacker-determined objects. Merely this act can lead to arbitrary code execution [4]. Here is our QL query for such problems:

```
import java
import semmle.code.java.dataflow.FlowSources
import UnsafeDeserialization

from UnsafeDeserializationSink sink, RemoteUserInput source
where source.flowsTo(sink)
select sink.getMethodAccess(), "Unsafe deserialization of $@.",
    source, "user input"
```

Most of the logic is encapsulated in the imported libraries, which stand ready to be extended. The query itself checks that a value in the `RemoteUserInput` class flows to `sink`, which is an `UnsafeDeserializationSink`. The most common Java APIs are already modelled by the QL libraries; for example, `RemoteUserInput` will cover HTTP servlet request objects and data read over network sockets, while `UnsafeDeserializationSink` models Java serialization, but also frameworks like XStream and Kryo. Each of these concepts, as well as, if necessary, the dataflow computation itself may be extended separately.

In the work that led to the discovery of CVE-2017-9805 [5], we were auditing Apache Struts and noticed that it had a somewhat convoluted code pattern for deserialization: implementors of the interface `ContentTypeHandler` would be responsible for deserializing data passed in via the first parameter of their `toObject` method. Adding support for this[1] was a simple matter of providing an additional kind of `UserInput` by adding this class definition:

```
/** Mark the first argument of 'toObject' as user input source **/
class ContentTypeHandlerInput extends UserInput {
  ContentTypeHandlerInput() {
    exists(Method m | m.asParameter() = m.getParameter(0) |
    m.getSignature() = "toObject(java.io.Reader,java.lang.Object)" and
    m.getDeclaringType().getASupertype+().hasQualifiedName(
        "org.apache.struts2.rest.handler", "ContentTypeHandler")
    )
  }
}
```

With this definition in scope, the remainder of the library will kick in and perform the additional tracking, leading us to the result.

A more general customization hook for variant analysis is provided by the libraries in the form of so-called *dataflow configurations*. The user can specify a set of sources, a set of sinks and (optionally) a set of sanitizers that should prevent flow. The libraries then take care of the rest.

An example of this in action can be seen in our work on CVE-2017-13782 [2], inspired by past issues with the `dtrace` component of Apple's MacOS kernel. This subsystem allows user-supplied dtrace scripts to perform various operations,

---

[1] More recent versions of the QL libraries are able to track this pattern out of the box, but the same customization mechanisms are still available.

with their data stored in an array of registers. Such data should not be used in sensitive operations like pointer arithmetic or array subscripting, at least without careful validation. The dataflow configuration that identified the vulnerability was defined as follows:

```
class DtraceRegisterFlow extends DataFlow::Configuration {
  DtraceRegisterFlow() { this = "DtraceRegisterFlow" }
  /** Our sources are register reads like 'regs[i]'. */
  override predicate isSource(DataFlow::Node node) {
    exists(ArrayExpr regRead | regRead = node.asExpr() |
      regRead.getArrayBase().(VariableAccess).getTarget().hasName("regs") and
      regRead.getEnclosingFunction().hasName("dtrace_dif_emulate")
    )
  }
  /** Our sinks are array index or pointer arithmetic operations. */
  override predicate isSink(DataFlow::Node node) {
    exists(Expr use | use = node.asExpr() |
      use = any(ArrayExpr ae).getArrayOffset() or
      use = any(PointerAddExpr add).getAnOperand()
    )
  }
}
```

This concern is much too codebase-specific to be flagged by a standard analysis, but the vulnerability leaks arbitrary kernel memory and is, therefore, of high severity. QL's approach of providing analysis building blocks makes it feasible to create bespoke checks in such cases.

4   Conclusion

We have discussed the idea of *variant analysis*: Given a bug or vulnerability, how can we find other variants of the same problem? QL makes it very easy to write simple analyses, and allows users to bring state-of-the-art flow analysis to bear when necessary, all while abstracting away the complexity. The underlying libraries are continuously evolving, and as they become more powerful existing queries written against them automatically increase in power as well.

In our experience, this approach resonates strongly with both security researchers and developers, who embrace the idea that program analysis should be everyone's concern. The analyses created during this process tend to distribute fairly evenly into three categories:

Codebase-specific. Concerns specific to a particular code base, its APIs and invariants, like our "bad use of `dtrace` data" example.

Domain-specific. Analyses that apply to code written for a particular domain, possibly while requiring some customization. A good example is unsafe deserialization, which is applicable to any code that serializes data.

General. Checks that are applicable to any code base, usually concerning common pitfalls of the target language, like the "bad overflow guard" query.

QL is used to analyze over 50,000 open-source projects on the https://lgtm.com portal, and a query console is available to run custom analyses. The default libraries are available as open-source at https://github.com/lgtmhq/lgtm-queries.

References

1. Avgustinov, P., de Moor O., Jones, M.P., Schäfer. M.: QL: object-oriented queries on relational data. In: Krishnamurthi, S., Lerner, B.S. (eds.) 30th European Conference on Object-Oriented Programming, ECOOP 2016, LIPIcs, Rome, Italy, 18–22 July 2016, vol. 56, pp. 2:1–2:25. Schloss Dagstuhl - Leibniz-Zentrum fuer Informatik (2016)
2. Backhouse, K.: Using QL to find a memory exposure vulnerability in Apple's macOS XNU kernel. In: lgtm.com blog (2017). https://lgtm.com/blog/apple_xnu_dtrace_CVE-2017-13782
3. Bravenboer, M., Smaragdakis, Y.: Strictly declarative specification of sophisticated points-to analyses. In: OOPSLA (2009)
4. Frohoff, C., Lawrence, G.: Deserialize My Shorts, Or How I Learned to Start Worrying and Hate Java Object Deserialization. In: AppSec California (2015)
5. Mo, M.Y.: Using QL to find a remote code execution vulnerability in Apache Struts. lgtm.com blog (2017). https://lgtm.com/blog/apache_struts_CVE-2017-9805
6. Whaley, J., Avots, D., Carbin, M., Lam, M.S.: Using datalog with binary decision diagrams for program analysis. In: Yi, K. (ed.) APLAS 2005. LNCS, vol. 3780, pp. 97–118. Springer, Heidelberg (2005). https://doi.org/10.1007/11575467_8

Object-Oriented Security Proofs

Ernie Cohen[✉]

Amazon Web Services, Wyncote, USA
ecohen@amazon.com

Abstract. We use standard program transformations to construct formal security proofs.

1 Security as Object Equivalence

A *security specification* is a functional specification that additionally bounds information flow. For example, a functional specification for a communication channel might say that messages are received in the order sent; its security specification might additionally say that sending a message can leak to an adversary only the length of the message, not its bits. Such precise specification allows the proof of useful security guarantees for practical designs under realistic environmental assumptions. Security proofs most commonly appear in the context of cryptographic protocols, but can handle a variety of security enforcement mechanisms, such as security policy checks, virtualization, and human operations.

We formalize a specification as a constructor producing fresh objects exhibiting permitted behaviors. The constructor parameters can include objects representing components of the (possibly adversarial) environment, providing to the constructed object both services to call and a way to explicitly leak information. For example, one possible ideal channel specification maintains the history of messages sent as a private field, with a send method that leaks to the adversary the length of the message, but not its bits. As demonic nondeterminism in the language would provide to an attacker an NP oracle, breaking all reasonable cryptographic assumptions, methods also delegate to the environment the resolution of nondeterminism. For example, the receive method of the channel would ask the environment to decide whether to fail the call or to return the next undelivered message from the history.

A specification C(_) *refines* a specification A(_) iff there is a function f such that C(x) and A(f(x)) are equivalent. Typically, A(x) will be an abstract specification of a service that describes security intent, while C(x) is a more concrete implementation of the service. This reduces security reasoning to object equivalence (or, more precisely, equivalence of two constructor calls).

This approach, a flavor of universal composability, bears some similarity to methods based on process algebra or higher-order functional programming, but has some practical advantages. One advantage is that object identity makes it easy to write first-order invariants about the program state. Another is that, unlike spi calculi, there are no cryptographic security assumptions built into the logic; they are formulated directly as equivalence assumptions.

ⓒ Springer International Publishing AG, part of Springer Nature 2018
K. Havelund et al. (Eds.): FM 2018, LNCS 10951, pp. 671–674, 2018.
https://doi.org/10.1007/978-3-319-95582-7_43

2   Reasoning About Object Equivalence

What does it mean for two objects to be equivalent? A natural definition is for every language-definable Boolean function of a single object reference to return the same value when called on the two objects. In a probabilistic language, the two function calls would have to have the same probability of returning true. This definition of equivalence, *semantic equivalence*, is suitable for constructions that do not use cryptography.

The basic tools for reasoning about semantic equivalence are mostly familiar ones used for modular reasoning about object-oriented programs. These include inlining method calls, introducing/eliminating auxiliary variables, type invariants, admissible object invariants, ownership (to justify admissibility of invariants depending on the state of owned objects), sequential code equivalence (leveraging object invariants), and simulation. To simplify such reasoning, it is useful to guarantee that a method call cannot result in a callback, so that we do not have to worry about changes to the local object state when making a method call. We achieve this by (1) requiring an object calling a method to hold a "reference" to the object (in addition to its address), (2) allowing only constructors to create new references, and (3) allowing references to be passed into constructors and returned from method calls, but not passed into method calls. In the absence of infinite loops/recursions within a single object, this discipline also guarantees that all method calls terminate.

Cryptography requires a more permissive and complex equivalence: *indistinguishability*. Indistinguishability assumes that objects are additionally parameterized by a security parameter. It requires that for every probabilistic function running in time polynomial in the security parameter, and given one of the two objects with equal probability, the advantage (probability in excess of 0.5) of the function guessing which of the two objects it is interacting with is negligible in the security parameter. (A real-valued function $f(n)$ is *negligible* iff for every polynomial $p(n)$, $\lim_{n \to \infty}(p(n) \cdot f(n)) = 0$.) Fortunately, indistinguishability is in practice not very different from semantic equivalence. It adds the side condition that the environment runs in probabilistic polynomial time. It also provides additional assumptions, e.g., that a uniformly chosen random number, of length linear in the security parameter, chooses a value not in any previously constructed set of polynomial size.

Our *simulations* are program terms that transform one state representation to another, with the usual forward simulation condition (simulation followed by a method of the first representation is equivalent to a method call of the second representation followed by simulation). This formulation is independent of semantic details of the language and the equivalence. In particular, it allows probabilistic simulations, which often eliminate explicit probability reasoning.

In a concurrent system, we want to allow internal steps, as many internal interactions with the environment might be required between successful external interactions. We do this by providing an additional method that performs an internal step. The method queries the adversary to choose which internal action to perform, performs the chosen action, and returns the result to the adversary. Timing side channels are easily modeled by leaking the time required to perform an operation. This also allows us to reason about transition systems.

A typical cryptographic assumption is that a concrete encryption functionality, which encrypts with a randomly generated key, is indistinguishable from an ideal encryption functionality (which zeroes message bits before encryption, but remembers the original plaintext). Proofs often revolve around transforming an implementation to encapsulating a key within a concrete encryption functionality, so as idealize it. If that ideal functionality is used to encrypt other keys, it can be transformed, through simulation, to instead map ciphertexts to concrete encryption functionalities encapsulating the encrypted keys, allowing them to be idealized also. Avoidance of key cycles thus arises naturally through the order in which encapsulations are done in the proof.

An important consideration in reasoning about key compromise using this style of proof (as opposed to direct game arguments) is the so-called *commitment problem*: when an encryption key is compromised, we can no longer justify the prior pretense that encryptions carried no information about the messages sent. Fortunately, it is still sound to use the ideal functionality to prove *safety* properties of the whole system that hold up to the point of key compromise. This allows the proof of properties like perfect forward secrecy.

3   Some Specification Examples

We write specifications in a simple, untyped, object language, where all values (including addresses) are bitstrings, fields are private, and method bodies are expressions. Calling a method that doesn't exist simply returns 0 (the empty string). We use ~ to denote indistinguishability on program terms. $Z(m)$ is the bitstring m with all bits replaced with 0's, and & is the C && operator.

As a simple example, here is a possible communication channel specification:

```
ChI(n) { new (n,s=0,r=0,h=0) {
    snd(m) { m & n.snd(Z(m)), h[s++] = m }
    rcv()  { n.rcv() & r<s & h[r++] }
}}
```

This defines a function ChI that returns the address of a freshly constructed object, with fields n (initialized to the parameter n), s, r, and h (each initialized to 0). These fields give the address of the environment/adversary object, the number of messages sent, the number of messages received, and the sequence of messages sent (represented as a sparse map). Since we use 0 to represent failure, messages must be nonzero. We leak to the adversary the length of the messages sent, and allow it to fail reception. If communication was to be only authenticated, m itself would be leaked instead of $Z(m)$. We could allow internal steps by adding the method step() { n.step() }.

ChI can be viewed as turning an arbitrary (insecure) service n into a secure, FIFO service. Since ChI is idempotent (i.e., ChI(ChI(n)) ~ ChI(n)), we say

an expression t returns a fresh, asymptotically computationally secure channel
iff ChI(t) ~ t.

We can implement ChI using AEAD (authenticated encryption with
associated data) as follows:

```
AEAD(n) { new (n,d=0) {
    enc(a,m) { m & c = n.enc(a,Z(m)) & d[a][c] = m & c }
    dec(a,c) { d[a][c] }
}}

ChC(n,e) { new (n,e,s=0,r=0) {
    snd(m) { m & n.snd(e.enc(s++,m)), m }
    rcv()  { m = e.dec(r, n.rcv()) & r++ & m }
}}
```

The correctness of this construction is given by the following theorem. For reasoning purposes, it matters little what the term inside ChI is:

Theorem: ChC(n,AEAD(e)) ~ ChI(ChC(n,AEAD(e)))

A typical AEAD implementation uses a uniformly chosen symmetric key k:

```
Enc(k) { new (k) {
    enc(a,m) { skEnc(k,a,m) }
    dec(a,c) { skDec(k,a,c) }
}}
```

where rnd() chooses uniformly a bitstring of length given by the security parameter. (The key is a parameter so that we can replace rnd() with any expression
indistinguishable from rnd(), such as the output of a key derivation function or a
pseudorandom generator.) This gives a computationally secure implementation,
i.e., ChC(n,Enc(rnd())) ~ ChI(ChC(n,Enc(rnd()))).

4 Conclusion

We have used the methodology to formally verify several security properties of
industrial protocols, including the following:

- We proved that a simple, TLS-like shared-key ciphersuite communication
  protocol provides a factory for secure communication channels.
- We proved that a distributed system design (using symmetric and asymmet-
  ric encryption, unauthenticted Diffie-Hellman agreement, KDFs, public-key
  signatures, envelope encryption, multiple encryption domains with mutually
  distrusting quorums, dynamically changing domain operator/server member-
  ships, and domain key rotation) provides an ideal encryption service.

Current work includes mechanization and proofs with concrete security bounds.

Acknowledgements. We thank Supriya Anand, James Bornholdt, Matt Campagna,
Byron Cook, Andres Erbsen, Ralf Küsters, Rustan Leino, Andrea Nedic, Jade
Philipoom, and Serdar Tasiran for their contributions.

Z3 and SMT in Industrial R&D

Nikolaj Bjørner[⊠]

Microsoft Research, Redmond, USA
nbjorner@microsoft.com

Abstract. Theorem proving has a proud history of elite academic pursuit and select industrial use. Impact, when predicated on acquiring the internals of a formalism or proof environment, is gated on skilled and idealistic users. In the case of automatic theorem provers known as Satisfiability Modulo Theories, SMT, solvers, the barrier of entry is shifted to tool builders and their domains. SMT solvers typically provide convenient support for domains that are prolific in software engineering and have in the past decade found widespread use cases in both academia and industry. We describe some of the background developing the Z3 solver, the factors that have played an important role in shaping its use, and an outlook on further development and use.

1 Introduction

SMT has been pursued for decades by logicians and in industrial laboratories. Decision procedures for selected logical theories have been studied by Presburger, who gave a decision procedure for quantified formulas over linear integer arithmetic, postulated by Hilbert in his famous 10th (unsolvable) problem on Diophantine equations to give two examples. They have been integrated with theorem provers NQTHM, Standford Pascal Verifier, EHDM starting in the 1970s and promoted in the context of PVS and Simplify in the 1990s. A set of important confluences materialized in the past 10–20 years for SMT: our understanding of efficient SAT solving advanced with conflict directed clause learning [5] and efficient data-structures [4], "killer" applications, such as dynamic symbolic execution [3], emerged; and a community around SMT benchmarks and formats formed thanks to initiatives by persistent stake-holders [1].

In the following we describe a set of *driving scenarios* that have shaped our development and use of Z3[1], the importance of the SMT *community efforts* to drive usage, the role of *engineering APIs* and *open sourcing*, and conclude by describing some current efforts on applying Z3 in industrial contexts.

2 Driving Scenarios and Research Synergy

Z3 had the fortune to be nurtured in an environment populated with researchers with synergistic pursuits. These initial driving scenarios and synergies with close

---

[1] https://github.com/Z3Prover/z3

© Springer International Publishing AG, part of Springer Nature 2018
K. Havelund et al. (Eds.): FM 2018, LNCS 10951, pp. 675–678, 2018.
https://doi.org/10.1007/978-3-319-95582-7_44

collaborators are significant enablers. Fortunately, the case for SMT and Z3 has broadened over time. In 2005 Dynamic Symbolic Execution introduced a sweet spot between fuzzing and model checking by applying symbolic solving to path conditions and coped with partial modeling of system calls or other unmodeled instructions using concrete run-time values. It facilitates an established part of software engineering, unit tests, exemplified by Pex, and enhances security fuzzing, exemplified by SAGE. Program verification and contract checking were established since the 90's using the Simplify SMT solver. Simplify had hit a performance barrier in its techniques for quantifier instantiation and our first advance with Z3 was to introduce efficient data-structures that would perform simultaneous E-matching on sets of terms and quantifiers [2]. Microsoft Research was also an incubator to the SLAM symbolic model checker, which had instigated the previous generations of SMT solvers at Microsoft: Zapatho solved integer difference logic and uninterpreted functions, Zap2 (dropping "atho") extended the scope to full linear arithmetic, uninterpreted functions, arrays and quantifiers, and Leonardo de Moura and I created a v. 3 from scratch, Z3, dropping "ap".

Further developments in Z3 and SMT solvers generally continue to be based on inspiration from driving scenarios, by improving their existing uses of constraint solving and enabling new uses through a combination of improved solvers and more expressive functionality. In the context of Z3, Christoph Wintersteiger added solvers for machine arithmetic with IEEE floating point theories. We added additional theories, such as for sequences and strings, plugins for adding custom theories, powerful quantifier instantiation engines that act as decision procedures for several quantified decidable theories, specialized solvers for a class of formulas characterized as constrained Horn clauses that serve as a logical layer for symbolic model checking of procedural languages, scalable linear programming by Lev Nachmanson, and optimization features for the case users need to retrieve models that optimize objectives. I like to characterize a common thread in these developments as one throws a new "toy" in the basket and typically smart minds put it to creative and useful uses. As a logical toolbox Z3 enjoys a cross-cut of application areas that go beyond initial uses. Conversely, users constantly put a growing feature set into increased stress-test, which helps raise the quality bar and inspire areas for further innovation.

Z3 had the benefit of an organization that invests in research tooling. While this is not similar to how products are managed, which include service level agreements and support, it allows for a longer term view compared to academic environments where students expire after a few years, or industrial environments that are driven by short term deliverables and therefore require leveraging existing tools.

3   SMT-LIB - A Research Community

The value of the academic initiative in the SMT community cannot be underestimated. It has produced a standard, SMT-LIB [1], which serves as a well designed and documented basis for community efforts. It has produced a large set of shared benchmarks from industrial and experimental use cases. The barrier of entry of using SMT tools has been reduced, perhaps at expense of the entry point for producing new solvers that can supersede previous solvers. A clear indication of success for the SMT-LIB efforts is that tools that use SMT solvers can cherry-pick solvers in a portfolio, as done in software model checking tools.

4   Tooling and Infrastructure

A fruit from the interaction with Jakob Lichtenberg from the SLAM/SDV model checker team, was an initial API for Z3, exposed as bindings from C, and on top of that with wrappers for OCaml and .NET. It enabled an initial direct integration, even though maintaining a text pipeline (Z3 originally supported a text-based front-end for the Simplify format) is easier to maintain and debug. A very significant development was the addition of Python based bindings. This enabled easy prototyping through high-level, intuitive, scripting. Together with the well-designed SMT-LIB2 text format, these accessible interfaces are possibly the most important enablers for SMT technologies. In comparison, SAT solvers use lower level formats where formulas are already converted to CNF, and variable names are replaced by numerals. Writing a parser for a SAT solver is trivial, but the barrier of entry of using a SAT solver then includes converting formulas to CNF, and tracking variable names as a separate process.

4.1   Development

A common question is: "who are you managing to develop Z3?". Perhaps this was inspired from institutions where professors are project managers, but not developers. While Z3 is over 300KLOC most was written by relatively few contributors, and development is synergistic with evaluating experimental research questions: e.g., develop more efficient decision procedures. Check-ins into GitHub are monitored by two services, Travis and VS-build, that compile to several target platforms and run unit tests. We use a couple of thousand Azure compute nodes to run full SMT-LIB regressions on check-ins. A custom distributed test infrastructure performs file-sweeping and presents SMT friendly output.

4.2   Open Sourcing

Z3 was open sourced in two stages. In the fist stage, the code was shared and open for academics to use and modify for any research purpose. In the second stage, Z3 was open sourced under an MIT license and moved to GitHub which opened up for significant traction, especially contributions around improved interfacing and later on solving internals. It eradicated several barriers for commercial uses, such as the one a researcher faced when he wanted to acquire Z3 for his company and went through a futile email thread of 7 different parties and 20+ emails because Z3 was only available from the Microsoft online store and not through re-sellers. The open license terms in place today mean that Z3 is integrated in commercial products without royalties. Open sourcing applies to a dominant number of other tools from Microsoft Research today and overall fits well into a modern era where code development is eased by online tools; and an environment where research code is shared as part of advancing science, advancing usage, and resulting in feedback and improvements.

5   Push, Pull and Confluences

Industrial uses of symbolic solving is a combination of push, pull, and confluences. Program verification has been mainly pushed as a scientific, academic pursuit of ideal software development, but thanks to an active community and tools it is taking inroads with systems such as the Verifying C Compiler, VCC, the Microsoft Research Everest project for verifying secure socket layer implementations. Z3 is part of crypto blockchain verification utilities, including Etherum. The LLVM toolsets, and a development version of the Visual Studio compiler, use Z3 for checking correctness of compiler transformations, and it is used for super-optimization of code snippets. Network Verification is an active area in the management of wide-area and corporate networks; with growth and complexity outpacing traditional lower level network management tools, Z3 and symbolic solving have become useful ingredients for managing networking based on *intents* with deployments in Azure, Amazon, startup code bases and in advanced academic prototypes. Broadly speaking, symbolic solving is being embraced as part of systems developments and deployments, perhaps resembling deployments of operations research optimization tools. New confluences are emerging with the software industry's quest for data-driven and learning-based experiences: operations research and SMT solvers add capabilities to integrate solving and optimization capabilities.

References

1. Barrett, C., Pascal, P., Tinelli, C.: The Satisfiability Modulo Theories Library (SMT-LIB) (2016). www.smt-lib.org
2. de Moura, L., Bjørner, N.: Efficient E-matching for SMT solvers. In: Pfenning, F. (ed.) CADE 2007. LNCS (LNAI), vol. 4603, pp. 183–198. Springer, Heidelberg (2007). https://doi.org/10.1007/978-3-540-73595-3_13
3. Godefroid, P., Klarlund, N., Sen, K.: DART: directed automated random testing. In: Proceedings of the ACM SIGPLAN 2005 Conference on Programming Language Design and Implementation, Chicago, IL, USA, June 12–15, pp. 213–223 (2005)
4. Moskewicz, M.W., Madigan, C.F., Zhao, Y., Zhang, L., Malik, S.: Chaff: engineering an efficient SAT solver. In: Proceedings of the 38th Design Automation Conference, DAC 2001, Las Vegas, NV, USA, June 18–22, pp. 530–535 (2001)
5. Marques Silva, J.P., Sakallah, K.A.: GRASP: a search algorithm for propositional satisfiability. IEEE Trans. Comput. **48**(5), 506–521 (1999)

Evidential and Continuous Integration of Software Verification Tools

Tewodros A. Beyene$^{(\boxtimes)}$ and Harald Ruess

fortiss — An-Institut Technische Universität München, Munich, Germany
beyene@fortiss.org

1 Introduction

The complexity of embedded software and increasing demands on dependability, safety, and security has outpaced the capabilities of current verification and certification methods. In particular traditional verification and certification methods based on manual reviews, process constraints, and testing, which are mandated by current safety standards such as DO-178C [1] and DO-278A [2] for airborne systems and air traffic management systems, ISO 26262 [11] in the automative domain, and IEC 61508 for industrial domains including factory automation and robotics are proving to be overly time- and resource-intensive. For example, costs for developing certification evidence in *safety cases* according to the DO-178C standard have been shown to range between $50 to $100 per executable line of code, depending on the required safety level [15]. Unless mission-critical embedded software can be developed and verified with less cost and effort, while still satisfying the highest dependability requirements, new mission-critical capabilities such as autonomous control may never reach the market.

In this short paper, we present an overview of our approach for automating the process of creating certification evidence for mission-critical software. This framework supports the *integrated verification* of a wide range of complementary approaches to software verification, including automated tools and methods such as model checking and static analysis [3,7], and manual and consensus-driven approaches such as code review processes [8]. A *workflow pattern* for a given verification activity (e.g., analysis, review or test) specifies which methods to be used and how the methods are integrated in the given verification activity [10]. Our framework takes a single *workflow pattern* as an input to perform such an integrated verification task.

The framework is said to be *evidential* as verification evidence, which form the basis for certification processes, are automatically generated from pre-defined *workflow patterns*. This is done by chaining evidence from combination of the formal software analysis methods [5] as given in the *workflow patterns* [12]. The framework also supports *continuous* verification by executing verification and by generating corresponding evidence during each iteration of an agile development process. For this, the framework is technically based on the widely used *Jenkins CI* [6]. Therefore, our framework supports integrated verification, where verification evidence are automatically generated and updated continuously as software development progresses.

K. Havelund et al. (Eds.): FM 2018, LNCS 10951, pp. 679–685, 2018.
https://doi.org/10.1007/978-3-319-95582-7_45

Our tool integration framework is inspired and also closely related to SRI's evidential toolbus (ETB) [4,14,16], which is a distributed workflow-based tool integration framework for constructing claims supported by evidence. A main difference is our choice of basing our integration framework on an widely used continuous integration framework. This design choice allows us to seamlessly integrate our verification framework into a large number of industrial software development infrastructures. Our prototype implementation uses *Jenkins CI*[1] as it provides the following crticial services for our integration framework: distributed computing capabilities, notion of analysis evidence, and Interaction mechanism with humans.

2   Verification Activities, Workflows and Patterns

The creation of assurance cases as the basis for certification is labour-intensive and largely manual. This process usually starts by developing a verification plan for determining adequate verification methods and tools together with acceptance criteria for successful verification runs. These verification plans are executed and verification results are, more or less manually, compiled into an assurance case as the basis for certification.

More generally, verification planning may be viewed as defining workflows for the selected verification activities such as analysis, review and test. A *verification workflow* is a sequence of steps applying verification methods and tools with the aim of ensuring that a system under verification satisfies its specification. Verification workflows, together with their verification methods and tools, are identified and defined during the verification planning phase of a project [10].

workflow CODEREVIEW
  input
    prog P **of type** SOURCECODE
  tools
    infer **of type** STATICANALYSIS
    cppCheck **of type** STATICANALYSIS
    CBMC **of type** MODELCHECKING
  begin
1:   $R_1 := \text{infer}(P)$
2:   $R_2 := \text{cppCheck}(P)$
3:   $R_3 := \text{MERGE}(R_1, R_2)$
4:   $R_4 := \text{REFINE}(\text{CBMC}, R_3, P)$
5:   **return** R_4
  end

Fig. 1. A code review workflow

workflow pattern CODEREVIEW
  input
    prog P **of type** SOURCECODE
  parameter
    tool set T **of type** STATICANALYSIS
    tool M **of type** MODELCHECKING
  begin
1:   $R := \{\}$
2:   **for each** $t \in T$ **do**
3:     $R_t := \text{APPLYSTATICANALYSIS}(t, P)$
4:     $R := \text{MERGE}(R, R_t)$
5:   **done**
6:   $R := \text{REFINE}(M, R, P)$
7:   **return** R
  end

Fig. 2. A code review workflow pattern

---

[1] https://jenkins.io.

An example code review workflow, which is inspired and extends Holzmann's [8,10] portfolio approach, is provided in Fig. 1. This code review workflow takes a program source code P as input and produces a review report R with potential defects. The workflow applies static analysis using $Infer^2$ and $cppCheck^3$ (Lines 1 & 2), and merges analysis results (Line 3). The merged result is further refined (e.g., false positives from static analysis are detected and therefore excluded from the review report) by calling the function REFINE, which employs the CBMC [13] model checker (Line 4).

These kinds of workflows are usually instantiations of given *verification workflow patterns*. An example workflow pattern for a code review verification process is specified in Fig. 2. Like the workflow in Fig. 1, the workflow pattern takes a program source code P as an input, and produces a review report R as an output. However, the specification of specific verification tools are not required in the definition of the workflow pattern. Instead, it is parameterised by a set of static analysis tools T and a model cheker M. The workflow pattern applies each static analysis tool over the source code (Lines 2–5), and collects the analysis results (Line 4). It also refines the collected report further by tagging, for example, false positives (Line 6).

The advantage of using *verification workflow patterns* is twofold: (1) choice of specific verification tools implementing verification methods in the workflow pattern can be made during the actual verification execution phase of the project, and (2) a given workflow pattern can be flexibly instantiated with different verification tools resulting in completely different verification workflows. In this way, our tool integration framework provides a flexible way of instantiating verification workflow patterns according to the heterogeneous needs and requirements of different industrial software development environments and supporting tool infrastructures. For example, the code review workflow pattern in Fig. 2 can be instantiated in a number of different ways by assigning different values for the parameters T and M. Consider, for example, the following three possible instantiations: $\{(T = \{\text{infer}, \text{cppCheck}\}, M = \text{CBMC}), (T = \{\text{infer}, \text{coverity}^4\}, M = \text{CBMC}), \text{ and } (T = \{\text{infer}, \text{coverity}\}, M = \text{SPIN [9]})\}$. The first instantiation is actually equivalent to the workflow in Fig. 1.

As verification methods form an integral part of *verification workflow patterns*, each verification method must be defined in terms of inputs and outputs. For example, the verification method *Static Analysis*, which is used in the *verification workflow pattern* of Fig. 2, can be defined as taking a *program source code* as an input and producing a *set of errors* as an output. Any verification tool implementing a given verification method must agree on inputs and outputs with the verification method.

---

[2] http://fbinfer.com.

[3] http://cppcheck.sourceforge.net.

[4] https://www.synopsys.com/software-integrity/security-testing/static-analysis-sast.html.

3   Structure of the Integration Framework

Our tool integration framework, as shown in Fig. 3, is built on top of a CI framework. It contains three additional components, namely *Patterns Database*, *Tools Server* and *Integration Engine*, for instrumenting and configuring the framework with the specific verification needs and available resources of a given software development project.

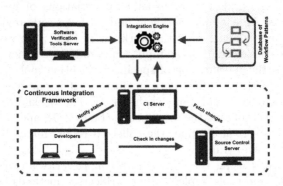

Fig. 3. The Integration Framework

One instrumentation deals with adding each verification tool, which implements certain verification method, to the *Tools Server* component. Another instrumentation deals with adding *workflow patterns*, which are created for the planned verification activities of the project, to the *Patterns Database* component. These instrumentations make the framework ready for integrated verification.

Users can perform an integrated verification by executing the framework with the appropriate *workflow pattern* and tools to instantiate the verification methods specified in the given *workflow pattern*. The *Integration Engine* is responsible for instantiating verification methods with the proper verification tools (as provided by the user), collecting outputs of each tool, and composing these outputs into high-level verification evidence.

4   Illustration

Let us run our framework with the *verification workflow pattern* in Fig. 2, parameter instantiations $T = \{\text{infer, coverity}\}$ and $M = \text{SPIN}$, and with the input program listed in Fig. 4. The generated review report is listed in Fig. 5. Let us consider two of the error entries in the report:

Error E1 is initially reported during static analysis by *Infer* and *Coverity* as a possible *dereference of null pointer on line 50 of the source file*. Then, the refinement procedure of our framework (implemented as function REFINE, and whose refinement logic depends on the type of error) tries to refute the error

```
 6:  struct BankInfo{ ... };
         ...
14:  int fileNotClosed(int fd){
15:    fd = open(csvFile, O_WRONLY | O_CREAT | O_TRUNC, 0600);
16:    if (fd != -1) {
17:      char buffer[256];
18:      write(fd,buffer,strlen(buffer));
19:    }
20     return fd;
21: }
         ...
46:  int main(){
47:    int fd;
48:    fileNotClosed(fd).close();
49:    BankInfo *PostB = 0;
50:    return PostB->Revenue;
51: }
```

No	Error Type	Location	Status
E1	*null dereference*	example.c (line 50)	verified error
	pointer PostB could be assigned null on line 49 and is dereferenced at line 50. [*code analysis tools: infer, coverity, model checking tool: SPIN*]		
E2	*resource leak*	example.c (line 20)	false positive
	resource acquired to fd at line 18 is not released. [static analysis tools: {*infer, coverity*}, model checking tool: *SPIN*]		
E3	*memory leak*	example.c (line 39)	not refined
	memory acquired by getMem at line 33 is never released. [*code analysis tools: infer, coverity*]		
E4	*division by zero*	example.c (line 43)	verified error
	variable count could be assigned 0 on line 41 and is used in division operation at line 43. [*code analysis tools: infer, coverity, model checking tool: SPIN*]		

Fig. 4. An example source code fragment   **Fig. 5.** Report generated by our framework

claim by adding the assertion '$max \neq$ NULL' on line 50 and running SPIN. Since SPIN proves the assertion does not hold and provides a counter-example, the process concludes that the error is a real violation. The counter-example from SPIN further supports the initial error claim. These kinds of additional evidence are added to the error report as the basis for further investigation, for example, in a code review meeting.

Error E2 is initially reported during static analysis as a possible *resource leak error* on line 20. The refinement procedure now encodes the eventual release of the file resource in LTL and applies SPIN. The model checking by SPIN actually succeeds as the resource is later released in the main function, i.e., the potential error does not actually materialize. Therefore, this error is marked as *false alarm* in the final review report. The set of applied tools as well as verification outputs will be kept as verification evidence for every verification decision made by the framework.

We have applied our framework with the code review workflow pattern on the Toyota static analysis benchmarks.[5] Although the refinement procedure of our framework is not defined for all type of possible defects addressed in this benchmark, the framework at least is able to refine many false positives for the type of errors it can handle (such as null dereference and division by zero errors). We have also used the framework in a project within the Airbus Group as a front end for a tool-based code review solution for Ada programs. In this project, the framework is able to integrate Ada code analysis tools, such as GNATProve and AdaCtl, with an in-house developed Ada model checker.

5 Conclusion

We have presented a tool integration framework for supporting the automated and continuous verification of mission-critical software. First, the framework supports *integrated verification* as it applies a workflow-based combination of complementary software analysis methods. Second, the framework is *evidential* as verification evidence, which form the basis for certification, are automatically generated from pre-defined *verification workflow patterns* by chaining results

---
[5] https://github.com/regehr/itc-benchmarks/.

from the integrated software analysis tools. Third, the framework is *continuous* as it is aimed at executing verification and generating corresponding evidence during each iteration of an agile development process.

We are in the process of launching and applying this tool integration framework in a number of industrial verification efforts for safety- and security-related software in the automotive and the aerospace domain. The ultimate goal here is to automatically generate assurance cases according to sector-specific safety standards such as ISO 26262, DO178C, or ECSS. In the future, we also plan to use this integrated verification framework for the on-line generation of certification evidence during operation, for example, for adaptive and learning-based control systems.

Benefits of using our tool integration framework include: (1) flexible and seamless integration into agile industrial software development processes, (2) integration of a number of complementary automated software verification tools with more process-oriented methods such as code review as mandated in industrial safety standards, (3) formal and automated process from verification planning down to producing corresponding verification evidence during development and in accordance with industrial safety standards; (4) considerable reduction of certification effort by means of automated generation of verification evidence; (5) instantaneous and up-to-date verification evidence and corresponding assurance cases as the basis for guiding agile development processes.

References

1. RTCA DO-178C Software Considerations in Airborne Systems and Equipment Certification. RTCA Standard, December 2011
2. RTCA DO-278A Software Integrity Assurance Considerations for Communication, Navigation and Air Traffic Management (CNS/ATM) Systems, December 2011
3. Ábrahám, E., Havelund, K.: Some recent advances in automated analysis. Int. J. Softw. Tools Technol. Transf. **18**(2), 121–128 (2016)
4. Cruanes, S., Hamon, G., Owre, S., Shankar, N.: Tool integration with the evidential tool bus. In: VMCAI (2013)
5. Denney, E., Pai, G.: Evidence arguments for using formal methods in software certification. In: Software Reliability Engineering Workshops (ISSREW), Nov 2013
6. Duvall, P., Matyas, S.M., Glover, A.: Continuous Integration: Improving Software Quality and Reducing Risk. Addison-Wesley Professional, Boston (2007)
7. Groce, A., Havelund, K., Holzmann, G., Joshi, R., Xu, R.-G.: Establishing flight software reliability: testing, model checking, constraint-solving, monitoring and learning. Ann. Math. Artif. Intell. **70**, 315–349 (2014)
8. Havelund, K., Holzmann, G.J.: Software certification: coding, code, and coders. In: EMSOFT 2011. ACM, New York, NY, USA (2011)
9. Holzmann, G.: The SPIN Model Checker: Primer and Reference Manual, 1st edn. Addison-Wesley Professional, Boston (2011)
10. Holzmann, G.J.: SCRUB: a tool for code reviews, December 2010
11. ISO: Road vehicles - Functional safety (2011)
12. Kelly, T.P., McDermid, J.A.: Safety case construction and reuse using patterns. In: Software Reliability Engineering Workshops (ISSREW) (1997)

13. Kroening, D., Tautschnig, M.: CBMC – C bounded model checker. In: Ábrahám, E., Havelund, K. (eds.) TACAS 2014. LNCS, vol. 8413, pp. 389–391. Springer, Heidelberg (2014). https://doi.org/10.1007/978-3-642-54862-8_26
14. Moura, L.D., Owre, S., Ruess, H., Rushby, J., Shankar, N.: Integrating verification components. Theories, Tools, Experiments. In: Verified Software (2005)
15. RTI Real-Time Innovations: DDS for Safety-Critical Applications (2014)
16. Rushby. J.: An evidential tool bus. In: Proceedings of ICFEM (2005)

Disruptive Innovations
for the Development and the Deployment
of Fault-Free Software

Thierry Lecomte[(✉)]

CLEARSY, 320 avenue Archimède, Aix en Provence, France
`thierry.lecomte@clearsy.com`

Abstract. Developing safety critical systems is a very difficult task. Such systems require talented engineers, strong experience and dedication when designing the safety principles of these systems. Indeed it should be demonstrated that no failure or combination of failures may lead to a catastrophic situation where people could be injured or could die because of that system. This article presents disruptive technologies that reduce the effort to develop such systems by providing integrated building blocks easier to use.

Keywords: Formal methods · Safety critical · Software development

1 Introduction

Developing safety critical systems [2] requires higher costs (advanced engineering, redundant architecture for SIL3/4[1] applications, extensive verification & validation, specific hardware, etc.). Using off-the-shelf hardware is often a nightmare as it requires to constraint the development cycle by using specific modeling and verification tools, software libraries (and imposed basic operators), etc. Lack of flexibility, requirement for expert practitioners, and resulting higher selling price could dramatically lower competitiveness. Even worse, from a societal point of view, means to improve population safety might not be put into existence because of economical reasons (costs).

To overcome this situation, a solution based on formal methods, the CLEARSY Safety Platform [3], has been designed to ease the development and the deployment of a function, by providing means to model the software, to prove its behavior regarding its specification, to verify mathematically the soundness and the correctness of its parameters, and to ensure a safe execution on a dedicated hardware.

The CLEARSY Safety Platform is made of an integrated software development environment (IDE) and a hardware platform that natively integrates

---

[1] Safety Integrity Level. 4 is the highest level, corresponding to a maximum of one catastrophic failure every hundred centuries.

© Springer International Publishing AG, part of Springer Nature 2018
K. Havelund et al. (Eds.): FM 2018, LNCS 10951, pp. 686–689, 2018.
https://doi.org/10.1007/978-3-319-95582-7_46

safety principles. Hence the developer only has to focus on the functional design while mathematical proof replaces unit and integration testing. There is no need for independent software development teams: redundant software is automatically produced from a single model. A certification kit allows the developer to build a safety case and as such ease the certification process. The final safety demonstration remains the responsibility of the developer.

2 Software Modeling

The B formal method is at the core of the software development process (Fig. 1). Mathematical proofs ensure that the software complies with its specification and guarantees the absence of programming errors while avoiding unit testing and integration testing.

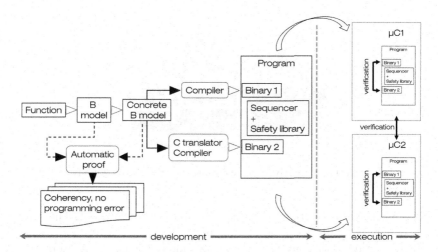

Fig. 1. Software development and deployment: a single formal model is used to generate diverse software. A sequencer and verification functions, developed with B, constitute the safety belt. The sequencer calls the software function every cycle while the verification functions ensure that any divergent behavior is detected and leads to reboot.

Moreover only one functional model is used to produce automatically the redundant software, avoiding the need to have two independent teams for its development. The formal model may be developed manually or be the by-product of a translation from a Domain Specific Language to B (BXml open API). A subset of the B formal language is supported to develop control-command applications. A software project is a B project already filled with an interface description with the board (inputs, outputs, current time), the supported types and operators. The developer only has to fill in the specification and design of the function *user_logic*. In its current form, the software integrated development environment allows developing cyclic applications (read inputs and current time, perform computations, command outputs), run directly on the hardware without any underlying operating system. There is no predefined cycle time to comply with: the application is run as fast as possible and the time information is managed directly by the application software. With PIC32 micro-controllers, the platform offers up to 100 MIPS for lightweight applications handling Boolean and integer data.

3 Low Cost High Integrity Platform

Software is not safe by itself as it is necessary to consider the processor (and its failures) that is going to execute it (Fig. 2).

The safety principles are built-in, both at software level and at hardware level (2oo2 hardware, 4oo4 software).

Fig. 2. The CLEARSY Safety Platform: the starter kit SK0

The functional correctness is ensured by mathematical proof. The software is also demonstrated to be programming error free.

The detection of any divergent behavior among the two processors and the four instances of the software is handled by the platform. The safety verifications include cross checks between software instances and between micro-controllers, memory integrity, micro-controller instruction checker, etc. In case of failure, the execution platform reboots. As the outputs require the two micro-controllers to be alive and running, it is not possible to have the outputs commanded in a permissive state in case of divergent behavior. The safety principles of the platform are out of reach of the developer who cannot alter them.

4 Formal Data Validation

Software applications are usually developed and validated independently from the parameters or constant data that fine-tune their behavior. In order to avoid a new compilation if the data are modified but not the software, two different processes define the software and the data validations. Data validation consists in checking a heterogeneous data collection against a set of properties/rules issued from diverse sources like technical constraints, regulation, exploitation constraints, etc. Manual data validation used to be entirely human, error-prone activities.

Formal data validation [1] is the natural evolution of this human-based process into a more secure one where the properties/rules are formalized, to constitute a formal data model (mathematical, based on the B language). It is built from natural language inputs. The verification of conformance between the data collection and the formal data model is performed by a formal tool, i.e. a model-checker (or by a combination of redundant formal tool if required). In the case of the applications developed with the CLEARSY Safety Platform, the parameters of the application but also the technical parameters of the implementation are formally verified.

5   Conclusion and Perspectives

The CLEARSY Safety Platform is aimed at easing the development and the deployment of safety critical applications, up to SIL4. It relies on the smart integration of formal methods, redundant code generation and compilation, and a hardware platform that ensures a safe execution of the software.

A starter kit SK0, developed with the support of the French R & D project FUI LCHIP (Low Cost High Integrity Platform), is available since Q4 2017 for experiment and education.

The building blocks of this technology have already been certified (SIL3/SIL4) in several railway projects worldwide, in particular the COPPILOT systems open and closing platform screen doors in São Paulo and Stockholm.

Together with the full automation of the proof, the connection with Domain Specific Languages, like Grafcet or Structured Text, is expected during this year 2018 to enable the development of functions independently of the B formal language, hence to ease the adoption of these new technologies in the industry.

References

1. Falampin, J., Le-Dang, H., Leuschel, M., Mokrani, M., Plagge, D.: Improving railway data validation with proB. In: Romanovsky, A., Thomas, M. (eds.) Industrial Deployment of System Engineering Methods, pp. 27–43. Springer, Heidelberg (2013)
2. Lecomte, T.: Applying a formal method in industry: a 15-Year trajectory. In: Alpuente, M., Cook, B., Joubert, C. (eds.) FMICS 2009. LNCS, vol. 5825, pp. 26–34. Springer, Heidelberg (2009). https://doi.org/10.1007/978-3-642-04570-7_3
3. Lecomte, T.: Double cœur et preuve formelle pour automatismes sil4. 8E-Modèles formels/preuves formelles-sûreté du logiciel (2016)

Author Index

Printed in the United States
By Bookmasters